Torts

Torts

Cases and Problems

FOURTH EDITION

Frank J. Vandall
PROFESSOR OF LAW
EMORY UNIVERSITY SCHOOL OF LAW

Ellen Wertheimer
PROFESSOR OF LAW
VILLANOVA UNIVERSITY CHARLES WIDGER SCHOOL OF LAW

Mark C. Rahdert
PROFESSOR OF LAW
TEMPLE UNIVERSITY JAMES E. BEASLEY SCHOOL OF LAW

CAROLINA ACADEMIC PRESS
Durham, North Carolina

ISBN: 978-1-5310-1146-8
eISBN: 978-1-53101-147-5
LCCN: 2018939849

Carolina Academic Press, LLC
700 Kent Street
Durham, North Carolina 27701
Telephone (919) 489-7486
Fax (919) 493-5668
www.cap-press.com

Printed in the United States of America

Dedications

I dedicate this book to my children Megan and Josh, and my grandchildren, Madison, Keegan and Emma. — *Frank Vandall*

We dedicate this book to our children, Chris and Lise. — *Ellen Wertheimer & Mark C. Rahdert*

Contents

Table of Cases

Preface

For the Fourth Edition, our goal was to "polish the apple" by replacing cases that were not effective in class and adding new and important ones. One of our goals was also to include cases with human interest in the book.

We have added many new cases and removed older cases that did not work well in class. We also shortened the casebook in an effort to reflect actual coverage in first year torts courses.

For this edition, we once again tried to incorporate comments we have received from those who have adopted the casebook. We hope to have been responsive.

Enjoy.

FRANK J. VANDALL
Professor of Law
Emory University School of Law

ELLEN WERTHEIMER
Professor of Law
Villanova University Charles Widger School of Law

MARK C. RAHDERT
Professor of Law
Temple University James E. Beasley School of Law
February, 2018

Acknowledgments

For the Fourth Edition, I am especially indebted to the organizational and computer expertise of Marianne D'Souza. I also appreciate the support and encouragement of Emory Law School. — *Frank Vandall*

For the Fourth Edition, I am deeply in the debt of Patricia Trask, my assistant, whose unfailing generosity with her time and expertise were invaluable. Christopher Merken, research assistant extraordinaire, provided crucial assistance for the Casebook and Teacher's Manual. — *Ellen Wertheimer*

For the Fourth Edition, I wish to acknowledge the encouragement and support I received from Dean Gregory Mandel and my faculty colleagues at Temple University Beasley School of Law. — *Mark C. Rahdert*

Torts

Chapter 1

Introduction

Torts is a deceptively simple subject because there is only one question in each case: who will pay the damages, plaintiff or defendant? This is a matter of justice and involves a weighing of numerous factors. Answering the question of whether the defendant will be liable or the loss left with the plaintiff in each case involves an evaluation of history, tort doctrine, and social policy. An examination of these subjects is the text of the course.

A tort is any civil action other than for breach of contract. The usual remedy sought is damages awarded after a jury trial. In fact, ninety-two percent of cases are settled before trial. Another six percent are "settled on the court house steps." Therefore ninety-eight percent are settled. Injunctions are rare. There are several fundamental purposes for tort law: to compensate the injured party, to prevent self-help (violence), and to deter the conduct in the future. Very simply, in today's world, the law of torts exists to give people an alternative to violence.

The foundation of tort law is absolute liability. Before 1300, the plaintiff merely had to prove that the defendant was a cause of his injury in order to prevail. Fault was not required:

> At your request I accompany you when you are about your own affairs; my enemies fall upon and kill me, you must pay for my death. You take me to see a wild beast show or that interesting spectacle, a mad man; beast or mad man kills me; you must pay. You hang up your sword; someone else knocks it down so that it cuts me; you must pay. In none of these cases can you honestly swear that you did nothing that helped to bring about death or wound.

W. Malone, *Ruminations on the Role of Fault in the History of the Common Law of Torts*, 31 La. L. Rev. 1, 3 (1970).

In torts as in most law school courses, you will learn the law by studying actual cases.

Before attorneys can take a case, they must first have an injured person as a client. The attorney, in consultation with the client, must then decide that the injury is worth the expense of a lawsuit. As you read the cases in this casebook, you should ask yourselves whether the plaintiffs might have reasons other than recovering damages to file lawsuits.

As in most torts casebooks, we will usually be reading appeals from trial courts to intermediate appellate courts or to the state supreme court. Occasionally, we will read a federal case, rarely one decided by the U.S. Supreme Court.

———————

1. What if, in Malone's examples, the defendant had exercised care or the plaintiff was careless?

2. In the above example, should not the attacker be liable rather than the invitor? Why not hold the circus liable for the attack of the wild beast? What is the basis of liability in the above example?

3. In *Weaver v. Ward*, Hobart 134, 80 Eng. Rep. 284 (1616), the court stated:

> Weaver brought an action of trespass of assault and battery against Ward. The defendant pleaded, that he was amongst others by the commandment of the Lords of the Council a trained soldier in London, of the band of one Andrews captain; and so was the plaintiff, and that they were skirmishing with their muskets charged with powder for their exercise in re militari, against another captain and his band; and as they were so skirmishing, the defendant casualiter & per infortunium & contra voluntatem suam, in discharging of his piece did hurt and wound the plaintiff, which is the same, &c. absque hoc, that he was guilty aliter sive alio modo. And upon demurrer by the plaintiff, judgment was given for him; for though it were agreed, that if men tilt or turney in the presence of the King, or if two masters of defence playing their prizes kill one another, that this shall be no felony; or if a lunatick kill a man, or the like, because felony must be done animo felonico: yet in trespass, which tends only to give damages according to hurt or loss, it is not so; and therefore if a lunatick hurt a man, he shall be answerable in trespass: and therefore no man shall be excused of a trespass (for this is the nature of an excuse, and not of a justification, prout ei bene licuit) except it may be judged utterly without his fault.
>
> As if a man by force take my hand and strike you, or if here the defendant had said, that the plaintiff ran cross his piece when it was discharging, or had set forth the case with the circumstances, so as it had appeared to the court that it had been inevitable, and that the defendant had committed no negligence to give occasion to the hurt.

What is a demurrer? What did the plaintiff plead? How did the defendant answer? What was the legal basis for the plaintiff's demurrer? How does the court respond to the demurrer? Why does the defendant lose? What message does the court provide for future cases? How does the court define fault?

4. Personal injury cases are often presented on the newspaper's front page. Torts is a "hot" topic and commonly the subject of legislative reform because of a perceived crisis (dramatic expansion in the number of cases and the size of the awards). Indeed, tort "reform" has become synonymous with legal changes that leave costs on the victims. A recent study suggests a need for facts and caution, however. Professors Thomas A. Eaton and Susette M. Talarico conclude that "[T]ort fights are fewer and simpler and end in victories for defendants more often than the public thinks." They conclude that "tort filings are level, not rising, and represent a much smaller

proportion [5%] of total civil litigation than is widely believed." Eaton stated that "there is [not an explosion of personal injury cases]. The general trend is really one of relative stability. We are not seeing an increase in the number of cases filed. And this holds true on a national level. Year-by-year, the tort filing levels [in Georgia] did not rise or fall dramatically. Federal and other available state court data indicate that tort filings have remained flat for 10 years." Eaton also made clear that "only 7 percent of tort claims filed ever get to trial." *Tort Crisis a Myth*, Fulton County Daily Report 1 (May 30, 1996), reporting of a speech based on Thomas A. Eaton & Susette M. Talarico, *A Profile of Tort Litigation in Georgia and Reflections on Tort Reform*, 30 Ga. L. Rev. 627 (1996).

5. Every lawyer, it is said, gets a dog case. Therefore, we present the following "simple" dog case for your elucidation and enjoyment.

Brown v. Kendall

Supreme Judicial Court of Massachusetts, 1850
6 Cush. (60 Mass.) 292

This was an action of trespass for assault and battery, originally commenced against George K. Kendall, the defendant. . . .

It appeared in evidence, on the trial, . . . that two dogs, belonging to the plaintiff and the defendant, respectively, were fighting in the presence of their masters; that the defendant took a stick about four feet long, and commenced beating the dogs in order to separate them; that the plaintiff was looking on, at the distance of about a rod, and that he advanced a step or two towards the dogs. In their struggle, the dogs approached the place where the plaintiff was standing. The defendant retreated backwards from before the dogs, striking them as he retreated; and as he approached the plaintiff, with his back towards him, in raising his stick over his shoulder, in order to strike the dogs, he . . . hit the plaintiff in the eye, inflicting upon him a severe injury.

Whether it was necessary or proper for the defendant to interfere in the fight between the dogs; whether the interference, if called for, was in a proper manner, and what degree of care was exercised by each party on the occasion; were the subject of controversy between the parties, upon all the evidence in the case, of which the foregoing is an outline.

The judge . . . left the case to the jury under the following instructions: "If the defendant, in beating the dogs, was doing a necessary act, or one which it was his duty under the circumstances of the case to do, and was doing it in a proper way; then he was not responsible in this action, provided he was using ordinary care at the time of the blow. If it was not a necessary act; if he was not in duty bound to attempt to part the dogs, but might with propriety interfere or not as he chose; the defendant was responsible for the consequences of the blow, unless it appeared that he was in the exercise of extraordinary care, so that the accident was inevitable, using the word inevitable not in a strict but a popular sense."

"If, however, the plaintiff, when he met with the injury, was not in the exercise of ordinary care, he cannot recover, and this rule applies, whether the interference of the defendant in the fight of the dogs was necessary or not. If the jury believe, that it was the duty of the defendant to interfere, then the burden of proving negligence on the part of the defendant, and ordinary care on the part of the plaintiff, is on the plaintiff. If the jury believes that the act of interference in the fight was unnecessary, then the burden of proving extraordinary care on the part of the defendant, or want of ordinary care on the part of the plaintiff, is on defendant."

The jury under these instructions returned a verdict for the plaintiff; whereupon the defendant alleged exceptions.

SHAW, C.J. . . .

The facts set forth in the bill of exceptions preclude the supposition, that the blow, inflicted by the hand of the defendant upon the person of the plaintiff, was intentional. The whole case proceeds on the assumption, that the damages sustained by the plaintiff, from the stick held by the defendant, was inadvertent and unintentional; and the case involves the question how far, and under what qualifications, the party by whose unconscious act the damage was done is responsible for it. We use the term "unintentional" rather than involuntary, because in some of the cases, it is stated, that the act of holding and using a weapon or instrument, the movement of which is the immediate cause of hurt to another, is a voluntary act, although its particular effect in hitting and hurting another is not within the purpose or intention of the party doing the act.

It appears to us, that some of the confusion in the cases on this subject has grown out of the long-vexed question, under the rule of the common law, whether a party's remedy, where he has one, should be sought in an action of the case, or of trespass. This is very distinguishable from the question, whether in a given case, any action will lie. The result of these cases is, that if the damage complained of is the immediate effect of the act of the defendant, trespass *vi et armis* lies; if consequential only, and not immediate, case is the proper remedy. . . .

In these discussions, it is frequently stated by judges, that when one receives injury from the direct act of another, trespass will lie. But we think this is said in reference to the question, whether trespass and not case will lie, assuming that the facts are such, that some action will lie. These *dicta* are no authority, we think, for holding, that damage received by a direct act of force from another will be sufficient to maintain an action of trespass, whether the act was lawful or unlawful, and neither wilful, intentional, or careless. . . .

We think, as the result of all the authorities, the rule is correctly stated by Mr. Greenleaf, that the plaintiff must come prepared with evidence to show either that the *intention* was unlawful, or that the defendant was *in fault;* for if the injury was unavoidable, and the conduct of the defendant was free from blame, he will not be liable. . . . If, in the prosecution of a lawful act, a casualty purely accidental arises, no action can be supported for an injury arising therefrom. . . . In applying these rules to the present case, we can perceive no reason why the instructions asked for by the defendant ought not to have been given; to this effect, that if both plaintiff and defendant at the time of the blow were using ordinary care, or if at that time the defendant was using ordinary care, and the plaintiff was not, or if at that time, both the plaintiff and defendant were not using ordinary care, then the plaintiff could not recover.

In using this term, ordinary care, it may be proper to state that what constitutes ordinary care will vary with the circumstances of cases. In general, it means that kind and degree of care which prudent and cautious men would use, such as is required by the exigency of the case, and such as is necessary to guard against probable danger. A man, who should have occasion to discharge a gun, on an open and extensive marsh, or in a forest, would be required to use less circumspection and care, than if he were to do the same thing in an inhabited town, village, or city. To make an accident, or casualty, or as the law sometimes states it, inevitable accident, it must be such an accident as the defendant could not have avoided by the use of the kind and degree of care necessary to the exigency, and in the circumstances in which he was placed.

We are not aware of any circumstances in this case, requiring a distinction between acts which it was lawful and proper to do, and acts of legal duty. There are cases, undoubtedly, in which officers are bound to act under process, for the legality of which they are not responsible, and perhaps some others in which this distinction would be important. We can have no doubt that the act of the defendant in attempting to part the fighting dogs, one of which was his own, and for the injurious acts of which he might be responsible, was a lawful and proper act, which he might do by proper and safe means. If, then, in doing this act, using due care and all proper precautions necessary to the exigency of the case, to avoid hurt to others, in raising his stick for that purpose, he accidentally hit the plaintiff in his eye, and wounded him, this was the result of pure accident, or was involuntary and unavoidable, and therefore the action would not lie. . . .

The court instructed the jury, that if it was not a necessary act, and the defendant was not duty bound to part the dogs, but might with propriety interfere or not as he chose, the defendant was responsible for the consequences of the blow, unless it appeared that he was in the exercise of extraordinary care, so that the accident was inevitable, using the word not in a strict but a popular sense. This is to be taken in connection with the charge afterwards given, that if the jury believed, that the act of interference in the fight was unnecessary (that is, as before explained, not a duty incumbent on the defendant), then the burden of proving extraordinary care on the part of the defendant, or want of ordinary care on the part of plaintiff, was on the defendant.

The court are of opinion that these directions were not conformable to law. If the act of hitting the plaintiff was unintentional, on the part of the defendant, and done in the doing of a lawful act, then the defendant was not liable, unless it was done in the want of exercise of due care, adapted to the exigency of the case, and therefore such want of due care became part of the plaintiff's case, and the burden of proof was on the plaintiff to establish it. . . .

Perhaps the learned judge, by the use of the term extraordinary care, in the above charge, explained as it is by the context, may have intended nothing more than that increased degree of care and diligence, which the exigency of particular circumstances might require, and which men of ordinary care and prudence would use under like circumstances, to guard against danger. If such was the meaning of this part of the charge, then it does not differ from our views, as above explained. But we are of opinion, that the other part of the charge, that the burden of proof was on the defendant, was incorrect. Those facts which are essential to enable the plaintiff to recover, he takes the burden of proving. The evidence may be offered by the plaintiff or by the defendant; the question of due care, or want of care, may be essentially connected with the main facts, and arise from the same proof; but the effect of the rule as to the burden of proof is this, that when the proof is all in, and before the jury, from whatever side it comes, and whether directly proved, or inferred from circumstances, if it appears that the defendant was doing a lawful act, and unintentionally hit and hurt the plaintiff, then unless it also appears to the satisfaction of the jury, that the defendant is chargeable with some fault, negligence, carelessness, or want of prudence, the plaintiff fails to sustain the burden of proof, and is not entitled to recover.

New trial ordered.

---

1. What did the plaintiff and the defendant apparently argue in the trial court?

2. Until *Brown*, what had been the rule for direct injuries? What did Judge Shaw say of this rule?

3. After *Brown*, what must a person show in order to recover for a physical injury?

4. What policy supports the decision in *Brown*? What would corporate America think of this case at the time it was decided?

5. Who has the burden of proving fault after *Brown*?

Hammontree v. Jenner

Court of Appeal of California, 1971
97 Cal. Rptr. 739

Lillie, J.

Plaintiffs Maxine Hammontree and her husband sued defendant for personal injuries and property damage arising out of an automobile accident. The cause was tried to a jury. Plaintiffs appeal from judgment entered on a jury verdict returned against them and in favor of defendant.

The evidence shows that on the afternoon of April 25, 1967, defendant was driving his 1959 Chevrolet home from work; at the same time plaintiff Maxine Hammontree was working in a bicycle shop owned and operated by her and her husband; without warning defendant's car crashed through the wall of the shop, struck Maxine and caused personal injuries and damage to the shop.

Defendant claimed he became unconscious during an epileptic seizure losing control of his car. He did not recall the accident but his last recollection before it, was leaving a stop light after his last stop, and his first recollection after the accident was being taken out of his car in plaintiffs' shop. Defendant testified he has a medical history of epilepsy and knows of no other reason for his loss of consciousness except an epileptic seizure; prior to 1952 he had been examined by several neurologists whose conclusion was that the condition could be controlled and who placed him on medication; in 1952 he suffered a seizure while fishing; several days later he went to Dr. Benson Hyatt who diagnosed his condition as petit mal seizure and kept him on the same medication; thereafter he saw Dr. Hyatt every six months and then on a yearly basis several years prior to 1967; in 1953 he had another seizure, was told he was an epileptic and continued his medication; in 1954 Dr. Kershner prescribed dilantin and in 1955 Dr. Hyatt prescribed phelantin; from 1955 until the accident occurred (1967) defendant had used phelantin on a regular basis which controlled his condition; defendant has continued to take medication as prescribed by his physician and has done everything his doctors told him to do to avoid a seizure; he had no inkling or warning that he was about to have a seizure prior to the occurrence of the accident.

In 1955 or 1956 the Department of Motor Vehicles was advised that defendant was an epileptic and placed him on probation under which every six months he had to report to the doctor who was required to advise it in writing of defendant's condition. In 1960 his probation was changed to a once-a-year report.

Dr. Hyatt testified that during the times he saw defendant, and according to his history, defendant "was doing normally" and that he continued to take phelantin; that "[the] purpose of the [phelantin] would be to react on the nervous system in such a way that where, without the medication, I would say to raise the threshold so that he would not be as subject to these episodes without the medication, so as not to have the seizures. He would not be having the seizures with the medication as he would without the medication compared to taking medication"; in a seizure it would be impossible for a person to drive and control an automobile; he believed it was safe for defendant to drive.

Appellants' contentions that the trial court erred in refusing to grant their motion for summary judgment on the issue of liability and their motion for directed verdict on the pleadings and counsel's opening argument are answered by the disposition of their third claim that the trial court committed prejudicial error in refusing to give their jury instruction on absolute liability.[1]

---

1. "When the evidence shows that a driver of a motor vehicle on a public street or highway loses his ability to safely operate and control such vehicle because of some seizure or health failure, that driver is nevertheless legally liable for all injuries and property damage which an innocent person may suffer as a proximate result of the defendant's inability to so control or operate his motor vehicle. This is true even if you find the defendant driver had no warning of any such impending seizure or health failure."

Under the present state of the law found in appellate authorities beginning with *Waters v. Pacific Coast Dairy, Inc.*, 55 Cal. App. 2d 789, 791–793 [131 P.2d 588] (driver rendered unconscious from sharp pain in left arm and shoulder) through *Ford v. Carew & English*, 89 Cal. App. 2d 199, 203–204 [200 P.2d 828] (fainting spells from strained heart muscles), *Zabunoff v. Walker*, 192 Cal. App. 2d 8, 11 [13 Cal. Rptr. 463] (sudden sneeze), and *Tanny-hill v. Pacific Motor Trans. Co.*, 227 Cal. App. 2d 512, 520 [38 Cal. Rptr. 774] (heart attack), the trial judge properly refused the instruction. The foregoing cases generally hold that liability of a driver, suddenly stricken by an illness rendering him unconscious, for injury resulting from an accident occcuring during that time rests on principles of negligence. However, herein during the trial plaintiffs withdrew their claim of negligence and, after both parties rested and before jury argument, objected to the giving of any instructions on negligence electing to stand solely on the theory of absolute liability. The objection was overruled and the court refused plaintiffs' requested instruction after which plaintiffs waived both opening and closing jury arguments. Defendant argued the cause to the jury after which the judge read a series of negligence instructions and, on his own motion, BAJI 4.02 (res ipsa loquitur).

Appellants seek to have this court override the established law of this state which is dispositive of the issue before us as outmoded in today's social and economic structure, particularly in the light of the now recognized principles imposing liability upon the manufacturer, retailer and all distributive and vending elements and activities which bring a product to the consumer to his injury, on the basis of strict liability in tort expressed first in Justice Traynor's concurring opinion in *Escola v. Coca Cola Bottling Co.*, 24 Cal. 2d 453, 461–468 [150 P.2d 436]; and then in *Greenman v. Yuba Power Products, Inc.*, 59 Cal. 2d 57 [27 Cal. Rptr. 697, 377 P.2d 897]; . . . These authorities hold that "A manufacturer [or retailer] is strictly liable in tort when an article he places on the market, knowing that it is to be used without inspection for defects, proves to have a defect that causes injury to a human being." (*Greenman v. Yuba Power Products, Inc.*, supra, 59 Cal. 2d 57, 62; . . .) Drawing a parallel with these products liability cases, appellants argue, with some degree of logic, that only the driver affected by a physical condition which could suddenly render him unconscious and who is aware of that condition can anticipate the hazards and foresee the dangers involved in his operation of a motor vehicle, and that the liability of those who by reason of seizure or heart failure or some other physical condition lose the ability to safely operate and control a motor vehicle resulting in injury to an innocent person should be predicated on strict liability.

We decline to superimpose the absolute liability of products liability cases upon drivers under the circumstances here. The theory on which those cases are predicated is that manufacturers, retailers and distributors of products are engaged in the business of distributing goods to the public and are an integral part of the over-all producing and marketing enterprise that should bear the cost of injuries from defective parts. (*Vandermark v. Ford Motor Co.*, 61 Cal. 2d 256, 262 [37 Cal. Rptr. 896, 391 P.2d 168]; . . .) This policy hardly applies here and it is not enough to simply say, as do appellants, that the insurance carriers should be the ones to bear the cost of injuries to innocent victims on a strict liability basis. In *Maloney v. Rath*, 69 Cal. 2d 442 [71 Cal. Rptr. 897, 445 P.2d 513], . . . appellant urged that defendant's violation of a safety provision (defective brakes) of the Vehicle Code makes the violator strictly liable for damages caused by the violation. While reversing the judgment for defendant upon another ground, the California Supreme Court refused to apply the doctrine of strict liability to automobile drivers. The situation involved two users of the highway but the problems of fixing responsibility under a system of strict liability are as complicated in the instant case as those in *Maloney v. Rath* (p. 447), and could only create uncertainty in the area of its concern. As stated in *Maloney*, at page 446: "To invoke a rule of strict liability on users of the streets and highways, however, without also establishing in substantial detail how the new rule should operate would only contribute confusion to the automobile accident problem. Settlement and claims adjustment procedures would become chaotic until the new rules were worked out on a case-by-case basis, and the hardships of delayed compensation would be seriously intensified. Only the Legislature, if it deems it wise to do so, can avoid such difficulties by enacting a comprehensive plan for the compensation of automobile accident victims in place of or in addition to the law of negligence."

The instruction tendered by appellants was properly refused for still another reason. Even assuming the merit of appellants' position under the facts of this case in which defendant knew he had a history of epilepsy, previously had suffered seizures and at the time of the accident was attempting to control the condition by medication, the instruction does not except from its ambit the driver who suddenly is stricken by an illness or physical condition which he had no reason whatever to anticipate and of which he had no prior knowledge.

The judgment is affirmed.

Wood, P.J., and Thompson, J., concur.

---

1. Who bears the loss in *Hammontree*? Why did the jury not find the defendant negligent?

2. What is the reasoning underlying the court of appeals decision? Construct an argument that would come out in the plaintiffs' favor. What advantages might there be for persons with disabilities that affect their ability to drive to a result in favor of the plaintiff? Why should the plaintiffs be obligated to cover the costs of the accident here? What caused the accident?

3. What is the policy underlying strict liability for defective products? Why does this court reject that policy?

4. What result if the defendant had been operating a taxi?

5. Argue that the plaintiff should or should not recover because the defendant has insurance. Note that few cases discuss insurance. Why? What if the defendant had been paying a surcharge on his insurance based on his diagnosis?

6. The cases often use the terms absolute liability and strict liability without drawing a distinction. To recover in absolute liability, the plaintiff need only prove causation. To recover under strict liability for a product, however, the plaintiff must prove causation and that the product is defective. He or she does not have to prove intent or negligence, but may be subject to defenses, such as assumption of risk or contributory negligence. This will be further considered in the Products Liability chapter.

Langan v. Valicopters, Inc.
Supreme Court of Washington, 1977
567 P.2d 218

DOLLIVER, J.

This is an appeal from a judgment against appellants for damages resulting from their crop spraying activities. Patrick and Dorothy Langan, respondents, own a small (2 1/2 to 3 acre) farm in the Yakima Valley. The Langans are organic farmers: that is, they use no nonorganic fertilizers, insecticides or herbicides to aid them in their farming but rely on natural fertilizers and natural pest control agents. They had planned to can and sell their produce to organic food buyers.

Valicopters, Inc., is a Washington corporation which engages in the aerial application of agricultural pesticides. Gene Bepple, one of the owners of Valicopters, Inc., was the helicopter pilot at the time of the incident giving rise to this lawsuit. The Thalheimers, doing business as Thalheimer Farms, owned and farmed the land adjoining that of the respondents. It was their land that was being sprayed by Valicopters. Simplot Soilbuilders sold the agricultural chemical to Thalheimers for aerial application.

On June 3, 1973, Bepple sprayed for Colorado beetle infestation on the Thalheimer farm with a chemical pesticide known as Thiodan. A small patch of the farm was sprayed with the chemical Guthion. While applying the pesticides to Thalheimers' property, Bepple traveled approximately 45 miles per hour while 6 to 8 feet off the ground with a 42-foot application boom extending from the sides of the helicopter. Patrick Langan testified that, during one spraying pass, the helicopter began spraying while it was over his property. This testimony was disputed. He further testified that the spray settled on the entire length of their tomato, bean, garlic, cucumber and Jerusalem artichoke rows.

The Langans and other organic farmers founded and are members of the Northwest Organic Food Producers' Association (NOFPA). The bylaws of NOFPA contain the following pertinent provisions:

> 7. No poisonous insecticides, repellents, herbicides, artificial fertilizers, stimulants or hormones may be used on food or in soil in which products are grown or animals are grazed. If any such item is applied by the grower to any committed acreage that has been previously committed and certified,

the acreage will be withdrawn from certification and this farmer cannot be recertified without approval of the Executive Committee.

9. No member shall be allowed to market foods or advertise food as certified organically grown by NOFPA if laboratory tests on the finished crop indicates [sic] the presence of more than ten percent (10%) of the maximum pesticide residue tolerances allowable by the Food and Drug Administration. In the event the finished crop reflects a residue higher than the allowable tolerances set forth in this section, the member's seal for any such crop shall immediately be suspended and public notice made thereof.

NOFPA Bylaws, art. 4, §§ 7, 9.

A laboratory test conducted after the spraying indicated the presence of 1.4 parts per million by weight of Thiodan on the Langans' crop tissue. The United States Department of Health Education and Welfare, Food and Drug Administration's tolerance for Thiodan on tomatoes and beans is 2.0 parts per million. Following the test results, the board of directors of NOFPA revoked the Langans' certification as organic food growers in conformance with bylaw No. 7. The Langans' entire property was decertified in conformance with the NOFPA rule which requires decertification when a portion of the land is contaminated.

Due to the decertification, the Langans did not grow their tomatoes and beans to fruition. Instead, they pulled them from the ground to prevent further contamination of the soil. The Langans had no contract to sell the contaminated tomatoes and beans commercially.

After a jury trial, a judgment in the amount of $5,500 was entered against appellants. They appealed to the Court of Appeals, Division Three. That court certified the case to this court and we accepted certification.

At the outset, it must be determined whether there was substantial evidence to support the jury's finding that respondents' damage occurred as a result of the spraying. Appellants contend that NOFPA erroneously interpreted its own bylaws. They argue that neither rule No. 7 nor rule No. 9 required immediate decertification of appellants' property and that the tomatoes and beans should have been tested for chemicals when those crops had fully matured. The bylaws of that organization are essentially a contract between NOFPA and its members. . . .

A director of NOFPA testified that their interpretation of rule No. 7, coupled with the basic purpose of NOFPA (to insure consumers that the products are organically grown if they are sold under the organization's seal) required decertification of respondents' farm. The Langans apparently agreed with this interpretation and did not question the legitimacy of the decertification. This decertification, which prompted the Langans to pull the crops, provided substantial evidence for the jury to conclude that they suffered damage as a result of crop spraying.

The next issue is whether the trial court erred by instructing the jury that appellants would be strictly liable for damage that was proximately caused by their aerial spraying. The trial judge gave the following instruction:

> If you find that defendants' chemicals fell upon plaintiffs' crops, you are instructed that as a matter of law the defendants are liable for such damage to plaintiffs' crops, if any, as you find was proximately caused by defendants' spray application.

Liability for damage caused by crop dusting or spraying generally is imposed on the basis of either negligence or strict liability. . . . The courts in most jurisdictions that have held crop dusters liable have used the theory of negligence. . . . However, other opinions which have ostensibly relied upon the principles of negligence have been criticized by legal writers because the reasoning is not clear or more nearly resembles strict liability.

Three jurisdictions have held crop dusting to be an activity to which the principles of strict liability apply. . . . In *Loe v. Lenhardt*, [227 Or. 242, 362 P.2d 312 (1961)] *supra*, Justice Goodwin, writing for the majority, noted that the dangers of spraying agricultural chemicals by aircraft has been the subject of considerable legislative attention nationwide, citing the laws of 29 states. These laws, he concluded, were evidence of the dangerous character of aerial spraying. The court recognized the activity was one capable of inflicting damage notwithstanding the exercise of utmost care by the applicator, and that the damage was within the scope of the risk created by spraying an adjoining field. The court cited *Bedell v. Goulter*, 199 Ore. 344, 362–63, 261 P.2d 842 (1953), a case involving strict liability for blasting, in which it stated:

> ". . . Basic to the problem is 'an adjustment of conflicting interests,' . . . of the right of the blaster, on the one hand, to pursue a lawful occupation and the right of an owner of land, on the other, to its peaceful enjoyment and possession. Where damage is sustained by the latter through the nonculpable activities of the former, who should bear the loss—the man who caused it or a 'third person,' as Judge Hand says, 'who has no relation to the explosion, other than that of injury'?"

Loe v. Lenhardt, supra at 253–54.

In Washington, this court has adopted the Restatement (Second) of Torts §§ 519, 520 (Tent. Draft No. 10, 1964). *Pacific Northwest Bell Tel. Co. v. Port of Seattle*, 80 Wn. 2d 59, 491 P.2d 1037 (1971); *Siegler v. Kuhlman*, 81 Wn. 2d 448, 502 P.2d 1181 (1972). Section 519 of the Restatement provides:

> (1) One who carries on an abnormally dangerous activity is subject to liability for harm to the person, land or chattels of another resulting from the activity, although he has exercised the utmost care to prevent such harm.

> (2) Such strict liability is limited to the kind of harm, the risk of which makes the activity abnormally dangerous.

Section 520 lists the factors to be used when determining what constitutes an abnormally dangerous activity:

> In determining whether an activity is abnormally dangerous, the following factors are to be considered:
>
> (a) Whether the activity involves a high degree of risk of some harm to the person, land or chattels of others;
>
> (b) Whether the gravity of the harm which may result from it is likely to be great;
>
> (c) Whether the risk cannot be eliminated by the exercise of reasonable care;
>
> (d) Whether the activity is not a matter of common usage;
>
> (e) Whether the activity is inappropriate to the place where it is carried on; and
>
> (f) The value of the activity to the community.

Whether an activity is abnormally dangerous is a question of law for the court to decide. *Siegler v. Kuhlman, supra;* Restatement (Second) of Torts § 520, comment (1) (Tent. Draft No. 10, 1964). In making this determination, we have considered each of the factors listed in the Restatement, section 520.

> The essential question is whether the risk created is so unusual, either because of its magnitude or because of the circumstances surrounding it, as to justify the imposition of strict liability for the harm which results from it, even though it is carried on with all reasonable care.

Restatement (Second) of Torts § 520, comment (f) (Tent. Draft No. 10, 1964). *See generally* Peck, "Negligence and Liability Without Fault in Tort Law," 46 Wash. L. Rev. 225 (1971). However, in this case, each test of the Restatement is met. [The court then applied the six Restatement factors to crop dusting.]

. . . .

There is no doubt that pesticides are socially valuable in the control of insects, weeds and other pests. They may benefit society by increasing production. Whether strict liability or negligence principles should be applied amounts to a balancing of conflicting social interest — the risk of harm versus the utility of the activity. In balancing these interests, we must ask who should bear the loss caused by the pesticides. . . .

In the present case, the Langans were eliminated from the organic food market for 1973 through no fault of their own. If crop dusting continues on the adjoining property, the Langens [sic] may never be able to sell their crops to organic food buyers. Appellants, on the other hand, will all profit from the continued application of pesticides. Under these circumstances, there can be an equitable balancing of social interests only if appellants are made to pay for the consequences of their acts.

We realize that farmers are statutorily bound to prevent the spread of insects, pests, noxious weeds and diseases. RCW 15.08.030 and RCW 17.10.140, 150. But the fulfillment of that duty does not mean the ability of an organic farmer to produce organic crops must be destroyed without compensation.

Thus, for the reasons mentioned above, we find that the trial court did not err by instructing the jury on strict liability.

. . . .

There is no reversible error; the judgment of the trial court is affirmed.

———————

1. What is the policy behind strict liability in *Langan*? Would the argument in *Langan* work in *Hammontree*? Why or why not?

2. Would it be fair to say that strict liability impedes progress? What do you think of the statement in *Spano v. Perini Corp.*, 25 N.Y.2d 11, 302 N.Y.S.2d 527, 250 N.E.2d 31 (1969): "The plaintiff . . . was not seeking, as the court implied, to 'exclude the defendant from blasting' . . . he was merely seeking compensation for the damage which was inflicted upon his own property as a result of that blasting. The question . . . was not *whether* it was lawful or proper to engage in blasting but *who* should bear the cost of any resulting damage—the person who engaged in the dangerous activity or the innocent neighbor injured thereby."

3. What could plaintiff or defendant have done to prevent the injury in *Langan*?

4. Note that the law has come full circle since the early middle ages. Wex Malone told us that, as of 1300, tort law was founded on absolute liability. In 1616, we saw a wisp of negligence in *Weaver v. Ward*. Negligence emerged as a fully feathered cause of action in 1850. Indeed, it appeared that absolute and strict liability were perhaps dead. Then strict liability emerged for abnormally dangerous activities, such as blasting and crop dusting, as presented in *Langan*. Strict liability for defective products, suggested in *Escola* (presented in *Hammontree*), became the dominant cause of action for cases involving defective products following the *Greenman* decision (also presented in *Hammontree*) in 1963. Strict liability and products liability will be discussed in later chapters. Much of our effort will now be devoted to the various aspects of intentional torts and negligence.

Chapter 2

Intentional Torts

The element of intent distinguishes the intentional torts from torts based on negligence or strict liability. Whether a tort is intentional or the product of negligence (accidental) has a major impact upon what the plaintiff must prove and upon what the defendants must pay should they be found liable.

The concept of intent has led to differences in treatment between intentional torts, on the one hand, and negligence and strict liability based torts, on the other. One difference of particular significance to plaintiffs seeking a substantial recovery is that the doctrine of respondeat superior is inapplicable in intentional tort cases. Under respondeat superior, an employer is liable for negligent torts committed by an employee when the employee is acting within the scope of his or her employment. Except in certain situations involving occupations like security guards and bouncers, intentional torts are, virtually by definition, only rarely within the scope of employment because of their intentional nature, and thus an employer who is liable when his or her employee commits a negligent tort is not liable when the tort is intentional. Another difference appears in the context of causation. There is no concept of proximate cause in the world of intentional torts: the defendant is simply liable for all of the consequences of his or her intentional act. Another difference appears in the realm of damages. If the tort was intentional, the courts do not generally require evidence of actual injury in order for the plaintiff to recover. Of course, if there was injury, the plaintiff will recover for that injury, but even if there was none, the plaintiff may recover nominal or other damages for the dignitary harm inflicted by the very fact that the intentional tort took place. Moreover, punitive damages, rarely available in negligence or strict liability contexts, may be awarded if the tort involved was intentional.

Perhaps because of the moral content inherent in the idea that the tort was committed at least to some extent on purpose, with the corollary availability of punitive damages, courts are adamant that the elements of each intentional tort be precisely proven in order for the plaintiff to prevail. In this respect, the intentional torts are easier to learn than the inherently more nebulous negligence or strict liability based torts. The court has its checklist of elements, and systematically marks off each one as the plaintiff makes his or her way through the case.

A. Intent in General

The element of intent divides the intentional torts from those which are the products of negligence. Thus, defining intent becomes central to the question of whether any intentional tort took place at all. Many courts use cases involving children as a vehicle for defining intent.

Garratt v. Dailey

Supreme Court of Washington, 1955
279 P.2d 1091

HILL, JUSTICE.

The liability of an infant for an alleged battery is presented to this court for the first time. Brian Dailey (age five years, nine months) was visiting with Naomi Garratt, an adult and a sister of the plaintiff, Ruth Garratt, likewise an adult, in the back yard of the plaintiff's home, on July 16, 1951. It is plaintiff's contention that she came out into the back yard to talk with Naomi and that, as she started to sit down in a wood and canvas lawn chair, Brian deliberately pulled it out from under her. The only one of the three persons present so testifying was Naomi Garratt. (Ruth Garratt, the plaintiff, did not testify as to how or why she fell.) The trial court, unwilling to accept this testimony, adopted instead Brian Dailey's version of what happened, and made the following findings:

> "III. . . . that while Naomi Garratt and Brian Dailey were in the back yard the plaintiff, Ruth Garratt, came out of her house into the back yard. Some time subsequent thereto defendant, Brian Dailey, picked up a lightly built wood and canvas lawn chair which was then and there located in the back yard of the above described premises, moved it sideways a few feet and seated himself therein, at which time he discovered the plaintiff, Ruth Garratt, about to sit down at the place where the lawn chair had formerly been, at which time he hurriedly got up from the chair and attempted to move it toward Ruth Garratt to aid her in sitting down in the chair; that due to the defendant's small size and lack of dexterity he was unable to get the lawn chair under the plaintiff in time to prevent her from falling to the ground. That plaintiff fell to the ground and sustained a fracture of her hip, and other injuries and damages as hereinafter set forth.

> "IV. That the preponderance of the evidence in this case establishes that when the defendant, Brian Dailey, moved the chair in question *he did not have any willful or unlawful purpose* in doing so; that *he did not have any intent to injure the plaintiff or any intent to bring about any unauthorized or offensive contact with her person* or any objects appurtenant thereto; that the circumstances which immediately preceded the fall of the plaintiff established that the defendant, *Brian Dailey, did not have purpose, intent or design to perform a prank or to effect an assault and battery upon the person of the plaintiff*" (Italics ours, for a purpose hereinafter indicated.)

It is conceded that Ruth Garratt's fall resulted in a fractured hip and other painful and serious injuries. To obviate the necessity of a retrial in the event this court determines that she was entitled to a judgment against Brian Dailey, the amount of her damage was found to be $11,000. Plaintiff appeals from a judgment dismissing the action and asks for the entry of a judgment in that amount or a new trial.

The authorities generally, but with certain notable exceptions, state that when a minor has committed a tort with force he is liable to be proceeded against as any other person would be.

In our analysis of the applicable law, we start with the basic premise that Brian, whether five or fifty-five, must have committed some wrongful act before he could be liable for appellant's injuries.

. . . .

It is urged that Brian's action in moving the chair constituted a battery. A definition (not all-inclusive but sufficient for our purpose) of a battery is the intentional infliction of a harmful bodily contact upon another. The rule that determines liability for battery is given in 1 Restatement, Torts, 29, § 13, as:

> "An act which, directly or indirectly, is the legal cause of a harmful contact with another's person makes the actor liable to the other, if
>
> "(a) the act is done with the intention of bringing about a harmful or offensive contact or an apprehension thereof to the other or a third person, and
>
> "(b) the contact is not consented to by the other or the other's consent thereto is procured by fraud or duress, and
>
> "(c) the contact is not otherwise privileged."

We have in this case no question of consent or privilege. We therefore proceed to an immediate consideration of intent and its place in the law of battery. In the comment on clause (a), the Restatement says:

> "*Character of actor's intention.* In order that an act may be done with the intention of bringing about a harmful or offensive contact or an apprehension thereof to a particular person, either the other or a third person, the act must be done for the purpose of causing the contact or apprehension or with knowledge on the part of the actor that such contact or apprehension is substantially certain to be produced." *See, also,* Prosser on Torts 41, § 8.

We have here the conceded volitional act of Brian, *i.e.,* the moving of a chair. Had the plaintiff proved to the satisfaction of the trial court that Brian moved the chair while she was in the act of sitting down, Brian's action would patently have been for the purpose or with the intent of causing the plaintiff's bodily contact with the ground, and she would be entitled to a judgment against him for the resulting damages.

The plaintiff based her case on that theory, and the trial court held that she failed in her proof and accepted Brian's version of the facts rather than that given by the eye-witness who testified for the plaintiff. After the trial court determined that the plaintiff had not established her theory of a battery (*i.e.,* that Brian had pulled the chair out from under the plaintiff while she was in the act of sitting down), it then became concerned with whether a battery was established under the facts as it found them to be.

In this connection, we quote another portion of the comment on the "Character of actor's intention," relating to clause (a) of the rule from the Restatement heretofore set forth:

> "It is not enough that the act itself is intentionally done and this, even though the actor realizes or should realize that it contains a very grave risk of bringing about the contact or apprehension. Such realization may make the actor's conduct negligent or even reckless but unless he realizes that to a substantial certainty, the contact or apprehension will result, the actor has not that intention which is necessary to make him liable under the rule stated in this section."

A battery would be established if, in addition to plaintiff's fall, it was proved that, when Brian moved the chair, he knew with substantial certainty that the plaintiff would attempt to sit down where the chair had been. If Brian had any of the intents which the trial court found, in the italicized portions of the findings of fact quoted above, that he did not have, he would of course have had the knowledge to which we have referred. The mere absence of any intent to injure the plaintiff or to play a prank on her or to embarrass her, or to commit an assault and battery on her would not absolve him from liability if in fact he had such knowledge. Without such knowledge, there would be nothing wrongful about Brian's act in moving the chair and, there being no wrongful act, there would be no liability.

While a finding that Brian had no such knowledge can be inferred from the findings made, we believe that before the plaintiff's action in such a case should be dismissed there should be no question but that the trial court had passed upon that issue; hence, the case should be remanded for clarification of the findings to specifically cover the question of Brian's knowledge, because intent could be inferred therefrom. If the court finds that he had such knowledge the necessary intent will be established and the plaintiff will be entitled to recover, even though there was no purpose to injure or embarrass the plaintiff. If Brian did not have such knowledge, there was no wrongful act by him and the basic premise of liability on the theory of a battery was not established.

It will be noted that the law of battery as we have discussed it is the law applicable to adults, and no significance has been attached to the fact that Brian was a child less than six years of age when the alleged battery occurred. The only circumstance where Brian's age is of any consequence is in determining what he knew, and there his experience, capacity, and understanding are of course material.

From what has been said, it is clear that we find no merit in plaintiff's contention that we can direct the entry of a judgment for $11,000 in her favor on the record now before us.

Nor do we find any error in the record that warrants a new trial.

. . . .

The cause is remanded for clarification, with instructions to make definite findings on the issue of whether Brian Dailey knew with substantial certainty that the plaintiff would attempt to sit down where the chair which he moved had been, and to change the judgment if the findings warrant it.

. . . .

Remanded for clarification.

SCHWELLENBACH, DONWORTH, and WEAVER, JJ., concur.

———————

1. Why didn't Ruth Garratt, the plaintiff, testify as to why she fell?

2. How does the court define intent? Did the court require that Brian know that the plaintiff might fall, or did the court require that Brian know that the plaintiff might be injured? If the plaintiff had not been injured, would Brian win?

3. If Brian had been an adult, what might this opinion have looked like?

4. In *Garratt*, the court focused on the fact question of whether, in fact, Brian had the intent necessary to treat the tort as an intentional one. Brian's age, as such, was irrelevant; what was important was whether he possessed the requisite intent. While his age may be significant in answering this question, it is only significant insofar as it contributes to the jury's ability to decide whether he, in fact, intended the results of his action.

Some courts treat children under seven as incapable of possessing the intent required for liability for an intentional tort as a matter of law, drawing the analogy to the rule in their jurisdictions that children under seven are, as a matter of law, incapable of contributory negligence. *DeLuca v. Bowden*, 329 N.E.2d 109 (Ohio 1975).

Garratt v. Dailey and *DeLuca v. Bowden* illustrate the alternative approaches to children taken in negligence cases as well as intentional tort cases. Some courts apply "bright line" rules, with the standard of care and potential liability of the child depending on that child's age. Other courts look at the individual child, irrespective of age, to determine whether *that* child has the capacity to act negligently or intentionally.

Wallace v. Rosen

Indiana Court of Appeals, Second District, 2002
765 N.E.2d 192

KIRSCH, JUDGE.

Mable Wallace appeals the jury verdict in favor of Indianapolis Public Schools (IPS) and Harriet Rosen, a teacher for IPS. On appeal, Wallace raises the following issues:

I. Whether the trial court erred in refusing to give her tendered jury instruction regarding battery.

II. Whether the trial court erred in instructing the jury regarding the defense of incurred risk.

We affirm.

FACTS AND PROCEDURAL HISTORY

In 1994, Rosen was a teacher at Northwest High School in Indianapolis. On April 22, 1994, the high school had a fire drill while classes were in session. The drill was not previously announced to the teachers and occurred just one week after a fire was extinguished in a bathroom near Rosen's classroom.

On the day the alarm sounded, Wallace was at the high school delivering homework to her daughter Lalaya. Because Wallace was recovering from foot surgery and Lalaya's class was on the second floor, Lalaya's boyfriend Eric Fuqua accompanied Wallace up the stairs. Wallace and Fuqua were near the top of the staircase when they saw Lalaya and began to speak with her. Jamie Arnold, a student who knew Lalaya and her mother, joined the conversation. The alarm then sounded and students began filing down the stairs while Wallace took a step or two up the stairs to the second floor landing.

In response to the alarm, Rosen escorted her class to the designated stairway and noticed three or four people talking together at the top of the stairway and blocking the students' exit. Rosen did not recognize any of the individuals but approached "telling everybody to move it." *Transcript* at 35. Wallace, with her back to Rosen, was unable to hear Rosen over the noise of the alarm and Rosen had to touch her on the back to get her attention. *Id.* at 259. Rosen then told Wallace, "you've got to get moving because this is a fire drill." *Id.* 259.

At trial, Wallace testified that Rosen pushed her down the stairs. *Id.* at 128. Rosen denied pushing Wallace and testified that Wallace had not fallen, but rather had made her way down the stairs unassisted and without losing her balance. *Id.* at 265–66.

At the close of the trial, Wallace tendered an instruction concerning civil battery. Over Wallace's objection, the court refused to read the instruction to the jury. IPS and Rosen tendered an instruction concerning the defense of incurred risk on the basis that Wallace had continued up the stairs after hearing the alarm, had stopped at the landing to talk, and had blocked the students' exit. Over Wallace's objection, the court gave the incurred risk instruction. The jury found in favor of IPS and Rosen, and Wallace now appeals.

I. Battery Instruction

Wallace first argues that it was error for the trial court to refuse to give the jury the following tendered instruction pertaining to battery:

> A battery is the knowing or intentional touching of one person by another in a rude, insolent, or angry manner.

Any touching, however slight, may constitute an assault and battery.

Also, a battery may be recklessly committed where one acts in reckless disregard of the consequences, and the fact the person does not intend that the act shall result in an injury is immaterial.

Wallace argues that the omission of the instruction was error because the instruction was an accurate statement of the law, was supported by the evidence, and was not covered by any other instruction read to the jury. Appellees respond that the instruction was properly omitted because there was no evidence presented that supported a battery instruction.

. . . .

[I]t is correct to tell the jury that, relying on circumstantial evidence, they may infer that the actor's state of mind was the same as a reasonable person's state of mind would have been. Thus, . . . the defendant on a bicycle who rides down a person in full view on a sidewalk where there is ample room to pass may learn that the factfinder (judge or jury) is unwilling to credit the statement, "I didn't mean to do it."

On the other hand, the mere knowledge and appreciation of a risk — something short of substantial certainty — is not intent. The defendant who acts in the belief or consciousness that the act is causing an appreciable risk of harm to another may be negligent, and if the risk is great the conduct may be characterized as reckless or wanton, but it is not an intentional wrong. In such cases the distinction between intent and negligence obviously is a matter of degree. The line has to be drawn by the courts at the point where the known danger ceases to be only a foreseeable risk which a reasonable person would avoid, and becomes in the mind of the actor a substantial certainty.

The intent with which tort liability is concerned is not necessarily a hostile intent, or a desire to do any harm. Rather it is an intent to bring about a result which will invade the interests of another in a way that the law forbids. The defendant may be liable although intending nothing more than a good-natured practical joke, or honestly believing that the act would not injure the plaintiff, or even though seeking the plaintiff's own good.

W. Page Keeton et al., Prosser and Keeton on the Law of Torts, § 8, at 33, 36–37 (5th ed. 1984) (footnotes omitted).

Wallace, Lalaya, and Fuqua testified that Rosen touched Wallace on the back causing her to fall down the stairs and injure herself. For battery to be an appropriate instruction, the evidence had to support an inference not only that Rosen intentionally touched Wallace, but that she did so in a rude, insolent, or angry manner, i.e., that she intended to invade Wallace's interests in a way that the law forbids.

Professors Prosser and Keeton also made the following observations about the intentional tort of battery and the character of the defendant's action:

> In a crowded world, a certain amount of personal contact is inevitable and must be accepted. *Absent expression to the contrary, consent is assumed to all those ordinary contacts which are customary and reasonably necessary to the common intercourse of life, such as a tap on the shoulder to attract attention*, a friendly grasp of the arm, or a casual jostling to make a passage....
>
> The time and place, and the circumstances under which the act is done, will necessarily affect its unpermitted character, and so will the relations between the parties. A stranger is not to be expected to tolerate liberties which would be allowed by an intimate friend. But unless the defendant has special reason to believe that more or less will be permitted by the individual plaintiff, the test is what would be offensive to an ordinary person not unduly sensitive as to personal dignity.

Keeton et al., § 9, at 42 (emphasis added).

. . . .

Viewed most favorably to the trial court's decision refusing the tendered instruction, the evidence ... indicates that Rosen placed her fingertips on Wallace's shoulder and turned her 90 degrees toward the exit in the midst of a fire drill. The conditions on the stairway of Northwest High School during the fire drill were an example of Professors Prosser and Keeton's "crowded world." Individuals standing in the middle of a stairway during the fire drill could expect that a certain amount of personal contact would be inevitable. Rosen had a responsibility to her students to keep them moving in an orderly fashion down the stairs and out the door. Under these circumstances, Rosen's touching of Wallace's shoulder or back with her fingertips to get her attention over the noise of the alarm cannot be said to be a rude, insolent, or angry touching. Wallace has failed to show that the trial court abused its discretion in refusing the battery instruction.

Furthermore, even if an instruction on battery was appropriate, Wallace's inclusion of language that "a battery may be recklessly committed" created an instruction that was likely to mislead or confuse the jury under the facts of this case.... *Mercer v. Corbin*, 117 Ind. 450, 20 N.E. 132 (1889) (the supreme court, ignoring the defendant's statement that he didn't mean to hit the plaintiff, found that the defendant committed assault and battery when he rode his bicycle over the plaintiff who was standing on one side of a fourteen-foot-wide sidewalk in broad daylight); *Reynolds v. Pierson*, 29 Ind. App. 273, 64 N.E. 484 (1902) ("horse play" in which the defendant jerked and pulled with sufficient force to throw the plaintiff off another's arm and injure him revealed a reckless disregard of the consequences and thus supplied grounds for inferring defendant's constructive intent and the willful act of battery).

The facts in this case can be distinguished from those cited by the Committee. Rosen's actions were clearly not intentional like the facts in *Kline*, nor can it be said that Rosen's touching arose from a recklessness or wanton disregard of human life and safety found in *Mercer*. Quite the contrary, the actions that Rosen took were intended to keep the student traffic flowing out of the building and away from any potential danger.... The inclusion of the reckless instruction with the intentional tort of battery under the facts of this case would have allowed the jury to use a lesser standard to convict Rosen and IPS of battery. We find that the inclusion of the "reckless" language in the battery instruction would have been misleading and made the instructions as a whole confusing to the jury.

A fire had been actually set in the bathroom on Rosen's floor less than a week before the fire alarm sounded. On April 22, 1994, with no prior knowledge whether the alarm signaled a drill or a fire, Rosen exercised ordinary and reasonable care when she tried to get the students to exit as quickly as possible. Finding Wallace and three others creating a bottleneck at the top of the staircase required Rosen to take quick action. It was necessary for Rosen to both raise her voice and touch Wallace's back to get her attention. When Wallace objected to being touched and did not move, it was also reasonable for Rosen to turn Wallace toward the stairs and tell her to get moving. Failing to give the battery instruction was not error because, even if given, the facts of this case would not have supported a claim for intentional battery.

. . . .

Affirmed.

SULLIVAN, J., concurs with separate opinion.

ROBB, J., concurs in part and concurs in result in part with separate opinion.

Vosburg v. Putney

Supreme Court of Wisconsin, 1891
50 N.W. 403

APPEAL from the Circuit Court for Waukesha County.

The action was brought to recover damages for an assault and battery, alleged to have been committed by the defendant upon the plaintiff on February 20, 1889. The answer is a general denial.

The injury complained of was caused by a kick inflicted by defendant upon the leg of the plaintiff, a little below the knee. The transaction occurred in a school-room in Waukesha, during school hours, both parties being pupils in the school. A former trial of the cause resulted in a verdict and judgment for the plaintiff for $2,800. The defendant appealed from such judgment to this court, and the same was reversed for error, and a new trial awarded.

The case has been again tried in the circuit court, and the trial resulted in a verdict for plaintiff for $2,500. The facts of the case, as they appeared on both trials, are sufficiently stated in the opinion by MR. JUSTICE ORTON on the former appeal, and require no repetition.

. . . .

Lyon, J.

[The facts of this case are included in the opinion of Orton, J. in an earlier appeal of this case at 47 N.W. 99 (Wise. 1890). They are briefly as follows: The plaintiff was about fourteen years of age, and the defendant about eleven years of age. On the 20th day of February, 1889, they were sitting opposite to each other across an aisle in the high school of the village of Waukesha. The defendant reached across the aisle with his foot, and hit with his toe the shin of the right leg of the plaintiff. The touch was slight. The plaintiff did not feel it, either on account of its being so slight or of loss of sensation produced by the shock. In a few moments he felt a violent pain in that place, which caused him to cry out loudly. The next day he was sick, and had to be helped to school. On the fourth day he was vomiting, and Dr. Bacon was sent for, but could not come, and he sent medicine to stop the vomiting, and came to see him the next day, on the 25th. There was a slight discoloration of the skin entirely over the inner surface of the tibia an inch below the bend of the knee. The doctor applied fomentations, and gave him anodynes to quiet the pain. This treatment was continued, and the swelling so increased by the 5th day of March that counsel was called, and on the 8th of March an operation was performed on the limb by making an incision, and a moderate amount of pus escaped. A drainage tube was inserted, and an iodoform dressing put on. On the sixth day after this, another incision was made to the bone, and it was found that destruction was going on in the bone, and so it has continued exfoliating pieces of bone. He will never recover the use of his limb. There were black and blue spots on the shin bone, indicating that there had been a blow. On the 1st day of January before, the plaintiff received an injury just above the knee of the same leg by coasting, which appeared to be healing up and drying down at the time of the last injury. The theory of at least one of the medical witnesses was that the limb was in a diseased condition when this touch or kick was given, caused by microbes entering in through the wound above the knee, and which were revivified by the touch, and that the touch was the exciting or remote cause of the destruction of the bone, or of the plaintiffs injury. It does not appear that there was any visible mark made or left by this touch or kick of the defendant's foot, or any appearance of injury until the black and blue spots were discovered by the physician several days afterwards, and then there were more spots than one. There was no proof of any other hurt, and the medical testimony seems to have been agreed that this touch or kick was the exciting cause of the injury to the plaintiff. The jury rendered a verdict for the plaintiff of $2,800.]

The rule of damages in actions for torts was held in *Brown v. C, M. & St. P. R. Co. 54 Wis. 342*, to be that the wrongdoer is liable for all injuries resulting directly from the wrongful act, whether they could or could not have been foreseen by him. . . .

––––––––––

1. What is the nature of the intent required as an element in intentional tort cases? Is it subjective or objective? What is recklessness?

2. The intent of a defendant is measured by his or her acts, and not by what the defendant happened to be thinking at the time of the acts. Why did the court in

Garratt v. Bailey focus on what the defendant actually knew or might actually have been thinking? Does the idea of the "crowded world" require some examination of intent? By what standard should the crowded world be measured?

3. A defendant may be liable for battery where no harm was intended. The intent required is the intent to make unconsented-to contact; the defendant is liable for the contact and any harm that results from the contact. *Vosburg v. Putney* is perhaps the best-known case standing for this proposition. Incidentally, there was a truly startling number of appeals and remands in this case before the litigation ended.

Vosburg also illustrates the rule that the defendant is liable for all of the consequences of his or her intentional tort, whether foreseeable or not. In negligence cases, the defendant is liable for all injury proximately caused by his or her negligent actions. The concept of proximate cause enables courts to sever the chain of causation in cases where the consequences were not foreseeable to the defendant. One acts negligently only in failing to avoid foreseeable dangers; one cannot be held liable for unreasonably failing to avoid a danger which no one could have predicted. In intentional tort cases, on the other hand, reasonable avoidance is not an issue because the act was intentional. Thus, the defendant is liable for all consequences of his or her intentional tort, no matter how farfetched those consequences may be. In negligence, the defendant's conduct is evaluated by its potential for harm. In intentional torts, the defendant's conduct is evaluated by its character, and its consequences are important only insofar as they cast light upon the intentional nature of the initial act itself and serve as the basis for an award of damages.

Another case illustrating the principle that the defendant is liable for all of the consequences of his or her actions, whether foreseeable or not, is *Caudle v. Betts*, 512 So. 2d 389 (La. 1987). In *Caudle*, the defendant, as a practical joke, caused a minor electrical shock to be administered to the plaintiff. This minor electrical shock caused severe and unforeseeable nerve damage to the plaintiff, for which the defendant had to pay.

The defendant may be liable for consequences that extend beyond the intended plaintiff. In *Keel v. Hainline*, 331 P.2d 397 (Okla. 1958), the court ruled that the defendants, who contrary to school rules were engaged in throwing erasers and other projectiles at each other, were liable for battery when the projectiles struck a classmate who was not participating in the activity. The intent of the defendants to strike each other was transferred to the person who was in fact struck, and the fact that the defendants had not intended to strike the plaintiff was irrelevant.

4. It is clear that not all contact should serve as the basis for a lawsuit. Where should courts draw the line between the kinds of contact individuals should be required to tolerate and the kinds of contact for which individuals should be able to file suit?

Problem

H, a ten-year-old child, decides to see what will happen if he throws a glass soda bottle against a telephone pole. He fails to look up before throwing the bottle. He throws the bottle, and it shatters. A piece of the bottle strikes a telephone company worker who is working at the top of the pole.

The telephone company worker files suit for battery. Assuming that the worker may sue H, what arguments will the parties make on the question of intent?

B. Battery

Battery is the classic intentional tort. What is particularly interesting about the following cases is the way in which an apparently archaic tort can fit modern contexts and needs.

Mink v. University of Chicago

United States District Court for the Northern District of Illinois, 1978
460 F. Supp. 713

Memorandum Opinion

GRADY, DISTRICT JUDGE.

Plaintiffs have brought this [diversity] action on behalf of themselves and some 1,000 women who were given diethylstilbestrol ("DES") as part of a medical experiment conducted by the defendants, University of Chicago and Eli Lilly & Company, between September 29, 1950, and November 20, 1952. The drug was administered to the plaintiffs during their prenatal care at the University's Lying-in Hospital as part of a double blind study to determine the value of DES in preventing miscarriages. The women were not told they were part of an experiment, nor were they told that the pills administered to them were DES. Plaintiffs claim that as a result of their taking DES, their daughters have developed abnormal cervical cellular formations and are exposed to an increased risk of vaginal or cervical cancer. Plaintiffs also allege that they and their sons have suffered reproductive tract and other abnormalities and have incurred an increased risk of cancer.

. . . .

The complaint seeks recovery on three causes of action. The first alleges that the defendants committed a series of batteries on the plaintiffs by conducting a medical experiment on them without their knowledge or consent. The administration of DES to the plaintiffs without their consent is alleged to be an "offensive invasion of their persons" which has caused them "severe mental anxiety and emotional distress due to the increased risk to their children of contracting cancer and other abnormalities." . . . Throughout the complaint plaintiffs claim the defendants intentionally concealed the fact of the experiment and information concerning the relationship between DES and cancer from the plaintiffs.

Both defendants have moved to dismiss the complaint for failure to state a claim. We will deny the motions as to the first cause of action. . . .

Battery

We must determine whether the administration of a drug, DES, to the plaintiffs without their knowledge or consent constitutes a battery under Illinois law. The defendants argue that the plaintiffs' first count is really a "lack of informed consent" case premised on negligence. Because the named plaintiffs have not alleged specific physical injury to themselves, the defendants contend they have failed to state a claim for negligence and the count should be dismissed. However, if we find the action to be based on a battery theory, it may stand notwithstanding the lack of an allegation of personal physical injury.

True "informed consent" cases concern the duty of the physician to inform his patient of risks inherent in the surgery or treatment to which he has consented. While early cases treated lack of informed consent as vitiating the consent to treatment so there was liability for battery, the modern view "is that the action . . . is in reality one for negligence in failing to conform to the proper standard, to be determined on the basis of expert testimony as to what disclosure should be made." W. Prosser, Law of Torts § 32, at 165 (4th ed. 1971). Nonetheless, a battery action may still be appropriate in certain circumstances. Where the patient has not consented to the treatment, it is meaningless to ask whether the doctor should have revealed certain risks necessary to make the consent an "informed" one. The distinction between battery and negligence is elucidated in *Trogun v. Fruchtman*, 58 Wis. 2d 569, 596, 207 N.W.2d 297, 311–12 (1973):

> The courts of this country have recognized essentially two theories of liability for allegedly unauthorized medical treatment or therapy rendered by physicians to their patients. The first of these theories is the traditional intentional tort of battery or assault and battery which is simply defined as the unauthorized touching of the person of another. Underlying this theory of liability is, of course, the general feeling that a person of sound mind has a right to determine, even as against his physician, what is to be done to his body. Under this theory, liability is imposed upon a physician who has performed non-emergency treatment upon a patient without his consent.
>
> . . . .
>
The second theory of liability, permitted by a majority of courts, is grounded upon negligence principles rather than on intentional tort. . . . "[This] doctrine of 'informed consent' . . . concerns the duty of the physician or surgeon to inform the patient of the risk which may be involved in treatment or surgery."

As for the application of the distinction, we find the analysis of the court in *Cobbs v. Grant*, 8 Cal. 3d 229, 104 Cal. Rptr. 505, 512, 502 P.2d 1, 8 (1972), persuasive:

> The battery theory should be reserved for those circumstances when a doctor performs an operation to which the patient has not consented. When the patient gives permission to perform one type of treatment and the doctor performs another, the requisite element of deliberate intent to deviate from the consent given is present. However, when the patient consents to certain

treatment and the doctor performs that treatment but an undisclosed inherent complication with a low probability occurs, no intentional deviation from the consent given appears; rather, the doctor in obtaining consent may have failed to meet his due care duty to disclose pertinent information. In that situation the action should be pleaded in negligence.

Illinois courts have adopted the modern approach to true informed consent cases, and have treated them as negligence actions. However, they have not overruled earlier cases which recognize a cause of action in battery for surgery performed without a patient's consent. Thus, it appears the two separate theories continue to exist in Illinois, and battery may be the proper cause of action in certain situations, for example, where there is a total lack of consent by the patient.[4]

The question thus becomes whether the instant case is more akin to the performance of an unauthorized operation than to the failure to disclose the potential ramifications of an agreed to treatment. We think the situation is closer to the former. The plaintiffs did not consent to DES treatment; they were not even aware that the drug was being administered to them. They were the subjects of an experiment whereby non-emergency treatment was performed upon them without their consent or knowledge.

. . . .

Battery is defined as the unauthorized touching of the person of another. To be liable for battery, the defendant must have done some affirmative act, intended to cause an unpermitted contact. "[I]t is enough that the defendant sets a force in motion which ultimately produces the result. . . . Proof of the technical invasion of the integrity of the plaintiff's person by even an entirely harmless, but offensive, contact entitles him to vindication of his legal right by an award of nominal damages, and the establishment of the tort cause of action entitles him also to compensation for the mental disturbance inflicted upon him." W. Prosser, Law of Torts § 9, at 35 (4th ed. 1971).

"The gist of the action for battery is not the hostile intent of the defendant, but rather the absence of consent to the contact on the part of the plaintiff." *Id.* at 36. "The essence . . . [of the] question in a battery case involving a physician is what did the patient agree with the physician to have done, and was the ultimate contact by the physician within the scope of the patient's consent." *Cathemer v. Hunter*, 27 Ariz. App. 780, 558 P.2d 975, 978 (1976). In sum, to state a cause of action for battery, the plaintiffs must allege intentional acts by the defendants resulting in offensive contact with the plaintiffs' persons, and the lack of consent to the defendants' conduct.

The administration of DES to the plaintiffs was clearly intentional. It was part of a planned experiment conducted by the defendants. The requisite element of intent

---

4. We disagree with defendants that the battery theory is applicable only in cases of unconsented operations. The gravamen of a battery action is the plaintiffs' lack of consent, not the form of the touching.

is therefore met, since the plaintiffs need show only an intent to bring about the contact; an intent to do harm is not essential to the action. Prosser at 36.

The act of administering the drug supplies the contact with the plaintiffs' persons. "It is not necessary that the contact with the other's person be directly caused by some act of the actor. All that is necessary is that the actor intend to cause the other, directly or indirectly, to come in contact with a foreign substance in a manner which the other will reasonably regard as offensive." Restatement (Second) of Torts § 18, Comment c at 31 (1965). We find the administration of a drug without the patient's knowledge comports with the meaning of offensive contact. Had the drug been administered by means of a hypodermic needle, the element of physical contact would clearly be sufficient. We believe that causing the patient to physically ingest a pill is indistinguishable in principle.

Finally, there is the question of consent. As previously stated, this is the real crux of the issue in cases involving a physician's treatment of his patient. If the patient has assented to the doctor's treatment, he may not later maintain an action in battery. The defendants argue that the plaintiffs consented to treatment when they admitted themselves to the University's Lying-in Hospital for prenatal care. The scope of the plaintiffs' consent is crucial to their ultimate recovery in a battery action. The defendants' privilege is limited at least to acts substantially similar to those to which the plaintiffs consented. If the defendants went beyond the consent given, to perform substantially different acts, they may be liable. The time, place and circumstances will affect the nature of the consent given. "It is . . . possible that the consent given will be sufficiently general in its terms to cover the particular operation [or treatment], or that the surgeon may be authorized with complete freedom to do whatever he thinks best to remedy whatever he finds, particularly where the patient has signed one of the written forms in common use in hospitals." Prosser at 104. These questions, however, are questions of fact which are to be determined by the jury, not by this court on a motion to dismiss. The plaintiffs have alleged sufficient lack of consent to the treatment involved to state a claim for battery against both defendants.

. . . .

Conclusion

The motions to dismiss of defendants University of Chicago and Eli Lilly & Co. are denied as to the plaintiffs' first cause of action. The first count states a claim for relief for battery and is not barred by the statute of limitations or the doctrine of charitable immunity.

. . . .

———————

1. What is the nature of the contact here? Why did the plaintiffs bring this suit as a battery case?

2. The concept of consent appears both here and in the Privileges chapter. This is because there is an inherent ambiguity in battery law: Is consent a defense or is its absence something the plaintiff must prove? As will appear further in the Privileges and Negligence chapters, there is also a wide gulf between those cases in which the plaintiff alleges that there was no consent whatever (which are adjudicated as battery cases) and those cases in which the plaintiff alleges that there was incomplete consent (which tend to be treated as negligence cases).

Fisher v. Carrousel Motor Hotel, Inc.

Supreme Court of Texas, 1967
424 S.W.2d 627

GREENHILL, JUSTICE.

This is a suit for actual and exemplary damages growing out of an alleged assault and battery. The plaintiff Fisher was a mathematician with the Data Processing Division of the Manned Spacecraft Center, an agency of the National Aeronautics and Space Agency, commonly called NASA, near Houston. The defendants were the Carrousel Motor Hotel, Inc., located in Houston, the Brass Ring Club, which is located in the Carrousel, and Robert W. Flynn, who as an employee of the Carrousel was the manager of the Brass Ring Club. Flynn died before the trial, and the suit proceeded as to the Carrousel and the Brass Ring. Trial was to a jury which found for the plaintiff Fisher. The trial court rendered judgment for the defendants notwithstanding the verdict. The Court of Civil Appeals affirmed. 414 S.W.2d 774. The questions before this Court are whether there was evidence that an actionable battery was committed, and, if so, whether the two corporate defendants must respond in exemplary [punitive] as well as actual damages for the malicious conduct of Flynn.

The plaintiff Fisher had been invited by Ampex Corporation and Defense Electronics to a one day's meeting regarding telemetry equipment at the Carrousel. The invitation included a luncheon. . . . After the morning session, the group of 25 or 30 guests adjourned to the Brass Ring Club for lunch. The luncheon was buffet style. . . . As Fisher was about to be served, he was approached by Flynn, who snatched the plate from Fisher's hand and shouted that he, a Negro, could not be served in the club. Fisher testified that he was not actually touched, and did not testify that he suffered fear or apprehension of physical injury; but he did testify that he was highly embarrassed and hurt by Flynn's conduct in the presence of his associates.

The jury found that Flynn "forceably dispossessed plaintiff of his dinner plate" and "shouted in a loud and offensive manner" that Fisher could not be served there, thus subjecting Fisher to humiliation and indignity. . . .

The Court of Civil Appeals held that there was no assault because there was no physical contact and no evidence of fear or apprehension of physical contact. However, it has long been settled that there can be a battery without an assault, and that actual physical contact is not necessary to constitute a battery, so long as there is contact with clothing or an object closely identified with the body. 1 Harper & James, The Law of Torts 216 (1956); Restatement of Torts 2d, §§ 18 and 19. In Prosser, Law of Torts 32 (3d Ed. 1964), it is said:

"The interest in freedom from intentional and unpermitted contacts with the plaintiff's person is protected by an action for the tort commonly called battery. The protection extends to any part of the body, or to anything which is attached to it and practically identified with it. Thus contact with the plaintiff's clothing, or with a cane, a paper, or any other object held in his hand will be sufficient; . . . The plaintiff's interest in the integrity of his person includes all those things which are in contact or connected with it."

Under the facts of this case, we have no difficulty in holding that the intentional grabbing of plaintiff's plate constituted a battery. The intentional snatching of an object from one's hand is as clearly an offensive invasion of his person as would be an actual contact with the body. "To constitute an assault and battery, it is not necessary to touch the plaintiff's body or even his clothing; knocking or snatching anything from plaintiff's hand or touching anything connected with his person, when done in an offensive manner, is sufficient." *Morgan v. Loyacomo*, 190 Miss. 656, 1 So. 2d 510 (1941).

. . . .

The rationale for holding an offensive contact with such an object to be a battery is explained in 1 Restatement of Torts 2d § 18 (Comment p. 31) as follows:

"Since the essence of the plaintiff's grievance consists in the offense to the dignity involved in the unpermitted and intentional invasion of the inviolability of his person and not in any physical harm done to his body, it is not necessary that the plaintiff's actual body be disturbed. Unpermitted and intentional contacts with anything so connected with the body as to be customarily regarded as part of the other's person and therefore as partaking of its inviolability is actionable as an offensive contact with his person. There are some things such as clothing or a cane or, indeed, anything directly grasped by the hand which are so intimately connected with one's body as to be universally regarded as part of the person."

We hold, therefore, that the forceful dispossession of plaintiff Fisher's plate in an offensive manner was sufficient to constitute a battery, and the trial court erred in granting judgment notwithstanding the verdict on the issue of actual damages.

. . . .

---

1. Under the Federal Civil Rights Act, 42 U.S.C. § 2000a *et seq.* (1964), all businesses accommodating the public and affecting interstate commerce must serve their customers "without discrimination or segregation on the ground of race, color, religion, or national origin."

2. In Texas, the employer can be held liable for the intentional torts of the employee if the actor was a manager, the act was "authorized," or if the employer "ratifies" the tortious acts, *Fisher* at 631.

Problem

Mrs. Clayton went roller skating at defendant's rink. While skating, she fell over some chewing gum on the rink surface and broke her arm. Defendant told Mrs. Clayton that he was not a doctor but that he had experience in dealing with injuries. In an effort to be helpful, he then tried to set the broken bone despite objections from Mrs. Clayton, causing her additional pain.

You are Mrs. Clayton's attorney. What will you allege in your suit against defendant?

Lambertson v. United States

United States Court of Appeals for the Second Circuit, 1976
528 F.2d 441

Before Moore, Oakes and Van Graafeiland, Circuit Judges.

Van Graafeiland, Circuit Judge:

This is an appeal from an order of Judge Edmund Port of the United States District Court for the Northern District of New York dismissing plaintiff's action against the United States as barred by 28 U.S.C. § 2680(h). We affirm.

Appellant, an employee of Armour & Co., sustained serious injuries to his mouth as a result of the actions of one William Boslet, a meat inspector for the United States Department of Agriculture [who was on duty at the time]. For the most part, the circumstances of the incident are not in dispute. . . .

On August 30, 1972, a truck shipment of beef arrived at the receiving dock of Armour's Syracuse plant. Plaintiff was one of the employees assigned to unload this truck. While he was so engaged, he was suddenly and without warning jumped by Boslet who, screaming "boo," pulled plaintiff's wool stocking hat over his eyes and, climbing on his back, began to ride him piggyback. As a result of this action, plaintiff fell forward and struck his face on some meat hooks located on the receiving dock [no more than six inches away] suffering severe injuries to his mouth and teeth.

It is apparently agreed by all witnesses that the mishap was the result of one-sided horseplay with no intention on Boslet's part to injure plaintiff. Indeed, immediately after the incident Boslet apologized to plaintiff, telling him that he was only playing around and meant no harm.

Seeking redress for his injuries, plaintiff commenced the instant action against the United States pursuant to the Federal Tort Claims Act, 28 U.S.C. § 1346(b).

Traditionally, the sovereign has always been immune from suit. To alleviate the harshness of this rule, Congress enacted the Federal Tort Claims Act which permits civil actions against the United States for personal injury and property damage caused by the "negligent or wrongful act or omission of any employee of the Government while acting within the scope of his office or employment." 28 U.S.C. § 1346(b). 28 U.S.C. § 2680, however, lists several claims expressly excepted from the purview of the Act, among which are any claims arising out of an assault or battery.[3] Since the United States has not consented to be sued for these torts, federal courts are without jurisdiction to entertain a suit based on them.

Although his order contains no express statement to that effect, the parties agree that the sole basis for Judge Port's dismissal was his conclusion that Boslet's actions constituted a battery.

Appellant contests this conclusion and steadfastly maintains that his complaint sounds in negligence.

. . . .

It is hornbook law in New York, as in most other jurisdictions, that the intent which is an essential element of the action for battery is the intent to make contact, not to do injury.

> A plaintiff in an action to recover damages for an assault founded on bodily contact must prove only that there was bodily contact; that such contact was offensive; and that the defendant intended to make the contact. The plaintiff is not required to prove that defendant intended physically to injure him. Certainly he is not required to prove an intention to cause the specific injuries resulting from the contact.

Harper and James put it that "it is a battery for a man . . . to play a joke upon another which involves a harmful or offensive contact." Prosser says that a "defendant may be liable where he has intended only a joke." *Accord* Restatement (Second) of Torts § 13, comment c (1965). Since there is not the remotest suggestion that Boslet's leap onto plaintiff's back, his piggy back ride and his use of plaintiff's hat as a blindfold might have been accidental, there was no error in the District Court's determination that it was a battery.

. . . .

Affirmed.

OAKES, CIRCUIT JUDGE (concurring):

Were we writing on a clean slate, a good argument could be made for the proposition that the 'battery" exclusion in 28 U.S.C. § 2680(h) was intended to apply only to cases where bodily harm was intended and not to cases involving a "technical battery."

---

1. What is a technical battery? What damages should be available for such a battery?

---

3. Section 2680 reads in pertinent part as follows: "The provisions of this chapter and section 1346(b) of this title shall not apply to— . . . (h) Any claim arising out of assault, battery, false imprisonment, false arrest, malicious prosecution, abuse of process, libel, slander, misrepresentation, deceit, or interference with contract rights."

2. Under what circumstances do you think that an employer should be liable for the intentional torts of an employee?

3. A corollary of the rule that the defendant is liable for all consequences of his or her intentional tort, no matter their foreseeability, is the principle that no actual damage is necessary in order for liability to attach. Even in the absence of actual damage, the plaintiff has been injured by the fact of the contact or other intentional tort. The defendant remains liable for the intentional tort, even if there is evidence that the intentional tort caused no actual damage to the plaintiff (or, indeed, evidence that the intentional tort benefited the plaintiff). *Harmony Ditch v. Sweeney*, 222 P. 577 (Wyo. 1924) (trespass to land).

Problem

Sally, sitting on her bike, flicks the ash off the end of her cigarette. It hits Jim's hand. He calls her a jackwood and hits her bike tire with a stick. Jim catches his thumb under the stick and breaks his thumb. Five weeks later, Jim's infected thumb must be amputated.

Consider both sides.

C. Assault

Conley v. Doe

Superior Court of Massachusetts, 2001
2001 Mass. Super. LEXIS 490

RALPH D. GANTS, JUSTICE OF THE SUPERIOR COURT.

The plaintiff, Mary Conley ("Ms. Conley"), is a sixth grade teacher at a suburban middle school in the Boston metropolitan area. The defendant John Doe ("John") was a sixth grade student in her English class and homeroom last school year. According to her Complaint, on Friday, January 12, 2001, in study hall, she saw John writing on a piece of paper with a black marker and observed that he had written the words, "People I Want to Kill," across the top of the paper. No names had been written on the paper. Ms. Conley confiscated the paper and brought John to the school office, informing school authorities of what she had found.

On Wednesday, January 17, Ms. Conley learned that school authorities had discovered on January 12 a second piece of paper that had been written by John and that also was entitled, "People I Want to Kill," but this paper included the names of nine people, including Ms. Conley. This second piece of paper was written less neatly than the piece of paper that Ms. Conley had found. Therefore, she inferred that John was either re-writing this first piece of paper onto a new page when she discovered him in study hall, or was seeking to add more names to the list, since he had run out of room on the second piece of paper. When Ms. Conley learned of the piece of paper that included her name on January 17, she left the school building and is "deathly afraid" of returning.

At roughly 1:30 p.m. on January 19, 2001, school officials met with John's parents, James Doe and Jane Moe ("John's parents" or "the parents"), telling them that John could not return to school until, among other things, he had completed a psychological evaluation. Early that same evening, one of John's parents accompanied John to school before a school dance and delivered to a school official what the parent contended was a full and complete psychological evaluation of John, as had been required by the school. Having received that evaluation, the school allowed John to attend the school dance that evening. Ms. Conley contends that this purported psychological evaluation could not have been a genuine full and complete psychological evaluation of John, because it was produced in too short a time. She alleges that the psychological evaluation submitted to the school was a misleading and fraudulent document, having been prepared by one or both of John's parents, or by another person who was under their control and supervision.

Ms. Conley alleges in her Complaint that the school failed to take any meaningful disciplinary action against John and allowed him to return to school, even though he may pose a serious risk of harm. She further alleges that the school's failure to take meaningful disciplinary action against John resulted from threats and intimidation by John's parents, including the threat by John's mother of a lawsuit if the school took strong disciplinary action or publicized what he had done.

Ms. Conley alleges eight counts in her complaint. . . .

The defendants now move to dismiss all eight counts of the Complaint, contending that each fails to state a claim under Mass.R.Civ.P. 12(b)(6). After hearing, for the reasons stated below, the motion to dismiss the Complaint is *ALLOWED*.

DISCUSSION

When evaluating the sufficiency of a complaint pursuant to Mass. R. Civ. P. 12(b)(6), the court must accept as true the factual allegations of the complaint and all reasonable inferences favorable to the plaintiff which can be drawn from those allegations. . . .

Count 2—Assault

For John to have committed the tort of assault, he must have engaged in conduct that put Ms. Conley in reasonable apprehension of an imminent harmful or offensive contact with her person. *Commonwealth v. Delgado*, 367 Mass. 432, 437 n.3 (1975), quoting Restatement 2d: Torts, § 31(1965). Words alone cannot constitute the tort of assault "unless together with other acts or circumstances they put the other in reasonable apprehension of an imminent harmful or offensive contact with his person." *Id.*

Here, the Complaint alleges nothing more than words written on two sheets of paper. These words cannot constitute even a criminal *threat* unless they were communicated by John to Ms. Conley. The Complaint does not allege that John communicated any words, orally or in writing, to Ms. Conley; she observed John writing the first piece of paper (which did not contain her name) in study hall and was informed by school authorities that the second piece of paper (which did contain her name) had been found. Nor is there any other conduct alleged, apart from the mere writing of these words, that put Ms. Conley in reasonable apprehension of an imminent harmful or offensive contact with John. Mere uncommunicated words, no matter how frightening, are not sufficient to constitute a tortious assault.

This Court is mindful that Ms. Conley alleges that she feared that John would carry out these words, and the Court respects that she is sincere in her fear. But the fact remains that a sixth grader does not assault a teacher by privately writing that he wants to kill her. Otherwise, a student writing such thoughts at home in his private journal would be assaulting a teacher once she somehow obtains a copy of the journal entry. At the very least, the student must in some fashion act to communicate that intention to the teacher before the expression of these private thoughts becomes a tortious assault. Here, since the Complaint makes clear that John did not act to communicate those thoughts to Ms. Conley, she has failed to state a claim for assault. . . .

What are some of the problems that might have arisen if the court had decided this case the other way?

Bouton v. Allstate Insurance Co.

Court of Appeal of Louisiana, First Circuit, 1986
491 So. 2d 56

SHORTESS, JUDGE.

This suit arose from the unfortunate events of Halloween night in 1981. Jeffrey Scott Trammel, aged 15, Robert Martin Landry, Jr., aged 13, and Daniel Breaux, aged 13, went trick-or-treating that evening. About 6:30 p.m., Trammel and Breaux rang Robert Bouton's (plaintiff) front door bell while Landry waited at the sidewalk. Plaintiff opened the door and saw Breaux standing before him. Breaux was dressed in military fatigues and was holding a plastic model submachine gun. Plaintiff shut the door immediately and locked it, then armed himself with a .357 magnum pistol. He returned to the door, opened it, and saw a flash of light, caused, he alleges, by Trammel's triggering a photographic flash. Plaintiff's pistol then discharged, the bullet striking and killing Breaux.

Plaintiff brought this suit against Allstate Insurance Company (Allstate), insurer of Landry and Breaux, and Independent Fire Insurance Company (Independent), insurer of Trammel. He alleged that the three boys' actions were tortious and caused him to be indicted and tried for second-degree murder,[1] incur substantial attorney

----

1. Plaintiff's trial ended with an acquittal.

fees, lose his job, and suffer unfavorable publicity. Allstate filed motions for summary judgment, and Independent raised the peremptory exception of no cause of action. LSA-C.C.P. arts. 966 and 927. The trial court granted the summary judgment motions and sustained the exception of no cause of action. From that action plaintiff brings this appeal.

If what these boys did on that Halloween night is to be deemed tortious, it must be either an intentional tort or one arising from their negligence.

Intentional Tort

Plaintiff claims that the boys committed an assault, causing him to become frightened and triggering the tragic series of events which ensued. Plaintiff must prove an intentional act by the defendants which would have put a person in reasonable apprehension of receiving a battery. We find that the pleadings and evidence fail to establish any right to relief because, under the facts as set out by the plaintiff, he could not have had a *reasonable* apprehension of an impending battery or physical harm. Although it is *possible* for one who opens his door to trick-or-treaters on Halloween to become so frightened that he believes a battery is imminent, under the circumstances here, such an apprehension is not reasonable. Any reasonable person expects to see an endless array of ghouls, beasts, and characters on this evening, especially when he is, as was plaintiff, passing out candy at his doorstep.

Plaintiff contends that "the sole determining issue in this case" is whether we judge the boys' actions from their point of view or from his. We do neither. Instead, "we place the average reasonable [person] . . . in the very situation which confronted the plaintiff and ask of him oracularly" if an apprehension of a battery could be reasonably expected to follow from such a situation. We do not believe that a reasonable person acting reasonably would have been apprehensive of a battery when confronted with this situation on Halloween.[2] Therefore, we hold that plaintiff was not the victim of an assault.

. . . .

For the foregoing reasons, the judgment of the trial court is affirmed at plaintiff's cost.

Affirmed.

———————

How much of a threat should be required before a defendant can be held liable for assault? Should mere words by themselves ever be enough?

———————

2. Because of this ruling, we need not address the question of the boys' intent, plaintiff being required to establish both the intentional act and the apprehension.

D. False Imprisonment

False imprisonment, in addition to requiring study of the defendant's intent, also necessitates examination of the plaintiff's perceptions. An unconscious plaintiff cannot seek recovery for false imprisonment, because the plaintiff was not aware that he or she was imprisoned. Because the test applied to the plaintiff is in this sense subjective, the analysis in the cases can begin to sound highly psychological. Courts in this area can easily become bogged down in the facts of who perceived what and how they felt about it.

Zavala v. Wal-Mart Stores, Inc.

United States District Court for the District of New Jersey, 2005
393 F. Supp. 2d 295

GREENAWAY, J., U.S. DISTRICT JUDGE.

Defendant Wal-Mart, by its own account, is the nation's largest private employer. The named plaintiffs are undocumented immigrants who worked as janitors in various Wal-Mart retail store locations across the country.

   . . . .

The Alleged Criminal Enterprise

Plaintiffs claim that the Wal-Mart Enterprise systematically employed, harbored, and trafficked in the labor of immigrants, aided and abetted violation of the immigration laws, failed to pay their wages and overtime and benefits as required, and concealed their profits and practices from detection.

More specifically, the Wal-Mart Enterprise operated as follows: participants in the Wal-Mart Enterprise violated the immigration laws to secure workers who could be exploited easily based on their undocumented status. It targeted, encouraged, harbored, trafficked, and employed undocumented aliens, specifically because they were a vulnerable population. The Wal-Mart Enterprise exploited them in any number of ways—by obligating them to work in excess of the statutory maximum number of hours, every day of the week, denying them of lawful pay and benefits under the [Fair Labor Standards Act], as well as time for sick leave, meals or breaks, and paying them in cash without withholding payroll taxes. The Wal-Mart Enterprise also easily could, and did, hide them from law enforcement authorities, by threatening them with deportation or locking them into the stores for the duration of their shifts.

DISCUSSION

Defendant Wal-Mart has moved to dismiss the complaint in its entirety. There are five counts to the complaint, [the fifth being] common law false imprisonment. For the reasons set forth below, this Court . . . denies the motion with respect to Count . . . 5.

Count 5—False Imprisonment Claim

Wal-Mart asserts that, despite the inflammatory allegations at Count 5, Plaintiffs have not alleged sufficient facts to state a claim for false imprisonment.

This Court disagrees. Assuming the truth of Plaintiffs' allegations and granting all favorable inferences to the non-moving party, . . . this Court concludes that Plaintiffs have stated a claim for false imprisonment. . . .

Plaintiffs allege that Wal-Mart intentionally engaged in a widespread, systematic practice of locking janitors into their stores during their shifts, against their will, causing them physical and emotional harm. The complaint further asserts that Wal-Mart:

> Compelled the labor of the janitors through its widespread and systematic practice of intentionally locking these vulnerable workers into its stores during its shifts. The [plaintiffs] knew they were so confined to the stores by Wal-Mart. Such confinement was against their will and resulted in physical and emotional injury of plaintiffs and coerced plaintiffs to work for Wal-Mart whether they wanted to or not.

For purposes of deciding this motion, this Court shall apply New Jersey law. . . . In New Jersey, a person "is falsely imprisoned when that person's freedom of movement is constrained . . . by force or by threats of force communicated through conduct or words. But for threats to be held to be a constraint, they must be such as would 'induce a reasonable apprehension of force and the means of coercion [must be] at hand.'"

> The essential thing is the constraint of the person. This constraint may be caused by threats as well as by actionable force, and the threats may be by conduct or by words. If the words or conduct are such as to induce a reasonable apprehension of force and the means of coercion is at hand, a person may be as effectually restrained and deprived of liberty as by prison bars. (101 A.2d at 539).

Physical force does not amount to an actionable restraint if there is a safe avenue of escape through an exit, but in the absence of a "reasonable means of escape," there may be an actionable restraint.

In order for allegations of threats of force to support a claim for false imprisonment, the threat of force must be sufficient for a person to be placed in reasonable apprehension of force, in order to state a claim. For example, the fact that an alarm might sound if a plaintiff exits through an employee exit, or that there is moral pressure, or that one's job is being threatened, is not sufficiently adequate to constitute an actionable constraint by threat of force. *Id.*

Plaintiffs' claim of false imprisonment appears to be rooted in their allegation that some of them were locked into their stores during their shifts, as part of a widespread practice and policy—against their will. . . . [B]ased on the allegations and granting all reasonable inferences therefrom in favor of Plaintiffs, Defendant's motion to dismiss Count 5 is denied.

As stated earlier, Plaintiffs allege that some of them were threatened with deportation. [T]he parties briefed the issue of whether or not the alleged threats of deportation are sufficient to state a claim for false imprisonment.

. . . .

In this Court's view, the authority is not decisive, one way or the other, in this matter. The Supreme Court has stated that "it is possible that threatening . . . an immigrant with deportation could constitute the threat of legal coercion that induces involuntary servitude, . . . "

───────────

1. These workers are potentially a vulnerable population, due to their immigration status and potential language or educational barrier. Should the law accord them any different treatment because of this vulnerability? What reasons might there be to take their vulnerability into account? Did their vulnerability enable Wal-Mart to act as it did?

2. In situations where there is an inherent imbalance of power and difference in privilege (employer vs. employee, legal status vs. undocumented status, business savvy vs. uninformed), do the courts have a role to play in leveling the playing field?

3. What policies does the court consider in deciding the case?

4. What if, instead of physically locking the plaintiffs in the stores, the defendant had threatened them with deportation or other legal action if they left the store during their shift? Would this constitute false imprisonment?

5. Did the workers consent to the confinement by accepting employment?

Whittaker v. Sandford
Supreme Judicial Court of Maine, 1912
85 A. 399

SAVAGE, J.

Action for false imprisonment. The plaintiff recovered a verdict for $1,100. The case comes up on defendant's exceptions and motion for a new trial.

The case shows that for several years prior to 1910, at a locality called "Shiloh," in Durham, in this state, there had been gathered together a religious sect, of which the defendant was at least the religious leader. They dwelt in a so-called colony. There was a similar colony under the same religious leadership at Jaffa, in Syria. The plaintiff was a member of this sect, and her husband was one of its ministers. For the promotion of the work of the "movement," as it is called, a Yacht Club was incorporated, of which the defendant was president. The Yacht Club owned two sailing yachts, the *"Kingdom"* and the *"Coronet"*. So far as this case is concerned, these yachts were employed in transporting members of the movement, back and forth, between the coast of Maine and Jaffa.

The plaintiff, with her four children, sailed on the *Coronet* to Jaffa in 1905. Her husband was in Jerusalem, but came to Jaffa, and there remained until he sailed, a year later, apparently to America. The plaintiff lived in Jerusalem and Jaffa, as a member of the colony, until March, 1909. At that time she decided to abandon the movement, and from that time on ceased to take part in its exercise or to be recognized as a member. She made her preparations to return to America by steamer, but did not obtain the necessary funds therefore until December 24, 1909. At that time the *Kingdom* was in the harbor at Jaffa, and the defendant was on board. . . . The plaintiff fearing, as she says, that if she came on board the defendant's yacht she would not be let off until she was "won to the movement" again, discussed that subject with the defendant, and he assured her repeatedly that under no circumstances would she be detained on board the vessel after they got into port, and that she should be free to do what she wanted to the moment they reached shore. Relying upon this promise, she boarded the *Kingdom* on December 28th and sailed for America. She had her four children with her. The defendant was also on board.

The *Kingdom* arrived in Portland Harbor on the afternoon of Sunday, May 8, 1910. The plaintiff's husband, who was at Shiloh, was telephoned to by someone, and went at once to Portland Harbor, reaching the yacht about midnight of the same day. The *Coronet* was also in Portland Harbor at that time. Later both yachts sailed to South Freeport, reaching there Tuesday morning, May 10th. From this time until June 6th following the plaintiff claims that she was prevented from leaving the *Kingdom*, by the defendant, in such manner as to constitute false imprisonment.

The Exceptions

. . . .

2. The plaintiff claimed and testified that on two or three occasions the defendant personally refused to furnish her with a boat so that she could leave the *Kingdom* — that when she wanted to go ashore "they," evidently referring to the defendant and her husband, "had talked against it"; that the defendant "had spoken plainly that it was out of the question"; that when she spoke to him about it he said he would leave it to her husband to do what he wanted to, that he would not take the responsibility of separating families, but that, when she asked her husband to take her ashore, he replied, "We will see Mr. Sandford about it and see what he says." The plaintiff contended that in this way the defendant and her husband in effect played into each other's hands, and shifted the responsibility from one to the other, while she was the victim of this play of battledore and shuttlecock. It was contended that by virtue of the peculiar religious character attributed to the defendant by those who were in the movement, of whom the plaintiff's husband was one, being a minister of that faith, he possessed and exercised supreme control over the members, both on sea and on land, and that his wish was law both to their wills and consciences, and that the

plaintiff's husband, whatever part he took in the matter, was either merely the defendant's instrument, or else was colleagued with him. . . .

The court instructed the jury that the plaintiff to recover must show that the restraint was physical, and not merely a moral influence; that it must have been actual physical restraint, in the sense that one intentionally locked into a room would be physically restrained but not necessarily involving physical force upon the person; that it was not necessary that the defendant, or any person by his direction, should lay his hand upon the plaintiff; that if the plaintiff was restrained so that she could not leave the yacht *Kingdom* by the intentional refusal to furnish transportation as agreed, she not having it in her power to escape otherwise, it would be a physical restraint and unlawful imprisonment. We think the instructions were apt and sufficient. If one should, without right, turn the key in a door, and thereby prevent a person in the room from leaving, it would be the simplest form of unlawful imprisonment. The restraint is physical. The four walls and the locked door are physical impediments to escape. . . . The boat is the key. By refusing the boat he turns the key. The guest is as effectually locked up as if there were walls along the sides of the vessel. The restraint is physical. The impassible sea is the physical barrier.

There are other exceptions, but the points involved are all covered by the foregoing discussion. The exceptions must all be overruled.

. . . .

———————

1. This classic case is perhaps one of the earliest religious cult cases on record. In modern times, the tort of false imprisonment has been revived in religious cult cases, both as a tool to combat those who would separate the individual from the cult and as a tool for those seeking to leave the cult.

2. Frank Weston Sandford, the founder of the cult in this case, died in 1948 at age 85. Life for those who followed him was far from easy; many died of disease and starvation. At the peak of his popularity, Sandford ran communities in Maine, England, Egypt, and Jerusalem. The cult went into decline after Sandford's arrest, trial, and three-year jail sentence for the deaths by starvation and disease of six of the crew on one of his ships. *See* Pamela Rohland, Book Review of *Fair, Clear, and Terrible: The Story of Shiloh* by Shirley Nelson (British American Publishing, 1996), Philadelphia Inquirer, July 9, 1996, at D9.

Dupler v. Seubert
Supreme Court of Wisconsin, 1975
230 N.W.2d 626

WILKIE, CHIEF JUSTICE.

This is a false imprisonment action. On April 23, 1971, plaintiff-appellant Ethel M. Dupler was fired from her job with the defendant-respondent Wisconsin Telephone

Company. She was informed of her discharge during an hour-and-a-half session with her two superiors, defendants-respondents Keith Peterson and Helen Seubert, who Dupler claims, falsely imprisoned her during a portion of this time period. A jury found that Peterson and Seubert did falsely imprison Dupler and fixed damages at $7,500. The trial court gave Dupler the option of accepting a lower amount — $500 — or a new trial on the issue of damages. The option was not exercised, judgment for $500 was entered, and Mrs. Dupler appeals. We reverse and remand for a new trial on the issue of damages, but give plaintiff-appellant an option to accept $1,000 damages in lieu of a new trial.

Dupler had worked for the Telephone Company as a customer service representative since 1960. At approximately 4:30 on April 23rd, Seubert asked Dupler to come to Peterson's office. When all three were inside, sitting down, with the door closed, Seubert told Dupler the Telephone Company would no longer employ her and that she could choose either to resign or be fired. Dupler testified that she refused to resign and that in the conversation that followed, Peterson discussed several alternatives short of dismissal, all of which had been considered but rejected.

At approximately five o'clock, Dupler testified, she began to feel sick to her stomach and said "You have already fired me. Why don't you just let me go." She made a motion to get up but Peterson told her to sit down in "a very loud harsh voice." Then, Dupler testified, she began to feel violently ill and stated "I got to go. I can't take this anymore. I'm sick to my stomach. I know I'm going to throw up." She got up and started for the door but Seubert also arose and stood in front of the door. After Dupler repeated that she was sick, Seubert allowed her to exit, but followed her to the men's washroom, where Dupler did throw up. Following this, at approximately 5:25, Seubert asked Dupler to return to Peterson's office where she had left her purse to discuss the situation further. Dupler testified that she went back to the office and reached for her purse; Seubert again closed the door and Peterson said "[i]n a loud voice 'Sit down. I'm still your boss. I'm not through with you.'" At approximately 5:40 Dupler told Peterson her husband was waiting for her outside in a car and Peterson told her to go outside and ask her husband to come inside. Dupler then went outside and explained the situation to her husband who said, "You get back in there and get your coat and if you aren't right out I'll call the police." Dupler returned to Peterson's office and was again told in a loud tone of voice to sit down. She said Seubert and Peterson were trying to convince her to resign rather than be fired and again reviewed the alternatives that had been considered. Dupler then said: "What's the sense of all this. Why keep torturing me. Let me go. Let me go."

Peterson replied: "No, we still aren't finished. We have a lot of things to discuss, your retirement pay, your vacation, other things." Finally, at approximately 6:00 Peterson told Dupler they could talk further on the phone or at her house, and Dupler left. When asked why she had stayed in Peterson's office for such a long time, Dupler replied:

> "Well, for one thing, Helen, Mrs. Seubert, had blocked the door, and tempers had been raised with all the shouting and screaming, I was just plain scared to make an effort. There were two against one."

The issue raised by a motion for review filed by defendants-respondents is: *Is the jury's verdict, finding that Dupler was falsely imprisoned, supported by the evidence?*

The essence of false imprisonment is the intentional, unlawful, and unconsented restraint by one person of the physical liberty of another. In *Maniaci v. Marquette University*, the court adopted the definition of false imprisonment contained in sec. 35 of the Restatement of Torts 2d, which provides in part:

"False Imprisonment

"(1) An actor is subject to liability to another for false imprisonment if

"(a) he acts intending to confine the other or a third person within boundaries fixed by the actor, and

"(b) his act directly or indirectly results in such a confinement of the other, and

"(c) the other is conscious of the confinement or is harmed by it."

Secs. 39[9] and 40[10] provide that the confinement may be caused by physical force or the threat of physical force, and the comment to sec. 40 indicates the threat may either be express, or inferred from the person's conduct. As Prosser comments:

"*Character of Defendant's Act*

"The restraint may be by means of physical barriers, or by threats of force which intimidate the plaintiff into compliance with orders. It is sufficient that he submits to an apprehension of force reasonably to be understood from the conduct of the defendant, although no force is used or even expressly threatened. . . . This gives rise, in borderline cases, to questions of fact, turning upon the details of the testimony, as to what was reasonably to be understood and implied from the defendant's conduct, tone of voice and the like, which seldom can be reflected accurately in an appellate record, and normally are for the jury."[11]

This is precisely such a case and we conclude that the record contains sufficient evidence from which the jury could have concluded that Mrs. Dupler was intentionally confined, against her will, by an implied threat of actual physical restraint. . . .

. . . .

We conclude . . . that the jury could properly find that defendants falsely imprisoned Dupler by compelling her to remain in Peterson's office against her will after

---

9. (1971), 50 Wis. 2d 287, 184 N.W.2d 168.

10. *Id.* at page 59:

"39. Confinement by Physical Force

"The confinement may be by overpowering physical force, or by submission to physical force.

"40. Confinement by Threats of Physical Force.

"The confinement may be by submission to a threat to apply physical force to the other's person immediately upon the other's going or attempting to go beyond the area in which the actor intends to confine him."

11. Prosser, Torts (4th ed. 1971), sec. 11, p. 44.

5 p.m. We conclude the imprisonment ceased when Dupler left the building to visit her husband, but resumed when she reentered Peterson's office to get her coat in order to leave, but was commanded to stay.

. . . .

Order affirmed; judgment modified with new trial ordered on the issue of damages unless, within twenty days of remittitur, plaintiff-appellant Ethel Dupler elects to accept judgment for $1,000, and, as modified affirmed.

———————

How is the imprisonment aspect of the tort established? In other words, what kind of escape attempts should be required of a plaintiff before that plaintiff can claim imprisonment? What about climbing out of the window of a school bus? Testing threats by ignoring them? What if you are pathologically frightened of cats, and someone aware of this put a cat between you and the door?

Problem

Two police officers are called to the scene of a noisy party. At the scene, they find one Parvi, who is intoxicated. Parvi claims that he has nowhere to go. The police officers load the semiconscious Parvi into their car, drive him to a golf course outside the city limits, and leave him there. In an effort to return home, Parvi, who has no idea where he is or what has happened, wanders out onto the highway which is near the golf course, is struck by an automobile, and is severely injured. While Parvi remembers nothing of the drive to the golf course, he resisted vigorously when being loaded into the police car.

Does Parvi have a cause of action for false imprisonment?

E. Intentional Infliction of Emotional Distress

The tort of intentional infliction of emotional distress has become an important tool in the modern world. It is perhaps the only intentional tort to be added to the list of intentional torts in modern times, and it fills the gap left when the elements of the other torts cannot be met, but when the message needs to be sent that certain conduct will not be tolerated in a civilized society.

Intentional infliction of emotional distress, like false imprisonment, requires an examination of the psychological facts of the case from the points of view of both parties. The defendant's acts must be reprehensible; the plaintiff's perceptions must be traumatic. Unlike false imprisonment, however, intentional infliction of emotional distress merges into negligence-based torts through the tort of negligent infliction of emotional distress. Intentional infliction of emotional distress lies on a continuum with the most grotesquely intentional acts on one end, and purely negligent acts on the other. Drawing the line between the intentional and the negligent can be difficult, as there is no easily perceived division between the two. The dividing line can be important in a particular case, however, because the plaintiff in the intentional tort context may recover damages for all injuries resulting from the commission of the tort, whether proximately caused by the defendant or not, and may also recover punitive damages which would be unavailable if the tort were based in negligence.

Intentional infliction of emotional distress applies where the defendant's conduct has been so appalling that to deny any recovery to the plaintiff would be unacceptable. The operative concept is that of intent: the defendant has intentionally caused suffering to the plaintiff and should be made to pay for the consequences of his or her behavior. The tort allows the courts to deter conduct that is simply not acceptable in a civilized society.

Harris v. Jones
Court of Appeals of Maryland, 1977
380 A.2d 611

Murphy, Chief Judge.

In *Jones v. Harris*, 35 Md. App. 556, 371 A.2d 1104 (1977), a case of first impression in Maryland, the Court of Special Appeals, in a scholarly opinion by Judge W. Albert Menchine, recognized intentional infliction of emotional distress as a new and independent tort in this jurisdiction. It found that a majority of the states now recognize intentional infliction of emotional distress as a separate and distinct basis of tort liability, apart from any other tort, thus repudiating earlier holdings that claims for emotional distress could not be sustained except as a parasitic element of damage accompanying a recognized tort. We granted certiorari to review the decision of the Court of Special Appeals and to decide whether, if intentional infliction of emotional distress is a viable tort in Maryland, the court erred in reversing judgments entered on jury verdicts for the plaintiff on that cause of action.

The plaintiff, William R. Harris, a 26-year-old, 8-year employee of General Motors Corporation (GM), sued GM and one of its supervisory employees, H. Robert Jones, in the Superior Court of Baltimore City. The declaration alleged that Jones, aware that Harris suffered from a speech impediment which caused him to stutter, and also aware of Harris' sensitivity to his disability, and his insecurity because of it, nevertheless "maliciously and cruelly ridiculed . . . [him] thus causing tremendous nervousness, increasing the physical defect itself and further injuring the mental attitude fostered by the Plaintiff toward his problem and otherwise intentionally inflicting emotional distress." It was also alleged in the declaration that Jones' actions occurred within the course of his employment with GM and that GM ratified Jones' conduct.

The evidence at trial showed that Harris stuttered throughout his entire life. While he had little trouble with one syllable words, he had great difficulty with longer words or sentences, causing him at times to shake his head up and down when attempting to speak.

During part of 1975, Harris worked under Jones' supervision at a GM automobile assembly plant. Over a five-month period, between March and August of 1975, Jones approached Harris over 30 times at work and verbally and physically mimicked his stuttering disability. In addition, two or three times a week during this period, Jones approached Harris and told him, in a "smart manner," not to get nervous. As a result of Jones' conduct, Harris was "shaken up" and felt "like going into a hole and hide."

. . . .

Harris had been under the care of a physician for a nervous condition for six years prior to the commencement of Jones' harassment. He admitted that many things made him nervous, including "bosses." Harris testified that Jones' conduct heightened his nervousness and his speech impediment worsened. He saw his physician on one occasion during the five-month period that Jones was mistreating him; the physician prescribed pills for his nerves.

Harris admitted that other employees at work mimicked his stuttering. Approximately 3,000 persons were employed on each of two shifts, and Harris acknowledged the presence at the plant of a lot of "tough guys," as well as profanity, name-calling and roughhousing among the employees. He said that a bad day at work caused him to become more nervous than usual. He admitted that he had problems with supervisors other than Jones, that he had been suspended or relieved from work 10 or 12 times, and that after one such dispute, he followed a supervisor home on his motorcycle, for which he was later disciplined.

. . . .

On this evidence, the case was submitted to the jury after the trial court denied the Defendants' motions for directed verdicts; the jury awarded Harris $3,500 compensatory damages and $15,000 punitive damages against both Jones and GM.

In concluding that the intentional infliction of emotional distress, standing alone, may constitute a valid tort action, the Court of Special Appeals relied upon Restatement (Second) of Torts, ch. 2, Emotional Distress, § 46 (1965), which provides, in pertinent part:

> "§ 46. Outrageous Conduct Causing Severe Emotional Distress
>
> (1) One who by extreme and outrageous conduct intentionally or recklessly causes severe emotional distress to another is subject to liability for such emotional distress, and if bodily harm to the other results from it, for such bodily harm."

The court noted that the tort was recognized, and its boundaries defined, in W. Prosser, Law of Torts § 12, at 56 (4th ed. 1971), as follows:

> "So far as it is possible to generalize from the cases, the rule which seems to have emerged is that there is liability for conduct exceeding all bounds usually tolerated by decent society, of a nature which is especially calculated to cause, and does cause, mental distress of a very serious kind."

. . . .

Illustrative of the cases which hold that a cause of action will lie for intentional infliction of emotional distress, unaccompanied by physical injury, is *Womack v. Eldridge*, 215 Va. 338, 210 S.E.2d 145 (1974). There, the defendant was engaged in the business of investigating cases for attorneys. She deceitfully obtained the plaintiff's photograph for the purpose of permitting a criminal defense lawyer to show it to the victims in several child molesting cases in an effort to have them identify the plaintiff as the perpetrator of the offenses, even though he was in no way involved in the crimes. While the victims did not identify the plaintiff, he was nevertheless questioned by the police, called repeatedly as a witness and required to explain the circumstances under which the defendant had obtained his photograph. As a result, plaintiff suffered shock, mental depression, nervousness and great anxiety as to what people would think of him and he feared that he would be accused of molesting the boys. The court, in concluding that a cause of action had been made out, said:

. . . .

> "In *Samms [v. Eccles*, 11 Utah 2d 289, 358 P.2d 344 (1961)], the Supreme Court of Utah aptly stated:
>
>> '. . . [T]he best considered view recognizes an action for severe emotional distress, though not accompanied by bodily impact or physical injury, where the defendant intentionally engaged in some conduct toward the plaintiff, (a) with the purpose of inflicting emotional distress, *or*, (b) where any reasonable person would have known that such would result; and his actions are of such a nature as to be considered outrageous and intolerable in that they offend against the generally accepted standards of decency and morality'" 210 S.E.2d at 147–148.

The court in *Womack* identified four elements which must coalesce to impose liability for intentional infliction of emotional distress:

(1) The conduct must be intentional or reckless;

(2) The conduct must be extreme and outrageous;

(3) There must be a causal connection between the wrongful conduct and the emotional distress;

(4) The emotional distress must be severe.

Essentially, these are the elements of the tort set forth in §46 of the Restatement, *supra*. We agree that the independent tort of intentional infliction of emotional distress should be sanctioned in Maryland. . . .

As to the first element of the tort, §46 of the Restatement, *supra*, comment i, states, and the cases generally recognize, that the defendant's conduct is intentional or reckless where he desires to inflict severe emotional distress, and also where he knows that such distress is certain, or substantially certain, to result from his conduct; or where the defendant acts recklessly in deliberate disregard of a high degree of probability that the emotional distress will follow.

Whether the conduct of a defendant has been "extreme and outrageous," so as to satisfy that element of the tort, has been a particularly troublesome question. Section 46 of the Restatement, comment d, states that "Liability has been found only where the conduct has been so outrageous in character, and so extreme in degree, as to go beyond all possible bounds of decency, and to be regarded as atrocious, and utterly intolerable in a civilized community." The comment goes on to state that liability does not extend, however:

> "to mere insults, indignities, threats, annoyances, petty oppressions, or other trivialities. The rough edges of our society are still in need of a good deal of filing down, and in the meantime plaintiffs must necessarily be expected and required to be hardened to a certain amount of rough language, and to occasional acts that are definitely inconsiderate and unkind."

. . . .

Comment f states that the extreme and outrageous character of the conduct "may arise from the actor's knowledge that the other is peculiarly susceptible to emotional distress, by reason of some physical or mental condition or peculiarity."

[Professor Calvert Magruder] observed at 1035 that "Against a large part of the frictions and irritations and clashing of temperaments incident to participation in a community life, a certain toughening of the mental hide is a better protection than the law could ever be."

. . . .

In determining whether conduct is extreme and outrageous, it should not be considered in a sterile setting, detached from the surroundings in which it occurred. The personality of the individual to whom the misconduct is directed is also a factor. "There is a difference between violent and vile profanity addressed to a lady, and the same language to a Butte miner and a United States marine." Prosser, *Intentional Infliction of Mental Suffering: A New Tort*, 37 Mich. L. Rev. 874, 887 (1939).

. . . .

It is for the court to determine, in the first instance, whether the defendant's conduct may reasonably be regarded as extreme and outrageous; where reasonable men may differ, it is for the jury to determine whether, in the particular case, the conduct has been sufficiently extreme and outrageous to result in liability.

The Court of Special Appeals found that Jones' conduct was intended to inflict emotional distress and was extreme and outrageous. As to the other elements of the tort, it concluded that the evidence was legally insufficient to establish either that a causal connection existed between Jones' conduct and Harris' emotional distress, or that Harris' emotional distress was severe.

While it is crystal clear that Jones' conduct was intentional, we need not decide whether it was extreme or outrageous, or causally related to the emotional distress which Harris allegedly suffered.[2] The fourth element of the tort—that the emotional

---

2. The fact that Harris may have had some pre-existing susceptibility to emotional distress does not necessarily preclude liability if it can be shown that the conduct intensified the pre-existing condition of psychological stress.

distress must be severe—was not established by legally sufficient evidence justifying submission of the case to the jury. That element of the tort requires the plaintiff to show that he suffered a *severely* disabling emotional response to the defendant's conduct. The severity of the emotional distress is not only relevant to the amount of recovery, but is a necessary element to any recovery. Comment j of § 46 of the Restatement, *supra*, elaborates on this requirement:

> "Emotional distress passes under various names, such as mental suffering, mental anguish, mental or nervous shock, or the like. It includes all highly unpleasant mental reactions, such as fright, horror, grief, shame, humiliation, embarrassment, anger, chagrin, disappointment, worry, and nausea. It is only where it is extreme that the liability arises.
>
> ". . . Severe distress must be proved; but in many cases the extreme and outrageous character of the defendant's conduct is in itself important evidence that the distress has existed. . . .
>
> "The distress must be reasonable and justified under the circumstances, and there is no liability where the plaintiff has suffered exaggerated and unreasonable emotional distress, unless it results from a peculiar susceptibility to such distress of which the actor has knowledge. . . .
>
> "It is for the court to determine whether on the evidence severe emotional distress can be found; it is for the jury to determine whether, on the evidence, it has in fact existed."

Assuming that a causal relationship was shown between Jones' wrongful conduct and Harris' emotional distress, we find no evidence, legally sufficient for submission to the jury, that the distress was "severe" within the contemplation of the rule requiring establishment of that element of the tort. The evidence that Jones' reprehensible conduct humiliated Harris and caused him emotional distress, which was manifested by an aggravation of Harris' preexisting nervous condition and a worsening of his speech impediment, was vague and weak at best. It was unaccompanied by any evidentiary particulars other than that Harris, during the period of Jones' harassment, saw his physician on one occasion for his nerves, for which pills were prescribed—the same treatment which Harris had been receiving from his physician for six years prior to Jones' mistreatment. The intensity and duration of Harris' emotional distress is nowhere reflected in the evidence. All that was shown was that Harris was "shaken up" by Jones' misconduct and was so humiliated that he felt "like going into a hole and hide." While Harris' nervous condition may have been exacerbated somewhat by Jones' conduct, his family problems antedated his encounter with Jones and were not shown to be attributable to Jones' actions. Just how, or to what degree, Harris' speech impediment worsened is not revealed by the evidence. Granting the cruel and insensitive nature of Jones' conduct toward Harris, and considering the position of authority which Jones held over Harris, we conclude that the humiliation suffered was not, as a matter of law, so intense as to constitute the "severe" emotional distress required to recover for the tort of intentional infliction of emotional distress.

Judgment affirmed; costs to be paid by appellant.

———————

1. Intentional infliction of emotional distress is the most subjective of the intentional torts by far. The availability of the tort depends on what the subjective effect on the plaintiff of defendant's conduct is, but it also depends on the specific and subjective intent of the defendant. Why is this the case? What is the court concerned about, besides deterring indefensible conduct?

2. The Americans with Disabilities Act, 42 U.S.C. § 12101 *et seq.* (1990), now provides some protection to disabled persons. Does this reflect an enhanced societal perception that conduct such as that in *Harris v. Jones* is inappropriate?

3. In *Taylor v. Vallelunga*, 339 P.2d 910 (Cal. Ct. App. 1959), the court dismissed the second count of a complaint for intentional infliction of emotional distress. In the dismissed count, the daughter of a man who had been beaten by the defendants sought damages against the defendants for the emotional distress she suffered as a result of watching the beating. The court dismissed her claim on the ground that she had failed to allege that the defendants had been aware of her presence as a witness to the beating. Thus, the defendants did not know that their conduct was likely to cause her to suffer severe emotional distress. Is this result consistent with the rule that a person who commits an intentional tort (in this case, battery) is liable for all the consequences of the tort, whether foreseeable or not?

4. If the defendant takes advantage of the victim's special sensitivity, he or she may be liable for intentional infliction of emotional distress, although a normal person would not experience distress.

In *Nickerson v. Hodges*, 84 So. 37 (La. 1920), several people buried a "pot of gold" and enabled the victim to find it. She was old and known to suffer from mental illness. They intended the victim to find the pot as a practical joke. She found it and passed out, withered and died when she discovered it was filled with manure. Her representatives recovered from the insensitive abusers.

———————

Hustler Magazine, Inc. v. Jerry Falwell
Supreme Court of the United States, 1988
485 U.S. 46

REHNQUIST, C.J., delivered the opinion of the Court, in which BRENNAN, MARSHALL, BLACKMUN, STEVENS, O'CONNOR, and SCALIA, JJ., joined. WHITE, J., filed an opinion concurring in the judgment. KENNEDY, J., took no part in the consideration or decision of the case.

CHIEF JUSTICE REHNQUIST delivered the opinion of the Court.

Petitioner Hustler Magazine, Inc., is a magazine of nationwide circulation. Respondent Jerry Falwell, a nationally known minister who has been active as a commentator on politics and public affairs, sued petitioner and its publisher, petitioner Larry Flynt, to recover damages for invasion of privacy, libel, and intentional infliction of emotional distress. The District Court directed a verdict against respondent on the privacy claim, and submitted the other two claims to a jury. The jury found for petitioners on the defamation claim, but found for respondent on the claim for intentional infliction of emotional distress and awarded damages. We now consider whether this award is consistent with the First and Fourteenth Amendments of the United States Constitution.

The inside front cover of the November 1983 issue of Hustler Magazine featured a "parody" of an advertisement for Campari Liqueur that contained the name and picture of respondent and was entitled "Jerry Falwell talks about his first time." This parody was modeled after actual Campari ads that included interviews with various celebrities about their "first times." Although it was apparent by the end of each interview that this meant the first time they sampled Campari, the ads clearly played on the sexual double entendre of the general subject of "first times." Copying the form and layout of these Campari ads, Hustler's editors chose respondent as the featured celebrity and drafted an alleged "interview" with him in which he states that his "first time" was during a drunken incestuous rendezvous with his mother in an outhouse. The Hustler parody portrays respondent and his mother as drunk and immoral, and suggests that respondent is a hypocrite who preaches only when he is drunk. In small print at the bottom of the page, the ad contains the disclaimer, "ad parody—not to be taken seriously." The magazine's table of contents also lists the ad as "Fiction; Ad and Personality Parody."

Soon after the November issue of Hustler became available to the public, respondent brought this diversity action . . . against Hustler Magazine, Inc., Larry C. Flynt, and Flynt Distributing Co. Respondent stated in his complaint that publication of the ad parody in Hustler entitled him to recover damages for libel, invasion of privacy, and intentional infliction of emotional distress. The case proceeded to trial. . . . The jury ruled for respondent on the intentional infliction of emotional distress claim. . . . Petitioners' motion for judgment notwithstanding the verdict was denied.

On appeal, the United States Court of Appeals for the Fourth Circuit affirmed the judgment against petitioners. . . . Given the importance of the constitutional issues involved, we granted certiorari. 480 U.S. 945 (1987).

This case presents us with a novel question involving First Amendment limitations upon a State's authority to protect its citizens from the intentional infliction of emotional distress. We must decide whether a public figure may recover damages for emotional harm caused by the publication of an ad parody offensive to him, and doubtless gross and repugnant in the eyes of most. Respondent would have us find that a State's interest in protecting public figures from emotional distress is sufficient to deny First Amendment protection to speech that is patently offensive and is intended to inflict emotional injury, even when that speech could not reasonably have been interpreted as stating actual facts about the public figure involved. This we decline to do.

At the heart of the First Amendment is the recognition of the fundamental importance of the free flow of ideas and opinions on matters of public interest and concern. "[T]he freedom to speak one's mind is not only an aspect of individual liberty—and thus a good unto itself—but also is essential to the common quest for truth and the vitality of society as a whole." *Bose Corp. v. Consumers Union of United States, Inc.*, 466 U.S. 485, 503–504 (1984). We have therefore been particularly vigilant to ensure that individual expressions of ideas remain free from governmentally imposed sanctions. The First Amendment recognizes no such thing as a "false" idea. *Gertz v. Robert Welch, Inc.*, 418 U.S. 323, 339 (1974). As Justice Holmes wrote, "when men have realized that time has upset many fighting faiths, they may come to believe even more than they believe the very foundations of their own conduct that the ultimate good desired is better reached by free trade in ideas—that the best test of truth is the power of the thought to get itself accepted in the competition of the market. . . ." *Abrams v. United States*, 250 U.S. 616, 630 (1919) (dissenting opinion).

The sort of robust political debate encouraged by the First Amendment is bound to produce speech that is critical of those who hold public office or those public figures who are "intimately involved in the resolution of important public questions or, by reason of their fame, shape events in areas of concern to society at large." *Associated Press v. Walker* decided with *Curtis Publishing Co. v. Butts*, 388 U.S. 130, 164 (1967) (Warren, C.J., concurring in result). Justice Frankfurter put it succinctly in *Baumgartner v. United States*, 322 U.S. 665, 673–674 (1944), when he said that "[o]ne of the prerogatives of American citizenship is the right to criticize public men and measures." Such criticism, inevitably, will not always be reasoned or moderate; public figures as well as public officials will be subject to "vehement, caustic, and sometimes unpleasantly sharp attacks," *New York Times, supra*, at 270. . . .

Of course, this does not mean that *any* speech about a public figure is immune from sanction in the form of damages. Since *New York Times Co. v. Sullivan*, 376 U.S. 254 (1964), we have consistently ruled that a public figure may hold a speaker liable for the damage to reputation caused by publication of a defamatory falsehood, but only if the statement was made "with knowledge that it was false or with reckless disregard of whether it was false or not." *Id.*, at 279–280. . . . "Freedoms of expression require 'breathing space.'" *Philadelphia Newspapers, Inc. v. Hepps*, 475 U.S. 767, 772 (1986) (quoting *New York Times, supra*, 376 U.S., at 272). This breathing space is provided by a constitutional rule that allows public figures to recover for libel or defamation only when they can prove *both* that the statement was false and that the statement was made with the requisite level of culpability.

. . . In respondent's view, and in the view of the Court of Appeals, so long as the utterance was intended to inflict emotional distress, was outrageous, and did in fact inflict serious emotional distress, it is of no constitutional import whether the statement was a fact or an opinion, or whether it was true or false. . . .

Thus while such a bad motive may be deemed controlling for purposes of tort liability in other areas of the law, we think the First Amendment prohibits such a result in the area of public debate about public figures.

Were we to hold otherwise, there can be little doubt that political cartoonists and satirists would be subjected to damages awards without any showing that their work falsely defamed its subject. Webster's defines a caricature as "the deliberately distorted picturing or imitating of a person, literary style, etc. by exaggerating features or mannerisms for satirical effect." . . . The appeal of the political cartoon or caricature is often based on exploitation of unfortunate physical traits or politically embarrassing events—an exploitation often calculated to injure the feelings of the subject of the portrayal. The art of the cartoonist is often not reasoned or even-handed, but slashing and one-sided. One cartoonist expressed the nature of the art in these words:

> "The political cartoon is a weapon of attack, of scorn and ridicule and satire; it is least effective when it tries to pat some politician on the back. It is usually as welcome as a bee sting and is always controversial in some quarters." Long, *The Political Cartoon: Journalism's Strongest Weapon*, The Quill, 56, 57 (Nov. 1962).

. . . .

Respondent contends, however, that the caricature in question here was so "outrageous" as to distinguish it from more traditional political cartoons. . . . "Outrageousness" in the area of political and social discourse has an inherent subjectiveness about it which would allow a jury to impose liability on the basis of the jurors' tastes or views, or perhaps on the basis of their dislike of a particular expression. An "outrageousness" standard thus runs afoul of our longstanding refusal to allow damages to be awarded because the speech in question may have an adverse emotional impact on the audience. . . .

> "[T]he fact that society may find speech offensive is not a sufficient reason for suppressing it. Indeed, if it is the speaker's opinion that gives offense, that consequence is a reason for according it constitutional protection. For it is a central tenet of the First Amendment that the government must remain neutral in the marketplace of ideas." *Id.*, at 745–746. . . .

. . . .

We conclude that public figures and public officials may not recover for the tort of intentional infliction of emotional distress by reason of publications such as the one here at issue without showing in addition that the publication contains a false statement of fact which was made with "actual malice," i.e., with knowledge that the statement was false or with reckless disregard as to whether or not it was true.

This is not merely a "blind application" of the *New York Times* standard, see *Time, Inc. v. Hill*, 385 U.S. 374, 390 (1967); it reflects our considered judgment that such a standard is necessary to give adequate "breathing space" to the freedoms protected by the First Amendment.

Here it is clear that respondent Falwell is a "public figure" for purposes of First Amendment law. The jury found against respondent on his libel claim when it decided that the Hustler ad parody could not "reasonably be understood as describing actual facts about [respondent] or actual events in which [he] participated." App. to Pet. for Cert. Cl. The Court of Appeals interpreted the jury's finding to be that the ad parody "was not reasonably believable," 797 F.2d, at 1278, and in accordance with our custom we accept this finding. Respondent is thus relegated to his claim for damages awarded by the jury for the intentional infliction of emotional distress by "outrageous" conduct. But for reasons heretofore stated this claim cannot, consistently with the First Amendment, form a basis for the award of damages when the conduct in question is the publication of a caricature such as the ad parody involved here. The judgment of the Court of Appeals is accordingly

Reversed.

How thick-skinned should we require public figures to be? Should there be a difference between public figures who seek the limelight and those who are dragged into the public eye? Do you think Jerry Falwell really suffered as a result of publication of this ad?

Problem

A national newpaper publishes a cartoon depicting X, a media star, as intoxicated. X sues the newspaper for intentional infliction of emotional distress. In the lawsuit, X points out that X's father died of alcoholism, and that X was therefore extremely distressed by the cartoon. In fact, X has made it part of her career to campaign against alcohol abuse. What result?

F. Trespass

1. In General

The entire social system of Western Europe in the middle ages revolved around land ownership. Thus, the tort of trespass to land attained early significance in the development of the common law. Much blood was spilled in resolving questions of land ownership, and many lives were saved when boundary conflicts moved into the courts. A lawsuit based on defendant putting a toe across the line where plaintiff thinks his or her property begins may seem silly. The issue is not really one of the damage caused to the plaintiff by the toe, however; the issue may well be the far more fundamental one of where the boundary line in fact should be drawn.

Dougherty v. Stepp

Supreme Court of North Carolina, 1835
18 N.C. 371

Every unauthorized intrusion into the land of another is a sufficient trespass to support an action for *breaking the close*, whether the land be actually enclosed or not. And from every such entry the law infers some damage; if nothing more, the treading down the grass or shrubbery.

Trespass quare clausum fregit, tried at Buncombe, on the last circuit, before his Honor, Judge Martin. The only proof introduced by the plaintiff to establish an act of trespass was, that the defendant had entered on the unenclosed land of the plaintiff, with a surveyor and chain-carriers, and actually surveyed a part of it, claiming it as his own, but without marking trees or cutting bushes. This, his Honor held not be a trespass, and the jury, under his instructions, found a verdict for the defendant, and the plaintiff appealed.

RUFFIN, C.J. In the opinion of the Court, there is error in the instructions given to the jury. The amount of damages may depend on the acts done on the land, and the extent of injury to it therefrom. But it is an elementary principle that every unauthorized, and therefore unlawful, entry into the close of another, is a trespass. From every such entry against the will of the possessor the law infers some damage; if nothing more, the treading down the grass or the herbage, or as here, the shrubbery. . . . It is the entry that constitutes the trespass. . . . Let the judgment be reversed and a new trial granted.

Per curiam.

Judgment reversed.

───────────

1. What amount of damages should a property owner receive in a case like *Dougherty v. Stepp*?

2. *Mistake?* Dean Prosser argues that mistake is not a defense to an intentional tort. This is because the result was intended and defendant "acted under an erroneous belief that circumstances existed which would justify his conduct." W. Page Keeton et al., Prosser and Keeton on Torts 110 (1984). What is the intent required to satisfy that element of the tort of trespass to land?

3. Under the common law, the owner of real estate owned from his or her parcel down to the center of the earth and up to the heavens. This rule has not remained intact. "The common law doctrine that ownership of land extends to the periphery of the universe has no place in the modern world." *United States v. Causby*, 328 U.S. 256, 260 (1946). While there has been no resistance to the idea that airplanes in flight are not trespassing, what about drones?

2. Trespass to Land and Nuisance

J.H. Borland, Sr. v. Sanders Lead Co.

Supreme Court of Alabama, 1979
369 So. 2d 523

JONES, JUSTICE.

This appeal involves the right of a property owner, in an action for trespass, to recover damages for pollution of his property. The case was tried *ore tenus* to the trial Judge without a jury, and judgment was rendered for the Defendant. We reverse and remand for a new trial.

J.H. Borland, Sr., and Sarah M. Borland, Appellants, own approximately 159 acres of land, located just south of Troy, Alabama, on Henderson Road. On this property, Appellants raise cattle, grow several different crops, and have a large pecan orchard.

In 1968, the Appellee, Sanders Lead Company, started an operation for the recovery of lead from used automobile batteries. This operation is conducted on property just east of the Borlands' property across Henderson Road. The Appellee's smelter was placed on the west edge of their property, that part nearest to the Appellants' property. The smelter is used to reduce the plates from used automobile batteries. It is alleged by Appellants that the smelting process results in the emission of lead particulates and sulfoxide gases.

It is undisputed that Appellee installed a filter system, commonly known as a "bag house," to intercept these lead particulates which otherwise would be emitted into the atmosphere. The "bag house" is a building containing fiber bags. The smoke emitting from the furnace is passed through two cooling systems before passing through the "bag house" so that the fiber bags will not catch fire. If properly installed and used, an efficient "bag house" will recover over 99% of the lead emitted. On two occasions, the cooling system at Appellee's smeltering plant has failed to function properly, resulting in the "bag house's" catching fire on both occasions. There is a dispute as to the efficiency of Appellee's "bag house" throughout its operation.

Appellants allege that, because of the problems with the "bag house," their property has been damaged by a dangerous accumulation of lead particulates and sulfoxide deposits on their property. . . .

It is apparent . . . that the trial Court was under the mistaken impression that compliance with the Alabama Air Pollution Control Act shielded the Defendant from liability for damages caused by pollutants emitting from its smelter. This is not the law in this State. Furthermore, the trial Court incorrectly applied the law of this State in concluding that, because there was evidence showing that the Plaintiffs' farm had increased in value as industrial property, due to its proximity to the lead plant, Plaintiffs could not recover of the Defendant. Such a rule, in effect, would permit private condemnation, which, unquestionably, is impermissible. A discussion of the applicable rule of damages appears later in this opinion.

The Alabama Air Pollution Control Act is codified at § 22-28-1, *et seq.*, Alabama Code 1975. § 22-28-23, Alabama Code 1975, specifically provides:

> *[N]othing in this section shall be construed to limit or abrogate any private remedies now available to any person* for the alleviation, abatement, control, correction or prevention of air pollution *or restitution for damage resulting therefrom.* (Emphasis added.)

Alabama law clearly provides an appropriate remedy for Plaintiffs who have been directly injured by the deleterious effects of pollutants created by another party's acts.

In *Rushing v. Hooper-McDonald, Inc.,* . . . a trespass need not be inflicted directly on another's realty, but may be committed by discharging foreign polluting matter at a point beyond the boundary of such realty. *Rushing* specifically held that a trespass is committed by one who knowingly discharges asphalt in such a manner that it will in due course invade a neighbor's realty and cause harm. . . .

Rushing further cited with approval the case of *Martin v. Reynolds Metals Co.,* 221 Or. 86, 342 P.2d 790, *cert. denied,* 362 U.S. 918, 80 S. Ct. 672, 4 L. Ed. 2d 739 (1959). In *Martin,* a case remarkably similar to the present case, the Plaintiffs sought recovery from the Defendant, aluminum company, for trespass. The Plaintiffs in *Martin* alleged that the operation by Defendants of an aluminum reduction plant caused certain fluoride compounds in the form of gases and particulates, invisible to the naked eye, to become airborne and settle on Plaintiffs' property, rendering it unfit for raising livestock. Plaintiffs in the present case allege that the operation of Defendant's lead reduction plant causes an emission of lead particulates, and S02, invisible to the naked eye, which emissions have settled on their property, making it unsuitable for raising cattle or growing crops.

The Defendants in *Martin* contended that there had not been a sufficient invasion of Plaintiffs' property to constitute trespass, but, at most, Defendant's acts constituted a nuisance. This would have allowed the Defendants to set up Oregon's two-year statute of limitations applicable to non-possessory injuries to land rather than Oregon's six-year statute for trespass to land.

The *Martin* Court pointed out that . . . trespass protects the possessor's interest in exclusive possession of property and nuisance protects the interest in use and enjoyment.

The confusion surrounding trespass and nuisance is due in a large part to the influence of common law forms of action. The modern action for trespass to land stemmed inexorably from the common law action for trespass which lay when the injury was both direct and substantial. Nuisance, on the other hand, would lie when injuries were indirect and less substantial. . . .

The *Martin* Court rejected the dimensional test and substituted in its place a force and energy test, stating:

... "[W]e prefer to emphasize the object's energy or force rather than its size. Viewed in this way we may define trespass as an intrusion which invades the possessor's protected interest in exclusive possession, whether that intrusion is by visible or invisible pieces of matter or by energy which can be measured only by the mathematical language of the physicist.

"We are of the opinion, therefore, that the intrusion of the fluoride particulates in the present case constituted a trespass."

In deciding what acts constitute a trespass, the Oregon Supreme Court cited earlier cases recognizing that a trespass is committed by a defendant's blasting operation when the vibrations and concussions to earth and air cause damage to the plaintiff's property. ...

... Suffice it to say that here we are not dealing with a vibration/concussion case. Moreover, it is clear from a thorough reading of *Martin* that the reliance by the Oregon Supreme Court on the trespass theory of the earlier blasting case was not essential to the *Martin* holding [that] deposits of fluoride particulates constituted a trespass upon the plaintiffs' land.

Having shown trespass and nuisance are not always mutually exclusive remedies, we do not wish to intimate that there is no longer a distinction in the two remedies. Indeed, this distinction is evident in the case of *Wilson v. Parent*, 228 Or. 354, 365 P.2d 72 (1961). There, Plaintiff alleged that her son-in-law, who resided on adjoining property, made vile and obscene gestures toward her and directed vile, obscene and profane language at her. The Plaintiff framed her complaint in nuisance, but a significant portion of the opinion was devoted to the question of whether the intrusions were trespasses. ...

... But we hasten to point out that there is a point where the entry is so lacking in substance that the law will refuse to recognize it, applying the maxim *de minimis non curat lex* — the law does not concern itself with trifles. In the present case, however, we are not faced with a trifling complaint.

The Plaintiffs in this case have suffered, if the evidence is believed, a real and substantial invasion of a protected interest.

... Whether an invasion of a property interest is a trespass or a nuisance does not depend upon whether the intruding agent is "tangible" or "intangible." Instead, an analysis must be made to determine the interest interfered with. If the intrusion interferes with the right to exclusive possession of property, the law of trespass applies. If the intrusion is to the interest in use and enjoyment of property, the law of nuisance applies. As previously observed, however, the remedies of trespass and nuisance are not necessarily mutually exclusive.

... Under the modern theory of trespass, the law presently allows an action to be maintained in trespass for invasions that, at one time, were considered indirect and, hence, only a nuisance. In order to recover in trespass for this type of invasion [i.e., the asphalt piled in such way as to run onto plaintiff's property, or the pollution emitting from a defendant's smoke stack, such as in the present case], a plaintiff must show 1) an invasion affecting an interest in the exclusive possession of his property; 2) an intentional doing of the act which results in the invasion; 3) reasonable foreseeability that the act done could result in an invasion of plaintiff's possessory interest; and 4) substantial damages to the *res.*

A further clarification of our nuisance/indirect trespass dichotomy is appropriate at this point. In the traditional sense, the law of nuisance applies where the invasion results in no substantial damage to the *res*, but where there is interference with the use and enjoyment of one's property. The classic cases of the barking dog, the neighboring bawdy house, noise, smoke, fumes, or obnoxious odors generally invoke the doctrine of the law of nuisance. These intrusions do not typically result in any actionable damage to the *res;* the injury caused by such acts usually results in a diminution of the use value of the property causally related to the harmful conduct made the basis of the claim.

We emphasize that these intrusions are not relegated to the nuisance remedy simply because of their indirect nature; rather, they do not constitute a trespass because all of the requisite elements of trespass to land are not present. For an indirect invasion to amount to an actionable trespass, there must be an interference with plaintiff's exclusive possessory interest; that is, through the defendant's intentional conduct, and with reasonable foreseeability, some substance has entered upon the land itself, affecting its nature and character, and causing substantial actual damage to the *res*. For example, if the smoke or polluting substance emitting from a defendant's operation causes discomfort and annoyance to the plaintiff in his use and enjoyment of the property, then the plaintiff's remedy is for nuisance; but if, as a result of the defendant's operation, the polluting substance is deposited upon the plaintiff's property, thus interfering with his exclusive possessory interest by causing substantial damage to the *res*, then the plaintiff may seek his remedy in trespass, though his alternative remedy in nuisance may co-exist.

Reversed and remanded.

All the Justices concur.

––––––––––

1. To what extent should nuisance law be available as an antipollution tool? Clearly, a property owner may file suit for trespass if some noxious substance crosses the boundary lines of his or her property, but what about odors? What about pollution of a stream with invisible chemicals upstream from the plaintiff's property?

2. In *Public Service Company of Colorado v. Van Wyk*, 27 P.3d 377 (Colo. 2001), the court held that for a trespass, the plaintiff must prove actual physical damages, and "noise, radiations, and electromagnetic fields" from high tension electric lines were not "physical intrusions" and not physical damages. Therefore, plaintiffs lost in trespass. How did the *Borland* court take care of the problem posed by ruling that

a trespass to land may be invisible? Did it alter trespass to land doctrine in order to accomplish its result?

Problem

Y, a homeowner, decides to install solar power on the roof of her house. Her neighbor, Z, dislikes the appearance of the solar panels, and plants trees on her (Z's) land so that the panels will not be visible to Z. The trees planted by Z block the sunlight which Y's panels need in order to generate power. Y sues Z to compel Z to trim the trees so that the sunlight may reach Y's panels. What arguments will the parties raise? What result?

3. Trespass to Chattels

Impairing the condition, quality, or value of a chattel upon brief interference can constitute a trespass to the chattel. Restatement (Second) of Torts § 226.

Huffman & Wright Logging Co. v. Wade

Supreme Court of Oregon, 1993
857 P.2d 101

GRABER, JUSTICE

In an action for trespass to chattels, the jury awarded compensatory and punitive damages to plaintiff. Defendants concede their liability for trespass and for compensatory damages, but argue that Article I, sections 8 and 26, of the Oregon Constitution, and the First and Fourteenth Amendments to the Constitution of the United States[2] prohibit an award of punitive damages against them, because their trespassory conduct was "expressive" political speech designed to change government policies. The Court of Appeals affirmed the judgment for punitive damages. *Huffman and Wright Logging Co. v. Wade*, 109 Or. App. 37, 817 P.2d 1334 (1991). We also affirm.

The material facts are not disputed. Plaintiff is a private corporation that operates a logging business. Defendants are six members of "Earth First!" In July 1987, defendants participated in a demonstration on a United States Forest Service logging road in the North Kalmiopsis area of the Siskiyou National Forest. The demonstration was organized to protest Forest Service policies regarding the area. During the demonstration, five of the six defendants climbed on, and chained themselves to, plaintiff's logging equipment. The sixth defendant climbed to the top of a yarder

---

2. The First Amendment provides in part:

   "Congress shall make no law . . . abridging the freedom of speech, or of the press; or the right of the people peaceably to assemble, and to petition the Government for a redress of grievances."

The First Amendment is made applicable to the states by the Due Process Clause of the Fourteenth Amendment. *New York Times Co. v. Sullivan*, 376 U.S. 254, 264 n. 4, 84 S. Ct. 710, 11 L. Ed. 2d 686 (1964).

belonging to plaintiff and hung a large banner that read: "FROM HERITAGE TO SAWDUST—EARTH FIRST!" The banner also depicted two trees being turned into sawdust. While defendants were attached to the equipment, they made statements, sang songs, and chanted slogans relating to their beliefs about the need for greater environmental protection of the North Kalmiopsis area. The demonstration was widely publicized.

Defendants did not have permission to be on, or otherwise to interfere with the use of, plaintiff's personal property, and they knew that they did not. Defendants' actions caused part of plaintiff's logging operation to be suspended for most of a day. Defendants were arrested and charged with criminal mischief in the third degree, ORS 164.345. After a trial to the court on stipulated facts, defendants were convicted. Each defendant served two weeks in jail, and each was ordered to pay a $250 fine and to make full restitution to plaintiff for its lost revenues resulting from Defendants' actions.

Plaintiff then filed this civil action against defendants. As material here, the complaint alleged that defendants committed a trespass by "intentionally and wrongfully interfering with and depriving Plaintiff of the use and possession of [its] logging equipment." Plaintiff sought compensatory damages for lost revenues in the amount of $7,818.26, plus punitive damages of $50,000.

Defendants conceded liability for compensatory damages (although they disputed the amount). As an affirmative defense to the claim for punitive damages, they asserted that Article I, sections 8 and 26, of the Oregon Constitution, and the First and Fourteenth Amendments to the Constitution of the United States precluded the imposition of punitive damages for their actions. . . . . The jury returned a verdict in plaintiff's favor, awarding $5,717.34 in compensatory damages and $25,000 in punitive damages. Defendants moved for judgment notwithstanding the verdict on the claim for punitive damages, continuing to assert the same constitutional theories. The trial court denied that motion and entered judgment for plaintiff.

Defendants sought review only with respect to the constitutionality of the award of punitive damages, and we allowed their petition.

Defendants contend that, as a matter of law, no punitive damages are recoverable, because *all* their activity was "expressive conduct" protected from an award of punitive damages by the state and federal constitutions.

. . . .

Article I, Section 8

The jury awarded compensatory and punitive damages for trespass to chattels. From the evidence presented, the jury could have found that the acts of trespass were Defendants' climbing on plaintiffs logging equipment, chaining themselves to it, affixing an object to it, and rendering the equipment inoperable during that time. Although those acts undoubtedly had a communicative effect, in the sense that most purposive human activity communicates something about the frame of mind of the actor, the acts were conduct, not speech. The question becomes, then, whether defendants are nonetheless constitutionally immune from potential responsibility for punitive damages because of the message that their conduct assertedly was trying to convey, the reason for their conduct, or the fact that speech accompanied their conduct.

Two lines of cases from this court demonstrate that the answer under Article I, section 8, is "no." . . .

We conclude that there are, indeed, some intentional torts that are concerned only with forbidden effects and that the tort that we consider in this case, trespass to chattels, is such a tort.

"In actions for trespass to personal property the gist of the action is the disturbance of the plaintiff's possession." *Swank v. Elwert*, 55 Or. 487, 496, 105 P. 901 (1910). That is, the tort of trespass to chattels focuses on the *effect*—the disturbance of the owner's possession. . . . [R]esponsibility for punitive damages may accompany an intentional tort—like the tort of trespass—that permits liability for harm not caused by speech. With respect to such a tort, liability for both compensatory and punitive damages rests on conduct. A defendant still may assert, however, that punitive damages cannot constitutionally be applied to the particular conduct involved. Where a defendant . . . makes such an assertion, the defendant—like a defendant in a second-category tort case—may be entitled to a limiting instruction.

If a tort permits liability for the content of speech, punitive damages are not recoverable. If a tort permits liability for speech-caused harm, then a defendant who requests it is entitled to an instruction limiting the tortious predicate for punitive damages to conduct not protected by the free speech provision of Article I, section 8.

. . . .

Defendants' conduct consisted of several acts: climbing on plaintiff's logging equipment, chaining themselves to the equipment, affixing an object to one piece of logging equipment, and thereby disrupting plaintiff's use of its property. We conclude that the jury was entitled to find that Defendants' acts caused the disturbance of plaintiff's possession of its personal property, wholly apart from any motivating opinion, underlying message, or accompanying speech. The trespassory acts were, therefore, "non-expressive conduct" within the meaning of Article I, section 8. The message that defendants sought to convey by their conduct, the reason for their conduct, and the spoken and written words accompanying their conduct did not transform Defendants' conduct into speech.

. . . Liability for Defendants' conduct in this case could have been assessed independently of any accompanying expression of views. A properly instructed jury could have awarded punitive damages based on the predicate of Defendants' trespassory conduct alone. Defendants did not choose to request a limiting instruction. Having failed to request such an instruction, defendants cannot prevail in their Article I, section 8, challenge to the award of punitive damages against them. . . .

First Amendment

Having rejected Defendants' state constitutional arguments, we turn to their arguments under the federal constitution. Defendants assert that the First Amendment to the Constitution of the United States protects them from an award of punitive damages in a case of this kind.

The Supreme Court of the United States recently reaffirmed the principle that "violence or other types of potentially expressive activities that produce special harms distinct from their communicative impact are entitled to no constitutional protection. . . ."

We already have held that the tort of trespass to chattels is aimed at conduct not protected by the free expression provision of the Oregon Constitution. The same conclusion obtains with respect to the First Amendment. In this case, Defendants' conduct, although accompanied by expressive activity, produced a special cognizable harm (an interference with plaintiff's possessory interest in its property), distinct from any communicative impact. "[T]he State, no less than a private owner of property, has power to preserve the property under its control for the use to which it is lawfully dedicated."

In addition, the First Amendment does not apply to private property that is not devoted to public use. For an owner of private property to be subject to the proscriptions of the First Amendment, the property must "assume to some significant degree the functional attributes of public property devoted to public use." *Central Hardware Co. v. NLRB*, 407 U.S. 539, 547, 92 S. Ct. 2238, 33 L. Ed. 2d 122 (1972). Devotion of private property to public use requires, at a minimum, the owner's invitation to the general public to enter the premises. *See Marsh v. Alabama*, 326 U.S. 501, 506, 66 S. Ct. 276, 90 L. Ed. 265 (1946) ("The more an owner . . . opens up his property for use by the public in general, the more do his rights become circumscribed by the statutory and constitutional rights of those who use it."). *See also Lloyd Corporation v. Whiffen, supra*, 315 Or. at 510–11, 849 P.2d 446 (citing and agreeing with the above-quoted passage from *Marsh v. Alabama).* Nothing in the First Amendment cases of the Supreme Court suggests that a different rule applies to private personal property than to private real property; the former, like the latter, is not subject to the proscriptions of the First Amendment unless it is devoted to public use. Here, plaintiff did not invite members of the general public to climb on or chain themselves to its equipment or otherwise subject itself to the proscriptions of the First Amendment.

Finally, defendants rely on the assembly and petition clauses of the First Amendment. They argue that the imposition of punitive damages violates their federally protected rights to assemble and to petition the government.

. . . .

The First and Fourteenth Amendments do not preclude an award of punitive damages against defendants in this case.

The jury's verdict awarding plaintiff $25,000 in punitive damages was permissible. The decision of the Court of Appeals and the judgment of the circuit court are affirmed.

———————

Why were punitive damages allowed in this case? When do you think that the First Amendment should serve as a defense in a case alleging trespass to chattels? Trespass to land? What about picketing in shopping malls? Are there kinds of private property which are so open to the public that they should lose their private character, at least for some purposes?

G. Conversion

The line between trespass to chattels and conversion can be difficult to perceive. One court defined the difference as follows:

> ... the difference between the two torts is fundamentally one of degree, trespass constituting a lesser interference with another's chattel, conversion a more serious exercise of dominion or control over it. *See* Restatement (Second) of Torts, § 222A, Comment (1965).

> Thus, a trespass has been defined as an intentional use or intermeddling with the chattel in possession of another, Restatement (Second) of Torts, § 217(b), such intermeddling occurring, *inter alia*, when "the chattel is impaired as to its condition, quality, or value." Restatement (Second) of Torts, § 218(b). *See also Walser v. Resthaven Memorial Gardens, Inc.*, 98 Md. App. 371, 395, 633 A.2d 466 (1993).

> A "conversion," on the other hand, has been defined as:

> [A]n intentional exercise of dominion or control over a chattel which so seriously interferes with the right of another to control it that the actor may justly be required to pay the other the full value of the chattel. Restatement (Second) of Torts, § 222A(1). Whereas impairing the condition, quality or value of a chattel upon brief interference can constitute a trespass, intentional destruction or material alteration of a chattel will subject the actor to liability for conversion. Restatement (Second) of Torts, § 226.

> A number of factors are considered in determining whether interference with a chattel is serious enough to constitute a conversion as opposed to a trespass. These include:

> a) the extent and duration of the actor's exercise of dominion or control;

> b) the actor's intent to assert a right in fact inconsistent with the other's right of control;

> c) the actor's good faith;

> d) the extent and duration of the resulting interference with the other's right of control;

e) the harm done to the chattel;

f) the inconvenience and expense caused to the other.[9]

[Citation], quoting Restatement (Second) of Torts, § 222A(2).

United States v. Arora, 860 F. Supp. 1091, 1097–98 (D. Md. 1994).

Dickens v. Debolt

Supreme Court of Oregon, 1979 (en banc)
602 P.2d 246

TONGUE, JUSTICE.

This is an action for conversion by a fisherman against a state police officer who seized a sturgeon which he mistakenly believed to have been caught illegally and may have then eaten most of the "evidence." The case was tried before a jury, which returned a verdict of $250 in general damages and $750 punitive damages. The Attorney General appealed from the resulting judgment on behalf of the state police officer. The Court of Appeals reversed the judgment upon the ground that Oregon statutes confer complete and absolute immunity upon a state police officer in such a case. 39 Or. App. 575, 592 P.2d 1082 (1979).[1] We allowed plaintiff's petition for review.

The facts are bizarre. On September 12, 1977, plaintiff with his wife, an uncle and an aunt, drove over 150 miles from their home to fish for sturgeon in the Columbia River below the John Day Dam.

At about sundown plaintiff hooked a fish. After a good fight lasting about 30 minutes he landed his prize, a sturgeon — a "royal fish" — 43 inches in length and weighing between 40 and 45 pounds.[2] Being concerned over the fish spoiling and it being too late to drive home, plaintiff put the end of a rope through the gills of the sturgeon and tied the other end of the rope to a cable under the platform, leaving the fish alive and in the river.

Because Golden and Elliot were still fishing and had a mobile home parked nearby, plaintiff asked them to "keep an eye" on his sturgeon. Plaintiff and his party then

---

9. It is inconsequential that the actor may have received no benefit from the act. *Maryland Casualty Co. v. Wolff*, 180 Md. 513, 25 A.2d 665 (1942).

1. ORS 496.620, relied upon by the Court of Appeals, provides:
  "No person authorized to enforce the wildlife laws shall suffer any civil liability for the enforcement or attempted enforcement of any provisions of the wildlife laws . . ."
ORS 30.265(3)(c), also referred to by the Court of Appeals, provides
    "(3) Every public body and its officers, employees and agents acting within the scope of their employment or duties are immune from liability for:
    "(c) Any claim based upon the performance of or the failure to exercise or perform a discretionary function or duty, whether or not the discretion is abused."

2. Under English common law, a sturgeon was a "royal fish" which belonged to the king and no subject could take such a fish without a royal grant. *Arnold v. Mundy*, 6 N.J.L. 1, 76 (1821).

went to a motel about one mile away in Rufus, where they had dinner and spent the night.

On returning to the river the next morning to get his sturgeon, plaintiff found the rope cut and the fish gone. He was then told by Rans Golden that a state police officer had taken the fish and had said that if plaintiff wanted it he "would have to call." Plaintiff testified that he then called the desk sergeant of the state police at Arlington, told him what had happened and asked for his fish, but was told that he would not get it back. Plaintiff also testified that he told the desk sergeant that he had witnesses who had seen him catch the fish, and was told that "if we went to court all seven of us could go to jail for perjury."

Plaintiff never saw his sturgeon again. He testified that the "going price" for the 40 to 45 pounds of meat, which he had planned to eat, was $5.65 per pound and that the rope was a ski rope worth from $10 to $15. He was never interviewed by the state police, much less arrested or charged with catching the sturgeon illegally.

Defendant was the state police officer who took plaintiff's sturgeon. He testified that on the evening of that day he observed two persons fishing on the platform below the dam and saw one of them catch a sturgeon at about 10:00 p.m., it then being illegal to fish for sturgeon. He also saw them tie a rope through its gills and tie the rope to a cable under the platform. Defendant arrested the two fishermen, Rans Golden and Gregory Elliot, for angling after hours. He then looked over the platform and saw one sturgeon tied to a cable. He testified that he took the fish "as evidence" in the case against Golden and Elliot. He admitted, however, that they told him that the sturgeon "belonged to some people that were in a motel in Rufus," but that he did not "check (that) out," apparently because he did not believe Golden and Elliot, who had not told him that there were two sturgeon tied to cables under the platform, including the one that he had seen them catch and which he believed to be the fish that he took "as evidence."

Defendant then took plaintiff's sturgeon to Arlington, where he lived. He testified that because the state police "didn't have any deep freeze facilities there," it "seemed like a reasonable thing to do" for him to put the sturgeon in the freezer at his home.

Before doing so, however, defendant skinned and fileted the sturgeon, and "packaged it up." He testified that he also put a state police evidence tag "on the package," with his name and number and also the names of Elliot and Golden and the charge against them. At the trial defendant produced a package of frozen fish with such a tag on it.

Defendant testified that after the fish was fileted, the meat weighed 8 pounds. He also testified that he had not eaten any of the sturgeon. A professional fish buyer called as a witness by the defense to testify to a market value of $.85 per pound for the sturgeon, if dressed, also testified that a 40 pound sturgeon, after dressing by removal of head and entrails, would "lose at least 15 percent," depending on the size of the head (or at least 6 pounds, with up to 34 pounds of the 40 pound fish remaining).

The answer filed by the Attorney General on behalf of defendant, in addition to denying most of the facts alleged in plaintiff's complaint for conversion, alleged the following affirmative defenses:

> "At all times material herein, defendant was acting in his official capacity as a trooper of the Oregon State Police, and seized said sturgeon and water ski rope as the fruits of a crime and at the time of and pursuant to a valid arrest." (ORS 496.620)

and,

> "At all times material herein, defendant, a trooper of the Oregon State Police, was performing a discretionary function." (ORS 30.265(3)(c)).

At the conclusion of the testimony defendant moved for a directed verdict upon the ground, among others, that ORS 496.620 conferred complete and absolute immunity upon defendant. Later, after the jury verdict in favor of plaintiff, defendant moved for a judgment notwithstanding the verdict on the same grounds. In the order denying that motion the trial judge held as follows:

> The storage of the fish in the private freezer might have been within the defendant's scope of employment, but there is no way a State Policeman's duties include the eating of filet of sturgeon.

We agree with the trial judge.

In holding that the trial judge erred in denying defendant's motion for directed verdict, the Court of Appeals recognized that the jury could have properly inferred from the facts that "there was an unexplained shrinkage in the amount of sturgeon still available at the time of trial," not only that "the officer had eaten a portion of the fish," but also that "the officer intended to do so when he seized the fish." (39 Or. App. at 580, 592 P.2d at 1085).

. . . .

As we analyze the problem presented by this case, however, the issue to be decided in determining whether ORS 496.620 provides immunity to the defendant is not whether he acted in good faith or in bad faith, but whether he was engaged in "the enforcement or attempted enforcement of . . . the wild life laws" or in "the exercise or attempted exercise of any of the duties or privileges granted to or imposed by law upon" the defendant when he "ate most of the evidence," as the jury was entitled to find.

We may agree that when a state police officer seizes a fish that he believes to have been caught illegally he is entitled to immunity under ORS 496.620. We do not believe, however, that this statute can properly be construed to mean when a state police officer "eats the evidence" he is then engaged in either the "enforcement or attempted enforcement" of the game laws or the "exercise or attempted exercise" of any of his "duties or privileges" as an officer. It follows, in our opinion, that the reasoning on which the Court of Appeals based its decision of this case is faulty and that it was in error in holding that ORS 496.620 granted an immunity to the defendant as a complete defense to this case.

For similar reasons, we hold that ORS 30.265(3)(c) of the Oregon Tort Claims Act does not confer immunity upon defendant as for the performance of a discretionary function or duty. Thus, we hold that when defendant ate most of the sturgeon, as the jury could properly find, he was not then acting "within the scope of (his) employment or duties," within the meaning of that statute.

. . . .

Both in instructions requested at the time of trial on behalf of the defendant and in the brief filed on his behalf in the Court of Appeals, it is contended by the Attorney General that a conversion in such a case is to be defined as held by this court in *Mustola v. Toddy*, 253 Or. 658, 456 P.2d 1004 (1969) (also an action for conversion against a state police officer), in which this court (at 663–64, 456 P.2d 1004) adopted Restatement (Second) of Torts § 222A (1965) as a definition of conversion for application in such a case and which reads as follows:

§ 222A. What Constitutes Conversion

"(1) Conversion is an intentional exercise of dominion or control over a chattel which so seriously interferes with the right of another to control it that the actor may justly be required to pay the other the full value of the chattel.

(2) In determining the seriousness of the interference and the justice of requiring the actor to pay the full value, the following factors are important: [The list of factors is presented earlier with the definition of conversion.]"

. . . .

ORS 496.620 would protect the officer from the legal consequences of that conversion only as long as he held the fish for the purpose which the statute protects; i.e., attempted enforcement of the wild life laws. The same is also true of ORS 30.265(3)(c). For reasons previously stated, we hold that those statutes do not confer such an immunity. It follows, in our opinion, that the trial court properly denied defendant's motion for a directed verdict and that the Court of Appeals erred in holding to the contrary.

. . . .

If, however, this defendant ate most of the sturgeon and at that time was *not* acting within the course and scope of his employment, as the jury was entitled to find from the evidence of this case, he would then be subject to punitive damages on the same basis as any other person who commits an act of conversion. This court has held that punitive damages may properly be awarded by a jury in actions for conversion when the circumstances are sufficiently aggravated.

Because the trial court erred in failing to give two of defendant's requested instructions, this case must be remanded to it for a new trial.

[Reversed] and remanded.

—————

The reasons for the reversal of the trial court had nothing to do with the substance of the opinion.

How did the court know that the defendant had eaten the fish? What should the defendant have done with the fish instead? What relationship did the fact that the defendant ate the fish bear to the conclusion that his employer would not be held liable for his conduct?

Pearson v. Dodd

United States Court of Appeals for the District of Columbia Circuit, 1969
410 F.2d 701

J. Skelly Wright, Circuit Judge:

This case arises out of the exposure of the alleged misdeeds of Senator Thomas Dodd of Connecticut by newspaper columnists Drew Pearson and Jack Anderson. The District Court has granted partial summary judgment to Senator Dodd, appellee here, finding liability on a theory of conversion. At the same time, the court denied partial summary judgment on the theory of invasion of privacy. Both branches of the court's judgment are before us on interlocutory appeal. We affirm the District Court's denial of summary judgment for invasion of privacy and reverse its grant of summary judgment for conversion.

The undisputed facts in the case were stated by the District Court as follows:

"... [O]n several occasions in June and July, 1965, two former employees of the plaintiff, at times with the assistance of two members of the plaintiff's staff, entered the plaintiff's office without authority and unbeknownst to him, removed numerous documents from his files, made copies of them, replaced the originals, and turned over the copies to the defendant Anderson, who was aware of the manner in which the copies had been obtained. The defendants Pearson and Anderson thereafter published articles containing information gleaned from these documents."[2]

. . . .

II

The District Court ruled that appellants' receipt and subsequent use of photocopies of documents which appellants knew had been removed from Appellee's files

—————

2. *Dodd v. Pearson*, D.D.C., 279 F. Supp. 101, 102 (1968).

without authorization established appellants' liability for conversion. We conclude that appellants are not guilty of conversion on the facts shown.

Dean Prosser has remarked that "[conversion is the forgotten tort."[21] That it is not entirely forgotten is attested by the case before us. History has largely defined its contours, contours which we should now follow except where they derive from clearly obsolete practices or abandoned theories.[22]

Conversion is the substantive tort theory which underlay the ancient common law form of action for trover. A plaintiff in trover alleged that he had lost a chattel which he rightfully possessed,[23] and that the defendant had found it and converted it to his own use. With time, the allegations of losing and finding became fictional, leaving the question of whether the defendant had "converted" the property the only operative one.

The most distinctive feature of conversion is its measure of damages, which is the value of the goods converted. The theory is that the "converting" defendant has in some way treated the goods as if they were his own, so that the plaintiff can properly ask the court to decree a forced sale of the property from the rightful possessor to the converter.

Because of this stringent measure of damages, it has long been recognized that not every wrongful interference with the personal property of another is a conversion. Where the intermeddling falls short of the complete or very substantial deprivation of possessory rights in the property, the tort committed is not conversion, but the lesser wrong of trespass to chattels.

The Second Restatement of Torts has marked the distinction by defining conversion as:

> "... [A]n intentional exercise of dominion or control over a chattel which so seriously interferes with the right of another to control it that the actor may justly be required to pay the other the full value of the chattel."[29]

Less serious interferences fall under the Restatement's definition of trespass.[30]

The difference is more than a semantic one. The measure of damages in trespass is not the whole value of the property interfered with, but rather the actual

---

21. Prosser, *The Nature of Conversion*, 42 Corn. L.Q. 168 (1957).

22. *Cf. id.* at 169: "The hand of history lies heavy upon the tort of conversion."

23. A threshold question, not briefed by either party and hence not decided by us, is the nature of the property right held by appellee in the contents of the files in his Senate office. Those files, themselves paid for by the United States, are maintained in an office owned by the United States, by employees of the United States. They are meant to contribute to the work of appellee as an officer of the United States. The question thus is not entirely free from doubt whether appellee has title to the contents of the files or has a right of exclusive possession of those contents, or is a bailee, or even a mere custodian of those contents.

29. Restatement (Second) of Torts § 222A(1) (1965).

30. *Id.*, § 217: "A trespass to a chattel may be committed by intentionally (a) dispossessing another of the chattel, or (b) using or intermeddling with a chattel in the possession of another."

diminution in its value caused by the interference. More important for this case, a judgment for conversion can be obtained with only nominal damages, whereas liability for trespass to chattels exists only on a showing of actual damage to the property interfered with.[32]

It is clear that on the agreed facts appellants committed no conversion of the physical documents taken from Appellee's files. Those documents were removed from the files at night, photocopied, and returned to the files undamaged before office operations resumed in the morning. Insofar as the documents' value to appellee resided in their usefulness as records of the business of his office, appellee was clearly not substantially deprived of his use of them.

This of course is not an end of the matter. It has long been recognized that documents often have value above and beyond that springing from their physical possession. They may embody information or ideas whose economic value depends in part or in whole upon being kept secret. The question then arises whether the information taken by means of copying Appellee's office files is of the type which the law of conversion protects. The general rule has been that ideas or information are not subject to legal protection,[34] but the law has developed exceptions to this rule.

Where information is gathered and arranged at some cost and sold as a commodity on the market, it is properly protected as property. Where ideas are formulated with labor and inventive genius, as in the case of literary works or scientific researches, they are protected. Where they constitute instruments of fair and effective commercial competition, those who develop them may gather their fruits under the protection of the law.

The question here is not whether appellee had a right to keep his files from prying eyes, but whether the information taken from those files falls under the protection of the law of property, enforceable by a suit for conversion. In our view, it does not. The information included the contents of letters to appellee from supplicants, and office records of other kinds, the nature of which is not fully revealed by the record. Insofar as we can tell, none of it amounts to literary property, to scientific invention, or to secret plans formulated by appellee for the conduct of commerce.

---

32. "To support an action of trespass to a chattel where the invasion of interests does not result in its destruction or in a dispossession thereof, it was early held there must be some physical harm to the chattel or to its possessor. Unlike the action of trespass quare clausum fregit in the case of land, no action could be maintained for a mere harmless intermeddling with goods. The possessor's proprietary interest in the inviolability of his personal property did not receive that protection which the similar interest in the possession of land or the dignitary interest in the inviolability of the person receives. . . ." 1 F. Harper & F. James, *supra* Note 25, § 2.3. (Footnotes omitted.)

34. The traditional rule has been that conversion will lie only for the taking of tangible property, or rights embodied in a tangible token necessary for the enforcement of those rights. [Citations.] This overly restrictive rule has recently been relaxed in favor of the reasonable proposition that any intangible generally protected as personal property may be the subject matter of a suit for conversion.

Nor does it appear to be information held in any way for sale by appellee, analogous to the fresh news copy produced by a wire service.

Appellee complains, not of the misappropriation of property bought or created by him, but of the exposure of information either (1) injurious to his reputation or (2) revelatory of matters which he believes he has a right to keep to himself. Injuries of this type are redressed at law by suit for libel and invasion of privacy respectively, where Defendants' liability for those torts can be established under the limitations created by common law and by the Constitution.

Because no conversion of the physical contents of Appellee's files took place, and because the information copied from the documents in those files has not been shown to be property subject to protection by suit for conversion, the District Court's ruling that appellants are guilty of conversion must be reversed.

So ordered.

TAMM, CIRCUIT JUDGE (concurring):

Some legal scholars will see in the majority opinion—as distinguished from its actual holding—an ironic aspect.

Conduct for which a law enforcement officer would be soundly castigated is, by the phraseology of the majority opinion, found tolerable; conduct which, if engaged in by government agents would lead to the suppression of evidence obtained by these means, is approved when used for the profit of the press. . . .

––––––––––

1. Must property be tangible in order to be converted? In *National Surety Corp. v. Applied Sys.*, 418 So. 2d 847 (Ala. 1982), the court decided that computer programs could be the subject of a suit for conversion. In an era when the most valuable property may well be intangible, the conclusion that conversion does not require tangibility is an important one.

2. What analytic difficulties does the application of conversion law to intangible property create?

H. Nuisance

Nuisance is, of course, an intentional tort. As was discussed earlier, it involves a defendant who is engaging in an activity on his or her own property that adversely affects other property owners and their ability to enjoy their own property. The following case provides a modern and creative approach to the problem of the appropriate remedy in nuisance cases. In the past, the remedy has tended to be injunctive, ordering the defendant to stop what he or she is doing. The balancing of the interests of the parties, however, may mean that an injunction is not the best way to approach the problem.

Spur Industries, Inc. v. Del E. Webb Development Co.

Supreme Court of Arizona, 1972
494 P.2d 700

In Banc.

CAMERON, VICE CHIEF JUSTICE

From a judgment permanently enjoining the defendant, Spur Industries, Inc., from operating a cattle feedlot near the plaintiff Del E. Webb Development Company's Sun City, Spur appeals. Webb cross-appeals. Although numerous issues are raised, we feel that it is necessary to answer only two questions. They are:

> 1. Where the operation of a business, such as a cattle feedlot is lawful in the first instance, but becomes a nuisance by reason of a nearby residential area, may the feedlot operation be enjoined in an action brought by the developer of the residential area?

> 2. Assuming that the nuisance may be enjoined, may the developer of a completely new town or urban area in a previously agricultural area be required to indemnify the operator of the feedlot who must move or cease operation because of the presence of the residential area created by the developer?

The facts necessary for a determination of this matter on appeal are as follows. The area in question is located in Maricopa County, Arizona, some 14 to 15 miles west of the urban area of Phoenix, on the Phoenix-Wickenburg Highway, also known as Grand Avenue. About two miles south of Grand Avenue is Olive Avenue which runs east and west. 111th Avenue runs north and south as does the Agua Fria River immediately to the west.

Farming started in this area about 1911. In 1929, with the completion of the Carl Pleasant Dam, gravity flow water became available to the property located to the west of the Agua Fria River, though land to the east remained dependent upon well water for irrigation. By 1950, the only urban areas in the vicinity were the agriculturally related communities of Peoria, El Mirage, and Surprise located along Grand Avenue. Along 111th Avenue, approximately one mile south of Grand Avenue and 1 1/2 miles north of Olive Avenue, the community of Youngtown was commenced in 1954. Youngtown is a retirement community appealing primarily to senior citizens.

In 1956, Spur's predecessors in interest, H. Marion Welborn and the Northside Hay Mill and Trading Company, developed feedlots, about 1/2 mile south of Olive Avenue, in an area between the confluence of the usually dry Agua Fria and New Rivers. The area is well suited for cattle feeding and in 1959, there were 25 cattle feeding pens or dairy operations within a 7 mile radius of the location developed by Spur's predecessors. In April and May of 1959, the Northside Hay Mill was feeding between 6,000 and 7,000 head of cattle and Welborn approximately 1,500 head on a combined area of 35 acres.

In May of 1959, Del Webb began to plan the development of an urban area to be known as Sun City. For this purpose, the Marinette and the Santa Fe Ranches, some

20,000 acres of farmland, were purchased for $15,000,000 or $750.00 per acre. This price was considerably less than the price of land located near the urban area of Phoenix, and along with the success of Youngtown was a factor influencing the decision to purchase the property in question.

By September 1959, Del Webb had started construction of a golf course south of Grand Avenue and Spur's predecessors had started to level ground for more feedlot area. In 1960, Spur purchased the property in question and began a rebuilding and expansion program extending both to the north and south of the original facilities. By 1962, Spur's expansion program was completed and had expanded from approximately 35 acres to 114 acres.

Accompanied by an extensive advertising campaign, homes were first offered by Del Webb in January 1960 and the first unit to be completed was south of Grand Avenue and approximately 2 1/2 miles north of Spur. By 2 May 1960, there were 450 to 500 houses completed or under construction. At this time, Del Webb did not consider odors from the Spur feed pens a problem and Del Webb continued to develop in a southerly direction, until sales resistance became so great that the parcels were difficult if not impossible to sell. . . .

By December 1967, Del Webb's property had extended south to Olive Avenue and Spur was within 500 feet of Olive Avenue to the north. Del Webb filed its original complaint alleging that in excess of 1,300 lots in the southwest portion were unfit for development for sale as residential lots because of the operation of the Spur feedlot.

Del Webb's suit complained that the Spur feeding operation was a public nuisance because of the flies and the odor which were drifting or being blown by the prevailing south to north wind over the southern portion of Sun City. At the time of the suit, Spur was feeding between 20,000 and 30,000 head of cattle, and the facts amply support the finding of the trial court that the feed pens had become a nuisance to the people who resided in the southern part of Del Webb's development. The testimony indicated that cattle in a commercial feedlot will produce 35 to 40 pounds of wet manure per day, per head, or over a million pounds of wet manure per day for 30,000 head of cattle, and that despite the admittedly good feedlot management and good housekeeping practices by Spur, the resulting odor and flies produced an annoying if not unhealthy situation as far as the senior citizens of southern Sun City were concerned. There is no doubt that some of the citizens of Sun City were unable to enjoy the outdoor living which Del Webb had advertised and that Del Webb was faced with sales resistance from prospective purchasers as well as strong and persistent complaints from the people who had purchased homes in that area.

Trial was commenced before the court with an advisory jury. The advisory jury was later discharged and the trial was continued before the court alone. Findings of fact and conclusions of law were requested and given. The case was vigorously contested, including special actions in this court on some of the matters. In one of the special actions before this court, Spur agreed to, and did, shut down its operation without prejudice to a determination of the matter on appeal. On appeal the many questions raised were extensively briefed.

It is noted, however, that neither the citizens of Sun City nor Youngtown are represented in this lawsuit and the suit is solely between Del E. Webb Development Company and Spur Industries, Inc.

MAY SPUR BE ENJOINED?

The difference between a private nuisance and a public nuisance is generally one of degree. A private nuisance is one affecting a single individual or a definite small number of persons in the enjoyment of private rights not common to the public, while a public nuisance is one affecting the rights enjoyed by citizens as a part of the public. To constitute a public nuisance, the nuisance must affect a considerable number of people or an entire community or neighborhood. *City of Phoenix v. Johnson*, 51 Ariz. 115, 75 P.2d 30 (1938).

Where the injury is slight, the remedy for minor inconveniences lies in an action for damages rather than in one for an injunction. *Kubby v. Hammond*, 68 Ariz. 17, 198 P.2d 134 (1948). Moreover, some courts have held, in the "balancing of conveniences" cases, that damages may be the sole remedy. See *Boomer v. Atlantic Cement Co.*, 26 N.Y.2d 219, 309 N.Y.S.2d 312, 257 N.E.2d 870, 40 AL.R.3d 590 (1970), and annotation comments, 40 A.L.R.3d 601.

Thus, it would appear from the admittedly incomplete record as developed in the trial court, that, at most, residents of Youngtown would be entitled to damages rather than injunctive relief.

We have no difficulty, however, in agreeing with the conclusion of the trial court that Spur's operation was an enjoinable public nuisance as far as the people in the southern portion of Del Webb's Sun City were concerned.

§ 36-601, subsec. A reads as follows:

"§ 36-601. Public nuisances dangerous to public health

"A. The following conditions are specifically declared public nuisances dangerous to the public health:

"1. Any condition or place in populous areas which constitutes a breeding place for flies, rodents, mosquitoes and other insects which are capable of carrying and transmitting disease-causing organisms to any person or persons."

By this statute, before an otherwise lawful (and necessary) business may be declared a public nuisance, there must be a "populous" area in which people are injured:

". . . [I]t hardly admits a doubt that, in determining the question as to whether a lawful occupation is so conducted as to constitute a nuisance as a matter of fact, the locality and surroundings are of the first importance (citations omitted). A business which is not per se a public nuisance may become such by being carried on at a place where the health, comfort, or convenience of a populous neighborhood is affected.... What might amount to a serious nuisance in one locality by reason of the density of the population, or character of the neighborhood affected, may in another place and under different surroundings be deemed proper and unobjectionable...." *MacDonald v. Perry*, 32 Ariz. 39, 49–50, 255 P. 494, 497 (1927).

It is clear that as to the citizens of Sun City, the operation of Spur's feedlot was both a public and a private nuisance. They could have successfully maintained an action to abate the nuisance. Del Webb, having shown a special injury in the loss of sales, had standing to bring suit to enjoin the nuisance. *Engle v. Clark*, 53 Ariz. 472, 90 P.2d 994 (1939); *City of Phoenix v. Johnson, supra.* The judgment of the trial court permanently enjoining the operation of the feedlot is affirmed.

MUST DEL WEBB INDEMNIFY SPUR?

A suit to enjoin a nuisance sounds in equity and the courts have long recognized a special responsibility to the public when acting as a court of equity:

"§ 104. Where public interest is involved.

"Courts of equity may, and frequently do, go much further both to give and withhold relief in furtherance of the public interest than they are accustomed to go when only private interests are involved. Accordingly, the granting or withholding of relief may properly be dependent upon considerations of public interest...." 27 Am. Jur. 2d, Equity, page 626.

In addition to protecting the public interest, however, courts of equity are concerned with protecting the operator of a lawfully, albeit noxious, business from the result of a knowing and willful encroachment by others near his business.

In the so-called "coming to the nuisance" cases, the courts have held that the residential landowner may not have relief if he knowingly came into a neighborhood reserved for industrial or agricultural endeavors and has been damaged thereby:

"Plaintiffs chose to live in an area uncontrolled by zoning laws or restrictive covenants and remote from urban development. In such an area plaintiffs cannot complain that legitimate agricultural pursuits are being carried on in the vicinity, nor can plaintiffs, having chosen to build in an agricultural area, complain that the agricultural pursuits carried on in the area depreciate the value of their homes. The area being primarily agricultural, any opinion reflecting the value of such property must take this factor into account. The standards affecting the value of residence property in an urban setting, subject to zoning controls and controlled planning techniques, cannot be the standards by which agricultural properties are judged.

"People employed in a city who build their homes in suburban areas of the county beyond the limits of a city and zoning regulations do so for a reason. Some do so to avoid the high taxation rate imposed by cities, or to avoid special assessments for street, sewer and water projects. They usually build on improved or hard surface highways, which have been built either at state or county expense and thereby avoid special assessments for these improvements. It may be that they desire to get away from the congestion of traffic, smoke, noise, foul air and the many other annoyances of city life. But with all these advantages in going beyond the area which is zoned and restricted to protect them in their homes, they must be prepared to take the disadvantages." *Dill v. Excel Packing Company*, 183 Kan. 513, 525, 526, 331 P.2d 539, 548, 549 (1958). See also *East St. Johns Shingle Co. v. City of Portland*, 195 Or. 505, 246 P.2d 554, 560–562 (1952).

And:

"... a party cannot justly call upon the law to make that place suitable for his residence which was not so when he selected it. ..." *Gilbert v. Showerman*, 23 Mich. 448, 455, 2 Brown 158 (1871).

Were Webb the only party injured, we would feel justified in holding that the doctrine of "coming to the nuisance" would have been a bar to the relief asked by Webb, and, on the other hand, had Spur located the feedlot near the outskirts of a city and had the city grown toward the feedlot, Spur would have to suffer the cost of abating the nuisance as to those people locating within the growth pattern of the expanding city:

"The case affords, perhaps, an example where a business established at a place remote from population is gradually surrounded and becomes part of a populous center, so that a business which formerly was not an interference with the rights of others has become so by the encroachment of the population. ..." *City of Ft. Smith v. Western Hide & Fur Co.*, 153 Ark. 99, 103, 239 S.W. 724, 726 (1922).

We agree, however, with the Massachusetts court that:

"The law of nuisance affords no rigid rule to be applied in all instances. It is elastic. It undertakes to require only that which is fair and reasonable under all the circumstances. In a commonwealth like this, which depends for its material prosperity so largely on the continued growth and enlargement of manufacturing of diverse varieties, 'extreme rights' cannot be enforced. ..." *Stevens v. Rockport Granite Co.*, 216 Mass. 486, 488, 104 N.E. 371, 373 (1914).

There was no indication in the instant case at the time Spur and its predecessors located in western Maricopa County that a new city would spring up, full-blown, alongside the feeding operation and that the developer of that city would ask the court to order Spur to move because of the new city. Spur is required to move not because of any wrongdoing on the part of Spur, but because of a proper and legitimate regard of the courts for the rights and interests of the public.

Del Webb, on the other hand, is entitled to the relief prayed for (a permanent injunction), not because Webb is blameless, but because of the damage to the people who have been encouraged to purchase homes in Sun City. It does not equitably or legally follow, however, that Webb, being entitled to the injunction, is then free of any liability to Spur if Webb has in fact been the cause of the damage Spur has sustained. It does not seem harsh to require a developer, who has taken advantage of the lesser land values in a rural area as well as the availability of large tracts of land on which to build and develop a new town or city in the area, to indemnify those who are forced to leave as a result.

Having brought people to the nuisance to the foreseeable detriment of Spur, Webb must indemnify Spur for a reasonable amount of the cost of moving or shutting down. It should be noted that this relief to Spur is limited to a case wherein a developer has, with foreseeability, brought into a previously agricultural or industrial area the population which makes necessary the granting of an injunction against a lawful business and for which the business has no adequate relief.

It is therefore the decision of this court that the matter be remanded to the trial court for a hearing upon the damages sustained by the defendant Spur as a reasonable and direct result of the granting of the permanent injunction. Since the result of the appeal may appear novel and both sides have obtained a measure of relief, it is ordered that each side will bear its own costs.

Affirmed in part, reversed in part, and remanded for further proceedings consistent with this opinion.

HAYS, C.J., STRUCKMEYER and LOCKWOOD, JJ., and UDALL, RETIRED JUSTICE.

––––––––––

Does the result in *Spur Industries* seem fair? In an era in which cities are sprawling and suburbs are transforming former farmlands, how should a court handle the inevitable conflicts? How important should a public priority—either developing or preserving farmlands—be in a court's analysis? What happens to the "coming to the nuisance" doctrine in *Spur Industries*? Didn't the homeowners, as well as Del Webb, come to the nuisance?

Chapter 3

Privileges

This chapter deals with the privileges which, if applicable, justify or exempt from liability the intentional act that is the basis of the underlying intentional tort suit. When arguing that an action was privileged, the defendant basically concedes that the facts as alleged are correct, but contends that he or she should not be liable for the reason covered by the privilege. The defendant in these cases is not arguing that any element of the intentional tort is missing. Rather, the argument is that the defendant's acts, which would subject the defendant to liability in the absence of a privilege, should not subject the defendant to liability because of the operation of the privilege. Under the privileges discussed in this chapter, the defendant basically agrees that the act that is the basis for the tort suit occurred, but contends that he or she should not be liable because the act was privileged.

A. Defenses to Battery

In the Intentional Torts chapter, we saw that the courts reject good intentions as a defense in battery cases. Similarly, the fact that the act at issue benefitted the plaintiff does not constitute a defense in an intentional tort suit. The injury in a battery case is the unconsented-to touching itself, irrespective of whether this touching benefitted the plaintiff. This contrasts sharply with torts based on negligence; in negligence-based jurisprudence, if there are no damages, there is no liability.

1. The Medical Arena

Mohr v. Williams

Supreme Court of Minnesota, 1905
104 N.W. 12,
overruled on an additur issue, *Genzel v. Halvorson*, 80 N.W.2d 854 (1957)

Brown, J.

Defendant is a physician and surgeon of standing and character, making disorders of the ear a specialty, and having an extensive practice in the city of St. Paul. . . . He informed plaintiff of the result of his examination [on her right ear], and advised an operation for the purpose of removing the polyp and diseased ossicles. After consultation with her family physician, and one or two further consultations with defendant, plaintiff decided to submit to the proposed operation. She was not informed that her left ear was in any way diseased, and understood that the necessity for an operation applied to her right ear only. She repaired to the hospital, and was placed under the influence of anesthetics; and, after being made unconscious, defendant made a thorough examination of her left ear, and found it in a more serious condition than her right one. A small perforation was discovered high up in the drum membrane, hooded, and with granulated edges, and the bone of the inner wall of the middle ear was diseased and dead. He called this discovery to the attention of Dr. Davis—plaintiff's family physician, who attended the operation at her request—who also examined the ear, and confirmed defendant in his diagnosis. Defendant also further examined the right ear, and found its condition less serious than expected, and finally concluded that the left, instead of the right, should be operated upon; devoting to the right ear other treatment. He then performed the operation of ossiculectomy on plaintiff's left ear; removing a portion of the drum membrane, and scraping away the diseased portion of the inner wall of the ear. The operation was in every way successful and skillfully performed. It is claimed by plaintiff that the operation greatly impaired her hearing, seriously injured her person, and, not having been consented to by her, was wrongful and unlawful, constituting an assault and battery; and she brought this action to recover damages therefor. The trial in the court below resulted in a verdict for plaintiff for $14,322.50. Defendant thereafter moved the court for judgment notwithstanding the verdict [or for a new trial], on the ground that, on the evidence presented, plaintiff was not entitled to recover. . . . The trial court denied the motion for judgment, but granted a new trial on the ground, as stated in the order, that the damages were excessive. Defendant appealed from the order denying the motion for judgment, and plaintiff appealed from the order granting a new trial.

2. We come then to a consideration of the questions presented by defendant's appeal from the order denying his motion for judgment notwithstanding the verdict. It is contended that final judgment should be ordered in his favor for the following reasons: (a) That it appears from the evidence received on the trial that plaintiff consented to the operation on her left ear. (b) If the court shall find that no such consent was given, that, under the circumstances disclosed by the record, no consent was necessary, (c) That, under the facts disclosed, an action for assault and battery will not lie; it appearing conclusively, as counsel urge, that there is a total lack of evidence showing or tending to show malice or an evil intent on the part of defendant, or that the operation was negligently performed.

We shall consider first the question whether, under the circumstances shown in the record, the consent of plaintiff to the operation was necessary. If, under the particular facts of this case, such consent was unnecessary, no recovery can be had, for the evidence fairly shows that the operation complained of was skillfully performed and of a generally beneficial nature. But if the consent of plaintiff was necessary, then the further questions presented become important. This particular question is new in this state. . . . [W]e are unable to concur with counsel for defendant in their contention that the consent of plaintiff was unnecessary. . . . It cannot be doubted that ordinarily the patient must be consulted, and his consent given, before a physician may operate upon him. It was said in the case *of Pratt v. Davis*, 37 Chicago Leg. News, 213, referred to and commented on in Cent. Law J. 452: "Under a free government, at least, the free citizen's first and greatest right, which underlies all others — the right to the inviolability of his person; in other words, the right to himself — is the subject of universal acquiescence, and this right necessarily forbids a physician or surgeon, however skillful or eminent, who has been asked to examine, diagnose, advise, and prescribe (which are at least necessary first steps in treatment and care), to violate, without permission, the bodily integrity of his patient by a major or capital operation, placing him under an anaesthetic for that purpose, and operating upon him without his consent or knowledge." 1 Kinkead on Torts, § 375, states the general rule on this subject as follows: "The patient must be the final arbiter as to whether he will take his chances with the operation, or take his chances of living without it. Such is the natural right of the individual, which the law recognizes as a legal one. Consent, therefore, of an individual, must be either expressly or impliedly given before a surgeon may have the right to operate." . . . It is not, however, contended by defendant that under ordinary circumstances consent is unnecessary, but that, under the particular circumstances of this case, consent was implied; that it was an emergency case, such as to authorize the operation without express consent or permission. If a person should be injured to the extent of rendering him unconscious, and his injuries were of such a nature as to require prompt surgical attention, a physician called to attend him would be justified in applying such medical or surgical treatment as might reasonably be necessary for the preservation of his life or limb, and consent on the part of the injured person would be implied. And again, if, in the course of an operation to which the patient consented, the physician should discover conditions not anticipated before the operation was commenced, and which, if not removed, would endanger the life or health of the patient, he would, though no express consent was obtained or given, be justified in extending the operation to remove and overcome them. But such is not the case at bar. The diseased condition of plaintiff's left ear was not discovered in the course of an operation on the right, which was authorized, but upon an independent examination of that organ, made after the authorized operation was found unnecessary. Nor is the evidence such as to justify the court in holding, as a matter of law, that it was such an affection as would result immediately in the serious injury of plaintiff, or such an emergency as to justify proceeding without her consent. She had experienced no particular difficulty with that ear, and the questions as to when its diseased condition would become alarming or fatal, and whether there was an immediate necessity for an operation, were, under the evidence, questions of fact for the jury.

3. The contention of defendant that the operation was consented to by plaintiff is not sustained by the evidence. . . .

4. The last contention of defendant is . . . [in] an entire absence of any evidence tending to show an evil intent, the court should say, as a matter of law, that no

assault and battery was committed, even though she did not consent to the operation. In other words, that the absence of a showing that defendant was actuated by a wrongful intent, or guilty of negligence, relieves the act of defendant from the charge of an unlawful assault and battery. We are unable to reach that conclusion, though the contention is not without merit. It would seem to follow from what has been said on the other features of the case that the act of defendant amounted at least to a technical assault and battery. If the operation was performed without plaintiff's consent, and the circumstances were not such as to justify its performance without, it was wrongful; and, if it was wrongful, it was unlawful. As remarked in 1 Jaggard on Torts, 437, every person has a right to complete immunity of his person from physical interference of others, except in so far as contact may be necessary under the general doctrine of privilege; and any unlawful or unauthorized touching of the person of another, except it be in the spirit of pleasantry, constitutes an assault and battery. In the case at bar, as we have already seen, the question whether defendant's act in performing the operation upon plaintiff was authorized was a question for the jury to determine. If it was unauthorized, then it was, within what we have said, unlawful. It was a violent assault, not a mere pleasantry; and, even though no negligence is shown, it was wrongful and unlawful. The case is unlike a criminal prosecution for assault and battery, for there an unlawful intent must be shown. But that rule does not apply to a civil action, to maintain which it is sufficient to show that the assault complained of was wrongful and unlawful or the result of negligence.

The amount of plaintiff's recovery, if she is entitled to recover at all, must depend upon the character and extent of the injury inflicted upon her, in determining which the nature of the malady intended to be healed and the beneficial nature of the operation should be taken into consideration, as well as the good faith of the defendant.

Order affirmed.

JAGGARD, J., took no part.

———

1. The court states that the beneficial nature of the procedure should be taken into account in assessing damages, and implies that a battery might occur but no damages be awarded. Is this consistent with the nature of the injury? What is the nature of the injury in *Mohr*?

2. What if the unconsented-to touching were entirely beneficial, such that there was no injury other than the unconsented-to touching itself? What might an award of damages look like in such a case?

3. A doctor may be liable for battery if he or she exceeds the scope of the consent given, even in the absence of negligence and the presence of good faith. *Rogers v. Lumbermens Mut. Cas. Co.*, 119 So. 2d 649 (La. Ct. App. 1960) (patient consented to appendectomy, doctor performed hysterectomy, no emergency).

What can a doctor do prior to an operation to foreclose such liability?

Pauscher v. Iowa Methodist Medical Center

Supreme Court of Iowa, 1987
408 N.W.2d 355

[The doctrine of informed consent has its roots in the tort of battery. Originally, the failure to inform the plaintiff about the proposed treatment vitiated the consent (if any), and the defendant would thus be liable for battery. Informed consent has, however, metamorphosed into a negligence doctrine. Thus, *Pauscher v. Iowa Methodist Medical Center* appears in Chapter 5, Negligence, and not in this chapter.]

In battery cases, the injury includes the unconsented-to contact itself. Because informed consent is now part of negligence doctrine, the concept of the injury has changed. Many informed consent cases are lost by plaintiffs because the plaintiffs cannot show that the lack of information caused them any harm: in order to recover for a failure of informed consent, the plaintiff must prove that he or she would have chosen differently had he or she possessed the information that the doctor neglected to provide.

Ashcraft v. King

California Court of Appeal, Second District, 1991
278 Cal. Rptr. 900

JOHNSON, ASSOCIATE JUSTICE.

Plaintiff appeals from a judgment for defendant in this medical malpractice case. Because plaintiff was erroneously nonsuited on her battery cause of action we reverse the judgment as to that cause of action. In all other respects the judgment is affirmed.

Facts and Proceedings Below

In 1983, plaintiff Daisy Ashcraft, age 16, was diagnosed as having scoliosis, a curvature of the spine, destined to become debilitating if not corrected. Ms. Ashcraft was referred to defendant John King, M.D., an orthopedic surgeon.

Ms. Ashcraft went to Dr. King's office for a consultation. She was accompanied by her mother, Lulu Ashcraft. At that meeting Dr. King recommended surgery and described the procedure generally. During the course of the consultation Dr. King and the Ashcrafts discussed the subject of blood transfusions, including the use of family donated blood in the operation.

. . . [P]laintiff's mother testified she insisted the operation be performed using only family donated blood. Dr. King conceded the subject of family donated blood was discussed but only in terms of whether it was "possible" for the family to donate blood to be used in Ms. Ashcraft's operation. Both parties agree Dr. King informed

Ms. Ashcraft and her mother they should contact officials at Children's Hospital, where the operation would be performed, to arrange for family donated blood.

Ms. Ashcraft's mother and father and several other relatives went to Children's Hospital and gave blood before and during the operation. None of this blood ever went to Daisy Ashcraft. Instead, all of the blood Ms. Ashcraft received during the operation came from the general supplies on hand at Children's Hospital.

At the time of this surgery, in 1983, no test was available to determine whether blood was contaminated with the Human Immuno-deficiency Virus (HIV), the cause of AIDS. It was not until 1987 the hospital discovered Daisy Ashcraft had been transfused during surgery with blood from an HIV positive donor. Ms. Ashcraft went to the hospital for a blood test the day she received this information. The test was positive.

In her medical malpractice suit against Dr. King, Ms. Ashcraft sought damages on the theories of negligence and battery. The battery theory rested on Ms. Ashcraft's contention she had specifically conditioned her consent to surgery on the understanding only family donated blood would be used in her transfusions but Dr. King willfully ignored that condition.

After all the evidence was received, the trial court granted Dr. King's motion for nonsuit on the battery cause of action. The case was submitted to the jury only on the negligence theory. After five days of deliberation, the jury returned a verdict in favor of defendant by a vote of nine to three.

I. A Patient Has the Right to Impose Express Limitations or Conditions on a Doctor's Authority to Perform an Operation.

A. Doctor Is Subject to Liability for Battery for Exceeding the Conditions Imposed by the Patient.

As a general rule, one who consents to a touching cannot recover in an action for battery. (Rest. 2d Torts, § 892A.) Thus, one who gives informed consent to a surgery cannot recover for resulting harm under a theory of battery. However, it is well-recognized a person may place conditions on the consent. If the actor exceeds the terms or conditions of the consent, the consent does not protect the actor from liability for the excessive act. (Rest. 2d Torts, § 89A(3), (4), comment h, p. 369.)

. . . .

In the present case, Ms. Ashcraft's claim of battery rested on the theory that although the operation was consented to, the consent was subject to a specific condition: only family donated blood would be used. If Ms. Ashcraft could establish the existence of this condition and its breach by Dr. King, she would establish a battery.

II. Plaintiff Introduced Sufficient Evidence of Battery to Have the Claim Determined by the Jury.

At the close of evidence from both parties the trial court granted defendant's motion for nonsuit as to the cause of action for battery. For the reasons discussed below, granting the motion was prejudicial error.

. . . .

It is equally well settled what elements Ms. Ashcraft had to introduce evidence of in order to survive a motion for nonsuit. A battery is any intentional, unlawful and harmful contact by one person with the person of another. A harmful contact, intentionally done is the essence of a battery. A contact is "unlawful" if it is unconsented to. In order to recover on a theory of battery, Ms. Ashcraft had to establish: (1) her consent to the operation was conditioned on the use of only family donated blood; (2) defendant intentionally violated this condition while performing the operation; (3) Ms. Ashcraft suffered harm as a result of defendant's violation of the condition.

At trial it was undisputed no family donated blood was used in the operation on Ms. Ashcraft. It was also undisputed some of the blood given Ms. Ashcraft in the operation was contaminated with the Human Immuno-deficiency Virus (HIV), the cause of AIDS, and that as a result Ms. Ashcraft is HIV positive. Therefore, the questions on appeal are whether, accepting all evidence favorable to the plaintiff as true, . . . there was sufficient evidence from which the jury could have determined Ms. Ashcraft's consent to the operation was conditioned on the use of family donated blood only and that defendant intentionally exceeded this condition in performing the operation.

We have concluded Ms. Ashcraft's evidence was sufficient to meet this test and, thereby, overcome the motion for nonsuit.

A. Consent Conditional on Family Donated Blood

Based on the testimony of Ms. Ashcraft and her mother that they wanted only "family blood" used in the operation and defendant's acknowledgement: "that's fine," and his instruction to the Ashcrafts to contact the hospital to make arrangements, the jury could have found Ms. Ashcraft's consent to the operation was conditioned on the use of "family blood."

B. Intent to Act in Excess of the Conditional Consent

In an action for civil battery the element of intent is satisfied if the evidence shows defendant acted with a "willful disregard" of the plaintiff's rights. In the context of battery in a medical procedure, "[w]hen the patient gives permission to perform one type of treatment and the doctor performs another, the requisite element of deliberate intent to deviate from the consent given is present."

Evidence in this case showed defendant had permission to operate on condition he used family donated blood but that he operated using blood from the hospital's general supply. . . . [T]his evidence was sufficient to allow the jury to infer an intent to willfully disregard plaintiff's conditional consent.

Disposition

The judgment is reversed only as to plaintiff's cause of action for battery and, as to that cause of action, the matter is remanded to the trial court for further proceedings consistent with this opinion. In all other respects, the judgment is affirmed. Each party to bear its own costs on appeal.

LILLIE, P.J., and FRED WOODS, J., concur.

———————

The court's list of the elements that the plaintiff had to prove included the requirement that she "suffered harm as a result of defendant's violation of the condition." What does the court mean by this? Would there have been an injury to the plaintiff if the blood had not been tainted? Usually, actual harm in addition to the touching itself is not required in battery cases. Why did the court require harm here?

2. The Sports Arena

Marchetti v. Kalish

Supreme Court of Ohio, 1990
559 N.E.2d 699

In June 1982, thirteen-year-old plaintiff-appellee, Angela Marchetti, had several neighborhood friends over to her house, including Richard Kalish, age fifteen, to play a game called "kick the can." . . .

On the day in question, the children were playing a modified version of the game. Their variations included the use of a ball instead of a can, and the first player captured immediately became the new "it." While appellee was the person designated "it," she spotted appellant and ran to home base. Appellee placed her left foot on the ball and shouted appellant's name. Under the rules of the game, appellant was supposed to stop and in turn become "it." Appellant, however, continued to run towards appellee, colliding with her and kicking the ball out from under her foot. Appellee fell to the ground, and her right leg was broken in two places.

Appellee filed a complaint on October 19, 1987, alleging appellant had "negligently and/or willfully, wantonly and maliciously" caused the above injury. The trial court granted appellant's motion for summary judgment, relying on *Hanson v. Kynast* (1987), 38 Ohio App. 3d 58, 526 N.E.2d 327, for the proposition that a participant in a recreational or athletic sporting event can recover only for an intentional tort. The trial court found that in the appellee's deposition she admitted that she did not believe that the defendant had intended to injure her during the game. The trial court also held that as a voluntary participant in the game, appellee had assumed the risk of her injury.

The court of appeals reversed the trial court and remanded the cause, holding that an issue of fact existed as to whether appellee consented to appellant's action through her participation in the game. The court adopted 1 Restatement of the Law 2d, Torts (1965), Section 50, and 4 Restatement of the Law 2d, Torts (1979), Section 892A, and rejected the holding in *Hanson, supra.* Finding its decision to be in conflict with the decision of the Fifth District Court of Appeals in *Hanson,* the court certified the record of this case to this court for review and final determination.

ALICE ROBIE RESNICK, JUSTICE.

The issue for this court's determination is whether a participant in a recreational or sporting activity can recover for personal injuries received during the course of the activity absent evidence of reckless or intentional conduct.[2] Stated differently, the question is whether a showing of negligence will suffice to allow recovery under these circumstances. The court of appeals adopted Sections 50 and 892A of the Restatement of Torts 2d, and essentially applied a negligence standard. Since these issues have not been previously addressed by this court, we must determine the proper standard as to the liability of persons engaging in a recreational or sporting activity.

I

Legal commentators have identified three distinct standards which are used by some jurisdictions to permit recovery for injuries received during sports and recreational activities: (1) intentional tort, i.e., assault and battery; (2) willful or reckless misconduct; and (3) negligence. However, courts traditionally have not been inclined to allow a cause of action for injuries received during participation in such activities. In *Kuehner v. Green* (Fla. 1983), 436 So. 2d 78, 81, Justice Boyd, concurring specially, noted that "[h]istorically, the courts have been reluctant to allow persons to recover money damages for injuries received while participating in a sport, especially a contact sport, unless there was a deliberate attempt to injure. In denying recovery, the courts have often explained that a person who participates in a sport assumes the risk that he or she may be injured. Only recently have some courts allowed a sport participant to recover damages for injuries resulting from unintentional but reckless misconduct. These courts reasoned that a sport participant does not assume the

---

2. We will employ the term "intentional" as it is defined in 1 Restatement of the Law 2d, Torts (1965) 15, Section 8A. Likewise, we shall employ the term "reckless" as it is defined in 2 Restatement of the Law 2d, Torts (1965) 587, Section 500. Respectively, these definitions are as follows:

"The word 'intent' is used throughout the Restatement of this Subject to denote that the actor desires to cause consequences of his act, or that he believes that the consequences are substantially certain to result from it." Restatement of Torts 2d, Section 8A.

"The actor's conduct is in reckless disregard of the safety of another if he does an act or intentionally fails to do an act which it is his duty to the other to do, knowing or having reason to know of facts which would lead a reasonable man to realize, not only that his conduct creates an unreasonable risk of physical harm to another, but also that such risk is substantially greater than that which is necessary to make his conduct negligent." Restatement of Torts 2d, Section 500.

risk of injuries resulting from bodily contact uncustomary to or prohibited by the rules of the particular sport."

Likewise, while allowing a recovery for a sports injury based on intentional tort, a Michigan court has stated that "[p]articipation in a game involves a manifestation of consent to those bodily contacts which are permitted by the rules of the game. Restatement of Torts, 2d, § 50, comment b. However, there is a general agreement that an intentional act causing injury, which goes beyond what is ordinarily permissible, is an assault and battery for which recovery may be had." *Overall v. Kadella* (1984), 138 Mich. App. 351, 361 N.W.2d 352, 355. Thus, courts generally allow a cause of action for injuries sustained in recreational or sports activities only under reckless or intentional tort theories.

In *Hanson, supra*, the court of appeals held that there is no liability for participants in an athletic competition for conduct which falls short of an intentional tort. The court in *Hanson* was confronted with a plaintiff injured while competing in a collegiate lacrosse match. The court stated that ". . . the only cause of action in the instant situation that can exist (and thus survive a summary judgment motion) is an intentional tort. . . ." *Id.*, 38 Ohio App. 3d at 60, 526 N.E.2d at 329. . . .

II

Appellee argues that [the] cases from other jurisdictions are distinguishable from the present case because here we are dealing with children involved in a simple neighborhood game rather than an organized contact sport. However, courts in other jurisdictions have not made this distinction as to whether the injury arises in an organized activity, neighborhood game, or whether it involves children or adults.

The common thread in [the cited] cases and the instant case is that the children involved were engaging in some type of recreational or sports activity. Whether the activity is organized, unorganized, supervised or unsupervised is immaterial to the standard of liability. To hold otherwise would open the floodgates to a myriad of lawsuits involving the backyard games of children. Furthermore, the courts in [the cited cases] did not differentiate between adults' and children's recreational and sports activities. Rather, the courts applied the same standard of liability to children's sports activities as to those of adults.

Additionally, appellee urges this court to follow the court of appeals in adopting the view taken in the Restatement of Torts 2d, Sections 50 and 892A. These sections provide as follows:

"892A. Effect of Consent

"(1) One who effectively consents to conduct of another intended to invade his interests cannot recover in an action of tort for the conduct or for harm resulting from it.

"(2) To be effective, consent must be

"(a) by one who has the capacity to consent or by a person empowered to consent for him, and

"(b) to the particular conduct, or to substantially the same conduct.

"(3) Conditional consent or consent restricted as to time, area or in other respects is effective only within the limits of the condition or restriction.

"(4) If the actor exceeds the consent, it is not effective for the excess.

"(5) Upon termination of consent its effectiveness is terminated, except as it may have become irrevocable by contract or otherwise, or except as its terms may include, expressly or by implication, a privilege to continue to act."

"50. Apparent Consent.

"The rule stated in § 892(2) as to apparent consent to the invasion of an interest applies to the intentional invasion of interests of personality."

Comment b to Section 50 of the Restatement provides as follows:

Taking part in a game. Taking part in a game manifests a willingness to submit to such bodily contacts or restrictions of liberty as are permitted by its rules or usages. Participating in such a game does not manifest consent to contacts which are prohibited by rules or usages of the game if such rules or usages are designed to protect the participants and not merely to secure the better playing of the game as a test of skill. This is true although the player knows that those with or against whom he is playing are habitual violators of such rules."

The position taken by the Restatement involves an examination of the injured person's scope of consent in the context of the particular rules of the recreational or sports activity involved. Hence, the emphasis under the Restatement would be initially on the consent of the plaintiff rather than on the conduct of the other player. The next step would entail an analysis by the trial court of the applicable rules of the game or sport, and then superimposing these rules on the plaintiff's state of mind to determine the scope of his or her consent. The present case, or indeed any case involving children's recreational or sport activities, demonstrates the difficulty associated with this standard. We believe that requiring courts to delve into the minds of children to determine whether they understand the rules of the recreational or sports activity they are engaging in could lead to anomalous results. In this context, we perceive no reason to distinguish between children and adults. The policy which we and other courts seek to advance was set forth in *Nabozny [v. Barnhill*, 31 Ill. App. 3d 212, 215, 334 N.E.2d 258, 260 (1975)]: "[T]he law should not place unreasonable burdens on the free and vigorous participation in sports by our youth. However, we also believe that organized, athletic competition does not exist in a vacuum. Rather, some of the restraints of civilization must accompany every athlete onto the playing field. One of the educational benefits of organized athletic competition to our youth is the development of discipline and self-control." . . . [O]ur goal is to strike a balance between encouraging vigorous and free participation in recreational or sports activities, while ensuring the safety of the players. The standard announced today does not curtail, but indeed enhances this objective, regardless of whether the participants are children or adults.

We therefore decline to adopt the analysis under the Restatement of Torts 2d, Sections 50 and 892A. Traditional tort concepts place the emphasis on the conduct or actions of the tort-feasor. Thus, we join the weight of authority set forth above and require that before a party may proceed with a cause of action involving injury resulting from a recreational or sports activity, reckless or intentional conduct must exist.[3] We hold that where individuals engage in recreational or sports activities, they assume the ordinary risks of the activity and cannot recover for any injury unless it can be shown that the other participant's actions were either "reckless" or "intentional" as defined in Sections 500 and 8A of the Restatement of Torts 2d.

In the present case, plaintiff-appellee's own testimony demonstrates that appellant did not act either recklessly or intentionally. Thus, there is no question of fact that needs to be resolved regarding this material issue. Additionally, appellee is deemed to have assumed the risk by voluntarily participating in the game. Since there has been no showing of reckless or intentional conduct on the part of appellant, the trial court was correct in granting summary judgment in appellant's favor. We reverse the judgment of the court of appeals and reinstate the trial court's judgment.

Judgment reversed.

---

3. Comments *f* and *g* to Section 500 of the Restatement of Torts 2d, *supra*, at 590, provide a concise analysis which differentiates between the three mental states of tortious conduct with which we are confronted. Without further discourse, we cite to these comments with approval. They provide as follows:

"*f. Intentional misconduct and recklessness contrasted.* Reckless misconduct differs from intentional wrongdoing in a very important particular. While an act to be reckless must be intended by the actor, the actor does not intend to cause the harm which results from it. It is enough that he realizes or, from facts which he knows, should realize that there is a strong probability that harm may result, even though he hopes or even expects that his conduct will prove harmless. However, a strong probability is a different thing from the substantial certainty without which he cannot be said to intend the harm in which his act results."

"*g. Negligence and recklessness contrasted.* Reckless misconduct differs from negligence in several important particulars. It differs from that form of negligence which consists in mere inadvertence, incompetence, unskillfulness, or a failure to take precautions to enable the actor adequately to cope with a possible or probable future emergency, in that reckless misconduct requires a conscious choice of a course of action, either with knowledge of the serious danger to others involved in it or with knowledge of facts which would disclose this danger to any reasonable man. It differs not only from the above-mentioned form of negligence, but also from that negligence which consists in intentionally doing an act with knowledge that it contains a risk of harm to others, in that the actor to be reckless must recognize that his conduct involves a risk substantially greater in amount than that which is necessary to make his conduct negligent. The difference between reckless misconduct and conduct involving only such a quantum of risk as is necessary to make it negligent is a difference in the degree of the risk, but this difference of degree is so marked as to amount substantially to a difference in kind."

Moyer, C.J., concurs separately.

Koffman v. Garnett

Supreme Court of Virginia, 2003
574 S.E.2d 258

Lacy, J.

In the fall of 2000, Andrew W. Koffman, a 13-year old middle school student at a public school in Botetourt County, began participating on the school's football team. It was Andy's first season playing organized football, and he was positioned as a third-string defensive player. James Garnett was employed by the Botetourt County School Board as an assistant coach for the football team and was responsible for the supervision, training, and instruction of the team's defensive players.

The team lost its first game of the season. Garnett was upset by the defensive players' inadequate tackling in that game and became further displeased by what he perceived as inadequate tackling during the first practice following the loss.

Garnett ordered Andy to hold a football and "stand upright and motionless" so that Garnett could explain the proper tackling technique to the defensive players. Then Garnett, without further warning, thrust his arms around Andy's body, lifted him "off his feet by two feet or more," and "slammed" him to the ground. Andy weighed 144 pounds, while Garnett weighed approximately 260 pounds. The force of the tackle broke the humerus bone in Andy's left arm. During prior practices, no coach had used physical force to instruct players on rules or techniques of playing football.

In his second amended motion for judgment, Andy, by his father and next friend, Richard Koffman, and Andy's parents, Richard and Rebecca Koffman, individually, (collectively "the Koffmans") alleged that Andy was injured as a result of Garnett's . . . intentional acts of assault and battery. Garnett filed a demurrer and plea of sovereign immunity, asserting that the second amended motion for judgment did not allege sufficient facts to support a lack of consent to the tackling demonstration and, therefore, did not plead causes of action for either, . . . assault, or battery. The trial court dismissed the action, finding that . . . the facts alleged were insufficient to state causes of action for gross negligence, assault, or battery because the instruction and playing of football are "inherently dangerous and always potentially violent."

In this appeal, the Koffmans . . . assert that they pled sufficient facts in their second amended motion for judgment to sustain their claims of . . . assault and battery. . . .

The second amended motion for judgment is sufficient, however, to establish a cause of action for the tort of battery. The Koffmans pled that Andy consented to physical contact with players "of like age and experience" and that neither Andy nor his parents expected or consented to his "participation in aggressive contact tackling by the adult coaches." Further, the Koffmans pled that, in the past, coaches had not tackled players as a method of instruction. Garnett asserts that, by consenting to play football, Andy consented to be tackled, by either other football players or by the coaches.

Whether Andy consented to be tackled by Garnett in the manner alleged was a matter of fact. Based on the allegations in the Koffmans' second amended motion for judgment, reasonable persons could disagree on whether Andy gave such consent. Thus, we find that the trial court erred in holding that the Koffmans' second amended motion for judgment was insufficient as a matter of law to establish a claim for battery.

For the above reasons, we will reverse the trial court's judgment that the Koffmans' second amended motion for judgment was insufficient as a matter of law to establish the cause of action for . . . battery and remand the case for further proceedings consistent with this opinion.

Reversed and remanded.

JUSTICE KINSER, concurring in part and dissenting in part.

I agree with the majority opinion except with regard to the issue of consent as it pertains to the intentional tort of battery. In my view, the second amended motion for judgment filed by the plaintiff was insufficient as a matter of law to state a claim for battery.

Absent fraud, consent is generally a defense to an alleged battery. In the context of this case, "taking part in a game manifests a willingness to submit to such bodily contacts or restrictions of liberty as are permitted by its rules or usages." Restatement (Second) of Torts § 50, cmt. b (1965), *quoted in Thompson v. McNeill,* 53 Ohio St. 3d 102, 559 N.E.2d 705, 708 (Ohio 1990). However, participating in a particular sport "does not manifest consent to contacts which are prohibited by rules or usages of the game if such rules or usages are designed to protect the participants and not merely to secure the better playing of the game as a test of skill." Restatement (Second) of Torts § 50, cmt. b (1965) *quoted in Thompson,* 559 N.E.2d at 708.

. . . .

---

1. How is this situation different from that in *Marchetti*? In other words, why can battery be alleged here and not in *Marchetti*?

2. Is this case more similar, in facts and reasoning, to *Marchetti* or *Hackbart, infra*?

3. Should the court consider Koffman's age (13 years) to show inability to consent? How does this case differ from *C.C.H* v. *Philadelphia Phillies, Inc., infra,* where the nature of the tort in question was sexual?

Hackbart v. Cincinnati Bengals, Inc.

United States Court of Appeals, Tenth Circuit, 1979
601 F.2d 516

Before Doyle, McKay and Logan, Circuit Judges.

Doyle, Circuit Judge,

The question in this case is whether in a regular season professional football game an injury which is inflicted by one professional football player on an opposing player can give rise to liability in tort where the injury was inflicted by the intentional striking of a blow during the game.

The injury occurred in the course of a game between the Denver Broncos and the Cincinnati Bengals, which game was being played in Denver in 1973. The Broncos' defensive back, Dale Hackbart, was the recipient of the injury and the Bengals' offensive back, Charles "Booby" Clark, inflicted the blow which produced it.

By agreement the liability question was determined by the United States District Court for the District of Colorado without a jury. The judge resolved the liability issue in favor of the Cincinnati team and Charles Clark. Consistent with this result, final judgment was entered for Cincinnati and the appeal challenges this judgment. In essence the trial court's reasons for rejecting plaintiff's claim were that professional football is a species of warfare and that so much physical force is tolerated and the magnitude of the force exerted is so great that it renders injuries not actionable in court; that even intentional batteries are beyond the scope of the judicial process.

Clark was an offensive back and just before the injury he had run a pass pattern to the right side of the Denver Broncos' end zone. The injury flowed indirectly from this play. The pass was intercepted by Billy Thompson, a Denver free safety, who returned it to mid-field. The subject injury occurred as an aftermath of the pass play.

As a consequence of the interception, the roles of Hackbart and Clark suddenly changed. Hackbart, who had been defending, instantaneously became an offensive player. Clark, on the other hand, became a defensive player. Acting as an offensive player, Hackbart attempted to block Clark by throwing his body in front of him. He thereafter remained on the ground. He turned, and with one knee on the ground, watched the play following the interception.

The trial court's finding was that Charles Clark, "acting out of anger and frustration, but without a specific intent to injure . . . stepped forward and struck a blow with his right forearm to the back of the kneeling plaintiff's head and neck with sufficient force to cause both players to fall forward to the ground." Both players, without complaining to the officials or to one another, returned to their respective sidelines since the ball had changed hands and the offensive and defensive teams of each had been substituted. Clark testified at trial that his frustration was brought about by the fact that his team was losing the game.

Due to the failure of the officials to view the incident, a foul was not called. However, the game film showed very clearly what had occurred. Plaintiff did not at the time report the happening to his coaches or to anyone else during the game. However, because of the pain which he experienced he was unable to play golf the next day. He did not seek medical attention, but the continued pain caused him to report this fact and the incident to the Bronco trainer who gave him treatment. Apparently he played on the specialty teams for two successive Sundays, but after that the Broncos released him on waivers. (He was in his thirteenth year as a player.) He sought medical help and it was then that it was discovered by the physician that he had a serious neck fracture injury.

Despite the fact that the defendant Charles Clark admitted that the blow which had been struck was not accidental, that it was intentionally administered, the trial court ruled as a matter of law that the game of professional football is basically a business which is violent in nature, and that the available sanctions are imposition of penalties and expulsion from the game. Notice was taken of the fact that many fouls are overlooked; that the game is played in an emotional and noisy environment; and that incidents such as that here complained of are not unusual.

The trial court spoke as well of the unreasonableness of applying the laws and rules which are a part of injury law to the game of professional football, noting the unreasonableness of holding that one player has a duty of care for the safety of others. He also talked about the concept of assumption of risk and contributory fault as applying and concluded that Hackbart had to recognize that he accepted the risk that he would be injured by such an act.

I.

THE ISSUES AND CONTENTIONS

1. Whether the trial court erred in ruling that as a matter of policy the principles of law governing the infliction of injuries should be entirely refused where the injury took place in the course of the game.

. . . .

II.

WHETHER THE EVIDENCE SUPPORTED THE JUDGMENT

The evidence at the trial uniformly supported the proposition that the intentional striking of a player in the head from the rear is not an accepted part of either the playing rules or the general customs of the game of professional football. The trial court, however, believed that the unusual nature of the case called for the consideration of underlying policy which it defined as common law principles which have evolved as a result of the case to case process and which necessarily affect behavior in various contexts. From these considerations the belief was expressed that even *intentional* injuries incurred in football games should be outside the framework of the law. The court recognized that the potential threat of legal liability has a significant deterrent effect, and further said that private civil actions constitute an important mechanism for societal control of human conduct. Due to the increase in severity of human conflicts, a need existed to expand the body of governing law more rapidly and with more certainty, but that this had to be accomplished by legislation and administrative regulation. The judge compared football to coal mining and railroading insofar as all are inherently hazardous. Judge Matsch said that in the case of football it was questionable whether social values would be improved by limiting the violence.

Thus the district court's assumption was that Clark had inflicted an intentional blow which would ordinarily generate civil liability and which might bring about a criminal sanction as well, but that since it had occurred in the course of a football game, it should not be subject to the restraints of the law; that if it were it would place unreasonable impediments and restraints on the activity. The judge also pointed out that courts are ill-suited to decide the different social questions and to administer conflicts on what is much like a battlefield where the restraints of civilization have been left on the sidelines.

We are forced to conclude that the result reached is not supported by evidence.

III.

WHETHER INTENTIONAL INJURY IS ALLOWED BY EITHER WRITTEN RULE OR CUSTOM

Plaintiff, of course, maintains that tort law applicable to the injury in this case applies on the football field as well as in other places. On the other hand, plaintiff does not rely on the theory of negligence being applicable. This is in recognition of the fact that subjecting another to unreasonable risk of harm, the essence of negligence, is inherent in the game of football, for admittedly it is violent. Plaintiff maintains that in the area of contributory fault, a vacuum exists in relationship to intentional infliction of injury. Since negligence does not apply, contributory negligence is inapplicable. Intentional or reckless contributory fault could theoretically at least apply to infliction of injuries in reckless disregard of the rights of others. This has some similarity to contributory negligence and undoubtedly it would apply if the evidence would justify it. But it is highly questionable whether a professional football player consents or submits to injuries caused by conduct not within the rules, and there is no evidence which we have seen which shows this. However, the trial court did not consider this question and we are not deciding it.

Contrary to the position of the court then, there are no principles of law which allow a court to rule out certain tortious conduct by reason of general roughness of the game or difficulty of administering it.

Indeed, the evidence shows that there are rules of the game which prohibit the intentional striking of blows. Thus, Article 1, Item 1, Subsection C, provides that:

> All players are prohibited from striking on the head, face or neck with the heel, back or side of the hand, wrist, forearm, elbow or clasped hands.

Thus the very conduct which was present here is expressly prohibited by the rule which is quoted above.

The general customs of football do not approve the intentional punching or striking of others. That this is prohibited was supported by the testimony of all of the witnesses. They testified that the intentional striking of a player in the face or from the rear is prohibited by the playing rules as well as the general customs of the game. Punching or hitting with the arms is prohibited. Undoubtedly these restraints are intended to establish reasonable boundaries so that one football player cannot intentionally inflict a serious injury on another. Therefore, the notion is not correct that all reason has been abandoned whereby the only possible remedy for the person who has been the victim of an unlawful blow is retaliation.

. . . .

The cause is reversed and remanded for a new trial in accordance with the foregoing views.

---

1. Is it possible to formulate a general rule for courts to apply where the injuries are incurred during a sporting event? If so, what would such a rule look like?

2. Should a rule for sporting events differentiate among professional, amateur, and informal contexts? If so, what is the basis for treating such contexts differently? If not, why not?

3. When a sporting event involves children, what standard should the court use? What if a child has no idea what the risks are?

4. What role should the rules and regulations of a game play in a court's decision? If the player has been penalized by an official such as a referee, should the imposition of the penalty have an impact upon the court's decision? If so, what should that impact be? The court in *Hackbart* rejected the idea that the game should be governed solely by referees, with the corollary that judges should stay out of it.

Problems

1. P, who is nine, plays softball with a league that uses a pitching machine instead of a person, so that each pitch will be perfect. One day, the pitching machine is out of order. The league officials agree that the teams which are scheduled to play that day will use their coaches as pitchers instead of the machine.

P, while up at bat, is struck in the chest by a pitch and severely injured. P sues the coach for battery. What result?

2. C and D play for different professional football teams. They have hated each other for years, and their rivalry, which is highly promoted by the television network which carries football games, is a source of higher television ratings for their teams,

as the viewers enjoy the enhanced competition and roughness of the games when C and D's teams play against each other.

C and D, who often end up brawling but who rarely hurt each other seriously, engage in a fight during a playoff game. This time, C is seriously injured. When an intrepid referee tries to stop the fight, he is trampled by both players, neither of whom sees him before stepping on him.

C sues D for battery. The referee sues C, D, their teams, and the network for battery. What arguments will the parties make? How will the court rule?

3. Consent in Other Arenas

Teolis v. Moscatelli

Supreme Court of Rhode Island, 1923
119 A. 161

RATHBURN, J.

This is an action of trespass for assault and battery. The trial in the superior court resulted in a verdict for plaintiff for $750. [The trial court denied defendants' motion for a new trial, and defendants appealed.] . . .

The assault resulted from a dispute between the plaintiff and defendants relative to a division fence. The plaintiff accepted the challenge of defendant Moscatelli to go into the highway and fight. After proceeding to the highway plaintiff removed his coat, and was immediately stabbed with a knife by defendant Moscatelli. Plaintiff testified that defendant Neri held him and told Moscatelli to "give it to him."

The defendants contend that the plaintiff, having agreed to fight, consented to the assault, and that such consent is a bar to recovery. The plaintiff agreed to engage in a fist fight. He never consented to being assaulted with a knife or held by Neri while Moscatelli wielded the knife.

The defendants' contention that an agreement to fight is a bar to recovery for injuries received in the course of combat by one of the participants and inflicted by the other is also untenable. As an agreement to break the peace is void, the maxim, "Volenti non fit injuria," does not apply. See authorities cited in 5 Corpus Juris, page 630, where the rule is stated as follows:

"By the weight of authority consent will not avail as a defense in a case of mutual combat, as such fighting is unlawful; and hence the acceptance of a challenge to fight, and voluntarily engaging in a fight by one party with another, because of the challenge, cannot be set up as a defense in a civil suit for damages for an assault and battery, although it seems that such consent may be shown in mitigation of damages."

. . . .

All of the defendants' exceptions are overruled, and the case is remitted to the superior court, with direction to enter Judgement on the verdict.

One of the most important reasons for the development of battery law (and, indeed, intentional tort law generally) was to keep the peace by preventing parties from taking the law into their own hands. Requiring that parties go to court to settle their differences accomplished this goal, because parties could obtain a remedy without the need to resort to violence. In order to make the availability of a remedy a complete cure for the problem of individual violence, however, the courts needed to penalize those who bypass the legal remedy and continue to take the law into their own hands.

In this case, the court states the rule applicable when one participant in an illegal fight sues the other. Under this rule, consent cannot operate as a defense in a battery action for injuries received in the fight, because one has no power to consent to an illegal act. On the hypothesis that the plaintiff will usually be the loser of the fight, does this rule deter illegal fighting? How should the situation be handled in order to accomplish the goal of deterring breaches of the peace?

C.C.H. v. Philadelphia Phillies, Inc.
Supreme Court of Pennsylvania, 2008
940 A.2d 336

Appellant T.G., a minor girl, was 11 years of age at the time she was allegedly sexually assaulted by Appellees Joseph Fabrizzio, John Scaruzzi, and Michael Ibbetson. She subsequently brought a civil action seeking damages against the individual defendants . . . The individual defendants defended, in part, by asserting that T.G. consented to sexual activities with them and, therefore, there was no sexual assault. There is no dispute that, given T.G.'s age, 11, consent would not be available as a defense if the individual defendants were charged criminally. The question before us regarding the individual defendants is whether the defense of consent may be asserted in this civil action. The trial court and the Superior Court concluded that, in the context of a civil trial, defendants are permitted to raise a minor victim's consent. For the following reasons, we conclude that, where the victim is less than 13 years of age, evidence of the victim's consent to sexual contact, like in criminal proceedings, is not an available defense in determining a defendant's civil liability. Accordingly, we reverse the Order of the Superior Court affirming the trial court with respect to the individual defendants, and remand the matter to the Superior Court with instructions to remand to the trial court for a new trial.

The Pennsylvania Criminal Code defines various crimes so as to make the defense of consent invalid where the victim is a minor under 13 years of age. For example, where a person commits rape of a child less than 13.

The relevant facts of this case are as follows. On August 9, 2000, T.G. was attending a Phillies baseball game at Veteran's Stadium in Philadelphia with an adult family friend. At some point during the game, T.G. was separated from her guardian and became lost inside the stadium. T.G. asserts that she then sought help from the Phillies' security personnel, who T.G. alleges failed to assist her in finding her guardian, in contravention to the team's "Lost People Policy." It is undisputed, however, that she eventually encountered the individual defendants, who were then 15 and 16 years old and employed at a concession stand at the stadium. According to T.G., these defendants offered to help her locate a telephone, but instead led her to a secluded area outside the stadium where they forcibly removed her clothes and sexually assaulted her. [W]hile the parties disagree on whether intercourse occurred, they all agree that some type of sexual contact took place.

Reversed and remanded.

————————

1. Would it matter if T.G. flirted with the boys or went outside with them voluntarily, as one of the defense attorneys stated? Do these actions have a strong enough relation with consent to sexual activity to matter in the court's analysis?

2. This is an intentional tort. Will the Philadelphia Phillies, Inc. be held liable for the acts of their employees? If respondeat superior does not apply, are there any other theories that might lead to liability on the part of Philadelphia Phillies, Inc.?

Thomas v. Bedford

Court of Appeal of Louisiana, Second Circuit, 1980
389 So. 2d 405

Before PRICE, JASPER E. JONES and FRED W. JONES, JR., JJ.

FRED W. JONES, JR., JUDGE.

Anna Spear Goff Thomas, as the natural tutrix of her minor son, Joseph A. Goff, filed this suit against Carter Bedford, a Caddo Parish school teacher, the Caddo Parish School Board, and the latter's liability insurance carrier, Reliance Insurance Company, for injuries allegedly sustained by the minor because of a battery committed by Bedford at a Caddo Parish School.

Plaintiff appeals from a district court judgment rejecting her demands. We reverse and render judgment for plaintiff.

The incident in question occurred in February 1979 at the Northwood High School in Caddo Parish. Goff, a student at the school, was 14 years of age, weighed between 95 and 100 pounds, and was 4 feet 9 inches in height. Bedford, a teacher at the school, was 26 years of age, weighed between 135 and 140 pounds, and was 5 feet 9 inches in height. The two had become acquainted the previous year when Goff was in one of Bedford's classes. The record indicated that, although not a serious disciplinary problem, Goff tended to engage in mischievous behavior, some of which had been occasionally directed at Bedford.

On the afternoon of February 15, 1979, while Bedford was standing outside a classroom at the high school conversing with two other teachers, Goff came up and struck Bedford a light blow in the back with his hand. Instead of going to his class as instructed by Bedford, Goff picked up a rubber band and from a distance of about two feet propelled it into Bedford's face. Goff then turned and ran into his classroom, chased by Bedford who threw a two foot long 1 by 2 board at the youngster, but missed him.

Bedford left and went to his classroom where he remained for ten or fifteen minutes. He then returned to Goff's classroom and pulled the youngster into an adjoining vacant "project" room where the altercation in question took place. Bedford testified that he gave Goff a "severe shaking." On the other hand, Goff stated that Bedford struck him three or four times on the body with his fist. The statement of the physician who examined Goff, finding that the youngster had contusions of the chest, arms and back, tended to corroborate Goff's version of the incident.

It is now recognized that "corporal punishment, reasonable in degree, administered by a teacher to a pupil for disciplinary reasons, is permitted in Louisiana." *Roy v. Continental Insurance Co.*, 313 So. 2d 349 (La. App. 3rd Cir. 1975). Further elaborating, the court in *Roy* commented:

> "It is also a well established rule in general tort law that a teacher is immune from civil liability for physical corporal punishment, reasonable in degree, administered to a student. But it is likewise clear under tort law that this discretionary right of a teacher to use physical punishment is a limited one and immunity or privilege from liability requires a showing that said punishment was administered neither unreasonably nor excessively, measured in part by such factors as the nature of the punishment itself, the misconduct of the child, the teacher's motive in the discipline, and the age and physical condition of the pupil. The question of 'reasonableness' or 'excessiveness' is determined on a case by case basis. . . ."

The rationale of these cases, which we adopt, is that a minor's school teacher, while the youngster is attending school, stands in the place of the parent for the purpose of enforcing discipline and, in connection therewith, may use a reasonable degree of corporal punishment. The factual question presented by each individual case is whether the punishment was unreasonable or excessive under the circumstances.

In his written reasons for judgment in this case the trial judge concluded that "although the teacher's action *greatly exceeded reasonable force* (emphasis added), nevertheless, there is sufficient provocation by plaintiff for Mr. Bedford to have lost his temper in rendering corporal punishment on Joseph Goff." In a previous portion of that opinion the minor had been characterized as the "aggressor."

The "aggressor doctrine" contemplates an altercation provoked by the aggressor against a party who defends himself. Even if, under the facts of this case, Goff's striking Bedford in the back and hitting him with a rubber band rendered him an aggressor, it is obvious that the subsequent altercation in the "project" room, some 10 or

15 minutes later after Bedford had admittedly calmed down, was in fact a separate incident and not a spontaneous reaction to the original provocation. Therefore, the "aggressor doctrine" is inapplicable. The pivotal issue here is whether the corporal punishment meted out by Bedford was unreasonable. The trial judge explicitly answered that question in the affirmative. Since this is a factual question and our review of the record does not show that the trial judge was clearly wrong in his conclusion, we must accept that ruling. Consequently, under our jurisprudence Bedford, his employer and the latter's insurance carrier are liable for Goff's injuries.

Legitimate concern for disciplinary problems in our schools ably articulated by the conscientious trial judge, does not permit us to disregard our responsibility to accord due deference to the rights of *all* those participants in the educational process, students as well as teachers and administrators. Needless to say, our law does not by any means render the latter impotent in the face of rule infractions. Where appropriate, corporal punishment may be administered in a reasonable manner as a measured, rational response to serious acts of misconduct.

. . . .

For the reasons set forth, we reverse the judgment of the trial court. . . .

---

1. Would the result in this case have been different if Bedford had immediately "punished" Goff instead of waiting the ten or fifteen minutes in question?

2. Should a school be able to administer corporal punishment over parental objections? *See Suits v. Glover*, 71 So. 2d 49 (Ala. 1954).

3. The Eighth Amendment to the United States Constitution forbids cruel and unusual punishment. Is it constitutional for teachers and administrators to administer corporal punishment for disciplinary purposes? *See Baker v. Owen*, 395 F. Supp. 294 (M.D.N.C.), *aff'd*, 423 U.S. 907 (1975).

4. Rules about deadly force, self defense, and privileges for protecting one's loved ones and property have been changing rapidly. Most of these changes are statutory.

B. Defenses to False Imprisonment

Noguchi v. Nakamura

Intermediate Court of Appeals of Hawaii, 1982
638 P.2d 1383

Before HAYASHI, C.J., and PADGETT and BURNS, JJ.

PER CURIAM.

This is an appeal from an order granting a directed verdict on a claim of false imprisonment. We reverse.

The complaint herein asserted two claims for relief: one based on negligence and one on false imprisonment. The court below directed a verdict on the false imprisonment claim and the jury found for the appellee on the negligence claim.

Basically, appellant testified that she and appellee had been girlfriend and boyfriend. She had come to the conclusion that she did not wish to go out with him anymore. On the day in question, he came to see her and asked her to go with him on a date that evening. She refused. After some conversation, he asked her to at least go to the store with him and she consented on the condition, which he agreed to, that he would bring her right back. She then entered his car and they proceeded to the store and returned, stopping in front of her house. She was seated in the car with the car door open when he suddenly drove off. At some point thereafter, she fell, was pushed or jumped from the car, sustaining the injuries complained of.

The tort of false imprisonment is defined in 2 Restatement of Torts 2d, § 35 (1965) as follows:

False Imprisonment

(1) An actor is subject to liability to another for false imprisonment if

(a) he acts intending to confine the other or a third person within boundaries fixed by the actor, and

(b) his act directly or indirectly results in such a confinement of the other, and

(c) the other is conscious of the confinement or is harmed by it.

Of course, it goes without saying that one who consents to being placed within a limited and enclosed space by the other is not legally confined.

Obviously, a moving automobile, because of the danger of any egress therefrom, can constitute a place of confinement. 2 Restatement of Torts 2d, § 36 (1965), ex. 9 at 56.

Appellee contends, however, that since appellant originally entered the car voluntarily, some threat against her to prevent her leaving must have been made or she was at least under an obligation when the car was stopped in front of her parents' home to express a refusal to go further. We do not regard such to be the law. She had refused to go anywhere on the day in question with the appellee but to the store and back. She was back; she was in front of her parents' house, and she had the car door open when appellee suddenly started off. A jury could well have found from her testimony that her consent to go anywhere with the appellee on the day in question was limited to going to the store and back; that she had previously expressly told him she would not go out with him that evening, so that the limited consent had expired; and that her having the door open in the stopped car in front of her parents' home reindicated her lack of consent to any further movement.

. . . .

[T]here was sufficient evidence to go to the jury on the claim of false imprisonment.

Because of our disposition of the question of the sufficiency of the evidence, we do not reach the other errors alleged.

Reversed and remanded for a new trial.

————————

1. How subjective should determinations of consent be? From whose perspective, the plaintiff's or defendant's, should the issue of consent be approached? Should a reasonable person standard simply be used for everyone involved?

2. What amount of damages should the plaintiff recover? Should the amount of recovery depend upon why the plaintiff fell from the car? If she jumped from the car, should her injuries be compensable? Does the answer to this depend upon why she jumped (if she did)?

Peterson v. Sorlien
Supreme Court of Minnesota, 1980
299 N.W.2d 123

SHERAN, CHIEF JUSTICE.

This action by plaintiff Susan Jungclaus Peterson for false imprisonment and intentional infliction of emotional distress arises from an effort by her parents, in conjunction with other individuals named as defendants, to prompt her disaffiliation from an organization known as The Way Ministry.

At trial, the Hennepin County District Court directed a verdict in favor of defendant Paul Sorlien, plaintiff's former minister, finding the evidence proffered against him insufficient as a matter of law. The jury returned a verdict exonerating Mr. and Mrs. Jungclaus and the other remaining defendants of the charge of false imprisonment; however, the jury found defendants Veronica Morgel and Kathy Mills liable for intentional infliction of emotional distress, assessing against each of them $1 compensatory damages and $4,000 and $6,000 respectively as punitive damages.

Plaintiff asserts that the trial court erred by 1) failing to grant a judgment notwithstanding the verdict on the claim of false imprisonment; 2) permitting the admission of evidence concerning her involvement in The Way and its activities. . . .

[W]e affirm the determination of the district court.

Viewing the evidence in the light most favorable to the prevailing defendants, this case marks the emergence of a new cultural phenomenon: youth-oriented religious or pseudo-religious groups which utilize the techniques of what has been termed "coercive persuasion" or "mind control" to cultivate an uncritical and devoted following. Commentators have used the term "coercive persuasion," originally coined to identify the experience of American prisoners of war during the Korean conflict to describe the cult-induction process. The word "cult" is not used pejoratively but in its dictionary sense to describe an unorthodox system of belief characterized by "[g]reat or excessive devotion or dedication to some person, idea, or thing." Webster's New International Dictionary of the English Language Unabridged 552 (1976). Coercive persuasion is fostered through the creation of a controlled environment that heightens the susceptibility of a subject to suggestion and manipulation through sensory deprivation, physiological depletion, cognitive dissonance, peer pressure, and a clear assertion of authority and dominion. The aftermath of indoctrination is a severe impairment of autonomy and the ability to think independently, which induces a subject's unyielding compliance and the rupture of past connections, affiliations and associations. *See generally* Delgado, *Religious Totalism: Gentle and Ungentle Persuasion under the First Amendment*, 51 S. Cal. L. Rev. 1 (1977). One psychologist characterized the process of cult indoctrination as "psychological kidnapping." *Id.* at 23.

At the time of the events in question, Susan Jungclaus Peterson was 21 years old. For most of her life, she lived with her family on a farm near Bird Island, Minnesota. In 1973, she graduated with honors from high school, ranking second in her class. She matriculated that fall at Moorhead State College. A dean's list student during her first year, her academic performance declined and her interests narrowed after she joined the local chapter of a group organized internationally and identified locally as The Way of Minnesota, Inc.

. . . .

The operation of The Way is predicated on the fund-raising activities of its members. The Way's fund-raising strategy centers upon the sale of prerecorded learning programs. Members are instructed to elicit the interest of a group of ten or twelve people and then play for them, at a charge of $85 per participant, a taped introductory course produced by The Way International. Advanced tape courses are then offered to the participants at additional cost, and training sessions are conducted to more fully acquaint recruits with the orientation of the group and the obligations of membership. Recruits must contribute a minimum of 10 percent of their earnings to the organization; to meet the tithe, student members are expected to obtain part-time employment. Members are also required to purchase books and other materials published by the ministry, and are encouraged to make larger financial contributions and to engage in more sustained efforts at solicitation.

By the end of her freshman year, Susan was devoting many hours to The Way, listening to instructional tapes, soliciting new members and assisting in training sessions. As her sophomore year began, Susan committed herself significantly, selling the car her father had given her and working part-time as a waitress to finance her contributions to The Way. Susan spent the following summer in South Dakota, living in conditions described as appalling and overcrowded, while recruiting, raising money and conducting training sessions for The Way.

As her junior year in college drew to a close, the Jungclauses grew increasingly alarmed by the personality changes they witnessed in their daughter; overly tired, unusually pale, distraught and irritable, she exhibited an increasing alienation from family, diminished interest in education and decline in academic performance. The Jungclauses, versed in the literature of youth cults and based on conversations with former members of The Way, concluded that through a calculated process of manipulation and exploitation Susan had been reduced to a condition of psychological bondage.

On May 24, 1976, defendant Norman Jungclaus, father of plaintiff, arrived at Moorhead to pick up Susan following the end of the third college quarter. Instead of returning to their family home, defendant drove with Susan to Minneapolis to the home of Veronica Morgel. Entering the home of Mrs. Morgel, Susan was greeted by Kathy Mills and several young people who wished to discuss Susan's involvement in the ministry. Each of those present had been in some way touched by the cult phenomenon. Kathy Mills, the leader of the group, had treated a number of former cult members, including Veronica Morgel's son. It was Kathy Mills[,] a self-styled professional deprogrammer, to whom the Jungclauses turned, and intermittently for the next sixteen days, it was in the home of Veronica Morgel that Susan stayed.

The avowed purpose of deprogramming is to break the hold of the cult over the individual through reason and confrontation. Initially, Susan was unwilling to discuss her involvement; she lay curled in a fetal position, in the downstairs bedroom where she first stayed, plugging her ears and crying while her father pleaded with her to listen to what was being said. This behavior persisted for two days during which she intermittently engaged in conversation, at one point screaming hysterically and flailing at her father. But by Wednesday Susan's demeanor had changed completely; she was friendly and vivacious and that night slept in an upstairs bedroom. Susan spent all day Thursday reading and conversing with her father and on Saturday night went roller-skating. On Sunday she played Softball at a nearby park, afterwards enjoying a picnic lunch. The next week Susan spent in Columbus, Ohio, flying there with a former cult member who had shared with her the experiences of the previous week. While in Columbus, she spoke every day by telephone to her fiancé who, playing tapes and songs from the ministry's headquarters in Minneapolis, begged that she return to the fold. Susan expressed the desire to extricate her fiancé from the dominion of the cult.

Susan returned to Minneapolis on June 9. Unable to arrange a controlled meeting so that Susan could see her fiancé outside the presence of other members of the ministry, her parents asked that she sign an agreement releasing them from liability for their past weeks' actions. Refusing to do so, Susan stepped outside the Morgel residence with the puppy she had purchased in Ohio, motioned to a passing police car and shortly thereafter was reunited with her fiancé in the Minneapolis headquarters of The Way. Following her return to the ministry, she was directed to counsel and initiated the present action.

1. Plaintiff seeks a judgment notwithstanding the verdict on the issue of false imprisonment, alleging that defendants unlawfully interfered with her personal liberty by words or acts which induced a reasonable apprehension that force would be used against her if she did not otherwise comply. The jury, instructed that an informed

and reasoned consent is a defense to an allegation of false imprisonment and that a nonconsensual detention could be deemed consensual if one's behavior so indicated, exonerated defendants with respect to the false imprisonment claim.

The period in question began on Monday, May 24, 1976, and ceased on Wednesday, June 9, 1976, a period of 16 days. The record clearly demonstrates that Susan willingly remained in the company of defendants for at least 13 of those days. During that time she took many excursions into the public sphere, playing softball and picnicking in a city park, roller-skating at a public rink, flying aboard public aircraft and shopping and swimming while relaxing in Ohio. Had Susan desired, manifold opportunities existed for her to alert the authorities of her allegedly unlawful detention; in Minneapolis, two police officers observed at close range the softball game in which she engaged; en route to Ohio, she passed through the security areas of the Twin Cities and Columbus airports in the presence of security guards and uniformed police; in Columbus she transacted business at a bank, went for walks in solitude and was interviewed by an F.B.I. agent who sought assurances of her safety. At no time during the 13-day period did she complain of her treatment or suggest that defendants were holding her against her will. If one is aware of a reasonable means of escape that does not present a danger of bodily or material harm, a restriction is not total and complete and does not constitute unlawful imprisonment. Damages may not be assessed for any period of detention to which one freely consents.

In his summation to the jury, the trial judge instructed that to deem consent a defense to the charge of false imprisonment for the entire period or for any part therein, a preponderance of the evidence must demonstrate that such plaintiff voluntarily consented. The central issue for the jury, then, was whether Susan voluntarily participated in the activities of the first three days. The jury concluded that her behavior constituted a waiver.

We believe the determination to have been consistent with the evidence. Were the relationship other than that of parent and child, the consent would have less significance.

To determine whether the findings of the jury can be supported upon review, the behavior Susan manifested during the initial three days at issue must be considered in light of her actions in the remainder of the period. Because, it is argued, the cult conditioning process induces dramatic and non-consensual change giving rise to a new temporary identity on the part of the individuals whose consent is under examination, Susan's volitional capacity prior to treatment may well have been impaired. Following her readjustment, the evidence suggests that Susan was a different person, "like her old self." As such, the question of Susan's consent becomes a function of time. We therefore deem Susan's subsequent affirmation of defendants' actions dispositive.

. . . .

In light of our examination of the record and rules of construction providing that upon review the evidence must be viewed in a manner most favorable to the prevailing party, we find that a reasonable basis existed for the verdict exonerating defendants of the charge of false imprisonment. Although carried out under colorably religious auspices, the method of cult indoctrination, viewed in a light most favorable to the prevailing party, is predicated on a strategy of coercive persuasion that undermines the capacity for informed consent. While we acknowledge that other social institutions may utilize a degree of coercion in promoting their objectives, none do so to the same extent or intend the same consequences. Society, therefore, has a compelling interest favoring intervention. The facts in this case support the conclusion that plaintiff only regained her volitional capacity to consent after engaging in the first three days of the deprogramming process. As such, we hold that when parents, or their agents, acting under the conviction that the judgmental capacity of their adult child is impaired, seek to extricate that child from what they reasonably believe to be a religious or pseudo-religious cult, and the child at some juncture assents to the actions in question, limitations upon the child's mobility do not constitute meaningful deprivations of personal liberty sufficient to support a judgment for false imprisonment. But owing to the threat that deprogramming poses to public order, we do not endorse self-help as a preferred alternative. In fashioning a remedy, the First Amendment requires resort to the least restrictive alternative so as to not impinge upon religious belief. *Cantwell v. Connecticut*, 310 U.S. 296, 60 S. Ct. 900, 84 L. Ed. 1213 (1940).

. . . .

Affirmed.

PETERSON, JUSTICE (concurring specially).

I concur in the result.

AMDAHL and SIMONETT, JJ., not having been members of this court at the time of the argument and submission, took no part in the consideration or decision of this case.

WAHL, JUSTICE (dissenting in part, concurring in part).

I must respectfully dissent. In every generation, parents have viewed their children's religious and political beliefs with alarm and dismay if those beliefs were different from their own. Under the First Amendment, however, adults in our society enjoy freedoms of association and belief. In my view, it is unwise to tamper with those freedoms and with longstanding principles of tort law out of sympathy for parents seeking to help their "misguided" offspring, however well-intentioned and loving their acts may be.

. . . .

OTIS, JUSTICE (dissenting in part).

I join in the views expressed by Justice Wahl, and particularly take issue with a rule which authorizes what is euphemistically described as "limitations upon the adult child's mobility" whenever a parent, or indeed a stranger acting for a parent, subjectively decides, without the benefit of a professional opinion or judicial intervention, that the adult child's "judgmental capacity" is impaired and that she should be "extricated" from what is deemed to be a religious or pseudo-religious cult.

At age 21, a daughter is no longer a child. She is an adult. Susan Peterson was not only an adult in 1976 but she was a bright, well-educated adult. For whatever reason, she was experiencing a period of restlessness and insecurity which is by no means uncommon in students of that age. But to hold that for seeking companionship and identity in a group whose proselyting tactics may well be suspect, she must endure without a remedy the degrading and humiliating treatment she received at the hands of her parents, is, in my opinion, totally at odds with the basic rights of young people to think unorthodox thoughts, join unorthodox groups, and proclaim unorthodox views. I would reverse the denial of recovery as to that cause of action.

How should courts balance the rights to freedom of belief against concerns that the individual no longer has the capacity to consent, whether to cult membership or to deprogramming? How can one tell whether the will of the individual has in fact been overborne? Who should make such a decision?

Bonkowski v. Arlan's Department Store

Court of Appeals of Michigan, Division No. 3, 1968
162 N.W.2d 347, rev'd on slander issue only, 174 N.W.2d 765 (1970)

NEAL E. FITZGERALD, JUDGE.

This appeal from a jury verdict for false arrest and slander, rendered against the defendant store whose agent stopped and questioned the plaintiff whom he suspected of larceny, surprisingly presents questions that are novel to the appellate courts of this jurisdiction.

The plaintiff, Mrs. Marion Bonkowski, accompanied by her husband, had left the defendant's Saginaw, Michigan store about 10:00 p.m. on the night of December 18, 1962 after making several purchases, when Earl Reinhardt, a private [uniformed] policeman on duty that night in the defendant's store, called to her to stop as she was walking to her car about 30 feet away in the adjacent parking lot. Reinhardt motioned to the plaintiff to return toward the store, and when she had done so, Reinhardt said that someone in the store had told him the plaintiff had put three pieces of costume jewelry into her purse without having paid for them. Mrs. Bonkowski denied she had taken anything unlawfully, but Reinhardt told her he wanted to see the contents of her purse. On a cement step in front of the store, plaintiff emptied the contents of her purse into her husband's hands. The plaintiff produced sales slips for the items she had purchased, and Reinhardt, satisfied that she had not committed larceny, returned to the store.

Plaintiff brought this action against Earl Reinhardt and Arlan's Department Store, seeking damages on several counts. She complains that as a result of defendant's tortious acts she has suffered numerous psychosomatic symptoms, including headaches, nervousness, and depression. Arlan's Department Store filed a third-party complaint against Earl Reinhardt's employer, Gerald Kaweck, doing business as Michigan Security Police Service, who defaulted. On the counts of false arrest and slander the case went to the jury, who returned a verdict of $43,750. The defendant's motions for judgment notwithstanding the verdict, remittitur, and new trial were denied by the trial court.

Numerous errors are alleged on appeal; we consider those necessary to the disposition of the case.

We conclude the plaintiff established a case entitling her to go to the jury on a charge of false arrest.[1]

But we conclude on the record before us that the cause of action on the ground of slander was not established. . . . Therefore, there must be a new trial.

We first consider briefly the issue whether defendant, Arlan's Department Store, can be held responsible for the acts of Earl Reinhardt, the private policeman employed by Michigan Security Police Service. Defendant Arlan's Department Store had contracted with the third-party defendant to provide private police protection in its Saginaw store. The record makes it clear that the apprehension of shoplifters was within the scope of Earl Reinhardt's authority and that, during the time he was on duty in the defendant's store, his activities were under the direction of Arlan's' supervisory employees. Therefore, we agree with the learned trial judge that Earl Reinhardt, with respect to the incident giving rise to this action, was acting within the scope of his authority as the agent of Arlan's Department Store, which must respond for his acts.

To the common-law tort of false arrest, privilege is a common-law defense, and we recognize as applicable here a privilege similar to that recognized by the American Law Institute in the Restatement of Torts, 2d. In section 120A, the Institute recognizes a privilege in favor of a merchant to detain for reasonable investigation a person whom he reasonably believes to have taken a chattel unlawfully. We adopt the concept embodied in section 120A, and we state the rule for this action as follows: if defendant Arlan's agent, Earl Reinhardt, reasonably believed the plaintiff had unlawfully taken goods held for sale in the defendant's store, then he enjoyed a privilege to detain her for a reasonable investigation of the facts.

The Commissioners' comment states the strong reason behind recognizing such a privilege:

> "The privilege stated in this section is necessary for the protection of a shopkeeper against the dilemma in which he would otherwise find himself when he reasonably believes that a shoplifter has taken goods from his counter. If

---

1. Although the distinctions are not always clearly set out in the authorities, false arrest, or unlawful arrest, is a species of the common-law action for false imprisonment.

there were no such privilege, he must either permit the suspected person to walk out of the premises and disappear, or must arrest him, at the risk of liability for false arrest if the theft could not be proved." 1 Restatement of Torts, 2d, page 202.

That the problem of shoplifting, faced by merchants, has reached serious dimensions is common knowledge, and we find compelling reason to recognize such a privilege, similar to that recognized in other jurisdictions.

. . . .

The privilege we recognize here goes beyond that set forth in the Restatement, for the Commissioners there stated a caveat that "the Institute expresses no opinion as to whether there may be circumstances under which this privilege may extend to the detention of one who has left the premises but is in their immediate vicinity." 1 Restatement of Torts, 2d, page 202.

In their comment, the Commissioners state that, by their caveat, in the absence of express authority, they intended to leave the question open. 1 Restatement of Torts, 2d, page 204. We think the privilege should be so extended here because we think it entirely reasonable to apply it to the circumstances of the case at bar, for the reason that a merchant may not be able to form the reasonable belief justifying a detention for a reasonable investigation before a suspected person has left the premises.

. . . .

On remand on the cause for false arrest, therefore, it will be the duty of the jury to determine in accordance with the rule we have set down, whether or not the defendant's agent, Earl Reinhardt, reasonably believed the plaintiff had unlawfully taken any goods held for sale at the defendant's store. If the jury finds the defendant's agent did so reasonably believe, then it must further determine whether the investigation that followed was reasonable under all the circumstances. If the jury finds the defendant does not come within this privilege, then from the facts as discussed above, it could find a false arrest.

. . . .

Reversed and remanded for new trial in accordance with this opinion. The award of costs to await final determination of the cause.

———————

If a plaintiff has the chance of escape, must he or she take it? How much danger should an imprisoned plaintiff be required to confront? What about jumping from a school bus window? Risking being fired from employment? Should the standard used by the courts be subjective (*this* plaintiff) or objective (a reasonable person)?

C. Privileges in Suits Alleging Trespass to Land and Chattels

Katko v. Briney

Supreme Court of Iowa, 1971
183 N.W.2d 657

MOORE, CHIEF JUSTICE.

The primary issue presented here is whether an owner may protect personal property in an unoccupied boarded-up farm house against trespassers and thieves by a spring gun capable of inflicting death or serious injury.

We are not here concerned with a man's right to protect his home and members of his family. Defendants' home was several miles from the scene of the incident to which we refer infra.

Plaintiff's action is for damages resulting from serious injury caused by a shot from a 20-gauge spring shotgun set by defendants in a bedroom of an old farm house which had been uninhabited for several years. Plaintiff and his companion, Marvin McDonough, had broken and entered the house to find and steal old bottles and dated fruit jars which they considered antiques.

At defendants' request plaintiff's action was tried to a jury consisting of residents of the community where defendants' property was located. The jury returned a verdict for plaintiff and against defendants for $20,000 actual and $10,000 punitive damages.

After careful consideration of defendants' motions for judgment notwithstanding the verdict and for new trial, the experienced and capable trial judge overruled them and entered judgment on the verdict. Thus we have this appeal by defendants.

. . . .

II. Most of the facts are not disputed. In 1957 defendant Bertha L. Briney inherited her parents' farm land in Mahaska and Monroe Counties. Included was an 80-acre tract in southwest Mahaska County where her grandparents and parents had lived. No one occupied the house thereafter. Her husband, Edward, attempted to care for the land. He kept no farm machinery thereon. The outbuildings became dilapidated.

For about 10 years, 1957 to 1967, there occurred a series of trespassing and housebreaking events with loss of some household items, the breaking of windows and "messing up of the property in general." The latest occurred June 8, 1967, prior to the event on July 16, 1967 herein involved.

Defendants through the years boarded up the windows and doors in an attempt to stop the intrusions. They had posted "no trespass" signs on the land several years before 1967. The nearest one was 35 feet from the house. On June 11, 1967 defendants set "a shotgun trap" in the north bedroom. After Mr. Briney cleaned and oiled his 20-gauge shotgun, the power of which he was well aware, defendants took it to the old house where they secured it to an iron bed with the barrel pointed at the bedroom door. It was rigged with wire from the doorknob to the gun's trigger so it would fire when the door was opened. Briney first pointed the gun so an intruder would be hit in the stomach but at Mrs. Briney's suggestion it was lowered to hit the legs. He admitted he did so "because I was mad and tired of being tormented" but "he did not intend to injure anyone." He gave no explanation of why he used a loaded shell and set it to hit a person already in the house. Tin was nailed over the bedroom window. The spring gun could not be seen from the outside. No warning of its presence was posted.

Plaintiff lived with his wife and worked regularly as a gasoline station attendant in Eddyville, seven miles from the old house. He had observed it for several years while hunting in the area and considered it as being abandoned. He knew it had long been uninhabited. In 1967 the area around the house was covered with high weeds. Prior to July 16, 1967 plaintiff and McDonough had been to the premises and found several old bottles and fruit jars which they took and added to their collection of antiques. On the latter date about 9:30 p.m. they made a second trip to the Briney property. They entered the old house by removing a board from a porch window which was without glass. While McDonough was looking around the kitchen area plaintiff went to another part of the house. As he started to open the north bedroom door the shotgun went off striking him in the right leg above the ankle bone. Much of his leg, including part of the tibia, was blown away. Only by McDonough's assistance was plaintiff able to get out of the house and after crawling some distance was put in his vehicle and rushed to a doctor and then to a hospital. He remained in the hospital 40 days [with very serious leg injuries].

. . . .

IV. The main thrust of defendants' defense in the trial court and on this appeal is that, "the law permits use of a spring gun in a dwelling or warehouse for the purpose of preventing the unlawful entry of a burglar or thief." They repeated this contention in their exceptions to the trial court's instructions 2, 5 and 6. They took no exception to the trial court's statement of the issues or to other instructions.

In the statement of issues the trial court stated plaintiff and his companion committed a felony when they broke and entered defendants' house.* In instruction 2 the court referred to the early case history of the use of spring guns and stated under the law their use was prohibited except to prevent the commission of felonies of violence and where human life is in danger. The instruction included a statement breaking and entering is not a felony of violence.

Instruction 5 stated: "You are hereby instructed that one may use reasonable force in the protection of his property, but such right is subject to the qualification that

---

*Plaintiff had pled guilty to larceny in the nighttime of property of less than $20 value.[Eds.]

one may not use such means of force as will take human life or inflict great bodily injury. Such is the rule even though the injured party is a trespasser and is in violation of the law himself."

Instruction 6 stated: "An owner of premises is prohibited from willfully or intentionally injuring a trespasser by means of force that either takes life or inflicts great bodily injury; and therefore a person owning a premise is prohibited from setting out 'spring guns' and like dangerous devices which will likely take life or inflict great bodily injury, for the purpose of harming trespassers. The fact that the trespasser may be acting in violation of the law does not change the rule. The only time when such conduct of setting a 'spring gun' or a like dangerous device is justified would be when the trespasser was committing a felony of violence or a felony punishable by death, or where the trespasser was endangering human life by his act."

Instruction 7, to which defendants made no objection or exception, stated: "To entitle the plaintiff to recover for compensatory damages, the burden of proof is upon him to establish by a preponderance of the evidence each and all of the following propositions:

1. That defendants erected a shotgun trap in a vacant house on land owned by defendant, Bertha L. Briney, on or about June 11, 1967, which fact was known only by them, to protect household goods from trespassers and thieves.

2. That the force used by defendants was in excess of that force reasonably necessary and which persons are entitled to use in the protection of their property.

3. That plaintiff was injured and damaged and the amount thereof.

4. That plaintiff's injuries and damages resulted directly from the discharge of the shotgun trap which was set and used by defendants.

The overwhelming weight of authority, both textbook and case law, supports the trial court's statement of the applicable principles of law.

Prosser on Torts, Third Edition, pages 116–118, states:

"... [T]he law has always placed a higher value upon human safety than upon mere rights in property, it is the accepted rule that there is no privilege to use any force calculated to cause death or serious bodily injury to repel the threat to land or chattels, unless there is also such a threat to the defendant's personal safety as to justify a self-defense.... [S]pring guns and other mankilling devices are not justifiable against a mere trespasser, or even a petty thief. They are privileged only against those upon whom the landowner, if he were present in person would be free to inflict injury of the same kind."

Restatement of Torts, section 85, page 180, states: "The value of human life and limb, not only to the individual concerned but also to society, so outweighs the interest of a possessor of land in excluding from it those whom he is not willing to admit thereto that a possessor of land has, as is stated in § 79, no privilege to use force intended or likely to cause death or serious harm against another whom the possessor sees about to enter his premises or meddle with his chattel, unless the intrusion threatens death or serious bodily harm to the occupiers or users of the premises. . . . A possessor of land cannot do indirectly and by a mechanical device that which, were he present, he could not do immediately and in person. Therefore, he cannot gain a privilege to install, for the purpose of protecting his land from intrusions harmless to the lives and limbs of the occupiers or users of it, a mechanical device whose only purpose is to inflict death or serious harm upon such as may intrude, by giving notice of his intention to inflict, by mechanical means and indirectly, harm which he could not, even after request, inflict directly were he present."

In Volume 2, Harper and James, The Law of Torts, section 27.3, pages 1440, 1441, this is found: "The possessor of land may not arrange his premises intentionally so as to cause death or serious bodily harm to a trespasser. The possessor may of course take some steps to repel a trespass. If he is present he may use force to do so, but only that amount which is reasonably necessary to effect the repulse. Moreover if the trespass threatens harm to property only—even a theft of property—the possessor would not be privileged to use deadly force, he may not arrange his premises so that such force will be inflicted by mechanical means. If he does, he will be liable even to a thief who is injured by such device."

Affirmed.

All Justices concur except LARSON, J., who dissents.

———————

1. How far should one be allowed to go to protect one's property? Should what constitutes reasonable force vary depending upon where the property one seeks to protect is located? Upon what is acceptable in the community? Upon whom is in the house?

2. What if Briney had posted a sign outside the property proclaiming the presence of a spring gun inside? Would he still be liable?

3. What should the contours of the privilege of self-defense be? Defense of property? What does *Katko* tell us about these privileges? Should the use of deadly force ever be privileged when it has been used to protect property and not human life? If the putative victim can run away rather than use deadly force to protect him or herself, should the privilege be applicable at all?

4. The law of Texas:

§ 9.41. Protection of One's Own Property

A person in lawful possession of land . . . is justified in using force against another when and to the degree the actor reasonably believes the force is immediately necessary to prevent or terminate the other's trespass. . . .

§ 9.42. Deadly Force to Protect Property

A person is justified in using deadly force against another to protect land . . .

(1) . . . to the degree he reasonably believes the deadly force is immediately necessary:

(A) to prevent the other's imminent commission of arson, burglary, robbery, . . . or theft during the nighttime; or

(B) to prevent the other who is fleeing immediately after committing burglary, robbery, . . . or theft during the nighttime from escaping with the property; and

(2) he reasonably believes that:

(A) the land . . . cannot be protected . . . by any other means; or

(B) the use of force other than deadly force to protect or recover the land or . . . would expose the actor . . . to a substantial risk of death or serious bodily injury.

§ 9.44. Use of Device to Protect Property

The justification afforded by Sections 9.41 and 9.43 applies to the use of a device to protect land . . . if:

(1) the device is not designed to cause . . . substantial risk of causing, death or serious bodily injury; and

(2) use of the device is reasonable under all the circumstances.

Vernon's Texas Statutes (2008). Many jurisdictions have statutes about the use of deadly force to protect persons or property.

D. Necessity

1. Private Necessity

Ploof v. Putnam

Supreme Court of Vermont, 1907
71 A. 188

Munson, J.

It is alleged as the ground of recovery that on the 13th day of November, 1904, the defendant was the owner of a certain island in Lake Champlain, and of a certain dock attached thereto, which island and dock were then in charge of the defendant's servant; that the plaintiff was then possessed of and sailing upon said lake a certain loaded sloop, on which were the plaintiff and his wife and two minor children; that there then arose a sudden and violent tempest, whereby the sloop and the property and persons therein were placed in great danger of destruction; that, to save these from destruction or injury, the plaintiff was compelled to, and did, moor the sloop to defendant's dock; that the defendant, by his servant, unmoored the sloop, whereupon it was drive[n] upon the shore by the tempest, without the plaintiff's fault; and that the sloop and its contents were thereby destroyed, and the plaintiff and his wife, and children cast into the lake and upon the shore, receiving injuries. This claim is set forth in two counts—one in trespass, charging that the defendant by his servant with force and arms willfully and designedly unmoored the sloop; the other in case, alleging that it was the duty of the defendant by his servant to permit the plaintiff to moor his sloop to the dock, and to permit it to remain so moored during the continuance of the tempest, but that the defendant by his servant, in disregard of this duty, negligently, carelessly, and wrongfully unmoored the sloop. Both counts are demurred to generally.

There are many cases in the books which hold that necessity, and an inability to control movements inaugurated in the proper exercise of a strict right, will justify entries upon land and interferences with personal property that would otherwise have been trespasses. A reference to a few of these will be sufficient to illustrate the doctrine. In *Miller v. Fandrye*, Poph. 161, trespass was brought for chasing sheep, and the defendant pleaded that the sheep were trespassing upon his land, and that he with a little dog chased them out, and that, as soon as the sheep were off his land, he called in the dog. It was argued that, although the defendant might lawfully drive the sheep from his own ground with a dog, he had no right to pursue them into the next ground; but the court considered that the defendant might drive the sheep from his land with a dog, and that the nature of a dog is such that he cannot be withdrawn in an instant, and that, as the defendant had done his best to recall the dog, trespass would not lie. In trespass of cattle taken in A., defendant pleaded that he was seised of C. and found the cattle there damage feasant, and chased them towards the pound, and they escaped from him and went into A., and he presently retook them; and this was held a good plea. If one have a way over the land of another for his beasts to pass, and the beasts, being properly driven feed the grass by morsels in passing, or run out of the way and are promptly pursued and brought back, trespass will not lie. A traveler on a highway who finds it obstructed from a sudden and temporary cause may pass upon the adjoining land without becoming a trespasser because of the necessity. An entry upon land to save goods which are in danger of being lost or destroyed by water or fire is not a trespass. In *Proctor v. Adams*, 113 Mass. 376, 18 Am. Rep. 500, the defendant went upon the plaintiff's beach for the purpose of saving and restoring to the lawful owner a boat which had been driven ashore, and was in danger of being carried off by the sea; and it was held no trespass.

This doctrine of necessity applies with special force to the preservation of human life. One assaulted and in peril of his life may run through the [land] of another to escape from his assailant. One may sacrifice the personal property of another to save his life or the lives of his fellows. In *Mouse's Case*, 12 Co. 63, the defendant was sued for taking and carrying away the plaintiff's casket and it[s] contents. It appeared that the ferryman of Gravesend took 47 passengers into his barge to pass to London, among whom were the plaintiff and defendant; and the barge being upon the water a great tempest happened, and a strong wind, so that the barge and all the passengers were in danger of being lost if certain ponderous things were not cast out, and the defendant thereupon cast out the plaintiff's casket. It was resolved that in case of necessity, to save the lives of the passengers, it was lawful for the defendant, being a passenger, to cast the plaintiff's casket out of the barge; that, if the ferryman surcharge the barge, the owner shall have his remedy upon the surcharge against the ferryman, but that if there be no surcharge, and the danger accrue only by the act of God, as by tempest, without fault of the ferryman, every one ought to bear his loss to safeguard the life of a man.

It is clear that an entry upon the land of another may be justified by necessity, and that the declaration before us discloses a necessity for mooring the sloop. But the defendant questions the sufficiency of the counts because they do not negative the existence of natural objects to which the plaintiff could have moored with equal safety. The allegations are, in substance, that the stress of a sudden and violent tempest compelled the plaintiff to moor to defendant's dock to save his sloop and the people in it. The averment of necessity is complete, for it covers not only the necessity of mooring, but the necessity of mooring to the dock; and the details of the situation which created this necessity, whatever the legal requirements regarding them are matters of proof, and need not be alleged. It is certain that the rule suggested cannot be held applicable irrespective of circumstance, and the question must be left for adjudication upon proceedings had with reference to the evidence or the charge.

. . . .

Judgment affirmed and cause remanded.

———————

Compare the following case with *Langan v. Valicopters* in Chapter 1. In what way(s) are they similar?

Vincent v. Lake Erie Transp. Co.
Supreme Court of Minnesota, 1910
124 N.W. 221

O'Brien, J.

The steamship *Reynolds*, owned by the defendant, was for the purpose of discharging her cargo on November 27, 1905, moored to plaintiffs' dock in Duluth. While the unloading of the boat was taking place a storm from the northeast developed, which at about 10 o'clock p.m., when the unloading was completed, had so grown in violence that the wind was then moving at 50 miles per hour and continued to increase during the night. There is some evidence that one, and perhaps two, boats were able to enter the harbor that night, but it is plain that navigation was practically suspended from the hour mentioned until the morning of the 29th, when the storm abated, and during that time no master would have been justified in attempting to navigate his vessel, if he could avoid doing so. After the discharge of the cargo the *Reynolds* signaled for a tug to tow her from the dock, but none could be obtained because of the severity of the storm. If the lines holding the ship to the dock had been cast off, she would doubtless have drifted away; but, instead, the lines were kept fast, and as soon as one parted or chafed it was replaced, sometimes with a larger one. The vessel lay upon the outside of the dock, her bow to the east, the wind and waves striking her starboard quarter with such force that she was constantly being lifted and thrown against the dock, resulting in its damage, as found by the jury, to the amount of $500.

We are satisfied that the character of the storm was such that it would have been highly imprudent for the master of the *Reynolds* to have attempted to leave the dock or to have permitted his vessel to drift away from it. . . . Nothing more was demanded of [the master] than ordinary prudence and care, and the record in this case fully sustains the contention of the appellant that, in holding the vessel fast to the dock, those in charge of her exercised good judgment and prudent seamanship.

. . . .

The appellant contends by ample assignments of error that, because its conduct during the storm was rendered necessary by prudence and good seamanship under conditions over which it had no control, it cannot be held liable for any injury resulting to the property of others, and claims that the jury should have been so instructed. An analysis of the charge given by the trial court is not necessary, as in our opinion the only question for the jury was the amount of damages which the plaintiffs were entitled to recover, and no complaint is made upon that score.

The situation was one in which the ordinary rules regulating properly [sic] rights were suspended by forces beyond human control, and if, without the direct intervention of some act by the one sought to be held liable, the property of another was injured, such injury must be attributed to the act of God, and not to the wrongful act of the person sought to be charged. If during the storm the *Reynolds* had entered the harbor, and while there had become disabled and been thrown against the plaintiffs' dock, the plaintiffs could not have recovered. Again, if which [sic] attempting to hold fast to the dock the lines had parted, without any negligence, and the vessel carried against some other boat or dock in the harbor, there would be no liability upon her owner. But here those in charge of the vessel deliberately and by their direct efforts held her in such a position that the damage to the dock resulted, and, having thus preserved the ship at the expense of the dock, it seems to us that her owners are responsible to the dock owners to the extent of the injury inflicted.

In *Depue v. Flatau*, 100 Minn. 299, 111 N.W. 1, 8 L.R.A. (N.S.) 485, this court held that where the plaintiff, while lawfully in the defendants' house, became so ill that he was incapable of traveling with safety, the defendants were responsible to him in damages for compelling him to leave the premises. If, however, the owner of the premises had furnished the traveler with proper accommodations and medical attendance, would he have been able to defeat an action brought against him for their reasonable worth?

In *Ploof v. Putnam*, 71 Atl. 188, 20 L.R.A. (N.S.) 152, the Supreme Court of Vermont held that where, under stress of weather, a vessel was without permission moored to a private dock at an island in Lake Champlain owned by the defendant, the plaintiff was not guilty of trespass, and that the defendant was responsible in damages because his representative upon the island unmoored the vessel, permitting it to drift upon the shore, with resultant injuries to it. If, in that case, the vessel had been permitted to remain, and the dock had suffered an injury, we believe the shipowner would have been held liable for the injury done.

Theologians hold that a starving man may, without moral guilt, take what is necessary to sustain life; but it could hardly be said that the obligation would not be upon such person to pay the value of the property so taken when he became able to do so. And so public necessity, in times of war or peace, may require the taking of private property for public purposes; but under our system of jurisprudence compensation must be made.

Let us imagine in this case that for the better mooring of the vessel those in charge of her had appropriated a valuable cable lying upon the dock. No matter how justifiable such appropriation might have been, it would not be claimed that, because of the overwhelming necessity of the situation, the owner of the cable could not recover its value.

This is not a case where life or property was menaced by any object or thing belonging to the plaintiff, the destruction of which became necessary to prevent the threatened disaster. Nor is it a case where, because of the act of God, or unavoidable accident, the infliction of the injury was beyond the control of the defendant, but is one where the defendant prudently and advisedly availed itself of the plaintiffs' property for the purpose of preserving its own more valuable property, and the plaintiffs are entitled to compensation for the injury done.

Order affirmed.

LEWIS, J.

I dissent.

. . . .

I am of the opinion that one who constructs a dock to the navigable line of waters, and enters into contractual relations with the owner of a vessel to moor at the same, takes the risk of damage to his dock by a boat caught there by a storm, which event could not have been avoided in the exercise of due care. . . .

JAGGARD, J., concurs herein.

———————

Shouldn't the defendant compensate the plaintiff for damage done by the defendant in the course of preserving his or her property? What if the defendant causes more damage to the plaintiff's property than the defendant would have suffered if the defendant had not made use of the plaintiff's property? In other words, suppose that the damage done by the defendant to the plaintiff's property is more extensive than the damage that would have been done to the defendant's property if the defendant had not used the plaintiff's property to save his or her own. Would this defeat a necessity defense?

Problem

A, while boating on a lake, decides that a severe storm is about to arise and, without B's consent, moors her boat to B's dock. In the mooring process, A causes severe damage to B's dock. The storm fails to materialize.

B sues A for damages to B's dock. What will A argue in defense of her actions?

2. Public Necessity

Wegner v. Milwaukee Mutual Insurance Co.

Supreme Court of Minnesota, 1991
479 N.W.2d 38

The salient facts are not in dispute. Around 6:30 p.m. on August 27, 1986, Minneapolis police were staking out an address in Northeast Minneapolis in the hope of apprehending two suspected felons who were believed to be coming to that address to sell stolen narcotics. The suspects arrived at the address with the stolen narcotics. Before arrests could be made, however, the suspects spotted the police and fled in their car at a high rate of speed with the police in pursuit. Eventually, the suspects abandoned their vehicle, separated and fled on foot. The police exchanged gunfire with one suspect as he fled. This suspect later entered the house of Harriet G. Wegner (Wegner) and hid in the front closet. Wegner's granddaughter, who was living at the house, and her fiancé then fled the premises and notified the police.

The police immediately surrounded the house and shortly thereafter called an "Operation 100" around 7:00 p.m. The term "Operation 100" refers to the calling of the Minneapolis Police Department's Emergency Response Unit (ERU) to the scene. The ERU, commonly thought of as a "SWAT" team, consists of personnel specially trained to deal with barricaded suspects, hostage-taking, or similar high-risk situations. Throughout the standoff, the police used a bullhorn and telephone in an attempt to communicate with the suspect. The police, receiving no response, continued efforts to establish contact with the suspect until around 10:00 p.m. At that time the police decided, according to ERU procedure, to take the next step in a barricaded suspect situation, which was to deliver chemical munitions. The police fired at least 25 rounds of chemical munitions or "tear gas" into the house in an attempt to expel the suspect. The police delivered the tear gas to every level of the house, breaking virtually every window in the process. In addition to the tear gas, the police cast three concussion or "flash-bang" grenades into the house to confuse the suspect. The police then entered the home and apprehended the suspect crawling out of a basement window.

The tear gas and flash-bang grenades caused extensive damage to the Wegner house. . . . Wegner alleges damages of $71,000. The City denied Wegner's request for reimbursement, so she turned to her insurance carrier, Milwaukee Mutual Insurance Company (Milwaukee Mutual) for coverage. Milwaukee Mutual paid Wegner $26,595.88 for structural damage, $1,410.06 for emergency board and glass repair and denied coverage for the rest of the claim. Milwaukee Mutual is subrogated to the claims of Wegner against the City to the extent of its payments under the policy.

Wegner commenced an action against both the City of Minneapolis and Milwaukee Mutual to recover the remaining damages. In conjunction with a trespass claim against the City, Wegner asserted that the police department's actions constituted a compensable taking under Minn. Const, art. I, § 13. Milwaukee Mutual cross-claimed against the City for its subrogation interest and any additional amounts the insurer may be found liable for in the future.

Milwaukee Mutual and the City both brought motions for summary judgment on all claims. The district court granted partial summary judgment in favor of the City on the "taking" issue, holding that "Eminent domain is not intended as a limitation on [the] police power." Both Wegner and Milwaukee Mutual appealed the trial court's determination.

The court of appeals affirmed the trial court, reasoning that although there was a "taking" within the meaning of Minn. Const, art. I, § 13, the "taking" was non-compensable under the doctrine of public necessity. *Wegner v. Milwaukee Mut. Ins. Co.*, 464 N.W.2d 543 (Minn. App. 1990).

I.

Article I, section 13, of the Minnesota Constitution provides: "Private property shall not be taken, destroyed or damaged for public use without just compensation, first paid or secured." This provision "imposes a condition on the exercise of the state's inherent supremacy over private property rights." *Johnson v. City of Plymouth*, 263 N.W.2d 603, 605 (Minn. 1978). This type of constitutional inhibition "was designed to bar Government from forcing some people alone to bear public burdens which, in all fairness and justice, should be borne by the public as a whole." *Armstrong v. United States*, 364 U.S. 40, 49, 80 S. Ct. 1563, 1569, 4 L. Ed. 2d 1554 (1960).

The purpose of the damage clause is to ensure that private landowners are compensated, not only for physical invasion of their property, but also damages caused by the state where no physical invasion has occurred. A more significant restriction on recovery under this provision is the requirement that the taking or damaging must be for a public use. What constitutes a public use under this provision is a judicial question which this court historically construes broadly.

The City contends there was no taking for a public use because the actions of the police constituted a legitimate exercise of the police power. The police power in its nature is indefinable.[2]

However, simply labeling the actions of the police as an exercise of the police power "cannot justify the disregard of the constitutional inhibitions." *Petition of Dreosch*, 233 Minn. 274, 282, 47 N.W.2d 106, 111 (1951).

The City argues that Wegner and Milwaukee Mutual are confusing the concept of police power and eminent domain. We agree that this is not an eminent domain action and should not be analyzed as such. This action is based on the plain meaning of the language of Minn. Const, art I, § 13, which requires compensation when property is damaged for a public use. Consequently, the issue in this case is not the reasonableness of the use of chemical munitions to extricate the barricaded suspect but rather whether the exercise of the city's admittedly legitimate police power resulted in a "taking."

In resolving this case of first impression, the well-reasoned decision of *Steele v. City of Houston*, 603 S.W.2d 786 (Tex. 1980) provides guidance. In *Steele*, the Texas Supreme Court addressed a constitutional taking claim involving facts strikingly similar to the present case. There, a group of escaped prisoners had taken refuge in a house apparently selected at random. After discovering the prisoners in the house, the Houston police discharged incendiary material into the house for the purpose of causing the house to catch fire. The police allegedly let the house burn, even after the fire department arrived, in order to ensure all the prisoners had been forced out. The court, interpreting the taking provision of the Texas Constitution, which is virtually identical to the Minnesota taking provision, stated, "this court has moved beyond the earlier notion that the government's duty to pay for taking property rights is excused by labeling the taking as an exercise of police powers." *Id.* at 789. In discussing the city's governmental immunity argument, the court stated:

> The Constitution itself is the authorization for compensation for the destruction of property and is a waiver of governmental immunity for the taking, damaging or destruction of property for public use.

The court further stated:

> The City argues that the destruction of the property as a means to apprehend escapees is a classic instance of police power exercised for the safety of the public. We do not hold that the police officers wrongfully ordered the destruction of the dwelling; we hold that the innocent third parties are entitled by the Constitution to compensation for their property.

---

2. One commentator explained:
[The police power] is used by the court to identify those state and local governmental restrictions and prohibitions which are valid and which may be invoked without payment of compensation. . . .
Sax, *Takings and the Police Power*, 74 Yale L.J. 36, n.6 (1966).

Id. at 791, 793. The court reversed the grant of summary judgment and remanded the case to the trial court so the plaintiffs could prove that the house was intentionally set on fire and that the destruction of the house and its contents was for a public use.

It is unnecessary to remand this case for a determination of whether the police intentionally damaged the Wegner house for a public use. It is undisputed the police intentionally fired tear gas and concussion grenades into the Wegner house. Similarly, it is clear that the damage inflicted by the police in the course of capturing a dangerous suspect was for a public use within the meaning of the constitution.

. . . .

We hold that where an innocent third party's property is damaged by the police in the course of apprehending a suspect, that property is damaged within the meaning of the constitution.

II.

We briefly address the application of the doctrine of public necessity to these facts. The Restatement (Second) of Torts § 196 describes the doctrine as follows:

> One is privileged to enter land in the possession of another if it is, or if the actor reasonably believes it to be, necessary for the purpose of averting an imminent public disaster.

See McDonald v. City of Red Wing, 13 Minn. 38 (Gil. 25) (1868) (city excused from paying compensation under the doctrine of "public safety" where city officers destroyed building to prevent the spread of fire). Prosser, apparently somewhat troubled by the potential harsh outcomes of this doctrine, states:

> It would seem that the moral obligation upon the group affected to make compensation in such a case should be recognized by the law, but recovery usually has been denied.

Prosser and Keeton, The Law of Torts, § 24 (5th ed. 1984); *see also* Restatement (Second) of Torts § 196 comment h. Here, the police were attempting to apprehend a dangerous felon who had fired shots at pursuing officers. The capture of this individual most certainly was beneficial to the whole community. In such circumstances, an individual in Wegner's position should not be forced to bear the entire cost of a benefit conferred on the community as a whole.

Although the court of appeals found there to be a "taking" under Minn. Const, art. I, § 13, the court ruled the "taking" was noncompensable based on the doctrine of public necessity. We do not agree. Once a "taking" is found, compensation is required by operation of law. Thus, if the doctrine of public necessity were to apply to a given fact situation, no taking could be found under Minn. Const, art. I, § 13.

We are not inclined to allow the city to defend its actions on the grounds of public necessity under the facts of this case. We believe the better rule, in situations where an innocent third party's property is taken, damaged or destroyed by the police in

the course of apprehending a suspect, is for the municipality to compensate the innocent party for the resulting damages. The policy considerations in this case center
around the basic notions of fairness and justice. At its most basic level, the issue is
whether it is fair to allocate the entire risk of loss to an innocent homeowner for the
good of the public. We do not believe the imposition of such a burden on the innocent citizens of this state would square with the underlying principles of our system
of justice. Therefore, the City must reimburse Wegner for the losses sustained.

As a final note, we hold that the individual police officers, who were acting in the
public interest, cannot be held personally liable. Instead, the citizens of the City should
all bear the cost of the benefit conferred.

The judgments of the courts below are reversed and the cause remanded for trial
on the issue of damages.

Affirmed in part, reversed in part and remanded.

Can a police officer "borrow" a car in order to pursue a fleeing bank robber? A
person who has run a red light? A fleeing murderer? If the police officer has an accident during the pursuit, who should pay for the damage to the borrowed car? For
the injuries to the bystanders caused by the accident?

Chapter 4

Duty

The negligence formula provides that five elements must be proven in order to win a negligence suit: duty, breach of duty, cause-in-fact, proximate cause, and damages. Many students have difficulty dealing with duty when it is presented at some other place (after proximate cause) in the book. They ask, "How can you limit or cut off duty by proximate cause before it has been established?" Therefore, duty is presented here. In truth, duty is a term of art, and the courts use it to find liability or to limit liability. Thus understood, duty is merely a branch of the social policy analysis considered in the proximate cause chapter. There is no rule for duty, and the courts consider many factors in deciding whether a duty exists. Thus the general duty theory presented in *Heaven v. Pender* has not been widely accepted, except perhaps in automobile collision cases:

> The proposition which these recognised cases suggest, and which is, therefore, to be deduced from them, is that whenever one person is by circumstances placed in such a position with regard to another that every one of ordinary sense who did think would at once recognise that if he did not use ordinary care and skill in his own conduct with regard to those circumstances he would cause danger of injury to the person or property of the other, a duty arises to use ordinary care and skill to avoid such danger.

11 Q.B.D. 503 (C.A. 1883).

While most cases in which duty is an issue involve discussions of when there is none, the chapter begins with two new scholarly opinions that endeavor to define the boundaries of the concept. This chapter will then turn to cases that analyze specific situations where the defendant has argued that the law does not extend a duty to this plaintiff for these injuries.

A. Duty in General

Kubert v. Best

Superior Court of New Jersey, 2013
75 A.3d 1214*

Ashrafi, J.A.D.

Plaintiffs Linda and David Kubert were grievously injured by an eighteen-year-old driver who was texting while driving and crossed the center-line of the road. Their claims for compensation from the young driver have been settled and are no longer part of this lawsuit. Plaintiffs appeal the trial court's dismissal of their claims against the driver's seventeen-year-old friend who was texting the driver much of the day and sent a text message to him immediately before the accident.

New Jersey prohibits texting while driving. A statute under our motor vehicle laws makes it illegal to use a cell phone that is not "hands-free" while driving, except in certain specifically-described emergency situations. N.J.S.A. 39:4-97.3. An offender is subject to a fine of $100. N.J.S.A. 39:4-97.3(d). For future cases like this one, the State Legislature enacted a law, called the "Kulesh, Kubert, and Bolis Law," to provide criminal penalties for those who are distracted by use of a cell phone while driving and injure others. The new law explicitly permits a jury to infer that a driver who was using a hand-held cell phone and caused injury in an accident may be guilty of assault by auto, a fourth-degree crime if someone was injured seriously, thus exposing the driver to a potential sentence in state prison.

The issue before us is not directly addressed by these statutes or any case law that has been brought to our attention. We must determine as a matter of civil common law whether one who is texting from a location remote from the driver of a motor vehicle can be liable to persons injured because the driver was distracted by the text. We hold that the sender of a text message can potentially be liable if an accident is caused by texting, but only if the sender knew or had special reason to know that the recipient would view the text while driving and thus be distracted.

In this appeal, we must also decide whether plaintiffs have shown sufficient evidence to defeat summary judgment in favor of the remote texter. We conclude they have not. We affirm the trial court's order dismissing plaintiffs' complaint against the sender of the text messages, but we do not adopt the trial court's reasoning that a remote texter does not have a legal duty to avoid sending text messages to one who is driving.

I.

The Kuberts' claims against defendant Shannon Colonna, the teenage sender of the texts, were never heard by a jury. Since this appeal comes to us from summary

---

* The editors have not indicated ellipses and have omitted most citations from this opinion.

judgment in favor of Colonna, we view all the evidence and reasonable inferences that can be drawn from the evidence favorably to plaintiffs, the Kuberts.

On the afternoon of September 21, 2009, David Kubert was riding his motorcycle, with his wife, Linda Kubert, riding as a passenger. As they came south around a curve on Hurd Street in Mine Hill Township, a pick-up truck being driven north by eighteen-year-old Kyle Best crossed the double center line of the roadway into their lane of travel. David Kubert attempted to evade the pick-up truck but could not. The front driver's side of the truck struck the Kuberts and their motorcycle. The collision severed, or nearly severed, David's left leg. It shattered Linda's left leg, leaving her fractured thighbone protruding out of the skin as she lay injured in the road.

Best stopped his truck, saw the severity of the injuries, and called 911. The time of the 911 call was 17:49:15, that is, fifteen seconds after 5:49 p.m. Best, a volunteer fireman, aided the Kuberts to the best of his ability until the police and emergency medical responders arrived. Medical treatment could not save either victim's leg. Both lost their left legs as a result of the accident.

After the Kuberts filed this lawsuit, their attorney developed evidence to prove Best's activities on the day of the accident. In September 2009, Best and Colonna were seeing each other socially but not exclusively; they were not boyfriend and girlfriend. Nevertheless, they texted each other many times each day. Best's cell phone record showed that he and Colonna texted each other sixty-two times on the day of the accident, about an equal number of texts originating from each. They averaged almost fourteen texts per hour for the four-and-a-half-hour, non-consecutive time-span they were in telephone contact on the day of the accident.

The telephone record also showed that, in a period of less than twelve hours on that day, Best had sent or received 180 text messages. In her deposition, Colonna acknowledged that it was her habit also to text more than 100 times per day. She said: "I'm a young teenager. That's what we do." She also testified that she generally did not pay attention to whether the recipient of her texts was driving a car at the time or not. She thought it was "weird" that plaintiffs' attorney was trying to pin her down on whether she knew that Best was driving when she texted him.

During the day of the accident, a Monday, Best and Colonna exchanged many text messages in the morning, had lunch together at his house, and watched television until he had to go to his part-time job at a YMCA in Randolph Township. The time record from the YMCA showed that Best punched in on a time clock at 3:35 p.m. At 3:49 p.m., Colonna texted him, but he did not respond at that time. He punched out of work at 5:41. A minute later, at 5:42, Best sent a text to Colonna. He then exchanged three text messages with his father, testifying at his deposition that he did so while in the parking lot of the YMCA and that the purpose was to notify his parents he was coming home to eat dinner with them.

The accident occurred about four or five minutes after Best began driving home from the YMCA. At his deposition, Best testified that he did not text while driving — meaning that it was not his habit to text when he was driving. He testified falsely at first that he did not text when he began his drive home from the YMCA on the day of the accident. But he was soon confronted with the telephone records, which he had seen earlier, and then he admitted that he and Colonna exchanged text messages within minutes of his beginning to drive.

The sequence of texts between Best and Colonna in the minutes before and after the accident is shown on the following chart. The first-listed text occurred immediately after Best left work, apparently while he was still at the YMCA, and the three texts in boldface type are those that were exchanged while Best was driving: [The chart, showing the list of texts and precisely when they were transmitted, has been omitted. Eds.]

This sequence indicates the precise time of the accident—within seconds of 5:48:58. Seventeen seconds elapsed from Best's sending a text to Colonna and the time of the 911 call after the accident. Those seconds had to include Best's stopping his vehicle, observing the injuries to the Kuberts, and dialing 911. It appears, therefore, that Best collided with the Kuberts' motorcycle immediately after sending a text at 5:48:58. It can be inferred that he sent that text in response to Colonna's text to him that he received twenty-five seconds earlier. Finally, it appears that Best initiated the texting with Colonna as he was about to and after he began to drive home.

After plaintiffs learned of Colonna's involvement and added her to their lawsuit, she moved for summary judgment. Her attorney argued to the trial court that Colonna had no liability for the accident because she was not present at the scene, had no legal duty to avoid sending a text to Best when he was driving, and further, that she did not know he was driving. The trial judge reviewed the evidence and the arguments of the attorneys, conducted independent research on the law, and ultimately concluded that Colonna did not have a legal duty to avoid sending a text message to Best, even if she knew he was driving. The judge dismissed plaintiffs' claims against Colonna.

II.

We conclude that a person sending text messages has a duty not to text someone who is driving if the texter knows, or has special reason to know, the recipient will view the text while driving. But we also conclude that plaintiffs have not presented sufficient evidence to prove that Colonna had such knowledge when she texted Best immediately before the accident.

A.

We first address generally the nature of a duty imposed by the common law.

In a lawsuit alleging that a defendant is liable to a plaintiff because of the defendant's negligent conduct, the plaintiff must prove four things: (1) that the defendant owed a duty of care to the plaintiff, (2) that the defendant breached that duty, (3) that the breach was a proximate cause of the plaintiff's injuries, and (4) that the plaintiff suffered actual compensable injuries as a result. The plaintiff bears the burden of proving each of these four "core elements" of a negligence claim.

Because plaintiffs in this case sued Best and eventually settled their claims against him, it is important to note that the law recognizes that more than one defendant can be the proximate cause of and therefore liable for causing injury. Whether a duty exists to prevent harm is not controlled by whether another person also has a duty, even a greater duty, to prevent the same harm. If more than one defendant breached his or her duty and proximately caused the injuries, the jury at a trial may determine relative fault and assign a percentage of responsibility to each under our comparative negligence statutes.

"A duty is an obligation imposed by law requiring one party 'to conform to a particular standard of conduct toward another.'" *Acuna v. Turkish*, 192 N.J. 399, 413, 930 A.2d 416 (2007) (quoting Prosser & Keeton on Torts: Lawyer's Edition § 53, at 356 (5th ed. 1984)), cert. denied, 555 U.S. 813, 129 S.Ct. 44, 172 L.Ed.2d 22 (2008); see also Restatement (Second) of Torts § 4 (1965) ("The word 'duty' . . . denote[s] the fact that the actor is required to conduct himself in a particular manner at the risk that if he does not do so he becomes subject to liability to another to whom the duty is owed for any injury sustained by such other, of which that actor's conduct is a legal cause.").

Whether a duty of care exists "is generally a matter for a court to decide," not a jury. The "fundamental question [is] whether the plaintiff's interests are entitled to legal protection against the defendant's conduct."

The New Jersey Supreme Court recently analyzed the common law process by which a court decides whether a legal duty of care exists to prevent injury to another. *Estate of Desir ex. rel. Estiverne v. Vertus*, 214 N.J. 303, 69 A.3d 1247 (2013). The Court reviewed precedents developed over the years in our courts and restated the "most cogent explanation of the principles that guide [the courts] in determining whether to recognize the existence of a duty of care":

> "[w]hether a person owes a duty of reasonable care toward another turns on whether the imposition of such a duty satisfies an abiding sense of basic fairness under all of the circumstances in light of considerations of public policy. That inquiry involves identifying, weighing, and balancing several factors — the relationship of the parties, the nature of the attendant risk, the opportunity and ability to exercise care, and the public interest in the proposed solution. . . . The analysis is both very fact-specific and principled; it must lead to solutions that properly and fairly resolve the specific case and generate intelligible and sensible rules to govern future conduct."

[(*Id.* at 322, 69 A.3d 1247) (alteration in original) (citations omitted) (quoting *Hopkins v. Fox & Lazo Realtors*, 132 N.J. 426, 439, 625 A.2d 1110 (1993)).]

The Court emphasized that the law must take into account "generally applicable rules to govern societal behaviors," not just an "outcome that reaches only the particular circumstances and parties before the Court today[.]" *Id.* at 323, 69 A.3d 1247. The Court described all of these considerations as "a full duty analysis" to determine whether the law recognizes a duty of care in the particular circumstances of a negligence case. *Id.* at 316, 69 A.3d 1247 (quoting *Rowe v. Mazel Thirty, LLC*, 209 N.J. 35, 44, 34 A.3d 1248 (2012)).

B.

In this case, plaintiffs argue that a duty of care should be imposed upon Colonna because she aided and abetted Best's violation of the law when he used his cell phone while driving. To support their argument, plaintiffs cite section 876 of the Restatement (Second) of Torts (1965), a compilation of common law principles. Under section 876 of the Restatement, an individual is liable if he or she knows that another person's "conduct constitutes a breach of duty and gives substantial assistance or encouragement to the other."

To illustrate this concept, the Restatement provides the following hypothetical example:

> A and B participate in a riot in which B, although throwing no rocks himself, encourages A to throw rocks. One of the rocks strikes C, a bystander. B is subject to liability to C.

[Restatement § 876, comment d, illustration 4.]

The example illustrates that one does not actually have to be the person who threw a rock to be liable for injury caused by the rock. In *Tarr v. Ciasulli*, 181 N.J. 70, 84, 853 A.2d 921 (2004), the New Jersey Supreme Court adopted the principle stated in Restatement § 876 as applicable to determine joint liability when persons act in concert and cause harm to another.

In this case, plaintiffs assert that Colonna and Best were acting in concert in exchanging text messages. Although Colonna was at a remote location from the site of the accident, plaintiffs say she was "electronically present" in Best's pick-up truck immediately before the accident and she aided and abetted his unlawful use of his cell phone.

In this case, Colonna did not have a special relationship with Best by which she could control his conduct. Nor is there evidence that she actively encouraged him to text her while he was driving. Colonna sent two texts to Best in the afternoon of September 21, 2009, one about two hours and the second about twenty-five seconds before the accident. What she said in those texts is unknown. Even if a reasonable inference can be drawn that she sent messages requiring responses, the act of sending such messages, by itself, is not active encouragement that the recipient read the text and respond immediately, that is, while driving and in violation of the law.

[T]he evidence in this case is not sufficient for a jury to conclude that Colonna took affirmative steps and gave substantial assistance to Best in violating the law. Plaintiffs produced no evidence tending to show that Colonna urged Best to read and respond to her text while he was driving.

The evidence available to plaintiffs is not sufficient to prove Colonna's liability to the Kuberts on the basis of aiding and abetting Best's negligent driving while using a cell phone.

C.

Plaintiffs argue alternatively that Colonna independently had a duty not to send texts to a person who she knew was driving a vehicle. They have not cited a case in New Jersey or any other jurisdiction that so holds, and we have not found one in our own research.

Having considered the competing arguments of the parties, we also conclude that liability is not established by showing only that the sender directed the message to a specific identified recipient, even if the sender knew the recipient was then driving. We conclude that additional proofs are necessary to establish the sender's liability, namely, that the sender also knew or had special reason to know that the driver would read the message while driving and would thus be distracted from attending to the road and the operation of the vehicle. We reach these conclusions by examining the law in analogous circumstances and applying "a full duty analysis."

A section of the Restatement that the parties have not referenced provides:

> An act is negligent if the actor intends it to affect, or realizes or should realize that it is likely to affect, the conduct of another, a third person, or an animal in such a manner as to create an unreasonable risk of harm to the other.

[Restatement § 303.]

To illustrate this concept, the Restatement provides the following hypothetical example:

> A is driving through heavy traffic. B, a passenger in the back seat, suddenly and unnecessarily calls out to A, diverting his attention, thus causing him to run into the car of C. B is negligent toward C.

[Restatement § 303, comment d, illustration 3.]

We have recognized that a passenger who distracts a driver can be held liable for the passenger's own negligence in causing an accident. In other words, a passenger in a motor vehicle has a duty "not to interfere with the driver's operations."

One form of interference with a driver might be obstructing his view or otherwise diverting his attention from the tasks of driving. It would be reasonable to hold a passenger liable for causing an accident if the passenger obstructed the driver's view of the road, for example, by suddenly holding a piece of paper in front of the driver's face and urging the driver to look at what is written or depicted on the paper. The same can be said if a passenger were to hold a cell phone with a text message or a picture in front of the driver's eyes. Such distracting conduct would be direct, independent negligence of the passenger, not aiding and abetting of the driver's negligent conduct. Here, of course, Colonna did not hold Best's cell phone in front of his eyes and physically distract his view of the road.

The more relevant question is whether a passenger can be liable not for actually obstructing the driver's view but only for urging the driver to take his eyes off the road and to look at a distracting object. We think the answer is yes, but only if the passenger's conduct is unreasonably risky because the passenger knows, or has special reason to know, that the driver will in fact be distracted and drive negligently as a result of the passenger's actions.

It is the primary responsibility of the driver to obey the law and to avoid distractions. Imposing a duty on a passenger to avoid any conduct that might theoretically distract the driver would open too broad a swath of potential liability in ordinary and innocent circumstances. [C]ourts must be careful not to "create a broadly worded duty and . . . run the risk of unintentionally imposing liability in situations far beyond the parameters we now face." "The scope of a duty is determined under 'the totality of the circumstances,' and must be 'reasonable' under those circumstances."

"Foreseeability of the risk of harm is the foundational element in the determination of whether a duty exists." "Foreseeability, in turn, is based on the defendant's knowledge of the risk of injury."*

It is foreseeable that a driver who is actually distracted by a text message might cause an accident and serious injuries or death, but it is not generally foreseeable that every recipient of a text message who is driving will neglect his obligation to obey the law and will be distracted by the text. Like a call to voicemail or an answering machine, the sending of a text message by itself does not demand that the recipient take any action. The sender should be able to assume that the recipient will read a text message only when it is safe and legal to do so, that is, when not operating a vehicle. However, if the sender knows that the recipient is both driving and will read the text immediately, then the sender has taken a foreseeable risk in sending a text at that time. The sender has knowingly engaged in distracting conduct, and it is not unfair also to hold the sender responsible for the distraction.

"When the risk of harm is that posed by third persons, a plaintiff may be required to prove that defendant was in a position to 'know or have reason to know, from past experience, that there [was] a likelihood of conduct on the part of [a] third person[]' that was 'likely to endanger the safety' of another."

Our conclusion that a limited duty should be imposed on the sender is supported by the "full duty analysis" described by the Supreme Court — identifying, weighing, and balancing "the relationship of the parties, the nature of the attendant risk, the opportunity and ability to exercise care, and the public interest in the proposed solution." When the sender knows that the text will reach the driver while operating a vehicle, the sender has a relationship to the public who use the roadways similar to that of a passenger physically present in the vehicle. As we have stated, a passenger must avoid distracting the driver. The remote sender of a text who knows the recipient is then driving must do the same.

When the sender texts a person who is then driving, knowing that the driver will immediately view the text, the sender has disregarded the attendant and foreseeable risk of harm to the public. The risk is substantial, as evidenced by the dire

---

* Citations for these quotations have been omitted. For those who wish to look them up, they may be found at 75 A.3d at 1227.

consequences in this and similar cases where texting drivers have caused severe injuries or death.

With respect to the sender's opportunity to exercise care, "[a] corresponding consideration is the practicality of preventing [the risk]." We must take into account "how establishing this duty will work in practice." It is easy for the sender of a text message to avoid texting to a driver who the sender knows will immediately view the text and thus be distracted from driving safely. "When the defendant's actions are 'relatively easily corrected' and the harm sought to be presented is 'serious,' it is fair to impose a duty."

At the same time, "[c]onsiderations of fairness implicate the scope as well as the existence of a duty." Limiting the duty to persons who have such knowledge will not require that the sender of a text predict in every instance how a recipient will act. It will not interfere with use of text messaging to a driver that one expects will obey the law. The limited duty we impose will not hold texters liable for the unlawful conduct of others, but it will hold them liable for their own negligence when they have knowingly disregarded a foreseeable risk of serious injury to others.

Finally, the public interest requires fair measures to deter dangerous texting while driving. Just as the public has learned the dangers of drinking and driving through a sustained campaign and enhanced criminal penalties and civil liability, the hazards of texting when on the road, or to someone who is on the road, may become part of the public consciousness when the liability of those involved matches the seriousness of the harm.

To summarize our conclusions, we do not hold that someone who texts to a person driving is liable for that person's negligent actions; the driver bears responsibility for obeying the law and maintaining safe control of the vehicle. We hold that, when a texter knows or has special reason to know that the intended recipient is driving and is likely to read the text message while driving, the texter has a duty to users of the public roads to refrain from sending the driver a text at that time.

D.

In this case, plaintiffs developed evidence pertaining to the habits of Best and Colonna in texting each other repeatedly. They also established that the day of the accident was not an unusual texting day for the two. But they failed to develop evidence tending to prove that Colonna not only knew that Best was driving when she texted him at 5:48:14 p.m. but that she knew he would violate the law and immediately view and respond to her text.

As our recitation of the facts shows, Colonna sent only one text while Best was driving. The contents of that text are unknown. No testimony established that she was aware Best would violate the law and read her text as he was driving, or that he would respond immediately. The evidence of multiple texting at other times when Best was not driving did not prove that Colonna breached the limited duty we have described.

Because the necessary evidence to prove breach of the remote texter's duty is absent on this record, summary judgment was properly granted dismissing plaintiffs' claims against Colonna.

Affirmed. [Concurrence by Judge Espinosa omitted.]

––––––––––––

What if a plaintiff could show that a text sender would get angry if there were a delay in responding, and the sender knew that the recipient was driving? What if the sender told the recipient that the situation of the sender was an emergency? What is the bottom line of all this?

Munn v. Hotchkiss School

Supreme Court of Connecticut, 2017
165 A.3d 1167

Rogers, C.J.

The issues in this case, which comes to us on certification from the United States Court of Appeals for the Second Circuit pursuant to General Statutes § 51-199b(d), are: (1) Does Connecticut public policy support imposing a duty on a school to warn about or protect against the risk of a serious insect-borne disease when it organizes a trip abroad? [Second issue related to the size of the damage award omitted.]

    . . . .

The following facts, which find support in the record certified by the Second Circuit and procedural history are relevant to our resolution of the certified issues. The defendant, The Hotchkiss School, is a private boarding school located in Lakeville. At the time of the events underlying this appeal, the plaintiff, Cara L. Munn, was a student there. In June and July of 2007, the plaintiff, who recently had turned fifteen years old and completed her freshman year, joined other students and faculty of the school on an educational trip to China. In July, she contracted tick-borne encephalitis, a viral infectious disease that attacks the central nervous system, as a result of being bitten by an infected tick during a hike on Mount Panshan, which is located in a forested area approximately sixty miles from Tianjin, a city in northeastern China. As a result of contracting tick-borne encephalitis, the plaintiff suffered permanent brain damage that has impacted severely the course of her life.

In 2009, the plaintiff filed a diversity action in the United States District Court for the District of Connecticut, alleging that the defendant had been negligent by, inter alia, failing to warn students and their parents of the risk of exposure to insect-borne diseases and failing to ensure that the students took protective measures against insect bites prior to visiting Mount Panshan. The case was tried to a jury in March, 2013. The jury returned a verdict in the plaintiff's favor, and it awarded her $10.25 million in economic damages and $31.5 million in noneconomic damages. The award was then reduced pursuant to a stipulated collateral source reduction.

The defendant thereafter challenged the verdict, moving for judgment as a matter of law; see Fed. R. Civ. P. 50(b); or, alternatively, for a new trial. See Fed. R. Civ.P. 59. The District Court rejected each of the claims the defendant made in support of those motions, including that the plaintiff's infection with tick-borne encephalitis was unforeseeable, that public policy precluded the imposition of a legal duty on the defendant and that the noneconomic portion of the damages award was excessive as a matter of law. The defendant appealed from the District Court's judgment to the Second Circuit Court of Appeals, challenging its determinations on each of those claims. The Second Circuit agreed with the plaintiff that there was sufficient evidence presented at trial for the jury to find that her illness was foreseeable; *Munn v. Hotchkiss School*, 795 F.3d 324, 330 (2d Cir. 2015); but, finding insufficient guidance in existing Connecticut law, certified to this court the issues of whether Connecticut public policy supports the imposition of a duty on a school to warn about or to protect against the foreseeable risk of a serious insect-borne disease when organizing a trip abroad and, if so, whether the jury's damages award, particularly the noneconomic portion, warranted a remittitur. *Id.*, at 337.

I

We first consider whether Connecticut public policy supports the imposition of a duty on a school to warn about or protect against the foreseeable risk of a serious insect-borne disease when it organizes a trip abroad. Because it is widely recognized that schools generally are obligated to exercise reasonable care to protect students in their charge from foreseeable dangers, and there is no compelling reason to create an exception for foreseeable serious insect-borne diseases, we conclude that the imposition of such a duty is not contrary to Connecticut public policy and, accordingly, answer the first certified question in the affirmative.

. . . .

We turn to the first certified question, which concerns the defendant's duty to the plaintiff. "Duty is a legal conclusion about relationships between individuals, made after the fact, and imperative to a negligence cause of action. The nature of the duty, and the specific persons to whom it is owed, are determined by the circumstances surrounding the conduct of the individual. . . . Although it has been said that no universal test for [duty] ever has been formulated . . . our threshold inquiry has always been whether the specific harm alleged by the plaintiff was foreseeable to the defendant. The ultimate test of the existence of the duty to use care is found in the foreseeability that harm may result if it is not exercised. . . . By that [it] is not meant that one charged with negligence must be found actually to have foreseen the probability of harm or that the particular injury [that] resulted was foreseeable. [T]he test for the existence of a legal duty entails (1) a determination of whether an ordinary person in the defendant's position, knowing what the defendant knew or should have known, would anticipate that harm of the general nature of that suffered was likely to result, and (2) a determination, on the basis of a public policy analysis, of whether the defendant's responsibility for its negligent conduct should extend to the particular consequences or particular plaintiff in the case." (Internal quotation marks omitted.) *Ruiz v. Victory Properties, LLC*, 315 Conn. 320, 328–29, 107 A.3d 381 (2015).

The second prong of the analysis is necessary because "[a] simple conclusion that the harm to the plaintiff was foreseeable . . . cannot by itself mandate a determination that a legal duty exists. Many harms are quite literally foreseeable, yet for pragmatic reasons, no recovery is allowed. . . . A further inquiry must be made, for we recognize that duty is not sacrosanct in itself . . . but is only an expression of the sum total of those considerations of policy [that] lead the law to say that the plaintiff is entitled to protection. . . . The final step in the duty inquiry, then, is to make a determination of the fundamental policy of the law, as to whether the defendant's responsibility should extend to such results. . . . [I]n considering whether public policy suggests the imposition of a duty, we . . . consider the following four factors: (1) the normal expectations of the participants in the activity under review; (2) the public policy of encouraging participation in the activity, while weighing the safety of the participants; (3) the avoidance of increased litigation; and (4) the decisions of other jurisdictions. . . . [This] totality of the circumstances rule . . . is most consistent with the public policy goals of our legal system, as well as the general tenor of our [tort] jurisprudence." (Citations omitted; internal quotation marks omitted.) *Id.*, at 336–37, 107 A.3d 381.

Before turning to the public policy analysis, we pause to examine the broader legal framework that encompasses the specific certified issue. Although the law of negligence typically does not impose a duty on one party to act affirmatively in furtherance of the protection of another, there are certain exceptions to that general proposition. See generally 2 Restatement (Third), Torts, Liability for Physical and Emotional Harm §§ 37 through 44 (2012). One exception applies when there is a "special relationship" between those parties; id., § 40, pp. 39–40; and one example of such a special relationship that has received wide recognition, along with a concomitant duty to protect, is the relationship between schools and their students.

As to the rationale for imposing an affirmative duty to protect in this context, "[t]he relationship between a school and its students parallels aspects of several other special relationships—it is a custodian of students, it is a land possessor who opens [its] premises to a significant public population, and it acts partially in the place of parents." (Internal quotation marks omitted.) *Monroe v. Basis School, Inc.*, 234 Ariz. 155, 157, 318 P.3d 871 (App. 2014). As a general matter, "[o]ne . . . who voluntarily takes the custody of another under circumstances such as to deprive the other of his normal opportunities for protection is under [a duty to protect the other against unreasonable risk of physical harm]." 2 Restatement (Second), Torts § 314A (4), p. 118 (1965). At heart, "the duty [to protect] derives from the simple fact that a school, in assuming physical custody and control over its students, effectively takes the place of parents and guardians . . . ." *Mirand v. New York, supra*, 84 N.Y.2d at 49, 614 N.Y.S.2d 372, 637 N.E.2d 263; see also 2 Restatement (Second), *supra*, § 320, comment (b), p. 131 ("[A] child while in school is deprived of the protection of his parents or guardian. Therefore, the actor who takes custody . . . of a child is properly required to give him the protection which the custody or the manner in which it is taken has deprived him.").

"[T]he scope of the duty imposed by the student-school relationship is not limitless. . . . [T]he duty is tied to expected activities within the relationship. Therefore, in the student-school relationship, the duty of care is bounded by geography and time, encompassing risks such as those that occur while the student is at school or otherwise under the school's control." (Citation omitted; internal quotation marks omitted.) *Boisson v. Arizona Board of Regents, supra,* 236 Ariz. at 623, 343 P.3d 931[.]

. . . .

Regarding the scope of the duty, standard negligence principles apply, within the context of the facts and circumstances of the particular case. "While [a] school is not an insurer of the safety of its students, it is obligated to exercise such care over students in its charge that a parent of ordinary prudence would exercise under comparable circumstances . . . ." (Citation omitted; internal quotation marks omitted.) *David v. New York,* 40 A.D.3d 572, 573, 835 N.Y.S.2d 377 (2007). The duty a school owes "to students and their parents is, on a general level, a duty to take whatever precautions are necessary reasonably to ensure the safety and welfare of the children entrusted to its custody and control against harm that the [school] anticipates, or reasonably should anticipate." *Doe Parents No. 1 v. State Dept. of Education, supra,* 100 Hawai'i at 80, 58 P.3d 545. What the duty quintessentially entails is "to exercise reasonable care in ensuring that students are educated in a safe environment free from any unreasonable risks of harm." *Id.,* at 81, 58 P.3d 545[.] The degree of care required will vary depending on the particular risk at issue, the ages of the students in the school's custody and all the attendant circumstances.

In light of the foregoing authorities, it is beyond dispute that, as a general matter, a school having custody of minor children has an obligation to use reasonable care to protect those children from foreseeable harms during school sponsored activities, including educational trips abroad. The question we must consider, then, is whether there is something unique and/or compelling about foreseeable insect-borne diseases that should excuse schools that are organizing educational trips abroad from exercising reasonable care to minimize the possibility that the minors entrusted to their custody will contract such diseases. Stated otherwise, does Connecticut public policy mandate that, when it comes to foreseeable insect-borne diseases, there should be an exception to the general rule that schools must refrain from negligently exposing minor students, whom they have agreed to supervise in the absence of their parents, to foreseeable dangers? To answer that question, we begin by considering the first public policy factor, the normal expectations of the participants in an educational trip abroad.

As this case amply demonstrates, insect-borne diseases can pose significant threats to human health. When insect-borne diseases present serious risks, they become the subject of government warnings and media attention. The reason for the provision of such information is clear: people are interested in having it. When a particular disease is brought to an individual's attention, he or she can learn about the disease's prevalence, the areas in which the disease is endemic, whether there is a vaccine available and, if not, what other measures may be effective to prevent it. Furthermore, he or she can become aware of the symptoms of the disease, the damage to one's health that the disease might cause, and whether and how the disease, if contracted, may be treated. With all of this information in hand, the individual can make educated choices about whether to travel to an area where the disease is present and, if so, what protective measures should be taken, in light of the individual's particular tolerance to risk.

Many measures are available to protect against insect- borne diseases. . . .

Information directed at travelers about insect-borne diseases, and the measures to protect against them, is not hard to come by. . . . Additionally, as the evidence in this case demonstrated, there are many commercially produced publications that track and compile information for travelers about insect-borne diseases and the areas in which they are endemic.

In light of the foregoing, we believe that the normal expectations of participants in a school sponsored educational trip abroad, involving minor children, are that the organizer of the trip would take reasonable measures to warn the participants and their parents about the serious insect-borne diseases that are present in the areas to be visited and to protect the children from those diseases. School personnel who are organizing an educational trip abroad typically will have superior knowledge of travel planning in general, and the trip itinerary in particular, and, as explained previously, have a general responsibility to protect the minors in their charge while they are away from the custody of their parents. Given the potential dangers posed by serious insect-borne diseases, the existence of methods by which to avoid such diseases and the availability of useful information about them, trip participants naturally would expect the organizer of the trip to pass along appropriate warnings and to use ordinary care to minimize the disease risks posed by the insects in the particular areas to be visited. Trip organizers, for their part, likely would agree that reasonable protective measures, tailored to the risk, are doable and appropriate. Accordingly, we conclude that the first factor of the public policy analysis supports the imposition of a duty on a school organizing a trip abroad to warn about, and to protect against, serious insect-borne diseases.

We turn next to the second and third factors of the analysis, namely, the public policy of encouraging participation in the activity at issue, while weighing the safety of the participants, and the avoidance of increased litigation. We recognize, as we must, that there are many benefits to international educational travel, and that it undeniably is the public policy of Connecticut to promote such travel. . . . We disagree, however, that recognizing that a school's general duty to protect its students includes the responsibility to take reasonable measures to warn about, and to protect against, serious insect-borne disease risks will have a chilling effect on such travel. Rather, it should have the salutary effect of promoting safety by ensuring that appropriate warnings are given and appropriate protective measures are taken. We emphasize that the duty to warn and protect does not amount to an absolute guaranty of safety, nor will it require, in every instance, that every possible precautionary measure be taken. Rather, the scope of the duty necessarily will vary, depending on the risk posed by the particular insect-borne illness at issue, the ages of the participants in the school sponsored trip, and all of the attendant circumstances.

In regard to the potential for increased litigation, we are skeptical that recognition of a school's duty to warn about, or protect against, a serious insect-borne illness when organizing an educational trip abroad will lead to a flood of similar actions. Our research has disclosed a dearth of claims with fact patterns similar to the present case, perhaps because the incidence of students contracting serious insect-borne diseases while on educational trips abroad, when appropriate protective measures are taken, is relatively uncommon. Again, information about insect-borne diseases, and the methods to protect against them, is readily available to travel professionals in a number of resources.

Additionally, the mere recognition of a legal duty by no means creates an open and shut case for every potential plaintiff who may contract an insect-borne disease while on an educational trip abroad. "A cause of action in negligence is comprised of four elements: duty; breach of that duty; causation; and actual injury." (Internal quotation marks omitted.) *Lawrence v. O & G Industries, Inc., supra*, 319 Conn. at 649, 126 A.3d 569. Thus, recognition of a duty affords students who contract insect-borne diseases on educational trips abroad only an opportunity to prove that the disease at issue was foreseeable, that the school failed to appropriately warn of the danger of the disease and/or to take reasonable precautionary measures and that such failure was a substantial cause of the illness. As always, principles of comparative negligence will apply. *Vendrella v. Astriab Family Ltd. Partnership*, 311 Conn. 301, 325, 87 A.3d 546 (2014). In the case of public institutions, discretionary act immunity may be invoked. See General Statutes § 52-557n(a)(2)(B). It is pure speculation, therefore, that our holding today will open the floodgates to let loose a wave of future litigants who inevitably will prevail.

. . . .

Notably, in several of the cases that we have cited herein in support of the general principle that a school has a duty to protect the students in its custody, the plaintiffs ultimately did not prevail due to their inability to satisfy other elements of their negligence claims.

We conclude that the second and third public policy factors support the imposition of a duty on a school to warn about, and protect against, the risk of serious insect-borne diseases when organizing a trip abroad. [The court ruled that the fourth public policy was "essentially neutral." Eds.]

. . . .

The defendant insists that there should be no duty to warn or to protect in the circumstances of this case because the chances of the plaintiff contracting tick-borne encephalitis were remote. Although, in a given case, the rarity of a particular illness should be weighed by the jury when determining whether its contraction was foreseeable, or whether the warnings given and protective measures taken by a school satisfied the duty of care, it is not relevant to a public policy analysis, which should be undertaken by a court without reference to the facts of a particular case.

Although the question of whether the defendant properly was proven to be negligent is not before us, we close with the following observation. Although we agree that tick-borne encephalitis is not a widespread illness, when it strikes, the results can be devastating. At the same time, some of the measures one might take to protect against it are simple and straightforward—covering exposed skin, applying insect repellent containing DEET, closely checking one's body for ticks and/or avoiding the woods in areas where the disease is known to be endemic. The case thus brings to mind the risk-benefit calculus articulated long ago by Judge Learned Hand to determine whether, in given circumstances, reasonable care has been exercised. Pursuant to that formulation, both the likelihood and the gravity of potential harm should be taken into consideration, as well as the burden of taking adequate precautions to prevent that harm from occurring. See *United States v. Carroll Towing Co.*, 159 F.2d 169, 173 (2d Cir. 1947). In short, "[g]iven a balancing approach to negligence, even if the likelihood of harm stemming from the actor's conduct is small, the actor can be negligent if the severity of the possible harm is great and the burden of precautions is limited." 1 Restatement (Third), *supra*, § 3, comment (f), p. 31; see also 3 F. Harper et al., Harper, James & Grey on Torts (3d Ed. 2007) § 16.9 (2), p. 523 ("[i]f the harm that may be foreseen is great, conduct that threatens it may be negligent even though the statistical probability of its happening is very slight indeed"); 3 F. Harper et al., *supra*, § 16.9 (3), p. 528 ("the law imposes liability for failure to take precautions, even against remote risks, if the cost of the precautions would be relatively low"). When schools are fulfilling their duty to supervise students in their custody, these admonitions should be taken into account.

In sum, we conclude that the public policy of Connecticut does not preclude imposing a duty on a school to warn about or to protect against the risk of a serious insect-borne disease when organizing a trip abroad. For that reason, we answer the first certified question in the affirmative.

. . . .

II

We answer the first certified question, "Yes."

In this opinion the other justices concurred.*

---

*On Feb. 6, 2018, the United States Court of Appeals for the Second Circuit dismissed Hotchkiss' remaining arguments and affirmed the District Court's decision. 2018 WL 722474.

B. The Obligation to Assist Others

Problem

Anna and Bob were both second-year law students. For their first date, they decided to go to a movie and then to a motel. At the motel, they took a shower together. Bob left the shower first. When Anna stepped from the shower, she slipped and fell, breaking her leg. She was bleeding and unable to move. Bob refused her requests to call for help. Two hours after the fall, Anna was able to crawl to the phone and call 911. Consider whether Bob had a duty to Anna to call for assistance.

Yania v. Bigan

Pennsylvania Supreme Court, 1959
155 A.2d 343

BENJAMIN R. JONES, JUSTICE.

A bizarre and most unusual circumstance provides the background of this appeal.

On September 25, 1957 John E. Bigan was engaged in a coal strip-mining operation in Shade Township, Somerset County. On the property being stripped were large cuts or trenches created by Bigan when he removed the earthen overburden for the purpose of removing the coal underneath. One cut contained water 8 to 10 feet in depth with side walls or embankments 16 to 18 feet in height; at this cut Bigan had installed a pump to remove the water.

At approximately 4 p.m. on that date, Joseph F. Yania, the operator of another coal strip-mining operation, and one Boyd M. Ross went upon Bigan's property for the purpose of discussing a business matter with Bigan, and, while there, were asked by Bigan to aid him in starting the pump. Ross and Bigan entered the cut and stood at the point where the pump was located. Yania stood at the top of one of the cut's side walls and then jumped from the side wall—a height of 16 to 18 feet—into the water and was drowned.

Yania's widow, in her own right and on behalf of her three children, instituted wrongful death and survival actions against Bigan contending Bigan was responsible for Yania's death. Preliminary objections, in the nature of demurrers, to the complaint were filed on behalf of Bigan. The court below sustained the preliminary objections; from the entry of that order this appeal was taken.

. . . .

Lastly, it is urged that Bigan failed to take the necessary steps to rescue Yania from the water. The mere fact that Bigan saw Yania in a position of peril in the water imposed upon him no legal, although a moral, obligation or duty to go to his rescue. . . .

Order affirmed.

1. What if a person on a bridge refused to throw a rope to a stranger drowning in the river below? Does a ship's captain have a duty to rescue a passenger who has fallen into the water? What if a doctor in Atlanta is the only doctor capable of saving a person in Chicago?

2. Courts often begin opinions involving rescue-type situations by stating that there is "no duty to rescue." Many of their decisions, however, conclude that there was a duty in the particular case, whether because of some relationship between the parties that allowed the one in need of rescue to expect the other to at least try to help or for some other reason. In *Soldano v. O'Daniels*, 190 Cal. Rptr. 310 (California Ct. App. 1983), the court decided that a bartender had a duty to allow a stranger who rushed into the bar and sought either to call 911 or to have the bartender call so that help could be summoned to deal with an incident that had nothing to do with the bar. The basis of the decision appeared to be the weighing of the risk (a shooting) against the burden of calling 911 (negligible).

3. The *Soldano* court cited several special relationships that might lead to a conclusion that there was a duty:

> . . . California courts have found special relationships in *Ellis v. D'Angelo* (1953) 116 Cal. App. 2d 310, 253 P.2d 675 (upholding a cause of action against parents who failed to warn a babysitter of the violent proclivities of their child), *Johnson v. State of California* (1968) 69 Cal. 2d 782, 73 Cal. Rptr. 240, 447 P.2d 352 (upholding suit against the state for failure to warn foster parents of the dangerous tendencies of their ward), *Morgan* v. *County of Yuba* (1964) 230 Cal. App. 2d 938, 41 Cal. Rptr. 508.

Are these really special relationships, or simply applications of the concept of foreseeability? How does the *Kubert* analysis fit here?

C. Privity: Suits by Third Parties

H.R. Moch Co. v. Rensselaer Water Co.

Court of Appeals of New York, 1928
159 N.E. 896

Cardozo, C.J.

The defendant, a water works company under the laws of this State, made a contract with the city of Rensselaer for the supply of water during a term of years. Water was to be furnished to the city for sewer flushing and street sprinkling; for service to schools and public buildings; and for service at fire hydrants, the latter service at the rate of $42.50 a year for each hydrant. Water was to be furnished to private takers within the city at their homes and factories and other industries at reasonable rates, not exceeding a stated schedule. While this contract was in force, a building caught fire. The flames, spreading to the plaintiff's warehouse nearby, destroyed it and its contents. The defendant according to the complaint was promptly notified of the fire, "but omitted and neglected after such notice, to supply or furnish sufficient or adequate quantity of water, with adequate pressure to stay, suppress or extinguish the fire before it reached the warehouse of the plaintiff, although the pressure and supply which the defendant was equipped to supply and furnish, and had agreed by said contract to supply and furnish, was adequate and sufficient to prevent the spread of the fire to and the destruction of the plaintiff's warehouse and its contents." By reason of the failure of the defendant to "fulfill the provisions of the contract between it and the city of Rensselaer," the plaintiff is said to have suffered damage, for which judgment is demanded. A motion, in the nature of a demurrer, to dismiss the complaint, was denied at Special Term. The Appellate Division reversed by a divided court.

We think the action is not maintainable as one for breach of contract.

No legal duty rests upon a city to supply its inhabitants with protection against fire. That being so, a member of the public may not maintain an action under *Lawrence v. Fox* against one contracting with the city to furnish water at the hydrants, unless an intention appears that the promisor is to be answerable to individual members of the public as well as to the city for any loss ensuing from the failure to fulfill the promise. No such intention is discernible here. . . .

We think the action is not maintainable as one for a common-law tort.

"It is ancient learning that one who assumes to act, even though gratuitously, may thereby become subject to the duty of acting carefully, if he acts at all." . . . A time-honored formula often phrases the distinction as one between misfeasance and nonfeasance. . . . If conduct has gone forward to such a stage that inaction would commonly result, not negatively merely in withholding a benefit, but positively or actively in working an injury, there exists a relation out of which arises a duty to go forward. . . . So the surgeon who operates without pay, is liable though his negligence is in the omission to sterilize his instruments; . . . the maker of automobiles, at the suit of someone other than the buyer, though his negligence is merely in inadequate inspection. . . . The query always is whether the putative wrongdoer has advanced to such a point as to have launched a force or instrument of harm, or has stopped where inaction is at most a refusal to become an instrument for good. . . .

The plaintiff would have us hold that the defendant, when once it entered upon the performance of its contract with the city, was brought into such a relation with everyone who might potentially be benefited through the supply of water at the hydrants as to give to negligent performance, without reasonable notice of a refusal to continue, the quality of a tort. . . . We are satisfied that liability would be unduly and indeed indefinitely extended by this enlargement of the zone of duty. . . . Every one making a promise having the quality of a contract will be under a duty to the promisee by virtue of the promise, but under another duty, apart from contract, to an indefinite number of potential beneficiaries when performance has begun. The assumption of one relation will mean the involuntary assumption of a series of new relations, inescapably hooked together. Again we may say in the words of the Supreme Court of the United States, "The law does not spread its protection so far."

. . . .

We think the action is not maintainable as one for the breach of a statutory duty.

. . . .

The judgment should be affirmed with costs.

————————

1. What is the holding in *Moch*? What is Cardozo's reasoning? Do you believe that the defendant's conduct had gone forward to such an extent as to work an injury? If so, what are the real reasons for the decision? Why didn't Cardozo state them?

2. If the true basis of *Moch* is lack of privity, in that the plaintiffs were not in contract with the defendants, the city (in privity) should be able to recover when its property is burned. A negative answer was provided in *Town of Ukiah v. Ukiah Water & Improvement Co.*, 142 Cal. 173, 75 P. 773 (1904).

If there is action, e.g., water containing typhoid is supplied, the plaintiff (not in privity) may be able to recover. *Hayes v. Torrington Water Co.*, 88 Conn. 609, 92 A. 406 (1914). Can *Moch, Ukiah*, and *Hayes* be synthesized?

3. Water companies have been held liable on facts similar to *Moch*, on the basis that the defendant began to perform, *Doyle v. South Pittsburgh Water Co.*, 414 Pa. 199, 199 A.2d 875 (1964), and the plaintiff was a third-party beneficiary of the water company's contract with the city. *See Harlan Water Co. v. Carter*, 220 Ky. 493, 295 S.W. 426 (1927).

Strauss v. Belle Realty Co.

Court of Appeals of New York, 1985
482 N.E.2d 34

Kaye, Judge.

On July 13, 1977, a failure of defendant Consolidated Edison's power system left most of New York City in darkness. In this action for damages allegedly resulting from the power failure, we are asked to determine whether Con Edison owed a duty of care to a tenant who suffered personal injuries in a common area of an apartment building, where his landlord—but not he—had a contractual relationship with the utility. We conclude that in the case of a blackout of a metropolis of several million residents and visitors, each in some manner necessarily affected by a 25-hour power failure, liability for injuries in a building's common areas should, as a matter of public policy, be limited by the contractual relationship.

. . . .

Plaintiff, Julius Strauss, then 77 years old, resided in an apartment building in Queens. Con Edison provided electricity to his apartment pursuant to agreement with him, and to the common areas of the building under a separate agreement with his landlord, defendant Belle Realty Company. As water to the apartment was supplied by electric pump, plaintiff had no running water for the duration of the blackout. Consequently, on the second day of the power failure, he set out for the basement to obtain water, but fell on the darkened, defective basement stairs, sustaining injuries. In this action against Belle Realty and Con Edison, plaintiff alleged negligence against the landlord, in failing to maintain the stairs or warn of their dangerous condition, and negligence against the utility in the performance of its duty to provide electricity.

. . . Con Edison cross-moved for summary judgment dismissing the complaint, maintaining it had no duty to a noncustomer.

. . . .

A defendant may be held liable for negligence only when it breaches a duty owed to the plaintiff. . . . The essential question here is whether Con Edison owed a duty to plaintiff, whose injuries from a fall on a darkened staircase may have conceivably been foreseeable, but with whom there was no contractual relationship for lighting in the building's common areas.

Duty in negligence cases is defined neither by foreseeability of injury nor by privity of contract. . . .

But while the absence of privity does not foreclose recognition of a duty, it is still the responsibility of courts, in fixing the orbit of duty, "to limit the legal consequences of wrongs to a controllable degree." . . . "In fixing the bounds of that duty, not only logic and science, but policy play an important role." . . . The courts' definition of an orbit of duty based on public policy may at times result in the exclusion of some who might otherwise have recovered for losses or injuries if traditional tort principles had been applied.

Considerations of privity are not entirely irrelevant in implementing policy. Indeed, in determining the liability of utilities for consequential damages for failure to provide service — a liability which could obviously be "enormous," and has been described as "sui generis," rather than strictly governed by tort or contract law principles — courts have declined to extend the duty of care to noncustomers. . . . The court denied recovery [in *Moch*], concluding that the proposed enlargement of the zone of duty would unduly extend liability. . . . In the view of the Appellate Division dissenter, *Moch* does not control because the injuries here were foreseeable and plaintiff was a member of a specific, limited, circumscribed class with a close relationship with Con Edison.

. . . .

Central to these decisions was an ability to extend the defendant's duty to cover specifically foreseeable parties but at the same time to contain liability to manageable levels. . . .

Additionally, we deal here with a system-wide power failure occasioned by what has already been determined to be the utility's gross negligence. If liability could be found here, then in logic and fairness the same result must follow in many similar situations. For example, a tenant's guests and invitees, as well as persons making deliveries or repairing equipment in the building, are equally persons who must use the common areas, and for whom they are maintained.

In sum, Con Edison is not answerable to the tenant of an apartment building injured in a common area as a result of Con Edison's negligent failure to provide electric service as required by its agreement with the building owner. Accordingly, the order of the Appellate Division should be affirmed, with costs.

---

1. What is the court's reasoning in *Strauss*? What role, if any, does privity play? What is the most important factor in the decision? What if a property owner who did have a contract with Con Ed sued for damage caused by the blackout? Do you think the result would have been different?

2. Why doesn't foreseeability or the fact that the plaintiff is a member of a "specific, limited, circumscribed class" control? Was *Moch* correctly decided? What is really the basis of the decisions in *Moch* and in *Strauss*?

D. Professionals

Lucas v. Hamm

Supreme Court of California, 1961
364 P.2d 685, *cert. denied*, 368 U.S. 987 (1962)

GIBSON, CHIEF JUSTICE.

The allegations of the first and second causes of action are summarized as follows: Defendant agreed with the testator, for a consideration, to prepare a will and codicils thereto for him by which plaintiffs were to be designated as beneficiaries of a trust. . . . Defendant . . . negligently prepared testamentary instruments containing phraseology that was invalid by virtue of . . . the rule against perpetuities.

The reasoning underlying the denial of tort liability in the *Buckley* case, i.e., the stringent privity test, was rejected in *Biakanja v. Irving*, 49 Cal. 2d 647, 648–650 [320 P.2d 16, 65 A.L.R.2d 1358], where we held that a notary public who, although not authorized to practice law, prepared a will but negligently failed to direct proper attestation was liable in tort to an intended beneficiary who was damaged because of the invalidity of the instrument. It was pointed out that since 1895, when *Buckley* was decided, the rule that in the absence of privity there was no liability for negligence committed in the performance of a contract had been greatly liberalized. . . . In restating the rule it was said that the determination whether in a specific case the defendant will be held liable to a third person not in privity is a matter of policy and involves the balancing of various factors, among which are the extent to which the transaction was intended to affect the plaintiff, the foreseeability of harm to him, the degree of certainty that the plaintiff suffered injury, the closeness of the connection between the defendant's conduct and the injury, and the policy of preventing future harm. . . . The same general principle must be applied in determining whether a beneficiary is entitled to bring an action for negligence in the drafting of a will when the instrument is drafted by an attorney rather than by a person not authorized to practice law.

. . . .

We are of the view that the extension of his liability to beneficiaries injured by a negligently drawn will does not place an undue burden on the profession, particularly when we take into consideration that a contrary conclusion would cause the innocent beneficiary to bear the loss.

It follows that the lack of privity between plaintiffs and defendant does not preclude plaintiffs from maintaining an action in tort against defendant. . . .

We conclude that intended beneficiaries of a will who lose their testamentary rights because of failure of the attorney who drew the will to properly fulfill his obligations under his contract with the testator may recover as third-party beneficiaries.

However, an attorney is not liable either to his client or to a beneficiary under a will for errors of the kind alleged in the first and second causes of action.

. . . The attorney is not liable for every mistake he may make in his practice; he is not, in the absence of an express agreement, an insurer of the soundness of his opinions or of the validity of an instrument that he is engaged to draft; and he is not liable for being in error as to a question of law on which reasonable doubt may be entertained by well-informed lawyers. . . .

The complaint, as we have seen, alleges that defendant drafted the will in such a manner that the trust was invalid because it violated the rules relating to perpetuities. . . . Of the California law on perpetuities and restraints it has been said that few, if any, areas of the law have been fraught with more confusion or concealed more traps for the unwary draftsman; that members of the bar, probate courts, and title insurance companies make errors in these matters. . . .

The judgment is affirmed.

———————

1. Why didn't the privity defense work in *Lucas v. Hamm*? What seems really to be the motivating factor in *Moch* and in *Strauss*?

2. As a law student, what do you think of the attorney's defense that the rule against perpetuities is very difficult to understand and to apply? What do you think of its success as a defense? Can you imagine a doctor winning a malpractice case solely on the ground that "the brain is very complicated"?

3. Note that the sole form of damage in cases like *Lucas v. Hamm* is economic harm, and that there is no risk to the plaintiff of any physical harm at all.

E. Duty to Control Others

Problem

Carl, a State University student, becomes a patient of Dr. Block, a psychiatrist, in the University health system. Carl says, "I will kill a female student." Dr. Block informs the campus police of Carl's statement, but does nothing more. Two weeks after the statement, Carl kills Helen, a University student. Discuss a suit by Helen's representatives against Dr. Block and the University.

Tarasoff v. The Regents of the University of California

Supreme Court of California, 1976
551 P.2d 334

Tobriner, Justice.

On October 27, 1969, Prosenjit Poddar killed Tatiana Tarasoff. Plaintiffs, Tatiana's parents, allege that two months earlier Poddar confided his intention to kill Tatiana to Dr. Lawrence Moore, a psychologist employed by the Cowell Memorial Hospital at the University of California at Berkeley. They allege that on Moore's request, the campus police briefly detained Poddar, but released him when he appeared rational. They further claim that Dr. Harvey Powelson, Moore's superior, then directed that no further action be taken to detain Poddar. No one warned plaintiffs of Tatiana's peril.

Concluding that these facts set forth causes of action against neither therapists and policemen involved, nor against the Regents of the University of California as their employer, the superior court sustained defendants' demurrers to plaintiffs' second amended complaints without leave to amend. This appeal ensued.

Plaintiffs' complaints predicate liability on . . . defendants' failure to warn plaintiffs of the impending danger. . . . Defendants, in turn, assert that they owed no duty of reasonable care to Tatiana. . . .

The second cause of action can be amended to allege that Tatiana's death proximately resulted from defendants' negligent failure to warn Tatiana or others likely to apprise her of her danger. Plaintiffs contend that as amended, such allegations of negligence and proximate causation, with resulting damages, establish a cause of action. Defendants, however, contend that in the circumstances of the present case they owed no duty of care to Tatiana or her parents. . . .

[L]iability should be imposed "for injury occasioned to another by his want of ordinary care or skill" . . . "Whenever one person is by circumstances placed in such a position with regard to another . . . that if he did not use ordinary care and skill in his own conduct . . . he would cause danger of injury to the person or property of the other, a duty arises to use ordinary care and skill to avoid such danger." [*Heaven v. Pender.*]

We depart from "this fundamental principle" only upon the "balancing of a number of considerations"; major ones "are the foreseeability of harm to the plaintiff, the degree of certainty that the plaintiff suffered injury, the closeness of the connection between the defendant's conduct and the injury suffered, the moral blame attached to the defendant's conduct, the policy of preventing future harm, the extent of the burden to the defendant and consequences to the community of imposing a duty to exercise care with resulting liability for breach, and the availability, cost and prevalence of insurance for the risk involved."

Although, as we have stated above, under the common law, as a general rule, one person owed no duty to control the conduct of another . . . nor to warn those endangered by such conduct the courts have carved out an exception to this rule in cases in which the defendant stands in some special relationship to either the person whose conduct needs to be controlled or in a relationship to the foreseeable victim of that conduct. . . .

Although plaintiffs' pleadings assert no special relation between Tatiana and defendant therapists, they establish as between Poddar and defendant therapists the special relation that arises between a patient and his doctor or psychotherapist. Such a relationship may support affirmative duties for the benefit of third persons. Thus, for example, a hospital must exercise reasonable care to control the behavior of a patient which may endanger other persons. A doctor must also warn a patient if the patient's condition or medication renders certain conduct, such as driving a car, dangerous to others.

Although the California decisions that recognize this duty have involved cases in which the defendant stood in a special relationship both to the victim and to the person whose conduct created the danger, we do not think that the duty should logically be constricted to such situations. Decisions of other jurisdictions hold that the single relationship of a doctor to his patient is sufficient to support the duty to exercise reasonable care to protect others against dangers emanating from the patient's illness. The courts hold that a doctor is liable to persons infected by his patient if he negligently fails to diagnose a contagious disease (*Hofmann v. Blackmon* (Fla. App. 1970) 241 So. 2d 752), or, having diagnosed the illness, fails to warn members of the patient's family. . . .

Defendants contend, however, that imposition of a duty to exercise reasonable care to protect third persons is unworkable because therapists cannot accurately predict whether or not a patient will resort to violence. In support of this argument amicus representing the American Psychiatric Association and other professional societies cites numerous articles which indicate that therapists, in the present state of the art, are unable reliably to predict violent acts; their forecasts, amicus claims, tend consistently to overpredict violence, and indeed are more often wrong than right. Since predictions of violence are often erroneous, amicus concludes, the courts should not render rulings that predicate the liability of therapists upon the validity of such predictions.

. . . .

We recognize the difficulty that a therapist encounters in attempting to forecast whether a patient presents a serious danger of violence. Obviously, we do not require that the therapist, in making that determination, render a perfect performance; the therapist need only exercise "that reasonable degree of skill, knowledge, and care ordinarily possessed and exercised by members of [that professional specialty] under similar circumstances." . . .

In the instant case, however, the pleadings do not raise any question as to failure of defendant therapists to predict that Poddar presented a serious danger of violence. On the contrary, the present complaints allege that defendant therapists did in fact predict that Poddar would kill, but were negligent in failing to warn.

Amicus contends, however, that even when a therapist does in fact predict that a patient poses a serious danger of violence to others, the therapist should be absolved of any responsibility for failing to act to protect the potential victim. In our view, however, once a therapist does in fact determine, or under applicable professional standards reasonably should have determined, that a patient poses a serious danger of violence to others, he bears a duty to exercise reasonable care to protect the foreseeable victim of that danger. While the discharge of this duty of due care will necessarily vary with the facts of each case, in each instance the adequacy of the therapist's conduct must be measured against the traditional negligence standard of the rendition of reasonable care under the circumstances. . . .

The risk that unnecessary warnings may be given is a reasonable price to pay for the lives of possible victims that may be saved. . . .

Defendants further argue that free and open communication is essential to psychotherapy . . . ; that "Unless a patient . . . is assured that . . . information [revealed by him] can and will be held in utmost confidence, he will be reluctant to make the full disclosure upon which diagnosis and treatment . . . depends." . . . The giving of a warning, defendants contend, constitutes a breach of trust which entails the revelation of confidential communications. We recognize the public interest in supporting effective treatment of mental illness and in protecting the rights of patients to privacy . . . and the consequent public importance of safeguarding the confidential character of psychotherapeutic communication. Against this interest, however, we must weigh the public interest in safety from violent assault. The Legislature has undertaken the difficult task of balancing the countervailing concerns. In Evidence Code section 1014, it established a broad rule of privilege to protect confidential communications between patient and psychotherapist. In Evidence Code section 1024, the Legislature created a specific and limited exception to the psychotherapist-patient privilege: "There is no privilege . . . if the psychotherapist has reasonable cause to believe that the patient is in such mental or emotional condition as to be dangerous to himself or to the person or property of another and that disclosure of the communication is necessary to prevent the threatened danger."

Our current crowded and computerized society compels the interdependence of its members. In this risk-infested society we can hardly tolerate the further exposure to danger that would result from a concealed knowledge of the therapist that his patient was lethal. If the exercise of reasonable care to protect the threatened victim requires the therapist to warn the endangered party or those who can reasonably be expected to notify him, we see no sufficient societal interest that would protect and justify concealment. The containment of such risks lies in the public interest. For the foregoing reasons, we find that plaintiffs' complaints can be amended to state a cause of action against defendants Moore, Powelson, Gold, and Yandell and against the Regents as their employer, for breach of a duty to exercise reasonable care to protect Tatiana.

. . . .

---

1. How is *Tarasoff* an extension of previous duty cases? What defenses did the psychotherapists raise?

2. How would you respond to a doctor who said that the courts have no understanding of the doctor's duty of confidentiality?

3. In California, therapists are immune from liability for failure to warn, "except when the patient has communicated to the psychotherapist a serious threat of physical violence against a reasonably identifiable victim or victims." Cal. Civ. Code § 43.92.

In *Thompson v. County of Alameda*, 27 Cal. 3d 741, 167 Cal. Rptr. 70, 614 P.2d 728 (1980), a juvenile was released from confinement although the county knew that he had said he would take the life of a child living in the neighborhood. He did, and the decedent's mother sued. The court distinguished *Tarasoff* on the basis that here no specific person was identified by the killer.

4. If the doctor discloses, he or she runs the risk of being sued by the patient. *See* Fleming & Maximov, *The Patient or His Victim: The Therapist's Dilemma*, 62 Cal. L. Rev. 1025 (1974).

5. Is there a duty to warn the parents of the child's threat to commit suicide? Yes, *Eisel v. Board of Educ., Montgomery County*, 324 Md. 376, 597 A.2d 447 (1991). No, *Bellah v. Greenson*, 81 Cal. App. 3d 614, 146 Cal. Rptr. 535 (1978).

6. What if you hear a classmate say, "I am going to kill Jim," also a classmate? Do you have a duty to inform Jim? What other action might you take?

Vince v. Wilson

Supreme Court of Vermont, 1989
561 A.2d 103

MAHADY, JUSTICE.

This personal injury action requires us to further refine our definition of the tort of negligent entrustment. Plaintiff, seriously injured in an automobile accident, brought suit against defendant Wilson, who had provided funding for her grand-nephew, the driver of the car in which plaintiff was a passenger at the time of the accident, to purchase the vehicle. Subsequently Ace Auto Sales, Inc. and its president Gary Gardner were added as defendants. Ace sold the vehicle to the driver; Gardner was the salesman of the vehicle.

At the close of plaintiff's case, the trial court directed verdicts in favor of defendants Ace and Gardner. Plaintiff appeals from this ruling. The claim against Wilson, on the other hand, was submitted to the jury, which returned a substantial verdict in favor of plaintiff. Wilson appeals from the judgment entered against her on the jury verdict. For the reasons stated below, we hold that the trial court erred in directing verdicts in favor of Ace and Gardner. As to the judgment against Wilson, we affirm the court's decision to submit the question to the jury, and remand for proceedings consistent with this opinion.

The tort of negligent entrustment has long been recognized in Vermont. *See Giguere v. Rosselot*, 110 Vt. 173, 179, 3 A.2d 538, 540 (1939). In *Dicranian v. Foster*, 114 Vt. 372, 45 A.2d 650 (1946), we noted that such "liability . . . arises out of the combined negligence of both, the negligence of one in entrusting the automobile to an incompetent driver and of the other in its operation." . . .

Plaintiff argues that the rule should be applied to a person who knowingly provides funding to an incompetent driver to purchase a vehicle and to a person who knowingly sells a vehicle to an incompetent driver. We have not previously had an opportunity to address this issue. In *Giguere*, the defendant negligently entrusted a firearm and ammunition to his child, who negligently discharged the firearm resulting in the death of the plaintiff's intestate. In *Dicranian*, the defendant negligently entrusted his motor vehicle to an incompetent operator whose negligent operation of the vehicle caused injury to the plaintiff.

Defendants urge us to follow those courts which have limited recovery under a claim of negligent entrustment to situations where the defendant "is the owner or has the right to control" the instrumentality entrusted. . . . These courts have denied liability where a father sold a car to his son who was known to have a drinking problem . . . ; where a vehicle was given to an incompetent operator; or where a bailee automobile dealer returned an automobile after repair to its obviously intoxicated owner. . . .

Other courts have applied the rule more broadly. For example, courts have allowed recovery against an automobile dealer who sold a vehicle to an inexperienced and incompetent driver whose driving injured several people when the seller knew or should have known of the incompetency. . . . These courts hold that the fact that a defendant had ownership and control over the instrumentality at the time it was turned over to an incompetent individual is sufficient. . . . Thus, a father was held liable for funding the purchase of an automobile by a son whom the father knew to be an irresponsible driver, . . . and a complaint against a father who purchased a vehicle for his epileptic son was held to state a cause of action. . . .

Both lines of cases derive their rule from the Restatement of Torts, which provides:

> One who supplies directly or through a third person a chattel for the use of another whom the supplier knows or has reason to know to be likely because of his youth, inexperience, or otherwise, to use it in a manner involving unreasonable risk of physical harm to himself and others whom the supplier should expect to share in or be endangered by its use, is subject to liability for physical harm resulting to them.

Restatement (Second) of Torts § 390 (1965). The comments to the Restatement support those decisions which extend the rule to individuals such as sellers:

> The rule stated applies to anyone who supplies a chattel for the use of another. It applies to sellers, lessors, donors or lenders, and to all kinds of bailors, irrespective of whether the bailment is gratuitous or for a consideration.

Id., comment a.

The cases noted above which restrict the rule to situations where the defendant is the owner or has the right to control the instrumentality have been severely criticized. *See, e.g.,* Notes, 32 Chi. Kent L. Rev. 237, 239 (1954) ("liability in these cases arises not from ownership or agency but from the combined negligence of the owner in entrusting the vehicle to the incompetent driver and of the driver in carelessly operating the same"); 43 Ky. L.J. 178, 183 (1954) ("mere passing of title does not change the character of the negligence of the defendant, and . . . the law should not operate to relieve him of his responsibility for the natural and probable consequences of his own negligent act"); 29 N.Y.U. L. Rev. 530 (1954); 33 B.U.L. Rev. 538 (1953).

[T]he leading commentators on the law of torts have said that such decisions "look definitely wrong," explaining: It is the negligent entrusting which creates the unreasonable risk; and this is none the less when the goods are conveyed. Prosser and Keeton on Torts § 104, at 718 (5th ed. 1984). Seen in this light, the issue is clearly one of negligence to be determined by the jury under proper instruction; the relationship of the defendant to the particular instrumentality is but one factor to be considered. The key factor is that "[t]he negligent entrustment theory requires a showing that the entrustor knew or should have known some reason why entrusting the item to another was foolish or negligent." . . .

With regard to plaintiff's claim against defendant Wilson, we must view the evidence in the light most favorable to plaintiff because of the jury's verdict in plaintiff's favor. . . . With regard to plaintiff's claims against defendants Ace and Gardner, the trial court directed a verdict in favor of the defendants; as such, we must view the evidence in the light most favorable to plaintiff, excluding the effect of any modifying evidence.

So viewed, the evidence indicates that Wilson knew that the operator for whom she provided funding to purchase the vehicle had no driver's license and had failed the driver's test several times. Indeed, she communicated this fact to defendant Gardner, an agent of defendant Ace, prior to the sale of the vehicle. Defendant Wilson was also aware of the fact that her grandnephew abused alcohol and other drugs. The evidence also tended to show that the operator's inexperience and lack of training contributed to the accident which caused plaintiff's injuries. The evidence was sufficient to make out a prima facie case of negligent entrustment, and the trial court properly submitted the question to the jury.

Verdicts should not have been directed in favor of defendants Ace and Gardner, however. There was evidence which, if believed by the jury, would establish that they knew the operator had no operator's license and that he had failed the driver's test several times. Viewed in the light most favorable to plaintiff, the evidence tends to demonstrate negligence on the part of Ace and Gardner, and the issue should have been determined by the jury. . . .

Cause remanded for further proceedings not inconsistent with this opinion.

----

1. What was Wilson's defense? What was the basis of the car dealer's liability? How would this decision be viewed by the general public?

2. Should liability be different, for one who sells, lends, or gives, from one who provides the money for the purchase? Explain.

3. Does *Vince* place a duty on a car dealer to inquire about the use of alcohol by the purchaser and the nature of the purchaser's driver's license? Don't car dealers already demand drivers' licenses and proof of insurance? Does a car dealer have a duty to inquire for whose use the car is being purchased?

4. In *Olivia N. v. National Broadcasting Co.*, 126 Cal. App. 3d 488, 178 Cal. Rptr. 888 (1981), *cert. denied*, 458 U.S. 1108 (1982), a young girl was raped on a beach by means of a soda bottle. She sued NBC, claiming that the rapist had imitated a rape scene on a recent television program where the actor had used a plumber's helper. The court rejected the plaintiff's tort duty argument and relied on the First Amendment:

> Appellant . . . asserts civil liability premised on traditional negligence concepts. But the chilling effect of permitting negligence actions for a television broadcast is obvious. "The fear of damage awards . . . may be markedly more inhibiting than the fear of prosecution under a criminal statute." . . . Realistically, television networks would become significantly more inhibited in the selection of controversial materials if liability were to be imposed on a simple negligence theory. "[T]he pall of fear and timidity imposed upon

those who would give voice to public criticism is an atmosphere in which the First Amendment freedoms cannot survive." . . . the deterrent effect of subjecting the television networks to negligence liability because of their programming choices would lead to self-censorship which would dampen the vigor and limit the variety of public debate. . . .

What are the arguments against this?

5. A duty may rest on a voluntary undertaking. In *Crowley v. Spivey*, 285 S.C. 397, 329 S.E.2d 774, 780 (1985), the defendant grandparents agreed to watch the grandchildren while the mother visited them. The defendants knew of the mother's mental instability and that she might have a gun. Indeed, they searched for it. The mother murdered her children, and the father (Timothy) sued the grandparents for negligence. The court found a duty:

> The duty of care in this case is grounded in the legal proposition that one who assumes to act, even though under no obligation to do so, may become subject to the duty to act with due care. . . . Timothy's testimony is unequivocal that he allowed visitation to resume because the Spiveys undertook to provide supervision over the children's visits with Lynette in Beaufort. The evidence also warrants the conclusion that Timothy was swayed to permit visitation because the Spiveys undertook a search for the pistol and were satisfied that Lynette no longer had it. Although the Spiveys were not obligated to so act, once their performance began, a common law duty to exercise reasonable care arose. . . .

F. Negligent Infliction of Emotional Distress

Quill v. Trans World Airlines

Court of Appeals of Minnesota, 1985
361 N.W.2d 438

LESLIE, JUDGE.

. . . .

On April 4, 1979, TWA flight 841 from New York to Minneapolis was cruising at an altitude of 39,000 feet when it suddenly rolled over and plunged downward. Its tailspin continued for the next 40 seconds at speeds just below the speed of sound, causing the plane to violently shake. At approximately 5,000 feet the pilots regained control of the plane, about 5 seconds before it would have struck ground. The force exerted on the plane and the passengers equalled approximately 6 G's. Testimony indicated that force wrinkled the fuselage skin of the aircraft and bent its wings.

Plaintiff is a medical doctor who does not practice; he teaches and consults on nuclear energy and environmental policy issues. He is 48 years old and married. His work requires him to make approximately 20 business trips per year, involving about 60 flights. On this flight he was returning to Minneapolis from Europe via New York. When the plane rolled over and started its accelerating dive, he believed that his death was certain. He testified that the G force was so strong that he could not lift his arm to reach the oxygen masks which had shaken loose. Plaintiff believed even if the child in the seat next to him had been screaming he could not have heard over the incredible noise generated.

. . . .

The pilot informed the passengers over the intercom that they had experienced some problems and that they would make an emergency landing in Detroit, Michigan. The flight crew, however, did not explain the problem, indicate the condition of the plane, or assure the passengers that they would land safely.

During the next forty minutes the plane continued to shake and make considerable noise. . . .

Since the incident, plaintiff has continued to fly for business purposes. On about 50 percent of the flights he experiences anxiety and recalls his feelings that night. His anxiety is often triggered by sudden changes in an aircraft's direction. Plaintiff's fear manifests itself physically in adrenaline surges, sweaty hands, elevated pulse and blood pressure. In a few instances plaintiff has not been able to take his scheduled flight, because of his concerns, and has taken a later plane instead. His wife says it sometimes takes him two days to relax after a flight. Plaintiff has not consulted any medical professionals about his problem because, as a doctor, he believes they could do nothing for him.

ISSUES

1. Did plaintiff present a prima facie case for negligent infliction of emotional distress?

. . . .

The seminal Minnesota case on negligent infliction of emotional distress is *Purcell v. St. Paul City Railway*, 48 Minn. 134, 50 N.W. 1034 (1892). In *Purcell* a pregnant woman was severely frightened when the cable car she was riding in nearly collided with another cable car. Her fear caused her to convulse violently, leading her to miscarry her child. She sued for damages for her miscarriage, alleging the railway company negligently caused the near collision. The supreme court said:

> The mind and body operate reciprocally on each other. Physical injury or illness sometimes causes mental disease. A mental shock or disturbance sometimes causes injury or illness of body, especially of the nervous system. Now, if the fright was the natural consequence of — was brought about, caused by — the circumstances of peril and alarm in which defendant's negligence placed plaintiff, and the fright caused the nervous shock and

convulsions and consequent illness, the negligence was the proximate cause
of those injuries. . . .

Later cases have modified the rules for recovery of damages for emotional distress.
In cases like the present one where the plaintiff did not suffer a contemporaneous
physical injury, the "zone of danger" rule applies. . . . In *Langeland v. Farmers State
Bank*, 319 N.W.2d 26 (Minn. 1982) the supreme court wrote:

> [T]he general rule regarding the negligent infliction of emotional distress has
> been that there can be no recovery absent some accompanying physical
> injury. See W. Prosser, Handbook of the Law of Torts § 54, at 328–29 (4th ed.
> 1971). In cases in which physical symptoms occur subsequent to and because
> of the plaintiff's emotional disturbance, many jurisdictions, including this
> one, require the plaintiff to have been in some personal physical danger
> caused by the defendant's negligence before awarding damages for emotional
> distress.

Id. at 31.

The Minnesota cases establish that damages for emotional distress are compensable under the zone of danger rule, but leave unanswered the narrower question
raised here: How severely must the emotional distress physically manifest itself before
the law will provide a remedy under the zone of danger theory?

Two Minnesota cases allowing recovery for emotional distress fit squarely under
the zone of danger rule: *Purcell* and *Okrina v. Midwestern Corp.*, 282 Minn. 400,
165 N.W.2d 259 (1969). In *Okrina* a wall of the store in which plaintiff was shopping
collapsed making a thunderous noise. Plaintiff was afraid the whole building would
collapse but she escaped without being struck by any debris. Following the incident
she felt numb and sought hospital care. She spent five days receiving treatment for
severe pain in her head, back and leg. Her doctor testified that her condition resulted
from her fright, that her personality had been altered, and that it was unlikely she
would improve. The court said:

> Here, there was a physical injury sustained as a result of Mrs. Okrina's fear
> and not merely mental anguish unaccompanied by symptoms of physical
> suffering. . . .

. . . .

TWA argues a recent decision should guide our analysis. In *Hubbard v. United Press
International, Inc.*, 330 N.W.2d 428 (Minn. 1983) the Minnesota Supreme Court recognized for the first time the independent tort of intentional infliction of emotional
distress. *Hubbard* ended a long period in Minnesota law where damages for emotional distress could only be recovered under the negligence theory outlined above,
or under a "parasitic tort" theory. *See* Note, "Minnesota's 'New Tort': Intentional
Infliction of Emotional Distress," 10 Wm. Mitchell L. Rev. 349 (1984) (recovery was
parasitic because the emotional suffering must have arisen out of an [sic] "host" tort
such as assault or mistreatment of a corpse).

. . . .

[W]e decide that the *Hubbard* standard does not apply to negligent infliction of emotional distress cases. . . .

Our issue remains whether plaintiff has satisfied the physical injury or symptom requirement. This requirement is a judicial obstacle designed to insure a plaintiff's claim is real. *See* Restatement (Second) of Torts, § 436A, com. b. (1965). Our task is problematic for no clear line can be drawn between mental and physical injury. Comment, *Negligently Inflicted Mental Distress: The Case for an Independent Tort*, 59 Geo. L.J. 1237, 1241 (1971). Cases taking varying positions on what meets the physical injury requirement illustrate the difficulty. *See Bowman v. Williams*, 164 Md. 397, 404, 165 A. 182, 184 (1933) (weakness and nervousness sufficient physical symptoms); *Cosgrove v. Beymer*, 244 F. Supp. 824, 826 (D. Del. 1965) (dizziness, mild headaches and nervousness insufficient symptoms of bodily harm). *See also Daley v. LaCroix*, 384 Mich. 4, 179 N.W.2d 390 (1970) (majority and dissenting views on what constitutes physical injury). The problem has led some jurisdictions to abandon altogether the physical injury or symptom requirement which Minnesota continues to employ. . . .

Although plaintiff's symptoms are less severe than those in *Okrina* and *Purcell*, we hold under the circumstances of this case that he has stated a prima facie case. The trial court upheld the jury's verdict finding that the "unique nature of the accident in this case [resolves] all doubts of the genuineness of the claim." This reasoning accords with Prosser's discussion of two types of cases allowing recovery for emotional distress without physical injury:

> What all of these cases appear to have in common is an especial likelihood of genuine and serious mental distress, arising from the special circumstances, which serves as a guarantee that the claim is not spurious. There may perhaps be other such cases. Where the guarantee can be found, and the mental distress is undoubtedly real and serious, there is no essential reason to deny recovery. But cases will obviously be rare in which "mental anguish," not so severe as to cause physical harm, will be so clearly a serious wrong worthy of redress, or sufficiently attested by the circumstances of the case.

Prosser, § 54, at 328.

This case does not fit in one of Prosser's recognized categories, but we believe the unusually disturbing experience plaintiff endured combined with his physical symptoms assure that his claim is real. There can be few experiences as terrifying as being pinned to a seat by gravity forces as an airplane twists and screams toward earth at just under the speed of sound. The nature of that experience guarantees plaintiff suffered severe emotional distress during the descent and the emergency detour to Detroit. This conclusion is supported by the suffering of many others who shared his experience. Plaintiff's recurring distress is no doubt genuine as well. His sweaty hands, elevated blood pressure and other signs of distress provide, in this case, sufficient physical symptoms to warrant the law's recognition of his claim. Therefore we hold that the law permits recovery of damages for plaintiff's emotional distress.

. . . .

———————

1. Why are the courts concerned about permitting recovery for the negligent infliction of emotional distress? Note that in this case, the airline was found 70% responsible and the manufacturer 30% for the initial dive.

2. Why do some courts require a resulting physical illness? How does *Quill* define the required physical injury? Examples?

3. Was Quill's spouse within the "zone of danger"? Was her mental distress foreseeable?

4. Does *Quill* require both resulting physical injury and "zone of danger"?

5. What was the key factor that led Quill's attorney to conclude that he had a good case? What is a court looking for in lawsuits for negligent infliction of emotional distress?

Potter v. Firestone Tire & Rubber Co.
Supreme Court of California, 1993
863 P.2d 795

BAXTER, JUSTICE.

We granted review in this case to consider:

> (1) whether emotional distress engendered by a fear of cancer or other serious physical illness or injury following exposure to a carcinogen or other toxic substance is an injury for which damages may be recovered in a negligence action in the absence of physical injury;

. . . .

Our analysis of existing case law and policy considerations relevant to the availability of damages for emotional distress leads us to conclude that, generally, in the absence of a present physical injury or illness, recovery of damages for fear of cancer in a negligence action should be allowed only if the plaintiff pleads and proves that the fear stems from a knowledge, corroborated by reliable medical and scientific opinion, that it is more likely than not that the feared cancer will develop in the future due to the toxic exposure.

. . . .

This is a toxic exposure case brought by four landowners living adjacent to a landfill. As a result of defendant Firestone's practice of disposing of its toxic wastes at the landfill, the landowners were subjected to prolonged exposure to certain carcinogens. While none of the landowners currently suffers from any cancerous or precancerous condition, each faces an enhanced but unquantified risk of developing cancer in the future due to the exposure.

. . . .

Crazy Horse, a class II sanitary landfill owned by the City of Salinas, covers approximately 125 acres suitable for the disposal of household and commercial solid waste. Unlike dump sites that are classified class I, class II landfills such as Crazy Horse prohibit toxic substances and liquids because of the danger that they will leach into the groundwater and cause contamination.

. . . .

Frank and Shirley Potter owned property and lived adjacent to Crazy Horse. . . .

. . . .

[T]he only damages at issue here are the fear of cancer component of the emotional distress award. . . .

"Fear of cancer" is a term generally used to describe a present anxiety over developing cancer in the future.

The availability of damages for fear of cancer as a result of exposure to carcinogens or other toxins in negligence actions is a relatively novel issue for California courts. Other jurisdictions, however, have considered such claims and the appropriate limits on recovery.

We must now consider whether, pursuant to California precedent, emotional distress engendered by the fear of developing cancer in the future as a result of a toxic exposure is a recoverable item of damages in a negligence action.

1. *Parasitic Recovery: Immune System Impairment and/or Cellular Damage as Physical Injury*

Because it initially appeared plaintiffs might have suffered damage to their immune systems, we solicited the views of the parties on whether such damage constitutes physical injury. We did so because it is settled in California that in ordinary negligence actions for physical injury, recovery for emotional distress caused by that injury is available as an item of parasitic damages. (*Crisci v. Security Insurance Co.* (1967), 66 Cal. 2d 425, 433 [58 Cal. Rptr. 13, 426 P.2d 173]; *Merenda v. Superior Court* (1992) 3 Cal. App. 4th 1, 8–9 [4 Cal. Rptr. 2d 87].) Where a plaintiff can demonstrate a physical injury caused by the defendant's negligence, anxiety specifically due to a reasonable fear of a future harm attributable to the injury may also constitute a proper element of damages. . . .

Although the availability of parasitic damages for emotional distress engendered by a fear of developing cancer in the future appears to be an issue of first impression in California, other jurisdictions have concluded that such damages are recoverable when they are derivative of a claim for serious physical injuries. For example, the court in *Ferrara v. Galluchio* (1958) 5 N.Y.2d 16, 21–22 [176 N.Y.S.2d 996, 1000, 152 N.E.2d 249, 253] upheld an award of emotional distress damages based on the plaintiff's fear of cancer where she had been negligently burned in X-ray treatments and later advised by a dermatologist to have her tissue examined every six months as cancer might develop. (*Accord, Dempsey v. Hartley* (E.D. Pa. 1951) 94 F. Supp. 918, 920–921 [fear of breast cancer due to traumatic breast injury]; *Alley v. Charlotte Pipe & Foundry Co.* (1912) 159 N.C. 327 [74 S.E. 885, 886] [fear stemming from sarcoma liable to ensue from burn wound].) In these cases, the existence of a present physical injury, rather than the degree of probability that the disease may actually develop, is determinative.

Plaintiffs, citing several such cases, contend that immune system impairment and cellular damage is a physical injury for which parasitic damages for emotional distress are available. . . .

Conversely, Firestone contends that mere subcellular changes that are unaccompanied by clinically verifiable symptoms of illness or disease do not constitute a physical injury sufficient to support a claim for parasitic emotional distress damages. . . .

It is not clear from the record in this case, however, that these plaintiffs' emotional distress is parasitic to this type of supposed injury. . . .

2. *Nonparasitic Fear of Cancer Recovery*

    . . . .

That is already the law in California. . . . The tort is negligence, a cause of action in which a duty to the plaintiff is an essential element. . . . Firestone did violate a duty imposed on it by law and regulation to dispose of toxic waste only in a class I landfill and to avoid contamination of underground water. The violation led directly to plaintiffs' ingestion of various known and suspected carcinogens, and thus to their fear of suffering the very harm which the Legislature sought by statute to avoid. Their fear of cancer was proximately caused by Firestone's unlawful conduct which threatened serious physical injury. . . .

B. *Absence of Physical Injury*

Amici curiae argue that no recovery for emotional distress arising from fear of cancer should be allowed in any case unless the plaintiff can establish a present physical injury such as a clinically verifiable cancerous or precancerous condition. . . . Amici curiae next contend that substantial policy reasons nevertheless support a physical injury requirement for recovery of fear of cancer damages where no preexisting relationship exists. They suggest that allowing recovery in the absence of a physical injury would create limitless liability and would result in a flood of litigation which thereby would impose onerous burdens on courts, corporations, insurers and society in general. Allowing such recovery would promote fraud and artful pleading, and would also encourage plaintiffs to seek damages based on a subjective fear of cancer. In amici curiae's view, a physical injury requirement is thus essential to provide meaningful limits on the class of potential plaintiffs and clear guidelines for resolving disputes over liability without the necessity for trial.

This argument overlooks the reasons for our decision to discard the requirement of physical injury. As we observed more than a decade ago, "[t]he primary justification for the requirement of physical injury appears to be that it serves as a screening device to minimize a presumed risk of feigned injuries and false claims. . . ."

In *Molien, supra*, 27 Cal. 3d 916, we perceived two significant difficulties with the physical injury requirement. First, "the classification is both overinclusive and underinclusive when viewed in the light of its purported purpose of screening false claims." (27 Cal. 3d at p. 928.) It is overinclusive in that it permits recovery whenever the suffering accompanies or results in physical injury, no matter how trivial (ibid.), yet underinclusive in that it mechanically denies court access to potentially valid claims that could be proved if the plaintiffs were permitted to go to trial (at p. 929).

Second, we observed that the physical injury requirement "encourages extravagant pleading and distorted testimony." . . .

Our reasons for discarding the physical injury requirement in *Molien, supra*, 27 Cal. 3d 916, remain valid today and are equally applicable in a toxic exposure case. That is, the physical injury requirement is a hopelessly imprecise screening device — it would allow recovery for fear of cancer whenever such distress accompanies or results in any physical injury, no matter how trivial, yet would disallow recovery in all cases where the fear is both serious and genuine but no physical injury has yet manifested itself.

Unless an express exception to this general rule is recognized, in the absence of a present physical injury or illness, damages for fear of cancer may be recovered only if the plaintiff pleads and proves that (1) as a result of the defendant's negligent breach of a duty owed to the plaintiff, the plaintiff is exposed to a toxic substance which threatens cancer; and (2) the plaintiff's fear stems from a knowledge, corroborated by reliable medical or scientific opinion, that it is more likely than not that the plaintiff will develop the cancer in the future due to the toxic exposure. Under this rule, a plaintiff must do more than simply establish knowledge of a toxic ingestion or exposure and a significant increased risk of cancer. The plaintiff must further show that based upon reliable medical or scientific opinion, the plaintiff harbors a serious fear that the toxic ingestion or exposure was of such magnitude and proportion as to likely result in the feared cancer.

        . . . .

D. Smoking and Comparative Fault

In this case, all four plaintiffs were long-time cigarette smokers. . . .

In other cases, however, when a defendant demonstrates that a plaintiff's smoking is negligent and that a portion of the plaintiff's fear of developing cancer is attributable to the smoking, comparative fault principles may be applied in determining the extent to which the plaintiff's emotional distress damages for such fear should be reduced to reflect the proportion of such damages for which the plaintiff should properly bear the responsibility. . . . .

Finally, we also observe that evidence of smoking by a plaintiff is relevant to whether the plaintiffs fear is reasonable and genuine. Thus, if a plaintiff had smoked heavily for 20 years without fearing cancer, the trier of fact may consider that evidence in assessing the legitimacy of the plaintiff's fear of cancer claim.

. . . .

1. What is the concern of the courts with cancerphobia? Has *Potter* kept the lid on the box, or will there be a flood of such suits?

2. What is the rule in regard to parasitic recovery? Absent physical injury, when is recovery for emotional distress permitted?

3. What policy reasons support a physical injury requirement? Why is it dropped? Is it out for all future cases? What role does a physical injury play in tort suits? Why is that role particularly relevant in suits for negligent infliction of emotional distress? What substitutes for the physical injury in cases like *Quill* and *Potter*?

Problems

1. An observant Jewish couple gave express instructions to the hospital that their newborn son was to be ritualistically circumcised, on his eighth day, by a *mohel*, in accordance with the tenets of their religion. Instead, due to the negligence of the hospital, the baby was circumcised on his fourth day by a physician. Discuss.

2. Carol sees and hears Nurse Smith negligently drop Carol's baby to the floor in the hospital. Carol suffers emotional distress and is not able to work for six months. Discuss whether Nurse Smith has a duty to Carol.

Thing v. La Chusa

Supreme Court of California, 1989 (en banc)
771 P.2d 814

EAGLESON, JUSTICE.

The narrow issue presented by the parties in this case is whether the Court of Appeal correctly held that a mother who did not witness an accident in which an automobile struck and injured her child may recover damages from the negligent driver for the emotional distress she suffered when she arrived at the accident scene. The more important question this issue poses for the court, however, is whether the "guidelines" enunciated by this court in *Dillon v. Legg* (1968) 68 Cal. 2d 728 [69 Cal. Rptr. 72, 441 P.2d 912, 29 A.L.R.3d 1316] are adequate, or if they should be refined to create greater certainty in this area of the law.

. . . It is in that context that we consider the appropriate application of the concept of "duty". . . .

On December 8, 1980, John Thing, a minor, was injured when struck by an automobile operated by defendant James V. La Chusa. His mother, plaintiff Maria Thing, was nearby, but neither saw nor heard the accident. She became aware of the injury to her son when told by a daughter that John had been struck by a car. She rushed to the scene where she saw her bloody and unconscious child, who she believed was dead, lying in the roadway. Maria sued defendants, alleging that she suffered great emotional disturbance, shock, and injury to her nervous system as a result of these events, and that the injury to John and emotional distress she suffered were proximately caused by defendants' negligence.

The trial court granted defendants' motion for summary judgment, ruling that, as a matter of law, Maria could not establish a claim for negligent infliction of emotional distress because she did not contemporaneously and sensorily perceive the accident. . . .

[I]n negligence cases the right to recover for emotional distress had been limited to circumstances in which the victim was himself injured and emotional distress was a "parasitic" item of damages, or if a plaintiff who had been in the "zone of danger" did not suffer injury from impact, but did suffer physical injury as a result of the emotional trauma.

But shortly before *Dillon*, in *Amaya v. Home Ice, Fuel & Supply Co., supra*, 59 Cal. 2d 295, the court had declined the opportunity to broaden the right to recover for emotional distress. *Amaya*, after confirming that the "impact rule" making a contemporaneous physical impact a prerequisite to recovery for negligently induced fright or shock was not applicable in California, held damages could not be recovered by persons outside the zone of danger created by the defendant's negligence even when that shock was reflected in physiological symptoms.

The *Amaya* view was short lived, however. Only five years later, the decision was overruled in *Dillon v. Legg*. . . .

In *Dillon* itself, the issue was limited. The mother and sister of a deceased infant each sought damages for "great emotional disturbance and shock and injury to her nervous system" which had caused them great mental pain and suffering. Allegedly these injuries were caused by witnessing the defendant's negligently operated vehicle collide with and roll over the infant as she lawfully crossed a street. The mother was not herself endangered by the defendant's conduct. The sister may have been. The trial court had therefore granted the defendant's motion for judgment on the pleadings as to the mother, but had denied it with respect to the sister of the decedent. Faced with the incongruous result demanded by the "zone of danger" rule which denied recovery for emotional distress and consequent physical injury unless the plaintiff himself had been threatened with injury, the court overruled *Amaya*.

. . . .

The difficulty in defining the limits on recovery anticipated by the *Amaya* court was rejected as a basis for denying recovery, but the court did recognize that "to limit the otherwise potentially infinite liability which would follow every negligent act, the law of torts holds defendant amenable only for injuries to others which to defendant at the time were reasonably foreseeable." (*Dillon, supra*, 68 Cal. 2d at p. 739.) Thus, while the court indicated that foreseeability of the injury was to be the primary consideration in finding duty, it simultaneously recognized that policy considerations mandated that infinite liability be avoided by restrictions that would somehow narrow the class of potential plaintiffs. But the test limiting liability was itself amorphous.

The expectation of the *Dillon* majority that the parameters of the tort would be further defined in future cases has not been fulfilled. Instead, subsequent decisions of the Courts of Appeal and this court, have created more uncertainty. And, just as the "zone of danger" limitation was abandoned in *Dillon* as an arbitrary restriction on recovery, the *Dillon* guidelines have been relaxed on grounds that they, too, created arbitrary limitations on recovery.

. . . .

Both the physical harm and accident or sudden occurrence elements were eliminated, however, in *Molien v. Kaiser Foundation Hospitals, supra*, 27 Cal. 3d 916, at least as to those plaintiffs who could claim to be "direct victims" of the defendant's negligence. The court held in *Molien* that a defendant hospital and doctor owed a duty directly to the husband of a patient who had been diagnosed erroneously as having syphilis, and had been told to so advise the husband in order that he could receive testing and, if necessary, treatment.

In finding the existence of a duty to the husband of the patient, the court reasoned that the risk of harm to the husband was reasonably foreseeable, and that the tortious conduct was directed to him as well as the patient. . . . The status of the plaintiff mother in *Dillon* was distinguished as she suffered her injury solely as a "percipient witness" to the infliction of injury on another. She was therefore a "bystander" rather than a "direct victim."

. . . .

The subtleties in the distinction between the right to recover as a "bystander" and as a "direct victim" created what one Court of Appeal has described as an "amorphous nether realm". . . . "The problem which arises from this cryptic explanation is: how are we to distinguish between 'direct victim' cases and 'bystander' cases? An impression is given that the foreseeability of the particular injury to the husband alone explains the result. The inference suggested is that a 'direct victim' is a person whose emotional distress is a reasonably foreseeable consequence of the conduct of the defendant. This does not provide criteria which delimit what counts as reasonable foreseeability. It leads into the quagmire of novel claims which the Supreme Court foresaw as an unacceptable consequence of a 'pure' foreseeability analysis. . . ."

. . . If the consequences of a negligent act are not limited an intolerable burden is placed on society. A "bright line in this area of the law is essential."

. . . .

The impact of personally observing the injury-producing event in most, although concededly not all, cases distinguishes the plaintiff's resultant emotional distress from the emotion felt when one learns of the injury or death of a loved one from another, or observes pain and suffering but not the traumatic cause of the injury. Greater certainty and a more reasonable limit on the exposure to liability for negligent conduct is possible by limiting the right to recover for negligently caused emotional distress to plaintiffs who personally and contemporaneously perceive the injury-producing event and its traumatic consequences.

Similar reasoning justifies limiting recovery to persons closely related by blood or marriage since, in common experience, it is more likely that they will suffer a greater degree of emotional distress than a disinterested witness to negligently caused pain and suffering or death. Such limitations are indisputably arbitrary since it is foreseeable that in some cases unrelated persons have a relationship to the victim or they are so affected by the traumatic event that they suffer equivalent emotional distress. As we have observed, however, drawing arbitrary lines is unavoidable if we are to limit liability and establish meaningful rules for application by litigants and lower courts.

No policy supports extension of the right to recover for [the negligent infliction of emotional distress] to a larger class of plaintiffs. Emotional distress is an intangible condition experienced by most persons, even absent negligence, at some time during their lives. Close relatives suffer serious, even debilitating, emotional reactions to the injury, death, serious illness, and evident suffering of loved ones. . . . The overwhelming majority of "emotional distress" which we endure, therefore is not compensable.

. . . In identifying those persons and the circumstances in which the defendant will be held to redress the injury, it is appropriate to restrict recovery to those persons who will suffer emotional impact beyond the impact that can be anticipated whenever one learns that a relative is injured, or dies, or the emotion felt by a "disinterested" witness. The class of potential plaintiffs should be limited to those who because of their relationship suffer the greatest emotional distress. When the right to recover is limited in this manner, the liability bears a reasonable relationship to the culpability of the negligent defendant.

We conclude, therefore, that a plaintiff may recover damages for emotional distress caused by observing the negligently inflicted injury of a third person if, but only if, said plaintiff: (1) is closely related to the injury victim; (2) is present at the scene of the injury producing event at the time it occurs and is then aware that it is causing injury to the victim; and (3) as a result suffers serious emotional distress—a reaction beyond that which would be anticipated in a disinterested witness and which is not an abnormal response to the circumstances.

. . . .

The undisputed facts establish that plaintiff was not present at the scene of the accident in which her son was injured. She did not observe defendant's conduct and was not aware that her son was being injured. She could not, therefore, establish a right to recover for the emotional distress she suffered when she subsequently learned of the accident and observed its consequences. The order granting summary judgment was proper.

The judgment of the Court of Appeal is reversed.

––––––––––

1. What are the policies for and against a recovery by a third party for the negligent infliction of emotional distress?

2. What was the function of the impact rule, and what problems did it create?

3. As plaintiff's attorney, apply the *Dillon* test to the *Thing* plaintiff prior to the *Thing* decision.

4. Was it foreseeable that the mother in the *Thing* case would suffer emotional distress? Why not permit a recovery? Why is "foreseeability alone" not a useful guideline?

5. Draw the line between a "bystander" (*Dillon*, mother) and a "direct victim" (*Molien*, husband).

6. In *St. Elizabeth Hosp. v. Garrard*, 730 S.W.2d 649 (Tex. 1987), the Texas Supreme Court appeared to give up after struggling with the physical injury requirement. The patient and her husband brought an action seeking damages for mental anguish after their stillborn daughter's body had been disposed of in an unmarked, common grave, without their knowledge or consent. The court stated:

> The question presented in this personal injury case is whether the physical manifestation requirement remains an element of claims for negligent infliction of mental anguish. . . . We hold that proof of physical injury is no longer required in order to recover for negligent infliction of mental anguish and therefore affirm the judgment of the court of appeals.
>
> . . . .
>
> By eliminating the physical manifestation requirement Texas joins an established trend in American jurisprudence which recognizes the tort of negligent infliction of mental anguish without imposing arbitrary restrictions on recovery in such actions. The distinction between physical injury and emotional distress is no longer defensible. The problem is one of proof, and to deny a remedy in all cases because some claims may be false leads to arbitrary results which do not serve the best interests of the public. Jurors

are best suited to determine whether and to what extent the defendant's conduct caused compensable mental anguish by referring to their own experience.

Thus, we hold that the Garrards' petition states a cause of action despite the absence of allegations that the mental anguish suffered resulted in physical injury.

Then came the following decision.

Boyles v. Kerr

Supreme Court of Texas, 1993
855 S.W.2d 593

Phillips, Chief Justice.

Respondent's motion for rehearing is overruled. Our opinion of December 2, 1992, is withdrawn and the following is substituted in its place.

This is a suit for the negligent infliction of emotional distress. We hold that there is no general duty in Texas not to negligently inflict emotional distress. A claimant may recover mental anguish damages only in connection with defendant's breach of some other legal duty. Because Respondent proceeded below only on the theory of negligent infliction of emotional distress, we reverse the judgment of the court of appeals in her favor. 806 S.W.2d 255. However, in the interest of justice, we remand for a new trial.

On August 10, 1985, Petitioner Dan Boyles, Jr., then seventeen, covertly videotaped nineteen-year-old Respondent Susan Leigh Kerr engaging in sexual intercourse with him. Although not dating steadily, they had known each other a few months and had shared several previous sexual encounters. Kerr testified that she had not had sexual intercourse prior to her relationship with Boyles.

. . . .

Boyles took possession of the tape shortly after it was made, and subsequently showed it on three occasions, each time at a private residence. Although he showed the tape to only ten friends, gossip about the incident soon spread among many of Kerr and Boyles' friends in Houston. Soon many students at Kerr's school, Southwest Texas State University, and Boyles' school, the University of Texas at Austin, also became aware of the story. . . .

The tape stigmatized Kerr with the reputation of "porno queen" among some of her friends, and she claimed that the embarrassment and notoriety affected her academic performance. Kerr also claimed that the incident made it difficult for her to relate to men, although she testified to having had subsequent sexually-active relationships. Eventually, she sought psychological counselling.

. . . Before the case was submitted to the jury, however, Kerr dropped all causes of action except for negligent infliction of emotional distress. The jury returned a verdict for Kerr on that claim, assessing $500,000 in actual damages. . . .

While the holding of *Garrard* was correct, we conclude that its reasoning was based on an erroneous interpretation *of Hill v. Kimball*, and is out of step with most American jurisdictions. Therefore, we overrule the language of *Garrard* to the extent that it recognizes an independent right to recover for negligently inflicted emotional distress. Instead, mental anguish damages should be compensated only in connection with defendant's breach of some other duty imposed by law. . . .

By overruling the language *of Garrard*, we hold only that there is no general duty not to negligently inflict emotional distress. Our decision does not affect a claimant's right to recover mental anguish damages caused by defendant's breach of some other legal duty. *See, e.g., Fisher v. Coastal Transp. Co.* (negligent infliction of direct physical injury); *Moore v. Lillebo* (wrongful death); *Fisher v. Carrousel Motor Hotel, Inc.* (battery); *Stuart v. Western Union Tel. Co.* (failure of telegraph company to timely deliver death message); *Billings v. Atkinson,* (invasion of privacy); *Leyendecker & Assocs., Inc., v. Wechter,* (defamation); *Pat H. Foley & Co. v. Wyatt* (negligent handling of corpse).

Also, our holding does not affect the right of bystanders to recover emotional distress damages suffered as a result of witnessing a serious or fatal accident. Texas has adopted the bystander rules originally promulgated by the California Supreme Court in *Dillon v. Legg*. . . .

We also are not imposing a requirement that emotional distress manifest itself physically to be compensable. . . .

Most other jurisdictions do not recognize a general duty not to negligently inflict emotional distress. Many limit recovery by requiring proof of a physical manifestation. Others allow recovery where the claimant establishes the breach of some independent duty. A few jurisdictions recognize a general right to recover for negligently inflicted emotional distress, but these jurisdictions are squarely in the minority.

We find the experience in California to be instructive. . . . *Thing v. La Chusa*. . . .

We therefore reverse the judgment of the court of appeals in favor of Kerr on the ground of negligent infliction of emotional distress.

. . . .

We denied recovery not because Boyles breached no duty toward Kerr, but because the only theory which she chose . . . negligent infliction of emotional distress—was overly broad and would encompass other cases involving merely rude or insensitive behavior. We reaffirm that conclusion today.

Kerr cannot recover based on the cause of action under which she proceeded. It may well be, however, that she failed to assert and preserve alternative causes of action because of her reliance on our holding in *Garrard*. . . . We therefore reverse the judgment of the court of appeals and remand this cause to the trial court for a new trial.

. . . .

Concurring Opinion on Motion for Rehearing

GONZALEZ, JUSTICE.

What happened to Ms. Kerr in this case is grossly offensive conduct which no one should tolerate. As such the law should, and does, provide a remedy. However, as a result of the posturing by the dissenting justices, what has been lost in the shuffle is the pivotal role that insurance played in this case.

The young men who videotaped Ms. Kerr's sexual encounter intentionally positioned the camera to capture the event on film. They intentionally showed the videotape to their friends. There was nothing accidental or careless about their outrageous conduct. However, Ms. Kerr intentionally gave up her right to receive redress under two other theories of recovery which she had pleaded: willful invasion of privacy, a cause of action which was recognized by this Court sixteen years before the jury verdict in this case in *Billings v. Atkinson*, 489 S.W.2d 858, 860–61 (Tex. 1973), and intentional infliction of emotional distress. . . . Her lawyers gambled when they made a strategic decision to proceed only with the questionable legal theory of negligent infliction of emotional distress.

. . . .

It does not take a rocket scientist to determine why Ms. Kerr's lawyers elected to proceed solely on the tort of negligent infliction of emotional distress. In fact, her lawyers explained their strategy to the trial court. At the close of the evidence, the defense attorneys made a motion for directed verdict on the negligence theories of recovery:

THE COURT: Under what basis?

MR. DRABECK [defendant's attorney]:

Under the basis that intentional tort cannot be the result of negligent conduct. That the case has been tried from start to finish as an intentional tort by the lawyers over here. We'd ask that the Court recognize that. There has never been one question asked of anybody as to whether or not they failed to exercise ordinary care on the occasion in question, whether they negligently inflicted some sort of mental distress on her. It would appear by virtue of the record as placed by the plaintiffs themselves that every single question was directed toward intentional conduct.

MR. KRIST: [plaintiff's attorney]:

Your Honor, the—to begin with, let the record reveal, for whatever purposes, it might be at a later date, that should the Court adopt counsel's suggestion, counsel would have dropped his client in the grease in that he would have gotten totally out of coverage.

THE COURT:

It's your case . . . and I am going to give you your requested charge. If you don't ask for an intentional tort, I ain't asking it, . . . I'm not going to make you prosecute a lawsuit that you didn't want to prosecute. So don't worry about that. Nobody is going to get intentional tort unless they ask for it.

In Texas, a home owners policy covers only accidents or careless conduct and excludes intentional acts. . . .

---

1. Why did plaintiff's attorneys limit the suit to negligent infliction of mental distress? What remains of the holding in *Garrard*? Is it limited to its facts, interference with dead bodies? Does this Texas decision change the law with respect to bystanders?

2. In Texas, after *Boyles v. Kerr*, when can a plaintiff recover for the negligent infliction of mental distress?

3. Some jurisdictions do not require a physical injury in two cases: (1) negligent interference with dead bodies and (2) mistakes in sending telegrams reporting death. *Lott v. State*, 32 Misc. 2d 296, 225 N.Y.S.2d 434 (Ct. Cl. 1962) (dead bodies); *Johnson v. State*, 37 N.Y.2d 378, 372 N.Y.S.2d 638, 334 N.E.2d 590 (1975) (death telegram).

4. Can the parents recover for emotional distress when their infant is abducted from the defendant hospital because of negligence? The court rejected the claim holding that the parents were not within the "zone of danger" and the hospital owed "no direct duty" to them. A direct duty was owed only to the child. *Johnson v. Jamaica Hosp.*, 62 N.Y.2d 523, 467 N.E.2d 502, 478 N.Y.2d 838 (1984).

The "no direct duty" rationale was extended to the misdiagnosis of disease in *Jacobs v. Horton Mem. Hosp.*, 130 A.D.2d 546, 515 N.Y.S.2d 281 (1987), where a wife had sued for the emotional distress resulting from the negligent diagnosis of pancreatic cancer in her husband. Have we returned to the privity of contract concept?

Binns v. Westminster Memorial Park

Court of Appeal of California, 2009
89 Cal. Rptr. 3d 890

Aronson, J.

In 1977, plaintiff's mother purchased a burial plot for plaintiff's deceased father in defendant's cemetery. A few months later, plaintiff's mother purchased three additional plots adjacent to the plot in which plaintiff's father was interred, intended for herself, plaintiff, and plaintiff's wife or, if plaintiff did not marry, plaintiff's brother. As part of the transaction, plaintiff's mother executed a purchase agreement with defendant. Plaintiff's mother died in 1986 and was interred in the plot next to plaintiff's father.

On Easter 2005, plaintiff visited his parents' graves and discovered a stranger, Maria Vallejo, buried in the plot immediately adjacent to his mother, which had been reserved for plaintiff. Plaintiff immediately brought the situation to the attention of Lydia Navas, defendant's family services counselor, who reviewed some records and promised to obtain further information. The following day, Navas contacted plaintiff, confirmed Vallejo had been buried in plaintiff's plot, and promised to rectify the problem. A few days later, Navas again contacted plaintiff to inform him the cemetery had removed Vallejo from plaintiff's plot and reinterred the corpse in another location. Defendant had not notified plaintiff it would disturb Vallejo's remains to rectify the situation.

. . . .

In awarding plaintiff emotional distress damages, the trial court relied exclusively on plaintiff's cause of action for negligent infliction of emotional distress. Damages for severe emotional distress are recoverable in a negligence action "when they result from the breach of a duty owed the plaintiff that is assumed by the defendant or imposed on the defendant as a matter of law, or that arises out of a relationship between the two." Defendant contends plaintiff's claim fails because it did not owe plaintiff a duty to prevent the temporary burial of Vallejo in his burial plot. We disagree.

Civil Code section 1714, subdivision (a), presents the general rule concerning a person's legal responsibility to others: "Everyone is responsible, not only for the result of his or her willful acts, but also for an injury occasioned to another by his or her want of ordinary care or skill in the management of his or her property or person, except so far as the latter has, willfully or by want of ordinary care, brought the injury upon himself or herself." The Supreme Court has observed that "'[i]n the absence of a statutory provision limiting this rule, exceptions to the general principle imposing liability for negligence are recognized only when clearly supported by public policy.'"

Generally, nonstatutory limitations on legal duty turn on (1) the reasonable foreseeability of the risk of injury, and (2) a weighing of policy considerations for and against imposition of liability. In elaborating upon the relationship between these two elements, the court in *Quesada v. Oak Hill Improvement Co.* (1989) 213 Cal. App.3d 596, 608 [261 Cal. Rptr. 769] (*Quesada*) explained that "although the court . . . utilize[s] foreseeability to begin a determination of duty, the final determination . . . is tempered by policy considerations."

The seminal case of *Rowland v. Christian* (1968) 69 Cal.2d 108 [70 Cal. Rptr. 97, 443 P.2d 561] set forth the major factors in determining the scope of a person's legal duty: "the foreseeability of harm to the plaintiff, the degree of certainty that the plaintiff suffered injury, the closeness of the connection between the defendant's conduct and the injury suffered, the moral blame attached to the defendant's conduct, the policy of preventing future harm, the extent of the burden to the defendant and consequences to the community of imposing a duty to exercise care with resulting liability for breach, and the availability, cost, and prevalence of insurance for the risk involved."

. . . . In *Christensen v. Superior Court* (1991) 54 Cal.3d 868 [2 Cal. Rptr. 2d 79, 820 P.2d 181] (*Christensen*), decided two years after *Quesada*, the mortuary defendants contracted with the cemetery defendants to perform cremations. The cemetery defendants mishandled the decedents' remains. The defendant mortuaries knew or should have known of the cemetery's malfeasance. (*Christensen*, at pp. 878–879.) The Supreme Court held family members could recover emotional distress damages because the mortuaries and crematories owed them an independent tort duty arising from a special relationship. (*Id.* at p. 891.) The court recognized that "'[o]nce a mortuary . . . undertakes to accept the care, custody and control of the remains, a duty of care must be found running to the members of decedent's bereaved family.'"

The *Christensen* court determined it was foreseeable that mishandling human remains likely would cause serious emotional distress to members of the decedent's immediate family.

. . . .

Although the issue is close, we conclude it is foreseeable a person could suffer severe emotional distress upon discovery a stranger had been buried in their family gravesite.

. . . Though unintentional, defendant's negligent interment of a stranger in plaintiff's family burial plot compromised the purpose underlying the agreement between the family and the cemetery, i.e., the emotional tranquility arising from the cemetery's promise that plaintiff will be buried next to his loved ones. While other relatives may be upset to discover a stranger buried in a family plot, it is the intended user of the plot who is most likely to suffer emotional distress from the incident.

. . . Finally, we note that recognizing a duty here supports the principle that "[a]s a society we want those who are entrusted with the bodies of our dead to exercise the greatest of care."

. . . "Emotional distress includes suffering, anguish, fright, horror, nervousness, grief, anxiety, worry, shock, humiliation, and shame." (CACI No. 1604; see also Black's Law Dict. (8th ed. 2004) p. 563 [defining emotional distress].) At trial, plaintiff presented evidence that when he discovered Vallejo's body buried in his own plot, he began trembling and felt as if he had been "struck by lightning." He was "horrified," believing he had been "spiritually violated." Plaintiff viewed the plot as having been desecrated because Vallejo's soul had been disturbed when she was moved from what was to have been her final resting place. As a result of defendant's error, plaintiff testified he suffered from nightmares, loss of appetite, and cold sweats. Plaintiff testified he did not seek medical care because he could not afford it.

. . . .

The judgment and order are affirmed. In the interests of justice, each side is to bear its own costs on appeal.

DISSENT

BEDSWORTH, Acting P. J., Concurring and Dissenting

. . . .

It seems to me we started out with a perfectly intelligible and easily applicable rule . . . that conduct amounting to a breach of contract becomes tortious only when it also violates an independent duty arising from principles of tort law. In applying this rule to funerary/mortuary services, it held that such an independent duty arises when one party agrees with another *to handle the remains* of a deceased loved one. It did not hold that such a duty arises when someone agrees to provide a plot for burial, and I see no reason to create such a rule.

————————

1. What is it about improperly handling the remains of dead bodies that makes it one of the only actions that consistently supports a claim for negligent infliction of emotional distress?

2. Aren't there other actions that can be seen as just as consistently disturbing? Couldn't the same be said for improperly handling the birth of a child, for example?

3. Make an argument in favor of the cemetery in this case. Do cases such as this one place too heavy a burden on those who are in the business of handling the deceased?

4. Should it be sufficient that the cemetery quickly moved Maria Vallejo's remains out of plaintiff's plot?

G. Injury to Unborn Children

Problem

Dale negligently crashes into Karen's car, causing Karen to give birth to Rick three months early. Because of the early birth, Rick suffers brain damage. Would you take Rick's suit against Dale? What if Rick had been stillborn?

Renslow v. Mennonite Hospital

Supreme Court of Illinois, 1977
367 N.E.2d 1250

MORAN, JUSTICE.

. . . .

There is but one issue: Does a child, not conceived at the time negligent acts were committed against its mother, have a cause of action against the tortfeasors for its injuries resulting from their conduct?

Plaintiff's six-count complaint for negligence . . . alleges that in October of 1965, when her mother was 13 years of age, the defendants, on two occasions, negligently transfused her mother with 500 cubic centimeters of Rh-positive blood. The mother's Rh-negative blood was incompatible with, and was sensitized by, the Rh-positive blood. Her mother had no knowledge of an adverse reaction from the transfusions and did not know she had been improperly transfused or that her blood had been sensitized. In December 1973 she first discovered her condition when a routine blood screening was ordered by her physician in the course of prenatal care. Plaintiff further asserts that the defendants discovered they had administered the incompatible blood, but at no time notified her mother or the mother's family.

The resulting sensitization of the mother's blood allegedly caused prenatal damage to plaintiff's hemolitic processes, which put her life in jeopardy and necessitated her induced premature birth. . . . It is further alleged that, as a result of the defendants' acts, plaintiff suffers from permanent damage to various organs, her brain, and her nervous system.

The trial court dismissed plaintiff's cause of action because she was not "at the time of the alleged infliction of the injury conceived." . . . [T]he appellate court found no reason to deny a cause of action to a person simply because he had not yet been conceived at the time of the wrongful conduct.

. . . [I]n *Allaire v. St. Luke's Hospital* (1900), 184 Ill. 359, 56 N.E. 638, 641, . . . Mr. Justice Boggs [dissent] pointed out that it was clearly demonstrable that "at a period of gestation in advance of . . . parturition the foetus is capable of independent and separate life, and that though within the [mother's body] it is not merely a part of her body, for her body may die in all of its parts and the child remain alive and capable of maintaining life when separated from the dead body of the mother." . . . [T]he impact of Mr. Justice Boggs' dissent eventually turned the tide toward prenatal recovery. *Bonbrest v. Kotz* (D.D.C. 1946), 65 F. Supp. 138, was the first decision to recognize a common law right of action for prenatal injuries. It relied heavily on Mr. Justice Boggs' reasoning—that an infant should be recognized as having a legal existence separate from its mother's at such time as it was capable of sustaining life separate from her. . . . This court in *Amann v. Faidy* . . . held that there is a right of action for the wrongful death of a viable child, injured in utero, who is born alive but thereafter dies. *Rodriguez v. Patti* . . . extended a common law right of action for personal injuries to an infant viable when wrongfully injured in utero. In *Chrisafogeorgis v. Brandenberg* . . . this rationale was further extended to permit a wrongful death action for a viable child wrongfully injured in utero and thereafter born dead. . . .

Although we have not decided whether a surviving infant has a right of action for injuries sustained in utero during a previable state of its development, our appellate courts have answered that question in the affirmative. *Sana v. Brown* (1962), 35 Ill. App. 2d 425; *Daley v. Meier* (1961), 33 Ill. App. 2d 218. *See also Rapp v. Hiemenz* (1969),

107 Ill. App. 2d 382, where an action for wrongful death as the result of prenatal injuries to a previable fetus, born dead, was denied.

The complaint in the case sub judice contains no allegation that the plaintiff was viable when her injuries were sustained. We, therefore, must consider whether the plaintiff must allege that she was viable at the time her injuries were sustained.

The rule permitting a cause of action only where the child is viable at the time of the injury has been criticized as a "most unsatisfactory criterion, since [viability] is a relative matter, depending on the health of mother and child and many other matters in addition to the stage of development." (Prosser, Torts sec. 55, at 337 (4th ed. 1971). . . .

Because the appellate court found the risk of harm reasonably foreseeable, it assumed duty was established, and concluded that the delay between the act and the injury was not a bar to the action.

The implication in the appellate court's opinion that duty and foreseeability are identical in scope is not altogether correct. In *Cunis v. Brennan* (1974), 56 Ill. 2d 372, 375, it was pointed out that "the existence of a legal duty is not to be bottomed on the factor of foreseeability alone." There, quoted with approval, was Dean Leon Green's observation:

> "[H]owever valuable the foreseeability formula may be in aiding a jury or judge to reach a decision on the negligence issue, it is altogether inadequate for use by the judge as a basis of determining the duty issue and its scope. The duty issue, being one of law, is broad in its implication; the negligence issue is confined to the particular case and has no implications for other cases. There are many factors other than foreseeability that may condition a judge's imposing or not imposing a duty in the particular case. . . ." Green, *Foreseeability in Negligence Law*, 61 Colum. L. Rev. 1401, 1417–18. . . .

The cases allowing relief to an infant for injuries incurred in its previable state make it clear that a defendant may be held liable to a person whose existence was not apparent at the time of his act. We therefore find it illogical to bar relief for an act done prior to conception where the defendant would be liable for this same conduct had the child, unbeknownst to him, been conceived prior to his act. We believe that there is a right to be born free from prenatal injuries foreseeably caused by a breach of duty to the child's mother.

The extension of duty in such a case is further supported by sound policy considerations. Medical science has developed various techniques which can mitigate or, in some cases, totally alleviate a child's prenatal harm. In light of these substantial medical advances it seems to us that sound social policy requires the extension of duty in this case.

. . . .

Since the liability announced herein represents an extension of duty to a new class of plaintiffs, we hold that it be given prospective application. Therefore, except as to the plaintiff herein, the rule shall apply only to cases arising out of future conduct. . . .

The decision of the appellate court, reversing the trial court's dismissal of this claim for failure to state a cause of action, is therefore affirmed and the cause remanded to the trial court for further proceedings.

———————

1. What factors influenced the court to find a duty in *Renslow*? What is the problem with foreseeability as a test?

2. Argue for the hospital that *Renslow* goes too far in permitting a nonexisting (at time of injury) infant to recover.

3. Why is it negligent to transfuse an Rh-negative girl or woman with Rh-positive blood? Does the risk to unconceived children create the duty?

Problem

Cheyanne, age fourteen, became pregnant following seduction by her biofeedback therapist. What damages can the child, Tom, who is healthy, recover from the therapist, Art?

Viccaro v. Milunsky

Supreme Judicial Court of Massachusetts, 1990
551 N.E.2d 8

WILKINS, JUSTICE.

A judge of the United States District Court for the District of Massachusetts has certified novel questions of Massachusetts law to this court. The judge asks whether a child who was born with a genetic defect and his parents have bases under Massachusetts law for recovery against a physician whose negligent preconception counseling led the parents to decide to conceive children.

The facts presented to us in association with the certified questions are brief. In November, 1976, not then married, the Viccaros consulted the defendant physician, a specialist in genetics, genetic disorders, and genetic counseling, concerning the possibility that Amy might have, or be a carrier of, a genetic disorder known as ectodermal dysplasia.[2] The defendant concluded that Amy did not have the disease and that there should be no likelihood of her developing the disorder or of having affected children. In October, 1977, the Viccaros were married. Relying on the defendant's assurances, they bore children. Their first child, a daughter, was born in July, 1980, apparently healthy, without manifestations of the disorder. On March 27, 1984, Adam

———————

2. For the purposes of certifying the questions to us, the judge accepted as correct the allegations of the complaint that several members of Amy's family were afflicted with ectodermal dysplasia, a severely disfiguring disorder that affects the skin, hair, nails, teeth, nerve cells, sweat glands, parts of the eyes and ears, and other organs of the body.

was born severely afflicted with anhidrotic ectodermal dysplasia. He will require special medical care throughout his life and will suffer substantial physical pain and mental anguish. The Viccaros have suffered and will continue to suffer severe emotional distress and substantial physical injuries (whose nature and cause are not disclosed on the record). Their complaint seeks, in addition to emotional distress damages, recovery of the extraordinary expenses for Adam's care, support, and education; their loss of companionship of a normal son; and their loss of the services and earnings of a normal son.[3]

The Parents' Claim

We think it preferable to consider and decide questions concerning the parents' claim first. . . .

If a child is born with a congenital or genetic disorder, almost all courts have allowed the parents to recover against a negligent physician the extraordinary medical, educational, and other expenses that are associated with and are consequences of the disorder.

We agree with the general rule that the Viccaros are entitled to recover the extraordinary medical and educational expenses and other extraordinary costs associated with caring for Adam. If the Viccaros prove that, when Adam attains his majority, they will remain liable for Adam's support, they will be entitled to recover for the extraordinary expenses they will incur during Adam's majority. In Massachusetts, a parent is liable for the support of an adult child if the child is physically or mentally impaired and incapable of supporting himself. The emotional distress the Viccaros sustain as a result of the defendant's negligence and any physical harm caused by that emotional distress are also recoverable. *See Burke v. Rivo, supra* at 768.

The Viccaros' claim for the loss of Adam's society and companionship as a normal child lacks merit. The defendant is not responsible for the fact that Adam is afflicted with a substantial genetic disease. Although the defendant may be liable for certain damages because, had he not been negligent, according to the complaint, the

---

3. In other jurisdictions, the claim that Adam asserts has generally been characterized as a "wrongful life" claim, one made by a child with a genetic defect who was born as a result of the defendant's negligence. The claim the Viccaros assert has generally been termed a "wrongful birth" claim, a claim by parents that, because of the defendant's negligence, they gave birth to a child with a genetic or other congenital defect. The claim asserted in *Burke v. Rivo, ante* 764 (1990), which we decide today, has often been placed in the category of "wrongful conception" or "wrongful pregnancy." That claim is that the birth of a normal, healthy child was a consequence of a negligently performed sterilization procedure or some other negligence without which the unwanted child would not have been born. These labels are not instructive. Any "wrongfulness" lies not in the life, the birth, the conception, or the pregnancy, but in the negligence of the physician. The harm, if any, is not the birth itself but the effect of the defendant's negligence on the parents' physical, emotional, and financial well-being resulting from the denial to the parents of their right, as the case may be, to decide whether to bear a child or whether to bear a child with a genetic or other defect. We abstained from using any label in the *Burke* opinion, such as wrongful pregnancy, and shall similarly abstain in this case from using the labels "wrongful life" or "wrongful birth."

Viccaros would not have conceived a child, the defendant cannot be liable for the Viccaros' loss of the companionship of a normal child.

We summarize our conclusions as to the parents' claims. Question 3, concerning the existence of a cause of action in the parents, we answer in the affirmative. There is one. We need not answer question 4(a) because the Viccaros do not press a claim for all financial burdens associated with raising Adam. In response to the two parts of question 4(b), we answer affirmatively that the Viccaros may recover for Adam's extraordinary medical needs and, as to the second question in question 4(b), in certain circumstances the Viccaros could recover for extraordinary expenses they may incur after Adam's majority. Because the Viccaros may recover damages for the cost of the extraordinary care that Adam needs, we answer the first question in question 4(c) in the affirmative. We do not have sufficient information, however, to answer the second part of question 4(c), concerning the parents' right to recover for wages they lost or will lose in providing extraordinary care to Adam. In general, damages should be measured by the fair market value of the necessary extraordinary services. Perhaps the parents' lost wages will be an appropriate measure of recovery in some special circumstance. As to question 4(d), the parents may recover for emotional distress and for physical harm caused by that emotional distress, offset by whatever emotional benefits they may derive from the existence of their first child and offset (as the Viccaros concede) by any benefits that may be derived from the existence of Adam. We do not know what other physical injuries this question may refer to. For completeness, although we are not asked to comment on the point, whatever emotional benefits the parents may derive from the children may also be offset against the extraordinary expenses the parents may incur.

We see no basis for the Viccaros to recover for the loss of Adam's society and companionship as a normal child, and thus we answer question 4(e) in the negative. Question 4(f) we answer in the negative because the Viccaros make no serious argument that they are entitled to recover for the loss of Adam's services as a normal child.

The Child's Claim

The judge has also asked us: "Does Massachusetts recognize a cause of action for wrongful life, where a minor child, afflicted with a genetic defect, alleges that the negligent preconception genetic counseling of his parents by a geneticist induced his parents to conceive and give birth to the child?" We answer the question in the negative. Because, as alleged by his parents, Adam would not have been born if the defendant had not been negligent, there is a fundamental problem of logic if Adam were allowed to recover against the defendant in a negligence-based tort action.

The almost universal rule in this country is that a physician is not liable to a child who was born because of the physician's negligence. . . .

A few courts, however, have allowed a child who was born with a defect to recover against a negligent physician the extraordinary expenses that he or she will incur during his or her lifetime because of the hereditary defect. . . .

We faced a somewhat similar, but not identical, question in *Payton v. Abbott Labs*, 386 Mass. 540, 557–560 (1982), where we concluded that a woman, who would not have been born but for her mother's use of a drug manufactured by the defendants, was barred from recovery for physical or emotional damage she suffered as a result of her mother's ingestion of the drug. We said that "[t]he provider of the probable means of a plaintiff's very existence should not be liable for unavoidable, collateral consequences of the use of that means." *Id.* at 560. By the same token, the defendant whose negligence (it is asserted) is a reason for Adam's very existence should not be liable for the unfortunate consequences of Adam's birth with a genetic disease, such as his pain and suffering, emotional distress, and loss of his parents' consortium.

On a theoretical basis, it is difficult to conclude that the defendant physician was in breach of any duty owed to Adam. It is alleged, however, that Adam does exist as a result of the defendant's negligence and that he may incur substantial and extraordinary expenses for medical care, educational, and other needs. It is this pragmatic consideration that has moved a few jurisdictions, as noted above, to allow a child like Adam to recover those extraordinary expenses that he will incur during his lifetime because of his genetic defect. As long, however, as Adam's parents are entitled to recover against the defendant for the extraordinary costs they will incur because of Adam's genetic disease, Adam need not have his own cause of action for those expenses. We do not know Adam's life expectancy nor whether he has a reasonable prospect of supporting himself in adulthood. We do not totally discount the possibility that we might impose liability for the extraordinary expenses of caring for a person like Adam after his parents' deaths, perhaps in order to keep such a person from being a public charge. That is not this case, as far as we are told, and certainly no question has been asked of us in these specific terms.

. . . .

---

1. What did the court mean in *Payton* when it said, "the provider of the probable means of a plaintiff's very existence should not be liable. . . ."?

2. Do Adam's extraordinary costs mirror those of his parents?

3. Should the emotional benefits that a parent receives from having a child be set off against the actual expenses of raising the child?

4. Should the parent's claim be denied because:

> [A]n assumption that a judge or jury can measure the net loss to parents of the birth of a normal child is so inconsistent with the reverence we should have for human life that the harm to society from such an inquiry, augmented by the harm to the family and child, outweighs the value of compensating parents for the wrong they allege. My position in this case is the same. Although I recognize that the burden of raising an impaired child may be considerably heavier than the burden associated with raising a normal child, the controlling values and principles are the same.

Viccaro dissent, 406 Mass. at 785–86. What if the family is very poor?

5. The calculation of damages in wrongful life cases has been viewed as impossible:

> The *Gleitman v. Cosgrove* Court found it impossible to compare the infant's condition if the doctor had not been negligent with the infant's impaired condition as a result of the negligence. Measurement of the value of life with impairments against the nonexistence of life itself was, the court declared, a logical impossibility. Consequently the Court rejected the infant's [entire] claim. . . .

> The *Berman v. Allan* Court also declined to recognize a cause of action in an infant born with birth defects. [E]ven a life with serious defects is more valuable than non-existence, the alternative for the infant plaintiff if his mother chose to have an abortion.

Procanik by Procanik v. Cillo, 97 N.J. 339, 478 A.2d 755 (1984). Does *Gleitman* or *Berman* have anything to recommend it?

6. What damages might Adam face in fact?

7. There may be substantial cause in fact issues, and a need for expert testimony in these cases, when the parents argue that the death or impairment of the child was caused by prescription drugs. The Supreme Court recently held:

> Faced with a proffer of expert scientific testimony, . . . the trial judge must determine . . . whether the expert is proposing to testify to (1) scientific knowledge that (2) will assist the trier of fact to understand or determine a fact in issue. This entails a preliminary assessment of whether the reasoning or methodology underlying the testimony is scientifically valid and of whether that reasoning or methodology properly can be applied to the facts in issue. . . . Many factors will bear on the inquiry. . . .

Daubert v. Merrell Dow Pharmaceuticals, Inc., 509 U.S. 579, 113 S. Ct. 2786 (1993).

Burke v. Rivo

Supreme Judicial Court of Massachusetts, 1990
551 N.E.2d 1

WILKINS, JUSTICE.

. . . .

In December, 1983, the plaintiff Carole Burke met with the defendant physician to discuss her desire not to have more children. The Burke family was experiencing financial difficulties. She wanted to return to work to support her family and to fulfil her career goals. The Burkes assert that the defendant recommended that Carole undergo a bipolar cauterization procedure and that he guaranteed that she would not again become pregnant if she did so. In February, 1984, the defendant performed a laparoscopic bilateral tubal ligation by bipolar cauterization.

On June 25, 1985, a pregnancy test confirmed that Carole was pregnant. On February 12, 1986, she give [sic] birth to a fourth child, and the next day she underwent a second sterilization procedure, known as bilateral salpingectomy. A pathology report showed that there had been a recanalization of the left fallopian tube. The Burkes assert that, if the defendant had told Carole of the risk of recanalization, however small, she would initially have selected a different sterilization procedure.

The judge has only reported questions concerning damages. . . . The matters of liability are, however, not before us, and remain to be proved.

. . . We reject his arguments that in Massachusetts there should be no liability for negligently performing a sterilization procedure when the result is the conception of a child; no liability for negligently failing to advise a patient of the risks of conceiving a child following a particular sterilization operation (where the patient, properly informed, would have selected a different and more certain sterilization operation); and no liability for breach of a guarantee that following a sterilization procedure there would be no further pregnancy.

The great weight of authority permits the parents of a normal child born as a result of a physician's negligence to recover damages directly associated with the birth (sometimes including damage for the parents' emotional distress), but courts are divided on whether the parents may recover the economic expense of rearing the child. . . .

The judge below recognized that damages properly would include the cost of the unsuccessful sterilization procedure and costs directly flowing from the pregnancy: the wife's lost earning capacity; medical expenses of the delivery and care following the birth; the cost of care for the other children while the wife was incapacitated; the cost of the second sterilization procedure and any expenses flowing from that operation; and the husband's loss of consortium. We would add the wife's pain and suffering in connection with the pregnancy and birth and with the second sterilization procedure. We also see no reason why the plaintiffs should not recover for emotional distress they sustained as a result of the unwanted pregnancy. Emotional distress could be the probable consequence of a breach of the duty the defendant owed directly to the plaintiffs. . . .

The principal issue is whether the plaintiffs are entitled, if they establish liability, to the cost of raising their child. Under normal tort and contract principles, that cost is both a reasonably foreseeable and a natural and probable consequence of the wrongs that the plaintiffs allege. The question is whether there is any public policy consideration to which we should give effect to limit traditional tort and contract damages. We conclude that there is none as to parents who have elected sterilization for economic reasons.

Many justifications often relied on for declining to allow recovery of the cost of rearing a healthy child born as a result of a physician's negligence are outstandingly unimpressive. . . . The judicial declaration that the joy and pride in raising a child always outweigh any economic loss the parents may suffer, thus precluding recovery for the cost of raising the child . . . simply lacks verisimilitude. The very fact that a person has sought medical intervention to prevent him or her from having a child demonstrates that, for that person, the benefits of parenthood did not outweigh the burdens, economic and otherwise, of having a child. The extensive use of contraception and sterilization and the performance of numerous abortions each year show that, in some instances, large numbers of people do not accept parenthood as a net positive circumstance. We agree with those courts that have rejected the theory that the birth of a child is for all parents at all times a net benefit. . . . While we firmly reject a universal rule that the birth of an unexpected healthy child is always a net benefit, we also firmly reject any suggestion that the availability of abortion or of adoption furnishes a basis for limiting damages payable by a physician but for whose negligence the child would not have been conceived. . . .

We are also unimpressed with the reasoning that child-rearing expenses should not be allowed because some day the child could be adversely affected by learning that he or she was unwanted and that someone else had paid for the expense of rearing the child. . . . Courts expressing concern about the effect on the child nevertheless allow the parents to recover certain direct expenses from the negligent physician without expressing concern about harm to the child when the child learns that he or she was unwanted. . . . The once unwanted child's knowledge that someone other than the parents had been obliged to pay for the cost of rearing him or her may in fact alleviate the child's distress at the knowledge of having been once unwanted. . . . In any event, it is for the parents, not the courts, to decide whether a lawsuit would adversely affect the child and should not be maintained.

We see no validity to the arguments, sometimes made, that the costs of child-rearing are too speculative or are unreasonably disproportionate to the doctor's negligence. . . . The determination of the anticipated costs of child-rearing is no more complicated or fanciful than many calculations of future losses made every day in tort cases. If a physician is negligent in caring for a newborn child, damage calculations would be made concerning the newborn's earning capacity and expected medical expenses over an entire lifetime. The expenses of rearing a child are far more easily determined. If there is any justification for denying recovery of normal tort damages in a case of this character, it is not that the cost of rearing a child is incapable of reasonable calculation or is too great to impose on a negligent physician.

A substantial number of jurisdictions have allowed recovery of the cost of rearing a normal child to adulthood, offset, however, by the benefits that the parents receive in having a normal, healthy child . . . . Such a balancing by the trier of fact requires a comparison of the economic loss of child-rearing with the emotional gains of having a normal, healthy child (converted into a dollar value). These courts have thought the comparison appropriate under the general principle expressed in Restatement

(Second) of Torts §920 (1979). A few courts have thought that, because the benefit conferred did not affect the economic interest that was harmed, no mitigation of the cost of child-rearing should be recognized. . . .

If the parents' desire to avoid the birth of a child was founded on eugenic reasons (avoidance of a feared genetic defect) or was founded on therapeutic reasons (concern for the mother's health) and if a healthy, normal baby is born, the justification for allowing recovery of the cost of rearing a normal child to maturity is far less than when, to conserve family resources, the parents sought unsuccessfully to avoid conceiving another child. *See University of Ariz. Health Sciences Center v. Superior Court*, 136 Ariz. 579, 585 (1983) ("For example, where the parent sought sterilization in order to avoid the danger of genetic defect, the jury could easily find that the uneventful birth of a healthy, non-defective child was a blessing rather than a 'damage'"). . . .

We conclude that, in addition to the recoverable damages described earlier in this opinion, parents may recover the cost of rearing a normal, healthy but (at least initially) unwanted child if their reason for seeking sterilization was founded on economic or financial considerations. In such a situation, the trier of fact should offset against the cost of rearing the child the benefit, if any, the parents receive and will receive from having their child. We discern no reason founded on sound public policy to immunize a physician from having to pay for a reasonably foreseeable consequence of his negligence or from a natural and probable consequence of a breach of his guarantee, namely, the parents' expenses in rearing the child to adulthood.

. . . .

———

1. Should a suit for loss of consortium be denied because the child might someday discover defendant paid for its upbringing? Justice O'Connor, in dissent, argued:

> The court states that it is "unimpressed with the reasoning [of several courts] that child-rearing expenses should not be allowed because some day the child could be adversely affected by learning that he or she was unwanted and that someone else had paid for the expense of rearing the child." The court concludes that "it is for the parents, not the courts, to decide whether a lawsuit would adversely affect the child and should not be maintained." I disagree. The State's interest in strengthening and encouraging family life for the protection and care of children is legitimate and strong. Indeed, it is for the State to determine whether to adopt a rule of damages that would encourage litigation harmful to families—litigation designed to produce the result, ultimately to be discovered by the child, that he or she was supported not by the parents, because they did not want him or her, but by an unwilling stranger.

Burke, 551 N.E.2d at 7, 8. Might the child say, "Cool"?

2. Is the jury capable of the "economic" balancing that the court requires? Should the courts decide that the birth of a child is always a benefit? Should the availability of abortion or adoption be relevant?

3. How is the argument in *Burke* different from other emotional harm actions in this chapter?

Chapter 5

Negligence

A. Introduction

Negligence has been the core concept in personal injury law since at least 1850. Substantial debate exists as to the nature of personal injury law before 1850, however. There are four different theories concerning the nature of tort law before 1850. First, Professor Wex Malone argues that the law rested on absolute liability. If the plaintiff was able to show cause in fact, the defendant was absolutely liable, and fault was not an issue:

> At your request I accompany you when you are about your own affairs; my enemies fall upon and kill me, you must pay for my death. You take me to see a wild beast show or that interesting spectacle, a mad man; beast or mad man kills me; you must pay. You hang up your sword; someone else knocks it down so that it cuts me; you must pay. In none of these cases can you honestly swear that you did nothing that helped to bring about death or wound.

W. Malone, *Ruminations on the Role of Fault in the History of the Common Law of Torts*, 31 La. L. Rev. 1, 3 (1970).

Second, Professor Robert Rabin argues that there was no tort law, merely a broad sea of immunities before 1850:

> Throughout the "heyday of negligence," the common law courts wrestled with issues that forced a choice between powerful no-liability principles and a fledgling doctrine of fault liability. Gradually the no-liability principles — immunities, privileges, and no-duty considerations imported from other conceptual systems (property, contract and such) — retreated, like a melting glacier in a hostile environment, before the successive onslaughts of fault and, later, strict liability rules.

Rabin, Perspectives on Tort Law 44 (2d ed. 1983).

Third, Professor Schwartz suggests a vacuum of knowledge; we just don't have enough information to evaluate the nature of the law:

> The meager quality of the English and American evidence counsels caution in making any dramatic assertions about pre-nineteenth century tort doctrine.

Schwartz, *Tort Law and the Economy in Nineteenth-Century America: A Reinterpretation*, 90 Yale L.J. 1722 (1981).

Fourth, Professor William Prosser suggests that prior to 1850, personal injury law rested on the distinction between two writs, trespass and case. Whenever someone wanted to bring a personal injury action, he or she obtained a writ of trespass to proceed before the king's common-law court. If the facts were outside the writ of trespass, he or she had to claim under the writ of trespass on the case. Trespass was available for direct and immediate injuries, while case was used for indirect injuries. Trespass did not require a showing of actual damages, but they were a requirement for case. W. Page Keeton et al., Prosser and Keeton on Torts 29–30 (5th ed. 1984).

The distinction between the writ of trespass and the writ of trespass on the case is shown in the following example:

> [I]f a man throws a log into the highway, and in that act it hits me; I may maintain trespass, because it is an immediate wrong; but if as it lies there I tumble over it, and receive an injury, I must bring an action upon the case; because it is only prejudicial in consequence, for which originally I could have no action at all.

Reynolds v. Clarke, 1 Strange 634, 92 Eng. Rep. 410 (1726).

Over the years, the intentional torts grew out of trespass, and many do not require a showing of damages. Negligence grew out of trespass on the case, and therefore damages must be shown to recover for negligence. *See Brown v. Kendall*, 6 Cush. (60 Mass.) 292 (1850).

B. The Core Concept

In order for a plaintiff to recover in negligence, he or she must show five elements:

1. *Duty.* The plaintiff must show that a legal obligation extends from the defendant to this plaintiff for this injury.

2. *Breach of Duty.* The plaintiff must show that the defendant breached his duty to the plaintiff. This is referred to as negligence and will be considered in this chapter.

3. *Cause-in-Fact.* The plaintiff must show that the defendant's conduct was a cause-in-fact of the plaintiff's injury. Cause-in-fact is often a matter of science. Did the defendant's conduct have something to do with the plaintiff's injury as a matter of science?

4. *Proximate Cause.* This is a matter of social policy, of practical politics. Liability cannot run-on or extend forever. A line must be drawn at some point, and proximate cause is the concept and the process for drawing that line. The question is whether the defendant's negligent conduct, although a cause-in-fact of the injury, is also the proximate cause. Proximate cause is often used to protect a negligent corporation from liability, especially when the damages caused were large.

5. *Damages.* In order to recover in negligence, the plaintiff must show that the defendant's conduct caused damages to the plaintiff.

Note that the term negligence is used in two ways: it refers both to the five elements collectively that must be shown to win in court and to the second requirement of the five-part negligence formula (2. Breach of Duty).

Problem

John (age nine), a little league baseball player, was shifted from second base to right field during a regular baseball game. (Second base is his usual position.) A fly ball was hit, and in John's attempt to catch the ball, he was hit in the eye by the ball and seriously injured. (John said the sun was in his eyes.)

John, by means of his parents, wants to sue the coach on the basis that the coach failed to instruct the boy how to shield his eyes from the sun when he caught a fly ball. Assume that the coach is a father of one of the players, a volunteer. John's parents have consulted you for advice. Discuss.

C. The Standard of Care

Blyth v. Birmingham Waterworks Co.

Court of Exchequer, 1856
11 Exch. 781, 156 Eng. Rep. 1047

[The defendant had installed water mains with fireplugs in the street. A large quantity of water escaped from a leak, where the fireplug joins the main, and forced its way through the ground into the plaintiff's house. One of the defendant's engineers stated that the leak might have been caused by the recent frost, one of the most severe frosts on record. The water main and fireplugs had been installed 25 years earlier and had functioned without problems. The judge left it to the jury to decide whether the defendant had used proper care. The jury found a verdict for the plaintiff. Defendant appealed.]

ALDERSON, B. I am of opinion that there was no evidence to be left to the jury. The case turns upon the question, whether the facts proved show that the defendants were guilty of negligence. Negligence is the omission to do something which a reasonable man, guided upon those considerations which ordinarily regulate the conduct of human affairs, would do, or doing something which a prudent and reasonable man would not do. The defendants might have been liable for negligence, if, unintentionally, they omitted to do, or doing something which a prudent and reasonable man would not do. The defendants might have been liable for negligence, if, unintentionally, they omitted to do that which a reasonable person would have done, or did that which a person taking reasonable precautions would not have done. A reasonable man would act with reference to the average circumstances of the temperature in ordinary years. The defendants had provided against such frosts as experience would have led men, acting prudently, to provide against; and they are not guilty of negligence, because their precautions proved insufficient against the effects of the extreme severity of the frost of 1855, which penetrated to a greater depth than any which ordinarily occurs south of the polar regions. Such a state of circumstances constitutes a contingency against which no reasonable man can provide. The result was an accident, for which the defendant cannot be held liable.

[The concurring opinions are omitted.] Verdict to be entered for the defendants.

––––––––––

1. Where did the court obtain the negligence concept?

2. What would it cost to rebury the water mains? How important is providing water to the community? How often would this injury occur?

3. Would it be helpful, in deciding whether the defendant was negligent, to know the exact damage to the plaintiff?

4. Should a drug manufacturer be liable for risks that premarket testing did not reveal?

United States v. Carroll Towing Co.

United States Court of Appeals, Second Circuit, 1947
159 F.2d 169

[During strong winds, a barge named the *Anna C.* broke loose, drifted down river, collided with a tanker and sank. Several acts contributed to the sinking. Because of the negligence of the harbormaster and a tug (the *Carroll)* deckhand, in adjusting the lines holding the *Anna C.*, she broke free while they were moving (drilling) another barge. This is a suit in admiralty to recover for the value of the *Anna C.* and her cargo (flour) owned by the United States. The issue discussed here is whether the recovery by the owners of the *Anna C.* should be reduced because the plaintiff's bargee was absent from his post (contributory negligence). If present, he could have reattached the lines and called for help to pump out the sinking *Anna C.*]

LEARNED HAND, CIRCUIT JUDGE.

. . . It appears from the foregoing review that there is no general rule to determine when the absence of a bargee or other attendant will make the owner of the barge liable for injuries to other vessels if she breaks away from her moorings. However, in any case where he would be so liable for injuries to others, obviously he must reduce his damages proportionately, if the injury is to his own barge. It becomes apparent why there can be no such general rule, when we consider the grounds for such a liability. Since there are occasions when every vessel will break from her moorings, and since, if she does, she becomes a menace to those about her; the owner's duty, as in other similar situations, to provide against resulting injuries is a function of three variables: (1) The probability that she will break away; (2) the gravity of the resulting injury, if she does; (3) the burden of adequate precautions. Possibly it serves to bring this notion into relief to state it in algebraic terms: if the probability be called P; the injury, L; and the burden, B; liability depends upon whether B is less than L multiplied by P: i.e., whether B < PL. Applied to the situation at bar, the likelihood that a barge will break from her fasts and the damage she will do, vary with the place and time; for example, if a storm threatens, the danger is greater; so it is, if she is in a crowded harbor where moored barges are constantly being shifted about. On the other hand, the barge must not be the bargee's prison, even though he lives aboard; he must go ashore at times. We need not say whether, even in such crowded waters as New York Harbor a bargee must be aboard at night at all; it may be that the custom is otherwise . . . and that, if so, the situation is one where custom should control. We leave that question open; but we hold that it is not in all cases a sufficient answer to a bargee's absence without excuse, during working hours, that he has properly made fast his barge to a pier, when he leaves her. In the case at bar the bargee left at five o'clock in the afternoon of January 3rd and the flotilla broke away at about two o'clock in the afternoon of the following day, twenty-one hours afterwards. The bargee had been away all the time, and we hold that his fabricated story was affirmative evidence that he had no excuse for his absence. At the locus in quo — especially during the short January days and in the full tide of war activity — barges were being constantly "drilled" in and out. Certainly it was not beyond reasonable expectation that, with the inevitable haste and bustle, the work might not be done with adequate care. In such circumstances we hold — and it is all that we do hold — that it was a fair requirement that the Conners Company should have a bargee aboard (unless he had some excuse for his absence), during the working hours of the daylight.

[The reduction of the recovery was affirmed.]

———————

1. Is this a negligence case, a proximate cause case, or a duty case? The court says that it is a duty case. Should it be placed in the duty chapter? Why is it here?

2. In applying Hand's formula, how do you obtain numbers for probability, gravity, burden, and injury (before the collision and sinking)?

3. Apply the Hand formula to *Blyth v. Birmingham Waterworks Co.* Is the formula helpful?

4. If you plan to marry, will you use such an equation to compare one choice with another? What factors will you weigh, and where will you get the numbers?

5. The cost-benefit nature of Judge Hand's formula has made it the keystone of the law and economics movement. *See* Richard Posner, *A Theory of Negligence*, 1 J. Legal Stud. 29, 32–33 (1972). For an evaluation of Posner's theory, see Frank Vandall, *Judge Posner's Negligence-Efficiency Theory: A Critique*, 35 Emory L.J. 383 (1986).

6. Seven years before *Carroll Towing*, Judge Learned Hand stated: "The degree of care demanded of a person by an occasion is the resultant of three factors: the likelihood that his conduct will injure others, taken with the seriousness of the injury if it happens, and balanced against the interest which he must sacrifice to avoid the risk.

All these are practically not susceptible of any quantitative estimate—even theoretically. For this reason a solution always involves some preference or choice among incommensurables, and is consigned to a jury. . . ." *Conway v. O'Brien*, 111 F.2d 611, 612 (2d Cir. 1940).

What does this mean?

7. Judge Posner has recently concluded that developing numerical values for tort policies may not be possible:

> Ordinarily, and here, the parties do not give the jury the information required to quantify the variables that the Hand Formula picks out as relevant. That is why the formula has greater analytic than operational significance. Conceptual as well as practical difficulties in monetizing personal injuries may continue to frustrate efforts to measure expected accident costs with the precision that is possible, in principle at least, in measuring the other side of the equation—the cost or burden of precaution.
>
> . . . For many years to come juries may be forced to make rough judgments of reasonableness, intuiting rather than measuring the factors in the Hand Formula; and so long as their judgment is reasonable, the trial judge has no right to set it aside, let alone substitute his own judgment.

McCarty v. Pheasant Run, Inc., 826 F.2d 1554 (7th Cir. 1987). What does Judge Posner mean by saying the Hand formula has "greater analytic than operational significance?" What has more predictive value, the Hand formula or a Torts hornbook? Is Judge Posner really saying anything new here?

Adams v. Bullock

Court of Appeals of New York, 1919
125 N.E. 93

Cardozo, J. The defendant runs a trolley line in the city of Dunkirk, employing the overhead wire system. At one point, the road is crossed by a bridge or culvert which carries the tracks of the Nickle Plate and Pennsylvania railroads. Pedestrians often use the bridge as a short cut between streets, and children play on it. On April 21, 1916, the plaintiff, a boy of twelve years, came across the bridge, swinging a wire about eight feet long. In swinging it, he brought it in contact with the defendant's trolley wire, which ran beneath the structure. The side of the bridge was protected by a parapet eighteen inches wide. Four feet seven and three-fourths inches below the top of the parapet, the trolley wire was strung. The plaintiff was shocked and burned when the wires came together. He had a verdict at Trial Term, which has been affirmed at the Appellate Division by a divided court.

We think the verdict cannot stand. The defendant in using an overhead trolley was in the lawful exercise of its franchise. Negligence, therefore, cannot be imputed to it because it used that system and not another. . . . There was, of course, a duty to adopt all reasonable precautions to minimize the resulting perils. We think there is no evidence that this duty was ignored. The trolley wire was so placed that no one standing on the bridge or even bending over the parapet could reach it. Only some extraordinary casualty, not fairly within the area of ordinary provision, could make it a thing of danger. Reasonable care in the use of a destructive agency imports a high degree of vigilance. . . . But no vigilance, however alert, unless fortified by the gift of prophecy, could have predicted the point upon the route where such an accident would occur. It might with equal reason have been expected anywhere else. At any point upon the route, a mischievous or thoughtless boy might touch the wire with a metal pole, or fling another wire across it. . . . If unable to reach it from the walk, he might stand upon a wagon or climb upon a tree. No special danger at this bridge warned the defendant that there was need of special measures of precaution. No like accident had occurred before. No custom had been disregarded. We think that ordinary caution did not involve forethought of this extraordinary peril. . . . There is, we may add, a distinction, not to be ignored, between electric light and trolley wires. The distinction is that the former may be insulated. Chance of harm, though remote, may betoken negligence, if needless. Facility of protection may impose a duty to protect. With trolley wires, the case is different. Insulation is impossible. Guards here and there are of little value. To avert the possibility of this accident and others like it at one point or another on the route, the defendant must have abandoned the overhead system, and put the wires underground. Neither its power nor its duty to make the change is shown. To hold it liable upon the facts exhibited in this record would be to charge it as an insurer.

The judgment should be reversed and a new trial granted.

---

1. What factors did the court weigh in deciding whether there was evidence of negligence to give to the jury?

2. Would the "lawful franchise" argument be effective today? Why not?

3. In *Gulf Refining Co. v. Williams*, 183 Miss. 723, 185 So. 234 (1938), the plaintiff was injured while removing the bung hole cap from a drum of gasoline. The drum exploded from a spark. The defense was that "no such happening had ever before been heard of." The "spark was produced by the condition of unrepair in the threads of the bung cap."

The court found for the plaintiff, because a reasonable person should have known of "the condition [of the bung threads] and should reasonably have anticipated . . . that a sudden fire or explosion would be caused by the stated condition of unrepair." Why did the Court in *Gulf Refining* decide for the plaintiff? What does this add to the negligence equation? Why did the court reach a verdict contrary to *Adams*?

4. Does a golfer, preparing to drive a ball, have a duty to warn persons not in the intended line of flight who are on another tee or fairway? No. *Rinaldo v. McGovern*, 587 N.E.2d 264 (N.Y. 1991). *See also Bolton v. Stone*, [1951] A.C. 850.

Rivera v. New York City Transit Authority

Court of Appeals of New York, 1991
569 N.E.2d 432

BELLACOSA, JUDGE.

In 1980, Milton Rivera fell from the platform of the 42nd Street and 6th Avenue Manhattan subway station onto the tracks and was struck by an arriving train. He died several hours later. His widow sued the New York City Transit Authority (TA) for damages. After a trial, the jury returned a verdict in plaintiff's favor. . . .

The theory of plaintiff's case was that the subway operator was negligent in speeding into the station and in not taking measures to stop the train as soon as he first observed the decedent on the platform. The defendant TA contends principally on this appeal that the trial court erred in refusing its requested instructions on the emergency doctrine. . . . This argument has merit and a new trial is required.

Viewing the evidence, as we must, in the light most favorably towards giving the requested emergency doctrine instruction to the jury, we conclude that it was reversible error for the trial court to deny the TA's request. . . . This doctrine recognizes that when an actor is faced with a sudden and unexpected circumstance which leaves little or no time for thought, deliberation or consideration, or causes the actor to be reasonably so disturbed that the actor must make a speedy decision without weighing alternative courses of conduct, the actor may not be negligent if the actions taken are reasonable and prudent in the emergency context. . . . A person in such an emergency situation "cannot reasonably be held to the same accuracy of judgment or conduct as one who has had full opportunity to reflect, even though it later appears that the actor made the wrong decision." . . . A party requesting the emergency instruction is entitled to have the jury so charged if some evidence of a qualifying emergency is presented. If, under some reasonable view of the evidence, an actor was confronted by a sudden and unforeseen occurrence not of the actor's own making, then the reasonableness of the conduct in the face of the emergency is for the jury, which should be appropriately instructed. . . .

The evidence in this case presents a person, awaiting the arrival of the train, suddenly and unexpectedly falling off the platform and onto the tracks. In light of defendant's expert's testimony that the operator was driving the train at a reasonable and prudent speed upon entering the station, the jury—if it believed that witness—could reasonably have concluded that the train was not traveling at an excessive speed and that the accident was unavoidable. Evidence was also adduced indicating that an operator entering the station can observe passengers within only 3 1/2 feet of the edge of the platform. Thus, a reasonable view of the evidence could support the conclusion that the accident was sudden and unexpected in that when the operator first saw Rivera he was standing normally near the edge of the platform but then staggered and fell onto the tracks without warning. A disinterested eyewitness confirmed these key details. Despite some conflicting testimony from other witnesses, the jury could reasonably have concluded that the operator released the brake handle as soon as he observed decedent's sudden, inseparable act of staggering and falling. The entire incident unfolded within seconds, during which flash of time the operator had to assess, deliberate, consider alternatives, and react to attempt to make the safest and speediest choice. The operator, in addition to everything else, also had to be mindful of the consequences to passengers on his train if the train were subjected to a sudden emergency stop. . . .

HANCOCK, JUDGE (dissenting).

I would affirm. The Appellate Division properly held that an emergency charge was not warranted. The emergency doctrine is predicated on the notion that an actor confronted with a sudden and unexpected event which leaves little or no time for thought, deliberation or consideration, or which reasonably causes the actor to make a quick decision without weighing alternative courses of action, cannot be judged in the same way as someone who has had a full opportunity to reflect before acting. . . .

That the actor is confronted with a sudden and unexpected event does not, without more, implicate the emergency doctrine. If that were the law, an emergency charge would be required in almost every accident case because an accident by its very nature is sudden and unexpected. What justifies the charge is the effect that the sudden and unexpected event has on the actor in the particular circumstances—i.e., whether it puts the actor in a position of having to make a split second choice or decision concerning the preferred course of conduct necessary to avoid harm to the endangered party. . . . In such a situation, there is no negligence if the choice or decision is reasonable under the circumstances, even though the actor did not use the best judgment. . . . In this case, neither plaintiff's nor defendant's version of the facts requires an assessment of the reasonableness of the motorman's choice of action in the face of an emergency.

According to plaintiff, the motorman saw or should have seen plaintiff's decedent staggering near the edge of the platform for several seconds prior to decedent's fall onto the tracks. The train then was still 200 to 344 feet away. Had the motorman taken steps then to stop or slow down, the accident could have been avoided. The claim of negligence is that he did not do so. This claim has nothing to do with the motorman's choice of action when confronted with an emergency. On the contrary, it involves the motorman's failure to act some seconds before any emergency arose. That this failure undoubtedly contributed to the emergency situation which later developed does not, of course, call for an emergency charge, but actually militates against it. . . . Thus, the emergency doctrine cannot apply if plaintiff's evidence is accepted.

---

1. Why did the trial court fail to charge on the emergency doctrine? Define the doctrine. Is it really necessary? Isn't it part of the "reasonable conduct in the circumstances" test? Why does it seem so important here?

2. What are the limits of the emergency doctrine? Why not raise it in every case? What if the defendant created the emergency?

Widmyer v. Southeast Skyways, Inc.

Supreme Court of Alaska, 1978
584 P.2d 1

Boochever, Chief Justice.

On November 15, 1974, a DeHavilland Beaver airplane, owned by Southeast Skyways, Inc, and piloted by Richard Norvell, crashed in the waters of False Bay, Chichagof Island, Alaska. The pilot and three passengers, Peggy Rae Welch, Joshua John Welch and Dermott R. O'Toole, were killed in the crash. Appellants, Carmelita Widmyer and A. Dermott OToole, personal representatives of the estates of the deceased passengers, brought this action for wrongful death against appellees, Southeast Skyways, Inc., and James Norvell, personal representative of the estate of Richard Norvell.

A jury returned a verdict for Skyways. . . .

It is not disputed that Skyways owed plaintiffs' deceased a duty of care. The controversy on appeal concerns the nature of that duty.

Plaintiffs submitted the following proposed instruction to the court:

> Common carriers owe a duty of utmost care and the vigilance of a very cautious person toward their passengers. They are responsible for any, even the slightest, negligence, and are required to do all that human care, vigilance and foresight reasonably can do under all the circumstances.

The instruction was not given. . . .

Although there is no Alaska statute to the contrary, we believe that a general duty of due care instruction is inadequate with respect to common carriers transporting passengers for hire. Singular treatment of common carriers is deeply rooted in common law and retains continuing validity in public policy.[10] Airline passengers are completely at the mercy of the carrier and are entitled to assume that the highest degree of care is being taken for their safety. . . .

Skyways cites no case in which the higher degree of care imposed on common carriers has been abandoned. Indeed, the rule has been repeatedly reaffirmed. We hold that the superior court erred in denying plaintiffs' proposed instruction.

. . . .

Reversed and remanded.

---

10. Congress has recognized this policy. 49 U.S.C. § 1421 provides in part:
    (a) the Administrator [of the Federal Aviation Administration] is empowered and it shall be his duty to promote safety of flight of civil aircraft in air commerce by prescribing and revising from time to time [various standards, rules and regulations]. . . .
    (b) in prescribing standards, rules, and regulations, and in issuing certificates under this subchapter, the Administrator shall give full consideration to perform [sic] their services with the highest possible degree of safety in the public interest. . . .

1. Draw the line between negligence and "utmost care." How is utmost care different from strict liability? How does the "utmost care" standard affect settlement negotiations?

2. Is a commercial bus or a cab a common carrier? Suppose your client's four-year-old child was being transported to the zoo in a nine-passenger van owned by the day-care center, does the carrier rule apply to the day-care center?

3. The standard of care in Georgia is: "Ordinary care and diligence is that care and diligence which every prudent man takes under the same and similar circumstances." *Sanders v. Central of Ga. Ry. Co.*, 123 Ga. 763, 51 S.E. 728 (1905).

4. Degrees of Negligence, Automobile Guest Passenger Statutes, and Good Samaritan Acts.

Degrees of Negligence

In order to make negligence analysis more precise, several jurisdictions divided negligence cases into categories. The three categories, based on degrees of negligence, were (1) slight negligence, (2) ordinary negligence, and (3) gross negligence. The courts applied the doctrine of degrees of negligence to automobile guest statutes and good Samaritan laws. Illinois and Kansas extended the doctrine to all negligence cases, however. *See Wabash R.R. Co. v. Henks*, 91 Ill. 406 (1879); *Wichita & Western Rwy. Co. v. Davis*, 37 Kan. 743, 16 P. 78 (1887). The distinctions are as follows:

1. *Slight negligence* involves a failure to exercise great care.

2. *Ordinary negligence* is the failure to exercise ordinary or reasonable care.

3. *Gross negligence* is the absence of the exercise of slight care or is the omission or commission of an act with a conscious indifference to consequences.

Some jurisdictions equate gross negligence with "recklessness," "willfulness," and "wantonness." *See* Edwin H. Byrd, *Reflections on Willful, Wanton, Reckless, and Gross Negligence*, 48 La. L. Rev. 1383 (1988).

Over the years of trying to apply degrees of negligence, courts were flooded with appeals as they attempted to differentiate among the categories. The degrees of negligence doctrine proved to be too burdensome for the courts, but some continue to refer to gross negligence when instructing the jury on punitive damages. *See* Nanette A. O'Donnell, *Punitive Damages in Florida Negligence Cases: How Much Negligence Is Enough?*, 42 U. Miami L. Rev. 803 (1988).

Automobile Guest Passenger Statutes

A guest passenger statute allows a guest passenger to recover for personal injury against his or her host driver *only* when the host's conduct amounts to more than ordinary negligence. This required higher degree of negligence must be willful, wanton, reckless, or gross negligence.

The policy behind these statutes, which originated in the early twentieth century, was (1) to prevent collusion and fraud between the host driver and the guest against insurance companies and (2) to preserve the hospitality of a host driver. The theory was that the insurance companies would be flooded with collusive claims, where the driver and the passenger would conceal the truth from the court.

However, definitional problems such as "who is a guest," "are family members guests," "what if the guest bought the gasoline," "what if the host had some social or business desire in providing the guest with a ride," plagued the statutes.

The most important guest passenger statute case is *Brown v. Merlo*, 8 Cal. 3d 855, 106 Cal. Rptr. 388, 506 P.2d 212 (1973). *Brown* found the California guest statute unconstitutional for violating the equal protection clauses of the California and U.S. Constitutions. The vast majority of states have repealed their guest statutes.

Good Samaritan Acts

A physician who sees an injured motorist in need of urgent medical attention can refuse to help without fear of liability. In response, courts created exceptions to the no duty to rescue rule. To encourage physicians to render assistance, all fifty states and the District of Columbia have enacted Good Samaritan Acts. These acts protect the physician from liability if he or she stops and provides aid. *See Colby v. Schwartz*, 78 Cal. App. 3d 885, 892, 144 Cal. Rptr. 624, 628 (1978). To complement these statutes, immunity statutes were also enacted to protect virtually every type of health care professional who offers his or her services in emergencies. Some states do not extend immunity to acts constituting gross negligence or willful and wanton misconduct. *See Dahl v. Turner*, 80 N.M. 564, 458 P.2d 816 (1969); *Ballou v. Sigma Nu General Fraternity*, 291 S.C. 140, 352 S.E.2d 488 (Ct. App. 1986).

Problem

Jennifer was robbed and shot at 10:00 p.m. while obtaining money from an automated teller machine (ATM). Is there evidence of the bank's negligence to give to the jury? What other facts do you need?

1. The Reasonable Person

Vaughan v. Menlove

Court of Common Pleas, 1837
3 Bing. (N.C.) 467, 132 Eng. Rep. 490

[A fire ignited on the defendant's land and spread causing damage to the plaintiff's buildings. The defendant had built a hay rick near the border of his property and had been told that the rick was likely to ignite, spread, and damage the plaintiff's cottages. The defendant denied that he was negligent.]

At the trial it appeared that the rick in question had been made by the defendant near the boundary of his own premises; that the hay was in such a state when put together, as to give rise to discussion on the probability of fire; that though there were conflicting opinions on the subject, yet during a period of five weeks, the Defendant was repeatedly warned of his peril; that his stock was insured; and that upon one occasion, being advised to take the rick down to avoid all danger, he said "he would chance it." He made an aperture or chimney through the rick; but in spite, or perhaps in consequence of this precaution, the rick at length burst into flames from the spontaneous heating of its materials; the flames communicated to the Defendant's barn and stables, and thence to the Plaintiff's cottages, which were entirely destroyed.

Patteson, J. before whom the cause was tried, told the jury that the question for them to consider was whether the fire had been occasioned by gross negligence on the part of the Defendant; adding, that he was bound to proceed with such reasonable caution as a prudent man would have exercised under such circumstances.

A verdict having been found for the Plaintiff, a rule nisi for a new trial was obtained, on the ground that the jury should have been directed to consider, not whether the Defendant had been guilty of gross negligence with reference to the standard of ordinary prudence, a standard too uncertain to afford any criterion; but whether he had acted bona fide to the best of his judgment; if he had, he ought not to be responsible for the misfortune of not possessing the highest order of intelligence. The action under such circumstances was of the first impression.

. . . .

TINDAL, C.J. I agree that this is a case primae impressionis. . . . [T]here is a rule of law which says you must so enjoy your own property as not to injure that of another; and according to that rule the Defendant is liable for the consequence of his own neglect; and though the Defendant did not himself light the fire, yet mediately, he is as much the cause of it as if he had himself put a candle to the rick; for it is well known that hay will ferment and take fire if it be not carefully stacked. . . .

It is contended, however, that the learned Judge was wrong in leaving this to the jury as a case of gross negligence, and that the question of negligence was so mixed up with reference to what would be the conduct of a man of ordinary prudence that the jury might have thought the latter the rule by which they were to decide; that such a rule would be too uncertain to act upon; and that the question ought to have been whether the Defendant had acted honestly and bona fide to the best of his own judgment. . . . The care taken by a prudent man has always been the rule laid down; and as to the supposed difficulty of applying it, a jury has always been able to say, whether taking that rule as their guide, there has been negligence on the occasion in question.

Instead, therefore, of saying that the liability for negligence should be coextensive with the judgment of each individual, which would be as variable as the length of the foot of each individual, we ought rather to adhere to the rule which requires in all cases a regard to caution such as a man of ordinary prudence would observe. That was in substance the criterion presented to the jury in this case, and therefore the present rule must be discharged. . . .

———————

1. How can a person hold himself or herself to a standard other than what he or she thinks is best?

2. The "reasonable man" was the standard, but the "reasonable person" is now the accepted term.

3. What policy is the law trying to promote with the reasonable person standard?

4. In *Delair v. McAdoo*, 324 Pa. 392, 188 A. 181 (1936), the court stated:

> The accident occurred when defendant, proceeding in the same direction as plaintiff, sought to pass him. As defendant drew alongside of plaintiff, the left rear tire of his car blew out, causing it to swerve and come into contact with the plaintiff's car. The latter's theory at trial was that defendant was negligent in driving with defective tires.
>
> . . . .
>
> There is always a duty of reasonable inspection.
>
> "Generally speaking, it is the duty of one operating a motor vehicle on the public highways to see that it is in reasonably good condition and properly equipped, so that it may be at all times controlled, and not become a source of danger to its occupants or to other travellers. To this end, the owner or operator of a motor vehicle must exercise reasonable care in the inspection of the machine and is chargeable with notice of everything that such inspection would disclose."
>
> It has been held in other states that the question whether a particular person is negligent in failing to know that his tires are in too poor a condition for ordinary operation on the highways is a question of fact for the jury. . . . In the instant case the testimony relative to the defect was as follows: A witness for the plaintiff stated that the tire "was worn pretty well through. You could see the tread in the tire — the inside lining." The witness later described this inside lining as the "fabric." The fact that the tire was worn through to and into the fabric over its entire area was corroborated by another witness. The repairman who replaced the tire which had blown out stated that he could see "the breaker strip" which is just under the fabric of a tire. This testimony was contradicted by the defendant.
>
> . . . It is apparent that a tire so worn that the fabric is exposed is not in a condition for safe driving, and that such a defect will support a finding by a jury of negligence.

Is an expert required to testify in regard to the nature of the bald tires? What other things will a reasonable person be held to know?

Berberian v. Lynn

Supreme Court of New Jersey, 2004
845 A.2d 122

WALLACE, J.

Plaintiffs, Mary Berberian, the head nurse in a long-term care facility, and her husband, Emmanuel Berberian, sued defendant Edmund Gernannt, an institutionalized patient with Alzheimer's dementia, his estate (defendant), Diane Lynn, in her capacity as Gernannt's guardian, and M.H. Rainey, M.D., to recover damages for personal injuries she sustained when Gernannt pushed her. After closing arguments, the trial court instructed the jury that the applicable standard of negligence was that of "a reasonably prudent person who has Alzheimer's dementia." The jury found in favor of defendant. On appeal, plaintiffs argued that the trial court should have applied an objective "reasonable person" standard without taking into account Gernannt's mental disability. The Appellate Division disagreed with plaintiffs and affirmed the trial court. . . .

I.

On October 3, 1997, Gernannt, now deceased, was involuntarily committed to Bergen Pines County Hospital (Bergen Pines) with a diagnosis of senile dementia, Alzheimer's type. On October 13, 1997, he was transferred from the long-term care unit to the acute geriatric psychiatric unit because he became increasingly agitated and assaultive towards the staff. On November 5, 1997, Gernannt was transferred to the eighth floor, where a number of other Alzheimer's and dementia patients were housed.

Plaintiff first met Gernannt on November 8, 1997. At that time, she was a nurse supervisor in the long-term care unit and had over twenty years of experience working with Alzheimer's patients. She knew that Gernannt had dementia and a history of agitation, including prior acts of violence towards staff. With respect to that behavior, plaintiff reported in her notes that Gernannt "refused to go to bed[,] . . . was combative, agitated," and "[t]ried to hit staff." Plaintiff was also aware of the Bergen Pines standard patient aggression policy. That policy stated that if a patient with dementia is violent, aggressive, resistant or unredirectable, the nurse should retreat from the patient and call security for assistance.

On November 11, 1997, Gernannt attempted to leave the unit by way of the fire exit and set off the alarm. Nurse Christine Schell tried to redirect him, but he began hitting her. Schell backed away and walked down the hall to call security. Plaintiff then approached him and extended her hand to help him to his room. Gernannt grabbed plaintiff's hand, pulled her toward him and then pushed her back, causing her to fall and fracture her right leg.

On January 26, 1998, plaintiffs filed a complaint against Lynn, Gernannt, . . . While not disputing that Gernannt was an adjudicated incompetent, plaintiffs alleged that he, "without provocation negligently, recklessly and carelessly" struck plaintiff, causing her injuries. . . .

. . . .

After the close of the evidence portion of the trial, plaintiffs requested a "reasonable man" standard instruction. The trial court denied the request and charged as follows:

Now in determining the standard of care that defendant, Edmund Gernannt should have used on November 11th, 1997, you must measure his actions as you would *a reasonably prudent person who has Alzheimer's dementia*

. . . .

The jury returned a verdict in favor of defendant.

Plaintiffs appealed. The Appellate Division affirmed, holding that "the appropriate capacity-based standard of care for mentally incompetent defendants, such as Gernannt, is that of a reasonable prudent person who has Alzheimer's disease in light of the defendant's capacity." . . . In a concurring opinion, Judge Lintner concluded that Gernannt had no duty of care because his "dementia and corresponding inability to act reasonably . . . is the very reason for his being institutionalized and under the care of plaintiff." Based on that reasoning, Judge Lintner concluded that the trial court should have granted defendant's motion for involuntary dismissal. *Ibid*.

II.

Plaintiffs contend that it was error to use a capacity-based standard of care for the mentally incompetent Gernannt. Plaintiffs urge that this Court's ruling in *Cowan v. Doering*, 111 N.J. 451, 545 A.2d 159 (1988), which held that capacity-based standards should be used in comparative negligence cases against mentally disturbed persons, does not apply here.

. . . .

A.

Generally, the reasonable person standard applies to a mentally deficient person. Restatement (Second) of Torts Section 283B (1965) provides that:

> Unless the actor is a child, his insanity or other mental deficiency does not relieve the actor from liability for conduct which does not conform to the standard of a reasonable man under like circumstances.

"The rule that a mentally deficient adult is liable for his torts is an old one, dating back at least to 1616, at a time when the action for trespass rested upon the older basis of strict liability, without regard to any fault of the individual." *Id.* at Section 283B comment b.

The rule's persistence in modern law has been justified on the following grounds:

> 1. The difficulty of drawing any satisfactory line between mental deficiency and those variations of temperament, intellect, and emotional balance which cannot, as a practical matter, be taken into account in imposing liability for damage done.

> 2. The unsatisfactory character of the evidence of mental deficiency in many cases, together with the ease with which it can be feigned. . . .

> . . .

> 3. The feeling that if mental defectives are to live in the world they should pay for the damage they do, and that it is better that their wealth, if any, should be used to compensate innocent victims than that it should remain in their hands.

> 4. The belief that their liability will mean that those who have charge of them or their estates will be stimulated to look after them, keep them in order, and see that they do not do harm.

. . . .

However, the Restatement limits the distinction with respect to the standards of care governing the tort liability of children and *physically* disabled persons, but *not mentally* disabled persons. *See id.* at Section 283a (providing that a child must conform his or her conduct to that of "a reasonable person of like age, intelligence, and experience under like circumstances"); *see also id.* at Section 283C (providing that a physically disabled individual must conform his or her conduct to "that of a reasonable man under like disability").

III.

. . . . We hold that a mentally disabled patient, who does not have the capacity to control his or her conduct, does not owe his or her caregiver a duty of care.

. . . .

Most important, Gernannt was involuntarily admitted to Bergen Pines to prevent the very type of injury that is at the center of this lawsuit.

Conversely, plaintiff had knowledge of Gernannt's potential for violence and was trained to enlist the assistance of security when necessary. Plaintiff could readily control her behavior to deal with the foreseeable harm. In these circumstances, it would not be fair to impose a duty of care on Gernannt to his professional caregiver when the caregiver's job duties included preventing Gernannt from injuring himself and others. Moreover, plaintiff has the benefit of worker's compensation for her work-related injuries.

. . . .

---

1. Did the third point under the given Restatement section sound punitive to you? "The feeling that if mental defectives are to live in the world they should pay for the damage they do, and that it is better that their wealth, if any, should be used to compensate innocent victims than that it should remain in their hands." Restatement (Second) of Torts § 283B, Comment B (1965).

2. Do you think it was intentional for the Restatement to allow for subjectivity in determining negligence of children (age) and physically disabled persons (blind), without mentioning the standard for mentally disabled persons? Why?

Roberts v. State of Louisiana

Court of Appeals of Louisiana, 1981
396 So. 2d 566

LABORDE, JUDGE.

In this tort suit, William C. Roberts sued to recover damages for injuries he sustained in an accident in the lobby of the U.S. Post Office Building in Alexandria, Louisiana. Roberts fell after being bumped into by Mike Burson, the blind operator of the concession stand located in the building.

Plaintiff sued the State of Louisiana, through the Louisiana Health and Human Resources Administration, advancing two theories of liability: respondeat superior and negligent failure by the State to properly supervise and oversee the safe operation of the concession stand. The stand's blind operator, Mike Burson, is not a party to this suit although he is charged with negligence. The trial court ordered plaintiff's suit dismissed. . . .

We affirm the trial court's decision for the reasons which follow.

On September 1, 1977, at about 12:45 in the afternoon, operator Mike Burson left his concession stand to go to the men's bathroom located in the building. As he was walking down the hall, he bumped into plaintiff who fell to the floor and injured his hip. Plaintiff was 75 years old, stood 5′6″ and weighed approximately 100 pounds. Burson, on the other hand, was 25 to 26 years old, stood approximately 6′ and weighed 165 pounds.

At the time of the incident, Burson was not using a cane nor was he utilizing the technique of walking with his arm or hand in front of him.

Even though Burson was not joined as a defendant, his negligence or lack thereof is crucial to a determination of the State's liability. Because of its importance, we begin with it.

Plaintiff contends that operator Mike Burson traversed the area from his concession stand to the men's bathroom in a negligent manner. To be more specific, he focuses on the operator's failure to use his cane even though he had it with him in his concession stand.

In determining an actor's negligence, various courts have imposed differing standards of care to which handicapped persons are expected to perform. Professor William L. Prosser expresses one generally recognized modern standard of care as follows:

"As to his physical characteristics, the reasonable man may be said to be identical with the actor. The man who is blind . . . is entitled to live in the world and to have allowance made by others for his disability, and he cannot be required to do the impossible by conforming to physical standards which he cannot meet . . . At the same time, the conduct of the handicapped individual must be reasonable in the light of his knowledge of his infirmity, which is treated merely as one of the circumstances under which he acts . . . It is sometimes said that a blind man must use a greater degree of care than one who can see; but it is now generally agreed that as a fixed rule this is inaccurate, and that the correct statement is merely that he must take the precautions, be they more or less, which the ordinary reasonable man would take if he were blind." . . .

A careful review of the record in this instance reveals that Burson was acting as a reasonably prudent blind person would under these particular circumstances.

Mike Burson is totally blind. Since 1974, he has operated the concession stand located in the lobby of the post office building. It is one of twenty-three vending stands operated by blind persons under a program funded by the federal government and implemented by the State through the Blind Services Division of the Department of Health and Human Resources. Burson hired no employees, choosing instead to operate his stand on his own.

Prior to running the vending stand in Alexandria, Burson attended Arkansas Enterprises for the blind where he received mobility training. In 1972, he took a refresher course in mobility followed by a course on vending stand training. In that same year, he operated a concession stand in Shreveport, his first under the vending stand program. He later operated a stand at Centenary before going to Alexandria in 1974 to take up operations there.

On the date of the incident in question, Mike Burson testified that he left his concession stand and was on his way to the men's bathroom when he bumped into plaintiff. He, without hesitancy, admitted that at the time he was not using his cane, explaining that he relies on his facial sense which he feels is an adequate technique for short trips inside the familiar building. Burson testified that he does use a cane to get to and from work.

Plaintiff makes much of Burson's failure to use a cane when traversing the halls of the post office building. Yet, our review of the testimony received at trial indicates that it is not uncommon for blind people to rely on other techniques when moving around in a familiar setting. For example George Marzloff, the director of the Division of Blind Services, testified that he can recommend to the blind operators that they should use a cane but he knows that when they are in a setting in which they are comfortable, he would say that nine out of ten will not use a cane and in his personal opinion, if the operator is in a relatively busy area, the cane can be more of a hazard than an asset. Mr. Marzloff further testified that he felt a reasonably functioning blind person would learn his way around his work setting as he does around his home so that he could get around without a cane. Mr. Marzloff added that he has several blind people working in his office, none of whom use a cane inside that facility.

The only testimony in the record that suggests that Burson traversed the halls in a negligent manner was that elicited from plaintiff's expert witness, William Henry Jacobson. Jacobson is an instructor in peripathology, which he explained as the science of movement within the surroundings by visually impaired individuals. Jacobson, admitting that he conducted no study or examination of Mike Burson's mobility skills and that he was unfamiliar with the State's vending program, nonetheless testified that he would require a blind person to use a cane in traversing the areas outside the concession stand. He added that a totally blind individual probably should use a cane under any situation where there in an unfamiliar environment or where a familiar environment involves a change, whether it be people moving through that environment or strangers moving through that environment or just a heavy traffic within that environment.

Upon our review of the record, we feel that plaintiff has failed to show that Burson was negligent. Burson testified that he was very familiar with his surroundings, having worked there for three and a half years. He had special mobility training and his reports introduced into evidence indicate good mobility skills. He explained his decision to rely on his facial sense instead of his cane for these short trips in a manner which convinces us that it was a reasoned decision. Not only was Burson's explanation adequate, there was additional testimony from other persons indicating that such a decision is not an unreasonable one. Also important is the total lack of any evidence in the record showing that at the time of the incident, Burson engaged in any acts which may be characterized as negligence on his part. For example, there is nothing showing that Burson was walking too fast, not paying attention, et cetera. Under all of these circumstances, we conclude that Mike Burson was not negligent.

Our determination that Mike Burson was not negligent disposes of our need to discuss liability on the part of the State.

For the above and foregoing reasons, the judgment of the trial court dismissing plaintiff's claims against defendant is affirmed and all costs of this appeal are assessed against the plaintiff-appellant.

Affirmed.

---

1. What other disabilities might qualify for this treatment? What about a short or weak man or woman? What policy is being applied here? *See* Restatement (Second) of Torts § 283C.

2. What result where the blind plaintiff suffers injury because he or she cannot see? *See Hill v. Glenwood*, 124 Iowa 479, 100 N.W. 522 (1904).

3. Whether the person with the disability is the plaintiff or the defendant makes a difference in the standard of care that will be applied to that person. As is the case with children, discussed below, the nature of the activity at issue also matters.

4. What if the defendant is drunk, or high on pot?

5. Does the result change if the plaintiff is intoxicated? In *Robinson v. Pioche, Bayerque & Co.*, 5 Cal. 460 (1855), the court stated: "A drunken man is as much entitled to a safe street as a sober one, and much more in need of it." What is required for this theory to apply? Does it make a difference to the standard of care if the intoxicated person is the plaintiff or the defendant?

6. A paraplegic, who is licensed to drive, runs a stoplight in a van because he or she is not paying attention. What standard applies?

Problem

A sixteen-year-old was shot while hunting deer by his seventeen-year-old companion, the defendant. Does an adult standard or the child standard for negligence apply? Assume that the case arose in Arkansas. What policies are applicable?

Robinson v. Lindsay

Supreme Court of Washington, 1979 (en banc)
598 P.2d 392

UTTER, CHIEF JUSTICE.

An action seeking damages for personal injuries was brought on behalf of Kelly Robinson who lost full use of a thumb in a snowmobile accident when she was 11 years of age. The petitioner, Billy Anderson, 13 years of age at the time of the accident, was the driver of the snowmobile. After a jury verdict in favor of Anderson, the trial court ordered a new trial.

The single issue on appeal is whether a minor operating a snowmobile is to be held to an adult standard of care. The trial court failed to instruct the jury as to that standard and ordered a new trial because it believed the jury should have been so instructed. We agree and affirm the order granting a new trial.

The trial court instructed the jury under WPI 10.05 that:

> In considering the claimed negligence of a child, you are instructed that it is the duty of a child to exercise the same care that a reasonably careful child of the same age, intelligence, maturity, training and experience would exercise under the same or similar circumstances.

Respondent properly excepted to the giving of this instruction and to the court's failure to give an adult standard of care.

. . . Children are traditionally encouraged to pursue childhood activities without the same burdens and responsibilities with which adults must contend. *See* Bahr, *Tort Law and the Games Kids Play*, 23 S.D.L. Rev. 275 (1978). As a result, courts evolved a special standard of care to measure a child's negligence in a particular situation.

In *Roth v. Union Depot Co.*, 13 Wash. 525, 43 P. 641 (1896), Washington joined "the overwhelming weight of authority" in distinguishing between the capacity of a child and that of an adult. As the court then stated, at page 544:

> [I]t would be a monstrous doctrine to hold that a child of inexperience — and experience can come only with years — should be held to the same degree of care in avoiding danger as a person of mature years and accumulated experience.

The court went on to hold, at page 545:

> The care or caution required is according to the capacity of the child, and this is to be determined ordinarily by the age of the child.
>
> > ". . . a child is held . . . only to the exercise of such degree of care and discretion as is reasonably to be expected from children of his age."

The current law in this state is fairly reflected in WPI 10.05, given in this case. In the past we have always compared a child's conduct to that expected of a reasonably careful child of the same age, intelligence, maturity, training and experience. This case is the first to consider the question of a child's liability for injuries sustained as a result of his or her operation of a motorized vehicle or participation in an inherently dangerous activity.

Courts in other jurisdictions have created an exception to the special child standard because of the apparent injustice that would occur if a child who caused injury while engaged in certain dangerous activities were permitted to defend himself by saying that other children similarly situated would not have exercised a degree of care higher than his, and he is, therefore, not liable for his tort. Some courts have couched the exception in terms of children engaging in an activity which is normally one for adults only. *See, e.g., Dellwo v. Pearson*, 259 Minn. 452, 107 N.W.2d 859, 97 A.L.R.2d 866 (1961) (operation of a motorboat). We believe a better rationale is that when the activity a child engages in is inherently dangerous, as is the operation of powerful mechanized vehicles, the child should be held to an adult standard of care.

Other courts adopting the adult standard of care for children engaged in adult activities have emphasized the hazards to the public if the rule is otherwise. We agree with the Minnesota Supreme Court's language in its decision in *Dellwo v. Pearson, supra* at 457–58:

> Certainly in the circumstances of modern life, where vehicles moved by powerful motors are readily available and frequently operated by immature individuals, we should be skeptical of a rule that would allow motor vehicles to be operated to the hazard of the public with less than the normal minimum degree of care and competence.

Dellwo applied the adult standard to a 12-year-old defendant operating a motorboat. Other jurisdictions have applied the adult standard to minors engaged in analogous activities. *Goodfellow v. Coggburn*, 98 Idaho 202, 203–04, 560 P.2d 873 (1977) (minor operating tractor); *Williams v. Esaw*, 214 Kan. 658, 668, 522 P.2d 950 (1974) (minor operating motorcycle); *Perricone v. DiBartolo*, 14 Ill. App. 3d 514, 520, 302 N.E.2d 637 (1973) (minor operating gasoline-powered minibike); *Krahn v. LaMeres*, 483 P.2d 522, 525–26 (Wyo. 1971) (minor operating automobile). The holding of minors to an adult standard of care when they operate motorized vehicles is gaining approval from an increasing number of courts and commentators. . . .

The operation of a snowmobile likewise requires adult care and competence. . . .

At the time of the accident, the 13-year-old petitioner had operated snowmobiles for about 2 years. When the injury occurred, petitioner was operating a 30-horsepower snowmobile at speeds of 10 to 20 miles per hour. The record indicates that the machine itself was capable of 65 miles per hour. Because petitioner was operating a powerful motorized vehicle, he should be held to the standard of care and conduct expected of an adult.

The order granting a new trial is affirmed.

---

1. What would happen if there were no special standard for children? What incentive would be created? What impact does the role of the child (plaintiff or defendant) play in the standard of care?

2. When you see a six-year-old on a bicycle coming at you, what thoughts go through your mind? What are your thoughts when you see a snowmobile coming at you at fifty miles per hour?

3. In a Pennsylvania case a five-year-old hit a six-year-old with a stick. The court held that the five-year-old was conclusively presumed incapable of negligence:

> The application of this standard is clarified by the use of several presumptions delineating convenient points to aid in drawing the uncertain line between capacity to appreciate and guard against danger and incapacity: (1) minors under the age of seven years are conclusively presumed incapable of negligence; (2) minors between the ages of seven and fourteen years are presumed incapable of negligence, but the presumption is a rebuttable one that weakens as the fourteenth year is approached; (3) minors over the age of fourteen years are presumptively capable of negligence, with the burden placed on the minor to prove incapacity.

Dunn v. Teti, 280 Pa. Super. 399, 421 A.2d 782 (1980). What is the policy behind *Dunn*? Argue for the plaintiff. Many courts have abandoned the age categories in favor of fact findings individual to the particular case.

2. The Professional

Boyce v. Brown

Supreme Court of Arizona, 1938
77 P.2d 455

LOCKWOOD, JUDGE. Berlie B. Boyce and Nannie E. Boyce, his wife, hereinafter called plaintiffs, brought suit against Edgar H. Brown, hereinafter called defendant, to recover damages for alleged malpractice by the defendant upon the person of Nannie E. Boyce. The case was tried to a jury and, at the close of the evidence for plaintiffs, the court granted a motion for an instructed verdict in favor of the defendant, ... Judgment was rendered on the verdict, and, after the usual motion for new trial was overruled, this appeal was taken.

About September 1, 1927, plaintiffs engaged the services of defendant, who for many years had been a practicing physician and surgeon in Phoenix, to reduce a fracture of Mrs. Boyce's ankle. This was done by means of an operation which consisted, in substance, of making an incision at the point of fracture, bringing the broken fragments of bone into apposition, and permanently fixing them in place by means of a metal screw placed in the bone. Defendant continued to attend Mrs. Boyce for three or four weeks following such operation until a complete union of the bone had been established, when his services terminated. There is no serious contention in the record that defendant did not follow the approved medical standard in the treatment of the fractured bone up to this time. No further professional relations existed between the parties until years later, in November, 1934, when Mrs. Boyce again consulted him, complaining that her ankle was giving her considerable pain. He examined the ankle, wrapped it with adhesive tape, and then filed the edge of an arch support, which he had made for her seven years before, and which, from use, had grown so thin that the edge was sharp. About a week later he removed the bandage. Her ankle, however, did not improve after this treatment, but continued to grow more painful until January, 1936, some two years later. At this last-mentioned time she returned to defendant, who again examined the ankle. A few days later she went to visit Dr. Kent of Mesa, who, on hearing the history of the case, and noticing some discoloration and swelling, caused an X-ray of the ankle to be made. This X-ray showed that there had been some necrosis of the bone around the screw. Dr. Kent operated upon Mrs. Boyce, removing the screw, and she made an uneventful recovery, the ankle becoming practically normal.

There are certain general rules of law governing actions of malpractice, which are almost universally accepted by the courts, and which are applicable to the present situation. We state them as follows: (1) One licensed to practice medicine is presumed to possess the degree of skill and learning which is possessed by the average member of the medical profession in good standing in the community in which he practices, and to apply that skill and learning, with ordinary and reasonable care, to cases which come to him for treatment. . . . (3) In order to sustain a verdict for the plaintiffs in an action for malpractice, the standard of medical practice in the community must be shown by affirmative evidence, and, unless there is evidence of such a standard, a jury may not be permitted to speculate as to what the required standard is, or whether the defendant has departed therefrom. *Butler* v. *Rule, supra; Rising v. Veatch,* 117 Cal. App. 404, 3 Pac. (2d) 1023; *Connelly v. Cone,* 205 Mo. App. 395, 224 S.W. 1011. (4) Negligence on the part of a physician or surgeon in the treatment of a case is never presumed, but must be affirmatively proven, and no presumption of negligence nor want of skill arises from the mere fact that a treatment was unsuccessful, failed to bring the best results, or that the patient died. 48 C.J. 1142, 1143, and cases cited. (5) The accepted rule is that negligence on the part of a physician or surgeon, by reason of his departure from the proper standard of practice, must be established by expert medical testimony, unless the negligence is so grossly apparent that a layman would have no difficulty in recognizing it. . . .

The . . . question is whether the examination and treatment given by defendant departed from the established standard for cases like that of Mrs. Boyce. The only testimony we have which, in any manner, bears upon medical standards or the proper treatment of Mrs. Boyce in November, 1934, is that of Dr. Kent, who performed the operation on the ankle in January, 1936, and of defendant. The latter testified that he did what was required by Mrs. Boyce's condition as it existed then. Dr. Kent's testimony as to the condition he found in 1936, and what he did, is clear and distinct. He was asked as to how long prior to that time the screw should have been removed, and stated that he could not answer; that, if the ankle was in the same condition as it was when he operated, he would say that the screw should have been removed, but that it was impossible for him to testify as to when the condition justifying removal arose. . . . On cross-examination he testified that the method of uniting bone used by defendant was a standard one, and that the screw was not removed, as a rule, unless it made trouble. Nowhere, however, did Dr. Kent testify as to what was the proper standard of medical care required at the time defendant treated Mrs. Boyce in 1934, or as to whether, in his opinion, the treatment given deviated from that standard. The nearest he came to such testimony was the statement that he personally would have had an X-ray taken, but he did not say the failure to do so was a deviation from the proper standard of treatment.

Counsel for plaintiffs . . . urge that this comes within the exception to the general rule, in that a failure to [take an X-ray] is such obvious negligence that even a layman knows it to be a departure from the proper standard. We think this contention cannot be sustained. It is true that most laymen know that the X-ray usually offers the best method of diagnosing physical changes of the interior organs of the body, and particularly of the skeleton, short of an actual opening of the body for ocular examination, but laymen cannot say that in all cases where there is some trouble with the internal organs that it is a departure from standard medical practice to fail to take and X-ray. Such things are costly and do not always give a satisfactory diagnosis, or even as good a one as other types of examination may give. . . . [W]e think it is going too far to say that the failure to take an X-ray of Mrs. Boyce's ankle at that time was so far a departure from ordinary medical standards that even laymen would know it to be gross negligence. Since, therefore, there was insufficient evidence in the record to show that defendant was guilty of malpractice, . . . the court properly instructed a verdict in favor of the defendant.

The judgment of the superior court is affirmed.

———————

1. The requirement of an expert witness in a medical malpractice case means that the plaintiff may lose if he or she cannot obtain one. Often doctors (and lawyers) do not wish to testify against their colleagues. *See Bernstein v. Alameda-Contra Costa Medical Assoc.*, 139 Cal. App. 2d 241, 293 P.2d 862 (1956). What are some solutions? While the old rule required that an expert be from the same locality as the defendant, this is no longer the case.

2. The expert witness must be able to testify to the standard of care of a reasonable physician in the circumstances, i.e., with the resources available to the defendant. Why is this important?

3. A professional is one whose work calls for special skills. They include doctors, dentists, psychiatrists, attorneys, architects, engineers and accountants. *See* W. Page Keeton et al., Prosser and Keeton on Torts (5th ed. 1984).

What about college teachers?

Jones v. O'Young

Supreme Court of Illinois, 1992
607 N.E.2d 224

Johnny Jones and Loretta Jones, plaintiffs, brought a medical malpractice action in the circuit court of Cook County against Roseland Community Hospital and Doctors Richard O'Young, Armanda Pacis, Ramasamy Kali-muthu and James So. . . . Dr. Kalimuthu is board certified in plastic surgery and general surgery. Dr. O'Young is an orthopedic surgeon and Dr. Pacis is a general surgeon. [The plaintiff, following a car crash, developed an infection that allegedly led to the amputation of his leg.]

. . . The court certified the following question of law:

> "In order to testify concerning the standard of care required of and deviations from the standard of care by a defendant physician specializing in an area of medicine, must the plaintiff's expert also specialize in the same area of medicine as the defendant, so that, in this case, the plaintiff's infectious disease specialist would not be qualified to testify against the defendant plastic surgeon, orthopedic surgeon, or general surgeon with regard to each defendant's care and treatment of the infectious disease, Pseudomonas osteomyelitis?"

We answer the question in the negative. We are not reviewing the trial court's decision as to the competency of Dr. Deam to testify and are considering only the question certified by the trial court. See *Purtill v. Hess*, 111 Ill. 2d 229, 251, 95 Ill. Dec. 305, 489 N.E.2d 867 (1986).

In *Purtill v. Hess*, 111 Ill. 2d 229, 95 Ill. Dec. 305, 489 N.E.2d 867 (1986), this court articulated the requirements necessary to demonstrate an expert physician's qualifications and competency to testify. First, the physician must be a licensed member of the school of medicine about which he proposes to testify. (*Purtill*, 111 Ill. 2d at 242–43, citing *Dolan v. Galluzzo*, 77 Ill. 2d 279, 32 Ill. Dec. 900, 396 N.E.2d 13 (1979).) Second, "the expert witness must show that he is familiar with the methods, procedures, and treatments ordinarily observed by other physicians, in either the defendant physician's community or a similar community." (*Purtill*, 111 Ill. 2d at 243.) Once the foundational requirements have been met, the trial court has the discretion to determine whether a physician is qualified and competent to state his opinion as an expert regarding the standard of care. *Purtill*, 111 Ill. 2d at 243.

By hearing evidence on the expert's qualifications and comparing the medical problem and the type of treatment in the case to the experience and background of the expert, the trial court can evaluate whether the witness has demonstrated a sufficient familiarity with the standard of care practiced in the case. The foundational requirements provide the trial court with the information necessary to determine whether an expert has expertise in dealing with the plaintiff's medical problem and treatment. Whether the expert is qualified to testify is not dependent on whether he is a member of the same specialty or subspecialty as the defendant but, rather, whether the allegations of negligence concern matters within his knowledge and observation.

If the plaintiff fails to satisfy either of the foundational requirements of *Purtill*, the trial court must disallow the expert's testimony. (*Purtill*, 111 Ill. 2d at 244.) The requirements are a threshold beneath which the plaintiff cannot fall without failing to sustain the allegations of his complaint. They monitor the course the plaintiff's action will take, and are sufficiently comprehensive in alerting the trial court to the concerns relevant in determining the admissibility of the expert's testimony.

If the trial court determines that the expert is qualified, the defendant is then in the position to direct the jury's attention to any infirmities in his testimony or his competency to testify. Cross-examination, argument and jury instructions provide defense counsel with the opportunity and means to challenge the expert's qualifications as well as the opinion he offers. Restricting the qualification of experts to those physicians who are members of the same specialty or subspecialty as the defendant would only upset the balance necessary to an adversarial system without any compensating benefit. Accordingly, we reaffirm this court's position in *Purtill* without qualification.

In its order, the trial court stated that "there is substantial ground for difference of opinion on this issue based upon the conflict" in the appellate court among the opinions in *Petkus, Northern Trust* and *Thomas*. We disagree.

. . . We believe the trial courts in these matters correctly applied the law as contained in *Purtill v. Hess*. We answer the question certified by the trial court in this matter in the negative and in so doing, reaffirm this court's decisions in *Purtill v. Hess*.

The cause is remanded to the circuit court for further proceedings.

———————

Avret v. McCormick, 246 Ga. 401, 271 S.E.2d 832 (1980), held that a nurse who had drawn blood over 2,000 times was qualified as an expert to testify against a doctor on the question of "standards of care in keeping sterile a needle used to draw blood from a patient."

Heath v. Swift Wings, Inc.

Court of Appeals of North Carolina, 1979
252 S.E.2d 526

On 3 August 1975 a Piper 180 Arrow airplane crashed immediately after takeoff from the Boone-Blowing Rock Airport. Killed in the crash was the pilot, Fred Heath; his wife, Jonna; their son, Karl; and a family friend, Vance Smathers. Valerie Heath, a daughter of Fred and Jonna Heath, and sister of Karl, became the sole survivor of the Heath family. This action was instituted by Richard E. Heath as ancillary administrator of the estates of Jonna and Karl Heath against (1) Swift Wings, Inc., the corporate owner of the aircraft, on the grounds of agency; (2) the four shareholders of Swift Wings, Inc.—Fred Heath, Frank Kish, Richard Kish, and Kermit

Rockett—alleging they actually constituted a de facto partnership, and (3) The Bank of Virginia Trust Company, Executor of the Estate of Frederick B. Heath, Jr.

Plaintiff's evidence, except to the extent it is quoted from the record, is briefly summarized as follows: Mary Payne Smathers Curry, widow of Vance Smathers, observed the takeoff of the Piper aircraft shortly after 5:00 o'clock on 3 August 1975. She observed Fred Heath load and reload the passengers and luggage, apparently in an effort to improve the balance of the aircraft. He also "walked around [the airplane] and looked at everything . . . She remembers seeing him and thinking that he's doublechecking it to be sure no one has slashed the tires." The airplane engine started promptly and the plane was taxied to the end of the runway where it paused for approximately five minutes before takeoff. The airplane came very close to the end of the runway before takeoff. However, "[t]he engine sounded good the entire time, and she did not recall hearing the engine miss or pop or backfire." After takeoff, the airplane "gained altitude but it didn't go up very high" and then "leveled off pretty low."

William B. Gough, Jr., a free-lance mechanical engineering consultant and pilot, testified concerning the operation and flight performance of the Piper 180 Arrow. He testified concerning the many factors affecting the takeoff capabilities of the Piper and the calculations to be made by the pilot before takeoff, utilizing flight performance charts. He testified that in his opinion, according to his calculations, the pilot should have used flaps to aid in the takeoff. Furthermore, he stated that in his opinion the reasonably prudent pilot should have made a controlled landing in the cornfield shortly after takeoff if he were experiencing difficulty attaining flight speed, and that if he had done so Jonna Heath and Karl Heath would have survived.

. . . .

After the customary motions at the conclusion of all the evidence, the case was submitted to the jury upon voluminous instructions by the trial court. The jury returned a verdict answering the following issue as indicated: "1. Was Fred Heath, Jr., negligent in the operation of PA—28R 'Arrow' airplane on August 3, 1975 as alleged in the complaint?" Answer: "No." Plaintiff appeals assigning error to the exclusion of certain evidence and to the charge to the jury. Defendants cross-appeal assigning error to the denial of the motions for a directed verdict by Swift Wings, Inc.

MORRIS, CHIEF JUDGE. . . .

Assignment of error No. 4 is directed to the trial court's charge concerning the definition of negligence and the applicable standard of care:

> "Negligence, ladies and gentlemen of the jury, is the failure of someone to act as a reasonably and careful and prudent person would under the same or similar circumstances. Obviously, this could be the doing of something or the failure to do something, depending on the circumstances. With respect to aviation negligence could be more specifically defined as the failure to exercise that degree of ordinary care and caution, which an ordinary prudent pilot having the same training and experience as Fred Heath, would have used in the same or similar circumstances."

It is a familiar rule of law that the standard of care required of an individual, unless altered by statute, is the conduct of the reasonably prudent man under the same or similar circumstances. . . . While the standard of care of the reasonably prudent man remains constant, the quantity or degree of care required varies significantly with the attendant circumstances. . . .

The trial court improperly introduced a subjective standard of care into the definition of negligence by referring to the "ordinary care and caution, which an ordinary prudent pilot having the same training and experience as Fred Heath, would have used in the same or similar circumstances." We are aware of the authorities which support the application of a greater standard of care than that of the ordinary prudent man for persons shown to possess special skill in a particular endeavor. . . . Indeed, our courts have long recognized that one who engages in a business, occupation, or profession must exercise the requisite degree of learning, skill, and ability of that calling with reasonable and ordinary care. . . . Furthermore, the specialist within a profession may be held to a standard of care greater than that required of the general practitioner. . . . Nevertheless, the professional standard remains an objective standard. For example, the recognized standard for a physician is established as "the standard of professional competence and care customary in similar communities among physicians engaged in his field of practice." . . .

Such objective standards avoid the evil of imposing a different standard of care upon each individual. The instructions in this case concerning the pilot's standard of care are misleading at best, and a misapplication of the law. They permit the jury to consider Fred Heath's own particular experience and training, whether outstanding or inferior, in determining the requisite standard of conduct, rather than applying a minimum standard generally applicable to all pilots. The plaintiff is entitled to an instruction holding Fred Heath to the objective minimum standard of care applicable to all pilots.

[F]or prejudicial errors in the charge, there must be a *New trial*.

---

1. What is the error in the charge to the jury? What is the appellate court's concern?

2. What is the standard of care for a pilot? Why?

3. What is the standard for the medical doctor? Without such a standard, what might the jury infer? With such a standard, what expense must the plaintiff bear?

4. What standard will be applied to an amateur mechanic who works on his friend's automobile?

5. The test for whether an expert must be provided to testify is whether a lay person can understand the nature of the defendant's work. If a lay person cannot understand, because the work is technical, an expert will be required. *See Aetna Ins. Co. v. Hellmuth, Obata & Kassabaum, Inc.*, 392 F.2d 472 (8th Cir. 1968):

Most of the cases stating the general rule on expert testimony to establish the standard of professional care required deal with physicians and surgeons, but the same principle is applicable to attorneys, architects and engineers and other professional men. . . .

Prosser notes that expert testimony is necessary to establish the standard of care required of those engaged in practicing medicine, as laymen are normally incompetent to pass judgment on questions of medical science or technique, but that

> "Where the matter is regarded as within the common knowledge of laymen, as where the surgeon saws off the wrong leg, or there is injury to a part of the body not within the operative field, it has been held that the jury may infer negligence without the aid of any expert." Prosser, Law of Torts 164 (3rd ed.)

It is a matter of common knowledge that it is often difficult to secure the services of a professional man to testify in a case involving a claim of dereliction of duty by a fellow member in the profession. This undoubtedly holds true in architectural circles as well as others. . . . It does appear that there are certain duties patently required of the architect that are within the common knowledge and experience of laymen serving as jurors. It requires no particular technical knowledge on the part of the jury to pass upon the failure to supervise the back-filling of the sewer ditch when specifically required under the contract, the failure to correct misaligned forms utilized in retaining and supporting a poured concrete wall, or the significance of a sewer pipe that is misaligned and crooked. The jury is competent to pass on these issues without knowledge of the professional skills and competency required of architects in the ordinary performance of their skilled duties. Questions relating to stress and strain and weight-bearing capacities of structural elements are beyond the ordinary comprehension of most laymen and the court and jury require expert enlightenment on issues of this type. It, therefore, appears that the general rule requiring expert testimony to establish a reasonable standard of professional care is necessary when issues are presented that are beyond the ordinary competency of laymen jurors, but is not necessary in passing on commonplace factual situations that the ordinary jury layman can readily grasp and understand.

6. In medical malpractice cases, the general rule is that the plaintiff's case will be dismissed, if the plaintiff does not provide an expert who will testify that the defendant doctor failed to exercise reasonable care. The Georgia Code provides:

Sec. 9-11-9.1. Affidavit to accompany charge of professional malpractice

(a) In any action for damages alleging professional malpractice, the plaintiff shall be required to file with the complaint an affidavit of an expert competent to testify, which affidavit shall set forth specifically at least one negligent act or omission claimed to exist and the factual basis for each such claim. . . .

. . . .

(e) . . . if a plaintiff fails to file an affidavit as required by this Code section contemporaneously with a complaint alleging professional malpractice and the defendant raises the failure to file such an affidavit in its initial responsive pleading, such complaint is subject to dismissal for failure to state a claim. . . .

O.C.G.A. § 9-11-9.1 (1995). What is the policy behind this? Why not obtain the standard from the defendant at trial? What policy is at work here? What does this requirement mean for the plaintiff? For the defendant?

7. *Furey v. Thomas Jefferson Univ. Hosp.*, 325 Pa. Super. 212, 472 A.2d 1083 (1984), presents the "two schools of thought" doctrine:

> This doctrine is called into play in medical malpractice cases where there is more than one method of accepted treatment for the patient's disease or injury. The rule is that, where competent medical authority is divided, a physician will not be liable if in the exercise of his judgment he followed a course of treatment supported by reputable, respectable, and reasonable medical experts.
>
> . . . .
>
> Here, the medical authority on the treatment of a severe bacterial infection was diametrically opposed. Dr. Bass testified that treatment should absolutely be limited to antibiotic therapy. The defense experts stated that surgical intervention was imperative, and that it would have constituted malpractice to have failed to operate at once.
>
> . . . .
>
> The testimony clearly showed a difference of medical opinion, expressed by physicians and surgeons of unquestioned standing and reputation, and the defendants were not negligent for having adopted the view held by the majority of their brethren who testified.

How if at all does this differ from the case where two experts disagree over the standard in the specific case?

Problem

Will broke his nose in a football game. He went to Dr. Callier to have it set. Will showed the doctor a picture of his face and said, "That is what my nose should look like."

Dr. Callier straightened the nose and took a little off the tip. He also removed an unsightly mole from Will's chin. There are dark marks where the skin was cut and stitched.

Will is furious because of the marks and because the nose on his face does not resemble his nose. To most observers, however, it looks very good. Discuss.

Pauscher v. Iowa Methodist Medical Center

Supreme Court of Iowa, 1987
408 N.W.2d 355

REYNOLDSON, CHIEF JUDGE.

August 1, 1982, Becky, age twenty-six, entered Iowa Methodist Medical Center (IMMC) to deliver her first child. The child, Brad, was born the next day and Becky was scheduled to be released August 6.

On the day she was to leave the hospital, Becky developed a fever and pain in her right side. She also began to discharge large amounts of blood in her urine. As a result, Becky's obstetrician, Dr. Mark, delayed her release and prescribed Macrodantin, a bacteriostatic drug.

Becky's symptoms continued on August 7, 1982. Dr. Mark telephoned defendant Dr. John Bardole, a urology specialist. The latter feared a potentially life-threatening obstruction might be present in Becky's urinary tract.

Bardole ordered intravenous administration of a more aggressive bacterial drug, Mandol. Blood tests were instituted. Bardole also ordered an intravenous pyelogram (IVP) to be run the next morning, August 8, to determine whether Becky's urinary tract was obstructed.

An IVP is a diagnostic procedure in which an iodine-containing contrast material, in this case Reno-M-60, is injected into the patient's veins. X-rays then taken of the urinary tract, highlighted by the dye material, often enable the physician to determine whether it is obstructed.

Administration of an IVP is not without risk. A relatively small percent of individuals will suffer some discomfort, including flushing, hives, and nausea. More serious reactions include significant trouble breathing and a severe drop in blood pressure. The record made in this trial also indicates 1 person in 100,000 to 1 person in 150,000 will die as a result of an IVP, less often than fatal reactions to penicillin.

Before the IVP was administered neither Dr. Bardole nor defendant Dr. Jeff Watters, the only radiologist present in IMMC's radiology department on the Sunday morning Becky died, ever saw or talked to her. Two of the shift nurses who had attended Becky testified they separately told Becky she was to have an IVP and briefly described its purpose. One told Becky she could get a mild reaction, like hives, or a severe reaction, like difficult breathing. The other nurse described only the possibility of a mild reaction, "just the warmth of the dye, that sort of thing."

These discussions were noted in Becky's charts four days after her death, as "a late entry," at the request of a supervisor. Neither nurse was acting at the direction of a doctor in visiting with Becky about the IVP, neither nurse told her a severe reaction could include anaphylactic shock and death, and neither asked Becky if she consented to the procedure.

. . . .

In this action the plaintiff, Becky's husband, the administrator of her estate, alleges Bardole and Watters failed to inform Becky about the possibility she could die from an IVP, and thus they failed to obtain her informed consent to the procedure. He also claims IMMC failed to adopt or carry out procedures sufficient to insure that Becky's informed consent was obtained before the IVP was administered.

At trial, plaintiff presented no expert testimony on the issue whether Bardole and Watters deviated from professional standards when they failed to inform Becky the administration of an IVP entailed a very remote risk of death. In the absence of such evidence the trial court, following our 1966 decision in *Grosjean v. Spencer*, 258 Iowa 685, 140 N.W.2d 139 (1966), granted the defendant doctors' motions for directed verdict. The court also granted IMMC's motion for directed verdict on the same ground, and apparently because the obligation to inform a patient of such risks is upon the doctor, not the hospital.

I. In this appeal we first address the issue whether the "patient rule" or the "professional rule" should apply in circumstances such as these. The two standards were identified and extensively discussed in *Cowman v. Hornaday*, . . . in which we applied the "patient rule" in a case of elective surgery. . . . We since have applied the same rule in *Moser v. Stallings*, . . . an elective cosmetic surgery situation, and, apparently without it becoming an issue, in *Van Iperen v. Van Bramer*, . . . a case that involved medication for a serious illness, not elective surgery.

As we noted in *Cowman*, the doctrine of informed consent arises out of the unquestioned principle that absent extenuating circumstances a patient has the right to exercise control over his or her body by making an informed decision concerning whether to submit to a particular medical procedure. . . . Thus, a doctor recommending a particular procedure generally has, among other obligations, the duty to disclose to the patient all material risks involved in the procedure. . . .

The "professional rule" we followed in *Grosjean* recognized the treating doctor's duty to "disclose danger of which he has knowledge and the patient does not — but should have — in order to determine whether to consent to the risk." . . . At the same time, however, we left the question whether that duty had been satisfied to the medical profession when we held this was "primarily a question of medical judgment." Because there was no expert testimony that the treating doctor "failed to do that which should have been done in . . . advising . . . plaintiff . . . [a] jury question on negligence was not created." We thus affirmed a judgment based on a directed verdict for the defendant doctor.

Recognizing the inherently paternalistic and authoritarian nature of the professional rule of disclosure, an expanding number of jurisdictions have rejected it for a judicially-fashioned standard [16 states]. . . .

Similarly, the professional rule has come under a barrage of criticism from current commentators. . . .

The authoritarian rationale that undergirds the professional rule is apparent in the record before us. Both defendant doctors testified the practice in the profession would be to avoid mentioning a risk of death to a patient scheduled for an IVP. Although both doctors took into consideration the remote chance of such a fatality—a factor we discuss later—both justified withholding this information on the ground it would produce an anxiety in the patient that might adversely affect the patient's condition during the procedure.

In this connection plaintiff's evidence disclosed the manufacturer's package insert accompanying the dye material contained no warning relating to a patient with anxiety, but did contain the following information:

> Adverse reactions accompanying the use of iodine-containing intravascular contrast agents are usually mild and transient although severe and life-threatening reactions, including fatalities, have occurred. . . .
>
> . . . The histamine-liberating effect of these compounds may induce an allergic-like reaction which may range in severity from rhinitis or angioneurotic edema to laryngeal or bronchial spasm or anaphylactoid shock.

Each doctor, however, testified that if the patient asked what might happen, he would reply that the patient could die from the IVP. The professional rule thus provides this information for the patient already apprehensive enough to ask, but denies it to one so lacking in anxiety that he or she is not motivated to inquire. A rule resulting in such anomalous treatment of patients has little to commend it.

On the other hand, under the patient rule we adopted for elective surgery in *Cowman*, the physician's duty to disclose is measured by the patient's need to have access to all information material to making a truly informed and intelligent decision concerning the proposed medical procedure. . . . In *Cowman* we concluded that in the elective surgery situation no valid reasons existed for allowing the medical community the exclusive determination of what information would be material to a patient's decision to consent to a particular medical procedure. . . . Today we confirm, as we implied in *Van Iperen*, . . . that the patient rule is applicable in all informed consent cases, in both elective and nonelective medical procedures.

Compelling grounds justify this conclusion. The patient's right to make an intelligent and informed decision cannot be exercised when information material to that decision is withheld. Although most aspects of the physician-patient relationship necessarily must be dominated by the superior skill and knowledge of the physician, the decision to consent to a particular medical procedure is not a medical decision. Instead, it ordinarily is a personal and often difficult decision to be made by the patient with the physician's advice and consultation. In order to make his or her informed decision, the patient has the right to expect the information reasonably necessary to that process will be made available by the physician. To force a layperson patient to prove the professional community's standard and its violation allows the exceptions to swallow the rule — the hallmark of the professional rule as demonstrated by this case — and forces the patient to prove the withholding of material information was not medically justified. In contrast, the patient rule makes full disclosure the rule but allows for numerous exceptions which the physician, who has access to the medical knowledge involved, can assert.

Adoption of the patient rule in all circumstances does not provide an easy burden for the patient, who generally must establish the following:

(1) The existence of a material risk unknown to the patient;

(2) A failure to disclose that risk on the part of the physician;

(3) Disclosure of the risk would have led a reasonable patient in plaintiff's position to reject the medical procedure or choose a different course of treatment;

(4) Injury.

. . . Further, the patient ordinarily will be required to present expert testimony relating to the nature of the risk and the likelihood of its occurrence, in order for the jury to determine, from the standpoint of the reasonable patient, whether the risk is in fact a material one. . . .

As we noted in *Cowman*, a number of situations may be established by the defendant physician as a defense to an informed consent action, constituting exceptions to the duty of disclosure. These include:

(1) Situations in which complete and candid disclosure might have a detrimental effect on the physical or psychological well-being of the patient;

(2) Situations in which a patient is incapable of giving consent by reason of mental disability or infancy;

(3) Situations in which an emergency makes it impractical to obtain consent;

(4) Situations in which the risk is either known to the patient or is so obvious as to justify a presumption on the part of the physician that the patient has knowledge of the risk;

(5) Situations in which the procedure itself is simple and the danger remote and commonly appreciated to be remote;

(6) Situations in which the physician does not know of an otherwise material risk and should not have been aware of it in the exercise of ordinary care. . . .

Dr. Bardole's brief contends for the professional rule "as a matter of public policy," on the ground the decision to withhold information from the patient, for the patient's best interests, is a uniquely medical judgment call to be measured by what physicians under similar circumstances do. . . .

Our holding that the patient rule is applicable in both elective and nonelective medical procedures and thus applicable here, means that trial court's basis for directed verdict in favor of the defendant doctors, although understandable in light of our former case law, was erroneous.

II. The above determination does not end our inquiry, however, for defendants' motions also asserted there was insufficient competent evidence from which a jury could find they were guilty of negligence.

As the evidence developed from plaintiff's use of defendant doctors as witnesses, Becky's symptoms indicated a strong possibility of a serious and life-threatening infection, gram-negative sepsis. On the other hand, the risk of death posed by the IVP was 1 in 100,000 to 1 in 150,000.

We here confront not an action for battery, which may lie when a patient consents to one type of treatment and the physician intentionally deviates from the consent and performs a substantially different treatment. . . . Rather, we view these situations as sounding in negligence and imposing upon the doctor a duty reasonably to disclose information material to the patient's decision.

. . . .

In this case there was little dispute about the operative facts. A patient with a potentially life-threatening illness was not told there was a 1 in 100,000 chance she could die from a diagnostic procedure. We must answer the question whether a jury reasonably could conclude this withheld information was material to Becky's decision. In *Cowman v. Hornaday*, . . . we discussed the "subjective test" and the "objective test."

The subjective test focuses on whether the particular patient would have considered the nondisclosed information sufficiently significant to affect his or her decision. Although embraced occasionally by commentators, . . . most courts have rejected the subjective test in favor of the objective test. . . .

In *Cowman*, 329 N.W.2d at 425, we quoted the definition of materiality, in this context, that was adopted by the court in *Wilkinson v. Vesey*, 110 R.I. 606, 295 A.2d 676 (1972): Materiality may be said to be the significance a reasonable person, in what the physician knows or should know is his [or her] patient's position, would attach to the disclosed risk or risks in deciding whether to submit . . . to surgery or treatment.

After careful consideration, we are unable to conclude, applying the above objective test for materiality, that a jury could reasonably find the withheld information relating to the extremely remote risk of death, shown by this record, would have been significant to a reasonable person in Becky's circumstances, or would have affected such a person's willingness to undergo the IVP. Plainly, the risk involved in every informed consent action is not so significant as to generate a jury question. It is generally acknowledged that not all risks need be disclosed, only the material risks. . . . Cases involving the remoteness of the risk, falling on both sides of a necessarily obscure line, are collected in *Canterbury*, 464 F.2d at 788. . . . Plaintiff's proof in this case, although reflecting a most tragic situation, does not generate a jury question under the principles above noted. Trial court thus properly granted the defendant doctors' motions for directed verdict. . . . ("No prudent juror could reasonably have considered the [1 in 100,000] risk of permanent paresthesia material to a decision on whether to consent to the procedure. . . .").

III. There remains the question whether the trial court properly granted IMMC's motion for directed verdict. Without the citation of any authority directly supporting the proposition, plaintiff argues IMMC "had a duty either to disseminate the necessary information and secure the patient's response or to adopt policies and procedures which allow physicians practicing in the hospital to perform medical procedures only with the patient's informed consent." In the circumstances of this case, we hold no jury issue relating to IMMC's liability was generated.

In Iowa as elsewhere a hospital does not practice medicine. . . . This court has not imposed on a hospital a duty to inform a patient of matters that lie at the heart of the doctor-patient relationship. . . . In similar situations other jurisdictions have held the responsibility of obtaining informed consent is the duty of the doctor and the hospital should not intervene. . . .

To the extent any of our prior decisions are inconsistent with our holding in division I of this opinion, the same are overruled. We affirm the judgment of the district court.

---

1. Define informed consent. What is a "material risk"? What is the problem with the "professional rule"? What is the problem with a "patient rule"?

2. What is the policy underlying the informed consent doctrine?

3. Why might a doctor want to avoid informing a patient of all the material risks? Should the rule be different for nonelective surgery? What kinds of risks would a patient want to know about for elective surgery?

4. What is the "objective" test? What would be an example of an emergency?

5. Note that the informed consent rule may allow a case to reach the jury without expert testimony.

6. If the doctor performs surgery without consent, or removes something without consent, the patient may sue in battery, *Mohr v. Williams*, 95 Minn. 261, 104 N.W. 12 (1905). What is the procedural difference between a battery suit and an informed consent (negligence) suit?

7. The doctor may be liable for failing to inform the patient of what might happen if the patient rejects the procedure. In *Truman v. Thomas*, 27 Cal. 3d 285, 165 Cal. Rptr. 308, 611 P.2d 902 (1980), the doctor was held liable for failing to inform the patient of the risk of death if the Pap smear test was rejected. The patient rejected the procedure, contracted cervical cancer, and died.

8. The doctor may have a duty to find the patient and warn her of risk that developed after he or she last saw her. Two years after inserting a Dalkon Shield (interuterine device) into the plaintiff, the doctor learned of the risks of migration, serious infection, and death. He was held liable for failing to notify his patient and to provide her with the opportunity to have it removed. *Tresemer v. Barke*, 86 Cal. App. 3d 656, 150 Cal. Rptr. 384 (1978).

9. In informed consent, the doctor is liable although he was not negligent in diagnosis or treatment. Is this fair to the doctor?

10. Some states have codified informed consent. The Georgia Code provides:

(a) [A]ny person who undergoes any surgical procedure under general anesthesia, spinal anesthesia, or major regional anesthesia or any person who undergoes an amniocentesis diagnostic procedure or a diagnostic procedure which involves the intravenous injection of a contrast material must consent to such procedure and shall be informed in general terms of the following:

(1) A diagnosis of the patient's condition requiring such proposed surgical or diagnostic procedure;

(2) The nature and purpose of such proposed surgical or diagnostic procedure;

(3) The material risks generally recognized and accepted by reasonably prudent physicians of infection, allergic reaction, severe loss of blood, loss or loss of function of any limb or organ, paralysis or partial paralysis, paraplegia or quadriplegia, disfiguring scar, brain damage, cardiac arrest, or death involved in such proposed surgical or diagnostic procedure which, if disclosed to a reasonably prudent person in the patient's position, could reasonably be expected to cause such prudent person to decline such proposed surgical or diagnostic procedure on the basis of the material risk of injury that could result from such proposed surgical or diagnostic procedure;

(4) The likelihood of success of such proposed surgical or diagnostic procedure;

(5) The practical alternatives to such proposed surgical or diagnostic procedure which are generally recognized and accepted by reasonably prudent physicians; and

(6) The prognosis of the patient's condition if such proposed surgical or diagnostic procedure is rejected.

. . . .

O.C.G.A. § 31-9-6.1 (1989). How is this different from the informed consent doctrine developed in *Pauscher v. Iowa Methodist Medical Center*?

11. In *Doreika*, the defendant was a chiropractor. He argued that informed consent did not apply, because it was not required by the Georgia statute (no anesthetic).

The court held that there was a common law and a constitutional right to informed consent and therefore he should have informed his patient of the risks of a neck adjustment. *Doreika v. Blotner* 666 S.E.2d 21 (Ga. Ct. App. 2008). What has this done to informed consent in Georgia?

John B. v. Superior Court of Los Angeles County
Supreme Court of California, 2006
137 P.3d 153

BAXTER, J.

This is a sad case. Bridget B., the plaintiff in the underlying action and real party in interest herein, is infected with the human immunodeficiency virus (HIV), the probable causative agent of acquired immune deficiency syndrome (AIDS). So is her husband, petitioner herein and defendant in the underlying action, John B.

Bridget alleges that John became infected with HIV first, as a result of engaging in unprotected sex with multiple men before and during their marriage, and that he then knowingly or negligently transmitted the virus to her. John, who now has full-blown AIDS, alleges in his answer that Bridget infected *him* and offers as proof a negative HIV test conducted in connection with his application for life insurance on August 17, 2000, six weeks before Bridget discovered she was infected with HIV.

This factual scenario raises a number of interesting questions: What duty does an HIV-positive individual have to avoid transmitting the virus? What level of awareness should be required before a court imposes a duty of care on an HIV-positive individual to avoid transmission of the virus? What responsibility does the victim have to protect himself or herself against possible infection with the virus? . . .

Bridget's complaint for damages alleges the following:

Plaintiff Bridget B. and defendant John B. met in September 1998 and began dating shortly thereafter. The couple became engaged in late 1999 and were married in July 2000. During this period, John represented to Bridget that he was healthy, disease-free, and monogamous. Indeed, it was John who insisted that the couple stop using condoms during intercourse. Based on John's representations, Bridget complied with his demand to engage in unprotected sex. In September 2000, however, Bridget began to suffer from exhaustion and high fevers.

On October 1, 2000, Bridget learned that she had tested positive for HIV. She was advised to undergo a second test and to have her husband tested as well. The second test confirmed that Bridget was HIV positive. John, too, was determined to be HIV positive. John's doctor told Bridget that she had "brought the HIV into the marriage." The doctor prescribed medications for John that made his viral load virtually undetectable. Bridget, on the other hand, was not offered treatment; she was informed that she had "had the illness for a long time." Bridget became depressed that she had infected her husband with this deadly disease.

In September 2001, John began telling others that Bridget had infected him with HIV. The next month, after defendant refused to continue his treatment, he became much sicker and developed sores on his face and scalp. Although he was diagnosed with AIDS, he refused all treatments and medications except those that treated the visible signs of the disease.

. . . .

The fourth cause of action (negligence) incorporates the foregoing allegations and alleges that John owed Bridget a duty of care to disclose the fact that he was HIV positive, that he breached this duty, and that he thereby infected her with HIV.

. . . .

This court has not yet had occasion to consider the tort of negligent transmission of a sexually transmitted disease, but the tort is far from novel. Our sister jurisdictions have long imposed liability on individuals who have harmed others by transmitting communicable diseases. . . . In particular, courts throughout the United States have recognized a cause of action for the negligent transmission of sexually transmitted diseases. . . . We agree with these courts that "[t]o be *stricken with disease* through another's negligence is in legal contemplation as it often is in the seriousness of consequences, no different from *being struck with an automobile* through another's negligence."

. . . .

John concedes that a person who actually knows he or she is infected with a sexually transmitted disease based on a test from an accredited laboratory or a medical diagnosis has a duty to use ordinary care to see that the disease is not transmitted to others. The foreseeability of harm in such a circumstance is manifest. John also concedes the viability of the tort of negligent transmission of HIV. In his view, though, a duty under this tort exists only when the actor has actual knowledge of being HIV positive; constructive knowledge of the infection is insufficient.

. . . Extending liability to those who have constructive knowledge of the disease, as [other] jurisdictions have done, comports with general principles of negligence. Indeed, the "very concept of negligence presupposes that the actor either does foresee an unreasonable risk of injury, or could foresee it if he conducted himself as a reasonably prudent person." (3 Harper et al., The Law of Torts (2d ed. 1986) Section 16.5, p. 397) . . . .

It must be noted, though, that "constructive knowledge," which means knowledge "that one using reasonable care or diligence should have, and therefore is attributed by law to a given person" (Black's Law Dict. (7th ed. 1999) p. 876), encompasses a variety of mental states, ranging from one who is deliberately indifferent in the face of an unjustifiably high risk of harm to one who merely should know of a dangerous condition. . . .

In this case, we conclude that the tort of negligent transmission of HIV does not depend solely on actual knowledge of HIV infection and would extend at least to those situations where the actor, under the totality of the circumstances, has *reason to know* of the infection. Under the reason-to-know standard, "the actor has information from which a person of reasonable intelligence or of the superior intelligence of the actor would infer that the fact in question exists, or that such person would govern his conduct upon the assumption that such fact exists."

Imposing liability for the transmission of HIV where the actor knows or has reason to know he or she is HIV positive is consistent with the general principle of California law that "'[a]ll persons are required to use ordinary care to prevent others being injured as the result of their conduct.'" The factor that "'plays a very significant role in this calculus'" is the foreseeability of the particular harm, which (like the reason-to-know standard) is assessed by an objective test.

. . . .

. . . . We need not consider the existence or scope of a duty for persons whose relationship does not extend beyond the sexual encounter itself, whose relationship does not contemplate sexual exclusivity, who have not represented themselves as disease-free, or who have not insisted on having sex without condoms.

. . . .

———————

1. Weigh the policy considerations in this case. Did the court get them right?

2. Do you agree with the assertion that, "[t]o be stricken with disease through another's negligence is in legal contemplation as it often is in the seriousness of consequences, no different from being struck with an automobile through another's negligence"? *Billo v. Allegheny Steel Co.*, 328 Pa. 97, 195 A. 110, 114 (1937). Does it depend on the severity of the specific disease?

3. Do you think the same rule should extend to casual sex?

Why does the court dodge this issue? Is contracting HIV through casual dating still "getting hit with a car"?

Moore v. The Regents of the University of California
Supreme Court of California, 1990
793 P.2d 479

[John Moore was diagnosed by his doctor, defendant Golde, at the U.C.L.A. Medical Center as having hairy-cell leukemia. He had his spleen removed and blood removed during his many visits to the medical center. From Moore's cells, Dr. Golde and others patented a cell line and "leased" it to Genetics Institute and Sandoz Pharmaceuticals.

Moore brought 13 causes of action, including informed consent, conversion and breach of fiduciary duty, against Golde, the University Regents, Genetics Institute and Sandoz.]

PENELLI, JUSTICE. . . .

A. *Breach of Fiduciary Duty and Lack of Informed Consent*

Moore repeatedly alleges that Golde failed to disclose the extent of his research and economic interests in Moore's cells before obtaining consent to the medical procedures by which the cells were extracted. These allegations, in our view, state a cause of action against Golde for invading a legally protected interest of his patient. This cause of action can properly be characterized either as the breach of a fiduciary duty to disclose facts material to the patient's consent or, alternatively, as the performance of medical procedures without first having obtained the patient's informed consent.

Our analysis begins with three well-established principles. First, "a person of adult years and in sound mind has the right, in the exercise of control over his own body, to determine whether or not to submit to lawful medical treatment." . . . Second, "the patient's consent to treatment, to be effective, must be an informed consent." . . . Third, in soliciting the patient's consent, a physician has a fiduciary duty to disclose all information material to the patient's decision. . . .

These principles lead to the following conclusions: (1) a physician must disclose personal interests unrelated to the patient's health, whether research or economic, that may affect the physician's professional judgment; and (2) a physician's failure to disclose such interests may give rise to a cause of action for performing medical procedures without informed consent or breach of fiduciary duty.

. . . "The scope of the physician's communication to the patient . . . must be measured by the patient's need, and that need is whatever information is material to the decision." . . .

Indeed, the law already recognizes that a reasonable patient would want to know whether a physician has an economic interest that might affect the physician's professional judgment. As the Court of Appeal has said, "[c]ertainly a sick patient deserves to be free of any reasonable suspicion that his doctor's judgment is influenced by a profit motive." . . . A physician who adds his own research interests to this balance may be tempted to order a scientifically useful procedure or test that offers marginal, or no, benefits to the patient.[8]

The possibility that an interest extraneous to the patient's health has affected the physician's judgment is something that a reasonable patient would want to know in deciding whether to consent to a proposed course of treatment. It is material to the patient's decision and, thus, a prerequisite to informed consent. . . .

Golde argues that the scientific use of cells that have already been removed cannot possibly affect the patient's medical interests. The argument is correct in one instance but not in another. If a physician has no plans to conduct research on a patient's cells at the time he recommends the medical procedure by which they are

---

8. This is, in fact, precisely what Moore has alleged with respect to the postoperative withdrawals of blood and other substances.

taken, then the patient's medical interests have not been impaired. In that instance the argument is correct. On the other hand, a physician who does have a preexisting research interest might, consciously or unconsciously, take that into consideration in recommending the procedure. In that instance the argument is incorrect: the physician's extraneous motivation may affect his judgment and is, thus, material to the patient's consent.

Accordingly, we hold that a physician who is seeking a patient's consent for a medical procedure must, in order to satisfy his fiduciary duty and to obtain the patient's informed consent, disclose personal interests unrelated to the patient's health, whether research or economic, that may affect his medical judgment.

. . . .

The decision of the Court of Appeal is affirmed in part and reversed in part. The case is remanded to the Court of Appeal, which shall direct the superior court to: (1) overrule Golde's demurrers to the causes of action for breach of fiduciary duty and lack of informed consent; (2) sustain, with leave to amend, the demurrers of the Regents, Quan, Sandoz, and Genetics Institute to the purported causes of action for breach of fiduciary duty and lack of informed consent; (3) sustain, without leave to amend, all defendants' demurrers to the purported cause of action for conversion; and (4) hear and determine all defendants' remaining demurrers.

[The concurring and dissenting opinions have been omitted.]

———————

1. Upon being informed of the physician's personal interest, as required by the opinion, is there a risk that the patient will be distracted from health considerations?

2. In some cases, might "a physician's research interest . . . play such an insignificant role in the decision . . . that disclosure should not be required because the interest is not material?" The court answered yes. What are examples of such trivial research interests?

3. The court held that the cause of action in conversion did not cover Moore's cells in part because there was no precedent. *Moore*, 793 P.2d at 487-97. Argue that the taking of his cells falls within conversion.

4. What will be the impact of the *Moore* decision on medical research? What damages, if any, should Moore recover? What do you think Moore really wants?

5. Assume that the physician sends the patient to a diagnostic lab for tests. Must the physician inform the patient of his or her part ownership in the lab?

3. Custom

Problem

Barbara took her car to Anita's Garage to have the transmission repaired. Anita removed the transmission, but parked the car in the adjacent unsecured parking lot overnight. During the night, the engine from the car was stolen. Anita has several local garage owners who will testify that they generally leave customers' cars parked outside overnight.

Will you take Barbara's suit against Anita's Garage?

The T.J. Hooper I

District Court, S.D. New York, 1931
53 F.2d 107

Coxe, District Judge.

These cases grow out of the foundering of the coal barges Northern 17 and Northern 30 in a storm off the New Jersey coast in March, 1928. Libels have been filed by the owners of the coal on the two barges for cargo loss against the barge owner. The owner of the tugs T. J. Hooper and Montrose has also instituted limitation proceedings, in which it seeks to be relieved from liability, and, at the same time, denies fault. In these limitation proceedings, the barge owner has answered, asserting negligent towage by the tugs, and claiming for the value of the barges. The cargo owners have also answered, alleging negligent towage, and contesting the right to limit. The cases have all been tried together as one action.

. . . .

This raises the question whether the Hooper and Montrose were required to have effective radio sets to pick up weather reports broadcast along the coast. Concededly, there is no statutory law on the subject applicable to tugs of that type, the radio statute applying only to steamers "licensed to carry, or carrying, fifty or more persons;" and excepting by its terms "steamers plying between ports, or places, less than two hundred miles apart." U.S. Code Annotated, title 46, §484. The standard of seaworthiness is not, however, dependent on statutory enactment, or condemned to inertia or rigidity, but changes "with advancing knowledge, experience, and the changed appliances of navigation." *The Titania* (D.C.) 19 F. 101, 106; *The Southwark*, 191 U.S. 1, 24 S. Ct. 1, 48 L. Ed. 65. It is particularly affected by new devices of demonstrated worth, which have become recognized as regular equipment by common usage.

Radio broadcasting was no new or untried thing in March, 1928. Everywhere, and in almost every field of activity, it was being utilized as an aid to communication, and for the dissemination of information. And that radio sets were in widespread use on vessels of all kinds is clearly indicated by the testimony in this case. Twice a day the government broadcast from Arlington weather reports forecasting weather conditions. Clearly this was important information which navigators could not afford to ignore.

Captain Powell, master of the Menominee, who was a witness for the tugs, testified that prior to March, 1928, his tug, and all other seagoing tugs of his company, were equipped by the owner with efficient radio sets, and that he regarded a radio as part "of the necessary equipment" of every reasonably well-equipped tug in the coastwise service. He further testified that 90 per cent of the coastwise tugs operating along the coast were so equipped. It is, of course, true that many of these radio sets were the personal property of the tug master, and not supplied by the owner. This was so with the Mars, Waltham, and Menominee; but, notwithstanding that fact, the use of the radio was shown to be so extensive as to amount almost to a universal practice in the navigation of coastwise tugs along the coast. I think therefore there was a duty on the part of the tug owner to supply effective receiving sets.

How have the tugs met this requirement? The Hooper had a radio set which belonged to her master, but was practically useless even before the tug left Hampton Roads, and was generally out of order. Similarly, the radio on the Montrose was the personal property of Captain Walton, and was "a home made set," which was not in very good working order, and was admittedly ineffective. Neither tug received any of the radio reports broadcast on March 8th. And Captain Savage of the Hooper admitted that if he had received such reports he would "quite likely" have turned into the breakwater. . . . Likewise, Captain Walton of the Montrose admitted that if he had received the weather reports on the 8th, which were received by the other tug captains, he "certainly would have gone into Breakwater." . . .

I hold therefore . . . (2) that the tugs T. J. Hooper and Montrose were unseaworthy in failing to have effective radio sets, capable of receiving weather reports on March 8th . . . (3) that the claims of the cargo owners against the tugs should be allowed. . . .

What was the custom of the tug owners? What was the custom of the tug captains?

The T.J. Hooper II

United States Court of Appeals, Second Circuit, 1932
60 F.2d 737

[This is the previous case now in the court of appeals. The court first held that the tugs would have sailed to the protection of the Delaware Breakwater if they had received the radio broadcasts.]

L. HAND, CIRCUIT JUDGE. . . .

They did not, because their private radio receiving sets, which were on board, were not in working order. These belonged to them personally, and were partly a toy, partly a part of the equipment, but neither furnished by the owner, nor supervised by it. It is not fair to say that there was a general custom among coastwise carriers to so equip their tugs. One line alone did it; as for the rest, they relied upon their crews, so far as they can be said to have relied at all. An adequate receiving set suitable for a coastwise tug can now be got at small cost and is reasonably reliable if kept up; obviously it is a source of great protection to their tows. Twice every day they can receive these predictions, based upon the widest possible information, available to every vessel within two or three hundred miles and more. Such a set is the ears of the tug to catch the spoken word, just as the master's binoculars are her eyes to see a storm signal ashore. Whatever may be said as to other vessels, tugs towing heavy coal laden barges, strung out for half a mile, have little power to maneuver, and do not, as this case proves, expose themselves to weather which would not turn back stauncher craft. They can have at hand protection against dangers of which they can learn in no other way.

Is it then a final answer that the business had not yet generally adopted receiving sets? There are, no doubt, cases where courts seem to make the general practice of the calling the standard of proper diligence; we have indeed given some currency to the notion ourselves. . . . Indeed in most cases reasonable prudence is in fact common prudence; but strictly it is never its measure; a whole calling may have unduly lagged in the adoption of new and available devices. It never may set its own tests, however persuasive be its usages. Courts must in the end say what is required; there are precautions so imperative that even their universal disregard will not excuse their omission. . . . But here there was no custom at all as to receiving sets; some had them, some did not; the most that can be urged is that they had not yet become general. Certainly in such a case we need not pause; when some have thought a device necessary, at least we may say that they were right, and the others too slack. The statute (section 484, title 46, U.S. Code [46 USCA § 484]) does not bear on this situation at all. It prescribes not a receiving, but a transmitting set, and for a very different purpose; to call for help, not to get news. We hold the tugs therefore [sic] because had they been properly equipped, they would have got the Arlington reports. The injury was a direct consequence of this unseaworthiness.

Decree affirmed. [The claims against the tugs were allowed.]

———————

1. Why would the owners decide not to supply radios? Is it the function of the courts to uphold the business decisions of the owners, the captains, or neither?

2. Argue that since this was a commercial case, the market decision by the owners should control.

3. Could it be that barges tend to sink, but tugs do not? In prior suits, perhaps the barges lost and tug owners won because storms were viewed as acts of God. Might the tug owners have reacted to the law (storms are acts of God), not the market (cheaper not to have radios)?

4. The plaintiff fell through a hole in the floor of a coal mine. Reflecting custom, the hole was unlit and unfenced. The court held that the custom was so careless that it was inadmissible as evidence. *Mayhew v. Sullivan Mining Co.*, 76 Me. 100 (1884).

5. In *Trimarco v. Klein*, 56 N.Y.2d 98, 451 N.Y.S.2d 52, 436 N.E.2d 502 (1982), the plaintiff was injured when the shower door shattered, and the court held that the custom was to replace the glass doors with safety glass. The landlord was negligent in replacing the non-safety glass with the same type.

D. The Relationship Between Judge and Jury

The judge has the opportunity and the responsibility to control the jury. In this section the judge does this by stating a rule of law. The judge may also look to a statute or the regulation for the standard (Section E, Violation of Statute), follow the standard of the reasonable person (Section C, Subsection 1), or apply the relevant custom (Section C, Subsection 3).

Baltimore & Ohio Railroad Co. v. Goodman

Supreme Court of the United States, 1927
275 U.S. 66

Mr. Justice Holmes delivered the opinion of the Court.

This is a suit brought by the widow and administratrix of Nathan Goodman against the petitioner for causing his death by running him down at a grade crossing. The defence is that Goodman's own negligence caused the death. At the trial, the defendant asked the Court to direct a verdict for it, but the request, and others looking to the same direction, were refused, and the plaintiff got a verdict and a judgment which was affirmed by the Circuit Court of Appeals. . . .

Goodman was driving an automobile truck in an easterly direction and was killed by a train running southwesterly across the road at a rate of not less than sixty miles an hour. The line was straight, but it is said by the respondent that Goodman 'had no practical view' beyond a section house two hundred and forty-three feet north of the crossing until he was about twenty feet from the first rail, or, as the respondent argues, twelve feet from danger, and that then the engine was still obscured by the section house. He had been driving at the rate of ten or twelve miles an hour, but had cut down his rate to five or six miles at about forty feet from the crossing. It is thought that there was an emergency in which, so far as appears, Goodman did all that he could.

We do not go into further details as to Goodman's precise situation, beyond mentioning that it was daylight and that he was familiar with the crossing, for it appears to us plain that nothing is suggested by the evidence to relieve Goodman from responsibility for his own death. When a man goes upon a railroad track he knows that he goes to a place where he will be killed if a train comes upon him before he is clear of the track. He knows that he must stop for the train, not the train stop for him. In such circumstances it seems to us that if a driver cannot be sure otherwise whether a train is dangerously near he must stop and get out of his vehicle, although obviously he will not often be required to do more than to stop and look. It seems to us that if he relies upon not hearing the train or any signal and takes no further precaution he does so at his own risk. If at the last moment Goodman found himself in an emergency it was his own fault that he did not reduce his speed earlier or come to a stop. It is true . . . that the question of due care very generally is left to the jury. But we are dealing with a standard of conduct, and when the standard is clear it should be laid down once for all by the courts. . . .

Judgment reversed.

---

1. Why did Justice Holmes state the standard? What is it? Was the standard reasonable?

2. Why does the Supreme Court rarely take a torts case? Was it appropriate here? Read on.

Pokora v. Wabash Railway Co.

Supreme Court of the United States, 1934
292 U.S. 98

Mr. Justice Cardozo delivered the opinion of the Court.

John Pokora, driving his truck across a railway grade crossing in the city of Springfield, Illinois, was struck by a train and injured. Upon the trial of his suit for damages, the District Court held that he had been guilty of contributory negligence, and directed a verdict for the defendant. The Circuit Court of Appeals (one judge dissenting) affirmed, 66 F.2d 166, resting its judgment on the opinion of this court in *B. & O. R. Co. v. Goodman*, 275 U.S. 66. A writ of certiorari brings the case here.

Pokora was an ice dealer, and had come to the crossing to load his truck with ice. The tracks of the Wabash Railway are laid along Tenth Street, which runs north and south. There is a crossing at Edwards Street running east and west. Two ice depots are on opposite corners of Tenth and Edward Streets, one at the northeast corner, the other at the southwest. Pokora, driving west along Edwards Street, stopped at the first of these corners to get his load of ice, but found so many trucks ahead of him that he decided to try the depot on the other side of the way. In this crossing of the railway, the accident occurred.

The defendant has four tracks on Tenth Street, a switch track on the east, then the main track, and then two switches. Pokora, as he left the northeast corner where his truck had been stopped, looked to the north for approaching trains. He did this at a point about ten or fifteen feet east of the switch ahead of him. A string of box cars standing on the switch, about five to ten feet from the north line of Edwards Street, cut off his view of the tracks beyond him to the north. At the same time he listened. There was neither bell nor whistle. Still listening, he crossed the switch, and reaching the main track was struck by a passenger train coming from the north at a speed of twenty-five to thirty miles an hour.

. . . .

The argument is made, however, that our decision in *B. & O. R. Co. v. Goodman, supra,* is a barrier in the plaintiff's path, irrespective of the conclusion that might commend itself if the question were at large. There is no doubt that the opinion in that case is correct in its result. Goodman, the driver, traveling only five or six miles an hour, had, before reaching the track, a clear space of eighteen feet within which the train was plainly visible. With that opportunity, he fell short of the legal standard of duty established for a traveler when he failed to look and see. This was decisive of the case. But the court did not stop there. It added a remark, unnecessary upon the facts before it, which has been a fertile source of controversy. "In such circumstances it seems to us that if a driver cannot be sure otherwise whether a train is dangerously near he must stop and get out of his vehicle, although obviously he will not often be required to do more than to stop and look."

There is need at this stage to clear the ground of brushwood that may obscure the point at issue. We do not now inquire into the existence of a duty to stop, disconnected from a duty to get out and reconnoitre. The inquiry, if pursued, would lead us into the thickets of conflicting judgments. Some courts apply what is often spoken of as the Pennsylvania rule, and impose an unyielding duty to stop, as well as to look and listen, no matter how clear the crossing or the tracks on either side. . . . Other courts, the majority, adopt the rule that the traveler must look and listen, but that the existence of a duty to stop depends upon the circumstances, and hence generally, even if not invariably, upon the judgment of the jury. . . . The subject has been less considered in this court, but in none of its opinions is there a suggestion that at any and every crossing the duty to stop is absolute, irrespective of the danger. Not even in *B. & O. R. Co. v. Goodman, supra,* which goes farther than the earlier cases, is there support for such a rule. To the contrary, the opinion makes it clear that the duty is conditioned upon the presence of impediments whereby sight and hearing become inadequate for the traveler's protection. . . .

Choice between these diversities of doctrine is unnecessary for the decision of the case at hand. Here the fact is not disputed that the plaintiff did stop before he started to cross the tracks. If we assume that by reason of the box cars, there was a duty to stop again when the obstructions had been cleared, that duty did not arise unless a stop could be made safely after the point of clearance had been reached. . . . For reasons already stated, the testimony permits the inference that the truck was in the zone of danger by the time the field of vision was enlarged. No stop would then have helped the plaintiff if he remained seated on his truck, or so the triers of the facts might find. His case was for the jury unless as a matter of law he was subject to a duty to get out of the vehicle before it crossed the switch, walk forward to the front, and then, afoot, survey the scene. We must say whether his failure to do this was negligence so obvious and certain that one conclusion and one only is permissible for rational and candid minds.

Standards of prudent conduct are declared at times by courts, but they are taken over from the facts of life. To get out of a vehicle and reconnoitre is an uncommon precaution, as everyday experience informs us. Besides being uncommon, it is very likely to be futile, and sometimes even dangerous. If the driver leaves his vehicle when he nears a cut or curve, he will learn nothing by getting out about the perils that lurk beyond. By the time he regains his seat and sets his car in motion, the hidden train may be upon him. . . . Often the added safeguard will be dubious though the track happens to be straight, as it seems that this one was, at all events as far as the station, about five blocks to the north. A train traveling at a speed of thirty miles an hour will cover a quarter of a mile in the space of thirty seconds. It may thus emerge out of obscurity as the driver turns his back to regain the waiting car, and may then descend upon him suddenly when his car is on the track. Instead of helping himself by getting out, he might do better to press forward with all his faculties alert. So a train at a neighboring station, apparently at rest and harmless, may be transformed in a few seconds into an instrument of destruction. At times the course of safety may be different. One can figure to oneself a roadbed so level and unbroken that getting out will be a gain. Even then the balance of advantage depends on many circumstances and can be easily disturbed. Where was Pokora to leave his truck after getting out to reconnoitre? If he was to leave it on the switch, there was the possibility that the box cars would be shunted down upon him before he could regain his seat. The defendant did not show whether there was a locomotive at the forward end, or whether the cars were so few that a locomotive could be seen. If he was to leave his vehicle near the curb, there was even stronger reason to believe that the space to be covered in going back and forth would make his observations worthless. One must remember that while the traveler turns his eyes in one direction, a train or a loose engine may be approaching from the other.

Illustrations such as these bear witness to the need for caution in framing standards of behavior that amount to rules of law. The need is the more urgent when there is no background of experience out of which the standards have emerged. They are then, not the natural flowerings of behavior in its customary forms, but rules artificially developed, and imposed from without. Extraordinary situations may not wisely or fairly be subjected to tests or regulations that are fitting for the common-place or normal. In default of the guide of customary conduct, what is suitable for the traveler caught in a mesh where the ordinary safeguards fail him is for the judgment of a jury. . . . The opinion in Goodman's case has been a source of confusion in the federal courts to the extent that it imposes a standard for application by the judge, and has had only wavering support in the courts of the states. We limit it accordingly.

The judgment should be reversed and the cause remanded for further proceedings in accordance with this opinion.

Reversed.

---

1. Why does Justice Cardozo object to the *Goodman* standard? What rule does he present in its place? Does he say that the courts should never state a firm rule?

2. If it was economically sound to subsidize the railroads in 1927, by placing the loss on the victim, had the strength of the railroads improved by 1933? Is Cardozo merely reflecting such strength? *See* Green, *The Duty Problem in Negligence Cases*, 29 Colum. L. Rev. 255 (1929). Does the court have a legitimate role in social engineering?

3. One case has rejected the professional standard of care as established by the customary practice of doctors. In spite of numerous office visits over several years, the defendant ophthalmologist did not test the patient for glaucoma. The accepted practice was to not give glaucoma tests to persons under age forty. The court rejected the medical standard and found for the plaintiff, stating:

> The incidence of glaucoma in one out of 25,000 persons under the age of 40 may appear quite minimal. However, that one person, the plaintiff in this instance, is entitled to the same protection, as afforded persons over 40, essential for timely detection of the evidence of glaucoma where it can be arrested to avoid the grave and devastating result of this disease. The test is a simple pressure test, relatively inexpensive. There is no judgment factor involved, and there is no doubt that by giving the test the evidence of glaucoma can be detected. The giving of the test is harmless if the physical condition of the eye permits.

> Under the facts of this case reasonable prudence required the timely giving of the pressure test to this plaintiff. The precaution of giving this test to detect the incidence of glaucoma to patients under 40 years of age is so imperative that irrespective of its disregard by the standards of the ophthalmology profession, it is the duty of the courts to say what is required to protect patients under 40 from the damaging results of glaucoma.

Helling v. Carey, 83 Wash. 2d 514, 518–19, 519 P.2d 981 (1974). What factors did the court balance in rejecting the professional standard? What did the standard adopted by the court require the defendant to have done? What advice would you give your eye doctor clients based on this decision?

Does the hard rule established in *Helling* fly in the face of *Pokora*? Would any other rule be unjust to those under age forty? What other policies are important? The *Helling* case led to a lot of statutory and other activity in Washington, and its current status is uncertain.

E. Violation of Statute

Hetherton v. Sears, Roebuck & Co.

United States Court of Appeals, Third Circuit, 1979
593 F.2d 526

A. Leon Higginbotham, Jr., Circuit Judge.

In this appeal we are asked to decide whether a retail store can be held liable under Delaware law when the ammunition it sold was used to injure an innocent person in an attempted murder and robbery.

We conclude that the district court was in error in granting a summary judgment for the defendant and therefore we will reverse the judgment.

I.

On February 25, 1976, Lloyd Fullman, Jr. purchased from Sears, Roebuck and Co. (Sears) a .22 caliber rifle and rifle cartridges. Six weeks later, in an attempted robbery of a Wilmington restaurant, Fullman, using the rifle and ammunition purchased at Sears, shot the plaintiff, James Hetherton, in the head. At the time, Hetherton, an off-duty police officer, was employed as a guard in the restaurant. Hetherton was injured seriously and, as of the time of the suit, still had "13 fragments of the projectile in his head." In the related criminal proceeding in state court, Fullman was convicted of attempted second degree murder, attempted robbery, possession of a deadly weapon during the commission of a felony, possession of a deadly weapon by a person prohibited and conspiracy of the second degree. These convictions, however, were not Fullman's first "brush with the law." He had been convicted previously of the felonies of attempted robbery, conspiracy of the second degree, and falsely reporting an incident. As a result of these prior felony convictions Fullman was prohibited under Delaware law from purchasing the rifle and cartridges obtained from Sears. Additionally, Delaware law required Sears, prior to sale, to receive from two freeholders the positive identification of a purchaser of any "deadly weapon." No freeholders identified Fullman when he made his purchase. He merely produced a Delaware driver's license and completed a Federal Firearms Transaction Record, Form 4473. Although Fullman had a criminal record, he indicated on Form 4473 that he had never been convicted of a felony.

Hetherton and his wife brought this suit alleging that Sears was negligent when it sold the gun and ammunition to Fullman and Sears was therefore liable for Hetherton's injuries. They asserted that Sears was negligent because it had failed to require at least two freeholders to identify Fullman before making the sale as required by 24 Del. C. § 904. . . .

A.

At least since 1911, Delaware has had a number of statutes regulating the sale and possession of guns and ammunition including 24 Del. C. § 904, on which the Hethertons rely for a theory of liability.

Section 904 provides that:

> Any person desiring to engage in the business described in this chapter shall keep and maintain in his place of business at all times a book which shall be furnished him by the State Tax Department. In such book he shall enter the date of the sale, the name and address of the person purchasing *any deadly weapon*, the number and kind of *deadly weapon* so purchased, the color of the person so purchasing the same, the apparent age of the purchaser, and the names and addresses of at least 2 freeholders resident in the county wherein the sale is made who shall positively identify the purchaser before the sale can be made (emphasis added).[6]

The starting point in this case has to be what is a "deadly weapon," or more specifically, was the ammunition Fullman purchased from Sears a "deadly weapon" under section 904. Sears argues that neither the rifle nor the ammunition it sold Fullman were "deadly weapons" within the meaning of the statute and therefore Sears was not required to comply with section 904 when it made the sale. While the plaintiffs agree that the rifle was not a "deadly weapon" as defined by the statute, they urge that the rifle cartridges were "deadly weapons" for the purpose of section 904.

Section 904 is a provision of chapter nine, title 24 of the Delaware Code. This chapter regulates "deadly weapons dealers." The chapter includes a definition of "deadly weapons" which is controlling for each of the chapter sections. "Deadly weapons" is defined in section 901 to mean "any pistol or revolver, or Revolver or pistol cartridges, stiletto, steel or brass knuckles, or other deadly weapon made especially for the defense of one's person." 24 Del. C. § 901 (emphasis added). The ammunition which Fullman purchased was sold as "Sears .22 Long Rifle Extra-Range Hollow Point Cartridges." These ".22 caliber rifle cartridges . . . can be used in many types of pistols and revolvers. Thus, although the ammunition which Fullman purchased was labeled as rifle cartridges, it can also be described as 'revolver or pistol cartridges.'" *Hetherton*, 445 F. Supp. at 297–98 (footnote omitted). Sears asserts that the sale of the ammunition did not fall within the statute because the ammunition was sold and labeled as rifle ammunition and not as pistol or revolver cartridges. As the district court noted:

---

6. We note that § 904 was amended after the Fullman purchase to strike the words "freeholders resident in the county wherein the sale is made" from the second sentence and to substitute the words "residents of the State of Delaware." House Bill No. 876, 66 Del. Laws 406 (June 30, 1978). This amendment does not change our disposition of this case. Moreover, it reinforces our belief that section 904 is not an obscure provision providing for an antiquated means of identification but one that reflects Delaware's current concerns with an important and sensitive problem.

> It is unlikely that the legislature intended to permit dealers to evade either the licensing requirements of § 901 or the recording requirements of § 904 merely by selling a product under one label rather than another.

Id. at 298. We agree and hold that cartridges which can be used, without alteration, as pistol cartridges are covered by section 904 regardless of the fortuity of labeling by the retailer.

B.

Having found that the ammunition was a "deadly weapon" covered by section 904, we must also decide whether Sears' violation of the statute results in liability to the Hethertons. First, it must be determined whether section 904 was enacted for the safety of others. If the statute was enacted for the safety of others, its violation is negligence per se. *See, e.g., Schwartzman v. Weiner,* 319 A.2d 48 (Del. Super. Ct. 1974) (landlord negligent when he failed to provide a handrail on a staircase in violation of housing code); *Farrow v. Hoffecker,* 23 Del. 223, 79 A. 920 (Del. Super. Ct. 1906) (defendant negligent when he violated ordinance prohibiting shooting within the city limits). Second, it must be determined whether Hetherton was among the group of individuals the legislature intended to protect. *Wealth v. Renai,* 49 Del. 289, 114 A.2d 809 (Del. Super. Ct. 1955) (pedestrians among the class of persons to be protected by statute prohibiting automobile passing at intersections.)

Recognizing the deadliness of firearms and their related components ammunition, it seems incomprehensible that the primary concern of the legislature in enacting provisions regulating "deadly weapons dealers" could have been anything other than the safety of citizens and the prevention of injuries caused by "deadly weapons." Yet, as so often occurs, our conclusions must be based on the logic of experience rather than any other indication of legislative intent. For in this case, we have found neither relevant legislative history nor pertinent Delaware cases construing the statute in issue.

However, our construction is consistent with cases reviewing gun control legislation from other jurisdictions. For example, in *State v. Sima,* 142 N.J. Super. 187, 192, 361 A.2d 58, 61 (1976), the New Jersey court noted that New Jersey's gun control legislation was designed "to prevent criminals and other unfit elements from acquiring firearms." The United States Supreme Court in construing federal gun control legislation in *Huddleston v. United States,* 415 U.S. 814, 94 S. Ct. 1262, 39 L. Ed. 2d 782 (1974) noted that:

> Information drawn from records kept by dealers was a prime guarantee of the Act's effectiveness in keeping "these lethal weapons out of the hands of criminals, drug addicts, mentally disordered persons, juveniles, and other persons whose possession of them is too high a price to pay in danger to us all to allow."

Id. at 825, 94 S. Ct. at 1269, quoting 114 Cong. Rec. 13219 (1968) (remarks of Sen. Tydings). *See also Franco v. Bunyard*, 261 Ark. 144, 547 S.W.2d 91 (Ark. 1977) (the purpose of federal gun control laws and regulations is to keep weapons out of the hands of criminals).

We therefore conclude that section 904 was enacted for the safety of others and that the legislature intended to protect innocent persons who might otherwise be injured during the commission of a crime. Thus, Sears' failure to require two freeholders to identify Fullman constituted negligence per se.

C.

The final question under section 904 liability is whether Sears' negligence was the proximate cause of the Hetherton's injuries. If not, the violation does not result in liability. . . .

Sears asserts and the district court agreed that Sears' failure to comply with the statute did not proximately cause Hetherton's injuries as a matter of law. It asserts that the requirement that a deadly weapons purchaser produce two freeholders serves *only* to verify the identity of the purchaser. It asserts that because Fullman properly identified himself, compliance with the statute would not have affected the sale.

We disagree. We note that the requirement that a purchaser produce two freeholders is a burdensome procedure which reduces the ease and simplicity of obtaining a "deadly weapon." It seems reasonable to conclude that the Delaware legislature was aware of the inconvenience of the requirement and that the legislature intended the inconvenience. It might have been difficult, if not impossible, for someone like Fullman, who could not legally purchase "deadly weapons," to meet the additional identification requirement. Compliance with the statute would have prevented consummation of the sale at least at that time because Fullman was not accompanied by two freeholders.

In *Franco v. Bunyard, supra*, the Arkansas court discussed issues somewhat similar to those presented by this case. In *Franco* the plaintiffs requested damages for the wrongful deaths and personal injuries which resulted from the defendant's sale of a weapon to an escaped convict. The defendant had sold the weapon without requiring the purchaser to complete Form 4473 as required by federal law. On the issue of proximate cause the court stated:

> (It) is enough to point out that the tragedies could not have occurred as they did if the federal rules had been obeyed. That is, Graham had no means of identification, an essential prerequisite to the purchase of a gun. This is not, as the appellees argue, a mere matter of record keeping. Form 4473 required the seller to obtain and record Graham's identification *before* handing over the gun. Graham had no identification. Thus, had the law been obeyed, he could not have obtained possession of the gun and could not have used it to shoot innocent men the next day. On the issue of foreseeability, we need say only that the very purpose of the law is to keep pistols out of the hands of

such persons as Graham, who was both a convicted criminal and a fugitive from justice. It certainly cannot be said that his use of the gun in such a way as to injure others was not foreseeable. Of course it is not required that the precise sequence of events leading to the injury be foreseeable.

547 S.W.2d at 93.

We do not conclude that as a matter of law a jury must find that Sears' failure to comply with the statute was the proximate cause of Hetherton's injuries. Proximate cause is usually a question for the jury and not an issue for the judge to decide. . . .

We will therefore reverse the judgment of the district court and will remand for further proceedings consistent with this opinion. In such proceedings, there will remain for the consideration of a jury the issues of proximate cause and damages.

---

1. *Hetherton* was reversed in the second appeal on the ground that the statute's "two freeholders" requirement was unconstitutional. 652 F.2d 1152 (3d Cir. 1981).

2. The plaintiff must be within the class intended to be protected by the statute. The plaintiff owned a hotel that was damaged when a car crashed into it. The defendant, heading north, turned left in front of a car heading south. The two cars collided, and the defendant's car hit the plaintiff's building. The statute prohibited left turns. The court refused to apply the negligence per se doctrine because the plaintiff was outside the class intended to be protected by the right-of-way statute. *Erickson v. Kongsli*, 40 Wash. 2d 79, 240 P.2d 1209 (1952).

3. The hazard must be the one intended to be protected against by the statute. The plaintiff's sheep were washed off the defendant's ship during a storm, and the plaintiff sued for failure to fence the sheep as required by statute. The court refused to apply negligence per se because the statute was intended to prevent the spread of disease, not protect against the perils of the sea. *Gorris v. Scott*, L.R. 9 Ex. 125 (1874). What hazard was the statute in *Hetherton* intended to prevent?

4. The Restatement (Second) of Torts § 288 provides that the court will not adopt, as the standard of the reasonable person, a statute intended to apply to a different class, interest, harm, or hazard than the one before the court.

5. Once the court decides that the statute applies to this plaintiff (class) for this injury (hazard), it will be difficult for the defendant to argue successfully that there was no proximate cause. Why should this be the case? What kind(s) of causation arguments will be available to the defendant even if the defendant violated the statute and the statute sets the standard of care?

In *Hetherton*, was Judge Higginbotham considering proximate cause, as he stated, or merely whether the statute applied to this class of persons? Was he considering whether violation of the statute was a cause in fact of the injury? What would the defendant argue in the trial court about this?

Tedla v. Ellman

Court of Appeals of New York, 1939
19 N.E.2d 987

LEHMAN, JUDGE.

While walking along a highway, Anna Tedla and her brother, John Bachek, were struck by a passing automobile, operated by the defendant Ellman. She was injured and Bachek was killed. Bachek was a deaf-mute. His occupation was collecting and selling junk. His sister, Mrs. Tedla, was engaged in the same occupation. They often picked up junk at the incinerator of the village of Islip. At the time of the accident they were walking along "Sunrise Highway" and wheeling baby carriages containing junk and wood which they had picked up at the incinerator. It was about six o'clock, or a little earlier, on a Sunday evening in December. Darkness had already set in. Bachek was carrying a lighted lantern, or, at least, there is testimony to that effect. The jury found that the accident was due solely to the negligence of the operator of the automobile. The defendants do not, upon this appeal, challenge the finding of negligence on the part of the operator. They maintain, however, that Mrs. Tedla and her brother were guilty of contributory negligence as a matter of law.

The Legislature in the first five subdivisions of section 85 of the Vehicle and Traffic Law has provided regulations to govern the conduct of pedestrians and of drivers of vehicles when a pedestrian is crossing a road. Until, by chapter 114 of the Laws of 1933, it adopted subdivision 6 of section 85, quoted above, there was no special statutory rule for pedestrians walking along a highway. Then for the first time it reversed, for pedestrians, the rule established for vehicles by immemorial custom, and provided that pedestrians shall keep to the left of the center line of a highway.

The plaintiffs showed by the testimony of a State policeman that "there were very few cars going east" at the time of the accident, but that going west there was "very heavy Sunday night traffic." [The plaintiffs were hit from behind while walking on the east side (right).] . . .

The analogy [to *Martin v. Herzog*] is, however, incomplete. The "established rule" should not be weakened either by subtle distinctions or by extension beyond its letter or spirit into a field where "by the very terms of the hypothesis" it can have no proper application. At times the indefinite and flexible standard of care of the traditional reasonably prudent man may be, in the opinion of the Legislature, an insufficient measure of the care which should be exercised to guard against a recognized danger; . . . . Then the Legislature may by statute prescribe additional safeguards and may define duty and standard of care in rigid terms; and when the Legislature has spoken, the standard of the care required is no longer what the reasonably prudent man would do under the circumstances but what the Legislature has commanded. That is the rule established by the courts and "by the very terms of the hypothesis" the rule applies where the Legislature has prescribed safeguards "for the benefit of another that he may be preserved in life or limb." In that field debate as to whether the safe-guards so prescribed are reasonably necessary is ended by the legislative fiat. . . .

The statute upon which the defendants rely is of different character. It does not prescribe additional safeguards which pedestrians must provide for the preservation of the life or limb or property of others, or even of themselves, nor does it impose upon pedestrians a higher standard of care. What the statute does provide is rules of the road to be observed by pedestrians and by vehicles, so that all those who use the road may know how they and others should proceed, at least under usual circumstances. . . .

Negligence is failure to exercise the care required by law. Where a statute defines the standard of care and the safeguards required to meet a recognized danger, then, as we have said, no other measure may be applied in determining whether a person has carried out the duty of care imposed by law. Failure to observe the standard imposed by statute is negligence, as matter of law. On the other hand, where a statu-tory general rule of conduct fixes no definite standard of care which would under all circumstances tend to protect life, limb or property but merely codifies or supple-ments a common-law rule, which has always been subject to limitations and excep-tions; or where the statutory rule of conduct regulates conflicting rights and obligations in manner calculated to promote public convenience and safety, then the statute, in the absence of clear language to the contrary, should not be construed as intended to wipe out the limitations and exceptions which judicial decisions have attached to the common-law duty; nor should it be construed as an inflexible com-mand that the general rule of conduct intended to prevent accidents must be followed even under conditions when observance might cause accidents. We may assume rea-sonably that the Legislature directed pedestrians to keep to the left of the center of the road because that would cause them to face traffic approaching in that lane and would enable them to care for their own safety better than if the traffic approached them from the rear. We cannot assume reasonably that the Legislature intended that a statute enacted for the preservation of the life and limb of pedestrians must be observed when observance would subject them to more imminent danger.

[A] pedestrian is, of course, at fault if he fails without good reason to observe the statutory rule of conduct. The general duty is established by the statute, and devia-tion from it without good cause is a wrong and the wrongdoer is responsible for the damages resulting from his wrong. . . .

In each action, the judgment [in favor of the plaintiffs] should be affirmed, with costs.

---

1. *Martin v. Herzog*, 228 N.Y. 164, 126 N.E. 814 (1920), referred to in *Tedla*, was a contributory negligence case. The defendant's car negligently ran into the front of the plaintiff's wagon, but the plaintiff was charged with contributory negligence for

not having lights on the front of his wagon as required by statute. Judge Cardozo wrote:

> We think the unexcused omission of the statutory signals is more than some evidence of negligence. It is negligence in itself. Lights are intended for the guidance and protection of other travelers on the highway. Highway Law, § 329a. By the very terms of the hypothesis, to omit, willfully or heedlessly, the safeguards prescribed by law for the benefit of another that he may be preserved in life or limb, is to fall short of the standard of diligence to which those who live in organized society are under a duty to conform. That, we think, is now the established rule in this state. . . .
>
> In the case at hand, we have an instance of the admitted violation of a statute intended for the protection of travelers on the highway, of whom the defendant at the time was one. Yet the jurors were instructed in effect that they were at liberty in their discretion to treat the omission of lights either as innocent or as culpable. They were allowed to "consider the default as lightly or gravely" as they would (Thomas, J., in the court below). . . . Jurors have no dispensing power, by which they may relax the duty that one traveler on the highways owes under the statute to another. It is error to tell them that they have. The omission of these lights was a wrong, and, being wholly unexcused, was also a negligent wrong. No license should have been conceded to the triers of the facts to find it anything else.

2. In *Martin* and *Tedla*, what do the judges think is the relationship between the legislature and the court?

3. Can the judge refuse to apply a statute or ordinance to which he or she has an objection? What is Cardozo's view in *Martin*? Lehman's view in *Tedla*?

4. Justice Traynor stated:

> A statute, that provides for a criminal proceeding only, does not create a civil liability; if there is no provision for a remedy by civil action to persons injured by a breach of the statute it is because the Legislature did not contemplate one. A suit for damages is based on the theory that the conduct inflicting the injuries is a common-law tort. . . . The decision as to what the civil standard should be still rests with the court, and the standard formulated by a legislative body in a police regulation or criminal statute becomes the standard to determine civil liability only because the court accepts it. In the absence of such a standard the case goes to the jury, which must determine whether the defendant has acted as a reasonably prudent man would act in similar circumstances. The jury then has the burden of deciding not only what the facts are but what the unformulated standard is of reasonable conduct. When a legislative body has generalized a standard from the experience of the community and prohibits conduct that is likely to cause harm, the court accepts the formulated standards and applies them. . . .

Clinkscales v. Carver, 22 Cal. 2d 72, 136 P.2d 777 (1943). How is Traynor's view different from Lehman's and Cardozo's? Are they fundamentally different, or will they vary with the statute and the facts of the case?

5. In these discussions we are assuming that the legislature provided no express civil standard. Why didn't the legislature provide a civil remedy?

6. Students often overlook the question of what weight should be given to the violation of the statute once the judge decides that the statutory standard applies to the case. There are three approaches: rebuttable presumption, negligence per se, and evidence of negligence.

A. *Violation of Statute as Rebuttable Presumption.* In a growing number of states, the rule concerning the proper role of a penal statute in a civil action for damages is that violation of the statute which has been found to apply to a particular set of facts establishes only a prima facie case of negligence, a presumption which may be rebutted by a showing on the part of the party violating the statute of an adequate excuse under the facts and circumstances of the case.

[An] attraction of this approach is that it is fair. "If there is sufficient excuse or justification there is ordinarily no violation of a statute and the statutory standard is inapplicable."

B. *Violation of Statute as Negligence Per Se.* While some Michigan cases seem to speak of negligence per se as a kind of strict liability ... an examination indicates that there are a number of conditions that attempt to create a more reasonable approach than would result from an automatic application of a per se rule.

Despite such limitations, the judge-made rule of negligence per se has still proved to be too inflexible and mechanical to satisfy thoughtful commentators and judges. It is forcefully argued that no matter how a court may attempt to confine the negligence per se doctrine, if defendant is liable despite the exercise of due care and the availability of a reasonable excuse, this is really strict liability, and not negligence. Prosser, The Law of Torts (4th ed.), §36, p. 197. . . .

C. *Violation of Statute as Evidence of Negligence.* Just as the rebuttable presumption approach to statutory violations in a negligence context arose, at least in part, from dissatisfaction with the result of a mechanical application of the per se rule, a parallel of administrative development in our state with respect to infractions of ordinances and regulations, has been that violations of these amount to only evidence of negligence. . . .

We have not chosen to join that small minority which has decreed that violation of a statute is only evidence of negligence. . . .

An accurate statement of our law is that when a court adopts a penal statute as the standard of care in an action for negligence, violation of that
statute establishes a prima facie case of negligence, with the determination
to be made by the finder of fact whether the party accused of violating the
statute has established a legally sufficient excuse. If the finder of fact determines such an excuse exists, the appropriate standard of care then becomes
that established by the common law.

Zeni v. Anderson, 397 Mich. 117, 243 N.W.2d 270 (1976). Which approach makes more
sense?

7. Why is the weight to be given a statutory violation "a tempest in a teapot" from
the plaintiff's perspective?

8. The defendant may argue that his or her compliance with a statute or ordinance
creates a presumption of due care. This is a common argument in products liability
litigation. In *Alvarado v. J.C. Penney Co.*, 735 F. Supp. 371 (D. Kan. 1990), the court
rejected a presumption of due care in the following statute:

> When the injury-causing aspect of the product was, at the time of manu
> facture, in compliance with legislative regulatory standards or administra
> tive regulatory safety standards relating to design or performance, the product
> shall be deemed not defective by reason of design or performance. . . .

> [W]e are now of the belief that we incorrectly interpreted [the statute] in
> our previous opinion. . . . This means that a plaintiff can attempt to dem
> onstrate by a preponderance of the evidence that a regulatory or adminis
> trative standard does not meet the necessary level of safety.

Problem

While carefully driving to work, Matt is hit by Niles' car. Niles was negligent but
claims that Matt was also negligent because he had no license. Matt's driver's license
expired three days before the crash.

What result and why?

Brown v. Shyne
Court of Appeals of New York, 1926
151 N.E. 197

LEHMAN, J.

The plaintiff employed the defendant to give chiropractic treatment to her for a
disease or physical condition. The defendant had no license to practice medicine, yet
he held himself out as being able to diagnose and treat disease, and under the provisions of the Public Health Law (Cons. Laws, ch. 45) he was guilty of a misdemeanor.
The plaintiff became paralyzed after she had received nine treatments by the defendant. She claims, and upon this appeal we must assume, that the paralysis was caused

by the treatment she received. She has recovered judgment in the sum of $10,000 for the damages caused by said injury.

The plaintiff in her complaint alleges that the injuries were caused by the defendant's negligence. If negligence on the part of the defendant caused the injury, the plaintiff may recover the consequent damages. Though the defendant held himself out, and the plaintiff consulted him, as a chiropractor and not as a regular physician, he claimed to possess the skill requisite for diagnosis and treatment of disease, and in the performance of what he undertook to do he may be held to the degree of skill and care which he claimed to possess. At the trial the plaintiff gave testimony in regard to the manner in which she was treated. . . .

At the close of the plaintiff's case the plaintiff was permitted to amend the complaint to allege "that in so treating the plaintiff the defendant was engaged in the practice of medicine contrary to and in violation of the provisions of the Public Health Law of the State of New York in such case made and provided, he at the time of so treating plaintiff not being a duly licensed physician or surgeon of the State of New York." Thereafter the trial judge charged the jury that they might bring in a verdict in favor of the plaintiff if they found that the evidence established that the treatment given to the plaintiff was not in accordance with the standards of skill and care which prevail among those treating disease. He then continued: "This is a little different from the ordinary malpractice case, and I am going to allow you, if you think proper under the evidence in the case, to predicate negligence upon another theory. The public health laws of this State prescribe that no person shall practice medicine unless he is licensed so to do by the Board of Regents of this State and registered pursuant to statute. . . . This statute to which I have referred is a general police regulation. Its violation, and it has been violated by the defendant, is some evidence, more or less cogent, of negligence which you may consider for what it is worth, along with all the other evidence in the case. . . ."

In so charging the jury that from the violation of the statute the jury might infer negligence which produced injury to the plaintiff, the trial justice in my opinion erred.

The provisions of the Public Health Law prohibiting the practice of medicine without a license granted upon proof of preliminary training and after examination intended to show adequate knowledge, are of course intended for the protection of the general public against injury which unskilled and unlearned practitioners might cause. If violation of the statute by the defendant was the proximate cause of the plaintiff's injury, then the plaintiff may recover upon proof of violation; if violation of the statute has no direct bearing on the injury, proof of the violation becomes irrelevant. For injury caused by neglect of duty imposed by the penal law there is civil remedy; but of course the injury must follow from the neglect.

Proper formulation of general standards of preliminary education and proper examination of the particular applicant should serve to raise the standards of skill and care generally possessed by members of the profession in this State; but the license to practice medicine confers no additional skill upon the practitioner; nor does it confer immunity from physical injury upon a patient if the practitioner fails to exercise care. Here, injury may have been caused by lack of skill or care; it would not have been obviated if the defendant had possessed a license yet failed to exercise the skill and care required of one practicing medicine. True, if the defendant had not practiced medicine in this State, he could not have injured the plaintiff, but the protection which the statute was intended to provide was against risk of injury by the unskilled or careless practitioner, and unless the plaintiff's injury was caused by carelessness or lack of skill, the defendant's failure to obtain a license was not connected with the injury. The plaintiff's cause of action is for negligence or malpractice. The defendant undertook to treat the plaintiff for a physical condition which seemed to require remedy. Under our law such treatment may be given only by a duly qualified practitioner who has obtained a license.

The defendant in offering to treat the plaintiff held himself out as qualified to give treatment. He must meet the professional standards of skill and care prevailing among those who do offer treatment lawfully. If injury follows through failure to meet those standards, the plaintiff may recover. The provisions of the Public Health Law may result in the exclusion from practice of some who are unqualified. Even a skilled and learned practitioner who is not licensed commits an offense against the State; but against such practitioners the statute was not intended to protect, for no protection was needed, and neglect to obtain a license results in no injury to the patient and, therefore, no private wrong. The purpose of the statute is to protect the public against unfounded assumption of skill by one who undertakes to prescribe or treat for disease. In order to show that the plaintiff has been injured by defendant's breach of the statutory duty, proof must be given that defendant in such treatment did not exercise the care and skill which would have been exercised by qualified practitioners within the State, and that such lack of skill and care caused the injury. Failure to obtain a license as required by law gives rise to no remedy if it has caused no injury. . . .

For these reasons the judgments should be reversed and a new trial granted, with costs to abide the event.

---

1. What did the court mean when it said: "We must assume that 'paralysis was caused by the treatment'"?

2. What evidence was there to show that the treatment was negligent? What is the narrow issue here?

3. If the "failure to obtain a license was not connected with the injury," what was the purpose of the statute?

4. Formerly, the rule in New Hampshire was that anyone driving on the road without a license was an outlaw and liable for injuries without a need to show negligence. This has been reversed. *See Fuller v. Sirois*, 97 N.H. 100, 82 A.2d 82 (1951). *Compare*

Mass. Laws ch. 250 (1959). For negligence, should failure to have an automobile driver's license be treated differently from failure to have a medical license?

Rushink v. Gerstheimer

Supreme Court of New York, 1981
440 N.Y.S.2d 738

Before MAHONEY, P.J., and SWEENEY, KANE, CASEY and WEISS, JJ.

Memorandum Decision.

Cross appeals from an order of the Supreme Court at Special Term (Miner, J.), entered October 21, 1980 in Sullivan County, which denied both plaintiff's and defendant's motions for summary judgment. On August 9, 1978, defendant Mary Jane Gerstheimer, a stenographer employed by the Letchworth Village Developmental Center, drove an automobile owned by her husband, defendant George F. Gerstheimer, to a pharmacy located on the grounds of the Middletown Psychiatric Center. After parking the automobile in front of the pharmacy, she left it unattended with the keys in the ignition. Moments later, Stephen E. Rushink, a resident patient at the facility, drove away in the vehicle and met his death soon thereafter when it left the road and struck a tree. After issue was joined, plaintiff moved at Special Term for summary judgment contending that there were no triable issues of fact since defendant Mary Jane Gerstheimer violated subdivision (a) of section 1210 of the Vehicle and Traffic Law and that the violation of the statute was the proximate cause of the occurrence. Defendants opposed the motion arguing that subdivision (a) of section 1210 of the Vehicle and Traffic Law is not applicable to the instant case and, assuming it was, that the alleged violation was not the proximate cause of plaintiff's decedent's accident. Defendants also moved for summary judgment to dismiss the complaint. Special Term denied both motions and these appeals ensued. Subdivision (a) of section 1210, which prohibits a person in charge of a vehicle from leaving it unattended without removing or hiding the key, was enacted to deter theft and injury from the operation of motor vehicles by unauthorized persons. . . . In our view, however, its provisions were plainly not designed to protect such unauthorized users from the consequences of their own actions. . . . That plaintiff's decedent may not have been capable of forming a larcenous intent is irrelevant to our conclusion that he could not have been within the class of persons the enactment was meant to protect. Of course, redress for wrongs suffered by one under a legal disability may be pursued in a common-law negligence action wholly apart from statutory considerations. The instant complaint is sufficient to support such a cause of action and, since there are obvious factual issues to be resolved in determining defendants' liability, if any, the motions for summary judgment were properly denied. Order affirmed, without costs.

SWEENEY, KANE and CASEY, JJ., concur.

MAHONEY, P.J., and WEISS, J., concur in the following memorandum by MAHONEY, P.J.

MAHONEY, PRESIDING JUDGE (concurring).

While we concur in the majority's holding that the order denying both plaintiff's and defendants' motions for summary judgment must be affirmed, we cannot accept the view that subdivision (a) of section 1210 of the Vehicle and Traffic Law does not create a class of persons entitled to be protected by the statute, and, further, that plaintiff's decedent is not among its membership. In recommending the enactment of section 1210, the Joint Legislative Committee on Motor Vehicle Problems stated that the proposed law was "designed to obviate the risk of a vehicle moving from the place where it was left parked and possibly injuring the person or property of others as well as itself being damaged. It serves to lessen the likelihood of theft" (NY Legis Doc, 1954, No. 36, pp. 106–107). Since at common law the owner was not liable, as a matter of law, for the negligence of a thief, on the basis that the use of the car by the thief intervened between the occurrence of the negligence of the owner and the unskillful operation of the car by the thief . . . , the statute changed the common law and made it clear that the intervention of an unauthorized person no longer operates to break the chain of causation. Where, as here, the legislative intent to protect the public generally from the consequences that foreseeably flow from unauthorized use of motor vehicles is clear, and, again as here, the violation of subdivision (a) of section 1210 is undisputed, it is patently unfair to deny to plaintiff the evidentiary weight of such violation and leave him to the more vigorous burden of establishing common-law negligence.

———————

1. Was the plaintiff within the hazard and class protected by the statute?

2. Why was Rushink not permitted to argue to the jury that the statute set the standard?

3. What is Rushink's course of action now? What problems lie ahead?

4. What would have been the result if Rushink had run into another car and injured the driver? *See Ney v. Yellow Cab Co.*, 2 Ill. 2d 74, 117 N.E.2d 74 (1954).

5. The plaintiff obtained drinks at the defendant's bar and was injured when her car later hit a tree. She alleged that she received the drinks after she was intoxicated. Although the statute provided that the sale of alcoholic beverages to a noticeably intoxicated person was a crime, the court found in favor of the bar: "[F]or at least 94 years it has been the law of this State that the statute . . . does not create any civil liability on the part of the sellers of alcoholic beverages." *Riverside Enters. v. Rahn*, 171 Ga. App. 674, 320 S.E.2d 595 (1984).

6. Some statutes are interpreted as providing strict liability without any excuses. *See*, for example, the Pure Food Act discussed in *Doherty v. S.S. Kresge Co.*, 227 Wis. 661, 278 N.W. 437 (1938). Child labor acts are another example. *See Blanton v. Kellioka Coal Co.*, 192 Ky. 220, 232 S.W. 614 (1921).

7. Statutory violations can be excused as follows: the actor is incapacitated, he or she does not know of the need for compliance, he or she exercises reasonable

diligence, there was an emergency, and compliance with the act involves a greater risk of harm than violation. Restatement (Second) of Torts § 288A.

8. A mentally ill plaintiff is only held to be contributorily negligent if he or she can appreciate the nature of the conduct. *See Emory Univ. v. Lee*, 97 Ga. App. 680, 104 S.E.2d 234 (1958).

9. Some states enact legislation holding the commercial providers of alcohol liable when an intoxicated customer injures someone. Such laws are called Dram Shop Acts. *See Ling v. Jan's Liquors*, 237 Kan. 629, 703 P.2d 731 (1985).

F. Proving the Negligence Case Before the Judge and the Jury

There are three types of evidence: direct, real, and circumstantial. Direct evidence is the statement of a witness about a fact in issue that he or she saw. The witness, for example, said that the defendant's car was traveling at 110 miles per hour when it hit the plaintiff's car. Real evidence is the knife used in the stabbing or a rug with a hole in it. Circumstantial evidence is evidence of fact A (not in issue) from which fact B (in issue) can be inferred. An example of this is the failure of the brakes in a new car. It can be inferred from the failure that there was something the matter with the car when it was sold.

Most evidence in torts cases is circumstantial. There are few smoking guns.

1. Circumstantial Evidence

Problem

Duane has an open-air market located beside a two-lane highway in Texas. About half the produce is displayed outside in boxes or on the ground. While "Bootsie" was picking up a pumpkin located outside, she was bitten by a rattlesnake. Discuss.

Negri v. Stop & Shop, Inc.
Court of Appeals of New York, 1985
480 N.E.2d 740

Memorandum.

. . . .

The record contains some evidence tending to show that defendant had constructive notice of a dangerous condition which allegedly caused injuries to its customer. There was testimony that the injured plaintiff, while shopping in defendant's store, fell backward, did not come into contact with the shelves, but hit her head directly on the floor where "a lot of broken jars" of baby food lay; that the baby food was "dirty and messy"; that a witness in the immediate vicinity of the accident did not hear any jars falling from the shelves or otherwise breaking during the 15 or 20 minutes prior to the accident; and that the aisle had not been cleaned or inspected for at least 50 minutes prior to the accident—indeed, some evidence was adduced that it was at least two hours.

Viewing the evidence in a light most favorable to the plaintiff and according plaintiff the benefit of every reasonable inference . . . , it cannot be said, as a matter of law, that the circumstantial evidence was insufficient to permit the jury to draw the necessary inference that a slippery condition was created by jars of baby food which had fallen and broken a sufficient length of time prior to the accident to permit defendant's employees to discover and remedy the condition. . . . Plaintiff having made out a prima facie case, it was error to dismiss the complaint.

––––––––––––

1. What kind of evidence did the plaintiff introduce? How convincing is it?

2. Compare *Negri* with *Goddard:*

> Action by Wilfred H. Goddard against the Boston & Maine Railroad Company for personal injuries received by falling upon a banana skin lying upon the platform at defendant's station at Boston. The evidence showed that plaintiff was a passenger who had just arrived, and was about the length of the car from where he alighted when he slipped and fell. There was evidence that there were many passengers on the platform. Verdict directed for defendant, and plaintiff excepts. Exceptions overruled.

> HOLMES, C.J. The banana skin upon which the plaintiff stepped and which caused him to slip may have been dropped within a minute by one of the persons who was leaving the train. It is unnecessary to go further to decide the case.

> Exceptions overruled.

Goddard v. Boston & Maine R.R. Co., 179 Mass. 52, 60 N.E. 486 (1901). Why did the plaintiff lose?

3. What inference in the following slip-and-fall case? Should the case be submitted to the jury?

> The plaintiff arrived on one of defendant's cars on the upper level of the Dudley Street terminal; other passengers arrived on the same car, but it does not appear how many. She waited until the crowd had left the platform, when she inquired of one of defendant's uniformed employees the direction to another car. He walked along a narrow platform, and she, following a few feet behind him toward the stairway he had indicated, was injured by slipping upon a banana peel. It was described by several who examined it in these terms: It "felt dry, gritty, as if there were dirt upon it," as if "trampled over a good deal," as "flattened down, and black in color," "every bit of it was black, there wasn't a particle of yellow," and as "black, flattened out and gritty." It

was one of the duties of employees of the defendant, of whom there was one at this station all the time, to observe and remove whatever was upon the platform to interfere with the safety of travelers. These might have been found to be the facts.

Anjou v. Boston Elevated R.R. Co., 208 Mass. 273, 94 N.E. 386 (1911). How is *Anjou* different from *Goddard* in regard to the weight of the evidence?

4. The constructive notice principle was clearly presented in *Gordon v. American Museum of Nat. History*, 67 N.Y.2d 836, 492 N.E.2d 774, 501N.Y.S.2d 646 (1986):

Plaintiff was injured when he fell on defendant's front entrance steps. He testified that as he descended the upper level of steps he slipped on the third step and that while he was in midair he observed a piece of white, waxy paper next to his left foot. He alleges that this paper came from the concession stand that defendant had contracted to have present and which was located on the plaza separating the two tiers of steps and that defendant was negligent insofar as its employees failed to discover and remove the paper before he fell on it. The case was submitted to the jury on the theory that defendant had either actual or constructive notice of the dangerous condition presented by the paper on the steps. The jury found against defendant on the issue of liability. A divided Appellate Division affirmed and granted defendant leave to appeal on a certified question.

There is no evidence in the record that defendant had actual notice of the paper and the case should not have gone to the jury on that theory. To constitute constructive notice, a defect must be visible and apparent and it must exist for a sufficient length of time prior to the accident to permit defendant's employees to discover and remedy it (*Negri v. Stop & Shop* . . .). The record contains no evidence that anyone including plaintiff, observed the piece of white paper prior to the accident. Nor did he describe the paper as being dirty or worn, which would have provided some indication that it had been present for some period of time *(cf. Negri v. Stop & Shop* . . .). Thus on the evidence presented, the piece of paper that caused plaintiff's fall could have been deposited there only minutes or seconds before the accident and any other conclusion would be pure speculation.

. . . The defect in plaintiff's case here, however, is not an inability to prove the causation element of his fall but the lack of evidence establishing constructive notice of the particular condition that caused his fall.

5. Suppose the plaintiff slips on a piece of freshly cooked pizza;

In her attempt to meet the requirement of notice, plaintiff did not claim or show that the alleged pizza was placed or dropped on the floor directly by the defendant or its employees, or that defendant knew of its presence. . . . Rather, it was her contention that defendant's method of selling pizza was one which leads inescapably to such mishaps as her own, and that in such a situation conventional notice requirements need not be met. We agree.

The dangerous condition was created by the store's method of sale. The steps taken to constantly clean the floor show that the store owner recognized the danger.

The practice of extensive selling of slices of pizza on waxed paper to customers who consume it while standing creates the reasonable probability that food will drop to the floor. Food on a terrazzo floor will create a dangerous condition. In such a situation, notice to the proprietor of the specific item on the floor need not be shown.

[Directed verdict in favor of defendant, reversed.] *Jasko v. F.W. Woolworth Co.*, 177 Colo. 418, 494 P.2d 839 (1972). How is this theory of liability different from the constructive notice cases?

Pietrone v. American Honda Motor Co.

Court of Appeals of California, 1987
235 Cal. Rptr. 137

Opinion by: GATES, J.

Defendant American Honda Motor Company, Inc., appeals from the judgment entered pursuant to a jury verdict in favor of plaintiff Alison Pietrone. . . .

Plaintiff presented evidence that she was a passenger on her husband's 1974 Honda CB 450 motorcycle on the afternoon of April 26, 1979. As they entered the intersection of Towne Avenue and Arrow Highway in the City of Pomona the driver of an oncoming automobile began a U-turn. Her husband moved to the right in an unsuccessful attempt to avoid the vehicle. The auto's bumper struck the lower portion of plaintiff's left leg, breaking it.

This impact was so slight it merely created a "wobbling sensation" in the motorcycle rather than causing it to overturn. Nonetheless, plaintiff's now unstable leg came into contact with the exposed spokes of its rear wheel behind the shock absorber, but "[not] very long, because it came out, and while it was coming out it was rotating." As it rotated two full revolutions, it "was also moving out and forward." As it did so her foot "caught the shock absorber, which brought it back in again," lodging it tightly into the equally open area located in front of the shock absorber and above the chain guard.

So powerful were the forces that had been exerted upon plaintiff's foot, she was required to sit, helplessly trapped, for many agonizing minutes. In fact, she was freed only after firemen arrived armed with an instrument known as the "jaws of life" with which they were able to cut away the shock absorber. As a result of her experience, it was necessary for this 21-year-old plaintiff to undergo a below-the-knee amputation of her leg.

After presenting the foregoing evidence, but before formally resting, counsel for plaintiff advised the court it was his "understanding of the law, as it exists now in product liability cases, that it is the responsibility of a plaintiff to meet her burden of proof that she present a prima facie case. That . . . a design feature, and in this case that would be the open, exposed, rotating wheel of this motorcycle, was a proximate cause of her injury. Having established a prima facie case to that extent, . . . the burden of proof then shifts to the defendant" who "must now prove and produce evidence that the benefit of this design feature outweighs the risk of injury, as has been presented by the plaintiff." Counsel expressed his belief that plaintiff had met this burden and sought the court's concurrence. He also informed the court that he had additional witnesses, specifically engineers, who could be called to defend "against whatever evidence the defendants present on their burden of proof."

The court declined to make an "anticipatory" ruling, but did indicate that in considering motions the defense might make, it "would see no prejudice to the defense to reopen in the event that [plaintiff] left something out which [the court] [deemed] critical." Plaintiff responded, "And I will rest, based upon that."

When proceedings commenced following a four-day recess, Honda's counsel opined that in his view plaintiff had failed to prove her case. He announced that . . . "the defendant will rest at this point of time without producing any additional evidence, other than that which has been produced on cross-examination of the witnesses called by plaintiff and will move this court for a directed verdict." He additionally advised the court, "one of the reasons that we have decided to rest, rather than move for non-suit, was the fact that there has been no expert testimony that would indicate any way, any method, that this motorcycle could have been designed, in order to prevent the unusual type of injury that occurred in this particular case."

In the instant case the evidence conclusively established that a design feature of Honda's product—the open, exposed, rotating rear wheel in close proximity to the passenger's foot pegs—was a proximate cause of plaintiff's injury. Without more, the burden then shifted to Honda to justify its adoption and utilization of that particular design. . . . Further, even were it to be assumed that plaintiff's burden under *Barker v. Lull* . . . exceeded such a showing and required that she demonstrate the existence of some alternative design which would have prevented or lessened her injury, this burden was met by the jury's mere inspection of the photographs introduced into evidence. That is to say, no more than a cursory examination of this machine's configuration makes apparent both the danger of its design and potential solutions thereto.

Given that such alternative designs were so self-evident as to obviate the need to present express testimony, expert or otherwise, on the subject, it is equally clear counsel for plaintiff did not commit misconduct by mentioning during argument that items which "would avoid contact" such as saddlebags, luggage racks, fairings, shields, etc., could be so placed as to partially enclose the motorcycle's rotating rear wheel.

The existence of such devices on other models is a matter of general knowledge and their potential effectiveness in preventing the sort of accident which occurred here is patent.

. . . .

The judgment is affirmed.

_____

1. Why did Honda rest without challenging plaintiff's evidence? Why did the court reject Honda's appellate argument?

2. Is this evidence real or circumstantial?

3. *Pietrone* rests on a strict liability cause of action. Would the result be different if it rested on negligence? Can't the jury conclude that the motorcycle was negligently designed? •

4. The Restatement (Third) of Products Liability, § 2(b), provides: A "product is defective in design when the foreseeable risks of harm posed by the product could have been reduced . . . by the adoption of a reasonable alternative design by the seller . . . and the omission . . . renders the product not reasonably safe."

How does this section of the Restatement affect what the plaintiff must prove in cases like *Pietrone*? For evaluations of the Restatement (Third) of Products Liability, see M.S. Shapo, *In Search of the Law of Products Liability: The ALI Restatement Project*, 48 Vand. L. Rev. 631 (1995); F.J. Vandall, *The Restatement (Third) of Torts, Products Liability, Section 2(b): Design Defect*, 68 Temp. L. Rev. 167 (1995).

2. Res Ipsa Loquitur

The plaintiff was bound to give affirmative proof of negligence. But there was not a scintilla of evidence, unless the occurrence is of itself evidence of negligence. . . . [Pollock, C.B. interrupted the defense's argument to say: "There are certain cases of which it may be said res ipsa loquitur, and this seems one of them. In some cases the Courts have held that the mere fact of the accident having occurred is evidence of negligence, . . ."]

The present case upon the evidence comes to this, a man is passing in front of the premises of a dealer in flour, and there falls down upon him a barrel of flour. I think it apparent that the barrel was in the custody of the defendant who occupied the premises, and who is responsible for the acts of his servants who had the control of it; and in my opinion the fact of its falling is prima facie evidence of negligence, and the plaintiff who was injured by it is not bound to show that it could not fall without negligence, but if there are any facts inconsistent with negligence it is for the defendant to prove them.

Byrne v. Boadle, 2 H & C 722, 159 Eng. Rep. 299 (Ct. Ex. 1863).

Problem

When Calla picked up her two-and-a-half-year-old daughter at the nursery room in her church, she discovered a serious eye injury. The two adults who supervised the children could not explain what happened, and an inspection of the toys in the nursery revealed no sharp objects. Is there an inference of negligence on the part of the supervisors and the church to give to the jury?

Escola v. Coca-Cola Bottling Co.

Supreme Court of California, 1944
150 P.2d 436

Opinion by: Gibson, J.

Plaintiff, a waitress in a restaurant, was injured when a bottle of Coca Cola broke in her hand. She alleged that defendant company, which had bottled and delivered the alleged defective bottle to her employer, was negligent in selling "bottles containing said beverage which on account of excessive pressure of gas or by reason of some defect in the bottle was dangerous . . . and likely to explode." This appeal is from a judgment upon a jury verdict in favor of plaintiff.

Defendant's driver delivered several cases of Coca-Cola to the restaurant, placing them on the floor, one on top of the other, under and behind the counter, where they remained at least thirty-six hours. Immediately before the accident, plaintiff picked up the top case and set it upon a near-by ice cream cabinet in front of and about three feet from the refrigerator. She then proceeded to take the bottles from the case with her right hand, one at a time, and put them into the refrigerator. Plaintiff testified that after she had placed three bottles in the refrigerator and had moved the fourth bottle about eighteen inches from the case "it exploded in my hand." The bottle broke into two jagged pieces and inflicted a deep five-inch cut, severing blood vessels, nerves and muscles of the thumb and palm of the hand. Plaintiff further testified that when the bottle exploded, "It made a sound similar to an electric light bulb that would have dropped. It made a loud pop." Plaintiff's employer testified, "I was about twenty feet from where it actually happened and I heard the explosion." A fellow employee, on the opposite side of the counter, testified that plaintiff "had the bottle, I should judge, waist high, and I know that it didn't bang either the case or the door or another bottle . . . when it popped. It sounded just like a fruit jar would blow up. . . ." The witness further testified that the contents of the bottle "flew all over herself and myself and the walls and one thing and another."

The top portion of the bottle, with the cap, remained in plaintiff's hand, and the lower portion fell to the floor but did not break. The broken bottle was not produced at the trial, the pieces having been thrown away by an employee of the restaurant shortly after the accident. Plaintiff, however, described the broken pieces, and a diagram of the bottle was made showing the location of the "fracture line" where the bottle broke in two.

. . . .

Plaintiff then rested her case, having announced to the court that being unable to show any specific acts of negligence she relied completely on the doctrine of res ipsa loquitur.

Defendant contends that the doctrine of res ipsa loquitur does not apply in this case, and that the evidence is insufficient to support the judgment.

Many jurisdictions have applied the doctrine in cases involving exploding bottles of carbonated beverages. . . . It would serve no useful purpose to discuss the reasoning of the foregoing cases in detail, since the problem is whether under the facts shown in the instant case the conditions warranting application of the doctrine have been satisfied.

Res ipsa loquitur does not apply unless (1) defendant had exclusive control of the thing causing the injury and (2) the accident is of such a nature that it ordinarily would not occur in the absence of negligence by the defendant. . . .

Many authorities state that the happening of the accident does not speak for itself where it took place sometime after defendant had relinquished control of the instrumentality causing the injury. Under the more logical view, however, the doctrine may be applied upon the theory that defendant had control at the time of the alleged negligent act, although not at the time of the accident, provided plaintiff first proves that the condition of the instrumentality had not been changed after it left the defendant's possession. . . . As said in *Dunn v. Hoffman Beverage Co.*, 126 N.J.L. 556 [20 A.2d 352, 354], "defendant is not charged with the duty of showing affirmatively that something happened to the bottle after it left its control or management; . . . to get to the jury the plaintiff must show that there was due care during that period." Plaintiff must also prove that she handled the bottle carefully. The reason for this prerequisite is set forth in Prosser on Torts, *supra*, at page 300, where the author states: "Allied to the condition of exclusive control in the defendant is that of absence of any action on the part of the plaintiff contributing to the accident. Its purpose, of course, is to eliminate the possibility that it was the plaintiff who was responsible." . . .

Upon an examination of the record, the evidence appears sufficient to support a reasonable inference that the bottle here involved was not damaged by any extraneous force after delivery to the restaurant by defendant. It follows, therefore, that the bottle was in some manner defective at the time defendant relinquished control, because sound and properly prepared bottles of carbonated liquids do not ordinarily explode when carefully handled.

. . . .

The judgment is affirmed. Concur by: Traynor, J.

1. Before the decision in *Byrne v. Boadle*, the plaintiff had to present affirmative evidence of negligence by means of witnesses who saw the occurrence. What is the import of res ipsa loquitur (the thing speaks for itself)?

2. If the defendant presents no evidence, after the court permits an inference of negligence, what may happen? Is this unfair to the defendant?

3. *Escola* is best known for the concurring opinion [omitted from this chapter] by Judge Traynor, where he presents the policy foundation for strict liability in products cases.

4. Isn't there a possibility that someone bumped the Coca-Cola bottle after it left the seller? Who should have the burden of proving that the bump occurred? What if such proof is not available?

5. Is it also possible that the plaintiff bumped the bottle? How does Judge Gibson deal with that possibility?

Cox v. Northwest Airlines

United States Court of Appeals, Seventh Circuit, 1967
379 F.2d 893

CASTLE, CIRCUIT JUDGE.

The appellant, Northwest Airlines, Inc., prosecutes this appeal from a judgment entered against it in an admiralty action instituted in the District Court by the libellant-appellee, Irene Cox, administratrix. Libellant sought recovery of damages under the Death on the High Seas Act (46 U.S.C.A. § 761 et seq.) for the death of her husband. The action was tried to the court without a jury. The court made and entered findings of fact and conclusions of law, and awarded judgment against the appellant for $329,956.59.

The record discloses that the libellant's decedent, her husband, Randall S. Cox, a Captain in the United States Army, 29 years of age, was a passenger on appellant's Douglas DC-7C airplane ... which crashed in the Pacific Ocean on June 3, 1963 during a flight from McChord Air Force Base, near Seattle, Washington, to Elmendorf, Alaska, at approximately 11:12 A.M. at a point about one hundred sixteen miles west-southwest of Annette Island off the west coast of Canada. The flight had taken off from McChord at about 8:32 A.M. after having been briefed on the weather by both its dispatch office at the Seattle Airport and by a U.S. Air Force weather specialist at McChord, and having followed the usual procedures in preparation for flight. The crew reported by radio at 11:07 A.M. that it had been over Domestic Annette at an altitude of 14,000 feet and requested clearance to climb to 18,000 feet. No reason for the requested change in altitude was given. Domestic Annette is a fix-point at which directional radio bearings are obtained along the air route from McChord to Elmendorf. This was the last known transmission made by the crew of the aircraft. On the following day, June 4, 1963, floating debris was sighted in the

Pacific Ocean about 35 nautical miles west of Domestic Annette. Approximately 1,500 pounds of wreckage identified as being from the aircraft, including life vests still encased in their plastic containers and extremely deformed seat frames, was recovered. The bodies of none of the crew or passengers were ever recovered.

. . . The court's conclusion that the negligence of appellant was the proximate cause of decedent's death is predicated upon the court's finding that:

"[A]s a result of the occurrence Randall S. Cox met his death. The instrumentality which produced the death of Randall S. Cox was under the exclusive control and management of the [appellant] and that the occurrence in question was such as does not ordinarily occur in the absence of negligence, and, further, that there is no possibility of contributing conduct which would make Randall S. Cox responsible; that the facts herein justify a finding of negligence."

The appellant recognizes that the doctrine of res ipsa loquitur may properly have application in actions involving airline accidents. But the appellant contends that in the instant case it was error to apply that doctrine in resolving the issue of liability because there is substantial proof of the exercise of due care by the appellant and no countervailing evidence of specific negligence or even of unusual circumstances. Appellant urges that evidence of due care on its part precludes any inference of negligence arising from the occurrence in the absence of at least minimal supporting evidence. . . .

The evidence of due care to which appellant alludes concerns its maintenance records and procedures with respect to the aircraft involved; the qualified and certified status, and the competence, of the operating personnel of the aircraft and of the dispatcher; the safety training received by the crew; and the evidence that the flight was properly dispatched and the weather normal.

There is no evidence as to the cause of the aircraft's crash into the ocean or concerning what happened to affect the operation of the aircraft during the period following 11:07 A.M. and prior to the crash. In the absence of such evidence, the probative value of appellant's general evidence of due care is not of substantial import. Whether due care was exercised by the operating personnel of the aircraft in the face of whatever occurred to affect the operation of the aircraft can be appraised only in the light of knowledge of what that occurrence was, whether human or mechanical failure or some other incident, and of what if anything was or could have been done about it.

We perceive nothing in appellant's due care evidence which precludes an application of the res ipsa loquitur doctrine or conditions such application upon the libellant's responding with evidence to support some specific negligent act or omission on the part of appellant. Here the cause of the crash which resulted in the death of Randall S. Cox is wholly unexplained. And, as was cogently observed in *Johnson v. United States*, 333 U.S. 46, 49 . . . .

"No act need be explicable only in terms of negligence in order for the rule of res ipsa loquitur to be invoked. The rule deals only with permissible inferences from unexplained events."

We are of the opinion that the court properly applied the doctrine of res ipsa loquitur and that its finding of negligence was a permissible one—warranted though not compelled . . . and that the court's conclusion on the issue of appellant's liability is thus supported by the evidence and the application of correct legal criteria. . . .

Affirmed in part and remanded with directions to modify damages awarded.

———

1. What inferences may be drawn from the plaintiff's evidence? Why does the court refuse to draw inferences from the defendant's evidence of due care? Why aren't the jury and the court merely guessing on the issue of negligence in *Cox*? Have tragic current events like plane crashes had an impact on the likelihood that a court will apply res ipsa loquitur in the case of an unexplained plane crash?

2. In another plane crash case brought by a passenger, the court refused to apply res ipsa loquitur against the pilot:

The record is barren of any demonstrable proof of what occurred after the aircraft disappeared from view. Except for the time and location of the crash, everything else relating to the fatal accident is a matter of conjecture and speculation. The scant evidence gathered at the crash site, at which fire followed impact, revealed nothing concerning the course and position of the plane or the actions of the pilot immediately before the crash.

Campbell v. First Nat'l Bank in Albuquerque, NM., 370 F. Supp. 1096 (D.N.M. 1973). The pilot had just rented the small plane in the morning, and there were difficult mountains around the airfield. Why a different result from *Cox*?

3. In contrast, res ipsa loquitur was applied to direct a verdict against the pilot in *Newing v. Cheatham*, 15 Cal. 3d 351, 124 Cal. Rptr. 193, 540 P.2d 33 (1975).

Ybarra v. Spangard

Supreme Court of California, 1944
154 P.2d 687

GIBSON, CHIEF JUSTICE.

This is an action for damages for personal injuries alleged to have been inflicted on plaintiff [Ybarra] by defendants during the course of a surgical operation. The trial court entered judgments of nonsuit as to all defendants and plaintiff appealed.

On October 28, 1939, plaintiff consulted defendant Dr. Tilley, who diagnosed his ailment as appendicitis, and made arrangements for an appendectomy to be performed by defendant Dr. Spangard at a hospital owned and managed by defendant Dr. Swift. Plaintiff entered the hospital, was given a hypodermic injection, slept, and later was awakened by Doctors Tilley and Spangard and wheeled into the operating room by a nurse whom he believed to be defendant Gisler, an employee of Dr. Swift. Defendant Dr. Reser, the anesthetist, also an employee of Dr. Swift, adjusted plaintiff for the operation, pulling his body to the head of the operating table and, according to plaintiff's testimony, laying him back against two hard objects at the top of his shoulders, about an inch below his neck. Dr. Reser then administered the anesthetic and plaintiff lost consciousness. When he awoke early the following morning he was in his hospital room attended by defendant Thompson, the special nurse, and another nurse who was not made a defendant.

Plaintiff testified that prior to the operation he had never had any pain in, or injury to, his right arm or shoulder, but that when he awakened he felt a sharp pain about half way between the neck and the point of the right shoulder. He complained to the nurse, and then to Dr. Tilley, who gave him diathermy treatments while he remained in the hospital. The pain did not cease, but spread down to the lower part of his arm, and after his release from the hospital the condition grew worse. He was unable to rotate or lift his arm, and developed paralysis and atrophy of the muscles around the shoulder. He received further treatments from Dr. Tilley until March, 1940, and then returned to work, wearing his arm in a splint on the advice of Dr. Spangard. . . .

Plaintiff's theory is that the foregoing evidence presents a proper case for the application of the doctrine of res ipsa loquitur. . . . Defendants take the position that, assuming that plaintiff's condition was in fact the result of an injury, there is no showing that the act of any particular defendant, nor any particular instrumentality, was the cause thereof. They attack plaintiff's action as an attempt to fix liability "en masse" on various defendants, some of whom were not responsible for the acts of others; and they further point to the failure to show which defendants had control of the instrumentalities that may have been involved. Their main defense may be briefly stated in two propositions: (1) that where there are several defendants, and there is a division of responsibility in the use of an instrumentality causing the injury, and the injury might have resulted from the separate act of either one of two or more persons, the rule of res ipsa loquitur cannot be invoked against any one of them; and (2) that where there are several instrumentalities, and no showing is made as to which caused the injury or as to the particular defendant in control of it, the doctrine cannot apply. We are satisfied, however, that these objections are not well taken in the circumstances of this case.

The doctrine of res ipsa loquitur has three conditions: "(1) the accident must be of a kind which ordinarily does not occur in the absence of someone's negligence; (2) it must be caused by an agency or instrumentality within the exclusive control of the defendant; (3) it must not have been due to any voluntary action or contribution on the part of the plaintiff." . . .

. . . If the doctrine is to continue to serve a useful purpose, we should not forget that "the particular force and justice of the rule, regarded as a presumption throwing upon the party charged the duty of producing evidence, consists in the circumstance that the chief evidence of the true cause, whether culpable or innocent, is practically accessible to him but inaccessible to the injured person." . . .

The present case is of a type which comes within the reason and spirit of the doctrine more fully perhaps than any other. The passenger sitting awake in a railroad car at the time of a collision, the pedestrian walking along the street and struck by a falling object or the debris of an explosion, are surely not more entitled to an explanation than the unconscious patient on the operating table. Viewed from this aspect, it is difficult to see how the doctrine can, with any justification, be so restricted in its statement as to become inapplicable to a patient who submits himself to the care and custody of doctors and nurses, is rendered unconscious, and receives some injury from instrumentalities used in his treatment. Without the aid of the doctrine a patient who received permanent injuries of a serious character, obviously the result of someone's negligence, would be entirely unable to recover unless the doctors and nurses in attendance voluntarily chose to disclose the identity of the negligent person and the facts establishing liability. . . . If this were the state of the law of negligence, the courts, to avoid gross injustice, would be forced to invoke the principles of absolute liability, irrespective of negligence, in actions by persons suffering injuries during the course of treatment under anesthesia. But we think this juncture has not yet been reached, and that the doctrine of res ipsa loquitur is properly applicable to the case before us.

The condition that the injury must not have been due to the plaintiff's voluntary action is of course fully satisfied under the evidence produced herein; and the same is true of the condition that the accident must be one which ordinarily does not occur unless someone was negligent. We have here no problem of negligence in treatment, but of distinct injury to a healthy part of the body not the subject of treatment, nor within the area covered by the operation. The decisions in this state make it clear that such circumstances raise the inference of negligence, and call upon the defendant to explain the unusual result. . . .

The argument of defendants is simply that plaintiff has not shown an injury caused by an instrumentality under a defendant's control, because he has not shown which of the several instrumentalities that he came in contact with while in the hospital caused the injury; and he has not shown that any one defendant or his servants had exclusive control over any particular instrumentality. Defendants assert that some of them were not the employees of other defendants, that some did not stand in any permanent relationship from which liability in tort would follow, and that in view of the nature of the injury, the number of defendants and the different functions performed by each, they could not all be liable for the wrong, if any.

We have no doubt that in a modern hospital a patient is quite likely to come under the care of a number of persons in different types of contractual and other relationships with each other. For example, in the present case it appears that Doctors Smith, Spangard and Tilley were physicians or surgeons commonly placed in the legal category of independent contractors; and Dr. Reser, the anesthetist, and defendant Thompson, the special nurse, were employees of Dr. Swift and not of the other doctors. But we do not believe that either the number or relationship of the defendants alone determines whether the doctrine of res ipsa loquitur applies. Every defendant in whose custody the plaintiff was placed for any period was bound to exercise ordinary care to see that no unnecessary harm came to him and each would be liable for failure in this regard. Any defendant who negligently injured him, and any defendant charged with his care who so neglected him as to allow injury to occur, would be liable. The defendant employers would be liable for the neglect of their employees; and the doctor in charge of the operation would be liable for the negligence of those who became his temporary servants for the purpose of assisting in the operation.

. . . .

It may appear at the trial that, consistent with the principles outlined above, one or more defendants will be found liable and others absolved, but this should not preclude the application of the rule of res ipsa loquitur. The control, at one time or another, of one or more of the various agencies or instrumentalities which might have harmed the plaintiff was in the hands of every defendant or of his employees or temporary servants. This, we think, places upon them the burden of initial explanation. Plaintiff was rendered unconscious for the purpose of undergoing surgical treatment by the defendants; it is manifestly unreasonable for them to insist that he identify any one of them as the person who did the alleged negligent act.

The other aspect of the case which defendants so strongly emphasize is that plaintiff has not identified the instrumentality any more than he has the particular guilty defendant. Here, again, there is a misconception which, if carried to the extreme for which defendants contend, would unreasonably limit the application of the res ipsa loquitur rule. It should be enough that the plaintiff can show an injury resulting from an external force applied while he lay unconscious in the hospital; this is as clear a case of identification of the instrumentality as the plaintiff may ever be able to make.

. . . .

In the face of these examples of liberalization of the tests for res ipsa loquitur, there can be no justification for the rejection of the doctrine in the instant case. As pointed out above, if we accept the contention of defendants herein, there will rarely be any compensation for patients injured while unconscious. A hospital today conducts a highly integrated system of activities, with many persons contributing their efforts. There may be, e.g., preparation for surgery by nurses and interns who are employees of the hospital; administering of an anesthetic by a doctor who may be an employee of the hospital, an employee of the operating surgeon, or an independent contractor; performance of an operation by a surgeon and assistants who may be his employees, employees of the hospital, or independent contractors; and post surgical care by the surgeon, a hospital physician, and nurses. The number of those in whose care the patient is placed is not a good reason for denying him all reasonable opportunity to recover for negligent harm. It is rather a good reason for re-examination of the statement of legal theories which supposedly compel such a shocking result.

. . . .

We . . . hold that where a plaintiff receives unusual injuries while unconscious and in the course of medical treatment, all those defendants who had any control over his body or the instrumentalities which might have caused the injuries may properly be called upon to meet the inference of negligence by giving an explanation of their conduct.

The judgment is reversed.

———————

1. What is the plaintiff's argument? What is the defendant's response to the plaintiff's contentions? Why does the court agree with the plaintiff?

2. If res ipsa had not applied in *Ybarra*, what would have been the result?

3. The remand was held before a judge sitting without a jury. The defendants all testified that they saw nothing, and the judge found for the plaintiff:

> All of the defendants except the owner of the hospital, who was not personally in attendance upon the respondent, gave evidence and each testified that while he was present he saw nothing occur which could have produced the injury to respondent's arm and shoulder. Upon this evidence appellants insist that the prima facie case made under the res ipsa doctrine was overcome. But it was for the trial judge to weigh the circumstantial evidence which made the prima facie case under the res ipsa rule against the positive testimony of the appellants and to determine whether the prima facie case had been met. . . . There is nothing inherent in direct testimony which compels a trial court to accept it over the contrary inferences which may reasonably be drawn from circumstantial evidence. The view taken of the evidence by the trial judge is illustrated by the following remark made at the hearing of the motion for new trial:
>
> > "I believe it arose from a traumatic condition. Now, where did it happen? That puts the court right back. Even though their explanations were honest, that there was something they did not appreciate happened in the course of the operation, in the course of handling the patient. That is the way I figured the case and that was my decision."

Ybarra v. Spangard, 93 Cal. App. 2d 43, 208 P.2d 445 (1949). Why did the court reach this result? What impact might this result have on future cases?

4. In medical malpractice cases, res ipsa loquitur has been applied to a sponge left in the body, *Truhitte v. French Hosp.*, 128 Cal. App. 3d 332, 180 Cal. Rptr. 152 (1982), and to severe burns the plaintiff received while unconscious following a Caesarean operation, *Timbrell v. Suburban Hosp.*, 4 Cal. 2d 68, 47 P.2d 737 (1935).

5. Does res ipsa loquitur apply when a patient undergoes abdominal surgery and receives a spinal anesthesia, but awakens with a paralyzed leg? No. Here the negligence must be grounded upon expert testimony. *Ayers v. Parry*, 192 F.2d 181 (3d Cir.

1951). If an injury like this one is not necessarily the result of negligence, might that affect an informed consent argument?

6. The plaintiff had a tumor removed from his spinal cord. In the recovery room it was discovered that he was hemorrhaging. He was returned to the operating room, and Gelfoam was applied to stop the bleeding. It failed. The defendant doctor therefore packed Surgicel into the area of the spine with the hemorrhage. Surgicel swells 10% to 20% when exposed to blood. It stopped the bleeding. In the recovery room, the plaintiff discovered that the lower portion of his body was paralyzed. Does res ipsa loquitur apply against the doctor? The court found for the defendant:

> This brings us to a consideration of whether the accident in this case is of a kind which ordinarily does not occur in the absence of someone's negligence. The plaintiff in his brief argues that the proper question is: "Is paralysis of the lower body as a result of surgery to remove a tumor from the chest the kind of an accident which ordinarily does not occur in the absence of negligence?" We cannot agree. [T]he question is: "Is paralysis of the lower body resulting from packing Surgicel against the spinal cord in an attempt to halt extensive hemorrhaging an accident of the kind which ordinarily does not occur in the absence of someone's negligence?"

> The test is not whether a particular injury rarely occurs, but rather, when it occurs, is it ordinarily the result of negligence. . . .

> The fact that a particular injury suffered by a patient as the result of an operation is something that rarely occurs does not in itself prove that the injury was probably caused by the negligence of those in charge of the operation.

> "To permit an inference of negligence under the doctrine of res ipsa loquitur solely because an uncommon complication develops would place too great a burden upon the medical profession and might result in an undesirable limitation on the use of operations or new procedures involving an inherent risk of injury even when due care is used. Where risks are inherent in an operation and an injury of a type which is rare does occur, the doctrine should not be applicable unless it can be said that, in light of past experience, such an occurrence is more likely the result of negligence than some cause for which the defendant is not responsible."

> We hold that it is not common knowledge that the result in this case does not ordinarily occur in the absence of negligence.

> There are risks inherent in the use of Surgicel against the spinal cord and, even though injury from this cause is rare, res ipsa loquitur is not applicable unless it can be shown through expert witnesses that the injury is more likely the result of negligence than some other cause. No doctor testified that under the facts of this case there was bad medical practice, and no doctor testified

that where, under the present facts, injury does occur it is more likely than not the result of negligence.

Brannon v. Wood, 251 Or. 349, 444 P.2d 558 (1968).

7. There are two situations where res ipsa loquitur does not apply. First, the "calculated risk." In *Brannon*, the doctor knew that paralysis was a risk of using Surgicel. Second, the "bad result." There is a risk of death whenever a general anesthetic is used, for example. The "calculated risk" and the "bad result" may occur in the absence of negligence. W. Page Keeton et al., Prosser and Keeton on Torts (5th ed. 1984).

What is the doctor's informational obligation when a "calculated risk" or "bad result" may occur during treatment?

Anderson v. Somberg

Supreme Court of New Jersey, 1975
338 A.2d 1

PASHMAN, JUSTICE.

These negligence-products liability actions had their inception in a surgery performed in 1967 on the premises of defendant St. James Hospital (Hospital). Plaintiff was undergoing a laminectomy, a back operation, performed by defendant Dr. Somberg. During the course of the procedure, the tip or cup of an angulated pituitary rongeur, a forceps-like instrument, broke off while the tool was being manipulated in plaintiff's spinal canal. The surgeon attempted to retrieve the metal but was unable to do so. After repeated failure in that attempt, he terminated the operation. The imbedded fragment caused medical complications and further surgical interventions were required. Plaintiff has suffered significant and permanent physical injury proximately caused by the rongeur fragment which lodged in his spine.

Plaintiff sued: (1) Dr. Somberg for medical malpractice, alleging that the doctor's negligent action caused the rongeur to break: (2) St. James Hospital, alleging that it negligently furnished Dr. Somberg with a defective surgical instrument; (3) Reinhold-Schumann, Inc. (Reinhold), the medical supply distributor which furnished the defective rongeur to the hospital, on a warranty theory, and (4) Lawton Instrument Company (Lawton), the manufacturer of the rongeur, on a strict liability in tort claim, alleging that the rongeur was a defective product. In short, plaintiff sued all who might have been liable for his injury, absent some alternative explanation such as contributory negligence.

. . . .

The position adopted by the Appellate Division majority seems to us substantially correct: that is, at the close of all the evidence, it was apparent that at least one of the defendants was liable for plaintiff's injury, because no alternative theory of liability was within reasonable contemplation. Since defendants had engaged in conduct which activated legal obligations by each of them to plaintiff, the jury should have been instructed that the failure of any defendant to prove his nonculpability would trigger liability; and further, that since at least one of the defendants could not sustain his burden of proof, at least one would be liable. A no cause of action verdict against all primary and third-party defendants will be unacceptable and would work a miscarriage of justice sufficient to require a new trial. . . .

In the ordinary case, the law will not assist an innocent plaintiff at the expense of an innocent defendant. However, in the type of case we consider here, where an unconscious or helpless patient suffers an admitted mishap not reasonably foreseeable and unrelated to the scope of the surgery (such as cases where foreign objects are left in the body of the patient), those who had custody of the patient, and who owed him a duty of care as to medical treatment, or not to furnish a defective instrument for use in such treatment can be called to account for their default. They must prove their nonculpability, or else risk liability for the injuries suffered.

This case resembles the ordinary medical malpractice foreign-objects case, where the patient is sewn up with a surgical tool or sponge inside him. In those cases, res ipsa loquitur is used to make out a prima facie case. . . .

The rule of evidence we set forth does not represent the doctrine of res ipsa loquitur as it has been traditionally understood. Res ipsa loquitur is ordinarily impressed only where the injury more probably than not has resulted from negligence of the defendant. . . . The doctrine has been expanded to include, as in the instant matter, multiple defendants . . . , although even this expansion has been criticized. . . . It has also been expanded to embrace cases where the negligence cause was not the only or most probable theory in the case, but where the alternate theories of liability accounted for the only possible causes of injury. . . . That is the situation in this case, where we find negligence, strict liability in tort and breach of warranty all advanced as possible theories of liability. In such cases, defendants are required to come forward and give their evidence. The latter development represents a substantial deviation from earlier conceptions of res ipsa loquitur and has more accurately been called "akin to res ipsa loquitur". . . .

We hold that in a situation like this, the burden of proof in fact does shift to defendants. All those in custody of that patient or who owed him a duty, as here, the manufacturer and the distributor, should be called forward and should be made to prove their freedom from liability. The rule would have no application except in those instances where the injury lay outside the ambit of the surgical procedure in question; for example, an injury to an organ, when that organ was itself the object of medical attention, would not by itself make out a prima facie case for malpractice or shift the burden of proof to defendants. . . .

The judgment of the Appellate Division is hereby affirmed, and the cause remanded for trial upon instructions consonant with this opinion.

MOUNTAIN, J., dissenting.

This Court has reached an extraordinary result in a very remarkable way. As I shall hope to make clear, the structure of argument as presented in the Court's opinion is rested upon an assumed factual premise which does not exist. In part because of this, the concluding and most significant part of the argument suffers from the defect of visiting liability, in a wholly irrational way, upon parties who are more probably than not totally free of blame. I respectfully dissent.

During the course of the Court's opinion there appear statements to the effect that all those who might have been in any way responsible for plaintiff's injury are before the court. Hence, the argument continues, a process of selection properly undertaken by the finder of fact cannot fail to implicate the true culprit or culprits. Indeed, as I read the opinion, the entire argument is made to rest upon this premise: each and every person who may have brought about the imperfection in the surgical instrument or who may have caused the injury by its misuse is before the court; it remains only to identify him.

And yet we know—and everyone who has been associated with this case has always known—that this assumption is not in fact true. The only four defendants in the case are: the surgeon, Dr. Harold Somberg, who performed the operation; St. James Hospital, the medical facility in which the operation took place; Lawton Instrument Co., which manufactured the rongeur; and Rheinhold-Schumann, Inc., the distributor which sold it to the hospital. There is no other defendant in the case. And yet the record is replete with testimony that other surgeons—perhaps as many as twenty—have used the rongeur during the four years that it has formed part of the surgical equipment of the hospital, and that any one or more of them may perfectly well have been responsible for so injuring the instrument that it came apart while being manipulated in plaintiff's incision; or that it may have been weakened to near breaking point by cumulative misuse, entirely by persons not now before the court. . . .

I would vote to reverse the judgment of the Appellate Division and to reinstate the judgment of the trial court.

---

1. Whom did the plaintiff sue? Why cast such a broad net? What were the causes of action?

2. As clerk for the trial court judge, formulate the charge to the jury on the remand of *Anderson*.

3. Is this a radical case? If so, why? If judges are generally conservative, why did these draft such an extreme decision?

4. What facts does the dissent overlook?

5. *Car crashes.* Res ipsa loquitur applies against the driver, in a suit brought by a passenger, when the car leaves the road and crashes into a tree. *Badela v. Karpowich*, 152 Conn. 360, 206 A.2d 838 (1965).

It does not apply against the other driver, when two cars crash into each other, because the jury would be required to guess as to negligence.

However, in a collision between a bus and a car, the bus passenger can go to the jury by arguing res ipsa loquitur. This is because the driver of a common carrier is held to the highest standard of care, and it is likely he or she violated this very high standard. *See* W. Page Keeton et al., Prosser and Keeton on Torts 252 (5th ed. 1984).

Problem

Over 100 high school juniors and seniors rent rooms in the Gobstopper Hotel, a huge hotel in a large city, for New Year's Eve. The hotel has an atrium 20 stories tall. In some cases, parents rented the rooms; in others, the students used fake identification. Tom, a junior, who is a guest of a senior who rented the room, gets drunk and jumps or falls from the 18th floor in the atrium. He dies.

Discuss a possible suit against the Gobstopper Hotel. What assumptions have you made?

Connolly v. Nicollet Hotel

Supreme Court of Minnesota, 1959
95 N.W.2d 657

MURPHY, JUSTICE.

Action by Marcella A. Connolly against The Nicollet Hotel, a copartnership, . . . for the loss of the sight of her left eye alleged to have been caused by defendants' negligence.

The accident occurred about midnight June 12, 1953, during the course of the 1953 National Junior Chamber of Commerce Convention which had its headquarters at The Nicollet Hotel in Minneapolis. It was occasioned when plaintiff was struck in her left eye by a substance falling from above her as she walked on a public sidewalk on Nicollet Avenue adjacent to the hotel.

The 1953 National Junior Chamber of Commerce Convention, Inc., was joined as a defendant in the action, but at the close of the testimony a verdict was directed in its favor. The jury returned a verdict against The Nicollet Hotel copartnership, which will hereinafter be designated defendants, in the sum of $30,000. This is an appeal from an order of the trial court granting judgment for such defendants notwithstanding the verdict. On appeal plaintiff contends that defendants were negligent in failing to maintain order and control the conduct of their guests . . . and that hence the court erred in granting judgment notwithstanding the verdict.

. . . .

Plaintiff, in company with one Margaret Hansen, had just left the hotel via its Nicollet Avenue entrance and was walking southerly toward Third Street on the west side of Nicollet Avenue. When she had traveled approximately six to ten steps from the canopy extending over such entrance, she observed two people walking toward her. She then heard a noise which sounded like a small explosion and saw something strike the walk in front of her. She observed that one of the persons approaching her was struck on the left shoulder by some substance. She then exclaimed, "We better get off this sidewalk, . . . or somebody is going to get hit." Immediately thereafter she glanced upward and was struck in the left eye by a substance she described as a mud-like substance or a "handful of dirt." Margaret Hansen testified that she also saw the substance falling from eye level to the sidewalk a step or two in front of her. She described the sound made by the striking object as explosive and accompanied by a splattering. The only place from which the article might have fallen from above was the hotel building.

The blow which struck plaintiff caused her to lose her balance but not to fall. Her knees buckled and she was caught by Margaret Hansen and held on her feet. Following the blow, she stated that she could not open her left eye and the left side of her face and head became numb, and her shoulders, hair, and the left side of her face were covered with dirt. A dark substance which looked like mud was found imbedded in her left eye. After the accident the assistant manager of the hotel attempted to remove a "mud like substance" from plaintiff's eye by using a cotton applicator. As a result of the foregoing accident, plaintiff lost the sight of the injured eye.

As stated above, the 1953 National Junior Chamber of Commerce Convention occupied a substantial portion of the hotel at the time of the accident. In connection therewith various delegates and firms maintained hospitality centers there where intoxicants, beer, and milk were served to guests and visitors. Two of such centers were located on the Nicollet Avenue side of the building.

The assistant manager of the hotel on duty at the time of the accident and in charge of maintaining order had received notice that water bags had been thrown from the hotel during the previous days of the convention. The night engineer testified that on the Hennepin Avenue side of the hotel he had observed liquor and beer bottles and cans on the sidewalk and described the accumulation in this area as greater than he had ever witnessed during the 18-month period he had been employed at the hotel. He also testified that he had found cans and beer bottles upon the fire escape at the third-floor level during the convention.

 . . . .

It is generally agreed that a hotel owner or innkeeper owes a duty to the public to protect it against foreseeable risk of danger attendant upon the maintenance and operation of his property . . . ; and to keep it in such condition that it will not be of danger to pedestrians using streets adjacent thereto. . . .

The failure of a hotel owner and operator to take reasonable precautions to eliminate or prevent conditions of which he is or should be aware and which might reasonably be expected to be dangerous to the public may constitute negligence. . . .

There are certain controlling principles of law which must be kept in mind in considering the merits of the plaintiff's claims as they are established by the record. It is recognized that one who assembles a large number of people upon his premises for the purpose of financial gain to himself assumes the responsibility for using all reasonable care to protect others from injury from causes reasonably to be anticipated.

In the exercise of this duty it is necessary for him to furnish a sufficient number of guards or attendants and to take other precautions to control the actions of the crowd. Whether the guards furnished or the precautions taken are sufficient is ordinarily a question for the jury to determine under all of the circumstances.

. . . .

The defendants contend that the proof is circumstantial and that there is no evidence that the object which struck the plaintiff came from the hotel. The plaintiff was struck in the eye by a mass of moist dirt or earth. The jury could find that this object was not an accumulation of dirt which fell from the structure. . . . We think that under the facts in this case the evidence presents inferences which make the question of where the mass of mud came from one for the jury.

. . . .

Reversed.

———————

1. At what point did the hotel's duty of care arise? For the hotel, what was reasonable care under these circumstances?

Notice the hotel's duty extends outside the boundary of the property.

2. Is there any evidence that the plaintiff was contributorily negligent?

3. Res ipsa loquitur was not applied against the hotel when an overstuffed chair was thrown out of a hotel window and hit the plaintiff, a pedestrian. The guests in the hotel were celebrating V-J Day, and the court held that the hotel lacked exclusive control. *Larson v. St. Francis Hotel*, 83 Cal. App. 2d 210, 188 P.2d 513 (1948). Compare *Larson* with *Connolly*. Why the different result?

4. The plaintiff ate turkey salad at a luncheon put on by eleven high school band mothers. She contracted food poisoning from the salad. The court refused to apply res ipsa loquitur against the eleven mothers:

> Some of the elements of res ipsa have been proved. The evidence leads to the conclusion that salmonella would not exist in the turkey salad without someone's negligence, but exclusive control in any one of the defendants or in the defendants collectively, on a theory of vicarious liability, has not been shown either by proof or by inference.

Samson v. Riesing, 62 Wis. 2d 698, 215 N.W.2d 662 (1974). What are the other reasons for the decision? Why is the result different from *Ybarra*? Is there anyone else in addition to those who contributed to the salad whom the plaintiff might sue?

5. In some jurisdictions there may be a debate as to the weight to be given to circumstantial evidence in a case where res ipsa loquitur applies:

> While we agree that these facts made a case of res ipsa loquitur, we do not agree that they, though unexplained, required an inference or finding of negligence, or that the jury could not reasonably refuse to find negligence

and return a verdict for defendant, or that there was no evidence to support their verdict for him.

It is true there has been confusion in the case as to the procedural effect of res ipsa loquitur, some cases giving it one and some another of these three different effects:

(1) It warrants an *inference* of negligence which the jury may draw or not, as their judgment dictates. . . .

(2) It raises a *presumption* of negligence which requires the jury to find negligence if defendant does not produce evidence sufficient to rebut the presumption. . . .

(3) It not only raises such a presumption but also *shifts the ultimate burden of proof to* defendant and requires him to prove by a preponderance of all the evidence that the injury was not caused by his negligence.

The effect of a case of res ipsa loquitur, like that of any other case of circumstantial evidence varies from case to case, depending on the particular facts of each case; and therefore such effect can no more be fitted into a fixed formula or reduced to a rigid rule than can the effect of other cases of circumstantial evidence. The only generalization that can be safely made is that, in the words of the definition of res ipsa loquitur, it affords "reasonable evidence," in the absence of an explanation by defendant, that the accident arose from this negligence.

The weight or strength of such "reasonable evidence" will necessarily depend on the particular facts of each case, and the cogency of the inference of negligence from such facts may of course vary in degree all the way from practical certainty in one case to reasonable probability in another.

In exceptional cases the inference may be so strong as to require a directed verdict for plaintiff, as in cases of objects falling from defendant's premises on persons in the highway, such as *Byrne v. Boadle*. . . .

In the ordinary case, however, res ipsa loquitur merely makes a case for the jury — merely permits the jury to choose the inference of defendant's negligence in preference to other permissible or reasonable inferences. . . .

Sullivan v. Crabtree, 36 Tenn. App. 469, 258 S.W.2d 782 (1953).

6. While chewing tobacco, the plaintiff's mouth began to burn. He found a human toe in the plug of tobacco. Does res ipsa loquitur apply? As judge would you direct a verdict for the plaintiff? The court said: "We can imagine no reason why, with ordinary care, human toes could not be left out of chewing tobacco, and if toes are found in chewing tobacco, it seems to us that somebody has been very careless." *Pillars v. R.J. Reynolds Tobacco Co.*, 117 Miss. 490, 78 So. 365 (1918).

7. Does res ipsa loquitur apply when two trains run into each other head-on? As the judge would you direct a verdict for the plaintiff? *See Moore v. Atchison, T. & S.F.R.*

Co., 28 Ill. App. 2d 340, 171 N.E.2d 393 (1960); *Rouse v. Hornsby*, 67 F. 219 (8th Cir. 1895).

8. What about a dental patient who has a tooth removed and emerges from the procedure with a broken finger? *See Wolfe v. Feldman*, 158 Misc. 656, 286 N.Y.S. 118 (1936).

Chapter 6

Cause in Fact

A. Introduction

Some authors include cause in fact and proximate cause in the same causation chapter. That leads to analytical confusion because cause in fact and proximate cause are not closely related. The only thing they have in common is the term "causation." Proximate cause is a matter of policy and answers the question of whether this particular defendant should be liable for this specific injury. Proximate cause should not be considered until cause in fact has been shown.

In contrast, cause in fact is a matter of science: did the defendant's act have something to do with the plaintiff's injury as a matter of science? There are two tests for cause in fact: the "but for" test and the "substantial factor" test. Cause in fact is necessary for liability, but it is not sufficient by itself to prove liability. For all injuries, there is more than one cause in fact. *See* Malone, *Ruminations on Cause-in-Fact*, 9 Stan. L. Rev. 60 (1958).

Problem

Marilyn was a guest at the Old Tyme Hotel when she received a cut on her forehead from a piece of glass that fell from the transom (a window above the door). The injury occurred when Marilyn opened the door to her room. Assume that the Old Tyme Hotel was negligent in regard to the maintenance of the transom. The wound would not heal, and a specialist found that at the point of injury, skin cancer had developed.

For what damages will Marilyn be able to recover?

Calhoun v. Honda Motor Company

United States Court of Appeals, Sixth Circuit, 1984
738 F.2d 126

I. Facts

On July 18, 1978 plaintiff, Richard Calhoun was driving his Honda 750 CB motorcycle to work when he collided with the rear of a stationary tractor trailer truck There were no witnesses to the accident and as a result of his injuries Calhoun does not recall what happened. A Kentucky state policeman was called to the scene and he later testified that the motorcycle had left forty feet of skid marks on the pavement.

Plaintiff filed an action against Honda alleging strict liability for his injuries under Restatement (Second) of Torts § 402A. The alleged product defect was poor wet braking performance due to a design defect present in all 1977 Honda 750 CB motorcycles. In support of his allegation, plaintiff relied upon a recall letter issued by Honda five months prior to the accident. The letter stated that the performance of the rear brake pad was reduced by heavy rain conditions. Although it had not rained the day of the accident, plaintiff had visited a car wash approximately thirty minutes prior to the collision.

In the pretrial order, Honda challenged the admissibility of the recall letter. A hearing was held in chambers. Both parties had already briefed the court on this issue and the trial judge ruled that the letter could go into evidence. Plaintiff took a deposition of Honda's Vice President for Legal Affairs, Doug Somers. Somers stated that the recall was a result of customer complaints. Honda found that the efficiency of the brakes was reduced by heavy rain conditions, which resulted in a longer stopping distance. To correct this problem, grooves were cut into the brake pads which allowed the captured water between the disc and puck of the brake to escape as pressure was applied.

After placing the Somers deposition into evidence, plaintiff called his expert witness, Stanley Klein, to testify. The witness read the recall letter into evidence. He testified he had examined the motorcycle after the accident. In response to trial counsel's question as to what in his opinion was the cause of the accident, he stated:

> [M]y opinion as to the cause of the accident was uncontrolled braking performance which caused the motorcycle's brakes to lock up and the driver lose steering control, an unexpected property of the braking performance, I would characterize it.

On cross-examination Klein was asked if he had an opinion as to whether the brakes were wet at the time of the accident. He replied:

> A. I do.

> Q. What is that based on?

> A. It is based on the fact that they were washed with a high-pressure hose just a short distance or short time interval prior to the accident.

II. Judgment Notwithstanding the Verdict

Calhoun argues that the district court's grant of a judgment notwithstanding the verdict was erroneous because the jury's verdict was supported by substantial evidence. Regretfully, we disagree.

A judgment notwithstanding the verdict has long been recognized as the legal equivalent of a directed verdict and both are governed by the same standards. To determine the sufficiency, "the court must draw all fair and rational inferences from the evidence in favor of the party opposing the motion and a verdict should not be directed unless the evidence is insufficient to sustain the verdict."

The Evidence Did Not Support the Verdict Because Plaintiff Failed to Establish Cause in Fact.

The jury found Honda liable for Calhoun's injuries on the theory of strict liability in torts. Restatement (Second) of Torts § 402A. In order to find a manufacturer liable for injury sustained by his product, the jury must have found that the product in question was defective and that this defect was the cause of plaintiff's injury.

Calhoun alleges that there was a defect in the rear brake of the motorcycle. Although Calhoun cannot remember what took place because of his injuries, he hypothesized that when he applied the brakes they did not perform properly. He claims this failure was the result of the brake pads becoming wet when he took his motorcycle to a car wash.

Plaintiff relied upon a recall letter sent by Honda to all owners of Honda 750 CB motorcycles as proof of a braking defect. The letter stated:

> Honda Motor Co. Ltd., has determined that a defect which related to motor vehicle safety exists in the rear brake pads of certain Honda motorcycles.

> When the rear disc brake is applied during operation in heavy rain, there may be noticeable initial reduction in effectiveness of the brake followed by gradual recovery to normal, dry condition effectiveness.

If we were to assume arguendo that the letter was admissible and established the existence of a defect, Calhoun failed to show where the defect was the cause in fact of the accident.

Calhoun's evidence never went further than to show that the claimed defect was a possible, not probable cause of the collision. This is insufficient to establish liability. The recall letter stated that the motorcycle's braking performance was reduced by heavy rain. However, it was not raining the day of the accident nor did plaintiff successfully prove that washing the motorcycle at a carwash was tantamount to a condition of heavy rain.

The Expert's Testimony Was Insufficient to Establish Causation.

Although plaintiff's expert [Klein] opined that the brakes were wet at the time of the accident, the evidence does not support his conclusion.

Klein testified under cross-examination that he assumed that the brakes were wet when applied by Calhoun due to the fact that the motorcycle had been washed some time before hand. His assumption, however, is not supported by the type of evidence necessary to reach this conclusion. For example, he did not know the amount of time that passed from when plaintiff washed his bike until he had his accident. He did not know how many stops plaintiff made before the accident. He did not know the material out of which the brake pad was made and therefore did not know the brake pad's drying time. Without knowledge of these facts, his assumption that the brakes were wet and therefore in a condition equivalent to that created by heavy rain, is baseless. An expert's testimony which expresses an opinion must be based on the evidence. As the court said in *Polk v. Ford Motor Co.*, (8th Cir. 1976), "[t]here must, of course, be sufficient facts already in evidence or disclosed by the witness as a result of his investigation to take the testimony out of the realm of guesswork and speculation."

Unfortunately, plaintiff does not recall the accident and there were no witnesses. Calhoun relies upon the fact that there were forty feet of skid marks which proved that he applied his brakes before the collision. These skid marks however are not dispositive of a brake defect. It is just as probable that they were the result of inattentiveness, as of brake failure. This fact was brought out during cross-examination of Mr. Klein:

> Q. But you don't know whether it was [rear brake lock up which caused the accident] as opposed to Mr. Calhoun just not reacting to the situation, do you?
>
> A. I have no way of knowing.

Mr. Klein, on cross-examination, also conceded that it would have been possible for the motorcycle to have left forty feet of skid marks with perfectly dry brakes.

The record reveals that very little is known about this tragic accident. It was estimated that approximately twenty minutes passed from the time plaintiff left the car wash until he had his accident. After leaving the car wash he drove to his aunt's house. The motorcycle sat outside his aunt's house for twenty minutes while he went inside to change clothes. Honda's expert, who retraced plaintiff's route, estimated he applied his brakes at least two times before the accident. Calhoun's mother estimated that it was several miles from the aunt's house to the scene of the accident; part of this distance retraced the route Calhoun had taken from the car wash. There was undisputed testimony at trial that the brake pads were in constant contact with the discs and therefore would be rubbed dry in approximately 125 feet. It would seem highly unlikely that the brake pads would still be wet after the aforementioned sequence of events. Even more unlikely is the possibility that they would be as wet as pads which were exposed to heavy rain conditions.

The evidence in this case has never risen to the level of establishing that the alleged defect was the probable cause of the accident. At best, it was a possible cause in a series of possibilities, of which plaintiff's inattentiveness cannot be excluded.

Plaintiff failed to prove that the defect was the cause of the accident and therefore the jury's verdict in his favor was not supported by the evidence.

This decision is a difficult one for our Court. It is not without heartfelt sympathy for Mr. Calhoun that we affirm the district court. We realize that as a result of his injury, plaintiff is of unsound mind and may be unable to care for himself the remainder of his days. However, the evidence failed to establish that the alleged defect was anything but a possible cause of his injury. Without more our hands are tied.

Therefore, taking all evidence in the light most favorable to the party against whom the motion was made and giving the non-moving party the benefit of all favorable inferences, the JNOV is affirmed.

————

1. As plaintiff's attorney, what questions would you have asked Stanley Klein prior to hiring him?

2. Does the court apply the "but for" test or the "substantial factor" test?

3. Why is it preferable to use the phrase "cause in fact" rather than merely "cause"?

4. The defendant was cutting ice on a lake and was negligent in failing to fence a large hole. The plaintiff's horses ran across the ice and into the hole and drowned. The court found that the horses were uncontrollable, and therefore would not have been stopped by the fence. The absence of a fence was not a cause in fact of the drownings. Is there anyone in the class who knows anything about horses? Is the court correct? *Stacy v. Knickerbocker Ice Co.*, 84 Wis. 614, 54 N.W. 1091 (1893).

5. A widow of a seaman who drowned while swimming in the ocean after jumping overboard brought a Jones Act action against the shipowner. The district court denied relief, and the widow appealed. The court of appeals held that (1) it was appropriate to conclude that the seaman was legally drunk at the time of his death; (2) the lack of the required line-throwing device, coupled with the shipowner's duty to rescue, established that the shipowner was negligent as a matter of law; (3) the existence of causation in fact was presumed, and the burden was on the shipowner to show that the ship's inaction and regulatory violations could not have been even a contributory cause of the seaman's death.

The Court of Appeals stated:

> From the foregoing discussion, it is apparent that the element of causation in this situation turns on a number of either ambiguous or hypothetical issues of fact. Determining the causation element in this case is made most difficult by the facts that (i) the ship lacked required equipment which could conceivably have been used for rescue and by (ii) the actual failure of the ship to even attempt a rescue. These omissions are solely the fault of the ship.

> We refuse to place such a difficult burden of proving causation on the widow of the deceased seaman. Instead, the District Court on remand is to presume the existence of causation and defendant-appellee shall have the burden of overcoming that presumption. A number of considerations support this allocation of the burden of proving causation.

> The "search and rescue" branch of the rescue doctrine already recognizes such a rebuttable presumption of causation in favor of a seaman's representative.

Reyes v. Vantage Steamship Co., 609 F.2d 140, 144 (5th Cir. 1980).

6. A father and his son drowned in the defendant's motel pool. The motel violated a statute that required a lifeguard and failed to warn of the absence of a lifeguard. The court held:

> [W]e have concluded that under the facts presented at trial, plaintiffs, in demonstrating defendants' failure to provide a lifeguard at the pool as required by statute, sustained their initial burden of proof and that defendants then bore the burden of showing that this statutory violation was not a cause of the deaths. Although defendants failed to meet this burden at the initial trial, we have determined that inasmuch as the parties' respective burdens were not clearly defined at that time, the judgment should be reversed and the cause be remanded for a new trial.

Haft v. Lone Palm Hotel, 3 Cal. 3d 756, 761, 91 Cal. Rptr. 745, 747, 478 P.2d 465, 467 (1970). On retrial, how will the motel prove that the failure to have a lifeguard and the failure to warn of the absence of a guard was not a cause in fact of the drownings?

7. A 250-pound woman fell down the steps at a railroad station and sued the railroad for failing to provide a handrail and failing to light the steps. The railroad argued that the cause in fact of her falling was her weight. The court held for the plaintiff, stating: "[W]here the negligence of the defendant greatly multiplies the chance of the accident . . . and is of a character naturally leading to its occurrence, the mere possibility that it might have happened without the negligence is not sufficient to break the chain of cause and effect. . . ." *Reynolds v. Texas & Pac. Ry. Co.*, 37 La. Ann. 694 (1885).

Sanchez v. Hillerich & Bradsby Co.

Court of Appeal, 2002
128 Cal. Rptr. 2d 529

Hastings, J.

Appellant Andrew Sanchez, a pitcher, was seriously injured when struck by a line drive hit by an aluminum bat. He filed suit against the bat manufacturer alleging that the design and use of this particular bat significantly increased the inherent risk in the sport of baseball that a pitcher would be hit by a line drive. Defendants moved for summary judgment asserting that appellant would be unable to prove causation. The trial court granted summary judgment when it concluded that appellant would be unable to prove that his injuries resulted from the alleged increased risk the bat posed to pitchers. We reverse.

FACTUAL AND PROCEDURAL BACKGROUND

On April 2, 1999, appellant, pitching for California State University, Northridge (CSUN), was struck by a line drive off the bat of a player for the University of Southern California (USC), Dominic Correa. Appellant suffered serious head injuries from the incident. Correa was using an aluminum bat, the Air Attack 2, designed and manufactured by respondent Hillerich & Bradsby Co. (H & B).

USC was a member of the Pac-10, a collegiate athletic conference. The Pac-10 was a member of the National Collegiate Athletic Association (NCAA), a non-profit organization of collegiate athletic conferences and other institutions. The NCAA establishes rules for equipment used in athletic events, including baseball bats. CSUN was a member of the NCAA, but not a member of the Pac-10.

The bat used by Correa was a newly-designed hollow aluminum alloy bat with a pressurized air bladder which, according to its designer, substantially increases the speed at which the ball leaves the surface of the bat. Correa was supplied with the bat pursuant to an agreement between USC and H & B, which provided that USC would receive compensation for using H & B's Louisville Slugger equipment exclusively. At the time of the accident, the NCAA rules allowed the use of metal bats, and the bat was made in compliance with NCAA standards.

At the time of the injury, appellant and all of his team members were using metal bats, and appellant had used a metal bat in organized baseball games since he was six years old.

On March 17, 2000, appellant filed a lawsuit against H & B, USC, NCAA and Pac-10 asserting causes of action for negligence.

Each defendant moved separately for summary judgment. H & B's motion was based on the following grounds: (1) that appellant could not establish causation as a matter of law. . . .

In support of its motion, H & B submitted portions of deposition testimony from various witnesses. Mike Batesole, one of appellant's coaches, testified that he saw the incident, he had seen other pitchers hit by batted balls before, and that the risk of a pitcher being hit by a batted ball is inherent in the sport of baseball. Dominic Correa, the batter, also testified that he saw the ball strike appellant in the temple and saw appellant fall to the ground. He had no opinion about the speed of the ball. Michael Gillespie, the head coach for USC, testified that the game was not videotaped. He also testified that in his opinion, metal bats do not perform differently from wood bats. He believed that the bat used by Correa met NCAA standards, but had no specific information to confirm whether it did nor not. Marty Archer, the president of H & B, testified that he had instructed his employees to make bats which conformed with the regulations of the various regulatory bodies involved and that H & B did so construct the bats. He also stated that H & B had never given money to the NCAA to influence it. Rhonda Hyatt, the head athletic trainer for CSUN, testified that when presenting the disclaimer form to baseball players, she normally would read to them the clause about assumption of risk word for word before they signed it. At deposition, appellant testified he was aware that pitchers were at risk for being hit by a line drive.

. . . .

Jack Mackay, the designer of the Air Attack 2, declared that he had been a designer and tester of bats for nine years and was a paid consultant for H & B's Louisville Slugger Division. Mackay was present when time studies were performed on the bat at a Louisville Slugger testing center. He stated that the invention allowed a batter to hit a ball at speeds in excess of that which would have given a pitcher time to avoid being hit. As a result, he opined that the Air Attack 2 *substantially* increased the risk of a pitcher being hit. Mackay complained to his employers at the Louisville Slugger division of H & B about the increased risks of injuries, but the complaints were ignored and Marty Archer, president of the division, warned Mackay that he should not publicly discuss issues of safety.

William Thurston, a college baseball coach and Editor of the NCAA Baseball Rules Committee from February 1985 to July 2000, had initiated an NCAA study tracking pitcher injuries from high performance aluminum bats. He concluded that the Air Attack 2 substantially increased the risk of a pitcher being hit by a line drive over the risk associated with wood bats or earlier generations of non-wood bats. He also compiled an analysis of statistics of college hitters and batters for the years 1997–2001, comparing their performance when using wooden bats versus aluminum bats and concluded there was a tremendous increase in hits and runs when aluminum bats were used.

The deposition transcript of Rhonda Hyatt was also submitted. She testified that Justin Kiersby, the student athletic trainer for appellant's team, was in the dugout when the ball was hit and wrote down his observation that the ball was sent back at appellant at over 100 miles per hour.

Appellant also submitted the declaration of James G. Kent, who had a Ph.D. in kinesiology. Based on his training and review of the evidence, he opined that the ball which struck appellant's head was traveling between 101 and 107.8 miles an hour, probably closer to the latter speed than the former. This would have left appellant a reaction time of .32 to .37 seconds to avoid the ball. This was below the minimum reaction time accepted by the NCAA and other organizations of .39 seconds. As a result, he concluded that appellant's head injury resulted from the increased danger posed by this particular bat.

The superior court granted the motions of H & B, USC and Pac-10 on the ground that appellant would not be able to prove causation. But it concluded that it could not grant summary judgment to NCAA because of NCAA's failure to submit admissible evidence. Instead, it treated the NCAA's motion as one for judgment on the pleadings and concluded that appellant would not be able to truthfully plead causation against the NCAA.

Causation

Respondents contended, and the trial court agreed, that because the speed of the ball leaving the bat was never established, no causation attributed to the increased risk of use of the Air Attack 2, if any, could be established. Respondents cite to *Saelzler v. Advanced Group* (2001) for the proposition that summary judgment cannot be granted when causation is not established. *Saelzler* does stand for that proposition. But application of *Saelzler to* the instant case is not as facile as argued by respondents. In *Saelzler,* a visitor to an apartment complex was attacked by three unidentified men at the complex, and she sought to impose liability on the owner for maintaining an unsafe premises. The Supreme Court concluded that without knowledge of who the attackers were it would be impossible to prove that any negligence on behalf of the owner of the complex was connected with the attack. Here, however, the connection is not so tenuous.

It is undisputed that Correa, using an Air Attack 2 manufactured by H & B, provided by USC, and approved by the NCAA, hit the ball that fractured appellants skull. It is also undisputed that the Air Attack 2 was designed to and did increase the speed at which the baseball leaves the bat compared to other metal and wood bats. Thus, absent other factors (none are suggested) it follows that the ball must have reached appellant sooner than if Correa had used a bat other than the Air Attack 2. Dr. Kent opined that the ball that hit Correa was traveling at a speed of up to 107.8 miles per hour, giving appellant a reaction time of between .32 and .37 seconds, below the acceptable minimum time recognized by the NCAA.

The trial court concluded that Dr. Kent's declaration was without foundation because he "saw no videotape of the incident, nor did he examine [appellant]. All he did was review the videotape of [appellant] pitching prior to the date of the injury and some deposition transcripts." This does not accurately reflect what was set out in his declaration:

> "Based upon my analysis of this matter, *it is more probable than not* that Mr. Sanchez's head injury resulted from the use of a baseball bat which possessed mechanical properties allowing a batted ball to attain a flight velocity in excess of a velocity that would allow for a reasonable reaction time by a pitcher in a post-delivery posture in a game situation." (Italics added.)

Respondents did not object to Dr. Kent's qualifications.

As previously noted, respondents did not challenge Dr. Kent's credentials. He is a kinesiologist who, since 1983, has specialized "in the analysis of biomechanics of trauma." His declaration establishes that in forming his opinions he reviewed appellant's medical records, relied upon "literature regarding skull fracture and traumatic brain injury biomechanics," undertook a quantitative analysis regarding "velocity necessary to cause Mr. Sanchez's injury pattern" and "utilizing basic principles of dynamics related to the flight of a baseball" reached an opinion about the range of speed of the ball which hit appellant. While he does not spell out the actual calculations he used, the declaration is not deficient for purposes of summary judgment. If respondents had desired to do so, they could have deposed Dr. Kent in an attempt to demonstrate his opinions had no basis in fact or science.

. . . .

Dr. Kent also relied upon literature from the NCAA regarding reaction times. The letter from the NCAA dated December 4, 1998, quoted above, also has a passage regarding reaction times:

> "Most of the experts providing information to the Baseball Rules Committee believe that a collegiate pitcher needs approximately .4 seconds to react and move to avoid being struck. . . . Most baseball experts believe that a

pitcher is between 51 and 52 feet away from the point of impact between the bat and ball at the time of impact, usually in an off-balance position with his glove down and back, and his weight moving forward. At 94 mph the ball will travel 52 feet in approximately .371 seconds. Game conditions using high-powered aluminum bats often result in speeds well in excess of 100 mph. At 100 mph, the ball will travel 52 feet in .354 seconds; at 110 mph, a ball will travel 52 feet in .321 seconds. The NCAA Baseball Rules Committee is aware that there is some risk even with wood bats, but believes that the increased risk of injury resulting from the use of high-powered aluminum bats is clear. To ignore this risk would, in our opinion, be irresponsible."

This provides independent corroboration for some of the facts relied upon by Dr. Kent and provides further facts relevant to the issue of causation.

We conclude the evidence presented by appellant is sufficient to create a triable issue of fact regarding causation in fact.

DISPOSITION

The judgment is reversed and the matter is remanded to the trial court.

———————

1. Why does the court permit the case to go forward on cause in fact against an iconic corporation, Louisville Slugger?

2. Is the court applying the "but for" or the "substantial factor" test for cause in fact?

3. Argue that plaintiff assumed the risk of being hit by the "returned" ball.

4. Is the NCAA careless in not mandating that college pitchers wear protective helmets?

B. Concurrent Causes

Anderson v. Minneapolis, St. Paul & Sault Ste. Marie Railway Co.

Supreme Court of Minnesota, 1920
179 N.W. 45

LEES, C. This is a fire case brought against the defendant railway company. . . . Plaintiff had a verdict. The appeal is from an order denying a motion in the alternative for judgment notwithstanding the verdict or for a new trial. . . .

Plaintiff's case in chief was directed to proving that in August, 1918, one of defendant's engines started a fire in a bog near the west side of plaintiff's land; that it smoldered there until October 12, 1918, when it flared up and burned his property shortly before it was reached by one of the great fires which swept through northeastern Minnesota at the close of that day.

Defendant introduced evidence to show that on and prior to October 12 fires were burning west and northwest of and were swept by the wind towards plaintiff's premises. . . .

In instructing the jury, the court said in part:

> If you find that other fire or fires not set by one of the defendant's engines mingled with one that was set by one of the defendant's engines, there may be difficulty in determining whether you should find that the fire set by the engine was a material or substantial element in causing plaintiff's damage. If it was, the defendant is liable, otherwise it is not. . . .

> If you find that bog fire was set by the defendant's engine and that some greater fire swept over it before it reached the plaintiff's land, then it will be for you to determine whether that bog fire . . . was a material or substantial factor in causing plaintiff's damage. If it was . . . defendant is liable. If it was not, defendant is not liable. . . .

The following proposition is stated in defendant's brief and relied on for a reversal:

> If plaintiff's property was damaged by a number of fires combining, one . . . being the fire pleaded . . . the others being of no responsible origin, but of such sufficient or such superior force that they would have produced the damage to plaintiff's property regardless of the fire pleaded, then defendant was not liable.

This proposition is based upon *Cook v. Minneapolis, St. P. & S.S.M. Ry. Co.* 98 Wis. 624, 74 N.W. 561. . . . If the *Cook* case merely decides that one who negligently sets a fire is not liable if another's property is damaged, unless it is made to appear that the fire was a material element in the destruction of the property, there can be no question about the soundness of the decision. But if it decides that if such fire combines with another of no responsible origin, and after the union of the two fires they destroy the property, and either fire independently of the other would have destroyed it, then, irrespective of whether the first fire was or was not a material factor in the destruction of the property, there is no liability, we are not prepared to adopt the doctrine as the law of this state. If a fire set by the engine of one railroad company unites with a fire set by the engine of another company, there is joint and several liability, even though either fire would have destroyed plaintiff's property. But if the doctrine of the *Cook* case is applied and one of the fires is of unknown origin, there is no liability. . . . We, therefore, hold that the trial court did not err in refusing to instruct the jury in accordance with the rule laid down in the *Cook* case.

We find no error requiring a reversal, and hence the order appealed from is affirmed.

---

1. The *Cook* case (cited in the principal case), decided in 1898, was also a suit against a railroad for damage from merged fires, one unknown and one caused by the railroad. The court found for the railroad. What happened to the railroads

between 1898 (*Cook*) and 1920 (Anderson)? What was the reason for the decision in *Cook*?

2. Suppose that Sally negligently drives into Tom, who is walking across the street, and severely injures his right leg. Carl negligently runs over Tom's same leg, as he is lying in the street awaiting an ambulance. Either contact would have been sufficient to necessitate amputation of the leg. The leg is amputated. Who is liable? *See People v. Lewis*, 124 Cal. 551, 57 P. 470 (1899) (criminal case).

3. California has adopted the "substantial factor" test by way of jury instructions as the test for cause in fact. *See Mitchell v. Gonzales*, 54 Cal. 3d 1041, 1 Cal. Rptr. 2d 913, 819 P.2d 872 (1991).

4. In contemporary products liability cases, only the substantial factor test is generally used by the courts. Why?

5. The Restatement (Third) of Torts provides:

§ 26: *Factual Cause*

Tortious conduct must be a factual cause of physical harm for liability to be imposed. Conduct is a factual cause of harm when the harm would not have occurred absent the conduct.

In 1993 the American Law institute (A.L.I.), publishers of the Restatement, began a campaign to make it more difficult for victims to sue corporations who manufactured toxic substance such as, tobacco, asbestos, and defective pharmaceuticals. The attack on victims took the form of removing strict liability from the attorney's arsenal. *See* Frank J. Vandall, *Constructing a Roof Before the Foundation Is Prepared: The Restatement (Third) Products Liability: Section 2(b) Design Defect*, 30 Mich. J.L.R. 261 (1997).

The second offensive by the A.L.I. was to argue that joint and several liability was unfair to corporate defendants. They advocated for several liability. This means the victims will lose a percentage or all of her damages. *See* Frank J. Vandall, *A Critique of the Restatement (Third), Apportionment as It Affects Joint and Several Liability*, 49 Emory L.J. 565 (2000).

A recent challenge by the A.L.I. to victims of toxic substance is to require proof of cause in fact solely by use of the "but for" test and to deep six the "substantial factor" test. The black letter of § 27 [Restatement (Third) of Torts] states: "If multiple acts occur, each of which under § 26 alone would have been a factual cause of the physical harm at the same time in the absence of the other act(s), each act is regarded as a factual cause of harm." *June v. Union Carbide Corp.*, 577 F.3d 1234 (10th Cir. 2009).

The problem is that when a smoker dies from cancer of the lungs, she very often also has other diseases. The same can be said of prescription drug victims, they are often sick from other illnesses. Therefore, use of the "but for" test makes it extremely difficult or impossible for the victim to win. The result is that the victims go uncompensated and corporate balance sheets are enhanced with a windfall. *See* Frank J. Vandall, A History of Civil Litigation: Political and Economic Perspectives (Oxford University Press 2011).

Problem

A developer would like to purchase Jane's property because it is located between two streams (A and B) that join to form a third stream. Strong odors emanate from stream A, because of the material that Alvin discharges into stream A upstream of Jane. Likewise, unpleasant odors waft up from stream B because of Ben's discharges into stream B upstream from Jane. The developer refuses to buy until the odors are abated. If Jane sues under the "but for" test, what result? (Assume the case occurred prior to 1972. What happened to the law in 1972?)

C. Failure to Identify the Specific Actor

Summers v. Tice
Supreme Court of California, 1948
199 P.2d 1

Actions by Charles A. Summers against Harold W. Tice and against Ernest Simonson for negligently shooting plaintiff while hunting. From judgments for plaintiff, defendants appeal, and the appeals were consolidated pursuant to stipulation.

CARTER, JUSTICE.

. . . .

Plaintiff's action was against both defendants for an injury to his right eye . . . as the result of being struck by bird shot discharged from a shotgun. . . . Defendant Tice flushed a quail which rose in flight to a 10-foot elevation and flew between plaintiff and defendants. Both defendants shot at the quail, shooting in plaintiff's direction. . . . One shot struck plaintiff in his eye. . . . [I]t was found by the court that as the direct result of the shooting by defendants the shots struck plaintiff . . . and that defendants were negligent in so shooting and plaintiff was not contributorily negligent.

. . . .

The problem presented in this case is whether the judgment against both defendants may stand. It is argued by defendants that they are not joint tort feasors, and thus jointly and severally liable, as they were not acting in concert, and that there is not sufficient evidence to show which defendant was guilty of the negligence which caused the injuries. . . . The one shot that entered plaintiff's eye was the major factor in assessing damages and that shot could not have come from the gun of both defendants. It was from one or the other only.

It has been held that where a group of persons are on a hunting party, or otherwise engaged in the use of firearms, and two of them are negligent in firing in the direction of a third person who is injured thereby, both of those so firing are liable for the injury suffered by the third person, although the negligence of only one of them could have caused the injury. . . . These cases speak of the action of defendants as being in concert as the ground of decision, yet it would seem they are straining that concept and the more reasonable basis appears in *Oliver v. Miles*, 110 So. 666. There two persons were hunting together. Both shot at some partridges and in so doing shot across the highway injuring plaintiff who was travelling on it. The court stated they were acting in concert and thus both were liable. The court then stated: "We think that . . . each is liable for the resulting injury to the boy, although no one can say definitely who actually shot him. *To hold otherwise would be to exonerate both from liability, although each was negligent, and the injury resulted from such negligence"* [Emphasis added.] . . . "The real reason for the rule that each joint tortfeasor is responsible for the whole damage is the practical unfairness of denying the injured person redress simply because he cannot prove how much damage each did, when it is certain that between them they did all; let them be the ones to apportion it among themselves." . . . (Wigmore, Select Cases on the Law of Torts, sec. 153.) . . .

When we consider the relative position of the parties and the results that would flow if plaintiff was required to pin the injury on one of the defendants only, a requirement that the burden of proof on that subject be shifted to defendants becomes manifest. They are both wrongdoers—both negligent toward plaintiff. They brought about a situation where the negligence of one of them injured the plaintiff, hence it should rest with them each to absolve himself if he can. The injured party has been placed by defendants in the unfair position of pointing to which defendant caused the harm. If one can escape the other may also and plaintiff is remediless. Ordinarily defendants are in a far better position to offer evidence to determine which one caused the injury. . . .

[I]t should be pointed out that the same reasons of policy and justice shift the burden to each of defendants to absolve himself if he can—relieving the wronged person of the duty of apportioning the injury to a particular defendant, apply here where we are concerned with whether plaintiff is required to supply evidence for the apportionment of damages. If defendants are independent tort feasors and thus each liable for the damage caused by him alone, and, at least, where the matter of apportionment is incapable of proof, the innocent wronged party should not be deprived of his right to redress. The wrongdoers should be left to work out between themselves any apportionment. . . .

We have seen that for the reasons of policy discussed herein, the case is based upon the legal proposition that, under the circumstances here presented, each defendant is liable for the whole damage whether they are deemed to be acting in concert or independently.

The judgment is affirmed.

––––––––––

1. Determining cause in fact in multiple-car crashes may be challenging. Suppose three cars negligently collide with each other and Barbara, a passenger in one of the cars, is injured. Does the rule in *Summers* apply? *See Murphy v. Taxicabs of Louisville, Inc.*, 330 S.W.2d 395 (Ky. 1959).

How is this different from the res ipsa loquitur car crashes we looked at in the Negligence chapter? There we said that res ipsa loquitur does not apply when the only evidence is that one car crashed into another and a passenger was injured.

2. Don negligently drove his car onto the railroad tracks after the crossing light began blinking. The gate operator negligently lowered both gates, trapping Don's car on the tracks. Wanda, a passenger in Don's car, jumped out and broke her leg trying to escape from the oncoming train. How is this case different from *Summers?* What result? *Washington & Georgetown R.R. Co. v. Hickey,* 166 U.S. 521 (1897).

3. In *Hill v. Edmonds,* 26 A.D.2d 554, 270 N.Y.S.2d 1020 (1966), the court held: "Where separate acts of negligence combine to produce directly a single injury each tortfeasor is responsible for the entire result, even though his act alone might not have caused it."

4. Thirty-seven Canadian families sued three corporations, located across the Detroit River in the United States, for emitting noxious pollutants. Does the *Summers* rule apply? Yes. The defendants were treated as joint tort-feasors because "the independent acts of several actors concur to produce indivisible harmful consequences." *Michie v. Great Lakes Steel Div., Nat'l Steel Corp.,* 495 F.2d 213 (1974).

5. The introductory paragraph to this chapter states that cause in fact is a question of fact, but proximate cause is a question of policy. What policies are involved in *Summers v. Tice?*

Hymowitz v. Eli Lilly & Co.

Court of Appeals of New York, 1989
539 N.E.2d 1069, *cert. denied,* 493 U.S. 944

WACHTLER, CHIEF JUDGE.

Plaintiffs in these appeals allege that they were injured by the drug diethylstilbestrol (DES) ingested by their mothers during pregnancy. They seek relief against defendant DES manufacturers. While not class actions, these cases are representative of nearly 500 similar actions pending in the courts in this State. . . . With this in mind, we now resolve the issue twice expressly left open by this court, and adopt a market share theory, using a national market, for determining liability and apportioning damages in DES cases in which identification of the manufacturer of the drug that injured the plaintiff is impossible. . . .

In 1947, the FDA began approving the NDAs (New Drug Application) of manufacturers to market DES for the purpose of preventing human miscarriages. . . . In 1971, however, the FDA banned the use of DES as a miscarriage preventative, when studies established the harmful latent effects of DES upon the offspring of mothers who took the drug. Specifically, tests indicated that DES caused vaginal adenocarcinoma, a form of cancer, and adenosis, a precancerous vaginal or cervical growth.

. . . [N]ot only is identification of the manufacturer of the DES ingested in a particular case generally impossible, but, due to the latent nature of DES injuries, many claims were barred by the Statute of Limitations before the injury was discovered.

The identification problem has many causes. All DES was of identical chemical composition. Druggists usually filled prescriptions from whatever was on hand. Approximately 300 manufacturers produced the drug, with companies entering and leaving the market continuously during the 24 years that DES was sold for pregnancy use. The long latency period of a DES injury compounds the identification problem; memories fade, records are lost or destroyed, and witnesses die. Thus the pregnant women who took DES generally never knew who produced the drug they took, and there was no reason to attempt to discover this fact until many years after ingestion, at which time the information is not available.

[I]n DES cases it is a "practical impossibility for most victims [to] pinpoint . . . the manufacturer directly responsible for their particular injury". . . .

The present appeals are before the court in the context of summary judgment motions. In all of the appeals defendants moved for summary judgment dismissing the complaints because plaintiffs could not identify the manufacturer of the drug that allegedly injured them. . . . The trial court denied all of these motions. . . .

In a products liability action, identification of the exact defendant whose product injured the plaintiff is, of course, generally required. . . . The record now before us, however, presents the question of whether a DES plaintiff may recover against a DES manufacturer when identification of the producer of the specific drug that caused the injury is impossible.

. . . [T]he accepted tort doctrines of alternative liability and concerted action are available in some personal injury cases to permit recovery where the precise identification of a wrongdoer is impossible. However, we agree with the near unanimous views of the high State courts that have considered the matter that these doctrines in their unaltered common-law forms do not permit recovery in DES cases. . . .

The paradigm of alternative liability is found in the case of *Summers v. Tice.* . . .

In DES cases, however, there is a great number of possible wrongdoers, who entered and left the market at different times, and some of whom no longer exist. Additionally, in DES cases many years elapse between the ingestion of the drug and injury. Consequently, DES defendants are not in any better position than are plaintiffs to identify the manufacturer of the DES ingested in any given case, nor is there any real prospect of having all the possible producers before the court. Finally, while it may be fair to employ alternative liability in cases involving only a small number of potential wrongdoers, that fairness disappears with the decreasing probability that any one of the defendants actually caused the injury. This is particularly true when applied to DES where the chance that a particular producer caused the injury is often very remote. . . . Alternative liability, therefore, provides DES plaintiffs no relief.

Nor does the theory of concerted action, in its pure form, supply a basis for recovery. This doctrine, seen in drag racing cases, provides for joint and several liability on the part of all defendants having an understanding, express or tacit, to participate in "a common plan or design to commit a tortious act". . . . There is nothing in the record, however, beyond this similar conduct to show any agreement, tacit or otherwise, to market DES for pregnancy use without taking proper steps to ensure the drug's safety. . . .

In short, extant common-law doctrines, unmodified, provide no relief for the DES plaintiff unable to identify the manufacturer of the drug that injured her. . . .

We conclude that the present circumstances call for recognition of a realistic avenue of relief for plaintiffs injured by DES. . . . [W]e perceive that here judicial action is again required to overcome the "'inordinately difficult problems of proof'" . . .

Indeed, it would be inconsistent with the reasonable expectations of a modern society to say to these plaintiffs that because of the insidious nature of an injury that long remains dormant, and because so many manufacturers, each behind a curtain, contributed to the devastation, the cost of injury should be borne by the innocent and not the wrongdoers. This is particularly so where the Legislature consciously created these expectations by reviving hundreds of DES cases. Consequently, the ever-evolving dictates of justice and fairness, which are the heart of our common-law system, require formation of a remedy for injuries caused by DES. . . .

We stress, however, that the DES situation is a singular case, with manufacturers acting in a parallel manner to produce an identical, generically marketed product, which causes injury many years later, and which has evoked a legislative response reviving previously barred actions. Given this unusual scenario, it is more appropriate that the loss be borne by those that produced the drug for use during pregnancy, rather than by those who were injured by the use, even where the precise manufacturer of the drug cannot be identified in a particular action. We turn then to the question of how to fairly and equitably apportion the loss occasioned by DES, in a case where the exact manufacturer of the drug that caused the injury is unknown. . . .

A narrower basis for liability, tailored more closely to the varying culpable-ness of individual DES producers, is the market share concept. . . . It first loosened the requirement that all possible wrongdoers be before the court, and instead made a "substantial share" sufficient. The court then held that each defendant who could not prove that it did not actually injure plaintiff would be liable according to that manufacturer's market share. The court's central justification for adopting this approach was its belief that limiting a defendant's liability to its market share will result, over the run of cases, in liability on the part of a defendant roughly equal to the injuries the defendant actually caused. . . .

In the recent case of *Brown v. Superior Ct.* (44 Cal. 3d 1049, 751 P.2d 470), the California Supreme Court resolved some apparent ambiguity in *Sindell v. Abbott Labs.* [26 Cal. 3d 588, 163 Cal. Rptr. 132, 607 P.2d 924], and held that a manufacturer's liability is several only, and, in cases in which all manufacturers in the market are not joined for any reason, liability will still be limited to market share, resulting in a less than 100% recovery for a plaintiff. Finally, it is noteworthy that determining market shares under *Sindell v. Abbott Labs*, proved difficult and engendered years of litigation. After attempts at using smaller geographical units, it was eventually determined that the national market provided the most feasible and fair solution. . . .

Turning to the structure to be adopted in New York, we heed both the lessons learned through experience in other jurisdictions and the realities of the mass litigation of DES claims in this State. Balancing these considerations, we are led to the conclusion that a market share theory, based upon a national market, provides the best solution. . . .

Consequently, for essentially practical reasons, we adopt a market share theory using a national market. We are aware that the adoption of a national market will likely result in a disproportion between the liability of individual manufacturers and the actual injuries each manufacturer caused in this State. Thus our market share theory cannot be founded upon the belief that, over the run of cases, liability will approximate causation in this State. . . . Nor does the use of a national market provide a reasonable link between liability and the risk created by a defendant to a particular plaintiff. . . . Instead, we choose to apportion liability so as to correspond to the over-all culpability of each defendant, measured by the amount of risk of injury each defendant created to the public-at-large. Use of a national market is a fair method, we believe, of apportioning defendants' liabilities according to their total culpability in marketing DES for use during pregnancy. Under the circumstances, this is an equitable way to provide plaintiffs with the relief they deserve, while also rationally distributing the responsibility for plaintiffs' injuries among defendants.

To be sure, a defendant cannot be held liable if it did not participate in the marketing of DES for pregnancy use; if a DES producer satisfies its burden of proof of showing that it was not a member of the market of DES sold for pregnancy use, disallowing exculpation would be unfair and unjust. Nevertheless, because liability here is based on the over-all risk produced, and not causation in a single case, there should be no exculpation of a defendant who, although a member of the market producing DES for pregnancy use, appears not to have caused a particular plaintiff's injury. It is merely a windfall for a producer to escape liability solely because it manufactured a more identifiable pill, or sold only to certain drugstores. These fortuities in no way diminish the culpability of a defendant for marketing the product, which is the basis of liability here.

Finally, we hold that the liability of DES producers is several only, and should not be inflated when all participants in the market are not before the court in a particular case. We understand that, as a practical matter, this will prevent some plaintiffs from recovering 100% of their damages. However, we eschewed exculpation to prevent the fortuitous avoidance of liability, and thus, equitably, we decline to unleash the same forces to increase a defendant's liability beyond its fair share of responsibility.[3]

---

3. The dissenter misapprehends the basis for liability here. We have not by the backdoor adopted a theory of concerted action. We avoided extending this theory, because its concomitant requirement of joint and several liability expands the burden on small manufacturers beyond a rational or

The constitutionality of the revival statute remains to be considered (see L. 1986, ch. 682, § 4). This section revives, for the period of one year, actions for damages caused by the latent effects of DES, tungsten-carbide, asbestos, chlordane, and polyvinylchloride. . . .

As it pertains to DES, surely the revival statute has a rational basis, and the Legislature acted within its broad range of discretion in enacting the law. . . . Accordingly, in each case the order of the Appellate Division should be affirmed, with costs, and the certified question answered in the affirmative.

MOLLEN, JUDGE (concurring in *Hymowitz* and *Hanfling*; and dissenting in part in *Tigue* and *Dolan*).

. . . .

The principle of market share liability in DES litigation was first espoused by the California Supreme Court in *Sindell v. Abbott Labs*, (*supra*), as a valid theory of manufacturer's liability based upon each manufacturer's share of the market. This approach provides DES plaintiffs with a means by which to recover damages for their injuries without the plaintiffs being held to the traditional tort requirement of identifying the actual wrongdoer. The public policy underpinnings of the *Sindell* rationale is that, from a perspective of fairness and equity, the DES manufacturers are in a better position than the innocent plaintiffs who have sustained grievous injuries to bear the cost of such injuries. Thus, the *Sindell* court held that once a plaintiff has joined a "substantial share" of the DES manufacturers of the relevant market in the action and has established that the sustained injuries were caused by the ingestion of DES by the plaintiff's mother during pregnancy, the burden of proof shifts to each defendant to demonstrate, by a preponderance of the evidence, that it did not produce or market the pill ingested by the plaintiff's mother. Those DES

---

fair limit. This result is reached by the dissent, not by the majority, so that criticism on this front is misplaced.

We are confronted here with an unprecedented identification problem, and have provided a solution that rationally apportions liability. We have heeded the practical lessons learned by other jurisdictions, resulting in our adoption of a national market theory with full knowledge that it concedes the lack of a logical link between liability and causation in a single case. The dissent ignores these lessons, and, endeavoring to articulate a theory it perceives to be closer to traditional law, sets out a construct in which liability is based upon chance, not upon the fair assessment of the acts of defendants. Under the dissent's theory, a manufacturer with a large market share may avoid liability in many cases just because it manufactured a memorably shaped pill. Conversely, a small manufacturer can be held jointly liable for the full amount of every DES injury in this State simply because the shape of its product was not remarkable, even though the odds, realistically, are exceedingly long that the small manufacturer caused the injury in any one particular case.

Therefore, although the dissent's theory based upon a "shifting the burden of proof" and joint and several liability is facially reminiscent of prior law, in the case of DES it is nothing more than advocating that bare fortuity be the test for liability. When faced with the novel identification problem posed by DES cases, it is preferable to adopt a new theory that apportions fault rationally, rather than to contort extant doctrines beyond the point at which they provide a sound premise for determining liability.

defendants who could not exculpate themselves, would then be liable for the proportion of the judgment which represented its share of the market. The intended result of the *Sindell* approach is that, "each manufacturer's liability for [a particular DES] injury would be approximately equivalent to the damage caused by the DES it manufactured".....

I cannot agree that the imposition of liability on drug companies, in this case DES manufacturers, solely upon their contribution, in some measure, to the risk of injury by producing and marketing a defective drug, without any consideration given to whether the defendant drug companies actually caused the plaintiffs' injuries, is appropriate or warranted. Rather, I would adopt a market share theory of liability, based upon a national market, which would provide for the shifting of the burden of proof on the issue of causation to the defendants and would impose liability upon all of the defendants who produced and marketed DES for pregnancy purposes, except those who were able to prove that their product could not have caused the injury. Under this approach, DES plaintiffs, who are unable to identify the actual manufacturer of the pill ingested by their mother, would only be required to establish, (1) that the plaintiff's mother ingested DES during pregnancy; (2) that the plaintiff's injuries were caused by DES; and (3) that the defendant or defendants produced and marketed DES for pregnancy purposes. Thereafter, the burden of proof would shift to the defendants to exculpate themselves by establishing, by a preponderance of the evidence, that the plaintiff's mother could not have ingested their particular pill. Of those defendants who are unable to exculpate themselves from liability, their respective share of the plaintiff's damages would be measured by their share of the national market of DES produced and marketed for pregnancy purposes during the period in question.

---

1. There have been numerous permutations of the *Sindell* decision. Wisconsin, for example, held that if the defendant manufactured the same color of DES pill as consumed by plaintiff's mother, the plaintiff could recover 100% of her damages from that single manufacturer. *Collins v. Eli Lilly Co.*, 116 Wis. 2d 166, 342 N.W.2d 37 (1984).

In Washington, the plaintiff was required to sue only one manufacturer of DES, and the burden was then shifted to the defendant to implead other manufacturers. *Martin v. Abbott Labs*, 102 Wash. 2d 581, 689 P.2d 368 (1984). *See also Conley v. Boyle Drug Co.*, 570 So. 2d 275 (Fla. 1990).

2. In terms of whether DES caused the cancer, the case is somewhat simple because the DES cancer is a "signature disease." Only DES causes that particular type of cancer.

3. What is the difference between joint liability and several liability? What makes more sense in DES cases? *See Brown v. Superior Ct.*, 44 Cal. 3d 1049, 245 Cal. Rptr. 412, 751 P.2d 470 (1988).

4. What percentage of damages does the plaintiff recover in *Hymowitz*? Under *Hymowitz*, does the plaintiff have to join a "substantial share" of the market?

5. Is it fair to not permit defendants to be dismissed from the suit if they can prove that they did not manufacture the DES pill that the plaintiff's mother took? (Different color, sold to other pharmacy.)

6. Courts have adopted market share theory outside the DES context. Most notable are Factor VIII (HIV-tainted blood clotting agents for hemophiliacs) in *Smith v. Cutter Biological, Inc.*, Div. of Miles, Inc., 823 P.2d 717 (Haw. 1991), *Ray v. Cutter Labs., Div. of Miles, Inc.*, 754 F. Supp. 193 (M.D. Fla. 1991), and *Doe v. Cutter Biological, Inc., A Division of Miles, Inc.*, 971 F.2d 375 (9th Cir. 1992) (applying Hawaii law); asbestos-lined brake pads in California in *Wheeler v. Raybestos-Manhattan*, 8 Cal. App. 4th 1152, 11 Cal. Rptr. 2d 109 (1992), and *Richie v. Bridgestone/Firestone, Inc.*, 22 Cal. App. 4th 335, 27 Cal. Rptr. 2d 418 (1994); lead paint in *Jackson v. Glidden Co.*, 98 Ohio App. 3d 100, 647 N.E.2d 879 (1995); and the vaccine for DPT in *Morris v. Parke, Davis & Co.*, 667 F. Supp. 1332 (C.D. Cal. 1987).

Many courts have been reluctant to extend market share liability outside the DES context, however. *See Skipworth v. Lead Indus. Assoc.*, 665 A.2d 1288 (Pa. Super. Ct. 1995) (lead paint); *White v. Celotex Corp.*, 907 F.2d 104 (9th Cir. 1990) (applying Arizona law) (asbestos); *In re New York State Silicone Breast Implant Litig.*, 166 Misc. 2d 85, 631 N.Y.S.2d 491 (Sup. Ct. 1995) (breast implants); *Doe v. Cutter Biological, A Div. of Miles, Inc.*, 852 F. Supp. 909 (D. Idaho 1994) (Factor VIII); *Miller v. Wyeth Labs.*, 43 F.3d 1483 (10th Cir. 1994) (applying Oklahoma law) (DPT vaccine); *Bixler v. Avondale Mills*, 405 N.W.2d 428 (Minn. Ct. App. 1987) (cotton flannel nightshirt).

The highest courts of the following states have rejected market share liability in the DES context and require the plaintiff to prove the identity of the tort-feasor: *Gorman v. Abbott Labs.*, 599 A.2d 1364 (R.I. 1991); *Smith v. Eli Lilly & Co.*, 137 Ill. 2d 222, 560 N.E.2d 324 (1990); *Mulcahy v. Eli Lilly & Co.*, 386 N.W.2d 67 (Iowa 1986); *Zafft v. Eli Lilly & Co.*, 676 S.W.2d 241 (Mo. 1984).

7. The first case to hold several defendants liable, including those who could not have caused the injury, was *Hall v. E.I. DuPont de Nemours & Co.*, 345 F. Supp. 353 (E.D.N.Y. 1972). Thirteen children were injured by the explosion of blasting caps in twelve separate incidents. The court held that the six manufacturers of blasting caps had acted in concert because they agreed on one formula and worked through a common trade association to produce an interchangeable and faulty product. *Sindell* and *Hymowitz* rejected *Hall* because there was no "concert of action" by the DES manufacturers.

8. The "market share" theory has its origin in a student note, Comment, *DES and a Proposed Theory of Enterprise Liability*, 46 Fordham L. Rev. 963 (1978). *See also* Fischer, *Products Liability—An Analysis of Market Share Liability*, 34 Vand. L. Rev. 1623 (1981); Schwartz & Mahshigian, *Failure to Identify the Defendant in Tort Law: Towards a Legislative Solution*, 73 Cal. L. Rev. 941 (1985).

D. Difficulties on Proof of Causation

Falcon v. Memorial Hospital

Supreme Court of Michigan, 1990
462 N.W.2d 44

LEVIN, JUSTICE.

The deposition testimony of plaintiff Ruby Falcon's[1] expert witness tended to show that had the defendant physician, S.N. Kelso, Jr., followed the procedures the expert witness claims should have been followed, the patient, Nena J. Falcon, would have had a 37.5 percent opportunity[2] of surviving the medical accident that was a cause of her death.

The trial court dismissed the complaint because Falcon's evidence did not show that Nena Falcon probably — defined as more than fifty percent — would have survived if the procedure had not been omitted. The Court of Appeals reversed, stating that Falcon need only "establish that the omitted treatment or procedure had the potential for improving the patient's recovery or preventing the patient's death." . . . The Court added that "while a plaintiff must show some probability that the treatment would be successful, that probability need not be greater than fifty percent." We affirm.

I

The defendants contend that because the proofs at a trial of Falcon's claim would not show that it was probable, measured as more than fifty percent, that Nena Falcon would have avoided physical harm had the procedure not been omitted, Falcon cannot show that the asserted negligence of defendants caused her physical harm. . . .

II

Under the more probable, measured as more than fifty percent, approach to causation, a plaintiff who establishes that the patient would have had more than a fifty percent opportunity of not suffering physical harm had the defendant not acted negligently, recovers one hundred percent of the damages. The better than even opportunity is compensated as if it were a certainty, although the patient's chances of a better result are significantly less than one hundred percent.

III

Other courts have permitted recovery for physical harm on a showing that the lost opportunity was a substantial, albeit fifty percent or less, factor in producing the harm. . . .

---

1. The plaintiff is Ruby Falcon, administratrix of the estate of her granddaughter, Nena Falcon.
2. While "chance" and "opportunity" can be used interchangeably, "chance" includes "the absence of any cause of events that can be predicted, understood, or controlled," Random House Dictionary of the English Language, 2d ed, unabridged, p. 344, and "opportunity" includes "a situation or condition favorable for attainment of a goal." *Id.*, 1359.

Some courts have held that the plaintiff need only show that the defendant's conduct was a substantial factor in producing the physical harm. Other courts allow recovery for loss of a fifty percent or less opportunity of achieving a better result without clearly articulating a standard of causation. A number of courts have so held on the basis of language in the Restatement Torts, 2d.

IV

Nena Falcon, a nineteen-year-old woman, gave birth to a healthy baby, Justice Eugene Falcon, in the early morning hours of March 21, 1973. Moments after delivery, Nena Falcon coughed, gagged, convulsed, became cyanotic, and suffered a complete respiratory and cardiac collapse. Attempts to revive her were unsuccessful. She was pronounced dead soon thereafter.

The autopsy report indicated that amniotic fluid embolism,[15] an unpreventable complication that occurs in approximately one out of ten or twenty thousand births, was the cause of death. The survival rate of amniotic fluid embolism is, according to Falcon's expert witness, 37.5 percent if an intravenous line is connected to the patient before the onset of the embolism. In this case, an intravenous line had not been established.

Falcon's theory . . . is the intravenous line could have been used to infuse life-saving fluids into Nena Falcon's circulatory system, providing her a 37.5 percent opportunity of surviving. By not inserting the intravenous line, the physician deprived her of a 37.5 percent opportunity of surviving the embolism.

V

The defendant's failure to act is largely responsible for the uncertainty regarding causation.

Had the defendants in the instant case inserted an intravenous line, one of two things would have happened, Nena Falcon would have lived, or she would have died. . . . The United States Court of Appeals for the Fourth Circuit, observed:

> "When a defendant's negligent action or inaction has effectively terminated a person's chance of survival, it does not lie in the defendant's mouth to raise conjectures as to the measure of the chances that he has put beyond the possibility of realization. If there was any substantial possibility of survival and the defendant has destroyed it, he is answerable. . . . The law does not in the existing circumstances require the plaintiff to show to a *certainty* that the

---

15. An amniotic fluid embolism occurs when the amniotic fluid infuses into the mother's circulatory system, most often through a rent in the uterus or through the mother's pelvic veins. The amniotic fluid is not clear. It may contain undissolved matter such as fetal skin cells, lanugo, mucus, or meconium (excrement from the fetus' intestinal tract). The debris-filled fluid is taken up into the mother's circulatory system, pumped through her heart and into her lungs where the embolus lodges, causing injury, and often, death. Amniotic fluid embolism may be diagnosed in an autopsy by the presence of amniotic debris in the body's lungs.

patient would have lived had she been hospitalized and operated on promptly. . . ." [Emphasis in original.]

VI

. . . .

The physician expects the patient to pay or provide payment for the services, whether the likelihood of there in fact being any benefit to the patient is only one through fifty percent or is greater than fifty percent.

. . . [The defendants] contend that they should be subject to liability only for acts or omissions likely, to the extent of more than fifty percent, to have caused physical harm to the patient:

> "The reasoning of the district court herein . . . in essence, declares open season on critically ill or injured persons as care providers would be free of liability for even the grossest malpractice if the patient had only a fifty-fifty chance of surviving the disease or injury even with proper treatment." . . .

. . . In reducing Nena Falcon's opportunity of living by failing to insert an intravenous line, her physician caused her harm, although it cannot be said, more probably than not, that he caused her death. A 37.5 percent opportunity of living is hardly the kind of opportunity that any of us would willingly allow our health care providers to ignore.

. . . .

VII

A number of courts have recognized, as we would, loss of an opportunity for a more favorable result, as distinguished from the unfavorable result, as compensable in medical malpractice actions. Under this approach, damages are recoverable for the loss of opportunity although the opportunity lost was less than even, and thus it is not more probable than not that the unfavorable result would or could have been avoided.

Under this approach, the plaintiff must establish more-probable-than-not causation. He must prove, more probably than not, that the defendant reduced the opportunity of avoiding harm.

VIII

We are persuaded that loss of a 37.5 percent opportunity of living constitutes a loss of a substantial opportunity of avoiding physical harm. We need not now decide what lesser percentage would constitute a substantial loss of opportunity.

IX

. . . In this case, 37.5 percent times the damages recoverable for wrongful death would be an appropriate measure of damages.

. . . .

We would affirm the Court of Appeals reversal of the entry of summary judgment for the defendants, and remand the case for trial.

———————

1. What damages does the plaintiff recover in *Falcon*? The dissenting opinion in
Falcon states:

> The lost chance theory is most fully explained in King, *Causation, Valu-
> ation, and Chance in Personal Injury Torts Involving Preexisting Conditions
> and Future Consequences*, 90 Yale L.J. 1353 (1981). The theory is premised
> on the reasoning that chance itself is an injury entitled to redress, and that
> chance should be measured by a mathematical percentage probability test:

> A plaintiff ordinarily should be required to prove by the applicable stan-
> dard of proof that the defendant caused the loss in question. *What* caused a
> loss, however, should be a separate question from what the *nature and extent*
> of the loss are. This distinction seems to have eluded the courts, with the
> result that lost chances in many respects are compensated either as certain-
> ties or not at all.

> To illustrate, consider the case in which a doctor negligently fails to diag-
> nose a patient's cancerous condition until it has become inoperable. Assume
> further that even with a timely diagnosis the patient would have had only a
> 30% chance of recovering from the disease and surviving over the long term.
> There are two ways of handling such a case. Under the traditional approach,
> this loss of a not-better-than-even chance of recovering from the cancer
> would not be compensable because it did not appear more likely [than] not
> that the patient would have survived with proper care. Recoverable damages,
> if any, would depend on the extent to which it appeared that cancer killed
> the patient sooner than it would have with timely diagnosis and treatment,
> and on the extent to which the delay in diagnosis aggravated the patient's
> condition, such as by causing additional pain. A more rational approach,
> however, would allow recovery for the loss of the chance of cure even though
> the chance was not better than even. The probability of long-term survival
> would be reflected in the amount of damages awarded for the loss of the
> chance. While the plaintiff here could not prove by a preponderance of
> the evidence that he was denied a cure by the defendant's negligence, he
> could show by a preponderance that he was deprived of a 30% chance of a
> cure. *Id.*, pp. 1363–1364.

> A number of cases adopting the lost chance of survival theory also adopt
> Professor King's statistical approach, holding that if a decedent had, for
> example, a thirty percent chance of survival, then compensation should be
> awarded for thirty percent of the value of the decedent's life.

Falcon, 462 N.W.2d at 63, 64.

2. Justice Boyle's concurring opinion in *Falcon* raises the issue of injuries other
than death:

> I concur in the recognition of "lost opportunity to survive" as injury for
> which tort law should allow recovery in proportion to the extent of the lost
> chance of survival, . . . provided that the negligence of the defendant more

probably than not caused the loss of opportunity. However, I would emphasize that the Court today is called upon to decide the viability of a claim for
"lost opportunity" only where the ultimate harm to the victim is death.
Thus, any language in the lead opinion suggesting that a similar cause of
action might lie for a lost opportunity of avoiding lesser physical harm is
dicta. Whether the social and policy factors which justify compensation for
a lost chance of survival would justify recovery for the loss of a chance to
avoid some lesser harm is a question for another day.

Falcon, 462 N.W.2d at 57, 58.

If Nena Falcon had suffered partial paralysis of her legs because of the embolism
and the failure to connect an intravenous line, should she be able to recover? Why
might the courts draw the line of recovery at death?

3. Does the lost chance of survival theory fundamentally alter the meaning of causation? Justice Riley (dissenting) argued:

The recognition of a lost chance as a cognizable injury is necessarily based
on the reasoning that but for the defendant's negligence, the plaintiff *might
possibly* have avoided an adverse result. Thus, recognition of lost chance as
a recoverable interest contradicts the very notion of cause in fact. Professor
King aptly characterizes a lost chance as a "raffle ticket" destroyed by the
defendant's negligence. King, *supra*, p. 1378. King advocates compensation
for "statistically demonstrable losses," *id.*, p. 1377, so that a person deprived
of a forty percent chance of survival should be compensated for forty percent
of the compensable value of his life. *Id.*, p. 1382. Thus, tort law is transformed
from a compensatory system to a payout scheme on the basis of a statistical
chance that the defendant caused the plaintiff's death.

Falcon, 462 N.W.2d at 65. Critique Riley's reasoning.

Following *Falcon*, Michigan statutory law was amended to include the following:
"In an action alleging medical malpractice, the plaintiff cannot recover for loss of
an opportunity to survive or an opportunity to achieve a better result unless the
opportunity was greater than 50%." M.C.L.A. 600.2912a (b)(2)(1994).

4. In *Herskovits v. Group Health Coop, of Puget Sound*, 99 Wash. 2d 609, 664 P.2d
474 (1983), the court permitted recovery for a 14% reduction in the opportunity for
survival. The case involved a failure to diagnose cancer in a patient who was certain
to die of the disease. The *Falcon* majority stated:

The Supreme Court of Washington permitted the personal representative
of the patient to maintain an action where there was expert testimony of a
fourteen percentage point reduction—from thirty-nine percent to twenty-
five percent—in the patient's opportunity for survival, which was claimed
to have resulted from a delay in diagnosis of lung cancer. *Herskovits v. Group
Health Cooperative of Puget Sound*, 99 Wash. 2d 609; 664 P.2d 474 (1983).
The majority, . . . agreed, that recovery for "[causing reduction of the

opportunity to recover] (loss of chance) by one's negligence, however, does not necessitate a total recovery against the negligent party for all damages caused by the victim's death."

Falcon, 462 N.W.2d at 54.

5. The loss of chance theory was rejected in *Fennell v. Southern Md. Hosp. Center, Inc.*, 320 Md. 776, 580 A.2d 206 (1990). The plaintiff sued for loss of a 40% chance of surviving meningitis. The majority reasoned:

> Since loss of chance damages are only permitted when the patient dies, it is also arguable that, when we strip away the rhetoric, damages are really being awarded for the *possibility* that the negligence was a cause of the death. Maryland law clearly does not allow damages based on mere possibilities.
>
> Another factor weighing against adoption of a loss of chance damages approach is its practical application in civil jury trials. Probabilities and statistical evidence comprise a substantial portion of the evidence submitted to the trier of fact in loss of chance actions. This evidence will generally be in the form of opinions based on statistics that show chance of survival of other individuals similarly situated to the victim. The use of statistics in trials is subject to criticism as being unreliable, misleading, easily manipulated, and confusing to a jury. When large damage awards will be based on the statistical chance of survival before the negligent treatment, minus the statistical chance of survival after the negligent treatment, times the value of the lost life, we can imagine the bewildering sets of numbers with which the jury will be confronted, as well as the difficulties juries will have in assessing the comparative reliability of the divergent statistical evidence offered by each side.

Id. at 213. Argue against the Maryland court's reasoning, or for it.

6. Informed consent, discussed in the Negligence chapter, may be important in these cases.

7. Suppose a singer, who is very popular with teenagers, records a song that says: "When your girlfriend leaves you, parents throw you out and you are failing math and gym, take a gun or pills and check out." Chucky, age 17, is found dead with the teenage angst CD in the player. Argue for cause in fact against the record company and the singer. *See McCollum v. CBS, Inc.*, 202 Cal. App. 3d 989, 249 Cal. Rptr. 187 (1988), where liability was rejected.

What about a rape that is presented on television and later imitated on the street? *See Olivia N. v. National Broadcasting Co.*, 126 Cal. App. 3d 488, 178 Cal. Rptr. 888 (1981) (rejecting liability on constitutional principles). *See* Krattenmaker & Powe, *Televised Violence: First Amendment Principles and Social Science Theory*, 64 Va. L. Rev. 1123 (1978).

Problem

Several states sued tobacco manufacturers to recover the medical costs of treating patients for sickness and disease allegedly caused by smoking. The manufacturers will likely argue that each patient must prove that smoking caused his or her specific illness. Argue for or against the proposition that the costs of treating numerous patients can be grouped together in one suit and that statistical proof (smoking caused 30% of these illnesses) is sufficient to send the case to the jury.

Georgia-Pacific Corp. v. Bostic

Court of Appeals of Texas, 2010
320 S.W.3d 588, *aff'd.* 439 S.W.3d 332 (Tex. 2014)

FILLMORE, J.

. . . In February 2003, Timothy Bostic's wife, son, father, and mother brought wrongful death claims and a survival action against Georgia-Pacific and numerous other entities alleging Timothy's death was caused by exposure to asbestos. At the time of trial, Georgia-Pacific was the sole remaining defendant, the other named defendants having settled or been dismissed. . . . The jury returned a verdict in favor of appellees, finding Georgia-Pacific seventy-five percent liable and Knox Glass, Inc., a non-party former employer of Timothy, twenty-five percent liable for Timothy's death. The jury awarded $7,554,907 in compensatory damages and $6,038,910 in punitive damages.

Georgia-Pacific appealed.

LEGAL SUFFICIENCY OF THE EVIDENCE

In its first issue, Georgia-Pacific asserts there is legally insufficient evidence that Georgia-Pacific asbestos-containing joint compound caused Timothy's mesothelioma, a form of cancer usually linked to asbestos exposure. Georgia-Pacific asserts there is no evidence Timothy was exposed to Georgia-Pacific asbestos-containing joint compound, and even if there was evidence of exposure, there is no evidence of dose. Further, Georgia-Pacific asserts that even if there was evidence of exposure and dose, the record contains no epidemiological studies showing that persons similar to Timothy with exposure to asbestos-containing joint compound had an increased risk of developing mesothelioma. . . . Georgia-Pacific asserts that for each of these reasons, appellees' negligence and defective marketing claims against Georgia-Pacific fail as a matter of law.

Joint compound, sometimes called "drywall mud," is used to connect and smooth the seams of adjoining pieces of drywall, also called sheetrock, and to cover nail heads on sheets of drywall. Joint compound is spread in a thin coat and then smoothed. After it dries, uneven areas are further smoothed by sanding. This process is sometimes carried out multiple times in further refining the surface.

. . . .

In 2002, Timothy was diagnosed with mesothelioma at the age of forty. He died in 2003. Appellees claim Timothy's mesothelioma was caused by his exposure to asbestos-containing joint compound manufactured by Georgia-Pacific. Georgia-Pacific acknowledged there is some evidence that Timothy used or was present during the use of joint compound between 1967 and 1977, but contends there is no evidence of exposure to Georgia-Pacific asbestos-containing joint compound. (Fundamental principle of products liability law is plaintiff must prove defendant supplied product which caused injury).

. . . .

Timothy testified he had been around drywall work his entire life, and he recalled that before the age of ten, he observed his father performing drywall work. He stated he mixed and sanded joint compound from the age of five. He testified he recalled at a young age helping his father "mud the holes" with joint compound. While he did not provide any more specifics of drywall work he performed with his father before 1977, he believed he used and was exposed to Georgia-Pacific joint compound before he graduated from high school in 1980. Timothy's work history sheets also indicate he worked with and around other brands of asbestos-containing joint compounds.

. . . .

Harold [Tim's father] testified he used Georgia-Pacific joint compound ninety-eight percent of the time that he did drywall work. He testified he tried one or two other brands of joint compound, but he always returned to Georgia-Pacific's product. With one exception listed below, Harold said he could not positively associate Georgia-Pacific's product with any specific drywall job. On this record, we disagree with Georgia-Pacific's argument that there is no evidence Timothy was exposed to Georgia-Pacific asbestos-containing joint compound.

Substantial-Factor Causation

. . . .

Georgia-Pacific contends that appellees failed to introduce evidence sufficient to satisfy the "substantial factor" standard of causation set forth in Flores, because appellees produced no evidence of cause-in-fact. In the context of an asbestos case, the Texas Supreme Court explained that "asbestos in the defendant's product [must be] a substantial factor in bringing about the plaintiff's injuries." *Flores*, 232 S.W.3d at 770. The court agreed that the "frequency, regularity, and proximity" test for exposure to asbestos set out in *Lohrmann v. Pittsburgh Corning Corp.*, 782 F.2d 1156 (4th Cir. 1986), is appropriate. *Flores*, 232 S.W.3d at 769; *see also Lohrmann*, 782 F.2d at 1162–63 (to support reasonable inference of substantial causation from circumstantial evidence, there must be evidence of exposure to specific product on regular basis over extended period of time in proximity to where plaintiff actually worked). The Supreme Court stated, however, that the terms "frequency," "regularity," and "proximity" do not "capture the emphasis [Texas] jurisprudence has placed on causation as an essential predicate to liability," and agreed with *Lohrmann*'s analysis that the asbestos exposure must be a substantial factor in causing the asbestos-related disease. *Fleers*, 232 S.W.3d at 769; *see also Lohrmann*, 782 F.2d at 1162.

. . . .

Appellees assert that *Flores* does not require "but-for" causation in proving specific causation and that *Flores* requires only that appellees prove Timothy's exposure to Georgia-Pacific asbestos-containing joint compound was a "substantial factor" in contributing to his risk of mesothelioma. We disagree. The Texas Supreme Court [has] recognized that [c]ommon to both proximate and producing cause is causation in fact, including the requirement that the defendant's conduct or product be a substantial factor in bringing about the plaintiff's injuries. Thus, to establish substantial-factor causation, a plaintiff must prove that the defendant's conduct was a cause-in-fact of the harm. *See Flores*, 232 S.W.3d at 770. "In asbestos cases, then, we must determine whether the asbestos in the defendant's product was a substantial factor in bringing about the plaintiff's injuries" and without which the injuries would not have occurred. *Id.; see also Stephens*, 239 S.W.3d at 308–09.

Appellees acknowledged in their brief and at oral submission that their only expert who opined on specific causation of Timothy's mesothelioma was pathologist Samuel Hammar, M.D. However, Dr. Hammar testified he could not opine that Timothy would not have developed mesothelioma absent exposure to Georgia-Pacific asbestos-containing joint compound. Because a plaintiff must prove that the defendant's conduct was a cause-in-fact of the harm, appellees' evidence is insufficient to satisfy the required substantial-factor causation element for maintaining this negligence and product liability suit. *See Flores, 232 S.W.3d at 770.*

. . . .

On this record, appellees' evidence is insufficient to provide quantitative evidence of Timothy's exposure to asbestos fibers from Georgia-Pacific's asbestos-containing joint compound or to establish Timothy's exposure was in amounts sufficient to increase his risk of developing mesothelioma. Therefore, appellees' evidence is legally insufficient to establish substantial-factor causation mandated by *Flores*.

. . . .

CONCLUSION

There is legally insufficient evidence of causation to support the verdict against Georgia-Pacific. We reverse the trial court's judgment and render judgment that appellees take nothing on their claims against Georgia-Pacific.

———————

1. How does the reasoning in this case contrast with that in *Falcon*? Is one case's reasoning more logical than the other, or are they both logical, but applicable to different circumstances?

2. What seems like the more reasonable test for mesothelioma: the "but for" test or the "substantial factor" test?

In *Bostic v. Georgia-Pacific Corp.*, 439 S.W.3d 332 (Tex. 2014), the Supreme Court of Texas affirmed the lower court's result but rejected its reasoning. The Court stated that "[W]e do not think the Restatements. . . would require the plaintiffs to meet a strict but for causation test in a case like today's case. . . . Accordingly, we hold that Plaintiffs were required to establish substantial factor causation, but were not required to prove that but for Bostic's exposure to Georgia-Pacific's products, he would not have contracted mesothelioma." *Id.* at 346.

3. Would you apply "market share liability" here?

Daubert v. Merrell Dow Pharmaceuticals, Inc.
United States Supreme Court, 1993
509 U.S. 579

Justice Blackmun delivered the opinion of the Court.

. . . Petitioners Jason Daubert and Eric Schuller are minor children born with serious birth defects. They and their parents sued respondent in California state court, alleging that the birth defects had been caused by the mothers' ingestion of Bendectin, a prescription anti-nausea drug marketed by respondent. Respondent removed the suits to federal court on diversity grounds.

After extensive discovery, respondent moved for summary judgment, contending that Bendectin does not cause birth defects in humans and that petitioners would be unable to come forward with any admissible evidence that it does. In support of its motion, respondent submitted an affidavit of Steven H. Lamm, physician and epidemiologist, who is a well-credentialed expert on the risks from exposure to various chemical substances. Doctor Lamm stated that he had reviewed all the literature on Bendectin and human birth defects—more than 30 published studies involving over 130,000 patients. No study had found Bendectin to be a human teratogen (i.e., a substance capable of causing malformations in fetuses). On the basis of this review, Doctor Lamm concluded that maternal use of Bendectin during the first trimester of pregnancy has not been shown to be a risk factor for human birth defects.

Petitioners did not (and do not) contest this characterization of the published record regarding Bendectin. Instead, they responded to respondent's motion with the testimony of eight experts of their own, each of whom also possessed impressive credentials. These experts had concluded that Bendectin can cause birth defects. Their conclusions were based upon "in vitro" (test tube) and "in vivo" (live) animal studies that found a link between Bendectin and malformations; pharmacological studies of the chemical structure of Bendectin that purported to show similarities between the structure of the drug and that of other substances known to cause birth defects; and the "reanalysis" of previously published epidemiological (human statistical) studies.

The District Court granted respondent's motion for summary judgment. The court stated that scientific evidence is admissible only if the principle upon which it is based is "sufficiently established to have general acceptance in the field to which it belongs." *Daubert v. Merrell Dow Pharmaceuticals, Inc.*, 727 F. Supp. 570, 572 (S.D. Cal. 1989), quoting *United States v. Kilgus*, 571 F.2d 508, 510 (9th Cir. 1978). The court concluded that petitioners' evidence did not meet this standard. Given the vast body of epidemiological data concerning Bendectin, the court held, expert opinion which is not based on epidemiological evidence is not admissible to establish causation. 727 F. Supp., at 575. Thus, the animal-cell studies, live-animal studies, and chemical-structure analyses on which petitioners had relied could not raise by themselves a reasonably disputable jury issue regarding causation. Petitioners' epidemiological analyses, based as they were on recalculations of data in previously published studies that had found no causal link between the drug and birth defects, were ruled to be inadmissible because they had not been published or subjected to peer review.

The United States Court of Appeals for the Ninth Circuit affirmed. 951 F.2d 1128 (1991). Citing *Frye v. United States*, 293 F. 1013, 1014, 54 App. D.C. 46, 47 (1923), the court stated that expert opinion based on a scientific technique is inadmissible unless the technique is "generally accepted" as reliable in the relevant scientific community. 951 F.2d, at 1129–1130.

. . . We granted certiorari in light of sharp divisions among the courts regarding the proper standard for the admission of expert testimony. . . .

In the 70 years since its formulation in the *Frye* case, the "general acceptance" test has been the dominant standard for determining the admissibility of novel scientific evidence at trial. Although under increasing attack of late, the rule continues to be followed by a majority of courts, including the Ninth Circuit.

. . . They contend that the *Frye* test was superseded by the adoption of the Federal Rules of Evidence. We agree.

. . . [T]here is a specific Rule that speaks to the contested issue. Rule 702, governing expert testimony, provides:

> If scientific, technical, or other specialized knowledge will assist the trier of fact to understand the evidence or to determine a fact in issue, a witness qualified as an expert by knowledge, skill, experience, training, or education, may testify thereto in the form of an opinion or otherwise.

That the *Frye* test was displaced by the Rules of Evidence does not mean, however, that the Rules themselves place no limits on the admissibility of purportedly scientific evidence. Nor is the trial judge disabled from screening such evidence. To the contrary, under the Rules the trial judge must ensure that any and all scientific testimony or evidence admitted is not only relevant, but reliable.

The primary locus of this obligation is Rule 702, which clearly contemplates some degree of regulation of the subjects and theories about which an expert may testify. "If scientific, technical, or other specialized knowledge will assist the trier of fact to understand the evidence or to determine a fact in issue" an expert "may testify thereto." The subject of an expert's testimony must be "scientific . . . knowledge." The adjective "scientific" implies a grounding in the methods and procedures of science.

Similarly, the word "knowledge" connotes more than subjective belief or unsupported speculation. The term "applies to any body of known facts or to any body of ideas inferred from such facts or accepted as truths on good grounds." Webster's Third New International Dictionary 1252 (1986). Of course, it would be unreasonable to conclude that the subject of scientific testimony must be "known" to a certainty; arguably, there are no certainties in science. But, in order to qualify as "scientific knowledge," an inference or assertion must be derived by the scientific method. Proposed testimony must be supported by appropriate validation, i.e., "good grounds," based on what is known. In short, the requirement that an expert's testimony pertain to "scientific knowledge" establishes a standard of evidentiary reliability.

Rule 702 further requires that the evidence or testimony "assist the trier of fact to understand the evidence or to determine a fact in issue." This condition goes primarily to relevance. . . .

Faced with a proffer of expert scientific testimony, then, the trial judge must determine at the outset, pursuant to Rule 104(a), whether the expert is proposing to testify to (1) scientific knowledge that (2) will assist the trier of fact to understand or determine a fact in issue. This entails a preliminary assessment of whether the reasoning or methodology underlying the testimony is scientifically valid and of whether that reasoning or methodology properly can be applied to the facts in issue. . . .

Ordinarily, a key question to be answered in determining whether a theory or technique is scientific knowledge that will assist the trier of fact will be whether it can be (and has been) tested. "Scientific methodology today is based on generating hypotheses and testing them to see if they can be falsified; indeed, this methodology is what distinguishes science from other fields of human inquiry." E. Green & C. Nesson, Problems, Cases, and Materials on Evidence 649, 645 (1983). See also C. Hempel, Philosophy of Natural Science 49 (1966) ([T]he statements constituting a scientific explanation must be capable of empirical test"). . . .

Another pertinent consideration is whether the theory or technique has been subjected to peer review and publication. Publication (which is but one element of peer review) is not a sine qua of admissibility; it does not necessarily correlate with reliability, and in some instances well-grounded but innovative theories will not have been published. Some propositions, moreover are too particular, too new, or of too limited interest to be published.

Finally, "general acceptance" can yet have a bearing on the inquiry. . . . Widespread acceptance can be an important factor in ruling particular evidence admissible, and "a known technique that has been able to attract only minimal support within the community," Downing, *supra*, at 1238, may be properly be viewed with skepticism.

To summarize: "general acceptance" is not a necessary precondition to the admissibility of scientific evidence under the Federal Rules of Evidence. . . .

The inquiries of the District Court and the Court of Appeals focused almost exclusively on "general acceptance," as gauged by publication and the decisions of other courts. Accordingly, the judgment of the Court of Appeals is vacated and the case is remanded for further proceedings consistent with this opinion.

It is so ordered.

———————

1. *The Scientific vs. The Technical Expert. In Kumho Tire Co., Ltd. v. Carmichael*, 526 U.S. 137 (1999), the Court held that the *Daubert* standard applied to expert testimony based on technical or other specialized knowledge, as well as testimony based on scientific knowledge.

Daubert and *Kumho* are binding on federal, but not state, courts. How does a trial court judge come to grips with questions of science that she may not understand?

2. In *Daubert v. Merrell Dow Pharmaceuticals, Inc.*, 43 F.3d 1311 (9th Cir. 1995), Judge Kozinski said:

> On remand from the United States Supreme Court, we undertake "the task of ensuring that an expert's testimony both rests on a reliable foundation and is relevant to the task at hand." . . .
>
> Two minors brought suit against Merrell Dow Pharmaceuticals, claiming they suffered limb reduction birth defects because their mothers had taken Benedectin, a drug prescribed for morning sickness to about 17.5 million pregnant women in the United States between 1957 and 1982. This appeal deals with an evidentiary question: whether certain expert scientific testimony is admissible to prove that Bendectin caused the plaintiffs' birth defects.
>
> For the most part, we don't know how birth defects come about. We do know they occur in 2–3% of births, whether or not the expectant mother has taken Benedectin. . . .
>
> Not knowing the mechanism whereby a particular agent causes a particular effect is not always fatal to a plaintiff's claim, . . . One method of proving causation in these circumstances is to use statistical evidence. . . .
>
> The opinions proffered by plaintiffs' expert do not, to understate the point, reflect the consensus within the scientific community. . . . Every published study here and abroad—and there have been many—concludes that Bendectin is not a teratogen. . . .
>
> It is largely because the opinions proffered by plaintiffs' experts run counter to the substantial consensus in the scientific community that we affirmed the district court's grant of summary judgment the last time the case appeared before us. . . .
>
> Federal judges ruling on the admissibility of expert scientific testimony face a far more complex and daunting task in a post-*Daubert* world than before. The judge's task under *Frye* was relatively simple: to determine whether the method employed by the experts is generally accepted in the scientific community. Under *Daubert*, we must engage in a difficult, two-part

analysis. First, we must determine nothing less than whether the experts' testimony reflects "scientific knowledge," whether their findings are "derived by the scientific method," and whether their work product amounts to "good science." Second, we must ensure that the proposed expert testimony is "relevant to the task at hand," i.e., that it logically advances a material aspect of the proposing party's case. The Supreme Court referred to this second prong of the analysis as the "fit" requirement. . . .

Our responsibility, then, unless we badly misread the Supreme Court's opinion, is to resolve disputes among respected, well-credentialed scientists about matters squarely within their expertise, in areas where there is no scientific consensus as to what is and is not "good science," and occasionally to reject such expert testimony because it was not "derived by the scientific method." . . .

Establishing that an expert's proffered testimony grows out of prelitigation research or that the expert's research has been subjected to peer review are the two principal ways the proponent of expert testimony can show that the evidence satisfies the first prong of Rule 702. Where such evidence is unavailable, the proponent of expert scientific testimony may attempt to satisfy its burden through the testimony of its own experts. For such a showing to be sufficient, the experts must explain precisely how they went about reaching their conclusions and point to some objective source—a learned treatise, the policy statement of a professional association, a published article in a reputed scientific method, as it is practiced by (at least) a recognized minority of scientists in their field. . . .

. . . We've been presented with only the experts' qualifications, their conclusions and their assurances of reliability. Under *Daubert*, that's not enough. . . .

[W]hat plaintiffs must prove is not that Bendectin causes some birth defects, but that it caused their birth defects. To show this, plaintiffs' experts would have had to testify either that Bendectin actually caused plaintiffs' injuries (which they could not say) or that Bendectin more than doubled the likelihood of limb reduction birth defects (which they did not say).

The district court's grant of summary judgment is AFFIRMED.

3. What are the cause in fact issues in a suit brought by a woman with silicone breast implants who sues to recover for connective tissue injury? *See Hopkins v. Dow Corning Corp.*, 33 F.3d 1116 (9th Cir. 1994). What are the cause in fact issues in a suit brought by the survivors of people shot by a person taking Prozac (a medication for depression)? *See Forsyth v. Eli Lilly & Co.*, 904 F. Supp. 1153 (D. Haw. 1995) (dismissing the Food and Drug Administration as a party).

4. Parents of children with severe limb deformities brought suit against Dow Chemical Company alleging that the fathers' exposures to Agent Orange (a defoliant) in Viet Nam caused the problems. Although the plaintiffs had substantial problems proving cause in fact, the judge urged both sides to settle:

> There are serious factual problems with plaintiffs' case, the chief one being doubt that present scientific knowledge would support a finding of causality. . . .

> Many plaintiffs suffer from diseases that can be caused by dioxin. . . . The logical and practical difficulty with their argument is that the diseases referred to may result from causes other than dioxin poisoning. . . .

> In conclusion, all that can be said is that persuasive evidence of causality has not been produced. . . .

> Defendants contend that even if anyone was injured by Agent Orange, plaintiffs cannot establish that the harm to any one of them was caused by any individual defendant. . . .

> Plaintiffs have several difficult legal hurdles to overcome. The first results from the conceded inability of any veteran to identify the manufacturer of the herbicide to which he was exposed. Second, all of the ailments and conditions class members allegedly suffer from, with the possible exception of chloracne, are not unique to Agent Orange or dioxin exposure and occur in the population at large. . . . Given the desirability of resolving the indeterminate plaintiff problem using a form of proportional liability or some other acceptable method, a dismissal of the class action would be unwarranted. The statistical theory, available data, and public policy are far from settled. Particularly during this period of rapidly changing scientific approaches and increased threats to the environment, we should not unduly restrict development of legal theory and practice—both substantive and procedural— by dismissing a class action such as the one now before us although the hazards of an ultimate dismissal must be considered in assessing the fairness of the settlement.

In re "Agent Orange" Prod. Liab. Litig., 597 F. Supp. 740, 775–843 (E.D.N.Y. 1984).

5. For a discussion of the cause in fact problems in suits brought by public hospitals and states to recover the costs of treating patients for tobacco-caused illnesses, see R.E. Gangarosa, F.J. Vandall & B.M. *Willis, Suits by Public Hospitals to Recover Expenditures for the Treatment of Disease, Injury and Disability Caused by Tobacco and Alcohol*, 22 Fordham Urb. L.J. 81 (1994).

6. Cause in fact may be a problem in fear of cancer cases and emotional distress cases that are discussed in the Duty chapter.

Chapter 7

Proximate Cause

The terms cause-in-fact and proximate cause are often confused by judges, attorneys and law students. Cause-in-fact is a matter of science: did the defendant's conduct have something to do with the plaintiff's injury as a matter of science? In contrast, proximate cause is a matter of social policy, and asks does the defendant's liability extend to this specific plaintiff for this particular injury? Proximate cause is based on or assumes that the defendant's conduct was the cause-in-fact of the plaintiff's injury. Proximate cause is a matter of line drawing and was developed by the courts to control the jury by taking a case from them. The court considers many factors in deciding the question of proximate cause. There is no rule for proximate cause, and the facts of each case are critical.

You will see that often, when proximate cause is a determinative issue, the party protected by it is a large corporation.

A. The Basic Theories

Problem

While adjusting his CD player, A crashes into B's car. B's car trunk explodes into flames, injuring B and destroying the car. C, standing beside the car, is injured by flying debris, and D, two blocks away, is hit on the head by a shingle that was dislodged by the blast.

E, an attorney located four blocks from the explosion, is frightened by the sound of the blast and therefore drops his infant, F. The child suffers brain damage, and E becomes depressed, can no longer work, loses his law practice, and then is divorced by his wife. Where would the proximate cause line be drawn, and why?

In re Arbitration Between Polemis & Furness, Withy & Co.

Court of Appeal, 1921
3 K.B. 560

BANKES L.J.

[T]he respondents chartered their vessel to the appellants. . . . The vessel was employed by the charterers to carry a cargo to Casablanca in Morocco. The cargo included a quantity of benzine or petrol in cases. While discharging at Casablanca a heavy plank fell into the hold in which the petrol was stowed, and caused an explosion, which set fire to the vessel and completely destroyed her. The owners claimed the value of the vessel from the charterers alleging that the loss of the vessel was due to the negligence of the charterers' servants. The charterers contended that . . . the damages claimed were too remote. The claim was referred to arbitration, and the arbitrators stated a special case for the opinion of the court. The arbitrators found that the ship was lost by fire; that the fire arose from a spark igniting the petrol vapour in the hold; that the spark was caused by the falling board coming into contact with some substance in the hold; and that the causing of the spark could not reasonably have been anticipated from the falling of the board, though some damage to the ship might reasonably have been anticipated. . . .

In the present case the arbitrators have found as a fact that the falling of the plank was due to the negligence of the defendants' servants. The fire appears to me to have been directly caused by the falling of the plank. Under these circumstances I consider that it is immaterial that the causing of the spark by the falling of the plank could not have been reasonably anticipated. The appellants' junior counsel sought to draw a distinction between the anticipation of the extent of damage resulting from a negligent act, and the anticipation of the type of damage resulting from such an act. He admitted that it could not lie in the mouth of a person whose negligent act had caused damage to say that he could not reasonably have foreseen the extent of the damage, but he contended that the negligent person was entitled to rely upon the fact that he could not reasonably have anticipated the type of damage which resulted from his negligent act. I do not think that the distinction can be admitted. Given the breach of duty which constitutes the negligence, and given the damage as a direct result of that negligence, the anticipations of the person whose negligent act has produced the damage appear to me to be irrelevant. I consider that the damages claimed are not too remote.

        . . . .

SCRUTTON L.J. The steamship *Thrasyvoulos* was lost by fire while being discharged by workmen employed by the charterers. Experienced arbitrators, by whose findings of fact we are bound, have decided that the fire was caused by a spark igniting petrol vapour in the hold, the vapour coming from leaks from cargo shipped by the charterers, and that the spark was caused by the . . . workmen employed by the charterers negligently knocking a plank out of a temporary staging erected in the hold, so that the plank fell into the hold, and in its fall by striking something made the spark which ignited the petrol vapour.

        . . . .

The . . . defence is that the damage is too remote from the negligence, as it could not be reasonably foreseen as a consequence. . . . To determine whether an act is negligent, it is relevant to determine whether any reasonable person would foresee that the act would cause damage; if he would not, the act is not negligent. But if the act would or might probably cause damage, the fact that the damage it in fact causes is not the exact kind of damage one would expect is immaterial, so long as the damage is in fact directly traceable to the negligent act, and not due to the operation of independent causes having no connection with the negligent act, except that they could not avoid its results. Once the act is negligent, the fact that its exact operation was not foreseen is immaterial. In the present case it was negligent in discharging cargo to knock down the planks of the temporary staging, for they might easily cause some damage either to workmen, or cargo, or the ship. The fact that they did directly produce an unexpected result, a spark in an atmosphere of petrol vapour which caused a fire, does not relieve the person who was negligent from the damage which his negligent act directly causes.

For these reasons the experienced arbitrators and the judge appealed from came, in my opinion, to a correct decision, and the appeal must be dismissed with costs.

Appeal dismissed.

[The concurring opinion of Warrington L.J. is omitted.]

————

1. What is the function of the term "foreseeable"? What does the court mean by "direct"?

2. In *Ryan v. New York Central R.R. Co.*, 35 N.Y. 210, 91 Am. Dec. 49 (1866), the railroad, through careless management of one of its engines, set fire to its woodshed. The plaintiff's house, located 130 feet from the railroad's shed, soon caught fire from the sparks and was consumed. In finding for the railroad, the court stated:

> Thus far the law is settled, and the principle is apparent. If, however, the fire communicates from the house of A. to that of B., and that is destroyed, is the negligent party liable for his loss? And if it spreads thence to the house of C., and thence to the house of D., and thence consecutively through the other houses, until it reaches and consumes the house of Z., is the party liable to pay the damages sustained by these twenty-four sufferers? The counsel for the plaintiff does not distinctly claim this, and I think it would not be seriously insisted, that the sufferers could recover in such case. Where, then, is the principle upon which A. recovers and Z. fails?
>
> . . . .
>
> Without deciding upon the importance of this distinction, I prefer to place my opinion upon the ground that, in the one case, to wit, the destruction of the building upon which the sparks were thrown by the negligent act of the party sought to be charged, the result was to have been anticipated, the moment the fire was communicated to the building; that its destruction was the ordinary and natural result of its being fired. In the second, third or twenty-fourth case, as supposed, the destruction of the building was not a natural and expected result of the first firing. That a building upon which sparks and cinders fall should be destroyed or seriously injured, must be expected, but that the fire should spread and other buildings be consumed, is not a necessary or an usual result. That it is possible, and that it is not

unfrequent, cannot be denied. The result, however, depends, not upon any necessity of a further communication of the fire, but upon a concurrence of accidental circumstances, such as the degree of the heat, the state of the atmosphere, the condition and materials of the adjoining structures and the direction of the wind. These are accidental and varying circumstances; the party has no control over them, and is not responsible for their effects.

My opinion, therefore, is, that this action cannot be sustained, for the reason that the damages incurred are not the immediate but the remote result of the negligence of the defendants. The immediate result was the destruction of their own wood and sheds; beyond that, it was remote.

. . . .

In a country where wood, coal, gas and oils are universally used, where men are crowded into cities and villages, where servants are employed, and where children find their home in all houses, it is impossible, that the most vigilant prudence should guard against the occurrence of accidental or negligent fires. A man may insure his own house, or his own furniture, but he cannot insure his neighbor's building or furniture for the reason that he has no interest in them. To hold that the owner must not only meet his own loss by fire, but that he must guaranty the security of his neighbors on both sides, and to an unlimited extent, would be to create a liability which would be the destruction of all civilized society. No community could long exist, under the operation of such a principle. In a commercial country, each man, to some extent, runs the hazard of his neighbor's conduct, and each, by insurance against such hazards, is enabled to obtain a reasonable security against loss.

Does this decision make sense in a community where insurance is available? What decision would you expect in a state where insurance was not available for crops such as grain? *See Atchison, T. & S.F. R.R. Co. v. Stanford*, 12 Kan. 354, 15 Am. Rep. 362 (1874).

3. *Ryan* is one of the earliest cases to mention insurance. What should be the role of insurance in proximate cause decisions? Today, it is rare to see insurance discussed as a decisional factor. Does that mean it is not a factor?

4. In *Ryan*, was the spread of fire natural, expected, usual, immediate, or remote?

5. "For an intended injury the law is astute to discover even very remote causation. For one which the defendant merely ought to have anticipated it has often stopped at an earlier stage of the investigation of causal connection." *Derosier v. New England Tel. & Tel. Co.*, 81 N.H. 451, 130 A. 145 (1925).

6. In *Bartolone v. Jeckovich*, 481 N.Y.S.2d 545 (1984), the court held that a car crash victim could suffer an acute psychotic breakdown from very minor injuries. He was not even hospitalized, but was "permanently disabled" and able to recover $500,000. The case was argued and won on the theory that the crash aggravated a preexisting paranoid schizophrenic condition.

7. What would a nonlawyer say of the plaintiff's recovery in *Bartolone*? How would you answer the nonlawyer?

8. The theory that you take the plaintiff as you find him or her (the thin skull rule) is supported by *Dulieu v. White*, [1901] 2 K.B. 669, where a pregnant woman recovered for a shock-induced premature birth of a child with mental illness. Plaintiff was behind the bar in a public house when the defendant's servant negligently drove his horse-drawn wagon into the house. There was no impact with the plaintiff. How would *Dulieu* be decided today in terms of cause-in-fact?

Overseas Tankship (U.K.) Ltd. v. Morts Dock & Engineering Co.

(The Wagon Mound No. 1)
Privy Council, 1961
[1961] A.C. 388

VISCOUNT SIMONDS:

Appeal from an order of the Full Court of the Supreme Court of New South Wales dismissing an appeal by the appellants, Overseas Tankship (U.K.) Ltd., from a judgment . . . in an action in which the appellants were defendants and the respondents, Morts Dock & Engineering Co. Ltd., were plaintiffs.

The plaintiffs at the relevant time carried on the business of ship-building, ship-repairing and general engineering at Morts Bay, Balmain, in the Port of Sydney. They owned and used for their business the Sheerlegs Wharf, a timber wharf about 400 feet in length and 40 feet wide, where there was a quantity of tools and equipment. In October and November, 1951, a vessel known as the *Corrimel* was moored alongside the wharf and was being refitted by the respondents. Her mast was lying on the wharf and a number of the respondents' employees were working both upon it and upon the vessel itself, using for that purpose electric and oxy-acetylene welding equipment.

At the same time the defendants were charterers . . . of the *S.S. Wagon Mound*, an oil-burning vessel, which was moored at the Caltex Wharf on the northern shore of the harbour at a distance of about 600 feet from the Sheerlegs Wharf. She was there . . . for the purpose of discharging gasolene products and taking in bunkering oil.

During the early hours of October 30, 1951, a large quantity of bunkering oil was, through the carelessness of the defendants' servants, allowed to spill into the bay, and by 10:30 on the morning of that day it had spread over a considerable part of the bay, being thickly concentrated in some places and particularly along the foreshore near the respondents' property. The defendants made no attempt to disperse the oil. The *Wagon Mound* unberthed and set sail very shortly after.

. . . .

For the remainder of October 30 and until about 2 p.m. on November 1 work was carried on as usual, the condition and congestion of the oil remaining substantially unaltered. But at about that time the oil under or near the wharf was ignited and a fire, fed initially by the oil, spread rapidly and burned with great intensity. The wharf and the *Corrimal* caught fire and considerable damage was done to the wharf and the equipment upon it.

The outbreak of fire was due, as the judge found, to the fact that there was floating in the oil underneath the wharf a piece of debris on which lay some smoldering cotton waste or rag which had been set on fire by molten metal falling from the wharf: that the cotton waste or rag burst into flames: that the flames from the cotton waste set the floating oil afire either directly or by first setting fire to a wooden pile coated with oil, and that after the floating oil became ignited the flames spread rapidly over the surface of the oil and . . . severely damaged the wharf.

. . . .

[The trial court found that the defendants did not know that the oil could be ignited while floating on top of the water. The plaintiff won in the trial court and this was affirmed by the Supreme Court of New South Wales. Defendants appealed to the Privy Council. They reversed the decision and stated:]

[T]he authority of *Polemis* has been severely shaken though lip-service has from time to time been paid to it. In their Lordships' opinion it should no longer be regarded as good law. It is not probable that many cases will for that reason have a different result, though it is hoped that the law will be thereby simplified, and that in some cases, at least, palpable injustice will be avoided. For it does not seem consonant with current ideas of justice or morality that for an act of negligence, however slight or venial, which results in some trivial foreseeable damage the actor should be liable for all consequences however unforeseeable and however grave, so long as they can be said to be "direct." It is a principle of civil liability, subject only to qualifications which have no present relevance, that a man must be considered to be responsible for the probable consequences of his act. To demand more of him is too harsh a rule, to demand less is to ignore that civilized order requires the observance of a minimum standard of behaviour.

This concept applied to the slowly developing law of negligence has led to a great variety of expressions which can, as it appears to their Lordships, be harmonised with little difficulty with the single exception of the so-called rule in *Polemis*. For, if it is asked why a man should be responsible for the natural or necessary or probable consequences of his act (or any other similar description of them) the answer is that it is not because, since they are natural or necessary or probable, but because, since they have this quality, it is judged by the standard of the reasonable man that he ought to have foreseen them. Thus it is that over and over again it has happened that in different judgments in the same case, and sometimes in a single judgment, liability for a consequence has been imposed on the ground that it was natural or necessary or probable. The two grounds have been treated as coterminous, and so they largely are. But, where they are not, the question arises to which the wrong answer was given in *Polemis*. For, if some limitation must be imposed upon the consequences for which the negligent actor is to be held responsible — and all are agreed that some limitation there must be—why should that test (reasonable foreseeability) be rejected which, since he is judged by what the reasonable man ought to foresee, corresponds with the common conscience of mankind, and a test (the "direct" consequence) be substituted which leads to nowhere by the never-ending and insoluble problems of causation. . . .

It is, no doubt, proper when considering tortious liability for negligence to analyze its elements and to say that the plaintiff must prove a duty owed to him by the defendant, a breach of that duty by the defendant, and consequent damage. But there can be no liability until the damage has been done. It is not the act but the consequences on which tortious liability is founded. Just as (as it has been said) there is no such thing as negligence in the air, so there is no such thing as liability in the air. Suppose an action brought by A for damage caused by the carelessness (a neutral word) of B, for example, a fire caused by the careless spillage of oil. It may, of course, become relevant to know what duty B owed to A, but the only liability that is in question is the liability for damage by fire. It is vain to isolate the liability from its context and to say that B is or is not liable, and then to ask for what damage he is liable. For his liability is in respect of that damage and no other. If, as admittedly it is, B's liability (culpability) depends on the reasonable foreseeability of the consequent damage, how is that to be determined except by the foreseeability of the damage which in fact happened—the damage in suit?

But, it is said, a different position arises if B's careless act has been shown to be negligent and has caused some foreseeable damage to A. Their Lordships have already observed that to hold B liable for consequences however unforeseeable of a careless act, if, but only if, he is at the same time liable for some other damage however trivial, appears to be neither logical nor just. This becomes more clear if it is supposed that similar unforeseeable damage is suffered by A and C but other foreseeable damage, for which B is liable, by A only. A system of law which would hold B liable to A but not to C for the similar damage suffered by each of them could not easily be defended. Fortunately, the attempt is not necessary. For the same fallacy is at the root of the proposition. It is irrelevant to the question whether B is liable for unforeseeable damage that he is liable for foreseeable damage, as irrelevant as would the fact that he had trespassed on Whiteacre be to the question whether he has trespassed on Blackacre. Again, suppose a claim by A for damage by fire by the careless act of B. Of what relevance is it to that claim that he has another claim arising out of the same careless act? It would surely not prejudice his claim if that other claim failed: it cannot assist it if it succeeds. Each of them rests on its own bottom, and will fail if it can be established that the damage could not reasonably be foreseen. . . .

Their Lordships will humbly advise Her Majesty that this appeal should be allowed, and the respondents' action so far as it related to damage caused by the negligence of the appellants be dismissed with costs. . . . The respondents must pay the costs of the appellants of this appeal and in the courts below.

———————

1. Why did the court dislike the rule in *Polemis*?

2. Does the court in *Wagon Mound* feel it is developing a rule or merely deciding the case before it?

3. What is the policy behind the new rule? What is left of *Polemis*?

4. When the defendant served "foul smelling" shrimp, could it be held to foresee that the plaintiff would slip on a customer's vomit? *Crankshaw v. Piedmont Driving Club*, 115 Ga. App. 820, 156 S.E.2d 208 (1967).

5. Will a doctor who negligently fails to identify a battered child be held to foresee the damage later inflicted by his parents? Should the criminal acts of the parents (beatings) cut off the doctor's liability? *See Landeros v. Flood*, 17 Cal. 3d 399, 131 Cal. Rptr. 69, 551 P.2d 389 (1976).

6. If a telephone company negligently places a phone booth too close to the road, will it be held to foresee that a drunk driver might run into the phone booth and cause the plaintiff (using the booth) serious injury? Should the drunk driver sever the phone company's liability? *See Bigbee v. Pacific Tel. & Tel. Co.*, 34 Cal. 3d 49, 192 Cal. Rptr. 857, 665 P.2d 947 (1983).

7. For articles discussing the *Wagon Mound* case, see Fleming, *The Passing of Polemis*, 39 Can. B. Rev. 489 (1961); Green, *Foreseeability in Negligence Law*, 61 Colum. L. Rev. 1401 (1961).

8. In a second suit, *Wagon Mound No. 2*, the owners of the *Corrimal* sued the charterers of the *Wagon Mound* on the same facts as found in *Wagon Mound No. 1*. The Privy Council reversed the trial court and held in favor of plaintiffs:

> In the present case the evidence led was substantially different from the evidence led in *The Wagon Mound (No. 1)* and the findings of Walsh J. are significantly different. That is not due to there having been any failure by the plaintiffs in *The Wagon Mound (No. 1)* in preparing and presenting their case. The plaintiffs there were no doubt embarrassed by a difficulty which does not affect the present plaintiffs. The outbreak of the fire was consequent on the act of the manager of the plaintiffs in *The Wagon Mound (No. 1)* in resuming oxy-acetylene welding and cutting while the wharf was surrounded by this oil. So if the plaintiffs in the former case had set out to prove that it was foreseeable by the engineers of the *Wagon Mound* that this oil could be set alight, they might have had difficulty in parrying the reply that this must also have been foreseeable by their manager. Then there would have been contributory negligence and at that time contributory negligence was a complete defence in New South Wales.
>
> . . . .
>
> In *The Wagon Mound (No. 1)* the Board were not concerned with degrees of foreseeability because the finding was that the fire was not foreseeable at all. So Lord Simonds had no cause to amplify the statement that the "essential factor in determining liability is whether the damage is of such a kind

as the reasonable man should have foreseen." But here the findings show that some risk of fire would have been present to the mind of a reasonable man in the shoes of the ship's chief engineer. So the first question must be what is the precise meaning to be attached in this context to the words "foreseeable" and "reasonably foreseeable."

. . . .

[I]t does not follow that, no matter what the circumstances may be, it is justifiable to neglect a risk of such a small magnitude. A reasonable man would only neglect such a risk if he had a valid reason for doing so, e.g., that it would involve considerable expense to eliminate the risk. He would weigh the risk against the difficulty of eliminating it.

. . . .

In the present case there was no justification whatever for discharging the oil into Sydney Harbour. Not only was it an offence to do so, but it involved considerable loss financially. If the ship's engineer had thought about the matter, there could have been no question of balancing the advantages and disadvantages. From every point of view it was both his duty and his interest to stop the discharge immediately.

It follows that in their Lordships' view the only question is whether a reasonable man having the knowledge and experience to be expected of the chief engineer of the *Wagon Mound* would have known that there was a real risk of the oil on the water catching fire in some way: if it did, serious damage to ships or other property was not only foreseeable but very likely.

. . . .

In the present case the evidence shows that the discharge of so much oil onto the water must have taken a considerable time, and a vigilant ship's engineer would have noticed the discharge at an early stage. The findings show that he ought to have known that it is possible to ignite this kind of oil on water, and that the ship's engineer probably ought to have known that this had in fact happened before. The most that can be said to justify inaction is that he would have known that this could only happen in very exceptional circumstances. But that does not mean that a reasonable man would dismiss such a risk from his mind and do nothing when it was so easy to prevent it. If it is clear that the reasonable man would have realised or foreseen and prevented the risk, then it must follow that the *[Wagon Mound]* is liable in damages.

Overseas Tankships [U.K.], Ltd. v. Miller Steamship Co. (Wagon Mound No. 2), [1967] 1 A.C. 617.

9. What rule was decided in *Wagon Mound No. 2*? What has happened to the *Polemis* rule?

10. For an article discussing the *Wagon Mound No. 2*, see Green, The Wagon Mound No. 2—*Foreseeability Revisited*, 1967 Utah L. Rev. 197.

Green v. Denney

Court of Appeals of Oregon, 1987
742 P.2d 639

WARREN, Judge

This is a product liability action arising out of a collision between a 1980 Ford Pinto automobile and a horse. Defendant Ford Motor Company (defendant) appeals the judgment in favor of plaintiff. We affirm.

On the evening of March 29, 1982, plaintiff was driving his 1980 Pinto at about 45–50 miles per hour on Highway 224 near Estacada. His wife, Kelly Sue, was in the front passenger seat. A horse suddenly appeared in front of the car, and plaintiff had no time to swerve or turn. The car's front bumper hit the horse's lower front legs, throwing the horse up over the car's hood, breaking the windshield and collapsing the roof rail (called the "header") above the windshield on the passenger side of the car. The roof collapsed, killing plaintiff's wife instantly.

. . . .

Plaintiff brought this action for the death of his wife against the owner of the horse, Denney, and defendant Ford. Plaintiff settled with Denney before trial. In his action against Ford, plaintiff alleged that the faulty design of the Pinto roof structure caused the fatal injury.

Defendant assigns error to the court's denial of its motion for directed verdict. We consider the evidence in the light most favorable to plaintiff and must affirm unless we can say that there is no evidence from which the jury could have found the facts necessary to establish the elements of plaintiff's claim. In deciding whether the evidence of defective design is sufficient to make a jury question, a trial court must balance the utility of the risk created by the unsafe feature of the product against the magnitude of the risk. In doing so, it should consider certain factors, *inter alia*, the product's usefulness, its safety and the feasibility of alternatives.

The parties' primary disagreement is about the safety factor, i.e., the likelihood that the product will cause injury. Defendant argues that the accident was freak and bizarre in that it involved an unusual concentration of forces and an abnormal load on the header, which resulted in the failure of the roof structure. It argues that the support structure is designed to work as a whole but that the horse hit the header at a point where the other roof components could not contribute to its support. According to defendant, plaintiff produced no evidence that would allow the jury to determine that a reasonable manufacturer, with knowledge of the risk that a load would fall on the roof in the particular manner that it did, would have designed the header differently. In sum, defendant contends that the design was not defective, because the force and impact of the accident were so unusual that it could not have reasonably been anticipated.

Product liability for defective design does not extend to cases where the risk of injury from the product's failure is so remote that a reasonable manufacturer would not consider it in design decisions. Plaintiff offered evidence that collisions with large animals, including horses, are common and foreseeable. Defendant countered that it was not foreseeable that such a collision would produce an impact on the roof concentrated at a particular point rather than being more evenly distributed. The problem with that argument is that its converse is equally true: It was just as unpredictable that the impact from a collision would fall evenly on the entire roof rather than land with greater force on its weakest part. That the horse landed with its full weight on the header did not make the accident any more a freak occurrence than if the weight had been distributed evenly.

There was evidence that the Pinto's roof design was unusual, because it eliminated numerous welds and the support beam across the roof, reduced the thickness of the metal and interrupted its integrity with a "lighting" hole in the center panel. Plaintiff's expert testified that reinforcement of the roof was technically and economically feasible and would have prevented its deformation so that it would not come into contact with a passenger's head. Plaintiff also introduced expert testimony that the amount of energy generated by the fall of the horse on the roof did not exceed the amount that it was required to sustain to pass a federal safety test. Other evidence was presented that defendant had experienced difficulties in testing the Pinto roof design. We conclude that the crash and the manner of injury were not unforeseeable, as a matter of law, and that plaintiff presented sufficient evidence of defective design to justify submission of the case to the jury.

––––––––––

1. Argue that Ford could foresee that a horse might be hit and kill Kelly Sue.

2. Argue that the death of Kelly Sue was the direct result of Ford's negligent design.

3. What "practical political" factors weigh against holding Ford liable? (See Judge Andrews' dissent in *Palsgraf, infra*.)

4. Argue that the death of Kelly Sue is a "freak accident."

Problem

Alex was walking along Main Street when he suddenly felt the call of nature. He saw a Porta-Potty looking device and stepped inside. As soon as he closed the door, the potty exploded. Alex was severely injured, as was his son who was standing outside the "Potty" door.

The device is not a true "Porta-Potty." Instead of a liquid chemical in the base of the potty, it drains into an underground sewer below. The sewer and the potty are owned by Salient Green, a private corporation.

Two weeks ago, Salient Green began to permit Hogs We Are (a large pig farm) to dump hog manure into the sewer.

Assume that Hogs We Are is judgment-proof. Assume also that Alex lit his cigarette as he stepped inside the "Potty".

Discuss.

Palsgraf v. The Long Island Railroad Co.

Court of Appeals of New York, 1928
162 N.E. 99

Appeal from a judgment of the Appellate Division of the Supreme Court in the second judicial department, entered December 16, 1927, affirming a judgment in favor of plaintiff entered upon a verdict.

CARDOZO, CH. J.

Plaintiff was standing on a platform of defendant's railroad after buying a ticket to go to Rockaway Beach. A train stopped at the station, bound for another place. Two men ran forward to catch it. One of the men reached the platform of the car without mishap, though the train was already moving. The other man, carrying a package, jumped aboard the car, but seemed unsteady as if about to fall. A guard on the car, who had held the door open, reached forward to help him in, and another guard on the platform pushed him from behind. In this act, the package was dislodged, and fell upon the rails. It was a package of small size, about fifteen inches long, and was covered by a newspaper. In fact it contained fireworks, but there was nothing in its appearance to give notice of its contents. The fireworks when they fell exploded. The shock of the explosion threw down some scales at the other end of the platform, many feet away. The scales struck the plaintiff, causing injuries for which she sues.

The conduct of the defendant's guard, if a wrong in its relation to the holder of the package, was not a wrong in its relation to the plaintiff, standing far away. Relatively to her it was not negligence at all. Nothing in the situation gave notice that the falling package had in it the potency of peril to persons thus removed. Negligence is not actionable unless it involves the invasion of a legally protected interest, the violation of a right. "Proof of negligence in the air, so to speak, will not do." . . .

If no hazard was apparent to the eye of ordinary vigilance, an act innocent and harmless, at least to outward seeming, with reference to her, did not take to itself the quality of a tort because it happened to be a wrong, though apparently not one involving the risk of bodily insecurity, with reference to someone else. "In every instance, before negligence can be predicated of a given act, back of the act must be sought and found a duty to the individual complaining, the observance of which would have averted or avoided the injury." . . . "The ideas of negligence and duty are strictly correlative." . . . The plaintiff sues in her own right for a wrong personal to her, and not as the vicarious beneficiary of a breach of duty to another.

A different conclusion will involve us, and swiftly too, in a maze of contradictions. A guard stumbles over a package which has been left upon a platform. It seems to be a bundle of newspapers. It turns out to be a can of dynamite. To the eye of ordinary vigilance, the bundle is abandoned waste, which may be kicked or trod on with impunity. Is a passenger at the other end of the platform protected by the law against the unsuspected hazard concealed beneath the waste? If not, is the result to be any different, so far as the distant passenger is concerned, when the guard stumbles over a valise which a truckman or a porter has left upon the walk? The passenger far away, if the victim of a wrong at all, has a cause of action, not derivative, but original and primary. His claim to be protected against invasion of his bodily security is neither greater nor less because the act resulting in the invasion is a wrong to another far removed. In this case, the rights that are said to have been violated, the interests said to have been invaded, are not even of the same order. The man was not injured in his person nor even put in danger. The purpose of the act, as well as its effect, was to make his person safe. If there was a wrong to him at all, which may very well be doubted, it was a wrong to a property interest only, the safety of his package. Out of this wrong to property, which threatened injury to nothing else, there has passed, we are told, to the plaintiff by derivation or succession a right of action for the invasion of an interest of another order, the right to bodily security. The diversity of interests emphasizes the futility of the effort to build the plaintiff's right upon the basis of a wrong to someone else. The gain is one of emphasis, for a like result would follow if the interests were the same. Even then, the orbit of the danger as disclosed to the eye of reasonable vigilance would be the orbit of the duty. One who jostles one's neighbor in a crowd does not invade the rights of others standing at the outer fringe when the unintended contact casts a bomb upon the ground. The wrongdoer as to them is the man who carries the bomb, not the one who explodes it without suspicion of the danger. . . .

The argument for the plaintiff is built upon the shifting meanings of such words as "wrong" and "wrongful," and shares their instability. What the plaintiff must show is "a wrong" to herself, i.e., a violation of her own right, and not merely a wrong to someone else, nor conduct "wrongful" because unsocial, but not "a wrong" to anyone. We are told that one who drives at reckless speed through a crowded city street is guilty of a negligent act and, therefore, of a wrongful one irrespective of the consequences. Negligent the act is, and wrongful in the sense that it is unsocial, but wrongful and unsocial in relation to other travelers, only because the eye of vigilance perceives the risk of damage. If the same act were to be committed on a speedway or a race course, it would lose its wrongful quality. The risk reasonably to be perceived defines the duty to be obeyed, and risk imports relation; it is risk to another or to others within the range of apprehension. . . . The range of reasonable apprehension is at times a question for the court, and at times, if varying inferences are possible, a question for the jury. Here, by concession, there was nothing in the situation to suggest to the most cautious mind that the parcel wrapped in newspaper would spread wreckage through the station. If the guard had thrown it down knowingly and willfully, he would not have threatened the plaintiff's safety, so far as appearances could warn him. His conduct would not have involved, even then, an unreasonable probability of invasion of her bodily security. Liability can be no greater where the act is inadvertent.

Negligence, like risk, is thus a term of relation. Negligence in the abstract, apart from things related, is surely not a tort, if indeed it is understandable at all. . . .

The law of causation, remote or proximate, is thus foreign to the case before us. The question of liability is always anterior to the question of the measure of the consequences that go with liability. If there is no tort to be redressed, there is no occasion to consider what damage might be recovered if there were a finding of a tort. We may assume, without deciding, that negligence, not at large or in the abstract, but in relation to the plaintiff, would entail liability for any and all consequences, however novel or extraordinary. . . . There is room for argument that a distinction is to be drawn according to the diversity of interests invaded by the act, as where conduct negligent in that it threatens an insignificant invasion of an interest in property results in an unforeseeable invasion of an interest of another order, as, e.g., one of bodily security. Perhaps other distinctions may be necessary. We do not go into the question now. The consequences to be followed must first be rooted in a wrong.

The judgment of the Appellate Division and that of the Trial Term should be reversed, and the complaint dismissed, with costs in all courts.

Andrews, J. (dissenting). Assisting a passenger to board a train, the defendant's servant negligently knocked a package from his arms. It fell between the platform and the cars. Of its contents the servant knew and could know nothing. A violent explosion followed. The concussion broke some scales standing a considerable distance away. In falling they injured the plaintiff, an intending passenger.

Upon these facts may she recover the damages she has suffered in an action brought against the master? The result we shall reach depends upon our theory as to the nature of negligence. Is it a relative concept—the breach of some duty owing to a particular person or to particular persons? Or where there is an act which unreasonably threatens the safety of others, is the doer liable for all its proximate consequences, even where they result in injury to one who would generally be thought to be outside the radius of danger? This is not a mere dispute as to words. We might not believe that to the average mind the dropping of the bundle would seem to involve the probability of harm to the plaintiff standing many feet away whatever might be the case as to the owner or to one so near as to be likely to be struck by its fall. If, however, we adopt the second hypothesis we have to inquire only as to the relation between cause and effect. We deal in terms of proximate cause, not of negligence. . . .

But we are told that "there is no negligence unless there is in the particular case a legal duty to take care, and this duty must be one which is owed to the plaintiff himself and not merely to others." . . . This, I think too narrow a conception. Where there is the unreasonable act, and some right that may be affected there is negligence whether damage does or does not result. That is immaterial. Should we drive down Broadway at a reckless speed, we are negligent whether we strike an approaching car or miss it by an inch. The act itself is wrongful. It is a wrong not only to those who happen to be within the radius of danger but to all who might have been there—a wrong to the public at large. Such is the language of the street. Such the language of the courts when speaking of contributory negligence. Such again and again their language in speaking of the duty of some defendant and discussing proximate cause in cases where such a discussion is wholly irrelevant on any other theory. . . .

It may well be that there is no such thing as negligence in the abstract. "Proof of negligence in the air, so to speak, will not do." In an empty world negligence would not exist. It does involve a relationship between man and his fellows. But not merely a relationship between man and those whom he might reasonably expect his act would injure. Rather, a relationship between him and those whom he does in fact injure. If his act has a tendency to harm someone, it harms him a mile away as surely as it does those on the scene. . . .

In the well-known *Polemis* Case (1921, 3 K. B. 560), Scrutton, L. J., said that the dropping of a plank was negligent for it might injure "workman or cargo or ship." Because of either possibility the owner of the vessel was to be made good for his loss. The act being wrongful the doer was liable for its proximate results. Criticized and explained as this statement may have been, I think it states the law as it should be and as it is. . . .

The proposition is this. Every one owes to the world at large the duty of refraining from those acts that may unreasonably threaten the safety of others. Such an act occurs. Not only is he wronged to whom harm might reasonably be expected to result, but he also who is in fact injured, even if he be outside what would generally be thought the danger zone. There needs be duty due the one complaining but this is not a duty to a particular individual because as to him harm might be expected. Harm to someone being the natural result of the act, not only that one alone, but all those in fact injured may complain. We have never, I think, held otherwise. . . .

If this be so, we do not have a plaintiff suing by "derivation or succession." Her action is original and primary. Her claim is for a breach of duty to herself—not that she is subrogated to any right of action of the owner of the parcel or of a passenger standing at the scene of the explosion.

. . . But there is one limitation. The damages must be so connected with the negligence that the latter may be said to be the proximate cause of the former.

These two words have never been given an inclusive definition. What is a cause in a legal sense, still more what is a proximate cause, depend in each case upon many considerations, as does the existence of negligence itself. . . .

As we have said, we cannot trace the effect of an act to the end, if end there is. Again, however, we may trace it part of the way. A murder at Serajevo may be the necessary antecedent to an assassination in London twenty years hence. An overturned lantern may burn all Chicago. We may follow the fire from the shed to the last building. We rightly say the fire started by the lantern caused its destruction.

A cause, but not the proximate cause. What we do mean by the word "proximate" is, that because of convenience, of public policy, of a rough sense of justice, the law arbitrarily declines to trace a series of events beyond a certain point. This is not logic. It is practical politics. Take our rule as to fires. Sparks from my burning haystack set on fire my house and my neighbor's. I may recover from a negligent railroad. He may not. Yet the wrongful act as directly harmed the one as the other. We may regret that the line was drawn just where it was, but drawn somewhere it had to be. We said the act of the railroad was not the proximate cause of our neighbor's fire. Cause it surely was. The words we used were simply indicative of our notions of public policy. Other courts think differently. But somewhere they reach the point where they cannot say the stream comes from any one source.

. . . .

It is all a question of expediency. There are no fixed rules to govern our judgment. . . .

There are some hints that may help us. The proximate cause, involved as it may be with many other causes, must be, at the least, something without which the event would not happen. The court must ask itself whether there was a natural and continuous sequence between cause and effect. Was the one a substantial factor in producing the other? Was there a direct connection between them, without too many intervening causes? Is the effect of cause on result not too attenuated? Is the cause likely, in the usual judgment of mankind, to produce the result? Or by the exercise of prudent foresight could the result be foreseen? Is the result too remote from the cause, and here we consider remoteness in time and space. . . . We draw an uncertain and wavering line, but draw it we must as best we can.

Once again, it is all a question of fair judgment, always keeping in mind the fact that we endeavor to make a rule in each case that will be practical and in keeping with the general understanding of mankind.

. . . .

This last suggestion is the factor which must determine the case before us. The act upon which defendant's liability rests is knocking an apparently harmless package onto the platform. The act was negligent. For its proximate consequences the defendant is liable. If its contents were broken, to the owner; if it fell upon and crushed a passenger's foot, then to him. If it exploded and injured one in the immediate vicinity, to him also as to A in the illustration. Mrs. Palsgraf was standing some distance away. How far cannot be told from the record—apparently twenty-five or thirty feet. Perhaps less. Except for the explosion, she would not have been injured. We are told by the appellant in his brief "it cannot be denied that the explosion was the direct cause of the plaintiff's injuries." So it was a substantial factor in producing the result—there was here a natural and continuous sequence—direct connection. The only intervening cause was that instead of blowing her to the ground the concussion smashed the weighing machine which in turn fell upon her. There was no remoteness in time, little in space. And surely, given such an explosion as here it needed no great foresight to predict that the natural result would be to injure one on the platform at no greater distance from its scene than was the plaintiff. Just how no one might be able to predict. Whether by flying fragments, by broken glass, by wreckage of machines or structures no one could say. But injury in some form was most probable.

Under these circumstances I cannot say as a matter of law that the plaintiff's injuries were not the proximate result of the negligence. That is all we have before us. The court refused to so charge. No request was made to submit the matter to the jury as a question of fact, even would that have been proper upon the record before us.

The judgment appealed from should be affirmed, with costs.

POUND, LEHMAN and KELLOGG, JJ., concur with CARDOZO, CH. J.; ANDREWS, J., dissents in opinion in which CRANE and O'BRIEN, JJ., concur.

Judgment reversed, etc.

---

1. What are Judge Cardozo's and Judge Andrew's theories in regard to duty, negligence, cause-in-fact, proximate cause, and damages?

2. What does Judge Cardozo mean when he says: "Negligence . . . is a term of relation"?

3. *Palsgraf* is probably the best known case in torts. Why?

4. Judge Cardozo may have obtained portions of his theory at a meeting of the American Law Institute. *See* Robert Keeton, *A* Palsgraf *Anecdote*, 56 Tex. L. Rev. 513 (1978).

5. For articles discussing *Palsgraf*, see William Prosser, Palsgraf *Revisited*, 52 Mich. L. Rev. 1 (1953); and Leon Green, *The* Palsgraf *Case*, 30 Colum. L. Rev. 789 (1930).

Petitions of the Kinsman Transit Co.

United States Court of Appeals, Second Circuit, 1964
338 F.2d 708, *cert. denied*, 380 U.S. 944 (1965)

FRIENDLY, CIRCUIT JUDGE:

We have here six appeals, from an interlocutory decree in admiralty adjudicating liability. The litigation, in the District Court for the Western District of New York, arose out of a series of misadventures on a navigable portion of the Buffalo River during the night of January 21, 1959. The owners of two vessels petitioned for exoneration from or limitation of liability. . . . The proceedings were consolidated for trial before Judge Burke. We shall summarize the facts as found by him:

The Buffalo River flows through Buffalo from east to west, with many turns and bends, until it empties into Lake Erie. Its navigable western portion is lined with docks, grain elevators, and industrial installations; during the winter, lake vessels tie up there pending resumption of navigation on the Great Lakes, without power and with only a shipkeeper aboard. About a mile from the mouth, the City of Buffalo maintains a lift bridge at Michigan Avenue. Thaws and rain frequently cause freshets to develop in the upper part of the river and its tributary, Cazenovia Creek; currents then range up to fifteen miles an hour and propel broken ice down the river, which sometimes overflows its banks.

. . . .

The *MacGilvray Shiras*, owned by The Kinsman Transit Company, was moored at the dock of the Concrete Elevator, operated by Continental Grain Company, on the south side of the river about three miles upstream of the Michigan Avenue Bridge.

She was loaded with grain owned by Continental. The berth, east of the main portion of the dock, was exposed in the sense that about 150' of the *Shiras'* forward end, pointing upstream, and 70' of her stern—a total of over half her length—projected beyond the dock. This left between her stem and the bank a space of water seventy-five feet wide where the ice and other debris could float in and accumulate. . . . From about 10 P.M. large chunks of ice and debris began to pile up between the *Shiras'* starboard bow and the bank; the pressure exerted by this mass on her starboard bow was augmented by the force of the current and of floating ice against her port quarter. The mooring lines began to part, and a 'deadman,' to which the No. 1 mooring cable had been attached, pulled out of the ground, the judge finding that it had not been properly constructed or inspected. About 10:40 P.M. the stern lines parted, and the *Shiras* drifted into the current.

Careening stern first down the S-shaped river, the *Shiras*, at about 11 P.M., struck the bow of the *Michael K. Tewksbury*. . . . Her shipkeeper had left around 5 P.M. and spent the evening watching television with a girl friend and her family. The collision caused the *Tewksbury's* mooring lines to part; she too drifted stern first down the river, followed by the *Shiras*. The collision caused damage to the Steamer *Druckenmiller* which was moored opposite the *Tewksbury*.

. . . [T]he Coast Guard, . . . called the city fire station on the river, which in turn warned the crew on the Michigan Avenue Bridge, this last call being made about 10:48 P.M. . . . [T]he bridge was just being raised when, at 11:17 P.M., the *Tewksbury* crashed into its center. . . .

The *Shiras* ended her journey with her stern against the *Tewksbury* and her bow against the north side of the river. So wedged, the two vessels substantially dammed the flow, causing water and ice to back up and flood installations on the banks with consequent damage as far as the Concrete Elevator, nearly three miles upstream. . . .

We see little similarity between the *Palsgraf* case and the situation before us. The point of *Palsgraf* was that the appearance of the newspaper-wrapped package gave no notice that its dislodgement could do any harm save to itself and those nearby, and this by impact, perhaps with consequent breakage, and not by explosion. In contrast, a ship insecurely moored in a fast flowing river is a known danger not only to herself but to the owners of all other ships and structures down-river, and to persons upon them. No one would dream of saying that a shipowner who "knowingly and willfully" failed to secure his ship at a pier on such a river "would not have threatened" persons and owners of property downstream in some manner. The shipowner and the wharfinger in this case having thus owed a duty of care to all within the reach of the ship's known destructive power, the impossibility of advance identification of the particular person who would be hurt is without legal consequence. . . . Similarly the foreseeable consequences of the City's failure to raise the bridge were not limited to the *Shiras* and the *Tewksbury*. Collision plainly created a danger that the bridge towers might fall onto adjoining property, and the crash of two uncontrolled lake vessels, one 425 feet and the other 525 feet long, into a bridge over a swift ice-ridden stream, with a channel only 177 feet wide, could well result in a partial damming that would flood property upstream. As to the City also, it is useful to consider, by way of contrast, Chief Judge Cardozo's statement that the Long Island would not have been liable to Mrs. Palsgraf had the guard wilfully thrown the package down. If the City had deliberately kept the bridge closed in the face of the onrushing vessels, taking the risk that they might not come so far, no one would give house-room to a claim that it "owed no duty" to those who later suffered from the flooding. Unlike Mrs. Palsgraf, they were within the area of hazard.

. . . .

Since all the claimants here met the *Palsgraf* requirement of being persons to whom the actors owed a "duty of care," we are not obliged to reconsider whether that case furnishes as useful a standard for determining the boundaries of liability in admiralty for negligent conduct. . . . But this does not dispose of the alternative argument that the manner in which several of the claimants were harmed, particularly by flood damage, was unforeseeable and that recovery for this may not be had. . . .

Although the obvious risks from not raising the bridge were damage to itself and to the vessels, the danger of a fall of the bridge and of flooding would not have been unforeseeable under the circumstances to anyone who gave them thought. And the same can be said as to the failure of Kinsman's shipkeeper to ready the anchors after the danger had become apparent. The exhibits indicate that the width of the channel between the Concrete Elevator and the bridge is at most points less than two hundred fifty feet. If the *Shiras* caught up on a dock or vessel moored along the shore, the current might well swing her bow across the channel so as to block the ice floes, as indeed could easily have occurred at the Standard Elevator dock where the stern of the *Shiras* struck the *Tewksbury's* bow. . . . Nor was it unforeseeable that the drawbridge would not be raised since, apart from any other reason, there was no assurance of timely warning. What may have been less foreseeable was that the *Shiras* would get that far down the twisting river, but this is somewhat negated both by the known speed of the current when freshets developed and by the evidence that, on learning of the *Shiras*' departure, Continental's employees and those they informed foresaw precisely that.

. . . Foreseeability of danger is necessary to render conduct negligent; whereas here the damage was caused by just those forces whose existence required the exercise of greater care than was taken — the current, the ice, and the physical mass of the *Shiras*, the incurring of consequences other and greater than foreseen does not make the conduct less culpable or provide a reasoned basis for insulation. . . . The oft encountered argument that failure to limit liability to foreseeable consequences may subject the defendant to a loss wholly out of proportion to his fault seems scarcely consistent with the universally accepted rule that the defendant takes the plaintiff as he finds him and will be responsible for the full extent of the injury. . . .

The weight of authority in this country rejects the limitation of damages to consequences foreseeable at the time of the negligent conduct when the consequences are "direct," and the damage, although other and greater than expectable, is of the same general sort that was risked. . . .

We see no reason why an actor engaging in conduct which entails a large risk of small damage and a small risk of other and greater damage, of the same general sort, from the same forces, and to the same class of persons, should be relieved of responsibility for the latter simply because the chance of its occurrence, if viewed alone, may not have been large enough to require the exercise of care. By hypothesis, the risk of the lesser harm was sufficient to render his disregard of it actionable; the existence of a less likely additional risk that the very forces against whose action he was required to guard would produce other and greater damage than could have been reasonably anticipated should inculpate him further rather than limit his liability. This does not mean that the careless actor will always be held for all damages for which the forces that he risked were a cause in fact. Somewhere a point will be reached when courts will agree that the link has become too tenuous — that what is claimed to be consequence is only fortuity. . . . [W]hat courts do in such cases makes better sense than what they, or others, say. Where the line will be drawn will vary from age to age; as society has come to rely increasingly on insurance and other methods of loss-sharing, the point may lie further off than a century ago. Here it is surely more equitable that the losses from the operators' negligent failure to raise the Michigan Avenue Bridge should be ratably borne by Buffalo's taxpayers than left with the innocent victims of the flooding; yet the mind is also repelled by a solution that would impose liability solely on the City and exonerate the persons whose negligent acts of commission and omission were the precipitating force of the collision with the bridge and its sequelae. We go only so far as to hold that where, as here, the damages resulted from the same physical forces whose existence required the exercise of greater care than was displayed and were of the same general sort that was expectable, unforeseeability of the exact developments and of the extent of the loss will not limit liability.

. . . .

---

1. How is the proximate cause issue facing the court in *Kinsman* different from *Palsgraf*? To what extent does the decision in *Kinsman* extend *Palsgraf*?

2. Compare the decision in *Kinsman* with *Polemis, Wagon Mound No. 1,* and *Wagon Mound No. 2*.

3. What factors does the court weigh in *Kinsman*?

Problem

Several years ago, Hemi Car Co. went into bankruptcy. This usually takes several years. Hemi emerged from bankruptcy in a few weeks after discontinuing many "small" dealers. This lightning-fast turnaround was assisted by the United States Government. Assume the small dealers lost millions of dollars each and were not compensated by Hemi.

Several small dealers, who were dropped, have asked you for assistance. Consider:

A. Under the Federal Torts Claims Act, should this be negligence on the part of government, or viewed as a "discretionary function" of high ranking government officials and therefore protected from suit?

B. In a tort suit (assume that you cannot sue Hemi), would proximate cause protect the government officials who designed and implemented the bankruptcy program for Hemi to discontinue the small dealers?

Hamblin v. State/Maricopa County Adult Probation Department

Court of Appeals of Arizona, 2006
143 P.3d 388

THOMPSON, J.

Appellants, the survivors of Russell Hamblin (the Hamblins), brought suit for his wrongful death against the State of Arizona and the Maricopa County Adult Probation Department (collectively MCAPD). The Hamblins appeal the summary judgment entered against them. Because we find that MCAPD was not the proximate cause of Russell Hamblin's death, we affirm.

FACTS AND RELEVANT PROCEEDINGS

Russell Hamblin was shot and killed by Roy Salinas (Salinas) during an armed robbery committed by Salinas and two others. At the time of the murder, fifteen-year-old Salinas was on adult probation with MCAPD for having assaulted a corrections officer while detained by the Arizona Department of Juvenile Corrections. Salinas pled guilty to attempted aggravated assault on a corrections officer, a class 6 offense, and was awaiting the start of his deferred jail term when he shot Russell Hamblin during a robbery.

The Hamblins alleged that MCAPD had a duty to supervise Salinas to ensure that he followed the terms of his probation, that MCAPD was grossly negligent when they failed to arrest Salinas or to seek a warrant for his arrest when Salinas violated his probationary terms, and that MCAPD's willful ignorance of Salinas's conduct allowed Salinas to murder Russell Hamblin.

We noted that there was an outstanding issue of causation urged below by MCAPD that the trial court had not ruled on. MCAPD argued that causation was lacking and that the Hamblins' claim required speculation that different supervision would have resulted in revocation of Salinas's probation, causing him to be incarcerated on the date that Russell Hamblin was killed. Our reversal of the dismissal order left the Hamblins with the task of developing evidence to support all of the allegations of their complaint and to establish the elements of their claim, including the element of causation.

Proximate Cause

. . . .

Causation is a two-part inquiry. Both elements, cause in fact and proximate cause, must be present for legal liability to attach. . . .

The second part of the causation inquiry is proximate cause. Our supreme court defines proximate cause as "that which, in a natural and continuous sequence, unbroken by any efficient intervening cause, produces an injury, and without which the injury would not have occurred." . . . That definition highlights the importance of the cause in fact element to proximate cause. Without cause in fact, proximate cause will never be shown. Whether a defendant's conduct that in-fact caused harm is too attenuated from the consequential harm is a question of proximate cause for the court.

In general, proximate cause embodies "ideas of what justice demands, or of what is administratively possible and convenient." Any examination of causation should recognize that "public policy undergirds concepts such as 'proximate cause'." "[P]roximate causation is a matter of public policy and therefore subject to the changing attitudes and needs of society." *See* Keeton, et al., *supra* P 11, Section 39, at p. 244.

. . . .

That there are policy limits inherent in proximate cause is neither a new nor a particularly revolutionary notion. The *Blue Shield* Court cited the seminal 1928 tort case *Palsgraf v. Long Island Railroad Company* for the proposition that:

> What we mean by the word 'proximate' is, that because of convenience, of public policy, of a rough sense of justice, the law arbitrarily declines to trace a series of events beyond a certain point.

. . . .

"Proximate cause" is not a logical proposition but a legal conclusion about when a party is to be held responsible for a loss; . . . proximate cause is a question of legal policy related directed at determining how far the protection of the law should extend; Leon Green, The Causal Relation Issue in Negligence Law, 60 Mich. L. Rev. 543, 548–49 (1960).

. . . .

As a policy matter, it is untenable to hold probation officers liable for all crimes committed by a person on probation. This is true even if the officer knows that the defendant has committed technical violations of his probation. To hold otherwise would give hindsight too much play and derogate the social utility of a probation officer's judgment and discretion. Our legislature outlined the powers and duties of probation officers in A.R.S. Section 12-253 (2005). Section 12-253(7) states that a probation officer has the power and duty to

> [b]ring defaulting probationers into court when in his judgment the conduct of the probationer justifies the court to revoke suspension of the sentence.

The plain language of A.R.S. Section 12-253(7) recognizes that not all probation violations warrant a change in status. The probation officer has a duty to bring probationers into court when "in his judgment" the violation would be likely to cause the court to alter the probationer's status.

. . . .

---

1. In general, courts tend to not hold governments liable for negligent acts such as this one. This seems appropriate in a practical sense. But in terms of checks on government, should there be the possibility of bringing such a tort against the government?

2. The trial court initially dismissed the Hamblins' claims against MCAPD for failure to state a claim on grounds of governmental immunity. On appeal from that decision this court reversed, holding that the alleged failure to supervise was not covered by immunity from civil liability, citing *Acevedo v. Pima County Adult Probation Department*, 142 Ariz. 319, 322, 690 P.2d 38, 41 (1984). Note that the Court's finding of "no proximate cause" accomplishes the same thing as immunity under the Federal Torts Claims Act.

B. Intervening Causes
Problem

Al was cleaning a coin-operated vending machine with a solvent in an eight-foot by ten-foot room when a rat ran out of the machine and sought refuge under a gas heater with an open flame, located in the room. The now-flaming rodent returned to the machine, which exploded into flames, and as a result Al was severely burned. Al is nineteen-years-old and sues the manufacturer of the vending machine whose instructions said that it could be cleaned with a solvent. What defense?

Weirum v. RKO General, Inc.
Supreme Court of California, 1975
539 P.2d 36

Mosk, Justice.

A rock radio station with an extensive teenage audience conducted a contest which rewarded the first contestant to locate a peripatetic disc jockey. Two minors driving in separate automobiles attempted to follow the disc jockey's automobile to its next stop. In the course of their pursuit, one of the minors negligently forced a car off the highway, killing its sole occupant. In a suit filed by the surviving wife and children of the decedent, the jury rendered a verdict against the radio station.

. . . .

On that day, Donald Steele Revert, known professionally as "The Real Don Steele," a KHJ disc jockey and television personality, traveled in a conspicuous red automobile to a number of locations in the Los Angeles metropolitan area. Periodically, he apprised KHJ of his whereabouts and his intended destination, and the station broadcast the information to its listeners. The first person to physically locate Steele and fulfill a specified condition received a cash prize. . . . The following excerpts from the July 16 broadcast illustrate the tenor of the contest announcements:

"9:30 and The Real Don Steele is back on his feet again with some money and he is headed for the Valley. Thought I would give you a warning so that you can get your kids out of the street."

. . . .

The primary question for our determination is whether defendant owed a duty to decedent arising out of its broadcast of the giveaway contest. The determination of duty is primarily a question of law. . . . It is the court's "expression of the sum total of those considerations of policy which lead the law to say that the particular plaintiff is entitled to protection." . . . Any number of considerations may justify the imposition of duty in particular circumstances, including the guidance of history, our continually refined concepts of morals and justice, the convenience of the rule, and social judgment as to where the loss should fall. . . . While the question whether one owes a duty to another must be decided on a case-by-case basis, every case is governed by the rule of general application that all persons are required to use ordinary care to prevent others from being injured as the result of their conduct. . . . [F]oreseeability of the risk is a primary consideration in establishing the element of duty. . . . Defendant asserts that the record here does not support a conclusion that a risk of harm to decedent was foreseeable.

While duty is a question of law, foreseeability is a question of fact for the jury. . . . The verdict in plaintiffs' favor here necessarily embraced a finding that decedent was exposed to a foreseeable risk of harm. . . .

We conclude that the record amply supports the finding of foreseeability. These tragic events unfolded in the middle of a Los Angeles summer, a time when young people were free from the constraints of school and responsive to relief from vacation tedium. Seeking to attract new listeners, KHJ devised an "exciting" promotion. Money and a small measure of momentary notoriety awaited the swiftest response. It was foreseeable that defendant's youthful listeners, finding the prize had eluded them at one location, would race to arrive first at the next site and in their haste would disregard the demands of highway safety.

. . . "The mere fact that a particular kind of an accident has not happened before does not . . . show that such accident is one which might not reasonably have been anticipated." . . . Thus, the fortuitous absence of prior injury does not justify relieving defendant from responsibility for the foreseeable consequences of its acts.

It is of no consequence that the harm to decedent was inflicted by third parties acting negligently. Defendant invokes the maxim that an actor is entitled to assume that others will not act negligently. . . . This concept is valid, however, only to the extent the intervening conduct was not to be anticipated. . . . If the likelihood that a third person may react in a particular manner is a hazard which makes the actor negligent, such reaction whether innocent or negligent does not prevent the actor from being liable for the harm caused thereby. . . . Here, reckless conduct by youthful contestants, stimulated by defendant's broadcast, constituted the hazard to which decedent was exposed.

   . . . .

Defendant's contention that the giveaway contest must be afforded the deference due society's interest in the First Amendment is clearly without merit. The issue here is civil accountability for the foreseeable results of a broadcast which created an undue risk of harm to decedent. The First Amendment does not sanction the infliction of physical injury merely because achieved by word, rather than act.

Defendant, relying upon the rule stated in section 315 of the Restatement Second of Torts, urges that it owed no duty of care to decedent. The section provides that, absent a special relationship, an actor is under no duty to control the conduct of third parties. As explained hereinafter, this rule has no application if the plaintiff's complaint, as here, is grounded upon an affirmative act of defendant which created an undue risk of harm.

The rule stated in section 315 is merely a refinement of the general principle embodied in section 314 that one is not obligated to act as a "good Samaritan." . . . This doctrine is rooted in the common law distinction between action and inaction, or misfeasance and nonfeasance. Misfeasance exists when the defendant is responsible for making the plaintiff's position worse, i.e., defendant has created a risk. Conversely, nonfeasance is found when the defendant has failed to aid plaintiff through beneficial intervention. As section 315 illustrates, liability for nonfeasance is largely limited to those circumstances in which some special relationship can be established. If, on the other hand, the act complained of is one of misfeasance, the question of duty is governed by the standards of ordinary care discussed above.

Here, there can be little doubt that we review an act of misfeasance to which section 315 is inapplicable. Liability is not predicated upon defendant's failure to intervene for the benefit of decedent but rather upon its creation of an unreasonable risk of harm to him. . . .

The judgment and the orders appealed from are affirmed. Plaintiffs shall recover their costs on appeal. The parties shall bear their own costs on the cross-appeal.

————————

1. In *Weirum*, who was the intervening cause? What arguments could you make for cutting off the radio station's liability?

2. How would you flesh out the court's First Amendment discussion?

3. How would you answer the following argument in *Weirum*: "Defendant is fearful that entrepreneurs will henceforth be burdened with an avalanche of obligations: an athletic department will owe a duty to an ardent sports fan injured while hastening to purchase one of a limited number of tickets . . ." (539 P.2d 36)? In *Riley v. Triplex Commun., Inc.*, 874 S.W.2d 333 (Tex. App. 1994), the radio station was found liable for negligently promoting a weekly Ladies' Night with ninety-four cent drinks at a local bar after a drunk customer injured two police officers.

4. In *Derdiarian v. Felix Contracting Corp.*, 51 N.Y.2d 308, 434 N.Y.S.2d 166, 414 N.E.2d 666 (1980), defendant Felix Contracting Corp. was excavating a worksite in a street when defendant Dickens suffered an epileptic seizure, allowing his vehicle to crash into the worksite and hit plaintiff, throwing him into the air. When plaintiff landed, he was splattered with boiling enamel from a kettle that had been struck by the automobile. Plaintiff Derdiarian was an employee of a subcontractor at the worksite. Defendant Felix argued that there was no causal link between Felix' breach of duty and plaintiff's injuries. Dickens' seizure and crash was held not to be a superseding cause of Felix' liability:

> Where the acts of a third person intervene between the defendant's conduct and the plaintiff's injury, the causal connection is not automatically severed. In such a case, liability turns upon whether the intervening act is a normal or foreseeable consequence of the situation created by the defendant's negligence. If the intervening act is extraordinary under the circumstances, not foreseeable in the normal course of events, or independent of or far removed from the defendant's conduct, it may well be a superseding act which breaks the causal nexus. Because questions concerning what is foreseeable and what is normal may be the subject of varying inferences, as is the question of negligence itself, these issues generally are for the fact finder to resolve.

> [I]n the present case, we cannot say as a matter of law that defendant Dickens' negligence was a superseding cause which interrupted the link between Felix's negligence and plaintiff's injuries. From the evidence in the record, the jury could have found that Felix negligently failed to safeguard the excavation site. A prime hazard associated with such dereliction is the possibility that a driver will negligently enter the work site and cause injury to a worker. That the driver was negligent, or even reckless, does not insulate Felix from liability. Nor is it decisive that the driver lost control of the vehicle through a negligent failure to take medication, rather than a driving mistake. The precise manner of the event need not be anticipated. The finder of fact could have concluded that the foreseeable, normal and natural result of the risk created by Felix was the injury of a worker by a car entering the improperly protected work area. An intervening act may not serve as a superseding cause, and relieve an actor of responsibility, where the risk of the intervening act occurring is the very same risk which renders the actor negligent.

> In a similar vein, plaintiff's act of placing the kettle on the west side of the excavation does not, as a matter of law, absolve defendant Felix of responsibility. Serious injury, or even death, was a foreseeable consequence of a vehicle crashing through the work area. The injury could have occurred in numerous ways, ranging from a worker being directly struck by the car to the car hitting an object that injures the worker. Placement of the kettle, or any object in the work area, could affect how the accident occurs and the extent of injuries. That defendant could not anticipate the precise manner of the accident or the exact extent of injuries, however, does not preclude

liability as a matter of law where the general risk and character of injuries are foreseeable.

Problem

Casey rents an apartment in an urban area from GHI, which has advertised night security. However, one night, an employee caretaker of the apartment complex walks into Casey's apartment with a key and murders one of Casey's guests, Jim. Casey and Jim's heirs sue the management of GHI and the security agency, claiming the negligent hiring of the employee and negligent security were the proximate cause of Jim's murder. What result?

Watson v. Kentucky & Indiana Bridge & Railroad Co.

Court of Appeals Kentucky, 1910
126 S.W. 146

[A gasoline tank car owned by defendant railroad was derailed because of a faulty roadbed thereby causing gasoline to flow into the streets of Louisville. The gasoline was ignited and damage done when Duerr lit a match. He said he was lighting a cigar. Others testified:

> Duerr, who had been a telegraph operator in the employ of the appellee Bridge & Railroad Company, was on the morning of the day of the explosion discharged from its service, and that 20 minutes before the explosion Duerr remarked to his companion, in the hearing of Giacometti and Darnall, "Let us go and set the damn thing on fire."

Plaintiff appeals a directed verdict in favor of the defendant.]

SETTLE, J. . . .

The lighting of the match of Duerr having resulted in the explosion, the question is, was that act merely a contributing cause, or the efficient and, therefore, proximate cause of appellant's injuries? The question of proximate cause is a question for the jury. In holding that Duerr in lighting or throwing the match acted maliciously or with intent to cause the explosion, the trial court invaded the province of the jury. There was, it is true, evidence tending to prove that it was inadvertently or negligently done by Duerr. It was therefore for the jury and not the court to determine from all the evidence whether the lighting of the match was done by Duerr inadvertently or negligently, or whether it was a wanton and malicious act.

. . . .

If the presence on Madison street in the city of Louisville of the great volume of loose gas that arose from the escaping gasoline was caused by the negligence of the appellee Bridge & Railroad Company, it seems to us that the probable consequences of its coming in contact with fire and causing an explosion was too plain a proposition to admit of doubt. Indeed, it was most probable that someone would strike a match to light a cigar or for other purposes in the midst of the gas. In our opinion, therefore, the act of one lighting and throwing a match under such circumstances cannot be said to be the efficient cause of the explosion. It did not of itself produce the explosion, nor could it have done so without the assistance and contribution resulting from the primary negligence, if there was such negligence, on the part of the appellee Bridge & Railroad company in furnishing the presence of the gas in the street. This conclusion, however, rests upon the theory that Duerr inadvertently or negligently lighted and threw the match in the gas.

If, however, the act of Duerr in lighting the match and throwing it into the vapor or gas arising from the gasoline was malicious, and done for the purpose of causing the explosion, we do not think appellees would be responsible, for while the appellee Bridge & Railroad Company's negligence may have been the efficient cause of the presence of the gas in the street, and it should have understood enough of the consequences thereof to have foreseen that an explosion was likely to result from the inadvertent or negligent lighting of a match by some person who was ignorant of the presence of the gas or of the effect of lighting or throwing a match in it, it could not have foreseen or deemed it probable that one would maliciously or wantonly do such an act for the evil purpose of producing the explosion. Therefore, if the act of Duerr was malicious, we quite agree with the trial court that it was one which the appellees could not reasonably have anticipated or guarded against, and in such case the act of Duerr, and not the primary negligence of the appellee Bridge & Railroad Company, in any of the particulars charged, was the efficient or proximate cause of appellant's injuries. The mere fact that the concurrent cause or intervening act was unforeseen will not relieve the defendant guilty of the primary negligence from liability, but if the intervening agency is something so unexpected or extraordinary as that he could not or ought not to have anticipated it, he will not be liable, and certainly he is not bound to anticipate the criminal acts of others by which damage is inflicted and hence is not liable therefor.

. . . .

[T]he judgment is . . . reversed as to the Bridge & Railroad Company, and cause remanded for a new trial consistent with the opinion.

---

1. In *Brower v. New York Central & H. R.R.*, 91 N.J.L. 190, 103 A. 166 (1918), the train, because of negligence, crashed into plaintiff's wagon. As a result, the barrels that were in the wagon were stolen. The court found that "the act of the thieves did not intervene between defendant's negligence and the plaintiff's loss."

2. Is the line between negligence and maliciousness drawn by the court in *Watson* clear?

3. Argue that the railroad should not escape liability even if Duerr's act was malicious.

4. Criminal behavior does not always break the chain of causation. *See* Restatement (Second) of Torts §§ 448–49. Examples:

a. Two minor students steal chemical explosives from defendant school's unlocked storage room. The plaintiff child is injured when the chemicals explode. Is the school liable? *Kush by Marszalek v. City of Buffalo*, 59 N.Y.2d 26, 462 N.Y.S.2d 831, 449 N.E.2d 725 (1983).

b. Defendant train misses plaintiff's stop and drops her one mile away from her stop in a dangerous area. The plaintiff, on her way home, is raped by two individuals. Is the railroad company liable? *Hines v. Garrett*, 108 S.E. 690 (Va. 1921).

c. The defendant pharmacist sold poison to the wife's husband, who then used it to kill her. The wife's survivors sue for wrongful death. Is the pharmacist liable? *January v. Peace*, 738 S.W.2d 355 (Tex. App. 1987).

d. The plaintiff freelance photographer is attacked and beaten while photographing a hotel in Mexico. The defendant newspaper had not informed the plaintiff that the newspaper had previously printed an article alleging that the owner of the hotel was a drug kingpin. Is the newspaper liable for plaintiff's injuries? *Gutierrez v. Scripps-Howard*, 823 S.W.2d 696 (Tex. App. 1992).

e. The defendant tenant violates a fire code by stacking trash next to a building. A fire destroys the building. Arson may have been the cause of fire, yet the plaintiff landlord sues the tenant for the loss of the building. Is the tenant liable? *Britton v. Wooten*, 817 S.W.2d 443 (Ky. 1991) (abrogating result in *Watson*).

Braun v. Soldier of Fortune Magazine, Inc.

United States Court of Appeals, Eleventh Circuit, 1992
968 F.2d 1110, *cert. denied*, 506 U.S. 1071 (1993)

[The sons of a murder victim brought this wrongful death action against *Soldier of Fortune* (S.O.F.) magazine and its parent company, alleging that the defendants negligently published an advertisement that created an unreasonable risk of solicitation of violent criminal activity. The jury awarded compensatory damages of $4.3 million.]

ANDERSON, CIRCUIT JUDGE:

. . . .

In January 1985, Michael Savage submitted a personal service advertisement to SOF. After several conversations between Savage and SOF's advertising manager, Joan Steel, the following advertisement ran in the June 1985 through March 1986 issues of SOF:

> GUN FOR HIRE: 37 year old professional mercenary desires jobs. Vietnam Veteran. Discrete [sic] and very private. Body guard, courier, and other special skills. All jobs considered. Phone (615) 436-9785 (days) or (615) 436-4335 (nights), or write: Rt. 2, Box 682 Village Loop Road, Gatlinburg, TN 37738.

Savage testified that, when he placed the ad, he had no intention of obtaining anything but legitimate jobs. Nonetheless, Savage stated that the overwhelming majority of the 30 to 40 phone calls a week he received in response to his ad sought his participation in criminal activity such as murder, assault, and kidnapping. The ad also generated at least one legitimate job as a bodyguard, which Savage accepted.

In late 1984 or early 1985, Bruce Gastwirth began seeking to murder his business partner, Richard Braun. Gastwirth enlisted the aid of another business associate, John Horton Moore, and together they arranged for at least three attempts on Braun's life, all of which were unsuccessful. Responding to Savage's SOF ad, Gastwirth and Moore contacted him in August 1985 to discuss plans to murder Braun.

On August 26, 1985, Savage, Moore, and another individual, Sean Trevor Doutre, went to Braun's suburban Atlanta home. As Braun and his sixteen year-old son Michael were driving down the driveway, Doutre stepped in front of Braun's car and fired several shots into the car with a MAC 11 automatic pistol. The shots hit Michael in the thigh and wounded Braun as well. Braun managed to roll out of the car, but Doutre walked over to Braun and killed him by firing two more shots into the back of his head as Braun lay on the ground.

. . . .

The district court, sitting in Alabama, properly looked to Georgia law in resolving appellees' negligence claims. . . .

. . . .

The district court found that publishers like SOF have a duty to the public when they publish an advertisement if "the ad in question contains a clearly identifiable unreasonable risk, that the offer in the ad is one to commit a serious violent crime, including murder." SOF argues that the district court erred in finding that a publisher has a duty "to reject ambiguous advertisements that pose a threat of harm," Brief for Appellants at 24, and contends that a publisher should be held liable for publishing an ad only if the ad explicitly solicits a crime. . . .

Georgia courts recognize a "general duty one owes to all the world not to subject them to an unreasonable risk of harm." . . . Accordingly, the district court properly found that SOF had a legal duty to refrain from publishing advertisements that subjected the public, including appellees, to a clearly identifiable unreasonable risk of harm from violent criminal activity. To the extent that SOF denies that a publisher owes any duty to the public when it publishes personal service ads, its position is clearly inconsistent with Georgia law. We believe, however, that the crux of SOF's argument is not that it had no duty to the public, but that, as a matter of law, the risk to the public presented when a publisher prints an advertisement is "unreasonable" only if the ad openly solicits criminal activity. . . .

. . . .

[W]e find that the district court properly . . . instructed that the jury could hold SOF liable for printing Savage's advertisement only if the advertisement on its face would have alerted a reasonably prudent publisher to the clearly identifiable unreasonable risk of harm to the public that the advertisement posed. . . . [T]he duty of care the district court imposed on publishers was an appropriate reconciliation of Georgia's interest in providing compensation to victims of tortious conduct with the First Amendment concern that state law not chill protected speech. Accordingly, we reject SOF's argument that the district court's instructions "placed an intolerable burden upon the press." . . . SOF's sole remaining claim is that the jury erred in finding that SOF's publication of Savage's ad was the proximate cause of appellees' injuries. SOF argues that the events that intervened between its publication of Savage's ad and the carrying out of the murder plot were entirely unforeseeable and, therefore, that SOF's publication of Savage's ad was too remote in the chain of events leading to appellees' injuries for the jury to hold SOF liable. Since the proximate cause issue does not implicate any constitutional values, we review the jury's factual finding under the traditional standard of deference to the fact finder. . . .

We find that the jury had ample grounds for finding that SOF's publication of Savage's ad was the proximate cause of appellees' injuries. Georgia law recognizes that, "generally, the intervening criminal act of a third party, without which the injury would not have occurred, will be treated as the proximate cause of the injury, superseding any negligence of the defendant . . ." . . . If, however, "the criminal act was a reasonably foreseeable consequence of the defendant's conduct, the casual connection between that conduct and the injury is not broken." . . . We have already held that the language of Savage's ad should have alerted a reasonably prudent publisher to the clearly identifiable unreasonable risk that Savage was soliciting violent and illegal jobs. It follows that a reasonable jury could conclude that the criminal act that harmed appellees was reasonably foreseeable and, accordingly, that the chain of causation was not broken.

For the foregoing reasons, we AFFIRM the district court's judgment.

Affirmed.

---

1. As compared with *Watson*, what makes *Braun* more challenging in dealing with proximate cause?

2. Liability of S.O.F. was denied in *Eimann v. Soldier of Fortune Magazine*, 880 F.2d 830 (5th Cir. 1989), *cert. denied*, 493 U.S. 1024 (1990), based on the following advertisement:

> EX-MARINES—67–69 'Nam Vets, Ex-DI, weapons specialist-jungle warfare, pilot, M.E., high risk assignments, U.S. or overseas. (404) 991-2684.

Compare this to the ad in *Braun*. What are the differences?

3. In *Way v. Boy Scouts of Am., Nat'l Shooting Sports Found., Inc.*, 856 S.W.2d 230 (Tex. App. 1993), for example, a mother sued a youth magazine publisher for advertising shooting sports, claiming the advertisement caused the death of her son. The mother claimed that her son, after having read the advertisement, was motivated to experiment with a rifle that discharged and killed him. The court found there was

no breach of duty and that Texas does not recognize a cause of action for negligent publication.

4. In *Braun*, the court rejected S.O.F.'s First Amendment arguments and concluded:

> Supreme Court cases discussing the limitations the First Amendment places on state defamation law indicate that there is no constitutional infirmity in Georgia Law holding publishers liable under a negligence standard with respect to the commercial advertisements they print.
>
> . . . .
>
> Based upon the foregoing authorities, we conclude that the First Amendment permits a state to impose upon a publisher liability for compensatory damages for negligently publishing a commercial advertisement where the ad on its face, and without the need for investigation, makes it apparent that there is a substantial danger of harm to the public. The absence of a duty requiring publishers to investigate the advertisements they print and the requirement that the substance of the ad itself must warn the publisher of a substantial danger of harm to the public guarantee that the burden placed on publishers will not impermissibly chill protected commercial speech. [968 F.2d 1110, 1119.]

5. In "Hit Man" the author wrote a manual for those who wished to kill someone. A reader committed a triple murder. In the civil suit, the publisher defended on the basis of free speech, but the U.S. Court of Appeals rejected that argument: "The mail-order book had no legitimate purpose beyond the promotion and teaching of murder." The court said, "In at least these circumstances, we are confident that the First Amendment does not erect an absolute bar to the imposition of civil liability . . ." Atlanta Journal Constitution A-10, Nov. 11, 1997.

6. If the owner of a car leaves the keys in the ignition, is he or she the proximate cause of the damage to the plaintiff where a thief steals the defendant's car and negligently runs into the plaintiff's car?

The answer may be yes where there is a statute on point. In *Ney v. Yellow Cab Co.*, 2 Ill. 2d 74, 117 N.E.2d 74 (1954), the statute provided: "No person driving . . . a motor vehicle shall permit it to stand unattended without first . . . removing the car key."

The answer may also be yes where the theft is especially foreseeable because of the neighborhood or the goods in the back of the truck, *Hergenrether v. East*, 61 Cal. 2d 440, 39 Cal. Rptr. 4, 393 P.2d 164 (1964).

The car thief is likely to be a superseding cause of the injury as indicated in cases without a statute and without strong facts suggesting foreseeability. *See Ross v. Nutt*, 177 Ohio St. 113, 203 N.E.2d 118 (1964).

Problem

Ann is the fourteen-year-old daughter of Jack. Jack went out of town for the weekend and left Ann with neighbors. Ann went home, allegedly to feed her cat. While there, she had a party for ten friends, which soon exploded to 100 teenagers. Everyone brought alcohol and consumed it. While driving home from the party, Bob (age seventeen) crashed into the plaintiff's car and seriously injured him. Bob was drunk. You represent the plaintiff. Discuss.

What if Jack had left a large amount of alcohol in the house and Ann had appropriated it for the party?

Kelly v. Gwinnell

Supreme Court of New Jersey, 1984
476 A.2d 1219

WILENTZ, C.J.

This case raises the issue of whether a social host who enables an adult guest at his home to become drunk is liable to the victim of an automobile accident caused by the drunken driving of the guest. Here the host served liquor to the guest beyond the point at which the guest was visibly intoxicated. We hold the host may be liable under the circumstances of this case. At the trial level, the case was disposed of, insofar as the issue before us is concerned, by summary judgment in favor of the social host. The record on which the summary judgment was based (pleadings, depositions, and certifications) discloses that defendant Donald Gwinnell, after driving defendant Joseph Zak home, spent an hour or two at Zak's home before leaving to return to his own home. During that time, according to Gwinnell, Zak, and Zak's wife, Gwinnell consumed two or three drinks of scotch on the rocks. Zak accompanied Gwinnell outside to his car, chatted with him, and watched as Gwinnell then drove off to go home. About twenty-five minutes later Zak telephoned Gwinnell's home to make sure Gwinnell had arrived there safely. The phone was answered by Mrs. Gwinnell, who advised Zak that Gwinnell had been involved in a head-on collision. The collision was with an automobile operated by plaintiff, Marie Kelly, who was seriously injured as a result.

After the accident Gwinnell was subjected to a blood test, which indicated a blood alcohol concentration of 0.286 percent. Kelly's expert concluded from that reading that Gwinnell had consumed not two or three scotches but the equivalent of thirteen drinks; that while at Zak's home Gwinnell must have been showing unmistakable signs of intoxication; and that in fact he was severely intoxicated while at Zak's residence and at the time of the accident.

Kelly sued Gwinnell and his employer; those defendants sued the Zaks in a third party action; and thereafter plaintiff amended her complaint to include Mr. and Mrs. Zak as direct defendants. The Zaks moved for summary judgment, contending that as a matter of law a host is not liable for the negligence of an adult social guest who has become intoxicated while at the host's home. The trial court granted the motion on that basis. . . .

Under the facts here defendant provided his guest with liquor, knowing that thereafter the guest would have to drive in order to get home. Viewing the facts most favorably to plaintiff (as we must, since the complaint was dismissed on a motion for summary judgment), one could reasonably conclude that the Zaks must have known that their provision of liquor was causing Gwinnell to become drunk, yet they continued to serve him even after he was visibly intoxicated. By the time he left, Gwinnell was in fact severely intoxicated. A reasonable person in Zak's position could foresee quite clearly that this continued provision of alcohol to Gwinnell was making it more and more likely that Gwinnell would not be able to operate his car carefully. Zak could foresee that unless he stopped providing drinks to Gwinnell, Gwinnell was likely to injure someone as a result of the negligent operation of his car. The usual elements of a cause of action for negligence are clearly present: an action by defendant creating an unreasonable risk of harm to plaintiff, a risk that was clearly foreseeable, and a risk that resulted in an injury equally foreseeable. Under those circumstances the only question remaining is whether a duty exists to prevent such risk or, realistically, whether this Court should impose such a duty.

In most cases the justice of imposing such a duty is so clear that the cause of action in negligence is assumed to exist simply on the basis of the actor's creation of an unreasonable risk of foreseeable harm resulting in injury. In fact, however, more is needed, "more" being the value judgment, based on an analysis of public policy, that the actor owed the injured party a duty of reasonable care. . . .

When the court determines that a duty exists and liability will be extended, it draws judicial lines based on fairness and policy. In a society where thousands of deaths are caused each year by drunken drivers, where the damage caused by such deaths is regarded increasingly as intolerable, where liquor licensees are prohibited from serving intoxicated adults, and where long-standing criminal sanctions against drunken driving have recently been significantly strengthened to the point where the Governor notes that they are regarded as the toughest in the nation, see Governor's Annual Message to the N. J. State Legislature, Jan. 10, 1984, the imposition of such a duty by the judiciary seems both fair and fully in accord with the State's policy. Unlike those cases in which the definition of desirable policy is the subject of intense controversy, here the imposition of a duty is both consistent with and supportive of a social goal—the reduction of drunken driving—that is practically unanimously accepted by society.

. . . .

The argument is made that the rule imposing liability on licensees is justified because licensees, unlike social hosts, derive a profit from serving liquor. We reject this analysis of the liability's foundation and emphasize that the liability proceeds from the duty of care that accompanies control of the liquor supply. Whatever the motive behind making alcohol available to those who will subsequently drive, the provider has a duty to the public not to create foreseeable, unreasonable risks by this activity.

We therefore hold that a host who serves liquor to an adult social guest, knowing both that the guest is intoxicated and will thereafter be operating a motor vehicle, is liable for injuries inflicted on a third party as a result of the negligent operation of a motor vehicle by the adult guest when such negligence is caused by the intoxication. We impose this duty on the host to the third party because we believe that the policy considerations served by its imposition far outweigh those asserted in opposition. While we recognize the concern that our ruling will interfere with accepted standards of social behavior; will intrude on and somewhat diminish the enjoyment, relaxation, and camaraderie that accompany social gatherings at which alcohol is served; and that such gatherings and social relationships are not simply tangential benefits of a civilized society but are regarded by many as important, we believe that the added assurance of just compensation to the victims of drunken driving as well as the added deterrent effect of the rule on such driving outweigh the importance of those other values. . . .

The liability we impose here is analogous to that traditionally imposed on owners of vehicles who lend their cars to persons they know to be intoxicated. . . . If, by lending a car to a drunk, a host becomes liable to third parties injured by the drunken driver's negligence, the same liability should extend to a host who furnishes liquor to a visibly drunken guest who he knows will thereafter drive away.

Some fear has been expressed that the extent of the potential liability may be disproportionate to the fault of the host. A social judgment is therein implied to the effect that society does not regard as particularly serious the host's actions in causing his guests to become drunk, even though he knows they will thereafter be driving their cars. We seriously question that value judgment; indeed, we do not believe that the liability is disproportionate when the host's actions, so relatively easily corrected, may result in serious injury or death. The other aspect of this argument is that the host's insurance protection will be insufficient. While acknowledging that homeowners' insurance will cover such liability, this argument notes the risk that both the host and spouse will be jointly liable. The point made is not that the level of insurance will be lower in relation to the injuries than in the case of other torts, but rather that the joint liability of the spouses may result in the loss of their home and other property to the extent that the policy limits are inadequate. If only one spouse were liable, then even though the policy limits did not cover the liability, the couple need not lose their home because the creditor might not reach the interest of the spouse who was not liable. . . . We observe, however, that it is common for both spouses to be liable in automobile accident cases. It may be that some special form of insurance could be designed to protect the spouses' equity in their homes in cases such as this one. In any event, it is not clear that the loss of a home by spouses who, by definition, have negligently caused the injury, is disproportionate to the loss of life of one who is totally innocent of any wrongdoing.

Given the lack of precedent anywhere else in the country, however, we believe it would be unfair to impose this liability retroactively. . . . Homeowners who are social hosts may desire to increase their policy limits; apartment dwellers may want to obtain liability insurance of this kind where perhaps they now have none. The imposition of retroactive liability could be considered unexpected and its imposition unfair. We therefore have determined that the liability imposed by this case on social hosts shall be prospective, applicable only to events that occur after the date of this decision. We will, however, apply the doctrine to the parties before us on the usual theory that to do otherwise would not only deprive the plaintiff of any benefit resulting from her own efforts but would also make it less likely that, in the future, individuals will be willing to claim rights, not yet established, that they believe are just.

. . . .

We are satisfied that our decision today is well within the competence of the judiciary. Defining the scope of tort liability has traditionally been accepted as the responsibility of the courts. Indeed, given the courts' prior involvement in these matters, our decision today is hardly the radical change implied by the dissent but, while significant, is rather a fairly predictable expansion of liability in this area.

It should be noted that the difficulties posited by the dissent as to the likely consequence of this decision are purely hypothetical. Given the facts before us, we decide only that where the social host directly serves the guest and continues to do so even after the guest is visibly intoxicated, knowing that the guest will soon be driving home, the social host may be liable for the consequences of the resulting drunken driving. We are not faced with a party where many guests congregate, nor with guests serving each other, nor with a host busily occupied with other responsibilities and therefore unable to attend to the matter of serving liquor, nor with a drunken host. We will face those situations when and if they come before us, we hope with sufficient reason and perception so as to balance, if necessary and if legitimate, the societal interests alleged to be inconsistent with the public policy considerations that are at the heart of today's decision. The fears expressed by the dissent concerning the vast impact of the decision on the "average citizen's" life are reminiscent of those asserted in opposition to our decisions abolishing husband-wife, parent-child, and generally family immunity. . . .

We recognize, however, that the point of view expressed by the dissent conforms, at least insofar as the result is concerned, with the view, whether legislatively or judicially expressed, of practically every other jurisdiction that has been faced with this question. It seems to us that by now it ought to be clear to all that the concerns on which that point of view is based are minor compared to the devastating consequences of drunken driving. This is a problem that society is just beginning to face squarely, and perhaps we in New Jersey are doing so sooner than others.

For instance, the dissent's emphasis on the financial impact of an insurance premium increase on the homeowner or the tenant should be measured against the monumental financial losses suffered by society as a result of drunken driving. By our decision we not only spread some of that loss so that it need not be borne completely by the victims of this widespread affliction, but, to some extent, reduce the likelihood that the loss will occur in the first place. Even if the dissent's view of the scope of our decision were correct, the adjustments in social behavior at parties, the burden put on the host to reasonably oversee the serving of liquor, the burden on the guests to make sure if one is drinking that another is driving, and the burden on all to take those reasonable steps even if, on some occasion, some guest may become belligerent: those social dislocations, their importance, must be measured against the misery, death, and destruction caused by the drunken driver. Does our society morally approve of the decision to continue to allow the charm of unrestrained social drinking when the cost is the lives of others, sometimes of the guests themselves?

If we but step back and observe ourselves objectively, we will see a phenomenon not of merriment but of cruelty, causing misery to innocent people, tolerated for years despite our knowledge that without fail, out of our extraordinarily high number of deaths caused by automobiles, nearly half have regularly been attributable to drunken driving.

. . . .

We therefore reverse the judgment in favor of the defendants Zak and remand the case to the Law Division for proceedings consistent with this opinion.

GARIBALDI, J., dissenting.

[T]he almost limitless implications of the majority's decision lead me to conclude that the Legislature is better equipped to effectuate the goals of reducing injuries from drunken driving and protecting the interests of the injured party, without placing such a grave burden on the average citizen of this state.

———————

1. Arguably, *Kelly* has had a substantial impact on how individuals, groups, and private clubs serve alcohol. Argue that the question is for the legislature or the courts.

2. What factors did the court consider in reaching its decision? Is the amount and availability of insurance an appropriate factor for consideration under proximate cause?

3. If you believe that the court would have reached a different decision twenty years ago, what has changed in the interim?

4. After the decision in *Kelly*, the New Jersey legislature passed a statute limiting the impact of the case. The statute provides social host liability for "willfully and knowingly" providing alcoholic beverages to "a person who was visibly intoxicated in the host's presence. . . ." An irrebutable presumption that the driver was not visibly intoxicated is provided if the blood alcohol concentration was less than .10%, and a rebuttable presumption of nonintoxication between .10% and .15%. The social host's liability is not joint and several. *See* N.J. Stat. Ann. §§ 2A:15-5.6 to 2A:15-5.8.

5. Dramshop Acts. Statutes often provide that commercial vendors of liquor are civilly and criminally liable for damages caused by intoxicated customers. For a summary of these acts, see *Ling v. Jan's Liquors*, 237 Kan. 629, 703 P.2d 731 (1985).

6. A majority of the courts, faced with the question, have refused to hold the social host liable for damages brought about by the guest. *See Overbaugh v. McCutcheon*, 396 S.E.2d 153 (W. Va. 1990). Why?

7. A mother purchased beer and supervised its consumption by teenagers, including her child. Although concerned, she permitted an intoxicated teen to drive home. He crashed into a car and killed the driver. The mother was held liable. *Sutter v. Hutchings*, 254 Ga. 194, 327 S.E.2d 716 (1985). When a drunken wedding guest injures someone, will the bride's parents be liable because they paid for the reception?

8. A bar owner who provided jumper cables to a visibly intoxicated person was held liable to third persons who suffered injuries in a collision. *Leppke v. Segura*, 632 P.2d 1057 (Colo. App. 1981). An extreme result?

9. Because "texting" now causes a large number of crashes and fatalities, should cell phone manufacturers be liable for not making the phone shut off automatically when the vehicle begins to move? What if texting is highly addictive? Consider assumption of risk.

In re September 11 Litigation

United States District Court, Southern District of New York, 2003
280 F. Supp. 2d 279

OPINION AND ORDER DENYING DEFENDANTS' MOTIONS TO DISMISS

HELLERSTEIN, District Judge.

The injured, and the representatives of the thousands who died from the terrorist- related aircraft crashes of September 11, 2001, are entitled to seek compensation. By act of Congress, they may seek compensation by filing claims with a Special Master established pursuant to the Air Transportation Safety and System Stabilization Act of 2001, ("the Act"). Or they may seek compensation in the traditional manner, by alleging and proving their claims in lawsuits, with the aggregate of their damages capped at the limits of defendants' liability insurance. If they choose the former alternative, their claims will be paid through a Victim Compensation Fund from money appropriated by Congress, within a relatively short period after filing. Claimants will not have to prove fault or show a duty to pay on the part of any defendant. The amount of their compensation, however, may be less than their possible recovery from lawsuits, for non-economic damages are limited to $250,000, economic damages are subject to formulas that are likely to be less generous than those often allowable in lawsuits, and punitive damages are unavailable.

Approximately seventy of the injured and representatives of those who died, and ten entities which sustained property damage, have chosen to bring lawsuits against defendants whom they claim are legally responsible to compensate them: the airlines, the airport security companies, the airport operators, the airplane manufacturer, and the operators and owners of the World Trade Center. The motions before me challenge the legal sufficiency of these lawsuits, and ask me to dismiss the complaints because no duty to the plaintiffs existed and because the defendants could not reasonably have anticipated that terrorists would hijack several jumbo jet airplanes and crash them, killing passengers, crew, thousands on the ground, and themselves. I discuss in this opinion the legal duties owed by the air carriers, United and American Airlines, and other airlines and airport security companies affiliated with the air carriers to the plaintiffs who were killed and damaged on the ground in and around the Twin Towers and the Pentagon; by the Port Authority of New York and New Jersey ("Port Authority") and World Trade Center Properties LLC ("WTC Properties") to those killed and injured in and around the Twin Towers; and by the Boeing Company, the manufacturer of the "757" jets that were flown into the Pentagon and the field near Shanksville, Pennsylvania, to those killed and injured in the two crashes. I hold in this opinion that each of these defendants owed duties to the plaintiffs who sued them.

. . . .

Motion to *Dismiss Claims Arising out of the Crash of American Airlines Flight 77*

Background

Thus far, three individual complaints have been filed with respect to the flight 77 crash. They charge Boeing with strict liability and negligent design based on an unreasonably dangerous design of the cockpit doors.

The Plaintiffs' First Amended Flight 77 Master Liability Complaint contains three counts applicable to Boeing. Count Six alleges strict tort liability for an unreasonably dangerous design of the cockpit doors. Count Seven alleges that Boeing breached its duty of care by failing to design the cockpit doors and accompanying locks in a manner that would prevent hijackers from accessing the cockpit.

. . . .

Proximate Causation

Boeing next argues that its design of the cockpit doors on its "757" passenger aircraft, even if held to constitute an "unreasonably dangerous condition," was not the proximate cause of plaintiffs' injuries. Boeing argues that the criminal acts of the terrorists in hijacking the airplanes and using the airplanes as weapons of mass destruction constituted an "efficient intervening cause" which broke the "natural and continuous sequence" of events flowing from Boeing's allegedly inadequate design. (a "proximate cause of an event is that 'act or omission which, in natural and continuous sequence, unbroken by an efficient intervening cause, produces the event, and without which that event would not have occurred.'") Plaintiffs have the burden to prove proximate cause and, generally, the issue is a question of fact to be resolved by a jury. However, when reasonable people cannot differ, the issue becomes a question of law for the court.

The record at this point does not support Boeing's argument that the invasion and take-over of the cockpit by the terrorists must, as a matter of law, be held to constitute an "efficient intervening act" that breaks the "natural and continuous sequence" flowing from Boeing's allegedly inadequate design. Plaintiffs allege that Boeing should have designed its cockpit door to prevent hijackers from invading the cockpit, that acts of terrorism, including hijackings of airplanes, were reasonably foreseeable, and that the lives of passengers, crew and ground victims would be imminently in danger from such hijackings. Virginia law does not require Boeing to have foreseen precisely how the injuries suffered on September 11, 2001 would be caused, as long as Boeing could reasonably have foreseen that "some injury" from its negligence "might probably result." "[A] reasonably prudent [person] ought under the circumstances to have foreseen that some injury might probably result from that negligence." Given the critical nature of the cockpit area, and the inherent danger of a crash when a plane is in flight, one cannot say that Boeing could not reasonably have foreseen the risk flowing from an inadequately constructed cockpit door.

Boeing relies heavily on *Baltimore & Ohio Railroad Co.* to support its argument that proximate causation was broken by an efficient intervening cause. The case, however, is distinguishable. The railroad had been using a certain type of switch for more than forty years. While a long freight train was stopped, with eight cars having passed over the switch and the balance of 51 freight cars still on the other side, a six-year old boy living at the side of the track surreptitiously came onto the tracks and threw the switch. When the train resumed its movement, a number of cars derailed, causing property damage to adjoining properties. The Virginia Supreme Court reversed the verdict for the plaintiff, holding that the railroad reasonably could not have foreseen the occurrence. The switch was of a standard type in use for more than forty years; it was used throughout the railroad's extensive system, and at the location in issue; it had consistently been operated in an identical manner for the forty years; the switch had never before been tampered with; and the railroad crew had not been negligent in monitoring the child or the tampered switch. The court held that an imposition of liability on the railroad would be unreasonable, for it would require the railroad to station employees at or near all its switches. The court ruled also that the boy's criminal conduct, not reasonably being foreseen by the railroad, constituted an independent and proximate cause of the adjoining property owner's damage. In contrast, the danger that a plane could crash if unauthorized individuals invaded and took over the cockpit was the very risk that Boeing should reasonably have foreseen. Privacy within a cockpit means very little if the door intended to provide security is not designed to keep out potential intruders.

Boeing's citation to cases in other jurisdictions are also distinguishable.

In re Korean Air Lines Disaster of September 1, 1983 (D.D.C.1985), involved lawsuits by the legal successors of passengers who died when Korean Airlines passenger flight 007 was shot down by Russian fighter planes. The passenger plane had flown off course and over a sensitive military zone in Russia. Russian fighter pilots intercepted the plane and, instead of following international protocol for causing the plane to return to international routes over the high seas or to land at a selected landing field, shot it down. Plaintiffs sued Boeing, the manufacturer of the airplane, alleging that a product defect in its navigation systems caused it to fly off course and over Soviet territory, and that Boeing's improper and unsafe design was therefore the proximate cause of plaintiffs' damages. The court dismissed the complaint, holding that Boeing could not foresee that the Soviet Union would destroy an intruding aircraft in violation of international conventions, and had no ability to guard against such conduct. The court held, consequently, that Boeing did not owe a duty to passengers with respect to such risks, and that the actions of the Russian pilots were independent and supervening causes that broke the chain of causation.

These three cases do not offer Boeing much support in its motion. In each, the acts of the third-parties were held to be superseding causes because they were not reasonably foreseeable to the product manufacturer. In *KAL,* the court held that the manufacturer of airplane navigational systems could not reasonably foresee that a passenger aircraft that strayed off course would be shot down by hostile military forces in violation of international conventions. In the cases before me, however, plaintiffs allege that Boeing could reasonably have foreseen that terrorists would try to invade the cockpits of airplanes, and that easy access on their part, because cockpit doors were not designed to prevent easy opening, would be imminently dangerous to passengers, crew and ground victims. Plaintiffs' allegations that duty and proximate cause existed cannot be dismissed as a matter of law on the basis of the record now before me. Accordingly, I deny Boeing's motion to dismiss the complaints against it arising from the crash of flight 77 into the Pentagon.

Negligent design claims

Boeing argues that the plaintiffs' negligent design claims must be dismissed because it did not owe a duty of care to the plaintiffs, and because its alleged negligence was not the proximate cause of plaintiffs' damages.

To determine whether proximate cause exists, "the court must determine whether the injury would have been foreseen by an ordinary person as the natural and probable outcome of the act complained of."

. . . .

"Among the factors to consider in determining whether a subsequent force is an intervening or superseding cause are whether the force is operating independently of any situation created by the first actor's negligence and whether it is a normal result of that situation." Plaintiffs allege that without defendant's negligence, the hijackers would not have been able to intrude into the cockpit and take over the airplane. Again, for the reasons previously discussed, the terrorists' unauthorized entry into the cockpit was not unforeseeable, and did not constitute an "intervening" or "superseding" cause that could, as a matter of law, break the chain of causation.

Accordingly, I deny Boeing's motion to dismiss the complaints against it arising from the crash of flight 93 into Shanksville.

––––––––––

1. Argue that Boeing did not foresee that terrorists would break through the airplane door into the front cockpit.

2. Argue, as in Andrews' dissent in *Palsgraf*, that as a matter of "practical politics," Boeing's negligence was severed. What are the relevant politics for the court in *In re September 11* . . . to weigh?

3. Argue that terrorists were foreseeable, as was their use of commercial airplanes to crash into tall buildings. Precedent?

Wagner v. International Railway Co.

Court of Appeals of New York, 1921
133 N.E. 437

CARDOZO, J.

The action is for personal injuries. The defendant operates an electric railway between Buffalo and Niagara Falls. There is a point on its line where an overhead crossing carries its tracks . . . upwards over a trestle. . . . A turn is then made to the left at an angle of from sixty-four to eighty-four degrees. After making this turn, the line passes over a bridge, which is about one hundred and fifty-eight feet long from one abutment to the other. Then comes a turn to the right at about the same angle down the same kind of an incline to grade. Above the trestles, the tracks are laid on ties, unguarded at the ends. There is thus an overhang of the cars, which is accentuated at curves. . . .

Plaintiff and his cousin Herbert boarded a car at a station near the bottom of one of the trestles. Other passengers, entering at the same time, filled the platform, and blocked admission to the aisle. The platform was provided with doors, but the conductor did not close them. Moving at from six to eight miles an hour, the car, without slackening, turned the curve. There was a violent lurch, and Herbert Wagner was thrown out, near the point where the trestle changes to a bridge. The cry was raised, "Man overboard." The car went on across the bridge, and stopped near the foot of the incline. Night and darkness had come on. Plaintiff walked along the trestle, a distance of four hundred and forty-five feet, until he arrived at the bridge, where he thought to find his cousin's body. He says that he was asked to go there by the conductor. He says, too, that the conductor followed with a lantern. Both these statements the conductor denies. Several other persons, instead of ascending the trestle, went beneath it, and discovered under the bridge the body they were seeking. As they stood there, the plaintiff's body struck the ground beside them. Reaching the bridge, he had found upon a beam his cousin's hat, but nothing else. About him, there was darkness. He missed his footing, and fell.

. . . .

Danger invites rescue. The cry of distress is the summons to relief. The law does not ignore these reactions of the mind in tracing conduct to its consequences. It recognizes them as normal. It places their effects within the range of the natural and probable. The wrong that imperils life is a wrong to the imperilled victim; it is a wrong also to his rescuer. The state that leaves an opening in a bridge is liable to the child that falls into the stream, but liable also to the parent who plunges to its aid. . . . The railroad company whose train approaches without signal is a wrongdoer toward the traveler surprised between the rails, but a wrongdoer also to the bystander who drags him from the path. . . . The risk of rescue, if only it be not wanton, is born of the occasion. The emergency begets the man. The wrongdoer may not have foreseen the coming of a deliverer. He is accountable as if he had. . . .

The defendant says that we must stop, in following the chain of causes, when action ceases to be "instinctive." By this, is meant, it seems, that rescue is at the peril of the rescuer, unless spontaneous and immediate. If there has been time to deliberate, if impulse has given way to judgment, one cause, it is said, has spent its force, and another has intervened. In this case, the plaintiff walked more than four hundred feet in going to Herbert's aid. He had time to reflect and weigh; impulse had been followed by choice; and choice, in the defendant's view, intercepts and breaks the sequence. We find no warrant for thus shortening the chain of jural causes. We may assume, though we are not required to decide, that peril and rescue must be in substance one transaction; that the sight of the one must have aroused the impulse to the other; in short, that there must be unbroken continuity between the commission of the wrong and the effort to avert its consequences. If all this be assumed, the defendant is not aided. Continuity in such circumstances is not broken by the exercise of volition. . . . The law does not discriminate between the rescuer oblivious of peril and the one who counts the cost. It is enough that the act, whether impulsive or deliberate, is the child of the occasion.

. . . The reason that was exacted of him was not the reason of the morrow. It was reason fitted and proportioned to the time and the event.

Whether Herbert Wagner's fall was due to the defendant's negligence, and whether plaintiff in going to the rescue, as he did, was foolhardy or reasonable in the light of the emergency confronting him, were questions for the jury.

The judgment of the Appellate Division and that of the Trial Term should be reversed, and a new trial granted, with costs to abide the event.

––––––––––

1. Note that *Wagner* was decided seven years before *Palsgraf* (1928). Does *Palsgraf* follow *Wagner*? Must it?

2. Suppose a cruise ship sinks because of negligence on the part of the captain. Would a private rescuer who is drowned in a hurricane be able to recover from the cruise line? What about a rescuing sailor who is a doctor and suffers a heart attack from overwork while treating the passengers? What if the doctor is employed by the cruise line for such emergencies and suffers a heart attack from strain after having been flown to the site of the sinking? *See Carter v. Taylor Diving & Salvage Co.*, 341 F. Supp. 628 (E.D. La. 1972), *aff'd mem.*, 470 F.2d 995 (5th Cir. 1973).

3. What limit does the court place on the rescuer's recovery?

4. The plaintiff fell and injured her leg while running from the defendant's railroad car that had jumped the track. The court rejected the argument that the plaintiff's fear was a superseding cause and upheld the plaintiff's verdict. *Tuttle v. Atlantic City R.R. Co.*, 66 N.J.L. 327, 49 A. 450 (1901).

5. Should a professional, i.e., firefighter, police officer, or doctor, who is injured in the line of duty be able to recover when defendant is negligent? The "fireman's rule," now more commonly referred to as the "professional rescuer" doctrine, bars recovery for a professional. However, some states have abolished or limited this rule. *See Christensen v. Murphy*, 296 Or. 610, 678 P.2d 1210 (1984) (holding the rule is no longer a bar to recovery for personal injury); *Bates v. McKeon*, 650 F. Supp. 476 (D. Conn. 1986) (holding that police officer could recover compensatory and punitive damages for intentional tort of assault and battery).

6. Suppose the plaintiff passenger is injured in a bus collision, resulting from the bus driver's negligence. The doctor treating the plaintiff performs unnecessary surgery on the plaintiff, whose injuries are therefore further aggravated. The plaintiff sues the bus driver and bus owner for all injuries. What result? *Ponder v. Cartmell*, 301 Ark. 409, 784 S.W.2d 758 (1990).

7. A recurring problem is where the first defendant injures the plaintiff in a car crash and on the way to the hospital, the plaintiff is injured by a second defendant, who crashes into the ambulance, or at the hospital, a doctor (defendant three) prescribes the wrong medicine or removes the wrong leg. The proximate cause issue becomes whether the first defendant is liable for the negligent acts of the later defendants.

In *Weber v. Charity Hospital*, 475 So. 2d 1047 (La. 1985), following a car crash, the plaintiff received a blood transfusion containing hepatitis. The negligent car driver was held liable for the damages from the hepatitis.

In *Pridham v. Cash & Carry*, 359 A.2d 193 (N.H. 1976), the plaintiff died when the ambulance driver had a heart attack and the ambulance crashed into a tree. The court said:

> "[I]f a [defendant's] negligence causes harm to another which requires the other to receive medical . . . services, and bodily harm results from a normal effort of persons rendering such services, whether done in a proper or

negligent manner, the [first defendant] is a legal cause of the injuries received. . . ."

The court held for the plaintiff on the intervening cause issue.

In *Anaya v. Superior Court*, 93 Cal. Rptr. 2d 228 (Ct. App. 2000), because of injuries caused by defendant one, the plaintiff was being rushed to the hospital in a helicopter when it crashed and killed her. In finding against the first defendant, the Court said:

> An actor may be liable if the actor's negligence is a substantial factor in caus-ing an injury, and the actor is not relieved of liability because of the inter-vening act of a third party if such act was reasonably foreseeable at the time of the original negligent conduct. . . . The allegations that the helicopter mal-functioned and the manufacturer is strictly liable . . . do not establish the manufacturer as a superseding actor.

Sometimes a line is drawn, however. *In Purchase v. Seelye*, 121 N.E. 413 (Mass. 1918), the first defendant's liability was severed when the hospital operated on the wrong patient. The Court said:

> It is well settled in this Commonwealth . . . that in an action for personal injuries arising out of the alleged negligence of the defendant, the plaintiff is entitled to recover for the injuries resulting from the defendant's negli-gence although such injuries are aggravated by the negligence of an attending physician if, in his selection and employment the plaintiff was in the exer-cise of reasonable care.
>
> . . . We are of opinion that the general rule as above stated is not appli-cable to the case at bar. There was sufficient evidence to show that the defen-dant made a mistake in the identity of the plaintiff at the time the operation was performed. . . . The reason why a wrongdoer is held liable for the negli-gence of a physician whose unskillful treatment aggravates an injury, is that such unskilled treatment is a result which reasonably ought to have been anticipated by him.

Fuller v. Preis

New York Court of Appeals, 1974
322 N.E.2d 263

BREITEL, CHIEF JUDGE.

. . . .

Decedent, Dr. Lewis, committed suicide some seven months after an automobile accident from which he had walked away believing he was uninjured. In fact he had suffered head injuries with consequences to be detailed later. The theory of the case was that defendants, owner and operator of the vehicle which struck decedent's auto-mobile, were responsible in tort for the suicide as a matter of proximate cause. . . . The issue is whether plaintiff's evidence of cause of the suicide was sufficient. . . .

On December 2, 1966, decedent Dr. Lewis, a 43-year-old surgeon, was involved in an intersection collision. Upon impact, the left side of his head struck the frame and window of his automobile. Suffering no evident injuries, he declined aid and drove himself home. . . .

Two days after the accident, Dr. Lewis had a seizure followed by others. . . .

Then ensued a period of deterioration and gradual contraction of his professional and private activities. . . .

On July 9, after experiencing three seizures that day, he went to the bathroom of his home, closed the door and shot himself in the head. He died the following day. . . .

[T]he act of suicide, as a matter of law, is not a superseding cause in negligence law precluding liability. . . .

That suicide may be encouraged by allowing recovery for suicide, a highly doubtful proposition in occidental society, is unpersuasive to preclude recovery for the suicide of a mentally deranged person. The remote possibility of fraudulent claims connecting a suicide with mental derangement affords no basis for barring recovery.

The obvious difficulty in proving or disproving causal relation should not bar recovery. . . .

Thus, there is neither public policy nor precedent barring recovery for suicide of a tortiously injured person driven "insane" by the consequence of the tortious act. . . .

[T]he jury was instructed, primarily, upon the theory of liability for a suicide by an accident victim suffering from ensuing mental disease, who was unable to control the "irresistible impulse" to destroy himself. . . .

Dr. Lewis was physically and mentally healthy immediately prior to the automobile accident in which he struck his head against the interior of his own vehicle. After the accident he suffered several epileptic seizures, often with unconsciousness. Before the accident he had never suffered a seizure. For seven months between the accident and his death, Dr. Lewis experienced no fewer than 38 separate seizures. . . .

The only authentic issue is whether the suicide was an "irresistible impulse" caused by traumatic organic brain damage. . . .

On the day of the suicide, only seven months after the accident, when Dr. Lewis had had three seizures, his daughter tried to speak with him but he did not respond. After the third seizure he seemed unable to recognize his wife, had a strange look, and locked himself in the bathroom. Twenty minutes later, his wife heard him mutter, "I must do it, I must do it," and then a gunshot rang out. Dr. Lewis had shot himself in the head and died the following day. . . .

In tort law, as contrasted with criminal law, there is recognition that one may retain the power to intend, to know, and yet to have an irresistible impulse to act and therefore be incapable of voluntary conduct. . . . The issue in this case was, precisely, whether Dr. Lewis, who obviously knew what he was doing and intended to do what he did, nevertheless, was because of mental derangement, incapable of resisting the impulse to destroy himself. Precedents and modern knowledge say that that could have been. The jury found that it was so.

When the suicide is preceded by a history of trauma, brain damage, epileptic seizures, aberrational conduct, depression and despair, it is at the very least a fair issue of fact whether the suicide was the rational act of a sound mind or the irrational act or irresistible impulse of a deranged mind evidenced by a physically damaged brain. . . .

Since the Appellate Division, in reversing, stated that in any event it would have set the verdict aside as contrary to the weight of the evidence, the verdict in favor of plaintiff may not be reinstated and a new trial is required.

Accordingly, the order of the Appellate Division should be reversed, with costs, and a new trial directed.

---

1. How does the court resolve the cause-in-fact issue?

2. What is the proximate cause issue? Would your thinking be affected by the fact that Dr. Lewis' mother-in-law was suffering from cancer and his wife was extremely sick?

3. Are you able to suggest a better test than "irresistible impulse" for suicides?

4. In older cases, courts found that suicide breaks the chain of causation. *See Scheffer v. Railroad Co.*, 105 U.S. 249 (1882). However, in more recent cases, the question is often left to the jury. *See Stafford v. Neurological Med., Inc.*, 811 F.2d 470 (8th Cir. 1987).

Enright v. Eli Lilly & Co.
Court of Appeals of New York, 1991
570 N.E.2d 198

WACHTLER, CHIEF JUDGE.

The question in this case is whether the liability of manufacturers of the drug diethylstilbestrol (DES) should extend to a so-called "third generation" plaintiff, the granddaughter of a woman who ingested the drug. According to the allegations of the complaint, the infant plaintiff's injuries were caused by her premature birth, which in turn resulted from damage to her mother's reproductive system caused by the mother's in utero exposure to DES. We hold, in accord with our decision in *Albala v. City of New York* (54 N.Y.2d 269), that in these circumstances no cause of action accrues in favor of the infant plaintiff against the drug manufacturers.

The plaintiffs in this case are Karen Enright, born August 9, 1981, and her parents, Patricia and Earl Enright. According to their complaint, the events underlying this action began more than 30 years ago, when Karen Enright's maternal grandmother ingested DES during a pregnancy which resulted in the birth of plaintiff Patricia Enright on January 29, 1960. Plaintiffs allege that because of her in utero exposure to DES, Patricia Enright developed a variety of abnormalities and deformities in her reproductive system. As a result, several of her pregnancies terminated in spontaneous abortions and another resulted in the premature birth of Karen Enright. Karen suffers from cerebral palsy and other disabilities that plaintiffs attribute to her premature birth and, ultimately, to her grandmother's ingestion of DES.

. . . .

We note that no issues are raised on this appeal regarding the still pending claims of Patricia and Earl Enright based on the injuries allegedly sustained by Patricia Enright due to her own in utero exposure to DES.

. . . .

The tragic DES tale is well documented in this Court's decisions and need not be recounted here. . . . It is sufficient to note that between 1947 and 1971, the drug, a synthetic estrogen-like substance produced by approximately 300 manufacturers, was prescribed for use and ingested by millions of pregnant women to prevent miscarriages. In 1971, the Food and Drug Administration banned the drug's use for the treatment of problems of pregnancy after studies established a link between in utero exposure to DES and the occurrence in teen-age women of a rare form of vaginal and cervical cancer. Plaintiffs allege that in utero exposure to DES has since been linked to other genital tract aberrations in DES daughters, including malformations or immaturity of the uterus, cervical abnormalities, misshapen Fallopian tubes and abnormal cell and tissue growth, all of which has caused in this population a marked increase in the incidence of infertility, miscarriages, premature births and ectopic pregnancies.

The Legislature and this Court have both expressed concern for the victims of this tragedy by removing legal barriers to their tort recovery—barriers which may have had their place in other contexts, but which in DES litigation worked a peculiar injustice because of the ways in which DES was developed, marketed and sold and because of the insidious nature of its harm.

For example, prior to 1986, the long-standing rule in this State was that a cause of action for personal injuries caused by a toxic substance accrued and the limitations period began to run upon exposure to the substance. . . . The Legislature, recognizing that under this rule claims for injuries caused by exposure to DES and other toxic substances were often time barred before the harmful effects of the exposure could be discovered, changed the law to provide that the limitations period in exposure cases begins to run upon discovery of the injury. . . . At the same time, the Legislature revived for one year previously time-barred causes of action based on exposure to DES and four other toxic substances. . . .

More recently, this Court responded to the fact that—for a variety of reasons unique to the DES litigation context—a DES plaintiff generally finds it impossible to identify the manufacturer of the drug that caused her injuries. We held that liability could be imposed upon DES manufacturers in accordance with their share of the national DES market, notwithstanding the plaintiff's inability to identify the manufacturer particularly at fault for her injuries. . . .

In the present case, we are asked to do something significantly different. We are asked, not to remove some barrier to recovery that presents unique problems in DES cases, but to recognize a cause of action not available in other contexts simply (or at least largely) because this is a DES case.

In *Albala v. City of New York* . . . , we were presented with the question "whether a cause of action lies in favor of a child for injuries suffered as a result of a preconception tort committed against the mother." There, the mother suffered a perforated uterus during the course of an abortion. Four years later, she gave birth to a brain-damaged child, whose injuries were allegedly attributable to the defendants' negligence in perforating the mother's uterus. We declined, as a matter of policy, to recognize a cause of action on behalf of the child, believing that to do so would "require the extension of traditional tort concepts beyond manageable bounds." . . . Among other things, we were concerned with "the staggering implications of any proposition which would honor claims assuming the breach of an identifiable duty for less than a perfect birth" and the difficulty, if such a cause of action were recognized, of confining liability by other than artificial and arbitrary boundaries. . . .

The case now before us differs from *Albala* only in that the mother's injuries in this case were caused by exposure to DES instead of by medical malpractice. A different rule is justified, therefore, only if that distinction alters the policy balance we struck in *Albala*.

The primary thrust of plaintiffs' argument and the Appellate Division's decision is that DES itself alters that balance. From the Legislature's actions in modifying the applicable Statute of Limitations and reviving time-barred DES cases and from our adoption of a market-share liability theory in *Hymowitz*, plaintiffs perceive a public policy favoring a remedy for DES-caused injuries sufficient to overcome the countervailing policy considerations we identified in *Albala*. The implication, of course, is that the public interest in providing a remedy for those injured by DES is stronger than the public interest in providing a remedy for those injured by other means— medical malpractice, for example. We do not believe that such a preference has been established.

To be sure, recent developments demonstrate legislative and judicial solicitude for the victims of DES, but they do not establish DES plaintiffs as a favored class for whose benefit all traditional limitations on tort liability must give way. To the extent that special rules have been fashioned, they are a response to unique procedural barriers and problems of proof peculiar to DES litigation.

. . . .

As in *Albala*, the cause of action plaintiffs ask us to recognize here could not be confined without the drawing of artificial and arbitrary boundaries. For all we know, the rippling effects of DES exposure may extend for generations. It is our duty to confine liability within manageable limits. . . . Limiting liability to those who ingested the drug or were exposed to it in utero serves this purpose. . . .

But in light of the FDA's responsibility in this area, the need for the tort system to promote prescription drug safety is at least diminished. . . .

More important, however, is recognition that public policy favors the availability of prescription drugs even though most carry some risks. . . . That is not to say that drug manufacturers should enjoy immunity from liability stemming from their failure to conduct adequate research and testing prior to the marketing of their products. They do not enjoy such immunity, as evidenced by our recognition of liability in favor of those who have been injured by ingestion or in utero exposure to DES. But we are aware of the dangers of overdeterrence—the possibility that research will be discouraged or beneficial drugs withheld from the market. These dangers are magnified in this context, where we are asked to recognize a legal duty toward generations not yet conceived.

In sum, the distinctions between this case and *Albala* provide no basis for a departure from the rule that an injury to a mother which results in injuries to a later-conceived child does not establish a cause of action in favor of the child against the original tort-feasor. For this reason, we decline to recognize a cause of action on behalf of plaintiff Karen Enright. Accordingly, the order of the Appellate Division should be modified, with costs to defendants, by granting defendants' motions for summary judgment dismissing the third cause of action and, as so modified, affirmed. The certified question should be answered in the affirmative.

---

1. This is a New York case with an issue as to whether the plaintiff is foreseeable. Why is there no discussion of *Palsgraf*, zone of danger, foreseeability, or directness?

2. What policies does the court present for not finding a duty, a "new" cause of action?

3. How would Judge Wachtler have decided *Polemis, Wagon Mound No. 1*, and *Palsgraf*? What is the difference in analytical approach between those three cases and *Enright*? Which approach do you prefer and why?

4. Why might a court be more accurate and clear in deciding proximate cause in products cases than other cases?

5. Is this a proximate cause or a products liability case? What is the distinction?

C. Economic Loss

Problem

Dr. Jones told Chuck that, because of cancer, Chuck had only six months to live. Chuck therefore retired early and suffered substantial financial loss because Dr. Jones was wrong and negligent. Will Chuck be able to recover his financial losses from Dr. Jones?

People Express Airlines v. Consolidated Rail Corp.

Supreme Court of New Jersey, 1985

495 A.2d 107

[The airline sued the various defendants including the railroad for damages it suffered due to evacuation of its offices following a tank car accident at a nearby railroad yard, although the airline suffered no physical damages. The Superior Court, Law Division, Essex County, entered summary judgment for the defendants, and the airline appealed. The Superior Court reversed and remanded, and defendants appealed.]

HANDLER, J.

. . . .

On July 22, 1981, a fire began in the Port Newark freight yard of defendant Consolidated Rail Corporation (Conrail) when ethylene oxide manufactured by defendant BASF Wyandotte Company (BASF) escaped from a tank car, punctured during a "coupling" operation with another rail car, and ignited. The tank car was owned by defendant Union Tank Car Company (Union Car) and was leased to defendant BASF.

The plaintiff asserted at oral argument that at least some of the defendants were aware from prior experiences that ethylene oxide is a highly volatile substance; further, that emergency response plans in case of an accident had been prepared. When the fire occurred that gave rise to this lawsuit, some of the defendants' consultants helped determine how much of the surrounding area to evacuate. The municipal authorities then evacuated the area within a one-mile radius surrounding the fire to lessen the risk to persons within the area should the burning tank car explode. The evacuation area included the adjacent North Terminal building of Newark International Airport, where plaintiff People Express Airlines' (People Express) business operations are based. Although the feared explosion never occurred, People Express employees were prohibited from using the North Terminal for twelve hours.

The plaintiff contends that it suffered business-interruption losses as a result of the evacuation. These losses consist of canceled scheduled flights and lost reservations because employees were unable to answer the telephones to accept bookings; also, certain fixed operating expenses allocable to the evacuation time period were incurred and paid despite the fact that plaintiff's offices were closed. No physical damage to airline property and no personal injury occurred as a result of the fire. . . .

The single characteristic that distinguishes parties in negligence suits whose claims for economic losses have been regularly denied by American and English courts from those who have recovered economic losses is, with respect to the successful claimants, the fortuitous occurrence of physical harm or property damage, however slight.

It is well-accepted that a defendant who negligently injures a plaintiff or his property may be liable for all proximately caused harm, including economic losses. *See Palsgraf.* . . . Nevertheless, a virtually *per se* rule barring recovery for economic loss unless the negligent conduct also caused physical harm has evolved throughout this century, based, in part, on *Robins Dry Dock & Repair Co. v. Flint*, 275 U.S. 303, 48 S. Ct. 134, 72 L. Ed. 2d 290 (1927). . . .

The reasons that have been advanced to explain the divergent results for litigants seeking economic losses are varied. Some courts have viewed the general rule against recovery as necessary to limit damages to reasonably foreseeable consequences of negligent conduct. This concern in a given case is often manifested as an issue of causation and has led to the requirement of physical harm as an element of proximate cause. In this context, the physical harm requirement functions as part of the definition of the causal relationship between the defendant's negligent act and the plaintiff's economic damages; it acts as a convenient clamp on otherwise boundless liability. . . . The physical harm rule also reflects certain deep-seated concerns that underlie courts' denial of recovery for purely economic losses occasioned by a defendant's negligence. These concerns include the fear of fraudulent claims, mass litigation, and limitless liability, or liability out of proportion to the defendant's fault. . . .

The troublesome concern reflected in cases denying recovery for negligently-caused economic loss is the alleged potential for infinite liability, or liability out of all proportion to the defendant's fault. . . .

Judicial discomfiture with the rule of nonrecovery for purely economic loss throughout the last several decades has led to numerous exceptions in the general rule. Although the rationalizations for these exceptions differ among courts and cases, two common threads run throughout the exceptions. The first is that the element of foreseeability emerges as a more appropriate analytical standard to determine the question of liability than a per se prohibitory rule. The second is that the extent to which the defendant knew or should have known the particular consequences of his negligence, including the economic loss of a particularly foreseeable plaintiff, is dispositive of the issues of duty and fault.

. . . .

Courts have found it fair and just in all of these exceptional cases to impose liability on defendants who, by virtue of their special activities, professional training or other unique preparation for their work, had particular knowledge or reason to know that others, such as the intended beneficiaries of wills . . . or the purchasers of stock who were expected to rely on the company's financial statement in the prospectus . . . would be economically harmed by negligent conduct. In this group of cases, even though the particular plaintiff was not always foreseeable, the particular class of plaintiffs was foreseeable as was the particular type of injury.

A very solid exception allowing recovery for economic losses has also been created in cases akin to private actions for public nuisance. Where a plaintiff's business is based in part upon the exercise of a public right, the plaintiff has been able to recover purely economic losses caused by a defendant's negligence. *See, e.g., Louisiana ex rel. Guste v. M/V Testbank*, 752 F.2d 1019 (5th Cir. 1985) (en banc) (defendants responsible for ship collision held liable to all commercial fishermen, shrimpers, crabbers and oystermen for resulting pollution of Mississippi River). . . . The theory running throughout these cases, in which the plaintiffs depend on the exercise of the public or riparian right to clean water as a natural resource, is that the pecuniary losses suffered by those who make direct use of the resource are particularly foreseeable because they are so closely linked, through the resource, to the defendants' behavior.

Particular knowledge of the economic consequences has sufficed to establish duty and proximate cause in contexts other than those already considered. . . .

These exceptions expose the hopeless artificiality of the *per se* rule against recovery for purely economic losses. When the plaintiffs are reasonably foreseeable, the injury is directly and proximately caused by defendant's negligence, and liability can be limited fairly, courts have endeavored to create exceptions to allow recovery. . . .

One thematic motif that may be extrapolated from these decisions to differentiate between those cases in which recovery for economic losses was allowed and denied is that of foreseeability as it relates to both the duty owed and proximate cause. . . .

We hold therefore that a defendant owes a duty of care to take reasonable measures to avoid the risk of causing economic damages, aside from physical injury, to particular plaintiffs or plaintiffs comprising an identifiable class with respect to whom defendant knows or has reason to know are likely to suffer such damages from its conduct. A defendant failing to adhere to this duty of care may be found liable for such economic damages proximately caused by its breach of duty.

We stress that an identifiable class of plaintiffs is not simply a foreseeable class of plaintiffs. For example, members of the general public, or invitees such as sales and service persons at a particular plaintiff's business premises, or persons travelling on a highway near the scene of a negligently-caused accident, such as the one at bar, who are delayed in the conduct of their affairs and suffer varied economic losses, are certainly a foreseeable class of plaintiffs. Yet their presence within the area would be fortuitous, and the particular type of economic injury that could be suffered by such persons would be hopelessly unpredictable and not realistically foreseeable. Thus, the class itself would not be sufficiently ascertainable. An identifiable class of plaintiffs must be particularly foreseeable in terms of the type of persons or entities comprising the class, the certainty or predictability of their presence, the approximate numbers of those in the class, as well as the type of economic expectations disrupted. . . .

In these cases, the courts will be required to draw upon notions of fairness, common sense and morality to fix the line limiting liability as a matter of public policy, rather than an uncritical application of the principle of particular foreseeability. . . .

. . . .

Among the facts that persuade us that a cause of action has been established is the close proximity of the North Terminal and People Express Airlines to the Conrail freight yard; the obvious nature of the plaintiff's operations and particular foreseeability of economic losses resulting from an accident and evacuation; the defendants' actual or constructive knowledge of the volatile properties of ethylene oxide; and the existence of an emergency response plan prepared by some of the defendants (alluded to in the course of oral argument), which apparently called for the nearby area to be evacuated to avoid the risk of harm in case of an explosion. We do not mean to suggest by our recitation of these facts that actual knowledge of the eventual economic losses is necessary to the cause of action; rather, particular foreseeability will suffice. The plaintiff still faces a difficult task in proving damages, particularly lost profits, to the degree of certainty required in other negligence cases. The trial court's examination of these proofs must be exacting to ensure that damages recovered are those reasonably to have been anticipated in view of the defendants' capacity to have foreseen that this particular plaintiff was within the risk created by their negligence. . . .

Accordingly, the judgment of the Appellate Division is modified, and, as modified, affirmed. The case is remanded for proceedings consistent with this opinion.

––––––––––

1. Define economic loss.

2. In *State of Louisiana ex rel. Guste v. M/V Testbank*, 752 F.2d 1019 (5th Cir. 1985), two ships collided, releasing an acidic white haze and forcing the closing of the Mississippi River. Owners of restaurants, vessels delayed upriver, and bait stores were not able to recover damages, such as lost business, because there was no physical damage to their property.

How would New Jersey decide *Testbank*? What is the built-in limit in *People Express*?

3. In *Kinsman II*, when the Buffalo River was closed due to the collision of two ships, the plaintiff had to purchase more grain and use trucks, rather than ships, to transport the grain. His suit for economic loss was rejected:

> On the previous appeal we stated aptly: "somewhere a point will be reached when courts will agree that the link has become too tenuous—that what is claimed to be consequence is only fortuity." . . . We believe that this point has been reached. . . . The instant claims occurred only because the downed bridge made it impossible to move traffic along the river. Under all the circumstances of this case, we hold that the connection between the defendants' negligence and the claimants' damages is too tenuous and remote to permit recovery. "The law does not spread its protection so far." Holmes, J., in *Robins Dry Dock, supra*, 275 U.S. at 309, 48 S. Ct. at 135.
>
> . . . As we have previously noted, . . . we return to Judge Andrews' frequently quoted statement in *Palsgraf* . . . (dissenting opinion): "It is all a question of expediency . . . of fair judgment, always keeping in mind the fact

that we endeavor to make a rule in each case that will be practical and in keeping with the general understanding of mankind."

Kinsman Transit Co. v. Buffalo, 388 F.2d 821 (2d Cir. 1968). Were the plaintiffs foreseeable under the *Palsgraf* test? Does *People Express* alter the guideline presented in Andrews' dissent in *Palsgraf*?

4. For articles on economic loss, see Bishop, *Economic Loss in Tort*, 2 Oxford J. Legal Stud. 1 (1982); Rizzo, *The Economic Loss Problem: A Comment on Bishop*, 2 Oxford J. Legal Stud. 197 (1982).

D. Duty Versus Proximate Cause: Green's Theory

1. Eliminate Proximate Cause

Over sixty years ago, Dean Leon Green suggested that proximate cause should be deleted from tort analysis. He reasoned that it created problems because proximate cause was often confused with cause-in-fact. He also wanted to make clear the limited but foundational role of cause-in-fact and to clarify the role of the judge in controlling the jury. He therefore advocated the elimination of proximate cause and the adoption of the duty concept.

2. Green's Duty Analysis

At the center of Green's duty theory is the question: Does the defendant's duty extend to this particular plaintiff for this particular injury? Green makes clear that negligence analysis cannot be done with a broad brush, but rather each plaintiff and each injury must be evaluated separately.

Dean Green also made clear that the concept of foreseeability has only a vestigial role in duty theory. He argued that foreseeability under proximate cause analysis carries too much baggage and that any careful reader should wonder whether foreseeability can carry the weight that is placed upon it by the courts. Its cure-all function is too broad. When the jury is given the negligence charge, under Green's theory, they are asked whether the defendant, as a reasonable person, could have foreseen this injury. That is all that remains of the foreseeability concept.

3. Three Questions

In applying the duty theory, Dean Green argued that before the duty question is considered, two other questions should be asked. First, is there evidence of cause-in-fact? In some cases where causation is discussed, what is at issue is cause-in-fact, not proximate cause or duty. If there is no evidence of cause-in-fact, the case is over. The second question that should be asked is: Is there evidence of negligence? In some of the proximate cause cases, the real question is was there any evidence of negligence. That is, the court is not actually talking about scope of liability but rather whether the defendant was at fault. If there is no such evidence, the case is over. If the cause-in-fact and the negligence question are both answered in the plaintiff's favor, the third question may be reached: Does the defendant's duty extend to this particular plaintiff for this particular injury?

4. Relevant Factors

In answering the question whether the defendant's duty extends to this particular plaintiff for this particular injury, the court must consider several factors such as the following: economics, the administrative role of the courts, loss shifting, who can best obtain insurance, the impact upon society of placing a duty on the defendant, precedent, justice, and prevention.

The administrative factor refers to the task of a court in deciding to take a case and the ability of the court to deal with the problems presented by the case. We see administrative problems most clearly in negligent infliction of mental distress cases. The court is there concerned about a flood of suits and where to draw the line in the next case. Faked claims are also a problem.

Loss shifting asks whether this loss should be placed on the actor rather than the victim. With the insurance factor, Dean Green asks the court to consider who among the parties is best able to insure. With the impact factor, he asks what might be the effect on society of making this defendant bear this loss.

With precedent, Dean Green asks the court to consider whether the question has been decided in a previous case. If it has, it should, by all means, be followed in this case, but if it has not, it is the responsibility of the court to weigh the various factors.

It must be noted, however, that Dean Green was loath to list the factors to be considered by the court and felt strongly that each case should be decided on its own merits. Indeed, he believed it was better for the court to decide the case and say nothing, rather than to mislead by using vague terms such as causation and foreseeability.

5. Conclusion

Why should we go through the duty analysis? The answer Dean Green gives is that it fosters clear analysis. It makes more sense to talk about social policy under duty, rather than cloud analysis with the term causation. Proximate cause (foreseeability) misleads attorneys, judges, and juries. Duty makes clear the role of the judge in guiding the jury and the demarcation between cause-in-fact and social policy.

While Dean Green's theory has struggled and not been widely accepted in ordinary negligence cases, it has leapfrogged to the forefront in products liability cases. The dominant issue in products liability cases is whether the product is defective. The most popular approach for answering this question is risk-utility analysis. Risk-utility analysis rests on a weighing of all relevant factors. To that extent, Dean Green's theory points us in the right direction for answering challenging products liability defect questions: weigh the relevant factors. On the other hand, foreseeability analysis is almost useless in products liability cases, because the injury that resulted is often foreseeable. For example, when an automobile manufacturer builds a car, he or she knows what will happen when the car rolls over at twenty, thirty or forty miles per hour. He or she knows precisely what forces will cause the roof to collapse. It is not helpful to ask if it was foreseeable that the roof would collapse. It is helpful, however, to ask what factors the manufacturer considered in designing the roof and if these were the appropriate factors.

For a further discussion of Dean Green's duty theory, see the following articles: Leon Green, *Proximate Cause in Texas Negligence Law*, 28 Tex. L. Rev. (I) 471, (II) 621, (III) 755 (1950); Leon Green, *The Duty Problem in Negligence Cases*, 29 Colum. L. Rev. 255 (1929); Leon Green, *The Duty Problem in Negligence Cases*, 28 Colum. L. Rev. 1014, 1034 (1928); Frank Vandall, *Duty: The Continuing Vitality of Dean Green's Theory*, 15 Quinnipiac L. Rev. 343 (1995).

Chapter 8

Multiple Defendants: Joint and Several Liability

Many cases involve multiple defendants. This reality creates numerous problems that can overlap into other aspects of tort law such as causation and comparative negligence. They can also involve other areas of law such as contracts (for example, the law of settlements and releases).

Many jurisdictions deal with allocating liability among multiple defendants by statute. It is therefore crucial to check the statutes when dealing with such matters. As the cases in this chapter illustrate, however, the statute may not answer all the questions about allocating liability. This area of the law is extraordinarily complex and arcane, as the more recent opinions included here make clear.

For reasons mired in the past, "joint and several liability" means that all the defendants are liable for all the damages (although the plaintiff collects only one full award, of course). "Several liability" refers to some division of liability between the defendants, and no one defendant will be liable for the total amount. Comparative negligence involves allocation of fault between the plaintiff, on the one hand, and the defendant(s), on the other. Joint and several liability deals with allocating damages among the defendants. It also deals, indirectly, with apportionment of financial responsibility in circumstances where one or more of the defendants is judgment-proof. Much of the current litigation about dividing liability centers on dealing with the relationship among all of these concepts. Once the jury has assessed percentages of fault among the defendants, the temptation to allow this assessment to affect what the plaintiff may recover can become irresistible, even though doing so may leave plaintiffs without the full recovery to which they are entitled by the facts.

Problem

Paul and Kathy negligently drive into each other's cars. Kathy's car then bounces into Tom's car. In the crash, Tom's leg is broken, and he suffers $100,000 in damages. Assume that Tom was also negligent, and Paul is 30% at fault, Kathy is 60% at fault, and Tom is 10% at fault. What result if Tom wants to sue both Paul and Kathy, but Kathy lacks insurance and is bankrupt? What result if the applicable jurisdiction has a statute providing: "Each party is liable only to the extent of his or her fault?"

Under the common law, where two or more persons plotted to injure or kill some-one, they could be liable as joint tortfeasors because of the conspiracy, even if only one actually did the deed. The injury or death was viewed as a single act. Over time, this concept was extended to include circumstances where two or more defendants acted "in concert" with one another and their joint action resulted in tortious injury. More recently, joint liability has also been extended to cases where multiple defendants have caused a single indivisible result. Each defendant may be liable for the whole amount (subject to what is known as a "right of contribution" from the other defendants) when there is no practical basis for apportioning the damages.

Bierczynski v. Rogers

Supreme Court of Delaware, 1968
239 A.2d 218

HERRMANN, JUSTICE.

This appeal involves an automobile accident in which the plaintiffs claim that the defendant motorists were racing on the public highway, as the result of which the accident occurred.

The plaintiffs Cecil B. Rogers and Susan D. Rogers brought this action against Robert C. Race and Ronald Bierczynski, ages 18 and 17 respectively, alleging con-current negligences in that they violated various speed statutes and various other stat-utory rules of the road, and in that they failed to keep a proper lookout and failed to keep their vehicles under proper control. The jury, by answer to interrogatories in its special verdict, expressly found that Race and Bierczynski were each negligent and that the negligence of each was a proximate cause of the accident. Substantial ver-dicts were entered in favor of the plaintiffs against both defendants jointly. The defen-dant Bierczynski appeals therefrom. The defendant Race does not appeal; rather, he joins with the plaintiffs in upholding the judgment below.

. . . .

Cecil Rogers testified as follows: He was returning from a Girl Scout trip with his daughter, headed for their home located about three blocks from the scene of the acci-dent. He entered Lore Avenue from Governor Printz Boulevard, thus driving in a westerly direction on Lore Avenue. At a point about 300 feet east of River Road, Rog-ers' car was struck by Race's car which approached him sideways, moving in an easterly direction on the westbound lane. Rogers saw Race's car coming at him; he stopped in the westbound lane; but he was unable to move out of the way because there was a guard rail along that part of the road and no shoulder. Rogers first saw the Race vehicle when it was about 550 feet up Lore Avenue — or about 250 feet west of River Road. At that point, the Race car was being driven easterly on Lore Avenue in the westbound lane, almost along-side the Bierczynski car which was moving east-erly in the eastbound lane. The front bumper of the Race car was opposite the back bumper of the Bierczynski car. Both cars were moving at about 55 or 60 m.p.h. down the hill. Before reaching River Road, Race swerved back into the eastbound lane behind Bierczynski, who was about a car length in front. As it crossed River Road, the Race automobile "bottomed on the road"; and it "careened down against the pavement and gave an impression of an explosion"; dust "flew everywhere" sufficiently to obscure the Race car momentarily from Rogers' view. At that point, the Race and Bierczynski automobiles were only "inches apart." The Race car then emerged from behind the Bierczynski car and careened sideways, at about 70 m.p.h., a distance of about 300 feet to the Rogers car standing in the westbound lane. The left side of the Race car struck the front of the Rogers car. Meanwhile, the Bierczynski car was brought to a stop in the eastbound lane, about 35 feet from the area of impact. The Bierczynski car did not come into contact with the Rogers vehicle.

Bierczynski's contention as to lack of proximate cause is based mainly upon the facts that his automobile remained in the proper lane at all times and was stopped about 35 feet before reaching the area of impact, without coming into contact with the Rogers car. These facts notwithstanding, the foregoing testimony of the plaintiff constituted sufficient evidence of proximate cause, in our opinion, to warrant the submission of that issue to the jury as to both drivers.

A reasonable inference capable of being drawn from the above testimony of Rogers, in the light of the surrounding circumstances, is that Race and Bierczynski were engaged in a speed contest as they came down the hill of Lore Avenue approaching its intersection with River Road. It is unimportant whether it was technically a "race," in the terminology of the defendants who deny that they were "racing." Clearly, the inference of a deliberate and intentional speed competition, as they came down the hill practically side-by-side at twice the legal speed, was permissible from Rogers' testimony; clearly, the inference that Bierczynski maintained his greatly excessive speed deliberately to prevent Race from passing him, was also permissible from Rogers' testimony. We classify both of these courses of conduct as improper racing on the highway. In either of the latter situations, the issue of whether Bierczynski's conduct was a proximate cause of Race's loss of control and collision with Rogers, was a proper issue for the jury.

In many States, automobile racing on a public highway is prohibited by statute, the violation of which is negligence per se. . . . Delaware has no such statute. Nevertheless, speed competition in automobiles on the public highway is negligence in this State, for the reason that a reasonably prudent person would not engage in such conduct. This conclusion is in accord with the general rule, prevailing in other jurisdictions which lack statutes on the subject, that racing motor vehicles on a public highway is negligence. . . .

It is also generally held that all who engage in a race on the highway do so at their peril, and are liable for injury or damage sustained by a third person as a result thereof, regardless of which of the racing cars directly inflicted the injury or damage. The authorities reflect generally accepted rules of causation that all parties engaged in a motor vehicle race on the highway are wrongdoers acting in concert, and that each participant is liable for harm to a third person arising from the tortious conduct of the other, because he has induced and encouraged the tort. . . .

We subscribe to those rules; and hold that, as a general rule, participation in a motor vehicle race on a public highway is an act of concurrent negligence imposing liability on each participant for any injury to a non-participant resulting from the race. If, therefore, Race and Bierczynski were engaged in a speed competition, each was liable for the damages and injuries to the plaintiffs herein, even though Bierczynski was not directly involved in the collision itself. Bierczynski apparently concedes liability if a race had, in fact, been in progress. Clearly there was ample evidence to carry to the jury the issue of a race — and with it, implicit therein, the issue of proximate cause as to Bierczynski.

The foregoing disposes of the appellant's contention that there was no evidence upon which it was proper for plaintiffs' counsel to argue to the jury that the defendants were racing.

. . . .

We find no error as asserted by the appellant. The judgments below are affirmed.

————————

1. In *Biercynski*, the activity of drag racing is a joint one, which essentially means that the parties jointly created the risk. They are thus defined as acting in concert, and both are equally liable for the whole amount of damages, although the plaintiff only recovers once. What if they had just happened to crash simultaneously into the plaintiff while driving negligently on a highway? Does the fact that the defendants were acting intentionally or even illegally play a role? What if two defendants cause a single injury, but only one of them was acting intentionally?

2. What result if during the race, but before the crash, Bierczynski's hubcap had come off and hit a bystander who was there for the purpose of watching the race? Are bystanders who attend an illegal drag race themselves acting negligently?

3. Why did Race not appeal? Why might he favor the imposition of joint and several liability here? Strategic decisions often determine the arguments that a defendant makes, creating many cross-arguments and even cross-suits in cases like this.

4. The first classification of joint tort is acting in concert, which was discussed above. The second classification involves two or more parties who fail in a common duty and cause injury to the plaintiff. An example would be where two defendants have the duty to maintain a party-wall. The wall collapses because they neglected their duty, and it injures the plaintiff. *See Johnson v. Chapman*, 43 W. Va. 639, 28 S.E. 744 (1897); *Schaffer v. Pennsylvania R.R. Co.*, 101 F.2d 369 (7th Cir. 1939) (jointly owned railway tracks).

5. The third classification of joint liability involves multiple defendants and a single indivisible result, which is taken up in the following case.

Ravo v. Rogatnick

Court of Appeals of New York, 1987
514 N.E.2d 1104

ALEXANDER, JUDGE.

In this medical malpractice action, defendant, Dr. Irwin L. Harris, appeals from an order of the Appellate Division unanimously affirming an amended judgment of Supreme Court, entered on a jury verdict, finding him jointly and severally liable with Dr. Sol Rogatnick for injuries negligently inflicted upon plaintiff, Josephine Ravo, and resulting in brain damage that has rendered her severely and permanently retarded. The issue presented is whether joint and several liability was properly imposed upon defendant under the circumstances of this case where, notwithstanding that the defendants neither acted in concert nor concurrently, a single indivisible injury—brain damage—was negligently inflicted. For the reasons that follow, we affirm.

I.

Uncontroverted expert medical evidence established that plaintiff, Josephine Ravo, who at the time of trial was 14 years of age, was severely and permanently retarded as a result of brain damage she suffered at birth. The evidence demonstrated that the child was born an unusually large baby whose mother suffered from gestational diabetes which contributed to difficulties during delivery. The evidence further established that Dr. Rogatnick, the obstetrician who had charge of the ante partum care of Josephine's mother and who delivered Josephine, failed to ascertain pertinent medical information about the mother, incorrectly estimated the size of the infant, and employed improper surgical procedures during the delivery. It was shown that Dr. Harris, the pediatrician under whose care Josephine came following birth, misdiagnosed and improperly treated the infant's condition after birth. Based upon this evidence, the jury concluded that Dr. Rogatnick committed eight separate acts of medical malpractice, and Dr. Harris committed three separate acts of medical malpractice.

Although Dr. Rogatnick's negligence contributed to Josephine's brain damage, the medical testimony demonstrated that Dr. Harris' negligence was also a substantial contributing cause of the injury. No testimony was adduced, however, from which the jury could delineate which aspects of the injury were caused by the respective negligence of the individual doctors. Indeed, plaintiff's expert, Dr. Charash, testified that while the hypoxia and trauma directly attributable to Dr. Rogatnick's negligence were two major villains—being the most common causes of perinatal difficulty—the hyperbilirubinemia and excessively high hematocrit level inadequately addressed by Dr. Harris could not be excluded as having a contributing effect. The expert concluded that neither he nor anybody else could say with certainty which of the factors caused the brain damage. Similarly, Dr. Perrotta, testifying on behalf of plaintiff, opined that she could not tell whether the excessively high hematocrit level contributed "10 percent, 20 percent, or anything like that" to the injury. Nor, as the Appellate Division found, did Dr. Harris adduce any evidence that could support a jury finding that he caused an identifiable percentage of the infant plaintiff's brain damage. Indeed, Dr. Harris' entire defense appears to have been that he was not responsible for the plaintiff's injury to any degree.

The trial court instructed the jury that if they found that both defendants were negligent, and that their separate and independent acts of negligence were direct causes of a single injury to the plaintiff, but that it was not possible to determine what proportion each contributed to the injury, they could find each responsible for the entire injury even though the act of one may not have caused the entire injury, and even though the acts of negligence were not equal in degree. The court further instructed the jury that if they found that both defendants were negligent, they would have "to compare their negligence on the basis of 100 percent." The court also instructed the jury that if they found both defendants responsible for the plaintiff's injury "then you will evaluate their respective faults in contributing to the infant's condition."

These instructions were explanatory of an interrogatory, previously accepted without objection by Dr. Harris, and submitted to the jury, that requested the standard *Dole v. Dow* [*Chem. Co.*, 30 N.Y.2d 143 (1972)] apportionment of fault. . . . Notwithstanding his failure to object to this interrogatory, Dr. Harris raised for the first time, after the jury was charged, an objection to the instructions, contending that he was only "liable for what injury he puts [sic] on top of the injury that exists," and therefore responsible only as a successive and independent tort-feasor. The trial court rejected defendant's contention, and the jury returned a verdict for plaintiff in the total amount of $2,750,000 attributing 80% of the "fault" to Dr. Rogatnick and 20% of the "fault" to Dr. Harris.

In a postverdict motion, Dr. Harris sought an order directing entry of judgment limiting the plaintiff's recovery against him to $450,000 (20% of the $2,250,000 base recovery—the court having set off $500,000 received by plaintiff in settlement of claims against other defendants) based upon his contention that his liability was not joint and several, but rather was independent and successive. This motion was denied. The Appellate Division dismissed Harris' appeal from the order denying the postverdict motion and affirmed the amended judgment entered on the jury's verdict.

II.

When two or more tort-feasors act concurrently or in concert to produce a single injury, they may be held jointly and severally liable. . . . This is so because such concerted wrongdoers are considered "joint tort-feasors" and in legal contemplation, there is a joint enterprise and a mutual agency, such that the act of one is the act of all and liability for all that is done is visited upon each. . . . On the other hand, where multiple tort-feasors "neither act in concert nor contribute concurrently to the same wrong, they are not joint tort-feasors; rather, their wrongs are independent and successive". . . . Under successive and independent liability, of course, the initial tort-feasor may well be liable to the plaintiff for the entire damage proximately resulting from his own wrongful acts, including aggravation of injuries by a successive tort-feasor. . . . The successive tort-feasor, however, is liable only for the separate injury or the aggravation his conduct has caused. . . .

It is sometimes the case that tort-feasors who neither act in concert nor concurrently may nevertheless be considered jointly and severally liable. This may occur in the instance of certain injuries which, because of their nature, are incapable of any reasonable or practicable division or allocation among multiple tort-feasors. . . .

We had occasion to consider such a circumstance in *Slater v. Mersereau* (64 N.Y. 138, *supra*), where premises belonging to the plaintiff were damaged by rainwater as a result of the negligent workmanship by a general contractor and a subcontractor. We held that where two parties by their separate and independent acts of negligence, cause a single, inseparable injury, each party is responsible for the entire injury: "Although they acted independently of each other, they did act at the same time in causing the damages . . . each contributing towards it, and although the act of each, alone and of itself, might not have caused the entire injury, under the circumstances presented, there is no good reason why each should not be liable for the damages caused by the different acts of all. . . . The water with which each of the parties were instrumental in injuring the plaintiffs was one mass and inseparable, and no distinction can be made between the different sources from whence it flowed, so that it can be claimed that each caused a separate and distinct injury for which each one is separately responsible . . . [the] contractor and subcontractors were separately negligent, and although such negligence was not concurrent, yet the negligence of both these parties contributed to produce the damages caused at one and the same time". . . .

Our affirmance in *Hawkes v. Goll* (281 N.Y. 808, *aff'g* 256 App. Div. 940, *supra*) demonstrates that simultaneous conduct is not necessary to a finding of joint and several liability when there is an indivisible injury. In that case, the decedent was struck by the vehicle driven by the defendant Farrell and was thrown across the roadway, where very shortly thereafter he was again struck, this time by the vehicle driven by the defendant Goll, and dragged some 40 to 50 feet along the highway. He was taken to the hospital where he expired within the hour. The Appellate Division stated (256 App. Div. 940): "As the result of his injuries the plaintiff's intestate died within an hour. There could be no evidence upon which the jury could base a finding of the nature of the injuries inflicted by the first car as distinguished from those inflicted by the second car. The case was submitted to the jury upon the theory that if both defendants were negligent they were jointly and severally liable. While the wrongful acts of the two defendants were not precisely concurrent in point of time, the defendants may nevertheless be joint tort feasors where, as here, their several acts of neglect concurred in producing the injury."

. . . .

Similarly, here the jury was unable to determine from the evidence adduced at trial the degree to which the defendants' separate acts of negligence contributed to the brain damage sustained by Josephine at birth. Certainly, a subsequent tort-feasor is not to be held jointly and severally liable for the acts of the initial tort-feasor with whom he is not acting in concert in every case where it is difficult, because of the nature of the injury, to separate the harm done by each tort-feasor from the others (. . . *see generally*, Prosser, *Joint Torts and Several Liability*, 25 Calif. L. Rev. 413). Here, however, the evidence established that plaintiff's brain damage was a single indivisible injury, and defendant failed to submit any evidence upon which the jury could base an apportionment of damage.

Harris argues, however, that since the jury ascribed only 20% of the fault to him, this was in reality an apportionment of damage, demonstrating that the injury was divisible. This argument must fail. Clearly, the court's instruction, and the interrogatory submitted in amplification thereof, called upon the jury to determine the respective responsibility in negligence of the defendants so as to establish a basis for an apportionment between them, by way of contribution, for the total damages awarded to plaintiff. . . .

As we said in *Schauer v. Joyce* (54 N.Y.2d 1, 5): " CPLR 1401, which codified this court's decision in *Dole v. Dow Chem. Co.* (30 N.Y.2d 143), provides that 'two or more persons who are subject to liability for damages for the same personal injury, injury to property or wrongful death, may claim contribution among them whether or not an action has been brought or a judgment has been rendered against the person from whom contribution is sought.' The section 'applies not only to joint tortfeasors, but also to concurrent successive, independent, alternative, and even intentional tortfeasors' (Siegel, New York Practice, § 172, p. 213)." The focus and purpose of the *Dole v. Dow* inquiry, therefore, is not whether, or to what degree, a defendant can be cast in damages to a plaintiff for a third party's negligence, . . . rather, it seeks to determine "whether each defendant owed a duty to plaintiff and whether, by breaching their respective duties, they contributed to plaintiff's ultimate injury" claimed to have been caused by each defendant. . . .

Here, the jury determined that the defendants breached duties owed to Josephine Ravo, and that these breaches contributed to her brain injury. The jury's apportionment of fault, however, does not alter the joint and several liability of defendants for the single indivisible injury. Rather, that aspect of the jury's determination of culpability merely defines the amount of contribution defendants may claim from each other, and does not impinge upon plaintiff's right to collect the entire judgment award from either defendant (CPLR 1402). As we stated in *Graphic Arts Mut. Ins. Co. v. Bakers Mut. Ins. Co.* (45 N.Y.2d 551, 557): "The right under the Dole-Dow doctrine to seek equitable apportionment based on relative culpability is not one intended for the benefit of the injured claimant. It is a right affecting the distributive responsibilities of tort-feasors inter sese. . . . It is elementary that injured claimants may still choose which joint tort-feasors to include as defendants in an action and, regardless of the concurrent negligence of others, recover the whole of their damages from any of the particular tort-feasors sued. . . ." This being so, in light of the evidence establishing the indivisibility of the brain injury and the contributing negligence of Dr. Harris, and of the manner in which the case was tried and submitted to the jury, we conclude that joint and several liability was properly imposed.

Accordingly, the order of the Appellate Division should be affirmed.

Since the development and widespread acceptance of comparative negligence, discussed in Chapter 13, it has become commonplace for juries, in cases where plaintiff's negligence is asserted as a defense, to assign percentages of responsibility to the parties in a tort suit. This development has raised the issue of how those percentages should be considered in terms of apportioning liability, whether similar assignments of responsibility should occur when the plaintiff is not subject to a comparative negligence defense, and how (if at all) those percentages should affect joint and several liability. The following cases take up these issues.

Banks v. Elks Club Pride of Tenneesee

Supreme Court of Tennessee, 2010
301 S.W.3d 214

William C. Koch, Jr., J., delivered the opinion of the court, in which Janice M. Holder, C.J., Cornelia A. Clark, Gary R. Wade, and Sharon G. Lee, JJ., joined.

William C. Koch, Jr., J.

This appeal involves the continuing viability in Tennessee of the common-law principle that imputes liability to an original tortfeasor for enhanced physical harm caused by the normal efforts of third persons to render aid which an injured party reasonably requires. A guest at a private club was injured on the club's premises. The injuries to the guest's back were compounded first by the conduct of her surgeon and second by the actions or inactions of a nursing home where the guest was a patient following her surgery. The guest filed separate lawsuits against the private club and her surgeon in the Circuit Court for Davidson County. After the cases were consolidated, the club and the surgeon moved to amend their answers to assert comparative fault claims against the nursing home. The trial court denied their motions but granted them permission to pursue an interlocutory appeal. After the Court of Appeals declined to consider the interlocutory appeal, the club and the surgeon sought this Court's permission for an interlocutory appeal. We granted their application. We now hold that an original tortfeasor is not jointly and severally liable for the further aggravation of an original injury caused by a subsequent tortfeasor's medically negligent treatment of the injury caused by the original tortfeasor's negligence. Therefore, we have determined that the trial court erred by denying the motions of the club and the surgeon to amend their complaints to assert comparative fault claims against the nursing home.

I.

Alice J. Banks attended a social event at an Elks Lodge in Nashville on March 24, 2006. While she was there, the chair on which she was seated collapsed, causing serious injuries to Ms. Banks's back. Ms. Banks consulted with Dr. Robert H. Boyce, a physician affiliated with Premier Orthopaedics and Sports Medicine, P.C. ("Premier Orthopaedics"), who recommended lumbar surgery at the L3-L4 and L4-L5 levels. The procedure consisted of a decompression laminectomy and fusion. Ms. Banks agreed to have the procedure performed.

On May 16, 2006, Ms. Banks underwent surgery at Centennial Medical Center. While Dr. Boyce's operative report indicates that he performed a lumbar laminectomy and fusion at the L3-L4 and L4-L5 vertebrae as intended, he actually performed the surgery upon the L2-L3 and L3-L4 vertebrae. It was only after the surgery was completed that Dr. Boyce realized he mistakenly performed the surgery at the L2-L3, rather than the L4-L5 vertebrae. As a result, Ms. Banks was required to undergo a second surgery on May 17, 2006.

Following Ms. Banks's surgeries, she was transferred to Cumberland Manor Nursing Home ("Cumberland Manor") for further recuperation and rehabilitation. While a patient at Cumberland Manor, Ms. Banks developed a serious staphylococcus infection that required additional surgeries and extensive care and treatment.

On March 23, 2007, Ms. Banks filed suit in the Circuit Court for Davidson County against the Elks Club Pride of Tennessee 1102, Pride of Tennessee Lodge of Elks No. 1102 Improved Benevolent, and Elks Lodge 1102 Pride of Tennessee ("Elks Lodge defendants"). She alleged that the negligence of the Elks Lodge defendants had caused her back injuries. The case was assigned to the Sixth Circuit Court.

On May 10, 2007, Ms. Banks filed a separate lawsuit against Dr. Boyce and Premier Orthopaedics ("Dr. Boyce") in the Circuit Court for Davidson County. She asserted claims of medical negligence and medical battery based on Dr. Boyce's performance of an unauthorized procedure. [The two cases were eventually consolidated]. . . .

On May 30, 2008, the Elks Lodge defendants filed a Tenn. R. Civ. P. 15.01 motion to amend their answer to assert a comparative fault defense against Cumberland Manor. They alleged that they had learned during the discovery process that Cumberland Manor's improper care and treatment had contributed to Ms. Banks's staphylococcus infection. They also asserted that this infection had aggravated Ms. Banks's injuries and damages and that Ms. Banks was seeking to hold them responsible for these additional injuries and damages. The Elks Lodge defendants also reserved the right "to amend their comparative fault defense to allege fault of others throughout the course of discovery and trial." On June 2, 2008, Dr. Boyce also sought to amend his answer to assert a comparative fault defense against Cumberland Manor, adopting the same language set forth in the Elks Lodge defendants' motion.

Ms. Banks opposed the defendants' motions to amend their answers to assert a comparative fault defense against Cumberland Manor. She argued that the defendants' efforts to assert a comparative fault defense "against a subsequent healthcare provider for alleged negligent medical treatment that was brought on by the injuries negligently caused by the named defendants is inappropriate." In their trial court briefs, the parties argued vigorously over whether what they referred to as the "original tortfeasor rule" or the "original tortfeasor doctrine"[3] survived this Court's decision in *McIntyre v. Balentine*, 833 S.W.2d 52 (Tenn. 1992) and its progeny.

On August 15, 2008, the trial court entered an order denying the Elks Lodge defendants' and Dr. Boyce's motion to amend their complaints to assert comparative fault claims against Cumberland Manor. The court reasoned that "the holdings in the cases of *Transports, Inc. v. Perry*, 220 Tenn. 57, 414 S.W.2d 1 (1967) and *Atkinson v. Hemphill*, 1994 Tenn. App. LEXIS 480 (Tenn.Ct.App.1994), [are] still good law and the proposed amendments would be futile and therefore must be denied under Rule 15, Tennessee Rules of Civil Procedure." [The defendants pursued an interlocutory appeal.] . . .

. . . We granted the application [for permission to appeal] on December 15, 2008. Following our decision to grant permission to appeal, Ms. Banks, seeking to avoid potentially adverse statute of limitations impact should this Court determine that the trial court erred in not permitting the Elks Lodge defendants or Dr. Boyce to amend their answers to assert an affirmative defense against Cumberland Manor, amended her complaint to name Cumberland Manor as a tortfeasor.

II.

Eighteen years ago, this Court produced a sea-change in Tennessee's tort law by replacing the common-law concept of contributory negligence with the concept of contributory fault. *McIntyre v. Balentine*, 833 S.W.2d at 56. We expressly recognized at that time that many of the issues arising from the transition to a comparative fault regime would be addressed in later cases. *McIntyre v. Balentine*, 833 S.W.2d at 57. Accordingly, it has come to pass that this Court has been presented with many opportunities since 1992 to revisit, refine, and clarify many of the central tenets of *McIntyre v. Balentine* and to address their impact on Tennessee tort law.

One of the central tenets of *McIntyre v. Balentine* is that the doctrine of joint and several liability was "obsolete" because it was inconsistent with the doctrine of comparative fault. *McIntyre v. Balentine*, 833 S.W.2d at 58. We explained that the doctrine of comparative fault, which would more closely link liability and fault, could

---

3. The terms "original tortfeasor rule" and "original tortfeasor doctrine" are actually shorthand references to a concatenation of two common-law principles. The first principle is that "if one is injured by the negligence of another, and these injuries are aggravated by medical treatment (either prudent or negligent), the negligence of the wrongdoer causing the original injury is regarded as the proximate cause of the damage subsequently flowing from the medical treatment." *Transports, Inc. v. Perry*, 220 Tenn. 57, 64–65, 414 S.W.2d 1, 4–5 (1967). The second principle is that the original tortfeasor is jointly and severally liable for the full extent of the injuries caused by the original tortfeasor and the successive tortfeasor. J.D. Lee & Barry A. Lindahl, *Modern Tort Law: Liability and Litigation* § 6:3 (2d ed. 2009) (hereinafter "Lee & Lindahl").

not be reconciled with joint and several liability which could "fortuitously impose a degree of liability that is out of all proportion to fault." *McIntyre v. Balentine*, 833 S.W.2d at 58.

The announcement that the doctrine of joint and several liability was obsolete, while later characterized as dictum, was not met with universal acceptance. Mr. McIntyre and one of the parties who filed an amicus curiae brief requested a rehearing to address "the advisability of retaining joint and several liability in certain limited circumstances." This Court declined to grant the petition for rehearing, stating that "such further guidance should await an appropriate controversy." *McIntyre v. Balentine*, 833 S.W.2d at 60.

Thus, the *McIntyre v. Balentine* decision left behind some ambiguity regarding the continuing viability of any application of the doctrine of joint and several liability. On one hand, the Court had declared the doctrine "obsolete." On the other hand, the Court had left open the possibility that it might retain the doctrine "in certain limited circumstances" in future cases. As a result, the practicing bar set out to create opportunities for the Court to decide in what circumstances, if any, the doctrine of joint and several liability could rise from the ashes of obsolescence.

In the first comparative fault cases considered by the Court, we reaffirmed that our decision in *McIntyre v. Balentine* "did abolish the doctrine of joint and several liability to the extent that it allows a plaintiff to sue and obtain a full recovery against any one or more of several parties against whom liability could be established." *Bervoets v. Harde Ralls Pontiac-Olds, Inc.*, 891 S.W.2d 905, 907 (Tenn. 1994). The following year, we repeated that "one of the corollaries to the adoption of comparative fault . . . was the abolition of the doctrine of joint and several liability," and we "confirm[ed] that the doctrine of joint and several liability was rendered obsolete by our decision in *McIntyre v. Balentine*." *Volz v. Ledes*, 895 S.W.2d at 680. We made the same point in 1995. *Whitehead v. Toyota Motor Corp.*, 897 S.W.2d 684, 686 (Tenn. 1995).

Thus, during the three years immediately following *McIntyre v. Balentine*, the Court exhibited little inclination to return the doctrine of joint and several liability, in any of its common-law applications, to useful service. The tide, however, began to turn in 1996. In the face of the broad obsolescence language in *McIntyre v. Balentine*, *Bervoets v. Harde Ralls Pontiac-Olds, Inc.*, *Volz v. Ledes*, and *Whitehead v. Toyota Motor Corp.*, the Court announced that it had "not . . . disapproved of the doctrine of joint and several liability *in a general sense* . . . it [had] disapproved joint and several liability *in a particular sense*, that is, where the defendants were charged with separate, independent acts of negligence." *Owens v. Truckstops of Am.*, 915 S.W.2d 420, 431 n. 13 (Tenn. 1996).

This change in direction prompted the author of *McIntyre v. Balentine* to point out in dissent that the Court was "resurrecting joint and several liability." *Owens v. Truckstops of Am., Inc.*, 915 S.W.2d at 437 (Drowota, J., dissenting in part). In response, the Court declared that "[j]oint and several liability need not be 'resurrected' . . . because it has continued to be an integral part of the law, except where specifically abrogated." *Owens v. Truckstops of Am.*, 915 S.W.2d at 431 n. 13. The Court then recalibrated the extent of the obsolescence of the doctrine of joint and several liability to circumstances "where the separate, independent negligent acts of more than one tortfeasor combine to cause a single, indivisible injury." *Owens v. Truckstops of Am.*, 915 S.W.2d at 430. In this circumstance, "each tortfeasor will be liable only for that proportion of the damages attributable to its fault. As to those tortfeasors, liability is not joint and several but several only, even though two or more tortfeasors are joined in the same action." *Owens v. Truckstops of Am.*, 915 S.W.2d at 430.

During the past fourteen years, this Court has reaffirmed its holding that the doctrine of joint and several liability, as it existed prior to 1992, is obsolete. *Ali v. Fisher*, 145 S.W.3d 557, 561 (Tenn. 2004); *Carroll v. Whitney*, 29 S.W.3d 14, 16 (Tenn. 2000); *Sherer v. Linginfelter*, 29 S.W.3d 451, 455 (Tenn. 2000). At the same time, however, we have determined that the doctrine remains viable in several well-defined circumstances. We approved joint and several liability for defendants in the chain of distribution of a product in a products liability action. *Owens v. Truckstops of Am.*, 915 S.W.2d at 433. We determined that the doctrine of joint and several liability was not obsolete in cases involving injury caused by multiple defendants who have breached a common duty. *Resolution Trust Corp. v. Block*, 924 S.W.2d 354, 355, 357 (Tenn. 1996). We have likewise approved the application of the doctrine in cases wherein the plaintiff's injury was caused by the concerted actions of the defendants. *Gen. Elec. Co. v. Process Control Co.*, 969 S.W.2d 914, 916 (Tenn. 1998).

To the extent that the doctrine of vicarious liability can be considered a species of joint and several liability, we have held that the adoption of comparative fault in *McIntyre v. Balentine* did not undermine the continuing viability of various vicarious liability doctrines, including the family purpose doctrine, *Camper v. Minor*, 915 S.W.2d 437, 447–48 (Tenn. 1996), "respondeat superior, or similar circumstance where liability is vicarious due to an agency-type relationship between the active, or actual wrongdoer and the one who is vicariously responsible." *Browder v. Morris*, 975 S.W.2d 308, 311–12 (Tenn. 1998). Finally, we determined that tortfeasors who have a duty to protect others from the foreseeable intentional acts of third persons are jointly and severally liable with the third person for the injuries caused by the third person's intentional acts. *Limbaugh v. Coffee Med. Ctr.*, 59 S.W.3d 73, 87 (Tenn. 2001); *White v. Lawrence*, 975 S.W.2d 525, 531 (Tenn. 1998); *Turner v. Jordan*, 957 S.W.2d 815, 823 (Tenn. 1997).

Ever since we handed down our decision in *McIntyre v. Balentine*, this Court's goal has been to assure that Tennessee's comparative fault regime strikes the proper balance between the plaintiff's interest in being made whole with the defendant's interest in paying only those damages for which the defendant is responsible. *Brown v. Wal-Mart Discount Cities*, 12 S.W.3d 785, 787 (Tenn. 2000). We have found this balance in proceedings that link liability to fault. *Biscan v. Brown*, 160 S.W.3d 462, 474 (Tenn. 2005); *Ali v. Fisher*, 145 S.W.3d at 563–64; *Carroll v. Whitney*, 29 S.W.3d at 16–17, 21. Thus, we have embraced an approach in which a tortfeasor may seek to reduce its proportional share of the damages by successfully asserting as an affirmative defense that a portion of the fault for the plaintiff's damages should be allocated to another tortfeasor.

Throughout this period, we have repeatedly emphasized four core principles of the comparative fault regime that we ushered in when we decided *McIntyre v. Balentine*. These principles are: (1) that when "the separate, independent negligent acts of more than one tortfeasor combine to cause a single, indivisible injury, all tortfeasors must be joined in the same action, unless joinder is specifically prohibited by law"; (2) that when "the separate, independent negligent acts of more than one tortfeasor combine to cause a single, indivisible injury, each tortfeasor will be liable only for that proportion of the damages attributed to its fault"; (3) that the goal of linking liability with fault is not furthered by a rule that allows a defendant's liability to be determined by the happenstance of the financial wherewithal of the other defendants; and (4) that the purpose of the comparative fault regime is to prevent fortuitously imposing a degree of liability that is out of all proportion to fault.

III.

This Court has not addressed the continuing viability of the original tortfeasor rule since deciding *McIntyre v. Balentine* in 1992. Despite the Court of Appeals's belief to the contrary, we do not view *McIntyre v. Balentine* as being incompatible with the common-law rule permitting a tortfeasor to be found liable for subsequent negligent conduct of third parties that is a foreseeable result of the original tortfeasor's negligence. Even though our decision in *McIntyre v. Balentine* altered the common-law rules for determining the apportionment of the liability among multiple tortfeasors, it did not alter the common-law rules for determining when tortfeasors are liable for the harm they cause.

A.

McIntyre v. Balentine did not require this Court to determine the role that the original tortfeasor rule would play following the advent of comparative fault. During the intervening years, the Court of Appeals has decided on three occasions that the original tortfeasor rule—embracing both the liability of the original tortfeasor for subsequent negligent acts and the concept of joint and several liability—was not affected by our decision in *McIntyre v. Balentine*.

In the first case presented to the Court of Appeals, the court observed that "to allow a tortfeasor to reduce his damages by alleging the subsequent negligence of a medical provider would for all practical purposes abolish the common law rule." *Atkinson v. Hemphill*, No. 01A01-9311-CV-00509, 1994 Tenn. App. LEXIS 480, at *2 (Tenn.Ct.App. Aug.24, 1994) (No Tenn. R.App. P. 11 application filed). Believing that the abolition of the common-law original tortfeasor rule would "penalize injured parties in several inequitable ways," the court concluded, "[w]e do not believe that the Supreme Court intended this result." *Atkinson v. Hemphill*, 1994 Tenn. App. LEXIS 480, at *2. [The other two decisions followed *Atkinson*.] . . .

We have concluded that the Court of Appeals analyses in the three cases it considered failed to differentiate between the two principles embodied in the original tortfeasor rule — the original tortfeasor's liability for subsequent negligent acts of third parties and the original tortfeasor's joint and several liability with the subsequent negligent actors. . . .

B.

The principles governing liability for successive injuries are settled. They recognize that there are circumstances in which an earlier tortfeasor may be held liable not only for the injury caused by its own negligent conduct but also for later injury caused by the negligent conduct of another tortfeasor. Restatement (Second) of Torts § 433A, cmt. c (1965); *Prosser and Keeton* § 52, at 352. Liability in these circumstances arises when the subsequent negligent conduct is a foreseeable or natural consequence of the original tortfeasor's negligence. 2 Jacob A. Stein, *Stein on Personal Injury Damages* § 11:7 (3d ed. 2009) (hereinafter "Stein"); *see also McClenahan v. Cooley*, 806 S.W.2d 767, 775 (Tenn. 1991) (noting that "[a]n intervening act, which is a normal response created by negligence, is not a superseding, intervening cause so as to relieve the original wrongdoer of liability, provided the intervening act could have reasonably been foreseen and the conduct was a substantial factor in bringing about the harm").

Negligence in subsequent medical treatment of a tortiously caused injury is the most common invocation of this rule. Lee & Lindahl, at § 6:3; *Prosser and Keeton* § 52, at 352; 2 Stein, at § 11:7. The first two Restatements of Torts recognized this principle. Restatement (Second) of Torts § 457, at 496; Restatement of Torts § 457, at 1214 (1934). It has also been carried forward in the Proposed Final Draft of the Restatement (Third) of Torts: Liability for Personal Injury in the following form:

> An actor whose tortious conduct is a factual cause of physical harm to another is subject to liability for any enhanced harm the other suffers due to the efforts of third persons to render aid reasonably required by the other's injury, so long as the harm arises from a risk that inheres in the effort to render aid.

Restatement (Third) of Torts: Liability for Physical Harm § 35, at 693 (Proposed Final Draft No. 12005) ("Restatement (Third) of Torts: Liability for Physical Harm").

Tennessee's courts have recognized and applied this principle for over one hundred years. This Court first alluded to it in *Arkansas River Packet Co. v. Hobbs*, 105 Tenn. 29, 44–46, 58 S.W. 278, 282 (1900). In 1931, we invoked it as an alternate basis for preventing an injured employee from filing a medical malpractice suit against an employer-provided physician after the employee obtained a judgment against the employer. *Revell v. McCaughan*, 162 Tenn. 532, 538, 39 S.W.2d 269, 271 (1931). In 1967, characterizing the principle as a "well settled principle of law," we employed it for the first time to decide a dispute that did not arise out of a workplace injury. *Transports, Inc. v. Perry*, 220 Tenn. at 64–65, 414 S.W.2d at 4–5. Ten years later in another case involving a workplace injury, we noted that this now well settled principle "applies to the general field of tort law." *McAlister v. Methodist Hosp.*, 550 S.W.2d 240, 242 (Tenn. 1977).

C.

McIntyre v. Balentine involved a straightforward intersection crash involving two intoxicated drivers. It did not raise an issue of liability for successive injuries, and thus, this Court had no occasion to determine how the new comparative fault regime would mesh with the principle that, in proper circumstances, an earlier tortfeasor could be liable for the later negligent acts of another tortfeasor. To understand the effect of *McIntyre v. Balentine* on the original tortfeasor rule, the two principles in that rule—the original tortfeasor's liability for subsequent negligent acts of third parties and the original tortfeasor's joint and several liability with the subsequent negligent actors—must be unraveled and considered separately.

Today, we state unequivocally that our decision regarding joint and several liability in *McIntyre v. Balentine* did not alter Tennessee's common-law rules with regard to liability of tortfeasors for injuries caused by subsequent medical treatment for the injuries they cause. That rule is a rule that determines "when defendants are liable for the harm they caused." Restatement (Third) of Torts: Liability for Physical Injury § 35, cmt. d, at 696–97. Thus, the rule in Tennessee is now, as it was before *McIntyre v. Balentine* was decided, that an actor whose tortious conduct causes physical harm to another is liable for any enhanced harm the other suffers due to the efforts of third persons to render aid reasonably required by the other's injury, as long as the enhanced harm arises from a risk that inheres in the effort to render aid. *See* Restatement (Third) of Torts: Liability for Physical Injury § 35, at 693.

However, at the same time, we again reaffirm our earlier decisions holding that following *McIntyre v. Balentine*, the doctrine of joint and several liability no longer applies to circumstances in which separate, independent negligent acts of more than one tortfeasor combine to cause a single, indivisible injury. *Sherer v. Linginfelter*, 29 S.W.3d at 455; *Samuelson v. McMurtry*, 962 S.W.2d at 476; *Owens v. Truckstops of Am., Inc.*, 915 S.W.2d at 430. This decision is not inconsistent with our decision to retain the rule imposing liability on tortfeasors for subsequent negligent medical care for the injuries caused by the original tortfeasor. As the drafters of the proposed Restatement (Third) of Torts: Liability for Physical Injury have explained:

> Nor does modification of joint and several liability require or imply any change in the rule contained in . . . Section [35]. Modern adoption of pure several liability limits the liability of each defendant liable for the same harm to that defendant's comparative share of the harm. See Restatement Third, Torts: Apportionment of Liability § 11.[12] Several liability, however, does not

---

12. Restatement (Third) of Torts: Apportionment of Liability § 11 (2000) provides: "When, under applicable law, a person is severally liable to an injured person for an indivisible injury, the injured person may recover only the severally liable person's comparative-responsibility share of the injured person's damages."

provide rules about when defendants are liable for harm that they caused. When two or more defendants are liable for the enhanced harm suffered by a plaintiff, as may occur under this Section, and the governing law imposes several liability, each of the defendants is held liable for the amount of damages reflecting the enhanced harm discounted by the comparative share responsibility assigned by the factfinder to that defendant.

Restatement (Third) of Torts: Liability for Physical Harm § 35, cmt. d., at 697.

The Court of Appeals in *Atkinson v. Hemphill* overstated the effect of *McIntyre v. Balentine* when it observed that applying the decision in circumstances such as this one would "penalize injured parties in several inequitable ways." *Atkinson v. Hemphill*, 1994 Tenn. App. LEXIS 480, at *3. To the contrary, as observed by the American Law Institute, "[c]omparative responsibility provides a different and easier method for apportioning liability among severally liable parties." Restatement (Third) of Torts: Apportionment of Liability § 11, at cmt. b., at 109. It spares injured plaintiffs, as well as the courts and other parties, the time and expense of multiple trials. As we noted over ten years ago, Tennessee's comparative fault regime "retains the efficiency of joint liability and the fairness of comparative fault." *Samuelson v. McMurtry*, 962 S.W.2d at 476.

Most of the states that have adopted the principles of comparative fault or comparative responsibility have done so by statute rather than by judicial decision. The substance of these statutes differs because states have balanced the rights and interests of the parties in different ways. Accordingly, decisions from other state courts construing their own comparative fault statute provide only limited guidance to us. However, we note that a significant number of state courts that have addressed the same question we address in this case have, like this Court, concluded that comparative fault does not prevent the continuing imposition of liability on an original tortfeasor for subsequent negligent medical care for the injuries caused by the original tortfeasor.

D.

Finally, Ms. Banks and the Tennessee Association for Justice assert that public policy dictates retaining joint and several liability in circumstances where an injured person suffers enhanced physical harm due to the efforts of third persons to render aid to the injured person for injuries caused by the defendant's negligence. They assert that joint and several liability is appropriate because (1) the original defendant is the proximate cause of the entire injury and (2) doing away with joint and several liability will require injured persons to make difficult choices with regard to filing suit against their treating physicians.

The proximate cause argument overlooks the fact that in cases of this sort, the original tortfeasor's conduct is not the sole proximate cause of the plaintiff's indivisible injury. To the contrary, the independent tortious conduct of the original tortfeasor and one or more other parties are both proximate causes of the injury. The tortfeasors are not acting in concert, have not breached common duty, and do not have a relationship triggering the application of vicarious liability. Therefore, this circumstance is governed by our consistent holding that joint and several liability is no longer applicable in circumstances "where the separate, independent negligent acts of more than one tortfeasor combine to cause a single, indivisible injury." *Sherer v. Linginfelter*, 29 S.W.3d at 455. As we noted more than one century ago, where "there is no intent that the combined acts of all shall culminate in the injury resulting therefrom, . . . it is just that each should only be held liable so far as his acts contribute to the injury." *Swain v. Tenn. Copper Co.*, 111 Tenn. 430, 439, 78 S.W. 93, 94 (1903).

Ms. Banks and the Tennessee Association for Justice also insist that not applying joint and several liability in circumstances like the one involved in this case will place plaintiffs in the difficult position of being forced to sue their treating physicians and, thereby, adding the complexity of a medical negligence claim to an otherwise straightforward ordinary negligence case. The force of this argument is somewhat undermined by the fact that Ms. Banks is not being drawn into reluctantly suing her treating physician because she has already sued Dr. Boyce. In any event, we have concluded that these concerns are overstated.

When a defendant tortfeasor files an answer asserting the affirmative defense[13] that a nonparty healthcare provider is at fault for the plaintiff's injuries, the plaintiff has two options. First, it can decide not to name the healthcare provider as a defendant under Tenn.Code Ann. §20-1-119(a) (2009) and run the risk of a diminished recovery if the defendant succeeds in convincing the trier of fact that the nonparty healthcare provider is partially or completely at fault. Second, the plaintiff can amend its complaint in accordance with Tenn.Code Ann. §20-1-119(a) and thereby preserve its opportunity for an undiminished recovery.

When a plaintiff elects to amend its complaint to name as a defendant a healthcare provider whom the original defendant identified as liable for the plaintiff's injury, the burden of proof regarding the healthcare provider's negligence does not shift entirely to the plaintiff. It remains with the original defendant who asserted the affirmative defense of comparative fault. Thus, the plaintiff is not required to shoulder the difficulty and expense of proving medical negligence unless, for some reason, it chooses to do so, just as Ms. Banks has already done in this case. That burden remains with the defendant who asserted the affirmative defense of comparative fault in the first place.[14]

---

13. One of the affirmative defenses included in Tenn. R. Civ. P. 8.03 is "comparative fault (including the identity or description of the other alleged tortfeasors)."

14. Accordingly, if a plaintiff amends its complaint to add a new defendant identified by the original defendant as contributing to the plaintiff's indivisible injuries, trial courts would not act on the new defendant's motion for a directed verdict until the close of all the proof in order to permit the original defendant to present its evidence regarding the new defendant's fault. A directed verdict at the close of the plaintiff's proof would be appropriate only when the original defendant states that it lacks sufficient evidence to send the issue of the new defendant's fault to the jury. If the

Leaving the burden of proof with the defendant asserting the comparative fault defense does not prejudice plaintiffs who elect to amend their complaint to name a healthcare provider as a defendant after the original defendant has asserted that the healthcare provider is comparatively at fault. If the original defendant is unable to prove that the healthcare provider is liable, the plaintiff may still obtain a complete recovery from the original defendant, just as it originally set out to do. If, however, the original defendant is successful in proving that the healthcare provider is liable, then the plaintiff may obtain a complete recovery apportioned between the original defendant and the healthcare provider based on their fault.

Plaintiffs are not required to amend their complaints to add as defendants third parties whom a defendant identifies as a contributing tortfeasor. That decision remains entirely in their control. Amending a complaint to add as a defendant a third-party tortfeasor identified by the original defendant also does not force the plaintiff to try a case it was not prepared to try. Therefore, amending a complaint pursuant to Tenn.Code Ann. § 20-1-119(a) to name as a defendant a third party named by a defendant as a contributing tortfeasor is neither burdensome nor costly.

IV.

In addition to their argument that they should have been permitted to assert a comparative fault defense against Cumberland Manor, the Elks Lodge defendants assert that the original tortfeasor principle is inconsistent with this Court's opinion in *Mercer v. Vanderbilt University, Inc.*, 134 S.W.3d 121 (Tenn. 2004). They argue that *Mercer v. Vanderbilt University, Inc.* stands for the proposition that a "negligent actor should not be held responsible for the subsequent negligence of a healthcare provider under Tennessee's law of comparative fault." The Elks Lodge defendants have placed more weight on the *Mercer* opinion than it can bear.

The principles that dictated the result in *Mercer v. Vanderbilt University, Inc.* do not apply to cases like this one for two reasons. First, unlike *Mercer* where we declined to extend comparative fault to patients who sue their physicians for negligence because doing so would prevent any recovery for injured patients who were found to be more than fifty percent at fault, applying comparative fault in this case will not prevent an injured plaintiff from recovering. *See Mercer v. Vanderbilt Univ., Inc.*, 134 S.W.3d at 129–30. It will simply enable the trier of fact to apportion the fault between the defendants whose conduct caused or contributed to the plaintiff's injuries.

Second, holding that original tortfeasors will not be liable for the enhanced injuries caused from the efforts of physicians or other healthcare providers to render aid to an injured plaintiff would be contrary to the basic tenets of Tennessee tort law, more than one century of Tennessee common-law precedents, and the general principles of liability reflected in the Restatement of Torts. Negligence is conduct that violates a person's obligation to exercise reasonable care to avoid engaging in behavior that creates

---

new defendant's motion for directed verdict is granted, the jury cannot be requested to allocate any portion of the fault to the now-dismissed defendant.

an unreasonable danger to others. *Satterfield v. Breeding Insulation Co.*, 266 S.W.3d 347, 363 (Tenn. 2008). Persons who are negligent are liable for the natural and probable consequences of their conduct, *Doe v. Linder Constr. Co.*, 845 S.W.2d 173, 181 (Tenn. 1992), as long as their conduct was a substantial factor in bringing about the plaintiff's injury, the injury was reasonably foreseeable, and there is no statute or policy relieving them of liability. *Naifeh v. Valley Forge Life Ins. Co.*, 204 S.W.3d 758, 771 (Tenn. 2006).

Ever since the advent of comparative fault in 1992, we have emphasized that the doctrine of joint and several liability no longer applies to circumstances in which separate, independent negligent acts of more than one tortfeasor combine to cause a single, indivisible injury. Today, we have explicitly held that the doctrine of joint and several liability does not apply in cases where the injuries caused by the negligence of the original tortfeasor are enhanced by the subsequent negligence of physicians and other healthcare providers. Nothing in *Mercer v. Vanderbilt University, Inc.* dictates a contrary result. Accordingly, we decline the Elks Lodge defendants' invitation to extend our ruling in *Mercer v. Vanderbilt University, Inc.* to entirely eliminate the original tortfeasor rule.

V.

Dr. Boyce has raised four other issues, only one of which merits discussion. He argues that the original tortfeasor principle cannot be applied to him because he "cannot be simultaneously branded the original tortfeasor and a successive tortfeasor." We respectfully disagree. Dr. Boyce can, in fact, be both an original tortfeasor and a successive tortfeasor.

In cases involving successive acts of malpractice, many courts have recognized that the original treating physician may be liable for the injuries caused by the negligence of subsequent physicians for medical treatment undertaken to mitigate the harm caused by the original physician's malpractice.

The specific circumstance in which a physician qualifies both as an "original tortfeasor" and a "successive tortfeasor" was well addressed in *State ex rel. Blond v. Stubbs*, 485 S.W.2d 152 (Mo.Ct.App.1972). The plaintiff was injured as a result of a dangerous condition at a building operated by the Tenth and Main Corporation and was treated by three different physicians. He alleged that each of the physicians had treated him negligently and that their treatment enhanced the injuries for which the Tenth and Main Corporation and the earlier treating physicians were responsible. Applying the original tortfeasor rule, the Missouri Court of Appeals concluded:

> By reason of the operation of the foregoing rule, defendant Tenth and Main Corporation is liable not only for its own alleged negligence, but also for the alleged negligence of all [three] doctors; likewise, [the first in time physician] is liable, not only for his own alleged negligence, but also for that of the two succeeding doctors; likewise, [the second in time physician] is liable for his own alleged negligence and also that of [the third in time physician]. The net result of all this is that the alleged negligence of [the third in time

physician] is a common occurrence for which all four defendants have potential liability.

State ex rel. Blond v. Stubbs, 485 S.W.2d at 154.

The continuing liability under the original tortfeasor rule is not tied to anything magical about being the "original" tortfeasor. It stems instead from being a proximate cause of an aggravated injury resulting from subsequent medical treatment of the negligent injury that one has caused or aggravated. *See Transports, Inc. v. Perry*, 220 Tenn. at 64–65, 414 S.W.2d at 4; Restatement (Third) of Torts: Liability for Physical Harm §35, at 693. We agree with the approach employed by the Missouri Court of Appeals in *State ex rel. Blond v. Stubbs*. Accordingly, we find that Dr. Boyce can, in fact, simultaneously be an original tortfeasor, for purposes of the aggravation that he allegedly caused and a subsequent aggravation resulting from the alleged medical negligence of Cumberland Manor, and a successive tortfeasor, for purposes of the injury allegedly negligently caused by the Elks Lodge and allegedly negligently aggravated by Dr. Boyce.

VI.

We reiterate that the doctrine of joint and several liability no longer applies to circumstances in which separate, independent negligent acts of more than one tortfeasor combine to cause a single, indivisible injury. We hold that an actor whose tortious conduct causes physical harm to another is liable for any enhanced harm the other suffers due to the efforts of third persons to render aid reasonably required by the other's injury, as long as the enhanced harm arises from a risk that inheres in the effort to render aid. In light of our consistent holding that the doctrine of joint and several liability no longer applies to circumstances in which separate, independent negligent acts of more than one tortfeasor combine to cause a single, indivisible injury, it is improper to maintain joint and several liability in cases involving subsequent medical negligence where there is even less cause. We find that the trial court erred by refusing to permit the Elks Lodge defendants and Dr. Boyce to amend their answers to assert a comparative fault defense against Cumberland Manor. [Remanded.]

---

1. What is the relationship (if any) between the various theories of joint and several liability, several liability, intervening causes and superseding causes? Does limiting liability for multiple defendants to their percentage of the negligence impinge on the concept of liability for injury caused by intervening negligent acts?

2. What is a successive tortfeasor? Why, in a successive tort, might the first tortfeasor be liable for later injuries? When might the second tortfeasor be liable for all the injuries?

3. What is the reason for holding two or more defendants liable when they produce a single indivisible injury? Should there be a difference between simultaneous and sequential acts?

4. If a joint defendant is required to pay the whole amount, how much should he recover from any codefendant? Should this affect his or her liability to the plaintiff?

Walt Disney World v. Wood

Supreme Court of Florida, 1987
515 So. 2d 198

GRIMES, JUSTICE.

Aloysia Wood was injured in November 1971 at the grand prix attraction at Walt Disney World (Disney), when her fiancé,[1] Daniel Wood, rammed from the rear the vehicle which she was driving. Aloysia Wood filed suit against Disney, and Disney sought contribution from Daniel Wood. After trial, the jury returned a verdict finding Aloysia Wood 14% at fault, Daniel Wood 85% at fault, and Disney 1% at fault. The jury assessed Wood's damages at $75,000. The court entered judgment against Disney for 86% of the damages. Disney subsequently moved to alter the judgment to reflect the jury's finding that Disney was only 1% at fault. The court denied the motion. On appeal, the fourth district affirmed the judgment on the basis of this Court's decision in *Lincenberg v. Issen*, 318 So. 2d 386 (Fla. 1975).

In *Hoffman v. Jones*, 280 So. 2d 431 (Fla. 1973), this Court discarded the rule of contributory negligence, which Florida had followed since at least 1886, and adopted the pure comparative negligence standard. . . .

Thereafter, in *Lincenberg v. Issen*, a faultless plaintiff obtained a verdict in which the jury determined that one defendant was 85% percent negligent and the other defendant was 15% negligent. The district court of appeal held that the jury should not have been asked to apportion fault between the defendants. *Issen v. Lincenberg*, 293 So. 2d 777 (Fla. 3d DCA 1974). On review, this Court concluded that the rationale of *Hoffman v. Jones* dictated the elimination of the rule against contribution among joint tortfeasors. The Court then said that since "'no contribution' is no longer a viable principle in Florida, we were confronted with the problem of determining what procedure will most fully effectuate the principle that each party should pay the proportion of the total damages he has caused to the other party, and we considered several alternatives." *Lincenberg*, 318 So. 2d at 392 (footnote omitted). At this point, the Court stated in footnote 2 that among the alternatives considered was pure apportionment whereby the plaintiff may recover judgment against codefendants only for the percentage of damages caused by the negligence of each individual defendant. However, the Court noted that the legislature had just passed section 738.31, Florida Statutes (1975), which provided for contribution among joint tortfeasors and interpreted the statute as retaining the "full, joint, and several liability of joint tortfeasors to the plaintiff." Thus, the Court held:

---

1. Wood married her fiancé prior to this action.

> The plaintiff is entitled to a measurement of his full damages and the liability for these damages should be apportioned in accordance with the percentage of negligence as it relates to the total of all the defendants. The negligence attributed to the defendants will then be apportioned on a pro rata basis without considering relative degrees of fault although the multiparty defendants will remain jointly and severally liable for the entire amount.

Lincenberg, 318 So. 2d at 393–94.

While arising in the context of a faultless plaintiff, it cannot reasonably be said that the Court in *Lincenberg* did not pass on the question now before us. Understandably, courts addressing the issue in subsequent decisions, including this Court, have interpreted *Lincenberg* as upholding the doctrine of joint and several liability. . . .

The real issue before us is whether we should now replace the doctrine of joint and several liability with one in which the liability of codefendants to the plaintiff is apportioned according to each defendant's respective fault. According to Disney, this Court in *Hoffman* set for itself the goal of creating a tort system that fairly and equitably allocated damages according to the degrees of fault. Therefore, a defendant should only be held responsible to the extent of his fault in the same way as a plaintiff under comparative negligence.

Joint and several liability is a judicially created doctrine. *Louisville & N.R.R. v. Allen*, 67 Fla. 257, 65 So. 8 (1914). This Court may alter a rule of law where great social upheaval dictates its necessity. *Hoffman*, 280 So. 2d 431. The "social upheaval" which is said to have occurred here is the fundamental alteration of Florida tort law encompassed by the adoption of comparative negligence. Following the adoption of comparative negligence, some states have passed laws eliminating joint and several liability,[4] and the courts of several others have judicially abolished the doctrine. . . . The Kansas Supreme Court in *Brown v. Keill* reasoned:

> There is nothing inherently fair about a defendant who is 10% at fault paying 100% of the loss, and there is no social policy that should compel defendants to pay more than their fair share of the loss. Plaintiffs now take the parties as they find them. If one of the parties at fault happens to be a spouse or a governmental agency and if by reason of some competing social policy the plaintiff cannot receive payment for his injuries from the spouse or agency, there is no compelling social policy which requires the codefendant to pay more than his fair share of the loss. The same is true if one of the defendants is wealthy and the other is not.

Brown, 224 Kan. at 203, 580 P.2d at 874.

---

4. Some statutes limit the judgment entered against each defendant to that defendant's percentage of the plaintiff's damages. *E.g.*, Ohio Rev. Code Ann. §2315.19(A) (Baldwin 1984); N.H. Rev. Stat. Ann. §507.7-d (1986 Supp.). Others only limit the defendant's liability to the percentage of his negligence when his negligence is less than that of the plaintiffs. *E.g.*, Or. Rev. Stat. §18.485 (1985); Tex. Civ. Prac. & Rem. Code Ann. §33.001(b) (Vernon 1986).

On the other hand, the majority of courts which have faced the issue in jurisdictions with comparative negligence have ruled that joint and several liability should be retained. . . . The Illinois Supreme Court in *Coney v. J.L.G. Industries, Inc.* gave four reasons justifying the retention of joint and several liability:

(1) The feasibility of apportioning fault on a comparative basis does not render an indivisible injury "divisible" for purposes of the joint and several liability rule. A concurrent tortfeasor is liable for the whole of an indivisible injury when his negligence is a proximate cause of that damage. In many instances, the negligence of a concurrent tortfeasor may be sufficient by itself to cause the entire loss. The mere fact that it may be possible to assign some percentage figure to the relative culpability of one negligent defendant as compared to another does not in any way suggest that each defendant's negligence is not a proximate cause of the entire indivisible injury.

(2) In those instances where the plaintiff is not guilty of negligence, he would be forced to bear a portion of the loss should one of the tortfeasors prove financially unable to satisfy his share of the damages.

(3) Even in cases where a plaintiff is partially at fault, his culpability is not equivalent to that of a defendant. The plaintiff's negligence relates only to a lack of due care for his own safety while the defendant's negligence relates to a lack of due care for the safety of others; the latter is tortious, but the former is not.

(4) Elimination of joint and several liability would work a serious and unwarranted deleterious effect on the ability of an injured plaintiff to obtain adequate compensation for his injuries.

Coney, 97 Ill. 2d at 121–22, 454 N.E.2d at 205 (citations omitted).

. . . .

While recognizing the logic in Disney's position, we cannot say with certainty that joint and several liability is an unjust doctrine or that it should necessarily be eliminated upon the adoption of comparative negligence. In view of the public policy considerations bearing on the issue, this Court believes that the viability of the doctrine is a matter which should best be decided by the legislature. Consequently, we approve the decision of the district court of appeal.

It is so ordered.

––––––––––

1. Chief Justice McDonald dissented in *Walt Disney World* as follows:

The majority opinion may make social sense, but it defies legal logic. The doctrines of joint and several liability and contributory negligence are consistent with each other. Each tortfeasor, as a part of the whole, is liable for the whole. Comparative negligence, which does not bar, but reduces a recovery to the extent of individual fault, requires a separation of fault between the injured party and the other tortfeasors. It would be a mismatch of legal concepts to have a separation theory for the plaintiffs and a joint liability responsibility for defendants. Comparative negligence recognized the ability of a court to determine and apportion damages in relation to the harm caused. Joint and several, in contrast, presumes the inability of the judiciary to divide fault among parties. We have now said that we can. Accordingly, when the comparative negligence doctrine comes into play, as it did in this case, the law of joint and several liability should be repudiated and each defendant held accountable for only the percentage of damages found by the trier of fact to have been caused by his conduct.

515 So. 2d 198, at 202 (McDonald, C.J., dissenting).

Has the adoption of comparative fault by the states eliminated the basis for joint liability, as Chief Justice McDonald and tort-reformers nationally suggest? What if one of the liable parties is bankrupt or otherwise unavailable? Who should bear the risk if part of the judgment is uncollectible? Is it appropriate for one or more of the defendants to benefit if a fellow-defendant cannot pay his or her share? What if one of the defendants in *Summers v. Tice* had been judgment-proof? Should the plaintiff only collect half of the judgment?

2. Subsequent to *Walt Disney World*, the Florida legislature adopted section 768.81(3) Florida Statutes, which states:

> (3) Apportionment of Damages. In cases to which this section applies, the court shall enter judgment against each party liable on the basis of such party's percentage of fault and not on the basis of the doctrine of joint and several liability; provided that with respect to any party whose percentage of fault equals or exceeds that of a particular claimant, the court shall enter judgment with respect to economic damages against that party on the basis of the doctrine of joint and several liability.

3. In 2003, the National Conference of Commissioners on Uniform State Laws adopted the Uniform Apportionment of Tort Responsibility Act. This Act deals with many of the issues raised in this chapter. While it seems not to have been adopted whole in any state, the comments in the Act discuss many of the approaches taken by the states to the problems raised in this chapter.

In the Preface, the Act notes that, with the exception of multiple defendants who engage in concerted action who cause damage to the environment, "many jurisdictions today . . . have abolished joint and several liability and, thereby, any necessity to recognize rights of contribution among joint tortfeasors." Some highlights of the Act of particular relevance to this chapter include adoption of the following approaches:

> 1. Comparative negligence on the part of the plaintiff reduces the plaintiff's recovery by a percentage equal to that of the plaintiff's negligence, and bars

any recovery if the plaintiff's negligence is greater than the sum of the combined negligence of the other parties (Section 3(a) and (b));

2. The jury or factfinder must make findings apportioning responsibility to all parties, including ones who have been released (Section 4 (a)(2));

3. Liability of each defendant is based on its percentage of responsibility (several liability), with the exception that uncollectible portions of the damages are reallocated to solvent defendants in proportion to their responsibility for the injuries (Section 5 (b)).

4. The Restatement of the Law Third: Torts: Apportionment of Liability (2000) also discusses many of the issues raised in this chapter. In the Introduction, the authors note that "there is no majority rule" on how to handle joint and several liability. Instead of restating the law, the authors present various alternative approaches, anticipating that legislatures will act on the matter. Many have done so, as joint and several liability has proven to be a popular target for those who wish to curtail tort liability.

5. *Release and Satisfaction.* Most personal injury actions are settled, either before trial or at some point in the proceedings. Releases, which are of course contracts, can bring with them major complications if the litigation proceeds against other parties. Under the Uniform Apportionment of Tort Responsibility Act, a release of one party in a multiple-defendant case reduces the potential liability of the other parties by the "percentage of responsibility attributed to the released person" (Section 8(b)).

A party that has settled with the plaintiff is very unlikely to continue to participate in the case after that point (indeed, avoiding litigation costs is a major incentive to settle). What difficulties may arise in terms of apportioning responsibility to that party? Within the bounds of the required honesty, might the other defendants be tempted to heap responsibility on the absent defendant, on the theory that the judgments against them are likely to be reduced under a several approach? Conversely, and also within the bounds of the required honesty, might the plaintiff be tempted to heap responsibility on the present parties, on the theory that minimizing the liability attributable to the absent party will maximize the judgment? Do these two incentives cancel each other out?

What if a plaintiff settles with one party in exchange for that party's testimony at trial? For example, in a medical malpractice case involving several physicians, the plaintiff might settle with one doctor with the testimony of that doctor against the other doctor(s) being part of the agreement. How, if at all, should this affect the allocation of responsibility and damages?

6. In a case involving admiralty law, the Supreme Court adopted a similar approach to the approach that would later be taken in the Uniform Apportionment of Tort Responsibility Act. *See McDermott, Inc. v. AmClyde,* 511 U.S. 202 (1994). Recognizing that judges and scholars vary in their approaches to how much credit a nonsettling defendant is entitled to after a plaintiff releases other defendants, the Supreme

Court reviewed the three major approaches, as identified by the Restatement (Second) of Torts § 886A:

> (1) The money paid extinguishes any claim that the injured party has against the party released and the amount of his remaining claim against the other tortfeasor is reached by crediting the amount received; but the transaction does not affect a claim for contribution by another tortfeasor who has paid more than his equitable share of the obligation. . . .

> (2) The money paid extinguishes both any claims on the part of the injured party and any claim for contribution by another tortfeasor who has paid more than his equitable share of the obligation and seeks contribution. [Pro Tanto Approach]. . . .

> (3) The money paid extinguishes any claim that the injured party has against the released tortfeasor and also diminishes the claim that the injured party has against the other tortfeasors by the amount of the equitable share of the obligation of the released tortfeasor. [Proportionate Share Rule].

511 U.S. at 208–09.

Basing its decision on the precedent of comparative fault, promotion of settlement, and judicial economy, the Supreme Court explained that under the proportionate share method:

> no suits for contribution from the settling defendants were permitted, nor are they necessary, because the nonsettling defendants pay no more than their share of the judgment. . . .

> [The first Restatement approach] is clearly inferior to the other two, because it discourages settlement and leads to unnecessary ancillary litigation. It discourages settlement, because settlement can only disadvantage the settling defendant. . . .

> The choice between [the pro tanto approach and the proportionate share method] is less clear. . . . Under the pro tanto approach, however, a litigating defendant's liability will frequently differ from its equitable share, because a settlement with one defendant for less than its equitable share requires the nonsettling defendant to pay more than its share. Such deviations from the equitable apportionment of damages will be common, because settlements seldom reflect an entirely accurate prediction of the outcome of the trial. . . .

> The rule encourages settlements by giving the defendant that settles first an opportunity to pay less than its fair share of the damages, thereby threatening the non-settling defendant with the prospect of paying more than its fair share of the loss. By disadvantaging the party that spurns settlement offers, the pro tanto rule puts pressure on all defendants to settle. While public policy wisely encourages settlements, such additional pressure to settle is unnecessary. The parties' desire to avoid litigation costs, to reduce uncertainty, and to maintain ongoing commercial relationships is sufficient to

ensure nontrial dispositions in the vast majority of cases. Under the proportionate share approach, such factors should ensure a similarly high settlement rate. The additional incentive to settlement provided by the pro tanto rule comes at too high a price in unfairness.

511 U.S. at 209 (footnotes omitted).

7. What if one of the participants in creating the injury is immune from suit for whatever reason? There are various approaches to this problem. The Uniform Apportionment of Tort Responsibility Act in Section 9 treats these situations as though the immune party had signed a release with the plaintiff. The *Restatement Third, Torts: Apportionment of Responsibility* presents alternative approaches without adopting one.

Richards v. Badger Mutual Insurance Co.

Supreme Court of Wisconsin, 2008
749 N.W.2d 581

PATIENCE DRAKE ROGGENSACK, J.*

We are asked to review a decision of the court of appeals that reversed the circuit court's decision, which concluded that the stipulated facts of this case present a "common scheme or plan" that invokes joint and several liability under Wis. Stat. § 895.045(2) (2005–06). [We affirm.]

We conclude as follows: (1) Wis. Stat. § 895.045(2) is the legislative codification of the concerted action theory of liability; (2) the damages in this case resulted from the consumption of beer to the point of intoxication and the subsequent decision to drive while intoxicated; and (3) although Robert Zimmerlee, David Schrimpf, and Tomakia Pratchet acted "in accordance with a common scheme or plan" to procure beer, they did not so act in consuming beer to the point of intoxication and in the subsequent act of driving while intoxicated, and, therefore, David Schrimpf is not jointly and severally liable under § 895.045(2) for the death of Chris Richards. Accordingly, Badger Mutual Insurance Company is relieved from making any further payment to Michelle Richards.

I. BACKGROUND

An ill-conceived idea between teenagers to "get some beer" one evening culminated in tragedy the next morning when an intoxicated Robert Zimmerlee, 19, failed to stop for a stop sign and smashed into the driver's side of Christopher Richards' vehicle, killing him instantly. Chris' wife, Michelle Richards (Richards), sought to recover damages. She initially pursued a negligence claim against Zimmerlee and his insurer. The parties settled on for $1,312,500,[4] and Zimmerlee is therefore not a party to this appeal. After Richards received the settlement, she then brought a wrongful

---

* Paragraph numbers in original have been omitted—Eds.
4. The parties stipulated that Richards' total damages equal $1,785,714.29.

death action against David Schrimpf, 19, who was the passenger in Zimmerlee's car, and Schrimpf's insurer, Badger Mutual Insurance Company, pursuant to Wis. Stat. § 895.04. Richards alleged that Schrimpf illegally procured beer and that Zimmerlee's consumption of the beer resulted in Christopher Richards' wrongful death. Schrimpf joined Tomakia Pratchet, who purchased the beer for Zimmerlee and Schrimpf, in the litigation.

The parties have stipulated to the facts in this case. Events leading to the accident unfolded the prior evening, when Schrimpf and Zimmerlee decided to "go get some beer." Schrimpf was employed at a West Allis restaurant, and he said that one of his co-workers, Pratchet, would be able to purchase the beer for them because she was of-age.

Zimmerlee and Schrimpf drove together to Schrimpf's employer, where Pratchet was working that evening. Schrimpf entered and spoke with Pratchet about her purchasing beer for him and Zimmerlee. Pratchet agreed. Schrimpf also spoke with another co-worker, Jennifer Spencer, who invited Schrimpf to a party at her home that evening.

From the restaurant, Zimmerlee, Schrimpf, and Pratchet traveled together to a nearby grocer, where Pratchet purchased an 18-pack of beer for Zimmerlee and Schrimpf with money Zimmerlee provided. The two dropped Pratchet off at a bus stop and Zimmerlee and Schrimpf went their separate ways for several hours, with the beer remaining in Zimmerlee's car.

Later that evening, Schrimpf and Zimmerlee reconnected, and with 18-pack in tow, arrived at Spencer's party between 12 midnight and 1:00 a.m. While Schrimpf drank "some" of the beer, Zimmerlee consumed "maybe half" of the 18 beers.

At approximately 7:30 a.m., the duo left Spencer's party. Schrimpf sat in the passenger seat, and Zimmerlee took the wheel of his car. They proceeded only half a block before colliding with Chris Richards' vehicle.

Two days before trial was set to commence, the parties entered into a settlement agreement. By the terms of that settlement agreement, the jury trial was waived and the parties agreed to allow the circuit judge to decide the question of whether Zimmerlee, Schrimpf, and Pratchet acted in accordance with a common scheme or plan that caused damage to Chris and Michelle Richards. The circuit court answered that question in the affirmative and held the parties jointly and severally liable for Richards' damages.

There is no dispute that Zimmerlee was negligent in the operation of his vehicle and that his negligence was a cause of the accident and death of Chris Richards. There is also no dispute that the beer was a substantial factor in causing the accident and the death. Both Schrimpf and Pratchet were "providers" of alcoholic beverages to Zimmerlee, as defined by Wis. Stat. § 125.035(2) and were therefore negligent under Wis. Stat. § 125.07(1)(a).

The parties also agreed to the apportionment of causal negligence among them: Zimmerlee at 72 percent; Schrimpf at 14 percent; and Pratchet at 14 percent. The parties stipulated . . . that Schrimpf's and Pratchet's combined causal negligence resulted in $500,000 of the total damages, or $250,000 each. . . . [T]he parties agreed that Richards was to be paid $250,000, as Schrimpf's share of the total damages, regardless of the outcome of this lawsuit. [The only remaining issue was Pratchet's responsibility, which turned on whether or not she participated with the others in a common scheme or plan.] If the final court decision in this case concluded that the parties did not act in accordance with a common scheme or plan that resulted in Richards' damages, Richards would not receive the 14 percent of the damages that remained unpaid. If, however, it was concluded that the parties did act in accordance with such common scheme or plan that caused Richards' damages, then Schrimpf and Pratchet would be jointly and severally liable to Richards and, therefore, Schrimpf, and [his insurer] Badger Mutual, would be required to pay Richards an additional $250,000 to cover the remainder of the damages.

What the parties dispute is whether the foregoing stipulated facts give rise to joint and several liability under Wis. Stat. § 895.045(2). The parties contest whether Zimmerlee, Schrimpf, and Pratchet acted in accordance with a common scheme or plan that resulted in Richards' damages, as those terms are used in § 895.045(2).

The court of appeals concluded that the parties were not jointly and severally liable under Wis. Stat. § 895.045(2) for Richards' damages. It held that, although the parties "had an agreement to purchase alcohol," that agreement did not include Zimmerlee's driving while intoxicated, which resulted in the damages. *Richards v. Badger Mut. Ins. Co.*, 297 Wis.2d 699, 727 N.W.2d 69, 2006 WI App 255, ¶ 27. Richards petitioned for review, which we granted.

II. DISCUSSION

A. Standard of Review

The outcome of this case hinges on the interpretation and application of Wis. Stat. § 895.045(2). . . .

B. The Parties' Positions

Both parties posit that Wis. Stat. § 895.045(2) is unambiguous; however, they offer differing interpretations and applications of it under the facts before us. Before turning to a discussion of the language of the statute, it is instructive to recount briefly the parties' respective arguments.

1. Richards' position

Richards argues that the parties agree that Zimmerlee, Schrimpf, and Pratchet acted in accordance with a common scheme or plan to purchase beer. She also asserts that the parties agree that "as a result of drinking the beer bought for [Zimmerlee] pursuant to his and Schrimpf's joint scheme and plan, Zimmerlee killed Mr. Richards by the intoxicated use of his vehicle." Further, Richards asserts that the parties have stipulated that the beer was a substantial factor in the cause of Chris Richards' death. Richards refers to Judge Fine's dissent as a succinct presentation of her argument: The stipulated facts require the conclusion that Chris Richards "would not have been killed by Zimmerlee if Zimmerlee had not been drunk as a result of drinking alcohol [bought] for him by Pratchet." *Richards*, 297 Wis.2d 699, ¶ 34, 727 N.W.2d 69 (Fine, J., dissenting). Richards contends that those facts evidence a common scheme or plan that falls within Wis. Stat. § 895.045(2), resulting in joint and several liability for all three defendants.

Furthermore, Richards argues that . . . (1) we have not adopted the concerted action theory of liability, as embodied in Restatement (Second) of Torts § 876, even though it is incorporated into Wisconsin Jury Instruction 1740 that attends § 895.045(2). Therefore, the so-called, but misnamed, "concerted action cases" that predate § 895.045(2) provide no guidance in interpreting the statute; and (2) the enactment of § 895.045(2) did not alter the law in Wisconsin that causal negligence is predicated on whether an act or omission is a substantial factor in causing harm. Here, it was stipulated that the beer was a substantial factor in causing the accident that killed Chris Richards.

2. Badger Mutual's position

In response, Badger Mutual argues that, while Richards correctly asserts that the statute is unambiguous, Richards nevertheless misapprehends the statute's meaning. First, Badger Mutual contends that . . . the concerted action theory of liability embodied in § 895.045(2) is the concerted action referred to in Wisconsin case law, [and that] subsection (2) requires that all parties have equal causal negligence. Consequently, because the parties stipulated to apportionment of causal negligence among Zimmerlee, Schrimpf, and Pratchet, their liability to Richards falls within subsection (1), not within subsection (2) of § 895.045.

Second, Badger Mutual acknowledges that while Schrimpf's conduct was a substantial factor in causing the accident, it did not also constitute concerted action, as is required before it falls within Wis. Stat. § 895.045(2). Badger Mutual contends that the Restatement (Second) of Torts § 876 and the common law in regard to concerted action support its position. Badger Mutual contends that the common scheme or plan to purchase beer did not damage Chris Richards. It was the reckless driving while intoxicated that resulted in damage to Chris Richards. However, the reckless driving was not part of a common scheme or plan in which Zimmerlee, Schrimpf, and Pratchet participated. Accordingly, it concludes that Schrimpf's liability to Richards falls within the parameters of § 895.045(1), not those of subsection (2).

C. Interpretation of Wis. Stat. § 895.045(2)

1. General principles

Statutory interpretation "begins with the language of the statute." We assume that the meaning of a statute is expressed in the words the legislature chose. The context in which the operative language appears is important too because a statute's meaning may be affected by the context in which the words chosen by the legislature are used. . . .

2. Statutory history

A review of statutory history is part of a plain meaning analysis. Statutory history encompasses the previously enacted and repealed provisions of a statute. By analyzing the changes the legislature has made over the course of several years, we may be assisted in arriving at the meaning of a statute. Therefore, statutory history is part of the context in which we interpret the words used in a statute. Accordingly, we examine the statutory history that underlies the current version of Wis. Stat. § 895.045.

The early common law rule of contributory negligence that existed prior to 1931, when the predecessor to Wis. Stat. § 895.045(1) was enacted, required that any contributory negligence of a plaintiff was a complete bar to recovery. *Brewster v. Ludtke*, 211 Wis. 344, 346, 247 N.W. 449 (1933). Also at common law, joint and several liability was the rule, such that when multiple tortfeasors caused injury to a plaintiff who was not contributorily negligent, the plaintiff could recover his or her entire damages from any tortfeasor. *Group Health Coop. of Eau Claire v. Hartland Cicero Mut. Ins. Co.*, 164 Wis.2d 632, 634–35, 476 N.W.2d 302 (Ct.App.1991).

In 1931, the legislature established statutory comparative negligence. This change in the law permitted a plaintiff who was contributorily negligent to recover damages if his or her negligence was less than the negligence of the person from whom recovery was sought. *Lupie v. Hartzheim*, 54 Wis.2d 415, 416, 195 N.W.2d 461 (1972). However, the adoption of comparative negligence did not change the common law rule of joint and several liability for the tortfeasors. *Walker v. Kroger Grocery & Baking Co.*, 214 Wis. 519, 535, 252 N.W. 721 (1934).

In 1971, the legislature renumbered the comparative negligence statute to Wis. Stat. § 895.045. It continued to permit a plaintiff who was not more negligent than the defendant from whom recovery was sought to recover damages, reduced by the amount of the plaintiff's negligence. Once again, this change did not affect the common law rule of joint and several liability. *Group Health*, 164 Wis.2d at 637, 476 N.W.2d 302. Therefore, in suits involving multiple tortfeasors, a comparison of the negligence of the plaintiff with that of any tortfeasor continued to be made and the full amount of damages[7] could be recovered from any tortfeasor who was more negligent than the plaintiff, even though a second tortfeasor may have been more negligent than the tortfeasor from whom recovery was sought. *Matthies v. Positive Safety Mfg. Co.*, 2001 WI 82, ¶ 10, 244 Wis.2d 720, 628 N.W.2d 842.

The current version of Wis. Stat. § 895.045 was created by 1995 Wis. Act 17. That Act amended comparative negligence in subsection (1) and created subsection (2). In subsection (1), the legislature chose to significantly change the law of joint and

---

7. The amount due the plaintiff was always first reduced by the percentage of plaintiff's negligence. *See Matthies v. Positive Safety Mfg. Co.*, 2001 WI 82, ¶ 10, 244 Wis.2d 720, 628 N.W.2d 842.

several liability by limiting the circumstances under which joint and several liability could be applied. *Id.* The relevant portion of § 895.045(1) provides:

> Comparative negligence. . . . The negligence of the plaintiff shall be measured separately against the negligence of each person found to be causally negligent. The liability of each person found to be causally negligent whose percentage of causal negligence is less than 51% is limited to the percentage of the total causal negligence attributed to that person. A person found to be causally negligent whose percentage of causal negligence is 51% or more shall be jointly and severally liable for the damages allowed.

Under revised subsection (1), a contributorily negligent plaintiff is precluded from recovering more of his or her damages from a tortfeasor than the tortfeasor's causal negligence bears to the total causal negligence. For those tortfeasors, the common law rule of joint and several liability is abrogated. Only when a tortfeasor is at least 51 percent causally negligent will the tortfeasor be jointly and severally liable for all damages attributed to all tortfeasors in the comparisons made under subsection (1). Therefore, in many cases involving joint tortfeasors and a contributorily negligent plaintiff, there no longer is joint and several liability.

In amending Wis. Stat. § 895.045 in 1995, the legislature also created subsection (2). This subsection retains the common law rule of joint and several liability in the circumstances described in the statute. Subsection (2) provides:

> **Concerted action.** Notwithstanding sub. (1), if 2 or more parties act in accordance with a common scheme or plan, those parties are jointly and severally liable for all damages resulting from that action, except as provided in § 895.043(5).[8]

Subsection (2), which the legislature chose to title "Concerted action," retains the common law rule of joint and several liability, if "that action" is taken in accordance with a common scheme or plan resulting in damages. However, while demonstrating a legislative choice to significantly reduce the occasions where joint and several liability may be awarded, the statutory history underlying § 895.045 does not resolve the meaning of the terms, "common scheme or plan" and "that action" "resulting" in damages that are before us in this review. Nor does it shed light on the title of subsection (2), "Concerted action." However, it does inform us that the legislature meant to proscribe the occasions for imposition of joint and several liability.[9]

---

8. Wisconsin Stat. § 895.043(5) provides: "The rule of joint and several liability does not apply to punitive damages."

9. The amicus brief of Wisconsin Academy of Trial Lawyers cites *Fuchsgruber v. Custom Accessories, Inc.*, 2001 WI 81, 244 Wis.2d 758, 628 N.W.2d 833, as support for its assertion that the 1995 amendments to Wis. Stat. § 895.045 did not intend to change the common law rule of joint and several liability. Reliance on *Fuchsgruber* for that proposition is misplaced. *Fuchsgruber* explained that a claim for strict products liability is not a negligence action under the common law; and therefore, because § 895.045(1) involves negligence, it has no application to claims of strict products liability. *Id.*, ¶¶ 1–3.

3. Ambiguity

Richards urges us to interpret Wis. Stat. § 895.045(2) such that it applies to persons engaged in a common scheme or plan to accomplish a result that in combination with other acts ultimately causes harm. Richards asserts that common law concerted action is not what the legislature meant to describe in subsection (2). Badger Mutual contends that the action that causes the harm must be undertaken to facilitate the common scheme or plan and that subsection (2) does embody common law concerted action. These competing interpretations of the terms and the title of § 895.045(2) are both reasonable interpretations. They indicate that the statute is "capable of being understood by reasonably well-informed persons in two or more senses" and is therefore ambiguous.

When confronted with an ambiguous statute, we may resort to extrinsic sources to help uncover the statute's meaning. The legislative history now available that relates to the creation of subsection (2) of Wis. Stat. § 895.045 is sparse. However, the Legislative Reference Bureau Analysis of an earlier version of the 1995 changes in § 895.045 that were eventually enacted states:

> This bill modifies the comparative negligence system in several ways. The bill requires that the negligence of the plaintiff be measured separately against each of the joint tort-feasors. Under this bill, a joint tort-feasor's liability is limited to the percentage of the total causal negligence attributed to that party.
>
> The bill specifies that the changes in the rule of joint and several liability do not apply to parties whose concerted action results in damages . . .

Drafting File for 1995 Wis. Act 17, *Analysis by the Legislative Reference Bureau* of 1995 S.B. 11, Legislative Reference Bureau, Madison, Wis. The LRB's analysis supports our conclusion that the 1995 changes to § 895.045 were meant to significantly change the common law rule of joint and several liability that had applied to negligence actions in the past. However, the legislative history provides limited guidance with respect to the statutory terms in subsection (2) that we must interpret.

The title is not part of a statute according to Wis. Stat. § 990.001(6); however, it may be used to assist in understanding a statute's meaning. We note that the title to Wis. Stat. § 895.045(2) is "Concerted action." Concerted action is a theory of liability that comes from the common law, as do key words the legislature chose to use in subsection (2), such as "common scheme or plan." Accordingly, we review Wisconsin's common law and the learned treatises cited therein for guidance in interpreting the title and terms of subsection (2).

4. Wisconsin appellate decisions

Four published appellate opinions offer potential guidance on the meaning of Wis. Stat. § 895.045(2). *Danks v. Stock Bldg. Supply, Inc.*, 298 Wis.2d 348, 727 N.W.2d 846, 2007 WI App 8; *Bruttig v. Olsen*, 154 Wis.2d 270, 453 N.W.2d 153 (Ct.App.1989);

Collins v. Eli Lilly Co., 116 Wis.2d 166, 342 N.W.2d 37 (1984); and *Ogle v. Avina*, 33 Wis.2d 125, 146 N.W.2d 422 (1966).

Danks provides only the briefest interpretation of Wis. Stat. § 895.045(2). . . .

However, *Danks* does interpret Wis. Stat. § 895.045(2) as pertaining only to tortfeasors who take concerted action. *Id.*, ¶ 39. *Danks* does not discuss the meanings of "Concerted action" or "common scheme or plan," but it does note that those who act "in concert" will come within the parameters of subsection (2):

> Subsection (2) simply modifies subsection (1) of the statute to provide that all defendants who are legally responsible for causing a plaintiff's damages, and who acted in concert in so doing, are jointly and severally liable for the plaintiff's damages, irrespective of whether a given defendant's apportioned causal negligence is less than 51%.

Id. Danks continues to conclude that "§ 895.045(2) plays no role to determine *whether* a given defendant may be held liable." *Id.*, ¶ 40 (emphasis in original). Rather, a defendant must be liable before subsection (2) may be applied. *Id.* . . .

Collins precedes *Danks* and the 1995 revisions of Wis. Stat. § 895.045. There we discussed concerted action as a theory of liability and relied on the explanation of that theory by Professor Prosser. *Collins*, 116 Wis.2d at 184, 342 N.W.2d 37. In it we explained that:

> The concerted action theory of liability rests upon the principle that "those who, in pursuance of a common plan or design to commit a tortious act, actively take part in it, or further it by cooperation or request, or who lend aid or encouragement to the wrongdoer, or ratify and adopt his acts done for their benefit, are equally liable with him. Express agreement is not necessary, and all that is required is that there be a tacit understanding."

Id. (quoting W. Prosser, *Handbook of The Law of Torts* § 46, at 292 (4th ed.1971)). However, we declined to apply the concerted action theory when the plaintiff, who sought damages from former manufacturers of the drug diethylstilbestrol (DES) that caused an aggressive form of cervical cancer, could not identify the specific manufacturer of the DES that was taken by her mother. *Id.* at 186, 342 N.W.2d 37.

. . . .

Collins is helpful to our analysis. For example, the specificity of the subject matter of the common plan in *Collins* that we concluded was necessary to support the concerted action theory of liability is important to our consideration of the specificity of the subject matter of the common plan at issue in the case before us. That is, the action that harmed Collins must have been that which was undertaken to further the drug companies' agreement. *Id.* In addition, *Collins* equated "concerted action," the title of Wis. Stat. § 895.045(2) with "pursuance of a common plan," terms employed in the text of subsection (2). *Id.* at 184, 342 N.W.2d 37.

Bruttig also tackled the topic of concerted action. There the plaintiff, Brian Bruttig who was a minor, and two friends, also minors, engaged in a game of "snowmobile tag." Brian was injured and recovery was denied because his liability was greater than that of either of the other two tortfeasors. *Bruttig*, 154 Wis.2d at 273, 453 N.W.2d 153. On appeal, Brian argued that he and the two defendants were equally negligent "because the tag game created a situation of mutual stimulation where the negligence of each participant [was] entirely interrelated with that of the others and therefore each should be charged with the causal negligence of the other." *Id.* at 280, 453 N.W.2d 153. The court of appeals recognized the argument as the theory of concerted action liability in which "the jury would not be permitted to apportion damages." *Id.* (citing W. Prosser, *Handbook of The Law of Torts* § 46, at 291 (4th ed.1971)).

The court of appeals noted that the concerted action theory of liability has never been "explicitly adopted" in Wisconsin. *Id.* at 280, 453 N.W.2d 153. It also noted that Brian had not raised this theory of liability in the circuit court. Therefore, it rejected his argument to apply it on appeal. *Id.* at 281, 453 N.W.2d 153.

Bruttig's discussion is helpful, as it reviews Brian's claim that the three boys "acted in concert," . . . *Bruttig* acknowledges that the theory that Brian is proffering is "a separate theory of liability, that of 'concerted action.'" *Id.* at 280, 453 N.W.2d 153. This is significant because Wis. Stat. § 895.045(2) requires proof of a separate theory of liability for one who may already be a tortfeasor under subsection (1), in order to accord joint and several liability. *Danks*, 298 Wis.2d 348, ¶ 39, 727 N.W.2d 846. That is, subsection (2) requires a plaintiff to prove that the tortfeasor acted "in accordance with a common scheme or plan" and also that the common scheme or plan the tortfeasor acted in accordance with resulted in damages. *Id.* Subsection (2) is not applicable in every case where joint tortfeasors are present.

Our review of Wisconsin case law that touches on the concerted action theory of liability concludes with *Ogle*. In *Ogle*, we held that both negligent participants in a "drag race" were equally liable for a fatal collision resulting from their negligence, even though only one of the tortfeasors struck a third automobile causing injury. *Ogle*, 33 Wis.2d at 135, 146 N.W.2d 422.

In *Ogle*, two cars were racing at a high rate of speed in the same direction down a highway, when the lead car collided with the plaintiff's car. *Id.* at 128–30, 146 N.W.2d 422. In holding both defendants equally liable for the collision without specifically referencing "concerted action," we applied the principles of concerted action:

> We think when there is an understanding to reach a common destination and in doing so illegal speed is used and the cars are driven so closely together as to be practically in tandem, or to constitute a unit, that we have a situation of mutual stimulation where the negligence of each participant is so related to the negligence of the other participants that the participants should each be chargeable with the causal negligence of the other as to speed and their percentage of causal negligence should be equal.

Id. at 135, 146 N.W.2d 422. The mutual agreement to use excessive speed to reach an agreed upon destination formed the basis for the tortfeasors' concerted action. *Id.*

This court went on to explain in *Ogle* that the usual rule of apportioning causal negligence between tortfeasors whose negligence combined or concurred in causing injury does not apply with "mutual fault" for the injury that occurred. *Id.* Rather, the tortfeasors in *Ogle* each assumed the fault of the other and causal negligence was apportioned equally between them. *Id.* Badger Mutual argues that the concept of equal fault for tortfeasors in concerted actions is significant to the case before us because the parties have agreed to apportioned causal negligence. Richards maintains it has no relevancy.

5. Learned treatises

Because discussions of the concerted action theory of liability in Professor Prosser's *The Law of Torts*, as well as those provided by The Restatement (Second) of Torts, are so prominent in the cases that discuss the concerted action theory of liability, we review those learned treatises as well, before interpreting and applying Wis. Stat. § 895.045(2). Prosser's explanation of the historic context of the concerted action theory of liability is helpful. It provides:

> The original meaning ... was that of vicarious liability for concerted action. All persons who acted in concert to commit a trespass, in pursuance of a common design, were held liable for the entire result. In such a case there was a common purpose, with mutual aid in carrying it out; in short, there was a joint enterprise, so that "all coming to do an unlawful act, and of one party, the act of one is the act of all of the same party being present." Each was therefore liable for the entire damage done. . . . [S]ince each was liable for all, the jury would not be permitted to apportion the damages.

W. Page Keeton, *Prosser and Keeton on The Law of Torts* § 46, at 322–23 (5th ed.1984) (quoted citations omitted). This historic framework for concerted action is helpful to our understanding of the mutuality of agreement that is necessary in order to have a common scheme or plan under the concerted action theory of liability, as well as to understanding the statutory terms used to express the concerted action theory of liability.

Section 876 of the Restatement (Second) of Torts is also helpful. It provides:

Persons Acting in Concert

For harm resulting to a third person from the tortious conduct of another, one is subject to liability if he

(a) does a tortious act in concert with the other or pursuant to a common design with him, or

(b) knows that the other's conduct constitutes a breach of duty and gives substantial assistance or encouragement to the other so to conduct himself, or

(c) gives substantial assistance to the other in accomplishing a tortious result and his own conduct, separately considered, constitutes a breach of duty to the third person.

Comment on Clause (a): Parties are acting in concert when they act in accordance with an agreement to cooperate in a particular line of conduct or to accomplish a particular result. The agreement need not be expressed in words and may be implied and understood to exist from the conduct itself. Whenever two or more persons commit tortious acts in concert, each becomes subject to liability for the acts of the others, as well as for his own acts. The theory of the early common law was that there was a mutual agency of each to act for the others, which made all liable for the tortious acts of any one.

Restatement (Second) of Torts § 876, at 315–16 (1979). The Comment to Clause (a) is particularly helpful in its description of mutual agency and that it was mutual agency that made all the actors liable for one another's tortious acts.

From our review of Wisconsin cases and learned treatises . . . we conclude that § 895.045(2) is the codification of the concerted action theory of liability. The statute is consistent with the concerted action theory as explained by Wisconsin courts and in learned treatises such as Prosser's *The Law of Torts* and the Restatement (Second) of Torts § 876. Our decision in this regard is supported by those who considered this question when drafting the Wisconsin Civil Jury Instruction 1740.

Our conclusion that Wis. Stat. § 895.045(2) is the codification of the concerted action theory of liability does not change Wisconsin law in regard to whether the actions of a tortfeasor were a substantial factor in causing harm sustained by another. This is so because in order to fit within the parameters of § 895.045(2), a tortfeasor must already be causally negligent under substantive law. *Danks*, 298 Wis.2d 348, ¶ 39, 727 N.W.2d 846. One is causally negligent when his or her conduct is a substantial factor in causing injury to another. *Johnson v. Misericordia Cmty. Hosp.*, 97 Wis.2d 521, 561, 294 N.W.2d 501 (Ct.App.1980). Accordingly, under our interpretation of § 895.045(2), a person who is causally negligent with regard to a recovering plaintiff will have proportionate liability under § 895.045(1), unless something more is proved about that tortfeasor's conduct that will bring it within the purview of subsection (2). *Danks*, 298 Wis.2d 348, ¶ 39, 727 N.W.2d 846.

6. Application of Wis. Stat. § 895.045(2)

There are two possible scenarios under the stipulated facts and the arguments made by Richards wherein she seeks to hold Schrimpf jointly and severally liable under Wis. Stat. § 895.045(2) for her damages: (1) Zimmerlee, Schrimpf, and Pratchet acted in accordance with a common scheme or plan to procure beer and that action resulted in her damages; or (2) Zimmerlee and Schrimpf acted in accordance with a common scheme or plan to drink to intoxication and then drive and that action resulted in her damages. Although Richards interweaves these two scenarios, we will examine them independently.

Concerted action liability is a separate theory of liability that does not apply to all who are proved to be causally negligent. *Danks*, 298 Wis.2d 348, ¶ 40, 727 N.W.2d 846; *see Bruttig*, 154 Wis.2d at 280, 453 N.W.2d 153; W. Page Keeton, *Prosser and Keeton on the Law of Torts* § 46, at 322–23 (5th ed.1984). Something more than causal negligence is required before the actions of a tortfeasor will come within the parameters of Wis. Stat. § 895.045(2). *Danks*, 298 Wis.2d 348, ¶ 40, 727 N.W.2d 846. Concerted action must be proved.

There are three factual predicates necessary to proving concerted action: First, there must be an explicit or tacit agreement among the parties to act in accordance with a mutually agreed upon scheme or plan. *See Collins*, 116 Wis.2d at 185, 342 N.W.2d 37. Parallel action, without more, is insufficient to show a common scheme or plan. *Id.* Second, there must be mutual acts committed in furtherance of that common scheme or plan that are tortious acts. *See Ogle*, 33 Wis.2d at 135, 146 N.W.2d 422. Third, the tortious acts that are undertaken to accomplish the common scheme or plan must be the acts that result in damages. *See Collins*, 116 Wis.2d at 184–85, 342 N.W.2d 37.

In regard to the actions of Zimmerlee, Schrimpf, and Pratchet, it is undisputed that they agreed to purchase beer. When Schrimpf asked Pratchet to purchase beer and Zimmerlee drove her to the grocery and gave her the money that she used to purchase the beer, they acted "in accordance with a common scheme or plan." Their procurement of beer was tortious. Wis. Stat. §§ 125.035(4)(b); 125.07(1). However, after that purchase, Pratchet had nothing further to do with the beer. She took a bus to an unnamed location. Zimmerlee and Schrimpf became parallel actors. Zimmerlee and Schrimpf separated, with Zimmerlee keeping the beer in his car. The scheme or plan that was common to these three defendants had been completed. Richards had suffered no damages because of actions taken to further that common plan. Something more was required. Therefore, the purchase of beer is insufficient to show concerted action, and to cause Schrimpf's conduct to fall within Wis. Stat. § 895.045(2).

In regard to concluding that there was concerted action between Zimmerlee and Schrimpf resulting in Zimmerlee's drinking until intoxicated and then driving, certainly, the consumption of the beer to the point of intoxication and Zimmerlee's driving while intoxicated resulted in Richards' damages. Moreover, the drinking by Zimmerlee and Schrimpf was tortious because they were both under age. Wis. Stat. § 125.07(4)(b). However, there is nothing in the record to show that their drinking was not merely parallel conduct and that Zimmerlee and Schrimpf did not have a common scheme or plan to drink until intoxicated and then to drive. Accordingly, Schrimpf's conduct does not bring him within the parameters of Wis. Stat. § 895.045(2).[13]

---

13. Schrimpf's involvement with Zimmerlee after the parties purchased the beer resembles the involvement of the defendants in *Blakeslee*. There, the drivers of two vehicles alternately changed lanes on a highway, and the rear driver crashed after dipping his tires onto the right-hand shoulder of the highway. *Blakeslee*, 37 A.D.3d at 1022, 831 N.Y.S.2d 556. The court held that there was insufficient proof to hold the drivers jointly and severally liable under a concerted action theory of

In addition, pursuant to the parties' stipulation, Zimmerlee was 72 percent caus-ally negligent in the death of Chris Richards; Schrimpf was 14 percent causally neg-ligent, and Pratchet was 14 percent causally negligent. The apportioned negligence here reflects Schrimpf's and Pratchet's respective several liability. However, with a concerted action theory of liability, each party assumes the causal negligence of the other so that all are equally liable. *See Ogle*, 33 Wis.2d at 135, 146 N.W.2d 422. There-fore, the parties' stipulation to differing percentages of causal negligence further supports our conclusion that Richards' injury was not the result of concerted action.

In sum, we reach the following conclusions: (1) Zimmerlee, Schrimpf, and Pratchet acted in accordance with a common scheme or plan to procure alcohol, but since the action undertaken to accomplish that common scheme or plan was not the act that resulted in Richards' damages, Wis. Stat. § 895.045(2) is inapplicable and therefore Schrimpf is not jointly and severally liable; and (2) the action that did result in Rich-ards' damages was Zimmerlee's drinking until he was intoxicated and his subsequent decision to drive while intoxicated, but since this action was not taken in accordance with a common scheme or plan, § 895.045(2) is again inapplicable and therefore Schrimpf is not jointly and severally liable in that context as well.

III. CONCLUSION

We conclude as follows: (1) Wis. Stat. § 895.045(2) is the legislative codification of the concerted action theory of liability; (2) the damages in this case resulted from the consumption of beer to the point of intoxication and the subsequent decision to drive while intoxicated; and (3) although Robert Zimmerlee, David Schrimpf, and Tomakia Pratchet acted "in accordance with a common scheme or plan" to procure beer, they did not so act in consuming beer to the point of intoxication and in the subsequent act of driving while intoxicated, and, therefore, David Schrimpf is not jointly and severally liable under § 895.045(2) for the death of Chris Richards. Accord-ingly, Badger Mutual Insurance Company is relieved from making any further pay-ment to Michelle Richards.

The decision of the court of appeals is affirmed.

SHIRLEY S. ABRAHAMSON, C.J. (dissenting).

The issue presented is whether the defendants Schrimpf and Pratchet are jointly and severally liable under Wis. Stat. § 895.045(2) for their combined 28 percent causal negligence for the plaintiff's injury. These two engaged in a common scheme or plan to procure alcohol for an underage drinker (Zimmerlee, the driver-defendant with 72 percent causal negligence) who became intoxicated and caused damage to an inno-cent third party (the plaintiff) by the intoxicated use of a motor vehicle. In other words, the issue is whether Schrimpf is liable to the plaintiff not only for the dam-ages attributed to his causal negligence but also for the damages attributed to Pratch-et's causal negligence. . . .

---

liability because the record did not demonstrate that the drivers had an express or implied agree-ment to engage in a "passing contest." *Id.* at 1022–23, 831 N.Y.S.2d 556.

The plain language of Wis. Stat. § 895.045(2) is that parties acting in accordance with a common scheme or plan are jointly and severally liable to the plaintiff for all the damages resulting to the plaintiff from that common scheme or plan. Wisconsin Stat. § 895.045(2) provides in full as follows:

> **(2) Concerted action.** Notwithstanding sub. (1), if 2 or more parties act in accordance with a common scheme or plan, those parties are jointly and severally liable for all damages resulting from that action, except as provided in § 895.043(5).

The parties, the circuit court, and the majority opinion agree that Schrimpf and Pratchet acted in accordance with a common scheme or plan to procure alcohol beverages for the underage driver in the present case. Furthermore, the parties, the circuit court, and the majority opinion agree that Schrimpf and Pratchet's procurement of the alcohol was tortious. Schrimpf and Pratchet stipulated that each was a "provider" of alcohol beverages to the underage driver for purposes of Wis. Stat. § 125.035(4), that is, that they each "procure[d] alcohol beverages for . . . an underage person in violation of § 125.07(1)(a)."

The parties, the circuit court, and the majority opinion also agree that Schrimpf and Pratchet's procurement of the alcohol caused damages to the plaintiff. Schrimpf and Pratchet stipulated that each was "causally negligent" with respect to the plaintiff's damages. Schrimpf and Pratchet stipulated that their combined negligence caused 28 percent of the total damages suffered by the plaintiff.[6]

Under these circumstances, the plain language of Wis. Stat. § 895.045(2) permits only one result: It provides that Schrimpf and Pratchet shall be jointly and severally liable for "all" damages resulting from their common scheme or plan to procure alcohol for the underage driver. No one disputes that 28 percent of the plaintiff's damages resulted from Schrimpf and Pratchet's procurement of alcohol for the underage driver. Wisconsin Stat. § 895.045(2) thus requires, about as clearly as any statute could, that Schrimpf and Pratchet be jointly and severally liable for 28 percent of the plaintiff's total damages.

The majority opinion errs. . . . in concluding that the question whether a common scheme or plan has resulted in damages for purposes of joint and several liability under Wis. Stat. § 895.045(2) is different from the question whether a common scheme or plan has resulted in damages for purposes of tort liability to the plaintiff. In other words, the majority opinion has concluded that Wis. Stat. § 895.045(2) changes the Wisconsin law on causation. Nothing in the text of Wis. Stat. § 895.045(2) states that the legislature is altering or modifying the substantial factor test of causation, as the majority opinions opine.

The end! No more need be said.

---

6. The parties stipulated that the plaintiff's total damages were $1,785,714.29. The parties further stipulated that the underage driver-defendant's share of the causal negligence was 72 percent, Schrimpf's share was 14 percent, and Pratchet's share was 14 percent.

I write more, however, because in addition to ignoring the text of the statute, the majority opinion rests . . . on "concepts that are not on point." The majority opinion errs by listening to the siren song of concerted action. The majority opinion errs by applying the common law doctrine of "concerted action" in a context in which it does not apply. The concept of concerted action in the Restatement (Second) of Torts § 876 and in the cases (upon which the majority opinion relies) is not on point in interpreting and applying Wis. Stat. § 895.045.

Concerted action in the Restatement and in the cases is a substantive rule of tort liability to determine which of multiple actors are causally negligent and liable to an injured plaintiff. Concerted action under the Restatement and in these cases relates to a theory of liability.[8]

The majority opinion lifts the doctrine of concerted action and applies it in a different legal context, namely in the allocation of damages among those tortfeasors already found at fault. Wisconsin Stat. § 895.045(2) does not determine fault; it apportions damages after liability has been determined.

The majority opinion compounds its mistake of applying the substantive doctrine of concerted action by treating the doctrine as one departing from Wisconsin's law of causation. According to the majority opinion, joint and several liability under Wis. Stat. § 895.045(2) applies only to tortfeasors who act in accordance with a common scheme or plan that is *the* direct and particular cause of the plaintiff's damages, rather than merely *a* cause of the plaintiff's damages. The majority opinion requires that

---

8. Section 876 of the Restatement (Second) of Torts (1979) is a specific application of the rule stated in § 875 of the Restatement, which provides as follows:

> Each of two or more persons whose tortious conduct is a legal cause of a single and indivisible harm to the injured party is subject to liability to the injured party for the entire harm.

Comment c explains that § 875 is consistent with the rules of causation in negligence; any one of a number of persons whose tortious conduct is a substantial factor in causing harm is liable for the harm in the absence of a superseding cause. Section 876 of the Restatement provides in relevant part as follows:

> For harm resulting to a third person from the tortious conduct of another, one is subject to liability if he . . . does a tortious act in concert with the other or pursuant to a common design with him. . . .

The Wisconsin cases upon which the majority relies similarly treat the common law doctrine of "concerted action" as a rule to determine causal negligence. *See Bruttig v. Olsen*, 154 Wis.2d 270, 280, 453 N.W.2d 153 (Ct.App.1989) (stating that concerted action is "a separate theory of liability"); *Collins v. Eli Lilly Co.*, 116 Wis.2d 166, 185, 342 N.W.2d 37 (1984) ("The concerted action theory typically is applied to situations in which . . . a particular defendant is already identified as causing the plaintiff's harm, and the plaintiff desires to extend liability to those acting in league with that defendant.") (citation omitted); *Ogle v. Avina*, 33 Wis.2d 125, 133–35, 146 N.W.2d 422 (1966) (participant in a drag race causally negligent even though plaintiff's injuries were caused most directly by another participant in the race).

damages be *the* direct and particular result of the common scheme or plan for purposes of § 895.045, rather than merely *a* result of the common scheme or plan.[9]

The majority opinion declares that for purposes of joint and several liability under § 895.045(2) the common scheme to procure the alcohol beverage in the instant case did not result in the plaintiff's damages, notwithstanding the parties' stipulation that the procurement of alcohol was a cause of damages to the plaintiff and that the providers were liable for their causal negligence. The majority opinion concludes that for purposes of joint and several liability under § 895.045(2), the only cause of the plaintiff's damages was the underage drinker's consumption of alcohol to the point of intoxication and subsequent decision to drive while intoxicated.

The majority opinion's reasoning is explained in a simple way in the third-party brief of the Wisconsin Insurance Alliance and Property Casualty Insurers Association of America. The brief urges that the words "that action" in Wis. Stat. § 895.045(2) mean that joint and several liability is applicable only in those cases where the damages result *solely* from the tortfeasors who act in accordance with a common scheme or plan. Applying this interpretation to the present case, the Alliance's brief concludes that "[i]n this case, the concerted action, or 'that action,' was buying beer, but the harm resulted from drunk driving—conduct different from 'that action.'"

I do not know on what basis the majority opinion determines that the common-law doctrine of concerted action (or Wis. Stat. § 895.045(2), which the majority opinion concludes is a codification of the common-law doctrine) applies only when damages result *solely* from acts that the tortfeasors undertake in accordance with a common scheme or plan. The majority opinion fails to cite any authority in support of its determination that for purposes of § 895.045(2), the plaintiff suffered no damages because of the defendants' common scheme or plan to procure alcohol. Even assuming that the majority opinion is correct to apply the substantive doctrine of concerted action to the present case, it does not appear that this doctrine distinguishes between "a" cause and "the" cause in the manner that the majority opinion does. The majority opinion cites no case or treatise dealing with a situation similar to the present case, in which the defendants' common scheme or plan caused some but not all of the plaintiff's damages.

In contrast to the majority opinion, I conclude that Wis. Stat. § 895.045 uses the concept of defendant tortfeasors acting in accordance with a common scheme or plan to allocate damages among the multiple tortfeasors already found to be at fault, not to determine (as § 876 of the Restatement does) whether each actor is liable to the

---

9. "The test of cause in Wisconsin is whether the defendant's negligence was a substantial factor in producing the injury. It need not be the sole factor or the primary factor, only a 'substantial factor.' The phrase 'substantial factor' denotes that the defendant's conduct has such an effect in producing the harm as to lead the trier of fact, as a reasonable person, to regard it as a cause, using that word in the popular sense. There may be several substantial factors contributing to the same result." *Clark v. Leisure Vehicles, Inc.*, 96 Wis.2d 607, 617–18, 292 N.W.2d 630 (1980) (internal citations omitted).

plaintiff under a theory of liability. The multiple tortfeasors in the present case have been identified as contributing to a single injury and the responsibility of each is based upon the causal fault. In other words, tort liability has already been decided when § 895.045 is applied. I conclude that under § 895.045, Schrimpf is liable for damages attributed to Pratchet's causal negligence.

. . . .

As I see it, Wis. Stat. § 895.045 directs that each of the multiple actors who has acted in accordance with a common scheme or plan and whose causal negligence has been apportioned at less than 51 percent is liable to the plaintiff not only for his or her own share of causal negligence but also for the share of causal negligence of another defendant with whom he acted in concert. Rather than decide the substantive tort liability of multiple actors, § 895.045 *apportions* damages after the liability of the multiple tortfeasors has already been determined. Section 895.045 does not change causal negligence.

. . . .

. . . Other states have similarly interpreted "concerted action" in joint and several liability statutes. The North Dakota Supreme Court, for example, held that its joint and several liability statute with a special provision for "concerted action" "does not create an independent basis of liability, rather it deals with the allocation of damages among those already at fault."[14]

. . . [M]y interpretation of Wis. Stat. § 895.045(2) comports with Restatement (Third) of the Law of Torts: Apportionment of Liability § 15 (2000), which does not replace Restatement (Second) § 876, but is an addition thereto. Section 15 provides for apportionment of liability when persons act in concert as follows:

> When persons are liable because they acted in concert, all persons are jointly and severally liable for the share of comparative responsibility assigned to each person engaged in concerted activity.

Comment *a* explains that § 15 applies when the "governing law determines that concerted activity took place and that the tortious acts of one or more of the participants in the concerted activity was a legal cause of the plaintiff's indivisible injury."

---

14. North Dakota has a statute similar to Wis. Stat. § 895.045(2). The North Dakota statute provides in part (and provided at the time of the *Hurt* decision):

> When two or more parties are found to have contributed to the injury, the liability of each party is several only, and is not joint, and each party is liable only for the amount of damages attributable to the percentage of fault of that party, *except that any persons who act in concert* in committing a tortious act or aid or encourage the act, or ratifies or adopts the act for their benefit, are jointly liable for all damages attributable to their combined percentage of fault. Under this section, fault includes negligence, malpractice, absolute liability, dram shop liability, failure to warn, reckless or willful conduct, assumption of risk, misuse of product, failure to avoid injury, and product liability, including product liability involving negligence or strict liability or breach of warranty for product defect.

N.D. Cent.Code § 32-03.2-02 (2006) (emphasis added).

The comment further explains that "[t]he joint and several liability of those engaged in concerted activity is for the total comparative responsibility assigned to all who engage in the concerted activity." The Reporters' Note to § 15 of the Restatement (Third) of Torts: Apportionment of Liability interprets Wis. Stat. § 895.045 as retaining "full joint and several liability for concerted actors." According to the comment, the American Law Institute does not take a position on "whether a concerted-action tortfeasor is also jointly and severally liable for the share of comparative responsibility assigned to an independent tortfeasor who is also liable for the same indivisible injury."

. . . [M]y interpretation of Wis. Stat. § 895.045(2) also comports with *Reilly v. Anderson*, 727 N.W.2d 102 (Iowa 2006), in which the Iowa Supreme Court had to decide whether the theory of concerted action is compatible with statutory comparative fault principles. The Iowa court explained, 727 N.W.2d at 109, that where an independent party (such as the underage drunken driver in the present case) had been assigned 55 percent fault and concerted actors # 1 and # 2 (here Schrimpf and Pratchet) had been assigned fault of 35 percent and 10 percent respectively, the concerted actors would at least be jointly and severally liable for 45 percent of plaintiff's damages. The Iowa court did not decide whether the concerted actors would be jointly and severally liable for the entire fault assigned to all defendants in the fact situation described.

For the reasons set forth, I dissent.

I am authorized to state that Justices Ann Walsh Bradley and Louis B. Butler, Jr. join this opinion.

Chapter 9

The Liability of Landowners

The ownership of property (by which is meant real estate, a definition of some significance), at one time a highly protected activity, has come to bring with it obligations as well as rights in the modern world. The courts have safeguarded the interests of owners and other lawful occupiers of real estate for centuries; much property law goes back hundreds of years to the English courts. At the dawning of property law, the property owner had close to absolute dominion over the land, and the person entering upon the property had few rights. As society changed, persons other than the property owner gained status, and the owner of the property no longer ruled that property absolutely. This chapter deals with the difficulties courts must face in balancing the rights of the owner, the lessee, etc. to use his or her property in any manner that he or she deems appropriate against the rights of others not to be injured by whatever the owner does.

Because the courts are always engaging in an implicit balancing of the rights of property owners and those affected by them, and because so much property law is ancient, the law in this arena can become tangled in complex definitions. Some courts in the modern era have elected to eliminate the accretion of centuries and apply the same negligence and reasonableness doctrines to land cases as are applied in many tort cases, but other courts, perceiving a value in the traditional rules, have been unwilling to eliminate them.

A. Liability to Those Who Enter on the Land

1. The Taxonomy of Plaintiffs

Rowland v. Christian

Supreme Court of California, 1968 (en banc)
443 P.2d 561

PETERS, JUSTICE.

Plaintiff appeals from a summary judgment for defendant Nancy Christian in this personal injury action.

In his complaint plaintiff alleged that about November 1, 1963, Miss Christian told the lessors of her apartment that the knob of the cold water faucet on the bathroom basin was cracked and should be replaced; that on November 30, 1963, plaintiff entered the apartment at the invitation of Miss Christian; that he was injured while using the bathroom fixtures, suffering severed tendons and nerves of his right hand; and that he has incurred medical and hospital expenses. He further alleged that the bathroom fixtures were dangerous, that Miss Christian was aware of the dangerous condition, and that his injuries were proximately caused by the negligence of Miss Christian. Plaintiff sought recovery of his medical and hospital expenses, loss of wages, damage to his clothing, and $100,000 general damages. It does not appear from the complaint whether the crack in the faucet handle was obvious to an ordinary inspection or was concealed.

Miss Christian filed an answer containing a general denial except that she alleged that plaintiff was a social guest and admitted the allegations that she had told the lessors that the faucet was defective and that it should be replaced. Miss Christian also alleged contributory negligence and assumption of the risk. In connection with the defenses, she alleged that plaintiff had failed to use his "eyesight" and knew of the condition of the premises. Apart from these allegations, Miss Christian did not allege whether the crack in the faucet handle was obvious or concealed.

Miss Christian's affidavit in support of the motion for summary judgment alleged facts showing that plaintiff was a social guest in her apartment when, as he was using the bathroom, the porcelain handle of one of the water faucets broke in his hand causing injuries to his hand and that plaintiff had used the bathroom on a prior occasion. In opposition to the motion for summary judgment, plaintiff filed an affidavit stating that immediately prior to the accident he told Miss Christian that he was going to use the bathroom facilities, that she had known for two weeks prior to the accident that the faucet handle that caused injury was cracked, that she warned the manager of the building of the condition, that nothing was done to repair the condition of the handle, that she did not say anything to plaintiff as to the condition of the handle, and that when plaintiff turned off the faucet the handle broke in his hands severing the tendons and medial nerve in his right hand.

The summary judgment procedure is drastic and should be used with caution so that it does not become a substitute for an open trial. . . .

In the instant case, Miss Christian's affidavit and admissions made by plaintiff show that plaintiff was a social guest and that he suffered injury when the faucet handle broke; they do not show that the faucet handle crack was obvious or even nonconcealed. Without in any way contradicting her affidavit or his own admissions, plaintiff at trial could establish that she was aware of the condition and realized or should have realized that it involved an unreasonable risk of harm to him, that defendant should have expected that he would not discover the danger, that she did not exercise reasonable care to eliminate the danger or warn him of it, and that he did not know or have reason to know of the danger. Plaintiff also could establish, without contradicting Miss Christian's affidavit or his admissions, that the crack was not obvious and was concealed. Under the circumstances, a summary judgment is proper in this case only if, after proof of such facts, a judgment would be required as a matter of law for Miss Christian. The record supports no such conclusion.

. . . .

One of the areas where this court and other courts have departed from the fundamental concept that a man is liable for injuries caused by his carelessness is with regard to the liability of a possessor of land for injuries to persons who have entered upon that land. It has been suggested that the special rules regarding liability of the possessor of land are due to historical considerations stemming from the high place which land has traditionally held in English and American thought, the dominance and prestige of the landowning class in England during the formative period of the rules governing the possessor's liability, and the heritage of feudalism.

The departure from the fundamental rule of liability for negligence has been accomplished by classifying the plaintiff either as a trespasser, licensee, or invitee and then adopting special rules as to the duty owed by the possessor to each of the classifications. Generally speaking a trespasser is a person who enters or remains upon land of another without a privilege to do so; a licensee is a person like a social guest who is not an invitee and who is privileged to enter or remain upon land by virtue of the possessor's consent, and an invitee is a business visitor who is invited or permitted to enter or remain on the land for a purpose directly or indirectly connected with business dealings between them.

Although the invitor owes the invitee a duty to exercise ordinary care to avoid injuring him, the general rule is that a trespasser and licensee or social guest are obliged to take the premises as they find them insofar as any alleged defective condition thereon may exist, and that the possessor of the land owes them only the duty of refraining from wanton or willful injury. The ordinary justification for the general rule severely restricting the occupier's liability to social guests is based on the theory that the guest should not expect special precautions to be made on his account and that if the host does not inspect and maintain his property the guest should not expect this to be done on his account.

An increasing regard for human safety has led to a retreat from this position.

. . . .

The cases dealing with the active negligence and the trap exceptions are indicative of the subtleties and confusion which have resulted from application of the common law principles governing the liability of the possessor of land. Similar confusion and complexity exist as to the definitions of trespasser, licensee, and invitee.

In refusing to adopt the rules relating to the liability of a possessor of land for the law of admiralty, the United States Supreme Court stated: ["] . . . [T]he common law has moved, unevenly and with hesitation, towards 'imposing on owners and occupiers a single duty of reasonable care in all circumstances.'" (Footnotes omitted.)

The courts of this state have also recognized the failings of the common law rules relating to the liability of the owner and occupier of land. . . .

There is another fundamental objection to the approach to the question of the possessor's liability on the basis of the common law distinctions based upon the status of the injured party as a trespasser, licensee, or invitee. Complexity can be borne and confusion remedied where the underlying principles governing liability are based upon proper considerations. Whatever may have been the historical justifications for the common law distinctions, it is clear that those distinctions are not justified in the light of our modern society and that the complexity and confusion which has arisen is not due to difficulty in applying the original common law rules—they are all too easy to apply in their original formulation—but is due to the attempts to apply just rules in our modern society within the ancient terminology.

Without attempting to labor all of the rules relating to the possessor's liability, it is apparent that the classifications of trespasser, licensee, and invitee, the immunities from liability predicated upon those classifications, and the exceptions to those immunities, often do not reflect the major factors which should determine whether immunity should be conferred upon the possessor of land. Some of those factors, including the closeness of the connection between the injury and the defendant's conduct, the moral blame attached to the defendant's conduct, the policy of preventing future harm, and the prevalence and availability of insurance, bear little, if any, relationship to the classifications of trespasser, licensee and invitee and the existing rules conferring immunity.

Although in general there may be a relationship between the remaining factors and the classifications of trespasser, licensee, and invitee, there are many cases in which no such relationship may exist. Thus, although the foreseeability of harm to an invitee would ordinarily seem greater than the foreseeability of harm to a trespasser, in a particular case the opposite may be true. The same may be said of the issue of certainty of injury. The burden to the defendant and consequences to the community of imposing a duty to exercise care with resulting liability for breach may often be greater with respect to trespassers than with respect to invitees, but it by no means follows that this is true in every case. In many situations, the burden will be the same, i.e., the conduct necessary upon the defendant's part to meet the burden of exercising due care as to invitees will also meet his burden with respect to licensees and trespassers. The last of the major factors, the cost of insurance, will, of course, vary depending upon the rules of liability adopted, but there is no persuasive evidence that applying ordinary principles of negligence law to the land occupier's liability will materially reduce the prevalence of insurance due to increased cost or even substantially increase the cost.

Considerations such as these have led some courts in particular situations to reject the rigid common law classifications and to approach the issue of the duty of the occupier on the basis of ordinary principles of negligence. And the common law distinctions after thorough study have been repudiated by the jurisdiction of their birth.

A man's life or limb does not become less worthy of protection by the law nor a loss less worthy of compensation under the law because he has come upon the land of another without permission or with permission but without a business purpose. Reasonable people do not ordinarily vary their conduct depending upon such matters, and to focus upon the status of the injured party as a trespasser, licensee, or invitee in order to determine the question whether the landowner has a duty of care, is contrary to our modern social mores and humanitarian values. The common law rules obscure rather than illuminate the proper considerations which should govern determination of the question of duty.

It bears repetition that the basic policy of this state set forth by the Legislature in section 1714 of the Civil Code is that everyone is responsible for an injury caused to another by his want of ordinary care or skill in the management of his property. The factors which may in particular cases warrant departure from this fundamental principle do not warrant the wholesale immunities resulting from the common law classifications, and we are satisfied that continued adherence to the common law distinctions can only lead to injustice or, if we are to avoid injustice, further fictions with the resulting complexity and confusion. We decline to follow and perpetuate such rigid classifications. The proper test to be applied to the liability of the possessor of land in accordance with section 1714 of the Civil Code is whether in the management of his property he has acted as a reasonable man in view of the probability of injury to others, and, although the plaintiff's status as a trespasser, licensee, or invitee may in the light of the facts giving rise to such status have some bearing on the question of liability, the status is not determinative.

Once the ancient concepts as to the liability of the occupier of land are stripped away, the status of the plaintiff relegated to its proper place in determining such liability, and ordinary principles of negligence applied, the result in the instant case presents no substantial difficulties. . . . Where the occupier of land is aware of a concealed condition involving in the absence of precautions an unreasonable risk of harm to those coming in contact with it and is aware that a person on the premises is about to come in contact with it, the trier of fact can reasonably conclude that a failure to warn or to repair the condition constitutes negligence. Whether or not a guest has a right to expect that his host will remedy dangerous conditions on his account, he should reasonably be entitled to rely upon a warning of the dangerous condition so that he, like the host, will be in a position to take special precautions when he comes in contact with it.

. . . .

The judgment is reversed.

TRAYNOR, C.J., and TOBRINER, MOSK and SULLIVAN, JJ., concur.

BURKE, JUSTICE (dissenting).

I dissent. In determining the liability of the occupier or owner of land for injuries, the distinctions between trespassers, licensees and invitees have been developed and applied by the courts over a period of many years. They supply a reasonable and workable approach to the problems involved, and one which provides the degree of stability and predictability so highly prized in the law.

. . . .

In my view, it is not a proper function of this court to overturn the learning, wisdom and experience of the past in this field. Sweeping modifications of tort liability law fall more suitably within the domain of the Legislature, before which all affected interests can be heard and which can enact statutes providing uniform standards and guidelines for the future.

I would affirm the judgment for defendant.

McComb, J., concurs.

Does *Rowland* change the range of appropriate landowner conduct? For what sorts of conduct might a landowner be liable under *Rowland* that would not subject him or her to liability under the system *Rowland* abolished? Is the impact of *Rowland* solely in favor of plaintiffs, or are there some forms of conduct for which a defendant might be not liable under *Rowland* but might have been under the earlier system? Note that this case involves a licensee, but the court extends coverage of the opinion to trespassers as well. What problems might that generate?

The Court's decision in *Rowland* was partly superseded in 1985 by Cal. Civ. Code § 847, which provides for partial owner-occupier immunity in suits brought by a trespasser who enters the property to commit one of 25 listed crimes. See *Calvillo-Silva v. Home Grocery*, 968 P.2d 65 (Cal. 1999).

Gerchberg v. Loney

Supreme Court of Kansas, 1978
576 P.2d 593

Fromme, Justice:

Rolf Gerchberg, a five year old boy, received burn injuries while playing on the premises of the neighbors, Mr. and Mrs. Roy Loney. At the close of plaintiff's evidence the district court directed a verdict in favor of defendants. The Court of Appeals reversed the judgment and remanded the case for trial on the theory of attractive nuisance. *See Gerchberg v. Loney*, 1 Kan. App. 2d 84, 562 P.2d 464.

The plaintiff-appellant urged the Court of Appeals to discard the traditional classification of trespassers, licensees and invitees, and to abolish the distinctions in our law as to the duty of care owed to each class. In place thereof he urged the court to adopt one duty of care owed to all who are on the premises of another, i.e., a duty of reasonable care under all facts and circumstances of the case. The Court of Appeals declined to do so and plaintiff-appellant sought review in this court.

. . . .

[In this case] the plaintiff Rolf Gerchberg, a five-year-old boy, received serious burns when he returned to an unattended smoldering fire in a barrel used by the defendants as an incinerator. Rodney Loney, the ten-year-old neighbor boy, had previously been directed to burn papers and had started the fire. Rolf was with him and saw Rodney place a stack of papers near the incinerator and start the fire. After a short while both boys left the premises. The fire had not been extinguished and was still smoldering on the Loney premises when Rolf returned to the barrel. He began putting the papers into the barrel. The fire blazed and his clothing caught on fire. Serious injuries resulted.

. . . .

Now let us turn our attention to plaintiff's argument that the traditional classification of trespassers, licensees and invitees should be discarded, and that the distinctions in our law covering the duty of care owed to each class be abandoned in favor of a single standard of reasonable care under the circumstances. Plaintiff contends there is no logical reason for protecting the possessor of premises by requiring his negligence to be wilful, wanton, or in reckless disregard for the safety of the trespasser or licensee before it is actionable.

Under the present law of Kansas a trespasser is one who enters on the premises of another without any right, lawful authority, or an express or implied invitation or license. The possessor of premises on which a trespasser intrudes owes a trespasser the duty to refrain from wilfully, wantonly, or recklessly injuring him.

A licensee is one who enters or remains on the premises of another by virtue of either the express or implied consent of the possessor of the premises, or by operation of law, so that he is not a trespasser thereon. The possessor of premises on which a licensee intrudes owes a licensee the duty to refrain from wilfully or wantonly injuring him. The parties agree that Rolf Gerchberg was a licensee under the facts of this case.

Under the law in this jurisdiction a social guest has the status of a licensee and his host owes him only the duty to refrain from wilfully, intentionally, or recklessly injuring him.

An invitee is one who enters or remains on the premises of another at the express or implied invitation of the possessor of the premises for the benefit of the inviter, or for the mutual benefit and advantage of both inviter and invitee. The possessor of premises on which an invitee enters owes a higher degree of care, that of reasonable or ordinary care for the invitee's safety. This duty is active and positive. It includes a duty to protect and warn an invitee against any danger that may be reasonably anticipated.

Under the law in this and other jurisdictions a child may be presumed conclusively incapable of contributory negligence. Children are not held to the same strict accountability to appreciate a danger and to care for themselves as persons of full age. Therefore the attractive nuisance exception has been recognized to accommodate for a child's incapacity to understand and appreciate the possible dangers to which he may be attracted.

. . . .

If the traditional classifications are discarded the legal distinctions which have heretofore governed the courts in imposing a particular standard of care are also discarded. In such case the standard, reasonable care under all the circumstances, would have to be applied by the jury to the specific facts of each case. Can a lay jury reasonably be expected to consider the proper relative effect of natural and artificial conditions on the premises which are or may be dangerous, the degree of danger inherent in such conditions, the extent of the burden which should be placed on the possessor of premises to alleviate the danger, the nature, use and location of the condition or force involved, the foreseeability of the presence of the plaintiff on the premises, the obviousness of such dangerous condition or the plaintiff's actual knowledge of the condition or force which resulted in injury? It would appear these considerations should be imparted to the jury if it is to be placed in a position to decide whether reasonable care was exercised by the possessor of the premises. Otherwise the jury will have a free hand to impose or withhold liability.

A majority of the members of this court do not feel that the traditional classifications of trespassers, licensees and invitees should be jettisoned. The traditional classifications were worked out and the exceptions were spelled out with much thought, sweat and even tears by generations of Kansas legal scholars who have gone before us. Should this body of law be discarded completely in favor of a free hand by a lay jury? We feel at this time there is too much of value in our premises law with respect to rights of possessors of premises to warrant its abandonment.

. . . .

It should be noted that the adoption of one standard of care not only will have the effect of lowering the standard of care owed to trespassers and licensees but also would lower the standard of care presently owed to invitees. Under our present law the duty owed to an invitee is active and positive. It includes a duty to protect and warn an invitee against any danger that may be reasonably anticipated. Not only does it extend to dangerous conditions known to the possessor but also to dangerous conditions discoverable in the exercise of a duty to inspect and keep the premises free of unreasonable risk of harm.

It has been suggested that the jury need not be left without guidance even though the traditional classifications are discarded. It is further suggested that after a jury is advised of the single standard of care the court can further instruct the jury by setting out the applicable rules found in the Restatement of the Law, Second, Torts, §§ 333 through 343B. The Restatement classifies these rules as follows: Title B. Liability of Possessors of Land to Trespassers; Title C. General Liability of Possessors of Land to Licensees and Invitees; Title D. Special Liability of Possessors of Land to Licensees; and Title E. Special Liability of Possessors of Land to Invitees. If such a suggestion is followed in advising the jury what if anything is gained by discarding the traditional rules? The traditional classifications (trespassers, licensees and invitees) are still to be considered by the court. If, as the appellant suggests, the traditional classifications are confusing, unreasonable and arbitrary any change which embraces the Restatement rules will be subject to similar charges. In such case we would be merely changing the extent of the duty owed by a possessor of premises. The extent of that duty would still be dictated by the circumstances surrounding entry on the premises, the danger involved and the burden to be placed on the possessor to make the premises reasonably safe. The traditional classifications would remain but the traditional rules worked out over so many years would be discarded and new rules governing a possessor's liability would have to be relearned.

A majority of this court feel if the mores and values of present society dictate changes such changes should be worked out individually as the circumstances of a particular case may warrant. Such changes will result in less general confusion and better understanding of each particular change.

. . . .

In conclusion we wish to acknowledge what has been referred to as a trend in this country toward abolition of the traditional classifications. Apparently the bellwether case in the United States was handed down in 1968, *Rowland v. Christian*, 69 Cal. 2d 108, 70 Cal. Rptr. 97, 443 P.2d 561. Our research indicates that in the ten years which have elapsed since *Rowland* only nine states have followed the lead. During this same period of time several states have elevated licensees to a common class with invitees, and five states have placed social guests in the category of invitees. During this same period of time a large majority of states have continued to follow the traditional common law classifications. At least six states have considered the advisability of following *Rowland v. Christian, supra*, and have declined to do so. The jurisdictions which have abolished all classifications are not sufficient in number to constitute a clear trend.

In the present case the plaintiff's evidence was sufficient to require submitting the case to a jury on the theory of attractive nuisance. . . .

Accordingly we approve the majority opinion of the Court of Appeals. The judgment of the District Court of Douglas County is reversed and the case is remanded for further proceedings.

PRAGER, JUSTICE, dissenting:

I respectfully dissent. Under the undisputed facts as shown in the record, the plaintiff has failed as a matter of law to establish that the defendants were negligent.

. . . .

I am also in disagreement with the position of the majority that the traditional classifications of trespassers, licensees, and invitees should be maintained and that the degree of care owed to each classification by a land occupier should be controlled solely by the status of the injured person. A cardinal principle of tort law today is that *all persons* should be required to use ordinary care under the circumstances to prevent others from being injured as the result of their conduct.

. . . .

MILLER, JUSTICE, dissenting:

I join in the dissent of Justice Prager. I would eliminate the distinction between licensees and invitees, and adopt reasonable care as the standard governing the duty of an occupier of land towards persons entering upon the land with consent. I would not abolish the trespasser classification, however, and would retain the present standard as to the duty owed to trespassers, i.e., the duty to refrain from the infliction of willful, wanton, or reckless injury.

OWSLEY, JUSTICE, concurring[.]

––––––––––

1. In *Jones v. Hansen*, 867 P.2d 303 (1994) the Kansas Supreme Court held that an occupier of land owes a full duty of reasonable care to both invitees and licensees.

The following case highlights the fact that wandering cattle cases remain a phenomenon of the present. *Wrinkle* involves issues that refer back to the intentional tort chapters and to privileges for people who might otherwise be considered to be trespassers, and forward to the strict liability and defenses chapters.

Wrinkle v. Norman

Supreme Court of Kansas, 2013
301 P.3d 312

PER CURIAM:

The appellant, Rodney Wrinkle, was injured in the course of providing aid to a calf that he was escorting onto a neighbor's property. He sued to recover medical damages from the neighbor, and the district court granted the Normans' motion for summary judgment. Because the district court applied the incorrect standard for the duty of care in this case, we remand for the submission of new arguments predicated on the proper duty.

Based on the pleadings and the record developed through deposition testimony, the circumstances of Wrinkle's injury were as follows:

On the afternoon of March 10, 2006, Wrinkle and his friend Raymond Lee observed four or five cows wandering loose in front of property belonging to Gene and Charlene Norman, and some of the cattle were straying toward the highway that ran between Wrinkle's and the Normans' property. Wrinkle was riding his lawn tractor, and he signaled to approaching cars to slow down. Initially riding on his lawn tractor and then going on foot, Wrinkle proceeded to herd the cattle into the Normans' yard. The Normans' gate was open, and Wrinkle herded the cows through the gate toward a pen. Wrinkle testified at his deposition that he had no reason to believe that the Normans consented to his entry onto their land.

A clothesline wire was attached in some fashion to a pole in the Normans' yard. According to his deposition testimony, Wrinkle did not see how it was attached when he entered the yard; it may have been hanging looped like a lasso over the pole, and some of it may have extended to the ground.

As Wrinkle herded the cattle across the Normans' yard toward the cow pen, one calf strayed into the clothesline wire, caught the line around its neck, and began to choke. Wrinkle grabbed the back of the clothesline and walked around to the other side, flipping the line several times in order to remove the line from the calf's neck. The calf took off running toward the gate of the pen, apparently catching the clothesline somehow, so that the clothesline caught Wrinkle from behind. Wrinkle's feet went out from under him, and he landed on his back on a concrete pad.

Wrinkle immediately experienced severe pain. ... Wrinkle eventually went to the hospital, where he was diagnosed with a broken back. He was hospitalized for 30 days. ...

Wrinkle then filed an action grounded in negligence alleging that the Normans had created a dangerous condition on their property that presented an unreasonable risk of harm by leaving their gate open and by leaving a clothesline wire running across the ground.

The Normans filed a motion for summary judgment. They maintained that Wrinkle was a trespasser on their land, that they were not negligent because they were unaware that their clothesline presented a danger, and that Wrinkle failed to proffer evidence that they did not take reasonable care for the safety of others.

The district court granted the Normans' motion for summary judgment, holding that Wrinkle was a trespasser on the Normans' property and they had breached no duty toward him. ...

[T]he Court of Appeals affirmed the district court. ... This court granted review without limitation.

The Duty of Care

A landowner's duty to both invitees and licensees is one of reasonable care under all the circumstances. *Jones v. Hansen*, 254 Kan. 499, Syl. ¶ 2, 867 P.2d 303 (1994). The landowner owes trespassers, on the other hand, only the duty "to refrain from willfully, wantonly, or recklessly injuring" the trespasser. 254 Kan. at 510, 867 P.2d 303.

The district court found that Wrinkle did not have express or implied permission to enter the Normans' property and he was therefore a trespasser. Because he was a trespasser, the Normans owed him a duty only to refrain from willfully, wantonly, or recklessly injuring him.

The Court of Appeals affirmed, holding that Wrinkle was a trespasser because "there was no evidence that the cattle were owned by the Normans." 44 Kan.App.2d at 956, 242 P.3d 1216. The court further held that, even if Wrinkle were privileged by private necessity to enter the Normans' property, the Normans owed no greater duty of care toward him than they would to a trespasser. ...

Wrinkle urges this court to adopt the Restatement (Second) of Torts § 197 (1965), relating to private necessity as an exception to the rules of trespass. Wrinkle contends that the Restatement section, if adopted in Kansas, would enhance the duty that the Normans owed him. Restatement (Second) of Torts § 197 creates a privilege in the event of necessity:

> "(1) One is privileged to enter or remain on land in the possession of another if it is or reasonably appears to be necessary to prevent serious harm to
>
> (a) the actor, or his land or chattels, or
>
> (b) the other or a third person, or the land or chattels of either, unless the actor knows or has reason to know that the one for whose benefit he enters is unwilling that he shall take such action.
>
> "(2) Where the entry is for the benefit of the actor or a third person, he is subject to liability for any harm done in the exercise of the privilege stated in Subsection (1) to any legally protected interest of the possessor in the land or connected with it, except where the threat of harm to avert which the entry is made is caused by the tortious conduct or contributory negligence of the possessor."

Kansas has not expressly adopted Restatement (Second) of Torts § 197. As the Court of Appeals noted, this section of the Restatement does not in itself change the duty of care owed to the actor. A review of the comments and illustrations accompanying § 197 make it clear that the section addresses only the liability of the actor to the possessor of the property; that is, it sets out under what situations may one enter the property of another without incurring liability for trespass or for damage resulting from the entry and use of the property. Section 197 by itself speaks to the opposite of the situation in the present case, in which an actor seeks damages from the possessor of the property.

A different section of the Restatement, Restatement (Second) of Torts § 345 (1965), addresses the kind of situation that the present case presents:

> "(1) Except as stated in Subsection (2), the liability of a possessor of land to one who enters the land only in the exercise of a privilege, for either a public or a private purpose, and irrespective of the possessor's consent, is the same as the liability to a licensee.
>
> "(2) The liability of a possessor of land to a public officer or employee who enters the land in the performance of his public duty, and suffers harm because of a condition of a part of the land held open to the public, is the same as the liability to an invitee."

In Kansas, the effect of these two provisions, when read together, is to create a presumption of implicit permission for one party to enter the property of another in order to prevent certain kinds of serious harm, and the possessor of the property has a duty of reasonable care to protect the wellbeing of the person exercising that privilege.

We regard the Restatement rules as sound and adopt them with modifications. In our view, they promote a willingness to assist others in times of need without taking on a greater burden of risk than others who enter property as merely casual visitors. Restatement (Second) of Torts § 197 makes it possible for a Good Samaritan to enter the property of another for the purpose of averting great property loss or personal injury without having to suffer the consequences of being deemed a trespasser.

Without passing judgment on the factual determinations to be made in the present case, it is not difficult to imagine scenarios in which the Restatement provisions provide the superior analytic framework. Suppose that an individual hears screams from across the street and sees a neighbor's house in flames. The individual rushes to the house and attempts to enter it in order to aid someone trapped inside but falls through a rotted step on the way in, injuring himself. Without the two Restatement sections, the would-be Good Samaritan could be found liable for trespass or would not be able to bring an action for negligently maintaining the premises. Applying the Restatement rules, the helpful neighbor would be protected from being the target of litigation himself and would be eligible for damages for the injuries that he suffered as a consequence of the hidden defect. See *Mercer v. Hawes*, No. 534,145, 1995 WL 506072 (Conn.Super.1995) (unpublished opinion); cf. Restatement (Second) of Torts § 345, comment d, illustration 1.

In adopting the Restatement provisions, we acknowledge that certain aspects of Kansas civil procedure and common law require modification of those rules. Restatement (Second) of Torts § 197, paragraph 2, limits the privilege where entry is for the benefit of the actor or a third person, except when the danger that justifies the entry is caused by the tortious conduct or contributory negligence of the possessor. That portion of the Restatement rule is modified to reflect principles of comparative fault that govern in Kansas.

Similarly, Restatement (Second) of Torts § 345 differentiates between the duty of care to public officers or employees who enter the land in the performance of a public duty and the duty of care to others exercising a privilege. Because Kansas no longer differentiates between the duty of care to a licensee and to an invitee, we adopt § 345 without distinguishing between the duties in paragraphs (1) and (2); the duty is always one of reasonable care under all circumstances.

The defendants based their motion for summary judgment on theories of trespass, and the district court likewise decided the motion without the benefit of the rules that we recognize in this opinion. The parties should not be penalized because this court has adopted a rule that has not been discussed in previous caselaw.

In addition, we find the plaintiff's theory of liability under K.S.A. 47-122 and K.S.A. 47-123 to be moot. The standard of care for actions under those statutes is one of reasonable precaution or due care in keeping cattle from running at large. *Clark v. Carson*, 188 Kan. 261, 265, 362 P.2d 71 (1961) (reasonable or due precaution); *Wilson v. Rule*, 169 Kan. 296, 303, 219 P.2d 690 (1950) (due care); *Walborn v. Stockman*, 10 Kan.App.2d 597, 599, 706 P.2d 465 (1985) (due care). The duty of reasonable care is essentially the same as the duty under the theory that the Normans were negligent in the manner of storing their clothesline. Because Wrinkle asserts that the injury occurred on the Normans' property and in the course of attempting to protect the Normans' calf, it is that theory of negligence that governs the duty of care.

The dissent raises several points that, if properly argued in the pleadings to the trial court and then advanced on appeal, might have provided grounds for us to reach a different result. Although the parties mentioned in their pleadings alternative grounds for summary judgment in passing, their focus was clearly on the question of whether Wrinkle was a trespasser. Other arguments were mentioned but were not supported by a developed legal analysis, and the district court did not address those peripheral arguments in its written decision. . . .

The judgment of the Court of Appeals is reversed. The judgment of the district court is reversed, and the case is remanded for further proceedings consistent with this opinion.

ROSEN, J., concurring in part and dissenting in part:

Although I agree with the majority that courts in Kansas should adopt the relevant Restatement sections, Restatement (Second) of Torts § 197 and Restatement (Second) of Torts § 345, I respectfully dissent from that portion of the opinion that remands the case to the district court for further proceedings.

My review of the record and the governing legal principles persuades me that summary judgment was appropriate even under the Restatement rules and it is unnecessary to return the case for further proceedings. I base my opinion on three factors.

First, the record and the pleadings show that a clothesline looped around a clothesline pole in plain view on a March afternoon constituted the asserted negligent condition on the defendants' property. I suggest that such a condition simply cannot serve as the basis of a negligence action. A duty to remove any object from one's property that could in any fashion somehow be a factor in an injury to another person entering one's property simply increases the possibility of liability and litigation to an absurd level. With some imagination, one can picture a flower pot, a drainpipe, a trash barrel, or a bicycle playing a role in a series of events leading to injury, even if those items are located in perfectly predictable and ordinary locations.

        . . . .

Furthermore, a landowner "is under no duty to remove known and obvious dangers." *Miller v. Zep Mfg. Co.*, 249 Kan. 34, 43, 815 P.2d 506 (1991). Either the clothesline, hanging in plain view from a clothesline pole in the afternoon, was an obvious danger, in which case the defendants were under no duty to remove it, or it was not in itself a danger, in which case the defendants simply were not negligent. . . .

My second concern with sending this case back for further proceedings is that the evidence that the plaintiff provided did not show that the defendants maintained the clothesline in such a way that they breached any duty of care. The record shows that the plaintiff at one time asserted that the clothesline was hanging looped around the pole and was off the ground; another time he asserted that the line partially lay on the ground; and another time he conceded that he never saw how the line was arranged before the calf became entangled in it. In other words, the plaintiff asserts that the defendants maintained a hazardous condition on their property, but he is unable to describe what that condition was. The only relevant fact question before the court or before a jury would be whether the clothesline was negligently strung from the pole, but the plaintiff's own testimony was that he had no idea how the clothesline was strung from the pole.

Finally, I suggest that this court can easily find from the pleadings and record that the plaintiff has failed to establish proximate causation of his injuries, even assuming that he can demonstrate some kind of breach of duty of care. Proximate cause is one necessary element of a successful tort action. . . .

. . . .

Although the courts below and Wrinkle make much of his status as trespasser or invitee/licensee, it is questionable whether that distinction matters in this case. . . .

In the present case, a bizarre series of events took place between the defendants' putative negligent acts of leaving the gate open and leaving a clothesline on a pole, and the ultimate unfortunate injury to the plaintiff. The plaintiff escorted cattle onto the defendants' property; a calf got caught in the clothesline; the plaintiff elected to set the calf free from the clothesline; the calf got caught in the line that the plaintiff chose to pull off of it; and the calf pulled the line in such a way that it knocked the plaintiff down on a concrete pad. It was a calf running free on the defendants' land and the plaintiff's decision to free the calf from the clothesline that immediately caused the injury. The placement of the clothesline was remote to the injury and its potential for causing harm was simply not foreseeable.

. . . .

In the case before us, the immediate cause of injury was a calf somehow knocking down a visitor on the defendants' property. The plaintiff saw the calf and saw the clothesline looped around the calf. The plaintiff elected to try to remove the clothesline from the calf. Nothing within that sequence of events hints at negligence on the part of the defendants. If the defendants were negligent in leaving a gate open and in leaving a clothesline on a clothesline pole, that negligence was so mitigated by subsequent, intervening, unforeseeable events that the plaintiff's burden of showing proximate causation could not be met. I suggest that this is a classic example of the doctrine of volenti non fit injuria, meaning that an individual who voluntarily risks danger cannot recover for any resulting injury. See Black's Law Dictionary 1605 (8th ed. 2004).

. . . .

I would decide this case as a matter of law on the basis of the pleadings and record developed before the district court, and I would affirm the judgment of the district court for reasons other than those on which the district court relied.

If you were a plaintiff, which would you prefer, the categories or a uniform reasonableness standard? If you were a defendant, which would you prefer? An insurance company selling homeowners' liability insurance? The question of the duty owed in a particular case is one for the judge; whether the defendant was negligent in light of that duty is for the jury. Does this allocation of responsibility at trial affect your answer?

Illinois Compiled Statutes Annotated Chapter 740. Civil Liabilities — Premises Liability Act
740 ILCS 130/2 (1996)

§ 740 ICLS 130/2. [Common law distinction abolished]

Sec.2. The distinction under the common law between invitees and licensees as to the duty owed by an owner or occupier of any premises to such entrants is abolished.

The duty owed to such entrants is that of reasonable care under the circumstances regarding the state of the premises or acts done or omitted on them. The duty of reasonable care under the circumstances which an owner or occupier of land owes to such entrants does not include any of the following: a duty to warn of or otherwise take reasonable steps to protect such entrants from conditions on the premises that are known to the entrant, are open and obvious, or can reasonably be expected to be discovered by the entrant; a duty to warn of latent defects or dangers or defects or dangers unknown to the owner or occupier of the premises; a duty to warn such entrants of any dangers resulting from misuse by the entrants of the premises or anything affixed to or located on the premises; or a duty to protect such entrants from their own misuse of the premises or anything affixed to or located on the premises . . .

§ 740 ILCS 13013. [Trespasser]

Sec. 3. Nothing herein affects the law as regards the trespassing child entrant. An owner or occupier of land owes no duty of care to an adult trespasser other than to refrain from willful and wanton conduct that would endanger the safety of a known trespasser on the property from a condition of the property or an activity conducted by the owner or occupier on the property.

---

1. Why did the Illinois legislature retain the trespasser classification?

2. The Second Restatement of Torts in Section 333 retains the trespasser classification and provides that "a possessor of land is not liable to trespassers for physical

harm caused by his failure to exercise reasonable care." The landowner is under no obligation either to make the land safe for trespassers or to take their presence into account when using his or her land. Section 333 states that this rule "applies although from past experience or otherwise the possessor has every reason to realize that there is a strong probability that trespassers will intrude upon his land." There are, of course, exceptions to this rule of nonliability. Sections 334–39 of the Second Restatement describe six types of trespasser to whom the owner of the land will be liable — in other words, six types of trespasser who are excepted from the general rule of nonliability to trespassers. Three of these are: (1) trespassers of whose constant presence the landowner is or should be aware, where the landowner's activity involves a risk of death or serious injury to the trespasser (Section 334), (2) trespassers of whose constant presence the landowner is or should be aware, where there is a highly dangerous artificial condition created or maintained by the landowner, where the trespassers are not likely to discover the condition, and where the landowner has failed to use reasonable care to warn the trespassers of the condition and the risk (Section 335), (3) trespassers of whose presence the landowner is or should be aware, where the landowner "fail[s] to carry on his activities upon the land with reasonable care for the trespasser's safety" (Section 336). How much of the nonliability principle remains after all these exceptions are applied? A court that has abandoned such classifications does not need to deal with the Restatement definitions; rather, that court will need to ask whether the landowner was negligent with respect to the plaintiffs involved.

3. The California and Kansas courts reach opposite conclusions about whether the classifications of plaintiff should remain in place. How often do you think that the classifications make a difference in the result of a case? Aren't the classifications really a rule-oriented effort to embody foreseeability concepts? If the classification of trespasser were unavailable, wouldn't the defendant argue that the presence of the plaintiff on his or her land was unforeseeable, or if foreseeable, that the defendant did not act unreasonably with respect to the plaintiff by failing to make his or her land safe for that plaintiff?

2. Natural and Unnatural Conditions On and Off the Land

Sprecher v. Adamson Cos.

Supreme Court of California, 1981 (en banc)
636 P.2d 1121

BIRD, CHIEF JUSTICE.

This case concerns the present validity of the old common law rule which immunized a possessor of land from liability for injury caused by a natural condition of his land to persons or property not on his land.

I.

The following facts are not in dispute. Respondent, South Winter Mesa Associates, a joint venture between respondents The Adamson Companies and Century-Malibu Ventures, Inc., owns a 90-acre parcel of land in Malibu, California. The parcel is bounded on the north by the Pacific Coast Highway and on the south by Malibu Road. Across Malibu Road and opposite the parcel are a number of beach front homes, including the home of appellant, Peter Sprecher.

Respondents' parcel of land contains part of an active landslide which extends seaward from the parcel for some 1,700 feet along Malibu Road and beyond the boundaries of respondents' property. The Sprecher property is situated within the toe of this slide. The landslide, which has been evident since the area was first developed in the early 1900's, is classified as active because it exhibits periodic cycles of activity and dormancy. The parties agree that the slide is a natural condition of the land which has not been affected by any of respondents' activities on the 90-acre parcel.

In March 1978, heavy spring rains triggered a major movement of the slide which caused appellant's home to rotate and to press against the home of his neighbor, Gwendolyn Sexton. As a result, Sexton filed an action against appellant, seeking to enjoin the encroachment of his home upon hers. Appellant cross-complained against Sexton, the County of Los Angeles and respondents. Specifically, appellant sought damages for the harm done to his home by the landslide. He alleged that such damage proximately resulted from respondents' negligent failure to correct or to control the landslide condition.

Respondents moved for summary judgment, arguing primarily that a possessor of land has no duty to remedy a natural condition of the land in order to prevent harm to property outside his premises. Since the landslide was a natural condition, they argued that they were not liable for the damage to appellant's home.

In opposition, appellant challenged the present validity of the common law rule of nonliability for a natural condition, arguing that the rule is neither premised upon sound public policy nor in accord with modern principles of tort liability.

The trial court ruled in favor of respondents and this appeal followed.

II.

Summary judgment is properly granted where the evidence in support of the moving party, here the respondents, is sufficient to establish a complete defense to appellant's claims and there is no triable issue of fact. Obviously, a rule of law, such as the traditional rule regarding natural conditions, which provides that a defendant has no duty to protect plaintiff is a complete defense to a claim of negligence. Its effect is to immunize or exempt the defendant from liability for negligence. Therefore, the first question this court must decide is whether a possessor of land should be immunized from liability for harm caused by a natural condition of his land to persons outside his premises. That is, should a possessor's exposure to liability be determined by reference to the origin of the condition causing harm or in accord with the ordinary principles of negligence.

Under the common law, the major important limitation upon the responsibility of a possessor of land to those outside his premises concerned the natural condition of the land.[3] While the possessor's liability for harm caused by artificial conditions[4] was determined in accord with ordinary principles of negligence, the common law gave him an absolute immunity from liability for harm caused by conditions considered natural in origin. No matter how great the harm threatened to his neighbor, or to one passing by, and no matter how small the effort needed to eliminate it, a possessor of land had no duty to remedy conditions that were natural in origin.

This court has held that it will not depart from the fundamental concept that a person is liable for injuries caused "by his want of ordinary care . . . in the management of his property or person . . ." (Civ. Code, § 1714) except when such a departure is "clearly supported by public policy." *(Rowland v. Christian* (1968) 69 Cal. 2d 108, 112, 70 Cal. Rptr. 97, 443 P.2d 561.) Accordingly, common law distinctions resulting in wholesale immunities have been struck down when such distinctions could not withstand critical scrutiny.

In *Rowland,* this court stated that "[a] departure from [the] fundamental principle [of Civil Code section 1714] involves the balancing of a number of considerations[.] [T]he major ones are the foreseeability of harm to the plaintiff, the degree of certainty that the plaintiff suffered injury, the closeness of the connection between the defendant's conduct and the injury suffered, the moral blame attached to the defendant's conduct, the policy of preventing future harm, the extent of the burden to the defendant and [the] consequences to the community of imposing a duty to exercise care with resulting liability for breach and the availability, cost, and prevalence of insurance for the risk involved." (*Rowland v. Christian, supra*, 69 Cal. 2d at pp. 112–113, 70 Cal. Rptr. 97, 443 P.2d 561.)

Th[e] progression of the law in California mirrors what appears to be a general trend toward rejecting the common law distinction between natural and artificial conditions. Instead, the courts are increasingly using ordinary negligence principles to determine a possessor's liability for harm caused by a condition of the land. The early case of *Gibson v. Denton* (1896) 4 A.D. 198, 38 N.Y.S. 554 was a precursor of this

---

3. The term "'[n]atural condition of the land' is used to indicate that the condition of land has not been changed by any act of a human being. . . . It is also used to include the natural growth of trees, weeds, and other vegetation upon land not artificially made receptive to them." (Rest. 2d Torts, § 363, com. b.

4. "[A] structure erected upon land is a non-natural or artificial condition, as are trees or plants planted or preserved, and changes in the surface by excavation or filling, irrespective of whether they are harmful in themselves or become so only because of the subsequent operation of natural forces." (Rest. 2d Torts, § 363, com. b.)

trend. In *Gibson*, the court held a possessor of land liable for damage caused when a decayed tree on her premises fell on the home of her neighbor during a storm. After noting that the defendant clearly would be liable for the fall of a dilapidated building, or artificial structure, the court observed that it could "see no good reason why she should not be responsible for the fall of a decayed tree, which she allowed to remain on her premises." *(Id.*, at p. 555.) "[T]he tree was on her lot, and was her property. It was as much under her control as a pole or building in the same position would have been." *(Ibid.)* Thus, "[t]he defendant had no more right to keep, maintain, or suffer to remain on her premises an unsound tree . . . than she would have had to keep a dilapidated and unsafe building in the same position." *(Id.*, at pp. 555–556.)

In more recent years, at least 13 other states and the District of Columbia have begun applying ordinary negligence principles in determining a possessor's liability for harm caused by a natural condition.

> . . . .

The courts are not simply creating an exception to the common law rule of non-liability for damage caused by trees and retaining the rule for other natural conditions of the land. Instead, the courts are moving toward jettisoning the common law rule in its entirety and replacing it with a single duty of reasonable care in the maintenance of property. This development is reflected in the Restatement Second of Torts, which now recognizes that a possessor of land may be subject to liability for harm caused not just by trees but by any natural condition of the land.

> . . . .

The latest formulation of the duty owed by a possessor of land to persons outside his premises with regard to natural conditions which is set forth in the Restatement Second of Torts still limits the reach of the duty to persons traveling on the public streets and highways. (Rest. 2d Torts, § 840, subd. (2).) The American Law Institute, however, noted that at the time this formulation was promulgated, the authority was insufficient to support a position regarding whether the duty was owed adjoining landowners as well. (See Rest. 2d Torts, § 840, com. c.) Nevertheless, a number of jurisdictions have held a possessor of land liable for harm caused an adjoining landowner by a natural condition of the land. It is difficult to discern any reason to restrict the possessor's duty to individuals using the highways. To do so would create an unsatisfying anomaly: a possessor of land would have a duty of care toward strangers but not toward his neighbor.

In rejecting the common law rule of nonliability for natural conditions, the courts have recognized the inherent injustice involved in a rule which states that "a landowner may escape all liability for serious damage to his neighbors [or those using a public highway], merely by allowing nature to take its course." (Prosser, [Law of Torts (4th ed. 1971) § 57], at p. 355.) As one commentator has observed: "[w]here a planted tree has become dangerous to persons on the highway or on adjoining land, and causes harm, the fault lies not in the planting of the tree but in permitting it to remain after it has become unsafe." (Noel, *Nuisances from Land in its Natural Condition* 56 Harv. L. Rev. 772, 796–797 (1943).)

Historically, the consideration most frequently invoked to support the rule of non-liability for natural conditions was that it was merely an embodiment of the principle that one should not be obligated to undertake affirmative conduct to aid or protect others. This doctrine rested on the common law distinction between the infliction of harm and the failure to prevent it, or misfeasance and nonfeasance. (Rest. 2d Torts, §314, com. c.) Misfeasance was determined to exist when a defendant played some part in the creation of a risk, even if his participation was innocent. Nonfeasance occurred when a defendant had merely failed to intervene in a plaintiff's behalf. Liability for nonfeasance, or the failure to take affirmative action, was ordinarily imposed only where some special relationship between the plaintiff and defendant could be established.

Proponents of the rule of nonliability for natural conditions argued that a defendant's failure to prevent a natural condition from causing harm was mere nonfeasance. A natural condition of the land was by definition, they argued, one which no human being had played a part in creating. Therefore, no basis for liability existed because a duty to exercise reasonable care could not arise out of possession alone. Since there was no special relationship between the possessor of land and persons outside the premises, there could be no liability. Conversely, a defendant's failure to prevent an artificial condition from causing harm constituted actionable misfeasance.

Whatever the rule may once have been, it is now clear that a duty to exercise due care can arise out of possession alone. One example is provided by modern cases dealing with the duty of a possessor of land to act affirmatively for the protection of individuals who come upon the premises. In days gone by, a possessor of land was deemed to owe such a duty of care only to invitees. That is, the duty to act affirmatively was grounded in the special relation between the possessor-invitor and the invitee. *Rowland* held that whether the individual coming upon the land was a trespasser, a licensee or an invitee made no difference as to the duty of reasonable care owed but was to be considered only as to the issue of whether the possessor had exercised reasonable care under all the circumstances. (*Rowland v. Christian, supra*, at pp. 118–119, 70 Cal. Rptr. 97, 443 P.2d 561.)

Modern cases recognize that after *Rowland*, the duty to take affirmative action for the protection of individuals coming upon the land is grounded in the possession of the premises and the attendant right to control and manage the premises.

. . . .

Thus, it becomes clear that the traditional characterization of a defendant's failure to take affirmative steps to prevent a natural condition from causing harm as nonactionable nonfeasance conflicts sharply with modern perceptions of the obligations which flow from the possession of land. Possession ordinarily brings with it the right of supervision and control. . . .

Another deficiency of the historical justification of the rule of nonliability is simply that it proves too much. Under the traditional analysis, a possessor of land should be excused from any duty to prevent harm to persons outside his land whenever he has played no part in the creation of the condition which threatens the harm, be it artificial or natural. However, most courts recognize that the possessor is under an affirmative duty to act with regard to a dangerous artificial condition even though the condition was created solely by some predecessor in title or possession (Rest. 2d Torts, § 366;[6] or by the unauthorized conduct of some other third person (Rest. 2d Torts, § 364, subd.(c)).[7]

. . . .

In addition, adherence to the rule in California would produce an anomalous result. A possessor of land would owe a duty of care to protect trespassers, invitees and licensees, but not his neighbor, from harms threatened by a natural condition of the land. It has long been established in California that a possessor of land is subject to liability for harm caused a person upon the land by a natural condition. It is difficult to see why this court should support a rule which would allow a trespasser to bring an action in negligence that would be denied a neighbor, where both were standing on either side of the possessor's boundary line and were both struck by a dead limb from his tree.

Finally, it is apparent that the distinction between artificial and natural conditions, and the immunity from liability predicated on that distinction, bears little relationship to the major factors which should determine whether immunity should be given the possessor of land for harm done by a natural condition of the land. The foreseeability of harm to the plaintiff, the degree of certainty that the plaintiff suffered injury, the closeness of the connection between the defendant's conduct and the injury suffered, the moral blame attached to the defendant's conduct, the policy of preventing future harm, and the extent of the burden to the defendant and the consequence to

---

6. Section 366 provides:

"One who takes possession of land upon which there is an existing structure or other artificial condition unreasonably dangerous to persons or property outside of the land is subject to liability for physical harm caused to them by the condition after, but only after,

"(a) the possessor knows or should know of the condition, and

"(b) he knows or should know that it exists without the consent of those affected by it, and

"(c) he has failed, after a reasonable opportunity, to make it safe or otherwise to protect such persons against it."

7. Section 364, subdivision (c), provides:

"A possessor of land is subject to liability to others outside of the land for physical harm caused by a structure or other artificial condition on the land, which the possessor realizes or should realize will involve an unreasonable risk of harm, if . . .

"(c) the condition is created by a third person without the possessor's consent or acquiescence, but reasonable care is not taken to make the condition safe after the possessor knows or should know of it."

the community of imposing a duty to exercise care have little, if any, relationship to the natural, as opposed to artificial, origin of the condition causing harm.

The remaining factors, the availability, cost, and prevalence of insurance may in some cases bear a relationship to the natural origin of the condition. Insurance may not be readily available for the risks posed by some natural conditions. On balance, however, it is clear that a departure from the fundamental concept that a person is liable for the harm caused "by his want of ordinary care . . . in the management of his property . . ." (Civ. Code, § 1714) is unwarranted as regards natural conditions of land.

The trend in the law is in the direction of imposing a duty of reasonable care upon the possessor of land with regard to natural conditions of land. The erosion of the doctrinal underpinning of the rule of nonliability is evident from even a cursory review of the case law. Also evident is the lack of congruence between the old common law rule of nonliability and the relevant factors which should determine whether a duty exists. All this leads to but one conclusion. The distinction between artificial and natural conditions should be rejected.

IV.

The judgment of the trial court is reversed and the cause remanded to the trial court for further proceedings consistent with the views expressed in this opinion.

TOBRINER, MOSK, NEWMAN, WORK and MCCLOSKY, JJ., concur.

RICHARDSON, JUSTICE, concurring.

I concur in the judgment of the court which reverses the trial court's entry of summary judgment in favor of respondents. It seems proper to require that landowners act reasonably with reference to their property, thus preventing damage to their neighbors. This is so regardless of whether the condition threatening the injury or damage is artificial or natural.

. . . .

---

1. What effect does extending liability to natural conditions have on insurance? What if you live on a mountaintop, and after a rainstorm, a mudslide runs from your property down onto your neighbor's house? How would you classify cattle?

2. As with many other areas of tort law, the concept of reasonable conduct in the circumstances may replace the proliferation of specific rules that the common law generated in the past. The issue becomes whether the defendant (and, for that matter, the plaintiff) acted reasonably; categorizing either party becomes unnecessary. This trend simplifies legal decisions enormously, not least because it creates a body of law that applies in all cases, no matter how bizarre or outside prior precedent the facts may be. Instead of having to figure out into which pigeonhole the facts fit, or having to invent a new pigeonhole if they don't fit anywhere, the court simply asks whether the parties acted reasonably.

One of the sets of pigeonholes that created problems involved natural and unnatural uses of or conditions on land. For example, the rules on trees could be unexpectedly complex. In some courts, any tree would be a natural condition; in others, a tree would be a natural condition only if it had grown by itself (as opposed to having been planted by the landowner). In still others, a tree would be a natural condition if it was of a native species, whether planted by the landowner or not. Any nonnative tree would then be an unnatural condition, however it appeared on the property. Just to add to the complexity, a native tree might be an unnatural condition if, for example, the forest around it had been removed, leaving it more exposed to wind and weather. Such a welter of definitional problems (similar to the complexities of automobile guest rules) can be eliminated when a rule-based standard is replaced by a reasonableness one.

3. T, the owner of real estate, builds a garage for his car on his land. Because he likes to be in the shade when working on his car, he builds his garage in such a way that a large healthy tree on the property of his next-door neighbor, R, will cast shade onto that garage.

During a storm, the tree on R's land, which is several hundred years old, falls onto T's garage. Will R be liable for damage to the garage? Would your answer change depending upon whether the tree had been planted by an ancestor of R or had grown at its location by itself?

B. Additional Categories of Plaintiffs

1. Attractive Nuisances, Artificial Conditions, and Children

Crawford v. Pacific Western Mobile Estates, Inc.
Missouri Court of Appeals, Kansas City District, 1977
548 S.W.2d 216

Before WASSERSTROM, P.J. and SOMMERVILLE and TURNAGE, JJ.

WASSERSTROM, PRESIDING JUDGE.

Plaintiffs seek damages for wrongful death of their six year old son, Mark, who drowned in a settlement tank maintained by defendant Pacific Western Mobile Estates, Inc., as part of its sewage treatment plant at Liberty Village Trailer Park in Clay County, Missouri. The jury returned a verdict of $30,000 against both Pacific Western and its resident manager Wilma Gilbert. However, the trial court, pursuant to after trial motions, set aside the verdict and entered judgment for defendants. Plaintiffs appeal. Reversed.

The sole issue presented is whether the evidence established a submissible case of negligence. . . .

The tragic accident in question occurred on November 22, 1973. Plaintiffs, together with their son Mark, were residents of Pacific Western's trailer park which accommodated 143 residential trailers. The southwest part of the park was reserved for non-family residents, while the southeast part was reserved for families with children. At the extreme northern part of the trailer park, and closer to the family portion than to the non-family section, Pacific Western maintained a sewage treatment plant of which the settlement tank was a part. The nearest trailer was approximately 200 yards from this sewage treatment facility.

The settlement tank itself resembled a swimming pool; it was approximately 25 feet long and 11 feet wide, with vertical concrete reinforced walls 7½ feet deep. The water level was maintained at a depth of 6 feet, which means that the surface of the effluent was 1½ feet below the top ledge of the tank (which is at ground level). There was no ladder or other device which would aid anyone who fell into the tank to climb out. The architect designed the tank with a cypress deck to completely cover the top of the tank. The deck was to rest upon a lip or indentation at either end of the tank and fit flush with the top. Although the tank does have the described lip or indentation, the tank has never been covered since the trailer park was acquired by Pacific Western in August, 1973, and manager Gilbert had never observed nor was she ever told about any covering of any kind.

The architect also designed a fence to be built around the tank, and a six foot tall solid wooden flat fence had been erected and was in place. Adjacent to this wooden fence and borrowing one side thereof, a rectangular area was fenced off with a chain link fence for use as a storage area. The chain link fence had a gate and there was also a gate between the storage area and the tank area. Gilbert testified that these gates were kept locked at all times.

After Pacific Western acquired the trailer park, the previous owner removed approximately 60 trailers from the trailer park, leaving behind on the ground concrete blocks which had been used to support those trailers. Pacific Western's maintenance employees gathered up these blocks and piled them against the wooden fence which enclosed the sewage settlement tank. These blocks were stacked in such a way so that "they were sort of like stairs going up" and reached to within 6 inches of the top of the fence. Although a child could not have gotten over the 6 foot wooden fence otherwise, the "stairway" of concrete blocks could be easily ascended by a child and there remained only a short jump to the ground inside of the sewage tank area.

A number of children lived in the trailer park with their parents, and they customarily played throughout the trailer park. There were no warning signs posted anywhere on the grounds to alert parents of any dangerous condition inside the wooden fence, nor were the tenants notified of the existence of the treatment facility. Mark's father testified that he did not know what was inside the fence until after the fatal accident. A neighbor who had lived in the court testified that she also was unaware of the sewage facility inside the fence until after the accident.

On the afternoon of the accident a number of children, aged six to ten, among whom Mark was one, were playing in the trailer park in the vicinity of the wooden fence described and they were seen playing on the concrete blocks piled next to the wooden fence. At about 3:30 an older boy walking by was hailed by the children and was told that someone was in the sewage tank. He climbed the blocks, but could see nothing but a ball floating on the surface of the murky effluent. Other children went to notify Mark's father, who was working beside his trailer, that someone was in the sewer. Mr. Crawford, unaware of the existence of a sewage treatment facility on the grounds, headed toward a storm sewer next to the street, but was corrected by the children. Mr. Crawford and a neighbor who had been summoned probed the pool with a rake and a two by twelve board and succeeded in locating and removing Mark's submerged body. Attempts at resuscitation were unsuccessful. In the course of these rescue attempts, Mr. Crawford saw a wooden ladder-like contraption lying across the width of the tank and which served as a bridge. Also lying across the width of the tank was a metal latticework which Mr. Crawford testified would probably not have borne the weight of a grown man but which might have borne the weight of a small child. Mr. Crawford also noticed small hand prints on one side of the concrete tank on the 1 1/2 foot vertical concrete wall above the surface of the effluent.

Defendants argue vigorously that defendants owed the deceased boy no duty which can be the foundation of recovery, because he was a trespasser when he entered the fenced area. Plaintiffs do not deny the classification of their son as a trespasser, but contend that the landowner nevertheless owed their son a duty of reasonable care under the standards of Section 339, 2 Restatement of the Law, Torts. Defendants deny that the facts here meet those requirements. The issue in this case accordingly narrows to the question of whether plaintiffs have brought this situation within the scope of the § 339 doctrine.

Section 339 of the Restatement (1965 Revision) provides as follows:

"§ 339. Artificial Conditions Highly Dangerous to Trespassing Children

"A possessor of land is subject to liability for physical harm to children trespassing thereon caused by an artificial condition upon the land if

(a) the place where the condition exists is one upon which the possessor knows or has reason to know that children are likely to trespass, and

(b) the condition is one of which the possessor knows or has reason to know and which he realizes or should realize will involve an unreasonable risk of death or serious bodily harm to such children, and

(c) the children because of their youth do not discover the condition or realize the risk involved in intermeddling with it or in coming within the area made dangerous by it, and

(d) the utility to the possessor of maintaining the condition and the burden of eliminating the danger are slight as compared with the risk to children involved, and

(e) the possessor fails to exercise reasonable care to eliminate the danger or otherwise to protect the children."

(a) *Reason to anticipate presence of children.* Treating these five requirements in order, the first question is whether defendants knew or had reason to know that children were likely to enter the fenced area. Defendants lay great stress upon the fact that the record contains no evidence that any children had ever before been in the sewage-treatment facility. That, however, misses the point. Merely because children had not trespassed in the past does not relieve the landowner from liability if there is some reasonable expectation that they might trespass. . . .

The evidence here shows that many of the families in the trailer court had young children who played all over the trailer court. . . . There was further evidence that children played on the concrete blocks which themselves allowed easy access to the sewage tank area itself. Defendant Gilbert, the resident manager of the trailer court, admitted that the kids "were like a bunch of damn monkeys and were down there all the time" and there was nothing she could do to keep them out.

Furthermore, the manager Gilbert had full knowledge of the piled up blocks which permitted of such easy access for children to get over the fence. . . .

The evidence in this case abundantly shows that defendants had good reason to know that children played in the immediate area of the settlement tank and that the conditions were such that the block stairway would provide easy access—if not an open invitation—for children to enter the sewage tank area. Defendants had ample reason to know that sooner or later some child was likely to enter the picket enclosure.

(b) *Reason to realize unreasonable risk.* The second requirement of § 339 is that defendants knew or had reason to know and which they realized or should have realized would involve an unreasonable risk of death *(sic)*. This requirement causes little difficulty under the facts of this case. The prospect of danger was so apparent from the beginning that the architect designed the settlement tank to be protected by both a wooden deck cover and also a six foot high fence. Although the deck cover was apparently never utilized, still the original owner of the trailer park showed a realization of the necessity of some protection by erecting the six foot fence and providing a locked gate to prevent inadvertent entrance into the area. After acquisition of the trailer park by Pacific Western, the necessity of such protection continued to be acknowledged by the defendants as shown by their custom, to which Mrs. Gilbert testified, of keeping the gate carefully locked at all times. Thus the general presence of danger requiring some protection has been established by the actions of defendants themselves. . . .

Yet, despite this awareness of danger against which the fence constituted the only protection, defendants permitted the piling up of concrete blocks against the fence in such a way as to completely negate the protection which the fence was designed to afford. No question is here presented about whether defendants knew of the location of those blocks—Pacific Western's own employees created that condition.

Moreover, the resident manager was reminded by her own eyesight of the danger-ous condition daily. The evidence amply shows that defendants had reason to know and to realize the unreasonable risk of death or injury.

(c) *Lack of realization of risk by trespassing child*. The third requirement for inquiry is whether Mark Crawford, because of his youth, failed to realize the risk involved. This element of plaintiffs' case represents by far the most difficult point of decision and it is the one which bears the heavy weight of defendant's attack. Defendants argue the Missouri courts have consistently denied recovery for the death of children who have drowned in ponds, pools or similar bodies of water and defendants contend that those cases decided under the attractive nuisance doctrine control here. As part of their reliance upon those cases, defendants insist in their brief that Restatement § 339 "is simply a rule setting forth the 'attractive nuisance doctrine.'"

Defendants' latter statement errs. The attractive nuisance doctrine originated as an effort by the courts to ameliorate the harsh rules relating to the extremely limited duty of a landowner to trespassers. The courts, however, confined that new doctrine to a very [narrow] scope, and legal thought grew in favor of further relief. Out of this current of thought grew § 339 of the Restatement. . . . Not until the decision in *Arbogast v. Terminal Railroad Assn. of St. Louis*, [452 S.W.2d 81 (Mo.)] in 1970, more than 35 years after the first publication of § 339, did the Missouri courts yield to the new rules of child trespasser liability. That this adoption would significantly extend the liability of the landowner was the very reason that the Missouri Supreme Court had for so long resisted the change. Now that the change has been accomplished, the old Mis-souri decisions applying the former attractive nuisance doctrine must be read with discrimination and applied only with the greatest of caution.

The pond and pool cases decided under the attractive nuisance doctrine, and upon which the defendants so heavily relied, went in part on the ground that these bodies of water constituted open and obvious danger which should be within the compre-hension of any child old enough to be permitted to roam at large. To this extent, the pool and pond cases still state the law, and a landowner is not now (just as he was not previously) required to "child-proof" his premises against an obvious danger. The underlying concept mentioned has been expressly stated in Comment j under § 339 as follows:

> "There are many dangers, such a [sic] those of fire and water, or of falling from a height, which under ordinary conditions may reasonably be expected to be fully understood and appreciated by any child of an age to be allowed at large. To such conditions the rule stated in this Section ordinarily has no application, in the absence of some other factor creating a special risk that the child will not avoid the danger, such as the fact that the condition is so hidden as not to be readily visible, or a distracting influence which makes it likely that the child will not discover or appreciate it." . . .

Analysis of the present situation must therefore take the next step of examining whether the facts here show distracting elements which kept Mark Crawford from realizing the danger inherent in the settlement tank. Such distracting factors did exist. First of all, the effluent in the tank was dark and murky so as to be opaque. No one could tell from looking whether the depth was a few inches or several yards. Next a ball was floating on top of the effluent. Whether Mark Crawford climbed over the wall to recover the ball which he may have been playing with outside the wall or whether he saw the ball floating in the tank only after he got inside the enclosure, in either event the ball represented a plaything which naturally became the focus of distracting attention to this six-year-old boy.

Added to that situation, there stretched across the tank a wooden bridge and a metal bridge which invited the child out over the pool to bring himself into a position better able to reach toward the ball. The combination of these factors readily support the inference that Mark Crawford was in fact distracted from and did not realize the danger. Under these circumstances, it is easy to understand why this young boy who knew how to swim would not notice that the concrete wall of the tank stood a sheer 1 1/2 feet above the surface of the effluent and that there was no ladder or similar device by which he could get out of the pool in the event he fell in.

. . . .

[The facts in this case meet the requirements of § 339.]

(d) *Comparison of the burden of eliminating the danger with the character of the risk.* The fourth element to be proved under § 339 requires that the burden to the landowner of eliminating the danger be slight as compared to the risk to the trespassing children. Satisfaction of this requirement presents no problem here. All that was necessary to protect against the danger created by the open tank was to eliminate the stacked pile of concrete blocks immediately alongside the wooden fence enclosing the sewage treatment area. Nothing at all appears which would require those blocks to be stored in this particular location. They could have been piled up anywhere else, thereby eliminating the danger which led to Mark Crawford's death. Even pulling down the height of the stack of blocks would probably have been enough. The cost of so doing would have been negligible.

(e) The final requirement of § 339 is a showing that the landowner failed to exercise reasonable care to protect the children. Comment *o* under this section says that the purpose of this requirement is to create liability "only if the possessor fails to take the steps which a reasonable man would take under such circumstances. If the possessor has exercised all reasonable care to make the condition safe, or otherwise to protect the children, and has still not succeeded, there is no liability." The Comment goes on to say that in some circumstances a warning would be all that could be expected of a reasonable man, and if so the giving of a warning may satisfy the landowner's duty.

No such problem complicates the instant case. Defendants had a safe condition if they themselves had not eliminated the safety feature of the fence by piling the concrete blocks against it. That danger was created by the affirmative acts of their own workmen, and defendants did nothing at all to offset the consequent danger. Even if a warning would have been sufficient, no warning, either written or oral, was ever given by defendants to anyone. No question can exist but what plaintiffs made a submissible case as to defendants' negligence.

. . . .

It follows from the foregoing that the trial court erred in setting aside the jury verdict. The judgment is therefore reversed with instructions to the trial court to reinstate the jury verdict.

All concur.

———————

1. How can landowners with ineradicable hazards on their property avoid liability to children? What is the standard of care to which a landowner should be held? A child? Would warning signs have been any use to the landowner in the above case? Why, or why not?

2. Children have for years presented special problems and issues in connection with so-called attractive nuisances. Certainly the structures which lure children into getting themselves injured on the property of others are attractive; the problem stems from the fact that the structures are often useful—like railroad trestles—and not true nuisances at all. The need to protect children (who are often highly creative at avoiding the protection), the cost of eliminating the dangers, and the general usefulness of the structure, in addition to the other factors involved, can lead to extremely involved calculations.

2. Public Employees: Firefighters and Police Officers

Rosa v. Dunkin' Donuts of Passaic

Supreme Court of New Jersey, 1991
583 A.2d 1129

GARIBALDI, J.

[In a 1960 case] we adopted the fireman's rule that "the owner or occupier is not liable to a paid fireman for negligence with respect to the creation of a fire." In [1960], we extended the rule to police officers.

This appeal concerns the scope of the immunity granted by the fireman's rule. The issue [here] is: does the fireman's rule bar liability only where the injuries arise from an ordinary act of negligence that is the reason for the firefighter or police officer being on the premises, or does it likewise bar liability where the injuries arise from an ordinary act of negligence that firefighters and police in the normal course of their duties should expect to meet?

I

The facts are essentially undisputed. While on duty, plaintiff, Jose Rosa, a police officer in Passaic, responded to a call for emergency medical assistance for a sick employee at defendants' Dunkin' Donuts store in Passaic. On arriving at the store Officer Rosa found an unconscious employee. While he was carrying the unconscious employee on a stretcher to the police ambulance, Officer Rosa's left foot slipped on a white powdery substance (presumably confectioner's sugar or flour) on the kitchen floor of the donut shop. Officer Rosa recalls no conscious recognition of the powder's presence before his fall; however, there is no indication or insinuation that it was not present when he arrived at the scene.

Officer Rosa received unspecified injuries as a result of slipping while transporting the sick employee to the ambulance. His injuries form the basis of a workers' compensation claim. His injuries also form the basis of this lawsuit.

On July 21, 1984, Officer Rosa filed a lawsuit based on these unspecified injuries against defendants Dunkin' Donuts of Passaic and Carmel Aditya, the owner of the franchise. He alleged that the defendants had caused him to slip and fall by negligently allowing the white powdery substance to remain scattered on the kitchen floor, thereby creating a slippery floor. He contended that the white powdery substance on the floor created a foreseeable risk of avoidable future harm. His contention forms a classic, ordinary negligence claim.

. . . .

In our view Rosa's fall was a risk inherent in the situation to which he responded (a rescue in the kitchen of a doughnut shop) and recovery was therein precluded under the "Fireman's Rule."

II

The fireman's rule is followed throughout the country. . . .

In adopting the rule, we eschewed the technical formalistic classifications used to define varying duties of care landowners owe to trespassers, licensees, or invitees. We recognized that the officer's "status being *sui generis*, justice is not aided by appending an inappropriate label and then visiting consequences which flow from a status artificially imputed." *Krauth v. Geller, supra*, 31 N.J. [270,] 273, 157 A.2d 129 [1960].

In *Krauth*, Chief Justice Weintraub set forth the policy underlying the fireman's rule:

> The rationale of the prevailing rule is sometimes stated in terms of "assumption of risk" used doubtless in the so-called "primary" sense of the term and meaning that the defendant did not breach a duty owed, rather than that the fireman was guilty of contributory fault in responding to his public duty. Stated affirmatively, what is meant is that it is the fireman's business to deal with that very hazard and hence, perhaps by analogy to the contractor engaged as an expert to remedy dangerous situations, he cannot complain of negligence in the creation of the very occasion for his engagement. In terms of duty, it may be said there is none owed the fireman to exercise care so as not to require the special services for which he is trained and paid. Probably most

fires are attributable to negligence and in the final analysis the policy decision is that it would be too burdensome to charge all who carelessly cause or fail to prevent fires with the injuries suffered by the expert retained with public funds to deal with those inevitable, although negligently created, occurrences. Hence, for that risk, the fireman should receive appropriate compensation from the public he serves, both in pay which reflects the hazard and in workmen's compensation benefits for the consequences of the inherent risks of the calling. [31 N.J. at 273–74, 157 A.2d 129 (citations omitted).]

We continue to recognize the fundamental fairness of the *Krauth* public-policy rationale that supports the fireman's rule. In *Berko v. Freda, supra,* we held that the rule barred a police officer's suit against a car owner who negligently left keys in his car for the injuries inflicted on the officer by the youth who stole the car. In *Berko,* we stated:

> We perceive more than mere dollars-and-cents considerations underpinning the fundamental justice of the "fireman's rule." There is at work here a public policy component that strongly opposes the notion that an act of ordinary negligence should expose the actor to liability for injuries sustained in the course of a public servant's performance of necessary, albeit hazardous, public duties. In the absence of a legislative expression of contrary policy, a citizen should not have to run the risk of a civil judgment against him for negligent acts that occasion the presence of a firefighter at the scene of a carelessly-set fire or of a police officer at a disturbance or unlawful incident resulting from negligent conduct. [*Id.* at 88–89, 459 A.2d 663].

> . . . .

The policies underlying the fireman's rule are simple, straightforward ones. The accidents and emergencies occasioning the presence of firefighters and police officers are a sad fact of life not soon to be eliminated. They are, however, also the very reason for the existence of the public forces of the "finest" and the "bravest." . . . A taxpayer who pays the fire and police departments to confront the risks should not have to pay again.

More significant, however, is the realization that the very nature of the profession that the officers have chosen embodies risks that the emergencies to which they will respond will neither be conveniently timed nor situated for rescuer, victim, or property-owner — they have assumed (and been trained to handle) those risks. Those professionals, whether firefighters or police officers, are charged with responding to a situation and effecting a rescue. They must measure the "situation" in the totality of the circumstances present at the scene. . . . It contravenes good sense and good policy to hold property owners liable to prepare for such unexpected arrivals.

> Ordinarily a firefighter or police officer is summoned in circumstances of emergency where the landowner has not had time to prepare the premises for his arrival. . . . A firefighter responding to such an emergency call has no reasonable expectation that the property has been made safe for his arrival. One engaged in this occupation does not determine whether to respond

based on weather conditions. This is because a firefighter is likely to enter at unforeseeable times under emergent circumstances. In other words weather is one of the "inherent risks of (this) calling." [*Maryland Casualty Co. v. Heiot, supra*, 224 N.J. Super, at 444–45, 540 A.2d 920.]

The noted commentator Dean Prosser stated:

> the most legitimate basis for [the firemen's rule] lies in the fact that firemen and policemen are likely to enter at unforeseeable times, upon unusual parts of the premises, and under circumstances of emergency where care in looking after the premises and in preparation for the visit, cannot reasonably be looked for. [W. Keeton, D. Dobbs, R. Keeton, D. Owen, Prosser and Keeton on the Law of Torts, §61 at 431 (5th ed. 1984)].

We agree. Firefighters and police officers must be held to assume the risks that are to be expected in encountering the hazards and risks of their job. They are risks inherent and incidental to the performance of the duties of a firefighter and police officer. Such risks properly include an ordinary act of negligence that an officer may encounter at the scene of the incident. To hold otherwise creates artificial distinctions between the negligence that occasioned one's presence and the negligence defining the scene at which one arrives (and with which one has been commissioned and empowered to deal). Such distinctions serve neither the rationale underlying the public-policy considerations for the fireman's rule nor the assumption of risk.

The policy rationale underlying the fireman's rule fully supports its application in this case. The conditions and responsibilities that Officer Rosa faced when he entered Dunkin' Donuts were those of a type inherent in the performance of his duties. Officer Rosa entered the kitchen to render medical assistance to an unconscious female employee. He is paid, trained, and expected to confront such emergencies and to remove those in peril.

His duty compelled him to traverse the area sprinkled with powder. He could not have fulfilled his duty without passing over the area in question. In carrying out that duty, the plaintiff must take the premises as he found them. Indeed, the unconscious woman could herself have knocked over the powder while falling. The intervening medical emergency could have disrupted normal cleaning procedures. Such conditions define one's role as a paid protector of the public. "Poor housekeeping is a hazard inherent or inevitable in firefighting," *Jackson v. Velveray Corp.*, 82 N.J. Super. 469, 480, 198 A.2d 115 (App. Div. 1964), or police work, whether it compounds the difficulty of extinguishing the flames or extricating the fallen.

. . . .

The fireman's rule still allows recovery in situations of willful or intentional misconduct traditionally outside of the cloak of the rule's immunity. As we stated clearly in *Mahoney v. Carus Chemical Co., supra*, 102 N.J. at 576, 510 A.2d 4, willful and wanton misconduct is an appropriate exception to most general rules of immunity. In the case of the fireman's rule it is perhaps most appropriate because according "immunity to one who deliberately and maliciously creates the hazard that injures the firemen or policemen stretches the policy underlying the fireman's rule beyond the logic and justifiable limits of its principle." *Id.* at 574, 510 A.2d at 4. By contrast, today's decision is well within the limits of that principle.

. . . .

Of course, the fireman's rule only applies to bar suit by a police officer or firefighter injured in the performance of his or her duty. It does not apply when the officer is acting as a normal citizen. . . .

In conclusion, we find that the policies and goals that bar a firefighter and police officer from recovering for injuries sustained from an ordinary act of negligence that occasioned the officer's presence on the premises are equally applicable to bar liability for injuries that arise from an act of ordinary negligence posing a hazard that is incidental to and inherent in the performance of the officer's duties. Such a rule would bar recovery to an injured firefighter who slipped on icy steps while responding to an emergency medical call from the owner of the premises; to an injured police officer who slipped into a hole in the owner's yard while investigating a burglar alarm at the home; to an injured police officer who, while checking the rear doors of a building, fell down a stairway because the handrail was too wide; to a police officer who was injured when he fell on ice in the early morning hours while investigating the presence of a suspicious car in the shopping center's parking lot. All those injuries arose out of the officer's normal performance of his duties. The relationship among the injuries, their causes, and the officers' duties is neither attenuated nor artificial. The officers in those cases came to the scene to inspect the area or to carry out the injured. Their injuries arose out of their inspections or out of passing over the very area providing access to and exit for the injured person.

Similarly, when a police officer responds to a medical emergency, he or she must anticipate attending to the victim, removing the victim from the present location, and facilitating the victim's transportation to the hospital. Lifting a stretcher under less-than-ideal conditions is not unfathomable. Indeed, it is so likely as to be considered an inherent part of the performance of the officer's rescue duty.

Accordingly, the judgment of the Appellate Division is affirmed.

HANDLER, J., filed a separate dissenting opinion.

HANDLER, J., dissenting.

. . . .

I strongly believe we should abrogate the fireman's rule. The rule, as currently formulated, is obtuse and abstruse. It needlessly extends an immunity that has a dubious value. We have, except in the face of the most compelling countervailing reasons, eliminated and restricted common-law immunities.

. . . .

For affirmance—CHIEF JUSTICE WILENTZ and JUSTICES CLIFFORD, POLLOCK, O'HERN, GARIBALDI and STEIN—6.

For reversal—JUSTICE HANDLER—1.

---

1. Why do the courts not adopt a reasonableness approach to the problems presented by firefighters and police officers? Under such an approach, the firefighter could sue the landowner if the hazard were not one within the reasonable contemplation of a firefighter under the circumstances. If the hazard were not within the contemplation of the firefighter, the firefighter would be under no obligation to protect him or herself from that hazard, and the landowner should be liable. Would such an approach fit the spirit of *Rowland*?

2. To what additional professions should the "firefighter's rule" apply? Should the rule apply only to professionals who are entering on the land to benefit the landowner? What about police officers executing a search warrant against the landowner, who are injured by a condition on the property while doing so? What if the police officer in *Rosa* had slipped on the sugar while arresting the owner of the Dunkin' Donuts?

It is clear that the firefighter's rule is not as uniformly applied as the *Rosa* majority thought. Indeed, New Jersey abrogated the *Rosa* result by statute, as follows:

> In addition to any other right of action or recovery otherwise available under law, whenever any law enforcement officer, firefighter, or member of a duly incorporated first aid, emergency, ambulance or rescue squad association suffers any injury, disease or death while in the lawful discharged of his official duties and that injury, disease or death is directly or indirectly the result of the neglect, willful omission, or willful or culpable conduct of any person or entity, other that that law enforcement officer, firefighter or first aid, emergency, ambulance or rescue squad member's employer or co-employee, the law enforcement officer, firefighter, or first aid emergency, ambulance or rescue squad member suffering that injury or disease, or, in the case of death, a representative of that law enforcement officer, firefighter or first aid, emergency, ambulance or rescue squad member's estate, may seek recovery and damages from the person or entity whose neglect, willful omission, or willful or culpable conduct resulted in that injury, disease for death.

N.J. Stat. § 2A:62A-21 (1993).

Problem

The fire department receives an alarm from TLC Pet Stores, Inc., and proceeds to the site. Seeing smoke pouring from the shop, the firefighters appropriately use their axes and enter the shop. M, a firefighter, is injured by a Rottweiler, which is one of the dogs for sale in the shop. What result if M sues the shop owner?

Same facts as above, except that there is no visible smoke coming from the shop, and upon entering the shop, the firefighters discover that there is no fire, and that the fire alarm went off because of a short circuit caused by the electric company. What result?

What if the shop were an electronics store, and the dog that injured the firefighter were a guard dog stationed in the store by the owner? Would this change your analysis?

3. Landlords and Tenants

McCutcheon v. United Homes Corp.

Supreme Court of Washington, 1971 (en banc)
486 P.2d 1093

STAFFORD, ASSOCIATE JUSTICE.

The two cases involved herein were considered separately by the trial court. Since the issues presented are identical, they have been consolidated on appeal.

Plaintiff Norma McCutcheon, a tenant of defendant United Homes Corporation, was injured one evening when she fell down an unlighted flight of stairs leading from her apartment. She alleged the defendant was negligent because the lights at the top and bottom of the stairwell were not operative.

Plaintiff Douglas R. Fuller, also defendant's tenant, was injured as he descended the outside stairs of his apartment on his way to work. A step pulled loose causing him to fall. He, too, alleged negligence on the part of defendant.

Defendant's answer alleged each plaintiff had executed a form "Month to Month Rental Agreement" which contained the following exculpatory clause:

> neither the Lessor, nor his Agent, shall be liable for any injury to Lessee, his family, guests or employees or any other person entering the premises or the building of which the demised premises are a part.

In each case the trial court granted a summary judgment of dismissal.

The question is one of first impression. The issue is whether the lessor of a residential unit within a multi-family dwelling complex may exculpate itself from liability for personal injuries sustained by a tenant, which injuries result from the lessor's own negligence in maintenance of the approaches, common passageways, stairways and other areas under the lessor's dominion and control, but available for the tenants' use. (Hereinafter called the "common areas.")

Basic to the entire discussion is the common law rule that one who leases a portion of his premises but retains control over the approaches, common passageways, stairways and other areas to be used in common by the owner and tenants, has a duty to use reasonable care to keep them in safe condition for use of the tenant in his enjoyment of the demised premises. The landlord is required to do more than passively refrain from negligent acts. He has a duty of affirmative conduct, an affirmative obligation to exercise reasonable care to inspect and repair the previously mentioned portions of the premises for protection of the lessee.

It is readily apparent that the exculpatory clause was inserted in defendant's form "Month to Month Rental Agreement" to bar its tenants from asserting actions for personal injuries sustained through the landlord's own negligence. It was adopted to negative the result of the lessor's failure to comply with its affirmative duty to the tenants.

The defendant asserts that a lessor may contract, in a rental agreement, to exculpate itself from liability to its lessee, for personal injuries caused by lessor's own negligence. It contends such exculpatory clauses are not contrary to public policy because the landlord-tenant relationship *is not a matter of public interest, but relates exclusively to the private affairs of the parties concerned and that the two parties stand upon equal terms. Thus, there should be full freedom to contract.*

. . . .

The importance of "freedom of contract" is clear enough. However, the use of such an argument for avoiding the affirmative duty of a landlord to its residential tenant is no longer compelling in light of today's multi-family dwelling complex wherein a tenant merely rents some space with appurtenant rights to make it more usable or livable. Under modern circumstances the tenant is almost wholly dependent upon the landlord to provide reasonably for his safe use of the "common areas" beyond the four walls demised to him.

As early as 1938 Williston recognized that while such exculpatory clauses were recognized as "legal," many courts had shown a reluctance to enforce them. Even then, courts were disposed to interpret them strictly so they would not be effective to discharge liability for the consequences of negligence in making or failing to make repairs.

. . . .

The key to our problem is found in Restatement of Contracts § 574, p. 1079 (1932) which reads:

> A bargain for exemption from liability for the consequences of negligence *not falling greatly below the standard established by law* for the protection of others against unreasonable risk of harm, is legal. . . .

(Italics ours.) In other words, such an exculpatory clause may be legal, when considered in the abstract. However, when applied to a specific situation, one may be exempt from liability for his own negligence *only when the consequences thereof do not fall greatly below the standard established by law.*

In the landlord-tenant relationship it is extremely meaningful to require that a landlord's attempt to exculpate itself, from liability for the result of its own negligence, *not fall greatly below the standard of negligence set by law.* As indicated earlier, a residential tenant who lives in a modern multi-family dwelling complex is almost wholly dependent upon the landlord for the reasonably safe condition of the "common areas." However, a clause which exculpates the lessor from liability to its lessee, for personal injuries caused by lessor's own acts of negligence, not only lowers the standard imposed by the common law, it effectively *destroys* the landlord's affirmative obligation or duty to keep or maintain the "common areas" in a reasonably safe condition for the tenant's use.

When a lessor is no longer liable for the failure to observe standards of affirmative conduct, or for *any* conduct amounting to negligence, by virtue of an exculpatory clause in a lease, *the standard ceases to exist.* In short, such a clause *destroys* the concept of negligence in the landlord-tenant relationship. Neither the standard nor negligence can exist in abstraction.

. . . .

[W]e are not faced merely with the theoretical duty of construing a provision in an isolated contract specifically bargained for by *one landlord and one tenant* as a ["] purely private affair." Considered realistically, we are asked to construe an exculpatory clause, the generalized use of which may have an impact upon thousands of potential tenants.

Under these circumstances it cannot be said that such exculpatory clauses are "purely a private affair" or that they are "not a matter of public interest." The real question is whether we should sanction a technique of immunizing lessors of residential units within a multi-family dwelling complex, from liability for personal injuries sustained by a tenant, which injuries result from the lessor's own negligence in maintaining the "common areas"; particularly when the technique employed destroys the concept of negligence and the standard of affirmative duty imposed upon the landlord for protection of the tenant.

An exculpatory clause of the type here involved contravenes long established common law rules of tort liability that exist in the landlord-tenant relationship. As so employed, it offends the public policy of the state and will not be enforced by the courts. It makes little sense for us to insist, on the one hand, that a workman have a safe place in which to work, but, on the other hand, to deny him a reasonably safe place in which to live.

The trial court is reversed and the cause is remanded for trial.

HAMILTON, C.J., and FINLEY, ROSELLINI, HUNTER, HALE, NEILL, and WRIGHT, JJ., concur.

SHARPE, J., did not participate.

———————

1. Would the courts uphold a contract in which the tenant agrees to assume the obligation of taking care of the common area surrounding his or her unit in exchange for a lower rent?

2. What is a real estate broker's responsibility for injury to potential buyers? Should a contract between the broker and the putative seller placing responsibility on the seller for any injuries to prospective buyers be valid?

3. What should be the relationship of tort and contract in cases like these?

4. Crime

Taco Bell, Inc. v. Lannon

Supreme Court of Colorado, 1987 (en banc)
744 P.2d 43

Lohr, Justice.

This is a negligence case arising from an incident in which the plaintiff, John P. Lannon, was injured by a shot fired by a robber when Lannon tried to leave the premises of the defendant, Taco Bell, Inc. (Taco Bell), during the course of a robbery. . . . The appellate court held that Taco Bell had a legal duty to take reasonable measures to protect its patrons from the consequences of criminal acts on the part of unknown third persons in this case, and further held that the issue of whether it breached that duty by failing to employ one or more armed security guards was properly submitted to the jury. We granted certiorari but limited our review to the issue of duty. We agree with the holdings of the court of appeals with respect to that issue and therefore affirm the judgment of that court.

I.

At approximately 10:30 p.m. on January 28, 1979, the plaintiff, John P. Lannon, entered a Taco Bell restaurant located on East Colfax Avenue in Denver. When the plaintiff approached the service counter, he noticed that the employees were off to one side of the counter and that a man was crouched behind the counter holding a handgun and going through a floor safe. The plaintiff deduced that a robbery was in progress. He then retreated toward the door, whereupon he encountered another robber apparently acting as a lookout for the robber behind the counter. The plaintiff brushed past the second robber and ran out the door into the Taco Bell parking lot. At that point, the robber behind the counter went toward the door and shot at the plaintiff, hitting him on the ring finger of his left hand. The plaintiff ran to a nearby laundromat and called the police. Police officers arrived within minutes but the robbers had already fled.

The plaintiff filed suit against Taco Bell in Denver District Court, alleging that Taco Bell had a duty to take adequate measures to protect him from the foreseeable criminal acts of third persons and that Taco Bell was negligent in failing to take such measures. The plaintiff also alleged that Taco Bell's negligence was the proximate cause of his injury. . . . Taco Bell later filed a motion to dismiss the plaintiff's claim, alleging that the plaintiff had failed to state a claim upon which relief could be granted because Taco Bell owed no legal duty to the plaintiff to protect him from the consequences of criminal acts on the part of third persons. The trial court denied Taco Bell's motion to dismiss, and the case proceeded to trial.

At trial, the plaintiff established, in addition to the facts previously set forth, that ten armed robberies had taken place at this same Taco Bell restaurant in the three years prior to the robbery giving rise to this case. One of these armed robberies had occurred only two nights before the robbery during which the plaintiff was injured. Furthermore, Detective William Martin of the Denver Police Department testified, on behalf of the plaintiff, that it was his opinion that this particular Taco Bell restaurant is located in a "high crime area." Detective Martin and two other Denver police officers called by the plaintiff also testified concerning security measures, including the use of security guards, that could be taken by this kind of restaurant to reduce the possibility of armed robberies. A management employee of a fast food restaurant also located on East Colfax Avenue testified on behalf of the plaintiff concerning that restaurant's practices with respect to hiring armed security guards.

Taco Bell moved for a directed verdict at the close of the plaintiff's case. Taco Bell based its motion on arguments that it had no duty, as a matter of law, to protect its customers from the consequences of criminal acts on the part of unknown third persons and that even if such a duty did exist, any failure on its part to employ armed security guards could not have been the proximate cause of the plaintiff's injuries. The trial court denied the motion.

Taco Bell called Richard Parson, an employee of the Taco Bell restaurant that had been robbed, as its sole witness. Parson testified concerning the robbery itself and the security measures that the restaurant took to discourage such robberies. At the conclusion of Parson's testimony, Taco Bell made a motion for a directed verdict which incorporated the arguments it had made on the earlier directed verdict motion. The plaintiff also moved for a directed verdict in his favor on the issue of Taco Bell's liability. The trial court denied both motions.

The trial court instructed the jury on negligence, including an instruction that the owner of premises has a duty to operate his business in a reasonably safe manner in view of the foreseeability, if any, of injury to others. The court specifically instructed the jury that the criminal act of a third party that causes injuries to the plaintiff does not relieve the defendant of liability if the act of the third party is reasonably and generally foreseeable. No specific instruction was given relating to the use of armed guards.

The jury returned a verdict in the plaintiff's favor, awarding him $40,000 in damages. Taco Bell appealed. . . .

As relevant to the issues before us on certiorari review, the court [of appeals] first held that the evidence established a duty on the part of the defendant to take "reasonable measures to prevent or deter reasonably foreseeable acts, and to alleviate known dangerous conditions"—specifically, the risks associated with armed robberies. Second, the court held that it was for the jury to decide whether the defendant had breached its duty by failing to employ armed, uniformed security guards. Additionally, the court rejected the defendant's argument that proximate cause was not established because the criminal acts of the robbers were not foreseeable. The court held that this view of foreseeability was too restrictive and that the evidence that the restaurant was located in a high crime area and that previous armed robberies had occurred on the premises and at other nearby establishments was sufficient to present a jury question as to foreseeability. . . .

Both parties petitioned this court for a writ of certiorari. We denied the plaintiff's petition but, based on the defendant's petition, we granted certiorari on the issue of "[w]hether a fast food restaurant in a 'high crime area' has a legal duty to take security measures, possibly including the use of armed guards, to protect its patrons from the consequences of criminal acts on the part of unknown third persons." We turn now to the resolution of that issue.

II.

A.

"The question of whether a defendant owes a plaintiff a duty to act to avoid injury is a question of law to be determined by the court." . . .

On a few occasions, this court has considered the duty that owners or occupiers of land owe to those who enter on their premises. In *Safeway Stores, Inc. v. Smith*, 658 P.2d 255 (Colo. 1983), a case in which the plaintiff had slipped and fallen in the defendant's grocery store, we held that "[a] store operator has a duty to his customers to use ordinary care to keep the floors used by them in a reasonably safe condition." *Id.* at 256. More generally, we also stated that a "proprietor is guilty of negligence only if he fails to use reasonable care under the circumstances to discover the foreseeable dangerous condition and to correct it or to warn customers of its existence." *Id.* at 258.

In *Mile High Fence Co. v. Radovich*, 175 Colo. 537, 489 P.2d 308 (1971), a case in which the plaintiff had stepped in a posthole located on the defendant's property, we held that foreseeability, rather than the status of the plaintiff as a trespasser, licensee, or invitee, is the primary factor in determining whether an owner or occupier of land owes a duty to persons who enter on the premises. *Id.* at 547–48, 489 P.2d at 314. "[I]t is the *foreseeability* of harm from the failure by the possessor to carry on his activities with reasonable care for the safety of the entrants which determines liability." *Id.* at 547, 489 P.2d at 314 (emphasis in original). "[T]he occupant, in the management of his property, should act as a reasonable man in view of the probability or foreseeability of injury to others." *Id.* at 548, 489 P.2d at 314.

Together, *Safeway* and *Mile High Fence* stand for the proposition that owners or occupiers of land have a duty to exercise reasonable and ordinary care to make their premises safe for those who may enter upon them. However, this court has never decided whether this duty encompasses taking reasonable measures to protect business patrons from injuries caused by the criminal acts of unknown third persons.

Other courts that have considered this issue have almost uniformly held that while owners or occupiers of land held open for business purposes are not insurers of their customers' safety, a duty arises on the part of the owner or occupier to take reasonable measures to protect customers from injuries caused by the criminal acts of unknown third persons when such acts are generally foreseeable.

The Restatement (Second) of Torts § 344 (1965) also recognizes that an owner or occupier of property has a duty to protect customers from injury caused by criminal conduct in such circumstances. Section 344 provides:

> Business Premises Open to Public: Acts of Third Persons or Animals
>
> A possessor of land who holds it open to the public for entry for his business purposes is subject to liability to members of the public while they are upon the land for such a purpose, for physical harm caused by the accidental, negligent, or intentionally harmful acts of third persons or animals, and by the failure of the possessor to exercise reasonable care to
>
> (a) discover that such acts are being done or are likely to be done, or
>
> (b) give a warning adequate to enable the visitors to avoid the harm, or otherwise to protect them against it.

Comment f to section 344 makes clear that the existence of this duty depends, to a great extent, on the foreseeability of criminal conduct by third persons.

> *Duty to police premises.* Since the possessor is not an insurer of the visitor's safety, he is ordinarily under no duty to exercise any care until he knows or has reason to know that the acts of the third person are occurring, or are about to occur. He may, however, know or have reason to know, from past experience, that there is a likelihood of conduct on the part of third persons in general which is likely to endanger the safety of the visitor, even though he has no reason to expect it on the part of any particular individual. If the place or character of his business, or his past experience, is such that he should reasonably anticipate careless or criminal conduct on the part of third persons, either generally or at some particular time, he *may* be under a duty to take precautions against it, and to provide a reasonably sufficient number of servants to afford a reasonable protection.

(Emphasis added.) We agree with the statement of the law contained in section 344 and comment f.

Turning to the facts of the present case, we conclude that the evidence of ten armed robberies at this particular Taco Bell restaurant in the three years prior to the incident at issue in this case sufficiently established that harm to customers as the result of criminal acts by third persons was foreseeable by Taco Bell.

Taco Bell argues, however, that the plaintiff's injury was not foreseeable since armed robberies of the type involved in this case occur randomly and without notice of the specific time and the specific manner in which they will take place. We reject this argument. The concept of foreseeability is simply not so limited. To establish that an incident is foreseeable, it is not necessary that an owner or occupier of land held open for business purposes be able to ascertain precisely when or how an incident will occur. Rather, foreseeability "includes whatever is likely enough in the setting of modern life that a reasonably thoughtful person would take account of it in guiding practical conduct." 3 F. Harper, F. James, & O. Gray, The Law of Torts § 18.2, at 658–59 (2d ed. 1986) (cited herein as "3 F. Harper"). The fact that ten armed robberies had occurred at the Taco Bell restaurant in a period of three years would certainly put a reasonable person on notice that such robberies would be likely to occur in the future and that the consequences of those robberies should be considered in determining how the restaurant should be run.

Taco Bell also argues that the plaintiff's injury was not foreseeable because none of the previous armed robberies at the restaurant had resulted in injury to any customer. This argument cannot withstand scrutiny. Simply because something has not yet happened does not mean that its happening is not foreseeable. Instead, foreseeability is based on common sense perceptions of the risks created by various conditions and circumstances. *See* Restatement (Second) of Torts § 289 (1965). We have little difficulty in concluding that armed robberies present a significant risk of injury to persons unfortunate enough to be present when one occurs. Therefore, the plaintiff's injury was foreseeable despite the absence of injuries from the previous armed robberies that had occurred at this particular Taco Bell restaurant.

We are satisfied that the risk of injury to the plaintiff was foreseeable in the present case. However, as noted earlier, foreseeability alone does not establish the existence of a duty. There are other considerations that we believe are relevant in helping to determine whether a duty arose in this case.

Armed robberies present a substantial degree of risk to the public. No evidence was presented in this case concerning the frequency of injuries to patrons resulting from armed robberies on business premises. However, we are persuaded that whatever the likelihood of armed robberies at this restaurant and of injuries resulting from those armed robberies may be, the gravity of the possible harm to patrons from such robberies is substantial. "As the gravity of the possible harm increases, the apparent likelihood of its occurrence need be correspondingly less to generate a duty of precaution." W. Keeton, § 31, at 171. *Accord* 3 F. Harper, § 16.2, at 471.

We also do not believe that imposition of a duty to take reasonable measures to protect patrons from the consequences of criminal acts on the part of unknown third persons would place an onerous burden on either Taco Bell or the community. . . .

Furthermore, we believe that it is equitable that the cost of taking reasonable measures to protect patrons from criminal activity be borne by the owner, operator, and, indirectly, the customers of the restaurant. As stated by the California Court of Appeals in *Cohen:*

> It is also not unfair that patrons pay a few cents more for items they purchase from such a store and gain the assurance of reasonable protection against criminal activity by shopping there, rather than allow the emotional and physical burden of a criminal attack to fall on the store patron who inadvertently finds himself or herself in the middle of a robbery invited by the store's failure to employ minimal crime deterrence measures.

Cohen, 703 Cal. Rptr. at 579. *See generally,* 3 F. Harper, § 16.9, at 475–80 (where cost of precautions is relatively low, social utility of not taking precautions is usually outweighed by the risk involved).

Taking all of these factors into consideration, we conclude that the court of appeals was correct in holding that Taco Bell had a legal duty, under the circumstances of this case, to take reasonable measures to protect its customers from the consequences of criminal acts on the part of unknown third persons.

. . . .

III.

In summary, we conclude that Taco Bell had a legal duty in this case to take reasonable measures to protect its patrons from the consequences of criminal acts on the part of unknown third persons. We further conclude that it was for the jury to decide whether Taco Bell breached its duty by failing to provide one or more armed security guards.

The judgment of the court of appeals is affirmed.

ERICKSON, J., dissents.

ROVIRA and VOLLACK, JJ., join in the dissent.

———————

1. The court in *Taco Bell* follows those cases which reject classification of the cast of characters. It also departs from the old rule that intervening criminal acts are inherently unforeseeable, preferring to view the entire case from the perspective of foreseeability. What impact might such a decision have on the question of whether the plaintiff was negligent in entering a restaurant which the plaintiff knows to be subject to a high risk of crime? Is this the kind of argument a place of business would make?

2. What if the restaurant hired armed guards, and a customer were injured by a guard in the course of a robbery? What if the presence of armed guards caused gunfire at a robbery to be more likely to occur than if no armed guards were present?

3. How far should the obligation of a business to protect its patrons extend? What are the obligations of a bank towards patrons of its twenty-four hour ATM machine?

5. Business Establishments and Danger to the Public

F.W. Woolworth v. Kirby

Supreme Court of Alabama, 1974
302 So. 2d 67

HEFLIN, CHIEF JUSTICE.

Defendant, F.W. Woolworth Company, appeals from a judgment rendered against it in a personal injury action.

As a promotional scheme, the appellant-defendant's Woolco store on University Drive in Huntsville, Alabama, planned a ping-pong ball drop. The idea was to drop balls from a passing airplane into the back parking lot of the store, each ball containing a certificate entitling the finder to a prize. Prizes ranged from a color television and a stereo set to ice cream cones. The ping-pong ball drop was held on the morning of November 17, 1971, in conjunction with a sale at the store, and as the result of extensive advertising—some nine full-page ads in the Huntsville Times and 200 thirty-second radio spots advertising the sale and promotional activities—there were, in the estimation of the manager, some 4,500 people in the back parking lot (300' [by] 350') at 9:00 o'clock that morning to catch the ping-pong balls.

Mr. Dall Shady, a Huntsville pilot with 30 years' experience, contracted with appellant (defendant) to drop the balls. Shady had a television camera installed in the airplane so he could see what was directly under him, and then made practice drops. Just before the actual drops he passed over the parking lot and dropped toilet paper to check the wind. Pilot Shady told the defendant he could not control where the balls would fall, so Woolco should put some employees on the buildings to get those balls that might fall there. Woolco did station employees on the buildings to catch balls and throw them to the crowd in the parking lot.

Plaintiff, Mrs. Lona Pearl Kirby, 70 years old at the time, having heard and seen the sale advertising, went to the store that morning with other people, including her small grandson. Evidence indicates that, finding the door of the store locked, she took her grandson toward the rear parking lot to watch the airplane, which was then coming over at 1,000 feet to make the third drop. (There were 768 balls dropped—approximately ⅓ on each of three passes.) Mrs. Kirby took several steps into the parking lot and, within a very short time after arrival, the ping-pong balls began falling around her. The crowd came after the balls. Someone in the crowd knocked her down and some members of the crowd ran over her. She was carried by ambulance to a hospital and treated for injuries, the most serious being a broken right hip.

There was testimony from a former employee of Woolco that he watched the drop from the top of the building and that he saw a man "on the ground after the second drop," and perhaps "knocked down." Another witness testified that on the third drop she was knocked down and stepped on, suffering a slightly injured ankle. Evidence indicated that during all three drops the crowd would run, or hurry around chasing the falling balls, watching them shift direction with the wind.

Mrs. Kirby sued the defendant, alleging negligent acts causing her injuries. The jury gave a verdict for $52,500.00. The trial court ordered a remittitur of $17,500.00, reducing the judgment to $35,000.00.

This case arose and was tried before the implementation of the new Alabama Rules of Civil Procedure.

The plaintiff's amended complaint alleged, among other things, three negligent acts, in the alternative, and that "as a proximate consequence of the negligent act or acts, the mob of people in the said back parking lot in their effort to catch the balls ran into the Plaintiff knocking her down and trampling her" and causing injuries. The alternative averments of negligent acts were that "at said time and place Defendant, F.W. Woolworth Company, (1) negligently failed to police or control the crowd that said Defendant had amassed at said time and place or (2) the said Defendant negligently dropped balls in close proximity to and around the Plaintiff or (3) negligently had an independent contractor to drop balls which balls fell in close proximity to and around the Plaintiff."

The defendant contends that the trial court erred in refusing its written request for the affirmative charge and in overruling its demurrers to the complaint as last amended. These contentions relate to all three alternative allegations and involve the question of the duty owed on the part of the defendant to the plaintiff. This raises a case of first impression in this state concerning the liability of a proprietor for injury to a customer or patron caused by other patrons through pushing, shoving or crowding during a promotional activity.

In 62 Am. Jur. 2d Premises Liability § 201 the following appears:

> ". . . [I]n accord with the concept of foreseeability, a duty to prevent the crowding of a business establishment may arise in those situations where the proprietor can foresee that a customer may suffer injuries through the pressure of the crowd, and a storekeeper will be held liable if he has failed to exercise ordinary care to protect a customer from the actions of a crowd which he should have foreseen or anticipated, and the customer is injured by the pushing, crowding, or jostling of other persons. Specifically, a storekeeper will be liable for injuries to a customer where he carries on a promotional activity which foreseeably will cause crowds to gather and push, notwithstanding a disorder in the crowd contributed to the injuries.
>
> "In regard to children and elderly persons who may be injured by being pushed by others while visiting a business establishment, the proprietor's duty of care requires the taking of precautions commensurate with the increased likelihood of injury to persons in those classes."

The closest case to the present factual situation that this court has been able to locate is *Hicks v. M.H.A. Inc.*, 107 Ga. App. 290, 129 S.E.2d 817 (1963). This case involved an action against owners of a shopping center for injuries sustained by a patron who was knocked down by a crowd trying to get paper plates (redeemable for merchandise) which were being dropped onto a parking lot from an airplane. The Georgia Court of Appeals held that foreseeability of the conduct of a crowd competing for "merchandise prizes" dropped from an airplane was for jury solution and that actual notice by the defendants of the danger to the particular plaintiff need not be alleged.

In *Lee v. National League Baseball Club of Milwaukee Inc.*, 4 Wis. 2d 168, 89 N.W.2d 811 (1958), a jury verdict was upheld where the plaintiff was injured when pushed off her chair and trampled upon by other spectators who were attempting to recover a foul ball which had landed in front of her chair. The Supreme Court of Wisconsin, in an action against the baseball club, stated:

> "It has generally been held that one who invites the public to a public amusement place operated by him is liable for injury sustained by an invitee as a result of acts of third persons, if such operator has not taken reasonable and appropriate measures to restrict the conduct of such third parties, of which he should have been aware and should have realized was dangerous."

In *Lane v. Fair Stores, Inc.*, 150 Tex. 566, 243 S.W.2d 683 (1951), a complaint was held sufficient which alleged that the defendant took no steps to police a crowd that had gathered at a store in response to advertising that ladies' hose would be given to the first 300 patrons on a particular morning where the plaintiff was injured when pushed by the crowd against the door and a glass showcase.

. . . .

Restatement, Second, Torts § 302 is as follows:

> "§ 302. Risk of Direct or Indirect Harm
>
> A negligent act or omission may be one which involves an unreasonable risk of harm to another through either
>
> (a) the continuous operation of a force started or continued by the act or omission, or
>
> (b) *the foreseeable action of the* other, *a third person*, an animal, or a force of nature." (Emphasis supplied)

Section 302 A of Restatement, Second, Torts recites:

> "§ 302 A. Risk of Negligence or Recklessness of Others
>
> An act or an omission may be negligent if the actor realizes or should realize that it involves an unreasonable risk of harm to another through the negligent or reckless conduct of the other or a third person."

In the case at hand the question arises as to whether or not the defendant should have foreseen or realized the probability of injury to the plaintiff or to a person similarly situated. Certainly it would be within the jury's province to determine that the defendant should have foreseen or realized that the crowd would run in unpredictable paths as the ping-pong balls were blown about with each gust of wind; that the crowd would push and shove in order to catch a ball and win a prize; and that dangerous conditions could develop for individuals in the crowd, including the elderly and children. Further the jury in this case had the right to determine that reasonable care under the circumstances required the defendant to take steps pertaining to the plaintiff and other persons similarly situated, including, but not limited to, giving warnings of the dangers involved, taking steps to control or police the crowd with supervisory personnel, and using loud speakers to warn the crowd not to run over people and to warn the elderly or children to stay out of the crowd.

. . . .

This court holds that when a proprietor or storekeeper causes a crowd of people to assemble pursuant to a promotional activity, then that person owes a duty to exercise reasonable care commensurate with foreseeable danger or injury to protect those assembled from injuries resulting from the pressure, pushing, shoving, jostling or other activities of the crowd or individuals within the crowd; that the foreseeability of danger or injury under such circumstances is for jury determination; and that reasonable care commensurate with the foreseeability of danger or injury may require greater precautions when children or the elderly are present.

. . . .

MERRILL, HARWOOD, BLOODWORTH, MADDOX, MCCALL, FAULKNER and JONES, JJ., concur.

COLEMAN, J., recuses himself.

JONES, JUSTICE (concurring specially).

. . . .

––––––––

1. In *Walt Disney World Co. v. Goode*, 501 So. 2d 622 (Fla. Dist. Ct. App. 1986), the court applied ordinary rules of negligence to the question of the defendant's liability for the death of a child who had fallen into a moat in the amusement park. The doctrine of attractive nuisance was ruled inapplicable because the child had been a business invitee and not a trespasser.

2. Does a shopping mall have a duty to protect patrons using its parking lots? What if the mall parking area is full, and the patrons must park some distance away from the mall? How far does the mall-owner's duty extend?

3. Should a pizza establishment that promises delivery of any pizza within half an hour be liable when its delivery persons become involved in car accidents while rushing pizzas to its patrons?

4. Is there a problem for a radio station that promises prizes to the eighth listener to call with the correct answer to a question if someone who has heard this announcement on his or her car radio is involved in an accident while attempting to call in on

a cell phone? At what point does the radio station (or other entity) become exempt from responsibility, even for foreseeable responses to their advertisements or offers?

C. Defenses and Plaintiff's Conduct

1. Comparative Negligence

Mathis v. Massachusetts Electric Co.
Supreme Judicial Court of Massachusetts, 1991
565 N.E.2d 1180

Before LIACOS, C.J., and WILKINS, ABRAMS, LYNCH AND GREANEY, JJ.

LIACOS, CHIEF JUSTICE.

During the evening of June 23, 1983, the plaintiff, Brian Mathis, sixteen years and eight months old, and three of his friends were gathered in front of the house located directly across from Brian's home in Franklin. Brian crossed the street and, to impress his friends, began climbing a utility pole, jointly owned by defendants Massachusetts Electric Company (MEC) and New England Telephone and Telegraph Company (NET). The pole was located on the property of the plaintiff's parents. It was supported by two guy wires, the upper one installed and owned by MEC, the lower one installed and owned by NET. As Brian climbed the pole, he came in contact with several telephone, cable television, and electrical wires which did not harm him. When Brian reached the top of the utility pole, he grabbed the primary electrical wire and received an electrical shock. Brian fell to the ground. He sustained severe injuries and burns.

In March, 1984, the plaintiff filed suit in Superior Court alleging that MEC's negligence caused his injuries. . . .

The case proceeded to trial before a jury. . . . The jury found that MEC violated its duty toward foreseeable child trespassers. The jury also found that the plaintiff was comparatively negligent. The jury determined that the plaintiff was 75% at fault, while MEC was 25% at fault. Thus, the plaintiff was barred, under the comparative negligence statute, G.L. c. 231, §85 (1988 ed.), from recovering any damages from MEC. The jury found that NET was not negligent. Judgment for the defendants was entered on November 30, 1988. MEC's third-party complaint and NET's cross claims against MEC were dismissed.

The plaintiff filed a motion for a new trial, and a motion to amend the judgment and for a new trial to assess damages. The judge denied both motions. The plaintiff appeals. He argues that . . . the lower court erred by denying his motion to amend the judgment and for a new trial on damages because the comparative negligence statute, G.L. c. 231, §85, is inapplicable to an action brought under the child trespasser statute, G.L. c. 231, §85Q[.]

1. *Comparative negligence.* The plaintiff claims that landowners who violate the child trespasser statute are strictly liable and therefore cannot avail themselves of the principle of comparative negligence. The child trespasser statute states:

. . . .

> "Any person who maintains an artificial condition upon his own land shall be liable for physical harm to children trespassing thereon if (a) the place where the condition exists *is one upon which the land owner knows or has reason to know* that children are likely to trespass, (b) the condition is one of which *the land owner knows or has reason to know and which he realizes or should realize will involve an unreasonable risk of death or serious bodily harm* to such children, (c) the children because of their youth do not discover the condition or realize the risk involved in intermeddling with it or in coming within the area made dangerous by it, (d) the utility to the land owner of maintaining the condition and the burden of eliminating the danger are slight as compared with the risk to children involved, and (e) *the land owner fails to exercise reasonable care* to eliminate the danger or otherwise to protect the children" (emphasis supplied). G.L. c. 231, § 85Q (1988).[6]

The plaintiff argues that once the five statutory conditions are met, the owners are strictly liable, and therefore negligence principles are inapplicable.

Neither the statute nor the common law doctrine of *Soule v. Massachusetts Elec. Co.,* 378 Mass. 177, 390 N.E.2d 716 (1979), imposes liability on landowners or others irrespective of their degree of fault or knowledge of the risk involved.

Under the traditional common law rule, a landowner did not have a duty toward a child trespasser, except to refrain from wanton and wilful conduct. The child trespasser statute softened the "Draconian" common law rule. By enacting the statute, the Legislature followed the national trend towards imposing on landowners a uniform standard of care regardless of the status of the injured party.[7]

---

6. The language of § 85Q is virtually identical to the language of § 339 of the Restatement (Second) of Torts (1965). We have previously recognized that the scope of § 85Q and § 339 of the Restatement is identical. Although, in our view, § 85Q is not applicable because the plaintiff's injuries did not occur in the defendants' "own land," and therefore the defendants are not "landowners" within the meaning of the statute, the parties have assumed throughout that § 85Q applies to utility poles. Since the parties have made this the "law of the case," we shall make the same assumption. We believe, however, that this case should be governed by common law principles and not by § 85Q. *See Soule v. Massachusetts Elec. Co., supra,* 378 Mass, at 182, 390 N.E.2d 716 ("we hold that there is a common law duty of reasonable care by a landowner or occupier to prevent harm to foreseeable child trespassers" [emphasis supplied]).

7. In *Mounsey v. Ellard,* 363 Mass. 693, 707, 297 N.E.2d 43 (1973), this court held that landowners owed the same duty of reasonable care to all lawful entrants regardless whether they were considered invitees or licensees at common law. Prior to *Mounsey,* landowners owed invitees a duty of reasonable care, while they owed licensees a duty not to inflict wanton or wilful harm. [Citations.] The court has refused, however, to extend the reasonable care standard to cases involving adult trespassers who are not helplessly trapped. [Citations.]

The child trespasser statute and the common law impose on landowners a duty of reasonable care, a negligence standard of liability.

Since the child trespasser statute, G.L. c. 231, § 85Q, imposes on landowners a duty of reasonable care, and creates liability based on negligence principles, the comparative negligence defense is available to defendants. "[T]he policy of negligence liability presumes that people will, or at least should, take reasonable measures to protect themselves and others from harm. . . . However, if the injured person's unreasonable conduct also has been a cause of his injury, his conduct will be accounted for in apportioning liability for damages." *Correia v. Firestone Tire & Rubber Co., supra,* 388 Mass, at 354, 446 N.E.2d 1033.

The plaintiff argues that a finding by a jury that children, because of their youth, did not "discover the condition or realize the risk involved in intermeddling" with the artificial condition, G.L. c. 231, § 85Q (c), is irreconcilable with the doctrine of comparative negligence. The plaintiff also argues that, even if such a finding by a jury is not irreconcilable with the doctrine of comparative negligence, the jury's answers to the special verdict questions in this case were inconsistent. The jury found that "the plaintiff, Brian Mathis, because of his youth, fail[ed] to appreciate the risk and danger involved or lack[ed] the understanding to evaluate the peril involved in intermeddling with the subject pole and its attachments." The jury also found that the plaintiff was negligent, and that his negligence was a proximate cause of his injuries. The plaintiff asks us to order a new trial because the jury's answers were inconsistent, and because they cannot be harmonized.

The child trespasser statute addresses a landowner's duty toward a child trespasser. In a case brought under the statute, a landowner's duty of reasonable care toward a foreseeable child trespasser will be breached only if the five conditions of the statute are satisfied. "[I]f the child is fully aware of the condition, understands the risk which it carries, and is quite able to avoid it, he stands in no better position than an adult with similar knowledge and understanding. This is not merely a matter of contributory negligence or assumption of risk, but of lack of duty to the child" (footnotes omitted). W. Prosser & W. Keeton, Torts, [§ 59] at 408–409. It is only after the jury determine that the landowner breached his or her duty toward the child that the child's possible negligence is taken into account.

The plaintiff is correct when he argues that an owner's liability under the child trespasser statute and a child's possible contributory negligence are two separate issues. "The question of the child's contributory negligence is a separate problem that must be carefully distinguished from that of the land occupier's duty." 5 F. Harper, F. James & O. Gray, Torts § 27.5 n. 60 (1986). The fact that they are two separate issues, however, does not make them irreconcilable.

The possible negligence of a child is "judged by the standard of behavior expected from a child of like age, intelligence, and experience." *Mann v. Cook,* 346 Mass. 174, 178, 190 N.E.2d 676 (1963). It is not inconsistent, therefore, for a jury to find that the landowner unreasonably created a dangerous condition, the risks of which would not ordinarily be discovered by children, while at the same time finding that even though the plaintiff failed to realize the risk, he or she acted without the degree of care expected from a child of similar age, intelligence, and experience. We cannot, as the plaintiff urges us, impose a judicially-created rule which would immunize child trespassers from their own negligence. The judge did not err in denying the plaintiff's motion to amend the judgment and for a new trial.

Judgment affirmed.

––––––––––

1. Comparative negligence doctrine is a modern version of contributory negligence. Under contributory negligence doctrine, a plaintiff who was at all negligent in looking after his or her safety would be barred from any recovery for injuries caused by defendant. Comparative negligence assigns a percentage of responsibility for injury to a negligent plaintiff rather than barring recovery altogether. This subject is covered in the chapter on defenses.

2. What sort of activity by a plaintiff should constitute contributory or comparative negligence? What should be the nature of the obligation of an institution of higher learning to intoxicated alumni wandering around the campus on reunion weekend? To intoxicated gate-crashers at a reunion party? What role do you think that the plaintiff's intoxication should play in the analysis? Should a defendant landowner have an obligation to protect intoxicated plaintiffs from themselves? Should intoxication ever be a defense against a charge of contributory or comparative negligence?

2. Assumption of Risk

Greenwood v. Lowe Chemical Co.

Court of Civil Appeals of Texas, Houston (14th Dist.), 1968
428 S.W.2d 358

BARRON, JUSTICE.

This suit was brought by Rebecca Greenwood under the Texas Death and Survival Statutes for damages resulting from the death of her husband, Charles F. Greenwood. Greenwood was a construction worker employed by a Richard Greenwood (no relation), who in turn had a contract to do certain work for the defendant, Lowe Chemical Company. On the day of the accident made the basis of this suit, Charles F. Greenwood was placing an aluminum ladder between a scrubbing tower and an open scrubbing pit or vat containing about 95% Hot water and 5% Acid and chemicals. The space was narrow between the tower and the pit, and deceased suddenly stepped backward causing one of his legs to enter the pit. He could not maintain his balance and he foundered and fell completely into the pit. He was critically burned and his death resulted some four days later.

The principal business of Lowe Chemical Company, appellee-defendant, was the manufacture and regeneration of chemicals and acid. In the manufacturing process appellee maintained on its premises, in the normal operation of its business, covered and uncovered concrete pits or vats containing various types of corrosive liquids. Appellee also maintained on its premises a complex device denominated a scrubber. In conjunction with the scrubber, and located approximately three to four feet from it, the appellee maintained two open concrete pits which were used to hold and circulate scrubber water back into the scrubber. These scrubber pits did not have a railing or cover and were completely open and exposed. The scrubber water solution was composed of approximately 95% water as well as certain amounts of corrosive chemicals. The exact temperature of the scrubber water was unknown but it was very hot, and on cold days the pits would emit steam. On January 19, 1965, the deceased, while working on the scrubber with a carpenter, Eddie Hergert, backed and fell into one of these scrubber pits.

Charles F. Greenwood, the deceased, was in the employ of an independent contractor doing work for Lowe Chemical Company. On the date of the accident contractor Greenwood and his employees, including decedent, had been working on appellee's premises for several months. All employees on appellee's premises had been warned of the dangers of the pits, and it was common knowledge that they contained hot water and harmful chemical liquids. Contractor Greenwood testified that both he and the decedent had warned other employees to be careful around the scrubber pits. Between the sidewall of the scrubber and the edge of the vats is about three or four feet, and one could narrowly walk between the scrubber and the vats. Work was proceeding on the north side of the scrubber, and Hergert, a co-worker, told the deceased just before the incident causing his death, to bring a section of a 16-foot extension ladder around to the south side of the scrubber. At the time Hergert had walked off about 20 feet away from the vat and had his back to the area where Charles F. Greenwood was working. The vat into which Greenwood inadvertently stepped and fell was between seven and eight feet square and about 30 to 36 inches deep; the sides were made of concrete, extending about six inches above the ground, and curved all the way around — the top of the curbing was rounded. The curbing on the vats was about five inches thick at the point where it extended above the ground. These vats were not covered over, and there was no fence or railing or any other type of protective device around them or near them. There was no paint on the curbing, no reflectors, and no signs to remind workmen of the danger involved. The surface area between the scrubber and the vat was concrete with a rough finish. The distance between the two vats was four feet. On the premises of appellee there were several other uncovered vats of a similar nature and type. Some of the vats were covered.

Appellant, Mrs. Greenwood, alleged that appellee failed to exercise care commensurate with the risk of harm and extent of injury likely to occur and that such was negligence; that appellee failed to place a fence or rail around the vat in question which would have been adequate to prevent the accident, and that appellee failed to roof-over the top of the vat with a cover which would have been adequate to prevent a person in the position of Charles F. Greenwood from falling into the vat. Appellant further alleged that each failure was negligence and a proximate cause of the accident and resulting death of decedent, Greenwood. Appellant alleged that the open vats checkerboarding the premises constituted exceedingly dangerous instrumentalities for workmen on the premises, and that the appellee had an affirmative duty to protect invitees and other such as Charles F. Greenwood from the extra-hazardous and dangerous conditions on the premises regardless of general knowledge of the dangers.

The appellee, Lowe Chemical Company, pleaded in its answer that the occupier of the land owed an invitee no duty to warn or protect invitees against dangers which were open and obvious, and it further pleaded that the condition was open and obvious to the decedent and invoked the defense of volenti non fit injuria. Contributory negligence and unavoidable accident were also pleaded by appellee. On a hearing appellee's motion for summary judgment was granted by the trial court on the basis of depositions and affidavit submitted to the court, and the trial court rendered judgment that appellant, Mrs. Greenwood, take nothing of defendant, Lowe Chemical Company. Mrs. Greenwood has properly perfected her appeal from the trial court's summary judgment.

It is clear to us that the maintenance of premises in such a manner as Lowe Chemical Company maintained its premises at the time of and prior to the sustaining of injuries and the death of Charles F. Greenwood is near the ultimate in danger to workmen on the property. Men were called upon to work around several unprotected vats of deadly hot water and lethal chemicals. The only protection the vats contained was a six-inch curb around each vat, which was probably a hindrance rather than a help. No handrails or guardrails or other protective devices were installed by appellee, and no reason for not installing them was shown. Any workman on the premises was required daily to be constantly alert, and every moment of his attention was required to guard against what to us appears to be sudden death or serious bodily injury. Such attention was hardly possible to a man with work on his mind. At any moment a failure to heed the dangers of the open pits might have spelled disaster. That was exactly what happened here and which had almost happened only a short time before on these identical premises.

It is undisputed that decedent was employed by Richard H. Greenwood, the contractor employed by appellee, and that the contractor was on appellee's premises to perform a contract with appellee. Accordingly, the contractor and his employee, the decedent, were invitees on the premises of appellee.

The law is clear that the occupier of land or premises is required to keep his land or premises in a reasonably safe condition for his invitees. But the cases hold that the landowner's duty is to protect his invitees from hidden dangers of which the landowner knows, or of which he should know in the exercise of ordinary care. The general rule is that if there are open and obvious dangers of which the invitees know, or of which they are charged with knowledge, then the occupier owes them "no duty" to warn or to protect the invitees. This is said to be so because there is "no duty" to warn a person of things he already knows, or of dangerous conditions or activities which are so open and obvious that as a matter of law he will be charged with knowledge and full appreciation thereof.

Based upon the undisputed facts, it is manifest that decedent knew generally of the location of the pits, knew generally that they were uncovered and unguarded, and he knew that they were filled with a hot, noxious liquid. It is not clear, however, whether decedent knew the deadly effect of a fall into one of the pits, though he knew it would be to some extent dangerous. He had been working on the premises for several months. These facts may be also applicable to the defense of volenti non fit injuria. The requirements of the latter defense were recently set out in *J. & W. Corp. v. Ball*, 414 S.W.2d 143, 146 (Tex. Sup.):

> "(1) the plaintiff has knowledge of facts constituting a dangerous condition or activity; (2) he knows the condition or activity is dangerous; (3) he appreciates the nature or extent of the danger; and (4) he voluntarily exposes himself to this danger."

The final element is not necessary in "no duty" cases because if there is no duty owed to the plaintiff, he cannot create a duty by voluntarily exposing himself to a known and appreciated risk.

But the rules and authorities above cited are based upon facts which require that a plaintiff voluntarily and directly encounter the known risk with full appreciation of the nature or extent of the danger. It is not sufficient that the plaintiff have knowledge that there is some danger in the particular undertaking. Decedent was not working on the vat. He must have knowledge of the particular risk which he voluntarily incurs and a full appreciation of the danger which leads to his injury. . . In the present case, the decedent was placing a ladder in the space between the scrubber and the vat to work on the scrubber when he somehow lost his balance and could not avoid stepping backward and falling into the unguarded and open vat nearby. He did not encounter the vat willfully and directly. The open and unprotected vat gave rise to a situation which rendered the premises more than ordinarily dangerous for workmen on the premises. A guardrail or protective cover around the vat probably would have prevented the injury and death of Greenwood. . . .

We cannot say as a matter of law that decedent took a known risk by stumbling or falling into the open vat involuntarily. The risk he was voluntarily encountering at the time had to do with the ladder and the scrubber. He did not "voluntarily" back into a deadly vat of hot water and chemicals, nor was an intelligent choice necessarily involved. The vat was incidental to and apart from decedent's activities at the time. Decedent fell and was fatally injured by reason of a fact originating separately and unconnected with the vat. We hold that there are jury issues presented concerning these questions and the alleged negligence of appellee in failing to provide decedent a safe place to work, to-wit: whether failure to provide guard rails or protective covering around the vats was negligence proximately causing or cooperating to cause the accident and other similar issues. Appellee owed decedent a duty of care unless under the circumstances decedent had a full understanding and appreciation of the extent of the danger.

. . . .

From the facts in this record it is plain to us that the premises belonging to appellee were exceptionally dangerous and extra-hazardous to an invitee regardless of a general knowledge of danger. At the time and place in question the decedent was required to work where he did under his employer's contract with Lowe Chemical Company. To quit his job would have been an unreasonable requirement. The facts show that he thought he could work in safety. But when he lost his balance he backed into the open vat unintentionally and received a fatal injury. Section 343A, Restatement of the Law of Torts (2d Ed.), says:

> "(1) A possessor of land is not liable to his invitees for physical harm caused to them by any activity or condition on the land whose danger is known or obvious to them, *unless the possessor should anticipate the harm despite such knowledge or obviousness.*" (Emphasis added).

We think the possessor-appellee should have anticipated harm to an invitee on the premises despite general knowledge of the dangers caused by the vats. Especially is this true when the invitee's balance was lost while he was working on something else, when his fall into the deadly vat was beyond his control, and when he may not have had, under the circumstances, a full appreciation of the extent of the danger. We think appellee had some duty to provide ordinary safety to invitees on its premises under these circumstances.

Appellant's decedent did not of necessity willfully and intelligently expose himself to such danger. To say that a landowner is required to keep his premises in a reasonably safe condition for his invitees is an empty phrase unless some minimal duty of care is required of him when he clearly should anticipate harm, regardless of knowledge, in a dangerous condition of this kind. Failure to provide any type of safety devices against this type of extreme danger is clearly unreasonable.

. . . .

The judgment of the trial court is reversed and remanded.

Tunks, Chief Justice (dissenting).

I respectfully dissent. . . .

———————

1. Does this case turn in any way upon the status of the plaintiff as an invitee? Should assumption of the risk doctrine look different in a workplace setting?

2. Should the doctrine of assumption of risk ever truly apply in a case where the plaintiff has accidentally exposed him or herself to danger? Is assumption of risk doctrine designed for plaintiffs who negligently injure themselves, however known the danger may be?

3. Can a court manipulate the assumption of risk doctrine in order to reach a given result? Does the doctrine lend itself to such manipulation?

Problem

G takes the ferry from Manhattan to Hoboken, New Jersey. Upon his arrival on the ferry pier, he discovers that a train has been left standing on its track, blocking the exit from the pier to Hoboken. After waiting a few minutes for the train to move, G, who has an appointment in Hoboken, decides to crawl between two of the cars in order to leave the pier. Inevitably, as soon as he is between two cars, the train starts up, and G is severely injured.

G sues the railroad, which admits that the train should not have been left standing where it was. What arguments will the railroad make in its defense? Be cynical.

D. The Taxonomy of Plaintiffs: The Modern Approach

Tantimonico v. Allendale Mutual Insurance Co.

Supreme Court of Rhode Island, 1994
637 A.2d 1056

SHEA, JUSTICE.

These consolidated cases are before the Supreme Court on the appeals of the plaintiffs from Superior Court orders granting the defendant's motions for summary judgment. For the reasons that follow we affirm.

The facts of this case are not in dispute. On May 5, 1985, Guy Tantimonico, Jr., and John McPhillips, Jr. (plaintiffs), were riding motorcycles on a piece of undeveloped property owned by Allendale Mutual Insurance Company (defendant) located near its corporate headquarters in Johnston, Rhode Island. While independently riding their motorcycles on the property, plaintiffs, both in their twenties, collided head on with each other. Neither plaintiff can recall the specifics of the accident, but both Tantimonico and McPhillips suffered severe injuries that required extensive hospitalization.

At the conclusion of the hearing on defendant's motions for summary judgment, the trial justice stated that he could find no legal duty that would support the actions against defendant and, that without a legal duty, no material facts were to be found because the question of law was dispositive of the entire matters.

The plaintiffs argue on appeal that in light of this court's holding in *Mariorenzi v. DiPonte, Inc.*, 114 R.I. 294, 333 A.2d 127 (1975), the trial justice erred in granting defendant's motions for summary judgment. In *Mariorenzi* a five-year-old trespasser at a construction site accidentally drowned in an excavation that had filled with water. On appeal, this court abolished the common-law distinctions between the duties owed to licensees, invitees, and trespassers and substituted the tort test of reasonableness. We now take this opportunity to depart from the holding in *Mariorenzi* as it pertains to trespassers.

Traditionally at common law the possessor of land owed a trespasser

> "no duty to discover, remedy, or warn of dangerous natural conditions. Perhaps if the possessor sees a trespasser about to encounter extreme danger from such a source, which is known to the possessor and perceptibly *not* known to the trespasser, there may be a duty to warn (as by shouting). That is about as far as the bystander's duty to a highway traveler would traditionally go, if indeed it would go that far." 4 Harper, James & Gray, The Law of Torts § 27.3 at 139 (2d ed. 1986).

Rhode Island followed the common law status categories, and in *Previte v. Wanskuck Co.*, 80 R.I. 1, 3, 90 A.2d 769, 770 (1952), this court stated that "in the ordinary case under the established law in this state no duty is owed a trespasser by a landowner except to refrain from injuring him wantonly or wilfully after discovering his peril."

Many jurisdictions carved out exceptions to the common-law status categories, and in 1957 Great Britain's Parliament enacted a statute abolishing the distinction between licensees and invitees.

In *Kermarec v. Compagnie Generale Transatlantique*, 358 U.S. 625, 79 S. Ct. 406, 3 L. Ed. 2d 550 (1959), the Supreme Court expressed its dissatisfaction with the common-law distinctions between licensees and invitees when it refused to extend them to maritime law. . . .

It was not until the Supreme Court of California issued its opinion in *Rowland v. Christian*, 69 Cal. 2d 108, 70 Cal. Rptr. 97, 443 P.2d 561 (1968), that the common-law categories were judicially abrogated in a United States jurisdiction.

. . . .

In the wake of *Rowland*, this court in *Mariorenzi* cited opinions from a limited number of jurisdictions that purportedly followed the California lead by totally abrogating the common-law status categories. *See* [cases from the United States Court of Appeals for the District of Columbia Circuit, Alaska, Colorado, Hawaii, Louisiana, New Hampshire, and New York]. As Justice Joslin pointed out in his dissent [in *Mariorenzi*], however, none of these cases involved an injury to a trespasser. . . .

Other jurisdictions repudiated the distinctions between licensee and invitee but retained limited-duty rules for trespassers. [Cases cited from Maine, Minnesota, North Dakota, and Wisconsin.]

Although repudiation or modification of the common-law status categories took effect in the above jurisdictions, by the late seventies an increasing number of courts had specifically rejected *Rowland. See* [cases from Alabama, Florida, Kansas, Maryland, Oklahoma, Texas, and Utah]. Others had postponed considering the repudiation of the categories, and still others simply reaffirmed the traditional classifications. *See* Page, The Law of Premises Liability at 139–40 (2d ed. 1988).

In *Mariorenzi* this court stated that it was giving a "final but fitting interment" to all three common-law categories. 114 R.I. at 307, 333 A.2d at 133. It also stated:

> "The time has come to extricate ourselves from a semantical quagmire that had its beginning in ancient and misleading phraseology. . . . The judiciary gave birth to the invitee, licensee, trespasser trio and the judiciary can lay this triptych to rest. Accordingly, we now give a final but fitting interment to the common-law categories of invitee, licensee, and trespasser as well as their extensions, exceptions, and extrapolations.

> "As we assign the trichotomy to the historical past, we substitute in its place the basic tort test of reasonableness. Hereafter, the common-law status of an entrant onto the land of another will no longer be determinative of the degree of care owed by the owner, but rather the question to be resolved will be whether the owner has used reasonable care for the safety of all persons reasonably expected to be upon his premises." *Id.* at 306–07, 333 A.2d at 133.

Justice Joslin, however, dissented, stating:

> "[T]he majority have made, in effect, a value judgment that it is more acceptable to our society that the risk of loss due to foreseeable injury sustained by a trespasser while on another's land—in any event a slight and readily insurable risk—be shifted from him to the land possessor.

> "If that judgment were premised more upon legal analysis and persuasive precedent and less upon presumed public acceptability, I would abide by my concurring opinion in *Henry v. J. W. Eshelman & Sons*, 99 R.I. 518, 527, 209 A.2d 46, 51 (1965). There I said that '[w]hile a deferral to the Legislature in the initiation of changes in matters affecting public policy may often be appropriate, it is not required where the concept demanding change is judicial in its origins.' But the majority's decision is not so premised. Instead, it rests purely on what in their judgment is a socially desirable policy." 114 R.I. at 309–10, 333 A.2d at 134–35.

At the time the *Mariorenzi* accident occurred, there was no statutory or case law in this state that addressed the special concerns for the infant trespasser. The so-called attractive-nuisance or trespassing-child doctrine was not recognized in this state until [1971, when] this court adopted the standard set out in the Restatement (Second) Torts § 339 (1965). . . .

The case at bar is the incarnation of the worst fears of many opponents to the movement away from common-law status categories. In *Ouellette v. Blanchard*, 116 N.H. 552, 364 A.2d 631 (1976), the Supreme Court of New Hampshire abolished the distinction among invitees, licensees, and trespassers. Justice Grimes of that court, in a vigorous dissent, wrote:

> "I fear that the elimination of the trespasser distinction in the determination of the landowner's duty of care will result in unreasonable, unrealistic and

unjust consequences. Every owner, lessee, and occupant of land will be faced with increased exposure to liability. If there are no good reasons for drawing a distinction between licensees and invitees, trespassers are in a fundamentally different position from those persons whom the landowner has expressly or by implication invited onto his property." *Id.* at 560, 364 A.2d at 636.

JUSTICE GRIMES continued:

"One difficulty I have with the court's decision is that it casts aside a whole body of law, built up over the years, which clearly defines the rights and obligations of the property owner on the basis of the relationship he has with those who came upon his land. It is fundamental in tort law that the duty is created by the relationship. Under this law, the owner knows in advance what his duty is. In place of this well-settled and reasonable set of rules, the court now substitutes a single vague duty of reasonable care, under which the property owner acts at his peril with no standard by which he can judge his obligations in advance. The kinds of trespassers are many. The only thing they have in common is that they have no right on the land. And yet it is to be determined after the event what the owner's duty was before the event with regard to each of these various kinds of trespassers who enter upon his land.

"Protesters who invade a company's property and are injured because of some condition of the premises will be able to have a jury decide after the event what duty the company owed to them. A burglar who is injured while scaling a fence in a high crime area where burglars are not unexpected would be able to put the owner to the risk of a jury decision on the question if he had used reasonable care toward the burglar. Such claims should of course be dismissed at the outset as they would be under our preexisting law." *Id.* at 561–62, 364 A.2d at 637.

Similarly, the Supreme Judicial Court of Massachusetts had stated in *Mounsey v. Ellard*, 363 Mass. 693, 297 N.E.2d 43 (1973):

"We feel that there is [a] significant difference in the legal status of one who trespasses on another's land as opposed to one who is on the land under some color of right — such as a licensee or invitee. For this reason, among others, we do not believe they should be placed in the same legal category. For example, one who jumps over a six foot fence to make use of his neighbor's swimming pool in his absence does not logically belong in the same legal classification as a licensee or invitee." *Id.* at 708 n.7, 297 N.E.2d at 51–52 n.7.

The more recent trend in premises-liability law is to uphold the traditional common-law categories. In *Kirschner v. Louisville Gas & Electric Co.*, 743 S.W.2d 840 (Ky. 1988), the Supreme Court of Kentucky stated:

"Historically, all tort law has been based on the theory of whether a defendant violated a duty owed to the injured party. There is nothing illogical or unfair in requiring violation of a duty before liability can be imposed, and we reject Kirschner's assertion that we should abolish the classifications of trespasser, licensee, and invitee." *Id.* at 844.

. . . .

Other recent cases that have upheld the common-law status categories are: [citing cases from Arizona, Maryland, Nebraska, New Jersey, and Oklahoma].

. . . .

In the case at bar we are presented with two adults who chose to ride their motorcycles on defendant's property without permission. Clearly plaintiffs were trespassers. . . . It is almost impossible to entertain the notion that anyone other than plaintiffs themselves is responsible for their injuries. To hold the property owner liable for injuries brought about by a plaintiff's negligent behavior would be patently ludicrous.

. . . .

Property owners have a basic right to be free from liability to those who engage in self-destructive activity on their premises without permission. The common-law rule developed over the centuries accomplishes this purpose clearly and without equivocation.

We conclude, therefore, that this landowner owed these plaintiffs no duty save to refrain from willful or wanton injury. To hold the defendant accountable would be tantamount to imposing strict liability upon every landowner in this jurisdiction. Consequently we depart from *Mariorenzi* as it applies to trespassers. We decline to comment on the other aspects of the holding in *Mariorenzi* as no issues involving invitees or licensees are before us.

For these reasons the plaintiffs' appeals are denied and dismissed, the judgments appealed from are affirmed, and the papers of the case are remanded to the Superior Court.

What does all this mean? Do you think that the courts which rejected the categories of plaintiff did not think through what their rejection would mean for landowners, particularly with respect to trespassers?

The Supreme Court of Iowa summarized the state of the law with respect to classifications of plaintiffs in *Alexander v. Medical Associates Clinic*, 646 N.W.2d 74, 77–78 (Iowa 2002), as follows:

> By the end of the 1970s, seven states had followed California's lead [in *Rowland*] and five states had not, the latter group choosing instead to retain the traditional rules based on the entrant's status. During that same period six states chose to abolish or modify the distinction made between invitees and licensees, but did not take the same step with respect to trespassers. Thus, in the twelve years after *Rowland*, a total of eleven states rejected California's rule that the liability of property owners to trespassers should be judged by the same standard as their liability to persons legally on their land.

Since 1980, the rejection of California's one-rule-fits-all approach has been even more overwhelming. In Rhode Island, the Rhode Island Supreme Court [in *Tantimonico*] partially overruled its earlier decision that had followed *Rowland* and held that the traditional rules governing liability to trespassers should be retained. In addition, the state legislatures in California and Colorado abrogated or partially abrogated court decisions adopting a negligence standard for all premises liability actions. In Colorado, the legislature passed a statute that reinstated a classification-based system of liability for landowners. See Colo.Rev.Stat. § 13-21-115 (1997). In California, in response to cases in which trespassing criminals had recovered for injuries incurred during their unlawful intrusions, the state legislature enacted a law that limited landowners' liability to trespassers who were on the property to commit a crime, essentially reinstating the common law duty in such cases. *See* 1985 Cal. Stat. ch. 1541, § 1 (codified at Cal. Civil Code § 847 (West 2002)).

In addition to those jurisdictions retreating from a prior, wholesale adoption of negligence principles, eight states refused to change their conventional principles of trespasser liability, even though they judicially abolished or modified the distinction between an invitee and a licensee. Additionally, two states, Maryland and Oklahoma, decided to retain their common law rules governing liability to trespassers, but left open the question whether they would discard the invitee and licensee classifications. Finally, seven more states chose to maintain the common law rules making the duty owed by a landowner dependent on the status of the injured party.

In stark contrast to this widespread rejection of negligence principles in trespasser cases, only one state since the 1970s has joined the minority position, abandoning all classifications.

In summary, presently six states use a negligence standard to govern trespasser liability; twenty-nine states have declined the opportunity to change their rule in such cases; and two state legislatures have reinstated the common law trespasser rule after it had been abolished by court decision. Given the fact that only one court in the last twenty-seven years has abandoned the common law trespasser rule, the so-called "trend" to adopt a universal standard of care for premises liability has clearly lost momentum.

See also Singleton v. Sherer, 659 S.E.2d 196 (S.C. Ct. App. 2008) (South Carolina has four categories of plaintiffs: trespassers, invitees, licensees, and children).

Chapter 10

Damages

In the introductory chapter we said that in many ways, torts is a deceptively simple subject dealing with the question of who pays. The second most important question is, how much does the losing party pay? Some aspects of this second question are covered in this chapter.

The basic theory of damages is to return the victim to the position that he or she was in just before the injury. Where the victim has suffered personal injury, dignitary harm (such as loss of reputation), or the loss of uniquely valuable property, that may not be actually possible, but the victim is nonetheless entitled to monetary compensation for his or her loss. Even when the defendant concedes liability, damages are sure to be challenged. The three types of damages that will be examined in this chapter are punitive damages (sometime called "exemplary" damages), pecuniary loss, and non-economic loss.

We have already studied some of the most challenging damage issues in the duty and proximate cause chapters. There we considered whether the actor had a duty to avoid the particular injury and whether the defendant's conduct was the proximate cause of the damage. Here we examine the Supreme Court's most important and most recent incursions into the punitive damage fray and some common damage questions.

A. Punitive Damages

Punitive damages are awarded by the jury to deter and punish intentional or malicious conduct by the defendant. Punitive damages are not available unless the defendant's conduct merits punishment. The jury awards punitive damages in its discretion, although its decisions are subject to review by the courts, which often reduce the amount of a punitive award. Until recently there were few standards for the amount of the award other than the character of the misconduct, the nature of the plaintiff's injury, and perhaps the defendant's wealth. This vagueness and the size of a few awards have caused problems and attracted attention. Ultimately, they led to the "constitutionalization" of punitive damages law by the Supreme Court of the United States.

Problem

In the crash of an economy car, the gas tank exploded; the driver was killed, and the passenger suffered severe burns. It was shown that the manufacturer was aware that the gas tank would explode in thirty mile per hour rear-end collisions.

The jury returned a verdict in favor of the plaintiff for $3.5 million compensatory damages and $125 million punitive damages. If you were the trial court judge, what, if anything, would you do with this verdict? As the appellate court judge, what would you do with the verdict, if the trial judge did nothing? What facts in addition to manufacturer knowledge of the risk might play a role in any decision with respect to punitive damages?

BMW of North America, Inc. v. Gore

Supreme Court of the United States, 1996

517 U.S. 559

Justice Stevens delivered the opinion of the Court.

The Due Process Clause of the Fourteenth Amendment prohibits a State from imposing a "grossly excessive" punishment on a tortfeasor. *TXO Production Corp. v. Alliance Resources Corp.*, 509 U.S. 443, 454, 113 S. Ct. 2711, 125 L. Ed. 2d 366 (1993) (and cases cited). The wrongdoing involved in this case was the decision by a national distributor of automobiles not to advise its dealers, and hence their customers, of predelivery damage to new cars when the cost of repair amounted to less than 3 percent of the car's suggested retail price. The question presented is whether a $2 million punitive damages award to the purchaser of one of these cars exceeds the constitutional limit.

I

In January 1990, Dr. Ira Gore, Jr. (respondent), purchased a black BMW sports sedan for $40,750.88 from an authorized BMW dealer in Birmingham, Alabama. After driving the car for approximately nine months, and without noticing any flaws in its appearance, Dr. Gore took the car to "Slick Finish," an independent detailer, to make it look "snazzier than it normally would appear." 646 So. 2d 619, 621 (Ala. 1994). Mr. Slick, the proprietor, detected evidence that the car had been repainted.[1] Convinced that he had been cheated, Dr. Gore brought suit against petitioner BMW of North America (BMW), the American distributor of BMW automobiles.[2] Dr. Gore alleged, inter alia, that the failure to disclose that the car had been repainted constituted suppression of a material fact.[3] The complaint prayed for $500,000 in compensatory and punitive damages, and costs.

---

1. The top, hood, trunk, and quarter panels of Dr. Gore's car were repainted at BMW's vehicle preparation center in Brunswick, Georgia. The parties presumed that the damage was caused by exposure to acid rain during transit between the manufacturing plant in Germany and the preparation center.

2. Dr. Gore also named the German manufacturer and the Birmingham dealership as defendants.

3. Alabama codified its common-law cause of action for fraud in a 1907 statute that is still in effect. H[a]ckmeyer v. Hackmeyer, 268 Ala. 329, 333, 106 So. 2d 245, 249 (Ala. 1958). The statute provides: "Suppression of a material fact which the party is under an obligation to communicate constitutes fraud. The obligation to communicate may arise from the confidential relations of the

At trial, BMW acknowledged that it had adopted a nationwide policy in 1983 concerning cars that were damaged in the course of manufacture or transportation. If the cost of repairing the damage exceeded 3 percent of the car's suggested retail price, the car was placed in company service for a period of time and then sold as used. If the repair cost did not exceed 3 percent of the suggested retail price, however, the car was sold as new without advising the dealer that any repairs had been made. Because the $601.37 cost of repainting Dr. Gore's car was only about 1.5 percent of its suggested retail price, BMW did not disclose the damage or repair to the Birmingham dealer.

Dr. Gore asserted that his repainted car was worth less than a car that had not been refinished. To prove his actual damages of $4,000, he relied on the testimony of a former BMW dealer, who estimated that the value of a repainted BMW was approximately 10 percent less than the value of a new car that had not been damaged and repaired. To support his claim for punitive damages, Dr. Gore introduced evidence that since 1983 BMW had sold 983 refinished cars as new, including 14 in Alabama, without disclosing that the cars had been repainted before sale at a cost of more than $300 per vehicle. Using the actual damage estimate of $4,000 per vehicle, Dr. Gore argued that a punitive award of $4 million would provide an appropriate penalty for selling approximately 1,000 cars for more than they were worth.

The jury returned a verdict finding BMW liable for compensatory damages of $4,000. In addition, the jury assessed $4 million in punitive damages, based on a determination that the nondisclosure policy constituted "gross, oppressive or malicious" fraud. *See* Ala. Code §§ 6-11-20, 6-11-21 (1993).

. . . .

BMW filed a post-trial motion to set aside the punitive damages award. The company introduced evidence to establish that its nondisclosure policy was consistent with the laws of roughly 25 States defining the disclosure obligations of automobile manufacturers, distributors, and dealers. . . .

BMW also drew the court's attention to the fact that its nondisclosure policy had never been adjudged unlawful before this action was filed. [BMW further noted that it had altered its policy in Alabama after being found liable in a separate fraud action, and that it had discontinued its policy nationally after the verdict in this case.]

In response to BMW's arguments, Dr. Gore asserted that the policy change demonstrated the efficacy of the punitive damages award. He noted that while no jury had held the policy unlawful, BMW had received a number of customer complaints relating to undisclosed repairs and had settled some lawsuits. [Gore also challenged the evidence of legality by noting that BMW had failed to prove whether the statutes it cited "had supplanted, rather than supplemented, existing causes of action for common law fraud."]

---

parties or from the particular circumstances of the case." Ala. Code § 6-5-102 (1993); see Ala. Code § 4299 (1907).

The trial judge denied BMW's post-trial motion, holding, *inter alia*, that the award was not excessive. On appeal, the Alabama Supreme Court also rejected BMW's claim that the award exceeded the constitutionally permissible amount.

The Alabama Supreme Court did, however, rule in BMW's favor on one critical point: The court found that the jury improperly computed the amount of punitive damages by multiplying Dr. Gore's compensatory damages by the number of similar sales in other jurisdictions. . . . Having found the verdict tainted, the court held that "a constitutionally reasonable punitive damages award in this case is $2,000,000," . . . and therefore ordered a remittitur in that amount. The court's discussion of the amount of its remitted award expressly disclaimed any reliance on "acts that occurred in other jurisdictions"; instead, the court explained that it had used a "comparative analysis" that considered Alabama cases, "along with cases from other jurisdictions, involving the sale of an automobile where the seller misrepresented the condition of the vehicle and the jury awarded punitive damages to the purchaser." . . .

Because we believed that a review of this case would help to illuminate "the character of the standard that will identify constitutionally excessive awards" of punitive damages . . . we granted certiorari.

II

Punitive damages may properly be imposed to further a State's legitimate interests in punishing unlawful conduct and deterring its repetition. In our federal system, States necessarily have considerable flexibility in determining the level of punitive damages that they will allow in different classes of cases and in any particular case. Most States that authorize exemplary damages afford the jury similar latitude, requiring only that the damages awarded be reasonably necessary to vindicate the State's legitimate interests in punishment and deterrence. *See TXO*, 509 U.S. at 456; *Haslip*, 499 U.S. at 21, 22. Only when an award can fairly be categorized as "grossly excessive" in relation to these interests does it enter the zone of arbitrariness that violates the Due Process Clause of the Fourteenth Amendment. *Cf. TXO*, 509 U.S. at 456. For that reason, the federal excessiveness inquiry appropriately begins with an identification of the state interests that a punitive award is designed to serve. We therefore focus our attention first on the scope of Alabama's legitimate interests in punishing BMW and deterring it from future misconduct.

. . . .

We think it follows from . . . principles of state sovereignty and comity that a State may not impose economic sanctions on violators of its laws with the intent of changing the tortfeasors' lawful conduct in other States. Before this Court Dr. Gore argued that the large punitive damages award was necessary to induce BMW to change the nationwide policy that it adopted in 1983.[18] But by attempting to alter BMW's

---

18. Brief for Respondent 11–12, 23, 27–28; Tr. of Oral Arg. 50–54. Dr. Gore's interest in altering the nationwide policy stems from his concern that BMW would not (or could not) discontinue the policy in Alabama alone. *Id.*, at 11. "If Alabama were limited to imposing punitive damages based

nationwide policy, Alabama would be infringing on the policy choices of other States. To avoid such encroachment, the economic penalties that a State such as Alabama inflicts on those who transgress its laws, whether the penalties take the form of legislatively authorized fines or judicially imposed punitive damages, must be supported by the State's interest in protecting its own consumers and its own economy. Alabama may insist that BMW adhere to a particular disclosure policy in that State. Alabama does not have the power, however, to punish BMW for conduct that was lawful where it occurred and that had no impact on Alabama or its residents. Nor may Alabama impose sanctions on BMW in order to deter conduct that is lawful in other jurisdictions.

. . . .

III

Elementary notions of fairness enshrined in our constitutional jurisprudence dictate that a person receive fair notice not only of the conduct that will subject him to punishment but also of the severity of the penalty that a State may impose. Three guideposts, each of which indicates that BMW did not receive adequate notice of the magnitude of the sanction that Alabama might impose for adhering to the nondisclosure policy adopted in 1983, lead us to the conclusion that the $2 million award against BMW is grossly excessive: the degree of reprehensibility of the nondisclosure; the disparity between the harm or potential harm suffered by Dr. Gore and his punitive damages award; and the difference between this remedy and the civil penalties authorized or imposed in comparable cases. We discuss these considerations in turn.

Degree of Reprehensibility

Perhaps the most important indicium of the reasonableness of a punitive damages award is the degree of reprehensibility of the defendant's conduct. . . . This principle reflects the accepted view that some wrongs are more blameworthy than others. Thus, we have said that "nonviolent crimes are less serious than crimes marked by violence or the threat of violence." *Solem v. Helm*, 463 U.S. 277, 292–293, 77 L. Ed. 2d 637, 103 S. Ct. 3001 (1983). Similarly, "trickery and deceit," *TXO*, 509 U.S. at 462, are more reprehensible than negligence. In *TXO*, both the West Virginia Supreme Court and the Justices of this Court placed special emphasis on the principle that punitive damages may not be "grossly out of proportion to the severity of the offense." *Id.*, at 453, 462. Indeed, for JUSTICE KENNEDY, the defendant's intentional malice was the decisive element in a "close and difficult" case. *Id.*, at 468.

In this case, none of the aggravating factors associated with particularly reprehensible conduct is present. The harm BMW inflicted on Dr. Gore was purely economic

---

only on BMW's gain from fraudulent sales in Alabama, the resulting award would have no prospect of protecting Alabama consumers from fraud, as it would provide no incentive for BMW to alter the unitary, national policy of nondisclosure which yielded BMW millions of dollars in profits." *Id.*, at 23. The record discloses no basis for Dr. Gore's contention that BMW could not comply with Alabama's law without changing its nationwide policy.

in nature. The presale refinishing of the car had no effect on its performance or safety features, or even its appearance for at least nine months after his purchase. BMW's conduct evinced no indifference to or reckless disregard for the health and safety of others. To be sure, infliction of economic injury, especially when done intentionally through affirmative acts of misconduct, *id.*, at 453, or when the target is financially vulnerable, can warrant a substantial penalty. But this observation does not convert all acts that cause economic harm into torts that are sufficiently reprehensible to justify a significant sanction in addition to compensatory damages.

. . . .

Dr. Gore's second argument for treating BMW as a recidivist is that the company should have anticipated that its actions would be considered fraudulent in some, if not all, jurisdictions. This contention overlooks the fact that actionable fraud requires a material misrepresentation or omission. This qualifier invites line drawing of just the sort engaged in by States with disclosure statutes and by BMW. We do not think it can be disputed that there may exist minor imperfections in the finish of a new car that can be repaired (or indeed, left unrepaired) without materially affecting the car's value. There is no evidence that BMW acted in bad faith when it sought to establish the appropriate line between presumptively minor damage and damage requiring disclosure to purchasers. For this purpose, BMW could reasonably rely on state disclosure statutes for guidance. In this regard, it is also significant that there is no evidence that BMW persisted in a course of conduct after it had been adjudged unlawful on even one occasion, let alone repeated occasions.

Finally, the record in this case discloses no deliberate false statements, acts of affirmative misconduct, or concealment of evidence of improper motive, such as were present in *Haslip* and *TXO*. *Haslip*, 499 U.S. at 5; *TXO*, 509 U.S. at 453. We accept, of course, the jury's finding that BMW suppressed a material fact which Alabama law obligated it to communicate to prospective purchasers of repainted cars in that State. But the omission of a material fact may be less reprehensible than a deliberate false statement, particularly when there is a good-faith basis for believing that no duty to disclose exists.

. . . Because this case exhibits none of the circumstances ordinarily associated with egregiously improper conduct, we are persuaded that BMW's conduct was not sufficiently reprehensible to warrant imposition of a $2 million exemplary damages award.

Ratio

The second and perhaps most commonly cited indicium of an unreasonable or excessive punitive damages award is its ratio to the actual harm inflicted on the plaintiff. *See TXO*, 509 U.S. at 459; *Haslip*, 499 U.S. at 23. The principle that exemplary damages must bear a "reasonable relationship" to compensatory damages has a long pedigree. Scholars have identified a number of early English statutes authorizing the award of multiple damages for particular wrongs. Some 65 different enactments during the period between 1275 and 1753 provided for double, treble, or quadruple damages. Our decisions in both *Haslip* and *TXO* endorsed the proposition that a comparison between the compensatory award and the punitive award is significant.

In *Haslip* we concluded that even though a punitive damages award of "more than 4 times the amount of compensatory damages," might be "close to the line," it did not "cross the line into the area of constitutional impropriety." *Haslip*, 499 U.S. at 23–24. *TXO*, following dicta in *Haslip*, refined this analysis by confirming that the proper inquiry is "'whether there is a reasonable relationship between the punitive damages award and the harm likely to result from the defendant's conduct as well as the harm that actually has occurred.'" *TXO*, 509 U.S. at 460 (emphasis in original), quoting *Haslip*, 499 U.S. at 21. Thus, in upholding the $10 million award in *TXO*, we relied on the difference between that figure and the harm to the victim that would have ensued if the tortious plan had succeeded. That difference suggested that the relevant ratio was not more than 10 to 1.

The $2 million in punitive damages awarded to Dr. Gore by the Alabama Supreme Court is 500 times the amount of his actual harm as determined by the jury[35] Moreover, there is no suggestion that Dr. Gore or any other BMW purchaser was threatened with any additional potential harm by BMW's nondisclosure policy. The disparity in this case is thus dramatically greater than those considered in *Haslip* and *TXO*.

Of course, we have consistently rejected the notion that the constitutional line is marked by a simple mathematical formula, even one that compares actual and potential damages to the punitive award. *TXO*, 509 U.S. at 458. Indeed, low awards of compensatory damages may properly support a higher ratio than high compensatory awards, if, for example, a particularly egregious act has resulted in only a small amount of economic damages. A higher ratio may also be justified in cases in which the injury is hard to detect or the monetary value of noneconomic harm might have been difficult to determine. It is appropriate, therefore, to reiterate our rejection of a categorical approach. . . . "'We can say, however, that [a] general concern of reasonableness . . . properly enters into the constitutional calculus.'" *TXO*, 509 U.S. at 458 (*quoting Haslip*, 499 U.S., at 18). In most cases, the ratio will be within a constitutionally acceptable range, and remittitur will not be justified on this basis. When the ratio is a breathtaking 500 to 1, however, the award must surely "raise a suspicious judicial eyebrow." *TXO*, 509 U.S. at 482 (O'CONNOR, J., dissenting).

Sanctions for Comparable Misconduct

Comparing the punitive damages award and the civil or criminal penalties that could be imposed for comparable misconduct provides a third indicium of excessiveness. . . . In this case the $2 million economic sanction imposed on BMW is substantially greater than the statutory fines available in Alabama and elsewhere for similar malfeasance.

---

35. Even assuming each repainted BMW suffers a diminution in value of approximately $4,000, the award is 35 times greater than the total damages of all 14 Alabama consumers who purchased repainted BMW's.

The maximum civil penalty authorized by the Alabama Legislature for a violation of its Deceptive Trade Practices Act is $2,000; other States authorize more severe sanctions, with the maxima ranging from $5,000 to $10,000. . . .

. . . In the absence of a history of noncompliance with known statutory requirements, there is no basis for assuming that a more modest sanction would not have been sufficient to motivate full compliance with the disclosure requirement imposed by the Alabama Supreme Court in this case.

. . . .

The fact that BMW is a large corporation rather than an impecunious individual does not diminish its entitlement to fair notice of the demands that the several States impose on the conduct of its business. Indeed, its status as an active participant in the national economy implicates the federal interest in preventing individual States from imposing undue burdens on interstate commerce. While each State has ample power to protect its own consumers, none may use the punitive damages deterrent as a means of imposing its regulatory policies on the entire Nation.

As in *Haslip*, we are not prepared to draw a bright line marking the limits of a constitutionally acceptable punitive damages award. Unlike that case, however, we are fully convinced that the grossly excessive award imposed in this case transcends the constitutional limit. Whether the appropriate remedy requires a new trial or merely an independent determination by the Alabama Supreme Court of the award necessary to vindicate the economic interests of Alabama consumers is a matter that should be addressed by the state court in the first instance.

The judgment is reversed, and the case is remanded for further proceedings not inconsistent with this opinion.

It is so ordered.

JUSTICE SCALIA, with whom JUSTICE THOMAS joins, dissenting:

Today we see the latest manifestation of this Court's recent and increasingly insistent "concern about punitive damages that 'run wild.'" *Pacific Mut. Life Ins. Co. v. Haslip*, 499 U.S. 1, 18, 111 S. Ct. 1032, 113 L. Ed. 2d 1 (1991). Since the Constitution does not make that concern any of our business, the Court's activities in this area are an unjustified incursion into the province of state governments.

In earlier cases that were the prelude to this decision, I set forth my view that a state trial procedure that commits the decision whether to impose punitive damages, and the amount, to the discretion of the jury, subject to some judicial review for "reasonableness," furnishes a defendant with all the process that is "due." See *TXO Production Corp. v. Alliance Resources Corp.*, 509 U.S. 443, 470, 113 S. Ct. 2711, 125 L. Ed. 2d 366 (1993). . . .

[T]oday's judgment represents the first instance of this Court's invalidation of a state-court punitive assessment as simply unreasonably large. . . .

. . . .

One might understand the Court's eagerness to enter this field, rather than leave it with the state legislatures, if it had something useful to say. In fact, however, its opinion provides virtually no guidance to legislatures, and to state and federal courts, as to what a "constitutionally proper" level of punitive damages might be.

. . . .

In Part III of its opinion, the Court identifies "three guideposts" that lead it to the conclusion that the award in this case is excessive: degree of reprehensibility, ratio between punitive award and plaintiff's actual harm, and legislative sanctions provided for comparable misconduct. . . . The legal significance of these "guideposts" is nowhere explored, but their necessary effect is to establish federal standards governing the hitherto exclusively state law of damages.

. . . .

These criss-crossing platitudes yield no real answers in no real cases. And it must be noted that the Court nowhere says that these three "guideposts" are the only guideposts; indeed, it makes very clear that they are not — explaining away the earlier opinions that do not really follow these "guideposts" on the basis of additional factors, thereby "reiterating our rejection of a categorical approach." . . . In other words, even these utter platitudes, if they should ever happen to produce an answer, may be overridden by other unnamed considerations. The Court has constructed a framework that does not genuinely constrain, that does not inform state legislatures and lower courts — that does nothing at all except confer an artificial air of doctrinal analysis upon its essentially ad hoc determination that this particular award of punitive damages was not "fair."

. . . .

JUSTICE GINSBURG, with whom the CHIEF JUSTICE [Rehnquist] joins, dissenting:

. . . The Court, I am convinced, unnecessarily and unwisely ventures into territory traditionally within the States' domain, and does so in the face of reform measures recently adopted or currently under consideration in legislative arenas. The Alabama Supreme Court, in this case, endeavored to follow this Court's prior instructions; and, more recently, Alabama's highest court has installed further controls on awards of punitive damages. . . . I would therefore leave the state court's judgment undisturbed, and resist unnecessary intrusion into an area dominantly of state concern.

————————

1. If you were the trial court judge, how would you interpret *BMW v. Gore*? Does the opinion provide any more guidance than "yikes" or "that is too much"? What is the standard that the trial court must now use in evaluating the size of punitive damage awards?

2. What do you think of BMW's argument that its policy had never been judged unlawful? Was there "no deliberate false statement" here?

3. Should a state adopt a "safe harbor" policy that sets a maximum ratio of punitive to compensatory awards?

4. How do damages verdicts affect the defendant's business in other states? Was there a market failure here? Did BMW provide what the consumer wanted and expected? In regard to minor repairs, are the expectations of a BMW consumer different from those of a Chevrolet consumer? What if there were evidence that repainting a car could in itself cause its value to drop by thousands of dollars because a buyer would assume that the repainting had been the product of damage to the vehicle?

5. In Justice Ginsburg's *Gore* dissent, she documented a great deal of activity by state legislatures intent on corralling punitive damages. In an appendix to her opinion, she identified pending or enacted measures in many states. These included various kinds of damages caps in 16 states, allocations of portions of a punitive award to state agencies in 13 states, and bifurcation of punitive damages from liability and compensatory damage proceedings in 12 states. State legislative activity to curb punitive damages has continued since *Gore* was decided.

Does the variation in state answers to the punitive damage question suggest that something is fundamentally wrong, that the answer to how to handle punitive damage awards depends on lobbyists, or that there may be numerous acceptable solutions to the problem? Which reforms do you prefer, if any? Why?

State Farm Mutual Automobile Ins. Co. v. Campbell

Supreme Court of the United States, 2003
538 U.S. 408

Justice Kennedy delivered the opinion of the Court.

We address once again the measure of punishment, by means of punitive damages, a State may impose upon a defendant in a civil case. The question is whether, in the circumstances we shall recount, an award of $145 million in punitive damages, where full compensatory damages are $1 million, is excessive and in violation of the Due Process Clause of the Fourteenth Amendment to the Constitution of the United States.

I

In 1981, Curtis Campbell (Campbell) was driving with his wife, Inez Preece Campbell, in Cache County, Utah. He decided to pass six vans traveling ahead of them on a two-lane highway. Todd Ospital was driving a small car approaching from the opposite direction. To avoid a head-on collision with Campbell, who by then was driving on the wrong side of the highway and toward oncoming traffic, Ospital swerved onto the shoulder, lost control of his automobile, and collided with a vehicle driven by Robert G. Slusher. Ospital was killed, and Slusher was rendered permanently disabled. The Campbells escaped unscathed.

In the ensuing wrongful death and tort action, Campbell insisted he was not at fault. Early investigations did support differing conclusions as to who caused the accident, but "a consensus was reached early on by the investigators and witnesses that Mr. Campbell's unsafe pass had indeed caused the crash." . . . Campbell's insurance company, petitioner State Farm Mutual Automobile Insurance Company (State

Farm), nonetheless decided to contest liability and declined offers by Slusher and Ospital's estate (Ospital) to settle the claims for the policy limit of $50,000 ($25,000 per claimant). State Farm also ignored the advice of one of its own investigators and took the case to trial, assuring the Campbells that "their assets were safe, that they had no liability for the accident, that [State Farm] would represent their interests, and that they did not need to procure separate counsel." . . . To the contrary, a jury determined that Campbell was 100 percent at fault, and a judgment was returned for $185,849, far more than the amount offered in settlement.

At first State Farm refused to cover the $135,849 in excess liability. Its counsel made this clear to the Campbells: "'You may want to put for sale signs on your property to get things moving.'" . . . Nor was State Farm willing to post a supersedeas bond to allow Campbell to appeal the judgment against him. Campbell obtained his own counsel to appeal the verdict. During the pendency of the appeal, in late 1984, Slusher, Ospital, and the Campbells reached an agreement whereby Slusher and Ospital agreed not to seek satisfaction of their claims against the Campbells. In exchange the Campbells agreed to pursue a bad-faith action against State Farm and to be represented by Slusher's and Ospital's attorneys.

. . . .

In 1989, the Utah Supreme Court denied Campbell's appeal in the wrongful-death and tort actions. *Slusher v. Ospital*, 777 P.2d 437. State Farm then paid the entire judgment, including the amounts in excess of the policy limits. The Campbells nonetheless filed a complaint against State Farm alleging bad faith, fraud, and intentional infliction of emotional distress. . . . At State Farm's request the trial court bifurcated the trial into two phases conducted before different juries. In the first phase the jury determined that State Farm's decision not to settle was unreasonable because there was a substantial likelihood of an excess verdict.

Before the second phase of the action against State Farm we decided *BMW of North America, Inc. v. Gore*. . . . The second phase addressed State Farm's liability for fraud and intentional infliction of emotional distress, as well as compensatory and punitive damages. The Utah Supreme Court aptly characterized this phase of the trial:

> "State Farm argued during phase II that its decision to take the case to trial was an 'honest mistake' that did not warrant punitive damages. In contrast, the Campbells introduced evidence that State Farm's decision to take the case to trial was a result of a national scheme [known as the "PP&R policy"] to meet corporate fiscal goals by capping payouts on claims company wide. . . . To prove the existence of this scheme, the trial court allowed the Campbells to introduce extensive expert testimony regarding fraudulent practices by State Farm in its nation-wide operations. Although State Farm moved prior to phase II of the trial for the exclusion of such evidence and continued to object to it at trial, the trial court ruled that such evidence was admissible to determine whether State Farm's conduct in the Campbell case was indeed intentional and sufficiently egregious to warrant punitive damages." 65 P. 3d, at 1143.

Evidence pertaining to the [PP&R scheme] concerned State Farm's business practices for over 20 years in numerous States. Most of these practices bore no relation to third party automobile insurance claims, the type of claim underlying the Campbells' complaint against the company. The jury awarded the Campbells $2.6 million in compensatory damages and $145 million in punitive damages, which the trial court reduced to $1 million and $25 million respectively. Both parties appealed.

The Utah Supreme Court sought to apply the three guideposts we identified in *Gore, supra,* . . . and it reinstated the $145 million punitive damages award. Relying in large part on the extensive evidence concerning the PP&R policy, the court concluded State Farm's conduct was reprehensible. The court also relied upon State Farm's "massive wealth" and on testimony indicating that "State Farm's actions, because of their clandestine nature, will be punished at most in one out of every 50,000 cases as a matter of statistical probability," 65 P. 3d, at 1153, and concluded that the ratio between punitive and compensatory damages was not unwarranted. Finally, the court noted that the punitive damages award was not excessive when compared to various civil and criminal penalties State Farm could have faced, including $10,000 for each act of fraud, the suspension of its license to conduct business in Utah, the disgorgement of profits, and imprisonment. *Id.,* at 1154–1155. We granted certiorari. . . .

II

We recognized in *Cooper Industries, Inc. v. Leatherman Tool Group, Inc.,* 532 U. S. 424 (2001), that in our judicial system compensatory and punitive damages, although usually awarded at the same time by the same decisionmaker, serve different purposes. *Id.,* at 432. Compensatory damages "are intended to redress the concrete loss that the plaintiff has suffered by reason of the defendant's wrongful conduct." *Ibid.* (citing Restatement (Second) of Torts § 903, pp. 453–454 (1979)). By contrast, punitive damages serve a broader function; they are aimed at deterrence and retribution. *Cooper Industries, supra,* at 432; see also *Gore, supra,* at 568. . . . While States possess discretion over the imposition of punitive damages, it is well established that there are procedural and substantive constitutional limitations on these awards. . . . The Due Process Clause of the Fourteenth Amendment prohibits the imposition of grossly excessive or arbitrary punishments on a tortfeasor. . . . The reason is that "[e]lementary notions of fairness enshrined in our constitutional jurisprudence dictate that a person receive fair notice not only of the conduct that will subject him to punishment, but also of the severity of the penalty that a State may impose." *Id.,* at 574. . . . To the extent an award is grossly excessive, it furthers no legitimate purpose and constitutes an arbitrary deprivation of property. . . .

Although these awards serve the same purposes as criminal penalties, defendants subjected to punitive damages in civil cases have not been accorded the protections applicable in a criminal proceeding. This increases our concerns over the imprecise manner in which punitive damages systems are administered. . . . Our concerns are heightened when the decisionmaker is presented, as we shall discuss, with evidence that has little bearing as to the amount of punitive damages that should be awarded. Vague instructions, or those that merely inform the jury to avoid "passion or prejudice," . . . do little to aid the decisionmaker in its task of assigning appropriate weight to evidence that is relevant and evidence that is tangential or only inflammatory.

In light of these concerns, in *Gore, supra,* we instructed courts reviewing punitive damages to consider three guideposts: (1) the degree of reprehensibility of the defendant's misconduct; (2) the disparity between the actual or potential harm suffered by the plaintiff and the punitive damages award; and (3) the difference between the punitive damages awarded by the jury and the civil penalties authorized or imposed in comparable cases. *Id.,* at 575. . . .

III

Under the principles outlined in *BMW of North America, Inc. v. Gore,* this case is neither close nor difficult. It was error to reinstate the jury's $145 million punitive damages award. We address each guidepost of *Gore* in some detail.

A

"[T]he most important indicium of the reasonableness of a punitive damages award is the degree of reprehensibility of the defendant's conduct." *Gore,* 517 U. S., at 575. We have instructed courts to determine the reprehensibility of a defendant by considering whether: the harm caused was physical as opposed to economic; the tortious conduct evinced an indifference to or a reckless disregard of the health or safety of others; the target of the conduct had financial vulnerability; the conduct involved repeated actions or was an isolated incident; and the harm was the result of intentional malice, trickery, or deceit, or mere accident. *Id.,* at 576–577. The existence of any one of these factors weighing in favor of a plaintiff may not be sufficient to sustain a punitive damages award; and the absence of all of them renders any award suspect. It should be presumed a plaintiff has been made whole for his injuries by compensatory damages, so punitive damages should only be awarded if the defendant's culpability, after having paid compensatory damages, is so reprehensible as to warrant the imposition of further sanctions to achieve punishment or deterrence. *Id.,* at 575.

Applying these factors in the instant case, we must acknowledge that State Farm's handling of the claims against the Campbells merits no praise. The trial court found that State Farm's employees altered the company's records to make Campbell appear less culpable. State Farm disregarded the overwhelming likelihood of liability and the near-certain probability that, by taking the case to trial, a judgment in excess of the policy limits would be awarded. State Farm amplified the harm by at first assuring the Campbells their assets would be safe from any verdict and by later telling them, postjudgment, to put a for-sale sign on their house. While we do not suggest there was error in awarding punitive damages based upon State Farm's conduct toward the Campbells, a more modest punishment for this reprehensible conduct could have satisfied the State's legitimate objectives, and the Utah courts should have gone no further. This case, instead, was used as a platform to expose, and punish, the perceived deficiencies of State Farm's operations throughout the country. The

Utah Supreme Court's opinion makes explicit that State Farm was being condemned for its nationwide policies rather than for the conduct directed toward the Campbells. . . .

The Campbells contend that State Farm has only itself to blame for the reliance upon dissimilar and out-of-state conduct evidence. The record does not support this contention. From their opening statements onward the Campbells framed this case as a chance to rebuke State Farm for its nationwide activities. . . . This was a position maintained throughout the litigation. In opposing State Farm's motion to exclude such evidence under *Gore*, the Campbells' counsel convinced the trial court that there was no limitation on the scope of evidence that could be considered under our precedents. . . . A State cannot punish a defendant for conduct that may have been lawful where it occurred. *Gore, supra*, at 572. . . .

Nor, as a general rule, does a State have a legitimate concern in imposing punitive damages to punish a defendant for unlawful acts committed outside of the State's jurisdiction. Any proper adjudication of conduct that occurred outside Utah to other persons would require their inclusion, and, to those parties, the Utah courts, in the usual case, would need to apply the laws of their relevant jurisdiction. *Phillips Petroleum Co. v. Shutts*, 472 U. S. 797, 821–822 (1985). Here, the Campbells do not dispute that much of the out-of-state conduct was lawful where it occurred. They argue, however, that such evidence was not the primary basis for the punitive damages award and was relevant to the extent it demonstrated, in a general sense, State Farm's motive against its insured. . . . This argument misses the mark. Lawful out-of-state conduct may be probative when it demonstrates the deliberateness and culpability of the defendant's action in the State where it is tortious, but that conduct must have a nexus to the specific harm suffered by the plaintiff. A jury must be instructed, furthermore, that it may not use evidence of out-of-state conduct to punish a defendant for action that was lawful in the jurisdiction where it occurred. *Gore*, 517 U. S., at 572–573. . . . A basic principle of federalism is that each State may make its own reasoned judgment about what conduct is permitted or proscribed within its borders, and each State alone can determine what measure of punishment, if any, to impose on a defendant who acts within its jurisdiction. *Id.*, at 569.

For a more fundamental reason, however, the Utah courts erred in relying upon this and other evidence: The courts awarded punitive damages to punish and deter conduct that bore no relation to the Campbells' harm. A defendant's dissimilar acts, independent from the acts upon which liability was premised, may not serve as the basis for punitive damages. A defendant should be punished for the conduct that harmed the plaintiff, not for being an unsavory individual or business. Due process does not permit courts, in the calculation of punitive damages, to adjudicate the merits of other parties' hypothetical claims against a defendant under the guise of the reprehensibility analysis, but we have no doubt the Utah Supreme Court did that here. . . . Punishment on these bases creates the possibility of multiple punitive damages awards for the same conduct; for in the usual case nonparties are not bound by the judgment some other plaintiff obtains. *Gore, supra*, at 593 (Breyer, J., concurring)

("Larger damages might also 'double count' by including in the punitive damages award some of the compensatory, or punitive, damages that subsequent plaintiffs would also recover").

The same reasons lead us to conclude the Utah Supreme Court's decision cannot be justified on the grounds that State Farm was a recidivist. Although "[o]ur holdings that a recidivist may be punished more severely than a first offender recognize that repeated misconduct is more reprehensible than an individual instance of malfeasance," *Gore, supra*, at 577, in the context of civil actions courts must ensure the conduct in question replicates the prior transgressions. . . .

The Campbells have identified scant evidence of repeated misconduct of the sort that injured them. Nor does our review of the Utah courts' decisions convince us that State Farm was only punished for its actions toward the Campbells. Although evidence of other acts need not be identical to have relevance in the calculation of punitive damages, the Utah court erred here because evidence pertaining to claims that had nothing to do with a third-party lawsuit was introduced at length. . . . The reprehensibility guidepost does not permit courts to expand the scope of the case so that a defendant may be punished for any malfeasance, which in this case extended for a 20-year period. In this case, because the Campbells have shown no conduct by State Farm similar to that which harmed them, the conduct that harmed them is the only conduct relevant to the reprehensibility analysis.

B

Turning to the second *Gore* guidepost, we have been reluctant to identify concrete constitutional limits on the ratio between harm, or potential harm, to the plaintiff and the punitive damages award. . . . We decline again to impose a bright-line ratio which a punitive damages award cannot exceed. Our jurisprudence and the principles it has now established demonstrate, however, that, in practice, few awards exceeding a single-digit ratio between punitive and compensatory damages, to a significant degree, will satisfy due process. . . . Single-digit multipliers are more likely to comport with due process, while still achieving the State's goals of deterrence and retribution, than awards with ratios in range of . . . 145 to 1.

Nonetheless, because there are no rigid benchmarks that a punitive damages award may not surpass, ratios greater than those we have previously upheld may comport with due process where "a particularly egregious act has resulted in only a small amount of economic damages." . . .

The converse is also true, however. When compensatory damages are substantial, then a lesser ratio, perhaps only equal to compensatory damages, can reach the outermost limit of the due process guarantee. The precise award in any case, of course, must be based upon the facts and circumstances of the defendant's conduct and the harm to the plaintiff.

In sum, courts must ensure that the measure of punishment is both reasonable and proportionate to the amount of harm to the plaintiff and to the general damages recovered. In the context of this case, we have no doubt that there is a presumption against an award that has a 145-to-1 ratio. The compensatory award in this case was substantial; the Campbells were awarded $1 million for a year and a half of emotional distress. This was complete compensation. The harm arose from a transaction in the economic realm, not from some physical assault or trauma; there were no physical injuries; and State Farm paid the excess verdict before the complaint was filed, so the Campbells suffered only minor economic injuries for the 18-month period in which State Farm refused to resolve the claim against them. The compensatory damages for the injury suffered here, moreover, likely were based on a component which was duplicated in the punitive award. Much of the distress was caused by the outrage and humiliation the Campbells suffered at the actions of their insurer; and it is a major role of punitive damages to condemn such conduct. Compensatory damages, however, already contain this punitive element. See Restatement (Second) of Torts § 908, Comment c, p. 466 (1977) ("In many cases in which compensatory damages include an amount for emotional distress, such as humiliation or indignation aroused by the defendant's act, there is no clear line of demarcation between punishment and compensation and a verdict for a specified amount frequently includes elements of both").

. . . .

The remaining premises for the Utah Supreme Court's decision bear no relation to the award's reasonableness or proportionality to the harm. They are, rather, arguments that seek to defend a departure from well-established constraints on punitive damages. While States enjoy considerable discretion in deducing when punitive damages are warranted, each award must comport with the principles set forth in *Gore*. Here the argument that State Farm will be punished in only the rare case, coupled with reference to its assets (which, of course, are what other insured parties in Utah and other States must rely upon for payment of claims) had little to do with the actual harm sustained by the Campbells. The wealth of a defendant cannot justify an otherwise unconstitutional punitive damages award. *Gore*, 517 U. S., at 585 ("The fact that BMW is a large corporation rather than an impecunious individual does not diminish its entitlement to fair notice of the demands that the several States impose on the conduct of its business"); see also *id.*, at 591 (Breyer, J., concurring) ("[Wealth] provides an open-ended basis for inflating awards when the defendant is wealthy. . . . That does not make its use unlawful or inappropriate; it simply means that this factor cannot make up for the failure of other factors, such as 'reprehensibility,' to constrain significantly an award that purports to punish a defendant's conduct"). The principles set forth in *Gore* must be implemented with care, to ensure both reasonableness and proportionality.

C

The third guidepost in *Gore* is the disparity between the punitive damages award and the "civil penalties authorized or imposed in comparable cases." *Id.*, at 575. We note that, in the past, we have also looked to criminal penalties that could be imposed. *Id.*, at 583; *Haslip*, 499 U.S., at 23. The existence of a criminal penalty does have bearing on the seriousness with which a State views the wrongful action. When used to determine the dollar amount of the award, however, the criminal penalty has less utility. Great care must be taken to avoid use of the civil process to assess criminal penalties that can be imposed only after the heightened protections of a criminal trial have been observed, including, of course, its higher standards of proof. Punitive damages are not a substitute for the criminal process, and the remote possibility of a criminal sanction does not automatically sustain a punitive damages award.

Here, we need not dwell long on this guidepost. The most relevant civil sanction under Utah state law for the wrong done to the Campbells appears to be a $10,000 fine for an act of fraud, 65 P. 3d, at 1154, an amount dwarfed by the $145 million punitive damages award. The Supreme Court of Utah speculated about the loss of State Farm's business license, the disgorgement of profits, and possible imprisonment, but here again its references were to the broad fraudulent scheme drawn from evidence of out-of-state and dissimilar conduct. This analysis was insufficient to justify the award.

IV

An application of the *Gore* guideposts to the facts of this case, especially in light of the substantial compensatory damages awarded (a portion of which contained a punitive element), likely would justify a punitive damages award at or near the amount of compensatory damages. The punitive award of $145 million, therefore, was neither reasonable nor proportionate to the wrong committed, and it was an irrational and arbitrary deprivation of the property of the defendant. . . .

The judgment of the Utah Supreme Court is reversed, and the case is remanded for further proceedings not inconsistent with this opinion.

It is so ordered.

[Justices Scalia and Thomas dissented]

Justice Ginsburg, dissenting

. . . .

In *Gore*, I stated why I resisted the Court's foray into punitive damages "territory traditionally within the States' domain." 517 U. S., at 612 (dissenting opinion). I adhere to those views. . . . It was once recognized that "the laws of the particular State must suffice [to superintend punitive damages awards] until judges or legislators authorized to do so initiate system-wide change." *Haslip*, 499 U. S., at 42 (Kennedy, J., concurring in judgment). I would adhere to that traditional view.

I

The large size of the award upheld by the Utah Supreme Court in this case indicates why damages-capping legislation may be altogether fitting and proper. Neither the amount of the award nor the trial record, however, justifies this Court's substitution of its judgment for that of Utah's competent decisionmakers. In this regard, I count it significant that, on the key criterion "reprehensibility," there is a good deal more to the story than the Court's abbreviated account tells.

Ample evidence allowed the jury to find that State Farm's treatment of the Campbells typified its "Performance, Planning and Review" (PP&R) program; implemented by top management in 1979, the program had "the explicit objective of using the claims-adjustment process as a profit center." . . . "[T]he Campbells presented considerable evidence," the trial court noted, documenting "that the PP&R program . . . has functioned, and continues to function, as an unlawful scheme . . . to deny benefits owed consumers by paying out less than fair value in order to meet preset, arbitrary payout targets designed to enhance corporate profits." . . . That policy, the trial court observed, was encompassing in scope; it "applied equally to the handling of both third-party and first-party claims." . . .

Evidence the jury could credit demonstrated that the PP&R program regularly and adversely affected Utah residents. Ray Summers, "the adjuster who handled the Campbell case and who was a State Farm employee in Utah for almost twenty years," described several methods used by State Farm to deny claimants fair benefits, for example, "falsifying or withholding of evidence in claim files." . . . A common tactic, Summers recounted, was to "unjustly attac[k] the character, reputation and credibility of a claimant and mak[e] notations to that effect in the claim file to create prejudice in the event the claim ever came before a jury." . . . State Farm manager Bob Noxon, Summers testified, resorted to a tactic of this order in the Campbell case when he "instruct[ed] Summers to write in the file that Todd Ospital (who was killed in the accident) was speeding because he was on his way to see a pregnant girlfriend." . . . In truth, "[t]here was no pregnant girlfriend." . . . Expert testimony noted by the trial court described these tactics as "completely improper." . . .

The trial court also noted the testimony of two Utah State Farm employees, Felix Jensen and Samantha Bird, both of whom recalled "intolerable" and "recurrent" pressure to reduce payouts below fair value. . . . When Jensen complained to top managers, he was told to "get out of the kitchen" if he could not take the heat; Bird was told she should be "more of a team player." . . . At times, Bird said, she "was forced to commit dishonest acts and to knowingly underpay claims." . . . Eventually, Bird quit. . . . Utah managers superior to Bird, the evidence indicated, were improperly influenced by the PP&R program to encourage insurance underpayments. For example, several documents evaluating the performance of managers Noxon and Brown "contained explicit preset average payout goals." . . .

Regarding liability for verdicts in excess of policy limits, the trial court referred to a State Farm document titled the "Excess Liability Handbook"; written before the Campbell accident, the handbook instructed adjusters to pad files with "self-serving" documents, and to leave critical items out of files, for example, evaluations of the insured's exposure. . . . Divisional superintendent Bill Brown used the handbook to train Utah employees. . . . While overseeing the Campbell case, Brown ordered adjuster Summers to change the portions of his report indicating that Mr. Campbell was likely at fault and that the settlement cost was correspondingly high. . . . The Campbells' case, according to expert testimony the trial court recited, "was a classic example of State Farm's application of the improper practices taught in the Excess Liability Handbook." . . .

The trial court further determined that the jury could find State Farm's policy "deliberately crafted" to prey on consumers who would be unlikely to defend themselves. . . . In this regard, the trial court noted the testimony of several former State Farm employees affirming that they were trained to target "the weakest of the herd"—"the elderly, the poor, and other consumers who are least knowledgeable about their rights and thus most vulnerable to trickery or deceit, or who have little money and hence have no real alternative but to accept an inadequate offer to settle a claim at much less than fair value." *Ibid.* (internal quotation marks omitted). The Campbells themselves could be placed within the "weakest of the herd" category. The couple appeared economically vulnerable and emotionally fragile. . . . At the time of State Farm's wrongful conduct, "Mr. Campbell had residuary effects from a stroke and Parkinson's disease."

To further insulate itself from liability, trial evidence indicated, State Farm made "systematic" efforts to destroy internal company documents that might reveal its scheme, . . . efforts that directly affected the Campbells. . . . For example, State Farm had "a special historical department that contained a copy of all past manuals on claim-handling practices and the dates on which each section of each manual was changed.". . . . Yet in discovery proceedings, State Farm failed to produce any claim-handling practice manuals for the years relevant to the Campbells' bad-faith case. . . .

State Farm's inability to produce the manuals, it appeared from the evidence, was not accidental. . . .

. . . State Farm admitted that it destroyed every single copy of claim-handling manuals on file in its historical department as of 1988, even though these documents could have been preserved at minimal expense. . . . Fortuitously, the Campbells obtained a copy of the 1979 PP&R manual by subpoena from a former employee. . . . Although that manual has been requested in other cases, State Farm has never itself produced the document. . . .

"As a final, related tactic," the trial court stated, the jury could reasonably find that "in recent years State Farm has gone to extraordinary lengths to stop damaging documents from being created in the first place." . . . State Farm kept no records at all on excess verdicts in third-party cases, or on bad-faith claims or attendant verdicts. . . . State Farm alleged "that it has no record of its punitive damage payments, even though such payments must be reported to the [Internal Revenue Service] and in some states may not be used to justify rate increases." . . . Regional Vice President Buck Moskalski testified that "he would not report a punitive damage verdict in [the Campbells'] case to higher management, as such reporting was not set out as part of State Farm's management practices." . . .

State Farm's "wrongful profit and evasion schemes," the trial court underscored, were directly relevant to the Campbells' case . . . : "The record fully supports the conclusion that the bad faith claim handling that exposed the Campbells to an excess verdict in 1983, and resulted in severe damages to them, was a product of the unlawful profit scheme that had been put in place by top management at State Farm years earlier. . . . There was ample evidence that the concepts taught in the Excess Liability Handbook, including the dishonest alteration and manipulation of claim files and the policy against posting any supersedeas bond for the full amount of an excess verdict, were dutifully carried out in this case. . . . There was ample basis for the jury to find that everything that had happened to the Campbells—when State Farm repeatedly refused in bad-faith to settle for the $50,000 policy limits and went to trial, and then failed to pay the 'excess' verdict, or at least post a bond, after trial—was a direct application of State Farm's overall profit scheme, operating through Brown and others." . . .

State Farm's "policies and practices," the trial evidence thus bore out, were "responsible for the injuries suffered by the Campbells," and the means used to implement those policies could be found "callous, clandestine, fraudulent, and dishonest." . . . The Utah Supreme Court, relying on the trial court's record-based recitations, understandably characterized State Farm's behavior as "egregious and malicious." . . .

II

The Court dismisses the evidence describing and documenting State Farm's PP&R policy and practices as essentially irrelevant, bearing "no relation to the Campbells' harm." . . . It is hardly apparent why that should be so. What is infirm about the Campbells' theory that their experience with State Farm exemplifies and reflects an overarching underpayment scheme, one that caused "repeated misconduct of the sort that injured them" . . . ? The Court's silence on that score is revealing: Once one recognizes that the Campbells did show "conduct by State Farm similar to that which harmed them," *ante* . . . it becomes impossible to shrink the reprehensibility analysis to this sole case, or to maintain, at odds with the determination of the trial court . . . that "the adverse effect on the State's general population was in fact minor," *ante*. . . .

Evidence of out-of-state conduct, the Court acknowledges, may be "probative [even if the conduct is lawful in the State where it occurred] when it demonstrates the deliberateness and culpability of the defendant's action in the State where it is tortious. . . ." *Ante* . . . "Other acts" evidence concerning practices both in and out of State was introduced in this case to show just such "deliberateness" and "culpability." The evidence was admissible, the trial court ruled: (1) to document State Farm's "reprehensible" PP&R program; and (2) to "rebut [State Farm's] assertion that [its] actions toward the Campbells were inadvertent errors or mistakes in judgment." . . . Viewed in this light, there surely was "a nexus" between much of the "other acts" evidence and "the specific harm suffered by [the Campbells]." *Ante*. . . .

III

When the Court first ventured to override state-court punitive damages awards, it did so moderately. The Court recalled that "[i]n our federal system, States necessarily have considerable flexibility in determining the level of punitive damages that they will allow in different classes of cases and in any particular case." *Gore*, 517 U. S., at 568. Today's decision exhibits no such respect and restraint. No longer content to accord state-court judgments "a strong presumption of validity," *TXO*, 509 U. S., at 457, the Court announces that "few awards exceeding a single-digit ratio between punitive and compensatory damages, to a significant degree, will satisfy due process." . . . Moreover, the Court adds, when compensatory damages are substantial, doubling those damages "can reach the outermost limit of the due process guarantee." *Ibid.* . . . In a legislative scheme or a state high court's design to cap punitive damages, the handiwork in setting single-digit and 1-to-1 benchmarks could hardly be questioned; in a judicial decree imposed on the States by this Court under the banner of substantive due process, the numerical controls today's decision installs seem to me boldly out of order.

----

1. *Philip Morris USA, Inc. v. Williams*, 549 U.S. 346 (2007), held that a punitive damages award that is based on the conduct of the defendant toward nonparties to the litigation amounts to an unconstitutional taking of property without due process, although conduct toward others can be used to assess reprehensibility. The case involved a suit alleging wrongful death of a smoker as a result of negligence and deceit by a tobacco manufacturer. In an opinion by Justice Breyer, the Court held that it was improper for the state courts to consider harm done to other smokers within the state in determining the amount of the punitive award. The Court reasoned that "to permit punishment for injuring a nonparty victim would add a near standardless dimension to the punitive damages equation." Justices Stevens, Scalia, Thomas, and Ginsburg dissented. In cases like *Gore, State Farm*, and *Philip Morris*, is the Court interpreting constitutional law or setting punitive damages policy?

2. Is there a punitive damages problem? In a watershed article, David G. Owen suggested that the problem, if any, has been overstated. For example, between 1960 and 1962, MER/29 was administered to 400,000 persons for the treatment of high levels of cholesterol. A side effect was that it allegedly caused injuries, such as cataracts, hair loss, and skin disorders, to a minimum of 5000 people. This led to 1500 suits against the manufacturer, Richardson-Merrell, for misrepresentation to the Food and Drug Administration. Only eleven suits resulted in jury verdicts, seven for the plaintiffs. Out of the 1500 suits there were only three awards of punitive damages, ranging from $100,000 to $250,000. One of these was set aside on appeal, leaving only two punitive damage awards standing. *See* David G. Owen, *Punitive Damages in Products Liability Litigation*, 74 Mich. L. Rev. 1257, 1329 (1976).

A later study of 220 federal cases found that punitive damages were awarded in only 2% of the cases. William Landes & Richard Posner, The Economic Structure of Tort Law 302-07 (1987).

3. A fundamental issue in punitive damages cases is whether the defendant must act with intent to harm the plaintiff. In *Taylor v. Superior Court*, involving a suit against a drunk driver, the California Supreme Court held:

> Section 3294 of the Civil Code authorizes the recovery of punitive damages in noncontract cases "where the defendant has been guilty of oppression, fraud, or malice, express or implied. . . ."

> Other authorities have amplified the foregoing principle. Thus it has been held that the "malice" required by section 3294 "implies an act conceived in

a spirit of mischief or with criminal indifference towards the obligations owed to others." (. . . Prosser, Law of Torts (4th ed. 1971) § 2, at pp. 9–10.) In Dean Prosser's words: "Where the defendant's wrongdoing has been intentional and deliberate, and has the character of outrage frequently associated with crime, all but a few courts have permitted the jury to award in the tort action 'punitive' or 'exemplary' damages. . . . Something more than the mere commission of a tort is always required for punitive damages. There must be circumstances of aggravation or outrage, such as spite or 'malice,' or a fraudulent or evil motive on the part of the defendant, or such a conscious and deliberate disregard of the interests of others that his conduct may be called wilful or wanton." . . .

Defendant's successful demurrer to the complaint herein was based upon plaintiff's failure to allege any actual intent of defendant to harm plaintiff or others. Is this an essential element of a claim for punitive damages? . . .

We discern no valid reason whatever for immunizing the driver himself from the exposure to punitive damages given the demonstrable and almost inevitable risk visited upon the innocent public by his voluntary conduct as alleged in the complaint. Indeed, under another recent amendment enacted following our *Coulter* decision, the Legislature has expressly acknowledged that "the consumption of alcoholic beverages is the proximate cause of injuries inflicted upon another by an intoxicated person." (Civ. Code, § 1714, subd. (b).)

Since the filing of *Coulter* we have had the enactment of section 25602. There also has appeared a graphic illustration of the magnitude of the danger in question. In June 1978, the Secretary of Health, Education, and Welfare filed the Third Special Report to the U.S. Congress on Alcohol and Health. We take judicial notice of, and extract the following from, this extensive and very recent official study: "Traffic accidents are the greatest cause of violent death in the United States, and approximately one-third of the ensuing injuries and one-half of the fatalities are alcohol related. In 1975, as many as 22,926 traffic deaths involved alcohol. . . .

. . . .

It is crystal clear to us that courts in the formulation of rules on damage assessment and in weighing the deterrent function must recognize the severe threat to the public safety which is posed by the intoxicated driver. The lesson is self-evident and widely understood. Drunken drivers are extremely dangerous people.

24 Cal. 3d 890, 157 Cal. Rptr. 693, 598 P.2d 854 (1979).

4. If malice is required for punitive damages, can one show malice in a products liability case resting on strict liability? In a suit by an injured asbestos worker for failure to warn of the danger, the New Jersey Supreme Court, in *Fischer v. Johns-Manville Corp.*, held that punitive damages could be recovered:

On this appeal Johns-Manville's position, succinctly stated, is that the punitive damages award against it is legally impermissible, ill-advised as a matter of public policy in litigation of this nature, and factually unwarranted.

. . . .

The "legally impermissible" argument rests on an asserted theoretical inconsistency between strict liability and punitive damages, which would preclude punitive damage claims when liability for compensatory damages is founded on strict products liability doctrine, if not in all situations at least in asbestos, strict liability lawsuits. We hold that there is no per se legal bar to pursuing a strict liability, failure-to-warn claim and a punitive damage claim in the same case. For this purpose there is no reason to distinguish asbestos litigation from other strict products liability actions. . . .

. . . .

. . . [A]lthough juries are asked in failure-to-warn cases to assess the reasonableness of a defendant's conduct, to prove a prima facie case of strict products liability a plaintiff need not introduce evidence relating to a manufacturer's or distributor's conduct, except to establish that the defendant did in fact put the offending article into the stream of commerce. This is in contrast to the quality of proofs required to establish a claim for punitive damages, in which a great deal must be shown about a defendant's conduct. "Punitive or exemplary damages are sums awarded apart from compensatory damages and are assessed when the wrongdoer's conduct is especially egregious." . . .

The type of conduct that will warrant an award of punitive damages has been described in various ways. The conduct must be "wantonly reckless or malicious. There must be an intentional wrongdoing in the sense of an 'evil-minded act' or an act accompanied by a wanton and willful disregard of the rights of another." *Nappe, supra*, 97 N.J. at 49 (citations omitted). "[T]he requirement may be satisfied upon a showing that there has been a deliberate act or omission with knowledge of a high degree of probability of harm and reckless indifference to consequences." *Berg v. Reaction Motors, supra*, 37 N.J. at 414, 181 A.2d 487. . . .

As should now be apparent, the proofs needed to establish a prima facie case of failure-to-warn, strict products liability differ markedly from the proofs that will support an award of punitive damages. Despite their differences — one going to the theory of liability, the other bearing on the form and extent of relief — they are not mutually exclusive nor even incompatible. There is no reason they cannot be litigated together. We agree with defendant's premises: strict products liability proofs center on the product; punitive damages proofs center on a defendant's conduct. We reject as wholly unwarranted the conclusion defendant draws — that these differences preclude punitive damages claims in failure-to-warn, strict product liability cases.

103 N.J. 643, 512 A.2d 466, 470–72 (1986).

5. Do punitive damage awards against corporations inappropriately punish shareholders?

> [An] argument, which ignores the legal nature of corporations, is that punitive damages unfairly punish innocent shareholders. This argument has been rejected repeatedly. . . . It is the corporation, not the individual shareholders, that is recognized as an ongoing legal entity engaged in manufacturing and distributing products. True, payment of punitive damages claims will deplete corporate assets, which will possibly produce a reduction in net worth and thereby result in a reduction in the value of individual shares. But the same is true of compensatory damages. Both are possible legal consequences of the commission of harmful acts in the course of doing business. To the same extent that damages claims may affect shareholders adversely, so do profitable sales of harmful products redound to their benefit (at least temporarily). These are the risks and rewards that await investors. Also, we would not consider it harmful were shareholders to be encouraged by decisions such as this to give close scrutiny to corporate practices in making investment decisions.

Fischer v. Johns-Manville, 103 N.J. 643, 512 A.2d 466, 476 (1986). What can be said of investing in tobacco stocks today? Punitive damage awards, if large enough, might attract shareholder attention and cause changes in the operation of the corporation. Should this be a reason to impose such awards?

6. Is it against public policy for insurance to cover punitive damages (so the loss is spread among the public, rather than visited upon the actor)? Yes, in California, *J.C. Penney Cas. Ins. v. M.K.*, 52 Cal. 3d 1009, 278 Cal. Rptr. 64, 804 P.2d 689 (1991). Yes, in New York, *Home Ins. Co. v. American Home Prods. Corp.*, 75 N.Y.2d 196, 551 N.Y.S.2d 481, 550 N.E.2d 930 (1990).

7. Does the criminal prosecution of corporations make more sense than punitive damages? One author has concluded that punitive damages are better, because criminal prosecution is unlikely, unsuccessful, and expensive. Frank J. Vandall, *Criminal Prosecution of Corporations for Defective Products*, 12 Int'l Legal Prac. 66 (Sept. 1987).

B. Pecuniary and Noneconomic Damages
Problem

What would someone have to pay you in order to obtain your consent to breaking your little finger (without anesthesia)? Is your answer to that question relevant to determining what damages you should receive if someone negligently breaks your little finger?

Seffert v. Los Angeles Transit Lines

Supreme Court of California, 1961
364 P.2d 337

PETERS, J.

Defendants appeal from a judgment for plaintiff for $187,903.75 entered on a jury verdict. Their motion for a new trial for errors of law and excessiveness of damages was denied.

At the trial plaintiff contended that she was properly entering defendants' bus when the doors closed suddenly catching her right hand and left foot. The bus started, dragged her some distance, and then threw her to the pavement. Defendants contended that the injury resulted from plaintiff's own negligence, that she was late for work and either ran into the side of the bus after the doors had closed or ran after the bus and attempted to enter after the doors had nearly closed.

The evidence supports plaintiff's version of the facts. Several eyewitnesses testified that plaintiff started to board the bus while it was standing with the doors wide open. Defendants do not challenge the sufficiency of the evidence. They do contend, however, that prejudicial errors were committed during the trial and that the verdict is excessive.

. . . .

One of the major contentions of defendants is that the damages are excessive, as a matter of law. There is no merit to this contention.

The evidence most favorable to the plaintiff shows that prior to the accident plaintiff was in good health, and had suffered no prior serious injuries. She was single, and had been self-supporting for 20 of her 42 years. The accident happened on October 11, 1957. The trial took place in July and August of 1959.

As already pointed out, the injury occurred when plaintiff was caught in the doors of defendants' bus when it started up before she had gained full entry. As a result she was dragged for some distance. The record is uncontradicted that her injuries were serious, painful, disabling and permanent.

The major injuries were to plaintiff's left foot. The main arteries and nerves leading to that foot, and the posterior tibial vessels and nerve of that foot, were completely severed at the ankle. The main blood vessel which supplies blood to that foot had to be tied off, with the result that there is a permanent stoppage of the main blood source. The heel and shin bones were fractured. There were deep lacerations and an avulsion[6] which involved the skin and soft tissue of the entire foot.

These injuries were extremely painful. They have resulted in a permanently raised left heel, which is two inches above the floor level, caused by the contraction of the

---

6. Defined in Webster's New International Dictionary (2d ed.) as a "tearing asunder; forcible separation."

ankle joint capsule. Plaintiff is crippled and will suffer pain for life.[7] Although this pain could, perhaps, be alleviated by an operative fusion of the ankle, the doctors considered and rejected this procedure because the area has been deprived of its normal blood supply. The foot is not only permanently deformed but has a persistent open ulcer on the heel, there being a continuous drainage from the entire area. Medical care of this foot and ankle is to be reasonably expected for the remainder of plaintiff's life.

Since the accident, and because of it, plaintiff has undergone nine operations and has spent eight months in various hospitals and rehabilitation centers. These operations involved painful skin grafting and other painful procedures. One involved the surgical removal of gangrenous skin leaving painful raw and open flesh exposed from the heel to the toe. Another involved a left lumbar sympathectomy in which plaintiff's abdomen was entered to sever the nerves affecting the remaining blood vessels of the left leg in order to force those blood vessels to remain open at all times to the maximum extent. Still another operation involved a cross leg flap graft of skin and tissue from plaintiff's thigh which required that her left foot be brought up to her right thigh and held at this painful angle, motionless, and in a cast for a month until the flap of skin and fat, partially removed from her thigh, but still nourished there by a skin connection, could be grafted to the bottom of her foot, and until the host site could develop enough blood vessels to support it. Several future operations of this nature may be necessary. One result of this operation was to leave a defective area of the thigh where the normal fat is missing and the muscles exposed, and the local nerves are missing. This condition is permanent and disfiguring.

Another operation called a debridement, was required. This involved removal of many small muscles of the foot, much of the fat beneath the skin, cleaning the end of the severed nerve, and tying off the severed vein and artery.

The ulcer on the heel is probably permanent, and there is the constant and real danger that osteomyelitis may develop if the infection extends into the bone. If this happens the heel bone would have to be removed surgically and perhaps the entire foot amputated.

Although plaintiff has gone back to work, she testified that she has difficulty standing, walking or even sitting, and must lie down frequently; that the leg is still very painful; that she can, even on her best days, walk not over three blocks and that very slowly; that her back hurts from walking; that she is tired and weak; that her sleep is disturbed; that she has frequent spasms in which the leg shakes uncontrollably; that she feels depressed and unhappy, and suffers humiliation and embarrassment.

Plaintiff claims that there is evidence that her total pecuniary loss, past and future, amounts to $53,903.75. This was the figure used by plaintiff's counsel in his argument to the jury, in which he also claimed $134,000 for pain and suffering, past and

---

7. Her life expectancy was 34.9 years from the time of trial.

future. Since the verdict was exactly the total of these two estimates, it is reasonable to assume that the jury accepted the amount proposed by counsel for each item. . . .

The summary of plaintiff as to pecuniary loss, past and future, is as follows: [doctor and hospital bills, drugs and other medical expenses, loss of earnings from accident to trial, future medical expenses, possible future lost earnings, totaling $53,903.75]. . . .

The amounts estimated for those various items [of pecuniary loss] are not out of line, and find support in the evidence.

This leaves the amount of $134,000 presumably allowed for the nonpecuniary items of damage, including pain and suffering, past and future. It is this allowance that defendants seriously attack as being excessive as a matter of law.

It must be remembered that the jury fixed these damages, and that the trial judge denied a motion for new trial, one ground of which was excessiveness of the award. These determinations are entitled to great weight. The amount of damages is a fact question, first committed to the discretion of the jury and next to the discretion of the trial judge on a motion for new trial. They see and hear the witnesses and frequently, as in this case, see the injury and the impairment that has resulted therefrom. As a result, all presumptions are in favor of the decision of the trial court. . . . The power of the appellate court differs materially from that of the trial court in passing on this question. An appellate court can interfere on the ground that the judgment is excessive only on the ground that the verdict is so large that, at first blush, it shocks the conscience and suggests passion, prejudice or corruption on the part of the jury. The proper rule was stated in *Holmes v. Southern Cal. Edison Co.*, 78 Cal. App. 2d 43, 51 [177 P.2d 32], as follows: "The powers and duties of a trial judge in ruling on a motion for new trial and of an appellate court on an appeal from a judgment are very different when the question of an excessive award of damages arises. The trial judge sits as a thirteenth juror with the power to weigh the evidence and judge the credibility of the witnesses. If he believes the damages awarded by the jury to be excessive and the question is presented it becomes his duty to reduce them. . . . When the question is raised his denial of a motion for new trial is an indication that he approves the amount of the award. An appellate court has no such powers. It cannot weigh the evidence and pass on the credibility of the witnesses as a juror does. To hold an award excessive it must be so large as to indicate passion or prejudice on the part of the jurors." In *Holder v. Key System*, 88 Cal. App. 2d 925, 940 [200 P.2d 98], the court, after quoting the above from the *Holmes* case added: "The question is not what this court would have awarded as the trier of the fact, but whether this court can say that the award is so high as to suggest passion or prejudice." In *Wilson v. Fitch*, 41 Cal. 363, 386, decided in 1871, there appears the oft-quoted statement that: "The Court will not interfere in such cases unless the amount awarded is so grossly excessive as to shock the moral sense, and raise a reasonable presumption that the jury was under the influence of passion or prejudice. In this case, whilst the sum awarded appears to be much larger than the facts demanded, the amount cannot be said to be so grossly excessive as to be reasonably imputed only to passion or prejudice in the jury. In such cases there is no accurate standard by which to compute the injury, and the jury must, necessarily, be left to the exercise of a wide discretion; to be restricted by the Court only when the sum awarded is so large that the verdict shocks the moral sense, and raises a presumption that it must have proceeded from passion or prejudice." This same rule was announced in *Johnston v. Long*, 30 Cal. 2d 54, 76 [181 P.2d 645], where it was stated that it "is not the function of a reviewing court to interfere with a jury's award of damages unless it is so grossly disproportionate to any reasonable limit of compensation warranted by the facts that it shocks the court's sense of justice and raises a presumption that it was the result of passion and prejudice." . . .

There are no fixed or absolute standards by which an appellate court can measure in monetary terms the extent of the damages suffered by a plaintiff as a result of the wrongful act of the defendant. The duty of an appellate court is to uphold the jury and trial judge whenever possible. . . . The amount to be awarded is "a matter on which there legitimately may be a wide difference of opinion". . . . In considering the contention that the damages are excessive the appellate court must determine every conflict in the evidence in respondent's favor, and must give him the benefit of every inference reasonably to be drawn from the record. . . .

While the appellate court should consider the amounts awarded in prior cases for similar injuries, obviously, each case must be decided on its own facts and circumstances. Such examination demonstrates that such awards vary greatly . . . Injuries are seldom identical and the amount of pain and suffering involved in similar physical injuries varies widely. These factors must be considered. . . . Basically, the question that should be decided by the appellate courts is whether or not the verdict is so out of line with reason that it shocks the conscience and necessarily implies that the verdict must have been the result of passion and prejudice.

In the instant case, the nonpecuniary items of damage include allowances for pain and suffering, past and future, humiliation as a result of being disfigured and being permanently crippled, and constant anxiety and fear that the leg will have to be amputated. While the amount of the award is high, and may be more than we would have awarded were we the trier of the facts, considering the nature of the injury, the great pain and suffering, past and future, and the other items of damage, we cannot say, as a matter of law, that it is so high that it shocks the conscience and gives rise to the presumption that it was the result of passion or prejudice on the part of the jurors.

Defendants next complain that it was prejudicial error for plaintiff's counsel to argue to the jury that damages for pain and suffering could be fixed by means of a mathematical formula predicated upon a per diem allowance for this item of damages. The propriety of such an argument seems never to have been passed upon in this state. In other jurisdictions there is a sharp divergence of opinion on the subject. . . . It is not necessary to pass on the propriety of such argument in the instant case because, when plaintiff's counsel made the argument in question, defendants' counsel did not object, assign it as misconduct or ask that the jury be admonished to disregard it. Moreover, in his argument to the jury, the defendants' counsel also adopted a mathematical formula type of argument. This being so, even if such argument were error (a point we do not pass upon), the point must be deemed to have been waived, and cannot be raised, properly, on appeal. *(State Rubbish etc. Assn. v. Siliznoff,* 38 Cal. 2d 330, 340 [240 P.2d 282].)

The judgment appealed from is affirmed.

Traynor, J.

I dissent.

Although I agree that there was no prejudicial error on the issue of liability, it is my opinion that the award of $134,000 for pain and suffering is so excessive as to indicate that it was prompted by passion, prejudice, whim, or caprice.[1]

Before the accident plaintiff was employed as a file clerk at a salary of $375 a month. At the time of the trial she had returned to her job at the same salary and her foot had healed sufficiently for her to walk. At the time of the accident she was 42 years old with a life expectancy of 34.9 years.

During closing argument plaintiff's counsel summarized the evidence relevant to past and possible future damages and proposed a specific amount for each item. His total of $187,903.75 was the exact amount awarded by the jury . . . .

The jury and the trial court have broad discretion in determining the damages in a personal injury case . . . A reviewing court, however, has responsibilities not only to the litigants in an action but to future litigants and must reverse or remit when a jury awards either inadequate or excessive damages.

. . . .

The crucial question in this case, therefore, is whether the award of $134,000 for pain and suffering is so excessive it must have resulted from passion, prejudice, whim or caprice. "To say that a verdict has been influenced by passion or prejudice is but another way of saying that the verdict exceeds any amount justified by the evidence." . . .

There has been forceful criticism of the rationale for awarding damages for pain and suffering in negligence cases. (Morris, *Liability for Pain and Suffering,* 59 Columb. L. Rev. 476; Plant, *Damages for Pain and Suffering,* 19 Ohio L. J. 200; Jaffe, *Damages for Personal Injury: The Impact of Insurance,* 18 Law and Contemporary Problems 219; Zelermyer, *Damages for Pain and Suffering,* 6 Syracuse L. Rev. 27.) Such damages originated under primitive law as a means of punishing wrongdoers and assuaging the

---

1. The award of $53,903.75 for pecuniary loss, past and future, is also suspect. The amount awarded for future medical expenses is $12,196.25 greater than the medical expenses incurred from the time of the accident to the time of trial, a period of nearly two years. The amount awarded for future loss of earnings is $4,500 greater than plaintiffs past loss of earnings. Yet the evidence indicates that plaintiff's medical care has been largely completed and that the future loss of earnings will not exceed the earnings lost by the prolonged stays in the hospital and the rehabilitation center.

feelings of those who had been wronged. (Morris, *Liability for Pain and Suffering*, *supra*, 59 Columb. L. Rev. at p. 478; Jaffe, *Damages for Personal Injury: The Impact of Insurance*, *supra*, 18 Law and Contemporary Problems at pp. 222–223.) They become increasingly anomalous as emphasis shifts in a mechanized society from ad hoc punishment to orderly distribution of losses through insurance and the price of goods or of transportation. Ultimately such losses are borne by a public free of fault as part of the price for the benefits of mechanization. . . .

Nonetheless, this state has long recognized pain and suffering as elements of damages in negligence cases (*Zibbell v. Southern Pacific Co.*, *supra*, 160 Cal. 237, 250; *Roedder v. Rowley*, *supra*, 28 Cal. 2d 820, 822); any change in this regard must await reexamination of the problem by the Legislature. Meanwhile, awards for pain and suffering serve to ease plaintiffs' discomfort and to pay for attorney fees for which plaintiffs are not otherwise compensated.

It would hardly be possible ever to compensate a person fully for pain and suffering. "No rational being would change places with the injured man for an amount of gold that would fill the room of the court, yet no lawyer would contend that such is the legal measure of damages." (*Zibbell v. Southern Pacific Co.*, *supra*, 160 Cal. 237, 255; *see* 2 Harper and James, The Law of Torts 1322.) "Translating pain and anguish into dollars can, at best, be only an arbitrary allowance, and not a process of measurement, and consequently the judge can, in his instructions give the jury no standard to go by; he can only tell them to allow such amount as in their discretion they may consider reasonable. . . . The chief reliance for reaching reasonable results in attempting to value suffering in terms of money must be the restraint and common sense of the jury. . . ." (McCormick, Damages, § 88, pp. 318–319.) Such restraint and common sense were lacking here.

A review of reported cases involving serious injuries and large pecuniary losses reveals that ordinarily the part of the verdict attributable to pain and suffering does not exceed the part attributable to pecuniary losses. . . . The award in this case of $134,000 for pain and suffering exceeds not only the pecuniary losses but any such award heretofore sustained in this state even in cases involving injuries more serious by far than those suffered by plaintiff. . . . In *McNulty v. Southern Pacific Co.*, *supra*, the court reviewed a large number of cases involving injuries to legs and feet, in each of which the total judgment, including both pecuniary loss and pain and suffering did not exceed $100,000[2] Although excessive damages is "an issue which is primarily factual and is not therefore a matter which can be decided upon the basis of awards made in other cases," . . . awards for similar injuries may be considered as one factor to be weighed in determining whether the damages awarded are excessive. . . .

The excessive award in this case was undoubtedly the result of the improper argument of plaintiff's counsel to the jury. Though no evidence was introduced, though

---

2. The verdicts in some of these cases were over $100,000 but in each case the award was reduced to $100,000 or less.

none could possibly be introduced on the monetary value of plaintiff's suffering, counsel urged the jury to award $100 a day for pain and suffering from the time of the accident to the time of trial and $2,000 a year for pain and suffering for the remainder of plaintiff's life.

The propriety of counsel's proposing a specific sum for each day or month of suffering has recently been considered by courts of several jurisdictions. . . . The reasons for and against permitting "per diem argument for pain and suffering" are reviewed in *Ratner v. Arrington* (Fla. App.), 111 So. 2d 82, 85–90 [1959 Florida decision holding such argument is permissible] and *Botta v. Brunner*, 26 N.J. 82 [138 A.2d 713, 718–725, 60 A.L.R.2d 1331] [1958 New Jersey decision holding such argument to be an "unwarranted intrusion into the domain of the jury"].

The reason usually advanced for not allowing such argument is that since there is no way of translating pain and suffering into monetary terms, counsel's proposal of a particular sum for each day of suffering represents an opinion and a conclusion on matters not disclosed by the evidence, and tends to mislead the jury and result in excessive awards. The reason usually advanced for allowing "per diem argument for pain and suffering" is that it affords the jury as good an arbitrary measure as any for that which cannot be measured.

Counsel may argue all legitimate inferences from the evidence, but he may not employ arguments that tend primarily to mislead the jury. . . . A specified sum for pain and suffering for any particular period is bound to be conjectural. Positing such a sum for a small period of time and then multiplying that sum by the number of days, minutes or seconds in plaintiff's life expectancy multiplies the hazards of conjecture. Counsel could arrive at any amount he wished by adjusting either the period of time to be taken as a measure or the amount surmised for the pain for that period.

> "The absurdity of a mathematical formula is demonstrated by applying it to its logical conclusion. If a day may be used as a unit of time in measuring pain and suffering, there is no logical reason why an hour or a minute or a second could not be used, or perhaps even a heart-beat since we live from heart-beat to heart-beat. If one cent were used for each second of pain this would amount to $3.60 per hour, to $86.40 per twenty-four hour day, and to $31,536 per year. The absurdity of such a result must be apparent, yet a penny a second for pain and suffering might not sound unreasonable. . . . The use of the formula was prejudicial error." . . .

The misleading effect of the per diem argument was not cured by the use of a similar argument by defense counsel. Truth is not served by a clash of sophistic arguments. . . . Had defendant objected to the improper argument of plaintiff's counsel this error would be a sufficient ground for reversal whether or not the award was excessive as a matter of law. Defendant's failure to object, however, did not preclude its appeal on the ground that the award was excessive as a matter of law or preclude this court's reversing on that ground and ruling on the impropriety of counsel's argument to guide the court on the retrial. . . .

I would reverse the judgment and remand the cause for a new trial on the issue of damages.

---

1. Why is the jury verdict on damages entitled to "great weight"? What is the test for setting aside the jury's award? Is the test helpful? What is Justice Traynor's reasoning for casting aside the jury verdict? How is Traynor's view of the role of the appellate court different from the majority's view?

2. The majority of personal injury damages are awarded in lump-sum amounts, not on a weekly or monthly basis, although tort settlements sometimes provide for periodic payments from a fund established by the settling defendant(s). Compensatory damage awards can be divided into two subcategories: special damages and general damages. Special damages are pecuniary losses and are objectively calculated, while general damages are noneconomic and subjectively determined. General damages will be discussed below in connection with damages for pain and suffering and loss of enjoyment of life.

Past Pecuniary Losses. Included in pecuniary losses are both past and future losses. Past pecuniary losses are relatively easy to calculate because bills and receipts are available, documenting past losses, such as medical expenses, lost earnings, and funeral expenses.

Future Pecuniary Losses. In personal injury cases, future losses to the plaintiff are recoverable. These losses include such items as future medical expenses, future earnings, and future lost pension benefits. Lost future earnings and benefits are also recoverable in wrongful death actions. These future losses are more problematic to calculate and usually require an economist to give expert testimony. Without reliable expert evidence, any type of future losses estimate will likely be found too speculative.

Future losses vary according to the injured party's age, gender, type of injury, occupation, life expectancy, work life expectancy, any discount rate and inflation factor which may be applicable, the annual wage rate increase, probable future earning capacity, and the loss of future earning ability and capacity. *Andrews v. Mosley Well Serv.*, 514 So. 2d 491, 499 (La. Ct. App. 1987). "An award for the loss of future earnings requires first a determination of the underlying facts influencing future earning capacity, and then a calculation of the loss based upon those facts." *Id.* Economists often refer to life expectancy and mortality tables to determine how much longer the victim will live.

3. *Per Diem Argument.* A per diem argument is a tool of persuasion used by a plaintiff's attorney to suggest to the jury how it can quantify plaintiff's damages for pain and suffering, as based on the evidence. *Debus v. Grand Union Stores of Vermont*, 159 Vt. 537, 539, 621 A.2d 1288, 1290 (1993). Counsel generally presents a dollar amount per unit of time to assist the jury in its calculation of the extent of the pain. For example, in closing argument, counsel may argue to the jury that it should award the plaintiff ten dollars a day every day for the next twenty-five years of the plaintiff's life. With this mathematical formula, the numbers quickly accrue, but it gives the jury something concrete to comprehend the amount of pain and suffering the plaintiff will endure for the next twenty-five years. Opposing counsel is allowed to rebut these arguments and can easily do so if the plaintiff's numbers are unreasonable.

Jurisdictions are split regarding the use of such per diem arguments. Those against the per diem approach insist that per diem arguments are merely argument, having never been entered into evidence, but nonetheless relied on by the jury to generate a jury award. An "illusion of certainty" is created. The plaintiff presents an illusion that pain is "constant, uniform, and continuous." Some courts believe that the jury will be too easily misled by the per diem argument. *See Botta v. Brunner*, 26 N.J. 82, 138 A.2d 713 (1958).

The courts that allow per diem arguments sometimes do so with the safeguard of cautionary instructions to the jury. *See Giant Food, Inc. v. Satterfield*, 90 Md. App. 660, 603 A.2d 877 (1992). As long as the trial court instructs the jury that the plaintiff's per diem arguments are arguments, and not evidence, the appellate court will likely uphold the jury's award.

4. *Pain and Suffering.* General damages refer "to those damages which may not be fixed with any degree of exactitude, but which involve mental or physical pain or suffering, inconvenience, loss of gratification or intellectual or physical enjoyment, or other losses of lifestyle which cannot be measured definitively in terms of money." *Foster v. Trafalgar House Oil & Gas*, 603 So. 2d 284 (La. Ct. App. 1992). Included in general damages are damages for pain and suffering. These nonpecuniary damages serve to give the plaintiff a full recovery for his injury. The majority rule is that damages are recoverable only for pain and suffering that is consciously experienced.

For demonstrative purposes, some plaintiffs submit "day in the life" films to show the jury the effects of the injury on the plaintiff. These films are generally admissible as long as they are an "accurate representation of the victim," *Wagner v. York Hosp.*, 415 Pa. Super. 1, 608 A.2d 496 (1992), and are not unduly prejudicial to the defendant. Other forms of demonstrative evidence are photographs, charts, diagrams, and other visual aids. Demonstrative evidence is admissible as long as it does not mislead or confuse the jury.

What is the function of damages for pain and suffering? If they drive up the cost of goods and services, is that a good reason to limit them?

Many recent tort reform proposals focus on pain and suffering and other forms of "noneconomic" damages. In some states, statutory caps limit the amount of noneconomic damages a tort plaintiff may recover. *See, e.g., DRD Pool Serv. v. Freed*, 5 A.3d 45 (Md. 2010) (upholding constitutionality of Md. Code Ann., Cts. & Jud. Proc. § 11-108, which put a statutory cap on noneconomic damages in Maryland tort suits). See note 13, *infra*. When noneconomic damages are capped, which victims are most acutely affected?

5. *Contingent Fees.* Personal injury attorneys representing plaintiffs are generally paid on a contingent fee basis, as opposed to an hourly rate. A contingent fee arrangement means that the attorney contracts with his or her client to be paid a certain percentage of the proceeds from settlement or a successful judgment. Fee agreements often specify a lower percentage if the case is settled and a higher one if it goes to trial. If the plaintiff loses at trial, the attorney is paid nothing for his or her services. Three main reasons support the contingency fee basis: (1) it enables the poor plaintiff, who may not be able to afford an hourly rate attorney, to pursue a claim; (2) it allows the plaintiff to shift his economic risk to the attorney, who has greater resources and is better able to spread the risk; and (3) it aligns the interests of the plaintiff with those of the attorney. Bradley L. Smith, Note, *Three Attorney Fee-Shifting Rules and Contingency Fees: Their Impact on Settlement Incentives*, 90 Mich. L. Rev. 2154, 2163 (1992). Those opposing the contingency fee arrangement argue that it produces high fees, encourages excessive litigation, and creates incentives for lawyers to accept settlement offers when settlement is contrary to their clients' best interests. *Id.*

The contingent fee arrangement is banned in many foreign countries, and its presence in the United States has generated much criticism. In response, many state legislatures have enacted tort reform statutes imposing fixed or sliding scale maxima for contingent fees in medical malpractice suits. A few states, via statute or court rules, have limited the contingent fee system in all or most tort suits. Most of these rules have been held constitutional. Richard M. Birnholz, *The Validity and Propriety of Contingent Fee Controls*, 37 UCLA L. Rev. 949, 950–53 (1990). *See* Conn. Gen. Stat. § 52-251c (sliding scale for all personal injury, wrongful death, and property damage actions: an attorney's fee on a contingency fee arrangement may not exceed "(1) Thirty-three and one-third per cent of the first three hundred thousand dollars; (2) twenty-five per cent of the next three hundred thousand dollars; (3) twenty per cent of the next three hundred thousand dollars; (4) fifteen per cent of the next three hundred thousand dollars; and (5) ten per cent of any amount which exceeds one million two hundred thousand dollars.") and Mich. Gen. Ct. R. 8.121 (1996) (maximum allowable fee is one-third of the amount recovered).

6. Who pays the plaintiff's attorney? One explanation for an award for pain and suffering is that it pays the plaintiff's attorney. Without an award for pain and suffering, the plaintiff would not be put back in the position he or she was in before the injury, because the attorney's fee would be subtracted from the plaintiff's economic damages. *See* Michael Horowitz, *Making Ethics Real, Making Ethics Work: A Proposal for Contingency Fee Reform*, 44 Emory L.J. 173 (1995).

7. What do you think of the following argument by Judge Posner?

> We disagree with those students of tort law who believe that pain and suffering are not real costs and should not be allowable items of damages in a tort suit. No one likes pain and suffering and most people would pay a good deal of money to be free of them. If they were not recoverable in damages,

the cost of negligence would be less to the tortfeasors and there would be
more negligence, more accidents, more pain and suffering, and hence higher
social costs.

Kwasny v. United States, 823 F.2d 194, 197 (7th Cir. 1987).

8. *Loss of Enjoyment of Life.* May a comatose person recover for an element of pain
and suffering called "loss of enjoyment of life"? Loss of enjoyment of life damages,
also known as hedonic damages, belong to the group of general damages. *See Thompson v. National R.R. Passenger Corp.*, 621 F.2d 814, 824 (6th Cir. 1980) (characterizing the types of damages as follows: "Permanent impairment compensates the victim
for the fact of being permanently injured whether or not it causes any pain or inconvenience; pain and suffering compensates the victim for the physical and mental discomfort caused by the injury; and loss of enjoyment of life compensates the victim
for the limitations on the person's life created by the injury.").

Courts vary in their approach to damages for the loss of enjoyment of life. Most
courts place hedonic damages in the same group as pain and suffering, while others
place them in a separate group, hedonic damages. A third category of courts completely disregards damages for the loss of enjoyment of life. Pamela J. Hermes, *Loss
of Enjoyment of Life—Duplication of Damages Versus Full Compensation*, 63 N.D. L.
Rev. 561 (1987). Unlike pain and suffering, courts may not require the victim to be
conscious or aware of his or her loss of enjoyment of life. *See Holston v. Sisters of Third
Order of St. Francis*, 247 Ill. App. 3d 985, 1005, 618 N.E.2d 334, 347 (1993) (holding
that damages may be awarded for "the loss of enjoyment of life to a disabled person
even if she was unaware of her loss because she had been deprived of her consciousness and therefore her ability to enjoy her life"). The award does not need to have
any meaning or utility to the injured person. *But see McDougald v. Garber*, 73 N.Y.2d
246, 538 N.Y.S.2d 937, 536 N.E.2d 372 (1989) (requiring the plaintiff to have some
level of cognitive awareness in order to recover for loss of enjoyment, because otherwise an award for such damages would be punitive and duplicative).

9. *Remittitur and Additur.* Remittitur and additur are procedural post-trial tools
courts use to reduce appeals and to promote efficiency. Courts reduce jury awards
through a remittitur. They increase a jury award through an additur. Before an additur or a remittitur is granted, however, the court examines the reasonableness of the
jury verdict to see if it is against the clear weight of the evidence. The standards courts
use are often dictated by statutes. However, a jury is given wide discretion in its award,
and a trial court is also given much deference in granting or denying an additur or
remittitur. One or both parties move for a new trial; then, if either party denies the
additur or remittitur, a motion for a new trial may be granted. The new trial may be
either a full-blown new trial or just a trial on the issue of damages.

Courts reduce jury awards considered excessive on the condition that the losing
defendant will not be granted a new trial. *Honda Motor Co. v. Oberg*, 512 U.S. 415,
114 S. Ct. 2331 (1994). Neither side is required to accept the remittitur. Two principal objectives are considered when calculating the amount of the remittitur. "The

first is to enable the parties to avoid the delay and expense of a new trial when the jury award is excessive. The second objective is to minimize the extent of the judicial interference with matter that is otherwise within the jury's domain." *Slade v. Whitco Corp.*, 811 F. Supp. 71, 77 (N.D.N.Y. 1993).

The *Slade* court described three possible methods for calculating a remittitur. The first method is to "reduce the verdict to the lowest amount that could reasonably be found by the jury." Second, the court can reduce the verdict only to the maximum amount not considered excessive and that would be upheld by the trial court. Third, the court can "reduce the jury award to what the trial court believes a properly functioning jury, acting free of suggestions by counsel will have awarded." *Slade*, 811 F. Supp. at 77. *See* Irene D. Sann, *Remittiturs (and Additurs) in the Federal Courts: An Evaluation with Suggested Alternatives*, 38 Case W. Res. L. Rev. 157 (1987).

Courts use additur to increase jury awards. However, the U.S. Supreme Court found additur to be unconstitutional in the federal courts. Finding additur to violate the Seventh Amendment right to a jury trial, the Court in *Dimick v. Schiedt*, 293 U.S. 474 (1935), held that additur invaded the jury's fact-finding authority. Some states allow additur, while others have found it unconstitutional under their state constitutions. The Supreme Court has not addressed the constitutional issue of remittiturs. *See* Fed. R. Civ. P. 59; David Baldus, John C. MacQueen, et al., *Improving Judicial Oversight of Jury Damages Assessments: A Proposal for the Comparative Additur/Remittitur Review of Awards for Nonpecuniary Harms and Punitive Damages*, 80 Iowa L. Rev. 1109 (1995).

10. *The Collateral Source Rule.* The plaintiff often has insurance that has paid for his or her medical care and property damage. In addition to insurance, the plaintiff may have received Social Security benefits, Medicare benefits, workers' compensation, or benefits from other sources. How states handle these in terms of calculating final damage awards is a highly statutory area of law.

11. *Substantial Damage Awards.* The fear of a "runaway jury" exists among many defendants today. Yet procedural devices exist to check the jury's discretion. Courts apply standards such as "unconscionable or outside reasonable bounds," "shock the judicial conscience," "so grossly excessive as to shock our sense of justice," and "tainted by passion or prejudice" in order to reduce or increase a jury's award. *See Wagner v. York Hosp.*, 415 Pa. Super. 1, 17, 608 A.2d 496, 504 (1992) (listing six factors used to determine excessiveness: (1) The severity of the injury; (2) whether plaintiff's injury is manifested by objective physical evidence instead of merely the subjective testimony of the plaintiff; (3) whether the injury will affect the plaintiff permanently; (4) whether the plaintiff can continue with his employment; (5) the size of the plaintiff's out-of-pocket expenses; and (6) the amount plaintiff demanded in the original complaint).

The Supreme Court has ruled that federal courts sitting in diversity in tort cases must apply state law when determining whether a jury award is excessive and a new trial is warranted. *Gasperini v. Center for Humanities, Inc.*, 518 U.S. 415 (1996).

12. *Tort Reform of Compensatory Damages.* Over the last two decades, numerous states have adopted statutes that limit or redefine the recovery of economic and non-economic losses.

For example, Oregon adopted a $500,000 cap on pain and suffering:

> [I]n any civil action seeking damages arising out of bodily injury, including emotional injury or distress, death or property damage of any one person including claims for loss of care, comfort, companionship and society and loss of consortium, the amount awarded for noneconomic damages shall not exceed $500,000.

Or. Rev. Stat. § 560.

The purpose "of imposing a cap on noneconomic damages was to stabilize insurance premiums and to decrease the costs associated with tort litigation." *Tenold v. Weyerhaeuser Co.*, 127 Or. App. 511, 873 P.2d 413 (1994). What does that mean?

The $500,000 cap was held unconstitutional in common-law tort actions by *Lakin v. Senco Products, Inc.*, 329 Or. 62, 987 P.2d 463 (1999), although the same court upheld it as applied to wrongful death actions in *Greist v. Phillips*, 322 Or. 281, 906 P.2d 789 (1995). Why the different outcomes?

Kansas passed a statute limiting noneconomic loss to $250,000:

> In any personal injury action, the total amount recoverable by each party from all defendants for all claims for pain and suffering shall not exceed a sum total of $250,000.

Kan. Stat. Ann. § 60-19a01. It was upheld as constitutional in *Samsel v. Wheeler Transp. Servs.*, 246 Kan. 336, 789 P.2d 541 (1990).

Many of the caps on pain and suffering have passed constitutional muster. Others have not. For example, a cap of $875,000 on pain and suffering was held to deny equal protection of the law in *Brannigan v. Usitalo*, 134 N.H. 50, 587 A.2d 1232 (1991):

> Although fewer tort plaintiffs would be affected by a $875,000 cap than a cap of $250,000, it seems to us even more "unfair and unreasonable to impose the burden of supporting the [insurance] industry solely upon those persons who are [even more] severely injured and therefore [even more] in need of compensation." *Carson*, 120 N.H. at 942, 424 A.2d at 837. . . . Finally, we note that society, through the courts, has developed a remedy to secure itself from the ills of a "run-away" jury that has imposed a disproportionally high award. That remedy is remittitur, to be exercised in the sound discretion of the trial court. *Hanlon v. Pomeroy*, 102 N.H. 407, 157 A.2d 646 (1960).
>
> RSA 508:4-d (Supp. 1990) is hereby declared unconstitutional. The case is remanded to the trial court.

Brannigan, 587 A.2d at 1236–37.

In *MacDonald v. City Hospital, Inc.*, 2011 W. Va. LEXIS 57 (June 22, 2011), the court upheld West Virginia's caps on noneconomic damages in medical malpractice cases. Collecting cases from other states, the court remarked that "our decision today is consistent with the majority of jurisdictions that have considered the constitutionality of caps on noneconomic damages in medical malpractice actions or in any personal injury action." It concluded that "now only a few states have declared such caps unconstitutional," and most of those decisions involved state constitutional provisions stating that "the right to trial by jury shall remain inviolate."

Some states have reformed compensatory damages by placing a cap on the total amount recovered. Virginia's one million dollar cap on the amount recovered in a medical malpractice case passed constitutional challenges. Va. Code Ann. § 8.01-581.15 provides:

> In any verdict returned against a health care provider in an action for malpractice . . . which is tried by a jury or in any judgment entered against a health care provider in such an action which is tried without a jury, the total amount recoverable for any injury . . . shall not exceed one million dollars.

The Supreme Court of Virginia, in *Fairfax Hosp. Sys. v. Nevitt*, held:

> Construing the language of the statutory recovery cap in a recent case, we said that "in a medical malpractice action, the total damages recoverable for injury to a 'patient' are limited to the statutory amount, regardless of the number of legal theories upon which the claims are based."
>
> . . . .
>
> We conclude that the plain meaning of the two statutes in issue, read together, is that where there is a verdict by a jury or a judgment by a court against a health care provider for "injury to . . . a patient" and the total amount recovered in that action and in all settlements related to the medical malpractice injury exceeds one million dollars, the total amount the plaintiff can recover for that injury is one million dollars. Accordingly, we hold that the trial court erred when it failed to apply the $600,000 credit for the PCA settlement against the $1,000,000 statutory recovery cap in determining the quantum of Nevitt's judgment.

457 S.E.2d 10, 14–15 (Va. 1995).

13. *The Role of Insurance in Tort Decisions.* Insurance, although often carried by both parties, is rarely mentioned in the opinions. There are two types of insurance: "first-party" and "third-party." First-party insurance, like property insurance, protects the owner from loss if his property is damaged. The owner's home burns, for example.

Third-party insurance, like automobile liability insurance, protects the insured from liability if he or she causes damage to a third party. Often, the insurance company has hired the attorney and is defending the insured in a suit brought by the injured third party. What conflicts might arise between the insurance company and the insured under third-party insurance? Would there be more such conflicts in a car crash case or a medical malpractice case?

Most of the cases in the book involve third-party insurance. The critical issue is the extent such insurance affects the tort decision. Although barely mentioned by the courts before 1960, insurance has become a factor that affects judicial decisions and influences the structure of tort law. *See* Mark C. Rahdert, Covering Accident Costs: Insurance, Liability, and Tort Reform (1995).

The first case to mention insurance was *Ryan v. New York Central R.R. Co.*, 35 N.Y. 210, 91 Am. Dec. 49 (1866): "A man may insure his own house. . . . In a commercial country each man . . . runs the hazard of his neighbor's conduct, and each, by insurance against such hazard, is enabled to obtain a reasonable security against loss."

In a series of books and articles beginning in the late 1920s, Dean Leon Green argued that the ability to bear the loss and insurance were two of the key factors to be weighed by a court in deciding whether a duty extended to a particular plaintiff. *See* Green, *Proximate Cause in Texas Negligence Law*, 28 Tex. L. Rev. 471, 628, 755 (1950); Green, *The Duty Problem in Negligence Cases*, 28 Colum. L. Rev. 1034 (1928).

This theme was reflected by Justice Traynor in his often-cited concurring opinion in *Escola v. Coca-Cola Bottling Co.*, 24 Cal. 2d 453, 150 P.2d 436, 441 (1944): "The cost of an injury and the loss of time or health may be an overwhelming misfortune to the person injured, and a needless one, for the risk of injury can be insured by the manufacturer and distributed among the public as a cost of doing business."

In the famous case *Kinsman I*, Judge Friendly had insurance foremost in his mind when he defined the limits of proximate cause:

> [P]erhaps in the long run one returns to Judge Andrews' statement in *Palsgraf*, 248 N.Y. at 354–355, 162 N.E. at 104 (dissenting opinion). "It is all a question of expediency, . . . of fair judgment, always keeping in mind the fact that we endeavor to make a rule in each case that will be practical and in keeping with the general understanding of mankind." It would be pleasant if greater certainty were possible, . . . but the many efforts that have been made at defining the locus of the "uncertain and wavering line," 248 N.Y. at 354, 162 N.E. 99, are not very promising; what courts do in such cases makes better sense than what they, or others, say. Where the line will be drawn will vary from age to age; as society has come to rely increasingly on insurance and other methods of loss-sharing, the point may lie further off than a century ago.

Petition of Kinsman Transit Co., 338 F.2d 708, 725–26 (2d Cir. 1964).

Four years later, the California Supreme Court made clear that insurance played a critical role in its decision to discard the traditional theories of property owner liability:

> Without attempting to labor all of the rules relating to the possessor's liability, it is apparent that . . . the major factors which should determine whether

immunity should be conferred upon the possessor of land . . . [include] the closeness of the connection between the injury and the defendant's conduct, the moral blame attached to the defendant's conduct, the policy of preventing future harm, and the prevalence and availability of insurance. . . .

Rowland v. Christian, 69 Cal. 2d 108, 70 Cal. Rptr. 97, 443 P.2d 561 (1968).

In *Kelly v. Gwinnell*, the New Jersey Supreme Court reflected on the limits of insurance in extending liability to the social host for the death caused by his intoxicated guest:

> Some fear has been expressed that the extent of the potential liability may be disproportionate to the fault of the host. A social judgment is therein implied to the effect that society does not regard as particularly serious the host's actions in causing his guests to become drunk, even though he knows they will thereafter be driving their cars. We seriously question that value judgment; indeed, we do not believe that the liability is disproportionate when the host's actions, so relatively easily corrected, may result in serious injury or death. The other aspect of this argument is that the host's insurance protection will be insufficient. While acknowledging that homeowners' insurance will cover such liability, this argument notes the risk that both the host and spouse will be jointly liable. The point made is not that the level of insurance will be lower in relation to the injuries than in the case of other torts, but rather that the joint liability of the spouses may result in the loss of their home and other property to the extent that the policy limits are inadequate. . . . We observe, however, that it is common for both spouses to be liable in automobile accident cases. It may be that some special form of insurance could be designed to protect the spouses' equity in their homes in cases such as this one. In any event, it is not clear that the loss of a home by spouses who, by definition, have negligently caused the injury, is disproportionate to the loss of life of one who is totally innocent of any wrongdoing.

96 N.J. 538, 549–50, 476 A.2d 1219, 1225 (1984).

The Supreme Court of West Virginia concluded in 1991 that the loss-spreading effect of insurance was a critical factor in products liability cases:

> What is obvious from the . . . court's discussion is that product liability is concerned with spreading the cost of inevitable accidents. Inherent in this cost-spreading function is the collection of what amounts to insurance premiums from all the purchasers of products, and the purchase by manufacturers of commercial insurance or the creation of self insurance funds.
>
> The defendant before us, General Motors, is the largest producer of automobiles in the world. . . . In light of the fact that all of our sister states have adopted a cause of action for lack of crashworthiness, General Motors is *already* collecting a product liability premium every time it sells a car anywhere in the world, including West Virginia. . . . West Virginians, then, are already paying the product liability insurance premium when they buy a

General Motors car, so this Court would be both foolish and irresponsible if we held that while West Virginians must pay the premiums, West Virginians can't collect the insurance after they're injured.

Blankenship v. General Motors Corp., 185 W. Va. 350, 406 S.E.2d 781 (1991). If you were an appellate court judge, how would you treat the issue of insurance?

Distinct from the treatment in the appellate courts, it may be reversible error to mention the defendant's insurance before the jury: "Evidence that a person was or was not insured against liability is not admissible upon the issue whether he acted negligently. . . ." Fed. R. Evid. 411. Why have this rule? May the trial court judge ask about your client's policy limits — in chambers? Why would the judge care?

14. *Structured Settlements.* The usual award in a tort case is a lump sum. This has the advantage of administrative simplicity, but involves substantial speculation as to future damages. A solution is the structured settlement. This provides for periodic payments in place of a single judgment. There are two different approaches to structured settlements. First, the future payments will vary with the health of the plaintiff, and second, the payments are set at the time of the agreement. The first approach will obviously offer little incentive for the plaintiff to improve. What risks are involved in structured settlements? What administrative costs are involved?

The constitutionality of a structured settlement statute for medical malpractice was upheld in *Bernier v. Burris*, 113 Ill. 2d 219, 497 N.E.2d 763 (1986):

> The provisions, applicable to actions for healing-art malpractice (*see* 111. Rev. Stat. 1985, ch. 110, pars. 2-1701, 2-1704), change the traditional rule of lump-sum awards by permitting the payment of large awards of future damages in periodic installments. The provisions do not apply in a particular case, however, unless an effective election has been made by a party. In general terms, this requires that a party make a timely motion for application of the provisions; the election is effective if the parties agree to have the provisions apply or fail to object to them or, once an objection is made, if it appears that the amount of future damages will exceed $250,000. . . .
>
> If the procedures apply in a case, the trier of fact is to make several special findings regarding both past damages and future damages, and must further specify as future damages medical and other health-care costs, other economic losses, and noneconomic loss. Under these provisions, economic loss is defined in terms of pecuniary harm, and noneconomic loss includes loss of consortium and all nonpecuniary harm for which damages are recoverable, including damages for pain and suffering (*see* 111. Rev. Stat. 1985, ch. 110, par. 2-1702). Past damages are "damages that have accrued when the damages findings are made" . . . and future damages are ones that will accrue after that time.
>
> . . . .

We do not believe that the provisions interfere with the right to trial by jury [nor do they violate due process].

Id. at 771.

Chapter 11

Strict Liability

The foundation of tort law is strict liability. The core of the concept is that the defendant will be liable for harm to another that the defendant caused, without a showing of fault. Professor Malone argued that before the Middle Ages, liability was absolute: for example, if you invited someone to the circus and an animal escaped and mauled your guest, you were strictly liable. W. Malone, *Ruminations on the Role of Fault in the History of the Common Law of Torts*, 31 La. L. Rev. 1, 3 (1970).

In one of the earliest reported cases, decided in 1466, the court stated: "[I]f a man does a thing he is bound to do it in such a manner that by his deed no injury or damage is inflicted upon others." *Anonymous*, Y.B. 5 Edw. IV, fol. 7, pi. 18 (1466). If you kept a wild animal and it injured someone, you were strictly liable. *See May v. Burdett*, 9 Q.B. 101 (1846).

A study of early strict liability cases suggests that social policy has always driven the law. In the late 1800s, when great value was placed on cattle, farmers were required by statute to fence-in their property as a condition to recovery for crop damage from trespassing cattle. *See Buford v. Houtz*, 133 U.S. 320 (1890). Later, as more value was placed on farming, the cattle ranchers were forced to fence-in their animals or risk strict liability for the trespass of their cattle. *See* W. Page Keeton et al., Prosser and Keeton on Torts 539–541 (5th ed. 1984). For further discussion, see W. Malone, *supra*; C.H.S. Fifoot, History and Sources of the Common Law: Tort and Contract 189 (1949); R. Rabin, Perspectives on Tort Law 44 (2d ed. 1983); M. Horwitz, The Transformation of American Law, 1780–1860 (1977).

Problem

Al lives on a hill. Bob's house is below and behind Al's house. Four years ago, Al purchased a large aboveground swimming pool and put it in his back yard. On numerous occasions Al has invited his next-door neighbor, Bob, to use the pool. Bob has often accepted the invitation.

One day, Al's seven-year-old son, John, started Al's pickup truck and drove it into the pool. The pool burst, and the water poured out. The water ran down the hill and into Bob's yard. In fact, it flooded Bob's living room and dining room. John was not injured.

In order to pump the water out of his house, Bob tried to start his portable gasoline water pump. Due to the exertion involved in trying to start the pump, Bob suffered a heart attack. As a result of his heart attack, Bob has lost the use of his right arm.

Discuss. Assume that, in purchasing, installing, and maintaining the pool, Al was not negligent.

Fletcher v. Rylands

Exchequer Chamber, 1866
L.R. 1 Ex. 265

[The facts are taken from the opinion in the House of Lords, *infra*.]

[I]n this case the Plaintiff . . . is the occupier of a mine and works under a close of land. The Defendants are the owners of a mill in his neighbourhood, and they proposed to make a reservoir for the purpose of keeping and storing water to be used about their mill upon another close of land, which, for the purposes of this case, may be taken as being adjoining to the close of the Plaintiff, although, in point of fact, some intervening land lay between the two. Underneath the close of land of the Defendants on which they proposed to construct their reservoir there were certain old and disused mining passages and works. There were five vertical shafts, and some horizontal shafts communicating with them. The vertical shafts had been filled up with soil and rubbish, and it does not appear that any person was aware of the existence either of the vertical shafts or of the horizontal works communicating with them. In the course of the working by the Plaintiff of his mine, he had gradually worked through the seams of coal underneath the close, and had come into contact with the old and disused works underneath the close of the Defendants.

In that state of things the reservoir of the Defendants was constructed. It was constructed by them through the agency and inspection of an engineer and contractor. Personally, the Defendants appear to have taken no part in the works. . . . As regards the engineer and the contractor, we must take it from the case that they did not exercise, as far as they were concerned, that reasonable care and caution which they might have exercised, taking notice, as they appear to have taken notice, of the vertical shafts filled up in the manner which I have mentioned. However, my Lords, when the reservoir was constructed, and filled, or partly filled, with water, the weight of the water bearing upon the disused and imperfectly filled-up vertical shafts, broke through those shafts. The water passed down them and into the horizontal workings, and from the horizontal workings under the close of the Defendants it passed on into the workings under the close of the Plaintiff, and flooded his mine, causing considerable damage, for which this action was brought.

BLACKBURN, J.:

It appears from the statement in the case, that the plaintiff was damaged by his property being flooded by water, which, without any fault on his part, broke out of a reservoir constructed on the defendants' land by the defendants' orders, and maintained by the defendants.

It appears from the statement in the case, that the coal under the defendants' land had, at some remote period, been worked out; but this was unknown at the time when the defendants gave directions to erect the reservoir, and the water in the reservoir would not have escaped from the defendants' land, and no mischief would have been done to the plaintiff, but for this latent defect in the defendants' subsoil. And it further appears that the defendants selected competent engineers and contractors to make their reservoir, and themselves personally continued in total ignorance of what we have called the latent defect in the subsoil; but that these persons employed by them in the course of the work became aware of the existence of the ancient shafts filled up with soil, though they did not know or suspect that they were shafts communicating with old workings.

It is found that the defendants, personally, were free from all blame, but that in fact proper care and skill was not used by the persons employed by them, to provide for the sufficiency of the reservoir with reference to these shafts. The consequence was, that the reservoir when filled with water burst into the shafts, the water flowed down through them into the old workings, and thence into the plaintiff's mine, and there did the mischief. The plaintiff, though free from all blame on his part, must bear the loss, unless he can establish that it was the consequence of some default for which the defendants are responsible. The question of law therefore arises, what is the obligation which the law casts on a person who, like the defendants, lawfully brings on his land something which, though harmless whilst it remains there, will naturally do mischief if it escape out of his land. It is agreed on all hands that he must take care to keep in that which he has brought on the land and keeps there, in order that it may not escape and damage his neighbours, but the question arises whether the duty which the law casts upon him, under such circumstances, is an absolute duty to keep it in at his peril, or is, as the majority of the Court of Exchequer have thought, merely a duty to take all reasonable and prudent precautions, in order to keep it in, but no more. If the first be the law, the person who has brought on his land and kept there something dangerous, and failed to keep it in, is responsible for all the natural consequences of its escape. If the second be the limit of his duty, he would not be answerable except on proof of negligence, and consequently would not be answerable for escape arising from any latent defect which ordinary prudence and skill could not detect.

. . . .

We think that the true rule of law is, that the person who for his own purposes brings on his lands and collects and keeps there anything likely to do mischief if it escapes, must keep it in at his peril, and, if he does not do so, is prima facie answerable for all the damage which is the natural consequence of its escape. He can excuse himself by showing that the escape was owing to the plaintiff's default; or perhaps that the escape was the consequence of vis major, or the act of God; but as nothing of this sort exists here, it is unnecessary to inquire what excuse would be sufficient. The general rule, as above stated, seems on principle just. The person whose grass or corn is eaten down by the escaping cattle of his neighbour, or whose mine is flooded by the water from his neighbour's reservoir, or whose cellar is invaded by the filth of his neighbour's privy, or whose habitation is made unhealthy by the fumes and noisome vapours of his neighbour's alkali works, is damnified without any fault of his own; and it seems but reasonable and just that the neighbour, who has brought something on his own property which was not naturally there, harmless to others so long as it is confined to his own property, but which he knows to be mischievous if it gets on his neighbour's, should be obliged to make good the damage which ensues if he does not succeed in confining it to his own property. . . .

The case that has most commonly occurred, and which is most frequently to be found in the books, is as to the obligation of the owner of cattle which he has brought on his land, to prevent their escaping and doing mischief. The law as to them seems to be perfectly settled from early times; the owner must keep them in at his peril. . . .

Judgment for the plaintiff.

---

1. Before the case reached the Exchequer Chamber, the judge in the Exchequer had held for the defendant, saying there was no trespass, because the damage was consequential and not immediate. A nuisance cause of action failed, because the defendants were engaged in a lawful act. According to the judge, the defendant must be shown to have been negligent in order for there to be liability. *Fletcher v. Rylands*, 3 H. & C. 774, 159 Eng. Rep. 737 (1865).

2. What was the holding in the Exchequer Chamber? What was the rationale? On what precedent does the decision rest? Are the animal cases appropriate precedent here?

3. Why not sue the defendant in negligence? Should the owner of the reservoir be liable for the negligence of the contractor?

Rylands v. Fletcher

House of Lords, 1868
L.R. 3 H.L. 330

[The facts are presented in *Fletcher v. Rylands, supra.*]

THE LORD CHANCELLOR (LORD CAIRNS):

. . . .

The Court of Exchequer, when the special case stating the facts to which I have referred, was argued, was of opinion that the Plaintiff had established no cause of action. The Court of Exchequer Chamber, before which an appeal from this judgment was argued, was of a contrary opinion, and the Judges there unanimously arrived at the conclusion that there was a cause of action, and that the Plaintiff was entitled to damages.

My Lords, the principles on which this case must be determined appear to me to be extremely simple. The Defendants, treating them as the owners or occupiers of the close on which the reservoir was constructed, might lawfully have used that close for any purpose for which it might in the ordinary course of the enjoyment of land be used; and if, in what I may term the natural user of that land, there had been any accumulation of water, either on the surface or underground, and if, by the operation of the laws of nature, that accumulation of water had passed off into the close occupied by the Plaintiff, the Plaintiff could not have complained that that result had taken place.

On the other hand if the Defendants, not stopping at the natural use of their close, had desired to use it for any purpose which I may term a non-natural use, for the purpose of introducing into the close that which in its natural condition was not in or upon it, for the purpose of introducing water either above or below ground in quantities and in a manner not the result of any work or operation on or under the land,—and if in consequence of their doing so, the water came to escape and to pass off into the close of the Plaintiff, then it appears to me that that which the Defendants were doing they were doing at their own peril; and, if in the course of their doing it, the evil arose to which I have referred, the evil, namely, of the escape of the water and its passing away to the close of the Plaintiff and injuring the Plaintiff, then for the consequence of that, in my opinion, the Defendants would be liable. . . .

My Lords, these simple principles, if they are well founded, as it appears to me they are, really dispose of this case.

The same result is arrived at on the principles referred to by Mr. Justice Blackburn in his judgment, in the Court of Exchequer Chamber, where he states the opinion of that Court as to the law in these words: "We think that the true rule of law is. . . ."

My Lords, in that opinion, I must say I entirely concur. Therefore, I have to move your Lordships that the judgment of the Court of Exchequer Chamber be affirmed, and that the present appeal be dismissed with costs.

LORD CRANWORTH (concurring):

My Lords, I concur with my noble and learned friend in thinking that the rule of law was correctly stated by Mr. Justice Blackburn in delivering the opinion of the Exchequer Chamber. If a person brings, or accumulates, on his land anything which, if it should escape, may cause damage to his neighbour, he does so at his peril. If it does escape, and cause damage, he is responsible, however careful he may have been, and whatever precautions he may have taken to prevent the damage.

. . . The Plaintiff had a right to work his coal through the lands of Mr. Whitehead, and up to the old workings. If water naturally rising in the Defendants' land (we may treat the land as the land of the Defendants for the purpose of this case) had by percolation found its way down to the Plaintiff's mine through the old workings, and so had impeded his operations, that would not have afforded him any ground of complaint. . . . The Defendants, in order to effect an object of their own, brought on to their land, or on to land which for this purpose may be treated as being theirs, a large accumulated mass of water, and stored it up in a reservoir. The consequence of this was damage to the Plaintiff, and for that damage, however skillfully and carefully the accumulation was made, the Defendants, according to the principles and authorities to which I have adverted, were certainly responsible.

Judgment of the Court of Exchequer Chamber affirmed.

———

1. Something was added by the holding of Lord Cairns; what is it? What subjects are missing from the opinions?

2. Early cases in the United States relied on the opinion of the Exchequer Chamber to reject the concept of strict liability. *See Losee v. Buchanan*, 51 N.Y 476 (1873) (exploding steam boiler); *Brown v. Collins*, 53 N.H. 442 (1873) (a runaway horse).

3. What is a "natural use" of the land? Does the phrase refer to flowers, rocks, and trees, or is it a term of art to be given definition by the court for each case? Is there a difference between naturally occurring trees and planted ones?

Turner v. Big Lake Oil Co.
Supreme Court of Texas, 1936
96 S.W.2d 221

CURETON, CHIEF JUSTICE.

The primary question for determination here is whether or not the defendants in error, without negligence on their part, may be held liable in damages for the destruction or injury to property occasioned by the escape of salt water from ponds constructed and used by them in the operation of their oil wells. . . .

The defendants in error in the operation of certain oil wells in Reagan County constructed large artificial earthen ponds or pools into which they ran the polluted waters from the wells. On the occasion complained of, water escaped from one or more of these ponds, and, passing over the grass lands of the plaintiffs in error, injured the turf, and after entering Garrison draw flowed down the same into Centralia draw. In Garrison draw there were natural water holes, which supplied water for the livestock of plaintiffs in error. The pond, or ponds, of water from which the salt water escaped were, we judge from the map, some six miles from the stock-water holes to which we refer. . . .

Upon both reason and authority we believe that the conclusion of the Court of Civil Appeals that negligence is a prerequisite to recovery in a case of this character is a correct one. There is some difference of opinion on the subject in American jurisprudence brought about by differing views as to the correctness or applicability of the decision of the English courts in *Rylands v. Fletcher*, L. R. 3 H. L. 330. . . .

In Texas we have conditions very different from those which obtain in England. A large portion of Texas is an arid or semi-arid region. West of the 98th meridian of longitude, where the rainfall is approximately 30 inches, the rainfall decreases until finally, in the extreme western part of the State, it is only about 10 inches. This land of decreasing rainfall is the great ranch or livestock region of the State, water for which is stored in thousands of ponds, tanks, and lakes on the surface of the ground. The country is almost without streams; and without the storage of water from rainfall in basins constructed for the purpose, or to hold waters pumped from the earth, the great live stock industry of West Texas must perish. No such condition obtains in England. With us the storage of water is a natural or necessary and common use of the land, necessarily within the contemplation of the State and its grantees when grants were made, and obviously the rule announced in *Rylands v. Fletcher*, predicated upon different conditions, can have no application here.

Again, in England there are no oil wells, no necessity for using surface storage facilities for impounding and evaporating salt waters therefrom. In Texas the situation is different. Texas has many great oil fields, tens of thousands of wells in almost every part of the State. Producing oil is one of our major industries. One of the by-products of oil production is salt water, which must be disposed of without injury to property or the pollution of streams. The construction of basins or pounds to hold this salt water is a necessary part of the oil business. . . .

The judgments of the Court of Civil Appeals and of the District Court are affirmed.

––––––––––

1. What are the reasons for the decision in *Turner*? What does "natural use" of water mean in Texas?

2. What will be the result in Texas if the plaintiff sues in negligence? *See* L. Green, *Hazardous Oil and Gas Operations: Tort Liability*, 33 Tex. L. Rev. 574 (1955).

3. In a Florida case, the facts were as follows:

The appellant, Cities Service Company (Cities Service), operates a phosphate rock mine in Polk County. On December 3, 1971, a dam break occurred in one of Cities Service's settling ponds. As a result, approximately one billion gallons of phosphate slimes contained therein escaped into Whidden Creek and thence into the Peace River, thereby killing countless numbers of fish and inflicting other damage.

Faced with the question of whether strict liability (*Rylands*) should apply, the Florida court held:

In early days it was important to encourage persons to use their land by whatever means were available for the purpose of commercial and industrial development. In a frontier society there was little likelihood that a dangerous use of land could cause damage to one's neighbor. Today our life has become more complex. Many areas are overcrowded, and even the non-negligent use of one's land can cause extensive damages to a neighbor's property. Though there are still many hazardous activities which are socially desirable, it now seems reasonable that they pay their own way. It is too much to ask an innocent neighbor to bear the burden thrust upon him as a consequence of an abnormal use of the land next door. The doctrine of *Rylands v. Fletcher* should be applied in Florida.

Cities Service Oil Co. v. Florida, 312 So. 2d 799 (Fla. Dist. Ct. App. 1975). Why did Florida reach a decision different from Texas?

4. In *Cities Service*, the court also considered the meaning of the term "non-natural" use:

> There have been many American cases which have passed upon the question of whether a particular use of the land was natural or non-natural for the purpose of applying the *Rylands v. Fletcher* doctrine. Thus, [W. Prosser, Law of Torts (4th ed. 1971)] states at page 510:
>
> > The conditions and activities to which the rule has been applied have followed the English pattern. They include water collected in quantity in a dangerous place, or allowed to percolate; explosives or inflammable liquids stored in quantity in the midst of a city; blasting; pile driving; . . . the fumigation of part of a building with cyanide gas; drilling oil wells or operating refineries in thickly settled communities; an excavation letting in the sea; factories emitting smoke, dust or noxious gases in the midst of a town; roofs so constructed as to shed snow into a highway; and a dangerous party wall.
> >
> > On the other hand the conditions and activities to which the American courts have refused to apply *Rylands v. Fletcher*, whether they purport to accept or to reject the case in principle, have been with few exceptions what the English courts would regard as a "natural" use of land, and not within the rule at all. They include water in household pipes, the tank of a humidity system or authorized utility mains; gas in a meter, electric wiring in a machine shop, and gasoline in a filling station; a dam in the natural bed of a stream; ordinary steam boilers; an ordinary fire in a factory; an automobile; Bermuda grass on a railroad right of way; a small quantity of dynamite kept for sale in a Texas hardware store; barnyard spray in a farmhouse; a division fence; the wall of a house left standing after a fire; coal mining operations regarded as usual and normal; vibrations from ordinary building construction; earth moving operations in grading a hillside; the construction of a railroad tunnel; and even a runaway horse.
>
> . . . .
>
> In the final analysis, we are impressed by the magnitude of the activity and the attendant risk of enormous damage. The impounding of billions of gallons of phosphatic slimes behind earthen walls which are subject to breaking even with the exercise of the best of care strikes us as being both "ultra-hazardous" and "abnormally dangerous," as the case may be.

Cities Service Co. v. Florida, 312 So. 2d at 801–03.

Yukon Equipment, Inc. v. Fireman's Fund Insurance Co.

Supreme Court of Alaska, 1978
585 P.2d 1206

[Thieves broke into an explosives storage magazine located in the suburbs of Anchorage and ignited 80,000 pounds of explosives, damaging homes within a two-mile radius. Yukon's magazine which exploded was located 3,820 feet from the nearest building not used to store explosives and 4,330 feet from the nearest public highway. Partial judgment on the issue of liability was granted in favor of Fireman's Fund. Yukon Equipment argued that strict liability and absolute liability do not apply.]

MATTHEWS, JUSTICE.

. . . .

I

The leading case on liability for the storage of explosives is *Exner v. Sherman Power Const. Co.*, 54 F.2d 510 (2d Cir. 1931). There dynamite stored by the defendant exploded causing personal injury and property damage to the plaintiffs who resided some 935 feet away from the storage site. A distinguished panel of the Circuit Court of Appeals for the Second Circuit held the defendant liable regardless of fault:

> Dynamite is of the class of elements which one who stores or uses in such a locality, or under such circumstances as to cause likelihood of risk to others, stores or uses at his peril. He is an insurer, and is absolutely liable if damage results to third persons, either from the direct impact of rocks thrown out by the explosion (which would be a common law trespass) or from concussion.

Id. at 512–13. The court pointed out that while the general principle of absolute liability expressed in the English case of *Rylands v. Fletcher* had been accorded a mixed reception at best in United States courts, there had been no such reluctance to impose absolute liability in blasting cases. The court then noted that some authorities had made a distinction between damage done by rocks or debris hurled by an explosion, as to which there would be absolute liability, and damage caused by a concussion, as to which a negligence standard applied. The court concluded that such a distinction was without a logical basis and rejected it. *Id.* at 514. The court also determined that there was no reason for attaching different legal consequences to the results of an explosion "whether the dynamite explodes when stored or when employed in blasting." The court expressed the policy behind the rule of absolute liability as follows:

> . . . . When, as here, the defendant, though without fault, has engaged in the perilous activity of storing large quantities of a dangerous explosive for use in his business, we think there is no justification for relieving it of liability, and that the owner of the business, rather than a third party who has no relation to the explosion, other than that of injury, should bear the loss.

Id. at 514. *Exner* has been widely followed, and was based on many earlier authorities imposing absolute liability for explosions.

As *Exner* reflects, the particular rule of absolute liability for blasting damage received earlier and more general acceptance in the United States than the generalized rule of absolute liability for unusually dangerous activity which has its antecedents in *Rylands v. Fletcher.* . . .

The Restatement (Second) of Torts [Section 520] (1977), adopted by the ALI after the explosion in this case, does not reflect a *per se* rule of liability for the storage of explosives. Instead it lists six factors to be considered in determining whether an activity is "abnormally dangerous" and therefore subject to the rule of absolute liability. The factors are:

(a) existence of a high degree of risk of some harm to the person, land or chattels of others;

(b) likelihood that the harm that results from it will be great;

(c) inability to eliminate the risk by the exercise of reasonable care;

(d) extent to which the activity is not a matter of common usage;

(e) inappropriateness of the activity to the place where it is carried on;

(f) extent to which its value to the community is outweighed by its dangerous attributes.

Based in large part on the Restatement (Second), petitioners argue that their use was not abnormally dangerous. Specifically they contend that their use of the magazine for the storage of explosives was a normal and appropriate use of the area in question since the storage magazine was situated on lands set aside by the United States for such purposes and was apparently located in compliance with applicable federal regulations. They point out that the storage served a legitimate community need for an accessible source of explosives for various purposes. They contend that before absolute liability can be imposed in any circumstance a preliminary finding must be made as to whether or not the defendant's activity is abnormally dangerous, that such a determination involves the weighing of the six factors set out in section 520 of the Restatement (Second) of Torts, and that an evaluation of those factors in this case could not appropriately be done on motion for summary judgment.

The factors specified by section 520 of the Restatement (Second) of Torts are for consideration of the court, not the jury. . . .

If we were to apply the Restatement (Second)'s six factor test to the storage of explosives in this case we would be inclined to conclude that the use involved here was an abnormally dangerous one. Comment (f) to section 520 makes it clear that all of the factors need not be present for an activity to be considered abnormally dangerous:

In determining whether the danger is abnormal, the factors listed in clauses (a) to (f) of this Section are all to be considered, and are all of importance. Any one of them is not necessarily sufficient to itself in a particular case, and ordinarily several of them will be required for strict liability. On the other hand it is not necessary that each of them be present, especially if others weigh heavily.

The first three factors, involving the degree of risk, harm, and difficulty of eliminating the risk, are obviously present in the storage of 80,000 pounds of explosives in a suburban area. The fourth factor, that the activity not be a matter of common usage, is also met. Comment (i) states:

> Likewise the manufacture, storage, transportation and use of high explosives, although necessary to the construction of many public and private works, are carried on by only a comparatively small number of persons and therefore are not matters of common usage.

The fifth factor, inappropriateness of the activity, is arguably not present, for the storage did take place on land designated by the United States government for that purpose. However, the designation took place at a time when the area was less densely populated than it was at the time of the explosion. Likewise, the storage reserve was not entirely appropriate to the quantity of explosives stored because the explosion caused damage well beyond the boundaries of the reserve. The sixth factor, value to the community, relates primarily to situations where the dangerous activity is the primary economic activity of the community in question. Thus comment (k) states that such factor applies

> particularly when the community is largely devoted to the dangerous enterprise and its prosperity largely depends upon it. Thus the interests of a particular town whose livelihood depends upon such an activity as manufacturing cement may be such that cement plants will be regarded as a normal activity for that community notwithstanding the risk of serious harm from the emission of cement dust.

The comment further states that

> in Texas and Oklahoma, a properly conducted oil or gas well, at least in a rural area, is not regarded as abnormally dangerous, while a different conclusion has been reached in Kansas and Indiana. California, whose oil industry is far from insignificant, has concluded that an oil well drilled in a thickly settled residential area in the City of Los Angeles is a matter of strict liability.

Since five of the six factors required by section 520 of the Restatement (Second) are met and the sixth is debatable, we would impose absolute liability here if we were to use that approach.

However, we do not believe that the Restatement (Second) approach should be used in cases involving the use or storage of explosives. Instead, we adhere to the rule of *Exner v. Sherman Power Constr. Co.* and its progeny imposing absolute liability in such cases. The Restatement (Second) approach requires an analysis of degrees of risk and harm, difficulty of eliminating risk, and appropriateness of place, before absolute liability may be imposed. Such factors suggest a negligence standard. The six factor analysis may well be necessary where damage is caused by unique hazards and the question is whether the general rule of absolute liability applies, but in cases involving the storage and use of explosives we take that question to have been resolved by more than a century of judicial decisions.

The reasons for imposing absolute liability on those who have created a grave risk of harm to others by storing or using explosives are largely independent of considerations of locational appropriateness. We see no reason for making a distinction between the right of a homesteader to recover when his property has been damaged by a blast set off in a remote corner of the state, and the right to compensation of an urban resident whose home is destroyed by an explosion originating in a settled area. In each case, the loss is properly to be regarded as a cost of the business of storing or using explosives. Every incentive remains to conduct such activities in locations which are as safe as possible, because there the damages resulting from an accident will be kept to a minimum.

II

The next question is whether the intentional detonation of the storage magazine was a superseding cause relieving petitioners from liability. In *Sharp v. Fairbanks North Star Borough*, 569 P.2d 178 (Alaska 1977), a negligence case, we stated. . . .

> [w]here the defendant's conduct threatens a particular kind of result which will injure the plaintiff and an intervening cause which could not have been anticipated changes the situation but produces the same result as originally threatened, such a result is within the scope of the defendant's negligence.

Id. at 183 n. 9. The considerations which impel cutting off liability where there is a superseding cause in negligence cases also apply to cases of absolute liability.

Prior to the explosion in question the petitioners' magazines had been illegally broken into at least six times. Most of these entries involved the theft of explosives. Petitioners had knowledge of all of this.

Applying the standards set forth in *Sharp, supra*, to these facts we find there to have been no superseding cause. The incendiary destruction of premises by thieves to cover evidence of theft is not so uncommon an occurrence that it can be regarded as highly extraordinary. Moreover, the particular kind of result threatened by the defendant's conduct, the storage of explosives, was an explosion at the storage site. Since the threatened result occurred it would not be consistent with the principles stated in *Sharp, supra*, to hold there to have been a superseding cause. Absolute liability is imposed on those who store or use explosives because they have created an unusual risk to others. As between those who have created the risk for the benefit of their own enterprise and those whose only connection with the enterprise is to have suffered damage because of it, the law places the risk of loss on the former. When the risk created causes damage in fact, insistence that the precise details of the intervening cause be foreseeable would subvert the purpose of that rule of law.

The partial summary judgment is *affirmed*.

---

1. Is the Restatement (Second) of Torts Section 520 the same as the rule in *Rylands v. Fletcher*? If not, how is it different? Why does the court reject the Restatement as a foundation of liability?

2. To what extent, if any, does Section 520 of the Restatement (Second) differ from negligence? *See* W. Page Keeton et al., Prosser and Keeton on Torts 555 (5th ed. 1984).

3. The term "common usage" [Section 520(d)] cut off policy analysis and created problems for the plaintiff in *Wood v. United Air Lines*, 32 Misc. 2d 955, 223 N.Y.S.2d 692 (Sup. Ct. 1961). In *Wood*, two planes crashed into each other, and then one of them crashed into the plaintiff's apartment. She sued the airline, but the court rejected her argument of strict liability, stating:

> I am of the opinion, in light of the technical progress achieved in the design, construction, operation and maintenance of aircraft generally, that flying should no longer be deemed to be an ultra-hazardous activity, requiring the imposition of absolute liability for any damage or injury caused in the course thereof. This view is in accord with the current trend of the law. . . .

> It is to be noted that the Restatement (First), which was adopted and promulgated in 1938, rested its view of flying, as being an ultra-hazardous activity, upon the state of development of aviation existing at that time. It is indisputable that aviation has since made tremendous strides, both technically and in its use as a common mode of transportation.

Id. at 697.

What result under *Rylands v. Fletcher*? Is flying over a congested city non-natural? Who should bear the loss, the actor or the innocent victim?

4. For a blasting case that accepts the superseding cause defense, see *Bridges v. Kentucky Stone Co.*, 425 N.E.2d 125 (Ind. 1981). The blast, set off by a thief, occurred three weeks after the theft, at a location 100 miles from the defendant's storage site. In *Yukon*, if thieves had never broken into the magazine previously, would the court have decided the case differently?

5. For a weaving of the lower court's strict liability decision into negligence, see Judge Posner's carefully crafted decision in *Indiana Harbor Belt R.R. Co. v. American Cyanamid Co.*, 916 F.2d 1174 (7th Cir. 1990). Prior to becoming a federal judge, Judge Posner had long been an opponent of strict liability. *See* Richard A. Posner, Tort Law: Cases and Economic Analysis 4, 5 (1982); Posner, *A Theory of Negligence*, 1 J. Legal Stud. 29, 32–34 (1972).

Spano v. Perini Corp.

Court of Appeals of New York, 1969
250 N.E.2d 31, *on remand*, 304 N.Y.S.2d 15 (1969)

FULD, CHIEF JUDGE.

The principal question posed on this appeal is whether a person who has sustained property damage caused by blasting on nearby property can maintain an action for damages without a showing that the blaster was negligent. Since 1893, when this court decided the case of *Booth v. Rome, W. & O.T.R.R. Co.*, 140 N.Y. 267 . . . it has been the law of this State that proof of negligence was required unless the blast was accompanied by an actual physical invasion of the damaged property — for example, by rocks or other material being cast upon the premises. We are now asked to reconsider that rule.

The plaintiff Spano is the owner of a garage in Brooklyn which was wrecked by a blast occurring on November 27, 1962. There was then in that garage, for repairs, an automobile owned by the plaintiff Davis which he also claims was damaged by the blasting. Each of the plaintiffs brought suit against the two defendants who, as joint venturers, were engaged in constructing a tunnel in the vicinity pursuant to a contract with the City of New York. The two cases were tried together, without a jury, in the Civil Court of the City of New York, New York County, and judgments were rendered in favor of the plaintiffs. The judgments were reversed by the Appellate Term and the Appellate Division affirmed that order, granting leave to appeal to this court.

It is undisputed that, on the day in question (November 27, 1962), the defendants had set off a total of 194 sticks of dynamite at a construction site which was only 125 feet away from the damaged premises. Although both plaintiffs alleged negligence in their complaints, no attempt was made to show that the defendants had failed to exercise reasonable care or to take necessary precautions when they were blasting. Instead, they chose to rely, upon the trial, solely on the principle of absolute liability. . . .

The concept of absolute liability in blasting cases is hardly a novel one. The overwhelming majority of American jurisdictions have adopted such a rule. . . .

We need not rely solely, however, upon out-of-state decisions in order to attain our result. Not only has the rationale of the *Booth* case (140 N.Y. 267, *supra*) been overwhelmingly rejected elsewhere but it appears to be fundamentally inconsistent with earlier cases in our own court which had held, long before *Booth* was decided, that a party was absolutely liable for damages to neighboring property caused by explosions. (*See, e.g., Hay v. Cohoes Co.*, 2 N.Y. 159; *Heeg v. Licht*, 80 N.Y. 579.) In the *Hay* case (2 N.Y. 159, *supra*), for example, the defendant was engaged in blasting an excavation for a canal and the force of the blasts caused large quantities of earth and stones to be thrown against the plaintiff's house, knocking down his stoop and part of his chimney. The court held the defendant absolutely liable for the damage caused, stating (2 N.Y., at pp. 160–161):

> It is an elementary principle in reference to private rights, that every individual is entitled to the undisturbed possession and lawful enjoyment of his own property. . . .

Although the court in *Booth* drew a distinction between a situation — such as was presented in the *Hay* case — where there was "a physical invasion" of, or trespass on, the plaintiff's property and one in which the damage was caused by "setting the air in motion, or in some other unexplained way" (140 N.Y., at pp. 279, 280), it is clear that the court, in the earlier cases, was not concerned with the particular manner by which the damage was caused but by the simple fact that any explosion in a built-up area was likely to cause damage. Thus, in *Heeg v. Licht* (80 N.Y. 579, *supra*), the court held that there should be absolute liability where the damage was caused by the accidental explosion of stored gunpowder, even in the absence of a physical trespass (p. 581). . . .

Such reasoning should, we venture, have led to the conclusion that the *intentional* setting off of explosives—that is, blasting—in an area in which it was likely to cause harm to neighboring property similarly results in absolute liability. However, the court in the *Booth* case rejected such an extension of the rule for the reason that "[to] exclude the defendant from blasting . . . would not be a compromise between conflicting rights, but an extinguishment of the right of the one for the benefit of the other" (140 N.Y., at p. 281). The court expanded on this by stating, "This sacrifice, we think, the law does not exact. Public policy is promoted by the building up of towns and cities and the improvement of property. Any unnecessary restraint on freedom of action of a property owner hinders this."

This rationale cannot withstand analysis. The plaintiff in *Booth* was not seeking, as the court implied, to "exclude the defendant from blasting" and thus prevent desirable improvements to the latter's property. Rather, he was merely seeking compensation for the damage which was inflicted upon his own property as a result of that blasting. The question, in other words, was not whether it was lawful or proper to engage in blasting but who should bear the cost of any resulting damage—the person who engaged in the dangerous activity or the innocent neighbor injured thereby. Viewed in such a light, it clearly appears that *Booth* was wrongly decided and should be forthrightly overruled.

. . . .

Even though the proof was not insufficient as a matter of law, however, the Appellate Division affirmed on the sole ground that no negligence had been proven against the defendants and thus had no occasion to consider the question whether, in fact, the blasting caused the damage. That being so, we must remit the case to the Appellate Division so that it may pass upon the weight of the evidence. . . .

The order appealed from should be reversed, with costs, and the matter remitted to the Appellate Division for further proceedings in accordance with this opinion.

Dyer v. Maine Drilling & Blasting, Inc.

Supreme Judicial Court of Maine, 2009
984 A.2d. 210

Silver, J.

Vera E., Paul, and Robert Dyer appeal from a summary judgment entered in the Superior Court (Waldo County, Hjelm, J.) in favor of Maine Drilling & Blasting, Inc. (Maine Drilling). The Dyers argue that: (1) we should follow the weight of authority and adopt a common law rule of strict liability for abnormally dangerous activities. . . . [W]e adopt the Second Restatement's imposition of strict liability for abnormally dangerous activities, see Restatement (Second) of Torts §§ 519–520 (1977)....

I. CASE HISTORY

Vera Dyer and her sons, Paul and Robert, have a home in Prospect that the family has owned since the 1950s. The home, believed to be over seventy years old, has a cement foundation and floor. A stand-alone garage with a cement floor was constructed in the 1980s.

On September 22, 2004, Maine Drilling distributed a form notice that informed the Dyers that Maine Drilling would begin blasting rock near the home on or about October 1, 2004, in connection with a construction project to replace the Waldo-Hancock Bridge and bridge access roads. The notice stated that Maine Drilling uses "the most advanced technologies available . . . to measure the seismic effect to the area," and assured the Dyers "that ground vibrations associated with the blasting [would] not exceed the established limits that could potentially cause damage."

As offered in the notice, Maine Drilling provided a pre-blast survey of the Dyer home. The survey report recorded the surveyor's observation of "some concrete deterioration to [the] west wall" and "cracking to [the] concrete floor," and a slight tilt to a retaining wall behind the garage. Richard Dyer, another son of Vera, thoroughly documented the condition of the home and garage by videotape before blasting began.

Maine Drilling conducted over 100 blasts between October 2004 and early August 2005. The closest blast was approximately 100 feet from the Dyer home. Vera was inside the home for at least two of the blasts and felt the whole house shake. During other blasts, she was not in the home because Maine Drilling employees advised her to go outside. Vera visited Florida from approximately January through April 2005, and so was absent from her home when blasting occurred during that period. Paul, however, checked on the home several times a week while Vera was in Florida.

In the early spring of 2005, after the blasting work had begun and while Vera remained in Florida, both Paul and Richard observed several changes from the pre-blasting condition of the home and the garage: (1) the center of the basement floor had dropped as much as three inches; (2) the center beam in the basement that supported part of the first floor was sagging, and as a result the first floor itself was noticeably unlevel; (3) there was a new crack between the basement floor and the cement pad that formed the foundation of the chimney in the basement; (4) new or enlarged cracks radiated out across the basement floor from the chimney foundation; and (5) cracks that had previously existed in the garage floor were noticeably wider and more extensive. The brothers also noticed that a flowerbed retaining wall that helped to support the rear wall of the garage had "moved demonstrably."

When she returned to Maine, Vera observed the same changes in the condition of the property as her sons had reported and also noted larger or new cracks or separations on the back wall of the home's foundation.

The Dyers engaged an expert in ground engineering and environmental services, Mark Peterson, who testified at a deposition that the U.S. Bureau of Mines has established a "safe operating envelope" for seismic impact of blasts to minimize property damage. Under these guidelines, a blast is considered unlikely to cosmetically damage fragile structures in a building if its velocity falls below the established envelope. Where, however, a structure is underlain by "uncontrolled fill" as opposed to "engineered fill," damage can potentially result even if blasting is within the Bureau of Mines's envelope. Peterson testified that the Dyer home might be built on top of uncontrolled fill. Assuming this, Peterson stated that "there is not 100% certainty how the [Dyers'] floor would behave" in response to vibrations from blasting, and that settlement of uncontrolled fill could occur as a result of blasting.

Readings from a seismograph that Maine Drilling placed adjacent to the Dyer residence showed that six blasts produced vibrations that "slightly" exceeded the Bureau of Mines's envelope. . . .

Peterson testified that it is common for Maine homes to have cracking in foundations or basement floors that appear "over the course of the years," which could be caused by such things as vibrations, earth pressure, ground settlement, temperature, and ground water. Peterson opined that settlement under the Dyer home could have taken place for reasons unrelated to Maine Drilling's blasting, but that he would have expected such settlement to have occurred prior to blasting. Conversely, Peterson concluded that settlement due to the blasting was possible because: (1) the Dyers observed changes in floor settlement after blasting; (2) the pre-blast survey and the Dyers' observations did not indicate that the current basement settlement conditions existed before blasting began; (3) uncontrolled fill could consolidate and cause settlement from blasting vibrations; and (4) the most severe vibrations from blasting occurred prior to observations that the basement floor had settled.

The Dyers filed a three-count complaint, subsequently amended, alleging causes of action in strict liability and negligence. Maine Drilling filed a motion for summary judgment as to all counts in the Dyers' complaint. The Dyers opposed Maine Drilling's motion and filed a statement of additional material facts.

The court granted Maine Drilling's motion for a summary judgment and awarded costs to Maine Drilling. The court found in favor of Maine Drilling on the Dyers' claim for strict liability, citing *Reynolds v. W.H. Hinman Co.*, 145 Me. 343, 75 A.2d 802 (1950) and other Maine precedent in support of its ruling. [We reverse and remand.]

II. DISCUSSION

A. Standard of Review

We review a grant of a summary judgment de novo, considering the evidence in the light most favorable to the non-moving party. . . .

B. Strict Liability

We adopt today the Second Restatement's imposition of strict liability for abnormally dangerous activities, and remand to the court to determine if the blasting in this case was an abnormally dangerous activity under the Restatement's six-factor test. See Restatement (Second) of Torts §§ 519–520 (1977). In doing so, we overrule our prior opinions requiring proof of negligence in blasting cases.

1. History of Strict Liability

Strict liability doctrine originated in the English case *Rylands v. Fletcher*, (1868) 3 L.R. 330 (H.L.), where the court held that a defendant was liable regardless of negligence when he used his land in a way that was non-natural and likely to cause injury, and injury in fact resulted. *Id.* ("If a person brings, or accumulates, on his land anything which, if it should escape, may cause damage to his neighbour, he does so at his peril. If it does escape, and cause damage, he is responsible, however careful he may have been."). This Court rejected *Rylands* in the 1950s, deciding that proof of negligence would be required in blasting cases. *Reynolds*, 145 Me. at 362, 75 A.2d at 811.

In *Reynolds*, we noted that strict liability was the historic rule, but that the majority of states had switched to a negligence approach in abnormally dangerous activities cases. *Id.* at 347–48, 75 A.2d at 804–05. Additionally, the opinion quoted a law review article arguing against strict liability based in part on the "difficulty of drawing the line between the danger which calls for care and the extra hazard. There are, as yet[,] no unanimously approved rules or criteria as to this subject." *Id.* at 349, 75 A.2d at 805 (quotation marks omitted). Finally, our *Reynolds* decision was supported by the conclusions that blasting is a reasonable and lawful use of land, *id.* at 361, 75 A.2d at 811, and that plaintiffs would generally be able to recover under a negligence scheme. *Id.* at 351, 75 A.2d at 806 ("At the present time, in an action for blasting, if the courts apply the modern law as to negligence, a plaintiff who has a meritorious case can generally recover without calling in aid the old rule of absolute liability." (quotation marks omitted)).

2. Modern Strict Liability

These rationales have been undermined in the last half-century. Policy approaches have shifted nationwide, leading almost every other state to adopt strict liability in blasting and other abnormally dangerous activity cases, and leading Maine to apply strict liability in other contexts. Additionally, the Second Restatement has provided a scheme of clear criteria for delineating which activities require a strict liability approach. In light of these changes, we overturn *Reynolds* and its progeny and adopt strict liability under the Restatement's six factor test.

Reynolds operated on the assumption that negligence liability would allow most plaintiffs to recover in blasting cases. However, we have recognized that blasting is inherently dangerous, and most courts have recognized that this inherent danger cannot be eliminated by the exercise of care. The Dyers' expert testified that blasting may cause damage even when it is within the Bureau of Mines's guidelines.

Consequently, although blasting is a lawful and often beneficial activity, the costs should fall on those who benefit from the blasting, rather than on an unfortunate neighbor. . . .

The negligence approach to abnormally dangerous activities initially taken by American courts was rooted in part in the idea that dangerous activities were essential to industrial development, "and it was considered that the interests of those in the vicinity of such enterprises must give way to them, and that too great a burden must not be placed upon them." But today, that attitude has changed, and strict liability seeks to encourage both cost-spreading and incentives for the utmost safety when engaging in dangerous activities. Additionally, blasters are already required by the rules of the Maine Department of Public Safety and by many town ordinances to have liability insurance covering damages that result from blasting. Thus, a strict liability scheme should not greatly increase costs for these businesses.

At least forty-one states have adopted some form of strict liability for blasting, with only two of those clearly limiting it to damage caused by debris. The other New England states are among those adopting strict liability, with the exception of New Hampshire, which has retained negligence liability for blasting damages . . .

Not only has the weight of authority shifted nationally, but we, acting pursuant to our common law authority, have applied forms of strict liability in certain circumstances. For example, we have adopted the Second Restatement approach to injuries caused by wild animals, analogizing those cases to blasting.

The Legislature has also been increasingly willing to apply strict liability in certain cases, imposing liability for explosions of natural gas, 14 M.R.S. § 165 (2008); for defective products, 14 M.R.S. § 221 (2008); and for oil spills and hazardous waste, 38 M.R.S. §§ 552(2), 1319-J (2008).

The Legislature has not, however, addressed the need for strict liability in abnormally dangerous activity cases. . . .

Under these circumstances, the application of strict liability or negligence to blasting "is a creation of our common law. . . . [I]ts applicability in Maine is controlled entirely by the precedents of this Court. It is therefore appropriate for this Court to continue to determine the scope of [the doctrine]." See *Picher v. Roman Catholic Bishop of Portland*, 974 A.2d 286, 295 (discussing doctrine of charitable immunity) (quotation marks omitted). . . .

We adopt the Second Restatement's approach to strict liability, imposing liability on defendants conducting an abnormally dangerous activity without requiring proof of negligence, although causation must still be proved. We believe that this approach strikes the right balance of policy interests by considering on a case-by-case basis which activities are encompassed by the rule, and by taking account of the social desirability of the activity at issue, see Restatement (Second) of Torts § 520(f) (1977), in contrast to the First Restatement approach, see Restatement (First) of Torts § 520 (1939).

Most jurisdictions have not adopted either the First or Second Restatement, and instead impose strict liability in blasting cases under a blanket rule that a blaster is always liable when causation is established. However, a number of courts that have re-examined the question since the adoption of the Second Restatement have chosen to apply the Restatement approach to abnormally dangerous activities. . . .

A person who creates a substantial risk of severe harm to others while acting for his own gain should bear the costs of that activity. Most of the courts of the nation have recognized this policy, and we now do as well. For these reasons we adopt strict liability and remand for a determination whether the activity in this case subjected Maine Drilling to liability under the Second Restatement approach.

———

1. What is the issue in *Spano* and *Dyer*? What are the holdings? What was the policy underlying the *Booth v. Rome* decision? Why was *Booth* overruled?

2. Compare the policy in *Spano* and *Rylands*, with Restatement (Second) Section 520. How, if at all, do they differ? Note Judge Fuld's observation that the question is "who should bear the cost of any resulting damage — the person who engaged in the dangerous activity or the innocent neighbor injured thereby." *Spano*, 250 N.E.2d at 34.

3. *Defenses to strict liability.* The following may be available as defenses to a suit in strict liability: proximate cause, *Foster v. Preston Mill Co.*, 44 Wash. 2d 440, 268 P.2d 645 (1954) (mother mink ate her kittens); act of Nature, *Golden v. Amory*, 329 Mass. 484, 109 N.E.2d 131 (1952) (hurricane caused dike to overflow); assumption of risk, *Sandy v. Bushey*, 124 Me. 320, 128 A. 513 (1925) (plaintiff kicked by defendant's vicious horse). Contributory negligence is generally rejected as a defense to strict liability, Restatement (Second) of Torts § 524.

Note on Additional Applications of Strict Liability

Strict liability applies in realms other than those specifically mentioned in this chapter. Recall *Langan v. Valicopters, Inc.*, 567 P.2d 218 (Wash. 1977), in which the court ruled that strict liability applied in a case involving crop dusting, and *Wrinkle v. Norman*, 242 P.3d 1216 (Kan. Ct. App. 2010), in which the court discussed statutes that impose strict liability for damage done by escaped animals. Liability for injuries caused by animals is further discussed in the Defenses chapter.

Strict liability may also have a new vitality in the realm of toxic torts. In *In re Hanford Nuclear Reservation Litigation, Phillips v. E.I. DuPont de Nemours & Co.*, 534 F.3d 986 (9th Cir.), *amended*, 521 F.3d 1028, *cert. denied*, 555 U.S. 1084 (2008), the Court of Appeals dealt with medical problems alleged to have been caused by emissions from a plutonium production facility in Washington. The Hanford facility had helped make the plutonium bomb that was dropped on Nagasaki in 1945. The emissions in question had been released into the area surrounding the facility as part of the production process.

The trial court decided that strict liability applied to the activity, and the Court of Appeals affirmed, stating that:

> We agree with the district court that Defendants' conduct at Hanford was an abnormally dangerous activity under factors [listed in the Restatement (Second) of Torts sections 519–520]. There was a high degree of risk to people and property associated with the Hanford facility and the gravity of any harm was likely to be great. Regardless of Defendants' efforts to exercise reasonable care, some [emissions] would be released, and developing plutonium is hardly an activity of common usage. While the value to the community at large, i.e., the nation, of developing an atomic bomb was perceived as high and there is pragmatically no very appropriate place to carry on such an activity, the [Section] 520 factors on balance support holding that Defendants' activities were abnormally dangerous.

The court rejected the argument that the defendants had been under a "public duty" to perform the work, ruling that the public duty exception to strict liability in Section 521 of the Restatement only applied to activities that the defendant was obligated to perform.

Chapter 12

Products Liability

This chapter is intended as an introduction to this highly complex subject. Many law schools have separate courses on products liability, which is an area of the law perpetually in a state of turmoil. This is largely because the doctrine, a relative late-comer, was the product of a policy decision about who should be responsible for the costs when a product causes injury. Thus, the doctrine is subject to change when the prevailing view about who should pay for product-related injuries alters. Strict products liability is likely to thrive in a political climate which puts a priority on compensating plaintiffs for injuries caused by products. On the other hand, strict liability is likely to be curtailed when other goals—such as a perceived need for product innovation—take center stage. Courts were never entirely comfortable with the idea of imposing liability in the absence of negligence, and the susceptibility of the doctrine to change reflects this judicial reality as well.

A. Food and Drink

The history of strict liability for products begins with food and drink. From an early date, courts demonstrated that they did not care how an impurity got into the product, provided that the product was designed to be eaten or for other intimate bodily use (like hair dye) and that the responsibility for the presence of the impurity could be laid at the manufacturer's door. Courts eventually realized that the reasoning behind strict liability for impure (defective) food and drink readily applied to other types of products as well, and the doctrine of strict products liability for defects was born.

Pillars v. R.J. Reynolds Tobacco Co.
Supreme Court of Mississippi, 1918
78 So. 365

Cook, P.J.

The appellant sued the Corr-Williams Tobacco Company, distributors, and R.J. Reynolds Tobacco Company, distributors, and R.J. Reynolds Tobacco Company, manufacturer, of "Brown Mule Chewing Tobacco," for damages resulting to the appellant from chewing a piece of Brown Mule tobacco in which was concealed a decomposed human toe. The evidence disclosed that R.J. Reynolds Tobacco Company was the sole manufacturer of the tobacco. . . . It seems that appellant consumed one plug of his purchase, which measured up to representations, that it was tobacco unmixed with human flesh, but when appellant tackled the second plug it made him sick, but, not suspecting the tobacco, he tried another chew, and still another, until he bit into some foreign substance, which crumbled like dry bread, and caused him to foam at the mouth, while he was getting "sicker and sicker." Finally, his teeth struck something hard; he could not bite through it. After an examination he discovered a human toe, with flesh and nail intact. We refrain from detailing the further harrowing and nauseating details. The appellant consulted a physician, who testified that appellant exhibited all of the characteristic symptoms of ptomaine poison. The physician examined the toe and identified it as a human toe in a state of putrefaction, and said, in effect, that his condition was caused by the poison generated by the rotten toe. At the close of the evidence for the plaintiff the trial judge, at the request of the defendants, directed a verdict for the defendants, and from a judgment responsive to this instruction, an appeal is prosecuted to this court.

Generally speaking, the rule is that the manufacturer is not liable to the ultimate consumer for damages resulting from the defects and impurities of the manufactured article. This rule is generally based upon the theory that there is no contractual relation existing between the ultimate consumer and the manufacturer. From time to time, the courts have made exceptions to the rule. The manufacturers of food, beverages, drugs, condiments, and confections have been held liable to ultimate consumers for damages resulting from the negligent preparation of their products. The contention of the defendants here is that the limit has been reached by the courts, and that the facts of this case do not warrant an exception in favor of the plaintiff, and this view was adopted by the learned trial court. The exceptions already made were for the protection of the health of the people, and to insure a scrupulous care in the preparation of those articles of commerce so as to reduce to a minimum all danger to those using them.

If poisons are concealed in food, or in beverages, or in confections or in drugs, death or the impairment of health will be the probable consequence. We know that chewing tobacco is taken into the mouth, and that some, at least, of the juice or pulp will and does find its way into the alimentary canal, there to be digested and ultimately to become a part of the blood. Tobacco may be relatively harmless, but decaying flesh, we are advised, develops poisonous ptomaines, which are certainly dangerous and often fatal. Anything taken into the mouth there to be masticated should be free of those elements which may endanger the life or health of the user. No one would be so bold as to contend that the manufacturer would be free from liability if it should appear that he purposely mixed human flesh with chewing tobacco, or chewing gum. If the manufacturer would be liable for intentionally feeding putrid human flesh to any and all consumers of chewing tobacco, does it not logically follow that he would be liable for negligently bringing about the same result? It seems to us that this question must be answered in the affirmative.

The fact that the courts have at this time made only the exceptions mentioned to the general rule does not prevent a step forward for the health and life of the public.

The principles announced in the cases which recognize the exceptions, in our opinion, apply, with equal force, to this case.

We believe that the way the tobacco is to be used furnishes the reason for great care in its preparation. If we eat food or drink beverages containing substances which under certain conditions may endanger our lives for obvious reasons, he who prepares the food or drink should be required to exercise great care to prevent the dangerous conditions. It appears sufficiently certain that chewing tobacco with poisonous ptomaines hidden in it is dangerous to the consumer, as was proven in this case.

We can imagine no reason why, with ordinary care, human toes could not be left out of chewing tobacco, and if toes are found in chewing tobacco, it seems to us that somebody has been very careless.

. . . .

Reversed in part and affirmed in part.

––––––––––

1. The court in this case states that the manufacturer is liable for "negligent preparation." What is the evidence of negligence in this case? On what basis did the court conclude that "somebody has been very careless"?

2. Was there any evidence that the manufacturer had acted unreasonably? Did the court conclude that the manufacturer had in fact been negligent?

Problem

What would the analysis in *Pillars* have looked like if the plaintiff had introduced evidence that chewing tobacco, even in the absence of extraneous contaminants, causes tongue cancer?

Matthews v. Campbell Soup Co.

United States District Court, S.D. Texas, 1974
380 F. Supp. 1061

MEMORANDUM AND ORDER:

SEALS, DISTRICT JUDGE.

This action is before the Court on a Motion for Summary Judgment filed by Defendant. In this diversity suit, 28 U.S.C. § 1332(a)(1), Plaintiff seeks to recover for injuries to his teeth and gums which were allegedly suffered while he was eating the contents of a can of Defendant's Oyster Stew Soup. Plaintiff claims that the injuries were caused by a small deleterious object in the soup. Plaintiff surrendered this object to Defendant for examination and it has been identified as a small irregularly shaped oyster pearl.

Plaintiff sets forth two theories of recovery: strict liability in tort and negligence in the manufacture and labeling of this product. Defendant contends that on the undisputed facts before the Court, Plaintiff cannot prevail on a theory of strict liability and that there is no evidence in the record to raise an issue of negligence. In ruling on Defendant's motion this Court is, of course, bound to apply those principles of products liability and negligence law which would be applied by the courts of this State. *Erie R.R. Co. v. Tompkins*, 304 U.S. 64, 58 S. Ct. 817, 82 L. Ed. 1188 (1938).

Texas courts have long recognized that the manufacturers of food products warrant that they are wholesome and fit for human consumption. The warranty was imposed by operation of law as a matter of public policy:

> It seems to be the rule that where food products sold for human consumption are unfit for that purpose, there is such an utter failure of the purpose for which the food is sold, and the consequences of eating unsound food are so disastrous to human health and life, that the law imposes a warranty of purity in favor of the ultimate consumer as a matter of public policy.

Jacob E. Decker & Sons, Inc. v. Capps, [164 S.W.2d 828, 829 (Tex. 1942)].

In *McKisson v. Sales Affiliates, Inc.*, 416 S.W.2d 787 (Tex. 1967), this strict liability concept applicable to foodstuffs was extended to include consumer products generally. *See also, Putnam v. Erie City Manufacturing Company*, 338 F.2d 911 (5th Cir. 1964). The *McKisson* court adopted the Restatement, Second, Torts § 402A which provides as follows:

> Special Liability of Seller of Product for Physical Harm to User or Consumer
>
> 1. One who sells any product in a defective condition unreasonably dangerous to the user or consumer or his property is subject to liability for physical harm thereby caused to the ultimate user or consumer, or to his property, if
>
> > (a) the seller is engaged in the business of selling such a product, and
> >
> > (b) it is expected to and does reach the user or consumer without substantial change in the condition in which it is sold.
>
> 2. The rule stated in Subsection (1) applies although
>
> > (a) the seller has exercised all possible care in the preparation and sale of his product, and
> >
> > (b) the user or consumer has not bought the product from or entered into any contractual relation with the seller.
>
> [Comment:
>
> a. This Section states a special rule applicable to sellers of products. The rule is one of strict liability, making the seller subject to liability to the user or consumer even though he has exercised all possible care in the preparation and sale of the product.]

In order to prevail under this strict liability standard Plaintiff must establish that: 1) the product in question was defective; 2) the defect existed at the time the products left the hands of the defendant; 3) that because of the defect the product was unreasonably dangerous to the user or consumer (plaintiff); 4) that the consumer was injured or suffered damages; 5) and that the defect (if proved) was the proximate cause of the injuries suffered.

Defendant argues that, as a matter of law, the can of Oyster Stew Soup at issue here was not unfit, unwholesome, defective, or unreasonably dangerous. As indicated in *Reyes v. Wyeth Laboratories,* [498 F.2d 1264 (5th Circ. 1974)], "defective condition" and "unreasonably dangerous" are essentially synonymous. Further, in light of the Texas Supreme Court's adoption of Section 402A of the Restatement in *McKisson, supra,* it is apparent that a food product is defective or unreasonably dangerous if it is unwholesome or unfit for human consumption and vice versa.

Defendant's position is bottomed on what may be labeled the "foreign-natural" doctrine. This doctrine, which has been neither accepted nor rejected by Texas courts, apparently first emerged in *Mix v. Ingersoll Candy Co.,* 6 Cal. 2d 674, 59 P.2d 144 (1936). There plaintiff brought suit for injuries caused by a fragment of chicken bone contained in a chicken pie. The court held that the chicken pie was not unfit for human consumption as a matter of law:

> "Although it may frequently be a question for a jury as the trier of facts to determine whether or not the particular defect alleged rendered the food not reasonably fit for human consumption, yet certain cases present facts from which the court itself may say, as a matter of law that the alleged defect does not fall within the terms of the statute. It is insisted that the court may so determine herein only if it is empowered to take judicial notice of the alleged fact that chicken pies usually contain chicken bones. It is not necessary to go so far as to hold that chicken pies usually contain chicken bones. It is sufficient if it may be said that as a matter of common knowledge chicken pies occasionally contain chicken bones. We have no hesitancy in so holding, and we are of the opinion that despite the fact that a chicken bone may occasionally be encountered in a chicken pie, such chicken pie, in the absence of some further defect, is reasonably fit for human consumption. *Bones which are natural to the type of meat served cannot legitimately be called a foreign substance, and a consumer who eats meat dishes ought to anticipate and be on his guard against the presence of such bones.* At least he cannot hold the restaurant keeper whose representation implied by law is that the meat dish is reasonably fit for human consumption, liable for any injury occurring as a result of the presence of a chicken bone in such chicken pie." At 148 (Emphasis supplied).

Probably a majority of jurisdictions having occasion to treat the problem have adopted the *Mix* rationale.

A relatively recent expression of the foreign-natural view is found in *Musso v. Picadilly Cafeterias, Inc.,* 178 So. 2d 421 (La. App. 1965). While eating at defendant's cafeteria, plaintiff encountered a cherry stone or pit in a slice of cherry pie. The court stated that vendors are strictly liable for injuries occasioned by the serving of food which is unwholesome or deleterious or which contains a vice or defect, but, held that a restauranteur is not liable for injuries resulting from substances natural to the food served and inadvertently left therein. The court's reasoning is attractively simple: if the food contains only natural substances it cannot be unfit or unwholesome.

The essence of the foreign-natural rule and the rationale behind it is captured in the following passage from *Musso:*

> The rationale of the majority rule as expressed in the cited authorities is that substances which are a natural part of the food served are not considered foreign matter or substances if inadvertently left therein. On this premise it is reasoned that the presence of substances natural to the ingredients or finished product does not constitute breach of the vendor's implied warranty that the food is wholesome and fit for human consumption. The cases further hold that the warranty implicit in the sale of food must be construed in the light of the common knowledge with reference to the nature and character of the food being served. In this respect it is further reasoned common experience dictates that one eating the meat of animals, fowl or fish should do so with the knowledge such foods may contain pieces of bone. At 426.

Not all jurisdictions have followed the foreign-natural view; it has been rejected by several courts in favor of a "reasonable expectation" test. In *Zabner v. Howard Johnson's Inc.*, 201 So. 2d 824 (Fla. App. 1967), a consumer was injured by a piece of walnut shell concealed in a dish of maple walnut ice cream. Following the foreign-natural test the trial court entered judgment for the defendant. After tracing the history of this doctrine and its application the appellate court opted in favor of a test of "reasonable expectation." "The test should be what is *'reasonably expected'* by the consumer in the food as served, not what might be natural to the ingredients of that food prior to preparation."

Observing that natural substances can often be as dangerous to the consumer as foreign objects such as a pebble or a piece of glass or wire, the *Zabner* court stated: "[The] naturalness of the substance to any ingredients in the food served is important only in determining whether the consumer may reasonably expect to find such substance in the particular type of dish or style of food served." The key question under the reasonable expectation test is whether the consumer ought to have anticipated the injury producing object in the final product not whether the object is foreign or natural. What the consumer might reasonably expect, the court noted, is a jury question in most cases.

The reasonable expectation view is also well stated in *Betehia v. Cape Cod Corp.*, 10 Wis. 2d 323, 103 N.E.2d 64 (1960):

> The test should be what is reasonably expected by the consumer in the food as served, not what might be natural to the ingredients of that food prior to preparation. What is to be reasonably expected by the consumer is a jury question in most cases; at least, we cannot say as a matter of law that a patron of a restaurant must expect a bone in a chicken sandwich either because chicken bones are occasionally found there or are natural to chicken.
>
> The test as applied to an action for breach of the implied warranty is keyed to what is "reasonably" fit. If it is found that the chicken bone the size alleged ought to be anticipated in a chicken sandwich and guarded against by the

consumer plaintiff, then the sandwich was reasonably fit under the implied warranty. At 69.

Texas courts have never been in a position requiring an election between these two competing doctrines. A great number of cases involving harmful objects have been litigated but the objects were so obviously "foreign" that the issue did not arise.

Making an *Erie* educated guess, this Court holds that, if faced with the problem, Texas courts would follow the reasonable expectation rule as it is stated in *Zabner*. It is obvious that the "reasonable expectation" approach is considerably more compatible and consistent with Section 402A which has been adopted as the law of Texas in product liability cases. Section 402A makes the seller liable for injuries caused by defective or unreasonably dangerous products. "Defective condition" is defined in Comment (g) as ". . . a condition not contemplated by the ultimate consumer, which will be unreasonably dangerous to him." An article is "unreasonably dangerous" according to Comment (i) if it is ". . . dangerous to an extent beyond that which would be contemplated by the ordinary consumer who purchases it, with the ordinary knowledge common to the community as to its characteristics." These Comments have been viewed as persuasive if not controlling in the application of Section 402A. *Garcia v. Sky Climber, Inc.*, 470 S.W.2d 261 (Tex. Civ. App. 1971).

If Texas courts were to follow the "reasonable expectation" test they logically should reach a result consistent in every case with the Restatement definitions of "defective condition" and "unreasonably dangerous." This would not necessarily be true under the foreign-natural doctrine. It would be possible under that approach only if it is assumed that consumers *always* contemplate the presence of every species of object which might be categorized as natural to the food they are eating regardless of how infrequently the object might appear in common experience. That is obviously a faulty assumption which Texas courts are not at all likely to make.

Andrews, J., concurring in *Zabner, supra*, suggests that the difficulty with the foreign-natural test as a problem solving device lies not in its theory but in its artificial application. He contends that courts too often apply it at a preliminary stage of production focusing on a single ingredient rather than the final consumer product. "By moving the focus of the test to the consumable item the foreign-natural distinction as measured by the consumer's reasonable expectations becomes a valid and relevant standard."

If this analysis is correct, the only way of avoiding misapplication of the foreign-natural theory is to focus on what the consumer might reasonably expect to find in the final product. This being the case it would make even more sense to discard the foreign-natural distinction and go directly to the reasonable expectation issue. The use of these labels does not advance the inquiry and unnecessarily increases the possibility of confusion on the ultimate issue.

Loyacano v. Continental Insurance Company, 283 So. 2d 302 (La. App. 1973) is an example of the confusion which adherence to the foreign-natural distinction can create. There the plaintiff sued for injuries caused by a bone fragment concealed in a ground meat patty. The court first professed adherence to the foreign-natural distinction of *Musso, supra,* and then stated:

> In *Musso* there was ample evidence to show the probability of expectancy of cherry pits in pitted cherries, but unfortunately there is no evidence in the present case concerning the probability of pieces of bone appearing in hamburger. Simply as a matter of general knowledge, we cannot say that we can take judicial notice that a hamburger patty should not contain any pieces of bone whatsoever . . . It may be said that a product can be considered defective if it does not meet the reasonable expectations of the ordinary consumer as to its safety. It is not the fact that a defect is a natural one which is important to this inquiry, but the fact that the ordinary consumer would expect that he might encounter it, and thus he would normally take his own precautions. A package of ground meat is not expected to be consumed from the sealed package as a bottle of soda water or milk, but is expected to be processed or otherwise altered before consumption by the purchaser. Therefore, it seems to us that the strict liability imposed upon vendors of sealed packages of that nature, cannot be imposed upon the vendor here, except insofar as a foreign object would be concerned. For a natural object, such as a bone, from the only evidence produced in this case, it appears that the inquiry should be directed to the size of the bone left in the ground meat. At 305.

The court went on to hold defendant liable for the injury stating that defendant had not presented sufficient evidence to prove its lack of negligence in handling the ground meat. Lemon, J., in a concurring opinion, indicates that *Musso* is the source of the problem and advocates a rethinking of the foreign-natural distinction, possibly portending changes to come in Louisiana jurisprudence. Texas courts have not descended into this quagmire and this Court is confident that they will not.

Having settled on the "reasonable expectation" standard the question before this Court can be restated. Can it be said, as a matter of law, that the consumer can reasonably expect to encounter a pearl in a can of Defendant's Oyster Stew Soup[?] This Court thinks not. It is clearly an issue for the jury to decide. With the undisputed facts reflected in the pleadings, interrogatories and affidavits on file herein it would be impossible for this Court to ascertain what the common consumer experience is with respect to pearls in canned oyster stew. Defendant's Motion For Summary Judgment on the issue of strict liability is therefore denied.

Defendant's motion going to Plaintiff's negligence theory of recovery is also denied. Even where there are no facts in dispute, it is usually for the jury to decide whether the conduct in question meets the reasonable man standard. *Cf.,* Wright & Miller, Federal Practice and Procedure, § 2729 at 572. On the facts reflected in this record the Court cannot say that Defendant was not negligent in the manufacture and labeling of this product as a matter of law.

———————

1. Is there any difference in result between the foreign/natural test and the reasonable expectation test? Wouldn't a consumer expect substances in food that naturally occur there? In what situations would the two tests produce different results? What role would a warning of possible bones serve?

2. This case introduces the reader to the Restatement (Second) of Torts § 402A. What significance does Section 402A have in this case?

Problem

B purchases a package of pork chops from a supermarket. He takes the pork chops home and prepares them for dinner by broiling them.

Some time later, B falls ill with trichinosis, a parasitic disease which results from eating pork which has not been thoroughly cooked. Cooking the meat thoroughly kills the trichinae and renders them unable to infest the person eating the pork. B's ailment was caused by the pork chops.

Assume that the supermarket is the appropriate entity for B to sue. What arguments would B make under the foreign/natural test? Under the reasonable expectation test? What do you think the supermarket will argue in response to either test?

B. Contract and Tort in Strict Products Liability

Before strict products liability theory could establish its identity as a separate doctrine, courts needed to define the relationship (if any) between contract and tort law in the cases they were adjudicating. The following case, in which the Supreme Court of New Jersey definitively discussed the problem, appears in courses dealing with contracts, torts, sales, and products liability.

Henningsen v. Bloomfield Motors, Inc.

Supreme Court of New Jersey, 1960
161 A.2d 69

FRANCIS, J.

Plaintiff Claus H. Henningsen purchased a Plymouth automobile, manufactured by defendant Chrysler Corporation, from defendant Bloomfield Motors, Inc. His wife, plaintiff Helen Henningsen, was injured while driving it and instituted suit against both defendants to recover damages on account of her injuries. Her husband joined in the action seeking compensation for his consequential losses. The complaint was predicated upon breach of express and implied warranties and upon negligence. At the trial the negligence counts were dismissed by the court and the cause was submitted to the jury for determination solely on the issues of implied warranty of merchantability. Verdicts were returned against both defendants and in favor of the plaintiffs. Defendants appealed and plaintiffs cross-appealed from the dismissal of their negligence claim. The matter was certified by this court prior to consideration in the Appellate Division.

The facts are not complicated, but a general outline of them is necessary to an understanding of the case.

On May 7, 1955 Mr. and Mrs. Henningsen visited the place of business of Bloomfield Motors, Inc., an authorized De Soto and Plymouth dealer, to look at a Plymouth. They wanted to buy a car and were considering a Ford or a Chevrolet as well as a Plymouth. They were shown a Plymouth which appealed to them and the purchase followed. The record indicates that Mr. Henningsen intended the car as a Mother's Day gift to his wife. He said the intention was communicated to the dealer. When the purchase order or contract was prepared and presented, the husband executed it alone. His wife did not join as a party.

The purchase order was a printed form of one page. On the front it contained blanks to be filled in with a description of the automobile to be sold, the various accessories to be included, and the details of the financing. The particular car selected was described as a 1955 Plymouth, Plaza "6," Club Sedan. The type used in the printed parts of the form became smaller in size, different in style, and less readable toward the bottom where the line for the purchaser's signature was placed. The smallest type on the page appears in the two paragraphs . . . on which great stress is laid by the defense in the case. These two paragraphs are the least legible and the most difficult to read in the instrument, but they are most important in the evaluation of the rights of the contesting parties. They do not attract attention and there is nothing about the format which would draw the reader's eye to them. In fact, a studied and concentrated effort would have to be made to read them. De-emphasis seems the motive rather than emphasis. . . .

The two paragraphs are:

"The front and back of this Order comprise the entire agreement affecting this purchase and no other agreement or understanding of any nature concerning same has been made or entered into, or will be recognized. I hereby certify that no credit has been extended to me for the purchase of this motor vehicle except as appears in writing on the face of this agreement.

"I have read the matter printed on the back hereof and agree to it as a part of this order the same as if it were printed above my signature. I certify that I am 21 years of age, or older, and hereby acknowledge receipt of a copy of this order."

On the right side of the form, immediately below these clauses and immediately above the signature line, and in 12 point block type, the following appears:

"CASH OR CERTIFIED CHECK ONLY ON DELIVERY."

On the left side, just opposite and in the same style type as the two quoted clauses, but in eight point size, this statement is set out:

"This agreement shall not become binding upon the Dealer until approved by an officer of the company."

The two latter statements are in the interest of the dealer and obviously an effort is made to draw attention to them.

The testimony of Claus Henningsen justifies the conclusion that he did not read the two fine print paragraphs referring to the back of the purchase contract. And it is uncontradicted that no one made any reference to them, or called them to his attention. With respect to the matter appearing on the back, it is likewise uncontradicted that he did not read it and that no one called it to his attention.

The reverse side of the contract contains 8 1/2 inches of fine print. . . . In the seventh paragraph, about two-thirds of the way down the page, the warranty, which is the focal point of the case, is set forth. It is as follows:

"7. It is expressly agreed that there are no warranties, express or implied, *made* by either the dealer or the manufacturer on the motor vehicle, chassis, of [sic] parts furnished hereunder except as follows.

"The manufacturer warrants each new motor vehicle (including original equipment placed thereon by the manufacturer except tires), chassis or parts manufactured by it to be free from defects in material or workmanship under normal use and service. Its obligation under this warranty being limited to making good at its factory any part or parts thereof which shall, within ninety (90) days after delivery of such vehicle *to the original purchaser* or before such vehicle has been driven 4,000 miles, whichever event shall first occur, be returned to it with transportation charges prepaid and which its examination shall disclose to its satisfaction to have been thus defective; *this warranty being expressly in lieu of all other warranties expressed or implied, and all other obligations or liabilities on its part*, and it neither assumes nor authorizes any other person to assume for it any other liability in connection with the sale of its vehicles. . . ." (Emphasis ours.)

After the contract had been executed, plaintiffs were told the car had to be serviced and that it would be ready in two days. . . .

. . . .

The new Plymouth was turned over to the Henningsens on May 9, 1955. . . . Thereafter, it was used for short trips on paved streets about the town. It had no servicing and no mishaps of any kind before the event of May 19. That day, Mrs. Henningsen drove to Asbury Park. On the way down and in returning the car performed in normal fashion until the accident occurred. She was proceeding north on Route 36 in Highlands, New Jersey, at 20–22 miles per hour. The highway was paved and smooth, and contained two lanes for northbound travel. She was riding in the right-hand lane. Suddenly she heard a loud noise "from the bottom, by the hood." It "felt as if something cracked." The steering wheel spun in her hands; the car veered sharply to the right and crashed into a highway sign and a brick wall. No other vehicle was in any way involved. A bus operator driving in the left-hand lane testified that he observed plaintiffs' car approaching in normal fashion in the opposite direction; "all of a sudden [it] veered at 90 degrees . . . and right into this wall." As a result of the impact, the front of the car was so badly damaged that it was impossible to determine if any of the parts of the steering wheel mechanism or workmanship or assembly were defective or improper prior to the accident. The condition was such that the collision insurance carrier, after inspection, declared the vehicle a total loss. It had 468 miles on the speedometer at the time.

The insurance carrier's inspector and appraiser of damaged cars, with 11 years of experience, advanced the opinion, based on the history and his examination, that something definitely went "wrong from the steering wheel down to the front wheels" and that the untoward happening must have been due to mechanical defect or failure; "something down there had to drop off or break loose to cause the car" to act in the manner described.

As has been indicated, the trial court felt that the proof was not sufficient to make out a *prima facie* case as to the negligence of either the manufacturer or the dealer. The case was given to the jury, therefore, solely on the warranty theory, with results favorable to the plaintiffs against both defendants.

I.

The Claim of Implied Warranty Against the Manufacturer.

In the ordinary case of sale of goods by description an implied warranty of merchantability is an integral part of the transaction. R.S. 46:30-20, N.J.S.A. . . . Th[is] type of warranty simply means that the thing sold is reasonably fit for the general purpose for which it is manufactured and sold.

. . . .

Of course . . . sales, whether oral or written, may be accompanied by an express warranty. Under the broad terms of the Uniform Sale of Goods Law any affirmation of fact relating to the goods is an express warranty if the natural tendency of the statement is to induce the buyer to make the purchase. R.S. 46:30-18, N.J.S.A. And over the years since the almost universal adoption of the act, a growing awareness of the tremendous development of modern business methods has prompted the courts to administer that provision with a liberal hand. Vold, Law of Sales, § 86, p. 429 (2d ed. 1959). Solicitude toward the buyer plainly harmonizes with the intention of the Legislature. That fact is manifested further by the later section of the act which preserves and continues any permissible implied warranty, despite an express warranty, unless the two are inconsistent. R.S. 46:30-21(6), N.J.S.A.

The uniform act codified, extended and liberalized the common law of sales. The motivation in part was to ameliorate the harsh doctrine *of caveat emptor,* and in some measure to impose a reciprocal obligation on the seller to beware. The transcendent value of the legislation, particularly with respect to implied warranties, rests in the fact that obligations on the part of the seller were imposed by operation of law, and did not depend for their existence upon express agreement of the parties. And of tremendous significance in a rapidly expanding commercial society was the recognition of the right to recover damages on account of personal injuries arising from a breach of warranty. The particular importance of this advance resides in the fact that under such circumstances strict liability is imposed upon the maker or seller of the product. Recovery of damages does not depend upon proof of negligence or knowledge of the defect.

As the Sales Act and its liberal interpretation by the courts threw this protective cloak about the buyer, the decisions in various jurisdictions revealed beyond doubt that many manufacturers took steps to avoid these ever increasing warranty obligations. Realizing that the act governed the relationship of buyer and seller, they undertook to withdraw from actual and direct contractual contact with the buyer. They ceased selling products to the consuming public through their own employees and making contracts of sale in their own names. Instead, a system of independent dealers was established; their products were sold to dealers who in turn dealt with the buying public, ostensibly solely in their own personal capacity as sellers. In the past in many instances, manufacturers were able to transfer to the dealers burdens imposed by the act and thus achieved a large measure of immunity for themselves. But, as will be noted in more detail hereafter, such marketing practices, coupled with the advent of large scale advertising by manufacturers to promote the purchase of these goods from dealers by members of the public, provided a basis upon which the existence of express or implied warranties was predicated, even though the manufacturer was not a party to the contract of sale.

The general observations that have been made are important largely for purposes of perspective. They are helpful in achieving a point from which to evaluate the situation now presented for solution. Primarily, they reveal a trend and a design in legislative and judicial thinking toward providing protection for the buyer. It must be noted, however, that the sections of the Sales Act, to which reference has been made, do not impose warranties in terms of unalterable absolutes. R.S. 46:30-3, N.J.S.A., provides in general terms that an applicable warranty may be negatived or varied by express agreement. As to disclaimers or limitations of the obligations that normally attend a sale, it seems sufficient at this juncture to say they are not favored, and that they are strictly construed against the seller.

With these considerations in mind, we come to a study of the express warranty on the reverse side of the purchase order signed by Claus Henningsen. At the outset we take notice that it was made only by the manufacturer and that by its terms it runs directly to Claus Henningsen. On the facts detailed above, it was to be extended to him by the dealer as the agent of Chrysler Corporation. The consideration for this warranty is the purchase of the manufacturer's product from the dealer by the ultimate buyer.

Although the franchise agreement between the defendants recites that the relationship of principal and agent is not created, in particular transactions involving third persons the law will look at their conduct and not to their intent or their words as between themselves but to their factual relation. Restatement (Second), Agency § 27 (1958). The normal pattern that the manufacturer-dealer relationship follows relegates the position of the dealer to the status of a way station along the car's route from maker to consumer. This is indicated by the language of the warranty. Obviously the parties knew and so intended that the dealer would not use the automobile for 90 days or drive it 4,000 miles. And the words "original purchaser," taken in their context, signify the purchasing member of the public. Moreover, the language of this warranty is that of the uniform warranty of the Automobile Manufacturers Association, of which Chrysler is a member. And it is the form appearing in the Plymouth Owner Service Certificate mentioned in the servicing instruction guide sent with the new car from the factory. The evidence is overwhelming that the dealer acted for Chrysler in including the warranty in the purchase contract.

The terms of the warranty are a sad commentary upon the automobile manufacturers' marketing practices. Warranties developed in the law in the interest of and to protect the ordinary consumer who cannot be expected to have the knowledge or capacity or even the opportunity to make adequate inspection of mechanical instrumentalities, like automobiles, and to decide for himself whether they are reasonably fit for the designed purpose. But the ingenuity of the Automobile Manufacturers Association, by means of its standardized form, has metamorphosed the warranty into a device to limit the maker's liability. . . . The manufacturer agrees to replace defective parts for 90 days after the sale or until the car has been driven 4,000 miles, whichever is first to occur, *if the part is sent to the factory, transportation charges prepaid, and if examination discloses to its satisfaction that the part is defective.* It is difficult to imagine a greater burden on the consumer, or less satisfactory remedy. Aside from imposing on the buyer the trouble of removing and shipping the part, the maker has sought to retain the uncontrolled discretion to decide the issue of defectiveness. . . .

Moreover, the guaranty is against defective workmanship. That condition may arise from good parts improperly assembled. There being no defective parts to return to the maker, is all remedy to be denied? . . . Must the purchaser return the car, transportation charges prepaid, over a great distance to the factory? . . .

The matters referred to represent only a small part of the illusory character of the security presented by the warranty. . . . [I]n this instance, after reciting that defective parts will be replaced at the factory, the alleged agreement relied upon by Chrysler provides that the manufacturer's "obligation under this warranty" is limited to that undertaking; further, that such remedy is "in lieu of all other warranties, express or implied, and all other obligations or liabilities on its part." The contention has been raised [in other cases] that such language bars any claim for personal injuries which may emanate from a breach of the warranty. . . .

Putting aside for the time being the problem of the efficacy of the disclaimer provisions contained in the express warranty, a question of first importance to be decided is whether an implied warranty of merchantability by Chrysler Corporation accompanied the sale of the automobile to Claus Henningsen.

Preliminarily, it may be said that the express warranty against defective parts and workmanship is not inconsistent with an implied warranty of merchantability. Such warranty cannot be excluded for that reason.

Chrysler . . . urges that since it was not a party to the sale by the dealer to Henningsen, there is no privity of contract between it and the plaintiffs, and the absence of this privity eliminates any such implied warranty.

There is no doubt that under early common-law concepts of contractual liability only those persons who were parties to the bargain could sue for a breach of it. In more recent times a noticeable disposition has appeared in a number of jurisdictions to break through the narrow barrier of privity when dealing with sales of goods in order to give realistic recognition to a universally accepted fact. The fact is that the dealer and the ordinary buyer do not, and are not expected to, buy goods, whether they be foodstuffs or automobiles, exclusively for their own consumption or use. Makers and manufacturers know this and advertise and market their products on that assumption; witness, the "family" car, the baby foods, etc. . . . With the advent of mass marketing, the manufacturer became remote from the purchaser, sales were accomplished through intermediaries, and the demand for the product was created by advertising media. In such an economy it became obvious that the consumer was the person being cultivated. Manifestly, the connotation of "consumer" was broader than that of "buyer." He signified such a person who, in the reasonable contemplation of the parties to the sale, might be expected to use the product. Thus, where the commodities sold are such that if defectively manufactured they will be dangerous to life or limb, then society's interests can only be protected by eliminating the requirement of privity between the maker and his dealers and the reasonably expected ultimate consumer. In that way the burden of losses consequent upon use of defective articles is borne by those who are in a position to either control the danger or make an equitable distribution of the losses when they do occur. . . .

. . . .

Although only a minority of jurisdictions have thus far departed from the requirement of privity, the movement in that direction is most certainly gathering momentum. Liability to the ultimate consumer in the absence of direct contractual connection has been predicated upon a variety of theories. Some courts hold that the warranty runs with the article like a covenant running with land; others recognize a third-party beneficiary thesis; still others rest their decision on the ground that public policy requires recognition of a warranty made directly to the consumer.

. . . .

Most of the cases where lack of privity has not been permitted to interfere with recovery have involved food and drugs. In fact, the rule as to such products has been characterized as an exception to the general doctrine. But more recently courts, sensing the inequity of such limitation, have moved into broader fields: home permanent wave set; soap detergent; inflammable cowboy suit (by clear implication); exploding bottle; defective emery wheel; defective wire rope; defective cinder blocks.

We see no rational doctrinal basis for differentiating between a fly in a bottle of beverage and a defective automobile. The unwholesome beverage may bring illness to one person, the defective car, with its great potentiality for harm to the driver, occupants, and others, demands even less adherence to the narrow barrier of privity. . . .

Under modern conditions the ordinary layman, on responding to the importuning of colorful advertising, has neither the opportunity nor the capacity to inspect or to determine the fitness of an automobile for use; he must rely on the manufacturer who has control of its construction, and to some degree on the dealer who, to the limited extent called for by the manufacturer's instructions, inspects and services it before delivery. In such a marketing milieu his remedies and those of persons who properly claim through him should not depend "upon the intricacies of the law of sales. The obligation of the manufacturer should not be based alone on privity of contract. It should rest, as was once said, upon "the demands of social justice." *Mazetti v. Armour & Co.*, 75 Wash. 622, 135 P. 633, 635, 48 L.R.A., N.S., 213 (Sup. Ct. 1913).

Accordingly, we hold that under modern marketing conditions, when a manufacturer puts a new automobile in the stream of trade and promotes its purchase by the public, an implied warranty that it is reasonably suitable for use as such accompanies it into the hands of the ultimate purchaser. Absence of agency between the manufacturer and the dealer who makes the ultimate sale is immaterial.

. . . .

IV.

Proof of Breach of the Implied Warranty of Merchantability.

Both defendants argue that the proof adduced by plaintiffs as to the happening of the accident was not sufficient to demonstrate a breach of warranty. Consequently, they claim that their motion for judgment should have been granted by the trial court. We cannot agree. In our view, the total effect of the circumstances shown from purchase to accident is adequate to raise an inference that the car was defective and that such condition was causally related to the mishap. Thus, determination by the jury was required.

The proof adduced by the plaintiffs disclosed that after servicing and delivery of the car, it operated normally during the succeeding ten days, so far as the Henningsens could tell. They had no difficulty or mishap of any kind, and it neither had nor required any servicing. It was driven by them alone. The owner's service certificate provided for return for further servicing at the end of the first 1,000 miles—less than half of which had been covered at the time of Mrs. Henningsen's injury.

The facts, detailed above, show that on the day of the accident, ten days after delivery, Mrs. Henningsen was driving in a normal fashion, on a smooth highway, when unexpectedly the steering wheel and the front wheels of the car went into the bizarre action described. Can it reasonably be said that the circumstances do not warrant an inference of unsuitability for ordinary use against the manufacturer and the dealer? Obviously there is nothing in the proof to indicate in the slightest that the most unusual action of the steering wheel was caused by Mrs. Henningsen's operation of the automobile on this day, or by the use of the car between delivery and the happening of the incident. Nor is there anything to suggest that any external force or condition unrelated to the manufacturing or servicing of the car operated as an inducing or even concurring factor.

. . . .

V.

The Defense of Lack of Privity Against Mrs. Henningsen.

Both defendants contend that since there was no privity of contract between them and Mrs. Henningsen, she cannot recover for breach of any warranty made by either of them. On the facts, as they were developed, we agree that she was not a party to the purchase agreement. Her right to maintain the action, therefore, depends upon whether she occupies such legal status thereunder as to permit her to take advantage of a breach of defendants' implied warranties.

For the most part the cases that have been considered dealt with the right of the buyer or consumer to maintain an action against the manufacturer where the contract of sale was with a dealer and the buyer had no contractual relationship with the manufacturer. . . . In our judgment, the principles of those cases and the supporting texts are just as proximately applicable to [Mrs. Henningsen's] situation. We are convinced that the cause of justice in this area of the law can be served only by recognizing that she is such a person who, in the reasonable contemplation of the parties to the warranty, might be expected to become a user of the automobile. Accordingly, her lack of privity does not stand in the way of prosecution of the injury suit against the defendant Chrysler.

The context in which the problem of privity with respect to the dealer must be considered, is much the same. Defendant Bloomfield Motors is chargeable with an implied warranty of merchantability to Claus Henningsen. There is no need to engage in a separate or extended discussion of the question. The legal principles which control are the same in quality. The manufacturer establishes the network of trade and the dealer is a unit utilized in that network to accomplish sales. He is the beneficiary of the same express and implied warranties from the manufacturer as he extends to the buyer of the automobile. If he is sued alone, he may implead the manufacturer. His understanding of the expected use of the car by persons other than the buyer is the same as that of the manufacturer. And so, his claim to the doctrine of privity should rise no higher than that of the manufacturer.

. . . .

It is important to express the right of Mrs. Henningsen to maintain her action in terms of a general principle. To what extent may lack of privity be disregarded in suits on such warranties? . . . [I]t is our opinion that an implied warranty of merchantability chargeable to either an automobile manufacturer or a dealer extends to the purchaser of the car, members of his family, and to other persons occupying or using it with his consent. It would be wholly opposed to reality to say that use by such persons is not within the anticipation of parties to such a warranty of reasonable suitability of an automobile for ordinary highway operation. Those persons must be considered within the distributive chain.

. . . .

VII.

Under all of the circumstances outlined above, the judgments in favor of the plaintiffs and against the defendants are affirmed.

For affirmance: CHIEF JUSTICE WEINTRAUB and JUSTICES BURLING, JACOBS, FRANCIS, PROCTOR and SCHETTINO — 6.

For reversal: None.

---

1. How does the court see the relationship between tort and contract law in cases involving defective products?

2. What was the product defect in *Henningsen*? How did the plaintiff prove that the automobile was defective?

3. It has long been settled law that the manufacturer that puts the fully assembled product into the stream of commerce is liable for any defects in the product, even when the defect lies in a component part of the product which the manufacturer did not make. *MacPherson v. Buick Motor Co.*, 111 N.E. 1050 (N.Y. 1916). The manufacturer may, of course, bring the producer of the component part into the lawsuit, but the injured consumer need not do so.

MacPherson, an extremely important opinion, involved a shattered wheel. In that case, the court rejected the idea that the plaintiff needed to be in some sort of privity with the seller, ruling that the consumer of the product (an automobile) could sue the manufacturer directly, even though there was no relationship between the manufacturer and the consumer.

C. Strict Products Liability in Tort

1. The Birth of the Doctrine

Escola v. Coca Cola Bottling Co.
Supreme Court of California, 1944
150 P.2d 436

GIBSON, CHIEF JUSTICE.

Plaintiff, a waitress in a restaurant, was injured when a bottle of Coca Cola broke in her hand. She alleged that defendant company, which had bottled and delivered the alleged defective bottle to her employer, was negligent in selling "bottles containing said beverage which on account of excessive pressure of gas or by reason of some defect in the bottle was dangerous . . . and likely to explode." This appeal is from a judgment upon a jury verdict in favor of plaintiff.

Defendant's driver delivered several cases of Coca Cola to the restaurant, placing them on the floor, one on top of the other, under and behind the counter, where they remained at least thirty-six hours. Immediately before the accident, plaintiff picked up the top case and set it upon a near-by ice cream cabinet in front of and about three feet from the refrigerator. She then proceeded to take the bottles from the case with her right hand, one at a time, and put them into the refrigerator. Plaintiff testified that after she had placed three bottles in the refrigerator and had moved the fourth bottle about 18 inches from the case "it exploded in my hand." The bottle broke into two jagged pieces and inflicted a deep five-inch cut, severing blood vessels, nerves and muscles of the thumb and palm of the hand. Plaintiff further testified that when the bottle exploded, "It made a sound similar to an electric light bulb that would have dropped. It made a loud pop." Plaintiff's employer testified, "I was about twenty feet from where it actually happened and I heard the explosion." A fellow employee, on the opposite side of the counter, testified that plaintiff "had the bottle, I should judge, waist high, and I know that it didn't bang either the case or the door or another bottle . . . when it popped. It sounded just like a fruit jar would blow up. . . ." The witness further testified that the contents of the bottle "flew all over herself and myself and the walls and one thing and another."

The top portion of the bottle, with the cap, remained in plaintiff's hand, and the lower portion fell to the floor but did not break. The broken bottle was not produced at the trial, the pieces having been thrown away by an employee of the restaurant shortly after the accident. Plaintiff, however, described the broken pieces, and a diagram of the bottle was made showing the location of the "fracture line" where the bottle broke in two.

One of defendant's drivers, called as a witness by plaintiff, testified that he had seen other bottles of Coca Cola in the past explode and had found broken bottles in the warehouse when he took the cases out, but that he did not know what made them blow up.

Plaintiff then rested her case, having announced to the court that being unable to show any specific acts of negligence she relied completely on the doctrine of res ipsa loquitur.

Defendant contends that the doctrine of res ipsa loquitur does not apply in this case, and that the evidence is insufficient to support the judgment. [For the court's discussion of the application of res ipsa loquitur, see Chapter 5, *supra*.] . . .

Upon an examination of the record, the evidence appears sufficient to support a reasonable inference that the bottle here involved was not damaged by any extraneous force after delivery to the restaurant by defendant. It follows, therefore, that the bottle was in some manner defective at the time defendant relinquished control, because sound and properly prepared bottles of carbonated liquids do not ordinarily explode when carefully handled.

The next question, then, is whether plaintiff may rely upon the doctrine of res ipsa loquitur to supply an inference that defendant's negligence was responsible for the defective condition of the bottle at the time it was delivered to the restaurant. Under the general rules pertaining to the doctrine, as set forth above, it must appear that bottles of carbonated liquid are not ordinarily defective without negligence by the bottling company. . . .

An explosion such as took place here might have been caused by an excessive internal pressure in a sound bottle, by a defect in the glass of a bottle containing a safe pressure, or by a combination of these two possible causes. The question is whether under the evidence there was a probability that defendant was negligent in any of these respects. If so, the doctrine of res ipsa loquitur applies.

The bottle was admittedly charged with gas under pressure, and the charging of the bottle was within the exclusive control of defendant. As it is a matter of common knowledge that an overcharge would not ordinarily result without negligence, it follows under the doctrine of res ipsa loquitur that if the bottle was in fact excessively charged an inference of defendant's negligence would arise. If the explosion resulted from a defective bottle containing a safe pressure, the defendant would be liable if it negligently failed to discover such flaw. . . .

Although it is not clear in this case whether the explosion was caused by an excessive charge or a defect in the glass there is a sufficient showing that neither cause would ordinarily have been present if due care had been used. Further, defendant had exclusive control over both the charging and inspection of the bottles. Accordingly, all the requirements necessary to entitle plaintiff to rely on the doctrine of res ipsa loquitur to supply an inference of negligence are present.

It is true that defendant presented evidence tending to show that it exercised considerable precaution by carefully regulating and checking the pressure in the bottles and by making visual inspections for defects in the glass at several stages during the bottling process. It is well settled, however, that when a defendant produces evidence to rebut the inference of negligence which arises upon application of the doctrine of res ipsa loquitur, it is ordinarily a question of fact for the jury to determine whether the inference has been dispelled.

The judgment is affirmed.

SHENK, CURTIS, CARTER, and SCHAUER, JJ., concurred.

TRAYNOR, JUSTICE.

I concur in the judgment, but I believe the manufacturer's negligence should no longer be singled out as the basis of a plaintiff's right to recover in cases like the present one. In my opinion it should now be recognized that a manufacturer incurs an absolute liability when an article that he has placed on the market, knowing that it is to be used without inspection, proves to have a defect that causes injury to human beings. *MacPherson v. Buick Motor Co.*, 217 N.Y. 382, 111 N.E. 1050, established the principle, recognized by this court, that irrespective of privity of contract, the manufacturer is responsible for an injury caused by such an article to any person who comes in lawful contact with it. In these cases the source of the manufacturer's liability was his negligence in the manufacturing process or in the inspection of component parts supplied by others. Even if there is no negligence, however, public policy demands that responsibility be fixed wherever it will most effectively reduce the hazards to life and health inherent in defective products that reach the market. It is evident that the manufacturer can anticipate some hazards and guard against the recurrence of others, as the public cannot. Those who suffer injury from defective products are unprepared to meet its consequences. The cost of an injury and the loss of time or health may be an overwhelming misfortune to the person injured, and a needless one, for the risk of injury can be insured by the manufacturer and distributed among the public as a cost of doing business. It is to the public interest to discourage the marketing of products having defects that are a menace to the public. If such products nevertheless find their way into the market it is to the public interest to place the responsibility for whatever injury they may cause upon the manufacturer, who, even if he is not negligent in the manufacture of the product, is responsible for its reaching the market. However intermittently such injuries may occur and however haphazardly they may strike, the risk of their occurrence is a constant risk and a general one. Against such a risk there should be general and constant protection and the manufacturer is best situated to afford such protection.

The injury from a defective product does not become a matter of indifference because the defect arises from causes other than the negligence of the manufacturer, such as negligence of a submanufacturer of a component part whose defects could not be revealed by inspection or unknown causes that even by the device of res ipsa loquitur cannot be classified as negligence of the manufacturer. The inference of negligence may be dispelled by an affirmative showing of proper care. If the evidence against the fact inferred is "clear, positive, uncontradicted, and of such a nature that it can not rationally be disbelieved, the court must instruct the jury that the nonexistence of the fact has been established as a matter of law." *Blank v. Coffin*, 20 Cal. 2d 457, 461, 126 P.2d 868, 870. An injured person, however, is not ordinarily in a position to refute such evidence or identify the cause of the defect, for he can hardly be familiar with the manufacturing process as the manufacturer himself is. In leaving it to the jury to decide whether the inference has been dispelled, regardless of the evidence against it, the negligence rule approaches the rule of strict liability. It is needlessly circuitous to make negligence the basis of recovery and impose what is in reality liability without negligence. If public policy demands that a manufacturer of goods be responsible for their quality regardless of negligence there is no reason not to fix that responsibility openly.

In the case of foodstuffs, the public policy of the state is formulated in a criminal statute. . . . The criminal liability under the statute attaches without proof of fault, so that the manufacturer is under the duty of ascertaining whether an article manufactured by him is safe. . . .

The statute may well be applicable to a bottle whose defects cause it to explode. In any event it is significant that the statute imposes criminal liability without fault, reflecting the public policy of protecting the public from dangerous products placed on the market, irrespective of negligence in their manufacture. While the Legislature imposes criminal liability only with regard to food products and their containers, there are many other sources of danger. It is to the public interest to prevent injury to the public from any defective goods by the imposition of civil liability generally.

The retailer, even though not equipped to test a product, is under an absolute liability to his customer, for the implied warranties of fitness for proposed use and merchantable quality include a warranty of safety of the product. This warranty is not necessarily a contractual one. . . . The courts recognize, however, that the retailer cannot bear the burden of this warranty, and allow him to recoup any losses by means of the warranty of safety attending the wholesaler's or manufacturer's sale to him. Such a procedure, however, is needlessly circuitous and engenders wasteful litigation. Much would be gained if the injured person could base his action directly on the manufacturer's warranty.

The liability of the manufacturer to an immediate buyer injured by a defective product follows without proof of negligence from the implied warranty of safety attending the sale. Ordinarily, however, the immediate buyer is a dealer who does not intend to use the product himself, and if the warranty of safety is to serve the purpose of protecting health and safety it must give rights to others than the dealer. In the words of Judge Cardozo in the *MacPherson* case [217 N.Y. 382, 111 N.E. 1053]: "The dealer was indeed the one person of whom it might be said with some approach to certainty that by him the car would not be used. Yet the defendant would have us say that he was the one person whom it was under a legal duty to protect. The law does not lead us to so inconsequent a conclusion." While the defendant's negligence in the *MacPherson* case made it unnecessary for the court to base liability on warranty, Judge Cardozo's reasoning recognized the injured person as the real party in interest and effectively disposed of the theory that the liability of the manufacturer incurred by his warranty should apply only to the immediate purchaser. It thus paves the way for a standard of liability that would make the manufacturer guarantee the safety of his product even when there is no negligence.

This court and many others have extended protection according to such a standard to consumers of food products, taking the view that the right of a consumer injured by unwholesome food does not depend "upon the intricacies of the law of sales" and that the warranty of the manufacturer to the consumer in absence of privity of contract rests on public policy. Dangers to life and health inhere in other consumers' goods that are defective and there is no reason to differentiate them from the dangers of defective food products.

In the food products cases the courts have resorted to various fictions to rationalize the extension of the manufacturer's warranty to the consumer. . . . They have also held the manufacturer liable on a mere fiction of negligence. . . . Such fictions are not necessary to fix the manufacturer's liability under a warranty if the warranty is severed from the contract of sale between the dealer and the consumer and based on the law of torts as a strict liability. Warranties are not necessarily rights arising under a contract. An action on a warranty "was, in its origin, a pure action of tort," and only late in the historical development of warranties was an action in assumpsit allowed. . . . As the court said in *Greco v. S. S. Kresge Co., supra* [277 N.Y. 26, 12 N.E.2d 561, 115 A.L.R. 1020], "Though the action may be brought solely for the breach of the implied warranty, the breach is a wrongful act, a default, and, in its essential nature, a tort." . . . "As an actual agreement to contract is not essential, the obligation of a seller in such a case is one imposed by law as distinguished from one voluntarily assumed. It may be called an obligation either on a quasi-contract or quasi-tort, because remedies appropriate to contract and also to tort are applicable." 1 Williston on Sales, 2d Ed. § 197.

As handicrafts have been replaced by mass production with its great markets and transportation facilities, the close relationship between the producer and consumer of a product has been altered. Manufacturing processes, frequently valuable secrets, are ordinarily either inaccessible to or beyond the ken of the general public. The consumer no longer has means or skill enough to investigate for himself the soundness of a product, even when it is not contained in a sealed package, and his erstwhile vigilance has been lulled by the steady efforts of manufacturers to build up confidence by advertising and marketing devices such as trade-marks. Consumers no longer approach products warily but accept them on faith, relying on the reputation of the manufacturer or the trade mark. Manufacturers have sought to justify that faith by increasingly high standards of inspection and a readiness to make good on defective products by way of replacements and refunds. The manufacturer's obligation to the consumer must keep pace with the changing relationship between them; it cannot be escaped because the marketing of a product has become so complicated as to require one or more intermediaries. Certainly there is greater reason to impose liability on the manufacturer than on the retailer who is but a conduit of a product that he is not himself able to test.

The manufacturer's liability should, of course, be defined in terms of the safety of the product in normal and proper use, and should not extend to injuries that cannot be traced to the product as it reached the market.

Rehearing denied; EDMONDS, J., dissenting.

———

1. What was the majority's basis for concluding that the manufacturer should be liable for the injury?

2. What is the difference between res ipsa loquitur and strict products liability? How do the differences between the two (if any) affect the proof a plaintiff must introduce? When would the two doctrines yield different results? Is there any evidence that the manufacturer could have introduced that would have resulted in a finding of nonliability?

Greenman v. Yuba Power Products, Inc.

Supreme Court of California, 1963 (en banc)
377 P.2d 897

TRAYNOR, JUSTICE.

Plaintiff brought this action for damages against the retailer and the manufacturer of a Shopsmith, a combination power tool that could be used as a saw, drill, and wood lathe. He saw a Shopsmith demonstrated by the retailer and studied a brochure prepared by the manufacturer. He decided he wanted a Shopsmith for his home workshop, and his wife bought and gave him one for Christmas in 1955. In 1957 he bought the necessary attachments to use the Shopsmith as a lathe for turning a large piece of wood he wished to make into a chalice. After he had worked on the piece of wood several times without difficulty, it suddenly flew out of the machine and struck him on the forehead, inflicting serious injuries. About ten and a half months later, he gave the retailer and the manufacturer written notice of claimed breaches of warranties and filed a complaint against them alleging such breaches and negligence.

After a trial before a jury, the court ruled that there was no evidence that the retailer was negligent or had breached any express warranty and that the manufacturer was not liable for the breach of any implied warranty. Accordingly, it submitted to the jury only the cause of action alleging breach of implied warranties against the retailer and the causes of action alleging negligence and breach of express warranties against the manufacturer. The jury returned a verdict for the retailer against plaintiff and for plaintiff against the manufacturer in the amount of $65,000. The trial court denied the manufacturer's motion for a new trial and entered judgment on the verdict. The manufacturer and plaintiff appeal. Plaintiff seeks a reversal of the part of the judgment in favor of the retailer, however, only in the event that the part of the judgment against the manufacturer is reversed.

Plaintiff introduced substantial evidence that his injuries were caused by defective design and construction of the Shopsmith. His expert witnesses testified that inadequate set screws were used to hold parts of the machine together so that normal vibration caused the tailstock of the lathe to move away from the piece of wood being turned permitting it to fly out of the lathe. They also testified that there were other more positive ways of fastening the parts of the machine together, the use of which would have prevented the accident. The jury could therefore reasonably have concluded that the manufacturer negligently constructed the Shopsmith. The jury could also reasonably have concluded that statements in the manufacturer's brochure were untrue, that they constituted express warranties,[1] and that plaintiff's injuries were caused by their breach.

---

1. In this respect the trial court limited the jury to a consideration of two statements in the manufacturer's brochure. (1) "WHEN SHOPSMITH IS IN HORIZONTAL POSITION—Rugged construction of frame provides rigid support from end to end. Heavy centerless-ground steel

The manufacturer contends, however, that plaintiff did not give it notice of breach of warranty within a reasonable time and that therefore his cause of action for breach of warranty is barred by section 1769 of the Civil Code. Since it cannot be determined whether the verdict against it was based on the negligence or warranty cause of action or both, the manufacturer concludes that the error in presenting the warranty cause of action to the jury was prejudicial.

Section 1769 of the Civil Code provides: "In the absence of express or implied agreement of the parties, acceptance of the goods by the buyer shall not discharge the seller from liability in damages or other legal remedy for breach of any promise or warranty in the contract to sell or the sale. But, if, after acceptance of the goods, the buyer fails to give notice to the seller of the breach of any promise or warranty within a reasonable time after the buyer knows, or ought to know of such breach, the seller shall not be liable therefor."

Like other provisions of the uniform sales act (Civ. Code, §§ 1721–1800), section 1769 deals with the rights of the parties to a contract of sale or a sale. It does not provide that notice must be given of the breach of a warranty that arises independently of a contract of sale between the parties. Such warranties are not imposed by the sales act, but are the product of common-law decisions that have recognized them in a variety of situations. It is true that in many of these situations the court has invoked the sales act definitions of warranties (Civ. Code, §§ 1732, 1735) in defining the defendant's liability, but it has done so, not because the statutes so required, but because they provided appropriate standards for the court to adopt under the circumstances presented.

The notice requirement of section 1769, however, is not an appropriate one for the court to adopt in actions by injured consumers against manufacturers with whom they have not dealt. "As between the immediate parties to the sale [the notice requirement] is a sound commercial rule, designed to protect the seller against unduly delayed claims for damages. As applied to personal injuries, and notice to a remote seller, it becomes a booby-trap for the unwary. The injured consumer is seldom 'steeped in the business practice which justifies the rule,' [James, *Product Liability*, 34 Texas L. Rev. 44, 192, 197] and at least until he has had legal advice it will not occur to him to give notice to one with whom he has had no dealings." (Prosser, *Strict Liability to the Consumer*, 69 Yale L.J. 1099, 1130, footnotes omitted.). . . . We conclude . . . that even if plaintiff did not give timely notice of breach of warranty to the manufacturer, his cause of action based on the representations contained in the brochure was not barred.

Moreover, to impose strict liability on the manufacturer under the circumstances of this case, it was not necessary for plaintiff to establish an express warranty as defined in section 1732 of the Civil Code. A manufacturer is strictly liable in tort when

---

tubing insures perfect alignment of components." (2) "SHOPSMITH maintains its accuracy because every component has positive locks that hold adjustments through rough or precision work."

an article he places on the market, knowing that it is to be used without inspection for defects, proves to have a defect that causes injury to a human being. Recognized first in the case of unwholesome food products, such liability has now been extended to a variety of other products that create as great or greater hazards if defective.

Although in these cases strict liability has usually been based on the theory of an express or implied warranty running from the manufacturer to the plaintiff, the abandonment of the requirement of a contract between them, the recognition that the liability is not assumed by agreement but imposed by law, and the refusal to permit the manufacturer to define the scope of its own responsibility for defective products make clear that the liability is not one governed by the law of contract warranties but by the law of strict liability in tort. Accordingly, rules defining and governing warranties that were developed to meet the needs of commercial transactions cannot properly be invoked to govern the manufacturer's liability to those injured by their defective products unless those rules also serve the purposes for which such liability is imposed.

We need not recanvass the reasons for imposing strict liability on the manufacturer. They have been fully articulated in the cases cited above. (*See also* 2 Harper and James, Torts, §§ 28.15-28,16, pp. 1569–1574; Prosser, *Strict Liability to the Consumer*, 69 Yale L.J. 1099; *Escola v. Coca Cola Bottling Co.*, 24 Cal. 2d 453, 461, 150 P.2d 436, concurring opinion.) The purpose of such liability is to insure that the costs of injuries resulting from defective products are borne by the manufacturers that put such products on the market rather than by the injured persons who are powerless to protect themselves. Sales warranties serve this purpose fitfully at best. In the present case, for example, plaintiff was able to plead and prove an express warranty only because he read and relied on the representations of the Shopsmith's ruggedness contained in the manufacturer's brochure. Implicit in the machine's presence on the market, however, was a representation that it would safely do the jobs for which it was built. Under these circumstances, it should not be controlling whether plaintiff selected the machine because of the statements in the brochure, or because of the machine's own appearance of excellence that belied the defect lurking beneath the surface, or because he merely assumed that it would safely do the jobs it was built to do. It should not be controlling whether the details of the sales from manufacturer to retailer and from retailer to plaintiff's wife were such that one or more of the implied warranties of the sales act arose. (Civ. Code, § 1735.) "The remedies of injured consumers ought not to be made to depend upon the intricacies of the law of sales." (*Ketterer v. Armour & Co.*, D.C., 200 F. 322, 323.) To establish the manufacturer's liability it was sufficient that plaintiff proved that he was injured while using the Shopsmith in a way it was intended to be used as a result of a defect in design and manufacture of which plaintiff was not aware that made the Shopsmith unsafe for its intended use.

The manufacturer contends that the trial court erred in refusing to give three instructions requested by it. It appears from the record, however, that the substance of two of the requested instructions was adequately covered by the instructions given and that the third instruction was not supported by the evidence.

The judgment is affirmed.

GIBSON, C.J., and SCHAUER, MCCOMB, PETERS, TOBRINER and PEEK, JJ., concur.

———————

1. How does the court in *Greenman* define defect?

2. Whom does the strict liability defined in *Greenman* protect? In other words, who may be a plaintiff?

2. Refining the Doctrine — Defining Defect

The central problem, once the courts had accepted the idea of liability without fault for defective products, was to define defect. Not all dangerous products are defective. A dangerous product is a product that causes injury. A defective product, on the other hand, is one that fails the applicable consumer expectation or risk/utility test. Classifying a product as defective means that the manufacturer will be liable for the injuries caused by that product. In other words, to classify a product as defective is to reach a legal conclusion about who pays for the injuries involved.

RESTATEMENT (SECOND) OF TORTS § 402A

402A. Special Liability of Seller of Product for Physical Harm to User or Consumer.

(1) One who sells any product in a defective condition unreasonably dangerous to the user or consumer or to his property is subject to liability for physical harm thereby caused to the ultimate user or consumer, or to his property, if

(a) the seller is engaged in the business of selling such a product, and

(b) it is expected to and does reach the user or consumer without substantial change in the condition in which it is sold.

(2) The rule stated in Subsection (1) applies although

(a) the seller has exercised all possible care in the preparation and sale of his product, and

(b) the user or consumer has not bought the product from or entered into any contractual relation with the seller.

As quoted in *Ex parte Chevron Chemical Co.*, 720 So. 2d 922, 927 (Ala. 1998).

———————

1. How does Section 402A define defect?

2. Who may be a plaintiff under Section 402A?

3. What if the product could not be made safer? Should this have an impact upon the decision as to whether the product is defective?

4. One strict products liability arena in which the courts tend to be sloppy involves terminology. A dangerous product is a product which has attributes that may cause harm. To say that a product is dangerous is to make a factual statement about that product. A defective product, on the other hand, is a product for the dangers of which the manufacturer will be held responsible. In other words, to rule that a product is defective is to reach a legal conclusion about that product and the implications of its dangers for the manufacturer. Courts often refer to dangers as defects, even though the former is a fact and the latter a legal conclusion.

Initially under Section 402A, courts treated all three types of defect — mismanufacture, design, and failure to warn — in an identical manner. This did not last long, however, and courts began dividing the three types of defect and applying different rules to each one.

Mismanufacture cases are relatively straightforward. In mismanufacture cases, there is something wrong with the individual product that makes it differ from the product line, and that defect causes injury. The plaintiff's case consists of evidence that the product differed from the product line and that the difference caused the injury. Res ipsa loquitur works in these cases; often, the individual product is not itself available, but the plaintiff can prove that it would not have behaved as it did if there had not been something the matter with it. Under a *Phillips* analysis, one can safely say that the manufacturer would not have sold the product in the form in which it was sold had the manufacturer known of the defect.

Design defect cases are more complex than mismanufacture cases, and the stakes are much higher: in a mismanufacture case, the manufacturer will be liable for injury done by the one product unit. In a design defect case, on the other hand, the manufacturer might be liable for the injuries caused by a whole line of products. In addition, while in mismanufacture, the product can be compared to the manufacturer's own standards and specifications to demonstrate the existence of a defect, in a design case, the claim is that those standards and specifications are themselves defective. This has made courts more wary about finding manufacturers liable, with a concomitant increase in care about what the plaintiff must prove. A mismanufactured product by definition fails a risk/utility test. A product with an allegedly defective design might not.

Phillips v. Kimwood Machine Co.

Supreme Court of Oregon, 1974 (en banc)
525 P.2d 1033

Holman, Justice.

Plaintiff was injured while feeding fiberboard into a sanding machine during his employment with Pope and Talbot, a wood products manufacturer. The sanding machine had been purchased by Pope and Talbot from defendant. Plaintiff brought this action on a products liability theory, contending the sanding machine was unreasonably dangerous by virtue of defective design. At the completion of the testimony, defendant's motion for a directed verdict was granted and plaintiff appealed.

As is required in such a situation, the evidence is recounted in a manner most favorable to the plaintiff. The machine in question was a six-headed sander. Each sanding head was a rapidly moving belt which revolved in the direction opposite to that which the pieces of fiberboard moved through the machine. Three of the heads sanded the top of the fiberboard sheet and three sanded the bottom. The top half of the machine could be raised or lowered depending upon the thickness of the fiberboard to be sanded. The bottom half of the machine had powered rollers which moved the fiberboard through the machine as the fiberboard was being sanded. The top half of the machine had pinch rolls, not powered, which, when pressed down on the fiberboard by use of springs, kept the sanding heads from forcefully ejecting it from the machine.

On the day of the accident plaintiff was engaged in feeding the sheets of fiberboard into the sander. Because of the defective operation of a press, a large group of sheets of extra thickness was received for sanding. These sheets could not be inserted into the machine as it was set, so the top half of the sander was adjusted upwards to leave a greater space between the top and bottom halves to accommodate the extra thick fiberboard sheets. During the sanding of the extra thick sheets, a thin sheet of fiberboard, which had become mixed with the lot, was inserted into the machine. The pressure exerted by the pinch rolls in the top half of the machine was insufficient to counteract the pressure which the sanding belts were exerting upon the thin sheet of fiberboard and, as a result, the machine regurgitated the piece of fiberboard back at plaintiff, hitting him in the abdomen and causing him the injuries for which he now seeks compensation.

Plaintiff asserts in his complaint that the machine was defective in its design and unreasonably dangerous because (1) "it . . . could not be operated in the manner and for the purpose for which it was manufactured and sold without throwing back towards the operator panels of material being sanded . . . ," and (2) ". . . it did not . . . contain . . . any guards, catches, shields, barricades or similar devices to protect the operator of said machine from being struck by panels of material thrown back out of the sanding machine. . . ." The two allegations assert substantially the same thing . . . . In effect, they allege the machine was defective and was unreasonably dangerous because there were no safety devices to protect the person feeding the machine from the regurgitation of sheets of fiberboard.

While we do not here attempt to recount all of the testimony presented by plaintiff concerning the defective design of the machine, there was evidence from which the jury could find that at a relatively small expense there could have been built into, or subsequently installed on, the machine a line of metal teeth which would point in the direction that the fiberboard progresses through the machine and which would press lightly against the sheet but which, in case of attempted regurgitation, would be jammed into it, thus stopping its backward motion. The evidence also showed that after the accident such teeth were installed upon the machine for that purpose by Pope and Talbot, whereupon subsequent regurgitations of thin fiberboard sheets were prevented while the efficiency of the machine was maintained. There was also evidence that defendant makes smaller sanders which usually are manually fed and on which there is such a safety device.

It was shown that the machine in question was built for use with an automatic feeder and that the one installed at Pope and Talbot is the only six-headed sander manufactured by defendant which is manually fed. There also was testimony that at the time of the purchase by Pope and Talbot, defendant had automatic feeders for sale but that Pope and Talbot did not purchase or show any interest in such a feeder. Pope and Talbot furnished a feeding device of their own manufacture for the machine which was partially automatic and partially manual but which, the jury could find, at times placed an employee in the way of regurgitated sheets.

There was testimony that at the time defendant's employee inspected the installation of the machine purchased by Pope and Talbot, which inspection was required by their contract, the inspecting employee became aware that the machine was being manually fed. There was no testimony of any warning given by defendant of the danger concerning regurgitated sheets to a person manually feeding the machine. Neither was there any evidence that Pope and Talbot was told that the machine was built for use with a fully automatic feeder and that it was not to be fed manually, nor was the recommendation made to plaintiff's employer that if the machine was to be used without a fully automatic feeder, some sort of safety device should be used for the protection of anyone who was manually feeding the machine. There was evidence that one of Pope and Talbot's representatives was told that the top of the machine should not be raised while sanding was taking place, but there was no evidence of the danger from doing so ever being mentioned.

. . . .

In defense of its judgment based upon a directed verdict, defendant contends there was no proof of a defect in the product, and therefore strict liability should not apply. This court and other courts continue to flounder while attempting to determine how one decides whether a product is "in a defective condition unreasonably dangerous to the user."[1] It has been recognized that unreasonably dangerous defects in products come from two principal sources: (1) mismanufacture and (2) faulty design.[2] Mismanufacture is relatively simple to identify because the item in question is capable of being compared with similar articles made by the same manufacturer. However, whether the mismanufactured article is dangerously defective because of the flaw is sometimes

---

1. 2 Restatement (Second) of Torts § 402A, at 347 (1965).

2. Wade, *On the Nature of Strict Tort Liability for Products*, 44 Miss. L.J. 825, 830 (1973) (including failure to warn as a design defect).

difficult to ascertain because not every such flaw which causes injury makes the article dangerously defective.[3]

The problem with strict liability of products has been one of limitation. No one wants absolute liability where all the article has to do is to cause injury. To impose liability there has to be something about the article which makes it dangerously defective without regard to whether the manufacturer was or was not at fault for such condition. A test for unreasonable danger is therefore vital.

A dangerously defective article would be one which a reasonable person would not put into the stream of commerce *if he had knowledge of its harmful character.* The test, therefore, is whether the seller would be negligent if he sold the article *knowing of the risk involved.* Strict liability imposed what amounts to constructive knowledge of the condition of the product.

On the surface such a test would seem to be different than the test of 2 Restatement (Second) of Torts § 402A, Comment i, of "dangerous to an extent beyond that which would be contemplated by the ordinary consumer who purchases it." This court has used this test in the past. These are not necessarily different standards, however. As stated in Welch v. Outboard Marine Corp. [481 F.2d 252, 254 (5th Cir. 1973)], where the court affirmed an instruction containing both standards:

> "We see no necessary inconsistency between a seller-oriented standard and a user-oriented standard when, as here, each turns on foreseeable risks. They are two sides of the same standard. A product is defective and unreasonably dangerous when a reasonable seller would not sell the product if he knew of the risk involved or if the risks are greater than a reasonable buyer would expect."

To elucidate this point further, we feel that the two standards are the same because a seller acting reasonably would be selling the same product which a reasonable consumer believes he is purchasing. That is to say, a manufacturer who would be negligent in marketing a given product, considering its risks, would necessarily be marketing a product which fell below the reasonable expectations of consumers who purchase it. The foreseeable uses to which a product could be put would be the same in the minds of both the seller and the buyer unless one of the parties was not acting reasonably. The advantage of describing a dangerous defect in the manner of Wade

---

3. The California Supreme Court recognized this problem and attempted to eliminate it by requiring only a defect that causes injury, and not an unreasonably dangerous defect. In *Cronin v. J.B.E. Olson Corp.*, 8 Cal. 3d 121, 104 Cal. Rptr. 433, 501 P.2d 1153 (1972), the court felt that requiring proof of an *unreasonably dangerous defect* would put an additional burden on plaintiff which the court deemed improper. We, however, feel that regardless of whether the term used is "defective," as in *Cronin,* or "defective condition unreasonably dangerous," as in the Restatement, or "dangerously defective," as used here, or "not duly safe," as used by Professor Wade, the same considerations will necessarily be utilized in fixing liability on sellers; and, therefore, the supposedly different standards will come ultimately to the same conclusion. *See* Wade, *Strict Tort Liability of Manufacturers,* 19 Sw. L.J. 5, 14–15 (1965); Wade, *supra* note 2.

and Keeton is that it preserves the use of familiar terms and thought processes with which courts, lawyers, and jurors customarily deal.

While apparently judging the seller's conduct, the test set out above would actually be a characterization of the product by a jury. If the manufacturer was not acting reasonably in selling the product, knowing of the risks involved, then the product would be dangerously defective when sold and the manufacturer would be subject to liability.

In the case of a product which is claimed to be dangerously defective because of misdesign, the process is not so easy as in the case of mismanufacture. All the products made to that design are the same. The question of whether the design is unreasonably dangerous can be determined only by taking into consideration the surrounding circumstances and knowledge at the time the article was sold, and determining therefrom whether a reasonably prudent manufacturer would have so designed and sold the article in question had he known of the risk involved which injured plaintiff. The issue has been raised in some courts concerning whether, in this context, there is any distinction between strict liability and negligence. The evidence which proves the one will almost always, if not always, prove the other. We discussed this matter recently in the case *of Roach v. Kononen*, 99 Or. Adv. Sh. 1092, 525 P.2d 125 (1974), and pointed out that there is a difference between strict liability for misdesign and negligence. We said:

> "However, be all this as it may, it is generally recognized that the basic difference between negligence on the one hand and strict liability for a design defect on the other is that in strict liability we are talking about the condition (dangerousness) of an article which is designed in a particular way, while in negligence we are talking about the reasonableness of the manufacturer's actions in designing and selling the article as he did. The article can have a degree of dangerousness which the law of strict liability will not tolerate even though the actions of the designer were entirely reasonable in view of what he knew at the time he planned and sold the manufactured article. As Professor Wade points out, a way of determining whether the condition of the article is of the requisite degree of dangerousness to be defective (unreasonably dangerous; greater degree of danger than a consumer has a right to expect; not duly safe) is to assume that the manufacturer knew of the product's propensity to injury as it did, and then to ask whether, with such knowledge, something should have been done about the danger before it was sold. In other words, a greater burden is placed on the manufacturer than is the case in negligence because the law assumes he has knowledge of the article's dangerous propensity which he may not reasonably be expected to have, had he been charged with negligence." 99 Or. Adv. Sh. at 1099, 525 P.2d at 129.

To some it may seem that absolute liability has been imposed upon the manufacturer since it might be argued that no manufacturer could reasonably put into the stream of commerce an article which he realized might result in injury to a user. This is not the case, however. The manner of injury may be so fortuitous and the chances of injury occurring so remote that it is reasonable to sell the product despite the danger. In design cases the utility of the article may be so great, and the change of design necessary to alleviate the danger in question may so impair such utility, that it is reasonable to market the product as it is, even though the possibility of injury exists and was realized at the time of the sale. Again, the cost of the change necessary to alleviate the danger in design may be so great that the article would be priced out of the market and no one would buy it even though it was of high utility. Such an article is not dangerously defective despite its having inflicted injury.

In this case defendant contends it was Pope and Talbot's choice to purchase and use the sander without an automatic feeder, even though it was manufactured to be used with one, and, therefore, it was Pope and Talbot's business choice which resulted in plaintiff's injury and not any misdesign by defendant. However, it is recognized that a failure to warn may make a product unreasonably dangerous. Comment j, Section 402A, 2 Restatement (Second) of Torts, has the following to say:

> "In order to prevent the product from being unreasonably dangerous, the seller may be required to give directions or warning, on the container, as to its use. The seller may reasonably assume that those with common allergies, as for example to eggs or strawberries, will be aware of them, and he is not required to warn against them. Where, however, the product contains an ingredient to which a substantial number of the population are allergic, and the ingredient is one whose danger is not generally known, or if known is one which the consumer would reasonably not expect to find in the product, the seller is required to give warning against it, if he had knowledge, or by the application of reasonable, developed human skill and foresight should have knowledge, of the presence of the ingredient and the danger. Likewise in the case of poisonous drugs, or those unduly dangerous for other reasons, warning as to use may be required."

Although the examples cited in the comment do not encompass machinery or such products, it has been recognized that a piece of machinery may or may not be dangerously defective, depending on the directions or warnings that may be given with it.

It is our opinion that the evidence was sufficient for the jury to find that a reasonably prudent manufacturer, knowing that the machine would be fed manually and having the constructive knowledge of its propensity to regurgitate thin sheets when it was set for thick ones, which the courts via strict liability have imposed upon it, would have warned plaintiff's employer either to feed it automatically or to use some safety device, and that, in the absence of such a warning, the machine was dangerously defective. It is therefore unnecessary for us to decide the questions that would arise had adequate warnings been given.

In *Anderson v. Klix Chemical*, 256 Or. 199, 472 P.2d 806 (1970), we came to the conclusion that there was no difference between negligence and strict liability for a product that was unreasonably dangerous because of failure to warn of certain characteristics. We have now come to the conclusion that we were in error. The reason we believe we were in error parallels the rationale that was expressed in the previously quoted material from *Roach v. Kononen, supra,* where we discussed the difference between strict liability for misdesign and negligence. In a strict liability case we are talking about the condition (dangerousness) of an article which is sold without any warning, while in negligence we are talking about the reasonableness of the manufacturer's actions in selling the article without a warning. The article can have a degree of dangerousness because of a lack of warning which the law of strict liability will not tolerate even though the actions of the seller were entirely reasonable in selling the article without a warning considering what he knew or should have known at the time he sold it. A way to determine the dangerousness of the article, as distinguished from the seller's culpability, is to assume the seller knew of the product's propensity to injure as it did, and then to ask whether, with such knowledge, he would have been negligent in selling it without a warning.

It is apparent that the language being used in the discussion of the above problems is largely that which is also used in *negligence* cases, i.e., "unreasonably dangerous," "have reasonably anticipated," "reasonably prudent manufacturer," etc. It is necessary to remember that whether the doctrine of negligence, ultrahazardousness, or strict liability is being used to impose liability, the same process is going on in each instance, i.e., weighing the utility of the article against the risk of its use. Therefore, the same language and concepts of reasonableness are used by courts for the determination of unreasonable danger in products liability cases.

. . . .

The case is reversed and remanded for a new trial.

---

1. What is the *Phillips* definition of defect?

2. Under the *Phillips* test, what dangerous products are nondefective?

3. What if the manufacturer does not know and could not have discovered the danger in the product prior to marketing it? To what extent is actual knowledge of the danger a factor in *Phillips*?

4. *Phillips'* "reasonable manufacturer" risk-utility analysis was overturned by statute in favor of a consumer expectation approach when the Oregon legislature codified product liability law in 1979. See ORS 30.920; *McCathern v. Toyota Motor Corp.,* 23P.3d 320 (Ore. 2001).

Barker v. Lull Engineering Co.

Supreme Court of California, 1978

573 P.2d 443

TOBRINER, ACTING CHIEF JUSTICE.

In August 1970, plaintiff Ray Barker was injured at a construction site at the University of California at Santa Cruz while operating a high-lift loader manufactured by defendant Lull Engineering Co. and leased to plaintiff's employer by defendant George M. Philpott Co., Inc. Claiming that his injuries were proximately caused, inter alia, by the alleged defective design of the loader, Barker instituted the present tort action seeking to recover damages for his injuries. The jury returned a verdict in favor of defendants, and plaintiff appeals from the judgment entered upon that verdict, contending primarily that in view of this court's decision in *Cronin v. J.B.E. Olson Corp.* (1972) 8 Cal. 3d 121, 104 Cal. Rptr. 433, 501 P.2d 1153, the trial court erred in instructing the jury "that strict liability for a defect in design of a product is based on a finding that the product was unreasonably dangerous for its intended use. . . ."

As we explain, we agree with plaintiff's objection to the challenged instruction and conclude that the judgment must be reversed. . . .

In addition, we take this opportunity to attempt to alleviate some confusion that our *Cronin* decision has apparently engendered in the lower courts. Although in *Cronin* we rejected the Restatement's "unreasonably dangerous" gloss on the defectiveness concept as potentially confusing and unduly restrictive, we shall explain that our *Cronin* decision did not dictate that the term "defect" be left undefined in jury instructions given in all product liability cases.

As *Cronin* acknowledged, in the past decade and a half California courts have frequently recognized that the defectiveness concept defies a simple, uniform definition applicable to all sectors of the diverse product liability domain. Although in many instances as when one machine in a million contains a cracked or broken part the meaning of the term "defect" will require little or no elaboration, in other instances, as when a product is claimed to be defective because of an unsafe design or an inadequate warning, the contours of the defect concept may not be self-evident. In such a case a trial judge may find it necessary to explain more fully to the jury the legal meaning of "defect" or "defective." We shall explain that *Cronin* in no way precluded such elucidation of the defect concept, but rather contemplated that, in typical common law fashion, the accumulating body of product liability authorities would give guidance for the formulation of a definition.

As numerous recent judicial decisions and academic commentaries have recognized, the formulation of a satisfactory definition of "design defect" has proven a formidable task; trial judges have repeatedly confronted difficulties in attempting to devise accurate and helpful instructions in design defect cases. . . .

As we explain in more detail below, we have concluded from this review that a product is defective in design either (1) if the product has failed to perform as safely as an ordinary consumer would expect when used in an intended or reasonably foreseeable manner, or (2) if, in light of the relevant factors discussed below, the benefits of the challenged design do not outweigh the risk of danger inherent in such design. In addition, we explain how the burden of proof with respect to the latter "risk-benefit" standard should be allocated.

This dual standard for design defect assures an injured plaintiff protection from products that either fall below ordinary consumer expectations as to safety, or that, on balance, are not as safely designed as they should be. At the same time, the standard permits a manufacturer who has marketed a product which satisfies ordinary consumer expectations to demonstrate the relative complexity of design decisions and the trade-offs that are frequently required in the adoption of alternative designs. Finally, this test reflects our continued adherence to the principle that, in a product liability action, the trier of fact must focus on the product, not on the manufacturer's conduct, and that the plaintiff need not prove that the manufacturer acted unreasonably or negligently in order to prevail in such an action.

1. *The facts of the present case*

Plaintiff Barker sustained serious injuries as a result of an accident which occurred while he was operating a Lull High-Lift Loader at a construction site. The loader, manufactured in 1967, is a piece of heavy construction equipment designed to lift loads of up to 5,000 pounds to a maximum height of 32 feet. The loader is 23 feet long, 8 feet wide and weighs 17,050 pounds; it sits on four large rubber tires which are about the height of a person's chest, and is equipped with four-wheel drive, an automatic transmission with no park position and a hand brake. Loads are lifted by forks similar to the forks of a forklift.

The loader is designed so that the load can be kept level even when the loader is being operated on sloping terrain. The leveling of the load is controlled by a lever located near the steering column, and positioned between the operator's legs. The lever is equipped with a manual lock that can be engaged to prevent accidental slipping of the load level during lifting.

The loader was not equipped with seat belts or a roll bar. A wire and pipe cage over the driver's seat afforded the driver some protection from falling objects. The cab of the loader was located at least nine feet behind the lifting forks.

On the day of the accident the regular operator of the loader, Bill Dalton, did not report for work, and plaintiff, who had received only limited instruction on the operation of the loader from Dalton and who had operated the loader on only a few occasions, was assigned to run the loader in Dalton's place. The accident occurred while plaintiff was attempting to lift a load of lumber to a height of approximately 18 to 20 feet and to place the load on the second story of a building under construction. The lift was a particularly difficult one because the terrain on which the loader rested sloped sharply in several directions.

Witnesses testified that plaintiff approached the structure with the loader, leveled the forks to compensate for the sloping ground and lifted the load to a height variously estimated between 10 and 18 feet. During the course of the lift plaintiff felt some vibration, and, when it appeared to several co-workers that the load was beginning to tip, the workers shouted to plaintiff to jump from the loader. Plaintiff heeded these warnings and leaped from the loader, but while scrambling away he was struck by a piece of falling lumber and suffered serious injury.

Although the above facts were generally not in dispute, the parties differed markedly in identifying the responsible causes for the accident. Plaintiff contended, inter alia, that the accident was attributable to one or more design defects of the loader. Defendant, in turn, denied that the loader was defective in any respect, and claimed that the accident resulted either from plaintiff's lack of skill or from his misuse of its product. We briefly review the conflicting evidence.

Plaintiff's principal expert witness initially testified that by reason of its relatively narrow base the loader was unstable and had a tendency to roll over when lifting loads to considerable heights; the witness surmised that this instability caused the load to tip in the instant case. The expert declared that to compensate for its instability, the loader should have been equipped with "outriggers," mechanical arms extending out from the sides of the machine, two in front and two in back, each of which could be operated independently and placed on the ground to lend stability to the loader. Evidence at trial revealed that cranes and some high lift loader models are either regularly equipped with outriggers or offer outriggers as optional equipment. Plaintiff's expert testified that the availability of outriggers would probably have averted the present accident.

The expert additionally testified that the loader was defective in that it was not equipped with a roll bar or seat belts. He stated that such safety devices were essential to protect the operator in the event that the machine rolled over. Plaintiff theorized that the lack of such safety equipment was a proximate cause of his injuries because in the absence of such devices he had no reasonable choice but to leap from the loader as it began to tip. If a seat belt and roll bar had been provided, plaintiff argued, he could have remained in the loader and would not have been struck by the falling lumber.

In addition, plaintiff's witnesses suggested that the accident may have been caused by the defective design of the loader's leveling mechanism. Several witnesses testified that both the absence of an automatic locking device on the leveling lever, and the placement of the leveling lever in a position in which it was extremely vulnerable to inadvertent bumping by the operator of the loader in the course of a lift, were defects which may have produced the accident and injuries in question. Finally, plaintiff's experts testified that the absence of a "park" position on the loader's transmission, that could have been utilized to avoid the possibility of the loader's movement during a lift, constituted a further defect in design which may have caused the accident.

Defendants, in response, presented evidence which attempted to refute plaintiff's claims that the loader was defective or that the loader's condition was the cause of the accident. Defendants' experts testified that the loader was not unstable when utilized on the terrain for which it was intended, and that if the accident did occur because of the tipping of the loader it was only because plaintiff had misused the equipment by operating it on steep terrain for which the loader was unsuited. In answer to the claim that the high-lift loader was defective because of a lack of outriggers, defendants' expert testified that outriggers were not necessary when the loader was used for its intended purpose and that no competitive loaders with similar height lifting capacity were equipped with outriggers; the expert conceded, however, that a competitor did offer outriggers as optional equipment on a high-lift loader which was capable of lifting loads to 40, as compared to 32, feet. The expert also testified that the addition of outriggers would simply have given the loader the functional capability of a crane, which was designed for use on all terrain, and that an experienced user of a high-lift loader should recognize that such a loader was not intended as a substitute for a crane.

The defense experts further testified that a roll bar was unnecessary because in view of the bulk of the loader it would not roll completely over. The witnesses also maintained that seat belts would have increased the danger of the loader by impairing the operator's ability to leave the vehicle quickly in case of an emergency. With respect to the claimed defects of the leveling device, the defense experts testified that the positioning of the lever was the safest and most convenient for the operator and that the manual lock on the leveling device provided completely adequate protection. Finally, defendants asserted that the absence of a "park" position on the transmission should not be considered a defect because none of the transmissions that were manufactured for this type of vehicle included a park position.

In addition to disputing plaintiff's contention as to the defectiveness of the loader, defendants' witnesses testified that the accident probably was caused by the plaintiff's own inexperience and consequent dangerous actions. Defendants maintained that if the lumber had begun to fall during the lift it did so only because plaintiff had failed to lock the leveling device prior to the lift. Defendants alternatively suggested that although the workers thought they saw the lumber begin to tip during the lift, this tipping was actually only the plaintiff's leveling of the load during the lift. Defendants hypothesized that the lumber actually fell off the loader only after plaintiff had leaped from the machine and that plaintiff was responsible for his own injuries because he had failed to set the hand brake, thereby permitting the loader to roll backwards.

After considering the sharply conflicting testimony reviewed above, the jury by a 10 to 2 vote returned a general verdict in favor of defendants. Plaintiff appeals from the judgment entered upon that verdict.

2. The trial court erred in instructing the jurors that "strict liability for a defect in design . . . is based on a finding that the product was unreasonably dangerous for its intended use."

Plaintiff principally contends that the trial court committed prejudicial error in instructing the jury "that strict liability for a defect in design of a product is based on a finding that the product was unreasonably dangerous for its intended use. . . ."

Plaintiff maintains that this instruction conflicts directly with this court's decision in *Cronin*, decided subsequently to the instant trial, and mandates a reversal of the judgment. Defendants argue, in response, that our *Cronin* decision should not be applied to product liability actions which involve "design defects" as distinguished from "manufacturing defects."

The plaintiff in *Cronin*, a driver of a bread delivery truck, was seriously injured when, during an accident, a metal hasp which held the truck's bread trays in place broke, permitting the trays to slide forward and propel plaintiff through the truck's windshield. Plaintiff brought a strict liability action against the seller, contending that his injuries were proximately caused by the defective condition of the truck. Evidence at trial established that the metal hasp broke during the accident "because it was extremely porous and had a significantly lower tolerance to force than a non-flawed aluminum hasp would have had" (8 Cal. 3d at p. 124, 104 Cal. Rptr. at p. 436, 501 P.2d at p. 1156), and, on the basis of this evidence, the jury returned a verdict in favor of plaintiff.

On appeal, defendant in *Cronin* argued that the trial court had erred "by submitting a definition of strict liability which failed to include, as defendant requested, the element that the defect found in the product be 'unreasonably dangerous.'" (8 Cal. 3d at pp. 127–128, 104 Cal. Rptr. at p. 438, 501 P.2d at p. 1158 (fns. omitted).) . . . [T]he defendant in *Cronin* maintained that a product's "unreasonable dangerousness" was an essential element that a plaintiff must establish in any product liability action.

After undertaking a thorough review of the origins and development of both California product liability doctrine and the Restatement's "unreasonably dangerous" criterion, we rejected the defendant's contention, concluding "that to require an injured plaintiff to prove not only that the product contained a defect but also that such defect made the product unreasonably dangerous to the user or consumer would place a considerably greater burden upon him than that articulated in *Greenman* [*v. Yuba Power Products, Inc.* (1963), 59 Cal. 2d 57, 27 Cal. Rptr. 697, 377 P.2d 897, California's seminal product liability decision]. . . . We are not persuaded to the contrary by the formulation of section 402A which inserts the factor of an 'unreasonably dangerous' condition into the equation of products liability." (8 Cal. 3d pp. 134–135, 104 Cal. Rptr. at p. 443, 501 P.2d at p. 1163.)

Plaintiff contends that the clear import of this language in *Cronin* is that the "unreasonably dangerous" terminology of the Restatement should not be utilized in defining defect in product liability actions, and that the trial court consequently erred in submitting an instruction which defined a design defect by reference to the "unreasonably dangerous" standard.

In attempting to escape the apparent force of *Cronin's* explicit language, defendants observe that the flawed hasp which rendered the truck defective in *Cronin* represented a manufacturing defect rather than a design defect, and they argue that *Cronin's* disapproval of the Restatement's "unreasonably dangerous" standard should be limited to the manufacturing defect context. . . .

. . . [D]efendants overlook the fact that our objection to the "unreasonably dangerous" terminology in *Cronin* . . . was based, more fundamentally, on a substantive determination that the Restatement's "unreasonably dangerous" formulation represented an undue restriction on the application of strict liability principles.

As we noted in *Cronin*, the Restatement draftsmen adopted the "unreasonably dangerous" language primarily as a means of confining the application of strict tort liability to an article which is "dangerous to an extent beyond that which would be contemplated by the ordinary consumer who purchases it, with the ordinary knowledge common to the community as to its characteristics." (Rest. 2d Torts, § 402A, com. i.) In *Cronin*, however, we flatly rejected the suggestion that recovery in a products liability action should be permitted *only* if a product is more dangerous than contemplated by the average consumer, refusing to permit the low esteem in which the public might hold a dangerous product to diminish the manufacturer's responsibility for injuries caused by that product. As we pointedly noted in *Cronin*, even if the "ordinary consumer" may have contemplated that Shopsmith lathes posed a risk of loosening their grip and letting a piece of wood strike the operator, "another Greenman" should not be denied recovery. (8 Cal. 3d at p. 133, 104 Cal. Rptr. 433, 501 P.2d 1153.) . . .

Accordingly, contrary to defendants' contention, the reasoning of *Cronin* does not dictate that decision be confined to the manufacturing defect context. Indeed, in *Cronin* itself we expressly stated that our holding applied to design defects as well as to manufacturing defects (8 Cal. 3d at pp. 134–135, 104 Cal. Rptr. 433, 501 P.2d 1153), and in *Henderson v. Harnischfeger Corp.* (1974) 12 Cal. 3d 663, 670, 117 Cal. Rptr. 1, 527 P.2d 353, we subsequently confirmed the impropriety of instructing a jury in the language of the "unreasonably dangerous" standard in a design defect case. (*See also Foglio v. Western Auto Supply* (1976) 56 Cal. App. 3d 470, 475, 128 Cal.

Rptr. 545.)[8] Consequently, we conclude that the design defect instruction given in the instant case was erroneous.[9]

3. *A trial court may properly formulate instructions to elucidate the "defect" concept in varying circumstances. In particular, in design defect cases, a court may properly instruct a jury that a product is defective in design if (1) the plaintiff proves that the product failed to perform as safely as an ordinary consumer would expect when used in an intended or reasonably foreseeable manner, or (2) the plaintiff proves that the product's design proximately caused injury and the defendant fails to prove, in light of the relevant factors, that on balance the benefits of the challenged design outweigh the risk of danger inherent in such design.*

Defendants contend, however, that if *Cronin* is interpreted as precluding the use of the "unreasonably dangerous" language in defining a design defect, the jury in all such cases will inevitably be left without any guidance whatsoever in determining whether a product is defective in design or not. Amicus California Trial Lawyer Association (CTLA) on behalf of the plaintiff responds by suggesting that the precise intent of our *Cronin* decision was to preclude a trial court from formulating any definition of "defect" in a product liability case, thus always leaving the definition of defect, as well as the application of such definition, to the jury. As we explain, neither of these contentions represents an accurate portrayal of the intent or effect of our *Cronin* decision.

In *Cronin*, we reaffirmed the basic formulation of strict tort liability doctrine set forth in *Greenman:* "A manufacturer is strictly liable in tort when an article he places on the market, knowing that it is to be used without inspection for defects, proves to have a defect that causes injury to a human being. . . ." We held in *Cronin* that a plaintiff satisfies his burden of proof under *Greenman*, in both a "manufacturing defect" and "design defect" context, when he proves the existence of a "defect" and that such defect was a proximate cause of his injuries. In reaching this conclusion, however, *Cronin* did not purport to hold that the term "defect" must remain undefined in all

---

8. One commentator has observed that, in addition to the deficiencies in the "unreasonably dangerous" terminology noted in *Cronin*, the Restatement's language is potentially misleading because "[i]t may suggest an idea like ultrahazardous, or abnormally dangerous, and thus give rise to the impression that the plaintiff must prove that the product was unusually or extremely dangerous." (Wade, *On the Nature of Strict Tort Liability for Products* (1973) 44 Miss. L.J. 825, 832.) We agree with this criticism and believe it constitutes a further reason for refraining from utilizing the "unreasonably dangerous" terminology in defining a defective product.

9. Indeed, the challenged instruction . . . was additionally erroneous because it suggested that in evaluating defectiveness, only the "intended use" of the product is relevant, rather than the product's "reasonably foreseeable use." In *Cronin*, we specifically held that the adequacy of a product must be determined in light of its reasonably foreseeable use, declaring that "[t]he design and manufacture of products should not be carried out in an industrial vacuum but with recognition of the realities of their everyday use." (8 Cal. 3d at p. 126, 104 Cal. Rptr. at p. 437, 501 P.2d at p. 1157.) Because, in the instant case, the jury may have concluded that the use of the loader by a relatively inexperienced worker was not an "intended use" of the loader, but was a "reasonably foreseeable use," this aspect of the instruction may well have prejudiced the plaintiff.

contexts, and did not preclude a trial court from framing a definition of defect, appropriate to the circumstances of a particular case, to guide the jury as to the standard to be applied in determining whether a product is defective or not.

As this court has recognized on numerous occasions, the term defect as utilized in the strict liability context is neither self-defining nor susceptible to a single definition applicable in all contexts. . . .

Resort to the numerous product liability precedents in California demonstrates that the defect or defectiveness concept has embraced a great variety of injury-producing deficiencies, ranging from products that cause injury because they deviate from the manufacturer's intended result . . . to products which, though "perfectly" manufactured, are unsafe because of the absence of a safety device . . . and including products that are dangerous because they lack adequate warnings or instructions . . . .

Commentators have pointed out that in view of the diversity of product deficiencies to which the defect rubric has been applied, an instruction which requires a plaintiff to prove the existence of a product defect, but which fails to elaborate on the meaning of defect in a particular context, may in some situations prove more misleading than helpful. As Professor Wade has written: "[The] natural application [of the term 'defective'] would be limited to the situation in which something went wrong in the manufacturing process, so that the article was defective in the sense that the manufacturer had not intended it to be in that condition. To apply [the term 'defective'] also to the case in which a warning is not attached to the chattel or the design turns out to be a bad one or the product is likely to be injurious in its normal condition . . . [and] [t]o use it without defining it to the jury is almost to ensure that they will be misled." (Wade, *On the Nature of Strict Tort Liability for Products, supra,* 44 Miss. L.J. 825, 831–832 (fns. omitted)).

Our decision in *Cronin* did not mandate such confusion. . . .

In general, a manufacturing or production defect is readily identifiable because a defective product is one that differs from the manufacturer's intended result or from other ostensibly identical units of the same product line. . . . A design defect, by contrast, cannot be identified simply by comparing the injury-producing product with the manufacturer's plans or with other units of the same product line, since by definition the plans and all such units will reflect the same design. Rather than applying any sort of deviation-from-the-norm test in determining whether a product is defective in design for strict liability purposes, our cases have employed two alternative criteria in ascertaining, in Justice Traynor's words, whether there is something "wrong, if not in the manufacturer's manner of production, at least in his product." (Traynor, *The Ways and Meanings of Defective Products and Strict Liability, supra,* 32 Tenn. L. Rev. 363, 366.)

First, our cases establish that a product may be found defective in design if the plaintiff demonstrates that the product failed to perform as safely as an ordinary consumer would expect when used in an intended or reasonably foreseeable manner. This initial standard, somewhat analogous to the Uniform Commercial Code's warranty of fitness and merchantability (Cal. U. Com. Code, § 2314), reflects the warranty heritage upon which California product liability doctrine in part rests. . . . When a product fails to satisfy such ordinary consumer expectations as to safety in its intended or reasonably foreseeable operation, a manufacturer is strictly liable for resulting injuries. Under this standard, an injured plaintiff will frequently be able to demonstrate the defectiveness of a product by resort to circumstantial evidence, even when the accident itself precludes identification of the specific defect at fault.

As Professor Wade has pointed out, however, the expectations of the ordinary consumer cannot be viewed as the exclusive yardstick for evaluating design defectiveness because "[i]n many situations . . . the consumer would not know what to expect, because he would have no idea how safe the product could be made." (Wade, *On the Nature of Strict Tort Liability for Products, supra*, 44 Miss. L.J. 825, 829.) Numerous California decisions have implicitly recognized this fact and have made clear, through varying linguistic formulations, that a product may be found defective in design, even if it satisfies ordinary consumer expectations, if through hindsight the jury determines that the product's design embodies "excessive preventable danger," or, in other words, if the jury finds that the risk of danger inherent in the challenged design outweighs the benefits of such design.[10]

A review of past cases indicates that in evaluating the adequacy of a product's design pursuant to this latter standard, a jury may consider, among other relevant factors, the gravity of the danger posed by the challenged design, the likelihood that such danger would occur, the mechanical feasibility of a safer alternative design, the financial cost of an improved design, and the adverse consequences to the product and to the consumer that would result from an alternative design.

Although our cases have thus recognized a variety of considerations that may be relevant to the determination of the adequacy of a product's design, past authorities have generally not devoted much attention to the appropriate allocation of the burden of proof with respect to these matters. The allocation of such burden is particularly significant in this context inasmuch as this court's product liability decisions, from *Greenman* to *Cronin*, have repeatedly emphasized that one of the principal purposes behind the strict product liability doctrine is to relieve an injured plaintiff of many of the onerous evidentiary burdens inherent in a negligence cause of action. Because most of the evidentiary matters which may be relevant to the determination of the adequacy of a product's design under the "risk-benefit" standard—e.g., the feasibility and cost of alternative designs—are similar to issues typically presented in a negligent design case and involve technical matters peculiarly within the knowledge of the

---

10. In the instant case we have no occasion to determine whether a product which entails a substantial risk of harm may be found defective even if no safer alternative design is feasible. As we noted in *Jiminez v. Sears, Roebuck & Co., supra*, 4 Cal. 3d 379, 383, 93 Cal. Rptr. 769, 772, 482 P.2d 681, 684, Justice Traynor has "suggested that liability might be imposed as to products whose norm is danger." (Citing Traynor, *The Ways and Meaning of Defective Products and Strict Liability, supra*, 32 Tenn. L. Rev. 363, 367 *et seq.*).

manufacturer, we conclude that once the plaintiff makes a prima facie showing that the injury was proximately caused by the product's design, the burden should appropriately shift to the defendant to prove, in light of the relevant factors, that the product is not defective. Moreover, inasmuch as this conclusion flows from our determination that the fundamental public policies embraced in *Greenman* dictate that a manufacturer who seeks to escape liability for an injury proximately caused by its product's design on a risk-benefit theory should bear the burden of persuading the trier of fact that its product should not be judged defective, the defendant's burden is one affecting the burden of proof, rather than simply the burden of producing evidence.

Thus, to reiterate, a product may be found defective in design, so as to subject a manufacturer to strict liability for resulting injuries, under either of two alternative tests. First, a product may be found defective in design if the plaintiff establishes that the product failed to perform as safely as an ordinary consumer would expect when used in an intended or reasonably foreseeable manner. Second, a product may alternatively be found defective in design if the plaintiff demonstrates that the product's design proximately caused his injury and the defendant fails to establish, in light of the relevant factors, that, on balance, the benefits of the challenged design outweigh the risk of danger inherent in such design.

. . . [W]e believe that the test for defective design set out above is appropriate in light of the rationale and limits of the strict liability doctrine, for it subjects a manufacturer to liability whenever there is something "wrong" with its product's design — either because the product fails to meet ordinary consumer expectations as to safety or because, on balance, the design is not as safe as it should be — while stopping short of making the manufacturer an insurer for all injuries which may result from the use of its product. This test, moreover, explicitly focuses the trier of fact's attention on the adequacy of the product itself, rather than on the manufacturer's conduct, and places the burden on the manufacturer, rather than the plaintiff, to establish that because of the complexity of, and trade-offs implicit in, the design process, an injury-producing product should nevertheless not be found defective. . . .

[P]ast design defect decisions demonstrate that, as a practical matter, in many instances it is simply impossible to eliminate the balancing or weighing of competing considerations in determining whether a product is defectively designed or not. . . .

In similar fashion, weighing the extent of the risks and the advantages posed by alternative designs is inevitable in many design defect cases. . . . Inasmuch as the weighing of competing considerations is implicit in many design defect determinations, an instruction which appears to preclude such a weighing process under all circumstances may mislead the jury.

Finally, contrary to the suggestion of amicus CTLA, an instruction which advises the jury that it may evaluate the adequacy of a product's design by weighing the benefits of the challenged design against the risk of danger inherent in such design is not simply the equivalent of an instruction which requires the jury to determine whether the manufacturer was negligent in designing the product. It is true, of course, that in many cases proof that a product is defective in design may also demonstrate that the manufacturer was negligent in choosing such a design. As we have indicated, however, in a strict liability case, as contrasted with a negligent design action, the jury's focus is properly directed to the condition of the product itself, and not to the reasonableness of the manufacturer's conduct.

Thus, the fact that the manufacturer took reasonable precautions in an attempt to design a safe product or otherwise acted as a reasonably prudent manufacturer would have under the circumstances, while perhaps absolving the manufacturer of liability under a negligence theory, will not preclude the imposition of liability under strict liability principles if, upon hindsight, the trier of fact concludes that the product's design is unsafe to consumers, users, or bystanders. *(See Foglio v. Western Auto Supply, supra*, 56 Cal. App. 3d 470, 477, 128 Cal. Rptr. 545.)

4. *Conclusion*

The technological revolution has created a society that contains dangers to the individual never before contemplated. The individual must face the threat to life and limb not only from the car on the street or highway but from a massive array of hazardous mechanisms and products. The radical change from a comparatively safe, largely agricultural, society to this industrial unsafe one has been reflected in the decisions that formerly tied liability to the fault of a tortfeasor but now are more concerned with the safety of the individual who suffers the loss. As Dean Keeton has written, "The change in the substantive law as regards the liability of makers of products and other sellers in the marketing chain has been from fault to defect. The plaintiff is no longer required to impugn the maker, but he is required to impugn the product." (Keeton, *Product Liability and the Meaning of Defect* (1973) 5 St. Mary's L.J. 30, 33.)

If a jury in determining liability for a defect in design is instructed only that it should decide whether or not there is "a defective design," it may reach to the extreme conclusion that the plaintiff, having suffered injury, should without further showing, recover; on the other hand, it may go to the opposite extreme and conclude that because the product matches the intended design the plaintiff, under no conceivable circumstance, could recover. The submitted definition eschews both extremes and attempts a balanced approach.

We hold that a trial judge may properly instruct the jury that a product is defective in design (1) if the plaintiff demonstrates that the product failed to perform as safely as an ordinary consumer would expect when used in an intended or reasonably foreseeable manner, or (2) if the plaintiff proves that the product's design proximately caused his injury and the defendant fails to prove, in light of the relevant factors discussed above, that on balance the benefits of the challenged design outweigh the risk of danger inherent in such design.

Because the jury may have interpreted the erroneous instruction given in the instant case as requiring plaintiff to prove that the high-lift loader was ultrahazardous or more dangerous than the average consumer contemplated, and because the instruction additionally misinformed the jury that the defectiveness of the product must be evaluated in light of the product's "intended use" rather than its "reasonably foreseeable use" (*see* fn. 9, *ante*), we cannot find that the error was harmless on the facts of this case. In light of this conclusion, we need not address plaintiff's additional claims of error, for such issues may not arise on retrial.

The judgment in favor of defendants is reversed.

MOSK, CLARK, RICHARDSON, WRIGHT (Retired Chief Justice of California assigned by the Acting Chairperson of the Judicial Council), and SULLIVAN (Retired Associate Justice of the Supreme Court sitting under assignment by the Chairperson of the Judicial Council), JJ., concur.

---

1. How does the *Barker* court define defect? What kinds of dangerous products will *not* subject their manufacturer to strict liability under *Barker*? What role, if any, does manufacturer knowledge of the danger play in *Barker* and *Cronin*?

2. The *Barker* court deals with an additional question that has caused much court and commentator ink to be spilled: the question of to what kinds of uses strict product liability will apply. What does Section 402A say about this subject? *Barker*? When will consumer misuse constitute a defense in a strict products liability action? Or is an absence of misuse part of the plaintiff's case?

---

3. The Third Restatement

In 1998, the American Law Institute promulgated the Third Restatement of Torts: Product Liability. The Third Restatement called for substantial change in product liability standards. While it retained strict liability for products with manufacturing defects, it changed the standards for proving product defects in both design and warning settings. For defects in design, Section 2(b) of the Third Restatement provides:

> A product . . . (b) is defective in design when the foreseeable risks of harm posed by the product could have been reduced or avoided by the adoption of a reasonable alternative design by the seller or other distributor, or a predecessor in the commercial chain of distribution, and the omission of the alternative design renders the product not reasonably safe[.]

How does this standard change the definition and proof of defect in product design cases?

In light of the substantial differences between the Third Restatement and Section 402A, courts have been called upon to decide which of these alternative standards to follow in both design and warning cases. In many instances, "adoption" of the

Third Restatement necessarily entails repudiation of several decades of decisional law that had accumulated through courts' attempts to interpret and apply Section 402A. Several jurisdictions have gravitated toward the Third Restatement, while others have elected to continue to follow Section 402A. The following case illustrates some of the challenges involved in deciding between these competing approaches.

Tincher v. Omega Flex, Inc.*
Supreme Court of Pennsylvania, 2014
104 A.3d 328

CASTILLE, CHIEF JUSTICE:

Omega Flex, Inc., appeals the decision of the Superior Court to affirm the judgment on the verdict entered in favor of [plaintiffs]. We reverse the Superior Court decision in part, upon reasoning different from that articulated by the courts below, and we remand to the trial court for further action consistent with the principles elucidated in this Opinion. We hold that:

1. This Court's decision in *Azzarello v. Black Brothers Company*, 391 A.2d 1020 (Pa. 1978) is hereby overruled.

2. [A] plaintiff pursuing a cause upon a theory of strict liability in tort must prove that the product is in a "defective condition." The plaintiff may prove defective condition by showing either that (1) the danger is unknowable and unacceptable to the average or ordinary consumer, or that (2) a reasonable person would conclude that the probability and seriousness of harm caused by the product outweigh the burden or costs of taking precautions. The burden of production and persuasion is by a preponderance of the evidence.

3. Whether a product is in a defective condition is a question of fact ordinarily submitted for determination to the finder of fact; the question is removed from the jury's consideration only where it is clear that reasonable minds could not differ on the issue. Thus, the trial court is relegated to its traditional role of determining issues of law, *e.g.*, on dispositive motions, and articulating the law for the jury, premised upon the governing legal theory, the facts adduced at trial and relevant advocacy by the parties.

4. To the extent relevant here, we decline to adopt the Restatement (Third) of Torts: Products Liability §§ 1 *et seq.*, albeit appreciation of certain principles contained in that Restatement has certainly informed our consideration of the proper approach to strict liability in Pennsylvania in the post-*Azzarello* paradigm.

I. Background

Around 2:30 a.m. on June 20, 2007, neighbors reported a fire that had erupted at the home of the Tinchers in Downingtown, Pennsylvania. The residence was the

---

* Extensive editing has been required due to the length of this scholarly and comprehensive opinion. Ellipses showing omissions have not been included.

central unit of a two-story triplex built in 1998–99, and purchased by the Tinchers in 2005. The fire was eventually extinguished and no persons were harmed. Subsequently, investigators concluded that a lightning strike near the Tinchers' home caused a small puncture in the corrugated stainless steel tubing ("CSST") transporting natural gas to a fireplace located on the first floor of the residence. The CSST installed in the Tinchers' home was manufactured and sold by Omega Flex as part of a gas transportation system marketed as the TracPipe System. The heat attending the melting of the CSST caused by the lightning strike ignited the natural gas and fueled a fire estimated to have burned for over an hour. The fire caused significant damage to the Tinchers' home and belongings.

In January 2008, the Tinchers filed a complaint against Omega Flex. The Tinchers asserted claims premised upon theories of strict liability, negligence, and breach of warranty.

In relevant part, the Tinchers' complaint relies upon the theory of strict liability articulated in Section 402A of the Second Restatement of Torts, but as followed and construed in Pennsylvania. The Tinchers alleged that Omega Flex is liable for damages to their home caused by the placement on the market and sale of the TracPipe System. According to the Tinchers, the CSST incorporated into the TracPipe System is defective, and unreasonably dangerous to intended users, because its walls are too thin to withstand the effects of lightning. Omega Flex answered the complaint denying the Tinchers' allegations.

In anticipation of trial, Omega Flex filed a motion in limine requesting the application of Sections 1 and 2 of the Third Restatement of Torts to the Tinchers' strict liability claim. Omega Flex also proposed jury instructions and findings of fact consistent with the provisions of the Third Restatement. The Tinchers opposed Omega Flex's motion in limine and offered proposed jury instructions and findings of fact consistent with the Second Restatement and *Azzarello, supra*. [The trial court did not rule on these motions.]

The parties proceeded to trial before a jury. The parties generally agreed that lightning had caused the fire, although they disagreed as to the sequence of events or the cause of ignition in the area of the fireplace. The Tinchers offered evidence that lightning transferred an electrical charge to parts of the home, including the TracPipe System; the electrical current then sought ground and created different electrical charges in the various metal components of the structure. The Tinchers' [introduced expert witness testimony supporting their theory].

By comparison, Omega Flex's witnesses testified that lightning measured near the Tinchers' home on the night of the fire did not carry sufficient energy to puncture the CSST. According to these witnesses, once lightning entered the house, lightning-related high voltages—although with low energy—broke down the insulation on electrical wires and, if the circuit breakers did not interrupt the current, the electrical current caused the fire. Omega Flex [also] offered evidence that an attempt had been made to bond the TracPipe System to the cold water pipe at the Tinchers' residence which, if successful, would have prevented the electrical arc—and the resulting fire—from occurring. Witnesses testified that, after the fire, a bonding clamp had been found connected to the CSST and near but disconnected from the cold water pipe. The parties offered competing testimony as to whether the clamp had been attached to the cold water pipe before the fire.

Relevant to their strict liability theory, the Tinchers offered testimony regarding a defect in the TracPipe from experts in electrical engineering and metallurgy, electrical arc physics, and material science. [They testified] that the probability was high that CSST would be punctured by occurrences within expected ranges of electrical current [based on phenomena that] are observable and predictable with equations developed in the Nineteenth Century. Nevertheless, the experts noted that Omega Flex had not conducted testing on the TracPipe's ability to withstand lightning strikes, although testing for resistance to lightning was necessary and available. Moreover, according to the Tinchers' evidence, the Omega Flex installation guide failed to direct compliance with lightning-related fire protection codes.

The Tinchers' witnesses also testified [concerning what they concluded was a lack of adequate grounding or bonding of] the TracPipe system at the Tinchers' residence. To be effective, the witnesses testified, bonding would be required every ten feet, which the experts deemed to be an impractical and unfeasible solution. The alternative would be to encase the CSST in black iron pipe.

Subsequently, Omega Flex introduced the testimony of its own experts relating to the defect in the TracPipe System alleged by the Tinchers. The Omega Flex experts opined that the TracPipe System is not defective or unreasonably dangerous. According to the defense experts, CSST is a technology with significant advantages, including resistance to corrosion, structural shifts, and mechanical ruptures; ease of installation, relocation, and retrofitting; and fewer joints accompanied by decreased susceptibility to natural gas leaks at any required joints. The experts noted that these net benefits are marked advantages over black iron pipe arising from the flexibility of CSST. If CSST's walls were thickened, according to the experts, there would be little practical difference between CSST and black iron pipe.

The defense witnesses also testified that the TracPipe System meets and exceeds all standards for minimum performance governing CSST developed by the American National Standards Institute, a clearinghouse for trade groups. Additionally, the witnesses stated, installation of the TracPipe System conforms with the Fuel Gas Code and the National Electric Code in force in 1998–99. The experts emphasized that these applicable standards did not anticipate intrusion by lightning as a possible safety concern, suggesting that it was unnecessary for Omega Flex to have foreseen any danger from lightning.

Finally, Omega Flex's experts noted that a disconnected clamp was consistent with Omega Flex's assessment of the circumstances surrounding the fire. The experts offered that the attempt to bond the TracPipe System to the cold water pipe was inadequate and that a successful attempt would have likely averted the resulting fire.

After the trial court concluded its instructions [to the jury] on the law, counsel for Omega Flex noted for the record that Omega Flex had proposed instructions based upon the Third Restatement with respect to the strict liability claim and that any Second Restatement instructions it proposed were offered in the alternative. The trial court responded that it had declined to instruct the jury in accordance with Third Restatement principles because Pennsylvania appellate courts, and the Supreme Court especially, had not adopted the Third Restatement.

The jury returned a verdict in favor of the Tinchers on the products liability claim, and awarded compensatory damages totaling $958,895.85. The trial court added $69,336.05 in delay damages, and entered judgment on the verdict.[2] Omega Flex filed a motion for post-trial relief requesting, among other things, a new trial premised upon trial court errors in denying its motion in limine and in failing to instruct the jury on the law as articulated in the Third Restatement. Additionally, Omega Flex sought judgment notwithstanding the verdict on the theory that the evidence introduced at trial was insufficient to prove a claim of strict liability under Third Restatement principles.

The trial court denied the [defendant's] motion [and] entered judgment on the verdict, in the amount of $1,028,231.90.

. . . [T]he Superior Court affirmed the judgment, among other things holding that the trial court did not err in declining to adopt the Third Restatement. [T]he court held that the Tinchers' claims implicated notions of strict liability, and the Tinchers had carried their burden of proof under the Second Restatement and *Azzarello*.

Omega Flex filed a petition for allowance of appeal, which this Court granted, limited to the following issue:

> Whether this Court should replace the strict liability analysis of Section 402A of the Second Restatement with the analysis of the Third Restatement.

In addition, the parties were directed to brief the question of whether, if the Court were to adopt the Third Restatement, that holding should be applied prospectively or retroactively.

II. Arguments

Omega Flex suggests an affirmative answer to the question accepted on appeal, and further argues that this Court should disapprove the decision in *Azzarello*, and abandon the Second Restatement articulation of the law of strict liability in Pennsylvania in favor of the approach in the Third Restatement. The Tinchers agree that *Azzarello* was wrongly decided but argue in favor of otherwise retaining the principles of liability of the Second Restatement.

---

2. The jury also returned a verdict in favor of Omega Flex on the negligence claim. There are no claims before this Court related to this part of the verdict.

III. Analysis

A. The Scope and Standard of Review

As a preliminary matter, we observe that the parties pose and argue a seemingly pristine question of law, regarding whether this Court should replace the strict liability analysis of the Second Restatement with the analysis of the Third Restatement.

The parties' present dispute implicates foundational notions in the law of strict liability. To decide the dispute, we necessarily address: (1) what evidence is sufficient under Pennsylvania law to prove a claim of strict liability in tort; (2) the proper role of the trial judge; and (3) the appropriate manner of instructing the jury. As we will explain, these questions can be further complicated by the particulars of the tort, or the product, at issue.

Furthermore, central to the parties' dispute are questions of whether this Court should disapprove the 1978 decision in *Azzarello*, and whether the Court should abandon the Second Restatement articulation of the strict liability cause of action and, in its place, "adopt" as the law of Pennsylvania the Third Restatement formulation of strict liability in tort. These questions implicate separate foundational principles of *stare decisis* and judicial restraint.

The doctrine of *stare decisis* "commands judicial respect for prior decisions of this Court and the legal rules contained in those decisions." *Stilp [v. Commonwealth]*, 905 A.2d at 954 n.31; *see also Kendrick v. District Attorney of Philadelphia County*, 916 A.2d 529, 539 (Pa. 2007). But, the Court's general faithfulness to precedent is not sufficient justification to buttress judicial decisions proven wrong in principle or "which are unsuited to modern experience and which no longer adequately serve the interests of justice." *In re Carney*, 79 A.3d 490, 505 (Pa. 2013); *Ayala v. Philadelphia Bd. of Public Ed.*, 305 A.2d 877, 888 (Pa. 1973) (quoting *Griffith v. United Air Lines, Inc.*, 203 A.2d 796, 806 (Pa. 1964)). Common law permits adjustment and development in the law, recognizing that precedent is not infallible and judicial honesty demands corrective action in appropriate cases. *See Ayala*, 305 A.2d at 888 (quoting *Olin Mathieson C. Corp. v. White C. Stores*, 199 A.2d 266, 268 (Pa. 1964)).

We have recently stressed in multiple cases that the common law "develops incrementally, within the confines of the circumstances of cases as they come before the Court." *Scampone [v. Highland Park Care Center, LLC]*, 57 A.3d at 604 (quoting *Maloney v. Valley Med. Facilities, Inc.*, 984 A.2d 478, 489–90 (Pa. 2009)).

Reliance upon the inherent and necessary flexibility of common law rules does not provide, however, the dispositive answer to the question of whether "adoption" of the American Law Institute's new formulation for tort law is appropriate or advisable. This Court has grown more careful over the years when presented with invitations to issue broad-based pronouncements in areas where it is apparent that such pronouncements are better suited to the information-gathering and give-and-take balancing of competing concerns available in the legislative arena. Thus, for example, it is difficult to imagine a modern court simply adopting something so broad-based and legislative in character as an outside organization's Restatement of the Law, even if it is the product of an esteemed organization.

Two other considerations are specific to the nature and recognized role of a "Restatement" of law in the development of Pennsylvania common law. Restatements of law published by the American Law Institute purport to offer a synthesis of American common law, which articulates the reasoned, mainstream, modern consensus on principles of broad application intended to govern large numbers of cases. *Scampone*, 57 A.3d at 606; *see also Coyle v. Richardson-Merrell, Inc.*, 584 A.2d 1383, 1385 (Pa. 1991). Consistent with its adjudicative rather than policy-making role, the Court has "adopted" or deemed sections of a restatement a proper statement of Pennsylvania law if the cause of action and its contours are consistent with the nature of the tort and Pennsylvania's traditional common law formulation. *See, e.g., Scampone*, 57 A.3d at 606; *Walnut Street Assocs.*, [*Inc. v. Brokerage Concepts, Inc.*,] 20 A.3d at 478–79; *Bilt-Rite Contractors, Inc. v. The Architectural Studio*, 866 A.2d 270, 285 (Pa. 2005). In this sense, the adoption of a restatement formulation intended to advance the law cannot be so unmoored from existing common law and produce such a policy shift that it amounts in actuality or public perception to a derogation of legislative authority, and the concomitant suggestion that such authority is reposed in the Judiciary or in the American Law Institute. Consistent with this principle, the Court must generally show restraint in altering existing allocations of risk created by long-tenured common law rules and resist the temptation of experimentation with untested social policies, especially where the individual record and the advocacy of the parties in the context of that record offer little more than abstract justifications.

Moreover, because the language of a provision of the restatement, even to the extent it was adopted by the Court *verbatim*, has not been vetted through the crucible of the legislative process, a court applying the restatement formulation should betray awareness that the language of an "adopted" restatement provision is not "considered controlling in the manner of a statute." A given restatement section simply states principles of the common law, general rules whose validity depends on the reasoning that supports them. *Coyle*, 584 A.2d at 1385. As with any other common law rules, the normative principles of an "adopted" section of a restatement are properly tested against the facts of each case. Thus, as to any particular claim in a disputed matter, a court should consider whether the application is logical and serves the interests of justice, and whether the general principle has been accepted elsewhere. "[T]he court always retains the right and the duty to test the reason behind a common law rule in determining the applicability of such rule to the facts before it. In the face of contrary arguments as to why the rule should not apply in a given case, it is not enough to say merely that the rule as stated contains no exceptions." *Coyle*, 584 A.2d at 1385. Stated otherwise, "[w]here the facts of a case demonstrate that the rule outruns the reason, the court has the power, indeed the obligation, to refuse to apply the rule, a power for the most part unavailable where the rule is legislatively ordained." *Id.*

B. Strict Liability in Pennsylvania: The Common Law

In the arena of strict liability, this Court does not write on a blank slate; the common law is the starting point of our explication of the conceptual framework for strict liability in tort in Pennsylvania. The evolution of strict liability jurisprudence has four distinct, relevant periods: early cases addressing the evolution of strict liability and the adoption of the Second Restatement's articulation of the cause of action; the advent of *Azzarello*; post-*Azzarello* jurisprudence; and recent judicial expressions addressing the Third Restatement.

At the outset, we note that disputes over liability for personal and economic harm caused by products, although perhaps not articulated in those same terms, likely accompanied the earliest division of labor. The resolution of these disputes in English and American jurisdictions over the several centuries created a rich body of experience-based common sensibilities and wisdom from which the modern principles of the common law of products liability evolved. Review of decisional law illustrates a general trend of gradual expansion of civil liability for harm to persons or property; as it happens, whether a particular development occurred in the context of injury caused by a product or not, the principles of liability were generally articulated in broad terms applicable to products.

By the 1960s, Pennsylvania was among those jurisdictions whose courts had accepted an application of civil liability without proof of negligence in cases of injury caused by food products. *See* William L. Prosser, *The Assault Upon the Citadel (Strict Liability to the Consumer)*, 69 Yale L.J. 1099, 1103–10 (1960) (citing, *inter alia*, *Caskie v. Coca-Cola Bottling Co.*, 96 A.2d 901 (Pa. 1953) (plaintiff who drank from bottle contaminated with hydrochloric acid established breach of implied warranty of fitness and did not have burden to prove that contamination was due to defendant's negligence or dereliction)). *See also Catani v. Swift & Co.*, 95 A. 931 (Pa. 1915) (where sale of food article is for immediate consumption, there is implied warranty that food is wholesome and fit for purpose intended, irrespective of seller's knowledge of disease or defects therein; "prima facie case is made out by proof that the meat sold by defendant was diseased and caused the death of plaintiff's husband"). Redress for injury caused by other products was available in tort (by asserting, *e.g.*, negligence, misrepresentation, or fraud claims) or by asserting breach of warranty claims. These causes of action, and their attendant respective forms of pleading, remain available to plaintiffs today, forming the greater body of products liability law.

By the 1960s, plaintiffs had sought to establish liability of sellers of products primarily via actions in negligence and breach of warranty, on the assumption that these recognized causes of action provided the best approximation of justice in individual cases then available. Negligence theory offered the convenience that it did not require proof of knowledge of a particular defect in the product, but simply the failure to exercise due care had the defect been foreseeable. Meanwhile, a breach of warranty action evolved to encompass the breach of an implied promise, and even of a fictitious promise. Elements of both the negligence and breach of warranty causes of action, as they had thus developed, foreshadowed the evolution of jurisprudence in the area of strict liability, and increasingly resonated with courts.

1. The Second Restatement and the Early Cases

Early decisional law in Pennsylvania explained the genesis and nature of the strict liability cause of action, with reference to Section 402A of the Second Restatement.

The commentary to the Second Restatement traces the roots of the higher degree of responsibility placed upon sellers of goods *See* Prosser, 69 Yale L.J. at 1104. Early American jurisprudence denominated the special civil responsibility as "warranty," imposed upon the seller of food in favor of the direct purchaser. At the beginning of the Twentieth Century, judicial decisions extended sellers' "strict liability" beyond the direct purchaser to injured consumers. *Id.* The decisions articulated an exception to the general rule of more direct liability premised upon proof of negligence or privity of contract. Later jurisprudence settled upon a theory of warranty "running with the goods" or made directly to the consumer; the alternative was strict liability in tort. After 1950, jurisdictions extended the rule of strict liability beyond the sale of food for human consumption, to other products intended for intimate bodily use. Finally, in the late 1950s, courts began applying these developed rules of strict liability to the sale of any product. *Id.*; *see also* Prosser, 69 Yale L.J. at 1103–14 (stating, *inter alia*, that Pennsylvania had extended application of a heightened responsibility to sellers of products other than food in *Jarnot v. Ford Motor Co.*, 156 A.2d 569 (Pa. Super. 1959), premised upon misconstruction of language in earlier cases).

In 1966, this Court took a major step by "adopting" the formulation of Section 402A of the Second Restatement of Torts as the common law of Pennsylvania. In *Webb* [*v. Zern*], 220 A.2d 853, the Court vacated the trial court's order to dismiss the case and remanded with instructions for the trial court to permit the plaintiff to amend his complaint to add a cause of action premised upon the theory of strict liability in tort as articulated by the Second Restatement. [T]he Court, in an opinion by Mr. Justice Cohen, offered little explanation of its reasoning for formally adopting the Second Restatement. [Instead it cited arguments that had been presented by the dissent in an earlier decision, *Miller v. Preis*.]

The several opinions filed in [*Miller v. Preis*, 221 A.2d 320 (Pa, 1966)] offer substantially more insight than *Webb* into the genesis of the strict liability tort in Pennsylvania and the Court's decision to adopt the Second Restatement to define its parameters. The *Miller* plaintiff was the estate administrator of a deceased infant, who was fatally injured when a vaporizer-humidifier used to relieve congestion in his nose shot boiling water on his body. The plaintiff filed a complaint asserting a breach of the implied warranty of merchantability against the manufacturer, the distributor, and the retail pharmacy that had sold the vaporizer-humidifier to the deceased infant's aunt. The infant had used the product in the aunt's home, next door to his family's home. In relevant part, the trial court sustained preliminary objections to the complaint, on the ground that the implied warranty did not extend to the deceased infant because he had not been in privity of contract with any of the defendants.

The *Miller* Court reversed the judgment as a matter of law entered in favor of a retailer because the deceased infant, who was harmed by the vaporizer-humidifier sold by the retailer, was "in the buyer's family" and, notwithstanding the infant's lack of privity with the retailer, his representative had met the prerequisites for pursuing a breach of warranty action under the plain language of the Uniform Commercial Code. Additionally, the *Miller* Court affirmed the judgment in favor of the manufacturer and of the distributor, reasoning that the Code's provisions did not extend warranty liability to remote sellers in the chain of distribution. *Id.* at 324 (citing 12A P.S. § 2-318). In both respects, according to the Court, the language of the Uniform Commercial Code was dispositive. The *Miller* Court viewed abandoning the requirement of privity in warranty actions as unnecessary, noting the expectation that strict liability in tort would vindicate public policy relating to products liability and accomplished a similar result to abandoning privity.

[The] dissent[ing Justices] would have reversed the summary judgment entered by the trial court as to all defendants. These dissenters reasoned that the majority's decision elevated form over substance, and they would have allowed the cause of action in the matter to proceed either in assumpsit, on the basis of a breach of warranty, or in trespass, on the basis of strict liability. In this regard, the dissent suggested that the same results would obtain whether a plaintiff chose to pursue his products liability claim on a breach of warranty theory or under the Second Restatement.

The dissent expressed its disapproval of the "conceptual abstractions and niceties of pleading" that had obscured what it believed was essentially a strict liability cause of action and the considerations that supported it, and encouraged the Court to adopt the Second Restatement. In the dissent's view:

> The public interest in affording the maximum protection possible under the law to human life, health and safety; the inability of the consumer to protect himself; the seller's implied assurance of the safety of a product on the open market; the superior ability of the manufacturer or seller to distribute the risk of loss; the needless circuity of recovery and the expensive, time consuming, wasteful and often unjust process which insistence upon privity frequently occasions — all support the extension of the protection of strict liability beyond the food cases to those involving other consumer goods as well.

221 A.2d at 338–39.

The commentary to the Second Restatement and the Court's decisional law over the subsequent decade reflect early foundational debates among members of the Court concerning the tort. In a series of cases, the Court addressed narrow applications of broader questions relating to burdens of proof, evidence, and jury instructions in strict liability litigation. To the extent these decisions necessitated explication of conceptual foundations, much like the Second Restatement and the commentary, the Court's efforts centered on describing in affirmative terms the theoretical basis for strict liability but lapsed, generally, into comparisons with the more familiar negligence and warranty causes of action in which strict liability was rooted. *See, e.g.,* Restatement (2d) of Torts § 402A(2) & cmt. a, c & m.

The Court revisited questions relating both to a plaintiff's burden of proving a strict liability claim, and relevant jury instructions, in *Berkebile v. Brantly Helicopter Corp.*, 337 A.2d 893 (Pa. 1975) (Opinion Announcing Judgment of Court [OAJC]). [Parts of] the OAJC later became law in *Azzarello. See* 391 A.2d at 1027 and discussion *infra*.

The *Berkebile* OAJC reiterated that strict liability, as a cause of action, implemented a policy of consumer protection. The OAJC explained that, in a strict liability matter, proof of a seller's due care and breach of due care are unnecessary because liability attaches "without fault." *Id.* (citing *Salvador* [*v. Atlantic Street Boiler Co.*], 319 A.2d at 907). Instead, to recover, a plaintiff must prove that the product was defective, and that the defect was a proximate cause of the plaintiff's injuries. In addition, according to the OAJC, the plaintiff has the burden to prove that the defect causing the injury existed at the time that the product left the seller's hands. The OAJC then warned of attempts by a defendant-seller at "indirectly . . . injecting negligence concepts into strict liability theory." *Id.* at 899.

The *Berkebile* OAJC also parsed the language of the Second Restatement, opining that the Restatement imposes a seemingly contradictory burden of proving that a "defect" is "unreasonably dangerous." According to the OAJC, the standards are reconcilable if the purpose of the "unreasonably dangerous" qualification is "to differentiate those products which are by their very nature unsafe but not defective from those which can truly be called defective." The OAJC rejected the notion that defect should be defined based upon the negligence-oriented reasonable man concept, which tended to dilute the strict liability concept, and offered that the "unreasonably dangerous clause" should be included in articulating the issue of proximate cause to the jury. As a result, the OAJC concluded that the jury should not be instructed as to the reasonable man standard or reasonableness "in any form." *Id.* at 900.

Finally, the *Berkebile* OAJC addressed the viability of the plaintiff's failure to warn claims, reasoning that the trial court had erred in failing to charge the jury on the point. Chief Justice Jones stated: "A 'defective condition' is not limited to defects in design or manufacture. *The seller must provide with the product every element necessary to make it safe for use.* One such element may be warnings and/or instructions concerning use of the product. A seller must give such warning and instructions as are required to inform the user or consumer of the possible risks and inherent limitations of his product." *Id.* at 902 (emphasis added) (citing Restatement (2d) of Torts § 402A cmt. c). The portion of the *Berkebile* lead opinion emphasized above was quoted subsequently out of context by the majority in *Azzarello* as the standard of proof in a strict liability action.

Looking back, it is now apparent that the first decade of applying the doctrine of strict liability in Pennsylvania offered a series of missed opportunities to develop a vibrant and coherent body of common law on the issue. [The early case law] suggested little in terms of an explication of essential foundational concepts or practical application, which are generally the *sine qua non* of common law decisions.

And so, much like the Second Restatement articulation of strict liability, Pennsylvania decisional law did not speak affirmatively to the plaintiff's burden of proof in strict liability cases but addressed it by negation, *i.e.*, as compared to then-more familiar theories of breach of warranty initially and, later, negligence. To the extent that the Court spoke to broader considerations, several trends became evident: the original prominence of warranty-related attempts to limit application of strict liability theory decreased, and the relevance of negligence-related encroachments commenced its ascent; rhetoric emerged not only to distinguish strict liability from its negligence roots, but also to excise negligence principles and terms (such as foreseeability) from strict liability theory; the reliance upon formulaic reiteration of consumer protection-related policies, offered as a bulwark against attempts to dilute the application of strict liability theory in individual cases; and then a focus in strict liability theory that ultimately turned upon a statutory construction-type of analysis of the Second Restatement. Experience suggests that these trends, and fits and starts, have proven antithetical to the orderly evolution of our decisional law, one that must be responsive to new problems, perspectives, and consequences.

2. *Azzarello*

In 1978, the Court was confronted with the question of whether the trial court had adequately charged a jury on the law of products liability in Pennsylvania. The *Azzarello* plaintiff had been injured when he pinched his hand between two hard rubber rolls in a coating machine manufactured by Black Brothers Company. The plaintiff proceeded on a theory of strict liability against the manufacturer, but the manufacturer also joined the plaintiff's employer as a co-defendant, asserting that the employer's negligence was the sole or contributing cause of the plaintiff's injuries. *See Azzarello*, 391 A.2d at 1022. In a unanimous opinion, the Court held that the jury charge issued by the trial court was misleading. The *Azzarello* Court approved an alternative charge. *Id*. at 1027 n.12.

The Court addressed two related and important questions: whether a determination as to the risk of loss in a strict liability case is a decision for the judge or the jury, and whether the words "unreasonably dangerous" have any place in the strict liability jury instruction. The Court concluded that the words "unreasonably dangerous" explain the term "defective" but have "no independent significance and merely represent a label to be used where it is determined that the risk of loss should be placed upon the supplier." [T]he difficulty with the use of the term in jury instructions, the Court reasoned, was that it signaled to the jury that the consumer has the burden to prove an element of negligence.

The *Azzarello* Court further reasoned that a change in terminology to avoid references to negligence principles would be insufficient to articulate instructions appropriate for a lay jury. The Court then concluded that the best means to implement the principles of the Second Restatement was to direct: (1) that the phrases "defective condition" and "unreasonably dangerous," which predict whether recovery would be justified, are issues of law and policy entrusted solely for decision to the trial court; and (2) that the inquiry into whether a plaintiff has proven the factual allegations in the complaint is a question for the jury. According to the Court, in cases of an alleged defective design, the dispositive question is whether the product is safe for its intended use. The Court emphasized that the seller is the "guarantor" of the product, and a jury could find a defect "where the product left the supplier's control lacking any element necessary to make it safe for its intended use or possessing any feature that renders it unsafe for the intended use." *Id.* at 1027 (citing *Berkebile*, 337 A.2d at 902).

3. Post-*Azzarello* Design Defect Jurisprudence

Following *Azzarello*, decisional focus in strict liability cases shifted to reflect an increasing concern with segregating strict liability and negligence concepts. The Court addressed several evidentiary questions, in the process touching upon foundational notions of strict liability relevant to a design defect claim.

In *Lewis v. Coffing Hoist Division, Duff-Norton Co.*, 528 A.2d 590 (Pa. 1987), the Court affirmed the Superior Court's decision to uphold a jury verdict in favor of a plaintiff who alleged that the design of a control box for an overhead electric hoist was defective because it lacked a safety mechanism to prevent accidental depression of the control buttons. The plaintiff had injured his legs when he accidentally depressed the control buttons, which caused the hoist to swing its load into his body. The Court rejected the defendant's claim that the trial court erred in excluding expert testimony relating to industry standards and practices.

Before addressing whether particular expert testimony was relevant to a strict liability cause of action, the *Lewis* Court set out its view of the applicable substantive law. The Court noted that [t]he Second Restatement does not provide a definition of the term "defect," and jurisdictions have articulated diverse formulas on the subject of design defect. The Court noted a "consumer expectations" approach, which is an inquiry into whether the product "failed to perform as safely as an ordinary consumer would expect when used in an intended or reasonably foreseeable manner." *Id.* at 593 (citing *Barker v. Lull Engineering Co.*, 573 P.2d 443 (Cal. 1978)). A second accepted approach, according to the Court, involves "risk-utility" balancing. *Id.* (citing *Barker, supra*, and A. Weinstein et al, Products Liability and the Reasonably Safe Product, at 43–59 (1978)). However, in Pennsylvania, *Azzarello* articulated a distinct approach: "the jury may find a defect where the product left the supplier's control lacking any element necessary to make it safe for its intended use or possessing any feature that renders it unsafe for the intended use." *Id.* (citing *Azzarello*, 391 A.2d 1027).

The *Lewis* Court observed that jurisdictions with various approaches agreed that relevant at trial is the condition of the product rather than the reasonableness of the manufacturer's conduct. As a result, the Court concluded, a strict liability claim does not sound in negligence. The Court held that, because "due care" has no bearing upon liability in a strict liability case, proof of industry standards—which go to a negligence concept of reasonable care—are irrelevant and "create[] a strong likelihood of diverting the jury's attention from [the product] to the reasonableness of the [manufacturer-defendant's] conduct in choosing its design." *Id.* at 593–94.

4. Recent Cases and the Third Restatement

In 1998, the ALI proposed a new restatement of the law relating specifically to products liability. *See* Restatement (3d) of Torts: Products Liability §§ 1–8 (1998) (Liability Rules Applicable to Products Generally). As is evident from the premise of this litigation, this Court has not yet determined whether to adopt the formulation of the Third Restatement as the law of Pennsylvania. However, the suggestion for a "move" to the Third Restatement, or adoption of certain of its principles, has been made in several non-precedential opinions. [The court then reviewed earlier cases that considered but failed to decide whether to adopt the Third Restatement, including *Phillips v. Cricket Lighters*, 841 A.2d 1000 (Pa. 2003); *Department of General Services v. United States Mineral Products Co.*, 898 A.2d 590 (Pa. 2008); and *Bugosh v. I.U. North Am., Inc.*, 942 A.2d 897 (Pa. 2008). The court noted that in separate opinions Justices in those cases vigorously advocated in favor of adopting the Third Restatement and also vigorously criticized *Azzarello*.]

In other relevant developments, the U.S. Court of Appeals for the Third Circuit has predicted that, if this Court were to directly confront the issue, we would adopt the Third Restatement's formulation of the strict liability doctrine. *See Berrier* [*v. Simplicity Mfg., Inc.*], 563 F.3d [38], 40 [(3d Cir. 2009)]. The Third Circuit reasoned that Justice Saylor's concurring opinion in *Phillips* foreshadowed this Court's adoption of Sections 1 and 2 of the Third Restatement's definition of the strict liability cause of action. *Id.* at 53. The *Berrier* Court went on to apply Third Restatement principles to permit a bystander, as distinguished from a user or consumer, to state a cause of action in strict liability. *Id.* at 61 (intended user doctrine does not bar strict liability claim; vacating trial court's decision to grant summary judgment). *See also Covell v. Bell Sports, Inc.*, 651 F.3d 357 (3d Cir. 2011) (Third Circuit applies Third Restatement, in accordance with which evidence of industry standards is admissible because such evidence is relevant to question of whether product is defective).[14]

---

14. Until *Berrier*, in diversity jurisdiction matters, the Third Circuit applied Pennsylvania law as articulated in *Azzarello*. The Third Circuit predicted that this Court would utilize a risk-utility analysis in making the *Azzarello* threshold determination of whether the risk of loss should be placed on the supplier.

C. The Continuing Viability of *Azzarello* and Its Progeny

In this case, the question is posed of whether the rationale of *Azzarello*, and its progeny, should retain viability.

Here, the parties agree that the decision in *Azzarello* articulates governing legal concepts which fail to reflect the realities of strict liability practice and to serve the interests of justice. Several members of this Court have suggested in the past this very assessment of *Azzarello*. *See, e.g., Phillips*, 841 A.2d at 1016–18 (Saylor, J., concurring, joined by Castille and Eakin, JJ.); *Berrier*, 959 A.2d at 901 (Saylor, J., concurring, joined by Castille, C.J.); *Bugosh*, 971 A.2d at 1236–37 (Saylor, J., dissenting, joined by Castille, C.J.). We agree that reconsideration of *Azzarello* is necessary and appropriate and, to the extent that the pronouncements in *Azzarello* are in tension with the principles articulated in this Opinion, the decision in *Azzarello* is overruled. We add the following observations.

The *Azzarello* Court premised its broad holding on the assumption that the term "unreasonably dangerous" is misleading to jurors because it "tends to suggest considerations which are usually identified with the law of negligence." 391 A.2d at 1025.

That the *Azzarello* Court keyed into a negligence-strict liability dichotomy may be explained by the Second Restatement's explicit reference to negligence in the negative. But, Section 402A does not articulate legal "requirements" as a statute may; and, moreover, the "intent" of the reporter is, of course, not due the same weight as a pronouncement of legislative intent in statutory construction. Yet, the *Azzarello* Court seemed to engage in a statutory-type construction of Section 402A, including by proceeding to presume every part of Section 402A effective.

The facts of *Azzarello*, when viewed with the appropriate judicial modesty, did not require such a broad pronouncement. [T]he *Azzarello* Court issued a decision that essentially perpetuated jury confusion in future strict liability cases, rather than dissipating it.

The greater difficulty is that the *Azzarello* standard is impracticable.

First, the notion that a legal inquiry into "whether that condition justifies placing liability upon the supplier" (product is unreasonably dangerous) is, albeit distinguishable, entirely separable from a factual inquiry into the predicate "condition of a product" (defective condition of product) when determining whether to affix liability upon a supplier is incompatible with basic principles of strict liability. Thus, in a jurisdiction following the Second Restatement formulation of strict liability in tort, the critical inquiry in affixing liability is whether a product is "defective"; in the context of a strict liability claim, whether a product is defective depends upon whether that product is "unreasonably dangerous." Yet, *Azzarello* divorced one inquiry from the other.

Second, the practical reality, as exemplified by the matter before us, is that trial courts simply do not necessarily have the expertise to conduct the social policy inquiry into the risks and utilities of a plethora of products and to decide, as a matter of law, whether a product is unreasonably dangerous except perhaps in the most obvious of cases (*e.g.*, where injury is caused by a knife), where a gate-keeper's function is hardly necessary. This matter illustrates that the assumptions upon which the *Azzarello* Court assigned the task of determining whether a product is unreasonably dangerous are impractical. In the alternative, a strict reading of *Azzarello* is undesirable because it would encourage trial courts to make either uninformed or unfounded decisions of social policy that then substantially determine the course and outcome of the trial.

D. The Strict Product Liability Cause of Action in Pennsylvania

Overruling *Azzarello* leaves a gap, going forward, in our strict liability jurisprudence. The preferable solution may be to have the General Assembly address this arena of substantive law. But, so long as the possibility of comprehensive legislative reform remains unlikely or uncertain, this Court retains the authority and duty at common law to take necessary action to avoid injustice, uncertainty, delay, and the possibility of different standards and procedures being employed in different courtrooms throughout the Commonwealth. This is particularly so when the underlying problem derives from our own decisional law.

Strict liability in tort for product defects is a cause of action which implicates the social and economic policy of this Commonwealth. The policy was articulated by the concurring and dissenting opinion of Justice Jones in *Miller*, upon which the *Webb* Court relied in "adopting" the strict liability theory as a distinct cause of action in tort: those who sell a product (*i.e.*, profit from making and putting a product in the stream of commerce) are held responsible for damage caused to a consumer by the reasonable use of the product. *See Miller*, 221 A.2d at 334–35 (Jones, J., concurring and dissenting). The risk of injury is placed, therefore, upon the supplier of products. *Azzarello*, 391 A.2d at 1023–24; *accord* Ellen Wertheimer, *Unknowable Dangers and the Death of Strict Products Liability: The Empire Strikes Back*, 60 U. Cin. L. Rev. 1183, 1184–85 (1992). No product is expressly exempt and, as a result, the presumption is that strict liability may be available with respect to any product, provided that the evidence is sufficient to prove a defect. *See* Restatement (2d) of Torts § 402A cmt. b (cause of action in strict liability "cover[s] the sale of *any product* which, if it should prove to be defective, may be expected to cause physical harm to the consumer or his property") (emphasis added); *accord* Prosser, 69 Yale L.J. 1103–04; *but see Hahn v. Richter*, 673 A.2d 888 (Pa. 1996) (manufacturer immune from strict liability defective design claim premised upon sale of prescription drugs without adequate warning).

A broad reading of this policy statement suggests that liability would attach absolutely, once the consumer or user suffers harm; indeed, early proponents supported such an application. *See, e.g., Escola v. Coca Cola Bottling Co. of Fresno*, 150 P.2d 436, 440 (Cal. 1944) (Traynor, J., concurring). But, experience has taught otherwise and, in modern application, strict liability doctrine is a substantially narrower theory. Prosser, 69 Yale L.J. at 1143–46 ("Few products can ever be made entirely safe, and the producer cannot be made an insurer of every one who may possibly be hurt.").

To explain its proper boundaries post-*Azzarello*, we address the fundamental underpinnings of the cause of action: the duty imposed by law and what constitutes a breach of the duty; and we also advert to additional matters such as causation, damages, defenses, and effects on other doctrines where necessary.

1. The Duty

Since the tide turned with New York's 1916 *MacPherson* decision,[16] all American jurisdictions have accepted the existence of a duty in tort arising from the supplier-consumer relationship. [T]he policy of those jurisdictions that have incorporated the Second Restatement into their common law is that those who engage in the business of selling a product are subject to both a duty of care in manufacturing and selling the product and a duty to sell a product free from a "defective condition." The duty spoken of in strict liability is intended to be distinct from the duty of due care in negligence. Restatement (2d) of Torts § 402A(2).

The duty in strict liability pertains to the duty of a manufacturer and of suppliers in the chain of distribution to the ultimate consumer. The Restatement offers a functional shorthand for the balancing of interests implicit in assessing the existence of the strict liability duty in tort between those in a consumer/user-supplier relationship. In incorporating the strict liability cause of action into Pennsylvania common law, the *Webb* Court expressly relied upon the Second Restatement and relevant scholarly commentary to supply its justification. 220 A.2d at 854. Indeed, comments b, c, g, and m to Section 402A of the Second Restatement offer reasoned consideration of factors relevant in Pennsylvania to explain the existence and nature of a seller's duty in tort to a consumer.

This reasoning explains the nature of the non-delegable duty articulated by the Second Restatement and recognized in *Webb*. Stated affirmatively, a person or entity engaged in the business of selling a product has a duty to make and/or market the product — which "is expected to and does reach the user or consumer without substantial change in the condition in which it is sold" — free from "a defective condition unreasonably dangerous to the consumer or [the consumer's] property." *Accord* Restatement (2d) of Torts § 402A(1).

2. Breach of Duty

Where a duty exists and, in the absence of a recognized immunity, the duty is breached, and the breach of the duty is causally connected to a compensable injury results, a tortious act results, regardless of whether the tortious act is construed

---

16. *MacPherson* [*v. Buick Motor Co.*], *supra*, 217 N.Y. [382] at 389 [(1916)] ("[i]f the nature of a thing is such that it is reasonably certain to place life and limb in peril when negligently made, it is then a thing of danger"; discarding requirement to prove that product was inherently dangerous (*e.g.*, "poisons, explosives, and things of like nature") to obtain compensation for harm caused by negligent conduct).

colloquially as fault. To demonstrate a breach of duty in a strict liability matter, a plaintiff must prove that a seller (manufacturer or distributor) placed on the market a product in a "defective condition."

In this context, the concept of defective condition is a legal term of art, which denotes neither its colloquial import nor a scientifically immutable fact. "The term 'defect' in design cases is 'an epithet—an expression for the legal conclusion rather than a test for reaching that conclusion.'" *Prentis* [*v. Yale Mfg. Co.*], 365 N.W.2d at 182 (quoting John W. Wade, *On Product "Design Defects" and Their Actionability*, 33 Van. L. Rev. 551, 552 (1980)); *accord* John W. Wade, *On the Nature of Strict Tort Liability for Products*, 44 Miss. L.J. 825, 831–32 (1973). Stated otherwise, evidentiary considerations (*e.g.*, what evidence tends to prove the existence of a legal defect) should not be mistaken for the question of whether a substantive duty in strict liability exists or should exist, or what constitutes a breach of that duty. In Pennsylvania, the question of whether those who make or market products have duties in strict liability (in addition to negligence) has been answered in the affirmative by the 1966 decision in *Webb*. The question which has proven substantially more difficult has been one of proof: what evidence is relevant to prove a "defective condition" and how should that evidence be weighed.

3. The Standard of Proving "Defective Condition" In the Context of a Design-Related Claim[18]

In addressing the disputed notion of "defective condition," we start with the assumption that, as with any other tort relationship, the supplier and the consumer are protecting legitimate but conflicting interests; the purpose of the court at common law is to evaluate the interests and articulate the principles based upon where the line is drawn in individual cases.

In the products liability arena, the individual consumer or user of the product retains primary interests in the safe continued use of a product and, relatedly, in the cost of any injury caused by the product. For the individual supplier, the assumed primary interest is to generate a sustained profit, above the cost of doing business. *Accord* Wertheimer, 60 U. Cin. L. Rev. at 1185. A supplier also retains complementary economic interests in maintaining a reputable name and in providing new or innovative products, which requires, among other things, financial flexibility beyond mere profitability. *See Beard* [*v. Johnson & Johnson Co,*], 41 A.3d at 837 & n.16; *Miller*, 221 A.2d at 334–35 (Second Restatement reflects expectation that manufacturers and sellers will stand behind their products). Another motivating factor may be a moral interest in providing a safe product with minimal negative externalities or spillover effects (*e.g.*, environmental impact). Concomitantly, suppliers across the same and/or

---

18. Our decision is limited to the context of a "design defect" claim by the facts of this matter, albeit the foundational principles upon which we touch may ultimately have broader implications by analogy.

related industries may share similar, albeit diluted, interests regarding profitability and reputability on industry-wide bases.

As they have been passed down to the present, the common law principles that delineate the strict liability cause of action, and the limits upon strict liability, reflect a balance of interests respecting what is socially or economically desirable. The calculus is sensitive to the varying magnitude of the interests and, sometimes perversely, to the force with which each interest is asserted from time to time.

Against this background, two standards have emerged, that purport to reflect the competing interests of consumers and sellers, upon which all American jurisdictions judge the adequacy of a product's design: one measures "consumer expectations," and articulates the standard more from the perspective of the reasonable consumer; the second balances "risk" and "utility," and articulates the standard more from the perspective of the reasonable seller. Other jurisdictions and the Third Restatement have combined the two standards. *See generally* Owen, 73 Mo. L. Rev. at 299–300. We describe the alternatives.

Consumer Expectations Standard

The consumer expectations test defines a "defective condition" as a condition, upon normal use, dangerous beyond the reasonable consumer's contemplations. *See, e.g., Welch*, 481 F.2d at 254; *see also* David G. Owen, Products Liability Law, at § 5.6 (Hornbook Series) (2d ed. 2008) (hereinafter referred to as "Owen, Hornbook") (describing provenance and alternative formulations). The test offers a standard of consumer expectations which, in typical common law terms, states that: the product is in a defective condition if the danger is unknowable and unacceptable to the average or ordinary consumer. The product is not defective if the ordinary consumer would reasonably anticipate and appreciate the dangerous condition of the product and the attendant risk of injury of which the plaintiff complains (*e.g.,* a knife). *See Vincer v. Esther Williams All-Aluminum Swimming Pool Co.*, 230 N.W.2d 794, 798 (Wis. 1975); *see also* Restatement (2d) of Torts § 402A cmt. i ("The article sold must be dangerous to an extent beyond that which would be contemplated by the ordinary consumer who purchases it, with the ordinary knowledge common to the community as to its characteristics."). The nature of the product, the identity of the user, the product's intended use and intended user, and any express or implied representations by a manufacturer or other seller are among considerations relevant to assessing the reasonable consumer's expectations.

The language of the consumer expectations test derives from the Second Restatement's commentary on the principles designated to limit liability, *i.e.,* "defective condition" and "unreasonably dangerous." Restatement (2d) of Torts § 402A cmts. g & i. Several commentators have suggested that this test reflects the warranty law roots of strict liability in tort, and serves to vindicate significant interests central to the public policy justifying the strict liability cause of action in the first place.

Application of the consumer expectations test in its purest form, however, has theoretical and practical limitations. First, products whose danger is obvious or within the ordinary consumer's contemplation would be exempt from strict liability; some therefore have said that related consumer safety expectations regarding the presence of the danger are too low. *See, e.g., Ahrens v. Ford Motor Co.*, 340 F.3d 1142 (10th Cir. 2003) (affirming district court decision that manufacturer not liable for defective design of tractor without seatbelt or for failing to warn of danger because plaintiff failed to adduce sufficient evidence that risk of danger was beyond contemplation of ordinary consumer). Second, a product whose danger is vague or outside the ordinary consumer's contemplation runs the risk of being subjected to arbitrary application of the strict liability doctrine; jury determinations of consumer expectations regarding the presence of danger are unpredictable. This difficulty is characteristic of products of relatively complex design. *See, e.g., Heaton v. Ford Motor Co.*, 435 P.2d 806 (Or. 1967). [S]*ee also Soule v. Gen. Motors Corp.*, 882 P.2d 298, 308 (Cal. 1994) ("[A] complex product, even when it is being used as intended, may often cause injury in a way that does not engage its ordinary consumers' reasonable minimum assumptions about safe performance. For example, the ordinary consumer of an automobile simply has 'no idea' how it should perform in all foreseeable situations, or how safe it should be made against all foreseeable hazards.").

The consumer expectations test, because of the "obvious defect" exception and vagueness concerns, has practical limitations in vindicating the basic public policy undergirding strict liability.

Risk-Utility Standard

The difficulty related to vindicating the salient public policy in cases in which the alleged defective condition is premised upon either an obvious danger or a danger outside the ordinary consumer's contemplation suggests that a different approach is necessary and appropriate for judging the reasonableness of danger, at least respecting some products. American jurisdictions, including Pennsylvania, apply a test balancing risks and utilities or, stated in economic terms, a cost-benefit analysis. *See* Owen, Hornbook, at § 5.7; *Azzarello*, 391 A.2d at 1026. The test offers a standard which, in typical common law terms, states that: a product is in a defective condition if a "reasonable person" would conclude that the probability and seriousness of harm caused by the product outweigh the burden or costs of taking precautions. *See, e.g., Denny v. Ford Motor Co.*, 662 N.E.2d 730, 735 (N.Y. 1995); *Barker*, 573 P.2d at 456; *accord Welch*, 481 F.2d at 256 (product is defective if reasonable seller would not sell product knowing of risks involved). Stated otherwise, a seller's precautions to advert [*sic*] the danger should anticipate and reflect the type and magnitude of the risk posed by the sale and use of the product. *See* Owen, Hornbook, at 315 (risk-utility standard "demands that manufacturers adopt precautions proportionate to the magnitude of the expected risk").

The risk-utility test offers courts an opportunity to analyze *post hoc* whether a manufacturer's conduct in manufacturing or designing a product was reasonable, which obviously reflects the negligence roots of strict liability. *See Blue v. Envt'l Eng'g, Inc.*, 828 N.E.2d 1128, 1140–41 (Ill. 2005) ("[I]t has been observed that the kind of hindsight analysis inherent in the risk-utility test, which requires juries to weigh the risk inherent in the product's design, has all the earmarks of determining negligence."); *see also U.S. v. Carroll Towing Co.*, 159 F.2d at 174 (Judge Learned Hand's formula). Other jurisdictions have generally cited favorably the works of Dean Wade, which articulated factors relevant to the manufacturer's risk-utility calculus implicated in manufacturing or designing a product. *See, e.g., Calles v. Scripto-Tokai Corp.*, 864 N.E.2d 249, 260–61 (Ill. 2007) (citing cases from multiple jurisdictions). The factors are:

1. The usefulness and desirability of the product—its utility to the user and to the public as a whole.

2. The safety aspects of the product—the likelihood that it will cause injury, and the probable seriousness of the injury.

3. The availability of a substitute product which would meet the same need and not be as unsafe.

4. The manufacturer's ability to eliminate the unsafe character of the product without impairing its usefulness or making it too expensive to maintain its utility.

5. The user's ability to avoid danger by the exercise of care in the use of the product.

6. The user's anticipated awareness of the dangers inherent in the product and their availability, because of general public knowledge of the obvious condition of the product, or of the existence of suitable warnings or instructions.

7. The feasibility, on the part of the manufacturer, of spreading the loss by setting the price of the product or carrying liability insurance.

Id. (quoting Wade, 44 Miss. L.J. at 837–38).

But, while these considerations may provide a holistic perspective on a manufacturer's choice to bring a product to market, they may not be immediately responsive in the (typical) case implicating allegations relating to a particular design feature. The difficulty in presenting the issue to the jury, Professor Owen suggests, is resolved by reference to Judge Learned Hand's formula, which "succinctly captures the common sense idea that products are unacceptably dangerous if they contain dangers that might cost-effectively (and practicably) be removed." Owen, Hornbook, at 315 (applying Hand formula in strict liability means that jury will decide whether seller "fails to adopt a burden of precaution of less magnitude than the harm it is likely to prevent").

Application of a risk-utility balancing test in its purest form likewise has theoretical and practical shortcomings. The goal and strength of a pure risk-utility test is to achieve efficiency or "to maximize the common good"; yet, this is also its perceived weakness. *See* Owen, Hornbook, at 316. For, while efficiency is certainly a salutary goal of the law, it is not its only purpose and, in some respects, it conflicts with bedrock moral intuitions regarding justice in determining proper compensation for injury to persons or property in individual cases. We should be mindful that public policy adjusts expectations of efficiency and intuitions of justice considerations, informing a seller's conduct toward consumers as a group, and ensuring proper compensation in individual cases by judicial application of the strict liability cause of action.

Combined Tests

A number of jurisdictions have expressly or implicitly combined the consumer expectations and risk-utility standards. One approach is to state the two standards in the alternative; a plaintiff's injury is compensable whether either test is met. *See, e.g., Barker*, 573 P.2d at 457–58 (discussed *infra*); *Calles*, 864 N.E.2d at 257; *Welch*, 481 F.2d at 254 ("A product is defective and unreasonably dangerous when a reasonable seller would not sell the product if he knew of the risks involved or if the risks are greater than a reasonable buyer would expect."). The combined standard, which states consumer expectations and risk-utility tests in the alternative, retains the features of each test, in practice, offering the parties a composite of the most workable features of both tests. *See Caterpillar Tractor Co. v. Beck*, 593 P.2d 871, 884–85 (Alaska 1979) *superseded in part by* Alaska Stat. §09.17.060 (1986); *accord Soule, supra*.

A second approach is to incorporate the risk calculus into a test of consumer expectations or, vice versa, to incorporate consumer expectations into the risk-utility determination.

Courts, moreover, have offered some variations on each of these approaches. In California, for example, the *Barker* court allocated to the supplier the burden to prove the adequacy of a product's design under the "risk-benefit" standard (*i.e.*, to disprove a plaintiff's *prima facie* case that a product is defective). Commentators have suggested that another California case, *see Soule, supra*, offered yet another variation by which the applicability of either prong of the combined *Barker* test depends upon the complexity of the product. *See* Owen, Hornbook, at 325; Henderson, 83 Cornell L. Rev. at 899.

It is questionable, however, that the *Soule* court sought to foreclose strict liability claims premised upon a simple/complex classification, as the commentators have suggested. Ourselves having had the experience of attempting to bring various principles to bear upon a single complex case, we believe that, placed into its proper context, *Soule* may be read as simply commenting upon the court's experience with analogous matters and offering guidance to aid trial courts in properly guiding the parties and the jury through the litigation process.

The Third Restatement also offers a variation upon those tests primarily based upon a risk-utility determination by requiring proof of a reasonable alternative design. *See* Henderson, 83 Cornell L. Rev. at 884–87 (explaining standard of proof premised upon risk-utility balancing and proof of alternative design). Restatement (3d) of Torts: Products Liability §§ 1–3 (1998) (Liability Rules Applicable to Products Generally).

Section 1 of the Third Restatement articulates the general policy of strict liability. Sections 2 through 4, as well as Sections 6 and 7, address evidentiary questions. Notably, Section 2 identifies three types of defects and, at least with respect to "design" defect (subsection (b)), states a general rule, which defines a defect by reference to the relative risk-utility calculi for the allegedly defective product and an alternatively designed product. *See also* Henderson, 83 Cornell L. Rev. at 888–89 (alternative design is proof of technological feasibility, "an empirical factor for courts to consider in the normative process of risk-utility balancing"). Application of this general rule is, as a result, limited — and compensation is available — only for those products for which an alternative design can be shown to exist. The Restatement illustrates its view that other evidence may be probative in a design defect case by articulating special rules. Thus, Sections 3, 4, and comment e to Section 2 of the Third Restatement establish alternative means for proving a design defect "in circumstances in which common experience teaches that an inference of defect may be warranted under the specific facts," where the seller or distributor violates statutory and regulatory norms, and "when the product design is manifestly unreasonable." Meanwhile, Sections 6 and 7 address special rules of liability for specific products: prescription drugs and medical devices, and food products. *See id.* at §§ 6–7; *see also* § 6 cmt. f (Section 6 principle articulates judgment that liability attaches only when certain type and quantum of evidence is adduced by plaintiff; noting expectation that, under "this very demanding objective standard, liability is likely to be imposed only under unusual circumstances"). In relation to prescription drugs, for example, the special rule reflects in part an understanding that, for some products, there is no alternative design.

4. The Appropriate Post-*Azzarello* Strict Liability Construct

a. The "Move" to the Third Restatement

Guided by this decisional and doctrinal universe, we address the parties' competing arguments, which rely, to a great extent, upon jurisprudential and policy assertions.

In essential part, both parties ask this Court to engage questions of whether their preferred iteration of the Restatement embodies a good, better, or more desirable public policy. As we have explained, as an adjudicative body, this Court is not particularly well-suited to such a broad task. The appropriate question is which, if either, Restatement articulates the standard of proof in terms that effectuate the public policy of this Commonwealth.

For the reasons that follow, we conclude that "adoption" of the Third Restatement approach is problematic. For one thing, articulating the burden of proof in terms of evidence (alternative design) deemed probative of the general principle of strict liability proscriptively limits the applicability of the cause of action to certain products as to which that sort of evidence is available. The approach suggests *a priori* categorical exemptions for some products—such as novel products with no alternative design—but not others. The Connecticut Supreme Court suggested a similar insight: "in some instances, a product may be in a defective condition unreasonably dangerous to the user even though no feasible alternative design is available." *Potter* [*v. Chicago Pneumatic Tool Co.*], 694 A.2d 1332 [(Conn.1997)].

Of course, the courts, legislatures, and the American Law Institute cannot foresee all the myriad products and circumstances that may arise. [T]his jurisdiction's experience with the repercussions of attempting to articulate specific principles of liability of broad application in implementing the strict liability cause of action make us reticent to go far beyond the necessities of an individual case and embrace a broad new approach premised upon what may prove to be procrustean categorical restrictions.

Our reticence respecting the Third Restatement scheme is not a judgment on our part that, as a matter of policy, articulating categorical exemptions from strict liability is not a viable or desirable alternative. Courts, which address evidence and arguments in individual cases, are neither positioned, nor resourced, to make the kind of policy judgments required to arrive at an *a priori* decision as to which individual products, or categories and types of products, should be exempt. Neither courts, nor the American Law Institute for that matter, are in the business of articulating general principles tailored to anoint special "winners" and "losers" among those who engage in the same type of conduct. In our view, the question of "special tort-insulated status" for certain suppliers—for example, manufacturers of innovative products with no comparable alternative design—optimally "requires an assessment and balancing of policies best left to the General Assembly." *Scampone*, 57 A.3d at 599; *Ayala, supra; but see, e.g., Hahn*, 673 A.2d 888 (where adequacy of warnings associated with prescription drugs is at issue, strict liability is not recognized as basis for liability).

The methodology employed by the reporters suggests additional potential weaknesses in the strict liability schemata of the Third Restatement that should caution courts against categorical pronouncements. This approach no doubt fulfills the role of the American Law Institute in its own salutary task of restating and clarifying a view of strict liability that can be reduced to decisive terms. But, what drives the Institute and treatise writers does not make comparative modesty, nuance, and reticence in the judiciary mistaken (much less indecisive) in a jurisdiction, like Pennsylvania, where the area, to date, has been the exclusive province of the common law.

That evidence of the existence and specifications of an alternative design is relevant and even highly probative to prove disputed issues in a products liability case, such as technological feasibility, cost, etc., is certainly true. That the more typical case implicates the type of products and circumstances in which evidence of an alternative product design is the most persuasive and efficient means of convincing the trier of fact may also be true. That offering evidence of an alternative product design may be the preferred legal strategy of the plaintiff's bar in certain cases—or may be a strategy the defense bar would like to impose on the plaintiff's bar in certain cases—again may also be true. But, while the reporters' intuition that meritorious cases are premised upon certain types of evidence may have some general validity and support in practice (and may prove helpful to litigants in articulating claims and preparing defenses), the reporters' commentary candidly betrays a problem—for the judiciary at least—of perspective. [I]t is our view that the reporters' "precise and categorical" perspective insufficiently accounts for the imperatives of the courts' more modest decisional role.

Insight into the reporters' perspective on how the nature of decisions at common law informs their consensus effort to speak otherwise, *i.e.*, to "speak precisely and categorically," should serve as a reminder of comparative judicial modesty. The Third Restatement approach presumes too much certainty about the range of circumstances, factual or otherwise, to which the "general rule" articulated should apply.

Additionally, the Third Restatement construct, because unmoored from guidance upon the broader legal issue, would likely impede the principled development of the law in this arena. Although "[b]right lines and broad rules always offer a superficially enticing option," they also risk elevating the lull of simplicity to doctrine. *See, e.g., Scampone*, 57 A.3d at 598; *Azzarello*. And, finally, our reticence respecting broad approval of the Third Restatement is separately explainable by looking no further than to the aftermath of *Azzarello*, whose negligence rhetoric-related doctrinal proscription arising from a peculiar set of circumstances had long-term deleterious effects on the development of strict liability law in Pennsylvania. *Azzarello* illustrate[s] how dogmatic pronouncements are difficult to apply in individual cases without guidance upon the broader legal issue and the result is often that litigation will derail into irrelevant, unreasoned, or unprincipled factual disputes. As a Court, in this dynamic area, we must settle for the incremental approach.

[T]he Third Restatement does not offer an articulation of the law sufficient to persuade us to simply abandon the Second Restatement formulation of the strict products liability cause of action and "move" to the Third Restatement. Unlike the Third Restatement, we believe that the Second Restatement already adopted, and properly calibrated, permits the plaintiffs to tailor their factual allegations and legal argumentation to the circumstances as they present themselves in the real-world crucible of litigation, rather than relying upon an evidence-bound standard of proof.

b. Prevailing Standard of Proof

Having overruled *Azzarello* and declined the invitation to fill the void by simply "adopting" the Third Restatement formulation, we proceed to address the appropriate standard of proof of a strict liability claim in Pennsylvania.

Initially, we note that, although Pennsylvania remains a Second Restatement jurisdiction, "adoption" of its principles into our common law is distinct in concept and application from the adoption of a statute by the General Assembly. Although the reporter's words have intrinsic significance because their purpose is to explain the legal principle clearly, they are not entitled to the fidelity due a legislative body's expression of policy, whose judgment and intent, wise or unwise, a court generally is obligated to effectuate, absent constitutional infirmity. The language of a restatement, as a result, is not necessarily susceptible to "statutory"-type construction or parsing.

With this qualification in mind, we explain: (1) that the strict liability cause of action sounds in tort; (2) that the notion of "defective condition unreasonably dangerous" is the normative principle of the strict liability cause of action, which reflects the standard of review or application of the tort, and its history; and (3) the appropriate interplay of principle and evidence.[23]

It is important to remember that the action sounds in tort, *i.e.* the cause involves breach of duties "imposed by law as a matter of social policy," rather than contract, *i.e.*, the cause involves breach of duties "imposed by mutual consensus agreements between particular individuals." *Ash* [*v. Continental Ins. Co.*], 932 A.2d at 884; *see* Restatement (2d) of Torts § 402A(2). Nevertheless, the tortious conduct at issue is not the same as that found in traditional claims of negligence and commonly associated with the more colloquial notion of "fault." In this sense, introducing a colloquial notion of "fault" into the conversation relating to strict product liability in tort detracts from the precision required to keep this legal proposition within rational bounds.

[W]e hold that, in Pennsylvania, the cause of action in strict products liability requires proof, in the alternative, either of the ordinary consumer's expectations or of the risk-utility of a product. To maintain the integrity and fairness of the strict products liability cause of action, each part of this standard of proof remains subject to its theoretical limitations, as explained above. We believe that the demands of strict liability policy are met because the composite standard retains the best functioning features of each test, when applied in the appropriate factual context. *See Caterpillar, supra.*

Thus, in placing a product on the market, a manufacturer acts to design (and manufacture) the product and, along with other distributors, to sell the product, including making the product attractive for sale by making implicit representations of the product's safety. A manufacturer, in designing the product, engages in a risk-utility calculus; the policy-driven *post hoc* risk-utility calculus necessary to determine whether the design choice thus made may justly require compensation for injury explains the relevance of that standard of proof in strict liability. Meanwhile, a seller of the product—whether the manufacturer or the supplier in the chain of distribution—implicitly represents by placing a product on the market that the product is not in a defective condition unreasonably dangerous.

---

23. While the Second Restatement formulation of the principles governing the strict liability cause of action in tort may have proven substantially less than clear, the policy that formulation embodies has not been challenged here and has largely remained uncontroverted.

The dual analytical structure also explains the historical ebb and flow of consumer expectations / risk-utility and warranty / negligence rhetoric that pervades decisional law. Essentially, given that a term like "defective condition unreasonably dangerous" is not self-defining, courts have offered multiple definitions applicable in the several contexts in which a definitional issue has arisen, all effectuating the single policy that those who sell a product are held responsible for damages caused to a consumer by the reasonable use of the product. *See, e.g., Miller*, 221 A.2d at 334–35 (Jones, J., concurring and dissenting); *accord Barker*, 573 P.2d at 453 ("term defect as utilized in the strict liability context is neither self-defining nor susceptible to a single definition applicable in all contexts").

Modern decisional law reflects that the focus of disputes making their way into the appellate courts has increasingly been upon the negligence-derived risk-utility alternative formulation of the standard. The prominence of the legal issue in decisional law coincides with the advent of design defect claims, in which issues of proof tend to more complexity than where a manufacturing defect is in dispute. This development reflected the complex litigation calculus implicated in a strict liability claim premised upon this type of defect resulting from either lack of proof (for example in the case of known or foreseeable risks for which an available cure may or may not have been available at the time of design) or the relative deterrent inefficacy of a theory of liability for unknowable risks, short of exiting the market. *Accord* Prosser, 69 Yale L.J. at 1116. Yet, some types of disputes are absent from the decisional law and may, indeed, provide rather strong evidence of strict liability as a deterrent by preventing bringing a product to market or encouraging settlement of claims—it must be remembered that an appellate expression is not necessary to illustrate the point that designers are properly deterred by strict liability from using consumers as guinea pigs.

[T]hat the theory of strict liability—like all other tort causes of action—is not fully capable of providing a sufficient deterrent incentive to achieve perfect safety goals is not a justification for jettisoning or restricting the duty in strict liability, whose compensatory objective remains part of the public policy of this Commonwealth.

Finally, we remark upon evidentiary issues necessarily implicated by the standard of proof we have articulated. Derived from its negligence-warranty dichotomy, the strict liability cause of action theoretically permits compensation where harm results from risks that are known or foreseeable (although proof of either may be unavailable)—a circumstance similar to cases in which traditional negligence theory is implicated—and also where harm results from risks unknowable at the time of manufacture or sale—a circumstance similar to cases in which traditional implied warranty theory is implicated. The difficulty is in cabining liability premised upon a risk unknowable at the time of manufacture / sale, which was logically unavoidable, in circumstances in which liability and attendant compensation was potentially limitless (in other words, 100 percent of risk would be shifted to suppliers). Because the circumstance is not before us, and in light of the complexities and dearth of persuasive authority, we will await the appropriate case to speak definitively to this issue.

By comparison, the Tinchers' claim was essentially premised upon the allegation that the risk of harm related to TracPipe's thickness was both foreseeable and avoidable, as illustrated by the resistance to lightning of black iron pipe. These allegations, at least, bear the indicia of negligence. Indeed, in some respects this is the "typical" case, which explains both the insight that in design cases, the character of the product and the conduct of the manufacturer are largely inseparable, and the Third Restatement's approach of requiring an alternative design as part of the standard of proof.

But, the point that we have stressed repeatedly in this Opinion, is that courts do not try the "typical" products case exclusively and a principle of the common law must permit just application to myriad factual circumstances that are beyond our power to conceive.

The delivery of justice in this area requires a recognition and appreciation of the appropriate and significant roles played by advocates, trial judges, and the appellate judiciary. Particularly relevant here, we note that the area of strict liability law remains complex and our decision here does not purport to foresee and account for the myriad implications or potential pitfalls as yet unarticulated or unappreciated. The principal point is that judicial modesty counsels that we be content to permit the common law to develop incrementally, as we provide reasoned explications of principles pertinent to factual circumstances of the cases that come before the Court.

5. Litigation Considerations Deriving from the New Strict Liability Construct

a. Judge and Jury; Jury Instructions

Having outlined these principles of strict liability law, we next offer the following guidance relating to the appropriate provinces of the judge and jury, and to adequate, targeted jury instructions in a strict liability case. We offer additional guidance to confirm our departure from that aspect of *Azzarello* that assigned these roles to the judge and jury in a strict liability case.

As is generally the case, the plaintiff is the master of the claim in the first instance. The immediate implication is that counsel must articulate the plaintiff's strict liability claim by alleging sufficient facts to make a *prima facie* case premised upon either a "consumer expectations" or "risk-utility" theory, or both. The calculus for a plaintiff and a plaintiff's advocate in choosing to pursue either theory or both will likely account, among other things, for the nature of the product, for the theoretical limitations of either alternative standard of proof, for whether pursuing both theories simultaneously is likely to confuse the finder of fact and, most importantly, for the evidence available or likely to become available for trial. The trial court is to act in its ordinary gate-keeper role, *e.g.*, monitoring litigation, mediating or adjudicating any subsidiary differences, and pending objections and motions, including those seeking to narrow, or expand, the theories of litigation to be pursued at trial. *See, e.g., Soule*, 882 P.2d at 303, 309.

One crucial aspect of the trial court's role is, of course, the task of defining the strict liability legal universe within which a particular jury operates for purposes of discharging its function.

Going forward, consistent with this decision, when a plaintiff proceeds on a theory that implicates a risk-utility calculus, proof of risks and utilities are part of the burden to prove that the harm suffered was due to the defective condition of the product. The credibility of witnesses and testimony offered, the weight of evidence relevant to the risk-utility calculus, and whether a party has met the burden to prove the elements of the strict liability cause of action are issues for the finder of fact, whether that finder of fact is judge or jury. A question of whether the party has met its burden of proof is properly "removed" — for example, via adjudication of a dispositive motion — "from the jury's consideration only where it is clear that reasonable minds [cannot] differ on the issue." *Hamil v. Bashline*, 392 A.2d 1280, 1284–85 (Pa. 1978). Thus, the strict liability construct we articulate today comfortably accommodates the gate-keeping role ordinarily relegated to the trial court in tort actions.

Our decision today allows for application of standards of proof in the alternative. Where evidence supports a party-requested instruction on a theory or defense, a charge on the theory or defense is warranted. At that point, "[t]he trial court has broad discretion in phrasing its instructions, and may choose its own wording so long as the law is clearly, adequately, and accurately presented to the jury for its consideration." [*Commonwealth v.*] *Sepulveda*, 55 A.3d at 1141.

It is essential for the bench and bar to recognize that the test we articulate today is not intended as a rigid formula to be offered to the jury in all situations. The alternate theories of proof contour the notion of "defective condition" in principled terms intended as comprehensive guidelines that are sufficiently malleable to account for product diversity and a variety of legal claims, products, and applications of theory. The crucial role of the trial court is to prepare a jury charge that explicates the meaning of "defective condition" within the boundaries of the law, *i.e.*, the alternative test standard, and the facts that pertain. *Cf. Soule*, 882 P.2d at 308–11.

b. The Burden of Proof

Another consideration derived from existing precedent implicates the burden of proof in a strict liability case. As we have noted, California pioneered the alternate consumer expectations / risk-utility balancing test as a prevailing standard of proof in strict liability cases. *See Barker*, 573 P.2d at 457–58. The *Barker* court also concluded that it was appropriate, when proceeding upon a risk-utility theory, to shift to the defendant the burden of production and persuasion to demonstrate that an injury-producing product is not defective in design. *Id.* at 455. Other jurisdictions have subscribed to the *Barker* standard of proof, although only some of those courts have also shifted the burden of proof to the defendant. *Compare, e.g., Lamkin v. Towner*, 563 N.E.2d 449, 457 (Ill. 1990) *with Knitz* [*v. Minster Mach. Co.*], 432 N.E.2d

[814] at 818 [(Ohio, 1982)]. The similarity of the approach we have approved to the *Barker* standard of proof may raise a question of whether Pennsylvania should also require a shifting of the burden of proof to the defendant when the plaintiff proceeds upon a risk-utility theory.

[T]he *Barker* court reasoned that placing the burden on the defendant was appropriate. According to *Barker*, the shift in the burden of proof reflected the policy judgment that "one of the principal purposes behind the strict product liability doctrine is to relieve an injured plaintiff of many of the onerous evidentiary burdens inherent in a negligence cause of action." 573 P.2d at 455.

The parties obviously have not briefed the question of burden-shifting in risk-utility cases—they had no reason to—and we need not decide it to resolve this appeal, nor is it apparent that it will matter upon remand. We note, however, that whatever may be the merit of the *Barker* court's concerns, countervailing considerations may also be relevant. For example, it is consistent with the treatment of tort causes of action generally, and the notion that Pennsylvania does not presume a product to be defective until proven otherwise, to assign the burden of proof in a strict liability case to the plaintiff. Moreover, proving a negative is generally not desirable as a jurisprudential matter because of fairness concerns related to anticipating and rebutting allegations, and because of the encumbrances placed upon the judicial system by an open-ended approach to pleading and trying a case. Finally, evidence relevant to a risk-utility test, including the feasibility and cost of alternative designs, while involving technical matters, would seem to be within the knowledge of expert witnesses available to either plaintiff or defendant in many cases; and liberal discovery may also aid the plaintiff.

These interests, and others that we may not perceive, are implicated in answering the question of whether the burden should be on the plaintiff or on the defendant, generally or in particular cases involving a risk-utility theory. The ultimate answer to the question best awaits balancing in an appropriate case, specifically raising the question, with attendant briefing from parties.

c. Related Legal Issues

We recognize that the decision to overrule *Azzarello* and articulate a standard of proof premised upon alternative tests in relation to claims of a product defective in design may have an impact upon other foundational issues regarding manufacturing or warning claims, and upon subsidiary issues, such as the availability of negligence-derived defenses, bystander compensation, or the proper application of the intended use doctrine. *Accord Bugosh*, 971 A.2d at 1244–45 & 1248–49. These considerations and effects are outside the scope of the facts of this dispute and, understandably, have not been briefed by the Tinchers or Omega Flex.

This Opinion does not purport to either approve or disapprove prior decisional law, or available alternatives suggested by commentators or the Restatements, relating to foundational or subsidiary considerations and consequences of our explicit holdings. In light of our prior discussion, the difficulties that justify our restraint should be readily apparent. The common law regarding these related considerations should develop within the proper factual contexts against the background of targeted advocacy.

IV. Conclusion / Mandate

[I]in light of the decision to overrule *Azzarello*, questions remain regarding whether Omega Flex should benefit from the application of our Opinion upon remand and, moreover, whether Omega Flex is entitled to a new trial. Here, Omega Flex preserved and presented its claim that *Azzarello* should be overruled to the trial court and on appeal; as a result, we hold that Omega Flex is entitled to the benefit of our decision in this regard. Whether Omega Flex is entitled to additional relief, including a new trial or judgment notwithstanding the verdict is not apparent upon the record before us.

For these reasons, we reverse in part the decision of the Superior Court in this matter, and remand to the trial court for further action upon post-trial motions.

Mr. Justice Saylor files a concurring and dissenting opinion in which Mr. Justice Eakin joins.

---

1. In *Aubin v. Union Carbide Corp.*, 177 So. 3d 489 (2015), the Florida Supreme Court agreed with *Tincher* in rejecting the Third Restatement's approach to cases involving design defects. In contrast, as *Tincher* acknowledged, there are several jurisdictions in which courts have embraced or followed significant portions of the Third Restatement. Among cases it cited are *Branham v. Ford Motor Co.*, 701 S.E.2d 5 (S.C. 2010); *Williams v. Bennett*, 921 So. 2d 1269 (Miss. 2006); *Wright v. Brooke Grp. Ltd.*, 652 N.W.2d 159 (Iowa 2002); *Jones v. NordicTrack, Inc.*, 550 S.E.2d 101 (Ga. 2001); and *Ruiz-Guzman v. Amvac Chem. Corp.*, 7 P.3d 795, 800 (Wash. 2000).

2. One of the many issues addressed in *Tincher* was the Third Restatement's requirement that plaintiffs in design defect cases produce evidence of an alternative design. Why does the *Tincher* court reject this requirement? What products might be defective under a risk/utility test but escape strict products liability on the ground that there is no alternative feasible design? Does the utility of cigarettes outweigh their dangers (cost)?

3. Can a cigarette ever be used safely? *See Bifolck v. Phillip Morris, Inc.*, 324 Conn. 402 (2016) (in a case alleging defective design of tobacco products, court refused to adopt Third Restatement standards under Connecticut product liability law, and specifically rejected Section 2(b)'s alternative design requirement).

4. The issue of alternative design also arose in *Mikolajczyk v. Ford Motor Co.*, 901 N.E. 329 (2008). The plaintiff's decedent died of injuries sustained when the Ford Escort he was driving was struck from behind by another vehicle. The seat had collapsed when the car was struck from behind, causing the victim to be propelled rearward and to strike his head on the backseat of the car. His widow, as special

administrator of his estate, sued the other driver claiming negligence, and Ford Motor Company and Mazda Motor Corporation claiming strict liability for defective design of the driver's seat. Relying in part on the on Section 2(b) of the Third Restatement, the defendant argued that the plaintiff should be required to present an alternative design in order to prove that the seat was defective. The court, however, rejected this argument. It concluded that Section 2(b) was inconsistent with Illinois product liability law, both because it required proof of an alternative design and because it required the plaintiff to prove that the product's design was "not reasonably safe." The court noted that in the mid-1990s, the state legislature had attempted to impose an alternative design requirement by statute, but that the court had struck the statute down on procedural state constitutional grounds, and the legislature had failed to re-enact the statute in terms that would have overcome the court's objections. In these circumstances, the court reasoned that the law presently did not include any such requirement, and it was up to the legislature whether or not to impose an alternative design requirement through a new statute.

4. Defining Defect When the Basis for Products Liability Is Failure to Warn

Failure to warn cases introduce an added complexity. In design defect cases, the manufacturer can argue that the product was not defective because its utility outweighs its actual risks. This balancing test includes the feasibility of eliminating or reducing the danger by a change in design, the expense of doing so, any reduction in utility resulting from the design change, and the ability of the consumer to avoid the danger. In a design defect case, all of these factors can provide the defendant with viable arguments against liability.

In a failure to warn case, on the other hand, the plaintiff is simply alleging that the product is defective because it did not contain a warning of the danger, one that is either informational (for dangers that cannot be avoided) or directional (for dangers that can be avoided if the product is used in accordance with the directions). Because warnings, unlike design changes, are cheap and do not directly affect the functioning of the product, it is much more difficult for a manufacturer to argue that a product without an adequate warning is not defective under a risk-utility type of analysis than it is for a manufacturer to argue that a design change would have been impractical or more expensive than it was worth.

The particular scenario that has caused the most trouble in warnings cases involves a dangerous product with what the manufacturer maintains are "unknowable" dangers. Such a product contains risks about which no one could have known at the time of manufacture or sale. Of course, many dangers that might be "unknown" are not truly "unknowable"—they could have been detected with additional testing or research at the time the product was made. But if a danger were truly unknowable, the manufacturer could not be negligent for failing to warn of the danger, because a reasonable manufacturer could not have known about it. Strict liability doctrine, at least as formulated, however, was not based on negligence, nor was it based on whether or not a reasonable manufacturer would have known of the danger at the time the product was distributed. Instead, it was based on the question whether the product's *actual* danger as marketed required a warning.

If one imputed knowledge of the danger to the manufacturer under a *Phillips v. Kimwood* test, the answer would be that a reasonable manufacturer, presumed to know of the product's actual danger, would not have sold the product without a warning. Thus, if the danger was truly unknowable, the manufacturer would be liable for failing to include a warning of a danger about which the manufacturer theoretically could not have known. To many courts and critics, this seemed entirely unfair, and it prompted a change in approach in warning cases.

This happened, for example, in a pair of prominent decisions in the Supreme Court of New Jersey. In *Beshada v. Johns-Manville Products Corp.*, 447 A.2d 539 (N.J. 1982), the court unanimously rejected an argument by asbestos manufacturers that they could not be held liable for "unknowable" dangers of that highly toxic substance. The court pointed out in that case that the difference between strict products liability and negligence-based liability was that in the former the manufacturer is irrebuttably presumed to know of the product's actual dangers, and therefore can be liable for failing to warn about them even if the manufacturer could not have known of the danger at the time the product was distributed. The manufacturer thus would not be allowed to introduce a so-called "state of the art" defense, pursuant to which the manufacturer would argue that it should not be liable because it could not have known of the danger. The court reasoned that to hold otherwise would be to shift the focus of the law away from the condition of the product and back toward the conduct of the manufacturer—in other words away from strict liability and back toward negligence.

The idea that a manufacturer could be held liable for failing to warn of dangers about which it could not have known, however, caused massive consternation. It took the Supreme Court of New Jersey only 23 months to back down from its decision in *Beshada*, which it did in the equally unanimous *Feldman v. Lederle Laboratories*, 479 A.2d 374 (N.J. 1984). In *Feldman*, the court ruled that a manufacturer of prescription pharmaceuticals had a duty to warn only of dangers about which the manufacturer could or should have known. Various other courts followed suit in various ways, ranging from exempting prescription pharmaceutical manufacturers from Section 402A altogether to holding that failure to warn law would be considered negligence-based, and not strict liability at all; thus, the manufacturer could only be liable for failing to warn of dangers about which a reasonable manufacturer could have known.

The Third Restatement of Products Liability provides that manufacturers are only liable for design and warning defects where the dangers were foreseeable. Thus, by definition, it excludes unknowable dangers from the scope of products liability altogether. Section 2(c) states that a product "is defective because of inadequate instructions or warnings when the foreseeable risks of harm posed by the product could have been reduced or avoided by the provision of reasonable instructions or warnings by the seller or other distributor, or a predecessor in the commercial chain of distribution, and the omission of the instructions or warnings renders the product not reasonably safe." As with the changes proposed by the Third Restatement on defects in design, this proposal has prompted courts to consider whether or not to "adopt" the Third Restatement approach.

The following two cases illustrate alternative approaches to this issue.

Sternhagen v. Dow Company
Supreme Court of Montana, 1997
935 P.2d 1139

Justice James C. Nelson delivered the Opinion of the Court.

The United States District Court for the District of Montana, Great Falls Division, has certified to this Court the following question:

> In a strict products liability case for injuries caused by an inherently unsafe product, is the manufacturer conclusively presumed to know the dangers inherent in his product, or is state-of-the-art evidence admissible to establish whether the manufacturer knew or through the exercise of reasonable human foresight should have known of the danger?

We conclude that Montana law precludes the admission of state-of-the-art evidence in products liability cases brought under the theory of strict liability.

FACTUAL AND PROCEDURAL BACKGROUND

The United States District Court for the District of Montana, Great Falls Division, found the following facts relevant to the question of law certified to this Court:

> 1. . . . [P]laintiff Marlene L. Sternhagen, as the personal representative of the estate of Charles J. Sternhagen, seeks recovery for injuries and damages allegedly sustained by Charles Sternhagen as a result of his exposure to the herbicide 2,4-D during the years 1948 through 1950. Plaintiff claims that the exposure of Charles Sternhagen to 2,4-D was the cause of the cancer that resulted in his death.

> 2. Plaintiff seeks recovery against the defendants under the doctrine of strict liability in tort. . . .

> 3. During the summer months of 1948, 1949 and 1950, Charles Sternhagen was employed by a crop spraying business in northeast Montana. Plaintiff claims that during that time, Charles Sternhagen was exposed to the herbicide, 2,4-D.

> 4. In 1981, Charles Sternhagen, a medical doctor specializing in radiology, was diagnosed as having a form of cancer which plaintiff claims was caused by his exposure to the herbicide 2,4-D during the years 1948 through 1950.

Defendants dispute the claim that there is a causal link between the herbicide 2,4-D and the type of cancer from which Charles Sternhagen died.

5. The defendants claim neither they, nor medical science, knew or had reason to know of any alleged cancer-causing properties of the herbicide 2,4-D during the years 1948 through 1950.

DISCUSSION

. . . .

The Chemical Companies next argue that if Restatement (Second) of Torts §402A (1965), is the applicable law, then state-of-the-art evidence is admissible because Montana law recognizes the state-of-the-art defense in failure to warn claims. The Chemical Companies contend that the certified question must be read in conjunction not only with Restatement (Second) of Torts §402A (1965) but also with the comments to §402A, including Comment j. Specifically, the Chemical Companies argue that the third sentence of Comment j applies, namely that "the seller is required to give warning . . . , if he has knowledge, or by the application of reasonably, developed human skill and foresight should have knowledge, of the presence of the . . . danger."

. . .

Furthermore, the Chemical Companies contend that in *Tacke v. Vermeer Mfg. Co.* (1986), 220 Mont. 1, 713 P.2d 527, the plaintiff offered state-of-the-art evidence on the issue of the feasibility in a design defect case. The Chemical Companies assert that if a plaintiff is allowed to offer state-of-the-art evidence to prove feasibility in a design defect case, a defendant may also offer state-of-the-art evidence to rebut feasibility as part of its defense. Therefore, the Chemical Companies argue a defendant should also be allowed to offer state-of-the-art evidence to disprove the feasibility of a warning in a failure to warn case.

Sternhagen responds that the certified question must be answered based on the fundamental principles underlying strict products liability in Montana. Sternhagen asserts that when this Court . . . adopted strict liability in tort for defective products as defined in Restatement (Second) of Torts §402A (1965), it did so based on substantial public interest and public policy grounds which included principles of fairness and economics, maximum protection for the consumer and placement of responsibility for injury on the manufacturer. Sternhagen asserts that over the past two-plus decades, this Court has consistently returned to and relied upon these core principles.

. . . .

Furthermore, Sternhagen contends that this Court has never adopted the state-of-the-art defense, but rather this Court has made it clear that even careful manufacturers may be strictly liable for unreasonably dangerous products which contained unforeseeable dangers. . . . Sternhagen urges this Court to again return to the core principles underlying the doctrine of strict liability and thereby reject the state-of-the-art defense. We agree with Sternhagen that we have not previously adopted the state-of-the-art defense. Further, we expressly reject the state-of-the-art defense, as this defense is contrary to the doctrine of strict products liability as that body of law has developed in Montana. . . .

. . . The Chemical Companies assert that we have either previously adopted or should now adopt the language of Comment j to § 402A. However, after researching Montana law on strict products liability, we conclude that the language in Comment j, which the Chemical Companies contend supports the state-of-the-art defense, is inconsistent with our established law concerning strict products liability and we therefore decline to adopt that language. Rather, we conclude that the imputation of knowledge doctrine, as discussed below, is more consistent with existing Montana law.

Furthermore, the Chemical Companies rely on only one part of the third sentence of Comment j which, when considered in its entirety, indicates that this sentence is not applicable to the question certified to this Court. The Chemical Companies rely on the language, "the seller is required to give warning . . . , if he has knowledge, or by the application of reasonably developed human skill and foresight should have knowledge, of the presence of the . . . danger." However, the third sentence of Comment j, from which that language is extracted, states:

> Where, however, the product contains **an ingredient to which a substantial number of the population are allergic**, *and the ingredient* is one whose danger is not generally known, or if known is one which the consumer would reasonably not expect to find in the product, the seller is required to give warning against *it* [the ingredient to which people are allergic], if he has knowledge, or by the application of reasonable, developed human skill and foresight should have knowledge, of the presence of *the ingredient* [to which people are allergic] and the danger. [Emphases [and parentheses] added [by the court in the original].]

The certified question before us involves an alleged cancer-causing ingredient, not one to which the decedent is alleged to have been allergic. Therefore, the third sentence of Comment j is not applicable to the certified question.

We adopted strict liability in torts for defective products based on important public policy considerations, to which we have consistently adhered for the past two-plus decades. "[T]he doctrine of strict liability was evolved to place liability on the party primarily responsible for the injury occurring, that is, the manufacturer of the defective product." *Brandenburger*, 513 P.2d at 273 (quoting *Lechuga, Inc. v. Montgomery* (1970), 12 Ariz. App. 32, 467 P.2d 256, 261 (Jacobson, J., concurring)). We, thereafter enumerated various public policy considerations supporting adoption of the strict liability doctrine:

1. The manufacturer can anticipate some hazards and guard against their recurrence, which the consumer cannot do.

2. The cost of injury may be overwhelming to the person injured while the risk of injury can be insured by the manufacturer and be distributed among the public as a cost of doing business.

3. It is in the public interest to discourage the marketing of defective products.

4. It is in the public interest to place responsibility for injury upon the manufacturer who was responsible for [the defective product] reaching the market.

5. That this responsibility should also be placed upon the retailer and wholesaler of the defective product in order that they may act as the conduit through which liability may flow to reach the manufacturer, where ultimate responsibility lies.

6. That because of the complexity of present day manufacturing processes and their secretiveness, the ability to prove negligent conduct by the injured plaintiff is almost impossible.

7. That the consumer does not have the ability to investigate for himself the soundness of the product.

8. That this consumer's vigilance has been lulled by advertising, marketing devices and trademarks.

Brandenburger, 513 P.2d at 273 (citations omitted). Furthermore, we stated:

The essential rationale for imposing the doctrine of strict liability in tort is that such imposition affords the consuming public the maximum protection from dangerous defects in manufactured products by requiring the manufacturer to bear the burden of injuries and losses enhanced by such defects in its products.

Brandenburger, 513 P.2d at 275.

Subsequent to our adoption of strict liability, we identified three elements essential to the establishment of a prima facie case in strict liability pursuant to § 402A:

(1) The product was in a defective condition, "unreasonably" dangerous to the user or consumer;

(2) The defect caused the accident and injuries complained of;

and

(3) The defect is traceable to the defendant.

Brown, 576 P.2d at 716.

The Chemical Companies argue that if this Court recognizes the imputation of knowledge doctrine, rather than the state-of-the-art defense, we will eliminate all of the elements that a plaintiff must prove to establish a strict products liability cause of action. Specifically, the Chemical Companies assert that the imputation of knowledge doctrine removes a plaintiff's burden of proving that a defect in the product caused the injury. In effect, the Chemical Companies are arguing that adoption of the imputation of knowledge doctrine will transform strict liability into absolute liability. We disagree.

From the time we initially adopted strict products liability, we have reassured defendants that strict liability is not absolute liability:

> The adoption of the doctrine of strict liability does not relieve the plaintiff from the burden of proving his case. Vital to that proof is the necessity of proving the existence of a defect in the product and that such defect caused the injury complained of.

Brandenburger, 513 P.2d at 274. We explained again, in *Brown*, that by imposing upon a plaintiff the burden of proving a traceable defect, causation, and damage or injury, even with a flexible rule of evidence, we assured "an appropriate limitation to a manufacturer's liability." *Brown*, 576 P.2d at 717. This has not changed.

Under the imputation of knowledge doctrine, which is based on strict liability's focus on the product and not the manufacturer's conduct, knowledge of a product's undiscovered or undiscoverable dangers shall be imputed to the manufacturer. Our adoption of the imputation of knowledge doctrine, and concomitant rejection of the state-of-the-art defense, does not change the requirements of plaintiff's prima facie case; it only reinforces our commitment to provide the maximum protection for consumers, while still assuring "an appropriate limitation to a manufacturer's liability."

In fact, for the past two-plus decades, we have consistently adhered to the core public policy principles underlying strict products liability as set forth in both *Brandenburger* and *Brown*. As stated in the certified question, state-of-the-art evidence is used to establish whether the manufacturer knew or through the exercise of reasonable human foresight should have known of the dangers inherent in his product. That is, the state-of-the-art defense raises issues of reasonableness and foreseeability—concepts fundamental to negligence law—to determine a manufacturer's liability. To recognize the state-of-the-art defense now would inject negligence principles into strict liability law and thereby sever Montana's strict products liability law from the core principles for which it was adopted—maximum protection for consumers against dangerous defects in manufactured products with the focus on the condition of the product, and not on the manufacturer's conduct or knowledge.

. . . .

Contrary to the Chemical Companies' assertion, our references to Comment j and our use of certain ambiguous language in previous case law does not support a conclusion that we have adopted the state-of-the-art defense. As discussed below, we conclude that in none of our prior cases was the state-of-the-art defense raised as an issue, much less adopted. Rather, these cases illustrate our strict adherence to the remedial policies underlying strict liability and our recognition of the basic differences between strict liability and negligence principles.

Attempting to demonstrate that we have adopted the state-of-the-art defense, the Chemical Companies cite to *Rost* and note that we referenced Comment j, and thereafter stated:

> Plaintiffs contend that this duty to warn is measured by an objective standard, the care which would be exercised by a reasonable seller or expected by the ordinary consumer. This standard focuses on the condition of the product and the degree of danger which would be tolerated by the reasonable manufacturer [who], *apprised of the danger*, would not sell the product without a warning.

Rost, 616 P.2d at 385 (citing *Phillips v. Kimwood Machine Co.* (1974), 269 Or. 485, 525 P.2d 1033, 1036–37) (emphasis added) (other citations omitted). The Chemical Companies assert that this language is synonymous with the state-of-the-art defense, and, therefore, that we recognized the state-of-the-art defense in *Rost*. We disagree. Rather, in making this assertion, the Chemical Companies take the language in *Rost* out of context from the authority cited.

To explain the nature of the duty to warn standard that the plaintiffs in *Rost* asserted, we cited *Phillips*. The Oregon Supreme Court stated in *Phillips* that to prevent strict liability from becoming absolute liability, a test for unreasonable danger is necessary to show that something about a product makes it dangerously defective without regard to whether the manufacturer was at fault for the condition. *Phillips*, 525 P.2d at 1036.

> A dangerously defective article would be one which a reasonable person would not put into the stream of commerce *if he had knowledge of its harmful character*. The test, therefore, is whether the seller would be negligent if he sold the article *knowing of the risk involved*. Strict liability imposes what amounts to constructive knowledge of the condition of the product.

Phillips, 525 P.2d at 1036. The Court in *Phillips* also explained that a difference exists between strict liability and negligence law because a product could be unreasonably dangerous even though the manufacturer's actions were reasonable in light of what he knew at the time he planned and sold the manufactured product. *Phillips*, 525 P.2d at 1037.

Furthermore, the Oregon Supreme Court explained that a way to determine if a product is unreasonably defective, is to assume that the manufacturer knew of the product's potential dangers and then ask whether a manufacturer with such knowledge should have done something about the danger before the product was sold. *Phillips*, 525 P.2d at 1037. When viewed in this context, it is apparent that this portion of the *Phillips* opinion to which we cited in *Rost* does not support the state-of-the-art defense, but rather describes the imputation of knowledge doctrine. . . .

Moreover, after citing *Phillips*, we further distinguished strict liability from negligence law and reiterated the public policy supporting strict products liability:

> This strict duty mandated by the theory of strict liability is warranted even though in some situations it may result in liability being imposed upon careful manufacturers. Unforeseeable product defects often cause severe physical injuries to members of the public. The manufacturer can distribute the risk from such accidents among the body of consumers, while the

individual consumer must bear the financial burden alone. Placing the risk of loss on the manufacturer provides an incentive to design and produce fail-safe products which exceed reasonable standards of safety. *Phillips, supra*, 525 P.2d at 1041. Nor can we ignore the fact that a manufacturer with research capabilities can anticipate hazards better than unsophisticated purchasers. Strict liability has its underpinnings in public policy.

Rost, 616 P.2d at 386 (other citations omitted).

. . . .

Alternatively, the Chemical Companies argue that even if the cases, discussed above, do not show that Montana has adopted the rule allowing state-of-the-art evidence, we should do so now based on the experience of other jurisdictions which favor the adoption of the rule. After discussing numerous cases from other jurisdictions, the Chemical Companies contend that an overwhelming majority of jurisdictions that have adopted § 402A also admit state-of-the-art evidence. Additionally, the Chemical Companies argue that the Restatement (Third) of the Law of Torts: Products Liability (Proposed Final Draft, Preliminary Version) (Oct. 18, 1996) would also allow state-of-the-art evidence. Furthermore, the Chemical Companies assert that public policy supports adoption of the state-of-the-art defense.

Despite the adoption of the state-of-the-art defense in other jurisdictions, recognition of the defense in the Restatement (Third) of the Law of Torts: Products Liability (Proposed Final Draft, Preliminary Version) (Oct. 18, 1996) and the Chemical Companies' assertion that public policy supports adoption of the defense, we choose to continue to adhere to the clear precedent we have heretofore established which focuses on the core principles and remedial purposes underlying strict products liability. Strict liability without regard to fault is the only doctrine that fulfills the public interest goals of protecting consumers, compensating the injured and making those who profit from the market bear the risks and costs associated with the defective or dangerous products which they place in the stream of commerce. As we discussed previously, no Montana case supports the Chemical Companies' position that state-of-the-art evidence is admissible when a product's inherent dangers are undiscovered or undiscoverable.

In fact, both our case law and statutory law make it clear that even careful manufacturers may be strictly liable for unreasonably dangerous products whose dangers could not be foreseen. Moreover, given strict liability's focus on the product and not on the manufacturer's conduct, knowledge of any undiscovered or undiscoverable dangers should be imputed to the manufacturer. That is, while a plaintiff must still prove the three prima facie elements set forth in *Brown*, evidence that a manufacturer knew or through the exercise of reasonable human foresight should have known of the dangers inherent in his product is irrelevant.

Accordingly, in answer to the question certified, we conclude that, in a strict products liability case, knowledge of any undiscovered or undiscoverable dangers should be imputed to the manufacturer. Furthermore, we conclude that, in a strict products liability case, state-of-the-art evidence is not admissible to establish whether the manufacturer knew or through the exercise of reasonable human foresight should have known of the danger.

TURNAGE, C.J., and GRAY, REGNIER, TRIEWEILER, LEAPHART and HUNT, JJ., concur.

Powers v. Taser International, Inc.

Court of Appeals of Arizona, 2007
174 P.3d 777

BARKER, JUDGE.

This Opinion addresses whether the hindsight test should be applied to a strict liability products claim alleging failure to warn as the defect. That test was adopted in *Dart v. Wiebe Manufacturing, Inc.* for strict liability products claims based on design defects. 147 Ariz. 242, 709 P.2d 876 (1985). The court expressly left open that issue as to strict liability products claims asserting a failure to warn. 147 Ariz. at 247 n. 2, 709 P.2d at 881 n. 2. For the reasons set forth below, we decline the invitation to adopt the hindsight test for such claims. . . .

I.

Plaintiff-Appellant Samuel E. Powers appeals a jury verdict in favor of Defendant-Appellee Taser International, Inc. ("Taser") on Powers' claim for strict products liability arising out of the alleged injury he suffered when shocked by the Advanced Taser M-26 ("M-26").

Taser manufactures and sells conducted energy weapons, including the M-26, which employs electro-muscular disruption (EMD) technology to stimulate a person's motor nerves, causing an involuntary muscle contraction. The evidence at trial was that earlier electric weapon devices affected only the sensory nervous system and relied primarily on pain compliance, which can be overcome by the recipient through focus or when he or she is under the effects of drugs or alcohol. The M-26, however, is designed to affect the sensory and motor nervous systems, overriding the central nervous system and causing uncontrollable muscle contractions that make it physically impossible for a person exposed to the M-26 to not respond to its effects.

On July 16, 2002, Powers was a sixteen-year veteran of the Maricopa County Sheriff's Office ("MCSO"), where he worked as a deputy sheriff. That morning, he participated in a training and certification course offered by the MCSO that was a prerequisite to being certified to carry the M-26. During the course, Powers received training materials prepared by Taser and viewed a PowerPoint Presentation regarding the M-26.

The materials described the M-26 as a "less-lethal" weapon and represented that the M-26 had been (1) tested on animals and found to have no effect on heart rhythms and (2) deployed on more than 3000 persons with no long-term effects. The materials warned, however, that short-term injuries could result from a fall associated with exposure to the M-26, noting that the most significant injuries to date had been "cuts, bruises and abrasions." In addition, as part of the training course, Powers viewed several videos showing individuals being exposed to the M-26.

As part of the course and as a prerequisite for certification to carry the M-26, the MCSO required all officers to be exposed to the electrical force of the M-26. Powers agreed to be exposed to the M-26 and was struck by the device. As a result of his exposure to the M-26, Powers allegedly suffered a compression fracture of his T-7 spinal disc.

Powers' physician, Dr. Terry McLean, discovered while treating Powers for this injury that Powers had severe osteoporosis, a quantitative loss of bone mass that weakens the bones. As a result of his osteoporosis and his physician's orders restricting him to light duty, Powers was unable to continue to work as a deputy sheriff and resigned from the MCSO in June 2003.

Powers filed suit against Taser, alleging that the M-26 was unreasonably dangerous and defective because it lacked adequate instructions and warnings. He alleged that as a direct and proximate result of the defective and unreasonably dangerous condition of the M-26, he suffered severe and permanent injuries for which he sought compensation. Taser argued at trial that because it did not know that the muscle contractions produced by the M-26 were strong enough to cause a fracture, it was not required to warn Powers about such a danger and contested his claimed damages.

The jury returned a general verdict in favor of Taser. Powers moved for a new trial, which was denied. . . .

Powers timely appealed. . . .

II.

A.

Powers argues that Arizona has adopted a "hindsight" approach in strict liability cases involving alleged informational defects and claims the trial court erroneously failed to instruct the jury that it could impute to Taser knowledge of the danger of the M-26 that was revealed subsequent to Taser's distribution of the product. . . .

The trial court ruled before trial that Taser's "duty to warn under a product liability claim for relief is . . . a foresight test, i.e., what the manufacturer of the product knew or reasonably should have known when the product was introduced into the stream of commerce, and not a hindsight test." Consistent with this ruling, throughout the trial the court excluded evidence of subsequent testing of the M-26, except as it pertained to the feasibility of having performed that testing prior to Powers' injury. Despite the court's position, at the conclusion of trial Powers requested that the court instruct the jury that it could impute to Taser knowledge of dangers associated with the M-26 that only became known after Powers' injury. Specifically, Powers requested that the trial court instruct the jury based on alternative 2 set forth in Revised Arizona Jury Instruction-Product Liability 4 (January 2005) ("RAJI 4"). RAJI 4 states:

[Name of plaintiff] claims that there was not (an) adequate [warning] [instruction] on/with the product. A product, even if faultlessly made, is defective and unreasonably dangerous if it would be unreasonably dangerous for use in a reasonably foreseeable manner without (an) adequate [warning(s)] [instruction(s)].

[RAJI 4 (2005). The RAJI Committee then gave a choice of two alternatives to complete the instruction. Alternative 1 states]:

A product is defective and unreasonably dangerous if a manufacturer or seller who knows or should know that a foreseeable use of its product may be unreasonably dangerous does not provide adequate [warning(s) of the danger] [instruction(s) for reasonably safe use].

Id. Alternative 2 provides:

[A manufacturer or seller is presumed to have known at all relevant times the facts that this accident and this trial have revealed about the harmful characteristics of the product and the consequences of its reasonably foreseeable use, whether or not the manufacturer or seller actually knew those facts. If you find that it would not be reasonable for a manufacturer or seller, with such presumed knowledge, to have put this product on the market without providing (an) adequate [warning(s) of the danger] [instruction(s) for reasonably safe use], then the product is defective and unreasonably dangerous.]

Id. Taser objected to Powers' proposed instruction, arguing that because the court had already ruled that it would not apply the hindsight test, the court should instruct the jury based upon alternative 1 to RAJI 4].

In the notes to RAJI 4, the Committee suggests that the court give the first paragraph of the instruction and either the second paragraph or the third paragraph, depending on the circumstances of the case, explaining:

The Committee was unable to determine, as a result of the Arizona Supreme Court's footnote 2 in *Dart v. Wiebe Manufacturing, Inc.*, 147 Ariz. 242, 709 P.2d 876 (1985), whether a hindsight test is applied in strict liability information defect cases. The court expressly reserved this question in *Dart.* Some members of the Committee hold to the view that *Gosewisch v. American Honda Motor Co.*, 153 Ariz. 400, 737 P.2d 376 (1987), resolves this issue in favor of using a hindsight test. Other members are of the view that until the Arizona Supreme Court actually addresses its reservation in *Dart*, it is reversible error to give a hindsight instruction in an information defect case. The [alternative 1] language is essentially a negligence instruction, but the Committee is unaware of any other alternatives to a hindsight instruction. If a hindsight test is not applicable, then the [alternative 1] language should be used. If a hindsight test is applicable, [alternative 2] language should be used.

RAJI 4, Use Note & Footnotes 1 & 2. The trial court gave a non-hindsight instruction similar to alternative 1, but included language that clarified what Taser should have known:

> Plaintiff claims that there was not an adequate warning on/with the product. A product, even if faultlessly made, is defective and unreasonably dangerous if it would be unreasonably dangerous for use in a reasonably foreseeable manner without an adequate warning(s).
>
> A product is defective and unreasonably dangerous if a manufacturer or seller who knows or should know that a foreseeable use of its product may be unreasonably dangerous does not provide adequate warning(s) of the danger for reasonably safe use.
>
> A seller of a product must warn of a particular risk that was known or knowable in light of the generally recognized and prevailing scientific and medical knowledge available at the time of its distribution.

Powers contends the trial court erred by refusing to instruct the jury to apply the hindsight test in this case, and by instead instructing the jury that it could only consider whether, at the time of the M-26's distribution, Taser knew or should have known that the M-26 was unreasonably dangerous unless accompanied by adequate warnings.

B.

The Arizona Supreme Court first adopted an imputed knowledge, or "hindsight," test in *Dart v. Wiebe Manufacturing, Inc.*, a case involving an alleged design defect. 147 Ariz. at 247, 709 P.2d at 881. In that case, the plaintiff sued the manufacturer of an industrial paper shredder after he was seriously injured by a shredding machine. *Id.* at 243, 709 P.2d at 877. The plaintiff alleged that the shredder was defectively designed because it lacked safety guards that would have prevented the injury. *Id.* The trial court gave the jury a single instruction regarding the plaintiff's separate theories of negligence and strict liability. *Id.* The Arizona Supreme Court reversed, ruling that in order to preserve the difference between negligence and strict liability theories, the applicable standard for each claim must be different. *Id.*

The court wrote that to prove negligence, a plaintiff must prove that the manufacturer acted unreasonably at the time of manufacture or design of the product. *Id.* at 247, 709 P.2d at 881. However, in a strict liability analysis, "it is not the conduct of the manufacturer or designer which is primarily in question, but rather the quality of the end result; the product is the focus of the inquiry." *Id.* The court thus held that with regard to the plaintiff's claim for strict liability, the jury should have been instructed that the "quality of the product may be measured not only by the information available to the manufacturer at the time of design, *but also by the information available to the trier of fact at the time of trial.*" *Id.* (emphasis added).

The Arizona Supreme Court did not extend this holding to failure to warn cases, and, in fact, expressly declined to reach the issue whether a hindsight test should be applied in strict liability cases involving the failure to warn or those involving inherently dangerous products. *Id.* at 247 n. 2, 709 P.2d at 881 n. 2, ("We do not reach the issue of whether a 'hindsight test' is to be applied to strict liability cases involving failure to warn or those involving unavoidably unsafe products."). Subsequent Arizona cases have reiterated the fundamental difference between negligence and strict products liability theories discussed in *Dart*, but have not extended the hindsight test to failure to warn cases.

In the absence of Arizona law specifically addressing the court's reservation in *Dart*, we would ordinarily follow pre-*Dart* authority, in which Arizona courts applied a foreseeability test in warning cases. *Schneider v. Cessna Aircraft Co.*, 150 Ariz. 153, 158–59, 722 P.2d 321, 326–27 (App.1985) (reversing jury verdict because trial court erroneously refused to instruct jury that defendant could be held strictly liable for failing to warn of product dangers that manufacturer had "reason to foresee"); *Shell Oil Co. v. Gutierrez*, 119 Ariz. 426, 434, 581 P.2d 271, 279 (App.1978) (holding that whether a product is defective or unreasonably dangerous because of a failure to warn depends on foreseeability, seriousness, and the cost of preventing injury). Such an approach would also be consistent with the Restatement (Third) of Torts: Products Liability ("Restatement Third") § 2(c)(1998), which provides that a product:

> [I]s defective because of inadequate instructions or warnings when the foreseeable risks of harm posed by the product could have been reduced or avoided by the provision of reasonable instructions or warnings by the [manufacturer], . . . and the omission of the instructions or warnings renders the product not reasonably safe.[5]

Absent controlling Arizona law to the contrary, we generally follow the Restatement, provided we deem it good legal authority. *In re Krohn*, 203 Ariz. 205, 210, 18, 52 P.3d 774, 779 (2002) (stating the Arizona Supreme Court has long followed the rule that it will follow the Restatement when not bound by previous decisions or legislative enactment); *Southwest Pet Prod., Inc., v. Koch Indus.*, 273 F. Supp. 2d 1041, 1052 n.17 (D.Ariz.2003) (stating reliance on Restatement Third is in keeping with "Arizona's long-standing policy to look to the Restatement absent contrary precedent."). However, we do not follow the Restatement blindly, *Barnes*, 192 Ariz. at 285, 6, 964 P.2d at 486, and will come to a contrary conclusion if Arizona law suggests otherwise. *Wilcox v. Waldman*, 154 Ariz. 532, 536, 744 P.2d 444, 448 (App.1987). Powers argues that we should not follow pre-*Dart* Arizona warning defect cases and the Restatement, and instead urges us to extend the Arizona Supreme Court's holding

---

5. This standard further develops the view set forth in the Restatement (Second) of Torts ("Restatement Second") § 402A (1965), which required that a manufacturer give warnings to prevent a product from being unreasonably dangerous only, "if [the manufacturer] has knowledge, or by the application of reasonable, developed human skill and foresight should have knowledge, of the presence of the . . . danger." Restatement Second § 402A cmt. j. The Restatement Third § 2 approach to warning defects thus parallels the standard set forth for determining design defects. Restatement Third § 2, cmt. i.

in *Dart* to warning defect cases, contending that the considerations the court relied on in *Dart* when adopting the hindsight test support the application of the same test in warning defect cases. We therefore consider whether the Restatement position is good legal authority under Arizona law, particularly in light of *Dart*.

C.

The court in *Dart* focused on the differences between the doctrine of negligence, which centers on the reasonableness of the manufacturer's conduct, and the doctrine of strict liability, which centers on the quality of the product. 147 Ariz. at 246–47, 709 P.2d at 880–81. The court ruled that by imposing on the manufacturer constructive knowledge of the condition of the product as revealed at trial, the inquiry would remain focused on the quality of the product, rather than on the reasonableness of the manufacturer's conduct in selecting the particular product design. *Id.* at 247, 709 P.2d at 881. In adopting this test, the court noted that it was "generally recommended by the commentators, and by precedent." *Id.* However, this circumstance has since changed, as the initial proponents of the hindsight doctrine later withdrew their support for the view, observing that a product's design should be measured in terms of the technology available at the time of manufacture. *See* Restatement Third § 2 cmt. m(1) (citing numerous academic articles taking issue with the validity of the hindsight approach).

Accordingly, the standard adopted by the Arizona Supreme Court in *Dart* is inconsistent with the recently adopted Restatement Third, which provides that a product is defective in design when "the *foreseeable* risks of harm posed by the product could have been reduced or avoided by the adoption of a reasonable alternative design." Restatement Third § 2(b) (emphasis added). In adopting this view, the American Law Institute expressly rejected the hindsight approach in design defect cases, citing widespread academic criticism of, and relatively thin judicial support for, the theory. Restatement Third § 2, note m.1 ("Given the criticism that has been leveled against the imputation of knowledge doctrine and the relatively thin judicial support for it, it is here rejected as a doctrinal matter."). We are, of course, bound by the Arizona Supreme Court's holding in *Dart* as it applies to design defect cases, even though the authorities the court relied upon in *Dart* have been modified. *City of Phoenix v. Leroy's Liquors Inc.*, 177 Ariz. 375, 378, 868 P.2d 958, 961 (App.1993) (stating court of appeals is bound by decisions of the supreme court and may not "overrule, modify or disregard them"). Nevertheless, we give due regard to this recent criticism and authority when evaluating whether we should extend the holding in *Dart* to warning defect cases.

There are other reasons not to extend *Dart* to warning defect cases. The nature of a design defect case is fundamentally different than a failure to warn case. *See Anderson v. Owens-Corning Fiberglas Corp.*, 53 Cal.3d 987, 1002, 281 Cal.Rptr. 528, 810 P.2d 549, 558 (1991) (positing that the warning defect theory is "rooted in negligence" to a greater extent than manufacturing or design defect theories). Accordingly, the same analysis applied by the court in *Dart* cannot simply be imported wholesale to determine the proper standard in a warnings defect case. "The 'warning defect' relates to a failure extraneous to the product itself. Thus, while a manufacturing or design defect *can be* evaluated without reference to the conduct of the manufacturer, the giving of a warning cannot." *Id.* (emphasis in original) (internal citations omitted). The Arizona Supreme Court impliedly recognized this essential distinction in *Dart* when it refused to extend the hindsight test to warning defect claims, citing *Kearl v. Lederle Labs.*, 172 Cal.App.3d 812, 218 Cal.Rptr. 453 (1985).

The California Court of Appeal ruled in *Kearl* that a products liability claim based on a failure to warn about an unavoidably dangerous product could not be brought in strict liability, only negligence, because the adequacy of the manufacturer's warning must be based on a determination regarding what it knew or should have known. *Id.* at 832–33, 218 Cal.Rptr. 453. Although the California Supreme Court later over-ruled *Kearl* in *Brown v. Superior Court*, 44 Cal.3d 1049, 1069, 245 Cal.Rptr. 412, 751 P.2d 470, 482–83 (1988), holding that a claim may be brought in strict liability for failure to warn of unavoidably dangerous products, the court in *Brown* reiterated that the applicable standard is *foreseeability*, stating that a product must be "accompanied by warnings of its dangerous propensities that were either known or reasonably scientifically knowable at the time of distribution." 44 Cal.3d at 1068–69, 245 Cal. Rptr. 412, 751 P.2d at 483.[6]

Moreover, as the California Supreme Court has recognized, applying a foresight test does not eliminate the distinction between negligence and strict liability:

> [D]espite its roots in negligence, failure to warn in strict liability differs markedly from failure to warn in the negligence context. Negligence law in a failure-to-warn case requires a plaintiff to prove that a manufacturer or distributor did not warn of a particular risk for reasons which fell below the acceptable standard of care, i.e., what a reasonably prudent manufacturer would have known and warned about. Strict liability is not concerned with the standard of due care or the reasonableness of a manufacturer's conduct. The rules of strict liability require a plaintiff to prove only that the defendant did not adequately warn of a particular risk that was known or knowable in light of the generally recognized and prevailing best scientific and medical knowledge available at the time of manufacture and distribution. *Thus, in strict liability, as opposed to negligence, the reasonableness of the defendant's failure to warn is immaterial.*

Anderson, 53 Cal.3d at 1002–03, 281 Cal.Rptr. 528, 810 P.2d at 558–59 (emphasis added). Thus, applying a foresight test in failure to warn cases would not eliminate the distinction between negligence and strict liability as the court in *Dart* was concerned would happen in design defect cases.

---

6. Both *Kearl* and *Brown* involved pharmaceutical products. In *Anderson*, the California Supreme Court extended its holding in *Brown* to cases not involving prescription drugs. 53 Cal.3d at 1000, 281 Cal.Rptr. 528, 810 P.2d at 557.

Finally, it is our view that employing the hindsight test in warning defect cases would be tantamount to imposing a duty on manufacturers to warn of unknowable dangers. *Id.* at 998, 281 Cal.Rptr. 528, 810 P.2d at 555 ("To exact an obligation to warn the user of unknown and unknowable allergies, sensitivities and idiosyncrasies would be for the courts to recast the manufacturer in the role of an insurer. . . ."). As the Arizona Supreme Court recognized in *Dart*, however, the doctrine of strict liability does not impose liability for every injury caused by a product. 147 Ariz. at 244, 709 P.2d at 878. *See also Anderson*, 53 Cal.3d at 994, 281 Cal.Rptr. 528, 810 P.2d at 552 ("From its inception, . . . strict liability has never been, and is not now, *absolute* liability . . . [U]nder strict liability the manufacturer does not thereby become the insurer of the safety of the product's use.") (citations omitted); Restatement Third § 2, note M ("Unforeseeable risks arising from foreseeable product use or consumption by definition cannot specifically be warned against. . . . A seller is charged with knowledge of what reasonable testing would reveal."). For this reason, a majority of jurisdictions reject the approach in warning defect cases, instead requiring a manufacturer to warn only of risks that were known or should have been known to a reasonable manufacturer. *See, e.g., Anderson*, 53 Cal.3d at 999, 281 Cal.Rptr. 528, 810 P.2d at 557 (holding that "knowledge, actual or constructive, is a requisite for strict liability for failure to warn."); *Fibreboard Corp. v. Fenton*, 845 P.2d 1168, 1172 (Colo.1993) ("We agree with the petitioners that state-of-the-art evidence is properly admissible to establish that a product is not defective and unreasonably dangerous because of a failure-to-warn. A manufacturer cannot warn of dangers that were not known to it or knowable in light of the generally recognized and prevailing scientific and technical knowledge available at the time of manufacture and distribution."); *Woodill v. Parke Davis & Co.*, 79 Ill.2d 26, 37 Ill.Dec. 304, 402 N.E.2d 194, 198 (1980) ("requiring a plaintiff to plead and prove that the defendant manufacturer knew or should have known of the danger that caused the injury, and that the defendant manufacturer failed to warn plaintiff of that danger, is a reasonable requirement, and one which focuses on the nature of the product and the adequacy of the warning, rather than on the conduct of the manufacturer").

Accordingly, we decline to extend Arizona law to adopt the hindsight test from *Dart* in failure to warn strict liability cases. The trial court did not err by instructing the jury that it could only consider whether, at the time of the M-26's distribution, Taser knew or should have known that the M-26 was unreasonably dangerous unless accompanied by an adequate warning. . . .

———————

1. In holding a manufacturer liable for failing to warn of an unknowable danger, is the court asking the manufacturer to do the impossible? Even if the answer to this question is "yes," does that mean that the manufacturer should not be liable? As between a non-negligent plaintiff and a non-negligent manufacturer, strict products liability at least in theory mandates that the loss should fall on the manufacturer, and not on the equally innocent plaintiff. Indeed, if the manufacturer is negligent

in failing to warn of a knowable danger, the plaintiff will not need strict liability in order to prevail.

2. What does "state of the art" mean? There are several possibilities, including (but not limited to) "state of industry knowledge of the danger" and "state of industry knowledge of the cure." Industry knowledge of the cure has never been imputed under Section 402A. How satisfactory is the *Powers* Court's analysis of the two concepts?

3. What impact does abolishing the imputation of knowledge have on Section 402A? On strict products liability generally? Many courts have used comment j in the way that the *Powers* Court did. Compare the quotation from comment j in *Powers* with the full comment, included in *Sternhagen*.

4. The Third Restatement of the Law, Torts: Products Liability makes several changes to the Second. These changes have proven to be of fundamental importance, particularly in the realms of design and warning defects. Section 2(c) of the Third Restatement defines defective warnings as follows: "A product is defective because of inadequate instructions or warnings when the foreseeable risks of harm posed by the product could have been reduced or avoided by the provision of reasonable instructions or warnings . . . and the omission of the instructions or warnings renders the product not reasonably safe." How does this differ from the Second Restatement concept of warning defect?

5. The Third Restatement leaves liability for mismanufacture basically intact: a plaintiff may use res ipsa loquitur doctrine in making his or her case that a product failed because the individual unit deviated from the norm for the particular product. The Third Restatement, in Section 3, makes clear, however, that in most cases plaintiffs may no longer use res ipsa loquitur doctrine in proving that a product suffered from a design or warning defect. Reporters' Note 2 states that "Section 3 applies in most instances to manufacturing defects only." *See Myrlak v. Port Authority of NY & NJ*, 723 A.2d 45 (NJ, 1999) (interpreting New Jersey product liability statute in accordance with Third Restatement approach).

6. There are products the dangers of which cannot be eliminated by the adoption of a reasonable alternative design, but which, unlike vaccines, fail any applicable risk/ utility test. The most familiar such product is the cigarette. Could a manufacturer be liable for such a product under the Second Restatement? Under the Third? Would a warning of such a product's dangers be sufficient to prevent a finding that the product was defective?

Problem

When C breaks his leg, the surgeons decide to attach the broken pieces together with a plate which screws directly to the bone. Several months later, one of the screws fails, and C is seriously injured.

C files suit against the manufacturer of the screw. He cannot show why the screw failed. He can prove that he followed all the directions he was given after the surgery, and that he was not informed prior to surgery that the screw might fail. He can also prove that, under magnification, the screw contained "inclusions," microscopic bits of substances other than that metal of which the screw was made. The manufacturer can prove that all screws—indeed, all objects made of metal—contain inclusions.

What will C argue in a lawsuit filed under the Second Restatement? Under the Third Restatement? How will the manufacturer respond? What result under each of the Restatements?

5. Defining Defect Where the Product Is a Prescription Drug

Freeman v. Hoffman-La Roche, Inc.

Supreme Court of Nebraska, 2000
618 N.W.2d 827

CONNOLLY, J.

In this appeal, we reconsider our approach to products liability for defects in prescription drugs in light of changes in the law and the release of Restatement (Third) of Torts: Products Liability §§ 1 to 21 (1997) (Third Restatement). . . .

I. BACKGROUND

Freeman's operative petition alleged the following facts: On or about September 23, 1995, Freeman presented herself to her physician for treatment of chronic acne. After examination, her physician prescribed 20 milligrams daily of Accutane. Hoffman is the designer, manufacturer, wholesaler, retailer, fabricator, and supplier of Accutane.

Freeman took the Accutane daily from September 27 through October 2, 1995, and from October 4 through November 20, 1995. Hoffman alleged that as a result of taking the Accutane, she developed multiple health problems. These problems included ulcerative colitis, inflammatory polyarthritis, nodular episcleritis OS, and optic nerve head drusen. As a result, Freeman alleged that she sustained various damages. . . .

IV. ANALYSIS

Freeman contends that she has stated a cause of action for products liability under a variety of theories of recovery. Before proceeding, we believe it helpful to set forth a brief history of the general principles of products liability law and its development since the adoption of Restatement (Second) of Torts § 402 A (1965) (Second Restatement).

In products liability litigation, the notion of a defective product embraces two separate concepts. The first, commonly labeled as a manufacturing defect, is one in which the product differs from the specifications and plan of the manufacturer. The second concept of a defective product is one in which the product meets the specifications of the manufacturer but the product nonetheless poses an unreasonable risk of danger. This condition is generally characterized as a design defect. A manufacturer may also be liable for a failure to warn.

In products liability cases, there is a significant distinction between a manufacturer's liability as the result of negligent manufacture and its liability for the manufactured product on account of strict liability in tort. In a cause of action based on negligence, the question involves the manufacturer's conduct, that is, whether the manufacturer's conduct was reasonable in view of the foreseeable risk of injury; whereas in a cause of action based on strict liability in tort, the question involves the quality of the product, that is, whether the product was unreasonably dangerous.

For organizational purposes, we address Freeman's allegations of product defects in terms of the defects which she attempts to allege: design, manufacturing, and warning.

1. DESIGN DEFECT

In her operative petition, Freeman alleges that Hoffman is strictly liable for her injuries on the bases that Accutane was not fit for its intended purpose, that the risks inherent in the design outweighed the benefits of its use, and that Accutane was more dangerous to Freeman than was anticipated due to undisclosed side effects. As facts supporting her allegations, Freeman alleges that Accutane is sold as an acne medication and that the side effects of Accutane present life-threatening conditions. Thus, Freeman's petition asserts that Hoffman is liable on the basis of a design defect. Hoffman, however, alleges that because Accutane was approved by the FDA, it is exempted from liability for a design defect pursuant to our decision in *McDaniel v. McNeil Laboratories, Inc.*, 196 Neb. 190, 241 N.W.2d 822 (1976).

(a) Second Restatement § 402 A

In dealing with products other than prescription drugs, this court has recognized a manufacturer's liability in tort for design defects. Liability arises when an article a manufacturer has placed in the market, knowing that it is to be used without inspection for defects, proves to have a defect which causes an injury to a human being rightfully using the product. We have also adopted and applied the test set out in the Second Restatement § 402 A.

Section 402 A at 347–48 provides:

(1) One who sells any product in a defective condition unreasonably dangerous to the user or consumer or to his property is subject to liability for physical harm thereby caused to the ultimate user or consumer, or to his property, if

(a) the seller is engaged in the business of selling such a product, and

(b) it is expected to and does reach the user or consumer without substantial change in the condition in which it is sold.

(2) The rule stated in Subsection (1) applies although

(a) the seller has exercised all possible care in the preparation and sale of his product, and

(b) the user or consumer has not bought the product from or entered into any contractual relation with the seller.

Comment *i*. at 352 provides that the rule stated in § 402 A

applies only where the defective condition of the product makes it unreasonably dangerous to the user or consumer. . . . The article sold must be dangerous to an extent beyond that which would be contemplated by the ordinary consumer who purchases it, with the ordinary knowledge common to the community as to its characteristics.

This is commonly referred to as the "consumer expectations test."

In *Rahmig v. Mosley Machinery Co.*, 226 Neb. 423, 412 N.W.2d 56 (1987), we discussed criticisms of the consumer expectations test as embodied in § 402 A and the application in other jurisdictions of a risk-utility test in determining whether a product is unreasonably dangerous. We noted, however, that the issue of whether to adopt a risk-utility test was not before us. We then specifically overruled cases indicating that a plaintiff must present evidence of a reasonable alternative design in cases involving design defects.

Since *Rahmig*, we have applied the consumer expectations test for strict liability. See, e.g., *Haag v. Bongers*, 256 Neb. 170, 589 N.W.2d 318 (1999). Under this test, "'[u]nreasonably dangerous' means that a product has the propensity for causing physical harm beyond that which would be contemplated by the ordinary user or consumer who purchases it, with ordinary knowledge common to the foreseeable class of users as to its characteristics." *Id.* at 184, 589 N.W.2d at 329. Thus, in regard to nonprescription drug products, we have generally followed the rule as set out in § 402 A of the Second Restatement. Prescription drugs, however, have been treated differently both by this court and by the Second Restatement.

(i) Comment K. Exception for Unavoidably Unsafe Products

Under the Second Restatement, prescription drugs are treated specially under § 402 A, comment *k*. Comment *k*. at 353–54 provides an exception from strict liability when a product is deemed to be "unavoidably unsafe" and states:

There are some products which, in the present state of human knowledge, are quite incapable of being made safe for their intended and ordinary use. These are especially common in the field of drugs. An outstanding example is the vaccine for the Pasteur treatment of rabies, which not uncommonly leads to very serious and damaging consequences when it is injected. Since the disease itself invariably leads to a dreadful death, both the marketing and the use of the vaccine are fully justified, notwithstanding the unavoidable high degree of risk which they involve. Such a product, properly prepared, and accompanied by proper directions and warning, is not defective, nor is it unreasonably dangerous. The same is true of many other drugs, vaccines, and the like, many of which for this very reason cannot legally be sold except to physicians, or under the prescription of a physician. It is also true in particular of many new or experimental drugs as to which, because of lack of time and opportunity for sufficient medical experience, there can be no assurance of safety, or perhaps even of purity of ingredients, but such experience as there is justifies the marketing and use of the drug notwithstanding a medically recognizable risk. The seller of such products, again with the qualification that they are properly prepared and marketed, and proper warning is given, where the situation calls for it, is not to be held to strict liability for unfortunate consequences attending their use, merely because he has undertaken to supply the public with an apparently useful and desirable product, attended with a known but apparently reasonable risk.

Application of comment *k.* has been justified under the law in some jurisdictions as a way to strike a balance between a manufacturer's responsibility and the encouragement of research and development of new products. Under certain instances, it is in the public interest to allow products to be marketed which are unsafe, because the benefits of the product justify its risks. See, *Hill v. Searle Laboratories*, 884 F.2d 1064 (8th Cir. 1989) (describing policy considerations); *Tansy v. Dacomed Corp.*, 890 P.2d 881 (Okla.1994).

We applied § 402 A, comment *k.*, to a products liability action involving a prescription drug in *McDaniel v. McNeil Laboratories, Inc.*, 196 Neb. 190, 241 N.W.2d 822 (1976). In *McDaniel*, a woman was rendered permanently comatose after being given doses of a prescription drug, Innovar, during surgery. At the time of her surgery, Innovar and the warnings and information contained in the package inserts had been approved for use by the FDA. At trial, it was contended that the manufacturer was negligent in failing to warn, strictly liable under § 402 A of the Second Restatement, and liable under a theory of either express or implied warranty. The trial court submitted the issue of negligence to the jury but did not submit the issue of strict liability or warranty to the jury. On appeal, we placed emphasis on FDA approval of the drug, and citing to § 402 A, comment *k.*, we held:

> An unavoidably unsafe drug which has been approved for marketing by the United States Food and Drug Administration, properly prepared, compounded, packaged, and distributed, and accompanied by proper approved directions and warnings, as a matter of law, is not defective nor unreasonably dangerous, in the absence of proof of inaccurate, incomplete, misleading, or fraudulent information furnished by the manufacturer in connection with such federal approval or later revisions thereof.

McDaniel, 196 Neb. at 201, 241 N.W.2d at 828. Under the evidence presented, we determined that it was not error for the trial court to refuse to submit the issue of strict liability or warranty either express or implied, to the jury.

(ii) Interpretation of Comment k. *in Other Jurisdictions*

Comment *k.*, however, has been interpreted in a variety of ways in other jurisdictions, and there has been a wide range of disagreement regarding its application.

Only a few jurisdictions have interpreted comment *k.* in a manner that strictly excepts all prescription drugs from strict liability. Under the minority view, a drug that is properly manufactured and accompanied by an adequate warning of the risks known to the manufacturer at the time of sale is not defectively designed as a matter of law. *Brown v. Superior Court (Abbott Laboratories)*, 44 Cal.3d 1049, 245 Cal.Rptr. 412, 751 P.2d 470 (1988); *Grundberg v. Upjohn Co.*, 813 P.2d 89 (Utah 1991); *Young v. Key Pharmaceuticals*, 130 Wash.2d 160, 922 P.2d 59 (1996) (en banc). These jurisdictions are commonly described by legal commentators as providing manufacturers with a "blanket immunity" from strict liability for design defects in prescription drugs. See, e.g., Winchester, *supra.* Our decision in *McDaniel, supra,* generally falls under this category of interpretation of comment *k.*

(iii) Cases Applying Risk-Utility Analysis Under Comment k.

An application of comment *k.* to provide a blanket immunity from strict liability is widely criticized. Comment *k.* has proved to be difficult to interpret and apply, thus, supporting the argument that it should not be applied so strictly. Further, it is said that an approach that entirely excepts manufacturers from [liability] limits the discretionary powers of the courts. Also, it is argued that a blanket immunity leads to patently unjust results. One court has stated:

> We believe that a more selective application [of comment *k.*] will encourage, rather than discourage, improvements in prescription products. Comment k was designed in part to protect new and experimental drugs. . . . "Comment k states: 'There are some products which, in the present state of human knowledge, are quite incapable of being made safe for their intended and ordinary use.' Obviously, for this to be true, the design must be as safe as the best available testing and research permits." . . . Thus, a product which is as safe as current testing and research permits should be protected. The reverse is also true; a product which is not as safe as current technology can make it should not be protected.

(Citation omitted.) *Adams v. G.D. Searle & Co., Inc.*, 576 So. 2d 728, 732 (Fla.App.1991).

The majority of jurisdictions that have adopted comment *k.* apply it on a case-by-case basis, believing that societal interests in ensuring the marketing and development of prescription drugs will be adequately served without the need to resort to a rule of blanket immunity. A few courts have not specifically adopted comment *k.* and have instead either fashioned their own rules or treated prescription drugs in the same manner as that of all other products.

Although a variety of tests are employed among jurisdictions that apply comment *k.* on a case-by-case basis, the majority apply the comment as an affirmative defense, with the trend toward the use of a risk-utility test in order to determine whether the defense applies. When a risk-utility test is applied, the existence of a reasonable alternative design is generally the central factor. Because the application of comment *k.* is traditionally viewed as an exception and a defense to strict liability, courts generally place the initial burden of proving the various risk utility factors on the defendant. Thus, under these cases, the plaintiff's burden of proof for his or her prima facie case remains the same as it is in any products liability case in the given jurisdiction.

At the time *McDaniel v. McNeil Laboratories, Inc.*, 196 Neb. 190, 241 N.W.2d 822 (1976), was decided, it reflected a minority view. Since that time, a clear majority of courts have decided on a case-by-case basis, through the application of a comment *k.* defense, the issue of liability of a manufacturer for a design defect in a prescription drug. On further reflection, we conclude that the rule of law expressed in *McDaniel* has not held up over time. We now believe that societal interests in ensuring the marketing and development of prescription drugs can be served without resorting to a rule which in effect amounts to a blanket immunity from strict liability for manufacturers. Accordingly, we overrule *McDaniel* to the extent it applies comment *k.* to provide a blanket immunity from strict liability for prescription drugs. Accordingly, we must address how, or if, comment *k.* should be applied, or whether we should consider adopting provisions of the Third Restatement. We next address those provisions in considering what test should be applied.

(b) Third Restatement

The provisions of the Second Restatement regarding products liability were changed dramatically in the Third Restatement, published by the American Law Institute in 1997. As stated in the introduction to the Third Restatement, the institute was required to answer questions that were not part of the products liability landscape when the Second Restatement was completed. Thus, the Third Restatement is a complete overhaul of the Second Restatement in the area of products liability.

Section 6 of the Third Restatement pertains specifically to prescription drugs, with § 6(c) applying to design defects. Section 6 at 144–45 states in part:

> (a) A manufacturer of a prescription drug or medical device who sells or otherwise distributes a defective drug or medical device is subject to liability for harm to persons caused by the defect. A prescription drug or medical device is one that may be legally sold or otherwise distributed only pursuant to a health-care provider's prescription.
>
> (b) For purposes of liability under Subsection (a), a prescription drug or medical device is defective if at the time of sale or other distribution the drug or medical device:
>
> > (1) contains a manufacturing defect as defined in § 2(a); or
> >
> > (2) is not reasonably safe due to defective design as defined in Subsection (c); or

(3) is not reasonably safe due to inadequate instructions or warnings as defined in Subsection (d).

(c) A prescription drug or medical device is not reasonably safe due to defective design if the foreseeable risks of harm posed by the drug or medical device are sufficiently great in relation to its foreseeable therapeutic benefits that reasonable health-care providers, knowing of such foreseeable risks and therapeutic benefits, would not prescribe the drug or medical device for any class of patients.

In addition, § 6, comment *b.* at 146–47, states in part:

The traditional refusal by courts to impose tort liability for defective designs of prescription drugs and medical devices is based on the fact that a prescription drug or medical device entails a unique set of risks and benefits. What may be harmful to one patient may be beneficial to another. Under Subsection (c) a drug is defectively designed only when it provides no net benefit to any class of patients. Courts have concluded that as long as a drug or medical device provides net benefits to some persons under some circumstances, the drug or device manufacturer should be required to instruct and warn health-care providers of the foreseeable risks and benefits. Courts have also recognized that the regulatory system governing prescription drugs is a legitimate mechanism for setting the standards for drug design. In part, this deference reflects concerns over the possible negative effects of judicially imposed liability on the cost and availability of valuable medical technology. This deference also rests on two further assumptions: first, that prescribing health-care providers, when adequately informed by drug manufacturers, are able to assure that the right drugs and medical devices reach the right patients; and second, that governmental regulatory agencies adequately review new prescription drugs and devices, keeping unreasonably dangerous designs off the market.

Nevertheless, unqualified deference to these regulatory mechanisms is considered by a growing number of courts to be unjustified. An approved prescription drug or medical device can present significant risks without corresponding advantages. At the same time, manufacturers must have ample discretion to develop useful drugs and devices without subjecting their design decisions to the ordinary test applicable to products generally under § 2(b). Accordingly, Subsection (c) imposes a more rigorous test for defect than does § 2(b), which does not apply to prescription drugs and medical devices. . . .

. . . .

. . . Subsections (c) and (d) recognize common-law causes of action for defective drug design and for failure to provide reasonable instructions or warnings, even though the manufacturer complied with governmental standards.

Section 6, comment *f.* at 149, states in part:

> A prescription drug or device manufacturer defeats a plaintiff's design claim by establishing one or more contexts in which its product would be prescribed by reasonable, informed health-care providers. That some individual providers do, in fact, prescribe defendant's product does not in itself suffice to defeat the plaintiff's claim. Evidence regarding the actual conduct of health-care providers, while relevant and admissible, is not necessarily controlling. The issue is whether, objectively viewed, reasonable providers, knowing of the foreseeable risks and benefits of the drug or medical device, would prescribe it for any class of patients. Given this very demanding objective standard, liability is likely to be imposed only under unusual circumstances. The court has the responsibility to determine when the plaintiff has introduced sufficient evidence so that reasonable persons could conclude that plaintiff has met this demanding standard.

As of this writing, no state court has faced the issue of whether to adopt § 6(c). A few federal courts have discussed this section, but only to the extent of either predicting whether the applicable state court would adopt § 6(c) or declining to apply it in the absence of state precedent.

There are several criticisms of § 6(c), which will be briefly summarized. First, it does not accurately restate the law. It has been repeatedly stated that there is no support in the case law for the application of a reasonable physician standard in which strict liability for a design defect will apply only when a product is not useful for any class of persons. Rather, as illustrated by the discussion of the treatment of comment *k.* under the Second Restatement in other jurisdictions, the majority of courts apply some form of risk-utility balancing that focuses on a variety of factors, including the existence of a reasonable alternative design. The few cases that the Third Restatement cites to as support for the reasonable physician test also apply a risk-utility test. Thus, § 6(c) does not restate the law and instead seeks to formulate new law with no precedential support.

Second, the reasonable physician test is criticized as being artificial and difficult to apply. The test requires fact finders to presume that physicians have as much or more of an awareness about a prescription drug product as the manufacturer. The test also ignores concerns of commentators that physicians tend to prescribe drugs they are familiar with or for which they have received advertising material, even when studies indicate that better alternatives are available.

A third criticism of particular applicability to Freeman's case is that the test lacks flexibility and treats drugs of unequal utility equally. For example, a drug used for cosmetic purposes but which causes serious side effects has less utility than a drug which treats a deadly disease, yet also has serious side effects. In each case, the drugs would likely be useful to a class of patients under the reasonable physician standard for some class of persons. Consequently, each would be exempted from design defect liability. But under a standard that considers reasonable alternative design, the cosmetic drug could be subject to liability if a safer yet equally effective design was available. As a result, the reasonable physician standard of § 6(c) of the Third Restatement has been described as a standard that in effect will never allow liability. However, a standard applying a risk-utility test that focuses on the presence or absence of a reasonable alternative design, although also rarely allowing liability, at least allows the flexibility for liability to attach in an appropriate case.

Fourth, the test allows a consumer's claim to be defeated simply by a statement from the defense's expert witness that the drug at issue had some benefit for any single class of people. Thus, it is argued that application of § 6(c) will likely shield pharmaceutical companies from a wide variety of suits that could have been brought under comment *k.* of the Second Restatement. As the Third Restatement, § 6(c), comment *f.* at 149, states in part: "Given this very demanding objective standard, liability is likely to be imposed only under unusual circumstances." Thus, even though the rule is reformulated, any application of § 6(c) will essentially provide the same blanket immunity from liability for design defects in prescription drugs as did the application of comment *k.* in the few states that interpreted it as such.

We conclude that § 6(c) has no basis in the case law. We view § 6(c) as too strict of a rule, under which recovery would be nearly impossible. Accordingly, we do not adopt § 6(c) of the Third Restatement. . . .

We conclude that § 402 A, comment *k.*, of the Second Restatement should be applied on a case-by-case basis and as an affirmative defense in cases involving prescription drug products. Under this rule, an application of the comment does not provide a blanket immunity from strict liability for prescription drugs. Rather, the plaintiff is required to plead the consumer expectations test, as he or she would be required to do in any products liability case. The defendant may then raise comment *k.* as an affirmative defense. The comment will apply to except the prescription drug product from strict liability when it is shown that (1) the product is properly manufactured and contains adequate warnings, (2) its benefits justify its risks, and (3) the product was at the time of manufacture and distribution incapable of being made more safe.

In this case, because the application of comment *k.* is an affirmative defense, Freeman was only required to plead that the Accutane she took was unreasonably dangerous under a consumer expectations test. Freeman alleged that Accutane was unreasonably dangerous for use, that it was not fit for its intended purpose, that the risks inherent in the design outweighed the benefits of its use, and that Accutane was more dangerous to Freeman than was anticipated due to undisclosed side effects. As facts supporting her allegations, Freeman alleged that Accutane is sold as an acne medication and that the side effects of Accutane present life-threatening conditions. Thus, Freeman alleged facts that the Accutane was dangerous to an extent beyond that which would be contemplated by the ordinary consumer who purchases it, with the ordinary knowledge common to the community as to its characteristics.

Accordingly, we conclude that Freeman has stated a theory of recovery based on a design defect. . . .

3. FAILURE TO WARN

Freeman alleges that Hoffman was negligent in failing to warn of dangers associated with the use of Accutane. Freeman also alleges that Hoffman failed to warn that Accutane was not adequately tested.

Under the Third Restatement § 2(c) at 14,

> [a product] is defective because of inadequate instructions or warnings when the foreseeable risks of harm posed by the product could have been reduced or avoided by the provision of reasonable instructions or warnings by the seller or other distributor, or a predecessor in the commercial chain of distribution, and the omission of the instructions or warnings renders the product not reasonably safe.

The Third Restatement reflects the same rule this court has applied in regard to a failure to warn. We have stated:

> In a products liability case based on negligence and the duty to warn: "A manufacturer or other seller is subject to liability for failing either to warn or adequately to warn about a risk or hazard inherent in the way a product is designed that is related to the intended uses as well as the reasonably foreseeable uses that may be made of the products it sells." . . . "[A] manufacturer's duty to produce a safe product, with appropriate warnings and instructions when necessary, is no different from the responsibility each of us bears to exercise due care to avoid unreasonable risks of harm to others. . . ."

Rahmig, 226 Neb. at 446, 412 N.W.2d at 72.

Pharmaceutical products have historically been treated differently in regard to a duty to warn. Although in ordinary product cases, a manufacturer's duty to warn runs directly to the consumer of the product, in cases involving prescription drugs, it is widely held that the duty to warn extends only to members of the medical profession and not to the consumer. This concept is known as the learned intermediary doctrine. . . .

The learned intermediary doctrine is provided for in § 6(d) of the Third Restatement. Section 6(d) at 145 states:

> A prescription drug or medical device is not reasonably safe due to inadequate instructions or warnings if reasonable instructions or warnings regarding foreseeable risks of harm are not provided to:
>
> (1) prescribing and other health-care providers who are in a position to reduce the risks of harm in accordance with the instructions or warnings; or

(2) the patient when the manufacturer knows or has reason to know that health-care providers will not be in a position to reduce the risks of harm in accordance with the instructions or warnings.

We have not specifically adopted the learned intermediary doctrine as the applicable test for determining whether a manufacturer may be liable for a warning defect in prescription drug cases. However, with a few exceptions for instances where special facts require a direct warning to the consumer, the doctrine is followed in virtually all jurisdictions that have considered whether to adopt it. The doctrine as stated in the Third Restatement has also been adopted in other jurisdictions. We adopt § 6(d) of the Third Restatement. Accordingly, we apply the learned intermediary doctrine to Freeman's case.

The section of Freeman's petition devoted to factual allegations alleges that Hoffman failed to warn of Accutane's dangers in the package insert provided to physicians, including Freeman's physician. Freeman makes further allegations regarding Hoffman's failure to provide her with warnings under the section specifically devoted to her theory of recovery for a failure to warn. Thus, we conclude that Freeman has stated a theory of recovery for liability based on a warning defect. . . .

Chapter 13

Defenses

This chapter deals with specific defenses in negligence-based, strict liability and strict products liability actions. The primary focus is on defenses that are based on plaintiff's conduct—negligence and assumption of the risk. These are "affirmative" defenses that the defendant must both plead and prove. They are in addition to any arguments that defendants might make concerning missing or incompletely proven elements of the plaintiff's case. For example, the argument that the defendant was not the proximate cause of the plaintiff's injury is not included in this chapter.

A. Comparative and Contributory Negligence and Assumption of Risk in Cases Where the Basis of Liability Is Negligence

1. Comparative Negligence: The Modern World

Li v. Yellow Cab Co. Of California

Supreme Court of California, 1975 (en banc)
532 P.2d 1226

SULLIVAN, JUSTICE.

In this case we address the grave and recurrent question whether we should judicially declare no longer applicable in California courts the doctrine of contributory negligence, which bars all recovery when the plaintiff's negligent conduct has contributed as a legal cause in any degree to the harm suffered by him, and hold that it must give way to a system of comparative negligence, which assesses liability in direct proportion to fault. As we explain in detail *infra*, we conclude that we should. In the course of reaching our ultimate decision we conclude that: (1) The doctrine of comparative negligence is preferable to the "all-or-nothing" doctrine of contributory negligence from the point of view of logic, practical experience, and fundamental justice; (2) judicial action in this area is not precluded by the presence of section 1714 of the Civil Code, which has been said to "codify" the "all-or-nothing" rule and to render it immune from attack in the courts except on constitutional grounds; (3) given the possibility of judicial action, certain practical difficulties attendant upon the adoption of comparative negligence should not dissuade us from charting a new course—leaving the resolution of some of these problems to future judicial or legislative action; (4) the doctrine of comparative negligence should be applied in this state in its so-called "pure" form under which the assessment of liability in proportion to fault proceeds in spite of the fact that the plaintiff is equally at fault as or more at fault than the defendant; and finally (5) this new rule should be given a limited retrospective application.

The accident here in question occurred near the intersection of Alvarado Street and Third Street in Los Angeles. At this intersection Third Street runs in a generally east-west direction along the crest of a hill, and Alvarado Street, running generally north and south, rises gently to the crest from either direction. At approximately 9 p.m. on November 21, 1968, plaintiff Nga Li was proceeding northbound on Alvarado in her 1967 Oldsmobile. She was in the inside lane, and about 70 feet before she reached the Third Street intersection she stopped and then began a left turn across the three southbound lanes of Alvarado, intending to enter the driveway of a service station. At this time defendant Robert Phillips, an employee of defendant Yellow Cab Company, was driving a company-owned taxicab southbound in the middle lane on Alvarado. He came over the crest of the hill, passed through the intersection, and collided with the right rear portion of plaintiff's automobile, resulting in personal injuries to plaintiff as well as considerable damage to the automobile.

The court, sitting without a jury, found as facts that defendant Phillips was traveling at approximately 30 miles per hour when he entered the intersection, that such speed was unsafe at that time and place, and that the traffic light controlling southbound traffic at the intersection was yellow when defendant Phillips drove into the intersection. It also found, however, that plaintiff's left turn across the southbound lanes of Alvarado "was made at a time when a vehicle was approaching from the opposite direction so close as to constitute an immediate hazard." The dispositive conclusion of law was as follows: "That the driving of Nga Li was negligent, that such negligence was a proximate cause of the collision, and that she is barred from recovery by reason of such contributory negligence." Judgment for defendants was entered accordingly.

I

"Contributory negligence is conduct on the part of the plaintiff which falls below the standard to which he should conform for his own protection, and which is a legally contributing cause cooperating with the negligence of the defendant in bringing about the plaintiff's harm." (Rest. 2d Torts, § 463.) Thus the American Law Institute, in its second restatement of the law, describes the kind of conduct on the part of one seeking recovery for damage caused by negligence which renders him subject to the doctrine of contributory negligence. What the effect of such conduct will be is left to a further section, which states the doctrine in its clearest essence: "Except where the defendant has the last clear chance, the plaintiff's contributory negligence *bars recovery* against a defendant whose negligent conduct would otherwise make him liable to the plaintiff for the harm sustained by him." (Rest. 2d Torts, § 467.) (Italics added.)

This rule, rooted in the long-standing principle that one should not recover from another for damages brought upon oneself, has been the law of this state from its beginning. Although criticized almost from the outset for the harshness of its operation, it has weathered numerous attacks, in both the legislative and the judicial arenas, seeking its amelioration or repudiation. We have undertaken a thorough reexamination of the matter, giving particular attention to the common law and statutory sources of the subject doctrine in this state. As we have indicated, this reexamination leads us to the conclusion that the "all-or-nothing" rule of contributory negligence can be and ought to be superseded by a rule which assesses liability in proportion to fault.

It is unnecessary for us to catalogue the enormous amount of critical comment that has been directed over the years against the "all-or-nothing" approach of the doctrine of contributory negligence. The essence of that criticism has been constant and clear: the doctrine is inequitable in its operation because it fails to distribute responsibility in proportion to fault.[3] Against this have been raised several arguments in justification, but none have proved even remotely adequate to the task.[4] The

---

3. Dean Prosser states the kernel of critical comment in these terms: "It [the rule] places upon one party the entire burden of a loss for which two are, by hypothesis, responsible." (Prosser, Torts (4th ed. 1971) §67, p. 433.) Harper and James express the same basic idea: "[T]here is no justification—in either policy or doctrine—for the rule of contributory negligence, except for the feeling that if one man is to be held liable because of his fault, then the fault of him who seeks to enforce that liability should also be considered. But this notion does not require the all-or-nothing rule, which would exonerate a very negligent defendant for even the slight fault of his victim. The logical corollary of the fault principle would be a rule of comparative or proportional negligence, not the present rule." (2 Harper & James, The Law of Torts (1956) §22.3, p. 1207.)

4. Dean Prosser, in a 1953 law review article on the subject which still enjoys considerable influence, addressed himself to the commonly advanced justificatory arguments in the following terms: "There has been much speculation as to why the rule thus declared found such ready acceptance in later decisions, both in England and in the United States. The explanations given by the courts themselves never have carried much conviction. Most of the decisions have talked about 'proximate cause,' saying that the plaintiff's negligence is an intervening, insulating cause between the defendant's negligence and the injury. But this cannot be supported unless a meaning is assigned to proximate cause which is found nowhere else. If two automobiles collide and injure a bystander, the negligence of one driver is not held to be a superseding cause which relieves the other of liability; and there is no visible reason for any different conclusion when the action is by one driver against the other. It has been said that the defense has a penal basis, and is intended to punish the plaintiff for his own misconduct; or that the court will not aid one who is himself at fault, and he must come into court with clean hands. But this is no explanation of the many cases, particularly those of the last clear chance, in which a plaintiff clearly at fault is permitted to recover. It has been said that the rule is intended to discourage accidents, by denying recovery to those who fail to use proper care for their own safety; but the assumption that the speeding motorist is, or should be, meditating on the possible failure of a lawsuit for his possible injuries lacks all reality, and it is quite as reasonable to say that the rule promotes accidents by encouraging the negligent defendant. Probably the true explanation lies merely in the highly individualistic attitude of the common law of the early nineteenth century. The period of development of contributory negligence was that of the industrial revolution, and there is reason to think that the courts found in this defense, along with the concepts of duty and proximate cause, a convenient instrument of control over the jury, by which the liabilities of rapidly growing industry were curbed and kept within bounds." (Prosser,

basic objection to the doctrine—grounded in the primal concept that in a system in which liability is based on fault, the extent of fault should govern the extent of liability—remains irresistible to reason and all intelligent notions of fairness.

Furthermore, practical experience with the application by juries of the doctrine of contributory negligence has added its weight to analyses of its inherent shortcomings: "Every trial lawyer is well aware that juries often do in fact allow recovery in cases of contributory negligence, and that the compromise in the jury room does result in some diminution of the damages because of the plaintiff's fault. But the process is at best a haphazard and most unsatisfactory one." (Prosser, *Comparative Negligence*, [(1953) 41 Cal. L. Rev. 1, 3–4,] p. 4; fn. omitted.) It is manifest that this state of affairs, viewed from the standpoint of the health and vitality of the legal process, can only detract from public confidence in the ability of law and legal institutions to assign liability on a just and consistent basis.

It is in view of these theoretical and practical considerations that to this date 25 states have abrogated the "all or nothing" rule of contributory negligence and have enacted in its place general apportionment *statutes* calculated in one manner or another to assess liability in proportion to fault. In 1973 these states were joined by Florida, which effected the same result by *judicial* decision. *(Hoffman v. Jones* (Fla. 1973) 280 So. 2d 431.) We are likewise persuaded that logic, practical experience, and fundamental justice counsel against the retention of the doctrine rendering contributory negligence a complete bar to recovery—and that it should be replaced in this state by a system under which liability for damage will be borne by those whose negligence caused it in direct proportion to their respective fault.

The foregoing conclusion, however, clearly takes us only part of the way. It is strenuously and ably urged by defendants and two of the amici curiae that whatever our views on the relative merits of contributory and comparative negligence, we are precluded from making those views the law of the state by judicial decision. Moreover, it is contended, even if we are not so precluded, there exist considerations of a practical nature which should dissuade us from embarking upon the course which we have indicated. We proceed to take up these two objections in order.

II

It is urged that any change in the law of contributory negligence must be made by the Legislature, not by this court. Although the doctrine of contributory negligence is of judicial origin—its genesis being traditionally attributed to the opinion of Lord Ellenborough in *Butterfield v. Forrester* (KB. 1809) 103 Eng. Rep. 926—the enactment

---

Comparative Negligence (1953) 41 Cal. L. Rev. 1, 3–4; fns. omitted. For a more extensive consideration of the same subject, see 2 Harper & James, [The Law of Torts (1956)], § 22.2, pp. 1199–1207.)

To be distinguished from arguments raised in justification of the "all or nothing" rule are practical considerations which have been said to counsel against the adoption of a fairer and more logical alternative. The latter considerations will be discussed in a subsequent portion of this opinion.

of section 1714 of the Civil Code[7] in 1872 codified the doctrine as it stood at that date and, the argument continues, rendered it invulnerable to attack in the courts except on constitutional grounds. Subsequent cases of this court, it is pointed out, have unanimously affirmed that—barring the appearance of some constitutional infirmity—the "all-or-nothing" rule is the law of this state and shall remain so until the Legislature directs otherwise. The fundamental constitutional doctrine of separation of powers, the argument concludes, requires judicial abstention.

. . . .

We have concluded that the foregoing argument, in spite of its superficial appeal, is fundamentally misguided. As we proceed to point out and elaborate below, it was not the intention of the Legislature in enacting section 1714 of the Civil Code, as well as other sections of that code declarative of the common law, to insulate the matters therein expressed from further judicial development; rather it was the intention of the Legislature to announce and formulate existing common law principles and definitions for purposes of orderly and concise presentation and with a distinct view toward continuing judicial evolution.

. . . .

[W]e hold that section 1714 of the Civil Code was not intended to and does not preclude present judicial action in furtherance of the purposes underlying it.

III

We are thus brought to the second group of arguments which have been advanced by defendants and the amici curiae supporting their position. Generally speaking, such arguments expose considerations of a practical nature which, it is urged, counsel against the adoption of a rule of comparative negligence in this state even if such adoption is possible by judicial means.

The most serious of these considerations are those attendant upon the administration of a rule of comparative negligence in cases involving multiple parties. One such problem may arise when all responsible parties are not brought before the court: it may be difficult for the jury to evaluate relative negligence in such circumstances, and to compound this difficulty such an evaluation would not be res judicata in a subsequent suit against the absent wrongdoer. Problems of contribution and indemnity among joint tortfeasors lurk in the background.

A second and related major area of concern involves the administration of the actual process of fact-finding in a comparative negligence system. The assigning of a specific percentage factor to the amount of negligence attributable to a particular party, while in theory a matter of little difficulty, can become a matter of perplexity

---

7. Section 1714 of the Civil Code has never been amended. It provides as follows: "Everyone is responsible, not only for the result of his willful acts, but also for an injury occasioned to another by his want of ordinary care or skill in the management of his property or person, *except so far as the latter has, willfully or by want of ordinary care, brought the injury upon himself.* The extent of liability in such cases is defined by the Title on Compensatory Relief." (Italics added.)

in the face of hard facts. The temptation for the jury to resort to a quotient verdict in such circumstances can be great. These inherent difficulties are not, however, insurmountable. Guidelines might be provided the jury which will assist it in keeping focussed upon the true inquiry, and the utilization of special verdicts or jury interrogatories can be of invaluable assistance in assuring that the jury has approached its sensitive and often complex task with proper standards and appropriate reverence.

The third area of concern, the status of the doctrines of last clear chance and assumption of risk, involves less the practical problems of administering a particular form of comparative negligence than it does a definition of the theoretical outline of the specific form to be adopted. Although several states which apply comparative negligence concepts retain the last clear chance doctrine, the better reasoned position seems to be that when true comparative negligence is adopted, the need for last clear chance as a palliative of the hardships of the "all-or-nothing" rule disappears and its retention results only in a windfall to the plaintiff in direct contravention of the principle of liability in proportion to fault. As for assumption of risk, we have recognized in this state that this defense overlaps that of contributory negligence to some extent and in fact is made up of at least two distinct defenses. "To simplify greatly, it has been observed . . . that in one kind of situation, to wit, where a plaintiff *unreasonably* undertakes to encounter a specific known risk imposed by a defendant's negligence, plaintiff's conduct, although he may encounter that risk in a prudent manner, is in reality a form of contributory negligence. . . . Other kinds of situations within the doctrine of assumption of risk are those, for example, where plaintiff is held to agree to relieve defendant of an obligation of reasonable conduct toward him. Such a situation would not involve contributory negligence, but rather a reduction of defendant's duty of care." (*Grey v. Fibreboard Paper Products Co.* (1966) 65 Cal. 2d 240, 245–246, 53 Cal. Rptr. 545, 548, 418 P.2d 153, 156). We think it clear that the adoption of a system of comparative negligence should entail the merger of the defense of assumption of risk into the general scheme of assessment of liability in proportion to fault in those particular cases in which the form of assumption of risk involved is no more than a variant of contributory negligence.

Finally there is the problem of the treatment of willful misconduct under a system of comparative negligence. In jurisdictions following the "all-or-nothing" rule, contributory negligence is no defense to an action based upon a claim of willful misconduct, and this is the present rule in California. . . . The thought is that the difference between willful and wanton misconduct and ordinary negligence is one of kind rather than degree in that the former involves conduct of an entirely different order, and under this conception it might well be urged that comparative negligence concepts should have no application when one of the parties has been guilty of willful and wanton misconduct. It has been persuasively argued, however, that the loss of deterrent effect that would occur upon application of comparative fault concepts to willful and wanton misconduct as well as ordinary negligence would be slight, and that a comprehensive system of comparative negligence should allow for the apportionment of damages in all cases involving misconduct which falls short of being intentional. The law of punitive damages remains a separate consideration.

The existence of the foregoing areas of difficulty and uncertainty has not diminished our conviction that the time for a revision of the means for dealing with contributory fault in this state is long past due and that it lies within the province of this court to initiate the needed change by our decision in this case. Two of the indicated areas (i.e., multiple parties and willful misconduct) are not involved in the case before us, and we consider it neither necessary nor wise to address ourselves to specific problems of this nature which might be expected to arise. . . .

Our previous comments relating to the remaining two areas of concern (i.e., the status of the doctrines of last clear chance and assumption of risk, and the matter of judicial supervision of the finder of fact) have provided sufficient guidance to enable the trial courts of this state to meet and resolve particular problems in this area as they arise. As we have indicated, last clear chance and assumption of risk (insofar as the latter doctrine is but a variant of contributory negligence) are to be subsumed under the general process of assessing liability in proportion to fault, and the matter of jury supervision we leave for the moment within the broad discretion of the trial courts.

. . . .

It remains to identify the precise form of comparative negligence which we now adopt for application in this state. Although there are many variants, only the two basic forms need be considered here. The first of these, the so-called "pure" form of comparative negligence, apportions liability in direct proportion to fault in all cases. . . . The second basic form of comparative negligence, of which there are several variants, applies apportionment based on fault *up to the point* at which the plaintiff's negligence is equal to or greater than that of the defendant—when that point is reached, plaintiff is barred from recovery. Nineteen states have adopted this form or one of its variants by statute. The principal argument advanced in its favor is moral in nature: that it is not morally right to permit one more at fault in an accident to recover from one less at fault. Other arguments assert the probability of increased insurance, administrative, and judicial costs if a "pure" rather than a "50 percent" system is adopted, but this has been seriously questioned.

We have concluded that the "pure" form of comparative negligence is that which should be adopted in this state. In our view the "50 percent" system simply shifts the lottery aspect of the contributory negligence rule[21] to a different ground. As Dean Prosser has noted, under such a system "[i]t is obvious that a slight difference in the

---

21. "The rule that contributory fault bars completely is a curious departure from the central principle of nineteenth century Anglo-American tort law—that wrongdoers should bear the losses they cause. Comparative negligence more faithfully serves that central principle by causing the wrongdoers to share the burden of resulting losses in reasonable relation to their wrongdoing, rather than allocating the heavier burden to the one who, as luck would have it, happened to be more seriously injured." (Comments on Maki v. Frelk, [21 Vand. L. Rev. 889], Comment by Keeton, pp. 912–913.)

proportionate fault may permit a recovery; and there has been much justified criticism of a rule under which a plaintiff who is charged with 49 percent of a total negligence recovers 51 percent of his damages, while one who is charged with 50 percent recovers nothing at all."[22] Prosser, *Comparative Negligence, supra*, 41 Cal. L. Rev. 1, 25; fns. omitted.)

. . . .

For all of the foregoing reasons we conclude that the "all-or-nothing" rule of contributory negligence as it presently exists in this state should be and is herewith superseded by a system of "pure" comparative negligence, the fundamental purpose of which shall be to assign responsibility and liability for damage in direct proportion to the amount of negligence of each of the parties. Therefore, in all actions for negligence resulting in injury to person or property, the contributory negligence of the person injured in person or property shall not bar recovery, but the damages awarded shall be diminished in proportion to the amount of negligence attributable to the person recovering. The doctrine of last clear chance is abolished, and the defense of assumption of risk is also abolished to the extent that it is merely a variant of the former doctrine of contributory negligence; both of these are to be subsumed under the general process of assessing liability in proportion to negligence. Pending future judicial or legislative developments, the trial courts of this state are to use broad discretion in seeking to assure that the principle stated is applied in the interest of justice and in furtherance of the purposes and objectives set forth in this opinion.

. . . .

CLARK, JUSTICE (dissenting).

. . . .

Contrary to the majority's assertions of judicial adequacy, the courts of other states — with near unanimity — have conceded their inability to determine the best system for replacing contributory negligence, concluding instead that the legislative branch is best able to resolve the issue.

. . . .

McCOMB, J., concurs.

––––––––––

1. In many jurisdictions, contributory negligence no longer exists as a defense. Courts and legislatures have instead replaced contributory negligence with comparative negligence. Comparative negligence doctrine is often perceived as helping plaintiffs, because plaintiffs will no longer be barred from recovery even if they were negligent. A system of comparative negligence can also help defendants, however,

––––––––––

22. This problem is compounded when the injurious result is produced by the combined negligence of several parties. For example in a three-car collision a plaintiff whose negligence amounts to one-third or more recovers nothing; in a four-car collision the plaintiff is barred if his negligence is only one-quarter of the total.

because it removes any temptation for jurors to find that the plaintiff was not negligent in order to allow the plaintiff to recover. Thus, instead of paying for 100% of the damage done, the defendant will be held liable for the percentage of the injury actually caused by the defendant. Additionally, in multiple-defendant cases where plaintiff's comparative negligence is a defense, defendants can in effect argue that their contribution to the accident was less than that of other defendants

2. There are three basic types of comparative negligence doctrine. Pure comparative negligence doctrine assesses damages proportional to fault; a plaintiff who is 90% responsible will still collect 10% of his or her damages from the defendant (when, of course, the jury has assessed 10% of the blame against that defendant). Under the "less than 50%" type, a plaintiff may recover provided the plaintiff's negligence was less than the defendant's. If the plaintiff and the defendant were each responsible for 50% of the negligence, the plaintiff will be barred from recovery. Under the "equal to or less than" type, the plaintiff may recover as long as the blame attached to the plaintiff is not greater than the blame attached to the defendant. In this third type of comparative negligence, the plaintiff may recover even when the plaintiff's negligence is equal to the defendant's.

Various questions remain, particularly under the latter two types of comparative negligence. For example, what if a plaintiff is 40% at fault and two codefendants are 30% at fault each? Jurisdictions have various rules for the application of comparative negligence in cases involving multiple parties.

3. Are the courts really comparing fault? Aren't they really comparing causation? Blame is apportioned to the various parties depending upon what percentage of the damages the conduct at issue caused. In other words, a defendant is 10% at fault if his or her conduct caused 10% of the damages. It is not the fault that is being divided; rather it is the causation of the damages. Viewing comparative negligence this way helps make the doctrine make sense as applied in strict liability or strict products liability cases, in which the defendant may not have been negligent at all. If the defendant has not been negligent, speaking of comparing the plaintiff's and the defendant's negligence makes no sense at all. But if the comparison is not between the negligence of the parties, but rather between the causative roles of the parties (or of the plaintiff and the product), applying what is somewhat misnamed as comparative negligence makes sense, even in the context of non-negligent defendants.

2. The Last Clear Chance Rule

Davies v. Mann

Exchequer, 1842
10 M.& W. 547, 152 Eng. Rep. 588

Exch. of Pleas. Nov. 4, 1842.—The general rule of law respecting negligence is, that, although there may have been negligence on the part of the plaintiff, yet unless he might by the exercise of ordinary care have avoided the consequences of the defendant's negligence, he is entitled to recover. Therefore, where the defendant negligently drove his horses and waggon against and killed an ass, which had been left in the highway fettered in the fore-feet, and thus unable to get out of the way of the defendant's waggon, which was going at a smartish pace along the road, it was held, that the jury were properly directed, that although it was an illegal act on the part of the plaintiff so to put the animal on the highway, the plaintiff was entitled to recover.

Case for negligence. The declaration stated, that the plaintiff theretofore, and at the time of the committing of the grievance thereinafter mentioned, to wit, on &c, was lawfully possessed of a certain donkey, which said donkey of the plaintiff was then lawfully in a certain highway, and the defendant was then possessed of a certain waggon and certain horses drawing the same, which said waggon and horses of the defendant were then under the care, government, and direction of a certain then servant of the defendant, in and along the said highway; nevertheless the defendant, by his said servant, so carelessly, negligently, unskillfully, and improperly governed and directed his said waggon and horses, that by and through the carelessness, negligence, unskillfulness, and improper conduct of the defendant, by his said servant, the said waggon and horses of the defendant then ran and struck with great violence against the said donkey of the plaintiff, and thereby then wounded, crushed, and killed the same.

The defendant pleaded not guilty.

At the trial, before Erskine, J., at the last Summer Assizes for the county of Worcester, it appeared that the plaintiff, having fettered the fore feet of an ass belonging to him, turned it into a public highway, and at the time in question the ass was grazing on the off side of a road about eight yards wide, when the defendant's waggon, with a team of three horses, coming down a slight descent, at what the witness termed a smartish pace, ran against the ass, knocked it down, and the wheels passing over it, it died soon after. The ass was fettered at the time, and it was proved that the driver of the waggon was some little distance behind the horses. The learned Judge told the jury, that though the act of the plaintiff, in leaving the donkey on the highway so fettered as to prevent his getting out of the way of carriages travelling along it, might be illegal, still, if the proximate cause of the injury was attributable to the want of proper conduct on the part of the driver of the waggon, the action was maintainable against the defendant; and his Lordship directed them, if they thought that the accident might have been avoided by the exercise of ordinary care on the part of the driver, to find for the plaintiff. The jury found their verdict for the plaintiff, damages 40s.

Godson now moved for a new trial, on the grounds of misdirection. The act of the plaintiff in turning the donkey into the public highway was an illegal one, and as the injury arose, principally from that act, the plaintiff was not entitled to compensation for that injury which, but for his own unlawful act, would never have occurred. [PARKE, B. The declaration states that the ass was lawfully on the highway, and the defendant has not traversed that allegation; therefore it must be taken to be admitted.] The principle of law, as deducible from the cases, is, that where an accident is the result of faults on both sides, neither party can maintain an action. Thus, in *Butterfield v. Forrester* (11 East, 60), it was held that one who is injured by an obstruction on a highway, against which he fell, cannot maintain an action, if it appear that he was riding with great violence and want of ordinary care, without which he might have seen and avoided the obstruction. So, in *Vennall v. Garner* (1 C. & M. 21), in case for running down a ship, it was held, that neither party can recover when both are in the wrong; and Bayley, B., there says, "I quite agree that if the mischief be the result of the combined negligence of the two, they must both remain in statu quo, and neither party can recover against the other." Here the plaintiff, by fettering the donkey, had prevented him from removing himself out of the way of accident; had his fore feet been free, no accident would probably have happened. *Pluckwell v. Wilson* (5 Carr. & P. 375), *Luxford v. Large (ibid.* 421) and *Lynch v. Nurdin* (1 Ad. & E. (N.S.), 29; 4 P. & D. 672), are to the same effect.

Lord Abinger, C.B. I am of opinion that there ought to be no rule in this case. The defendant has not denied that the ass was lawfully there; but even were it otherwise, it would have made no difference, for as the defendant might, by proper care, have avoided injuring the animal, and did not, he is liable for the consequences of his negligence, though the animal may have been improperly there.

Parke, B. This subject was fully considered by this Court in the case of *Bridge v. The Grand Junction Railway Company* (3 M. & W. 246), where, as appears to me, the correct rule is laid down concerning negligence, namely, that the negligence which is to preclude a plaintiff from recovering in an action of this nature, must be such as that he could, by ordinary care, have avoided the consequences of the defendant's negligence. I am reported to have said in that case, and I believe quite correctly, that "the rule of law is laid down with perfect correctness in the case of *Butterfield v. Forrester*, that, although there may have been negligence on the part of the plaintiff, yet unless he might, by the exercise of ordinary care, have avoided the consequences of the defendant's negligence, he is entitled to recover; if by ordinary care he might have avoided them he is the author of his own wrong." In that case of *Bridge v. Grand Junction Railway Company*, there was a plea imputing negligence on both sides; here it is otherwise; and the Judge simply told the jury, that the mere fact of negligence on the part of the plaintiff in leaving his donkey on the public highway, was no answer to the action, unless the donkey's being there was the immediate cause of the injury; and that, if they were of opinion that it was caused by the fault of the defendant's servant in driving too fast, or, which is the same thing, at a smartish pace, the mere fact of putting the ass upon the road would not bar the plaintiff of his action. All that is perfectly correct; for, although the ass may have been wrongfully there, still the defendant was bound to go along the road at such a pace as would be likely to prevent mischief. Were this not so, a man might justify the driving over goods left on a public highway, or even over a man lying asleep there, or the purposely running against a carriage going on the wrong side of the road.

Gurney, B., and Rolfe, B., concurred.

Rule refused.

———————

In this case, the court deals with what came to be called the last clear chance rule. Under the last clear chance rule, a party, usually the defendant, is liable if that party fails to take reasonable steps to avoid the consequences of the negligent act of another (usually the plaintiff). In general, of course, a party is not entitled to recover for the consequences of another's negligence when those consequences could have been avoided. Avoidable consequences are caused not by the original negligence, but rather by the negligence of the party in failing to avoid them. Doesn't the last clear chance rule really represent the application of proximate causation principles in cases where both parties have been negligent, and the negligence of the injured party consists in failing to avoid the consequences of the negligence of the other party?

Problems

1. D is proceeding in her automobile down a quiet street and is approaching a stop light, which is green in her direction. E, approaching the crossroads from right angles, goes through the red light, and D and E make contact in the intersection. D saw E approaching the intersection before contact was made. Assuming D could have stopped, what arguments will E make to avoid liability? Will E be able to avoid liability altogether? If so, would this be an appropriate result? What would the arguments of the parties be in a jurisdiction that had abolished the last clear chance rule by statute?

2. G negligently causes a car crash in which H is injured. The injury might have been cured if H's doctor had not been negligent in treating H; as it is, however, H has developed a permanent limp. Do these facts lend themselves to a last clear chance analysis at all? Should G be exempt from liability for injuries caused by the doctor's negligence? Isn't it foreseeable, if one causes another to need medical attention, that the doctor administering that attention might be negligent?

The "Seatbelt Defense"

The role that a plaintiff's non-use of an available, working seatbelt should play in a lawsuit where the defendant's negligent driving caused an accident has generated many cases and much statutory law. Should such non-use serve as a defense? If so, how should it be weighed against the negligent driving that caused the non-use to produce injuries? Failure to use an available seatbelt is, of course, not really a manifestation of the last clear chance rule. In a way, seatbelts are a "first clear chance" to reduce injuries from the foreseeable, albeit regrettable, risk of car accidents. Fastening one's seatbelt (or not) occurs before the accident, not after.

For a detailed and somewhat confusing discussion of this subject, see *Ridley v. Safety Kleen*, 693 So. 2d 934 (Fla. 1996). In that case, the court worked hard to reconcile the common law with various statutes enacted in Florida to try to resolve the problems posed in tort cases by non-use of seatbelts. In *Hodges v. Mack Trucks, Inc.*, 474 F.3d 188 (5th Cir. 2006), whether the plaintiff truck driver, who had been ejected from the vehicle, had been wearing a seatbelt at the time of the accident was in dispute. The court ruled that defendant Mack's evidence of the plaintiff's non-use of the seatbelt was admissible, despite the prohibition on such evidence imposed by the state statute in effect at the time. The court stated (at 202):

> Subsection (g) [of the statute] prohibits the introduction of seatbelt evidence to show the plaintiff was contributorily negligent. On the other hand, in secondary-collision product-liability actions, such evidence may be admissible to show, or, as in this action, rebut, the essential element of causation. Seatbelt evidence was necessary for Mack to rebut the essential element of causation—whether its door latch was the proximate cause of [plaintiff's] injuries, and, ultimately, to defeat a crashworthiness claim.

In many jurisdictions, non-use of seatbelts is a citable motor vehicle offense, which adds to the layers of complication. In such jurisdictions, the plaintiff who has failed to use an available seatbelt is guilty of at least a misdemeanor, which may mean that the plaintiff has acted unreasonably as a matter of law. Such unreasonableness may play a role in evaluating that plaintiff's comparative negligence in contributing to any injury caused by the crash and exacerbated by the seatbelt nonuse.

Many states have reduced the impact that the offense of failing to "click it" can have on any tort judgments that may result from the accident in question. For example, in *Lowe v. Estate Motors, Ltd.*, 410 N.W.2d 706 (Mich. 1987), the court cited Michigan's mandatory seatbelt statute. Under the statute, failure to use a seatbelt constituted evidence of negligence, but the plaintiff's recovery could be reduced by a maximum of 5%. Justice Levin, in a separate opinion, stated that, "A large majority of the statutes requiring adults to wear seatbelts provide either that a violation cannot be grounds for reducing an award on the basis of comparative or contributory negligence, or limit the possible reduction to a small percentage of the award." *Lowe*, 410 N.W.2d at 727–28 n.9 (Levin, J., separate opinion).

Does it make sense to limit the reduction in damages for failure to wear a seatbelt? What if there would have been no injury had the plaintiff been wearing a seatbelt? One of the worst things that can happen in an accident is ejection from the vehicle, which cannot occur if the injured party is wearing a seatbelt. Why might a legislature adopt a statute limiting the effect of failure to wear a seat belt?

3. Assumption of Risk

Assumption of risk doctrine is a complex network of competing concerns which arise, at least in part, out of the fact that assumption of the risk is a complete defense. Courts are reluctant to let negligent defendants avoid liability altogether. On the other hand, they are equally reluctant to allow plaintiffs to recover damages when the plaintiffs have taken on the risk themselves. Compounding the complexity of the doctrine is the possibility that assumption of risk can be based either on the plaintiff's conduct, which evinces undertaking of a particular risk, or on some sort of anticipatory agreement between the plaintiff and defendant regarding how the risks of a particular activity should be allocated. In the context of such an agreement, tort and contract law policies intersect, sometimes in conflicting ways.

a. The Elements

Goepfert v. Filler

Supreme Court of South Dakota, 1997
563 N.W.2d 140

Konenkamp, Justice.

Michael Goepfert lost his life shortly after he jumped from a moving car. His parents sued the driver and others, and the circuit court granted summary judgment for the driver. Ordinarily, assumption of the risk is a question of fact for a jury, but under these circumstances, can it be decided as a matter of law? Because he voluntarily alighted from a moving vehicle without warning, we conclude Goepfert assumed the risk, and thus we uphold the summary judgment.

Facts

On Friday evening, October 29, 1993, several friends, including Chris Stethem and Michael Goepfert, began celebrating the annual "Hobo Day" homecoming at South Dakota State University in Brookings. After dinner and a few beers at a friend's home, the group of six left for downtown. Stethem drove. Goepfert was in the front passenger seat, another man sat between them, and the remaining three were in the backseat. As they neared their destination, the Chevy Lounge on Main Street, they approached an intersection with a red traffic light. Stethem slowed, but never stopped. About fifty feet from the intersection, a passenger in the back told Stethem, "Let us out. Let us out right here." Goepfert said nothing, but others joined in, wanting to be dropped off near the bar, so they would not have to walk back from where they would park. Stethem replied, "No, we'll all walk up there." One passenger persisted, and Stethem said, "If you want to get out, get out." They were still moving at approximately 10 to 15 miles per hour when the light turned green. Stethem began to accelerate normally. According to everyone in the car, at the moment of acceleration, Goepfert simultaneously, without a word, opened the car door and jumped out. When his feet hit the roadway, he flipped over backwards, causing his head to strike the pavement. He came to rest in the crosswalk where the car entered the intersection. Stethem pulled over on the other side, and all ran back to help their friend.

Goepfert was unconscious. He was taken by ambulance to Brookings Hospital, treated and released. Concerned friends watched him through the night to monitor his condition. In the morning, they took him back to the hospital when he became unresponsive. Doctors then discovered a skull fracture and intracranial hemorrhaging. Goepfert was rushed by air ambulance to a hospital in Sioux Falls, where he died the next day. His parents brought a wrongful death action against Stethem and certain medical providers. The malpractice claims are not part of this appeal. Stethem moved for summary judgment. Concluding as a matter of law Goepfert assumed the risk of injury by exiting a moving car, negating any duty Stethem owed to him, the circuit judge granted the motion.

Standard of Review

The framework for determining summary judgment questions is set forth in S.D.CL 15-6-56(c): "The judgment sought shall be rendered forthwith if the pleadings, depositions, answers to interrogatories, and admissions on file, together with the affidavits, if any, show that there is no genuine issue of material fact and that the moving party is entitled to a judgment as a matter of law." *Id.* (reproduced in part). . . .

Analysis and Decision

The circuit court ruled from the bench:

> [I]n looking at everything in the light most favorable to the plaintiff here, the scenario I get is that the driver of the car was driving by the Chevy Lounge, the passengers were saying, "Let us out here and so we don't have to walk all the way back to the Chevy Lounge after you find a place to park." The driver of the car said, "No," and then because he was getting badgered about it, he says, "Well, if you want to get out, get out now," but the car had not stopped; that is undisputed. It was going slow, but it had not stopped, and even looking at it from the perspective of the decedent here, that the defendant was slowing down and that he took the defendant's statement seriously, that "If you want to get out, get out now," that that was permission to exit the car, no reasonable person exits a moving car until it is stopped. I think that anytime somebody exits a moving vehicle, he is assuming a known risk. He is assuming there is a good chance that he is going to get injured. He has got to wait until it stops. And so to me, as a matter of law, I conclude that there was assumption of the risk here.

To learn whether the judge decided correctly, we now examine the concept of assumption of the risk with the facts viewed in a light most favorable to Goepfert. We review this question under the de novo standard. *Boever v. State Board of Accountancy*, 526 N.W.2d 747, 749 (S.D. 1995) (Boever I).

Assumption of the risk embodies three elements. It must be shown that Goepfert: (1) had actual or constructive knowledge of the risk; (2) appreciated its character; and (3) voluntarily accepted the risk, with the time, knowledge, and experience to make an intelligent choice. . . .

Though assumption of the risk is most often an issue for the jury, we have occasionally held summary judgment appropriate. . . . In *Myers v. Lennox Co-op. Ass'n*, 307 N.W.2d 863 (S.D. 1981), for example, we affirmed summary judgment on assumption of the risk against a plaintiff who was injured after stepping on an unstable pile of lumber while loading a garbage truck. No facts were in dispute; he had reasonable alternatives to stepping on the lumber; and reasonable persons could not differ over the risk the plaintiff assumed. "His decision to walk on the lumber was made under such circumstance that he must be held to have made an intelligent choice to encounter the risk presented by that course of action." *Id.* at 865. Has each required element been satisfied in this case?

First, to assume a risk, one must have actual or constructive knowledge of the peril involved. Constructive knowledge will be imputed if the risk is so plainly observable that "anyone of competent faculties [could be] charged with knowledge of it." *Westover* [*v. East River Elec. Power Co-op., Inc.*, 488 N.W.2d 892 (S.D. 1992)], at 901 (internal citations omitted). Risk is intrinsic to some acts. Considering these facts and exercising ordinary common sense, reasonable minds cannot differ on the jeopardy involved in stepping from a moving vehicle. *See Nix v. Williams*, 35 A.D.2d 188, 316 N.Y.S.2d 321, 324 (1970) (passenger who suddenly and unexpectedly jumped out of moving vehicle without saying anything barred from recovery as a matter of law); *Groshek v. Groshek*, 263 Wis. 515, 57 N.W.2d 704, 706 (1953) (where plaintiff driver allowed a passenger to drive while he reached into the backseat, it cannot be reasonably said that plaintiff did not know the danger in such activity).

Next, an individual will be held to have appreciated the danger undertaken if it was "a risk that no adult person of average intelligence can deny." *Bell*, 535 N.W.2d at 754; *Nelson*, 513 N.W.2d at 905. Obviously, "there are some risks to which no adult will be believed if he says he did not understand them." *Staats by Staats v. Lawrence*, 576 A.2d 663, 668 (Del. Super. Ct. 1990), *affd*, 582 A.2d 936 (Del. 1990). Michael Goepfert, a twenty-two year old college student, had to know and appreciate the hazard he faced in leaping from a moving car. "[One] may not close his eyes to obvious dangers, and cannot recover where he was in possession of facts from which he would be legally charged with appreciation of the danger." *Herod v. Grant*, 262 So. 2d 781, 783 (Miss. 1972) (quoting 57 Am. Jur. 2d *Negligence* § 282 (1971)). No testimony from anyone in the car suggests Goepfert was unaware of what he was doing or that he misperceived the car was moving.

Finally, assumption of the risk requires voluntarily acceptance, having had the time, knowledge, and experience to make an intelligent choice. [According to testimony from one of the passengers, as] he leapt from the car, Goepfert may not have known the light had turned green and Stethem was just then accelerating.

. . . .

Consistent with the others, this same witness testified:

Q. — "Were you surprised that Mike jumped out of the vehicle?"

A. — "Yeah, I was very much so."

Everyone in the car felt Stethem spoke in jest or was acting the "smart aleck" when he said, "If you want to get out, get out." Even if Goepfert took this comment seriously, he still gave no sign of his intent, other than, as one passenger said, to glance at his friends in the backseat: "It was like he was joking like he was going to. Kind of acting like he was going to do it and then not really do it. Then he went ahead and did it." Automobile passengers have a duty of care for their own safety. *Glandon v. Fiala*, 261 Iowa 750, 156 N.W.2d 327, 331 (1968); *Atwood v. Holland*, 267 N.C. 722,

148 S.E.2d 851, 854 (N.C. 1966) ("A gratuitous passenger in an automobile is required to use that care for his own safety that a reasonably prudent person would employ under the same or similar circumstances."); *Rutz v. Iacono*, 229 Minn. 591, 40 N.W.2d 892, 895 (1949); *White v. Huffmaster*, 326 Mich. 108, 40 N.W.2d 87, 89 (1949).* Goepfert's decision surpassed mere negligence.

Acceptance of risk necessarily connotes attention to reasonable alternatives. Here "reasonable" refers to whether one had a fair opportunity to elect whether to subject oneself to danger. Acceptance is not voluntary if another's tortious conduct leaves no reasonable alternative to avert harm or to exercise or protect a right or privilege, which another has no right to deny. Everyone agreed Stethem drove normally. The car may have been moving faster than Goepfert anticipated when he jumped, but that cannot erase the reality that he still elected to jump while the car was moving. On this point the evidence is unrefuted. Goepfert's only reasonable alternative was to stay in the car until it reached a complete stop. No one's wrongful conduct forced him to make his fateful choice.

As a matter of law, Goepfert assumed the risk. We see no genuine issues of material fact for trial. By jumping from the car, Goepfert voluntarily and unfortunately accepted the peril inherent in such act, and, to the sorrow of his family and friends, his decision ended in tragedy.

Affirmed.

MILLER, CHIEF JUSTICE, and SABERS, AMUNDSON, and GILBERTSON, JUSTICES, concur.

Ray v. Downes

Supreme Court of South Dakota, 1998
576 N.W.2d 896

GILBERTSON, JUSTICE.

On October 16, 1995 Donald Ray (Ray) was injured in a farm accident when a semi-tractor/trailer rolled over his legs while he was attempting to position an auger under a trailer to unload crops into a large storage bin. Ray then brought a

---

* Compare cases involving passengers engaged in horseplay in and around moving vehicles. *See, e.g.*, Brown v. Derry, 10 Wash. App. 459, 518 P.2d 251, 253 (Wash. Ct. App. 1974) (considering sixteen-year-old who rode on the trunk of a car, "The risk of harm in attempting to ride on the exterior of an automobile for even a short distance in such a fashion is plainly a foreseeable risk, and reasonable minds could not differ with respect to it"); Miller v. General Accident Fire & Life Assur. Corp., Ltd., 280 So. 2d 280, 282 (La. Ct. App. 1973) (man riding on a car fender, "The general rule when one is an outrider on a vehicle is that he only assumes such risks as are ordinarily incident to his position"); Vaughn v. Cortez, 180 So. 2d 796 (La. Ct. App. 1965) ("playing cowboy" while riding on the front of a moving car is so dangerous, a risk is assumed); Irwin v. Klaeren, 4 Ill. App. 2d 114, 123 N.E.2d 743, 744 (Ill. App. Ct. 1954) (holding as a matter of law and noting that "it is hard to conceive of a more reckless disregard for his own safety" than a man who holds his head and shoulders outside of the window of a moving car).

negligence action against his employer, the owner of the farm. He also sued the custom harvester hired by his employer and the custom harvester's driver. Ray's wife, Levena Ray, joined in the suit by submitting a loss of consortium claim. The trial court granted defendants' motion for summary judgment after finding, as a matter of law, that Ray had assumed the risk of his injuries. Ray appeals. We affirm as to his employer, Downes, and reverse as to the custom harvester, Wieczorek and his employee, Waldner.

FACTS AND PROCEDURE

Harold Downes (Downes), the owner of a farm near Pierre, South Dakota, hired Ray in May of 1995 as a farm laborer. Ray was 39 years old at the time and had many years of farm experience. As the fall 1995 harvest approached, Downes hired a custom harvester, John Wieczorek, to harvest his soybeans and corn. Wieczorek then assigned one of his employees to combine the fields and another, Phillip Waldner (Waldner), to drive a large 18-wheeled semi-tractor/trailer (semi) from the fields to the storage bins on Downes' farm and unload the crops into the bins. Wieczorek's two employees spent approximately one week harvesting soybeans. Ray was not directed by Downes to assist the harvesters but observed Waldner unloading the crops from the semi into the bins during the previous day's harvesting. During this process Waldner would drive the semi close to the bin, get out of the semi and position a swing-type auger directly underneath the openings in the bottom of the trailer. The crops would then fall through the bottom doors of the trailer into the auger to be transported into the bins.

On October 16, 1995, it became apparent that the ground near one of the bins was too high to allow sufficient clearance to get the auger under the semi trailer. Downes asked Ray to use a front-end loader to scrape smooth the ground near one of the bins so that the auger could be positioned. Downes did not direct Ray to assist Waldner in the actual unloading of the corn. After Ray scraped the ground, he volunteered to help Waldner position the auger under the trailer. Ray and Waldner agreed that Waldner would drive the truck and Ray would shove the auger underneath the trailer while the truck was moving. Ray would use hand signals and then "holler" for Waldner to stop when the auger was in place.

As Waldner was entering the truck Ray positioned himself three to four feet in front of the protruding rear set of wheels on the trailer. After the auger was in position Ray "hollered" for Waldner to stop. Either Ray did not signal or Waldner did not see Ray's signals or hear Ray "holler" and the wheels of the trailer caught Ray's left foot and ran over his left leg.[1] Downes was nearby and was alerted to the scene when he heard Ray urgently scream for Waldner to back up. Downes found Ray pinned under the trailer's wheels, got Waldner's attention, who then drove the trailer off of Ray.

---

1. The location was fairly noisy at the time because the engines of the semi and a tractor, which was used to power the auger, were running in addition to the grain bin dryers. Ray was aware that some of the truck's windows were rolled up prior to the accident.

Ray brought a personal injury suit against Waldner and Waldner's employer Wieczorek (under respondeat superior principles). Ray also alleged that Downes had maintained an unsafe workplace because the noise from the grain bin dryers prevented Waldner from hearing Ray's shouting to stop. Ray's wife, Levena, also filed a claim for loss of consortium. Downes brought a cross-claim against Waldner and Wieczorek. The circuit court granted summary judgment in favor of all defendants on the basis that Ray had assumed the risk of his injury based on his own admissions. The Rays appeal.

. . . .

ANALYSIS AND DECISION

. . . .

2. Whether summary judgment in favor of Waldner and Wieczorek was proper.

Although assumption of the risk is generally a jury issue, this Court has occasionally held summary judgment appropriate in those rare cases "where the essential elements are conclusively established that the plaintiff may be charged with assumption of the risk as a matter of law." *Goepfert*, 1997 S.D. 56 at ¶ 7, 563 N.W.2d at 142 (citation omitted). We examine the affirmative defense of assumption of the risk with the facts viewed in a light most favorable to Ray. This question is reviewed under the *de novo* standard.

Assumption of the risk is composed of three elements. It must be shown that Ray: (1) had actual or constructive knowledge of the risk; (2) appreciated its character; and (3) voluntarily accepted the risk, with the time, knowledge, and experience to make an intelligent choice. We have held that the failure to establish any of these elements will preclude summary judgment. At the pretrial hearing which addressed the motion for summary judgment, the circuit court held:

> [I]t's this court's reluctant view that this is one of those rare cases where [Ray's] own testimony establishes as a matter of law assumption of the risk. I don't believe there can be any reasonable dispute that when the deposition and the depositions of the other people are read together, even with the supplementary affidavit that was just filed by [Ray], I don't believe that reasonable people can disagree that the first two elements of the assumption of the risk doctrine were clearly satisfied and [Ray's] testimony, . . . in his deposition clearly establishes the voluntariness and the availability of reasonable alternatives.

b. Actual or Constructive Knowledge of the Risk

Generally, both knowledge and appreciation of danger are jury questions. However, "where it is clear that any person in [plaintiff's] position must have understood the danger, the issue may be decided by the court." W. Page Keeton et al., Prosser and Keeton on the Law of Torts § 68, at 481 (5th ed. 1984). Waldner argues that "[reasonable men] could not differ that [Ray] had actual knowledge of the risk" of being run over by the rear wheels. *Mack*, 1996 S.D. 63 at ¶ 11, 548 N.W.2d at 814. Waldner cites Ray's deposition testimony to support his argument that Ray had *actual* knowledge of the risk of danger involved at the time he positioned himself near the rear wheels in his attempt to push the auger underneath the moving semi:

> . . . .
>
> Q: And you knew that if you didn't move, that the wheels on that trailer would drive over your leg?
>
> A: Yes, I knew it. *But if he would have stopped when I motioned for him to stop, he wouldn't have got me.*
>
> . . . .

(Emphasis added). "Risk is intrinsic to some acts." *Goepfert*, 1997 S.D. 56 at H8, 563 N.W.2d 140, 143. However this intrinsic risk is not unlimited. Certainly, Ray put himself in harm's way by standing in a position to be run over. He frankly admitted as much. Nonetheless, he did not consent to relieve the driver of his subsequent duty to act with reasonable care. In the words of Prosser, "This is a distinction which has baffled a great many law students, some judges, and unhappily a few very learned legal writers." Prosser & Keeton, The Law of Torts § 68, at 485.

> It is here that there is the greatest misapprehension and confusion as to assumption of risk, and its most frequent misapplication. It is not true that in any case where the plaintiff voluntarily encounters a known danger he necessarily consents to any future negligence of the defendant. A pedestrian who walks across the street in the middle of a block, through a stream of traffic traveling at excessive speed, cannot by any stretch of the imagination be found to consent that the drivers shall not use care to watch for him and avoid running him down. On the contrary, he is insisting that they shall. This is contributory negligence pure and simple; it is not assumption of the risk. And if A leaves an automobile stopped at night on the traveled portion of the highway, and his passenger remains sitting in it, it can readily be found that there is consent to the prior negligence of A, whose control over the risk has terminated, but not to the subsequent negligence of B, who thereafter runs into the car from the rear.

Id.

Looking at the evidence in a light most favorable to Ray, as we must when reviewing summary judgments, Ray and Waldner had agreed upon certain "signals." According to Ray, Waldner so disregarded their understanding that he did not even realize he had run over Ray until Downes intervened. Nothing in the record even suggests that Ray anticipated Waldner would disregard his signals when moving the truck. Ray's awareness of danger was not consent to relieve Waldner of his duty of care. Not every acceptance of known danger may reasonably be interpreted as evidence of such consent. Prosser & Keeton, *supra* at 490. "[Although one may assume the risk of the negligence of another if he is fully informed of such negligence, one is not, under the doctrine of assumption of risk, bound to anticipate the negligent conduct of others." *Garcia v. City of South Tucson*, 131 Ariz. 315, 640 P.2d 1117, 1121 (Ct.

App. 1981) rev'd on other grounds, *Garcia v. City of South Tucson*, 135 Ariz. 604, 663 P.2d 596 (Ct. App. 1983)).

. . . .

We . . . reverse and remand for trial as to Waldner and his employer, Wieczorek. In so doing, our disposition preserves the opportunity for Waldner and Wieczorek to pursue traditional tort defenses such as assumption of the risk at trial.

Sabers, Amundson and Konenkamp, Justices, concur.

Miller, Chief Justice (concurring in part and dissenting in part).

I would affirm the circuit court's grant of summary judgment in its entirety.

. . . .

The majority grounds its holding, and ceases any further analysis of assumption of the risk, principally relying on secondary authority (a Prosser and Keeton hornbook) and an old decision by the intermediate court of appeals in Arizona. That simply is not an adequate analysis. I will next examine the three elements necessary to a proper assumption of the risk analysis. . . .

. . . Unlike the majority, I agree with Waldner and would hold that Ray's deposition clearly established that he had *actual* knowledge of the danger involved at the time he positioned himself near the rear wheels of the truck. . . .

. . . It is important to observe that although Ray had only worked for Downes for a short time, he did have considerable farm experience. Additionally, he had approximately ten years' experience driving and maneuvering heavy trucks with fellow co-workers in close proximity. Ray admitted that any adult person of average intelligence would understand the danger of getting in front of the wheels of a truck while it was moving.

. . . .

As evidenced by [his] testimony, Ray has conceded that he voluntarily put himself in a position of danger.

. . . .

Ray admits that he was not compelled by Waldner to use the particular method he did. Rather, Ray felt the method of moving the auger that he employed was more convenient.[2] In utilizing this method, Ray was acting under no compulsion of

---

2. There is no evidence in the record indicating that either Downes or Waldner gave Ray the impression that they were in a hurry. Setting up the auger took several minutes and it cannot be said that Ray did not have a reasonable opportunity to reconsider his approach. *See Berg v. Sukup Mfg. Co.*, 355 N.W.2d 833, 835 (S.D. 1984) (in considering available alternatives, "reasonableness refers to whether the plaintiff had a reasonable opportunity to elect whether or not to subject himself to the danger."). Safer alternatives should not be held unreasonable merely because they entail duplicative effort.

circumstances created by Waldner. The Restatement (Second) of Torts § 496E cmt. b provides in part:

> The plaintiff's acceptance of the risk is to be regarded as voluntary even though he is acting under the compulsion of circumstances, not created by the tortious conduct of the defendant, which have left him no reasonable alternative. Where the defendant is under no independent duty to the plaintiff, and the plaintiff finds himself confronted by a choice of risks, or is driven by his own necessities to accept a danger, the situation is not to be charged against the defendant.

> . . . .

Ray also contends that . . . he should not have been held to have assumed the risk because of Waldner's alleged negligence in driving the semi. In other words, Ray argues that Waldner's alleged negligence was the proximate cause of his injury. . . . Ray has admitted he knew that it is difficult to move large vehicles short distances and that he was aware he might be injured. Simply put, Waldner's actions were not unforeseeable or unexpected . . . . There is no allegation that Waldner suddenly turned or accelerated . . . . Upon Ray's command, Waldner drove the vehicle straight ahead only three or four feet. . . . Ray admit[ted] "I knew it was unsafe to be there" and that he was taking the risk of injuring his legs or hip.

Ray argues that Waldner failed to utilize his mirrors properly and failed to see his hand signals. Yet before Waldner entered the semi, Ray knew that he would be required to simultaneously use his hands to move the auger and signal Waldner. Furthermore, before the accident Ray knew that some of the windows were up in the semi and that there was a significant amount of noise which could have prevented Waldner from hearing him shout to stop. Where a plaintiff has impliedly consented to the negligence, and agrees to take his own chances, "[t]he legal result is that the defendant is simply relieved of the duty which would otherwise exist." W. Page Keeton et al., *Prosser and Keeton on the Law of Torts* § 68, at 481 (5th ed. 1984).

Since I agree with the trial court that there exists no genuine issue of material fact as to whether Ray assumed the risk of his injury, I would affirm.

---

1. In *Fred Harvey Corp. v. Mateas*, 170 F.2d 612 (9th Cir. 1948), the plaintiff was injured when he was thrown by an unusually rambunctious Grand Canyon tour mule named Chiggers. He argued (successfully) that he had assumed the risk of a well-behaved mule, not a fractious one. If a livery stable asks its customers about their skill, and assigns them horses to ride based on their answers, will they be protected from liability? What if it is a well-known phenomenon that people questioned about their skill at a given activity will tend to exaggerate their ability? How can a livery stable protect itself from liability? Should it be able to protect itself from liability for providing skittish horses to its customer?

2. What kinds of risk are assumable? If you are teaching teenagers to drive, and are injured in an accident which occurs during a lesson, should you be able to sue the driver? Should a patient be able to exchange a promise not to sue a doctor, even for negligent treatment, in exchange for a reduced bill?

Bass v. Aetna Insurance Co.

Supreme Court of Louisiana, 1979
370 So. 2d 511

DIXON, JUSTICE.

Mr. and Mrs. Loyd Bass sued Aetna Insurance Company, insurer of Mr. Kenneth Fussell under a homeowner's policy, and Southern Farm Bureau Casualty Insurance Company, insurer of Shepard's Fold Church of God, seeking damages for personal injuries suffered by Mrs. Bass when Mr. Fussell, a member of the Shepard's Fold Church, ran down the church aisle and collided with Mrs. Bass, also a member of the church, who was in the aisle praying. The defendants denied all allegations of negligence on the part of their insureds, and, alternatively, pleaded the affirmative defenses of assumption of the risk and contributory negligence. After trial on the merits, the Twenty-Second Judicial District Court for the Parish of St. Tammany dismissed plaintiffs' suit and on appeal the First Circuit Court of Appeal affirmed the dismissal in an unpublished opinion. Upon plaintiffs' application we granted writs.

On the evening of February 12, 1974, during a revival service, the Shepard's Fold Church of God was very crowded with not enough seats to accommodate all the parishioners. Consequently, Mrs. Bass and other parishioners who could not find seats were standing in the aisles of the church. Reverend Rodney Jeffers, in the course of preaching to the congregation, stated that the doors of the church should be opened and referred to the possibility of "running." Immediately afterward, Mr. Fussell began running up the aisle and ran into Mrs. Bass, who was in the aisle praying with her head bowed. As a result, Mrs. Bass fell and was injured.

The issues are whether Mr. Fussell was negligent, whether the Shepard's Fold Church of God was negligent, and, if so, whether the plaintiffs' action is barred by either the defenses of assumption of the risk or contributory negligence. Although Mr. Fussell testified that he was "trotting" under the Spirit of the Lord and does not remember actually running into Mrs. Bass, another witness testified that she saw Mr. Fussell run into Mrs. Bass and knock her down. If Fussel's defense is that he was not in control of his actions, it can be compared to voluntary intoxication, which will not exonerate one from delictual responsibility. A worshiper in church has no more right to run over a fellow worshiper in the aisle than a passerby on the sidewalk. Mr. Fussell breached this duty and was negligent when he trotted or run [sic] down the aisle of the church without regard for the safety of other parishioners in the aisles.

Actionable negligence also results from the creation or maintenance of an unreasonable risk of injury to others. In determining whether the risk is unreasonable, not only the seriousness of the harm that may be caused is relevant, but also the likelihood that harm may be caused. In the instant case, according to both Mrs. Bass and Reverend Jeffers, there were approximately three hundred fifty to three hundred seventy-five parishioners in the church on the night of the accident, and many of the parishioners were standing in the aisles. Reverend Jeffers recognized the likelihood that harm might be caused by this crowded condition because he testified that he asked that the aisles be cleared, that he encouraged "open response to the Spirit," and that running or moving "in the Spirit" were common forms of religious expression in Shepard's Fold Church. Another defense witness testified that Reverend Jeffers, recognizing the crowded aisles, asked if somebody would run for him (which apparently is what Mr. Fussell did). Reverend Jeffers did not stop the service to clear the aisles, but continued to maintain an unreasonable risk of injury to the parishioners. The Shepard's Fold Church is responsible for the negligence of its pastor, Reverend Jeffers, under these circumstances. C.C. 2320.

Concluding that both Mr. Fussell and the church were negligent, we next consider the defenses of assumption of the risk and contributory negligence. The Court of Appeal, in affirming the trial court, concluded that Mrs. Bass assumed the risk by remaining in the aisle with her eyes closed, and that she was contributorily negligent by remaining after having been alerted that running might occur.

Assumption of the risk and contributory negligence are affirmative defenses, C.C.P. 1005, and as we stated in *Langlois v. Allied Chemical Corp.*, 258 La. 1067, 249 So. 2d 133, 141 (1971):

> "The determination of whether a plaintiff has assumed a risk is made by subjective inquiry, whereas contributory negligence is determined objectively under the reasonable man standard. *See* Restatement (Second), Torts § 496 (1965); Symposium: *Assumption of Risk*, 22 La. L. Rev. 1–166. . . ."

Knowledge is the mainstay of this assumption of the risk defense, and this court will impute knowledge to a plaintiff, not because he was in a position to make certain observations, but only when the plaintiff *actually* made those observations and from those observations should reasonably have known that a risk was involved. Assumption of the risk therefore is properly applicable to those situations where the plaintiff, with knowledge of the peril, *voluntarily* enters into a relationship with defendant involving danger to himself because of defendant's contemplated conduct.

We cannot agree with the Court of Appeal's conclusion that Mrs. Bass assumed the risk. Although Mrs. Bass had belonged to the Church of God faith for approximately fifty-five years and the Shepard's Fold Church for approximately twenty-five years, neither she nor any other witness had seen or heard of any injury or collision in any Church of God church. Before the accident, no one, including Mrs. Bass, felt endangered by worshiping in this church. Mrs. Bass unequivocally testified that she had never seen anyone run in the church. The evidence fails to persuade us that Mrs. Bass actually, subjectively comprehended that by praying in the aisle she was incurring a risk of being run over, or that she could or should have known or understood that she was incurring such a risk.

The defense failed to prove that Mrs. Bass voluntarily assumed or exposed herself to this risk. Movement in the aisles was not an extraordinary condition in this church because worshipers frequently went to the altar, "the very central focal point in the church," for prayer. Heedless running in the aisle was an unusual and extraordinary hazard, to which plaintiff did not knowingly expose herself. *Rosenberger v. Central Louisiana District Livestock Show*, 312 So. 2d 300 (La. 1975).[4]

Contributory negligence is also an affirmative defense; the defendants bear the burden of proving contributory negligence by a preponderance of the evidence. Contributory negligence is objectively determined under the "reasonable [person]" standard. It is not contributory negligence to bow one's head when praying in a church, whether in the pew or in the aisle.

. . . .

For the reasons assigned, the judgments of the district court and of the Court of Appeal are reversed; the case is remanded to the Court of Appeal, First Circuit, to fix the damages to which plaintiffs are entitled. All costs are taxed against the defendants.

MARCUS, J., concurs in part and dissents in part and assigns reasons.

SUMMERS, C.J., dissents.

BLANCHE, J., dissents and assigns reasons.

MARCUS, JUSTICE (concurring in part and dissenting in part).

I consider that Mr. Fussell was negligent and that his negligence was the sole proximate cause of the accident. Moreover, I do not feel that Mrs. Bass either assumed the risk or was contributorily negligent. I do not find that Reverend Jeffers was negligent; however, even assuming that he was, I do not consider that his negligence was a proximate cause of the accident. Hence, I concur in part and dissent in part.

BLANCHE, JUSTICE, dissenting.

I respectfully dissent.

I believe that Mrs. Bass assumed the risk of the injury which she suffered because she knew, or reasonably should have known, from her own personal experience the demonstrative nature of the church service which she understood and in which she was a willing participant.

Problem

F, who was raised in the country and still lives there, decides to spend a day at a car race. He takes his seat in the stands, and the race begins. Fairly shortly thereafter, he begins to wheeze. He has so much trouble breathing that the paramedics at the track need to rescue him, and he is forced to spend some time in the hospital. It

---

4. In *Rosenberger*, the plaintiff was injured in a bareback bronco riding contest when the horse ran the plaintiff into the gatepost of a gate in the arena negligently left open during the contest. This court found that the plaintiff had assumed the natural and ordinary risks ancillary to bronco riding but not the extraordinary risks created by negligent operation or maintenance of the rodeo premises.

turns out that he is allergic to automobile exhaust in the large quantities that racing cars produce. F files suit against the race track. What will he argue? What defenses will the track raise?

Castello v. County of Nassau

Supreme Court, Appellate Division, Second Department, 1996
636 N.Y.S.2d 817

Before BRACKEN, J.P., and O'BRIEN, RITTER, FRIEDMANN and GOLDSTEIN, JJ.

MEMORANDUM BY THE COURT

In an action to recover damages for personal injuries, the plaintiff appeals from an order of the Supreme Court, Nassau County (Roberto, J.), dated July 29, 1994, which, upon reargument, granted the motion by the defendant Incorporated Village of Freeport to dismiss the complaint insofar as it is asserted against it.

ORDERED that the order is affirmed, with costs.

The plaintiff, an experienced softball player, was injured during the eighth inning of a softball game when he slid head-first into home plate and jammed his shoulder on a protruding corner of home plate. The plaintiff admitted that, prior to the accident, he had noticed that the third-base side of home plate was "being dug" by the batters.

It is well settled that those who voluntarily participate in a sporting activity "may be held to have consented, by their participation, to those injury-causing events which are known, apparent or reasonably foreseeable consequences of the participation" (*Turcotte v. Fell*, 68 N.Y.2d 432, 439, 510 N.Y.S.2d 49, 502 N.E.2d 964). "If the risks of the activity are fully comprehended or perfectly obvious, plaintiff has consented to them and defendant has performed its duty" (*Pascucci v. Town of Oyster Bay*, 186 A.D.2d 725, 726, 588 N.Y.S.2d 663). In the present case, the plaintiff admitted that he knew that the third-base side of home plate was "dug out". In addition, because the plaintiff, a right-handed batter, had batted several times during the game from that side of home plate, he had actually stood in the "ditch" next to the protruding corner of home plate. Under these circumstances, the risk presented by the "protruding home plate" was not a concealed one, and the plaintiff consciously assumed that risk by his voluntary participation in the game. Accordingly, the court properly dismissed the complaint insofar as it is asserted against the Incorporated Village of Freeport.

We have considered the plaintiff's remaining contentions and find them to be without merit.

BRACKEN, J.P., and O'BRIEN, RITTER, FRIEDMANN and GOLDSTEIN, JJ., concur.

———————

Was there any negligence on the part of the defendant in this case? Is the court even interested in the possibility?

Problem

G visits a new zoo on its opening day to see the polar bears. She is particularly fond of polar bears and knows a good deal about them. The bear enclosure is made of an inner chain link fence and an outer iron fence. G climbs over the outer fence and reaches her arm into the enclosed area under the chain link fence. One of the bears bites her arm severely. Whom may G sue, and for what? What defenses will be raised? Irrespective of the law, should G be able to recover anything?

b. Assumption of Risk by Agreement — The Anticipatory Release

As has been noted, express assumption of risk is typically a contractual matter. In contemporary society, businesses and other entities often attempt to secure assumption of risk by their patrons by insisting that the patrons sign some form of written "release" that exonerates the business in advance from liability for any injury the patron may experience. Whenever one goes horseback riding on a rented horse, uses a skateboard park, or participates in a rock-climbing class, the entity providing the resource will normally require that a release be signed before allowing access to the facilities. In other instances, an entity might post a warning to those entering its premises that by doing so certain risks are assumed. When one is informed of the risks of a non-negligently performed medical procedure, one might be characterized as assuming those risks.

There are, however, certain types of risk that one should not be able to accept, whether tacitly or by contract. In *Tunkl v. The Regents of the University of California*, 383 P.2d 441 (Cal. 1963), the Supreme Court of California ruled that a contract in which the plaintiff had released the defendants from the consequences of their own negligence was void as against public policy. The plaintiff in that case had been required to sign the release upon his admission to a hospital emergency room, and the court concluded that such a release was invalid as a matter of law. How should courts distinguish between circumstances where an anticipatory release should be enforced and those in which it is contrary to public policy?

Jones v. Dressel

Supreme Court of Colorado, 1981 (en banc)
623 P.2d 370

ERICKSON, Justice.

We granted certiorari to review the decision in *Jones v. Dressel*, 40 Colo. App. 459, 582 P.2d 1057 (1978). In an action for damages by the plaintiff for personal injuries sustained in an airplane crash, the trial court granted the defendants' motion for partial summary judgment. Summary judgment was based upon the execution of an exculpatory agreement which the court held insulated the defendants from liability for simple negligence involving the crash of an airplane. A claim alleging willful and wanton negligence is at issue in the trial court. The court of appeals affirmed. We affirm the court of appeals.

On November 17, 1973, the plaintiff, William Michael Jones, who was then seventeen years old, signed a contract with the defendant, Free Flight Sport Aviation, Inc. (Free Flight).[1] The contract allowed Jones to use Free Flight's recreational skydiving facilities, which included use of an airplane to ferry skydivers to the parachute jumping site. A covenant not to sue and a clause exempting Free Flight from liability were included in the contract:

> "2A. EXEMPTION FROM LIABILITY. The [plaintiff] exempts and releases the Corporation, its, owners, officers, agents, servants, employees, and lessors from any and all liability, claims, demands or actions or causes of action whatsoever arising out of any damage, loss or injury to the [plaintiff] or the [plaintiff's] property while upon the premises or aircraft of the Corporation or while participating in any of the activities contemplated by this Agreement, whether such loss, damage, or injury results from the negligence of the Corporation, its officers, agents, servants, employees, or lessors or from some other cause."

The contract also contained an alternative provision which would have permitted Jones to use Free Flight's facilities at an increased cost, but without releasing Free Flight from liability for negligence.[2]

On December 28, 1973, Jones attained the age of eighteen.[3] Ten months later, on October 19, 1974, he suffered serious personal injuries in an airplane crash which occurred shortly after takeoff from Littleton Airport. Free Flight furnished the airplane as part of its skydiving operation.[4]

On November 21, 1975, nearly two years after attaining his majority, Jones filed suit against Free Flight alleging negligence and willful and wanton misconduct as the cause of the airplane crash. The defendants included the owners and operators of the airplane, the airport, and Free Flight. Based upon the exculpatory agreement, the trial court granted summary judgment in favor of the defendants. The court of appeals affirmed the trial court.

---

1. Even though Jones' mother had ratified the terms of this contract on November 16, 1973, it should be noted that the approval by a parent does not necessarily validate an infant child's contract. See generally, *Kaufman v. American Youth Hostels*, 13 Misc. 2d 8, 174 N.Y.S.2d 580 (1957); *Fedor v. Mauwehu Council, Boy Scouts of America*, 21 Conn. Super. Ct. 38, 143 A.2d 466 (1958).

2. The record indicates that the alternative provision of the contract was crossed out when Jones signed the contract. However, the record does not establish that Free Flight would have prohibited Jones from participating in skydiving activities if the alternative provision had not been crossed out. . . .

3. Section 13-22-101(1)(a), C.R.S. 1973 provides: "Notwithstanding any other provision of law enacted or any judicial decision made prior to July 1, 1973, every person, otherwise competent, shall be deemed to be of full age at the age of eighteen years or older for the following specific purposes: To enter into any legal contractual obligation and to be legally bound thereby to the full extent as any other adult person. . . ."

4. Inferences can be gleaned from the record that indicate that Jones used Free Flight's services on several occasions between November 17, 1973, the date that the contract was signed, and October 19, 1974, the date of the crash . . . .

Jones asserts three grounds for reversal of the summary judgment. First, he claims that he disaffirmed the contract with Free Flight within a reasonable time after he attained his majority by filing suit. Second, he asserts that the exculpatory agreement is void as a matter of public policy. Third, he contends that inasmuch as an exculpatory agreement must be strictly construed against the party seeking to avoid liability for negligence, the injuries which he sustained as a result of the airplane crash were beyond the scope of the agreement.

I.

. . . [O]ur review of the order granting summary judgment necessarily involves a determination of whether a genuine issue as to any material fact exists which would foreclose the defendants from obtaining summary judgment as a matter of law.

II.

Ratification

As a matter of public policy, the courts have protected minors from improvident and imprudent contractual commitments by declaring that the contract of a minor is voidable at the election of the minor after he attains his majority. . . . *Doenges-Long Motors v. Gillen*, 138 Colo. 31, 328 P.2d 1077 (1958). A minor may disaffirm a contract made during his minority within a reasonable time after attaining his majority or he may, after becoming of legal age, by acts recognizing the contract, ratify it. *Keser v. Chagnon*, 159 Colo. 209, 410 P.2d 637 (1966); *Fellows v. Cantrell*, 143 Colo. 126, 352 P.2d 289 (1960); *Doenges-Long v. Gillen, supra*; *Kendrick v. Neisz*, 17 Colo. 506, 30 P. 245 (1892).

Affirmance is not merely a matter of intent. It may be determined by the actions of a minor who accepts the benefits of a contract after reaching the age of majority, or who is silent or acquiesces in the contract for a considerable length of time. . . . We conclude . . . that the trial court properly determined that Jones ratified the contract, as a matter of law, by accepting the benefits of the contract when he used Free Flight's facilities on October 19, 1974.

Thus, since Jones ratified the contract, the factual issue of whether his suit for personal injuries was filed within a reasonable time after attaining his majority and constituted disaffirmance of the contract, is not relevant. Accordingly, the entry of summary judgment on the issue of ratification was not error.

III.

The Contract

Jones' assertion that his contract with Free Flight is void as a matter of public policy, raises two issues: (A) whether the contract with Free Flight is an adhesion contract; and (B) the validity of the exculpatory provisions of the contract. Our consideration of the two issues necessarily involves a determination, as a matter of law, whether summary judgment was properly granted based upon the undisputed facts in this case.

A.

Adhesion Contract

An adhesion contract is a contract drafted unilaterally by a business enterprise and forced upon an unwilling and often unknowing public for services that cannot readily be obtained elsewhere. *See Chandler v. Aero Mayflower Transit Company*, 374 F.2d 129 (1967); A. Ehrenzweig, *Adhesion Contracts in the Conflict of Laws*, 53 Col.L.Rev. 1072. An adhesion contract is generally not bargained for, but is imposed on the public for a necessary service on a take or leave it basis. *See generally Clinic Masters v. District Court*, 192 Colo. 120, 556 P.2d 473 (1976); *Standard Oil Company of California v. Perkins*, 347 F.2d 379 (9th Cir. 1965).

In *Clinic Masters v. District Court, supra*, this Court stated that even though a contract is a printed form and offered on a "take-it-or-leave-it" basis, those facts alone do not cause it to be an adhesion contract. There must be a showing "that the parties were greatly disparate in bargaining power, that there was no opportunity for negotiation, or that [the] services could not be obtained elsewhere." *Id*. at 124, 556 P.2d 473. *See also, W. C. James Inc. v. Phillips Petroleum Company*, 347 F. Supp. 381 (D.Colo.1972); *Weaver v. American Oil Company*, 257 Ind. 458, 276 N.E.2d 144 (1971); *Williams v. Walker-Thomas Furniture Company*, 350 F.2d 445 (D.C.Cir. 1965).

The various elements of an adhesion contract may be characterized as substantive (those that appear in the contract) and procedural (those that must be identified by resort to evidence relating to the formation of the contract). *Matter of Friedman*, 64 A.D.2d 70, 407 N.Y.S. 999 (1978). However, whether the issue is substantive or procedural, the determination of whether the contract is an adhesion contract is a matter of law for the court to resolve. *Wilson Trading Corp. v. David Ferguson Ltd.*, 23 N.Y.2d 398, 297 N.Y.S.2d 108, 244 N.E.2d 685 (1968). Thus, in the absence of any genuine issue of material fact, the issue of whether a contract is an adhesion contract, does not preclude the entry of summary judgment.

We conclude that the record in the instant case supports the trial court's determination that the contract between Jones and Free Flight was not an adhesion contract as a matter of law.[7]

---

7. Jones asserts that *Rosen v. LTV Recreational Development, Inc.*, 569 F.2d 1117 (10th Cir. 1978), requires a different conclusion. In *Rosen*, the court characterized a season ski pass which contained a waiver of liability for negligence as an adhesion contract. The court stated that where an adhesion contract is involved, the contract will be strictly construed, and the court cannot imply provisions not expressed in the agreement. The agreement in *Rosen* attempted to exonerate a ski area for injuries resulting from the negligence and carelessness of fellow skiers, but did not specifically waive injuries resulting from the negligence of the ski area. Consequently, the court affirmed the trial court's determination that the scope of the agreement was a material issue of fact for the fact finder to determine. In the instant case, the contract expressly exempts Free Flight from liability for negligence "while upon the aircraft of the Corporation." Consequently, even if Jones could successfully argue that the contract was an adhesion contract, the wording of the exculpatory agreement, under the rationale of *Rosen*, did not preclude the trial court from granting the defendant's motion for summary judgment.

Jones contends that this was an adhesion contract because he was not allowed to select the alternative provision which would have allowed him to participate in the activities without releasing Free Flight from liability for its negligence, and that a genuine issue as to his lack of choice precluded the entry of summary judgment. We disagree. As we stated in *Clinic Masters v. District Court, supra,* the fact that a contract is a printed form contract and offered on a "take-it-or-leave-it" basis does not alone cause it to be an adhesion contract.

We also agree with the court of appeals' conclusion that nothing in the record establishes a disparity in bargaining power, or that the services provided by Free Flight could not be obtained elsewhere.

B.

The Exculpatory Provisions

Jones asserts that the exculpatory agreement is void as a matter of public policy. We disagree. The defendants contend that *Barker v. Colorado Region,* 35 Colo. App. 73, 532 P.2d 372 (1974), is dispositive of the issue of the validity of the exculpatory agreement. In *Barker,* the court of appeals held that an exculpatory clause in a contract relating to recreational activities will be given effect where the intention of the parties is expressed in sufficiently clear and unequivocal language and does not fall within any of the categories where the public interest is directly involved.

Jones, however, claims that summary judgment should not have been granted for three reasons. First, he argues that because exculpatory agreements must be strictly construed against the party seeking exemption, the agreement here does not insulate the defendants from liability for negligence in connection with a crash that occurred prior to the time that Jones made a parachute jump. Second, he claims that Free Flight was acting as a common carrier when it carried Jones, for compensation, to an altitude from which he could make a parachute jump, and that a common carrier by air cannot compel a passenger to release or limit the carrier's legal liability for its own negligence. Third, he contends that Free Flight, which is engaged in the private air charter business and operates under a Part 135 Certificate, is subject to FAA regulations which impose standards of safety upon the pilot of an airplane, and that Free Flight cannot contract away its liability for negligence in the performance of a duty imposed by law or where the public interest requires performance.[9]

The determination of the sufficiency and validity of an exculpatory agreement is a question of law for the court to determine. . . .

---

9. 14 C.F.R., § 135.5 provides: "Certificate and operations specifications required. No person may operate an aircraft under this part without, or in violation of, an air taxi/commercial operator (ATCO) operating certificate and appropriate operations specifications issued under this part, or, for operations with large aircraft having a maximum passenger seating configuration, excluding any pilot seat, of more than 30 seats, or a maximum payload capacity of more tha[n] 7,500 pounds, without, or in violation of, appropriate operations specifications issued under Part 121 of this chapter."

An exculpatory agreement, which attempts to insulate a party from liability from his own negligence, must be closely scrutinized, and in no event will such an agreement provide a shield against a claim for willful and wanton negligence. *Barker v. Colorado Region, supra*; *Kansas City Power & Light Company v. United Telephone Company of Kansas, Inc.*, 458 F.2d 177 (1972); *Ciofalo v. Vic Tanney Gyms, Inc.*, [10 N.Y.2d 294, 220 N.Y.S.2d 962, 177 N.E.2d 925 (1961)], *supra*. In determining whether an exculpatory agreement is valid, there are four factors which a court must consider: (1) the existence of a duty to the public; (2) the nature of the service performed; (3) whether the contract was fairly entered into; and (4) whether the intention of the parties is expressed in clear and unambiguous language. *See Rosen v. LTV Recreational Development, Inc.*, 569 F.2d 1117 (10th Cir. 1978); *Barker v. Colorado Region, supra*; *Threadgill v. Peabody Coal Co.*, 34 Colo. App. 203, 526 P.2d 676 (1974); *Ciofalo v. Vic Tanney Gyms, Inc., supra*.

Measured against the four factors which determine the validity of an exculpatory agreement, we conclude that the trial court correctly held, as a matter of law, that the exculpatory agreement was valid. Therefore, the granting of defendants' motion for summary judgment was not error.

The duty to the public factor is not present in this case. In *Tunkl v. Regents of University of California*, 60 Cal. 2d 92, 32 Cal. Rptr. 33, 383 P.2d 441 (1963), the California Supreme Court stated:

> "In placing particular contracts within or without the category of those affected with a public interest, the courts have revealed a rough outline of that type of transaction in which exculpatory provisions will be held invalid. Thus the attempted but invalid exemption involves a transaction which exhibits some or all of the following characteristics. It concerns a business of a type generally thought suitable for public regulation. The party seeking exculpation is engaged in performing a service of great importance to the public, which is often a matter of practical necessity for some members of the public. The party holds himself out as willing to perform this service for any member of the public who seeks it, or at least for any member coming within certain established standards. As a result of the essential nature of the service, in the economic setting of the transaction, the party invoking exculpation possesses a decisive advantage of bargaining strength against any member of the public who seeks his services. In exercising a superior bargaining power the party confronts the public with a standardized adhesion contract of exculpation, and makes no provision whereby a purchaser may pay additional reasonable fees and obtain protection against negligence. Finally, as a result of the transaction, the person or property of the purchaser is placed under the control of the seller, subject to the risk of carelessness by the seller or his agents." *Id.* 32 Cal. Rptr. at 36, 383 P.2d at 444.

In light of the foregoing factors, we conclude that the contract between Jones and Free Flight does not fall within the category of agreements affecting the public interest.

Jones relies on the Federal Aviation Regulations as a basis for disregarding the exculpatory provisions of the contract. He contends that the regulations governing private air charter business, as well as the F.A.A. regulation governing common carriers, prevents the enforcement of the exculpatory provision in the contract. Private Air Charter Business, 14 C.F.R. § 135.1.

Admittedly, a commercial air operation is a business that is subject to extensive regulation. 14 C.F.R. § 135, et seq. We note, however, that 14 C.F.R. § 135.1(a)(3) provides that the rules governing operation of air carriers apply to: "[t]he carrying in air commerce by any person, other than an air carrier, of persons or property for compensation or hire [commercial operations] in small aircraft. . . ." Therefore, the standards of care and safety for private air charter services set forth in the Code of Federal Regulations apply only if Free Flight was engaged in "commercial operations" at the time of the airplane crash.

Jones also claims that Free Flight was operating as a common carrier when it accepted funds and provided an aircraft to ferry him to an altitude from which he could make a parachute jump. He is correct in his statement that releases or limitations of liability in airline tickets issued by a common carrier have uniformly been held invalid. *Conklin v. Canadian Colonial Airways, Inc.*, 266 N.Y. 244, 194 N.E. 692 (1935); *Curtiss-Wright Flying Service, Inc. v. Glose*, 66 F.2d 710 (3d Cir. 1933), *cert. denied*, 290 U.S. 696, 54 S. Ct. 132, 78 L. Ed. 599 (1938). See L. Kreindler, I. Aviation Accident Law § 3.13 (rev.1977). He is in error, however, in his contention that Free Flight was operating as a common carrier or was engaged in "commercial operations" as defined by 14 C.F.R. § 135.1(a)(3).[10] 14 C.F.R. § 1.1 provides:

> "'Commercial operator' means a person who, for compensation or hire, engages in the carriage by aircraft in air commerce of persons or property, other than as an air carrier or foreign air carrier or under the authority of Part 375 of this Title. Where it is doubtful that an operation is for 'compensation or hire,' the test applied is whether the carriage by air is merely incidental to the person's other business or is, in itself, a major enterprise for profit."

Here, the facts are clear that Free Flight was not engaged in "commercial operations" or acting as a common carrier in connection with this skydiving flight. Paragraph four of Jones' complaint alleges that the defendants were "engaged in the business of operating a service for the general aviation public involving parachuting, soaring, and aerobatics. . . ." Carriage by air was incidental to Free Flight's principal business. The standards of care and safety for private air charter services set forth in the Code of Federal Regulations do not apply.

---

10. Jones argues that the applicable definition of "common carrier" is found at section 40-1-102, C.R.S. 1973. We note, however, that the definition of "common carrier" used in that portion of the statute applies only to articles 1 through 7 of the "Public Utilities Law," sections 40-1-101 to 40-7-111, C.R.S. 1973.

While it is not necessary for a contract to embody all of the characteristics set forth in *Tunkl, supra*, to meet the test, we conclude that an insufficient number of these characteristics are present in the instant case to establish that the contract between Jones and Free Flight affected the public interest. The service provided by Free Flight was not a matter of practical necessity for even some members of the public; because the service provided by Free Flight was not an essential service, it did not possess a decisive advantage of bargaining strength over Jones; and the contract was not an adhesion contract.

Finally, in our consideration of the remaining factors that must be reviewed in considering the validity of an exculpatory agreement, we note that there was no disagreement between the parties that the contract was fairly entered into. Likewise, the agreement expressed the parties' intention in clear and unambiguous language; the contract used the word "negligence" and specifically included injuries sustained "while upon the aircraft of the Corporation." *See generally, Gross v. Sweet,* 49 N.Y.2d 102, 424 N.Y.S.2d 365, 400 N.E.2d 306 (1979); *Kaufman v. American Youth Hostels,* 13 Misc. 2d 8, 174 N.Y.S.2d 580 (1957).

We conclude that the exculpatory agreement was not void as a matter of public policy, and that there was no genuine issue as to any material fact.

Accordingly, the trial court properly granted a partial summary judgment on the simple negligence issue and we, therefore, affirm the decision of the court of appeals.

LEE, J., does not participate.

Bagley v. Mt. Bachelor, Inc.

Supreme Court of Oregon, 2014
340 P.3d 27

BREWER, J.

The issue on review in this case is whether an anticipatory release[1] of a ski area operator's liability for its own negligence in a ski pass agreement is enforceable in the face of an assertion that the release violates public policy and is unconscionable. Plaintiff suffered serious injuries while snowboarding over a jump in defendant ski area operator's "terrain park," and brought this action alleging that defendant was negligent in the design, construction, maintenance, and inspection of the jump. Defendant moved for summary judgment based on an affirmative defense of release; plaintiff filed a cross-motion for partial summary judgment on the ground that the release was unenforceable as a matter of law. The trial court granted defendant's summary judgment motion and denied plaintiff's cross-motion. . . . The Court of Appeals affirmed. . . . Because we conclude that enforcement of the release would be unconscionable, we reverse and remand.

---

1. By "anticipatory release," we refer to an exculpatory agreement that purports to immunize — before an injury occurs — the released party from liability for its own tortious conduct.

FACTS AND PROCEDURAL BACKGROUND

. . . The historical facts in the record largely relate to the enforceability of the release at issue. Defendant's summary judgment motion did not address the issues of negligence, causation, or damages. Therefore, insofar as those issues are relevant to the enforceability of the release, we accept as true the allegations in plaintiff's complaint. . . .

On September 29, 2005, plaintiff purchased a season pass from defendant for use at defendant's ski area. Plaintiff was a skilled and experienced snowboarder, having purchased season passes from defendant for each of the preceding three years and having classified his skill level as of early 2006, before being injured, as an "advanced expert." Upon purchasing the season pass, plaintiff executed a written "release and indemnity agreement" that defendant required of all its patrons.

That document provided, in pertinent part:

> "In consideration of the use of a Mt. Bachelor pass and/or Mt. Bachelor's premises, I/we agree to release and indemnify Mt. Bachelor, Inc., . . . from any and all claims for property damage, injury, or death which I/we may suffer or for which I/we may be liable to others, in any way connected with skiing, snowboarding, or snowriding. This release and indemnity agreement shall apply to any claim even if caused by negligence. The only claims not released are those based upon intentional misconduct.

> "* * * * *

> "The undersigned(s) have carefully read and understand this agreement and all of its terms on both sides of this document. This includes, but is not limited to, the duties of skiers, snowboarders, or snowriders. The undersigned(s) understand that this document is an agreement of release and indemnity which will prevent the undersigned(s) or the undersigneds' estate from recovering damages from Mt. Bachelor, Inc. in the event of death or injury to person or property. The undersigned(s), nevertheless, enter into this agreement freely and voluntarily and agree it is binding on the undersigned(s) and the undersigneds' heirs and legal representatives.

> "By my/our signature(s) below, I/we agree that this release and indemnity agreement will remain in full force and effect and I will be bound by its terms throughout this season and all subsequent seasons for which I/we renew this season pass.

> "See reverse side of this sheet * * * for duties of skiers, snowboarders, or snow riders which you must observe." (Capitalization omitted.)[2]

---

2. Although defendant relies on several documents that, it asserts, separately and collectively released it from liability for plaintiff's injuries, for convenience we refer to those documents in the singular throughout this opinion as "the release." . . .

The reverse side of the document detailed the "Duties of Skiers' under ORS 30.985 and ORS 30.990 and also included a printed notification that "Skiers/Snowboarders/Snowriders Assume Certain Risks" under ORS 30.975 — the "inherent risks of skiing."[3]

On November 18, 2005, plaintiff began using the pass, which stated, in part:

"Read this release agreement.

"In consideration for each lift ride, the ticket user releases and agrees to hold harmless and indemnify Mt. Bachelor, Inc., and its employees and agents from all claims for property damage, injury or death even if caused by negligence. The only claims not released are those based upon intentional misconduct."

(Capitalization omitted.) Further, the following sign was posted at each of defendant's ski lift terminals:

"YOUR TICKET IS A RELEASE

"The back of your ticket contains a release of all claims against Mt. Bachelor, Inc. and its employees or agents. Read the back of your ticket before you ride any lifts or use any of the facilities of Mt. Bachelor, Inc. If you purchase a ticket from someone else, you must provide this ticket release information to that person or persons.

"Skiers and lift passengers who use tickets at this resort release and agree to hold harmless and indemnify Mt. Bachelor, Inc., its employees and agents from all claims for property damage, injury or death which he/she may suffer or for which he/she may be liable to others, arising out of the use of Mt. Bachelor's premises, whether such claims are for negligence or any other theory of recovery, except for intentional misconduct.

"If you do not agree to be bound by the terms and conditions of the sale of your ticket, please do not purchase the ticket or use the facilities at Mt. Bachelor.

"Presentation of this ticket to gain access to the premises and facilities of this area is an acknowledgment of your agreement to the terms and conditions outlined above."

(Capitalization in original.)

Beginning on November 18, 2005, plaintiff used his season pass to ride defendant's lifts at least 119 times over the course of 26 days that he spent snowboarding at the ski area. On February 16, 2006, while snowboarding over a human-made jump in

---

3. As elaborated below, Oregon has enacted statutes specifically pertaining to skiing and ski areas. *See* ORS 30.970–30.990. Those statutes, among other provisions, set out the 'duties' of skiers, require that ski area operators inform skiers of those duties, establish notice requirements and a statute of limitations pertaining specifically to injury or death while skiing, and provide that those who engage in the sport of skiing accept and assume the risks inherent in that activity.

defendant's "air chamber" terrain park, plaintiff sustained serious injuries resulting in his permanent paralysis. . . . [P]laintiff brought this action; his complaint alleged negligence on defendant's part in designing, constructing, maintaining, and inspecting the jump on which plaintiff was injured. Defendant answered, in part, by invoking the affirmative defense of release, pointing to the above-quoted documents.

In its summary judgment motion, defendant asserted that plaintiff "admittedly understood that he [had] entered into a release agreement and was snowboarding under its terms on the date of [the] accident." Defendant argued that the release conspicuously and unambiguously disclaimed its future liability for negligence, and that the release was neither unconscionable nor contrary to public policy under Oregon law, because "skiers and snowboarders voluntarily choose to ski and snowboard and ski resorts do not provide essential public services." Thus, defendant reasoned, there was no material issue of fact as to whether the release barred plaintiff's action, and defendant was entitled to judgment as a matter of law.

In his cross-motion for partial summary judgment, plaintiff asserted that the release was unenforceable because it was contrary to public policy and was "both substantively and procedurally unconscionable." The trial court rejected plaintiff's public policy and unconscionability arguments, . . . granted summary judgment in defendant's favor and denied plaintiff's cross-motion for partial summary judgment. . . .

ANALYSIS

The parties' dispute in this case involves a topic — the validity of exculpatory agreements — that this court has not comprehensively addressed in decades. Although the specific issue on review — the validity of an anticipatory release of a ski area operator's liability for negligence — is finite and particular, it has broader implications insofar as it lies at the intersection of two traditional common law domains — contract and tort — where, at least in part, the legislature has established statutory rights and duties that affect the reach of otherwise governing common law principles.

It is a truism that a contract validly made between competent parties is not to be set aside lightly. . . . The right to contract privately is part of the liberty of citizenship, and an important office of the courts is to enforce contractual rights and obligations. . . . As this court has stated, however, "contract rights are [not] absolute; . . . [e]qually fundamental with the private right is that of the public to regulate it in the common interest." *Christian v. La Forge*, 194 Ore. 450, 469, 242 P.2d 797 (1952) (internal quotation marks omitted).

That "common," or public, interest is embodied, in part, in the principles of tort law. As a leading treatise explains:

> "It is sometimes said that compensation for losses is the primary function of tort law * * * [but it] is perhaps more accurate to describe the primary function as one of determining when compensation is to be required.

> "* * * * *

> "[Additionally, t]he 'prophylactic' factor of preventing future harm has been quite important in the field of torts. The courts are concerned not only with compensation of the victim, but with admonition of the wrongdoer."

W. Page Keeton, *Prosser and Keeton on the Law of Torts* § 4, 20–25 (5th ed. 1984). See also Dan B. Dobbs, *The Law of Torts*, § 8, 12 (2000) (most commonly mentioned aims of tort law are compensation of injured persons and deterrence of undesirable behavior). A related function of the tort system is to distribute the risk of injury to or among responsible parties. *Prosser and Keeton*, § 4, 24–25.[4]

One way in which courts have placed limits on the freedom of contract is by refusing to enforce agreements that are illegal. *Uhlmann v. Kin Daw,* 97 Ore. 681, 688, 193 P. 435 (1920) (an illegal agreement is void and unenforceable). According to *Uhlmann*:

> "An agreement is illegal if it is contrary to law, morality or public policy. Plain examples of illegality are found in agreements made in violation of some statute; and, stating the rule broadly, an agreement is illegal if it violates a statute or cannot be performed without violating a statute."

Id. at 689 (internal citation omitted . . . .

In determining whether an agreement is illegal because it is contrary to public policy, "[t]he test is the evil tendency of the contract and not its actual injury to the public in a particular instance." *Pyle v. Kernan,* 148 Ore. 666, 673–74, 36 P.2d 580 (1934). The fact that the effect of a contract provision may be harsh as applied to one of the contracting parties does not mean that the agreement is, for that reason alone, contrary to public policy, particularly where "the contract in question was freely entered into between parties in equal bargaining positions and did not involve a contract of adhesion, such as some retail installment contracts and insurance policies." [*W.J. Seufert Land Co. v. Greenfield*], 262 Ore. [83,] at 92 [(1972)].

As we discuss in more detail below, courts determine whether a contract is illegal by determining whether it violates public policy as expressed in relevant constitutional and statutory provisions and in case law, *see, e.g., Delaney v. Taco Time Int'l, Inc.,* 297 Ore. 10, 681 P.2d 114 (1984) (looking to those sources to determine whether discharge of at-will employee violated public policy), and by considering whether it is unconscionable. With respect to the doctrine of unconscionability, one commentator has explained:

> "The concept of unconscionability was meant to counteract two generic forms of abuses: the first of which relates to procedural deficiencies in the contract formation process, such as deception or a refusal to bargain over contract terms, today often analyzed in terms of whether the imposed-upon

---

4. *See also Rizutto v. Davidson Ladders, Inc.,* 280 Conn. 225, 235, 905 A.2d 1165 (2006) (fundamental purposes of the tort system are "compensation of innocent parties, shifting the loss to responsible parties or distributing it among appropriate entities, and deterrence of wrongful conduct.").

party had meaningful choice about whether and how to enter the transaction; and the second of which relates to the substantive contract terms themselves and whether those terms are unreasonably favorable to the more powerful party, such as terms that impair the integrity of the bargaining process or otherwise contravene the public interest or public policy; terms (usually of an adhesion or boilerplate nature) that attempt to alter in an impermissible manner fundamental duties otherwise imposed by the law, fine-print terms, or provisions that seek to negate the reasonable expectations of the nondrafting party, or unreasonably and unexpectedly harsh terms having nothing to do with price or other central aspects of the transaction."

Richard A. Lord, 8 *Williston on Contracts* § 18.10, 91 (4th ed. 2010). As that passage suggests, the doctrine of unconscionability reflects concerns related specifically to the parties and their formation of the contract, but it also has a broader dimension that converges with an analysis of whether a contract or contract term is illegal because it violates public policy.

Recognizing that convergence, this court often has relied on public policy considerations to determine whether a contract or contract term is sufficiently unfair or oppressive to be deemed unconscionable.

... [N]either party has suggested that different legal standards apply in determining whether the release at issue in this case violates public policy or is unconscionable. Thus, for the sake of convenience—if not doctrinal convergence—we address the parties' public policy arguments in the context of our analysis of whether, in the particular circumstances of this case, enforcement of the release would be unconscionable.[6]

Oregon courts have recognized their authority to refuse to enforce unconscionable contracts since the nineteenth century. . . . Unconscionability is "assessed as of the time of contract formation," and the doctrine "applies to contract terms rather than to contract performance." *Best v. U.S. National Bank,* 303 Ore. 557, 560, 739 P.2d 554 (1987) ("Unconscionability is a legal issue that must be assessed as of the time of contract formation."); *Tolbert v. First National Bank,* 312 Ore. 485, 492 n. 4, 823 P.2d 965 (1991) (same).

Unconscionability may be procedural or substantive. Procedural unconscionability refers to the conditions of contract formation and focuses on two factors: oppression and surprise. *See, e.g.,* John Edward Murray, Jr., *Murray on Contracts* § 96(b), 555–56 (4th ed. 2001) (describing components of procedural unconscionability). Oppression exists when there is inequality in bargaining power between the parties, resulting in no real opportunity to negotiate the terms of the contract and the absence

---

6. We emphasize that it is not necessary to decide in this case whether the doctrines always are identical in practical effect or whether they may vary in their application depending on the particular circumstances of a given case. It suffices to say that we discern no difference in their practical application in this case and, therefore, for the sake of convenience, we consider plaintiff's violation of public policy theory in the context of his unconscionability arguments.

of meaningful choice. *Vasquez-Lopez v. Beneficial Oregon, Inc.,* 210 Ore. App. 553, 566–567, 152 P.3d 940, 948 (2007); *Acorn v. Household Intern. Inc.,* 211 F. Supp. 2d 1160, 1168 (ND Cal. 2002). Surprise involves whether terms were hidden or obscure from the vantage of the party seeking to avoid them. *Id.* Generally speaking, factors such as ambiguous contract wording and fine print are the hallmarks of surprise. In contrast, the existence of gross inequality of bargaining power, a take-it-or-leave-it bargaining stance, and the fact that a contract involves a consumer transaction, rather than a commercial bargain, can be evidence of oppression.

Substantive unconscionability, on the other hand, generally refers to the terms of the contract, rather than the circumstances of formation, and focuses on whether the substantive terms contravene the public interest or public policy.[7] *See* Restatement § 208 comment a; *Williston on Contracts* § 18.10 at 91. Both procedural and substantive deficiencies — frequently in combination — can preclude enforcement of a contract or contract term on unconscionability grounds. Restatement § 208 comment a.

Identifying whether a contract is procedurally unconscionable requires consideration of evidence related to the specific circumstances surrounding the formation of the contract at issue. By contrast, the inquiry into substantive unconscionability can be more complicated. To discern whether, in the context of a particular transaction, substantive concerns relating to unfairness or oppression are sufficiently important to warrant interference with the parties' freedom to contract as they see fit, courts frequently look to legislation for relevant indicia of public policy. When relevant public policy is expressed in a statute, the issue is one of legislative intent. *See Uhlmann,* 97 Ore. at 689–90 (so stating). In that situation, the court must examine the statutory text and context to determine whether the legislature intended to invalidate the contract term at issue.[9] *Id.*

---

7. It sometimes can be difficult to categorize the factors on which a determination of unconscionability may be based as distinctly procedural or substantive, and even factors usually considered in assessing procedural unconscionability can help establish a violation of public policy....

9. Many jurisdictions that limit or prohibit the use of anticipatory releases from negligence liability on public policy grounds do so as a matter of statutory enactment, rather than common law. For example, Great Britain and the States of Louisiana and Montana have statutory provisions that forbid contracts exculpating one party from liability for negligence that results in personal injury. Unfair Contract Terms Act of 1977, ch. 50, § 2(1) (Eng.) ("A person cannot by reference to any contract term or to a notice given to persons generally or to particular persons exclude or restrict his liability for death or personal injury resulting from negligence."); La. Civ. Code Ann. Art. 2004 ("Any clause is null that, in advance, excludes or limits the liability of one party for causing physical injury to the other party."); Mont. Code Ann. § 28-2-702 ("All contracts that have for their object, directly or indirectly, to exempt anyone from responsibility ... for violation of law, whether willful or negligent, are against the policy of the law."); *see also Miller v. Fallon County,* 222 Mont. 214, 221, 721 P.2d 342 (1986) (under statute, prospective release from liability for negligence is against the policy of the law and illegal, despite being a private contract between two persons without significant public implications).

Some states use statutes to make anticipatory releases from liability for negligence void as against public policy as to businesses providing recreational activities to the public. N.Y. Gen.

Frequently, however, the argument that a contract term is sufficiently unfair or oppressive as to be unenforceable is grounded in one or more factors that are not expressly codified; in such circumstances, the common law has a significant role to play. As the commentary to the Restatement (Second) of Contracts explains:

> "Only infrequently does legislation, on grounds of public policy, provide that a term is unenforceable. When a court reaches that conclusion, it usually does so on the basis of a public policy derived either from its own perception of the need to protect some aspect of the public welfare or from legislation that is relevant to the policy although it says nothing explicitly about enforceability."

Restatement § 178 comment b.

This court has considered whether enforcement of an anticipatory release would violate an uncodified public policy in only a few cases. Although, in those cases, this court has not expressly analyzed the issue through the lens of unconscionability, it has followed an approach that is generally consistent with the application of that doctrine. That is, the court has not declared such releases to be *per se* invalid, but

---

Oblig. Law § 5-326 (every contract between recreational business owner and user of facility, pursuant to which owner receives payment for use of facilities, that exempts owner from liability for damages resulting from owner's negligence "shall be deemed void as against public policy and wholly unenforceable"); Haw. Rev. Stat. § 663-1.54(a) ("Any person who owns or operates a business providing recreational activities to the public . . . shall be liable for damages resulting from negligent acts or omissions of the person which cause injury.").

Other states have enacted more narrowly crafted statutes that deal with specific recreational activities, including skiing. For example, an Alaska statute specifically prohibits ski area operators from requiring skiers to enter into agreements releasing them from liability in exchange for the use of the facilities. Alaska Stat. Ann. § 05.45.120. In North Carolina, a statute imposes a duty on ski area operators "[n]ot to engage willfully or negligently in any type of conduct that contributes to or causes injury to another person or his properties." N.C. Gen. Stat. § 99C-2(c)(7); N.C. Gen. Statute § 99C-3 (violation of duties of ski area operator that causes injury or damage shall constitute negligence); *see also Strawbridge v. Sugar Mountain Resort, Inc.*, 320 F. Supp. 2d 425, 433 (W.D. N.C. 2004) (in light of statutory duty imposed on ski area operators not to negligently engage in conduct that causes injury, exculpatory clause on back of lift ticket was unenforceable).

Still other states have statutes that pertain specifically to skiing and, although not addressing releases, prescribe ski area operator duties and provide that operators will be liable for a violation of those duties. Colo. Rev. Stat. § 33-44-104(1) (violation of duties of ski area operator constitutes negligence to extent such violation causes injury to any person or damage to property); *see also Anderson v. Vail Corp.*, 251 P.3d 1125, 1129-30 (Colo. App. 2010) (if ski area operator violated statutory duties, exculpatory agreement would not release operator from liability); Idaho Code § 6-1107 ("Any ski area operator shall be liable for loss or damages caused by its failure to follow the duties set forth in [other sections of the Idaho Code pertaining to duties of ski area operators], where the violation of duty is causally related to the loss or damage suffered."); N.M. Stat. Ann. § 24-15-11 (to same effect); N.D. Cent. Code § 53-09-07 (same); W. Va. Code § 20-3A-6 (same); Utah Code Ann. § 78B-4-401 (public policy of Utah Inherent Risks of Skiing Act is to make ski area operators better able to insure themselves against the risk of loss occasioned by their negligence); *see also Rothstein v. Snowbird Corp.*, 2007 UT 96, 175 P.3d 560, 564 (Utah 2007) (by extracting a pre-injury release from plaintiff for liability due to ski resort's negligent acts, resort breached public policy underlying Utah Inherent Risks of Skiing Act).

neither has it concluded that they are always enforceable. Instead, the court has followed a multi-factor approach:

> "Agreements to exonerate a party from liability or to limit the extent of the party's liability for tortious conduct are not favorites of the courts but neither are they automatically voided. The treatment courts accord such agreements depends upon the subject and terms of the agreement and the relationship of the parties."

K-Lines v. Roberts Motor Co., 273 Ore. 242, 248, 541 P.2d 1378 (1975).

In *K-Lines*, this court upheld a limitation of liability contained in a commercial sales agreement. The court held that the fact

> "[t]hat one party may possess greater financial resources than the other is not proof that such a disparity of bargaining power exists that a limitation of liability provisions should be voided. "When the parties are business concerns dealing in a commercial setting and entering into an unambiguous agreement with terms commonly used in commercial transactions, the contract will not be deemed a contract of *adhesion* in *the* absence of evidence of unusual circumstances."

Id. at 252–53. The court also noted that, in an earlier decision, it had stated:

> "'There is nothing inherently bad about a contract provision which exempts one of the parties from liability. The parties are free to contract as they please, unless to permit them to do so would contravene the public interest.'"

Id. at 248 (quoting *Irish & Swartz Stores v. First Nat'l Bk.*, 220 Ore. 362, 375, 349 P.2d 814 (1960), *overruled on other grounds by Real Good Food v. First National Bank*, 276 Ore. 1057, 557 P.2d 654 (1976)).

Soon after deciding *K-Lines*, this court, in *Real Good Food*, held that a bank — serving as a bailee for depositors — could not limit its liability for the negligence of its employees. Relying on the Restatement (Second) of Torts, the court held:

> "Where the defendant is a common carrier, an innkeeper, a public warehouseman, a public utility, or is otherwise charged with a duty of public service, and the agreement to assume the risk relates to the defendant's performance of any part of that duty, it is well settled that it will not be given effect. Having undertaken the duty to the public, which includes the obligation of reasonable care, such defendants are not free to rid themselves of their public obligation by contract, or by any other agreement."

Id. at 1061 (quoting Restatement (Second) of Torts § 496B comment g (1965)).[11] The court in *Real Good Food* concluded that "[b]anks, like common carriers and utility

---

11. Restatement (Second) of Torts § 496B provides:
    "A plaintiff who by contract or otherwise expressly agrees to accept a risk of harm arising from the defendant's negligent or reckless conduct cannot recover for such harm, unless the agreement is invalid as contrary to public policy."

companies, perform an important public service," and the release therefore violated public policy and was unenforceable. 276 Ore. at 1061.

Finally, this court has held that another factor for determining whether an anticipatory release may be unenforceable is the possibility of a harsh or inequitable result for the releasing party. . . .

We glean from those decisions that relevant procedural factors in the determination of whether enforcement of an anticipatory release would violate public policy or be unconscionable include whether the release was conspicuous and unambiguous; whether there was a substantial disparity in the parties' bargaining power; whether the contract was offered on a take-it-or-leave-it basis; and whether the contract involved a consumer transaction. Relevant substantive considerations include whether enforcement of the release would cause a harsh or inequitable result to befall the releasing party; whether the release serves an important public interest or function; and whether the release purported to disclaim liability for more serious misconduct than ordinary negligence. Nothing in our previous decisions suggests that any single factor takes precedence over the others or that the listed factors are exclusive. Rather, they indicate that a determination whether enforcement of an anticipatory release would violate public policy or be unconscionable must be based on the totality of the circumstances of a particular transaction. The analysis in that regard is guided, but not limited, by the factors that this court previously has identified; it is also informed by any other considerations that may be relevant, including societal expectations.

With those principles in mind, we first consider the factors that usually are described as procedural, *viz.*, those pertaining to the formation of the agreement. Plaintiff does not contend that the release was inconspicuous or ambiguous; that is, plaintiff does not contend that he was surprised by its terms. Thus, that factor weighs in favor of enforcement. Other procedural factors, however, point in a different direction. This was not an agreement between equals. Only one party to the contract— defendant—was a commercial enterprise, and that party exercised its superior bargaining strength by requiring its patrons, including plaintiff, to sign an anticipatory release on a take-it-or-leave-it basis as a condition of using its facilities. As the Restatement (Second) of Torts, section 496B, explains, a release may not be enforced

> "where there is such a disparity in bargaining power between the parties that the agreement does not represent a free choice on the part of the plaintiff. The basis for such a result is the policy of the law which relieves the party

---

According to the comments to that section, an exculpatory agreement should be upheld if it is freely and fairly made, if it is between parties who are in an equal bargaining position, and if there is no societal interest with which it interferes. Restatement (Second) of Torts § 496B comment b. Comments e-j set out a non-exclusive list of situations in which releases may interfere with societal interests, insofar as they are contrary to public policy. Among other things, in addition to situations like those described in the passage quoted above, the Restatement refuses to give effect to express liability releases where there is a substantial disparity in bargaining power. Restatement (Second) of Torts § 496B comment j.

who is at such a disadvantage from harsh, inequitable, and unfair contracts which he is forced to accept by the necessities of his situation. The disparity in bargaining power may arise from the defendant's monopoly of a particular field of service, *from the generality of use of contract clauses insisting upon assumption of risk by those engaged in such a field, so that the plaintiff has no alternative possibility of obtaining the service without the clause;* or it may arise from the exigencies of the needs of the plaintiff himself, which leave him no reasonable alternative to the acceptance of the offered terms."

Id. comment j (emphasis added).

Also, plaintiff had no opportunity in this case to negotiate for different terms or pay an additional fee for protection against defendant's negligence. What makes the substantial disparity in the parties' bargaining positions even more significant in this circumstance is the limited number of ski areas that provide downhill skiing and snow-boarding opportunities in Oregon, and the generality of the use of similar releases among that limited commercial cohort.[13] Simply put, plaintiff had no meaningful alternative to defendant's take-it-or-leave-it terms if he wanted to participate in downhill snowboarding. Although that factor is not, by itself, dispositive,

"[w]hen one party is in such a superior bargaining position that it totally dictates all terms of the contract and the only option presented to the other party is to take it or leave it, some quantum of procedural unconscionability is established. The party who drafts such a contract of adhesion bears the responsibility of assuring that the provisions of the contract are not so one-sided as to be unconscionable."

Strand v. U.S. Bank Nat. Ass'n, 2005 ND 68, 693 N.W.2d 918, 925 (N.D. 2005).

We next consider the substantive factors that are relevant to our inquiry ... whether enforcement of the release would cause a harsh or inequitable result; whether defendant's recreational business operation serves an important public interest or function; and whether the release purported to disclaim liability for more serious misconduct than ordinary negligence.

We begin with the question whether enforcement of the release would cause a harsh and inequitable result to befall the releasing party, in this case, plaintiff. . . . [W]e conclude that the result would be harsh because, accepting as true the allegations in plaintiff's complaint, plaintiff would not have been injured if defendant had exercised reasonable care in designing, constructing, maintaining, or inspecting the jump on which he was injured. And that harsh result also would be inequitable because defendant, not its patrons, has the expertise and opportunity to foresee and control hazards of its own creation on its premises, and to guard against the negligence

---

13. In an excerpt from the transcript of plaintiff's deposition that was included in the summary judgment record, plaintiff testified that he had never been to a ski resort where a release such as the one at issue here was not required.

of its employees. Moreover, defendant alone can effectively spread the cost of guarding and insuring against such risks among its many patrons.

Those public policy considerations are embodied in the common law of business premises liability. Business owners and operators have a heightened duty of care toward patrons — invitees — with respect to the condition of their premises that exceeds the general duty of care to avoid unreasonable risks of harm to others. *Hagler v. Coastal Farm Holdings, Inc.*, 354 Ore. 132, 140–41, 309 P.3d 1073 (2013); *Garrison v. Deschutes County*, 334 Ore. 264, 272, 48 P.3d 807 (2002) (business invitee rule is a "special duty"). . . .

Furthermore, a business operator's obligation to make its premises reasonably safe for its invitees includes taking into account the use to which the premises are put. *See, e.g., Ragnone v. Portland School Dist. No. 1J*, 291 Ore. 617, 621 n. 3, 633 P.2d 1287 (1981) (so stating); *Mickel v. Haines Enterprises, Inc.*, 240 Ore. 369, 371–72, 400 P.2d 518 (1965) (owner must "take reasonable precautions to protect the invitee from dangers which are foreseeable from the arrangement or use of the premises.").

The legislature has statutorily modified those duties to some extent in the Skier Responsibility Law, ORS 30.970 to 30.990. Under ORS 30.975, skiers assume certain risks:

> "In accordance with ORS 31.600 [pertaining to contributory negligence] and notwithstanding ORS 31.620 (2) [abolishing the doctrine of implied assumption of risk], an individual who engages in the sport of skiing, alpine or nordic, accepts and assumes the inherent risks of skiing insofar as they are reasonably obvious, expected or necessary."

ORS 30.970(1) describes "inherent risks of skiing":

> "'Inherent risks of skiing' includes, but is not limited to, those dangers or conditions which are an integral part of the sport, such as changing weather conditions, variations or steepness in terrain, snow or ice conditions, surface or subsurface conditions, bare spots, creeks and gullies, forest growth, rocks, stumps, lift towers and other structures and their components, collisions with other skiers and a skier's failure to ski within the skier's own ability."

ORS 30.985 prescribes the duties of skiers, which generally deal with behaving safely while skiing.

By providing that a skier assumes the "inherent risks of skiing," ORS 30.975 reduced ski area operators' heightened common law duty to discover and guard against certain natural and inherent risks of harm. However, the Skier Responsibility Law did not abrogate the common-law principle that skiers do not assume responsibility for unreasonable conditions created by a ski area operator insofar as those conditions are not inherent to the activity. . . . It follows that the public policy underlying the common-law duty of a ski area operator to exercise reasonable care to avoid creating risks of harm to its business invitees remains applicable in this case.

In short, because (1) accepting as true the allegations in plaintiff's complaint, plaintiff would not have been injured if defendant had exercised reasonable care in designing, constructing, maintaining, or inspecting the jump on which he was injured; and (2) defendant, not its patrons, had the expertise and opportunity—indeed, the common law duty—to foresee and avoid unreasonable risks of its own creation on its business premises, we conclude that the enforcement of the release would cause a harsh and inequitable result, a factor that militates against its enforcement.

To continue our analysis, we next consider whether defendant's business operation serves an important public interest or function. The parties sharply disagree about the importance of that factor to our resolution of this case. According to defendant, that factor is paramount here, because, as a matter of law, anticipatory releases of negligence liability are unenforceable only when a defendant provides an "essential" public service.

Although this court has not previously addressed that precise issue in the context of a release involving a recreational activity, other courts have done so. As defendant observes, courts in several jurisdictions that lack statutory prohibitions of anticipatory releases of liability for negligence have upheld such releases (at least in part) on the ground that the activity at issue did not involve an "essential" public service.[15] However, courts in other jurisdictions have taken the opposite approach, concluding that, regardless of whether the release involves an essential public service.

For example, in *Dalury v. S-K-I, Ltd.*, 164 Vt. 329, 670 A.2d 795 (1995), the Vermont Supreme Court rejected the argument that anticipatory releases of negligence liability necessarily are enforceable in the context of recreational activities because such activities are not essential. 670 A.2d at 799. In that case, the plaintiff sustained serious injuries when he collided with a metal pole that formed part of the control maze for a ski-lift line. He brought a negligence action against the defendant ski area operator, alleging that it had negligently designed, built, and placed the maze pole. The trial court granted the defendant's motion for summary judgment based on an anticipatory release that the plaintiff had signed absolving the defendant of liability for negligence.

On appeal, the court noted that the release was conspicuous and unambiguous, but it nevertheless concluded that the release violated public policy. *Id.* at 797. . . . The court found a significant public policy consideration in the case in the law of premises liability; in particular, the court stated, business owners—including ski area

---

15. *See, e.g., Malecha v. St. Croix Valley Skydiving Club, Inc.*, 392 N.W. 2d 727 (Minn. App. 1986) (upholding an exculpatory agreement entered into between a skydiving operation and a patron); *Chepkevich v. Hidden Valley Resort*, 607 Pa. 1, 2 A.3d 1174 (2010) (skiing); *Pearce v. Utah Athletic Foundation*, 2008 UT 13, 179 P.3d 760 (Utah 2008) (bobsledding); *Benedek v. PLC Santa Monica, LLC*, 104 Cal. App. 4th 1351, 129 Cal. Rptr. 2d 197 (2002) (health club); *Henderson v. Quest Expeditions, Inc.*, 174 S.W.3d 730 (Tenn. Ct. App. 2005) (whitewater rafting).

operators—owe a duty of care to make their premises safe for patrons where their operations create a foreseeable risk of harm. *Id.* at 799. The court observed that

> "[d]efendants, not recreational skiers, have the expertise and opportunity to foresee and control hazards, and to guard against the negligence of their agents and employees. They alone can properly maintain and inspect their premises, and train their employees in risk management. They alone can insure against risks and effectively spread the cost of insurance among their thousands of customers. Skiers, on the other hand, are not in a position to discover and correct risks of harm, and they cannot insure against the ski area's negligence. If defendants were permitted to obtain broad waivers for their liability, an important incentive for ski areas to manage risk would be removed with the public bearing the cost of the resulting injuries. . . . It is illogical, in these circumstances, to undermine the public policy underlying business invitee law and allow skiers to bear risks they have no ability or right to control."

Id.

Turning to the defendant's argument that the release was enforceable because ski resorts do not provide an essential public service, the court stated that, "[w]hile interference with an essential public service surely affects the public interest, those services do not represent the universe of activities that implicate public concerns." *Id.* The court held that, "when a facility becomes a place of public accommodation, it 'render[s] a service which has become of public interest in the manner of the innkeepers and common carriers of old.'" *Id.* at 799–800 (quoting *Lombard v. Louisiana,* 373 U.S. 267, 279, 83 S. Ct. 1122, 10 L. Ed. 2d 338 (1963)) (internal quotation marks omitted).

Finally, the court's analysis was informed by a statute that placed the "inherent risks" of any sport on the participant, insofar as the risks were obvious and necessary. The court stated that "[a] ski area's own negligence . . . is neither an inherent risk nor an obvious and necessary one in the sport of skiing," and, therefore, "a skier's assumption of the inherent risks of skiing does not abrogate the ski area's duty to warn of or correct dangers which in the exercise of reasonable prudence in the circumstances could have been foreseen and corrected." *Dalury,* 670 A2d at 800 (internal quotation marks omitted).[17]

---

17. For similar reasons, the Connecticut Supreme Court also has declined to enforce an anticipatory release of negligence liability in the face of the defendant's contention that recreational activities do not implicate the public interest. *Hanks v. Powder Ridge Restaurant Corp.*, 276 Conn. 314, 885 A.2d 734 (2005). *Hanks* was a negligence action brought by a plaintiff who was injured when his foot was caught between his snowtube and the artificial bank of a snowtubing run at a ski resort operated by the defendant. The defendant relied on an anticipatory release that the plaintiff had signed that purported to absolve the defendant from liability for its negligence. The court acknowledged that the release was conspicuous and unambiguous, but ultimately agreed with the Vermont Supreme Court that determining what constitutes the public interest required consideration of all relevant circumstances, including that the plaintiff lacked sufficient knowledge and

We, too, think that the fact that defendant does not provide an essential public service does not compel the conclusion that the release in this case must be enforced. . . . It is true that ski areas do not provide the kind of public service typically associated with government entities or heavily regulated private enterprises such as railroads, hospitals, or banks. . . . However, like other places of public accommodation such as inns or public warehouses, defendant's business premises—including its terrain park—are open to the general public virtually without restriction, and large numbers of skiers and snowboarders regularly avail themselves of its facilities. To be sure, defendants' business facilities are privately owned, but that characteristic does not overcome a number of legitimate public interests concerning their operation.

The major public interests at stake are those underlying the law of business premises liability. The policy rationale is to place responsibility for negligently created conditions of business premises on those who own or control them, with the ultimate goal of mitigating the risk of injury-producing accidents. *Hagler,* 354 Ore. at 140–41; *Garrison,* 334 Ore. at 272. In that setting, where a business operator extends a general invitation to enter and engage in activities on its premises that is accepted by large numbers of the public, and those invitees are subject to risks of harm from conditions of the operator's creation, their safety is a matter of broad societal concern. . . . Accordingly, we reject defendant's argument that the fact that skiing and snowboarding are "non-essential" activities compels enforcement of the release in this case. Instead, we conclude that defendant's business operation is sufficiently tied to the public interest as to require the performance of its private duties to its patrons.

Finally, we consider the nature of the conduct to which the release would apply in this case. Defendant makes a fair point that, although the release purports to immunize it from liability for any misconduct short of intentional conduct, plaintiff's claim is based on ordinary negligence. Defendant notes that this court has held that an anticipatory release violates public policy where it purports to immunize the releasee from liability for gross negligence, reckless, or intentional conduct, but a release that disclaims liability only for ordinary negligence more often is enforced. *K-Lines,* 273 Ore. at 249. That statement is correct as a general comment on the validity of anticipatory releases, but, of course, whether any particular release will be enforced depends on the various factors that we discuss in this opinion. In the circumstances of this transaction, the fact that plaintiff's claim is based on negligence rather than on more egregious conduct carries less weight than the other

---

authority to discern whether, much less ensure that, the snowtubing runs were maintained in a reasonably safe condition. *Id*. at 331. Thus, the court held, "it is illogical to permit snowtubers, and the public generally, to bear the costs of risks that they have no ability or right to control." *Id.* at 332.

substantive factors that we have considered or than it would, for example, in a commercial transaction between parties of relatively equal bargaining power.[19]

SUMMARY AND APPLICATION

To summarize, our analysis leads to the conclusion that permitting defendant to exculpate itself from its own negligence would be unconscionable. As discussed, important procedural factors supporting that conclusion include the substantial disparity in the parties' bargaining power in the particular circumstances of this consumer transaction, and the fact that the release was offered to plaintiff and defendant's other customers on a take-it-or-leave-it basis.

There also are indications that the release is substantively unfair and oppressive. First, a harsh and inequitable result would follow if defendant were immunized from negligence liability, in light of (1) defendant's superior ability to guard against the risk of harm to its patrons arising from its own negligence in designing, creating, and maintaining its runs, slopes, jumps, and other facilities; and (2) defendant's superior ability to absorb and spread the costs associated with insuring against those risks. Second, because defendant's business premises are open to the general public virtually without restriction, large numbers of skiers and snowboarders regularly avail themselves of its facilities, and those patrons are subject to risks of harm from conditions on the premises of defendant's creation, the safety of those patrons is a matter of broad societal concern. The public interest, therefore, is affected by the performance of defendant's private duties toward them under business premises liability law.

In the ultimate step of our unconscionability analysis, we consider whether those procedural and substantive considerations outweigh defendant's interest in enforcing the release at issue here. Restatement (Second) of Contracts § 178 comment b ("[A] decision as to enforceability is reached only after a careful balancing, in the light of all the circumstances, of the interest in the enforcement of the particular promise against the policy against the enforcement of such terms."). Defendant argues that, in light of the inherent risks of skiing, it is neither unfair nor oppressive for a ski area operator to insist on a release from liability for its own negligence. As defendant explains,

> "[W]hen the plaintiff undertook this activity, he exposed himself to a high risk of injury. Only he controlled his speed, course, angle, 'pop' and the difficulty of his aerial maneuver. Skiing and snowboarding requires [sic] the skier to exercise appropriate caution and good judgment. Sometimes, even despite the exercise of due care, accidents and injuries occur."

Further, defendant contends, denying enforcement of such a release

> "improperly elevates premises liability tort law above the freedom to contract, fails to take into account the countervailing policy interest of

---

19. Defendant does not contend that the release would be enforceable against a claim based on alleged gross negligence or reckless conduct.

providing recreational opportunities to the public, fails to recognize that certain recreational activities are inherently dangerous and fails to consider the fact that the ski area operator has little, if any, control over the skier/snowboarder."

Defendant's arguments have some force. After all, skiing and snowboarding are activities whose allure and risks derive from a unique blend of factors that include natural features, artificial constructs, and human engagement. It may be difficult in such circumstances to untangle the causal forces that lead to an injury-producing accident. . . .

That said, the release is very broad; it applies on its face to a multitude of conditions and risks, many of which (such as riding on a chairlift) leave defendant's patrons vulnerable to risks of harm of defendant's creation. Accepting as true the allegations in plaintiff's complaint, defendant designed, created, and maintained artificial constructs, including the jump on which plaintiff was injured.[20] Even in the context of expert snowboarding in defendant's terrain park, defendant was in a better position than its invitees to guard against risks of harm created by its own conduct.

A final point deserves mention. It is axiomatic that public policy favors the deterrence of negligent conduct. . . . Although that policy of deterrence has implications in any case involving the enforceability of an anticipatory release of negligence liability, here, that policy bolsters the other considerations that weigh against enforcement of the release. As the parties readily agree, the activities at issue in this case involve considerable risks to life and limb. Skiers and snowboarders have important legal inducements to exercise reasonable care for their own safety by virtue of their statutory assumption of the inherent risks of skiing. By contrast, without potential exposure to liability for their own negligence, ski area operators would lack a commensurate legal incentive to avoid creating unreasonable risks of harm to their business invitees. *See Alabama Great Southern Railroad Co. v. Sumter Plywood Corp.*, 359 So. 2d 1140, 1145 (Ala. 1978) (human experience shows that exculpatory agreements induce a lack of care). Where, as here, members of the public are invited to participate without restriction in risky activities on defendant's business premises (and many do), and where the risks of harm posed by operator negligence are appreciable, such an imbalance in legal incentives is not conducive to the public interest.

Because the factors favoring enforcement of the release are outweighed by the countervailing considerations that we have identified, we conclude that enforcement of the release at issue in this case would be unconscionable. . . .

The decision of the Court of Appeals is reversed. The judgment of the trial court is reversed and the case is remanded to that court for further proceedings.

---

20. We reiterate that the issues of whether defendant actually was negligent in one or more of the particulars alleged by plaintiff, whether and the extent to which plaintiff was comparatively negligent, and the extent to which either party's negligence actually caused plaintiff's injuries, are not before us on review.

c. Assumption of Risk in the Context of Other Defenses

i. Abolishing Assumption of Risk

Blackburn v. Dorta

Supreme Court of Florida, 1977

348 So. 2d 287

SUNDBERG, JUSTICE.

These three consolidated cases are before the Court under our conflict certiorari jurisdiction as provided by Article V, Section 3(b)(3), Florida Constitution, and Florida Appellate Rule 4.5(b)....

Since our decision in *Hoffman v. Jones*, [280 So. 2d 431 (Fla. 1973),] contributory negligence no longer serves as a complete bar to plaintiff's recovery but is to be considered in apportioning damages according to the principles of comparative negligence. We are now asked to determine the effect of the *Hoffman* decision on the common law doctrine of assumption of risk. If assumption of risk is equivalent to contributory negligence, then *Hoffman* mandates that it can no longer operate as a complete bar to recovery. However, if it has a distinct purpose apart from contributory negligence, its continued existence remains unaffected by *Hoffman*. This question was expressly reserved in *Hoffman* as being not ripe for decision. 280 So. 2d 431, 439.

At the outset, we note that assumption of risk is not a favored defense. There is a puissant drift toward abrogating the defense. The argument is that assumption of risk serves no purpose which is not subsumed by either the doctrine of contributory negligence or the common law concept of duty. It is said that this redundancy results in confusion and, in some cases, denies recovery unjustly. The leading case in Florida dealing with the distinction between the doctrines recognizes that "[a]t times the line of demarcation between contributory negligence and assumption of risk is exceedingly difficult to define." *Byers v. Gunn*, 81 So. 2d 723, 727 (Fla. 1955). The issue is most salient in states which have enacted comparative negligence legislation. Those statutes provide that the common law defense of contributory negligence no longer necessarily acts as a complete bar to recovery. The effect of these statutes upon the doctrine of assumption of risk has proved to be controversial. Joining the intensifying assault upon the doctrine, a number of comparative negligence jurisdictions have abrogated assumption of risk. Those jurisdictions hold that assumption of risk is interchangeable with contributory negligence and should be treated equivalently. Today we are invited to join this trend of dissatisfaction with the doctrine. For the reasons herein expressed, we accept the invitation.

At the commencement of any analysis of the doctrine of assumption of risk, we must recognize that we deal with a potpourri of labels, concepts, definitions, thoughts, and doctrines. The confusion of labels does not end with the indiscriminate and interchangeable use of the terms "contributory negligence" and "assumption of risk." In the case law and among text writers, there have developed categories of assumption of risk. Distinctions exist between *express* and *implied;* between *primary* and *secondary;* and between *reasonable* and *unreasonable* or, as sometimes expressed, *strict* and *qualified.* It will be our task to analyze these various labels and to trace the historical basis of the doctrine to unravel what has been in the law an "enigma wrapped in a mystery."

It should be pointed out that we are not here concerned with express assumption of risk which is a contractual concept outside the purview of this inquiry and upon which we express no opinion herein. Included within the definition of express assumption of risk are express contracts not to sue for injury or loss which may thereafter be occasioned by the covenantee's negligence as well as situations in which actual consent exists such as where one voluntarily participates in a contact sport.

The breed of assumption of risk with which we deal here is that which arises by implication or implied assumption of risk. Initially it may be divided into the categories of *primary* and *secondary.* The term primary assumption of risk is simply another means of stating that the defendant was not negligent, either because he owed no duty to the plaintiff in the first instance, or because he did not breach the duty owed. Secondary assumption of risk is an affirmative defense to an established breach of a duty owed by the defendant to the plaintiff.

The concept of primary assumption of risk is the basis for the historical doctrine which arose in the master-servant relationship during the late nineteenth century. The master was held not to be negligent if he provided a reasonably safe place to work; the servant was said to have assumed the inherent risks that remained. In this context assumption of risk was not an affirmative defense at all. Rather, it was another way of expressing that the master was not negligent, for the servant had the burden of proving that his injury resulted from a risk other than one inherent in a facility or location that was a reasonably safe place to work. As is often the case in the common law, however, the doctrine mutated into an affirmative defense, with the burden of pleading and proof upon the master. Consequently, even if the servant could show that the master owed and had breached a duty to provide a reasonably safe place to work, the master could escape liability if he could establish that the servant had voluntarily exposed himself to a risk negligently created by the master. Thus, two distinct concepts came to bear the same label with inevitable confusion which has persisted to the present.

It is apparent that no useful purpose is served by retaining terminology which expresses the thought embodied in primary assumption of risk. This branch (or trunk) of the tree of assumption of risk is subsumed in the principle of negligence itself. Under our Florida jury instructions, the jury is directed first to determine whether the defendant has been negligent, i.e., did he owe a duty to the plaintiff and, if so, did he breach that duty? To sprinkle the term assumption of risk into the equation can only lead to confusion of a jury. An example of this concept is presented in the operation of a passenger train. It can be said that a passenger assumes the risk of lurches and jerks which are ordinary and usual to the proper operation of the train, but that he does not assume the risk of extraordinary or unusual lurches and jerks resulting from substandard operation of the train. The same issue can be characterized in terms of the standard of care of the railroad. Thus, it can be said that the railroad owes a duty to operate its train with the degree of care of an ordinary prudent person under similar circumstances which includes some lurching and jerking while a train is in motion or commencing to move under ideal circumstances. So long as the lurching or jerking is not extraordinary due to substandard conduct of the railroad, there is no breach of duty and, hence, no negligence on the part of the railroad. The latter characterization of the issue clearly seems preferable and is consistent with the manner in which the jury is instructed under our standard jury instructions.

Having dispensed with *express* and *primary-implied* assumption of risk, we recur to *secondary-implied* assumption of risk which is the affirmative defense variety that has been such a thorn in the judicial side. The affirmative defense brand of assumption of risk can be subdivided into the type of conduct which is reasonable but nonetheless bars recovery (sometimes called *pure* or *strict* assumption of risk), and the type of conduct which is unreasonable and bars recovery (sometimes referred to as *qualified* assumption of risk). Application of pure or strict assumption of risk is exemplified by the hypothetical situation in which a landlord has negligently permitted his tenant's premises to become highly flammable and a fire ensues. The tenant returns from work to find the premises a blazing inferno with his infant child trapped within. He rushes in to retrieve the child and is injured in so doing. Under the pure doctrine of assumption of risk, the tenant is barred from recovery because it can be said he voluntarily exposed himself to a known risk. Under this view of assumption of risk, the tenant is precluded from recovery notwithstanding the fact that his conduct could be said to be entirely reasonable under the circumstances. There is little to commend this doctrine of implied-pure or strict assumption of risk, and our research discloses no Florida case in which it has been applied. Certainly, in light of *Hoffman v. Jones, supra*, there is no reason supported by law or justice in this state to give credence to such a principle of law.

There remains, then, for analysis only the principle of implied-qualified assumption of risk, and it can be demonstrated in the hypothetical recited above with the minor alteration that the tenant rushes into the blazing premises to retrieve his favorite fedora. Such conduct on the tenant's part clearly would be unreasonable. Consequently, his conduct can just as readily be characterized as contributory negligence. It is the failure to exercise the care of a reasonably prudent man under similar circumstances. It is this last category of assumption of risk which has caused persistent confusion in the law of torts because of the lack of analytic difference between it and contributory negligence. If the only significant form of assumption of risk (implied-qualified) is so readily characterized, conceptualized, and verbalized as contributory negligence, can there be any sound rationale for retaining it as a separate affirmative defense to negligent conduct which bars recovery altogether? In the absence of any historical imperative, the answer must be no. . . .

We find no discernible basis analytically or historically to maintain a distinction between the affirmative defense of contributory negligence and assumption of risk.

The latter appears to be a viable, rational doctrine only in the sense described herein as implied-qualified assumption of risk which connotes unreasonable conduct on the part of the plaintiff. This result comports with the definition of contributory negligence appearing in Restatement (Second) of Torts, § 466 (1965). Furthermore, were we not otherwise persuaded to elimination of assumption of risk as a separate affirmative defense in the context herein described, the decision of this Court in *Hoffman v. Jones, supra*, would dictate such a result. As stated therein:

> ... A primary function of a court is to see that legal conflicts are equitably resolved. In the field of tort law, the most equitable result that can ever be reached by a court is the equation of liability with fault. Comparative negligence does this more completely than contributory negligence, and we would be shirking our duty if we did not adopt the better doctrine. 280 So. 2d 431, 438.

Is liability equated with fault under a doctrine which would totally bar recovery by one who voluntarily, but reasonably, assumes a known risk while one whose conduct is unreasonable but denominated "contributory negligence" is permitted to recover a proportionate amount of his damages for injury? Certainly not. Therefore, we hold that the affirmative defense of implied assumption of risk is merged into the defense of contributory negligence and the principles of comparative negligence enunciated in *Hoffman v. Jones, supra*, shall apply in all cases where such defense is asserted.

. . . .

OVERTON, C.J., and ADKINS, BOYD, ENGLAND and HATCHETT, JJ., concur.

What is the difference between assumption of risk and contributory or comparative negligence? Could a jurisdiction consistently maintain both an assumption of risk and a comparative negligence defense?

ii. Retaining Assumption of Risk

Patterson v. Sacramento City Unified School District

California Court of Appeal, 2007
66 Cal. Rptr. 3d 337

CANTIL-SAKAUYE, J.

Plaintiff James Patterson was injured while participating in a truck driver training course. Defendant Sacramento City Unified School District (District) offered the course as part of its adult education program. Patterson sued the District for negligent supervision. The trial court granted the District's motion for summary judgment, ruling that the doctrine of primary assumption of risk barred Patterson's negligence claim.

On appeal, Patterson contends judgment must be reversed because: (1) the court improperly overruled a finding of duty in the District's first summary judgment motion; (2) assumption of risk does not apply in the circumstances of this case; and (3) even if the assumption of risk doctrine applies, there are triable issues of fact on whether the District acted recklessly. We agree with plaintiff that assumption of the risk does not apply in these circumstances and shall reverse the judgment.

FACTUAL BACKGROUND

In spring 2003, Patterson enrolled in the District's California Heavy Duty Truck Driving Program. The truck driving course provided students with the training and hands-on experience they needed to become professional truck drivers. It consisted of three six-week segments: classroom instruction; hands-on training; and on-the-road experience. In order to pass the course, students were required to participate in community service projects as part of their hands-on training and on-the-road experience.

The District assigned credentialed heavy-duty truck driving instructors to teach each segment of the course. Joe Arcuri and Ward Allen taught the second and third segments. Allen also served as field instructor and supervisor for the community service projects.

On May 9, 2003, during the first week of the hands-on segment of the training course, Patterson and several other students participated in a community service project which involved picking up bleachers from several locations, loading them onto a flat bed trailer attached to a tractor, and transporting them to the site of a rugby tournament. The classroom curriculum covered freight loading in a basic sense, but did not cover the specifics of loading flat bed trucks or trailers. According to the instructors, a primary goal of the community service assignment was to teach students how to load the trailers safely. The instructors described the loading of cargo as a "hands-on kind of thing" that involved common sense. The instructors typically critiqued the students after they loaded the cargo.

Allen was responsible for instructing Patterson and the other students on loading the bleachers on the flat bed trailer. The bed of the trailer was between 96 and 102 inches wide and approximately five feet off the ground. Allen was present when the students picked up aluminum bleachers at the first location and loaded them on the trailer without incident. He told the students to pick up the bleachers at the second location on their own. Allen did not know how much prior training or experience his students had in loading trailers.

The bleachers at the second location were made of heavy wood. Allen had not seen the wooden bleachers before assigning the students to pick them up. Because there were no teachers present, and none of the students was considered to be in charge, the unsupervised students decided as a group how to load the wooden bleachers. It took six students to carry each section of wooden bleachers. Patterson and a student named Don Cruse stood on the trailer bed. Patterson had never climbed on the flat bed trailer before he and the other students arrived at the second pick-up location. Patterson and Cruse pulled on the wooden bleachers while the remaining students pushed the bleachers from below. Patterson cautioned the students who were pushing to slow down when he recognized that he was running out of room at the edge of the trailer. Instead, the students gave the bleachers "one big push," and Patterson fell backward off the trailer.

DISCUSSION

. . . .

Duty of Care and Assumption of Risk

Patterson's complaint alleges that the District "had a duty to supervise, train, educate, instruct, and oversee the conduct of its [truck driver training] students" on proper techniques for loading and unloading flat bed trucks and trailers and "to exercise ordinary care to protect students from the type of injury" that Patterson suffered. The District maintains that under the doctrine of assumption of risk, it owed Patterson no duty of care.

Historically, the concept of duty developed in the late 19th century as a legal device was "designed to curtail the feared propensities of juries toward liberal awards." (*Dillon v. Legg* (1968) 68 Cal.2d 728, 734, 69 Cal.Rptr. 72, 441 P.2d 912 (*Dillon*).) The essential question in a duty analysis is "'whether the plaintiff's interests are entitled to legal protection against the defendant's conduct. . . . [Duty] is a shorthand statement of a conclusion, rather than an aid to analysis in itself. . . . But it should be recognized that "duty" is not sacrosanct in itself, but only an expression of the sum total of those considerations of policy which lead the law to say that the particular plaintiff is entitled to protection.' [Citation.]" (*Ibid.*; accord, *Avila v. Citrus Community College Dist.* (2006) 38 Cal.4th 148, 160–161, 41 Cal.Rptr.3d 299, 131 P.3d 383 (*Avila*).)

In deciding whether to depart from the general principle that a person is liable for injuries caused by his or her failure to exercise reasonable care, courts balance the now classic list of policy considerations which include "the foreseeability of harm to the plaintiff, the degree of certainty that the plaintiff suffered injury, the closeness of the connection between the defendant's conduct and the injury suffered, the moral blame attached to the defendant's conduct, the policy of preventing future harm, the extent of the burden to the defendant and consequences to the community of imposing a duty to exercise care with resulting liability for breach, and the availability, cost, and prevalence of insurance for the risk involved." (*Rowland v. Christian* (1968) 69 Cal.2d 108, 113, 70 Cal.Rptr. 97, 443 P.2d 561; see *Stockinger v. Feather River Community College* (2003) 111 Cal.App.4th 1014, 1035, 4 Cal.Rptr.3d 385 (*Stockinger*).)

This case presents competing policy considerations. On one hand, as an adult student at a public school, is Patterson entitled to legal protection against the alleged negligence of the District employees in failing to supervise and instruct him on how to load wooden bleachers on a flat bed trailer? As we explained, the court denied the District's first summary judgment motion on grounds it owed Patterson a duty of care under statutory law. On the other hand, does the doctrine of assumption of risk relieve the District of any duty of care based on the nature of the class activity and the potentially chilling effect of imposing a duty of care on the District's truck driving instructors? Although this case may not fit neatly into either line of author-ity, we conclude that Patterson was not engaged in an inherently dangerous activity as a matter of law. Nor do policy considerations favor application of the doctrine of assumption of risk. Accordingly, the court erred in ruling that assumption of risk barred Patterson's negligence claims. . . .

Primary and Secondary Assumption of Risk:

In *Knight [v. Jewett*, 834 P.2d 696 (Cal. 1992) (en banc)] the Supreme Court rec-onciled the doctrine of assumption of risk, which completely bars a plaintiff's recov-ery in a negligence action, with comparative negligence principles announced in *Li v. Yellow Cab Co.* (1975) 13 Cal.3d 804, 119 Cal.Rptr. 858, 532 P.2d 1226 (*Li*). The discussion in *Knight* provides the necessary background for our decision that assump-tion of risk does not apply in this case. We quote *Knight* at length.

"In *Li*, our court undertook a basic reexamination of the common law doctrine of contributory negligence. As *Li* noted, contributory negligence generally has been defined as '"conduct on the part of the plaintiff which falls below the standard to which he should conform for his own protec-tion, and which is a legally contributing cause cooperating with the negli-gence of the defendant in bringing about the plaintiff's harm."' (*Li, supra*, 13 Cal.3d at p. 809, 119 Cal.Rptr. 858, 532 P.2d 1226, quoting Rest.2d Torts, § 463.) Prior to *Li*, the common law rule was that '"[e]xcept where the defendant has the last clear chance, the plaintiff's contributory negligence *bars recovery* against a defendant whose negligent conduct would otherwise make him liable to the plaintiff for the harm sustained by him."' (*Li, supra*, at pp. 809–810, 119 Cal.Rptr. 858, 532 P.2d 1226, italics added, quoting Rest.2d Torts, § 467.)

"In *Li, supra*, 13 Cal.3d 804[, 119 Cal.Rptr. 858, 532 P.2d 1226], we observed that '[i]t is unnecessary for us to catalogue the enormous amount of critical comment that has been directed over the years against the "all-or-nothing" approach of the doctrine of contributory negligence. The essence of that criticism has been constant and clear: the doctrine is ineq-uitable in its operation because it fails to distribute responsibility in pro-portion to fault. . . . *The basic objection to the doctrine—grounded in the primal concept that in a system in which liability is based on fault, the extent of fault should govern the extent of liability—remains irresistible to reason and all intelligent notions of fairness.*' (At pp. 810–811[, 119 Cal.Rptr. 858, 532 P.2d 1226], italics added.) After taking additional note of the untoward practical consequences of the doctrine in the litigation of cases and the increasing rejection of the doctrine in other jurisdictions, the *Li* court con-cluded that '[w]e are likewise persuaded that logic, practical experience, and fundamental justice counsel against the retention of the doctrine ren-dering contributory negligence a complete bar to recovery—and that it should be replaced in this state by a system under which liability for dam-age will be borne by those whose negligence caused it in direct proportion to their respective fault.' (At pp. 812–813[, 119 Cal.Rptr. 858, 532 P.2d 1226].)

"After determining that the 'all-or-nothing' contributory negligence doctrine should be replaced by a system of comparative negligence, the *Li* court went on to undertake a rather extensive discussion of the effect that the adoption of comparative negligence would have on a number of related tort doctrines, including the doctrines of last clear chance and assumption of risk. (*Li, supra*, 13 Cal.3d at pp. 823–826, 119 Cal.Rptr. 858, 532 P.2d 1226.)

"With respect to the effect of the adoption of comparative negligence on the assumption of risk doctrine—the issue before [the *Knight* court]—the *Li* decision, *supra*, 13 Cal.3d 804[, 119 Cal.Rptr. 858, 532 P.2d 1226], stated as follows: 'As for assumption of risk, we have recognized in this state that this defense overlaps that of contributory negligence to some extent and in fact is made up of at least two distinct defenses. "To simplify greatly, it has been observed . . . that in one kind of situation, to wit, where a plaintiff *unreasonably* undertakes to encounter a specific known risk imposed by a defendant's negligence, plaintiff's conduct, although he may encounter that risk in a prudent manner, is in reality a form of contributory negligence. . . . Other kinds of situations within the doctrine of assumption of risk are those, for example, where plaintiff is held to agree to relieve defendant of an obligation of reasonable conduct toward him. Such a situation would not involve contributory negligence, but rather a reduction of defendant's duty of care." [Citations.] We think it clear that the adoption of a system of comparative negligence should entail the merger of the defense of assumption of risk into the general scheme of assessment of liability in proportion to fault in those particular cases in which the form of assumption of risk involved is no more than a variant of contributory negligence. [Citation.]' (*Li, supra*, 13 Cal.3d at pp. 824–825, 119 Cal.Rptr. 858, 532 P.2d 1226, original italics.)

"As this passage indicates, the *Li* decision, *supra*, 13 Cal.3d 804[, 119 Cal. Rptr. 858, 532 P.2d 1226], clearly contemplated that the assumption of risk doctrine was to be *partially* merged or subsumed into the comparative negligence scheme. Subsequent Court of Appeal decisions have disagreed, however, in interpreting *Li*, as to what category of assumption of risk cases would be merged into the comparative negligence scheme.

"A number of appellate decisions, focusing on the language in *Li* indicating that assumption of risk is in reality a form of contributory negligence 'where a plaintiff *unreasonably* undertakes to encounter a specific known risk imposed by a defendant's negligence' (13 Cal.3d at p. 824[, 119 Cal.Rptr. 858, 532 P.2d 1226]), have concluded that *Li* properly should be interpreted as drawing a distinction between those assumption of risk cases in which a plaintiff 'unreasonably' encounters a known risk imposed by a defendant's negligence and those assumption of risk cases in which a plaintiff 'reasonably' encounters a known risk imposed by a defendant's negligence. (See, e.g., *Ordway v. Superior Court* [1988] 198 Cal.App.3d 98, 103–105[, 243 Cal. Rptr. 536].)

"In our view, these decisions—regardless whether they reached the correct result on the facts at issue—have misinterpreted *Li* by suggesting that our decision contemplated less favorable legal treatment for a plaintiff who reasonably encounters a known risk than for a plaintiff who unreasonably encounters such a risk. . . .

"Indeed, particularly when the relevant passage in *Li, supra*, 13 Cal.3d at pages 824–825, 119 Cal.Rptr. 858, 532 P.2d 1226, is read as a whole and in conjunction with the authorities it cites, we believe it becomes clear that the distinction in assumption of risk cases to which the *Li* court referred in this passage was not a distinction between instances in which a plaintiff unreasonably encounters a known risk imposed by a defendant's negligence and instances in which a plaintiff reasonably encounters such a risk. Rather, the distinction to which the *Li* court referred was between (1) those instances in which the assumption of risk doctrine embodies a legal conclusion that there is 'no duty' on the part of the defendant to protect the plaintiff from a particular risk—the category of assumption of risk that the legal commentators generally refer to as 'primary assumption of risk'—and (2) those instances in which the defendant does owe a duty of care to the plaintiff but the plaintiff knowingly encounters a risk of injury caused by the defendant's breach of that duty—what most commentators have termed 'secondary assumption of risk.' Properly interpreted, the relevant passage in *Li* provides that the category of assumption of risk cases that is not merged into the comparative negligence system and in which the plaintiff's recovery continues to be completely barred involves those cases in which the defendant's conduct did not breach a legal duty of care to the plaintiff, i.e., 'primary assumption of risk' cases, whereas cases involving 'secondary assumption of risk' properly are merged into the comprehensive comparative fault system adopted in *Li*.

"Although the difference between the 'primary assumption of risk'/'secondary assumption of risk' nomenclature and the 'reasonable implied assumption of risk'/'unreasonable implied assumption of risk' terminology embraced in many of the recent Court of Appeal decisions may appear at first blush to be only semantic, the significance extends beyond mere rhetoric. First, in 'primary assumption of risk' cases—where the defendant owes no duty to protect the plaintiff from a particular risk of harm—a plaintiff who has suffered such harm is not entitled to recover from the defendant, whether the plaintiff's conduct in undertaking the activity was reasonable *or unreasonable*. Second, in 'secondary assumption of risk' cases—involving instances in which the defendant has breached the duty of care owed to the plaintiff—the defendant is not entitled to be entirely relieved of liability for an injury proximately caused by such breach, simply because the plaintiff's conduct in encountering the risk of such an injury was *reasonable* rather than unreasonable. Third and finally, the question whether the defendant owed a legal duty to protect the plaintiff from a particular risk of harm does not turn on the reasonableness or unreasonableness of the plaintiff's conduct, but rather on the nature of the activity or sport in which the defendant is engaged and the relationship of the defendant and the plaintiff to that activity or sport. For these reasons, use of the 'reasonable implied assumption of risk'/unreasonable implied assumption of risk' terminology, as a means of differentiating between the cases in which a plaintiff is barred from bringing an action and those in which he or she is not barred, is more misleading than helpful." (*Knight, supra,* 3 Cal.4th at pp. 304–309, 11 Cal.Rptr.2d 2, 834 P.2d 696, fns. omitted.)

In our view, the case before us involves classic secondary assumption of risk—where the District owed a duty of care but, at most, Patterson may have unreasonably encountered the risk of climbing onto the flat bed truck to load the wooden bleachers. As we shall explain, the record and the policy reasons underlying primary assumption of risk demonstrate that the doctrine should not be applied in the circumstances of this case. Accordingly, Patterson's negligence claim survives the District's motion for summary judgment.

Assumption of Risk Does Not Trump the District's Duty:

The Supreme Court observed in *Knight* that, "the phrase 'assumption of risk' traditionally has been used in a number of very different factual settings involving analytically distinct legal concepts." (*Knight, supra,* 3 Cal.4th at p. 303, 11 Cal.Rptr.2d 2, 834 P.2d 696.) Two different species of assumption of risk are candidates for application in the case before us. One type of assumption of risk arose in the context of active sports and evolved to include similar activities in the school and employment setting. The other type of assumption of risk, more commonly known as the firefighter's rule, arose and developed in the context of the public service professions. As we shall explain, neither species of assumption of risk applies here.

1. The Firefighter's Rule:

The firefighter's rule is a variation on the doctrine of primary assumption of risk based on different policy concerns than those found in the sports context. "In its most classic form, the firefighter's rule involves the question whether a person who negligently has started a fire is liable for an injury sustained by a firefighter who is summoned to fight the fire; the rule provides that the person who started the fire is not liable under such circumstances. [Citation.] Although a number of theories have been cited to support this conclusion, the most persuasive explanation is that the party who negligently started the fire had no legal duty to protect the firefighter from the very danger that the firefighter is employed to confront. [Citations.]" (*Knight, supra,* 3 Cal.4th at p. 309, fn. 5, 11 Cal.Rptr.2d 2, 834 P.2d 696; see also, *Priebe v. Nelson*

(2006) 39 Cal.4th 1112, 47 Cal.Rptr.3d 553, 140 P.3d 848 [employee of boarding kennel]; *Calatayud v. State of California* (1998) 18 Cal.4th 1057, 77 Cal.Rptr.2d 202, 959 P.2d 360 [police officer] (*Calatayud*).)

In *Calatayud*, the Supreme Court discussed the policies underlying the firefighter's rule. First, "'"In terms of duty, it may be said there is none owed the fireman to exercise care so as not to require the special services for which he is trained and paid."' [Citations.]" (*Calatayud, supra*, 18 Cal.4th at p. 1061, 77 Cal.Rptr.2d 202, 959 P.2d 360.) Second, "[t]he rule is equally grounded in considerations of public policy '"distilled from the relevant factors involved upon an inquiry into what is fair and just. . . . [¶] [I]t is the fireman's business to deal with that very hazard [the fire] and hence, perhaps by analogy to the contractor engaged as an expert to remedy dangerous situations, he cannot complain of negligence in the creation of the very occasion for his engagement."' [Citations.] Moreover, 'public safety employees receive special public compensation for confronting the dangers posed by the defendants' negligence.' [Citation.] 'Firemen and policemen are paid for the work they perform including preparation for facing the hazards of their professions and dealing with perils when they arise. When injury occurs, liberal compensation is provided. In addition to the usual medical and disability benefits ordinarily provided all employees covered by the Workers' Compensation Act, firemen and policemen are provided special benefits [including special statutory presumptions of industrial causation, special death benefits, optional paid leaves of absence, and fully paid disability benefits despite retirement].' [Citations.]" (*Id.* at pp. 1061–1062, 77 Cal.Rptr.2d 202, 959 P.2d 360.)

None of the policy reasons undergirding the firefighter's rule applies to a student like Patterson who attends adult education courses offered by a public school district. The student receives no advance training to deal with the danger; rather, he is attending the adult education class to obtain that training. The student receives no compensation in the form of wages; instead, he ordinarily pays fees to the district in order to participate in its educational program. Finally, the adult education student receives no special public benefits when he is injured. . . . Because none of the policy reasons advanced for the firefighter's rule applies in the circumstances of the present case, we conclude the rule is inapplicable.

2. Assumption of Risk in the Sports Context:

The *Knight* court described primary assumption of risk as an exception to the general rule that people "have a duty to use due care to avoid injury to others, and may be held liable if their careless conduct injures another person." (*Knight, supra*, 3 Cal.4th at p. 315, 11 Cal.Rptr.2d 2, 834 P.2d 696.) As we explained earlier, the doctrine applies "where, by virtue of the nature of the activity and the parties' relationship to the activity, the defendant owes no legal duty to protect the plaintiff from the particular risk of harm that caused the injury. . . ." (*Id.* at pp. 314–315, 11 Cal. Rptr.2d 2, 834 P.2d 696.) *Knight* instructs that where "the careless conduct of others is treated as an 'inherent risk' of a sport" or activity, recovery is barred. (*Id.* at p. 316, 11 Cal.Rptr.2d 2, 834 P.2d 696.)

The classic assumption of risk cases arose in the active sports context where California courts ruled that the doctrine barred participants from suing co-participants or coaches for their injuries. (See, e.g., *Avila, supra,* 38 Cal.4th 148, 41 Cal.Rptr.3d 299, 131 P.3d 383 [student baseball game]; *Cheong v. Antablin* (1997) 16 Cal.4th 1063, 68 Cal.Rptr.2d 859, 946 P.2d 817 [skier]; *Knight, supra,* 3 Cal.4th 296, 11 Cal.Rptr.2d 2, 834 P.2d 696 [touch football game]; *Fortier v. Los Rios Community College Dist.* (1996) 45 Cal.App.4th 430, 52 Cal.Rptr.2d 812 [football practice]; *Regents of the University of California v. Superior Court* (1996) 41 Cal.App.4th 1040, 48 Cal.Rptr.2d 922 [rock climbing class]; *Galardi v. Seahorse Riding Club* (1993) 16 Cal.App.4th 817, 20 Cal.Rptr.2d 270 [horse jumping instruction]; *Tan v. Goddard* (1993) 13 Cal. App.4th 1528, 17 Cal.Rptr.2d 89 [jockey school]; compare *Kahn v. East Side Union High School Dist.* (2003) 31 Cal.4th 990, 4 Cal.Rptr.3d 103, 75 P.3d 30 [primary assumption of risk applied to novice swimmer, but summary judgment reversed because the record established reckless conduct by the coach as a matter of law].)

Knight articulated the policy basis for applying the assumption of risk doctrine in the active sports setting. "In reaching the conclusion that a coparticipant's duty of care should be limited in this fashion, the cases have explained that, in the heat of an active sporting event like baseball or football a participant's normal energetic conduct often includes accidentally careless behavior. The courts have concluded that vigorous participation in such sporting events likely would be chilled if legal liability were to be imposed on a participant on the basis of his or her ordinary careless conduct. The cases have recognized that, in such a sport, even when a participant's conduct violates a rule of the game and may subject the violator to internal sanctions prescribed by the sport itself, imposition of *legal liability* for such conduct might well alter fundamentally the nature of the sport by deterring participants from vigorously engaging in activity that falls close to, but on the permissible side of, a prescribed rule." (*Knight, supra,* 3 Cal.4th at pp. 318–319, 11 Cal.Rptr.2d 2, 834 P.2d 696.)

If the assumption of risk doctrine were limited to the sports context, there would be little question that it is inapplicable in the circumstances of the present case. However, by expanding application of the doctrine to the school and employment setting, California courts have provided the District with a rationale to justify its argument that assumption of risk bars Patterson's negligence claim here. As we explain, the policy basis for applying the doctrine is still lacking.

3. Assumption of Risk in Other Contexts:

California courts have expanded the scope of the assumption of risk doctrine to encompass dangerous activities in other contexts where the activity is inherently dangerous. (*See, e.g., Saville, supra,* 133 Cal.App.4th 857, 36 Cal.Rptr.3d 515 [training in peace officer takedown maneuvers]; *Hamilton v. Martinelli & Associates* (2003) 110 Cal.App.4th 1012, 2 Cal.Rptr.3d 168 (*Hamilton*) [training on physical restraint methods]; *Aaris v. Las Virgenes* Unified School Dist. (1998) 64 Cal.App.4th 1112, 75 Cal.

Rptr.2d 801 (*Aaris*) [cheerleader practice]; and *Bushnell v. Japanese-American Religious & Cultural Center* (1996) 43 Cal.App.4th 525, 50 Cal.Rptr.2d 671 (*Bushnell*) [practice of moves in judo class].) Two of these cases deserve special mention.

The first is *Hamilton*. In that case, plaintiff worked as a probation corrections officer (and peace officer) in a youth detention center. Her duties included supervising and counseling children between the ages of 10 and 18, including violent offenders. Plaintiff participated in an "Unarmed Defensive Tactics" training course taught by defendant Martinelli and Associates. She injured her neck and back when she performed a "maneuver . . . designed to teach [her how] to extricate herself if she was attacked, landed on her stomach, and was being choked by an assailant straddling her back." (*Hamilton, supra,* 110 Cal.App.4th at p. 1018, 2 Cal.Rptr.3d 168.) In holding that the doctrine of primary assumption of risk applied, the court found that the injuries plaintiff suffered in a training course for probation corrections officers were an inherent risk of performing the training maneuver. (*Id.* at pp. 1017–1018, 1023, 2 Cal.Rptr.3d 168.) "Moreover, plaintiff's employment duties entailed the very risk of injury of which she complains. Plaintiff's employment duties included restraining violent juvenile offenders. She was required to wear a uniform and carry pepper spray. And since 1997, her job philosophy emphasized physical restraint of juveniles. Thus, the ability to physically restrain juveniles was a necessary tool in plaintiff's employment. By continuing in this employment capacity, plaintiff assumed the risk that she would be injured by a violent juvenile offender. And by participating in an employer-required training course, she assumed the risk that she would be injured while training to restrain a violent juvenile offender." (*Id.* at p. 1023, 2 Cal.Rptr.3d 168.)

Unlike the activity described in *Hamilton*, which satisfied one requirement for applying assumption of risk, loading a flat bed trailer is not an inherently dangerous activity. We reject the District's suggestion, based on language in *Aaris, supra,* 64 Cal.App.4th at p. 1114, 75 Cal.Rptr.2d 801, that "[w]henever gravity is at play, . . . the risk of injury in inherent." This case involves standing on the bed of the trailer, albeit five feet above the ground. Gravity is similarly "at play" when a person climbs up a ladder, walks across a bridge or leans against a porch railing. The District cites no case that holds assumption of risk applies to such common, everyday work activities. We conclude that loading wooden bleachers on a flat bed trailer is not inherently dangerous as a matter of law.

Moreover, the court's rationale in *Hamilton* is really a mixture of the firefighter's rule and assumption of risk based on competitive or violent sports announced in *Knight.* Because plaintiff incurred the injury in connection with her employment, all the policy reasons supporting application of the firefighter's rule would apply, including the provision of care and treatment under the workers' compensation scheme. In the case before us, Patterson was not an employee who would be covered by workers' compensation or (so far as the record shows) by any other insurance. Patterson, a student, simply signed up for a truck driver training class. We conclude that the policy reasons for applying primary assumption of risk in *Hamilton* are completely absent here.

The second case deserving special mention is *Saville, supra,* 133 Cal.App.4th 857, 36 Cal.Rptr.3d 515, an opinion from this court. The plaintiff in *Saville* enrolled in a certified peace officer training class offered by the defendant community college. The course consisted of three parts: lectures, arrest and control methods, and firearms. Students were required to attend and pass all three parts of the course. (*Id.* at p. 861, 36 Cal.Rptr.3d 515.) They learned arrest and control methods from the local police chief "in as realistic an experience as possible . . . [by] 'modeling' the actions an actual police officer would take when performing a takedown in the field." (*Id.* at p. 862, 36 Cal.Rptr.3d 515.) Three police officers demonstrated four takedown maneuvers. (*Id.* at pp. 862–863, 36 Cal.Rptr.3d 515.) The officers then moved around the room to observe the students as they practiced the maneuvers. Plaintiff injured his back while practicing what was described as a forehead sweep. (*Id.* at p. 863, 36 Cal.Rptr.3d 515.) This court concluded that the takedown maneuvers bore "similar risks of injury inherent in many sports. The maneuvers are inherently dangerous. One person is intentionally throwing another to the ground. 'Whenever gravity is at play with the human body, the risk of injury is inherent.'" (*Ibid.,* quoting *Aaris, supra,* 64 Cal. App.4th at p. 1114, 75 Cal.Rptr.2d 801.) "Careless conduct by others is also an inherent risk in performing the maneuvers. Plaintiff acknowledged both he and his partner were inexperienced and had not learned or practiced these maneuvers before the class. Even with the steps taken by the officers to minimize the risk of injury — personal training, placing mats on the floors, demonstrating the moves, observing the students perform the moves — the risk of harm from participating in the actual maneuvers with an inexperienced person remained obvious, and plaintiff suffered injury from that particular risk. Grabbing someone's face from behind, pushing his head into his spine, and throwing him back and down to the ground with an elbow in his back, even at half speed, could hurt someone." (*Saville, supra,* at p. 867, 36 Cal.Rptr.3d 515.)

Once again, there is a vast difference between the activity described as inherently dangerous in *Saville* and the activity at issue in the present case. Driving a truck, or even loading a truck, does not involve the same risk of injury as the violent take-down maneuver at issue in that case. Inherent danger is measured by more than the number or inches or feet between the plaintiff and the ground. (Compare *Aaris, supra,* 64 Cal.App.4th at p. 1114, 75 Cal.Rptr.2d 801.)

We also concluded in *Saville* that "[i]mposing a duty to eliminate the risk of injury from the activity in [that] particular classroom situation would invariably chill vigorous participation in learning the maneuvers." (*Saville, supra,* 133 Cal.App.4th at p. 867, 36 Cal.Rptr.3d 515.) What the instructors allegedly did — or did not do — in the present case is conduct that we want to chill. As a matter of policy, we do not want truck driver training instructors to send inexperienced students out to load flat bed trailers without instruction and supervision.

In deciding that primary assumption of risk does not apply in the case before us, we cite *Knight* one last time: "It may be helpful at this point to summarize our general conclusions as to the current state of the doctrine of assumption of risk in light of the adoption of comparative fault principles in *Li, supra*, 13 Cal.3d 804, 119 Cal. Rptr. 858, 532 P.2d 1226, general conclusions that reflect the view of a majority of the justices of the court (i.e., the three justices who have signed this opinion and Justice Mosk (see conc. and dis. opn. by Mosk, J., *post*, p. 321, 11 Cal.Rptr.2d 2, 834 P.2d 696)). In cases involving 'primary assumption of risk'—where, by virtue of the nature of the activity and the parties' relationship to the activity, the defendant owes no legal duty to protect the plaintiff from the particular risk of harm that caused the injury—the doctrine continues to operate as a complete bar to the plaintiff's recovery. In cases involving 'secondary assumption of risk'—where the defendant does owe a duty of care to the plaintiff, but the plaintiff proceeds to encounter a known risk imposed by the defendant's breach of duty—the doctrine is merged into the comparative fault scheme, and the trier of fact, in apportioning the loss resulting from the injury, may consider the relative responsibility of the parties." (*Knight, supra*, 3 Cal.4th at pp. 314–315, 11 Cal.Rptr.2d 2, 834 P.2d 696.)

The wise and just rule to be applied in this case is one that imposes a duty of reasonable care upon the District to Patterson and apportions responsibility for damages between the District and Patterson according to their respective degrees of fault. Given the nature of the instructors' alleged breach of duty in this case, there is no reason in law, equity or policy to absolve the District entirely from liability for damages suffered by Patterson. Although it might be argued that the District will decline to provide truck driving classes in the future, that argument is speculative and therefore untenable on this record. (See *City of Santa Barbara v. Superior Court of Santa Barbara County* (2007) 41 Cal.4th 747, 773–776, 62 Cal.Rptr.3d 527, 161 P.3d 1095.) For all these reasons, we conclude the court erred in finding that the doctrine of assumption of risk applied.

Given this resolution of the case, we need not address Patterson's argument that even if primary assumption of risk applied in this case, the undisputed evidence suggests that the District's conduct recklessly increased the risks inherent in loading the flat bed trailer.

[Reversed.]

———————

Knight v. Jewett, 834 P.2d 696 (Cal. 1992) (en banc), from which the court quoted extensively in the preceding case, remains a leading analysis of assumption of the risk doctrine. *Knight* involved a touch football game played by the protagonists during the half-time break of the 1987 Super Bowl. During the game, the defendant ran into the plaintiff, who told him to stop playing so vigorously. On the next play, he ran into the plaintiff again, knocked her over, and stepped on her hand, an injury that led to three operations on and ultimately to the amputation of the plaintiff's little finger.

After a lengthy analysis, the Supreme Court of California ruled that a participant in an "active sport" only breaches a legal duty to a fellow participant if that participant intentionally or recklessly causes injury to the fellow participant. In other words, a person participating in an active sport has no duty not to be negligent; the only duty is not to cause injury recklessly or intentionally. Thus, those who engage in an active sporting activity assume the risk of all injury except injury caused by the intentional or reckless misconduct of a fellow participant.

What does *Knight* do to the rule that one cannot assume the risk of someone else's negligence? What does it do to the concept that one always has an obligation to act reasonably? If there are no consequences for unreasonable conduct that causes injury, is there any incentive to be reasonable? What social policies might (or might not) outweigh the obligation to act reasonably?

d. Assumption of Risk as a Duty Doctrine

Vinikoor v. Pedal Pennsylvania, Inc.

Commonwealth Court of Pennsylvania, 2009
974 A.2d 1233

SENIOR JUDGE FLAHERTY.

Paul M. Vinikoor (Vinikoor) appeals from an order of the Court of Common Pleas of Blair County (trial court) which denied the motion for summary judgment filed by the Department of Transportation (Department) but granted the motion for summary judgment filed by Pedal Pennsylvania, Inc. (Pedal). We affirm.

Vinikoor commenced this action by filing a writ of summons on July 17, 2006. In the negligence action, Vinikoor sought to recover damages resulting from a bicycle accident which occurred while he was participating in a tour organized by Pedal. Vinikoor alleged in his complaint that his bike's right front tire became locked in a groove on a public roadway. As a result, Vinikoor's bicycle was trapped and Vinikoor was unable to steer, causing him to fall from his bicycle. Vinikoor suffered injuries including a central dislocation of his right pelvis and a loss of cartilage in that joint.

Vinikoor asserts that Pedal was negligent, in that Pedal represented to Vinikoor that the route was safe when in fact there was a hidden danger, consisting of a curved groove on the roadway. Additionally, Vinikoor alleged that Pedal failed to make an inspection of the route, or alternatively, failed to notice the defect in the road during its inspection, and thus failed to provide a safe route. Vinikoor alleged that Pedal assured Vinikoor that it had inspected the route and that it was safe. Additionally, Vinikoor was provided a cue sheet and route description, which noted cautions at certain locations where there were dangers. A caution was not noted at the intersection where the incident occurred. Vinikoor also alleged that Department was negligent with respect to construction of the road in the area where the fall occurred.

Pedal filed an answer and new matter. In the new matter, Pedal asserted that Vinikoor's claims were released and discharged based upon a release signed by Vinikoor prior to the tour. Additionally, Pedal claimed that it had no duty to Vinikoor and that Vinikoor had voluntarily assumed the risk. Department also filed an answer and new matter. Vinikoor replied to all new matters.

. . . .

The trial court set the matter down for a hearing. According to Vinikoor's deposition, he was an experienced bicyclist who had been on numerous bicycle tours. The tour at issue, organized by Pedal, was a week long bike tour covering over four hundred miles. Vinikoor had previously been on a tour organized by Pedal. In his complaint and in his deposition testimony, Vinikoor claimed that he was assured by Pedal that the route had been inspected and was safe. Further, Pedal provided Vinikoor with a cue sheet and route description, which included detailed directions and noted cautions at various locations where there were dangers. No caution was noted at the intersection where the accident occurred. . . .

Although the trial court did not address the issue of whether Vinikoor's claim was barred under the voluntary assumption of the risk/no duty rule, which was raised in Pedal's motion for summary judgment, Pedal states that this court may, however, affirm on that basis. In *Howell v. Clyde*, 533 Pa. 151, 620 A.2d 1107 (1993), the defendant's grandfather had made a fireworks cannon. The plaintiff expressed an interest in firing the cannon and went to his house next door to retrieve black powder. The plaintiff held a flashlight while the defendant filled the cannon with powder. The plaintiff stood back while defendant ignited the cannon, which then exploded and injured both of them.

The court held that a non-suit in favor of defendant was proper because, as a matter of law, the plaintiff had assumed the risk of injury by voluntarily participating in a dangerous activity, as the ignition of gunpowder is inherently dangerous and might cause injury to oneself or others. A court may determine, as a matter of law, that a defendant owed plaintiff no duty of care where "reasonable minds could not disagree that the plaintiff deliberately and with the awareness of specific risks inherent in the activity nonetheless engaged in the activity that produced his injury." *Id.* at 162–163, 620 A.2d at 1113.

Similarly, in *Zachardy v. Geneva College*, 733 A.2d 648 (Pa.Super.1999), *appeal denied*, 561 Pa. 700, 751 A.2d 193 (2000), the court affirmed the granting of defendant's motion for summary judgment under the assumption of the risk analysis. Therein a baseball player voluntarily and knowingly proceeded to play on a baseball field which had depressions/unevenness and injured himself while stepping into a hole.

Here, Vinikoor knew that falling and encountering irregular road conditions were risks of bicycling. In fact, Vinikoor was involved in a bicycle accident in 1993, during which he injured his leg. Vinikoor nonetheless assumed the risks involved in bicycling.

The no-duty rule provides that a defendant owes no duty of care to warn, protect or insure against risks which are common, frequent, expected and inherent in an activity. *Craig v. Amateur Softball Association of America*, 951 A.2d 372 (Pa.Super.2008). In *Pakett v. The Phillies L.P.*, 871 A.2d 304 (Pa.Cmwlth.2005), the plaintiff attended a major league baseball game and was struck by a foul ball while sitting in the stands. The plaintiff had sat in the seat before and knew that foul balls reached that area. This court affirmed the grant of summary judgment determining that the risk of being hit by a foul ball during a baseball game was an inherent risk of attending a game. Additionally, the team did not assume additional duties by placing a protective screen behind home plate.

Likewise, in this case, even if Pedal engaged in actions such as planning the route, painting arrows on the road and warning of "rumble strips", these activities do not preclude application of the voluntary assumption of the risk/no duty rule with respect to the risk of falling from a bicycle or encountering an irregular surface.

In his reply brief, Vinikoor states that the doctrine of the assumption of the risk has been supplanted by the Pennsylvania General Assembly's adoption of a system of recovery based on comparative fault in the Comparative Negligence Act, 42 Pa.C.S. § 7102(a)–(b); *Hughes v. Seven Springs Farm, Inc.*, 563 Pa. 501, 762 A.2d 339 (2000). The doctrine of assumption of the risk is preserved only "in cases involving express assumption of risk, or cases brought pursuant to 402A (strict liability theory), or cases in which assumption of risk is specifically preserved by statute." *Duquesne Light Company v. Woodland Hills School District*, 700 A.2d 1038, 1054 (Pa.Cmwlth.1997), *appeal denied*, 555 Pa. 722, 724 A.2d 936 (1998) (citation omitted).

The issue of whether Vinikoor contractually waived his right to recover has been argued by the parties in terms of the exculpatory release at issue herein. Because this is not a strict liability case, nor has it been argued that any statutory exception applies, the only remaining question is whether Pedal owed a duty to Vinikoor. Here, the assertion by Pedal that it had no duty to Vinikoor is based solely on the claim that bicycling has inherent dangers. Vinikoor maintains that his acknowledgement that he was aware of the general risks of injury is not sufficient to grant summary judgment, unless it also appears that he consciously appreciated the specific risk that attended a certain endeavor, assumed the risk of injury by engaging in the endeavor despite the appreciation of the risk and that the injury sustained was the same risk of injury that was appreciated and assumed. *Hadar v. AVCO Corporation*, 886 A.2d 225, 229 (2005), *appeal denied*, 586 Pa. 758, 895 A.2d 550 (2006).

Here, we conclude that as acknowledged by Vinikoor, he was aware of the general risks of riding a bicycle, including uneven surfaces, voluntarily chose to participate, voluntarily signed a waiver releasing Pedal from all liability, and acknowledged by voluntarily signing the waiver that he was aware that riding a bicycle could result in serious bodily injury. Vinikoor deliberately engaged in the bicycle tour with knowledge and awareness of the specific risks inherent in riding a bicycle, including bodily injury.

In accordance with the above, the decision of the trial court is, therefore, affirmed.

---

1. Are the results in *Knight* and *Vinikoor* really different? Putting aside all legal analysis for a moment, what would a purely common-sense approach to the facts in these cases look like? What should be the goal of assumption of risk theory?

2. Assumption of risk doctrine clearly involves difficulties for the courts which must deal with it. Do you have any theory as to why this doctrine seems, more than others, to present problems? In reading the cases, the fact that plaintiffs sometimes do unbelievably stupid things forcibly strikes the reader. (Think about *Howell*, cited in *Vinikoor*, in which the plaintiff supplied the gunpowder.) Maybe this has something to do with the reaction of the courts in dealing with assumption of the risk: it is difficult to impose liability on the defendant when the plaintiff has voluntarily done something surpassingly risky. On the other hand, the "defense" of lack of causation remains available to defendants, even where assumption of the risk has been abolished. At some point, the courts will sever the chain of causation from the defendant to the plaintiff's injury. If the plaintiff has been appallingly stupid, the courts may rule that the defendant's act (or product) can no longer be considered the proximate cause of the injury to the plaintiff, and the defendant will not be liable.

3. To what extent has assumption of the risk doctrine really been abolished? Many courts continue to apply the doctrine in its conventional form. See, for example, *Baker v. Harcon*, 694 S.E.2d 673 (Ga. Ct. App. 2010), in which a construction worker fell through an opening for a trash chute. See also *Ervin v. Continental Conveyor and Equipment Co.*, 674 F. Supp. 2d 709 (D.S.C. 2009), in which the court analyzed comparative negligence and assumption of the risk as two separate doctrines, with the conventional elements of assumption of the risk fully in effect.

B. Comparative and Contributory Negligence and Assumption of Risk in Cases Where the Basis of Liability Is Strict Liability

Marshall v. Ranne

Supreme Court of Texas, 1974
511 S.W.2d 255

Pope, Justice.

Paul Marshall instituted this suit against John C. Ranne seeking damages for injuries he sustained when Ranne's vicious hog attacked him and severely injured his hand. The jury made findings that plaintiff Marshall was contributorily negligent and also that he voluntarily assumed the risk of the hog. The trial court rendered judgment for the defendant on the verdict. The court of civil appeals ruled that the findings of the jury concerning the plaintiff's assumption of the risk supported the judgment and affirmed. 493 S.W.2d 533. We reverse the judgments of the courts below and render judgment for the plaintiff Marshall.

The opinion of the court of civil appeals correctly states these operative facts:

> The only witness to the occurrence was plaintiff. He and defendant both lived in Dallas, but they owned neighboring farms in Van Zandt County. Plaintiff's principal occupation was raising hogs. At the time of the injury he had about two hundred on his farm. The hog in question was a boar which had escaped from defendant's farm and had been seen on plaintiff's land during several weeks before the day of the injury. According to plaintiff, defendant's boar had charged him ten to twelve times before this occurrence, had held him prisoner in his outhouse several times, and had attacked his wife on four or five occasions. On the day of the injury plaintiff had hauled in several barrels of old bread in his pickup and had put it out for his hogs at the barn. At that time he saw defendant's boar about a hundred yards behind the barn, but it came no nearer. After feeding his hogs, he went into the house and changed clothes to get ready to go back to Dallas. On emerging from the house, he looked for the boar because, as he testified, he always had to look before he made a move, but he did not see it. He started toward his pickup, and when he was about thirty feet from it, near the outhouse, he heard a noise behind him, turned around and saw the boar charging toward him. He put out his hand defensively, but the boar grabbed it and bit it severely.

> Plaintiff testified that the first time the hog had jeopardized his safety was about a week or ten days before he was hurt. He did not shoot the hog because he did not consider that the neighborly thing to do, although he was an expert with a gun and had two available. He made no complaint about the hog to defendant until the day of the injury, when he wrote a note and put it on defendant's gate. The note read:

> > "John, your boar has gone bad. He is trying to chase me off the farm. He stalks us just like a cat stalks a mouse every time he catches us out of the house. We are going to have to get him out before he hurts someone."

> This note did not come to defendant's attention until he came in late that afternoon, and the evidence does not reveal whether he saw it before plaintiff was injured. Plaintiff testified that he and defendant had previously discussed the hog's viciousness on several occasions.

The answers to the special issues were: (1) defendant's boar hog bit the plaintiff's right hand on January 21, 1970, (2) immediately prior to that date, the boar hog had vicious propensities and was likely to cause injury to persons, (3) [the jury] refused to find that at any time before plaintiff's injury, the defendant actually knew that the defendant's boar hog was vicious and was likely to cause injury to persons,

(4) the defendant prior to plaintiff's injury in the exercise of ordinary care should have known that the boar hog was vicious and likely to cause injury to persons, (5) defendant permitted his boar hog to run at large after he knew or should have known that the hog was vicious and likely to cause injury to persons, (6) plaintiff, Paul Marshall, had knowledge of the vicious propensities of the defendant's boar hog and that it was likely to cause injury to persons at and prior to the time the hog bit him, (7) plaintiff, Paul Marshall, with knowledge of the nature of defendant's boar hog voluntarily exposed himself to the risk of attack by the animal, (8) plaintiff's failure to shoot the defendant's boar hog prior to the time the hog bit plaintiff was negligence, (9) which failure was a proximate cause of plaintiff's injuries, (10) plaintiff failed to maintain a fence about his premises sufficiently close to prevent hogs passing through, (11) which was negligence, and (12) a proximate cause of plaintiff's injuries, (13) plaintiff was damaged in the amount of $4,146.00.

The questions presented by this cause are (1) the true nature of an action for damages caused by a vicious animal, (2) whether contributory negligence is a defense to this action, and (3) whether plaintiff Marshall was, as a matter of law, deprived of a voluntary and free choice in confronting the risk.

Nature of Vicious Animal Cases

A correct classification of this case is important, since that decision also controls the nature of the acceptable defenses to the action. In Texas, actions for damages caused by vicious domestic animals have sometimes been cast as common law negligence cases, at other times as strict liability cases, and sometimes as either.

. . . .

We approve the rule expressed in *Moore v. McKay*, [55 S.W.2d 865 (Tex. Civ. App. 1933, no writ)], that suits for damages caused by vicious animals should be governed by principles of strict liability, and disapprove the cases which hold the contrary. The correct rule is expressed in Restatement of Torts §§ 507, 509 (1938):

§ 507. LIABILITY OF POSSESSOR OF WILD ANIMAL.

Except as stated in §§ 505 and 517, a possessor of a wild animal is subject to liability to others, except trespassers on his land, for such harm done by the animal to their persons, lands or chattels as results from a dangerous propensity which is characteristic of wild animals of its class or of which the possessor has reason to know, although he has exercised the utmost care to confine the animal or otherwise prevent it from doing harm.

§ 509. HARM DONE BY ABNORMALLY DANGEROUS DOMESTIC ANIMALS.

Except as stated in § 517, a possessor of a domestic animal which he has reason to know has dangerous propensities abnormal to its class, is subject to liability for harm caused thereby to others, except trespassers on his land, although he has exercised the utmost care to prevent it from doing the harm.

The jury in this case refused to find that the defendant actually knew that the hog was vicious and was likely to cause injury to persons, but it did find in answer to special issue four that the defendant prior to plaintiff's injury should have known that fact. Defendant Ranne does not challenge the finding to issue four.

The Restatement, quoted above, uses the phrase "has reason to know" and the fourth special issue submitted in this case used the phrase "should have known." There is no essential distinction between the two terms as explained in Restatement (Second) of Torts § 12 (1965):

§ 12. Reason to Know; Should Know

(1) The words "reason to know" are used throughout the Restatement of this Subject to denote the fact that the actor has information from which a person of reasonable intelligence or of the superior intelligence of the actor would infer that the fact in question exists, or that such person would govern his conduct upon the assumption that such fact exists.

(2) The words "should know" are used throughout the Restatement of this Subject to denote the fact that a person of reasonable prudence and intelligence or of the superior intelligence of the actor would ascertain the fact in question in the performance of his duty to another, or would govern his conduct upon the assumption that such fact exists.

Contributory Negligence is No Defense to Strict Liability

The trial court over plaintiff's objection, submitted contributory negligence issues and the jury found that plaintiff Marshall was negligent in several particulars. We hold that contributory negligence is not a defense to this action. The court in *Copley v. Wills*, 152 S.W. 830 (Tex. Civ. App. 1913, no writ), confronted this question and rejected contributory negligence as an applicable defense to an action for strict liability for keeping a vicious animal which one knew or had reason to know was vicious. This is also the view expressed in Restatement (Second) of Torts § 515, Comment b (Tent. Draft No. 10, 1964):

b. Since the strict liability of the possessor of an animal is not founded on his negligence, the ordinary contributory negligence of the plaintiff is not a defense to such an action. The reason is the policy of the law which places the full responsibility for preventing the harm upon the defendant. Thus where the plaintiff merely fails to exercise reasonable care to discover the presence of the animal, or to take precautions against the harm which may result from it, his recovery on the basis of strict liability is not barred.

We conclude that the findings of plaintiff's contributory negligence as contained in the answers to special issues eight through twelve have no place in this case and did not bar the plaintiff from recovery. 2 F. Harper & F. James, The Law of Torts

§ 14.12, at 843 (1956). We do not hold that negligence and contributory negligence can never be a correct theory in a case which concerns animals. All animals are not vicious and a possessor of a non-vicious animal may be subject to liability for his negligent handling of such an animal.

Did Marshall Voluntarily Assume the Risk?

Plaintiff Marshall does not contend that voluntary assumption of risk is no defense to an action which asserts the defendant's strict liability. He alludes to the truth that it has been abolished as a defense in a number of states in actions grounded upon negligence. Marshall's argument is that he did not, as a matter of law voluntarily expose himself to the risk of the attack by the hog. The jury found that plaintiff Marshall had knowledge of the vicious propensities of the hog and that it was likely to cause injury to persons, and also found that plaintiff, with knowledge of the nature of defendant's boar hog, voluntarily exposed himself to the risk of attack by the animal. We hold that there was no proof that plaintiff had a free and voluntary choice, because he did not have a free choice of alternatives. He had, instead, only a choice of evils, both of which were wrongfully imposed upon him by the defendant. He could remain a prisoner inside his own house or he could take the risk of reaching his car before defendant's hog attacked him. Plaintiff could have remained inside his house, but in doing so, he would have surrendered his legal right to proceed over his own property to his car so he could return to his home in Dallas. The latter alternative was forced upon him against his will and was a choice he was not legally required to accept. W. Prosser, Law of Torts § 68, at 450–453 (4th ed. 1971). We approve and follow the rule expressed in Restatement (Second) of Torts § 496E (1965):

(1) A plaintiff does not assume a risk of harm unless he voluntarily accepts the risk.

(2) The plaintiff's acceptance of a risk is not voluntary if the defendant's tortious conduct has left him no reasonable alternative course of conduct in order to

(a) avert harm to himself or another, or

(b) exercise or protect a right or privilege of which the defendant has no right to deprive him.

The dilemma which defendant forced upon plaintiff was that of facing the danger or surrendering his rights with respect to his own real property, and that was not, as a matter of law the voluntary choice to which the law entitled him.

. . . .

Defendant Ranne argues also that the plaintiff Marshall had yet another alternative, that of shooting the hog. The proof showed that Marshall was an expert marksman and had a gun in his house with which he could have killed the hog. Plaintiff Marshall testified that he was reluctant to destroy his neighbor's animal because he did not know how Ranne would react. We do not regard the slaughter of the animal as a reasonable alternative, because plaintiff would have subjected himself arguably to charges under the provision of two criminal statutes.

We accordingly hold that contributory negligence is not a defense in a strict liability action. Voluntary assumption of risk, if established, would be a valid defense. In this case as a matter of law, the proof shows that plaintiff Marshall did not voluntarily encounter the vicious hog. We, therefore, reverse the judgments of the courts below and render judgment that plaintiff recover the sum of $4,146.00 the amount of damages found by the jury.

ON REHEARING

[Rehearing granted on ground of inadequate damages.]

------

1. How important is it that the plaintiff is on his own property when he is attacked? What if he had been on public property? What if he had been on the defendant's property for the purpose of complaining about the hog?

2. What if the hog had no prior history of viciousness?

3. The fact that liability for injuries caused by animals is strict does not exempt the plaintiff from any obligation to look after his or her own safety. In *Sandy v. Bushey*, 128 A. 513, 514 (Me. 1925), the court stated that a defendant would not be liable if "the injury is attributable, not to the keeping of the animal but to the injured party's unnecessarily and voluntarily putting himself in a way to be hurt knowing the probable consequences of his act, so that he may fairly be deemed to have brought the injury upon himself." The court also adopted the rule that the owner of an animal would not be liable when the plaintiff "knowingly" incites or provokes the animal. Negligence on the plaintiff's part would be insufficient to act as a defense.

C. Comparative and Contributory Negligence and Assumption of Risk in Cases Where the Basis of Liability Is Strict Products Liability

McCown v. International Harvester Co.

Supreme Court of Pennsylvania, 1975
342 A.2d 381

JONES, CHIEF JUSTICE.

Appellant, manufacturer of large over-the-road tractors, was held liable under Section 402A of Restatement (Second) of Torts (1965) for the injuries sustained by the appellee in a one-vehicle accident. The Superior Court affirmed and we granted allocatur limited to the issue of the availability of contributory negligence as a defense to a 402A action.

Appellee was injured while driving a tractor manufactured by appellant. The design of the steering mechanism of the tractor made the vehicle unusually difficult to maneuver. Specifically, twelve to fifteen percent more mechanical effort than that normally expended had to be applied to the steering wheel to accomplish any given turn. Appellee, after driving the vehicle for several hours, stopped for an equipment check on the blacktopped shoulder of the Pennsylvania Turnpike. After completing the inspection the appellee proceeded to reenter the Turnpike.

Unrelated to any steering difficulty appellee struck a guardrail adjoining the shoulder with the right front tire of the tractor. This collision caused the steering wheel to spin rapidly in the direction opposite to the turn. The spokes of the spinning steering wheel struck appellee's right arm, fracturing his wrist and forearm. Evidence adduced at trial indicated that the force and speed of the steering wheel's counter-rotation were directly related to the design of the steering mechanism.

For the purposes of this appeal appellant concedes the defect in the steering system's design, but argues that appellee's contributory negligence in colliding with the guardrail should at least be considered in determining appellee's recovery. We disagree and affirm.

In *Webb v. Zern*, 422 Pa. 424, 220 A.2d 853 (1966), this Court adopted Section 402A of the Restatement and in *Ferraro v. Ford Motor Co.*, 423 Pa. 324, 223 A.2d 746 (1966), permitted the assertion of assumption of the risk as a defense to a 402A action, citing with approval comment *n* to Section 402A. Today, we complete our acceptance of the principles delineated in comment *n*[1] by rejecting contributory negligence as an available defense in 402A cases.

Appellant's position that contributory negligence should affect 402A liability could have two possible applications. Either contributory negligence should serve to diminish any recovery in an amount adjudged equal to a plaintiff's lack of care or, as in most other tort actions, contributory negligence should be available as a complete defense to liability.

Acceptance of the appellant's first alternative would create a system of comparative assessment of damages for 402A actions. Neither the General Assembly by statute nor this Court by case law has established such a scheme of comparative negligence in other areas of tort law. Without considering the relative merits of comparative negligence, we think it unwise to embrace the theory in the context of an appeal involving Section 402A.[3]

---

1. The portion of comment *n* relevant to this opinion is as follows:
   "Contributory negligence of the plaintiff is not a defense when such negligence consists merely in a failure to discover the defect in the product, or to guard against the possibility of its existence."
3. To initially apply a theory of comparative negligence to an area of the law in which liability is not premised on negligence seems particularly inappropriate.

Adoption of contributory negligence as a complete defense in 402A actions would defeat one theoretical basis for our acceptance of Section 402A. "Our courts have determined that a manufacturer by marketing and advertising his products [*sic*] impliedly represents that it is safe for its intended use." *Salvador v. Atlantic Steel Boiler Co.*, 457 Pa. 24, 32, 319 A.2d 903, 907 (1974). Based on that implied representation is the consumer's assumption that a manufacturer's goods are safe. Recognition of consumer negligence as a defense to a 402A action would contradict this normal expectation of product safety. One does not inspect a product for defects or guard against the possibility of product defects when one assumes the item to be safe. The law should not require such inspection or caution when it has accepted as reasonable the consumer's anticipation of safety. We reject contributory negligence as a defense to actions grounded in Section 402A.

Judgment affirmed.

MR. JUSTICE ROBERTS did not participate in the consideration or decision of this case.

POMEROY, JUSTICE (CONCURRING).

I agree with the Court that negligence by the plaintiff should not necessarily bar recovery in a products liability action brought pursuant to Section 402A of the Restatement (Second) of Torts; I also agree that McCown's conduct in the instant case—misjudging whether the tractor he was driving would clear a guard rail as he was leaving the parking area—should not bar his recovery from the appellant. The purpose of this opinion is to place the Court's decision in what I perceive as its proper perspective.

Contrary to what the opinion of the Court seems to suggest, the answer to the question presented by this appeal is not to be found altogether in the language of Comment *n* to Section 402A. Comment *n* provides, on the one hand, that the negligent failure to discover a defect in a product or to guard against the possibility of its existence is not defense to a strict liability action, and, on the other hand, that assumption of risk is a defense. But the conduct of John McCown, the appellee, fits into neither of the above categories. His negligence, if any, was the manner of his operation of an International Harvester tractor. Although Comment *n* is silent with regard to the consequences of negligent use of a product, it points to a resolution of the issue by referring to Section 524 of the Restatement (Second) of Torts. That section provides that in general "the contributory negligence of the plaintiff is not a defense to the strict liability of one who carries on an abnormally dangerous activity."[2] Neither the Comments to Section 524 nor Comment *n* to Section 402A

---

2. In their treatise on the law of Torts, Professors Harper and James state as follows the rationale for the rule that contributory negligence is not a defense to the strict liability of one engaged in an extra-hazardous activity:

"Society has, in effect, permitted defendant's activity on the condition that he compensate those injured by its peculiar hazards and has thereby transferred some of the duty that protects potential victims from the victims themselves to the entrepreneur. In such a context ordinary questions of negligence on either side of the scale become irrelevant.

offer a rationale for the application of this rule in products liability cases, but I am satisfied that the elimination of the defense of plaintiff's negligence is in accord not only with the weight of authority in other jurisdictions but also with the policy which underlies the concept of strict liability in tort.

The strict liability of Section 402A is founded in part upon the belief that as between the sellers of products and those who use them, the former are the better able to bear the losses caused by defects in the products involved. This greater loss-bearing capacity is unrelated to negligence in the manufacture or marketing of products. Indeed, retail and wholesale sellers of chattels are themselves often in no position to discover or avoid defects in their inventories, even by the exercise of a high degree of care. Thus, defendants in Section 402A actions are subjected to liability without regard to fault. It is a proper corollary to this principle that the lesser loss-bearing capacity of product users exists independently of their negligence or lack of it. It follows that such negligence should not ordinarily or necessarily operate to preclude recovery in a strict liability case. On the other hand, where assumption of risk is involved, the "loss-bearing" policy underlying Section 402A is outweighed by a countervailing policy, one which refuses recovery to persons who consciously expose themselves to known dangers. This policy is deemed stronger than the one, reflected in the normal law of contributory negligence, which denies recovery to individuals whose conduct is merely lacking in due care under the circumstances.

This is not to say, however, that evidence of ordinary negligence on the part of a plaintiff is never relevant in a Section 402A action; such evidence may bear directly upon the determination of whether the plaintiff has proved all the elements necessary to make out a cause of action. Thus, negligence in the use of a product may tend to show that the plaintiff caused a defect and therefore that the product was not defective when sold. See Comment g to Section 402A. Again, if the negligent use of a product amounts to abnormal use, it may be inferred that the product was not defective at all, for a product is not defective if it is safe for normal handling and use. See Comment h to Section 402A. Similarly, negligence in the use of a product may have a bearing on the question whether a defect in a product was the legal cause of the plaintiff's injury.

What has been said is not intended as an exhaustive listing of the purposes for which evidence of the plaintiff's negligence may be relevant in Section 402 A cases. It is intended merely to indicate that, although such negligence is not per se a bar to recovery, it may nevertheless have that effect in a proper case where it negates an essential element of the cause of action. I do not read the opinion of the Court as suggesting anything to the contrary.

Human failings like inadvertence are simply part of the setting that makes a toll of the enterprise inevitable." (Footnotes omitted). 2 F. Harper & F. James, The Law of Torts, §22.7 at 1216–17 (1956).

1. Was the tractor safe for its intended use? What if the tractor had had a warning on it stating that the driver should avoid sudden turns?

2. Should a consumer's negligent use of a product be a defense when the claimed defect is the failure to prevent injury from just such a negligent use?

Culpepper v. Hermann Weihrauch KG

Middle District of Alabama, 1997

991 F. Supp. 1397

MYRON H. THOMPSON, CHIEF JUDGE.

ORDER

Plaintiff Ann Culpepper brought this [diversity] action against defendant Hermann Weihrauch KG on August 12, 1996, seeking damages for injuries she sustained as a result of accidentally shooting herself with a handgun manufactured by Weihrauch. . . . The court now has before it Culpepper's motions for summary judgment, filed July 11, 1997, as to Weihrauch's three affirmative defenses: assumption of risk, misuse of the product, and contributory negligence. For the reasons set forth below, the court grants Culpepper's motions for summary judgment in their entirety.

. . . .

FACTUAL BACKGROUND

Culpepper purchased a handgun, manufactured by Weihrauch, in 1968 as a gift for her then husband. After her divorce in 1977, she kept the gun for personal protection. In the early 1990's, after obtaining the necessary permit, she began carrying the gun to work in her automobile. She kept the gun in a leather zippered pouch; it was her custom to store the gun either in her bedside table when she was home or in the glove compartment of her car while she was at work.

On March 5, 1996, after going to work, to her parents' house, and to the supermarket, Culpepper returned home. She had placed the gun in the glove compartment of her car when she left for work in the morning and did not remove it until she came home in the afternoon. Culpepper does not remember how the accident occurred; she only remembers that she got out of the car, heard a shot, and felt pain. She does not remember how she attempted to carry the gun, along with her purse or her groceries, out of the car. When she was found by people who had heard the shot, her gun was lying on the ground out of its pouch, about one or two feet away from the driver's seat. One witness saw an indentation on the dirt in the driveway that looked as if it had been made by the hammer spur of the handgun. Culpepper was struck by the bullet in the lower right side of her abdomen; the injury required the removal of her right kidney, and parts of her small intestine and colon.

Culpepper brought this lawsuit against Weihrauch on August 12, 1996, under several different products liability theories, including allegations of design and manufacturing defects, warning defects, negligent assembly and sale, negligent failure to warn, wanton failure to warn, and breach of implied warranty. The crux of these claims is that the hammerblock safety, a device on the gun which prevents "drop fire" accidents such as the one described above, was improperly designed and manufactured. A hammerblock safety, according to Culpepper, is designed to "hold the hammer face off of the firing pin and prevent force applied to the back of the hammer spur from driving the hammer face into the firing pin and . . . eliminate the possibility of drop-fire except under extraordinary circumstances."

Weihrauch filed its answer on December 5, 1996, asserting general denials and seven affirmative defenses. . . .

. . . Weihrauch conceded that summary judgment [for the plaintiff] should be granted as to the assumption-of-risk and misuse-of-product defenses. Therefore, the only issue requiring this court's review is Culpepper's motions for summary judgment on the contributory-negligence defense. . . .

DISCUSSION

Culpepper seeks to impose liability on Weihrauch under the Alabama Extended Manufacturer's Liability Doctrine (AEMLD). The AEMLD provides for such liability if "the defendant manufactured or designed or sold a defective product which, because of its unreasonably unsafe condition, injured the plaintiff or damaged his property when such product, substantially unaltered, was put to its intended use." *Atkins v. American Motors Corp.*, 335 So. 2d 134, 139 (Ala. 1976). The AEMLD is similar to a strict liability tort action under §402(A) of the Restatement (Second) of Torts. However, the Alabama Supreme Court has rejected the Restatement's no-fault strict liability concept for products liability. *Atkins*, 335 So. 2d at 139. Rather, certain affirmative defenses and general denials are available to defendant manufacturers in an AEMLD action.

Contributory negligence is one such viable affirmative defense under the AEMLD. *Sears v. Waste Processing Equip., Inc.*, 695 So. 2d 51, 53 (Ala. Civ. App. 1997); *see also Hicks v. Commercial Union Ins. Co.*, 652 So. 2d 211 (Ala. 1994). A plaintiff is contributorily negligent when she fails to use reasonable care with regard to that product. *Williams v. Delta Int'l Machinery Corp.*, 619 So. 2d 1330 (Ala. 1993). Contributory negligence can be roughly divided into two categories: first, the plaintiff's negligence, or failure to use reasonable care, in actually using the product; second, the plaintiff's negligence in causing the accident in which the product is used. *Campbell v. Robert Bosch Power Tool Corp.*, 795 F. Supp. 1093, 1097 (M.D. Ala. 1992). In an AEMLD action, the contributory negligence defense is limited to acts within the first category. That is, the plaintiff's acts with regard to negligence or failure to use reasonable care in handling the product are admissible; the plaintiff's acts regarding the cause of the accident itself are not. *Dennis v. American Honda Motor Co.*, 585 So. 2d 1336, 1339 (Ala. 1991) ("To allow a plaintiff's negligence relating to accident causation to bar recovery would go against the purpose of the AEMLD, which is to protect consumers from defective products."); *see also Campbell v. Cutler Hammer, Inc.*, 646 So. 2d 573, 574 (Ala. 1994) (answering in the affirmative the Eleventh Circuit's certified

question whether contributory negligence bars recovery if unreasonably dangerous condition of product was proximate cause of injury, but contributing proximate
cause was plaintiff's failure to exercise reasonable care in using the product).

Failure to use reasonable care in the context of the contributory negligence defense
is distinct from the separate affirmative defense of product misuse. *See General Motors
Corp. v. Saint*, 646 So. 2d 564, 568 (Ala. 1994). In *Saint*, the court distinguished the
two defenses by stating "A plaintiff misuses a product when he or she uses it in a manner not intended or foreseen by the manufacturer ... A plaintiff is contributorily
negligent in handling a defective product when he or she fails to use reasonable care
with regard to that product." *Id.*

Culpepper argues that Weihrauch cannot avail itself of the contributory negligence
defense because (1) there is no evidence to suggest that Culpepper was negligent in
using the hammerblock safety on the gun, and (2) any evidence of negligence related
to the causation of the accident cannot be used to support Weihrauch's defense pursuant to *Dennis*. Culpepper argues that in an AEMLD action involving a safety feature of a product, the only admissible evidence to support a finding of contributory
negligence is the plaintiff's mishandling of the safety feature, rather than the product as a whole. Weihrauch admits that evidence of negligence related to accident causation is impermissible to support a claim of contributory negligence, but maintains
that the issue is whether Culpepper failed to use due care in handling the gun, not
the hammerblock safety. Because the law in Alabama is clear that only negligence
related to use of the product, as opposed to negligence in accident causation, is admissible to prove contributory negligence, the only issues the court must decide on Culpepper's motions for summary judgment are (1) whether "product" refers to the
hammerblock safety on the gun or the gun itself, and (2) whether Weihrauch has
met its burden in demonstrating why summary judgment is inappropriate.

A.

Although contributory negligence serves as a total bar against recovery in AEMLD
cases, the Alabama Supreme Court diminished its effect in *Dennis*, where the court
held that contributory negligence related to accident causation was an invalid defense:
"A plaintiff's mere inadvertence or carelessness in causing an accident should not be
available as an affirmative defense to an AEMLD action." 585 So. 2d at 1339. In *Dennis*, the plaintiff brought suit against the manufacturer of a motorcycle helmet, alleging that the helmet was defective and not fit for its intended purpose. In charging
the jury, the trial court gave instructions regarding the defendant's burden of proof
for the defense of contributory negligence. The court stated that the defendant could
meet its burden "by proving to [the jurors'] reasonable satisfaction that [plaintiff]
violated a rule or rules of the road during the operation of the motorcycle at the time
of the accident in question." 585 So. 2d at 1338. The Alabama Supreme Court rejected
this instruction and stated that contributory negligence could be used as a defense
to an AEMLD action only under certain circumstances, such as "plaintiff's misuse
of the product." Id. at 1339. In *Saint*, which the court noted was "just the reverse of
that in *Dennis*," 646 So. 2d at 566, the Alabama Supreme Court held that an

automobile manufacturer was entitled to jury instructions regarding plaintiff's contributory negligence where the defendant contended plaintiff either did not wear or improperly wore a seatbelt at the time of a car accident. Culpepper interprets these two cases as holding that, in AEMLD cases involving safety devices, only mishandling of the safety feature can be used to support a contributory negligence defense. Culpepper cites two cases as supporting this interpretation: *Williams v. Delta Int'l Machinery Corp.*, 619 So. 2d 1330 (Ala. 1993), and *Gibson v. Norfolk Southern Corp.*, 878 F. Supp. 1455 (N.D. Ala. 1994), aff'd, 48 F.3d 536 (11th Cir. 1995) (table opinion). In *Williams*, the Alabama Supreme Court rejected application of the *Dennis* rule to a products liability case where the products, a table saw and dado blade, were not safety features and because "the only contributory negligence alleged in this case involved the use of the table saw and the dado blade." 619 So. 2d at 1332–33. In *Gibson*, the court held that contributory negligence could be asserted as a defense where the plaintiff failed to "stop, look, and listen" at the railroad's warning light and sign. 878 F. Supp. at 1461. Neither case directly supports the proposition of law Culpepper has advanced.

Arguing against Culpepper's interpretation, Weihrauch cites to *Haisten v. Kubota Corp.*, 648 So. 2d 561 (Ala. 1994). In *Haisten*, the plaintiff brought an AEMLD action against the manufacturer of a tractor alleging that the manufacturer's failure to include a rollover protection system rendered the tractor defective. The Alabama Supreme Court held that the trial judge correctly charged the jury with instructions to consider the plaintiff's contributory negligence as a defense to the AEMLD claim. *Haisten*, 648 So. 2d at 565. Weihrauch concludes that, since *Haisten* is factually analogous to the present case, the contributory negligence defense should be permitted. The court disagrees. The issue involved in *Haisten* was whether the tractor was defective for not having a rollover safety device, rather than a defect in the safety device rendering the product unreasonably dangerous, as was the case in *Dennis, Saint*, and the action presently before this court.

In grappling with the issue of whether misuse of the product for the purpose of proving contributory negligence refers to the handgun or the hammerblock safety, the court first notes that in her complaint, Culpepper alleges that "the handgun was unreasonably dangerous and therefore defective." The fact that Culpepper has alleged the product as a whole was unreasonably dangerous does not, however, end the court's inquiry. In *Saint*, the plaintiff brought an AEMLD action alleging that her automobile was unreasonably dangerous—because the seatbelt failed to protect her during the accident—and the court permitted evidence of only her negligence in misusing the seatbelt, rather than the automobile itself. The seatbelt in the automobile in *Saint* is sufficiently analogous to the hammerblock safety in the handgun here: both are designed to protect the user of the product in case of an accident. The court therefore concludes that Weihrauch may assert the contributory negligence defense only as to Culpepper's misuse of the hammerblock safety, rather than the handgun. To hold otherwise would permit Weihrauch to introduce evidence going to Culpepper's contributory negligence related to accident causation, and would directly contravene the Alabama Supreme Court's decision in *Dennis*.

B.

The second issue for the court to decide is whether Weihrauch has alleged sufficient facts to defeat Culpepper's motion for summary judgment. In order to find contributory negligence as a matter of law, there must be a finding that the plaintiff put herself in danger's way, a finding that the plaintiff appreciated the danger confronted, and that such appreciation of the danger was conscious at the moment the incident occurred. *Hicks v. Commercial Union Ins. Co.*, 652 So. 2d 211, 219 (Ala. 1994). A court may decide the issue of contributory negligence as a matter of law "only when the facts are such that all reasonable [people] must draw the same conclusion therefrom." *Caterpillar Tractor Co. v. Ford*, 406 So. 2d 854, 857 (Ala. 1981).

. . . .

Weihrauch offers the following facts to support its argument that the jury should be able to decide whether Culpepper was contributorily negligent: Culpepper either had the gun in her hand or "under [her] arm," and Culpepper may have been trying to carry the gun, her purse, and her groceries at the same time. While these facts could support a conclusion that Culpepper failed to exercise due care in handling the gun, the facts do not support a conclusion that Culpepper failed to exercise due care in handling the hammerblock safety on the handgun. Moreover, these facts go directly to the issue of accident causation which, as discussed above, cannot be used to support a contributory negligence defense in an AEMLD case involving a safety device. Weihrauch has not provided evidence of the existence of any facts to support a finding of contributory negligence in Culpepper's use of the hammerblock safety. Culpepper's motions will therefore be granted in their entirety. . . .

CONCLUSION

For the above reasons, it is ORDERED that plaintiff Ann Culpepper's motions for summary judgment . . . regarding defendant Hermann Weihrauch KG's affirmative defenses of contributory negligence, misuse of the product, and assumption of risk, are granted.

---

1. What would a seatbelt defense argument look like under the AEMLD?

2. Does the contributing negligence doctrine described in the court's opinion really sound like contributory negligence?

3. The federal government has enacted a statute that provides gun manufacturers with partial tort immunity, although it contains several exceptions, including an exception for some cases alleging a defect in design. See 15 U.S.C. §§ 7901–7903. Several states also have statutes establishing partial gun manufacturer tort immunity. What factors justify special protections for gun manufacturers, if any?

Daly v. General Motors Corp.

Supreme Court of California, 1978
575 P.2d 1162

Richardson, Justice.

The most important of several problems which we consider is whether the principles of comparative negligence expressed by us in *Li v. Yellow Cab Co.* (1975) 13 Cal. 3d 804, 119 Cal. Rptr. 858, 532 P.2d 1226, apply to actions founded on strict products liability. We will conclude that they do. . . .

The Facts and the Trial

Although there were no eyewitnesses, the parties agree, generally, on the reconstruction of the accident in question. In the early hours of October 31, 1970, decedent Kirk Daly, a 36-year-old attorney, was driving his Opel southbound on the Harbor Freeway in Los Angeles. The vehicle, while travelling at a speed of 50–70 miles per hour, collided with and damaged 50 feet of metal divider fence. After the initial impact between the left side of the vehicle and the fence the Opel spun counterclockwise, the driver's door was thrown open, and Daly was forcibly ejected from the car and sustained fatal head injuries. It was equally undisputed that had the deceased remained in the Opel his injuries, in all probability, would have been relatively minor.

Plaintiffs, who are decedent's widow and three surviving minor children, sued General Motors Corporation, Boulevard Buick, Underwriter's Auto Leasing, and Alco Leasing Company, the successive links in the Opel's manufacturing and distribution chain. The sole theory of plaintiffs' complaint was strict liability for damages allegedly caused by a defective product, namely, an improperly designed door latch claimed to have been activated by the impact. It was further asserted that, but for the faulty latch, decedent would have been restrained in the vehicle and, although perhaps injured, would not have been killed. Thus, the case involves a so-called "second collision" in which the "defect" did not contribute to the original impact, but only to the "enhancement" of injury.

At trial the jury heard conflicting expert versions as to the functioning of the latch mechanism during the accident. Plaintiffs' principal witness testified that the Opel's door was caused to open when the latch button on the exterior handle of the driver's door was forcibly depressed by some protruding portion of the divider fence. It was his opinion that the exposed push button on the door constituted a design "defect" which caused injuries greatly in excess of those which Daly would otherwise have sustained. Plaintiffs also introduced evidence that other vehicular door latch designs used in production models of the same and prior years afforded substantially greater protection. Defendants' experts countered with their opinions that the force of the impact was sufficiently strong that it would have caused the door to open resulting in Daly's death even if the Opel had been equipped with door latches of the alternative designs suggested by plaintiffs.

Over plaintiffs' objections, defendants were permitted to introduce evidence indicating that: (1) the Opel was equipped with a seat belt-shoulder harness system, and a door lock, either of which if used, it was contended, would have prevented Daly's ejection from the vehicle; (2) Daly used neither the harness system nor the lock; (3) the 1970 Opel owner's manual contained warnings that seat belts should be worn and doors locked when the car was in motion for "accident security"; and (4) Daly was intoxicated at the time of collision, which evidence the jury was advised was admitted for the limited purpose of determining whether decedent had used the vehicle's safety equipment. After relatively brief deliberations the jury returned a verdict favoring all defendants, and plaintiffs appeal from the ensuing adverse judgment.

Strict Products Liability and Comparative Fault

In response to plaintiffs' assertion that the "intoxication-nonuse" evidence was improperly admitted, defendants contend that the deceased's own conduct contributed to his death. Because plaintiffs' case rests upon strict products liability based on improper design of the door latch and because defendants assert a failure in decedent's conduct, namely, his alleged intoxication and nonuse of safety equipment, without which the accident and ensuing death would not have occurred, there is thereby posed the overriding issue in the case, should comparative principles apply in strict products liability actions?

It may be useful to refer briefly to certain highlights in the historical development of the two principles—strict and comparative liability. Tort law has evolved from a legal obligation initially imposed without "fault," to recovery which, generally, was based on blameworthiness in a moral sense. For reasons of social policy and because of the unusual nature of defendants' acts, liability without fault continued to be prescribed in a certain restricted area, for example, upon keepers of wild animals, or those who handled explosives or other dangerous substances, or who engaged in ultrahazardous activities. Simultaneously, and more particularly, those who were injured in the use of personal property were permitted recovery on a contract theory if they were the purchasers of the chattel or were in privity. Subsequently, liability was imposed in negligence upon the manufacturer of personalty in favor of the general consumer. Evolving social policies designed to protect the ultimate consumer soon prompted the extension of legal responsibility beyond negligence to express or implied warranty. Thus, in the area of food and drink a form of strict liability predicated upon warranty found wide acceptance. Warranty actions, however, contained their own inherent limitations requiring a precedent notice to the vendor of a breach of the warranty, and absolving him from loss if he had issued an adequate disclaimer.

General dissatisfaction continued with the conceptual limitations which traditional tort and contract doctrines placed upon the consumers and users of manufactured products, this at a time when mass production of an almost infinite variety of goods and products was responding to a myriad of ever-changing societal demands stimulated by wide-spread commercial advertising. From an historic combination of economic and sociological forces was born the doctrine of strict liability in tort.

We, ourselves, were perhaps the first court to give the new principle judicial sanction. In *Greenman v. Yuba Power Products, Inc.* (1963) 59 Cal. 2d 57, 27 Cal. Rptr. 697, 377 P.2d 897, confronted with injury to an ultimate consumer caused by a defective power tool, we fastened strict liability on a manufacturer who placed on the market a defective product even though both privity and notice of breach of warranty were lacking. We rejected both contract and warranty theories, express or implied, as the basis for liability. Strict liability, we said, did not rest on a consensual foundation but, rather, on one created by law. The liability was created judicially because of the economic and social need for the protection of consumers in an increasingly complex and mechanized society, and because of the limitations in the negligence and warranty remedies. Our avowed purpose was "to insure that the costs of injuries resulting from defective products are borne by the manufacturer that put such products on the market rather than by the injured persons who are powerless to protect themselves." (*Id.*, at p. 63, 27 Cal. Rptr. at p. 701, 377 P.2d at p. 901.) Subsequently, the *Greenman* principle was incorporated in section 402A of the Restatement Second of Torts, and adopted by a majority of American jurisdictions. (Prosser, [Law of Torts (4th ed. 1971) § 96], at pp. 657–658.)

From its inception, however, strict liability has never been, and is not now, *absolute* liability. As has been repeatedly expressed, under strict liability the manufacturer does not thereby become the insurer of the safety of the product's user. On the contrary, the plaintiff's injury must have been caused by a "defect" in the product. Thus the manufacturer is not deemed responsible when injury results from an unforeseeable use of its product. Furthermore, we have recognized that though most forms of contributory negligence do not constitute a defense to a strict products liability action, plaintiff's negligence is a complete defense when it comprises assumption of risk. As will thus be seen, the concept of strict products liability was created and shaped judicially. In its evolution, the doctrinal encumbrances of contract and warranty, and the traditional elements of negligence, were stripped from the remedy, and a new tort emerged which extended liability for defective product design and manufacture beyond negligence but short of absolute liability.

In *Li v. Yellow Cab Co., supra*, 13 Cal. 3d 804, 119 Cal. Rptr. 858, 532 P.2d 1126, we introduced the other doctrine with which we are concerned, comparative negligence. We examined the history of contributory negligence, the massive criticism directed at it because its presence in the slightest degree completely barred plaintiff's recovery, and the increasing defection from the doctrine. We then weighed the two principal arguments against its removal from California law, namely, that such a sharp change in direction required legislative action, and that there existed a cluster of asserted practical obstacles relating to multiple parties, the apportionment burdens on a jury and the uncertain effect on the defenses of last clear chance, assumption of risk, and wilful misconduct. Concluding that none of the obstacles was insurmountable, we announced in *Li* the adoption of a "pure" form of comparative negligence which, when present, reduced but did not prevent plaintiff's recovery. (Pp. 828–829, 119 Cal. Rptr. 858, 532 P.2d 1126.) We held that the defense of assumption of risk, insofar as it is no more than a variant of contributory negligence, was merged into the assessment of liability in proportion to fault. (Pp. 824–825, 119 Cal. Rptr. 858, 532 P.2d 1126.) Within the broad guidelines therein announced, we left to trial courts discretion in the particular implementation of the new doctrine. (Pp. 826–827, 119 Cal. Rptr. 858, 532 P.2d 1126.)

We stand now at the point of confluence of these two conceptual streams, having been greatly assisted by the thoughtful analysis of the parties and the valuable assistance of numerous amici curiae. We are by no means the first to consider the interaction of these two developing principles. As with the litigants before us, responsible and respected authorities have reached opposing conclusions stressing in various degrees the different considerations which we now examine.

Those counseling against the recognition of comparative fault principles in strict products liability cases vigorously stress, perhaps equally, not only the conceptual, but also the semantic difficulties incident to such a course. The task of merging the two concepts is said to be impossible, that "apples and oranges" cannot be compared, that "oil and water" do not mix, and that strict liability, which is not founded on negligence or fault, is inhospitable to comparative principles. The syllogism runs, contributory negligence was only a defense to negligence, comparative negligence only affects contributory negligence, therefore comparative negligence cannot be a defense to strict liability. While fully recognizing the theoretical and semantic distinctions between the twin principles of strict products liability and traditional negligence, we think they can be blended or accommodated.

The inherent difficulty in the "apples and oranges" argument is its insistence on fixed and precise definitional treatment of legal concepts. In the evolving areas of both products liability and tort defenses, however, there has developed much conceptual overlapping and interweaving in order to attain substantial justice. The concept of strict liability itself, as we have noted, arose from dissatisfaction with the wooden formalisms of traditional tort and contract principles in order to protect the consumer of manufactured goods. Similarly, increasing social awareness of its harsh "all or nothing" consequences led us in *Li* to moderate the impact of traditional contributory negligence in order to accomplish a fairer and more balanced result. We acknowledged an intermixing of defenses of contributory negligence and assumption of risk and formally effected a type of merger. "As for assumption of risk, we have recognized in this state that this defense overlaps that of contributory negligence to some extent. . . ." (Li, *supra*, 13 Cal. 3d at p. 824, 119 Cal. Rptr. at p. 872, 532 P.2d at p. 1240.) In *Li*, we further reaffirmed our observation in *Grey v. Fibreboard Paper Products Co.* (1966) 65 Cal. 2d 240, 245, 53 Cal. Rptr. 545, 418 P.2d 153. "[T]hat in one kind of situation, to wit, where a plaintiff unreasonably undertakes to encounter a specific known risk imposed by a defendant's negligence, plaintiff's conduct, although he may encounter that risk in a prudent manner, is in reality a form of contributory negligence. . . .' We think it clear that the adoption of a system of comparative negligence should entail the merger of the defense of assumption of risk into the general scheme of assessment of liability in proportion to fault in those particular cases in which the form of assumption of risk involved is no more than a variant of contributory negligence." (13 Cal. 3d at pp. 824–825, 119 Cal. Rptr. at pp. 872–873, 532 P.2d at pp. 1240–1241, quoting *Grey, supra*, 65 Cal. 2d at pp. 245–246, 53 Cal. Rptr. 545, 418 P.2d 153, italics in orig.)

Furthermore, the "apples and oranges" argument may be conceptually suspect. It has been suggested that the term "contributory negligence," one of the vital building blocks upon which much of the argument is based, may indeed itself be a misnomer since it lacks the first element of the classical negligence formula, namely, a duty of care owing to another. A highly respected torts authority, Dean William Prosser, has noted this fact by observing, "It is perhaps unfortunate that contributory negligence is called negligence at all. 'Contributory fault' would be a more descriptive term. Negligence as it is commonly understood is conduct which creates an undue risk of harm to others. Contributory negligence is conduct which involves an undue risk of harm to the actor himself. Negligence requires a duty, an obligation of conduct to another person. Contributory negligence involves no duty, unless we are to be so ingenious as to say that the plaintiff is under an obligation to protect the defendant against liability for the consequences of his own negligence." (Prosser, Law of Torts, *supra*, § 65, p. 418.)

We think, accordingly, the conclusion may fairly be drawn that the terms "comparative negligence," "contributory negligence" and "assumption of risk" do not, standing alone, lend themselves to the exact measurements of a micrometer-caliper, or to such precise definition as to divert us from otherwise strong and consistent countervailing policy considerations. Fixed semantic consistency at this point is less important than the attainment of a just and equitable result. The interweaving of concept and terminology in this area suggests a judicial posture that is flexible rather than doctrinaire.

We pause at this point to observe that where, as here, a consumer or user sues the manufacturer or designer alone, technically, neither fault nor conduct is really compared functionally. The conduct of one party in combination with the product of another, or perhaps the placing of a defective article in the stream of projected and anticipated use, may produce the ultimate injury. In such a case, as in the situation before us, we think the term "equitable apportionment or allocation of loss" may be more descriptive than "comparative fault."

Given all of the foregoing, we are, in the wake of *Li*, disinclined to resolve the important issue before us by the simple expedient of matching linguistic labels which have evolved either for convenience or by custom. Rather, we consider it more useful to examine the foundational reasons underlying the creation of strict products liability in California to ascertain whether the purposes of the doctrine would be defeated or diluted by adoption of comparative principles. We imposed strict liability against the manufacturer and in favor of the user or consumer in order to relieve injured consumers "from *problems of proof* inherent in pursuing negligence . . . and warranty . . . remedies, . . ." *(Cronin v. J.B.E. Olson Corp.*, 8 Cal. 3d at p. 133, 104 Cal. Rptr. at p. 442, 501 P.2d at p. 1162, italics added.) As we have noted, we sought to place the burden of loss on manufacturers rather than "... injured persons *who are powerless to protect themselves. . . ." (Greenman, supra*, 59 Cal.2d at p. 63, 27 Cal.Rptr. at p. 701, 377 P.2d at p. 901, italics added; see *Escola*, 24 Cal. 2d at p. 462, 150 P.2d 436; *Price v. Shell Oil Co.* (1970) 2 Cal. 3d 245, 251, 85 Cal. Rptr. 178, 182, 466 P.2d 722, 726 [*"protection of otherwise defenseless victims of* manufacturing defects and the spreading throughout society of the cost of compensating them"] italics added.)

The foregoing goals, we think, will not be frustrated by the adoption of comparative principles. Plaintiffs will continue to be relieved of proving that the manufacturer or distributor was negligent in the production, design, or dissemination of the article in question. Defendant's liability for injuries caused by a defective product remains strict. The principle of protecting the defenseless is likewise preserved, for plaintiff's recovery will be reduced *only* to the extent that his own lack of reasonable care contributed to his injury. The cost of compensating the victim of a defective product, albeit proportionately reduced, remains on defendant manufacturer, and will, through him, be "spread among society." However, we do not permit plaintiff's own conduct relative to the product to escape unexamined, and as to that share of plaintiff's damages which flows from his own fault we discern no reason of policy why it should, following *Li*, be borne by others. Such a result would directly contravene the principle announced in *Li*, that loss should be assessed equitably in proportion to fault.

We conclude, accordingly, that the expressed purposes which persuaded us in the first instance to adopt strict liability in California would not be thwarted were we to apply comparative principles. What would be forfeit is a degree of semantic symmetry. However, in this evolving area of tort law in which new remedies are judicially created, and old defenses judicially merged, impelled by strong considerations of equity and fairness we seek a larger synthesis. If a more just result follows from the expansion of comparative principles, we have no hesitancy in seeking it, mindful always that the fundamental and underlying purpose of *Li* was to promote the equitable allocation of loss among all parties legally responsible in proportion to their fault.

A second objection to the application of comparative principles in strict products liability cases is that a manufacturer's incentive to produce safe products will thereby be reduced or removed. While we fully recognize this concern we think, for several reasons, that the problem is more shadow than substance. First, of course, the manufacturer cannot avoid its continuing liability for a defective product even when the plaintiff's own conduct has contributed to his injury. The manufacturer's liability, and therefore its incentive to avoid and correct product defects, remains; its exposure will be lessened only to the extent that the trier finds that the victim's conduct contributed to his injury. Second, as a practical matter a manufacturer, in a particular case, cannot assume that the user of a defective product upon whom an injury is visited will be blameworthy. Doubtless, many users are free of fault, and a defect is at least as likely as not to be exposed by an entirely innocent plaintiff who will obtain full recovery. In such cases the manufacturer's incentive toward safety both in design and production is wholly unaffected. Finally, we must observe that under the present law, which recognizes assumption of risk as a complete defense to products liability, the curious and cynical message is that it profits the manufacturer to make his product so defective that in the event of injury he can argue that the user had to be aware of its patent defects. To that extent the incentives are inverted. We conclude, accordingly, that no substantial or significant impairment of the safety incentives of defendants will occur by the adoption of comparative principles.

In passing, we note one important and felicitous result if we apply comparative principles to strict products liability. This arises from the fact that under present law when plaintiff sues in negligence his own contributory negligence, however denominated, may diminish but cannot wholly defeat his recovery. When he sues in strict products liability, however, his "assumption of risk" *completely bars* his recovery. Under *Li*, as we have noted, "assumption of risk" is merged into comparative principles. (13 Cal. 3d at p. 825, 119 Cal. Rptr. 858, 533 P.2d 1226.) The consequence is that after *Li* in a negligence action, plaintiff's conduct which amounts to "negligent" assumption of risk no longer defeats plaintiff's recovery. Identical conduct, however, in a strict liability case acts as a complete bar under rules heretofore applicable. Thus, strict products liability, which was developed to free injured consumers from the constraints imposed by traditional negligence and warranty theories, places a consumer plaintiff in a worse position than would be the case were his claim founded on simple negligence. This, in turn, rewards adroit pleading and selection of theories. The application of comparative principles to strict liability obviates this bizarre anomaly by treating alike the defenses to both negligence and strict products liability actions. In each instance the defense, if established, will reduce but not bar plaintiff's claim.

A third objection to the merger of strict liability and comparative fault focuses on the claim that, as a practical matter, triers of fact, particularly jurors, cannot assess, measure, or compare plaintiff's negligence with defendant's strict liability. We are unpersuaded by the argument and are convinced that jurors are able to undertake a fair apportionment of liability.

. . . .

We note that the majority of our sister states which have addressed the problem, either by statute or judicial decree, have extended comparative principles to strict products liability.

. . . .

Moreover, we are further encouraged in our decision herein by noting that the apparent majority of scholarly commentators has urged adoption of the rule which we announce herein.

. . . .

Having examined the principal objections and finding them not insurmountable, and persuaded by logic, justice, and fundamental fairness, we conclude that a system of comparative fault should be and it is hereby extended to actions founded on strict products liability. In such cases the separate defense of "assumption of risk," to the extent that it is a form of contributory negligence, is abolished. While, as we have suggested, on the particular facts before us, the term "equitable apportionment of loss" is more accurately descriptive of the process, nonetheless, the term "comparative fault" has gained such wide acceptance by courts and in the literature that we adopt its use herein.

In *Li*, we announced a system of pure comparative negligence "the fundamental purpose of which shall be to assign responsibility and liability for damage in direct proportion to the amount of negligence of each of the parties." *(Id.,* 13 Cal. 3d at p. 829, 119 Cal. Rptr. at p. 875, 532 P.2d at p. 1243.) Those same underlying considerations of policy which moved us judicially in *Li* to rescue blameworthy plaintiffs from a 100-year-old sanction against *all* recovery persuade us now to extend similar principles to the strict products liability area. Legal responsibility is thereby shared. We think that apportioning tort liability is sound, logical and capable of wider application than to negligence cases alone. To hold otherwise, in our view, would be to perpetuate a system which, as we noted in *Li*, Dean Prosser describes as placing ". . . upon one party the entire burden of a loss for which two are, by hypothesis, responsible." (Prosser, *supra,* § 67, p. 433.) We reiterate that our reason for extending a full system of comparative fault to strict products liability is because it is fair to do so. The law consistently seeks to elevate justice and equity above the exact contours of a mathematical equation. We are convinced that in merging the two principles what may be lost in symmetry is more than gained in fundamental fairness.

. . . .

By extending and tailoring the comparative principles announced in *Li, supra,* to the doctrine of strict products liability, we believe that we move closer to the goal of the equitable allocation of legal responsibility for personal injuries. We do so by relying on what Professor Schwartz aptly terms a "predicate of fairness." In making liability more commensurate with fault we undermine neither the theories nor the policies of the strict liability rule. In *Li* we took "a first step in what we deem to be a proper and just direction, . . ." (13 Cal. 3d at p. 826, 119 Cal. Rptr. at p. 874, 532 P.2d at p. 1242.) We are convinced that the principles herein announced constitute the next appropriate and logical step in the same direction.

The judgment is reversed.

TOBRINER, CLARK and MANUEL, JJ., concur.

CLARK, JUSTICE, concurring.

The reasoning of *Li v. Yellow Cab. Co.* (1975) 13 Cal. 3d 804, 119 Cal. Rptr. 858, 532 P.2d 1226, as the majority point out, is equally applicable to strict liability cases and compels applying comparative fault in those cases. Under the compulsion of *Li*, I have signed the majority opinion.

. . . .

Having undertaken the legislative function by repudiating contributory negligence and adopting comparative fault, we have abandoned our traditional deference to legislative province and to stare decisis. Having done so, we, like the Legislature, should reconsider our bold decisions from time to time, performing the legislative process to the best of our ability—until the Legislature awakens to reclaim and exercise its historic power.

JEFFERSON, [assigned], JUSTICE, concurring and dissenting.

I concur in part and dissent in part.

I agree with the majority's result that the judgment should be reversed because of the prejudicial error in admitting evidence of decedent's intoxication and of his failure to use available safety devices. Otherwise, I part company with the majority's views.

The majority rejects what I consider to be a sound criticism of its holding that it is illogical and illusory to compare elements or factors that are not reasonably subject to comparison. The majority states that it is convinced that jurors will be able to compare the noncomparables—plaintiff's negligence with defendant's strict liability for a defective product—and still reach a fair apportionment of liability.

I consider the majority conclusion a case of wishful thinking and an application of an impractical, ivory-tower approach. The majority's assumption that a jury is capable of making a fair apportionment between a plaintiff's negligent conduct and a defendant's defective product is no more logical or convincing than if a jury were to be instructed that it should add a quart of milk (representing plaintiff's negligence) and a metal bar three feet in length (representing defendant's strict liability for a defective product), and that the two added together equal 100 percent—the total fault for plaintiff's injuries; that plaintiff's quart of milk is then to be assigned its percentage of the 100 percent total and defendant's metal bar is to be assigned the remaining percentage of the total.

. . . .

BIRD, C.J., concurs.

MOSK, JUSTICE, dissenting.

I dissent.

This will be remembered as the dark day when this court, which heroically took the lead in originating the doctrine of products liability *(Greenman v. Yuba Power Products, Inc.* 59 Cal. 2d 57, 27 Cal. Rptr. 697, 377 P.2d 897 (1963)) and steadfastly resisted efforts to inject concepts of negligence into the newly designed tort *(Cronin v. J.B.E. Olson Corp.* 8 Cal. 121, 104 Cal. Rptr. 433, 501 P.2d 1153 (1972)), inexplicably turned 180 degrees and beat a hasty retreat almost back to square one. The pure concept of products liability so pridefully fashioned and nurtured by this court for the past decade and a half is reduced to a shambles.

. . . .

Transferring the liability, or part of the liability, from the party responsible for putting the article in the stream of commerce to the consumer is precisely what the majority propose to do. They do this by employing a euphemism: the victim's recovery is to be "proportionately reduced." The result, however delicately described, is to dilute the defect of the article by elevating the conduct of the wounded consumer to an issue of equal significance. We can be as certain as tomorrow's daylight that every defendant charged with marketing a defective product will hereafter assert that the injured plaintiff did something, anything, that conceivably could be deemed contributorily negligent: he drove the vehicle with a defective steering mechanism 56 miles an hour instead of 54; or he should have discovered a latent defect hidden in the machinery; or perhaps he should not have succumbed to the salesman's persuasion and purchased the defective object in the first instance. I need no crystal ball to foresee that the pleading of affirmative defenses alleging contributory negligence — or the currently approved substitute terminology will now become boilerplate.

. . . .

The best reasoned authorities decline to inject negligence, contributory or comparative, into strict products liability litigation. . . . In *Kirkland v. General Motors Corp.*, 521 P.2d 1353 (Okl. 1974), the Oklahoma Supreme Court refused to apply a comparative negligence statute to products liability because it consistently determined that "manufacturers' products liability is not negligence, nor is it to be treated as a negligence action" (*id.* at p. 1367). A similar result followed in *Melia v. Ford Motor Co.*, 534 F.2d 795, 802 (8th Cir. 1976), in which the court held application of a comparative negligence statute would be "inappropriate in a strict liability case." Even more emphatic was the court in *Kinard v. Coats Co., Inc.*, 553 P.2d 835, 837 (Colo. App. 1976): "Although some other jurisdictions have chosen to apply comparative negligence to products liability cases in our view the better-reasoned position is that comparative negligence has no application to products liability actions under §402A. Products liability under §402A does not rest upon negligence principles, but rather is premised on the concept of enterprise liability for casting a defective product into the stream of commerce. Thus, the focus is upon the nature of the product, and the consumer's reasonable expectations with regard to that product, rather than on the conduct either of the manufacturer or of the person injured because of the product." The Colorado Supreme Court completely eliminated negligence from products liability actions, declaring in such proceedings it "'shifts the focus from the conduct of the manufacturer to the nature of the product.'" (*Hiigel v. General Motors Corp.*, 544 P.2d 983 (Colo. 1975)).

We also declared in *Ault v. International Harvester Co.*, 13 Cal. 3d 113 (1974), that the focus is not on the conduct of the defendant, but on the nature of the product. That being so, the majority create an impossible dilemma for trial courts. If comparative negligence is to be applied, how can the trier of fact rationally weigh the conduct of the plaintiff against the defective product? I know of no other instance in American jurisprudence in which the antagonists are the conduct of a human being versus an inanimate object.

. . . .

The majority note one "felicitous result" of adopting comparative negligence to products liability: the merger of assumption of risk—which they term a "bizarre anomaly"—into their innovative defense. I find that result neither felicitous nor tenable. In *Barker v. Lull Engineering Co.*, 20 Cal. 3d at page 429, 143 Cal. Rptr. 225, 573 P.2d 443, we defined a defective product as one which failed to perform safely when used in an intended or foreseeable manner. If a consumer elects to use a product patently defective when other alternatives are available, or to use a product in a manner clearly not intended or foreseeable, he assumes the risks inherent in his improper utilization and should not be heard to complain about the condition of the object. One who employs a power saw to trim his fingernails—and thereafter finds the number of his fingers reduced—should not prevail to any extent whatever against the manufacturer even if the saw had a defective blade. I would retain assumption of risk as a total defense to products liability, as it always has been.

The majority deny their opinion diminishes the therapeutic effect of products liability upon producers of defective products. It seems self-evident that procedures which evaluate the injured consumer's conduct in each instance, and thus eliminate or reduce the award against the producer or distributor of a defective product, are not designed as an effective incentive to maximum responsibility to consumers. The converse is more accurate: the motivation to avoid polluting the stream of commerce with defective products increases in direct relation to the size of potential damage awards.

In sum, I am convinced that since the negligence of the defendant is irrelevant in products liability cases, the negligence—call it contributory or comparative—of the plaintiff is also irrelevant. The majority, by considering the comparative negligence of a plaintiff in an action in which defendant's negligence is not an issue, apply an untenable double standard. Their error is grievously unsettling to the law of torts. More significantly, this decision seriously erodes the pattern of the law which up to now reflected a healthy concern for consumers victimized by defective products placed on the market in this mechanized age through the dynamics of mass production, national and international distribution, and psychologically subtle marketing.

. . . .

I would affirm the judgment.

----

1. The concept of applying comparative negligence in strict products liability actions—where the defendant was not negligent at all—makes it all the more clear that the courts are in fact comparing causation and not negligence. But what about those products that are defective because they fail to prevent (or minimize the effect of) negligent misuse? Can *Daly* be reconciled with *Culpepper*?

2. *Daly* is, in a way, a seatbelt case. It is unusual in that the driver, the plaintiff, caused the accident by reckless driving. Presumably, he was too intoxicated to fasten his seatbelt.

3. On the surface, *Daly* sounds like a pro-defendant opinion, because the court is opening the door to a new defense in strict products liability cases. In this connection, it is worth noting that the plaintiff had lost the case in the trial court.

4. *Culpepper, McCown,* and *Daly* are all "crashworthiness" cases, in which the issue is not whether the product caused the accident, but rather whether the product caused injuries from the accident to be exacerbated. Negligence in failing to use an available safety device or, as in *Culpepper,* misusing an available safety device, may become the issue. In other words, manufacturers have a duty to make a product that is safe in the face of foreseeable misuse, such as being crashed, whatever the cause of the crash. What about misuse of the safety device itself?

5. After *Daly,* how should a court handle the fact that a plaintiff's negligence was the sole cause of an accident? If the plaintiff in *Daly* had not negligently crashed his car, he would not have been injured at all. In this respect, his own negligence was the sole cause of the accident. If this fact bars recovery, how can safety devices included on a product to minimize the effects of user negligence ever be challenged as defective in a jurisdiction that applies comparative negligence in products liability cases, when the plaintiff's own negligence has set the chain of events in motion? Clearly, the Court in *Daly* did not intend this result, although the court fails to explain how the plaintiff's negligence should be treated in a crashworthiness case. What would a reasonable analysis of the relationship between causing an accident and causing the resulting injury to be exacerbated look like? It is perhaps worth noting here that courts have consistently held that user conduct that causes safety devices to be necessary is all too foreseeable.

Ford v. Polaris Industries, Inc.

California Court of Appeal, 2006
43 Cal. Rptr. 3d 215

REARDON, J.

Susan Ford sustained severe orifice injuries after falling off the rear of a two-seater Polaris personal watercraft. The jet-powered nozzle propelled a high-pressure stream of water that tore apart her internal organs. Today she uses a colostomy bag, she urinates through a catheter, and her lower right torso and leg are numb from nerve damage. Susan and her husband sued the manufacturer and distributor of the watercraft on a strict products liability theory.

This appeal frames the question whether the doctrine of primary assumption of risk applies to the manufacturer of the personal watercraft so as to preclude the injured jet skier from raising a defective design claim. We conclude that the trial court properly ruled that primary assumption of the risk did not bar plaintiff's suit. The appeal also addresses the propriety of instructions in a strict products liability case where the plaintiff alleges that the personal watercraft was defectively designed and caused her injury. We determine that the standard instructions on defective design were adequate.

Finally, defendant manufacturer insists that the court below erred in refusing to permit the jury to allocate fault to the watercraft operator for giving misleading instructions to the injured skier and to the owners and operator for failure to pass on safety warnings. This assertion begs the questions: Did the operator owe a duty not to deliver misleading instructions and did the owners and operator have a duty to convey the manufacturer's warnings? Finding no such duties, we reject these contentions as well and affirm the judgment.

I. FACTS AND PROCEDURE

A. *The Accident, Injuries and Aftermath*

In April 2001 Steve and Laura Nakamura bought two 2-seater Polaris SLH-700 personal watercraft.[3]

On September 9, 2001, the Fords and Nakamuras and various family members went to Lake Berryessa for a picnic. Laura took Susan for a ride on the watercraft. Susan was wearing a one-piece swimsuit and a life jacket. This was her first time riding a personal watercraft.

Susan held onto Laura's waist. After about five minutes, Laura stopped to tell Susan she was holding on too tight and to hold onto the grips behind her instead. Susan looked around; all she saw were the grab handles. She had to lean back and could only hook a couple fingers into each handle.

They started out again in a straight line. The jet ski was "bumping up and down." Susan lost her grip, was lifted off the seat and fell backward off the rear of the watercraft. As Susan hit the water she felt "a lot" of pain and vomited. Laura saw Susan floating in a pool of blood. Paramedics rushed Susan by helicopter to University of California Davis Medical Center.

Susan sustained a severe hernial and rectal injury. Her internal bleeding required multiple transfusions. Two surgeries were required to prepare and establish a colostomy. Medical records indicate she also required "massive resuscitation . . . from her initial operation."

Susan was in the hospital for 10 days, followed by a five-day postoperative stay at North Bay Medical Center.

Susan has no control over her bowels. She was evaluated for rectal-colon reconstructive surgery, but the specialist concluded there was no possibility of reconstruction. When Susan learned this, she "basically fell apart."

---

3. A personal watercraft is a small jet-propelled vessel. The sport of riding a personal watercraft is referred to as jet skiing.

The injuries also created urological complications such that Susan must self-catheterize in order to urinate. As well, Susan is numb from her right kneecap to her waist; her buttocks and pelvic area are also numb. She can no longer engage in such activities as playing softball and dancing. And, because of loss of sensation and the physical limitations she endures, Susan and Anthony's sex life has suffered. Susan used to work at Raley's Superstore but was unable to keep up with her responsibilities after she returned to work. She now takes care of her father-in-law.

B. *Cause of the Accident*

Michael Burleson, an industrial engineer and safety professional with extensive experience on personal watercraft concerns, testified that the jet nozzle is centrally positioned in back of the Polaris watercraft and protrudes two and five-eighths inches beyond the rear deck. The position of the jet increases the chance of high-pressure exposure should a passenger be ejected to the rear of the watercraft. Susan landed less than a foot from the back of the jet nozzle.

When a watercraft is accelerating and encounters a wave, the passenger can "get some lift" off the seat, and if the passenger is not well coupled to the craft he or she may lose balance and roll off. When there is a rearward ejection into the stream of water thrust by a jet nozzle such as occurred with Susan, the high pressure of the water penetrates the body, causing internal injuries.

C. *Design Defect*

1. *Plaintiffs' Case*

Burleson explained that because it is important that nothing interfere with the operator's ability to control a personal watercraft, a passenger cannot always hold onto the operator. Sometimes passengers pull more than is comfortable for the operator. In some situations it may not be feasible to hold on, for example if the operator stands up to move around. As well there may be social constraints to holding onto the operator. A significant difference in size may also militate against holding on.

In Burleson's opinion there was a defect in the design of the SLH Polaris watercraft because this particular craft lacked adequate design safeguards to protect against a rearward ejection injury. In other words, there was no easily identifiable alternative means for the passenger to hold on when it was not feasible to hold onto the operator.

Several feasible design features were available to Polaris to protect against rear ejections. A seatback is one alternative to prevent the passenger from "coming off" the back.[4]

---

4. No originally equipped watercraft were sold with a seatback in 2001. Polaris offered evidence that a seatback would be in the way if installed on a two-person watercraft, and would increase the risk of back injuries.

Another solution would be recognizable and accessible handgrips that the passenger can "grasp completely." The grips Burleson proffered protruded from the side of the craft. Many manufacturers have switched from protruding handles to the recessed handles that were on the Polaris craft.[5, 6]

For fifty cents at most, a simple seat strap that goes around the seat would provide a secure handhold for passenger stability. Several models in the Polaris manual for this machine had a seat strap, and there were bolt holes for such a strap on the craft but it had not been installed. Had the machine been equipped with a seat strap, Burleson did not think the accident would have occurred.[7]

Dr. Edward Karnes was the Fords' human factors engineer. That discipline concerns the evaluation of human factors involved in the design and use of products, including how people understand risks and respond to warnings. He described the hazard in this case as falling off the rear of the watercraft and being struck by the jet thrust. The manufacturer's job is to identify and evaluate hazards and make decisions about remedies according to a safety hierarchy. The first tier on the hierarchy is to design out the hazard. If that cannot be accomplished, the next tier would be to provide some type of guard to prevent access to the hazardous situation. Warning—the last tier—is an appropriate remedy only if the hazard cannot be eliminated by design or guard.

Polaris's solution to orifice injuries was to admonish participants to wear protective clothing. The rear and front on-craft labels for the SLH warned that the passenger must wear a wetsuit or equivalent protective clothing to avoid orifice injuries. The owner's manual reproduced the rear decal, in bigger typeface, as well as the front warning label, and instructed elsewhere to wear protective clothing for body or orifice protection. Susan did not notice the warning decal and, being a guest, she never saw the owner's manual.

In Dr. Karnes's opinion, warnings alone were not an appropriate remedy for the hazard that creates the risk of orifice injury. He regarded the cost of compliance—or the effort required to comply with warning—as high for wearing a wetsuit. First, they are not comfortable when worn in warm weather conditions. Second, the likelihood that owner-operators would have wetsuits on hand for recreational passengers such as friends or family members is "going to be about nil." Third, the person

---

5. Polaris's expert testified that in 2001 there were not any personal watercraft marketed with protruding side handles. The purpose of recessed handles is "to minimize inadvertent contact with the handles."

6. Apparently the Polaris watercraft was equipped with sculpted outside handles, also referred to as detents or fingerholds, with a rear grip handle primarily used for reboarding from the water. Susan reached for this grip handle.

7. On cross-examination, Burleson stated that although the seat strap can provide a way to hold on, it was not the best solution for rearward ejection. The strap is an active device, meaning the passenger has to use it. On the other hand a seatback, for example, would provide passive safety that would be there all the time.

at greatest risk—the passenger—is also the person least likely to have read the vehicle warning label.

Moreover, although the Polaris decal warning provided correct basic risk factor information about the need to wear protective clothing, the forceful entry of water into orifices and the need for all riders to wear protective clothing, Karnes considered the warning inadequate because it did not identify the risk (falling off the rear of the craft) or pinpoint those who were at greatest risk, namely passengers. Additionally, had the decal been placed on the seat, it would be more conspicuous to the passenger. From the operators' perspective, the warning label fails to tell them directly not to give a ride to someone who is not wearing protective clothing, and why this is important. Further, the admonition to wear protective clothing was undermined by the safety video which did not discuss orifice injuries or the special risk to passengers, and indeed portrayed passengers in bathing suits, never in protective clothing.

3. *Defendants' Case*

Kevin Breen, Polaris's forensic engineer, concurred that it was likely Susan would not have been injured had she been holding onto a seat strap. The force required to dislodge a passenger holding onto a seat strap compares favorably with the force to dislodge the operator: It is the same or a bit greater. Indeed, the Polaris manual states that the passenger should hold onto the operator or seat strap.

Breen also stated that although orifice injuries are exceedingly rare, watercraft manufacturers cannot ignore them and have a responsibility to try to design features that would prevent or minimize the risk.

Breen tested different fabrics to determine whether other materials would have prevented Susan's injuries by reducing the water pressure behind the fabric below five pounds per square inch, the threshold for sphincter muscle tension. Both the neoprene wetsuit and blue jeans sufficiently reduced the water pressure. Susan wore denim shorts to the lake, but not when she boarded the watercraft.

Polaris designated Daniel Schroepher as the employee most qualified to address safety features on the SLH such as rear passenger seating, safety testing and safety studies. He testified that Polaris designed the SLH in-house. By the time of the 1996 model year, the label warned against orifice injuries. Polaris did not conduct tests to distinguish the risk of falling off the back of the craft as opposed to the side.

Schroepher identified several design features intended to prevent the passenger from sliding off the back. The driver's seat and handgrips were of nonslippery material so the driver could stay put as well as the passenger who was hanging on. The foot pad was also of grippy material, and there was a spot where the passenger could put his or her heels. Grab handles were an option to stay on board if there was discomfort with holding onto the operator. Schroepher testified that Polaris had been aware of the possibility of falling off the watercraft and the nature of injuries that could be sustained, and had done everything it could to address the situation.

Schroepher was not sure if Polaris ever provided seat straps for the two-person SLH. They were not offered as an optional feature because there was "no safety need" and "engineering got busy and was never able to get it done."

By 2001 Polaris was aware that the thrust of the jet pump would be dangerous to someone who fell off the rear of a moving watercraft. Yet the Polaris safety video did not refer to the risk of orifice injury. Schroepher offered as a rationale for this omission that Polaris "wanted to provide adequate information but not drag out the video so it's so long so people won't watch it." Therefore, the video "hit the highlights" such as wearing proper gear, avoiding collisions and the most common injuries. "And if you do those things, then it would avoid orifice injuries. . . ."

D. *The Nakamuras' Interaction with Polaris*

Prior to completing the purchase of the SLH-700 watercraft, Steve and Laura Nakamura watched a safety video at the dealership as required by Polaris. Neither the video nor representatives of the dealership mentioned the need to wear protective clothing or the risk of falling backward and sustaining orifice injuries. As described by Schroepher, the marketing product manager for Polaris, the safety video highlighted issues such as common injuries and how to avoid collisions.

The Polaris dealer went through the owner's manual with Steve Nakamura, pointing out all the warnings and stressing the importance of reading the manual. Polaris required Steve to sign a warranty registration certifying that he received and would read the owner's manual and warning labels before using the watercraft, and would ask anyone he allowed to use the craft to also read the labels and manual. Steve skimmed through the manual, focusing on maintenance issues. Prior to the accident he did not read the warning decals, including the decal advising "SEVERE INJURY or DEATH. . . . [¶] WEAR PROTECTIVE CLOTHING." Nor was it his practice to have guests read the manual and labels. The Nakamuras did not have any discussion with Susan about what to wear when riding the watercraft.

E. *Procedural History*

In September 2002 the Fords filed suit, alleging causes of action for "products liability" against Polaris and negligence against Laura Nakamura. Polaris cross-complained against Laura for equitable indemnity.

Laura moved for summary judgment asserting that the doctrine of primary assumption of risk barred the Fords' action against her. Laura argued that she owed no duty to eliminate, or protect Susan against, "the risk of falling while the water craft was engaged in its maneuvers[,] as those maneuvers constitute a risk inherent in, if not the very purpose of, the sport itself." The Fords did not oppose the motion but Polaris did, arguing that Laura failed to communicate to Susan the instructions and warnings provided by the company, and wrongfully instructed her to ride the watercraft in an unsafe manner.

Granting the motion and directing that judgment be entered in Laura's favor, the trial court concluded that the activity that Laura and Susan were engaged in was subject to the doctrine of primary assumption of the risk: "[T]his . . . personal water craft operation was being done for enjoyment or thrill. It does require physical exertion as well as elements of skill, and involves a challenge containing a potential risk of injury. [¶] And, in addition, even though there is no competition . . . or race going on with other operators of personal water craft, there was a kind of competition going on with the elements including waves [set up] by other boats and the testing of oneself against the challenges of speed and sudden turns." As to Polaris's claims, the court ruled that although Laura did not communicate to Susan the Polaris warning to wear protective clothing, and told her to hang onto the handles, contrary to Polaris instructions and warnings, these lapses at most amounted to mere negligence. Therefore under the doctrine of primary assumption of the risk Laura owed Susan no duty of care.

Polaris also moved for summary judgment, arguing that under principles of collateral estoppel, the court must apply primary assumption of the risk to the Fords' claims against it. Denying the motion, the trial court explained that reliance on the ruling in favor of Laura was misplaced because the Fords' allegations against Polaris concerned its duty to provide products free of design defects, a duty that did not attach to Laura. Moreover, while the court acknowledged that primary assumption of the risk may be applied to the activity of jet skiing, there was no finding that "'rearward ejection jet thrust injuries'" were inherent in the sport.

At the close of evidence Polaris moved unsuccessfully for nonsuit, arguing that plaintiffs did not prove that Polaris increased the risks inherent in jet skiing. As well, Polaris proposed a special instruction to the effect that plaintiffs must prove "[t]hat the defects increased the risk of harm beyond those risks that are a normal part of the sport of jet skiing." The court denied the instruction, ruling that if plaintiffs prove a defect, "that ipso facto raises the risk beyond those normally inherent in jet skiing and, therefore, requiring the jury to return a finding on that would not only be a redundancy but would be a confusing factor." Polaris also proposed a special verdict that asked whether the design defect increased the risk of harm. The court rejected this verdict form.

Additionally, Polaris sought to allocate fault to the Nakamuras pursuant to Civil Code section 1431.2, proposing a verdict form permitting such allocation. The court declined this request.

The jury returned a special verdict against Polaris on the design defect claim, awarded Susan $382,024 in economic losses and $3,262,500 in noneconomic losses, and awarded Anthony $115,000 for loss of consortium. The jury also found that Susan was not comparatively negligent. This appeal followed.

II. DISCUSSION

A. *Assumption of the Risk Meets Strict Products Liability on a Recreational Equipment Design Defect Claim.*

1. *Introduction; Standards of Review*

Although Polaris frames the primary issue on appeal in terms of the court's failure to require Susan to prove not only that there was a design defect, but that the defect increased the inherent risks of jet skiing—an error manifest in denied instructions, denied nonsuit motion and rejected verdict form—the heart of its argument is that the court erred in deciding the lawsuit did not fall within the doctrine of primary assumption of the risk. We address both concerns.

The existence and scope of a defendant's duty of care in the context of primary assumption of the risk is a legal question to be decided by the court. (*Knight v. Jewett* (1992) 3 Cal.4th 296, 313, 11 Cal.Rptr.2d 2, 834 P.2d 696 (*Knight*); see *Kahn v. East Side Union High School Dist.* (2003) 31 Cal.4th 990, 1004, 4 Cal.Rptr.3d 103, 75 P.3d 30 (*Kahn*).) Therefore, we review, de novo, the trial court's decision denying Polaris's motion for summary judgment on primary assumption of the risk. (Code Civ. Proc., § 437c, subd. (p)(2); *American Golf Corp. v. Superior Court* (2000) 79 Cal. App.4th 30, 35, 93 Cal.Rptr.2d 683.) However, as we conclude that primary assumption of the risk does not bar the Fords' action, we next evaluate the nature of Polaris's duty as the manufacturer of recreational equipment, and whether the jury instructions on products liability/design defect were adequate in this context. The standard of review for a claim of instructional error of this type is also de novo because the question is one of law, involving the determination of the applicable legal principles. (*National Medical Transportation Network v. Deloitte & Touche* (1998) 62 Cal.App.4th 412, 427, 72 Cal.Rptr.2d 720.)

2. *Legal Framework*

Under the general umbrella of strict products liability, the case went to the jury on the risk-benefit test for design defect.[9] Pursuant to this test, a manufacturer is strictly liable in tort where "the plaintiff demonstrates that the product's design proximately caused his injury and the defendant fails to establish, in light of the relevant factors, that, on balance, the benefits of the challenged design outweigh the risk of danger inherent in such design." (*Barker v. Lull Engineering Co.* (1978) 20 Cal.3d 413, 432, 143 Cal.Rptr. 225, 573 P.2d 443.) Relevant factors pertinent to the risk-benefit analysis include "the gravity of the danger posed by the challenged design, the likelihood that such danger would occur, the mechanical feasibility of a safer alternative design, the financial cost of an improved design, and the adverse consequences to the product and to the consumer that would result from an alternative design." (*Id.* at p. 431, 143 Cal.Rptr. 225, 573 P.2d 443.)

In *Daly v. General Motors Corp.* (1978) 20 Cal.3d 725, 736, 144 Cal.Rptr. 380, 575 P.2d 1162, our Supreme Court reiterated that the purposes underlying the strict products liability doctrine are to relieve injured consumers from problems of proof inherent in pursuing negligence remedies, and to protect otherwise defenseless victims of manufacturing defects by spreading the cost of compensation throughout society. The court concluded that these purposes would not be diluted or frustrated

---

9. As a second strand, the Fords also pursued a defective warning theory. Since the jury found that there was a defect in the design of the watercraft that caused Susan's injuries, it did not reach the issue of the adequacy of warnings.

by adoption of comparative fault principles and proceeded to extend these principles to actions founded on strict products liability. At the same time and with respect to such cases, it abolished the separate defense of assumption of the risk, to the extent it served as a form of contributory negligence. (*Id.* at p. 742, 144 Cal.Rptr. 380, 575 P.2d 1162.)

Years later in *Knight*, involving coparticipants in a game of touch football, our Supreme Court differentiated between cases involving primary assumption of the risk — where, in view of the nature of the activity and the parties' relationship to it, the defendant owes no legal duty to protect the plaintiff from a particular risk of harm — and those involving secondary assumption of the risk, in which the defendant owes a duty of care but the plaintiff knowingly encounters the risk. (*Knight, supra,* 3 Cal.4th at pp. 314–315, 11 Cal.Rptr.2d 2, 834 P.2d 696.) In the former situation, the absence of a duty operates as a complete bar to recovery whereas in the latter, the trier of fact apportions liability under comparative fault principles. (*Id.* at p. 315, 11 Cal.Rptr.2d 2, 834 P.2d 696.)

The determination whether the defendant owes a legal duty to protect the plaintiff from a particular risk of harm turns on the *nature of the activity in which the defendant is engaged and the relationship of the defendant and the plaintiff to that activity.* (*Knight, supra,* 3 Cal.4th at p. 309, 11 Cal.Rptr.2d 2, 834 P.2d 696.) As to any given active sport, "defendants generally have no legal duty to eliminate (or protect a plaintiff against) risks inherent in the sport itself, [although] defendants generally do have a duty to use due care not to increase the risks to a participant over and above those inherent in the sport." (*Id.* at pp. 315–316, 11 Cal.Rptr.2d 2, 834 P.2d 696.) As explained in *Kahn, supra,* 31 Cal.4th at page 1004, 4 Cal.Rptr.3d 103, 75 P.3d 30, this passage from *Knight* reflects a policy that in a sports setting it is not appropriate to "recognize a duty of care when to do so would require that an integral part of the sport be abandoned, or would discourage vigorous participation in sporting events." Further, because the duty question also hinges on the role of the defendant whose conduct is at issue, duties with respect to the same risk may vary depending on whether the defendant is a coparticipant, coach, recreation provider, manufacturer, and the like. (See *ibid.*)

Shortly after *Knight*, the reviewing court in *Milwaukee Electric Tool Corp. v. Superior Court* (1993) 15 Cal.App.4th 547, 19 Cal.Rptr.2d 24 (*Milwaukee Tool*), responding to the Supreme Court's direction to vacate and reconsider its prior opinion in light of *Knight*, applied the newly announced rules to a cause of action against a tool manufacturer sounding in strict products liability. (*Id.* at p. 550, 19 Cal.Rptr.2d 24.) The plaintiff in *Milwaukee Tool* was an experienced glazier who was injured while using a heavy-duty variable-speed drill. The manufacturer claimed he misused the tool.

The reasoning of *Milwaukee Tool* is instructive. Extensively reviewing the development of the strict product liability doctrine in California (*Milwaukee Tool, supra,* 15 Cal.App.4th at pp. 555–558, 19 Cal.Rptr.2d 24), the court concluded that although the doctrine is not pled in terms of classic negligence, unquestionably a manufacturer has a duty to provide consumers with defect-free products, and that duty is inherent in a strict liability cause of action (*id.* at p. 559, 19 Cal.Rptr.2d 24). Indeed, courts have viewed the doctrine of strict products liability theory—which focuses on the product itself rather than the conduct of the manufacturer—"as a 'short cut' to liability where negligence may be present but may be difficult to prove. [Citations.]" (*Id.* at pp. 556–557, 19 Cal.Rptr.2d 24.) Against this background, the *Milwaukee Tool* court did not hesitate to apply the duty analysis set forth in *Knight* to the question of whether the tool company in question could assert primary assumption of the risk as a complete defense to liability. (*Ibid.*)

First, the nature of the activity asserted in the action was the manufacturer's alleged production of a defective product. There was nothing "in the nature of the manufacturing activity to indicate that a finding of no duty on the manufacturer's part should be made. To the contrary, we believe there is a sound basis in the development of strict products liability doctrine to support analysis of a products liability case, even one involving an assertion of assumption of the risk, in terms of a duty on the part of the manufacturer to produce defect-free products." (*Milwaukee Tool, supra,* 15 Cal.App.4th at p. 562, 19 Cal.Rptr.2d 24.)

Second, looking at the relationship of the defendant and the plaintiff to the activity, namely the use of the tool, the court noted that the accident occurred in an employment setting. Therefore, the court examined the rationale of the firefighter's rule[10] and the related situation where a professional, such as a veterinary assistant, accepts employment involving a known risk of danger. In both cases, primary assumption of the risk has barred recovery. Notwithstanding parallels to the case at hand, the court concluded that an injury asserted to have been caused by a dangerously defective power tool is not "'a risk that is inherent' in a worker's job." (*Milwaukee Tool, supra,* 15 Cal.App.4th at pp. 562–563, 19 Cal.Rptr.2d 24.) Moreover, "[i]n the relationship of the defendant and the plaintiff to the activity, the use of the tool, it cannot be said that the plaintiff user undertook to act as a product tester or guinea pig." (*Id.* at p. 563, 19 Cal.Rptr.2d 24.) In other words, the user of the tool which causes the injury is "not necessarily a professional employed to confront the very danger posed by the injury-causing agent." (*Ibid.*) Summing it up, the court stated: "[W]e believe that the purposes of strict products liability doctrine will be well served by a finding that a manufacturer owes a duty to a user of its product, thus making the primary assumption of the risk doctrine inapplicable, absent some extraordinary circumstance not reflected by this record." (*Id.* at p. 565, 19 Cal.Rptr.2d 24.)

---

10. The *Knight* court explained that this rule "involves the question whether a person who negligently has started a fire is liable for an injury sustained by a firefighter who is summoned to fight the fire; the rule provides that the person who started the fire is not liable under such circumstances. [Citation.] . . . [T]he most persuasive explanation [to support this conclusion] is that the party who negligently started the fire had no legal duty to protect the firefighter from the very danger that the firefighter is employed to confront." (*Knight, supra,* 3 Cal.4th at pp. 309–310, fn. 5, 11 Cal.Rptr.2d 2, 834 P.2d 696.)

More recently, the reviewing court in *Bunch v. Hoffinger Industries, Inc.* (2004) 123 Cal.App.4th 1278, 20 Cal.Rptr.3d 780 (*Bunch*) applied *Milwaukee Tool* in the context of a sports injury. There, a girl suffered catastrophic injuries when she dove into a shallow pool. She recovered against the manufacturer of the replacement pool liner on a product liability/failure to warn theory. (*Id.* at pp. 1281–1282, 1289–1290, 20 Cal.Rptr.3d 780.) The reviewing court recognized that under *Knight* and the rule of primary assumption of the risk, a participant in a sporting activity generally may not recover damages for injuries resulting from risks inherent in the sport. (*Id.* at p. 1300, 20 Cal.Rptr.3d 780.) However, the test for liability for equipment providers is different from that of coparticipant in a sport, and hence the doctrine of primary assumption of risk "does not insulate equipment suppliers from liability for injury from providing defective equipment." (*Ibid.*) Moreover, "under products liability, the manufacturer does owe a duty to produce defect-free products. [Citation.] In addition, in using a defective product, the user does not intend to confront a risk that is inherent in its use. [Citation.]" (*Id.* at p. 1301, 20 Cal.Rptr.3d 780.)

3. *The Trial Court Correctly Ruled That Primary Assumption of the Risk Did Not Foreclose the Fords' Strict Products Liability Claim.*

Polaris's refrain on appeal, expressed in various ways throughout the briefs, is as follows: Falling off a watercraft and coming into contact with the surface of water are inherent risks of the sport of jet skiing. As well, suffering orifice injuries is an inherent, but rare, risk of the sport. Polaris owed Susan no duty to eliminate or protect against these risks and therefore primary assumption of the risk absolves it of any liability. Finally, *Milwaukee Tool* and *Bunch* "were wrongly decided" because products liability claims are not exempt from application of primary assumption of the risk principles.

a. *Polaris's Criticism of* Milwaukee Tool *and* Bunch

Milwaukee Tool and *Bunch* stand for the proposition that a manufacturer's duty to produce defect-free products is not obliterated by primary assumption of the risk, absent extraordinary circumstances. Polaris criticizes these decisions, asserting that they conflict with *Lipson v. Superior Court* (1982) 31 Cal.3d 362, 182 Cal.Rptr. 629, 644 P.2d 822, *Kelhi v. Fitzpatrick* (1994) 25 Cal.App.4th 1149, 31 Cal.Rptr.2d 182 and *Sanchez v. Hillerich & Bradsby Co.* (2002) 104 Cal.App.4th 703, 128 Cal.Rptr.2d 529. Polaris's authority does not undermine *Milwaukee Tool* and *Bunch*.

Lipson was a pre- *Knight* case entailing application of the firefighter's rule to a claim of strict liability for an ultrahazardous activity. The court focused on the petitioners' conduct, and did not engage in the analysis of duty set forth in *Knight*. (*Lipson v. Superior Court, supra*, 31 Cal.3d at pp. 375–376, 182 Cal.Rptr. 629, 644 P.2d 822.) *Kelhi* also involved the firefighter's rule. . . . The present case does not involve the firefighter's rule and therefore the primary assumption of risk doctrine is not invoked automatically. Moreover, as emphasized in *Neighbarger v. Irwin Industries, Inc.* (1994) 8 Cal.4th 532, 546, 34 Cal.Rptr.2d 630, 882 P.2d 347, "[t]he most substantial justifications for the firefighter's rule are those based on the public nature of the service provided by firefighters and the relationship between the public and the public firefighter." Those concerns are not present here.

Nor does *Sanchez* aid Polaris. In *Sanchez* the injured college pitcher pursued negligence and products liability claims against a bat manufacturer. He alleged that the newly design[ed] bat, made of hollow aluminum alloy with a pressurized air bladder, significantly increased the inherent risk that a pitcher would be hit by a line drive. (*Sanchez v. Hillerich & Bradsby Co., supra*, 104 Cal.App.4th at p. 707, 128 Cal.Rptr.2d 529.) The reviewing court *rejected* primary assumption of the risk as shielding the manufacturer and *reversed* summary judgment because the plaintiff's evidence raised a triable issue whether the design increased the inherent risk. (*Id.* at p. 715, 128 Cal. Rptr.2d 529.) As the court further explained: "If it is ultimately determined primary assumption of the risk does not apply here, the issue then becomes one of secondary assumption of the risk." (*Ibid.*) Moreover, as pointed out in *Bunch, supra*, 123 Cal. App.4th at pages 1301–1302, 20 Cal.Rptr.3d 780, the court in *Sanchez* "did not discuss the interplay between products liability and primary assumption of risk. Nor did the court discuss or distinguish *Milwaukee* [*Tool*]." (*Id.* at p. 1302, 20 Cal.Rptr.3d 780.)

While we do not agree with Polaris that *Milwaukee Tool* and *Bunch* were "wrongly decided" and in conflict with the above opinions, we are mindful that these decisions are not exact templates for the instant case: *Milwaukee Tool* was not a sports case and thus there was no need for the court to address the issue of inherent risks in assessing the scope and existence of the defendant's duty. *Bunch* was a sports case, but the issue was inadequate warnings, not design defect. There was no charge in *Bunch* that imposing on the manufacturer a duty to provide effective and adequate warnings *would change* the nature of the sport or chill participation in it. The premise of these decisions is sound: Manufacturers have an independent duty to make nondefective products that as a general rule will withstand application of primary assumption of risk principles. However, in a recreational equipment defect case such as this, the *scope* of that duty may be at issue as when, for example, the defendant asserts that the purported defect is the very failure of the product to eliminate or provide protection against an inherent risk of the sport. Under such circumstances, the court must also assess the risks inherent in the sport as part and parcel of ascertaining the *scope* of the manufacturer's duty.

b. Analysis of Inherent Risks

To reiterate, in the context of an active sport, the "existence and scope of a defendant's duty of care ... depends on *the nature of the sport or activity* in question and on the parties' general relationship to the activity...." (*Knight, supra*, 3 Cal.4th at p. 313, 11 Cal.Rptr.2d 2, 834 P.2d 696, italics added.) Defining the risks inherent in a particular sport thus is integral to determining whether a particular defendant owes a duty of care. (*Staten v. Superior Court* (1996) 45 Cal.App.4th 1628, 1633, 1635, 53 Cal.Rptr.2d 657.) "Inherent" means "involved in the constitution or essential character of something: belonging by nature or habit: intrinsic." (Merriam-Webster's

Collegiate Dict. (10th ed.2001) p. 600.) The court in *Freeman v. Hale* (1994) 30 Cal. App.4th 1388, 1394–1395, 36 Cal.Rptr.2d 418 articulated the test this way: An inherent risk is one that, if eliminated, would fundamentally alter the nature of the sport or deter vigorous participation. (See also *Distefano v. Forester* (2001) 85 Cal. App.4th 1249, 1261, 102 Cal.Rptr.2d 813.)

Here, the general risk of falling and coming into contact with water is inherent in jet skiing. However, Polaris asks us to evaluate its potential for liability under a rubric that includes the specific risk of suffering orifice injuries within the inherent risks of jet skiing, thereby eliminating its duty of care. The trial court specifically declined to find that such injuries are inherent in the sport. We agree.

Orifice injuries and the conduct that causes them do not belong to the "fundamental nature or habit" of the sport. Such injuries occur by way of rearward ejection into a very dangerous, defined space, namely the high-pressure stream of water thrust by the jet nozzle of the watercraft. Polaris's role with respect to the sport of jet skiing is as the manufacturer and designer of the Polaris SLH-700 personal watercraft. The Fords asserted that the watercraft was defective because Polaris did not consider or utilize appropriate alternative designs that would reduce the chances of rearward ejection into the jet propulsion. *The norm in jet skiing is to hold on.* Providing an alternative to hanging on while jet skiing in circumstances where holding onto the operator is not feasible would not alter the fundamental nature of the sport or deter vigorous participation. The Fords submitted Burleson's declaration on summary judgment to the effect that the watercraft was defectively designed and substantially increased the risk of harm because "Polaris continue[d] to manufacture personal watercraft without passenger protection against rearward ejection injuries incorporated into the design of the machines."[11] Under these facts the trial court properly denied Polaris's motion for summary judgment on primary assumption of the risk.

Citing *American Golf Corp. v. Superior Court, supra*, 79 Cal.App.4th at page 37, 93 Cal.Rptr.2d 683, Polaris also maintains that what is standard in the industry defines the nature of the sport and its inherent risks. Since the designs of other watercraft are essentially the same as the Polaris craft, the standard is established and cannot be attacked without running afoul of the doctrine of primary assumption of the risk. This argument is not sustainable in the context of a strict product liability/design defect case. None of the cases cited by Polaris stand for the proposition that primary assumption of the risk will preclude a strict products liability/design defect claim

---

11. Specifically, Burleson referred to the alternative of a passenger seatback. At trial, three possible alternative designs were advanced. Polaris found fault with all three of them, but it is not the plaintiff's burden in a design defect case to prove the existence of a feasible alternative design. (*Bernal v. Richard Wolf Medical Instruments Corp.* (1990) 221 Cal.App.3d 1326, 1335, 272 Cal.Rptr. 41, overruled on another point in *Soule v. General Motors Corp.* (1994) 8 Cal.4th 548, 574, 34 Cal. Rptr.2d 607, 882 P.2d 298.) Nonetheless, seat straps, while perhaps not the best solution to rearward ejection into the high-pressure jet stream, are feasible and inexpensive, and do not alter the fundamental nature of the sport or deter active participation. Had Susan been able to grasp one, the evidence supports a finding that she would not have been injured.

against a recreational equipment manufacturer simply because its equipment is "essentially the same" in design as that of other manufacturers.[12] To reiterate, a risk is inherent if its absence would significantly change the sport or deter enthusiastic participation. Not all design features that are "essentially the same" throughout an industry would meet this definition. Moreover, the evidence does not support Polaris's proposition: Its own expert testified that "roughly half" of watercraft sold have seat straps, and roughly half do not!

c. *Analysis of Defendant's Role*

Polaris ignores a key principle of *Knight* and *Kahn*, namely that the examination of duty under a primary assumption of risk inquiry also takes into account the defendant's role in, or relationship to, the sport in question. (*Knight, supra,* 3 Cal.4th at pp. 317–318, 11 Cal.Rptr.2d 2, 834 P.2d 696; see *Kahn, supra,* 31 Cal.4th at p. 1004, 4 Cal.Rptr.3d 103, 75 P.3d 30.) The same risk may pose different duties according to the function of a particular defendant with respect to a particular sport. Thus, while a batter owes no duty to avoid carelessly throwing the bat after making a hit, a stadium owner has a duty to provide a reasonably safe stadium and may be held responsible "for its failure to provide the patron 'protection from flying bats, at least in the area where the greatest danger exists and where such an occurrence is reasonably to be expected.'" (*Knight, supra,* 3 Cal.4th at p. 317, 11 Cal.Rptr.2d 2, 834 P.2d 696, quoting *Ratcliff v. San Diego Baseball Club* (1938) 27 Cal.App.2d 733, 736, 81 P.2d 625 [spectator hit by accidentally thrown bat while walking in stands between home plate and first base].) The *Knight* court *approved* of *Ratcliff* and other cases which, in the process of analyzing the duty of proprietors of sports facilities, defined "the risks inherent in the sport not only by virtue of the nature of the sport itself, *but also by reference to the steps the sponsoring business entity reasonably should be obligated to take in order to minimize the risks without altering the nature of the sport.*" (*Knight, supra,* at p. 317, 11 Cal.Rptr.2d 2, 834 P.2d 696, italics added.)

A number of courts have taken their cue from this language in defining the duty of the owner or operator of a sporting venue. (See, for example, *Morgan v. Fuji*

---

12. See *American Golf Corp. v. Superior Court, supra,* 79 Cal.App.4th at pages 38–39, 93 Cal. Rptr.2d 683 [primary assumption of risk foreclosed action against golf course for *negligent* design and placement of yardage markers: Errant shots are inherent risk of sport, yardage markers are integral to sport, and golf course as recreational provider did not increase risk of injury by its design and placement of yardage markers according to system standard]; *Ferrari v. Grand Canyon Dories* (1995) 32 Cal.App.4th 248, 256–257, 38 Cal.Rptr.2d 65 [plaintiff's negligence claim against commercial rafting trip sponsors and operators barred by primary assumption of risk: Defendants owed duty to provide customers with properly equipped raft made of materials adequate for intended purpose; rafts configured with exposed metal frames were standard in industry and defined sport such that significant change in watercraft to enhance safety would necessarily reduce challenge of whitewater rafting]; *Balthazor v. Little League Baseball, Inc.* (1998) 62 Cal.App.4th 47, 52, 72 Cal.Rptr.2d 337 [claim that league breached its duty not to increase risks inherent in baseball by failing to provide helmet with faceguard did not survive primary assumption of risk: Faceguard was not part of league's normal safety equipment and failure to require it did not increase risk of being struck by carelessly thrown ball].

Country USA, Inc. (1995) 34 Cal.App.4th 127, 134–135, 40 Cal.Rptr.2d 249 [duty of golf course owner/operator to provide reasonably safe golf course requires owner to minimize risks without changing nature of game . . .]; *Branco v. Kearny Moto Park, Inc.* (1995) 37 Cal.App.4th 184, 190, 193, 43 Cal.Rptr.2d 392 [operator of motocross bicycle course has duty to refrain from using jumps which by design create extreme risk of injury]; *Vine v. Bear Valley Ski Co.* (2004) 118 Cal.App.4th 577, 597–598, 13 Cal.Rptr.3d 370 [. . . *Knight* articulated appropriate standard of care by which liability of ski resort charged with designing and constructing defective snowboard jump should be determined].)

While the above passage from *Knight* at first glance may seem at odds with the assertion that defendants have no duty to *protect against* inherent risks, it accurately acknowledges and articulates the appropriate standard for assessing liability of proprietors and operators of sports venues whose relationship to the sport is not that of coparticipant, trainer or coach. Indeed, it is the very existence of the independent duties of such entities with respect to the design and operation of sports venues that, if renounced, *would increase* the risks inherent in a particular sport. In other words, the scope of an inherent risk of a given sport does not incorporate the additional level of risk that would be accounted for within the duty of care of proprietors and operators of sports venues to take reasonable steps to minimize those risks without changing the nature of the sport. Thus, whether the standard is stated in terms of a duty not to increase the inherent risks, or in terms of taking reasonable steps to minimize risks while not altering the sport, the import is the same. And, it goes without saying that application of such a standard propels a case out of the purview of primary assumption of the risk.

We see no reason why the logic of the above cited cases would not apply equally to the role of manufacturing, supplying or distributing defective recreational equipment. Thus, by analogy to the duty of sports venue proprietors and operators, in a case such as this where the asserted design defect is the failure to incorporate protection against a serious injury into the design of the recreational equipment, the manufacturer's duty to design nondefective products could be rephrased as a duty to take reasonable steps to minimize inherent risks without altering the nature of the sport, at least under circumstances where the risk poses the gravest danger.

3. The Trial Court Did Not Err in Refusing to Deliver Polaris's Special Instructions or Granting Nonsuit in its Favor.

The question remains whether, once the trial court determined that primary assumption of the risk did not operate as a complete bar to the Fords' recovery, the court erred in refusing to instruct that in addition to proving a defective design that harmed her, Susan had to prove that the defect increased the risk of harm beyond those risks that are a normal part of the sport. . . .

Here, the trial court determined that a finding of a design defect would in itself establish that Polaris increased the risk of harm inherent in jet skiing, and therefore instructions also requiring plaintiffs to prove that the defect increased those risks would be redundant and confusing. We agree. The inherent risk is falling into the water. The Fords' theory was that the Polaris SLH-700 watercraft was defectively designed because it did not provide a way for the passenger to hang on securely when it was not feasible to hold onto the operator. We have concluded that the asserted design defect did not attack an inherent risk of the sport because protecting against rearward ejection into the jet stream, thereby preventing orifice injury, would not alter the sport or deter vigorous participation. The very nature of the defect necessarily increased the likelihood that a passenger would fall rearward and suffer the extreme harm of orifice injuries. Thus as a matter of law the defect escalated the risk of harm beyond the inherent risk of falling into the water.

. . . Here, . . . the absence of an alternative mechanism to help avoid rearward ejection increased the risk of serious injury. And again, while Susan did not have to prove a feasible alternative design, the seat strap was cheap, feasible and provided an alternative to holding onto the operator without any meaningful alteration of the watercraft.

. . . .

[Risk-utility] criteria, stated in black-letter strict products liability terms, essentially encompass the criteria that would be assessed in determining whether a defendant breached the duty not to increase the inherent risks of a sport; or, stated in the more particular terms of the standard of care announced in *Knight* and its progeny for proprietors of sports venues, whether defendant breached the duty to pursue reasonable steps to minimize inherent risks without altering the nature of the sport. Determination of whether a particular design increased the inherent risks — or of what steps a manufacturer reasonably should take to minimize risks without altering the sport — would necessarily focus on the ingredients of a risk/benefit analysis, namely the feasibility and cost of an alternative design, the gravity and likelihood of the danger to be avoided by such alternative, and the consequences flowing from it. On this latter point, adverse consequences to the product and consumer would include changes that alter the nature of the sport or activity.

B. *The Trial Court Did Not Err in Precluding Allocation of Fault to Laura as Operator/Coparticipant and to the Nakamuras as Suppliers of the Watercraft.*

Polaris faults the trial court for rejecting a verdict form that would have permitted the jury to allocate some fault to Laura as operator/coparticipant and to the Nakamuras as the owners and suppliers of the personal watercraft. There was no basis to assign liability to them and therefore the trial court properly declined this request.

1. *Polaris Cannot Allocate Fault to Laura as Operator/Coparticipant.*

Notwithstanding that the trial court absolved Laura of liability under the doctrine of primary assumption of the risk, Polaris insists that the jury should have been allowed to assign fault to her as operator of the watercraft. Specifically, Polaris argues the jury could have apportioned some fault to her upon finding she negligently failed to relay the manufacturer's warnings to Susan and provided misleading instructions. Laura was not a tortfeasor and hence no fault could be allocated to her.

. . . .

. . . Laura prevailed on summary judgment based on primary assumption of the risk. The judgment in her favor was a judgment that as a matter of law, Laura, as operator/coparticipant, owed no duty of care to Susan. Because Laura breached no duty and committed no tort, there is no legal fault to apportion to her.

Nonetheless, Polaris urges that the nature of the assumption of risk doctrine triggers a different rule. Specifically, Polaris posits that the negligence of Laura as a coparticipant is an inherent risk that Susan assumed and damages attributable to that negligence should rest with her, not the manufacturer. Polaris's proposal would eviscerate a central principle of *Knight* and *Kahn*, namely that in the context of an active sport, the question whether defendant has a legal duty to protect plaintiff from a particular risk of harm *does not depend* on the reasonableness or unreasonableness of plaintiff's conduct in subjecting him or herself to the risks of the game, including the risk of a coparticipant's conduct. Rather, the question of duty hinges on the nature of the sport and the relationship of plaintiff and defendant to that sport. (*Knight, supra*, 3 Cal.4th at pp. 309, 315, 11 Cal.Rptr.2d 2, 834 P.2d 696; see *Kahn, supra*, 31 Cal.4th at p. 1004, 4 Cal.Rptr.3d 103, 75 P.3d 30.)

. . . Polaris has elected to engage in the industry of manufacturing recreational equipment for use in active sports. Because some risk of injury is inherent in active sports, our Supreme Court has recognized that it is inappropriate to hold coparticipants in sports activities liable for ordinary careless behavior. To do so would tend to deter vigorous participation in the sport or alter its fundamental character. (*Knight, supra*, 3 Cal.4th at pp. 315–316, 318–320, 11 Cal.Rptr.2d 2, 834 P.2d 696; see *Kahn, supra*, 31 Cal.4th at pp. 995–996, 1004, 4 Cal.Rptr.3d 103, 75 P.3d 30.) Thus liability will attach to a sports participant "only if the participant intentionally injures another player or engages in conduct that is so reckless as to be totally outside the range of the ordinary activity involved in the sport." (*Knight, supra*, 3 Cal.4th at p. 320, 11 Cal.Rptr.2d 2, 834 P.2d 696, fn. omitted.) The same general standard applies to sports instructors or coaches. (*Kahn, supra*, 31 Cal.4th at pp. 996, 1011, 4 Cal.Rptr.3d 103, 75 P.3d 30.) In the arena that Polaris operates, the standard of care imposed on coparticipants, coaches and instructors is lower than the standard for ordinary negligence. There is a sound basis for this distinction. It would be anomalous if Laura could be assigned "fault" for her actions as a jet skiing coparticipant/watercraft operator in Susan's suit against Polaris, while as a matter of sound public policy she nevertheless has no direct liability to Susan for those actions. . . .

2. The Nakamuras Had No Duty to Call Susan's Attention to the Manufacturer's Warnings.

As owners of the watercraft supplied for the family jet skiing activities on the day of the accident, the Nakamuras had a duty not to supply faulty equipment. (*Bjork v. Mason* (2000) 77 Cal.App.4th 544, 553–554, 92 Cal.Rptr.2d 49.) However, the

Nakamuras played no role in the watercraft's defective condition and thus *Bjork* does not apply. They also had a duty to warn of the watercraft's defective condition if they had, or reasonably should have had, such knowledge. (*Yamaha Motor Corp. v. Paseman* (1990) 219 Cal.App.3d 958, 968, 268 Cal.Rptr. 514.) Again, they had no knowledge of the defective condition.

Nevertheless, Polaris asserts Steve Nakamura also had a duty to call to Susan's attention the warnings on the craft and in the owner's manual. Polaris maintains that a jury could find that Steve was on notice of the "'SEVERE INJURY OR DEATH/ WEAR PROTECTIVE CLOTHING'" warning, and knowing this was Susan's first time on the watercraft should reasonably have called her attention to it. The trial court determined that the law did not impose on the owner "a manufacturer's duty to warn."

Polaris first relies on the fact that Steve Nakamura signed a warranty registration form agreeing to ask anyone who used the watercraft to read the manual and labels. However, Polaris does not explain how any representation made in the warranty registration form could create a duty to third parties.

Polaris also cites section 388 of the Restatement Second of Torts (Restatement), which provides that a person who supplies "a chattel for another to use is subject to liability . . . for physical harm caused by the use of the chattel in the manner for which . . . it is supplied, if the supplier [¶] (a) knows or has reason to know that the chattel is or is likely to be dangerous for the use for which it is supplied, and [¶] (b) has no reason to believe that those for whose use the chattel is supplied will realize its dangerous condition, and [¶] (c) fails to exercise reasonable care to inform them of its dangerous condition or of the facts which make it likely to be dangerous."

Comment k to Restatement section 388 indicates that the supplier's duty to warn is limited, as follows: "One who supplies a chattel to others to use for any purpose is under a duty to exercise reasonable care to inform them of its dangerous character in so far as it is known to him, or of facts which to his knowledge make it likely to be dangerous, if, but only if, he has no reason to expect that those for whose use the chattel is supplied will discover its condition and realize the danger involved. It is not necessary for the supplier to inform those for whose use the chattel is supplied of a condition which a mere casual looking over will disclose, unless the circumstances under which the chattel is supplied are such as to make it likely that even so casual an inspection will not be made."

Here, the warning about the potential for orifice injuries and the need to wear protective clothing appeared on the body of the watercraft and in the owner's manual. There were two warning labels on the craft itself. One was located on the rear of the craft above the boarding platform where riders could board, and one was located in the front under the handlebars. The Nakamuras had not removed or altered the on-craft decals. Although Susan stepped onto the craft from the side and did not board from the rear, there were no special conditions that would have deterred her from casually taking notice of the labels as she approached and looked around the craft.

Oftentimes, as was the case here, those who supply the watercraft are also participating in the sport. The Nakamuras did not lend the watercraft to someone else to use and operate. In such a situation they might have been inclined to call the borrower's attention to the owner's manual. Instead, Laura and Susan went out on the craft together to have a good time. Polaris is attempting to foist onto suppliers/coparticipants the extra job of being the company's representative with the responsibility of nudging every passenger to read the label and owner's manual. This is unrealistic given the nature of the activity and the role of suppliers/coparticipants to that activity. As between the supplier/coparticipant and the manufacturer of the watercraft, the Nakamuras should be able to rely on the manufacturer's placement, design and content of warning labels to communicate its safety concerns to passengers. By not altering or removing the label, and in the absence of any special conditions, including any mental or physical limitations presented by the passenger, the supplier/coparticipant has no further duty with respect to the manufacturer warnings.

III. DISPOSITION

The judgment is affirmed.

Problem

N decides to lay a new tile floor, and purchases a can of glue with which to fasten the tiles to the floor. The can sets forth a warning, in large letters, to the effect that the product will give off toxic fumes, and should only be used in a well-ventilated location or with a fan to dissipate the fumes. N is laying the tile floor in the bathroom during the winter. Concerned about the risk that the pipes will freeze, N does not open the windows or ventilate the bathroom. N is injured by the fumes and sues the manufacturer of the glue. Assume that the warning on the can is adequate. N contends that the glue is defective because it could have been made with a less toxic substance which would have reduced the risk of injury. Can this argument prevail? What defenses will the manufacturer raise?

D. Preemption

Federal statutory preemption can be an important defense in products liability lawsuits. This is a constitutional doctrine, based on the U.S. Constitution's Supremacy Clause, which states that when federal and state laws are in conflict, federal law must control and therefore contrary state law is unenforceable. Under preemption doctrine, the defendant argues that it cannot be held liable under state tort law because it complied with the federal regulatory standards applicable to the particular aspect of whatever product or industry is involved. Not all federal standards necessarily preempt state tort law—it depends on the degree to which the laws conflict and on the intentions of Congress in enacting the federal statute. When this defense arises, the court must decide whether the federal standards cover the claimed defect sufficiently to warrant dismissing the state tort suit. Most preemption cases involve prescription pharmaceuticals, medical devices, cigarettes, and automobiles.

Preemption is an extraordinarily difficult and complex area of the law. For those who want to investigate it more fully, see *Wyeth v. Levine*, 555 U.S. 555 (2009), and *PLIVA, Inc. v. Mensing*, 564 U.S. 604 (2011), both of which involved failures to warn in medical contexts. In *Wyeth*, the Court decided that the failure to warn lawsuit was not preempted by federal regulations. In *PLIVA*, the Court decided that the failure to warn lawsuit was preempted by federal regulations. This subject tends to be covered in courses on constitutional law, health law, and regulation.

E. Immunities and Defenses Based Upon the Status of the Defendant

A variety of defenses have nothing to do with the conduct of the parties, but rather depend upon the nature of the defendant, the relationship between the plaintiff and the defendant, or particular statutory grants of immunity. Many traditional common-law immunities, such as charitable immunity and spousal immunity, have been abolished as antiquated and unnecessary to serve any valuable goal. Others, such as the tort immunity of employers in workplace injury suits by employees, reflect the fact that an alternative system of compensation (workers' compensation) has been devised as a replacement for tort liability. Still others, such as the immunity of judges and prosecutors for their official duties, reflect public policy judgments that certain individuals must be able to make official decisions without fear of potential liability if they make a mistake. Sovereign immunity protects governments from tort liability; it has often been either eliminated or reduced by statute, particularly at the state and local levels. At the federal level, potential tort liability is determined under the Federal Tort Claims Act, 28 U.S.C. § 1346(b).

While immunity defenses can figure prominently in some tort cases, they often function independently of tort law itself and thus lie beyond the scope of this casebook.

F. Statutes of Limitation and Repose

Like virtually all legal claims, tort claims are generally subject to statutes of limitation and repose.

Statutes of limitation generally require that claims of a particular sort must be filed in court within a particular time frame. In the case of tort claims, the time frame is typically calculated from the time that the tort was committed. Most jurisdictions, however, also recognize that in some instances, the statute of limitation may be "tolled"—that is, held in abeyance—in special circumstances. One such circumstance is where the victim is a minor; in that case, the statute may be tolled until the victim reaches majority and can decide for him- or herself whether or not to bring suit. Another, more complicated, circumstance known as the "discovery rule" arises when the statute is tolled until the victim learns of the existence of the tort. This can often be important in cases such as fraud, where the fact of the tort may have been deliberately hidden from detection by the tortfeasor. It can also be important in cases such as DES or asbestos litigation, where the ultimate injury to the victim does not arise until many years after the tortious exposure to a dangerous product.

In the distant past, when statutes of limitation were born, there was no particular problem about setting a time limit within which the plaintiff had to file his or her suit. The horse ran over a pedestrian: the injury was known from the start, and the time limit placed no burden on the plaintiff. The same sort of clarity exists today in most auto accidents. But as the relationships between people grew more complex, it grew increasingly possible that an injury might be inflicted, and the plaintiff not know about it for years. One classic example of this is a medical operation where the surgeon leaves a sponge behind in the patient. If the limitations period begins to run on the date of the surgery, and if the patient does not have any ill effects for years, it is possible that the limitations period would run out before the plaintiff has found out about the negligent act of the surgeon. The discovery rule was developed in response to such cases, to protect the plaintiff from being cut off from access to the courts before he or she even knows such access is needed.

In contrast to statutes of limitation, statutes of repose set an absolute time limit within which a suit must be filed. They override the discovery rule and other doctrines that might otherwise toll the limitation period. Under a statute of repose, the fact that the infliction of the injury was unknown until after the repose period has run will not protect the plaintiff. Some states have enacted statutes of repose that set outside liability limits (typically ten or fifteen years) for certain kinds of product liability claims.

Once again, statutes of limitation or repose can figure prominently in tort actions, but they are beyond the scope of this casebook.

Chapter 14

Defamation

Problem

Bertha edits a newsletter that she posts on her website and sends free by email to 50 families in Pigskin County. All the families have children who play on the public Pigskin High School football team. In her newsletter (called *The Squeeeel*), Bertha wrote in regard to the Friday night football game that "the coach was a 'weenie.'" Coach has come to you for advice. He wants to know whether he can sue Bertha for defamation, and if so with what prospects for success. In addition to being the coach of the Pigskin H.S. football team, he ran for mayor of Pigskin County five years ago.

Libel and slander have their roots in the middle ages and England's Star Chamber, where they were used to protect the Crown and government from criticism. Both are concerned with protection from injury to reputation by false or misleading statements. Until 1964, defamation was a very technical tort dealing with the subtle issues involved in whether the statement was "libel" or "slander," what damages must be shown and what privileges were available as defenses. Roughly, libel applied to "published" defamation, while slander applied to spoken defamation. Although technically an intentional tort, defamation rested effectively on strict liability since publication or utterance of the defamatory statement itself proved intent. Damages, often "presumed," were determined by the whim of the jury. In many jurisdictions, truth of the statements in question was an affirmative defense that had to be proved by the defendant.

The Supreme Court's decision in *New York Times v. Sullivan*, 376 U.S. 254 (1964), fundamentally changed the nature of defamation. The Court held that actions for defamation are subject to constitutional limitation under the First Amendment's protections for freedom of speech and press. The issues shifted to whether the plaintiff was a public official or a public figure and whether "actual malice," the constitutionally required standard for liability in public official and public figure cases, had been shown. Different standards have developed for private persons. The Court also held that plaintiffs must prove the falsehood of the statements in question as part of their case, and that they must prove "actual damages." The Court has extended analogous constitutional limitations to actions for "false light" invasions of privacy and to actions for infliction of emotional distress, when they are based on constitutionally protected speech or publication. *See Time, Inc. v. Hill*, 385 U.S. 374 (1967); *Hustler Magazine, Inc. v. Falwell*, 485 U.S. 46 (1988), *supra*. All these changes have been driven by the importance of free speech and the media in the United States. Collectively they have effectively transformed defamation into a tort-based branch of federal constitutional law.

The chapter will reflect these changes in defamation doctrine. We will first consider the historic torts of libel and slander. Then we will view some of the changes wrought by the Supreme Court after 1964.

A. What Constitutes a Defamatory Statement?

Romaine v. Kallinger

Supreme Court of New Jersey, 1988
537 A.2d 284

HANDLER, J.

More than ten years ago Joseph Kallinger and his son went on a criminal rampage in Pennsylvania and New Jersey. The offenses were vicious, involving physical threats and sexual abuse of victims during the course of robberies of suburban homes. Kallinger murdered his victims on three occasions. In 1983, approximately eight years after Kallinger and his son had been apprehended, the defendant Simon & Schuster Publishing Inc. published a book entitled "The Shoemaker," written by the defendant Flora Rheta Schreiber, depicting the life and crimes of Joseph Kallinger. The book gave rise to this litigation.

The plaintiffs . . . were victims of Kallinger, whose criminal acts against them resulted in the murder of a young woman, Maria Fasching. Plaintiffs sued the defendants Kallinger, Elizabeth Kallinger, his wife, Schreiber, Simon & Schuster, and Paul J. Giblin, claiming to have been legally injured by defamatory and offensively intrusive statements relating to these crimes contained in "The Shoemaker." Plaintiffs sought in separate counts the award of compensatory and punitive damages based respectively on libel and invasion of privacy by being cast in a false light; they also claimed that their privacy had been invaded through the unreasonable publication of private facts. . . .

Defendants Simon & Schuster and Schreiber filed motions for summary judgment seeking dismissal of the action. . . . The trial court granted defendants' motion for summary judgment with respect to the defamation and privacy claims. . . .

Plaintiffs filed a notice of appeal. . . .

I

The factual context of this litigation is important. Ms. Schreiber, the author of "The Shoemaker," is a professor at the City University of New York, John Jay College of Criminal Justice. . . .

According to defendants, Professor Schreiber's work is an in-depth study of the psychological make-up of a killer. Specifically, the book explores the relationship between the abuse suffered by Kallinger as a child and the psychotic behavior that led to his criminal acts. *"The Shoemaker"* received a significant amount of critical praise and Schreiber was named "Author of the Year" by the American Society of Journalists and Authors in 1985 in recognition of her work.

The complaint focuses on a chapter of "The Shoemaker" called "The Hunting Knife." The chapter . . . describes the murder of Maria Fasching on January 8, 1975, in Leonia, New Jersey. The chapter relates that Kallinger and his son broke into the home of Mr. and Mrs. DeWitt Romaine. . . . While this was occurring, Maria Fasching, a friend of one of the victims, the plaintiff Randi Romaine, came into the house. She was also captured by Kallinger. He directed Ms. Fasching, a nurse, to perform an act of sexual mutilation on plaintiff Frank Welby, who was tied up and helpless. When she refused to do so, he killed her by slashing her throat several times. . . .

On the second page of "The Hunting Knife" chapter this passage appears relating the circumstances leading up to Maria Fasching's visit to the Romaine house:

> . . . .
>
> A militant women's libber, Maria Fasching was famous among her friends for her battles on behalf of the weak and downtrodden. She would always try to rescue someone a bully had attacked, and she could not tolerate racists.
>
> Maria thought of herself as a "free spirit." She resisted anything that she considered a restriction on her freedom. She cared for cats that had been hit by cars and for birds with broken wings.
>
> Today, Maria Fasching was on the four-to-midnight shift at Hackensack Hospital, and she wore her nurse's uniform under her coat. In the morning Maria's friend Randi Romaine, who lived in the stucco house, had called Maria and asked her to drop over for coffee. The two women had not seen each other for a long time, for, between hospital duties and preparations for her wedding, Maria's schedule was full.
>
> At first Maria said that she couldn't visit because she had to go to a wake. The wake, however, was only for an acquaintance. Randi and her twin sister, Retta, had been Maria's friends since they were all in the first grade. Besides, Maria was eager for news from Randi about a junkie they both knew who was doing time in prison. . . .

According to plaintiffs, one sentence in the passage falsely depicts the reason for Ms. Fasching's visit: "Besides, Maria was eager for news from Randi about a junkie they both knew who was doing time in prison." This sentence, it is claimed, is defamatory as a matter of law and constitutes a false-light invasion of privacy.[1] The

---

1. The trial court dismissed the defamation claims of plaintiffs Edwin Wiseman, Retta Romaine Welby, and Frank Welby, finding that the statement did not concern these individuals. Plaintiffs

chapter's general narration of the criminal events, from which this passage is taken, is in turn the basis for plaintiffs' invasion of privacy by unreasonable publication of private facts claim.

II

Plaintiff Randi Romaine asserts that the particular sentence is defamatory as a matter of law, or alternatively, that the statement's defamatory content was at least a question for the jury. She claims this sentence falsely accuses her of criminality or associations with criminals. Plaintiff also contends that the false accusation was particularly damaging because it injured Ms. Romaine's professional reputation as a drug counsellor and a social worker, interfering with her ability to obtain future employment.

A defamatory statement is one that is false and "injurious to the reputation of another" or exposes another person to "hatred, contempt or ridicule" or subjects another person to "a loss of the good will and confidence" in which he or she is held by others. *Leers v. Green*, 24 N.J. 239, 251 (1957); *see* W. Keeton, D. Dobbs, R. Keeton & D. Owen, Prosser and Keeton on the Law of Torts, para. III at 773–78 (5th ed. 1984); *see also* Restatement (Second) of Torts § 559 (1977) (a defamatory communication is one that "tends so to harm the reputation of another so as to lower him in the estimation of the community or to deter third persons from associating or dealing with him.").

The threshold issue in any defamation case is whether the statement at issue is reasonably susceptible of a defamatory meaning. *Kotlikoff v. The Community News*, 89 N.J. 62, 67 (1982); *Mosler v. Whelan*, 28 N.J. 397, 404 (1958). This question is one to be decided first by the court. In making this determination, the court must evaluate the language in question "according to the fair and natural meaning which will be given it by reasonable persons of ordinary intelligence." In assessing the language, the court must view the publication as a whole and consider particularly the context in which the statement appears.

If a published statement is susceptible of one meaning only, and that meaning is defamatory, the statement is libelous as a matter of law. *See Mosler v. Whelan, supra*, 28 N.J. at 40; *Herrmann v. Newark Morning Ledger Co., supra*, 48 N.J. Super, at 430. Conversely, if the statement is susceptible of only a non-defamatory meaning, it cannot be considered libelous, justifying dismissal of the action. *See Pierce v. Capital Cities Communications Inc.*, 576 F.2d 495, 501–04 (3d Cir.) (applying Pennsylvania law), *cert. denied*, 439 U.S. 861, 99 S. Ct. 181, 58 L. Ed. 2d 170 (1978); *Cibenko v. Worth Publishers, supra*, 510 F. Supp. at 764–65. However, in cases where the statement is capable of being assigned more than one meaning, one of which is defamatory and

---

Wiseman, Welby, and Welby conceded before the Appellate Division that this ruling was correct, hence the only remaining defamation claim is that of Randi Romaine. All plaintiffs, however, continue to press the false-light invasion of privacy claim caused by this same statement.

another not, the question of whether its content is defamatory is one that must be resolved by the trier of fact.

Certain kinds of statements denote such defamatory meaning that they are considered defamatory as a matter of law. A prime example is the false attribution of criminality. *See Hoagburg v. Harrah's Marina Hotel Casino*, 585 F.Supp. 1167, 1170 (D.N.J.1984); *Karnell v. Campbell, supra*, 206 N.J. Super. at 88–89; *cf. Lawrence v. Bauer Publishing & Printing Ltd., supra*, 89 N.J. at 459–60 (statement that plaintiff might be charged with criminal conduct defamatory as a matter of law). Relying essentially on this example of defamation, plaintiff Randi Romaine contends in this case that the published offending statement must be considered libelous *per se.* According to Ms. Romaine, the sentence has only a defamatory meaning, in that it accuses her of having engaged in criminal conduct or having associated with criminals relating to drugs.

The trial court concluded, and the Appellate Division agreed, that only the most contorted reading of the offending language could lead to the conclusion that it accuses plaintiff of illegal drug use or criminal associations. We concur in the determinations of the courts below. "[A]ccording to the fair and natural meaning which will be given [this statement] by reasonable persons of ordinary intelligence," *Herrmann v. Newark Morning Ledger Co., supra*, 48 N.J. Super, at 431, it does not attribute any kind of criminality to plaintiff. A reasonable and fair understanding of the statement simply does not yield an interpretation that the plaintiff was or had been in illegal possession of drugs or otherwise engaging in any illegal drug-related activity. . . .

At most, the sentence can be read to imply that plaintiff knew a junkie. Even if we assume that a commonly accepted and well-understood meaning of the term "junkie" is "a narcotics peddler or addict," Webster's Third New International Dictionary 1227 (1981), *see also* Dictionary of American Slang 300 (2d ed. 1975) (defining "junkie" as a "drug addict"), the statement still does not suggest either direct or indirect involvement by plaintiff herself in any criminal drug-related activities. Absent exceptional circumstances, the mere allegation that plaintiff knows a criminal is not defamatory as a matter of law. . . .

Beyond the language itself, we are satisfied that the statement in its contextual setting cannot fairly and reasonably be invested with any defamatory meaning. Maria Fasching, we note, is described in the chapter as a person who had compassion for others and who would care for less fortunate persons. The reasonable meaning of the critical sentence that is implied from this context is that Ms. Fasching's interest in the "junkie" stemmed from sympathy and compassion, not from any predilection toward or involvement in criminal drug activity. As extended to Randi Romaine, the only fair inference to be drawn from the larger context is that Ms. Romaine shared her friend's feelings, attitudes and interests, and that her own interest in the junkie was similar to that of Ms. Fasching's.

We note the further contention that this statement had a defamatory meaning because it implied that the only reason for Ms. Fasching's visit to the Romaine home was her "interest" in news about a "junkie." A review of the full text, however, indicates that there were several reasons for the visit, only one of which was Ms. Fasching's interest in the "junkie." The lower courts soundly rejected this contention.

We conclude that the statement is not defamatory as a matter of law and accordingly uphold the ruling of the lower court on this point.

. . . .

—————

1. Where a published statement is defamatory on its face, it is sometimes called libel *per se*. Where the published statement is capable of more than one meaning, it is sometimes called libel *per quod* and special damages must be shown. Special damages will be considered *infra. Gertz v. Robert Welch, infra*, by requiring the showing of actual damages and fault, reduces the importance of special damages.

2. In *Belli v. Orlando Daily Newspapers*, 389 F.2d 579 (5th Cir. 1967), *cert. denied*, 393 U.S. 825 (1968), the court defined libel as "a false and unprivileged publication by letter . . . which exposes a person to distrust, hatred, contempt, ridicule . . . or which has a tendency to injure such person in his office, occupation, business, or employment." The court held: "It is for the court in the first instance to determine whether the words are reasonably capable of a particular interpretation . . . it is then for the jury to say whether they were in fact understood as defamatory. If the language used is open to two meanings . . . it is for the jury to determine whether the defamatory sense was the one conveyed."

Matherson v. Marchello

Supreme Court of New York, Appellate Division, 1984
473 N.Y.S.2d 998

TITONE, JUSTICE presiding

On October 28, 1980, radio station WBAB conducted an interview with the members of a singing group called "The Good Rats". Following a commercial which advertised a Halloween party at an establishment known as "OBI", a discussion ensued in which various members of the group explained that they are no longer permitted to play at OBI South because:

"Good Rat #1:   Well, you know, we had that law suit with Mr. Matherson.

"A Good Rat: And we used to fool around with his wife.

"Good Rat #1:   And we won.

"A Good Rat: One of us used to fool around with his wife. He wasn't into that too much.

"D.J.:   Oh yea.

"Good Rat #1:   (interrupted and joined by another Good Rat) We used to start off our gigs over there with the National Anthem, and he was very upset about that, now all of a sudden he's very patriotic and he's using it in his commercials.

"A Good Rat: I don't think it was his wife that he got so upset about, I think it was when somebody started messing round with his boyfriend that he really freaked out. Really. (Laughter) That did it man."

Plaintiffs, who are husband and wife, subsequently commenced this action against "The Good Rats" (as individuals and against their record company), alleging that the words "we used to fool around with his wife" and "I don't think it was his wife that he got upset about, I think it was when somebody started messing around with his boyfriend that he really freaked out," were defamatory. They seek compensatory and punitive damages for humiliation, mental anguish, loss of reputation and injury to their marital relationship as well as for the loss of customers, business opportunities and good will allegedly suffered by Mr. Matherson. . . .

Preliminarily, we observe that if special damages are a necessary ingredient of plaintiffs' cause of action, Special Term properly found the allegations of the complaint to be deficient.

Special damages consist of "the loss of something having economic or pecuniary value" (Restatement, Torts 2d, § 575, Comment *b*) which "must flow directly from the injury to reputation caused by the defamation; not from the effects of defamation" (Sack, Libel, Slander, and Related Problems, § VII.2.2, 345–346; see, also, 1 Harper and James, The Law of Torts, § 5.14) and it is settled law that they must be fully and accurately identified "with sufficient particularity to identify actual losses" (*Lincoln First Bank v. Siegel*, 60 A.D.2d 270, 280). When loss of business is claimed, the persons who ceased to be customers must be named and the losses itemized (*Reporters' Assn. v. Sun Print. & Pub. Assn.*, 186 N.Y. 437; *Continental Air Ticketing Agency v. Empire Int. Travel*, 51 A.D.2d 104, 108). "Round figures" or a general allegation of a dollar amount as special damages do not suffice (*Drug Research Corp. v. Curtis Pub. Co.*, 7 N.Y.2d 435, 440; *Continental Air Ticketing Agency v. Empire Int. Travel*, *supra*, p. 108). Consequently, plaintiffs' nonspecific conclusory allegations do not meet the stringent requirements imposed for pleading special damages (*Zausner v. Fotochrome*, 18 A.D.2d 649; Fuchsberg, 9 Encyclopedia of N.Y. Law, Damages, § 243).

We must, therefore, determine whether an allegation of special damages is necessary. In large measure, this turns on which branch of the law of defamation is involved. As a result of historical accident, which, though not sensibly defensible today, is so well settled as to be beyond our ability to uproot it (*Ostrowe v. Lee*, 256 N.Y. 36, 39), there is a schism between the law governing slander and the law governing libel (see Restatement, Torts 2d, § 568, Comment *b*; see, also, *Gurtler v. Union Parts Mfg. Co.*, 1 N.Y.2d 5; 2 N.Y. PJI 84 [1983 Supp]).[1]

---

1. The historical development is traced in Franklin, *Cases and Materials on Tort Law and Alternatives* (pp. 884–886), and Veeder, *The History and Theory of the Law of Defamation* (3 Col. L. Rev.

A plaintiff suing in slander must plead special damages unless the defamation falls into any one of four per se categories (see Prosser, Torts [4th ed], § 112, pp. 751–760; Restatement, Torts 2d, § 570). Those categories consist of allegations (1) that the plaintiff committed a crime, (2) that tend to injure the plaintiff in his or her trade, business or profession, (3) that plaintiff has contracted a loathsome disease, and (4) that impute unchastity to a woman.[2]

The exceptions were established apparently for no other reason than a recognition that by their nature the accusations encompassed therein would be likely to cause material damage (Prosser, Torts [4th ed], § 112, p. 754).

On the other hand, a plaintiff suing in libel need not plead or prove special damages if the defamatory statement "'tends to expose the plaintiff to public contempt, ridicule, aversion or disgrace, or induce an evil opinion of him in the minds of right-thinking persons, and to deprive him of their friendly intercourse in society.'"[3] Thus,

---

546; 4 Col. L. Rev 33). The distinction has, moreover, not gone unchallenged. As early as 1812, a defendant urged that a libel read by one person should not be treated more harshly than a slander spoken to hundreds in a crowd. While the Judge conceded the merits of the argument, he refused to overturn the firmly rooted contrary precedents (Thorley v. Lord Kerry, 128 Eng. Rep. 367; see 1 Harper and James, The Law of Torts, § 5.9, p 372; Comment, *The Pre-Thorley v. Kerry Case Law of The Libel-Slander Distinction*, 23 U Chi. L. Rev 132).

2. The first three categories were established relatively early. The fourth is of more recent vintage, having first been put into effect in England by the Slander of Women Act of 1891 (54 & 55 Viet, ch 51); similar statutory additions to the common law were made in this country (e.g., Civil Rights Law, § 77, derived from L 1871, ch 219, § 1; see, generally, 1 Harper and James, The Law of Torts, §§ 5.10–5.13; Prosser, Torts [4th ed], pp. 754–760). We do not view these categories as fixed or rigid and, in appropriate circumstances, a new category may be judicially established (see, e.g., Privitera v. Town of Phelps, 79 A.D.2d 1, 3; 2 N.Y. PJI 85–86, 101–102 [1983 Supp], listing the imputation of homosexual behavior as a separate category of per se slander; contra, Stein v. Trager, 36 Misc. 2d 227).

3. We have avoided the use of the terms libel per se and libel per quod because, as explained in this footnote, the cases and commentators are divided on the question of whether any meaningful distinction exists between the two.

It is clear that when the defamatory import is apparent from the face of the publication itself without resort to any other source, the libel, often referred to as libel per se, is actionable without proof of special harm (2 NY PJI 86 [1983 Supp]). Libel per quod, on the other hand, has been traditionally defined as an encompassing libel in which the defamatory import can only be ascertained by reference to facts not set forth in the publication (Prosser, Libel Per Quod, 46 Va. L. Rev. 839).

In the view of some writers, libel per quod does not exist in New York. Under their reasoning, special harm is a necessary component only under the so-called "single instance" rule, i.e., where the statement charges the plaintiff with a single dereliction in connection with his or her trade or profession (*see* Lyons v. New Amer. Lib., 78 A.D.2d 723, app withdrawn 53 N.Y.2d 704). They read Hinsdale v. Orange County Pub. (17 N.Y.2d 284) as establishing that all other libel, whether defamatory on its face or by extrinsic fact, is actionable without proof of special harm (see Prosser, Torts [4th ed], § 112, p 762; 2 N.Y. PJI 706–707).

Other commentators decline to interpret Hinsdale (*supra*) as obliterating the special harm requirements in extrinsic fact cases, viewing the pleading and proof of special damages as necessary both under the "single instance" rule and in extrinsic fact cases unless, with respect to extrinsic fact cases, it is "reasonably likely" that the plaintiff's reputation will be impaired among readers who are aware of the extrinsic facts (2 N.Y. PJI 95–96 [1983 Supp]; see, e.g., Samore, *New York Libel Per Quod: Enigma Still?*, 31 Albany L. Rev. 250).

unlike the law of slander, in the law of libel the existence of damage is conclusively presumed from the publication itself and a plaintiff may rely on general damages (compare Restatement, Torts 2d, §569 with §570; but see Excessiveness or Inadequacy of Damages for Defamation, Ann., 35 A.L.R.2d 218, which suggests, by its scheme of classification, how relatively few cases of libel actually do arise which are not more or less easily referrable to the categories of slander per se).

On the question of whether the allegedly defamatory statements are actionable, our scope of review is limited. "If the contested statements are reasonably susceptible of a defamatory connotation, then 'it becomes the jury's function to say whether that was the sense in which the words were likely to be understood by the ordinary and average reader'"(*James v. Gannett Co.* 40 N.Y.2d 415, 419, quoting *Mencher v. Chesley*, 297 N.Y. 94, 100; *cf. Gurda v. Orange County Pub. Div.*, 81 A.D.2d 120, 130 [dissenting opn of MOLLEN, P.J., and TITONE, J.], *revd* 56 N.Y.2d 705 on dissent at App. Div.). We must accord the words their natural meaning and we cannot strain to interpret them in their mildest and most inoffensive sense in order to render them nondefamatory (e.g., *November v. Time Inc.*, 13 N.Y.2d 175, 178–179; *Schermerhorn v. Rosenberg*, 73 A.D.2d 276, 283–284; *Nowark v. Maguire*, 22 A.D.2d 901). Unless we can say, as a matter of law, that the statements could not have had a defamatory connotation, it is for the jury to decide whether or not they did (*Schermerhorn v. Rosenberg, supra; Greenberg v. CBS Inc.*, 69 A.D.2d 693).

Taken in the context of a rock and roll station's interview with musicians, and taking note of contemporary usage, we have no difficulty in concluding that the words "fooling around with his wife" could have been interpreted by listeners to mean that Mrs. Matherson was having an affair with one of the defendants. Such charges are clearly libelous on their face, thus obviating any need to prove special damages (see Civil Rights Law, §77; *James v Gannett Co.*, supra, p 419). While it may be possible to construe the words in an inoffensive manner, since they are susceptible of a defamatory connotation, the cause of action should stand (*cf. Schermerhorn v. Rosenberg, supra; Greenberg v. CBS Inc., supra; Jordon v. Lewis*, 20 A.D.2d 773, 774).

The second comment—"I don't think it was his wife that he got upset about, I think it was when somebody started messing around with his boyfriend that he really freaked out"—presents a far more subtle and difficult question (see Imputation of Homosexuality as Defamation, Ann., 3 A.L.R. 4th 752). It is plaintiffs' contention that this statement constitutes an imputation of homosexuality which should be recognized as defamatory. Defendants, on the other hand, basically do not deny that such reading is plausible. Rather, they claim that many public officials have acknowledged their homosexuality and, therefore, no social stigma may be attached to such an allegation. We are constrained to reject defendants' position at this point in time.

The cases simply state that if a libel is not per se, a plaintiff must plead and prove special damages as part of the prima facie case, without drawing a line of demarcation between them. Since neither the single instance rule nor extrinsic fact libel is involved, we have no opportunity to resolve the conflict.

It cannot be said that social opprobrium of homosexuality does not remain with us today. Rightly or wrongly, many individuals still view homosexuality as immoral (*see Newsweek*, Aug. 8, 1983, p. 33, containing the results of a Gallup poll; *cf. People v. Onofre*, 51 N.Y.2d 476, 488, n. 3, *cert. den*, 451 U.S. 987). Legal sanctions imposed upon homosexuals in areas ranging from immigration (*Matter of Longstaff*, 716 F.2d 1439) to military service (*Watkins v. United States Army*, 721 F.2d 687) have recently been reaffirmed despite the concurring Judge's observation in *Watkins* (p. 691) that it "demonstrates a callous disregard for the progress American law and society have made toward acknowledging that an individual's choice of life style is not the concern of government, but a fundamental aspect of personal liberty."

In short, despite the fact that an increasing number of homosexuals are publicly expressing satisfaction and even pride in their status, the potential and probable harm of a false charge of homosexuality, in terms of social and economic impact, cannot be ignored. Thus, on the facts of this case, where the plaintiffs are husband and wife, we find, given the narrow scope of review, that the imputation of homosexuality is "reasonably susceptible of a defamatory connotation" (*James v. Gannett Co.*, 40 N.Y.2d 415, 419, *supra*) and is actionable without proof of special damages (*cf. Nowark v. Maguire*, 22 AD2d 901, *supra*).

For these reasons, the order should be reversed insofar as appealed from, with costs, the defendants' motion to dismiss should be denied and the complaint should be reinstated.

––––––––––

1. Note the court's treatment of defamation, libel, slander, slander *per se*, and libel *per quod*.

2. Is it slander *per se* to call a secretary a coward? What about calling a soldier a coward?

3. Is it slander *per se* to say that someone has AIDS? What about mono?

4. The special damage rule arose from *Terwilliger v. Wands*, 17 N.Y. 54 (1858), which held that the plaintiff could not recover for slander because his only damage was to his health and ability to work. Neither mental nor physical injury constitutes special damage. Special damages are essentially a loss of business.

5. Can a statue be defamatory? What test do you apply?

6. In *Agnant v. Shakur*, 30 F. Supp. 2d 420 (S.D.N.Y. 1998), the plaintiff alleged that Tupac Shakur's rap song had libeled him. The district court held for the defendant's estate that the statement the plaintiff had worked as a federal undercover informant was not defamatory, the lyrics did not constitute libel *per se*, and plaintiff failed to plead and prove special damages.

7. If the statement is not defamatory on its face, plaintiff must plead extrinsic facts in order to prove the defamatory meaning of the statement. See *Barter v. Wilson*, 512 N.E.2d 816 (Ill. App. Ct. 1987), where defendant said in regard to developer's application for a permit, "the fix was in." The court held that the reasonable interpretation of the statement was not defamatory.

8. In deciding whether a statement is defamatory, who is the relevant public to consider? Should a court take into consideration widely shared attitudes, even if they are unfair or prejudiced? What if a defendant writes that the plaintiff is gay, or that the plaintiff reported being the victim of a crime? In *Stern v. Cosby*, 645 F. Supp. 2d 258 (S.D.N.Y. 2009), in a defamation suit brought by the attorney of controversial television personality Anna Nicole Smith, the court refused to follow *Matherson's* conclusion that imputation of homosexuality can be defamatory. Among other factors, the court reasoned that the conclusion was questionable after the Supreme Court's decision in *Lawrence v. Texas*, 539 U.S. 558 (2003), establishing constitutional protection for same-sex intimate relations.

9. For a gender-neutral approach, perhaps "serious sexual misconduct" should replace "chastity." *See Nazeri v. Missouri Valley College*, 860 S.W.2d 303 (Mo. 1993).

10. The defamatory statement must be published. This is a term of art and means that the statement must be communicated to someone other than the plaintiff. In *Economopoulos v. A. G. Pollard Co.*, 218 Mass. 294, 105 N.E. 896 (1914), liability failed because although the statement was communicated to a third party, that person did not understand English.

11. Dictating a letter to a secretary is often considered to be a publication. *Rickbeil v. Grafton Deaconess Hosp*, 74 N.D. 525, 23 N.W.2d 247 (1946). Sending the defamatory statement on a postcard is presumed to be publication. *Ostro v. Safir*, 165 Misc. 647, 1 N.Y.S.2d 377 (Sup. Ct. 1937). Sending a sealed letter to the plaintiff, however, is not a publication. *Barnes v. Clayton House Motel*, 435 S.W.2d 616 (Tex. Civ. App. 1968). What forms of electronic communication involve a publication?

B. The Defamatory Statement Must Be Understood to Have Been Made "Of and Concerning" the Plaintiff

Neiman-Marcus Co. v. Lait

United States District Court for the Southern District of New York, 1952
13 F.R.D. 311

IRVING R. KAUFMAN, DISTRICT JUDGE

The defendants are authors of a book entitled "U.S.A. Confidential." The plaintiffs are the Neiman-Marcus Company, a Texas corporation operating a department store at Dallas, Texas, and three groups of its employees. They allege that the following matter libeled and defamed them:

. . . .

"He [Stanley Marcus, president of plaintiff Neiman-Marcus Company] may not know that some Neiman models are call girls—the top babes in town. The guy who escorts one feels in the same league with the playboys who took out Ziegfeld's glorified. Price, a hundred bucks a night."

"The salesgirls are good, too—pretty, and often much cheaper—twenty bucks on the average. They're more fun, too, not as snooty as the models. We got this confidential, from a Dallas wolf."

"Neiman-Marcus also contributes to the improvement of the local breed when it imports New York models to make a flash at style shows. These girls are the cream of the crop. Oil millionaires toss around thousand-dollar bills for a chance to take them out."

"Neiman's was a women's specialty shop until the old biddies who patronized it decided their husbands should get class, too. So Neiman's put in a men's store. Well, you should see what happened."

"Houston is faced with a serious homosexual problem. It is not as evident as Dallas', because there are no expensive imported faggots in town like those in the Neiman-Marcus set." . . .

The individual plaintiffs . . . state that they were employed by the Neiman-Marcus Company at the time the alleged libel was published and that the groups of individual plaintiffs are composed as follows:

(1) Nine individual models who constitute the entire group of models at the time of the publication . . . ;

(2) Fifteen salesmen of a total of twenty-five suing on their own behalf and on behalf of the others pursuant to Rule 23(a)(3) of the Federal Rules of Civil Procedure . . . ;

(3) Thirty saleswomen of a total of 382 suing on their own behalf and on behalf of the others . . .

The first part of defendants' motion is to dismiss the amended complaint as to the salesmen and saleswomen for failure to state a cause of action for libel since, it is alleged, no ascertainable person is identified by the words complained of.

. . . .

An examination of the case and text law of libel reveals that the following propositions are rather widely accepted:

(1) Where the group or class libeled is large, none can sue even though the language used is inclusive.

(2) Where the group or class libeled is small, and each and every member of the group or class is referred to, then any individual member can sue.

Conflict arises when the publication complained of libels *some* or *less than all* of a designated small group. Some courts say no cause of action exists in any individual of the group. Other courts in other states would apparently allow such an action.

. . . .

The Court of Appeals for this Circuit has referred to the Restatement of Torts for the "general law." *Mattox v. News Syndicate Co., supra*, 176 F.2d at page 901. If we do so in this instance, we find that Illustration 2 of § 564, Comment (c) reads as follows:

> "A newspaper publishes the statement that some member of B's household has committed murder. In the absence of any circumstances indicating that some particular member of B's household was referred to, the newspaper has defamed each member of B's household."

Thus the Restatement of Torts would authorize suit by each member of a small group where the defamatory publication refers to but a portion of the group. This result seems to find support in logic and justice, as well as the case law mentioned above. See Riesman, *Group Libel*, 42 Col. Law Review 727, 768 (1942). An imputation of gross immorality to *some* of a small group casts suspicion upon all, where no attempt is made to exclude the innocent.[1]

Applying the above principles to the case at bar, it is the opinion of this Court that the plaintiff salesmen, of whom it is alleged that "most . . . are fairies" have a cause of action in New York and most likely other states . . . . Defendants' motion to dismiss as to the salesmen for failure to state a claim upon which relief can be granted is denied.

The plaintiff saleswomen are in a different category. The alleged defamatory statement in defendants' book speaks of the saleswomen generally. While it does not use the word "all" or similar terminology, yet it stands unqualified. However, the group of saleswomen is extremely large, consisting of 382 members at the time of publication. No specific individual is named in the alleged libelous statement. I am not cited to a single case which would support a cause of action by an individual member of any group of such magnitude.

. . . .

[W]here the group or class disparaged is a large one, absent circumstances pointing to a particular plaintiff as the person defamed, no individual member of the group or class has a cause of action. Restatement of Torts, § 564(c); Gatley, Libel and Slander (3rd Ed. 1938) pp. 123–124. . . .

Giving the plaintiff saleswomen the benefit of all legitimate favorable inferences, the defendants' alleged libel cannot reasonably be said to concern more than the saleswomen as a class. There is no language referring to some ascertained or ascertainable person. Nor is the class so small that it follows that defamation of the class infects the individual of the class. This Court so holds as a matter of law since it is of the

---

1. It should be noted that defendants have not moved to dismiss as to the plaintiff models. If this is a concession of a valid cause of action on the part of the models, it is difficult to perceive a legalistic distinction between the statements that 'some Neiman models are call girls' and 'most of the sales staff are fairies.'

opinion that no reasonable man would take the writers seriously and conclude from the publication a reference to any individual saleswoman. *Weston v. Commercial Advertiser Ass'n, supra*, 184 N.Y. at page 485, 77 N.E. 660; *Watts-Wagner Co. v. General Motors Corp., supra.*

While it is generally recognized that even where the group is large, a member of the group may have a cause of action if some particular circumstances point to the plaintiff as the person defamed, no such circumstances are alleged in the amended complaint. This further exception is designed to apply only where a plaintiff can satisfy a jury that the words referred solely or especially to himself. Odgers, Libel and Slander (6th Ed.) p. 128. The plaintiffs' general allegation that the alleged libellous and defamatory matter was written "of and concerning . . . each of them" is insufficient to satisfy this requirement. *Cf. Noral v. Hearst Publications, supra.*

Accordingly it is the opinion of this Court that as a matter of law the individual saleswomen do not state a claim for libel upon which relief can be granted and the motion to dismiss their cause of action is granted.

---

1. The plaintiff must show that the statement was made "of and concerning" her. What if the statement is: "She burned her car."?

2. One of the problems with common law defamation is that if the defendant intended to make the statement and it is defamatory, she is strictly liable, regardless of whether she intended to defame the plaintiff. For example, in *Hutton v. Jones*, [1920] A.C. 20, the defendant Newspaper published: "[T]here is Artemus Jones with a woman who is not his wife, who must be the other thing." The name was invented by the author without realizing that there actually was such a man. The true Artemus Jones, an attorney, came forward, sued, and won.

In *New York Times v. Sullivan, infra*, a newspaper advertisement refers to the chief of police, but does not name him, and makes some trivial factual errors. Because of strict liability, the commissioner of police won $500,000 before the Alabama courts.

Pring v. Penthouse International

United States Court of Appeals for the Tenth Circuit, 1982
695 F.2d 438, *cert. denied*, 462 U.S. 1132 (1983)

SETH, CHIEF JUDGE.

This defamation case concerns an article which appeared in defendant's magazine *Penthouse*. It was written about a "Charlene," a Miss Wyoming at the Miss America contest and about the contest. The defendants argue that the story is a spoof of the contest, ridicule, an attempt to be humorous, "black humor," a complete fantasy which could not be taken literally.

The basic question which had to be resolved at the trial was in two parts—whether the publication was about the plaintiff, that is, whether it was of and concerning her as a matter of identity; and secondly, whether the story must reasonably be understood as describing actual facts or events about plaintiff or actual conduct of the plaintiff.

. . . .

[T]he story must reasonably be understood as describing actual facts about the plaintiff or her actual conduct. . . . In some opinions it is treated as part of the "of and concerning" requirement. It is really part of the basic ingredient of any defamation action; that is, a false representation of fact. In the case before us this requirement that the story must reasonably be understood to describe actual facts about the plaintiff has become the central issue.

. . . .

The article had its setting at a Miss America contest and described Charlene, a Miss Wyoming at the contest, who was a baton twirler. The article began with a description of Charlene with other contestants at a bar during the course of the contest. It quotes a conversation between Charlene and her coach, a man referred to as Corky. The story then switches to the contest as Charlene is about to perform her talent as a baton twirler. She is about to go on stage and her thoughts are described. She thinks of Wyoming and an incident there when she was with a football player from her school. It describes an act of fellatio whereby she causes him to levitate. . . .

The complaint, as amended, refers to these incidents and limits the consequences to:

"The net effect of the aforementioned article was to create the impression throughout the United States, Wyoming and the world that the Plaintiff committed fellatio on one Monty Applewhite and also upon her coach, Corky Corcoran, in the presence of a national television audience at the Miss America Pageant. The article also creates the impression that Plaintiff committed fellatio like acts upon her baton at the Miss America contest."

. . . .

The author of the article was the defendant Cioffari, a Ph.D. who was a professor of English at a university in New Jersey.

. . . Here, the underlying event described was the Miss America Pageant, but it was readily apparent, with the extended description of thoughts of Charlene and other indications, that it was all fanciful and did not purport to be a factual account. In this context there are the particular three incidents which are in themselves fantasy and present levitation as the central theme and as a device to "save the world." We have impossibility and fantasy within a fanciful story. Also of significance is the fact that some of the incidents were described as being on national television and apparently before the audience at the pageant or part of the audience. This in itself would seem to provide a sufficient signal that the story could not be taken literally, and the portions charged as defamatory could not reasonably be understood as a statement of fact. . . .

The test is not whether the story is or is not characterized as "fiction," "humor," or anything else in the publication, but whether the charged portions in context could be reasonably understood as describing actual facts about the plaintiff or actual events in which she participated. If it could not be so understood, the charged portions could not be taken literally. . . .

All the testimony from plaintiff's lay witnesses was that it could not be about the plaintiff. An "expert" witness testified that some individuals might attach a broader subliminal meaning of sexual permissiveness, but this does not represent an applicable standard and cannot be regarded as much more than a contradiction of the testimony of her witnesses.

The charged portions of the story described something physically impossible in an impossible setting. In these circumstances we must reach the same conclusion . . . that it is simply impossible to believe that a reader would not have understood that the charged portions were pure fantasy and nothing else. It is impossible to believe that anyone could understand that levitation could be accomplished by oral sex before a national television audience or anywhere else. The incidents charged were impossible. The setting was impossible.

This does not leave, on the record before us, any alternative but to decide as a matter of law . . . "even the most careless reader must have perceived that" the descriptions were "no more than rhetorical hyperbole." Here, they were obviously a complete fantasy.

. . . .

The judgment must be reversed with directions to set aside the verdict of the jury and to dismiss the action.

IT IS SO ORDERED.

Breitenstein, Circuit Judge, dissenting:

The majority holds that as a matter of law this defamation action must be dismissed because the publication was pure fantasy protected by the First Amendment. I do not agree.

On overwhelming evidence the jury found that the plaintiff Pring was the "Miss Wyoming" about whom the Penthouse article was written. The majority accept that jury finding. The question is whether Penthouse can escape liability by the claim that the article was fiction and fantasy.

The article contains both fact and fiction. The article says that Miss Wyoming performed fellatio with a male companion and caused him to levitate. . . . I consider levitation, dreams, and public performance as fiction. Fellatio is not. It is a physical act, a fact, not a mental idea. . . .

Penthouse cannot escape liability by relying on the fantasy used to embellish the fact. Penthouse did not present the article as fiction. It did not make the usual disclaimer of reference to no person living or dead. In the table of contents, the article is characterized as "Humor."

1. If Ms. Pring were a married woman with children, would she likely have suffered shame and humiliation? Why then did the court refuse to provide a remedy? How would you have decided the case?

2. Hyperbole has been discussed earlier in *Hustler Magazine v. Falwell*, Chapter 2, *supra*.

C. Defenses to Defamation

1. Truth

An action for defamation cannot be maintained for truthful statements. Absolute truth is not required and substantial truth is sufficient. *See Kilian v. Doubleday & Co.*, 367 Pa. 117, 79 A.2d 657 (Pa. 1951). In *Kilian*, which involved an account of alleged mistreatment of American soldiers in a camp in England during World War II, the defendant lost because he failed to prove that the statements were substantially true. In many jurisdictions, truth used to be an affirmative defense, but it is now established that the First Amendment usually requires the plaintiff to prove the falsehood of the statements in question. *See Masson v. New Yorker Magazine* and *Philadelphia Newspapers v. Hepps, infra*.

2. Privileges

Carradine v. Minnesota

Supreme Court of Minnesota, 1994
511 N.W.2d 733

COYNE, JUSTICE.

We agreed to review this case, which has not yet been tried, in order to address whether a state trooper enjoys an absolute privilege that affords him or her absolute immunity from a defamation suit for anything said in preparing an arrest report or in responding to press inquiries about the arrest.

On July 9, 1987, plaintiff, Robert Reed Carradine, was stopped and arrested by a state trooper, defendant Patrick Chase, as he was driving to the airport to catch a flight. In his arrest report and in statements to jail personnel, to prosecutors and to a reporter, Chase said that Carradine's conduct involved speeding, reckless driving, fleeing an officer, and impersonating an officer. Carradine was booked, finger printed, strip-searched and held in custody for 10 hours before being released. News accounts of Carradine's alleged conduct appeared in newspapers throughout the county and on television because Carradine, in addition to "racing" cars professionally, is an actor who has appeared in a number of movies, the most well-known being "Revenge of the Nerds."

. . . .

Carradine then filed suit against Chase and his employer, the State of Minnesota, claiming unreasonable search and seizure, denial of due process, assault and battery, false imprisonment, excessive use of force, negligent infliction of emotional distress, defamation, malicious prosecution, negligence, trespass to personal property, conversion, and vicarious liability.

. . . .

The trial court granted summary judgment to the defendants on all of Carradine's federal claims and all of his state claims except for three: negligent infliction of emotional distress, defamation and vicarious liability. Defendants appealed from the denial of summary judgment as to those three claims. Carradine noticed review of the award of partial summary judgment.

The court of appeals, in affirming, said, inter alia, that Chase lacked an absolute privilege to make defamatory statements in preparing the arrest report and in subsequently talking with the press about the arrest. *Carradine v. State*, 494 N.W.2d 77, 81 (Minn. App. 1992).

The history of absolute privilege for defamatory statements made by public officials in the course of duty is "a story of uneven development." *Barr v. Matteo*, 360 U.S. 564, 579, 79 S. Ct. 1335, 3 L. Ed. 2d 1434 (1959) (Warren, C.J., dissenting). Absolute legislative privilege "dates back to at least 1399." Id., citing Van Vechten Veeder, *Absolute Immunity in Defamation: Legislative and Executive Proceedings*, 10 Colum. L. Rev. 131, 132 (1910). "The Constitution itself gives an absolute privilege to members of both Houses of Congress in respect to any speech, debate, vote, report, or action done in session." *Barr v. Matteo*, 360 U.S. at 569 (Harlan, J.), citing U.S. Const., Art. I, §6. Moreover, the privilege is given by our state constitution to the legislative branch. Minn. Const., Art. IV, §10.

Absolute immunity for defamatory statements made by participants in the course of a judicial proceeding dates back at least to the sixteenth century. Van Vechten Veeder, *Absolute Immunity in Defamation: Judicial Proceedings*, 9 Colum. L. Rev. 463, 474 (1909). The United States Supreme Court "early held that judges of courts of superior or general authority are absolutely privileged as respects civil suits to recover for actions taken by them in the exercise of their judicial functions, irrespective of the motives with which those acts are alleged to have been performed," *Bradley v. Fisher*, 80 U.S. 335, 20 L. Ed. 646, 13 Wall 335, and that a like immunity extends to other officers of government whose duties are related to the judicial process.

Barr v. Matteo, 360 U.S. 564, 79 S. Ct. 1335, 3 L. Ed. 2d 1434, is the leading case recognizing absolute privilege in the executive branch. The officer there, Acting Director of the Office of Rent Stabilization, issued a press release announcing his intention to suspend certain employees because of the part they had played in formulating a controversial plan for the use of certain agency funds. The employees sued the Acting Director for libel, alleging malice. The United States Supreme Court, by a split decision, held that the statements in the press release were absolutely privileged.

There is now considerable agreement among state courts that "high level" executive officers have absolute immunity from suit for defamatory statements made in the course of their duties. . . .

It is no answer to the question whether an executive branch employee has absolute immunity to say that the employee is not a "high level" employee but a "low level" employee. Immunity "is not a badge or emolument of exalted office, but an expression of a policy designed to aid in the effective functioning of government. The complexities and magnitude of governmental activity have become so great that there must of necessity be a delegation and redelegation of authority as to many functions, and we cannot say that these functions become less important simply because they are exercised by officers of lower rank in the executive hierarchy." *Barr v. Matteo*, 360 U.S. at 572–73.

In other words, the purpose of extending absolute immunity to an officer performing a certain governmental function is not primarily to protect the officer personally from civil liability (although that is the effect of absolute immunity). Rather, the rationale is that unless the officer in question is absolutely immune from suit, the officer will timorously, instead of fearlessly, perform the function in question and, as a result, government—that is, the public—will be the ultimate loser. *Barr v. Matteo*, 360 U.S. at 571. . . .

Whether an executive officer is absolutely immune from defamation liability depends on many factors, including the nature of the function assigned to the officer and the relationship of the statements to the performance of that function.

The issue in this case, therefore, is not whether police officers have absolute immunity from civil suit for all allegedly defamatory statements made in the performance of their duties. Instead, we address two much more specific issues: (a) whether Trooper Chase has absolute immunity from civil suit for allegedly defamatory statements made in an arrest report; and (b) whether this officer has absolute immunity from civil suit for allegedly defamatory statements made in response to press inquiries about the arrest. We believe that the proper answers are "yes" to the first question and "no, with qualification" to the second.

In answering "yes" to the first question, we attach great significance to the following factors: (a) It is a key part of an arresting officer's job to prepare a written arrest report accurately summarizing the circumstances leading to and surrounding the arrest; (b) the report typically is useful not only to the officer's departmental superiors but also to the prosecutor in determining whether to charge the arrestee and, if so, what offenses to charge; (c) moreover, the police report often plays a significant role in the trial of a criminal defendant, with the prosecutor using the report to refresh the officer's recollection and with defense counsel using the report to cross-examine and attempt to impeach the officer; and (d) the knowledge that making statements in the report subjects the officer to possible civil liability in a defamation or similar action may well deter the honest officer from fearlessly and vigorously preparing a detailed, accurate report and increase the likelihood that the officer will hesitate to prepare anything more than a bland report that will be less useful within the department and in any subsequent prosecution and trial. . . . Given these and other factors, we conclude that Trooper Chase has absolute immunity from a civil suit in defamation for the statements made in the written police report.[2]

Whether Chase has absolute immunity from civil suit for allegedly defamatory statements made in response to press inquiries is another matter. An arresting officer's freedom of expression in making an arrest report is essential to the performance of his function as an officer, whereas it is not at all essential to the officer's performance of his duties as an officer that he respond to press inquiries about the circumstances leading up to and surrounding an arrest. . . . It appears that there is evidence that statements to the media by state troopers are "allowed" by state patrol policy but that officers are not required to give statements when requested. In fact, there is evidence that state troopers are encouraged to refer questions to a public affairs officer in well-publicized cases.

Since we must presume on this record that responding to press inquiries was not one of the officer's duties and because of the greater risk of publication to a large number of people that accompanies the making of public statements about the arrestee, we conclude that not all statements made to the press by an arresting officer such as Trooper Chase are absolutely privileged.

To the extent, however, that Chase's statements to the press merely amounted to an exact repetition or a substantial repetition, without amplification or comment, of the statements made in the arrest report, which is a matter of public record available to the press pursuant to Minn. Stat. § 13.82 (1993 Supp.), the statements to the press may not support liability. *Johnson v. Dirkswager*, 315 N.W.2d at 222. Plaintiff Carradine argues that Chase's statements to the press did not merely amount to a substantial repetition of the statements in the arrest report. We believe that the trial court is in a better position at this time than we are to determine whether this is so. If it is so and if a jury properly might find that the additional statements significantly added to any injury sustained by plaintiff over and above any injury sustained as a result of the absolutely privileged statements, then plaintiff should be allowed to proceed to trial against Chase;[3] otherwise, not.

The only remaining issue is whether any absolute immunity of the officer also extends to protect the state in its capacity as the officer's employer. We hold that, in

---

2. For similar reasons, we conclude that, on the facts as we understand them, Chase also has absolute immunity from civil suit for any other intradepartmental statements he made in the course of his duties.

3. Moreover, in order to be entitled to proceed to trial on the basis of any significantly different statements made to the press, plaintiff must first satisfy the trial court that he has evidence to establish actual malice by the officer in the making of the statements, because, to the extent the statements by the officer are not protected by an absolute privilege, they are protected by a qualified privilege. Plaintiff must therefore establish that he has actual evidence of malice; it is not enough for him to argue that malice may be inferred from the mere making of the statements in question. We also leave this determination to the trial court at this time.

this context, the immunity enjoyed by the officer extends to the state. *Pletan v. Gaines*, 494 N.W.2d 38, 41–43 (Minn. 1992).

Affirmed in part and reversed in part; remanded to trial court for further proceedings.

---

1. Absolute immunity extends to the judge, the attorney, and witnesses as long as the statements are relevant to the case. *See Irwin v. Ashurst*, 158 Or. 61, 74 P.2d 1127 (1938).

2. Some states would not extend absolute immunity to a low ranking official, such as a police officer. She would receive a qualified immunity instead. *See Chamberlain v. Mathis*, 151 Ariz. 551, 729 P.2d 905 (1986).

3. Although Senator William Proxmire had an absolute privilege under the Speech or Debate Clause to speak on the Senate floor, he lost it by speaking to the press outside the Senate. He defamed a scientist by giving him the "Golden Fleece Award" (a device Proxmire used to ridicule wasteful government spending) for his research on emotional behavior. *Hutchinson v. Proxmire*, 443 U.S. 111 (1979).

Liberman v. Gelstein

Court of Appeals of New York, 1992
605 N.E.2d 344

KAYE, J.

In this action for slander, we consider whether the plaintiff has stated a viable claim without any showing of special damages, whether the alleged slander is protected by qualified privilege, and whether there is a triable issue of fact as to malice. We conclude that plaintiff's claims were correctly dismissed on summary judgment.

I

Before us is one of eight actions, consolidated for disposition by the motion court, centering on a luxury apartment building in Manhattan. Plaintiff, Barnet L. Liberman, is the building's landlord. Defendant, Leonard Gelstein (a tenant), is on the board of governors of the tenants' association. . . .

This defamation action against Gelstein is one of three suits brought by Liberman against individual members of the tenant association's board of governors. . . .

The present complaint alleged five causes of action sounding in slander. Only two—the second and fifth—are pressed by plaintiff on this appeal. . . .

In his second cause of action, plaintiff alleged that in July 1986, the following conversation took place between defendant and another tenant of the building, Robert Kohler.

"Gelstein: Can you find out from your friend at the precinct which cop is on the take from Liberman?

"Kohler: What are you talking about?

"Gelstein: There is a cop on the take from Liberman. That's why none of the building's cars ever get tickets—they can park anywhere because Liberman's paid them off. He gives them a hundred or two hundred a week."

The fifth cause of action alleged that in May 1986 defendant made the following statement in the presence of employees of the building:

"Liberman threw a punch at me. He screamed at my wife and daughter. He called my daughter a slut and threatened to kill me and my family."

Plaintiff claimed $5 million damages on each cause of action for injury to his reputation and emotional distress. . . .

II

We next consider whether the courts below properly concluded that defendant's conversation with Kohler was conditionally privileged and that plaintiff failed to raise an issue of fact on malice.

Courts have long recognized that the public interest is served by shielding certain communications, though possibly defamatory, from litigation, rather than risk stifling them altogether (*see, Bingham v. Gaynor*, 203 NY 27, 31). When compelling public policy requires that the speaker be immune from suit, the law affords an absolute privilege, while statements fostering a lesser public interest are only conditionally privileged.

One such conditional, or qualified, privilege extends to a "communication made by one person to another upon a subject in which both have an interest" (*Stillman v. Ford*, 22 N.Y.2d 48, 53). This "common interest" privilege (*see*, Restatement § 596) has been applied, for example, to employees of an organization (*see, Loughry v. Lincoln First Bank*, 67 N.Y.2d 369, 376), members of a faculty tenure committee (*Stukuls v. State of New York*, 42 N.Y.2d 272) and constituent physicians of a health insurance plan (*Shapiro v. Health Ins. Plan*, 7 N.Y.2d 56, 60–61). The rationale for applying the privilege in these circumstances is that so long as the privilege is not abused, the flow of information between persons sharing a common interest should not be impeded.

We thus agree with the motion court and Appellate Division that defendant's conversation with Kohler was conditionally privileged (*see*, Restatement § 596, comment *d* ["Tenants in common . . . are included within the rule stated in this Section as being conditionally privileged to communicate among themselves matter defamatory of others which concerns their common interests"]). Gelstein and Kohler were members of the governing body of an association formed to protect the tenants' interests. If Liberman was in fact bribing the police so that his cars could occupy spaces in front of the building, that would be inimical to those interests. Thus, Gelstein had a qualified right to communicate his suspicions—though defamatory of Liberman—to Kohler.

The shield provided by a qualified privilege may be dissolved if plaintiff can demonstrate that defendant spoke with "malice." Under common law, malice meant spite or ill will. In *New York Times Co. v. Sullivan* (376 U.S. 254), however, the Supreme

Court established an "actual malice" standard for certain cases governed by the First Amendment: "knowledge that [the statement] was false or . . . reckless disregard of whether it was false or not." Consequently, the term "malice" has become somewhat confused. . . . Indeed, as the Supreme Court itself recently acknowledged:

> "Actual malice under the *New York Times* standard should not be confused with the concept of malice as an evil intent or a motive arising from spite or ill will . . . We have used the term actual malice as a shorthand to describe the First Amendment protections for speech injurious to reputation and we continue to do so here. But the term can confuse as well as enlighten. In this respect, the phrase may be an unfortunate one."

Nevertheless, malice has now assumed a dual meaning, and we have recognized that the constitutional as well as the common-law standard will suffice to defeat a conditional privilege.

Under the *Times* malice standard, the plaintiff must demonstrate that the "statements [were] made with [a] high degree of awareness of their probable falsity" (*Garrison v. Louisiana*, 379 U.S. 64, 74). In other words, there "must be sufficient evidence to permit the conclusion that the defendant in fact entertained serious doubts as to the truth of [the] publication" (*St. Amant v. Thompson*, 390 U.S. 727, 731; *see also*, Restatement §600, comment *b*).

Applying these principles, we conclude that there is no triable malice issue under the *Times* standard. Although the dissenter below suggested that Gelstein's admission that he did not know whether the bribery charge was true raised a triable issue on malice, there is a critical difference between not knowing whether something is true and being highly aware that it is probably false. Only the latter establishes reckless disregard in a defamation action. Moreover, as the motion court correctly observed, plaintiff's mere characterization of Gelstein's informants as "disgruntled" is insufficient to raise a triable issue. Although plaintiff criticizes defendant for not producing affidavits from the informants—arguing that "it has never been factually established that Gelstein had any source"—it was plaintiff's burden to raise a factual issue on malice, and he did not seek to depose the employees either. In sum, this record is insufficient to raise a triable issue of fact under the *Times* standard of malice.

Similarly, there is insufficient evidence of malice under the common-law definition. A jury could undoubtedly find that, at the time Gelstein discussed his bribery suspicions with Kohler, Gelstein harbored ill will toward Liberman. In this context, however, spite or ill will refers not to defendant's general feelings about plaintiff, but to the speaker's motivation for making the defamatory statements (*see*, Restatement §603, and comment *a*). If the defendant's statements were made to further the interest protected by the privilege, it matters not that defendant *also* despised plaintiff. Thus, a triable issue is raised only if a jury could reasonably conclude that "malice was the one and only cause for the publication."

Plaintiff has not sustained that burden. Significantly, Gelstein did not make a public announcement of his suspicions—from which an inference could be drawn that his motive was to defame Liberman—but relayed them to a colleague who was in a position to investigate. As noted, the conversation was within the common interest of Gelstein and Kohler, and there is nothing in this record from which a reasonable jury could find that Gelstein was not seeking to advance that common interest.

Thus, the courts below properly concluded that defendant's conversation with Kohler was qualifiedly privileged, and plaintiff failed to raise a fact issue on malice.

Accordingly, the order of the Appellate Division should be affirmed, with costs.

———————

1. *Liberman* defines the concept of qualified privilege and how it may be lost.

2. A common application of the qualified privilege is an employer's reply to an inquiry from a prospective employer regarding the qualifications of a job applicant. *Erickson v. Marsh & McLennan*, 569 A.2d 793 (N.J. 1990), suggests a three-part test for whether the qualified privilege applies:

> The critical elements of this test are the appropriateness of the occasion on which the defamatory information is published, the legitimacy of the interest thereby sought to be protected or promoted, and the pertinence of the receipt of that information by the recipient.

Applying that test *Erickson* held that a qualified privilege extended to statements made to Erickson's prospective employers where they "were made in response to inquiries . . . [and] not simply volunteered," the "prospective employers had a legitimate and obvious interest in the professional qualifications, skill, and experience" of the plaintiff "including the reasons for his termination," and the information provided "specifically addressed the questions posed" making it "directly relevant to their inquiry."

3. Some jurisdictions recognize a qualified privilege for reports to the police of potentially criminal behavior. *See Kennedy v. Sheriff of E. Baton Rouge*, 935 So. 2d 669 (La. 2006) (report to sheriff by fast-food outlet's employees erroneously claiming that plaintiff was using counterfeit money held subject to qualified privilege).

Brown & Williamson Tobacco Corporation v. Jacobson and CBS

United States Court of Appeals for the Seventh Circuit, 1983
713 F.2d 262

POSNER, CIRCUIT JUDGE.

This diversity suit brought by Brown & Williamson, the manufacturer of Viceroy cigarettes, charges CBS and Walter Jacobson with libel and other violations of Illinois law. Jacobson is a news commentator for WBBM-TV, a Chicago television station owned by CBS. . . .

In 1975, Ted Bates, the advertising agency that had the Viceroy account, hired the Kennan market-research firm to help develop a new advertising strategy for Viceroy. Kennan submitted a report which stated that for "the young smoker," "a cigarette, and the whole smoking process, is part of the illicit pleasure category. . . . In the young smoker's mind a cigarette falls into the same category with wine, beer, shaving, wearing a bra (or purposely not wearing one), declaration of independence and striving for self-identity. . . . To the best of your ability, (considering some legal constraints), relate the cigarette to 'pot', wine, beer, sex, etc. *Don't* communicate health or health-related points." Ted Bates forwarded the report to Brown & Williamson. According to the allegations of the complaint, which on this appeal we must accept as true, Brown & Williamson rejected the "illicit pleasure strategy" proposed in the report, and fired Ted Bates primarily because of displeasure with the proposed strategy.

Years later the Federal Trade Commission conducted an investigation of cigarette advertising, and in May 1981 it published a report of its staff on the investigation. The FTC staff report discusses the Kennan report, correctly dates it to May 1975, and after quoting from it the passages we have quoted states that "B&W adopted many of the ideas contained in this report in the development of a Viceroy advertising campaign." . . .

Walter Jacobson's "Perspective" on the tobacco industry was broadcast on November 11 and rebroadcast on November 12 and again on March 5, 1982. In the broadcast, Jacobson, after stating that "pushing cigarettes on television is prohibited," announces his theme: "Television is off limits to cigarettes and so the business, the killer business, has gone to the ad business in New York for help, to the slicksters on Madison Avenue with a billion dollars a year for bigger and better ways to sell cigarettes. Go for the youth of America, go get'em guys. . . . Hook'em while they are young, make'em start now—just think how many cigarettes they'll be smoking when they grow up." Various examples of how cigarette marketing attempts "to addict the children to poison" are given. The last and longest concerns Viceroy.

. . . .

Under contemporary as under traditional Illinois law, Jacobson's broadcast is libelous per se. Accusing a cigarette company of what many people consider the immoral strategy of enticing children to smoke—enticing them by advertising that employs themes exploitive of adolescent vulnerability—is likely to harm the company. It may make it harder for the company to fend off hostile government regulation and may invite rejection of the company's product by angry parents who smoke but may not want their children to do so. These harms cannot easily be measured, but so long as some harm is highly likely the difficulty of measurement is an additional reason, under the modern functional approach of the Illinois courts, for finding libel per se rather than insisting on proof of special damage. . . .

The defendants . . . argue and the district court also found that the libel was privileged as a fair and accurate summary of the Federal Trade Commission staff's report on cigarette advertising. The parties agree as they must that Illinois recognizes a privilege for fair and accurate summaries of, or reports on, government proceedings and investigations. They agree that the privilege extends to a public FTC staff report on an investigation. But they disagree over whether Jacobson's summary of the FTC staff report was "fair," that is, whether the overall impression created by the summary was no more defamatory than that created by the original. See Restatement (Second) of Torts § 611, Comment f (1977). Since this is a question of fact . . . and the case was dismissed on the pleadings, all we need decide is whether the fairness of the Jacobson summary emerges so incontrovertibly from a comparison of the FTC staff report with the broadcast that no rational jury considering these documents with the aid of whatever additional evidence Brown & Williamson might introduce could consider the summary unfair.

. . . .

The fact that there are discrepancies between a libel and the government report on which it is based need not defeat the privilege of fair summary. Unless the report is published verbatim it is bound to convey a somewhat different impression from the original, no matter how carefully the publisher attempts to summarize or paraphrase or excerpt it fairly and accurately. An unfair summary in the present context is one that amplifies the libelous effect that publication of the government report verbatim would have on a reader who read it carefully—that carries a "greater sting," . . . The Jacobson broadcast conveys the following message: Brown & Williamson currently is advertising cigarettes in a manner designed to entice children to smoke by associating smoking with drinking, sex, marijuana, and other illicit pleasures of youth. So at least a rational jury might interpret the source and the summary, and if it did it would be entitled to conclude that the summary carried a greater sting and was therefore unfair.

---

1. Aren't there always going to be "discrepancies" between the media report and the government record? How does a court determine whether those discrepancies "amplif[y] the libelous effect"? Won't a media report almost always carry more "sting"?

2. Why was the CBS report libelous? Why didn't CBS argue truth? Is the tobacco industry viewed differently today?

3. Other Defenses

A full and fair retraction by the newspaper may reduce the amount of damages. *See Burnett v. National Enquirer, Inc.*, 144 Cal. App. 3d 991, 193 Cal. Rptr. 206 (1983). The California Code provides:

Section 48a:

1. In any action for damages for the publication of a libel in a newspaper, or of a slander by radio broadcast, plaintiff shall recover no more than special damages unless a correction be demanded and be not published or broadcast, as hereinafter provided. Plaintiff shall serve upon the publisher, at the place of publication or broadcaster at the place of broadcast, a written notice

specifying the statements claimed to be libelous and demanding that the same be corrected. Said notice and demand must be served within 20 days after knowledge of the publication or broadcast of the statements claimed to be libelous.

A defamatory statement cannot be enjoined because to do so would involve a "prior restraint" violating the defendant's right to free speech, protected by the First Amendment. *Near v. Minnesota*, 283 U.S. 697 (1931); *New York Times v. United States*, 403 U.S. 713 (1971).

Sometimes a defendant argues that the plaintiff's reputation is so bad (*e.g.*, if the plaintiff were a mass murderer) that he is libel-proof and cannot be defamed. *See Jackson v. Long-Cope*, 476 N.E.2d 617 (Mass. 1985). However, it may still be possible to defame bad people, on the theory that "[t]he law . . . proceeds upon the optimistic premise that there is a little bit of good in all of us—or perhaps upon the pessimistic assumption that no matter how bad someone is, he can always be worse." *Liberty Lobby v. Anderson*, 746 F.2d 1563 (D.C. Cir. 1984) (Scalia, J.)

The single publication rule is now widely accepted: "The publication of a book, periodical, or newspaper containing defamatory matter gives rise to one cause of action for libel which accrues at the time of the original publication." The previous rule that each sale gives rise to a separate cause of action is no longer followed. *Ogden v. Association of the United States Army*, 177 F. Supp. 498 (D.D.C. 1959).

A vendor or distributor of newspapers, magazines, or books is known as a "secondary publisher" and is not liable unless it can be shown that the distributor knew of the defamatory material in the publication. *See Balabanoff v. Fossani*, 81 N.Y.S.2d 732 (Sup. Ct. 1948). Under federal law, internet providers are similarly immune from suits based on the content of information they transmit. The Communications Decency Act, 47 U.S.C. § 230(c)(1), states: "No provider of an interactive computer service shall be treated as the publisher or speaker of information provided by another content provider."

In recent years, some jurisdictions have experienced a phenomenon known as "SLAPP" suits (Strategic Lawsuits Against Public Participation). These are actions, frequently claiming defamation, that are brought against individuals, not with the expectation of success on the merits, but to deter plaintiffs (or others like them) from seeking legal redress or engaging in various forms of public criticism of an individual or entity. They are sometimes brought as a counterclaim, sometimes as an original action. In an attempt to counteract these suits, some jurisdictions have established procedures for summary dismissal of SLAPP suits and have allowed successful defendants to recover attorneys' fees and costs from the plaintiffs or counterclaimants who bring them. For cases applying California's anti-SLAPP legislation, see *Simpson Strong-Tie Co., Inc. v. Gore*, 49 Cal. 4th 12 (2010) (finding defamation suit brought against individual who questioned safety of plaintiff's products within scope of anti-SLAPP legislation); *Kibler v. Northern Inyo County Local Hospital Dist.*, 39 Cal. 4th 192 (2006) (applying anti-SLAPP legislation to suit by doctor suspended by hospital for abusive behavior). For general discussion, see Kathryn Tate, *California's Anti-SLAPP Legislation: A Summary of and Commentary on Its Operation and Scope*, 33 Loy. L.A. L. Rev. 801 (2000).

D. Constitutional Issues

In 1964, an action was brought in Alabama against the *New York Times* and numerous civil rights leaders, based on an advertisement carried in the *Times* that criticized police handling of civil rights protests in Montgomery, Alabama. The libel action, resting on strict liability, led to a $500,000 jury verdict, based on assumed damages. The defendants argued constitutional freedom of speech as a defense, and the Supreme Court's decision in their favor changed the nature of defamation law.

1. Public Officials

New York Times Co. v. Sullivan

Supreme Court of the United States, 1964
376 U.S. 254

MR. JUSTICE BRENNAN delivered the opinion of the Court.

We are required in this case to determine for the first time the extent to which the constitutional protections for speech and press limit a State's power to award damages in a libel action brought by a public official against critics of his official conduct.

Respondent L. B. Sullivan is one of the three elected Commissioners of the City of Montgomery, Alabama. He testified that he was "Commissioner of Public Affairs and the duties are supervision of the Police Department, Fire Department, Department of Cemetery and Department of Scales." He brought this civil libel action against the four individual petitioners, who are Negroes and Alabama clergymen, and against petitioner the New York Times Company, a New York corporation which publishes the *New York Times*, a daily newspaper. A jury in the Circuit Court of Montgomery County awarded him damages of $500,000, the full amount claimed, against all the petitioners, and the Supreme Court of Alabama affirmed. 273 Ala. 656, 144 So. 2d 25.

Respondent's complaint alleged that he had been libeled by statements in a full-page advertisement that was carried in the *New York Times* on March 29, 1960. Entitled "Heed Their Rising Voices," the advertisement began by stating that "As the whole world knows by now, thousands of Southern Negro students are engaged in widespread non-violent demonstrations in positive affirmation of the right to live in human dignity as guaranteed by the U.S. Constitution and the Bill of Rights." It went on to charge that "in their efforts to uphold these guarantees, they are being met by an unprecedented wave of terror by those who would deny and negate that document which the whole world looks upon as setting the pattern for modern freedom. . . ."

The text appeared over the names of 64 persons, many widely known for their activities in public affairs, religion, trade unions, and the performing arts. Below these names, and under a line reading "We in the South who are struggling daily for dignity and freedom warmly endorse this appeal," appeared the names of the four individual petitioners and of 16 other persons, all but two of whom were identified as clergymen in various Southern cities. The advertisement was signed at the bottom of the page by the "Committee to Defend Martin Luther King and the Struggle for Freedom in the South," and the officers of the Committee were listed.

Of the 10 paragraphs of text in the advertisement, the third and a portion of the sixth were the basis of respondent's claim of libel. They read as follows:

Third paragraph:

"In Montgomery, Alabama, after students sang 'My Country/Tis of Thee' on the State Capitol steps, their leaders were expelled from school, and truckloads of police armed with shotguns and tear-gas ringed the Alabama State College Campus. When the entire student body protested to state authorities by refusing to re-register, their dining hall was padlocked in an attempt to starve them into submission."

Sixth paragraph:

"Again and again the Southern violators have answered Dr. King's peaceful protests with intimidation and violence. They have bombed his home almost killing his wife and child. They have assaulted his person. They have arrested him seven times—for 'speeding,' 'loitering' and similar 'offenses.' And now they have charged him with 'perjury'—a *felony* under which they could imprison him for *ten years.* . . ."

Although neither of these statements mentions respondent by name, he contended that the word "police" in the third paragraph referred to him as the Montgomery Commissioner who supervised the Police Department, so that he was being accused of "ringing" the campus with police. He further claimed that the paragraph would be read as imputing to the police, and hence to him, the padlocking of the dining hall in order to starve the students into submission. As to the sixth paragraph, he contended that since arrests are ordinarily made by the police, the statement "They have arrested [Dr. King] seven times" would be read as referring to him; he further contended that the "They" who did the arresting would be equated with the "They" who committed the other described acts and with the "Southern violators." Thus, he argued, the paragraph would be read as accusing the Montgomery police, and hence him, of answering Dr. King's protests with "intimidation and violence," bombing his home, assaulting his person, and charging him with perjury. Respondent and six other Montgomery residents testified that they read some or all of the statements as referring to him in his capacity as Commissioner.

It is uncontroverted that some of the statements contained in the two paragraphs were not accurate descriptions of events which occurred in Montgomery. Although Negro students staged a demonstration on the State Capitol steps, they sang the

National Anthem and not "My Country, 'Tis of Thee." Although nine students were expelled by the State Board of Education, this was not for leading the demonstration at the Capitol, but for demanding service at a lunch counter in the Montgomery County Courthouse on another day. Not the entire student body, but most of it, had protested the expulsion, not by refusing to register, but by boycotting classes on a single day; virtually all the students did register for the ensuing semester. The campus dining hall was not padlocked on any occasion, and the only students who may have been barred from eating there were the few who had neither signed a preregistration application nor requested temporary meal tickets. Although the police were deployed near the campus in large numbers on three occasions, they did not at any time "ring" the campus, and they were not called to the campus in connection with the demonstration on the State Capitol steps, as the third paragraph implied. Dr. King had not been arrested seven times, but only four; and although he claimed to have been assaulted some years earlier in connection with his arrest for loitering outside a courtroom, one of the officers who made the arrest denied that there was such an assault.

On the premise that the charges in the sixth paragraph could be read as referring to him, respondent was allowed to prove that he had not participated in the events described. Although Dr. King's home had in fact been bombed twice when his wife and child were there, both of these occasions antedated respondent's tenure as Commissioner, and the police were not only not implicated in the bombings, but had made every effort to apprehend those who were. Three of Dr. King's four arrests took place before respondent became Commissioner. Although Dr. King had in fact been indicted (he was subsequently acquitted) on two counts of perjury, each of which carried a possible five-year sentence, respondent had nothing to do with procuring the indictment.

Respondent made no effort to prove that he suffered actual pecuniary loss as a result of the alleged libel. . . .

The manager of the Advertising Acceptability Department testified that he had approved the advertisement for publication because he knew nothing to cause him to believe that anything in it was false, and because it bore the endorsement of "a number of people who are well known and whose reputation" he "had no reason to question." Neither he nor anyone else at the Times made an effort to confirm the accuracy of the advertisement, either by checking it against recent Times news stories relating to some of the described events or by any other means.

. . . .

The trial judge submitted the case to the jury under instructions that the statements in the advertisement were "libelous per se" and were not privileged, so that petitioners might be held liable if the jury found that they had published the advertisement and that the statements were made "of and concerning" respondent. . . . The judge rejected petitioners' contention that his rulings abridged the freedoms of speech and of the press that are guaranteed by the First and Fourteenth Amendments.

. . . [T]he Supreme Court of Alabama sustained the trial judge's rulings and instructions in all respects. . . . [T]he court said that malice could be inferred from the Times' "irresponsibility" in printing the advertisement while "the Times in its own files had articles already published which would have demonstrated the falsity of the allegations in the advertisement"; from the Times' failure to retract for respondent while retracting for the Governor, whereas the falsity of some of the allegations was then known to the Times and "the matter contained in the advertisement was equally false as to both parties"; and from the testimony of the Times' Secretary that, apart from the statement that the dining hall was padlocked, he thought the two paragraphs were "substantially correct." . . .

II

Under Alabama law as applied in this case, a publication is "libelous per se" if the words "tend to injure a person . . . in his reputation" or to "bring [him] into public contempt"; the trial court stated that the standard was met if the words are such as to "injure him in his public office, or impute misconduct to him in his office, or want of official integrity, or want of fidelity to a public trust. . . ." The jury must find that the words were published "of and concerning" the plaintiff, but where the plaintiff is a public official his place in the governmental hierarchy is sufficient evidence to support a finding that his reputation has been affected by statements that reflect upon the agency of which he is in charge. Once "libel per se" has been established, the defendant has no defense as to stated facts unless he can persuade the jury that they were true in all their particulars. *Alabama Ride Co. v. Vance*, 235 Ala. 263, 178 So. 438 (1938); *Johnson Publishing Co. v. Davis*, 271 Ala. 474, 494–495, 124 So. 2d 441, 457–458 (1960). His privilege of "fair comment" for expressions of opinion depends on the truth of the facts upon which the comment is based. *Parsons v. Age-Herald Publishing Co.*, 181 Ala. 439, 450, 61 So. 345, 350 (1913). Unless he can discharge the burden of proving truth, general damages are presumed, and may be awarded without proof of pecuniary injury. A showing of actual malice is apparently a prerequisite to recovery of punitive damages, and the defendant may in any event forestall a punitive award by a retraction meeting the statutory requirements. Good motives and belief in truth do not negate an inference of malice, but are relevant only in mitigation of punitive damages if the jury chooses to accord them weight.

The question before us is whether this rule of liability, as applied to an action brought by a public official against critics of his official conduct, abridges the freedom of speech and of the press that is guaranteed by the First and Fourteenth Amendments.

Respondent relies heavily, as did the Alabama courts, on statements of this Court to the effect that the Constitution does not protect libelous publications. Those statements do not foreclose our inquiry here. None of the cases sustained the use of libel laws to impose sanctions upon expression critical of the official conduct of public officials.

. . . .

The general proposition that freedom of expression upon public questions is secured by the First Amendment has long been settled by our decisions. The constitutional safeguard, we have said, "was fashioned to assure unfettered inter-change of ideas for the bringing about of political and social changes desired by the people." . . . The First Amendment, said Judge Learned Hand, "presupposes that right conclusions are more likely to be gathered out of a multitude of tongues, than through any kind of authoritative selection. To many this is, and always will be, folly; but we have staked upon it our all."

. . . .

Thus we consider this case against the background of a profound national com-mitment to the principle that debate on public issues should be uninhibited, robust, and wide-open, and that it may well include vehement, caustic, and sometimes unpleasantly sharp attacks on government and public officials. The present advertise-ment, as an expression of grievance and protest on one of the major public issues of our time, would seem clearly to qualify for the constitutional protection. The question is whether it forfeits that protection by the falsity of *some* of its factual statements and by its alleged defamation of respondent.

Authoritative interpretations of the First Amendment guarantees have consistently refused to recognize an exception for any test of truth—whether administered by judges, juries, or administrative officials—and especially one that puts the burden of proving truth on the speaker. *Cf. Speiser v. Randall*, 357 U.S. 513, 525–526. The constitutional protection does not turn upon "the truth, popularity, or social utility of the ideas and beliefs which are offered." *NAACP v. Button*, 371 U.S. 415, 445. As Madison said, "Some degree of abuse is inseparable from the proper use of every thing; and in no instance is this more true than in that of the press."

. . . .

[E]rroneous statement is inevitable in free debate, and . . . it must be protected if the freedoms of expression are to have the "breathing space" that they "need . . . to survive," *NAACP v. Button*. . . .

Injury to official reputation affords no more warrant for repressing speech that would otherwise be free than does factual error. . . . Criticism of their official con-duct does not lose its constitutional protection merely because it is effective criticism and hence diminishes their official reputations.

If neither factual error nor defamatory content suffices to remove the constitu-tional shield from criticism of official conduct, the combination of the two elements is no less inadequate. This is the lesson to be drawn from the great controversy over the Sedition Act of 1798, 1 Stat. 596, which first crystallized a national awareness of the central meaning of the First Amendment. See Levy, Legacy of Suppression (1960), at 258 *et seq.;* Smith, Freedom's Fetters (1956), at 426, 431, and *passim*. That statute made it a crime, punishable by a $5,000 fine and five years in prison, "if any person shall write, print, utter or publish . . . any false, scandalous and malicious writing or writings against the government of the United States, or either house of the Con-gress . . . , or the President . . . , with intent to defame . . . or to bring them, or either of them, into contempt or disrepute; or to excite against them, or either or any of them, the hatred of the good people of the United States." The Act allowed the defendant the defense of truth, and provided that the jury were to be judges both of the law and the facts. Despite these qualifications, the Act was vigorously condemned as unconstitutional in an attack joined in by Jefferson and Madison. . . .

Madison prepared the Report in support of the protest. His premise was that the Constitution created a form of government under which "The people, not the government, possess the absolute sovereignty." The structure of the government dispersed power in reflection of the people's distrust of concentrated power, and of power itself at all levels. This form of government was "altogether different" from the British form, under which the Crown was sovereign and the people were subjects. "Is it not natural and necessary, under such different circumstances," he asked, "that a different degree of freedom in the use of the press should be contemplated?" *Id.*, pp. 569–570. . . . On this footing the freedom of the press has stood; on this foundation it yet stands. . . ." 4 Elliot's Debates, *supra*, p. 570. The right of free public discussion of the stewardship of public officials was thus, in Madison's view, a fundamental principle of the American form of government.

Although the Sedition Act was never tested in this Court [the Act expired by its terms in 1801], the attack upon its validity has carried the day in the court of history. . . . These views reflect a broad consensus that the Act, because of the restraint it imposed upon criticism of government and public officials, was inconsistent with the First Amendment.

The constitutional guarantees require, we think, a federal rule that prohibits a public official from recovering damages for a defamatory falsehood relating to his official conduct unless he proves that the statement was made with "actual malice"—that is, with knowledge that it was false or with reckless disregard of whether it was false or not. . . .

III

We hold today that the Constitution delimits a State's power to award damages for libel in actions brought by public officials against critics of their official conduct. Since this is such an action, the rule requiring proof of actual malice is applicable. While Alabama law apparently requires proof of actual malice for an award of punitive damages, where general damages are concerned malice is "presumed." Such a presumption is inconsistent with the federal rule. . . .

Since respondent may seek a new trial, we deem that considerations of effective judicial administration require us to review the evidence in the present record to determine whether it could constitutionally support a judgment for respondent. This Court's duty is not limited to the elaboration of constitutional principles; we must also in proper cases review the evidence to make certain that those principles have been constitutionally applied. . . .

Applying these standards, we consider that the proof presented to show actual malice lacks the convincing clarity which the constitutional standard demands, and hence that it would not constitutionally sustain the judgment for respondent under the proper rule of law. . . .

As to the *Times*, we similarly conclude that the facts do not support a finding of actual malice. The statement by the *Times'* Secretary that . . . he thought the advertisement was "substantially correct," affords no constitutional warrant for the Alabama Supreme Court's conclusion that it was a "cavalier ignoring of the falsity of the advertisement" . . . "[E]ven if the advertisement was not "substantially correct" — although respondent's own proofs tend to show that it was — that opinion was at least a reasonable one, and there was no evidence to impeach the witness' good faith in holding it. The Times' failure to retract upon respondent's demand . . . is likewise not adequate evidence of malice for constitutional purposes. . . .

Finally, there is evidence that the Times published the advertisement without checking its accuracy against the news stories in the Times' own files. The mere presence of the stories in the files does not, of course, establish that the Times "knew" the advertisement was false, since the state of mind required for actual malice would have to be brought home to the persons in the Times' organization having responsibility for the publication of the advertisement. With respect to the failure of those persons to make the check, the record shows that they relied upon their knowledge of the good reputation of many of those whose names were listed as sponsors of the advertisement, and upon the letter from A. Philip Randolph, known to them as a responsible individual, certifying that the use of the names was authorized. . . . We think the evidence against the Times supports at most a finding of negligence in failing to discover the misstatements, and is constitutionally insufficient to show the recklessness that is required for a finding of actual malice.

We also think the evidence was constitutionally defective in another respect: it was incapable of supporting the jury's finding that the allegedly libelous statements were made "of and concerning" respondent. Respondent relies on the words of the advertisement and the testimony of six witnesses to establish a connection between it and himself. . . .

There was no reference to respondent in the advertisement, either by name or official position. A number of the allegedly libelous statements — the charges that the dining hall was padlocked and that Dr. King's home was bombed, his person assaulted, and a perjury prosecution instituted against him — did not even concern the police; despite the ingenuity of the arguments which would attach this significance to the word "They," it is plain that these statements could not reasonably be read as accusing respondent of personal involvement in the acts in question. . . . Although the statements may be taken as referring to the police, they did not on their face make even an oblique reference to respondent as an individual. Support for the asserted reference must, therefore, be sought in the testimony of respondent's witnesses. But none of them suggested any basis for the belief that respondent himself was attacked in the advertisement beyond the bare fact that he was in overall charge of the Police Department and thus bore official responsibility for police conduct . . .

The judgment of the Supreme Court of Alabama is reversed and the case is remanded to that court for further proceedings not inconsistent with this opinion.

Reversed and remanded.

Mr. Justice Black, with whom Mr. Justice Douglas joins, concurring.

I concur in reversing this half-million-dollar judgment against the New York Times Company and the four individual defendants. In reversing the Court holds that "the Constitution delimits a State's power to award damages for libel in actions brought by public officials against critics of their official conduct." . . . I base my vote to reverse on the belief that the First and Fourteenth Amendments not merely "delimit" a State's power to award damages to "public officials against critics of their official conduct" but completely prohibit a State from exercising such a power. The Court goes on to hold that a State can subject such critics to damages if "actual malice" can be proved against them. "Malice," even as defined by the Court, is an elusive, abstract concept, hard to prove and hard to disprove. The requirement that malice be proved provides at best an evanescent protection for the right critically to discuss public affairs and certainly does not measure up to the sturdy safeguard embodied in the First Amendment. Unlike the Court, therefore, I vote to reverse exclusively on the ground that the Times and the individual defendants had an absolute, unconditional constitutional right to publish in the Times advertisement their criticisms of the Montgomery agencies and officials. . . .

We would, I think, more faithfully interpret the First Amendment by holding that at the very least it leaves the people and the press free to criticize officials and discuss public affairs with impunity. . . . An unconditional right to say what one pleases about public affairs is what I consider to be the minimum guarantee of the First Amendment.

I regret that the Court has stopped short of this holding indispensable to preserve our free press from destruction.

---

1. As the Court struggled to define the scope *of New York Times*, it was faced with a case brought by a University of Georgia football coach and athletic director (*Curtis Publishing Co. v. Butts*) and a retired Army General (*Associated Press v. Walker*) for libel. The cases were consolidated for decision. The opinions offer several different tests for liability. An important point is that both Butts and Walker were held to be public figures who should be treated the same as public officials for purposes of "actual malice." *Curtis Publishing Co. v. Butts*, 388 U.S. 130 (1967).

2. *Malice.* A great deal of caution must be exercised in using the word "malice." At common law, malice was imputed if the statement was intended. *Bromage v. Prosser*, (1825) 4 B. & C. 247, 107 Eng. Rep. 1051 (K.B.). Often "malice" means spite or ill will and may be used to defeat a privilege. *New York Times* presents and defines the term "actual malice" in a way that is quite different from spite and ill will. It focuses instead on whether the defendant either knew of a statement's falsehood or showed "reckless disregard" of the truth.

The Supreme Court later moved away from this position in *Gertz, infra*.

3. What is the scope of *New York Times*? If "actual malice" applies to public officials and public figures, should it apply to all matters of "public interest"? In 1971, a plurality of the Supreme Court answered in the affirmative in *Rosenbloom v. Metromedia, Inc.*, 403 U.S. 29 (1971):

> The instant case presents the question whether the *New York Times'* knowing-or-reckless-falsity standard applied in a state civil libel action brought not by a "public official" or a "public figure" but by a private individual for a defamatory falsehood uttered in a news broadcast by a radio station about the individual's involvement in an event of public or general interest. The Court of Appeals for the Third Circuit held that the *New York Times* standard did apply and reversed the judgment for damages awarded to petitioner by the jury. We granted certiorari. We agree with the Court of Appeals and affirm that court's judgment.

4. *Public Officials.* A public (county) recreation supervisor was held to be a public official in *Rosenblatt v. Baer*, 383 U.S. 75 (1966). What about a high school athletic coach? *See O'Connor v. Burningham*, 165 P.3d 1214 (Utah 2007) (distinguishing *Butts* and holding that coach of a high school girls' basketball team was not a public official because he was "not likely to influence matters of public policy in the civil, as distinguished from the cultural, educational or sports realms").

5. Police officers are considered public officials, *Rotkiewicz v. Sadowsky*, 730 N.E.2d 282 (Mass. 2000), but not firefighters, *Jones v. Palmer Communications*, 440 N.W.2d 884 (Iowa 1989). Why not? Should the treatment of firefighters change after 9/11/2001?

6. *Kassel v. Gannett Co.*, 875 F.2d 935 (1st Cir. 1989), presents a three part test for public official:

> Read together, the Court's defamation opinions reveal that the "public official" rule rests on a tripodal base. The trio of policy concerns which undergirds the caselaw can be instructive in attempting to assess the rule's range and reach.

> . . . The Three-Legged Stool.

> The first leg of the stool is a frank recognition that the First Amendment requires maximum latitude for "uninhibited, robust, and wide-open" discourse on issues of public importance. That philosophy necessarily implies "a strong interest in debate about those persons who are in a position significantly to influence the resolution of [such] issues." The public official doctrine provides an extra measure of protection for speakers who dare to voice "[c]riticism of those responsible for government operations." Id. Policymakers, upper-level administrators, and supervisors are caught up in the "public official" net for that reason: such plenipotentiaries occupy niches of

"apparent importance" sufficient to give the public "an independent interest in the qualifications and performances of the person[s] who hold[] [them], beyond the general public interest in the qualifications and performance of all government employees."

. . . .

The second leg of the stool implicates communication. Those who hold public office are frequently able to defend themselves in the media. That ability is tantamount to the ability to engage in self-help. When the need arises to respond to charges, such officeholders "usually enjoy significantly greater access to the channels of effective communication and hence have a more realistic opportunity to counteract false statements than private individuals normally enjoy."

. . . .

The last leg of the stool recognizes the reality of assumed risks. Persons who actively seek positions of influence in public life do so with the knowledge that, if successful in attaining their goals, diminished privacy will result. The classic case, of course, is the aspirant to elective office: a candidate is on fair notice that adverse, even negligent, press coverage is a "necessary consequence[] of that involvement in public affairs." The same can be said of individuals who accept appointments to powerful government positions.

2. The Actual Malice Standard

St. Amant v. Thompson

Supreme Court of the United States, 1968
390 U.S. 727

MR. JUSTICE WHITE delivered the opinion of the Court.

The question presented by this case is whether the Louisiana Supreme Court, in sustaining a judgment for damages in a public official's defamation action, correctly interpreted and applied the rule of *New York Times Co. v. Sullivan*, 376 U.S. 254 (1964), that the plaintiff in such an action must prove that the defamatory publication "was made with 'actual malice' — that is, with knowledge that it was false or with reckless disregard of whether it was false or not." 376 U.S., at 279–280.

On June 27, 1962, petitioner St. Amant, a candidate for public office, made a televised speech in Baton Rouge, Louisiana. In the course of this speech, St. Amant read a series of questions which he had put to J. D. Albin, a member of a Teamsters Union local, and Albin's answers [in an affidavit] to those questions. The exchange concerned the allegedly nefarious activities of E. G. Partin, the president of the local, and the alleged relationship between Partin and St. Amant's political opponent. . . .

Thompson promptly brought suit for defamation, claiming that the publication had "impute[d] . . . gross misconduct" and "infer[red] conduct of the most nefarious nature." The case was tried prior to the decision in *New York Times Co. v. Sullivan, supra.* The trial judge ruled in Thompson's favor and awarded $5,000 in damages. Thereafter, in the course of entertaining and denying a motion for a new trial, the Court considered the ruling in *New York Times,* finding that rule no barrier to the judgment already entered. The Louisiana Court of Appeal reversed because the record failed to show that St. Amant had acted with actual malice. . . . The Supreme Court of Louisiana reversed the intermediate appellate court. . . . In its view, there was sufficient evidence that St. Amant recklessly disregarded whether the statements about Thompson were true or false. We granted a writ of certiorari. . . .

For purposes of this case we accept the determinations of the Louisiana courts that the material published by St. Amant charged Thompson with criminal conduct, that the charge was false, and that Thompson was a public official and so had the burden of proving that the false statements about Thompson were made with actual malice as defined in *New York Times Co. v. Sullivan* and later cases. We cannot, however, agree with either the Supreme Court of Louisiana or the trial court that Thompson sustained this burden.

Purporting to apply the *New York Times* malice standard, the Louisiana Supreme Court ruled that St. Amant had broadcast false information about Thompson recklessly, though not knowingly. . . . St. Amant had no personal knowledge of Thompson's activities; he relied solely on Albin's affidavit although the record was silent as to Albin's reputation for veracity; he failed to verify the information with those in the union office who might have known the facts; he gave no consideration to whether or not the statements defamed Thompson and went ahead heedless of the consequences; and he mistakenly believed he had no responsibility for the broadcast because he was merely quoting Albin's words.

These considerations fall short of proving St. Amant's reckless disregard for the accuracy of his statements about Thompson. "Reckless disregard," it is true, cannot be fully encompassed in one infallible definition. . . . Our cases, however, have furnished meaningful guidance for the further definition of a reckless publication. In *New York Times, supra,* the plaintiff did not satisfy his burden because the record failed to show that the publisher was aware of the likelihood that he was circulating false information. . . . Mr. Justice Harlan's opinion in *Curtis Publishing Co. v. Butts,* 388 U.S. 130, 153 (1967), stated that evidence of either deliberate falsification or reckless publication "despite the publisher's awareness of probable falsity" was essential to recovery by public officials in defamation actions. These cases are clear that reckless conduct is not measured by whether a reasonably prudent man would have published, or would have investigated before publishing. There must be sufficient evidence to permit the conclusion that the defendant in fact entertained serious doubts as to the truth of his publication. Publishing with such doubts shows reckless disregard for truth or falsity and demonstrates actual malice.

It may be said that such a test puts a premium on ignorance, encourages the irresponsible publisher not to inquire, and permits the issue to be determined by the defendant's testimony that he published the statement in good faith and unaware of its probable falsity. Concededly the reckless disregard standard may permit recovery in fewer situations than would a rule that publishers must satisfy the standard of the reasonable man or the prudent publisher. But *New York Times* and succeeding cases have emphasized that the stake of the people in public business and the conduct of public officials is so great that neither the defense of truth nor the standard of ordinary care would protect against self-censorship and thus adequately implement First Amendment policies. . . . But to insure the ascertainment and publication of the truth about public affairs, it is essential that the First Amendment protect some erroneous publications as well as true ones. We adhere to this view and to the line which our cases have drawn between false communications which are protected and those which are not.

The defendant in a defamation action brought by a public official cannot, however, automatically insure a favorable verdict by testifying that he published with a belief that the statements were true. The finder of fact must determine whether the publication was indeed made in good faith. Professions of good faith will be unlikely to prove persuasive, for example, where a story is fabricated by the defendant, is the product of his imagination, or is based wholly on an unverified anonymous telephone call. Nor will they be likely to prevail when the publisher's allegations are so inherently improbable that only a reckless man would have put them in circulation. Likewise, recklessness may be found where there are obvious reasons to doubt the veracity of the informant or the accuracy of his reports.

By no proper test of reckless disregard was St. Amant's broadcast a reckless publication about a public officer. Nothing referred to by the Louisiana courts indicates an awareness by St. Amant of the probable falsity of Albin's statement about Thompson. Failure to investigate does not in itself establish bad faith. *New York Times Co. v. Sullivan, supra,* at 287–288. St. Amant's mistake about his probable legal liability does not evidence a doubtful mind on his part. . . .

Because the state court misunderstood and misapplied the actual malice standard which must be observed in a public official's defamation action, the judgment is reversed and the case remanded for further proceedings not inconsistent with this opinion.

Reversed and remanded.

––––––––

1. *Westmoreland v. CBS*, 601 F. Supp. 66 (S.D.N.Y. 1984), held that the presentation of "one-sided attacks" does not constitute actual malice, if the publisher honestly believes in the truth of his statements:

> The fairness of the broadcast is not at issue in the libel suit. Publishers and reporters do not commit a libel in a public figure case by publishing unfair one-sided attacks. The issue in the libel suit is whether the publisher recklessly or knowingly published false material. The fact that a commentary is one sided and sets forth categorical accusations has no tendency to prove that the publisher believed it to be false. The libel law does not require the publisher to grant his accused equal time or fair reply. It requires only that the

publisher not slander by known falsehoods (or reckless ones). A publisher who honestly believes in the truth of his accusations (and can point to a non-reckless basis for his beliefs) is under no obligation under the libel law to treat the subject of his accusations fairly or evenhandedly.

Masson v. New Yorker Magazine, Inc.

Supreme Court of the United States, 1991
501 U.S. 496

JUSTICE KENNEDY delivered the opinion of the Court.

In this libel case, a public figure claims he was defamed by an author who, with full knowledge of the inaccuracy, used quotation marks to attribute to him comments he had not made. The First Amendment protects authors and journalists who write about public figures by requiring a plaintiff to prove that the defamatory statements were made with what we have called "actual malice," a term of art denoting deliberate or reckless falsification. We consider in this opinion whether the attributed quotations had the degree of falsity required to prove this state of mind, so that the public figure can defeat a motion for summary judgment and proceed to a trial on the merits of the defamation claim.

I

Petitioner Jeffrey Masson trained at Harvard University as a Sanskrit scholar, and in 1970 became a professor of Sanskrit & Indian Studies at the University of Toronto. . . . Through his professional activities, he came to know Dr. Kurt Eissler, head of the Sigmund Freud Archives, and Dr. Anna Freud, daughter of Sigmund Freud and a major psychoanalyst in her own right. The Sigmund Freud Archives . . . serves as a repository for materials about Freud, including his own writings, letters, and personal library. The materials, and the right of access to them, are of immense value to those who study Freud and his theories, life, and work.

In 1980, Eissler and Anna Freud hired petitioner as projects director of the archives. After assuming his post, petitioner became disillusioned with Freudian psychology. In a 1981 lecture before the Western New England Psychoanalytical Society in New Haven, Connecticut, he advanced his theories of Freud. Soon after, the board of the archives terminated petitioner as projects director.

Respondent Janet Malcolm is an author and a contributor to respondent *The New Yorker*, a weekly magazine. She contacted petitioner in 1982 regarding the possibility of an article on his relationship with the archives. He agreed, and the two met in person and spoke by telephone in a series of interviews. Based on the interviews and other sources, Malcolm wrote a lengthy article. One of Malcolm's narrative devices consists of enclosing lengthy passages in quotation marks, reporting statements of Masson, Eissler, and her other subjects.

During the editorial process, Nancy Franklin, a member of the fact-checking department at *The New Yorker*, called petitioner to confirm some of the facts underlying the article. According to petitioner, he expressed alarm at the number of errors in the few passages Franklin discussed with him. Petitioner contends that he asked permission to review those portions of the article which attributed quotations or information to him, but was brushed off with a never-fulfilled promise to "get back to [him]." . . .

The New Yorker published Malcolm's piece in December 1983, as a two-part series. In 1984, with knowledge of at least petitioner's general allegation that the article contained defamatory material, respondent Alfred A. Knopf, Inc., published the entire work as a book, entitled In the Freud Archives.

Malcolm's work received complimentary reviews. But this gave little joy to Masson, for the book portrays him in a most unflattering light. According to one reviewer:

> "Masson the promising psychoanalytic scholar emerges gradually, as a grandiose egotist — mean-spirited, self-serving, full of braggadocio, impossibly arrogant and, in the end, a self-destructive fool. But it is not Janet Malcolm who calls him such: his own words reveal this psychological profile — a self-portrait offered to us through the efforts of an observer and listener who is, surely, as wise as any in the psychoanalytic profession." Coles, Freudianism Confronts Its Malcontents, Boston Globe, May 27, 1984, pp. 58, 60.

Petitioner brought an action for libel under California law in the United States District Court for the Northern District of California. . . .

Each passage before us purports to quote a statement made by petitioner during the interviews. Yet in each instance no identical statement appears in the more than 40 hours of taped interviews. Petitioner complains that Malcolm fabricated all but one passage; with respect to that passage, he claims Malcolm omitted a crucial portion, rendering the remainder misleading.

Malcolm submitted to the District Court that not all of her discussions with petitioner were recorded on tape, in particular conversations that occurred while the two of them walked together or traveled by car, while petitioner stayed at Malcolm's home in New York, or while her tape recorder was inoperable. She claimed to have taken notes of these unrecorded sessions, which she later typed, then discarding the handwritten originals. Petitioner denied that any discussion relating to the substance of the article occurred during his stay at Malcolm's home in New York, that Malcolm took notes during any of their conversations, or that Malcolm gave any indication that her tape recorder was broken.

Respondents moved for summary judgment. The parties agreed that petitioner was a public figure and so could escape summary judgment only if the evidence in the record would permit a reasonable finder of fact, by clear and convincing evidence, to conclude that respondents published a defamatory statement with actual malice as defined by our cases. The District Court analyzed each of the passages and held that the alleged inaccuracies did not raise a jury question. The court found that the allegedly fabricated quotations were either substantially true, or were "'one of a number of possible rational interpretations' of a conversation or event that 'bristled with ambiguities,'" and thus were entitled to constitutional protection. The court also ruled that the "he had the wrong man" passage involved an exercise of editorial judgment upon which the courts could not intrude. 686 F. Supp. at 1403–1404.

The Court of Appeals affirmed, with one judge dissenting. 895 F.2d 1535 (CA9 1989). The court assumed for much of its opinion that Malcolm had deliberately altered each quotation not found on the tape recordings, but nevertheless held that petitioner failed to raise a jury question of actual malice, in large part for the reasons stated by the District Court. . . .

The dissent argued that any intentional or reckless alteration would prove actual malice, so long as a passage within quotation marks purports to be a verbatim rendition of what was said, contains material inaccuracies, and is defamatory. 895 F.2d at 1562–1570. We granted certiorari, 498 U.S. 808 (1990), and now reverse.

II

A

Under California law, "libel is a false and unprivileged publication by writing . . . which exposes any person to hatred, contempt, ridicule, or obloquy, or which causes him to be shunned or avoided, or which has a tendency to injure him in his occupation." Cal. Civ. Code Ann. §45 (West 1982). False attribution of statements to a person may constitute libel, if the falsity exposes that person to an injury comprehended by the statute. It matters not under California law that petitioner alleges only part of the work at issue to be false. "The test of libel is not quantitative; a single sentence may be the basis for an action in libel even though buried in a much longer text," though the California courts recognize that "while a drop of poison may be lethal, weaker poisons are sometimes diluted to the point of impotency."

B

In general, quotation marks around a passage indicate to the reader that the passage reproduces the speaker's words verbatim. They inform the reader that he or she is reading the statement of the speaker, not a paraphrase or other indirect interpretation by an author. By providing this information, quotations add authority to the statement and credibility to the author's work. Quotations allow the reader to form his or her own conclusions and to assess the conclusions of the author, instead of relying entirely upon the author's characterization of her subject.

A fabricated quotation may injure reputation in at least two senses, either giving rise to a conceivable claim of defamation. First, the quotation might injure because it attributes an untrue factual assertion to the speaker. An example would be a fabricated quotation of a public official admitting he had been convicted of a serious crime when in fact he had not.

Second, regardless of the truth or falsity of the factual matters asserted within the quoted statement, the attribution may result in injury to reputation because the manner of expression or even the fact that the statement was made indicates a negative personal trait or an attitude the speaker does not hold. John Lennon once was quoted as saying of the Beatles, "We're more popular than Jesus Christ now." Time, Aug. 12, 1966, p. 38. Supposing the quotation had been a fabrication, it appears California law could permit recovery for defamation because, even without regard to the truth of the underlying assertion, false attribution of the statement could have injured his reputation. Here, in like manner, one need not determine whether petitioner is or is not the greatest analyst who ever lived in order to determine that it might have injured his reputation to be reported as having so proclaimed.

. . . .

Of course, quotations do not always convey that the speaker actually said or wrote the quoted material. "Punctuation marks, like words, have many uses. Writers often use quotation marks, yet no reasonable reader would assume that such punctuation automatically implies the truth of the quoted material." . . .

The work at issue here, however, as with much journalistic writing, provides the reader no clue that the quotations are being used as a rhetorical device or to paraphrase the speaker's actual statements. To the contrary, the work purports to be nonfiction, the result of numerous interviews. At least a trier of fact could so conclude. The work contains lengthy quotations attributed to petitioner, and neither Malcolm nor her publishers indicate to the reader that the quotations are anything but the reproduction of actual conversations. Further, the work was published in *The New Yorker*, a magazine which at the relevant time seemed to enjoy a reputation for scrupulous factual accuracy. These factors would, or at least could, lead a reader to take the quotations at face value. A defendant may be able to argue to the jury that quotations should be viewed by the reader as nonliteral or reconstructions, but we conclude that a trier of fact in this case could find that the reasonable reader would understand the quotations to be nearly verbatim reports of statements made by the subject.

C

The constitutional question we must consider here is whether, in the framework of a summary judgment motion, the evidence suffices to show that respondents acted with the requisite knowledge of falsity or reckless disregard as to truth or falsity. . . . We must consider whether the requisite falsity inheres in the attribution of words to the petitioner which he did not speak.

In some sense, any alteration of a verbatim quotation is false. But writers and reporters by necessity alter what people say, at the very least to eliminate grammatical and syntactical infelicities. If every alteration constituted the falsity required to prove actual malice, the practice of journalism, which the First Amendment standard is designed to protect, would require a radical change, one inconsistent with our precedents and First Amendment principles.

. . . .

We reject the idea that any alteration beyond correction of grammar or syntax by itself proves falsity in the sense relevant to determining actual malice under the First Amendment. An interviewer who writes from notes often will engage in the task of attempting a reconstruction of the speaker's statement. That author would, we may assume, act with knowledge that at times she has attributed to her subject words other than those actually used.

. . . .

Even if a journalist has tape-recorded the spoken statement of a public figure, the full and exact statement will be reported in only rare circumstances. The existence of both a speaker and a reporter; the translation between two media, speech and the printed word; the addition of punctuation; and the practical necessity to edit and make intelligible a speaker's perhaps rambling comments, all make it misleading to suggest that a quotation will be reconstructed with complete accuracy. The use or absence of punctuation may distort a speaker's meaning, for example, where that meaning turns upon a speaker's emphasis of a particular word. In other cases, if a speaker makes an obvious misstatement, for example by unconscious substitution of one name for another, a journalist might alter the speaker's words but preserve his intended meaning. And conversely, an exact quotation out of context can distort meaning, although the speaker did use each reported word.

In all events, technical distinctions between correcting grammar and syntax and some greater level of alteration do not appear workable, for we can think of no method by which courts or juries would draw the line between cleaning up and other changes, except by reference to the meaning a statement conveys to a reasonable reader. To attempt narrow distinctions of this type would be an unnecessary departure from First Amendment principles of general applicability, and, just as important, a departure from the underlying purposes of the tort of libel as understood since the latter half of the 16th century. From then until now, the tort action for defamation has existed to redress injury to the plaintiff's reputation by a statement that is defamatory and false. See *Milkovich v. Lorain Journal Co.*, 497 U.S. 1, 11, 110 S. Ct. 2695, 111 L. Ed. 2d 1 (1990). As we have recognized, "the legitimate state interest underlying the law of libel is the compensation of individuals for the harm inflicted on them by defamatory falsehood." *Gertz v. Robert Welch, Inc.*, 418 U.S. 323, 341, 94 S. Ct. 2997, 41 L. Ed. 2d 789 (1974). If an author alters a speaker's words but effects no material change in meaning, including any meaning conveyed by the manner or fact of expression, the speaker suffers no injury to reputation that is compensable as a defamation.

. . . .

The common law of libel takes but one approach to the question of falsity, regardless of the form of the communication. See Restatement (Second) of Torts § 563, Comment *c* (1977); W. Keeton, D. Dobbs, R. Keeton, & D. Owen, Prosser and Keeton on Law of Torts 776 (5th ed. 1984). It overlooks minor inaccuracies and concentrates upon substantial truth. As in other jurisdictions, California law permits the defense of substantial truth and would absolve a defendant even if she cannot "justify every word of the alleged defamatory matter; it is sufficient if the substance of the charge be proved true, irrespective of slight inaccuracy in the details." 5 B. Witkin, Summary of California Law § 495 (9th ed. 1988) (citing cases). . . . Minor inaccuracies do not amount to falsity so long as "the substance, the gist, the sting, of the libelous charge be justified." Put another way, the statement is not considered false unless it "would have a different effect on the mind of the reader from that which the pleaded truth would have produced." R. Sack, Libel, Slander, and Related Problems 138 (1980); see, *e.g., Wehling v. Columbia Broadcasting System*, 721 F.2d 506, 509 (CA5 1983); see generally R. Smolla, Law of Defamation § 5.08 (1991). Our definition of actual malice relies upon this historical understanding.

We conclude that a deliberate alteration of the words uttered by a plaintiff does not equate with knowledge of falsity for purposes of *New York Times Co. v. Sullivan*, 376 U.S. at 279–280, and *Gertz v. Robert Welch, Inc., supra*, at 342, unless the alteration results in a material change in the meaning conveyed by the statement. The use of quotations to attribute words not in fact spoken bears in a most important way on that inquiry, but it is not dispositive in every case . . .

III

. . . .

Because of the Court of Appeals' disposition with respect to Malcolm, it did not have occasion to address petitioner's argument that the District Court erred in granting summary judgment to The New Yorker Magazine, Inc., and Alfred A. Knopf, Inc., on the basis of their respective relations with Malcolm or the lack of any independent actual malice. These questions are best addressed in the first instance on remand.

The judgment of the Court of Appeals is reversed, and the case is remanded for further proceedings consistent with this opinion.

It is so ordered.

JUSTICE WHITE, with whom JUSTICE SCALIA joins, concurring in part and dissenting in part.

I join Parts I, II-A, II-D, and III-A, but cannot wholly agree with the remainder of the opinion. My principal disagreement is with the holding . . . that "a deliberate alteration of the words uttered by a plaintiff does not equate with knowledge of falsity . . . unless the alteration results in a material change in the meaning conveyed by the statement."

. . . .

[T]he Court states that deliberate misquotation does not amount to *New York Times* malice unless it results in a material change in the meaning conveyed by the statement. This ignores the fact that, under *New York Times*, reporting a known falsehood—here the knowingly false attribution—is sufficient proof of malice. The falsehood, apparently, must be substantial; the reporter may lie a little, but not too much.

This standard is not only a less manageable one than the traditional approach, but it also assigns to the courts issues that are for the jury to decide. For a court to ask whether a misquotation substantially alters the meaning of spoken words in a defamatory manner is a far different inquiry from whether reasonable jurors could find that the misquotation was different enough to be libelous. In the one case, the court is measuring the difference from its own point of view; in the other it is asking how the jury would or could view the erroneous attribution.

———————

Does *Masson* introduce a constitutional definition of truth or is it *sui generis*? Does it set the standard for accuracy in quotation too high? Too low? Could the author and publisher avoid liability by putting a disclaimer regarding quotations at the front of a book or article? If so, what should the disclaimer say?

3. Private Plaintiffs

Gertz v. Robert Welch, Inc.

Supreme Court of the United States, 1974
418 U.S. 323

MR. JUSTICE POWELL delivered the opinion of the Court.

. . . We granted certiorari to reconsider the extent of a publisher's constitutional privilege against liability for defamation of a private citizen. . . .

I

In 1968 a Chicago policeman named Nuccio shot and killed a youth named Nelson. The state authorities prosecuted Nuccio for the homicide and ultimately obtained a conviction for murder in the second degree. The Nelson family retained petitioner Elmer Gertz, a reputable attorney, to represent them in civil litigation against Nuccio.

Respondent publishes *American Opinion*, a monthly outlet for the views of the John Birch Society. Early in the 1960's the magazine began to warn of a nationwide conspiracy to discredit local law enforcement agencies and create in their stead a national police force capable of supporting a Communist dictatorship. As part of the continuing effort to alert the public to this assumed danger, the managing editor of *American Opinion* commissioned an article on the murder trial of Officer Nuccio. . . . In March 1969 respondent published the resulting article under the title "FRAME-UP: Richard Nuccio And The War On Police." The article purports to demonstrate that the testimony against Nuccio at his criminal trial was false and that his prosecution was part of the Communist campaign against the police.

In his capacity as counsel for the Nelson family in the civil litigation, petitioner attended the coroner's inquest into the boy's death and initiated actions for damages, but he neither discussed Officer Nuccio with the press nor played any part in the criminal proceeding. Notwithstanding petitioner's remote connection with the prosecution of Nuccio, respondent's magazine portrayed him as an architect of the "frame-up." According to the article, the police file on petitioner took "a big, Irish cop to lift." The article stated that petitioner had been an official of the "Marxist League for Industrial Democracy, originally known as the Intercollegiate Socialist Society, which has advocated the violent seizure of our government." It labeled Gertz a "Leninist" and a "Communist-fronter." It also stated that Gertz had been an officer of the National Lawyers Guild, described as a Communist organization that "probably did more than any other outfit to plan the Communist attack on the Chicago police during the 1968 Democratic Convention."

These statements contained serious inaccuracies. The implication that petitioner had a criminal record was false. Petitioner had been a member and officer of the National Lawyers Guild some 15 years earlier, but there was no evidence that he or that organization had taken any part in planning the 1968 demonstrations in Chicago. There was also no basis for the charge that petitioner was a "Leninist" or a "Communist-fronter." And he had never been a member of the "Marxist League for Industrial Democracy" or the "Intercollegiate Socialist Society."

The managing editor of *American Opinion* made no effort to verify or substantiate the charges against petitioner. Instead, he appended an editorial introduction stating that the author had "conducted extensive research into the Richard Nuccio Case." And he included in the article a photograph of petitioner and wrote the caption that appeared under it: "Elmer Gertz of Red Guild harrasses Nuccio." Respondent placed the issue of American Opinion containing the article on sale at newsstands throughout the country and distributed reprints of the article on the streets of Chicago.

Petitioner filed a diversity action for libel in the United States District Court for the Northern District of Illinois. He claimed that the falsehoods published by respondent injured his reputation as a lawyer and a citizen. . . .

After answering the complaint, respondent filed a pretrial motion for summary judgment, claiming a constitutional privilege against liability for defamation. It asserted that petitioner was a public official or a public figure and that the article concerned an issue of public interest and concern. For these reasons, respondent argued, it was entitled to invoke the privilege enunciated in *New York Times Co. v. Sullivan*, 376 U.S. 254 (1964). Under this rule respondent would escape liability unless petitioner could prove publication of defamatory falsehood "with 'actual malice' — that is, with knowledge that it was false or with reckless disregard of whether it was false or not." *Id.*, at 280. . . .

The District Court denied respondent's motion for summary judgment in a memorandum opinion of September 16, 1970. . . . After all the evidence had been presented but before submission of the case to the jury, the court ruled in effect that petitioner was neither a public official nor a public figure. It added that, if he were, the resulting application of the *New York Times* standard would require a directed verdict for respondent. Because some statements in the article constituted libel *per se* under Illinois law, the court submitted the case to the jury under instructions that withdrew from its consideration all issues save the measure of damages. The jury awarded $50,000 to petitioner.

Following the jury verdict and on further reflection, the District Court concluded that the *New York Times* standard should govern this case even though petitioner was not a public official or public figure. It accepted respondent's contention that that privilege protected discussion of any public issue without regard to the status of a person defamed therein. Accordingly, the court entered judgment for respondent notwithstanding the jury's verdict. . . .

Petitioner appealed to contest the applicability of the *New York Times* standard to this case. Although the Court of Appeals for the Seventh Circuit doubted the correctness of the District Court's determination that petitioner was not a public figure, it did not overturn that finding. It agreed with the District Court that respondent could assert the constitutional privilege because the article concerned a matter of public interest . . . After reviewing the record, the Court of Appeals endorsed the District Court's conclusion that petitioner had failed to show by clear and convincing evidence that respondent had acted with "actual malice" as defined by *New York Times*. . . . The Court of Appeals therefore affirmed, 471 F.2d 801 (1972). For the reasons stated below, we reverse.

II

The principal issue in this case is whether a newspaper or broadcaster that publishes defamatory falsehoods about an individual who is neither a public official nor a public figure may claim a constitutional privilege against liability for the injury inflicted by those statements. . . .

Three years after *New York Times*, a majority of the Court agreed to extend the constitutional privilege to defamatory criticism of "public figures." This extension was announced in *Curtis Publishing Co. v. Butts* and its companion, *Associated Press v. Walker*, 388 U.S. 130, 162 (1967). . . .

III

We begin with the common ground. Under the First Amendment there is no such thing as a false idea. However pernicious an opinion may seem, we depend for its correction not on the conscience of judges and juries but on the competition of other ideas. But there is no constitutional value in false statements of fact. Neither the intentional lie nor the careless error materially advances society's interest in "uninhibited, robust, and wide-open" debate on public issues. *New York Times Co. v. Sullivan*, 376 U.S., at 270. . . .

Although the erroneous statement of fact is not worthy of constitutional protection, it is nevertheless inevitable in free debate. . . . Our decisions recognize that a rule of strict liability that compels a publisher or broadcaster to guarantee the accuracy of his factual assertions may lead to intolerable self-censorship. Allowing the media to avoid liability only by proving the truth of all injurious statements does not accord adequate protection to First Amendment liberties. . . .

The legitimate state interest underlying the law of libel is the compensation of individuals for the harm inflicted on them by defamatory falsehood. We would not lightly require the State to abandon this purpose, for, as Mr. Justice Stewart has reminded us, the individual's right to the protection of his own good name

> "reflects no more than our basic concept of the essential dignity and worth of every human being—a concept at the root of any decent system of ordered liberty. The protection of private personality, like the protection of life itself, is left primarily to the individual States under the Ninth and Tenth Amendments. But this does not mean that the right is entitled to any less recognition by this Court as a basic of our constitutional system." *Rosenblatt v. Baer*, 383 U.S. 75, 92 (1966) (concurring opinion).

Some tension necessarily exists between the need for a vigorous and uninhibited press and the legitimate interest in redressing wrongful injury. . . . To that end this Court has extended a measure of strategic protection to defamatory falsehood.

The *New York Times* standard defines the level of constitutional protection appropriate to the context of defamation of a public person. Those who, by reason of the notoriety of their achievements or the vigor and success with which they seek the public's attention, are properly classed as public figures and those who hold governmental office may recover for injury to reputation only on clear and convincing proof that the defamatory falsehood was made with knowledge of its falsity or with reckless disregard for the truth. This standard administers an extremely powerful antidote to the inducement to media self-censorship of the common-law rule of strict liability for libel and slander. And it exacts a correspondingly high price from the victims of defamatory falsehood. Plainly many deserving plaintiffs, including some intentionally subjected to injury, will be unable to surmount the barrier of the *New York Times* test. Despite this substantial abridgment of the state law right to compensation for wrongful hurt to one's reputation, the Court has concluded that the protection of the *New York Times* privilege should be available to publishers and broadcasters of defamatory falsehood concerning public officials and public figures. *New York Times Co. v. Sullivan, supra; Curtis Publishing Co. v. Butts, supra.* We think that these decisions are correct, but we do not find their holdings justified solely by reference to the interest of the press and broadcast media in immunity from liability. Rather, we believe that the *New York Times* rule states an accommodation between this concern and the limited state interest present in the context of libel actions brought by public persons. For the reasons stated below, we conclude that the state interest in compensating injury to the reputation of private individuals requires that a different rule should obtain with respect to them.

Theoretically, of course, the balance between the needs of the press and the individual's claim to compensation for wrongful injury might be struck on a case-by-case basis. . . . Because an *ad hoc* resolution of the competing interests at stake in each particular case is not feasible, we must lay down broad rules of general application. Such rules necessarily treat alike various cases involving differences as well as similarities. . . .

With that caveat we have no difficulty in distinguishing among defamation plaintiffs. The first remedy of any victim of defamation is self-help—using available opportunities to contradict the lie or correct the error and thereby to minimize its adverse impact on reputation. Public officials and public figures usually enjoy significantly greater access to the channels of effective communication and hence have a more realistic opportunity to counteract false statements than private individuals normally enjoy. Private individuals are therefore more vulnerable to injury, and the state interest in protecting them is correspondingly greater.

More important than the likelihood that private individuals will lack effective opportunities for rebuttal, there is a compelling normative consideration underlying the distinction between public and private defamation plaintiffs. An individual who decides to seek governmental office must accept certain necessary consequences of that involvement in public affairs. He runs the risk of closer public scrutiny than might otherwise be the case. And society's interest in the officers of government is not strictly limited to the formal discharge of official duties. As the Court pointed out in *Garrison v. Louisiana*, 379 U.S., at 77, the public's interest extends to "anything which might touch on an official's fitness for office. . . . Few personal attributes are more germane to fitness for office than dishonesty, malfeasance, or improper motivation, even though these characteristics may also affect the official's private character."

Those classed as public figures stand in a similar position. Hypothetically, it may be possible for someone to become a public figure through no purposeful action of his own, but the instances of truly involuntary public figures must be exceedingly rare. For the most part those who attain this status have assumed roles of special prominence in the affairs of society. Some occupy positions of such persuasive power and influence that they are deemed public figures for all purposes. More commonly, those classed as public figures have thrust themselves to the forefront of particular public controversies in order to influence the resolution of the issues involved. In either event, they invite attention and comment.

Even if the foregoing generalities do not obtain in every instance, the communications media are entitled to act on the assumption that public officials and public figures have voluntarily exposed themselves to increased risk of injury from defamatory falsehood concerning them. No such assumption is justified with respect to a private individual. He has not accepted public office or assumed an "influential role in ordering society." *Curtis Publishing Co. v. Butts*, 388 U.S., at 164 (Warren, C. J., concurring in result). He has relinquished no part of his interest in the protection of his own good name, and consequently he has a more compelling call on the courts for redress of injury inflicted by defamatory falsehood. Thus, private individuals are not only more vulnerable to injury than public officials and public figures; they are also more deserving of recovery.

For these reasons we conclude that the States should retain substantial latitude in their efforts to enforce a legal remedy for defamatory falsehood injurious to the reputation of a private individual. . . . The "public or general interest" test for determining the applicability of the *New York Times* standard to private defamation actions inadequately serves both of the competing values at stake. On the one hand, a private individual whose reputation is injured by defamatory falsehood that does concern an issue of public or general interest has no recourse unless he can meet the rigorous requirements *of New York Times*. This is true despite the factors that distinguish the state interest in compensating private individuals from the analogous interest involved in the context of public persons. On the other hand, a publisher or broadcaster of a defamatory error which a court deems unrelated to an issue of public or general interest may be held liable in damages even if it took every reasonable precaution to ensure the accuracy of its assertions. And liability may far exceed compensation for any actual injury to the plaintiff, for the jury may be permitted to presume damages without proof of loss and even to award punitive damages.

We hold that, so long as they do not impose liability without fault, the States may define for themselves the appropriate standard of liability for a publisher or broadcaster of defamatory falsehood injurious to a private individual. This approach provides a more equitable boundary between the competing concerns involved here. It recognizes the strength of the legitimate state interest in compensating private individuals for wrongful injury to reputation, yet shields the press and broadcast media from the rigors of strict liability for defamation. At least this conclusion obtains where, as here, the substance of the defamatory statement "makes substantial danger to reputation apparent." . . .

IV

Our accommodation of the competing values at stake in defamation suits by private individuals allows the States to impose liability on the publisher or broadcaster of defamatory falsehood on a less demanding showing than that required by *New York Times*. This conclusion is not based on a belief that the considerations which prompted the adoption of the *New York Times* privilege for defamation of public officials and its extension to public figures are wholly inapplicable to the context of private individuals. Rather, we endorse this approach in recognition of the strong and legitimate state interest in compensating private individuals for injury to reputation. But this countervailing state interest extends no further than compensation for actual injury. For the reasons stated below, we hold that the States may not permit recovery of presumed or punitive damages, at least when liability is not based on a showing of knowledge of falsity or reckless disregard for the truth.

The common law of defamation is an oddity of tort law, for it allows recovery of purportedly compensatory damages without evidence of actual loss. Under the traditional rules pertaining to actions for libel, the existence of injury is presumed from the fact of publication. Juries may award substantial sums as compensation for supposed damage to reputation without any proof that such harm actually occurred. The largely uncontrolled discretion of juries to award damages where there is no loss unnecessarily compounds the potential of any system of liability for defamatory falsehood to inhibit the vigorous exercise of First Amendment freedoms. Additionally, the doctrine of presumed damages invites juries to punish unpopular opinion rather than to compensate individuals for injury sustained by the publication of a false fact.

More to the point, the States have no substantial interest in securing for plaintiffs such as this petitioner gratuitous awards of money damages far in excess of any actual injury.

We would not, of course, invalidate state law simply because we doubt its wisdom, but here we are attempting to reconcile state law with a competing interest grounded in the constitutional command of the First Amendment. It is therefore appropriate to require that state remedies for defamatory falsehood reach no farther than is necessary to protect the legitimate interest involved. It is necessary to restrict defamation plaintiffs who do not prove knowledge of falsity or reckless disregard for the truth to compensation for actual injury. We need not define "actual injury," as trial courts have wide experience in framing appropriate jury instructions in tort actions. Suffice it to say that actual injury is not limited to out-of-pocket loss. Indeed, the more customary types of actual harm inflicted by defamatory falsehood include impairment of reputation and standing in the community, personal humiliation, and mental anguish and suffering. Of course, juries must be limited by appropriate instructions, and all awards must be supported by competent evidence concerning the injury, although there need be no evidence which assigns an actual dollar value to the injury.

We also find no justification for allowing awards of punitive damages against publishers and broadcasters held liable under state-defined standards of liability for defamation. In most jurisdictions jury discretion over the amounts awarded is limited only by the gentle rule that they not be excessive. Consequently, juries assess punitive damages in wholly unpredictable amounts bearing no necessary relation to the actual harm caused. And they remain free to use their discretion selectively to punish expressions of unpopular views. Like the doctrine of presumed damages, jury discretion to award punitive damages unnecessarily exacerbates the danger of media self-censorship, but, unlike the former rule, punitive damages are wholly irrelevant to the state interest that justifies a negligence standard for private defamation actions. They are not compensation for injury. Instead, they are private fines levied by civil juries to punish reprehensible conduct and to deter its future occurrence. In short, the private defamation plaintiff who establishes liability under a less demanding standard than that stated by *New York Times* may recover only such damages as are sufficient to compensate him for actual injury.

V

Notwithstanding our refusal to extend the *New York Times* privilege to defamation of private individuals, respondent contends that we should affirm the judgment below on the ground that petitioner is either a public official or a public figure. There is little basis for the former assertion. Several years prior to the present incident, petitioner had served briefly on housing committees appointed by the mayor of Chicago, but at the time of publication he had never held any remunerative governmental position. Respondent admits this but argues that petitioner's appearance at the coroner's inquest rendered him a "de facto public official." Our cases recognize no such concept. Respondent's suggestion would sweep all lawyers under the *New York Times* rule as officers of the court and distort the plain meaning of the "public official" category beyond all recognition. We decline to follow it.

Respondent's characterization of petitioner as a public figure raises a different question. That designation may rest on either of two alternative bases. In some instances an individual may achieve such pervasive fame or notoriety that he becomes a public figure for all purposes and in all contexts. More commonly, an individual voluntarily injects himself or is drawn into a particular public controversy and thereby becomes a public figure for a limited range of issues. In either case such persons assume special prominence in the resolution of public questions.

Petitioner has long been active in community and professional affairs. He has served as an officer of local civic groups and of various professional organizations, and he has published several books and articles on legal subjects. Although petitioner was consequently well known in some circles, he had achieved no general fame or notoriety in the community. . . . We would not lightly assume that a citizen's participation in community and professional affairs rendered him a public figure for all purposes. Absent clear evidence of general fame or notoriety in the community, and pervasive involvement in the affairs of society, an individual should not be deemed a public personality for all aspects of his life. It is preferable to reduce the public-figure question to a more meaningful context by looking to the nature and extent of an individual's participation in the particular controversy giving rise to the defamation.

In this context it is plain that petitioner was not a public figure. He played a minimal role at the coroner's inquest, and his participation related solely to his representation of a private client. He took no part in the criminal prosecution of Officer Nuccio. Moreover, he never discussed either the criminal or civil litigation with the press and was never quoted as having done so. He plainly did not thrust himself into the vortex of this public issue, nor did he engage the public's attention in an attempt to influence its outcome. We are persuaded that the trial court did not err in refusing to characterize petitioner as a public figure for the purpose of this litigation.

We therefore conclude that the *New York Times* standard is inapplicable to this case and that the trial court erred in entering judgment for respondent. Because the jury was allowed to impose liability without fault and was permitted to presume damages without proof of injury, a new trial is necessary. We reverse and remand for further proceedings in accord with this opinion.

It is so ordered.

MR. JUSTICE BLACKMUN, concurring.

. . . .

The Court today refuses to apply *New York Times* to the private individual, as contrasted with the public official and the public figure. . . . It thereby fixes the outer boundary of the *New York Times* doctrine and says that beyond that boundary, a State is free to define for itself the appropriate standard of media liability so long as it does not impose liability without fault. As my joinder in *Rosenbloom's* plurality opinion would intimate, I sense some illogic in this.

. . . Although the Court's opinion in the present case departs from the rationale of the *Rosenbloom* plurality, . . . I am willing to join, and do join, the Court's opinion and its judgment for two reasons:

> . . . By removing the specters of presumed and punitive damages in the absence of *New York Times* malice, the Court eliminates significant and powerful motives for self-censorship that otherwise are present in the traditional libel action. . . . What the Court has done, I believe, will have little, if any, practical effect on the functioning of responsible journalism.

. . . .

Mr. Chief Justice Burger, dissenting.

. . . In today's opinion the Court abandons the traditional thread so far as the ordinary private citizen is concerned and introduces the concept that the media will be liable for negligence in publishing defamatory statements with respect to such persons. . . . I am frank to say I do not know the parameters of a "negligence" doctrine as applied to the news media. Conceivably this new doctrine could inhibit some editors, as the dissents of Mr. Justice Douglas and Mr. Justice Brennan suggest. But I would prefer to allow this area of law to continue to evolve as it has up to now with respect to private citizens rather than embark on a new doctrinal theory which has no jurisprudential ancestry.

. . . .

I would reverse the judgment of the Court of Appeals and remand for reinstatement of the verdict of the jury and the entry of an appropriate judgment on that verdict.

Mr. Justice Douglas, dissenting.

. . . .

With the First Amendment made applicable to the States through the Fourteenth, I do not see how States have any more ability to "accommodate" freedoms of speech or of the press than does Congress. . . . Like Congress, States are without power "to use a civil libel law or any other law to impose damages for merely discussing public affairs." [*New York Times v. Sullivan* 364 U.S.] at 295 (Black, J., concurring).

Continued recognition of the possibility of state libel suits for public discussion of public issues leaves the freedom of speech honored by the Fourteenth Amendment a diluted version of First Amendment protection. . . .

Since in my view the First and Fourteenth Amendments prohibit the imposition of damages upon respondent for this discussion of public affairs, I would affirm the judgment below.

Time, Inc. v. Firestone

Supreme Court of the United States, 1976
424 U.S. 448

Mr. Justice Rehnquist delivered the opinion of the Court.

Petitioner is the publisher of *Time*, a weekly news magazine. . . .

I

Respondent, Mary Alice Firestone, married Russell Firestone, the scion of one of America's wealthier industrial families, in 1961. In 1964, they separated, and respondent filed a complaint for separate maintenance in the Circuit Court of Palm Beach County, Fla. Her husband counterclaimed for divorce on grounds of extreme cruelty and adultery. After a lengthy trial the Circuit Court issued a judgment granting the divorce requested by respondent's husband. In relevant part the court's final judgment read:

. . . .

"According to certain testimony in behalf of the defendant, extramarital escapades of the plaintiff were bizarre and of an amatory nature which would have made Dr. Freud's hair curl. Other testimony, in plaintiff's behalf, would indicate that defendant was guilty of bounding from one bed partner to another with the erotic zest of a satyr. The court is inclined to discount much of this testimony as unreliable. Nevertheless, it is the conclusion and finding of this court that neither party is domesticated within the meaning of that term as used by the Supreme Court of Florida. . . .

"In the present case, it is abundantly clear from the evidence of marital discord that neither of the parties has shown the least susceptibility to domestication, and that the marriage should be dissolved."

. . . .

Time's editorial staff, headquartered in New York, was alerted by a wire service report and an account in a New York newspaper to the fact that a judgment had been rendered in the Firestone divorce proceeding. The staff subsequently received further information regarding the Florida decision from *Time's* Miami bureau chief and from a "stringer" working on a special assignment basis in the Palm Beach area. On the basis of these four sources, *Time's* staff composed the following item, which appeared in the magazine's "Milestones" section the following week:

"DIVORCED. By Russell A. Firestone Jr., 41, heir to the tire fortune: Mary Alice Sullivan Firestone, 32, his third wife; a onetime Palm Beach schoolteacher; on grounds of extreme cruelty and adultery; after six years of marriage, one son; in West Palm Beach, Fla. The 17-month intermittent trial produced enough testimony of extramarital adventures on both sides, said the judge, 'to make Dr. Freud's hair curl.'"

Within a few weeks of the publication of this article respondent demanded in writing a retraction from petitioner, alleging that a portion of the article was "false, malicious and defamatory." Petitioner declined to issue the requested retraction.[1]

Respondent then filed this libel action against petitioner in the Florida Circuit Court. Based on a jury verdict for respondent, that court entered judgment against petitioner for $100,000, and after review in both the Florida District Court of Appeal and the Supreme Court of Florida the judgment was ultimately affirmed. 305 So. 2d 172 (1974). . . .

II

Petitioner initially contends that it cannot be liable for publishing any falsehood defaming respondent unless it is established that the publication was made "with actual malice," as that term is defined in *New York Times Co. v. Sullivan*, 376 U.S. 254 (1964). Petitioner advances two arguments in support of this contention: that respondent is a "public figure" within this Court's decisions extending New York Times to defamation suits brought by such individuals, see, e.g., *Curtis Publishing Co. v. Butts*, 388 U.S. 130 (1967); and that the *Time* item constituted a report of a judicial proceeding, a class of subject matter which petitioner claims deserves the protection of the "actual malice" standard even if the story is proved to be defamatorily false or inaccurate. We reject both arguments.

Respondent did not assume any role of especial prominence in the affairs of society, other than perhaps Palm Beach society, and she did not thrust herself to the forefront of any particular public controversy in order to influence the resolution of the issues involved in it.

Petitioner contends that because the Firestone divorce was characterized by the Florida Supreme Court as a "cause celebre," it must have been a public controversy and respondent must be considered a public figure. But in so doing petitioner seeks to equate "public controversy" with all controversies of interest to the public. Were we to accept this reasoning, we would reinstate the doctrine advanced in the plurality opinion in *Rosenbloom v. Metromedia, Inc.*, 403 U.S. 29 (1971), which concluded that the *New York Times* privilege should be extended to falsehoods defamatory of private persons whenever the statements concern matters of general or public interest. In *Gertz*, however, the Court repudiated this position, stating that "extension of the *New York Times* test proposed by the *Rosenbloom* plurality would abridge [a] legitimate state interest to a degree that we find unacceptable." 418 U.S., at 346.

. . . .

Dissolution of a marriage through judicial proceedings is not the sort of "public controversy" referred to in *Gertz*, even though the marital difficulties of extremely

---

1. Under Florida law the demand for retraction was a prerequisite for filing a libel action, and permits defendants to limit their potential liability to actual damages by complying with the demand. Fla. Stat. Ann. §§ 770.01–770.02 (1963).

wealthy individuals may be of interest to some portion of the reading public. Nor did respondent freely choose to publicize issues as to the propriety of her married life. She was compelled to go to court by the State in order to obtain legal release from the bonds of matrimony. We have said that in such an instance "[r]esort to the judicial process . . . is no more voluntary in a realistic sense than that of the defendant called upon to defend his interests in court." *Boddie v. Connecticut*, 401 U.S. 371, 376–377 (1971). Her actions, both in instituting the litigation and in its conduct, were quite different from those of General Walker in *Curtis Publishing Co., supra.*[3] She assumed no "special prominence in the resolution of public questions." *Gertz, supra,* at 351. We hold respondent was not a "public figure" for the purpose of determining the constitutional protection afforded petitioner's report of the factual and legal basis for her divorce.

It may be argued that there is still room for application of the *New York Times* protections to more narrowly focused reports of what actually transpires in the courtroom. But even so narrowed, the suggested privilege is simply too broad. Imposing upon the law of private defamation the rather drastic limitations worked by *New York Times* cannot be justified by generalized references to the public interest in reports of judicial proceedings. The details of many, if not most, courtroom battles would add almost nothing toward advancing the uninhibited debate on public issues thought to provide principal support for the decision in *New York Times. See* 376 U.S., at 270; *cf. Rosenblatt v. Baer*, 383 U.S. 75, 86 (1966). And while participants in some litigation may be legitimate "public figures," either generally or for the limited purpose of that litigation, the majority will more likely resemble respondent, drawn into a public forum largely against their will in order to attempt to obtain the only redress available to them or to defend themselves against actions brought by the State or by others. There appears little reason why these individuals should substantially forfeit that degree of protection which the law of defamation would otherwise afford them simply by virtue of their being drawn into a courtroom. . . .

III

Petitioner's theory seems to be that the only compensable injury in a defamation action is that which may be done to one's reputation, and that claims not predicated upon such injury are by definition not actions for defamation. But Florida has obviously decided to permit recovery for other injuries without regard to measuring the effect the falsehood may have had upon a plaintiff's reputation. This does not transform the action into something other than an action for defamation as that term is

---

3. Nor do we think the fact that respondent may have held a few press conferences during the divorce proceedings in an attempt to satisfy inquiring reporters converts her into a "public figure." Such interviews should have had no effect upon the merits of the legal dispute between respondent and her husband or the outcome of that trial, and we do not think it can be assumed that any such purpose was intended. Moreover, there is no indication that she sought to use the press conferences as a vehicle by which to thrust herself to the forefront of some unrelated controversy in order to influence its resolution. *See* Gertz v. Robert Welch, Inc., 418 U.S. 323, 345 (1974).

meant in *Gertz*. In that opinion we made it clear that States could base awards on elements other than injury to reputation, specifically listing "personal humiliation, and mental anguish and suffering" as examples of injuries which might be compensated consistently with the Constitution upon a showing of fault. Because respondent has decided to forgo recovery for injury to her reputation, she is not prevented from obtaining compensation for such other damages that a defamatory falsehood may have caused her.

The trial court charged, consistently with *Gertz*, that the jury should award respondent compensatory damages in "an amount of money that will fairly and adequately compensate her for such damages," and further cautioned that "[i]t is only damages which are a direct and natural result of the alleged libel which may be recovered." App. 509. There was competent evidence introduced to permit the jury to assess the amount of injury. Several witnesses[6] testified to the extent of respondent's anxiety and concern over Time's inaccurately reporting that she had been found guilty of adultery, and she herself took the stand to elaborate on her fears that her young son would be adversely affected by this falsehood when he grew older. The jury decided these injuries should be compensated by an award of $100,000. We have no warrant for re-examining this determination. Cf. *Lincoln v. Power*, 151 U.S. 436 (1894).

IV

. . . .

It may well be that petitioner's account in its "Milestones" section was the product of some fault on its part, and that the libel judgment against it was, therefore, entirely consistent with *Gertz*. But in the absence of a finding in some element of the state-court system that there was fault, we are not inclined to canvass the record to make such a determination in the first instance. Cf. *Rosenblatt v. Baer*, 383 U.S., at 87–88. Accordingly, the judgment of the Supreme Court of Florida is vacated and the case remanded for further proceedings not inconsistent with this opinion.

So ordered.

---

1. Why wasn't Mrs. Firestone held to be a public figure? What must she prove as a private person in order to recover?

2. While the Court refused to recognize a constitutional privilege for reporting judicial proceedings, in many jurisdictions a "fair report" privilege is recognized under state law for reasonably accurate reports of various official proceedings, including court matters. The privilege "extends to publication of defamatory matter concerning another in a report of an official action or proceeding, or of a meeting open to the public that deals with a matter of public concern." It is based on "the right of

---

6. These included respondent's minister, her attorney in the divorce proceedings, plus several friends and neighbors, one of whom was a physician who testified to having to administer a sedative to respondent in an attempt to reduce discomfort wrought by her worrying about the article.

the public, in a democratic society, to be informed about a wide variety of official matters" and "attaches where the report is accurate and complete or a fair abridgement of the occurrence that is recounted." *Salzano v. North Jersey Media Group, Inc.*, 993 A.2d 778 (N.J. 2010) (applying privilege to report on complaint filed in bankruptcy proceedings).

4. The Limited Purpose Public Figure

Waldbaum v. Fairchild Publications, Inc.

United States Court of Appeals, District of Columbia Circuit, 1980
627 F.2d 1287, *cert. denied*, 449 U.S. 898

Tamm, Circuit Judge:

In this action we must determine when an individual not a public official has left the relatively safe harbor that the law of defamation provides for private persons and has become a public figure within the meaning of the Supreme Court's decision in *Gertz v. Robert Welch, Inc.*, 418 U.S. 323, 94 S. Ct. 2997, 41 L. Ed. 2d 789 (1974)....
[T]he United States District Court for the District of Columbia concluded that the plaintiff was a limited public figure under *Gertz*. Because the plaintiff admitted that he could not prove "actual malice" on the part of the defendant, which *Gertz* requires public figures to do, [the court] entered summary judgment for the defendant. Having reviewed the facts in light of the criteria that govern the status of a defamation plaintiff, we . . . affirm.

I

Although the parties in this case differ over how to classify the plaintiff, they fundamentally agree on the underlying facts. Eric Waldbaum, the plaintiff, became president and chief executive officer of Greenbelt Consumer Services, Inc. (Greenbelt) in January of 1971. Greenbelt is a diversified consumer cooperative that, during Waldbaum's tenure, ranked as the second largest cooperative in the country.[1]

While serving as Greenbelt's president, Waldbaum played an active role not only in the management of the cooperative but also in setting policies and standards within the supermarket industry. He battled the traditional practices in the industry and fought particularly hard for the introduction of unit pricing and open dating in supermarkets. He held several meetings, to which press and public were invited, on topics varying from supermarket practices to energy legislation and fuel allocation. He pursued a vigorous policy of consolidating Greenbelt's operations to eliminate unprofitable outlets. These actions generated considerable comment on both Greenbelt and Waldbaum in trade journals and general-interest publications.

---

1. When Waldbaum left as Greenbelt's president, the cooperative had approximately 38,500 members. The company owns retail supermarkets (Co-op Supermarkets), furniture and gift outlets (SCAN stores), and automobile service stations (Exval stations).

On March 16, 1976, Greenbelt's board of directors dismissed Waldbaum as the cooperative's president and chief executive officer. *Supermarket News*, a trade publication owned by the defendant, Fairchild Publications, Inc. (Fairchild), ran an item on Waldbaum's ouster on page 35 of its March 22 issue. The five-sentence article stated at one point that Greenbelt "has been losing money the past year and retrenching."[5]

On September 27, 1976, Waldbaum filed a libel action in the district court based upon this comment in the article. He contended that in fact Greenbelt had not been losing money or retrenching and that this allegedly false report damaged his reputation as a businessman. Waldbaum sought actual and exemplary damages totaling $75,000.

After discovery, Fairchild moved for summary judgment. It argued that Waldbaum was a public figure and, because he had admitted the absence of "actual malice," he could not recover damages for defamation. Waldbaum countered that he was not a public figure and thus would have to prove only negligence on the part of Fairchild in researching and publishing the article. On February 15, 1979, Judge Corcoran granted Fairchild's motion. He concluded that although Waldbaum could not be considered a public figure for all purposes, he was a public figure for the limited range of issues concerning "Greenbelt's unique position within the supermarket industry and Waldbaum's efforts to advance that position."

. . . .

In *Gertz*, decided in 1974, the Court focused on the public or private status of the plaintiff. . . . It therefore held that a state may allow a private person to recover for defamation under any standard, as long as that standard does not impose liability without fault.

. . . .

In trying to define who is a public figure, the Court in *Gertz* created two subclassifications, persons who are public figures for all purposes and those who are public figures for particular public controversies. An individual may have attained a position "of such persuasive power and influence," *id.*, and of "such pervasive fame or notoriety," *id.* at 351, 94 S. Ct. at 3013, that he has become a public figure in all situations. This test is a strict one. The Court stated flatly that "(a)bsent clear evidence of general fame or notoriety in the community, and pervasive involvement in the

---

5. The story in its entirety read:

GREENBELT OUSTS ERIC WALDBAUM

WASHINGTON Eric Waldbaum has been replaced as president of Greenbelt Consumer Services. Rowland Burnstan will serve as acting chief executive office(r) until a new president is named. Burnstan, an independent management consultant and economist, has worked for various Government agencies and businesses.

Greenbelt said part of his interim job will be to locate a new president for the co-op, which has been losing money the past year and retrenching.

affairs of society, an individual should not be deemed a public personality for all aspects of his life."

The Court in *Gertz* acknowledged freely that under this definition the general public figure is a rare creature. More common are persons who "have thrust themselves to the forefront of particular public controversies in order to influence the resolution of the issues involved." 418 U.S. at 345, 94 S. Ct. at 3009. Put slightly differently, this limited-purpose public figure is "an individual (who) voluntarily injects himself or is drawn into a particular public controversy and therefore becomes a public figure for a limited range of issues." *Id.* at 351, 94 S. Ct. at 3013. The relevant examination turns on "the nature and extent of an individual's participation in the particular controversy giving rise to the defamation." *Id.* at 352, 94 S. Ct. at 3013.

III

. . . From analyzing *Gertz* and more recent defamation cases, we believe that a person can be a general public figure only if he is a "celebrity[,]" his name a "household word" whose ideas and actions the public in fact follows with great interest. We also conclude that a person has become a public figure for limited purposes if he is attempting to have, or realistically can be expected to have, a major impact on the resolution of a specific public dispute that has foreseeable and substantial ramifications for persons beyond its immediate participants. . . .

Given these considerations, a court[12] analyzing whether a given plaintiff is a public figure must look at the facts, taken as a whole, through the eyes of a reasonable person. This objective approach should enable both the press and the individual in question to assess the individual's status, in advance, against the same yardstick. . . . Resolving these questions based upon what a reasonable person, looking at the entire situation, would conclude allows the press and the individual to evaluate public-figure status against a single, discoverable norm and from there to act as they see fit, understanding the consequences of their conduct under *New York Times*.

. . . A court first must ask whether the plaintiff is a public figure for all purposes. . . . In other words, a general public figure is a well-known "celebrity," his name a "household word." The public recognizes him and follows his words and deeds, either because it regards his ideas, conduct, or judgment as worthy of its attention or because he actively pursues that consideration.

. . . .

In determining whether a plaintiff has achieved the degree of notoriety and influence necessary to become a public figure in all contexts, a court may look to several factors.[19] The judge can examine statistical surveys, if presented, that concern the

---

12. Whether the plaintiff is a public figure is a question of law for the court to resolve.

19. The court must examine these factors as they existed before the defamation was published. Otherwise, the press could convert a private individual into a general public figure simply by publicizing the defamation itself and creating a controversy surrounding it and, perhaps, litigation arising out of it. *See Hutchinson v. Proxmire*, 443 U.S. Ill, 99 S. Ct. 2675, 2688, 61 L. Ed. 2d 411 (1979)

plaintiff's name recognition. Previous coverage of the plaintiff in the press also is relevant....

    . . . .

Newsworthiness alone will not suffice, for the alleged defamation itself indicates that someone in the press believed the matter deserved media coverage. Moreover, a court may not question the legitimacy of the public's concern; such an approach would turn courts into censors of "'what information is relevant to self-government.'" A vital part of open public debate is deciding what should be debated. No arm of the government, including the judiciary, should be able to set society's agenda.

Trivial or tangential participation is not enough. The language of *Gertz* is clear that plaintiffs must have "thrust themselves to the forefront" of the controversies so as to become factors in their ultimate resolution. The plaintiff either must have been purposely trying to influence the outcome or could realistically have been expected, because of his position in the controversy, to have an impact on its resolution....

Finally, the alleged defamation must have been germane to the plaintiff's participation in the controversy. His talents, education, experience, and motives could have been relevant to the public's decision whether to listen to him. Misstatements wholly unrelated to the controversy, however, do not receive the *New York Times* protection.

Those who attempt to affect the result of a particular controversy have assumed the risk that the press, in covering the controversy, will examine the major participants with a critical eye. Occasionally, someone is caught up in the controversy involuntarily and, against his will, assumes a prominent position in its outcome.... In short, the court must ask whether a reasonable person would have concluded that this individual would play or was seeking to play a major role in determining the outcome of the controversy and whether the alleged defamation related to that controversy.

IV

With the foregoing analysis in mind, we now must determine whether Judge Corcoran correctly concluded that Waldbaum was a public figure. As noted above, Fairchild concedes that he was not a general-purpose public figure, and Waldbaum concedes that he cannot prove "actual malice" within the meaning of *New York Times*. ... After examining the facts, we do agree and, therefore, affirm.

Evidence submitted with Fairehild's motion for summary judgment indicates clearly that Greenbelt was an innovative company often the subject of news reports. As the second largest cooperative in the nation it attracted attention, and its pathbreaking marketing policies... became the subject of public debate with the supermarket industry and beyond....

("those charged with defamation cannot, by their own conduct, create their own defense by making the claimant a public figure").

Waldbaum was known as a leading advocate of certain precedent-breaking policies before coming to Greenbelt. . . .

Being an executive within a prominent and influential company does not by itself make one a public figure.[36]. . . . [Waldbaum's] own deposition indicates that he was the mover and shaper of many of the cooperative's controversial actions. He made it a leader in unit pricing and open dating. . . .

Thus, it would appear to a reasonable person that Waldbaum had thrust himself into the public controversies concerning unit pricing, open dating, the cooperative form of business, and other issues. . . . Looking at the overall picture, we conclude that Waldbaum was a public figure for the limited purpose of comment on Greenbelt's and his own innovation policies and that the article giving rise to this action was within the protected sphere of reporting. Because Fairchild concededly did not act with "actual malice," it was entitled to summary judgment.

V

. . . Nevertheless, when one assumes a position of great influence within a specific area and uses that influence to advocate and practice controversial policies that substantially affect others, he becomes a public figure for that debate. Waldbaum was such a person, and comment on his termination as president and chief executive officer of Greenbelt falls within the range of reports protected under *New York Times*. Therefore, the judgment of the district court is

Affirmed.

Foretich v. Capital Cities/ABC, Inc.

United States Court of Appeals for the Fourth Circuit, 1994
37 F.3d 1541

MURNAGHAN, CIRCUIT JUDGE

Vincent and Doris Foretich filed a defamation action against the producers and broadcasters of an ABC docudrama in which a character apparently referred to one or both of them as "abusers" of their granddaughter, Hilary A. Foretich, who had been the subject of a prolonged and highly publicized child-custody dispute.

. . .

On November 29, 1992, American Broadcasting Companies, Inc. aired, as its "ABC Sunday Night Movie," a 91-minute docudrama entitled "A Mother's Right: The Elizabeth Morgan Story." . . . In the scene, Hilary is initially agitated, gradually warms to her grandparents, and eventually climbs into her grandfather's lap after joining in the singing of "Row, Row, Row Your Boat." There immediately follows a conversation between Dr. Morgan and her friend, as they are leaving Washington by car. The friend had brought Hilary to the psychiatrist's office and had remained in an

---

36. Sometimes position alone can make one a public figure.

adjacent room during the visit. He describes to Dr. Morgan what he heard: "It was like a circus pony going through her tricks. You know, she even giggled on cue." Dr. Morgan responds, "It's just like the therapist said. . . . Classic response. She's being kind to her abusers so she won't be hurt again" (emphasis added).

. . . Plaintiffs' entire case is based on the utterance of a single sound—the "s" in the word "abusers," which allegedly indicated that Hilary was being abused not only by her father but also by one or both of her paternal grandparents. At the present stage of the litigation, it is undisputed that the "s" that converted the singular "abuser" into the plural "abusers" was included unintentionally.. . . .

II

Because the question of whether a defamation plaintiff is a "limited-purpose public figure" is an issue of law, we review de novo. In conducting our review, we "must look through the eyes of a reasonable person at the facts taken as a whole."

. . . .

In *Fitzgerald* [*v. Penthouse Int'l, Ltd.*, 691 F.2d 666 (4th Cir. 1982), *cert. denied*, 460 U.S. 1024 (1983)] and again in our en banc opinion in *Reuber* [*v. Food Chemical News*, 925 F.2d 703 (4th Cir.), *cert. denied*, 501 U.S. 1212 (1991)], we set forth five requirements that the defamation defendant must prove before a court can properly hold that the plaintiff is a public figure for the limited purpose of comment on a particular public controversy: (1) the plaintiff had access to channels of effective communication; (2) the plaintiff voluntarily assumed a role of special prominence in the public controversy; (3) the plaintiff sought to influence the resolution or outcome of the controversy; (4) the controversy existed prior to the publication of the defamatory statement; and (5) the plaintiff retained public-figure status at the time of the alleged defamation.

. . . .

IV

The first question we must address is whether there was a particular public controversy that gave rise to the alleged defamation.

Gertz provided no express definition of a "public controversy," but the Court's subsequent decisions on limited-purpose public figure status provide some useful guidance. . . .

In 1980, after carefully sifting through the Supreme Court cases, the United States Court of Appeals for the District of Columbia Circuit enunciated an express definition of a "public controversy":

> A public controversy is not simply a matter of interest to the public; it must be a real dispute, the outcome of which affects the general public or some segment of it in an appreciable way. . . . Essentially private concerns or disagreements do not become public controversies simply because they attract attention. . . . Rather, a public controversy is a dispute that in fact has received

public attention because its ramifications will be felt by persons who are not direct participants.

. . . .

. . . Dr. Morgan's prolonged contempt incarceration for refusing to divulge Hilary's whereabouts raised a special set of public policy issues. . . . The public discussion of those issues ultimately prompted Congress and the President to secure Dr. Morgan's release through federal legislation limiting the power of the District of Columbia courts to impose contempt in child custody cases. . . .

V

Having concluded that there was indeed a public controversy that gave rise to the alleged defamation, we must next examine "the nature and extent of [Vincent Foretich's and Doris Foretich's] participation in [that] controversy." . . . Because we find that neither Vincent nor Doris Foretich voluntarily assumed a role of special prominence in the Morgan-Foretich controversy in order to influence its outcome, we need not consider the other elements of the *Fitzgerald/Reuber* test. *See Reuber*, 925 F. 2d at 708–09 . . . ; *Fitzgerald*, 691 F. 2d at 668.

The bare words of the legal test — whether the plaintiff "voluntarily assumed a role of special prominence in a public controversy in order to influence its outcome" can best be illuminated by reference to *Gertz* and subsequent Supreme Court cases . . . .

. . . ABC has argued that Vincent and Doris Foretich voluntarily participated in the public controversy when they chose to support their son by publicly criticizing Dr. Morgan, by speaking with news reporters, and by appearing on television, at press conferences, and at public gatherings. . . . ABC has argued, both Vincent and Doris Foretich voluntarily assumed special roles of prominence in the Morgan-Foretich controversy in order to influence its outcome, and they may not now claim the protections of purely "private" persons.

We reject ABC's argument because it pays inadequate attention to the context . . . The resultant publicity doubtless had the potential to destroy Vincent Foretich's and Doris Foretich's reputations, and that potential may well have been realized.

The common law of defamation has long recognized that charges such as those leveled against the Foretich grandparents are so obviously and materially harmful to reputational interests that they must be deemed defamatory per se. We, too, recognize the devastation that public accusations of child sexual abuse can wreak, and we are extremely reluctant to attribute public-figure status to otherwise private persons merely because they have responded to such accusations in a reasonable attempt to vindicate their reputations.

In determining the reasonableness of a reply, we need not plow entirely new ground: the common law on the conditional (or qualified) privilege of reply, also known as the privilege to speak in self-defense or to defend one's reputation, can help guide our discussion. . . .

Because the Foretiches' public responses to Dr. Morgan's accusations were responsive, proportionate, and not excessively published, they were "reasonable." . . . [W]e conclude that the Foretiches' primary motive was to defend their own good names against Dr. Morgan's accusations and that their public statements can most fairly be characterized as measured defensive replies to her attacks, rather than as efforts to thrust themselves to the forefront of a public controversy in order to influence its outcome. Therefore, we hold that Vincent and Doris Foretich were private individuals, not limited-purpose public figures.

. . . At first blush, one might characterize our decision today as favoring [reputation] over [free expression]. But such a characterization would miss the point. We see no good reason "why someone dragged into a controversy should be able to speak publicly only at the expense of foregoing a private person's protection from defamation." *Clyburn* [*v. News World Communications*], 903 F.2d [29,] at 32 [(D.C. Cir. 1990)]. By allowing the Foretiches to defend their good names without succumbing to public-figure status, we protect not only their own interests in reputation, but also society's interest in free speech. . . . By freely permitting the Foretiches to respond to Dr. Morgan's charges against them—charges that have never been proved in any court of law—we foster both the individual interest in self-expression and the social interest in the discovery and dissemination of truth—the very goals that animate our First Amendment jurisprudence.

. . . .

Affirmed and remanded.

———————

1. Why do the Foretiches escape the "public figure" classification?

2. Is this a situation in which the *Rosenbloom* test ("matter in the public interest") would be helpful?

3. In *Mzamane v. Winfrey*, 693 F. Supp. 2d 442 (E.D. Pa. 2010), the headmistress of the Oprah Winfrey Leadership Academy for Girls (OWLAG) in South Africa sued television celebrity and OWLAG founder Winfrey for defamation, based on statements Winfrey made to parents of students at the academy, and later at a press conference, in response to allegations of student abuse by some OWLAG staff members. The court distinguished *Foretich* and held that the headmistress was a limited purpose public figure. She "voluntarily held a significant position in a high-profile public institution" so that "even before she went public with her version of the facts, she was already a limited purpose public figure."

4. *Erickson v. Jones Street Publishers, LLC*, 629 S.E.2d 653 (S.C. 2006), held that an individual serving as a private guardian *ad litem* assigned by the court to represent the interests of a minor child in a divorce/custody proceeding is not a limited purpose public figure. Do you agree?

5. The Nonmedia Defendant

Greenmoss Builders, Inc. v. Dun & Bradstreet, Inc.

Supreme Court of Vermont, 1983
461 A.2d 414

HILL, J.

Plaintiff, a residential and commercial building contractor, brought this defamation action against defendant as a result of an erroneous credit report issued to defendant's subscribers (plaintiff's creditors). The credit report alleged that plaintiff had filed a voluntary petition in bankruptcy and, in addition, grossly misrepresented plaintiff's assets and liabilities. The false nature of the report's allegations has never been disputed.

In its complaint, plaintiff asserted that the consequences of defendant's report, which it insisted was published with reckless disregard for truth and accuracy, were a damaged business reputation, loss of company profits, and loss of money expended to correct the error. In response, defendant claimed both a constitutional and common law qualified privilege against defamation actions, and on that basis contended that since its report was published in good faith, it could not be held liable.

After a trial by jury, a verdict was returned in favor of plaintiff for $50,000 in compensatory or actual damages, and $300,000 in punitive damages. Thereafter, defendant filed timely motions for judgment notwithstanding the verdict, V.R.C.P. 50, and for new trial, V.R.C.P. 59, on the issues of liability and damages. The trial court, persuaded that the evidence was sufficient as a matter of law to create issues of fact for the jury as to both liability and damages, denied defendant's motions for judgment notwithstanding the verdict. Upon reviewing its jury instructions, however, the trial court concluded that it had incorrectly charged those standards of liability enunciated in *Gertz v. Robert Welch, Inc.*, 418 U.S. 323 (1974), and granted defendant's motions for new trial on all issues.

This action is before us pursuant to an interlocutory order by the Washington Superior Court, V.R.A.P. 5(b)(1), certifying five questions of law for our resolution. . . .

We begin with a review of the record. Defendant operates a business in which factual and financial reports about individual business enterprises are issued exclusively to subscribers of defendant's service. These subscribers, usually creditors of the reported enterprises, may contract for "continuous service reports" which enable them to receive all report updates about a particular business over a year's time from the subscriber's initial inquiry. The reports are based on information solicited from the business itself, the business' banking and credit sources, from trade suppliers, and from public records such as annual reports filed with the Secretary of State and reports of bankruptcy petitions.

On or about July 26, 1976, plaintiff's president met with a representative of its principal creditor, a bank, to discuss the possibility of future financing. During the meeting, the bank's representative informed plaintiff's president that he had just received a credit report issued by defendant indicating that plaintiff had recently filed a voluntary petition in bankruptcy. Plaintiff's president testified that he was both shocked and confused when confronted with the report, since plaintiff had never filed such a petition and, at the time the report was published, plaintiff's business was steadily expanding. In fact, plaintiff's president later testified that prior to the issuance of the credit report, plaintiff had never suffered a major economic reversal and its financial condition was sound. Nevertheless, despite the bank representative's trial testimony that he never really believed the report, the bank put off any future consideration of credit to plaintiff until the discrepancy was cleared up. The bank later terminated plaintiff's credit allegedly for reasons unrelated to the report.

. . . .

The basis of the error was established at trial: a former employee of plaintiff, and not plaintiff, had filed a voluntary petition in bankruptcy. Defendant's employee, a seventeen-year-old high school student, paid $200 annually to review Vermont's bankruptcy petitions, had inadvertently attributed the former employee's bankruptcy petition to plaintiff itself, and reported the information as such to defendant. A representative of defendant testified that prior to the issuance of a credit report indicating a bankrupt business, it was defendant's routine practice first to check the report's accuracy with the business itself. No prepublication verification was ever attempted in the present case.

On or about August 3, 1976, having satisfied itself that its credit report on plaintiff was wrong, defendant issued a corrective notice to the five subscribers who had received the initial report. In substance, the corrective notice stated that it was a former employee of plaintiff, not plaintiff itself, who had filed the petition in bankruptcy, and that plaintiff "continued in business as usual." Plaintiff informed defendant that it was dissatisfied with the corrective notice, since it implied that the initial mistake was attributable to plaintiff, not defendant. Plaintiff again demanded a list of subscribers who had seen the report, but its request was once again denied.

Thereafter, plaintiff refused to provide defendant with any further financial data, and requested that defendant inform anyone seeking such data that they were being withheld pending the outcome of plaintiff s defamation action against defendant. Instead, defendant issued plaintiff a "blank rating," indicating that plaintiff's circumstances were "difficult to classify" within defendant's rating system, and such information was distributed to those creditors who requested a current indication of plaintiff's financial status. A short while later, plaintiff commenced its defamation action.

I

. . . Although *Gertz* permitted a "private individual" to recover actual damages, presumed or punitive damages were not permitted absent proof of the *New York Times* standard "of knowledge of falsity or reckless disregard for the truth." *Id.* at 348.

The critical issue underlying the certified questions presented, a matter of first impression for this Court, is whether the First and Fourteenth Amendments to the United States Constitution require that the qualified protections afforded the media in "private" defamation actions, as set forth in *Gertz*, be extended to actions involving nonmedia defendants.

. . . .

[I]n carefully surveying the decisions of those jurisdictions which have specifically addressed the issue of whether *Gertz* should be applied to non-media defendants, we note that the majority have refused such an extension. Although we are not bound by these decisions, their reasoning is both persuasive and compelling. In nonmedia defamation actions, "[the] crucial elements . . . which brought the United States Supreme Court into the field of defamation law are missing. There is no threat to the free and robust debate of public issues; there is no potential interference with a meaningful dialogue of ideas concerning self-government; and there is no threat of liability causing a reaction of self-censorship by the press."

. . . .

In light of the above, we are convinced that the balance must be struck in favor of the private plaintiff defamed by a nonmedia defendant. "Neither the intentional lie nor the careless error materially advances society's interest in 'uninhibited, robust, and wide-open' debate on public issues." *Gertz v. Robert Welch, Inc., supra*, 418 U.S. at 340 (quoting *New York Times Co. v. Sullivan, supra*, 376 U.S. at 270). Accordingly, we hold that as a matter of federal constitutional law, the media protections outlined in *Gertz* are inapplicable to nonmedia defamation actions.

. . . .

III

With regard to the question of damages, we note that "the availability of both general and punitive damages in libel actions has not been rejected as a matter of constitutional law." "When the defamation is actionable per se the plaintiff can recover general damages without proof of loss or injury, which is conclusively presumed to result from the defamation, but he is not required to rely solely upon the implications that are applicable and may present any evidence of a competent character that is authorized by his pleadings, for the purpose of showing the extent of the injury and the amount of the compensation that should be awarded."

Likewise, in accordance with this Court's belief that "[punitive] damages are awarded to 'stamp the condemnation of the jury upon the acts of defendant on account of their malicious character,'" . . . we have indicated that malice "may be shown by conduct manifesting personal ill will or carried out under circumstances evidencing insult or oppression, or even by conduct showing a reckless or wanton disregard of one's rights."

Since "punitive damages are incapable of precise determination, their assessment is 'largely discretionary with the jury'" . . .

IV

. . . .

We are not persuaded that the trial court abused its discretion in denying defendant's motion to set aside the verdict as to the issue of punitive damages. There was ample evidence in the record to enable the jury to conclude that defendant's conduct was insulting, reckless, and in total disregard of plaintiff's rights. . . .

---

1. Why doesn't *Gertz* apply?

2. What damages may Plaintiff recover? What proof of these damages is required?

Dun & Bradstreet v. Greenmoss Builders, Inc.

Supreme Court of the United States, 1985
472 U.S. 749

JUSTICE POWELL announced the judgment of the Court and delivered an opinion, in which JUSTICE REHNQUIST and JUSTICE O'CONNOR joined.

In *Gertz v. Robert Welch, Inc.*, 418 U.S. 323 (1974), we held that the First Amendment restricted the damages that a private individual could obtain from a publisher for a libel that involved a matter of public concern. More specifically, we held that in these circumstances the First Amendment prohibited awards of presumed and punitive damages for false and defamatory statements unless the plaintiff shows "actual malice," that is, knowledge of falsity or reckless disregard for the truth. The question presented in this case is whether this rule of *Gertz* applies when the false and defamatory statements do not involve matters of public concern.

I

Petitioner Dun & Bradstreet, a credit reporting agency, provides subscribers with financial and related information about businesses. All the information is confidential; under the terms of the subscription agreement the subscribers may not reveal it to anyone else. On July 26, 1976, petitioner sent a report to five subscribers indicating that respondent, a construction contractor, had filed a voluntary petition for bankruptcy. This report was false and grossly misrepresented respondent's assets and liabilities. That same day, while discussing the possibility of future financing with its bank, respondent's president was told that the bank had received the defamatory report. He immediately called petitioner's regional office, explained the error, and asked for a correction. In addition, he requested the names of the firms that had received the false report in order to assure them that the company was solvent. Petitioner promised to look into the matter but refused to divulge the names of those who had received the report.

After determining that its report was indeed false, petitioner issued a corrective notice on or about August 3, 1976, to the five subscribers who had received the initial report. The notice stated that one of respondent's former employees, not respondent itself, had filed for bankruptcy and that respondent "continued in business as usual." Respondent told petitioner that it was dissatisfied with the notice, and it again asked for a list of subscribers who had seen the initial report. Again petitioner refused to divulge their names.

Respondent then brought this defamation action in Vermont state court. It alleged that the false report had injured its reputation and sought both compensatory and punitive damages. The trial established that the error in petitioner's report had been caused when one of its employees, a 17-year-old high school student paid to review Vermont bankruptcy pleadings, had inadvertently attributed to respondent a bankruptcy petition filed by one of respondent's former employees. Although petitioner's representative testified that it was routine practice to check the accuracy of such reports with the businesses themselves, it did not try to verify the information about respondent before reporting it.

After trial, the jury returned a verdict in favor of respondent and awarded $50,000 in compensatory or presumed damages and $300,000 in punitive damages. Petitioner moved for a new trial. It argued that in *Gertz v. Robert Welch, Inc., supra*, at 349, this Court had ruled broadly that "the States may not permit recovery of presumed or punitive damages, at least when liability is not based on a showing of knowledge of falsity or reckless disregard for the truth," and it argued that the judge's instructions in this case permitted the jury to award such damages on a lesser showing. The trial court indicated some doubt as to whether *Gertz* applied to "non-media cases," but granted a new trial "[because] of . . . dissatisfaction with its charge and . . . conviction that the interests of justice [required]" it. App. 26.

The Vermont Supreme Court reversed. 143 Vt. 66, 461 A. 2d 414 (1983). Although recognizing that "in certain instances the distinction between media and nonmedia defendants may be difficult to draw," the court stated that "no such difficulty is presented with credit reporting agencies, which are in the business of selling financial information to a limited number of subscribers who have paid substantial fees for their services." . . . Relying on this distinguishing characteristic of credit reporting firms, the court concluded that such firms are not "the type of media worthy of First Amendment protection as contemplated by *New York Times [Co. v. Sullivan*, 376 U.S. 254 (1964),] and its progeny." . . . It held that the balance between a private plaintiff's right to recover presumed and punitive damages without a showing of special fault and the First Amendment rights of "nonmedia" speakers "must be struck in favor of the private plaintiff defamed by a nonmedia defendant." . . . Accordingly, the court held "that as a matter of federal constitutional law, the media protections outlined in *Gertz* are inapplicable to nonmedia defamation actions."

Recognizing disagreement among the lower courts about when the protections *of Gertz* apply, we granted certiorari. . . . We now affirm, although for reasons different from those relied upon by the Vermont Supreme Court.

. . . .

In Gertz, we held that the fact that expression concerned a public issue did not by itself entitle the libel defendant to the constitutional protections *of New York Times*. These protections, we found, were not "justified solely by reference to the interest of the press and broadcast media in immunity from liability." 418 U.S., at 343. Rather, they represented "an accommodation between [First Amendment] [concerns] and the limited state interest present in the context of libel actions brought by public persons." *Ibid.* In libel actions brought by private persons we found the competing interests different. Largely because private persons have not voluntarily exposed themselves to increased risk of injury from defamatory statements and because they generally lack effective opportunities for rebutting such statements, *id.*, at 345, we found that the State possessed a "strong and legitimate . . . interest in compensating private individuals for injury to reputation." *Id.*, at 348–349. Balancing this stronger state interest against the same First Amendment interest at stake in *New York Times*, we held that a State could not allow recovery of presumed and punitive damages absent a showing of "actual malice." Nothing in our opinion, however, indicated that this same balance would be struck regardless of the type of speech involved.

IV

We have never considered whether the *Gertz* balance obtains when the defamatory statements involve no issue of public concern. To make this determination, we must employ the approach approved in *Gertz* and balance the State's interest in compensating private individuals for injury to their reputation against the First Amendment interest in protecting this type of expression. This state interest is identical to the one weighed in *Gertz*. There we found that it was "strong and legitimate." . . .

The First Amendment interest, on the other hand, is less important than the one weighed in *Gertz*. We have long recognized that not all speech is of equal First Amendment importance. It is speech on "'matters of public concern'" that is "at the heart of the First Amendment's protection." . . . In contrast, speech on matters of purely private concern is of less First Amendment concern. . . .

While such speech is not totally unprotected by the First Amendment, its protections are less stringent. In *Gertz*, we found that the state interest in awarding presumed and punitive damages was not "substantial" in view of their effect on speech at the core of First Amendment concern. 418 U.S., at 349. This interest, however, *is* "substantial" relative to the incidental effect these remedies may have on speech of significantly less constitutional interest. The rationale of the common-law rules has been the experience and judgment of history that "proof of actual damage will be impossible in a great many cases where, from the character of the defamatory words and the circumstances of publication, it is all but certain that serious harm has resulted in fact." W. Prosser, Law of Torts § 112, p. 765 (4th ed. 1971); accord, *Rowe v. Metz, supra*, at 425–426, 579 P. 2d, at 84; Note, *Developments in the Law—Defamation*, 69 Harv. L. Rev. 875, 891–892 (1956). As a result, courts for centuries have allowed juries to presume that some damage occurred from many defamatory utterances and publications. This rule furthers the state interest in providing remedies for defamation by ensuring that those remedies are effective. In light of the reduced constitutional value of speech involving no matters of public concern, we hold that the state interest adequately supports awards of presumed and punitive damages—even absent a showing of "actual malice.

V

The only remaining issue is whether petitioner's credit report involved a matter of public concern. In a related context, we have held that "[whether] . . . speech addresses a matter of public concern must be determined by [the expression's] content, form, and context . . . as revealed by the whole record." *Connick v. Myers, supra,* at 147–148. These factors indicate that petitioner's credit report concerns no public issue. It was speech solely in the individual interest of the speaker and its specific business audience. Cf. *Central Hudson Gas & Elec. Corp. v. Public Service Comm'n of New York*, 447 U.S. 557, 561 (1980). This particular interest warrants no special protection when—as in this case—the speech is wholly false and clearly damaging to the victim's business reputation. Cf. *id.*, at 566; *Virginia Pharmacy Bd. v. Virginia Citizens Consumer Council, Inc.*, 425 U.S. 748, 771–772 (1976). Moreover, since the credit report was made available to only five subscribers, who, under the terms of the subscription agreement, could not disseminate it further, it cannot be said that the report involves any "strong interest in the free flow of commercial information." *Id.*, at 764. There is simply no credible argument that this type of credit reporting requires special protection to ensure that "debate on public issues [will] be uninhibited, robust, and wide-open." *New York Times Co. v. Sullivan*, 376 U.S., at 270.

In addition, the speech here, like advertising, is hardy and unlikely to be deterred by incidental state regulation. . . . Arguably, the reporting here was also more objectively verifiable than speech deserving of greater protection. See *ibid.* In any case, the market provides a powerful incentive to a credit reporting agency to be accurate, since false credit reporting is of no use to creditors. Thus, any incremental "chilling" effect of libel suits would be of decreased significance.[9]

VI

We conclude that permitting recovery of presumed and punitive damages in defamation cases absent a showing of "actual malice" does not violate the First Amendment when the defamatory statements do not involve matters of public concern. Accordingly, we affirm the judgment of the Vermont Supreme Court.

It is so ordered.

CHIEF JUSTICE BURGER, concurring in the judgment.

. . . .

---

9. The Court of Appeals for the Fifth Circuit has noted that, while most States provide a qualified privilege against libel suits for commercial credit reporting agencies, in those States that do not there is a thriving credit reporting business and commercial credit transactions are not inhibited.

I dissented in *Gertz* because I believed that, insofar as the "ordinary private citizen" was concerned, 418 U.S., at 355, the Court's opinion "[abandoned] the traditional thread," *id.*, at 354–355, that had been the theme of the law in this country up to that time. I preferred "to allow this area of law to continue to evolve as it [had] up to [then] with respect to private citizens rather than embark on a new doctrinal theory which [had] no jurisprudential ancestry." *Ibid. Gertz*, however, is now the law of the land, and until it is overruled, it must, under the principle of *stare decisis*, be applied by this Court.

The single question before the Court today is whether *Gertz* applies to this case. . . . I agree that *Gertz* is limited to circumstances in which the alleged defamatory expression concerns a matter of general public importance, and that the expression in question here relates to a matter of essentially private concern. I therefore agree with the plurality opinion to the extent that it holds that *Gertz* is inapplicable in this case for the two reasons indicated. No more is needed to dispose of the present case.

---

1. What is the difference between matters of "public concern" and matters of "public interest," *Rosenbloom v. Metromedia*?

2. What defamation rules apply to private persons when the matter is not of "public concern"?

6. The Burden of Proving Truth

Philadelphia Newspapers, Inc. v. Hepps

Supreme Court of the United States, 1986
475 U.S. 767

JUSTICE O'CONNOR delivered the opinion of the Court.

This case requires us once more to "[struggle] . . . to define the proper accommodation between the law of defamation and the freedoms of speech and press protected by the First Amendment." *Gertz v. Robert Welch, Inc.*, 418 U.S. 323, 325 (1974). In *Gertz*, the Court held that a private figure who brings a suit for defamation cannot recover without some showing that the media defendant was at fault in publishing the statements at issue. *Id.*, at 347. Here, we hold that, at least where a newspaper publishes speech of public concern, a private-figure plaintiff cannot recover damages without also showing that the statements at issue are false.

I

Maurice S. Hepps is the principal stockholder of General Programming, Inc. (GPI), a corporation that franchises a chain of stores—known at the relevant time as "Thrifty" stores—selling beer, soft drinks, and snacks. Mr. Hepps, GPI, and a number of its franchisees are the appellees here. Appellant Philadelphia Newspapers, Inc., owns the Philadelphia Inquirer (Inquirer). The Inquirer published a series of articles, . . . containing the statements at issue here. The general theme of the five articles, which appeared in the Inquirer between May 1975 and May 1976, was that appellees had links to organized crime and used some of those links to influence the State's governmental processes, both legislative and administrative. The articles discussed a state legislator, described as "a Pittsburgh Democrat and convicted felon," . . . whose actions displayed "a clear pattern of interference in state government by [the legislator] on behalf of Hepps and Thrifty," . . . The stories reported that federal "investigators have found connections between Thrifty and underworld figures," . . . ; that "the Thrifty Beverage beer chain . . . had connections . . . with organized crime" . . . ; and that Thrifty had "won a series of competitive advantages through rulings by the State Liquor Control Board". . . . A grand jury was said to be investigating the "alleged relationship between the Thrifty chain and known Mafia figures," and "[whether] the chain received special treatment from the [state Governor's] administration and the Liquor Control Board." . . .

Appellees brought suit for defamation against appellants in a Pennsylvania state court. Consistent with *Gertz, supra,* Pennsylvania requires a private figure who brings a suit for defamation to bear the burden of proving negligence or malice by the defendant in publishing the statements at issue. 42 Pa. Cons. Stat. §8344 (1982). As to falsity, Pennsylvania follows the common law's presumption that an individual's reputation is a good one. Statements defaming that person are therefore presumptively false, although a publisher who bears the burden of proving the truth of the statements has an absolute defense. . . .

After all the evidence had been presented by both sides, the trial court concluded that Pennsylvania's statute giving the defendant the burden of proving the truth of the statements violated the Federal Constitution. . . . . The trial court therefore instructed the jury that the plaintiffs bore the burden of proving falsity. . . .

. . . The jury ruled for appellants and therefore awarded no damages to appellees.

[T]he appellees here brought an appeal directly to the Pennsylvania Supreme Court. That court viewed *Gertz* as simply requiring the plaintiff to show fault in actions for defamation. It concluded that a showing of fault did not require a showing of falsity, held that to place the burden of showing truth on the defendant did not unconstitutionally inhibit free debate, and remanded the case for a new trial. 506 Pa., at 318–329, 485 A. 2d, at 382–387. We noted probable jurisdiction, 472 U.S. 1025 (1985), and now reverse.

II

In *New York Times Co. v. Sullivan,* 376 U.S. 254 (1964), the Court "[determined] for the first time the extent to which the constitutional protections for speech and press limit a State's power to award damages in a libel action brought by a public official against critics of his official conduct." . . .

The Court therefore held that the Constitution "prohibits a public official from recovering damages for a defamatory falsehood relating to his official conduct unless he proves that the statement was made with 'actual malice'—that is, with knowledge that it was false or with reckless disregard of whether it was false or not." *Id.,* at

279–280. That showing must be made with "convincing clarity," *id.*, at 285–286, or, in a later formulation, by "clear and convincing proof," *Gertz*, 418 U.S., at 342. The standards of *New York Times* apply not only when a public official sues a newspaper, but also when a "public figure" sues a magazine or news service.

A decade after *New York Times*, the Court examined the constitutional limits on defamation suits by private-figure plaintiffs against media defendants. . . . *Gertz, supra*, at 344–345, the Court held that the Constitution "allows the States to impose liability on the publisher or broadcaster of defamatory falsehood on a less demanding showing than that required by *New York Times*," 418 U.S., at 348: "[So] long as they do not impose liability without fault, the States may define for themselves the appropriate standard of liability for a publisher or broadcaster of defamatory falsehood injurious to a private individual." *Id.*, at 347. . . . In addition, the Court in *Gertz* expressly held that, although a showing of simple fault sufficed to allow recovery for actual damages, even a private-figure plaintiff was required to show actual malice in order to recover presumed or punitive damages. *Id.*, at 348–350.

The Court most recently considered the constitutional limits on suits for defamation in *Dun & Bradstreet, Inc. v. Greenmoss Builders, Inc.*, 472 U.S. 749 (1985). In sharp contrast to *New York Times, Dun & Bradstreet* involved not only a private-figure plaintiff, but also speech of purely private concern. 472 U.S., at 751–752. A plurality of the Court in *Dun & Bradstreet* was convinced that . . . the showing of actual malice needed to recover punitive damages under either *New York Times* or *Gertz* was unnecessary.

. . . .

One can discern in these decisions two forces that may reshape the common-law landscape to conform to the First Amendment. The first is whether the plaintiff is a public official or figure, or is instead a private figure. The second is whether the speech at issue is of public concern. When the speech is of public concern and the plaintiff is a public official or public figure, the Constitution clearly requires the plaintiff to surmount a much higher barrier before recovering damages from a media defendant than is raised by the common law. When the speech is of public concern but the plaintiff is a private figure, as in *Gertz*, the Constitution still supplants the standards of the common law, but the constitutional requirements are, in at least some of their range, less forbidding than when the plaintiff is a public figure and the speech is of public concern. When the speech is of exclusively private concern and the plaintiff is a private figure, as in *Dun & Bradstreet*, the constitutional requirements do not necessarily force any change in at least some of the features of the common-law landscape.

Our opinions to date have chiefly treated the necessary showings of fault rather than of falsity. Nonetheless, as one might expect given the language of the Court in *New York Times*, see *supra*, at 772–773, a public-figure plaintiff must show the falsity of the statements at issue in order to prevail in a suit for defamation. . . .

Here, as in *Gertz*, the plaintiff is a private figure and the newspaper articles are of public concern. . . . We believe that the common law's rule on falsity—that the defendant must bear the burden of proving truth—must similarly fall here to a constitutional requirement that the plaintiff bear the burden of showing falsity, as well as fault, before recovering damages.

. . . .

We recognize that requiring the plaintiff to show falsity will insulate from liability some speech that is false, but unprovably so. Nonetheless, the Court's previous decisions on the restrictions that the First Amendment places upon the common law of defamation firmly support our conclusion here with respect to the allocation of the burden of proof. . . . We therefore do not break new ground here in insulating speech that is not even demonstrably false.

We note that our decision adds only marginally to the burdens that the plaintiff must already bear as a result of our earlier decisions in the law of defamation. The plaintiff must show fault. A jury is obviously more likely to accept a plaintiff's contention that the defendant was at fault in publishing the statements at issue if convinced that the relevant statements were false. As a practical matter, then, evidence offered by plaintiffs on the publisher's fault in adequately investigating the truth of the published statements will generally encompass evidence of the falsity of the matters asserted. See Keeton, *Defamation and Freedom of the Press*, 54 Texas L. Rev. 1221, 1236 (1976). See also Franklin & Bussel, *The Plaintiff's Burden in Defamation: Awareness and Falsity*, 25 Wm. & Mary L. Rev. 825, 856–857 (1984).

. . . .

For the reasons stated above, the judgment of the Pennsylvania Supreme Court is reversed, and the case is remanded for further proceedings not inconsistent with this opinion.

It is so ordered.

JUSTICE BRENNAN, with whom JUSTICE BLACKMUN joins, concurring.

I believe that where allegedly defamatory speech is of public concern, the First Amendment requires that the plaintiff, whether public official, public figure, or private individual, prove the statements at issue to be false, and thus join the Court's opinion. Cf. *Rosenbloom v. Metromedia, Inc.*, 403 U.S. 29 (1971). I write separately only to note that, while the Court reserves the question whether the rule it announces applies to nonmedia defendants, *ante*, at 779, n. 4, I adhere to my view that such a distinction is "irreconcilable" with the fundamental First Amendment principle that "'[the] inherent worth of . . . speech in terms of its capacity for informing the public does not depend upon the identity of the source, whether corporation, association, union, or individual.'"

JUSTICE STEVENS, with whom THE CHIEF JUSTICE, JUSTICE WHITE, and JUSTICE REHNQUIST join, dissenting.

The issue the Court resolves today will make a difference in only one category of cases—those in which a private individual can prove that he was libeled by a defendant who was at least negligent. For unless such a plaintiff can overcome the burden imposed by *Gertz v. Robert Welch, Inc.*, 418 U.S. 323, 347 (1974), he cannot recover regardless of how the burden of proof on the issue of truth or falsity is allocated. By definition, therefore, the only litigants—and the only publishers—who will benefit from today's decision are those who act negligently or maliciously.

The Court . . . decides to override "the common-law presumption" retained by several States that "defamatory speech is false" because of the need "[to] ensure that true speech on matters of public concern is not deterred." . . . I do not agree that our precedents require a private individual to bear the risk that a defamatory statement—uttered either with a mind toward assassinating his good name or with careless indifference to that possibility—cannot be proven false. By attaching no weight to the State's interest in protecting the private individual's good name, the Court has reached a pernicious result.

7. Opinion

Steinhausen v. Homeservices of Nebraska, Inc.

Supreme Court of Nebraska, 2015*
857 N.W.2d 816

CONNOLLY, J.

. . . Shelly J. Nitz is a real estate agent affiliated with HomeServices of Nebraska, Inc. (HomeServices). Matthew M. Steinhausen is a home inspector who inspected a house that one of Nitz' clients owned. More than 2 years after the inspection, Nitz sent an e-mail to HomeServices real estate agents and employees stating that Steinhausen was a "[t]otal idiot." Steinhausen . . . sued Nitz and HomeServices, alleging claims of libel, false light invasion of privacy, and tortious interference with a business relationship or expectancy.** The district court sustained Nitz' and HomeServices' motions for summary judgment . . . . We affirm the court's judgment as it relates to the claims asserted by Steinhausen in his personal capacity . . . .

HomeServices is a brokerage firm whose business includes real estate sales . . . . Nitz is a real estate agent affiliated with HomeServices.

Steinhausen began performing home inspections in 1999 . . . .

In 2008, Nitz represented the seller of a home in Seward, Nebraska. A potential buyer exercised her right to a home inspection, and Steinhausen performed the inspection. Nitz testified that some of the items in Steinhausen's report "were unquestionably beyond the scope of a typical home inspection." Nitz felt that Steinhausen's comments on "non-condition related items" were "likely to tear apart transactions when property condition was not a real issue, to the detriment of a seller."

---

* [Footnote citations in original opinion omitted.]

** [Court's discussion of privacy and business interference claims omitted.]

HomeServices provides its real estate agents with access to a company e-mail network. The network uses "group email lists," or listservs, including the "HRE-HOTSHEET" and "WBR-HOTSHEET" lists (collectively the Hotsheets). The Hotsheets include the e-mail addresses of current HomeServices real estate agents and employees and are accessed through their individual e-mail accounts.

HomeServices' vice president stated that agents use the Hotsheets as a forum to share information and opinions on topics related to the real estate business: It is common for HomeServices Sales Associates to use the Hotsheets to send emails to other HomeServices Sales Associates to obtain information, market properties, and discuss current issues or questions on which they share a common interest, for example, questions or comments about particular aspects of real estate transactions, availability of properties and developments, real estate rules, regulations and practices and how they relate to real estate transactions, or questions or comments about vendors who work in the real estate sales community.

Nitz averred that, in her experience, HomeServices agents use the Hotsheets to communicate amongst themselves their opinions of other Realtors and vendors in the real estate business.

On January 14, 2011, Nitz posted a reply to an e-mail on the Hotsheets with the subject "RE: Steinhausen inspections." Nitz' e-mail stated in its entirety: "He did an inspection in Seward for the agent that sold one of my listings. I will never let him near one of my listings ever again!!! Total idiot."

The record shows that at least two other HomeServices agents sent e-mails on the same subject to the Hotsheets before Nitz sent her e-mail. The author of the first e-mail stated, "IN MY OPINION," Steinhausen was not qualified to inspect residential structures. The author of the second e-mail stated that inspections performed by Steinhausen were poor and that Steinhausen addressed issues unrelated to structural soundness. After Nitz sent her e-mail, another HomeServices agent replied that Steinhausen was "not professional."

Nitz stated that she "did not have any specific facts in mind" when she wrote her e-mail. Nitz did "recall[] having a generally negative impression of . . . Steinhausen and the inspection he conducted" and used the phrase "'total idiot'" to "express that generally negative opinion."

At some point in January 2011, Steinhausen received an anonymous letter in the U.S. mail that included a copy of Nitz' e-mail. Steinhausen testified that the letter had no return address and that he did not know who had sent the letter.

After requesting a retraction from Nitz, Steinhausen filed a complaint with the State Real Estate Commission in February 2011 alleging that Nitz' e-mail violated Neb.Rev.Stat. § 81-885.24(22) and (29) (Cum.Supp.2010). Section 81-885.24 authorizes the commission to discipline real estate brokers who commit certain unfair trade practices, including . . . "[m]aking any substantial misrepresentations" and . . . "[d]emonstrating negligence, incompetency, or unworthiness to act as a broker . . . ." Nitz signed a consent order with the commission that determined that she had violated § 81-885.24(29). The commission ordered Nitz to complete 6 hours of ethics courses.

Steinhausen claimed . . . that he suffered $30,000 per year in lost business following Nitz' e-mail and would continue to suffer the same losses for the next 25 years.

Steinhausen testified that Nitz' e-mail and its aftermath also weighed on him personally. According to Steinhausen, he "was physically ill" after learning about Nitz' e-mail and "went through a period of depression, anger, [and] sadness." Steinhausen testified that he had trouble sleeping but that he had not visited a medical doctor or been diagnosed with depression. [The trial court granted summary judgment in favor of Nitz, from which Steinhausen appealed.]

. . . .

On appeal, Nitz argues that the [trial] court should have determined whether her statement was capable of defamatory meaning before deciding whether it was privileged. Nitz contends that "[i]n today's parlance, 'idiot' is merely a subjective pejorative term." Nitz argues that in the context of the Hotsheets—which she refers to as a place for HomeServices agents to "express their opinions without pulling punches"—the phrase "total idiot" is not "a factual statement that [Steinhausen] is mentally defective." Steinhausen responds that "[i]diocy is verifiable" and "can be defined and proved." He notes that "idiot" is defined in one dictionary as "a stupid person or a mentally handicapped person" and asserts that he "is neither stupid nor mentally handicapped."

In the ordinary case, a defamation claim has four elements: (1) a false and defamatory statement concerning the plaintiff, (2) an unprivileged publication to a third party, (3) fault amounting to at least negligence on the part of the publisher, and (4) either actionability of the statement irrespective of special harm or the existence of special harm caused by the publication. A communication is defamatory if it tends so to harm the reputation of another as to lower him in the estimation of the community or to deter third persons from associating or dealing with him.

The threshold question in a defamation suit is whether a reasonable fact finder could conclude that the published statements imply a provably false factual assertion. Statements of fact can be defamatory whereas statements of opinion—the publication of which is protected by the First Amendment—cannot. Put another way, "subjective impressions" cannot be defamatory, as contrasted with objective "expressions of verifiable facts." Distinguishing the two presents a question of law for the trial judge to decide. In making this distinction, courts apply a totality of the circumstances test. Relevant factors include (1) whether the general tenor of the entire work negates the impression that the defendant asserted an objective fact, (2) whether the defendant used figurative or hyperbolic language, and (3) whether the statement is susceptible of being proved true or false.

And context is important to whether an ordinary reader would view a statement as one of fact or opinion. In addition to the content of the communication, a court looks to the knowledge, understanding, and reasonable expectations of the audience to whom the communication was directed, taking cues from "the broader setting in which the statement appears." Words, particularly the pejorative ones, often have both a literal and figurative meaning. Whether the statement is capable of being defamatory depends on which meaning was used, which can be answered only by examining the context in which the language appears.

As noted, whether the language is hyperbolic is relevant to distinguishing fact from opinion. Rhetorical hyperbole—"language that, in context, was obviously understood as an exaggeration, rather than a statement of literal fact"—is not actionable. In particular, "[t]he ad hominem nature of abusive epithets, vulgarities, and profanities," which some writers "use to enliven their prose," indicates that the statement is hyperbole.

Exercises in "name calling" generally fall under the category of rhetorical hyperbole. For example, courts have held that "'idiot,'" "'raving idiot,'" "'[i]diots [a] float,'" and more vulgar variants were rude statements of opinion, rather than lay diagnoses of mental capacity. Similarly, courts have held that statements calling the plaintiff "'stupid,'" a "'moron,'" and a "'nincompoop'" were not actionable. Courts have also held that statements potentially referring to the plaintiff's mental health, such as "'raving maniac'"; "'pitiable lunatics,'" "wacko," "nut job," and "'hysterical'"; "'crazy'"; and "crank," were statements of opinion.

To analyze Nitz' communication, we begin with the context in which it was made. Nitz sent the e-mail to the Hotsheets, which the evidence shows are accessed by HomeServices real estate agents and used, among other purposes, as a forum to express their thoughts on vendors in the real estate community. The reasonable expectations of the audience of Nitz' e-mail (members of the Hotsheets) depend on how members used the forum, particularly whether the Hotsheets were a "place[] that invited exaggeration and personal opinion." At least two other e-mails on the subject of "Steinhausen inspections" preceded Nitz' e-mail. The first, prefaced by "IN MY OPINION," suggested that Steinhausen "should never be allowed to inspect even a dog house." The second called inspections performed by Steinhausen "horrendous."

We next turn to the language of Nitz' e-mail itself. To recap, Nitz stated: "He did an inspection in Seward for the agent that sold one of my listings. I will never let him near one of my listings ever again!!! Total idiot." The word "total" means "complete in extent or degree" or "absolute." In some contexts, "idiot" might refer to an objective state of mental capacity and particularly to a person "lacking the capacity to develop beyond the mental age of three or four years." But "idiot" can also refer to "an utterly foolish or senseless person," and we conclude that Nitz used this meaning. The broad setting of Nitz' statement—along with the superfluous exclamation marks and the adjective "[t]otal"—shows that the statement was hyperbolic rhetoric rather than a reference to arrested intellectual development. Whether a person is "foolish" or "senseless" is a "subjective impression[]" and not an objective "expression[] of verifiable facts." Nitz' e-mail might have been distasteful, but it was a statement of opinion and, therefore, not defamatory.

. . . .

. . . We conclude that the e-mail sent by Nitz stated an opinion and, therefore, was not actionable as libel. The false light invasion of privacy claim was subsumed within the libel claim because both claims were based on the same statement. . . .

Affirmed in part, reversed in part, and remanded with directions.

WRIGHT, J., not participating.

Mr. Chow of New York v. Ste. Jour Azur S.A.

United States Court of Appeals for the Second Circuit, 1985
759 F.2d 219

MESKILL, CIRCUIT JUDGE:

On February 19, 1982 Mr. Chow of New York, the joint venture that owns Mr. Chow, commenced the instant action. In the complaint, Ste. Jour, Gault and Millau were named as defendants and jurisdiction was based on diversity of citizenship. The complaint alleged that the review [in the defendants' restaurant guide] contained false and defamatory statements and sought compensatory damages in excess of $10,000 and punitive damages in excess of $250,000.

. . . .

The district court submitted six statements to the jury. It instructed the jury that, as a matter of law, these were statements of fact and that if any one of them was false, defamatory and made with malice it would support a finding that the review had libeled Mr. Chow. The six statements submitted were:

(1) "It is impossible to have the basic condiments . . . on the table."

(2) "The sweet and sour pork contained more dough . . . than meat."

(3) "The green peppers . . . remained still frozen on the plate."

(4) The rice was "soaking . . . in oil."

(5) The Peking Duck "was made up of only one dish (instead of the traditional three)."

(6) The pancakes were "the thickness of a finger."

The jury returned a general verdict, finding that the review was libelous. It awarded $20,000 in compensatory and $5 in punitive damages. Appellants' motion for judgment notwithstanding the verdict was denied without opinion.

DISCUSSION

On appeal, appellants raise a host of grounds for reversal. Among them are a claim that the statements submitted to the jury are opinion and thus protected speech and a claim that the evidence on the issue of malice is insufficient to support the jury's findings. Because we find these two claims dispositive of this appeal, we do not consider appellants' other claims.

A. *Opinion*

Appellants' initial argument is that the district court erred when it failed to hold that the statements submitted to the jury were opinion and thus privileged. Appellants' argument stems from the Supreme Court's decision in *Gertz v. Robert Welch, Inc.*, 418 U.S. 323, 94 S. Ct. 2997, 41 L. Ed. 2d 789 (1974), . . .

We begin with the common ground. Under the First Amendment there is no such thing as a false idea. However pernicious an opinion may seem, we depend for its correction not on the conscience of judges and juries but on the competition of other ideas. But there is no constitutional value in false statements of fact. *Id*, at 339–40 (footnote omitted). We have recognized that *Gertz* made crucial the distinction between statements of fact and opinions. And, we have held that generally one cannot be liable simply for expressing an opinion. The Supreme Court has also made clear that the constitutional protection afforded statements of opinion is not lost simply because the opinion is expressed through the use of figurative or hyperbolic language. . . .

Although it is clear that expressions of opinion are constitutionally protected, the determination of whether a specific statement is one of opinion or fact is difficult. As an initial matter, the inquiry into whether a statement should be viewed as one of fact or one of opinion must be made from the perspective of an "ordinary reader" of the statement. *Buckley v. Littell*, 539 F.2d at 894. It is also clear that the determination of whether a statement is opinion or rhetorical hyperbole as opposed to a factual representation is a question of law for the court. . . .

. . . .

Although none of [our prior] decisions can be said to establish an actual test for determining if a statement is protected opinion or unprotected fact, they do provide guidance. Thus, it is clear that we must examine both the context in which the statements are made and the circumstances surrounding the statements. . . . We must also look at the language itself to determine if it is used in a precise, literal manner or in a loose, figurative or hyperbolic sense. . . . Related to this inquiry, we must examine the statements to determine if they are objectively capable of being proved true or false. . . . Finally, if the above analysis indicates that the statement is opinion, we must determine if it implies the allegation of undisclosed defamatory facts as the basis for the opinion. . . .

In the recent en banc decision of the D.C. Circuit in *Ollman v. Evans*, 750 F.2d 970, 242 U.S. App. D.C. 301 (D.C. Cir. 1984), Judge Starr, writing for the court, developed a similar guide to aid in the determination of whether the average reader would view a statement as one of fact or one of opinion.

. . . .

Turning to the instant case, we believe that application of the guidelines culled from our previous opinions and Judge Starr's opinion in *Ollman* mandates a holding that five of the six statements submitted to the jury were opinion rather than fact. Only the statement that Mr. Chow served Peking Duck in one dish rather than the traditional three can be considered factual.

1. Context

As indicated earlier, both the immediate and broader context in which a statement occurs can indicate that what appears to be a statement of fact is in reality protected opinion. . . .

Restaurant reviews are also the well recognized home of opinion and comment. Indeed, "by its very nature, an article commenting upon the quality of a restaurant or its food, like a review of a play or movie, constitutes the opinion of the reviewer." *Greer v. Columbus Monthly Publishing Corp.*, 4 Ohio App. 3d 235, 238, 448 N.E.2d 157, 161 (1982). The natural function of the review is to convey the critic's opinion of the restaurant reviewed: the food, the service, the decor, the atmosphere, and so forth. Such matters are to a large extent controlled by personal tastes. The average reader approaches a review with the knowledge that it contains only one person's views of the establishment. And importantly, "as is essential in aesthetic criticism . . . the object of the judgment is available to the critic's audience." *Myers*, 380 Mass. at 341, 403 N.E.2d at 379. Appellee does not cite a single case that has found a restaurant review libelous. Appellants and *amici*, on the other hand, cite numerous decisions that have refused to do so. Although the rationale underlying each of these decisions is different, they all recognize to some extent that reviews, although they may be unkind, are not normally a breeding ground for successful libel actions.

2. Language Used

Recognizing that reviews are normally conveyors of opinion, we turn to the language in the review before us to see if it makes factual representations. Examining the language in the review itself, we cannot say that it would cause the average reader to believe that the writer in five of the six contested remarks had gone beyond statements of opinion. . . .

The average reader would understand the author's statements to be attempts to express his opinions through the use of metaphors and hyperbole. Because the average reader would understand the statements involved to be opinion, the statements are entitled to the same constitutional protection as a straight-forward expression of opinion would receive.

3. Truth/Falsity

The final factor that our previous decisions indicate should be examined is whether the statement is objectively capable of being proved true or false. As Judge Starr stated in *Ollman*, "a reader cannot rationally view an unverifiable statement as conveying actual facts."

. . . .

When viewed in the entire context and given a reasonable rather than a literal reading, only the statement that Mr. Chow served Peking Duck in one dish instead of the traditional three can be viewed as an assertion of fact. The statement is not metaphorical or hyperbolic; it clearly is laden with factual content. . . .

. . . .

CONCLUSION

We conclude that five of the six statements submitted to the jury were statements of opinion and thus constitutionally protected. Plaintiff has failed to prove by clear and convincing evidence that the sixth statement, even if false and defamatory, was made with actual malice. Moreover, Mr. Chow points to no statements that could support a jury verdict in a new trial. Therefore, the judgment below is vacated and the case is remanded to the district court with instructions to dismiss the complaint.

––––––––––

1. The common law recognized a privilege known as fair comment to allow critique of the arts, restaurants, candidates for public office, anything presented to the public. As you see in *Mr. Chow*, the Second Circuit believes this has changed into a constitutional privilege to comment. Both rest on protected opinion.

2. Did *Gertz* establish that the Constitution protects all opinions?

Milkovich v. Lorain Journal Co.

Supreme Court of the United States, 1990
497 U.S. 1

CHIEF JUSTICE REHNQUIST delivered the opinion of the Court.

Respondent J. Theodore Diadiun authored an article in an Ohio newspaper implying that petitioner Michael Milkovich, a local high school wrestling coach, lied under oath in a judicial proceeding about an incident involving petitioner and his team which occurred at a wrestling match. Petitioner sued Diadiun and the newspaper for libel, and the Ohio Court of Appeals affirmed a lower court entry of summary judgment against petitioner. This judgment was based in part on the grounds that the article constituted an "opinion" protected from the reach of state defamation law by the First Amendment to the United States Constitution. We hold that the First Amendment does not prohibit the application of Ohio's libel laws to the alleged defamations contained in the article.

This lawsuit is before us for the third time in an odyssey of litigation spanning nearly 15 years. Petitioner Milkovich, now retired, was the wrestling coach at Maple Heights High School in Maple Heights, Ohio. In 1974, his team was involved in an altercation at a home wrestling match with a team from Mentor High School. Several people were injured. In response to the incident, the Ohio High School Athletic Association (OHSAA) held a hearing at which Milkovich and H. Don Scott, the Superintendent of Maple Heights Public Schools, testified. Following the hearing, OHSAA placed the Maple Heights team on probation for a year and declared the team ineligible for the 1975 state tournament. OHSAA also censured Milkovich for his actions during the altercation. Thereafter, several parents and wrestlers sued OHSAA in the Court of Common Pleas of Franklin County, Ohio, seeking a restraining order against OHSAA's ruling on the grounds that they had been denied due process in the OHSAA proceeding. Both Milkovich and Scott testified in that proceeding. The court overturned OHSAA's probation and ineligibility orders on due process grounds.

The day after the court rendered its decision, respondent Diadiun's column appeared in the News-Herald, a newspaper which circulates in Lake County, Ohio, and is owned by respondent Lorain Journal Co. The column bore the heading "Maple beat the law with the 'big lie,'" beneath which appeared Diadiun's photograph and the words "TD Says." The carryover page headline announced ". . . Diadiun says Maple told a lie." The column contained the following passages:

". . . [A] lesson was learned (or relearned) yesterday by the student body of Maple Heights High School, and by anyone who attended the Maple-Mentor wrestling meet of last Feb. 8."

"A lesson which, sadly, in view of the events of the past year, is well they learned early."

"It is simply this: If you get in a jam, lie your way out."

"If you're successful enough, and powerful enough, and can sound sincere enough, you stand an excellent chance of making the lie stand up, regardless of what really happened."

"The teachers responsible were mainly head Maple wrestling coach, Mike Milkovich, and former superintendent of schools H. Donald Scott."

". . . ."

"Anyone who attended the meet, whether he be from Maple Heights, Mentor, or impartial observer, knows in his heart that Milkovich and Scott lied at the hearing after each having given his solemn oath to tell the truth."

"But they got away with it."

"Is that the kind of lesson we want our young people learning from their high school administrators and coaches?"

"I think not."

Petitioner commenced a defamation action against respondents . . . alleging that the headline of Diadun's article and the nine passages quoted above "accused plaintiff of committing the crime of perjury. . . ."

Meanwhile, Superintendent Scott had been pursuing a separate defamation action through the Ohio courts. [In the *Scott* case], the Ohio Supreme Court . . . [concluded] that the column was "constitutionally protected opinion." *Scott v. News-Herald*, 25 Ohio St. 3d 243, 254, 496 N.E.2d 699, 709 (1986). Consequently, the court upheld a lower court's grant of summary judgment against Scott.

The *Scott* court decided that the proper analysis for determining whether utterances are fact or opinion was set forth in the decision of the United States Court of Appeals for the District of Columbia Circuit in *Ollman v. Evans* (1985). . . . Under that analysis, four factors are considered to ascertain whether, under the "totality of circumstances," a statement is fact or opinion. These factors are: (1) "the specific language used"; (2) "whether the statement is verifiable"; (3) "the general context of the statement"; and (4) "the broader context in which the statement appeared." . . . The court found that application of the first two factors to the column militated in favor of deeming the challenged passages actionable assertions of fact. . . . That potential outcome was trumped, however, by the court's consideration of the third and fourth factors. With respect to the third factor, the general context, the court explained that "the large caption 'TD Says' . . . would indicate to even the most gullible reader that the article was, in fact, opinion." . . . As for the fourth factor, the "broader context," the court reasoned that because the article appeared on a sports page—"a traditional haven for cajoling, invective, and hyperbole"—the article would probably be construed as opinion.

Subsequently, considering itself bound by the Ohio Supreme Court's decision in *Scott*, the Ohio Court of Appeals in the instant proceedings affirmed a trial court's grant of summary judgment in favor of respondents, concluding that "it has been decided, as a matter of law, that the article in question was constitutionally protected opinion." . . . The Supreme Court of Ohio dismissed petitioner's ensuing appeal for want of a substantial constitutional question. . . . We granted certiorari . . . to consider the important questions raised by the Ohio courts' recognition of a constitutionally required "opinion" exception to the application of its defamation laws. We now reverse.

. . . Defamation law developed not only as a means of allowing an individual to vindicate his good name, but also for the purpose of obtaining redress for harm caused by such statements. . . . As the common law developed in this country, apart from the issue of damages, one usually needed only allege an unprivileged publication of false and defamatory matter to state a cause of action for defamation. . . . The common law generally did not place any additional restrictions on the type of statement that could be actionable. Indeed, defamatory communications were deemed actionable regardless of whether they were deemed to be statements of fact or opinion. See, *e.g.*, Restatement of Torts, *supra*, §§ 565–567. As noted in the 1977 Restatement (Second) of Torts § 566, Comment *a:*

"Under the law of defamation, an expression of opinion could be defamatory if the expression was sufficiently derogatory of another as to cause harm to his reputation, so as to lower him in the estimation of the community or to deter third persons from associating or dealing with him. . . . The expression of opinion was also actionable in a suit for defamation, despite the normal requirement that the communication be false as well as defamatory. . . . This position was maintained even though the truth or falsity of an opinion—as distinguished from a statement of fact—is not a matter that can be objectively determined and truth is a complete defense to a suit for defamation."

However, due to concerns that unduly burdensome defamation laws could stifle valuable public debate, the privilege of "fair comment" was incorporated into the common law as an affirmative defense to an action for defamation. "The principle of 'fair comment' afforded legal immunity for the honest expression of opinion on matters of legitimate public interest when based upon a true or privileged statement of fact." 1 F. Harper & F. James, Law of Torts § 5.28, p. 456 (1956) (footnote omitted). As this statement implies, comment was generally privileged when it concerned a matter of public concern, was upon true or privileged facts, represented the actual opinion of the speaker, and was not made solely for the purpose of causing harm. See Restatement of Torts, *supra*, § 606. "According to the majority rule, the privilege of fair comment applied only to an expression of opinion and not to a false statement of fact, whether it was expressly stated or implied from an expression of opinion." . . .

Respondents would have us recognize, in addition to the established safeguards discussed above, still another First-Amendment-based protection for defamatory statements which are categorized as "opinion" as opposed to "fact." For this proposition they rely principally on the following dictum from our opinion in *Gertz:*

"Under the First Amendment there is no such thing as a false idea. However pernicious an opinion may seem, we depend for its correction not on the conscience of judges and juries but on the competition of other ideas. But there is no constitutional value in false statements of fact."

. . . Read in context, though, the fair meaning of the passage is to equate the word "opinion" in the second sentence with the word "idea" in the first sentence. Under this view, the language was merely a reiteration of Justice Holmes' classic "marketplace of ideas" concept. . . .

Thus, we do not think this passage from *Gertz* was intended to create a wholesale defamation exemption for anything that might be labeled "opinion." Not only would such an interpretation be contrary to the tenor and context of the passage, but it would also ignore the fact that expressions of "opinion" may often imply an assertion of objective fact.

If a speaker says, "In my opinion John Jones is a liar," he implies a knowledge of facts which lead to the conclusion that Jones told an untruth. Even if the speaker states the facts upon which he bases his opinion, if those facts are either incorrect or incomplete, or if his assessment of them is erroneous, the statement may still imply a false assertion of fact. Simply couching such statements in terms of opinion does not dispel these implications; and the statement, "In my opinion Jones is a liar," can cause as much damage to reputation as the statement, "Jones is a liar." As Judge Friendly aptly stated: "[It] would be destructive of the law of libel if a writer could escape liability for accusations of [defamatory conduct] simply by using, explicitly or implicitly, the words 'I think.'" See *Cianci, supra*, at 64. It is worthy of note that at common law, even the privilege of fair comment did not extend to "a false statement of fact, whether it was expressly stated or implied from an expression of opinion." Restatement (Second) of Torts, §566, Comment *a* (1977).

Apart from their reliance on the *Gertz* dictum, respondents do not really contend that a statement such as, "In my opinion John Jones is a liar," should be protected by a separate privilege for "opinion" under the First Amendment. But they do contend that in every defamation case the First Amendment mandates an inquiry into whether a statement is "opinion" or "fact," and that only the latter statements may be actionable. They propose that a number of factors developed by the lower courts (in what we hold was a mistaken reliance on the *Gertz* dictum) be considered in deciding which is which. But we think the "'breathing space'" which "'freedoms of expression require in order to survive,'" *Hepps*, 475 U.S. at 772 (quoting *New York Times*, 376 U.S. at 272), is adequately secured by existing constitutional doctrine without the creation of an artificial dichotomy between "opinion" and fact.

Foremost, we think *Hepps* stands for the proposition that a statement on matters of public concern must be provable as false before there can be liability under state defamation law, at least in situations, like the present, where a media defendant is involved. Thus, unlike the statement, "In my opinion Mayor Jones is a liar," the statement, "In my opinion Mayor Jones shows his abysmal ignorance by accepting the teachings of Marx and Lenin," would not be actionable. *Hepps* ensures that a statement of opinion relating to matters of public concern which does not contain a provably false factual connotation will receive full constitutional protection.

. . . .

The *New York Times-Butts-Gertz* culpability requirements further ensure that debate on public issues remains "uninhibited, robust, and wide-open." *New York Times*, 376 U.S. at 270. Thus, where a statement of "opinion" on a matter of public concern reasonably implies false and defamatory facts regarding public figures or officials, those individuals must show that such statements were made with knowledge of their false implications or with reckless disregard of their truth. Similarly, where such a statement involves a private figure on a matter of public concern, a plaintiff must show that the false connotations were made with some level of fault as required by *Gertz*.

. . . .

We are not persuaded that, in addition to these protections, an additional separate constitutional privilege for "opinion" is required to ensure the freedom of expression guaranteed by the First Amendment. The dispositive question in the present case then becomes whether a reasonable factfinder could conclude that the statements in the Diadiun column imply an assertion that petitioner Milkovich perjured himself in a judicial proceeding. We think this question must be answered in the affirmative. . . . This is not the sort of loose, figurative, or hyperbolic language which would negate the impression that the writer was seriously maintaining that petitioner committed the crime of perjury. Nor does the general tenor of the article negate this impression.

We also think the connotation that petitioner committed perjury is sufficiently factual to be susceptible of being proved true or false. A determination whether petitioner lied in this instance can be made on a core of objective evidence by comparing, *inter alia*, petitioner's testimony before the OHSAA board with his subsequent testimony before the trial court. . . .

We believe our decision in the present case holds the balance true. The judgment of the Ohio Court of Appeals is reversed, and the case is remanded for further proceedings not inconsistent with this opinion.

Reversed.

Justice Brennan, with whom Justice Marshall joins, dissenting.

 . . . .

[W]hile the Court today dispels any misimpression that there is a so-called opinion privilege *wholly in addition* to the protections we have already found to be guaranteed by the First Amendment, it determines that a protection for statements of pure opinion is dictated by *existing* First Amendment doctrine. As the Court explains, "full constitutional protection" extends to any statement relating to matters of public concern "that cannot 'reasonably [be] interpreted as stating actual facts' about an individual."

———————

1. The Court refuses to recognize a blanket exemption for all opinion. Why?

2. *Sullivan v. Conway*, 157 F.3d 1092 (7th Cir. 1998), holds that the statement he is a "very poor lawyer" is protected opinion, not a verifiable fact:

> It is one thing to say that a lawyer is dishonest, or has falsified his credentials, or has lost every case he has tried, or can never file suit within the statute of limitations. These are all readily verifiable statements of fact. But to say that he is a very poor lawyer is to express an opinion that is so difficult to verify or refute that it cannot feasibly be made a subject to inquiry by a jury. It is true that prefacing a defamatory statement with the qualification, "In my opinion," does not shield a defendant from liability for defamation. The test is whether a reasonable listener would take him to be basing his "opinion" on knowledge of facts of the sort that can be evaluated in a defamation suit. Here the answer is "no." Legal representation is attended by a great deal of

uncertainty. Excellent lawyers may lose most of their cases because they are hired only in the most difficult ones, while poor lawyers may win cases because they turn away all the ones that would challenge their meager abilities. Many lawyers are good at some things and poor at others, so that the evaluation of them will depend on what the evaluator is interested in. It would be unmanageable to ask a court, in order to determine the validity of the defendants' defense of truth, to determine whether "in fact" Sullivan is a poor lawyer.

3. Courts continue to distinguish between fact and opinion. In *Flamm v. American Assoc. of Univ. Women*, 201 F.3d 144 (2d Cir. 2000), the court held that statements in a nonprofit organization's directory of lawyers willing to accept referrals, where at least one client had described the attorney as an "ambulance chaser" who was interested only in "slam dunk" cases was not necessarily opinion and could support an action in defamation. By contrast, in *Imperial Apparel, Ltd. v. Cosmo's Designer Direct, Inc.*, 882 N.E.2d 1011 (Ill. 2008), the court held that an advertisement which disparaged a commercial rival by claiming that "they brazenly attempt pulling polyester over their customer's eyes by conjuring up a low rent imitation [to the defendant's 3-for-1 promotion] that has the transparency of a hooker's come on" amounted to constitutionally protected opinion because the reasonable reader would recognize the ad as nothing more than "colorful hyperbole" meant only to attract the reader's attention. And in *State v. Carpenter*, 171 P.3d 41 (Alaska, 2007), the court ruled that sexually explicit derogatory comments made on air by a radio talk show personality about a complaining listener "were pure insults that were not factually verifiable" and hence not defamatory as a matter of law.

E. Summing Up: A Contemporary Example

Palin v. The New York Times Co.*
Southern District of New York, 2017
17-Civ-4583 (JSR)

Rakoff, J.

Nowhere is political journalism so free, so robust, or perhaps so rowdy as in the United States. In the exercise of that freedom, mistakes will be made, some of which will be hurtful to others Responsible journals will promptly correct their errors; others will not. But if political journalism is to achieve its constitutionally endorsed role of challenging the powerful, legal redress by a public figure must be limited to those cases where the public figure has a plausible factual basis for complaining that

---

*[As this edition goes to press, this decision has been appealed to the United States Court of Appeals for the Second Circuit, but that court has not yet ruled on the appeal. Eds.]

the mistake was made maliciously, that is, with knowledge it was false or with reckless disregard of its falsity. Here, plaintiff's complaint, even when supplemented by facts developed at an evidentiary hearing convened by the Court, fails to make that showing. Accordingly, the complaint must be dismissed.

BACKGROUND

In her one-count complaint filed on June 27, 2017, plaintiff Sarah Palin,** an acknowledged public figure, alleged that The New York Times Company (the "Times") defamed her in an editorial published on June 14, 2017, the defamatory statements in which were not corrected until the next day. On July 14, 2017, the Times moved to dismiss the complaint for failure to state a claim as a matter of law, and the matter was promptly briefed by both sides. [The Court' discussion of various deficiencies in pleading is omitted.]

Although, therefore, if the Court were to solely limit its evaluation to the face of the complaint, it would readily grant the motion to dismiss, the Court has instead evaluated the plausibility of the complaint in light of such background facts developed during the evidentiary hearing that, as shown by the parties' post-hearing briefs, were either undisputed (at least for purposes of the instant motion) or, where disputed, are taken most favorably to plaintiff.

In brief, the pertinent factual allegations are as follows [citations to the record are omitted]:

On the morning of June 14, 2017, James Hodgkinson opened fire on members of Congress and current and former congressional aides playing baseball at a field in Virginia. That same day, Elizabeth Williamson, an editorial writer at the Times, proposed that the Times editorial board write a piece about the shooting. Before she began writing, James Bennet - the Times' editorial page editor, asked Ms. Williamson to look at editorials the Times had previously published in the aftermath of a January 7, 2011 attack carried out by Jared Lee Loughner at a political event in Tucson, Arizona. In this shooting spree, Loughner shot nineteen people, severely wounding United States Congresswoman Gabrielle Giffords and killing six others, including Chief U.S. District Court Judge John Roll and a nine-year-old girl. Mr. Bennet asked a researcher to send Ms. Williamson these editorials, which the researcher did, copying Mr. Bennet.

Shortly following Loughner's attack, speculation arose about a connection between the crime and plaintiff Palin. This speculation focused on a map (the "SarahPAC Map") circulated by plaintiff's political action committee, SarahPAC, prior to the shooting. The map depicted stylized crosshairs placed over the geographic locations of congressional districts that Republicans were targeting in an upcoming election, including Representative Gabrielle Giffords' district, as well as photos

---

** [Plaintiff Sarah Palin is a former governor of Alaska, Republican Vice-Presidential candidate in 2008, and an active political speaker and commentator. Eds.]

(below the map) of the incumbent Democrats. In the end, however, articles published in the Times and elsewhere stated that no such connection had been established between the circulation of the SarahPAC Map and the Loughner shooting.

Ms. Williamson sent a first draft of the editorial to Mr. Bennet around 5:00 pm on June 14. The original draft stated, in relevant part, that "[n]ot all the details [of the Hodgkinson shooting] are known yet, but a sickeningly familiar pattern is emerging: a deranged individual with a gun — perhaps multiple guns — and scores of rounds of ammunition uses politics as a pretense for a murderous shooting spree .... Just as in 2011, when Jared Lee Loughner opened fire in a supermarket parking lot, grievously wounding Representative Gabby Giffords and killing six people, including a nine year-old girl, Mr. Hodgkinson's rage was nurtured in a vile political climate. Then, it was the pro-gun right being criticized: in the weeks before the shooting Sarah Palin's political action committee circulated a map of targeted electoral districts that put Ms. Giffords and 19 other Democrats under stylized crosshairs." The word "circulated" was highlighted as above in the manner indicating that a hyperlink would take the reader to an ABC News article published the day after Loughner's attack, which stated, inter alia, that "[n]o connection has been made between [the SarahPAC Map] and the Arizona shooting."

After receiving Ms. Williamson's draft, Mr. Bennet "effectively rewr[o]te the piece." Mr. Bennet's revised version of the editorial was published online on the evening of June 14, 2017 and in print on June 15, 2017 under the title "America's Lethal Politics. The two paragraphs here relevant read as follows:

> Was this attack [by Hodgkinson] evidence of how vicious American politics has become? Probably. In 2011, when Jared Lee Loughner opened fire in a supermarket parking lot, grievously wounding Representative Gabby Giffords and killing six people, including a 9-year-old girl, the link to political incitement was clear. Before the shooting, Sarah Palin's political action committee circulated a map of targeted electoral districts that put Ms. Giffords and 19 other Democrats under stylized cross hairs.

> Conservatives and right-wing media were quick on Wednesday to demand forceful condemnation of hate speech and crimes by anti-Trump liberals. They're right. Though there's no sign of incitement as direct as in the Giffords attack, liberals should of course hold themselves to the same standard of decency that they ask of the right.

The published version of the editorial retained the hyperlink to the ABC News article.

However, within a day or so of publication, the Times twice revised (and corrected) the text of the editorial, and separately also issued two corrections online beginning on or about 11:15 am on June 15. The corrections were also in the print editions of the Times on June 16. Specifically, the Times revised the editorial text online by deleting the phrases "the link to political incitement was clear" and "[t]hough there's no sign of incitement as direct as in the Giffords attack," and adding the sentence "But no connection to that crime was ever established." As to the corrections, published both online and in print, the first correction read: "An earlier version of this editorial incorrectly stated that a link existed between political incitement and the 2011 shooting of Representative Gabby Giffords. In fact, no such link was established." The second correction read: "An editorial on Thursday about the shooting of Representative Steve Scalise incorrectly stated that a link existed between political rhetoric and the 2011 shooting of Representative Gabby Giffords. In fact, no such link was established. The editorial also incorrectly described a map distributed by a political action committee before that shooting. It depicted electoral districts, not individual Democratic lawmakers, beneath stylized crosshairs."

Despite these corrections, plaintiff, less than three weeks later, filed the instant complaint alleging that the Times defamed her by including within the original version of the editorial the subsequently-corrected errors. As noted, the Times then promptly moved to dismiss the complaint. The motion was fully briefed by both sides, and the Court heard oral argument, after which it convened the aforementioned evidentiary hearing. The hearing was followed, in turn, by still more briefing. As a result, the motion is now fully ripe for decision.

DISCUSSION

On a motion to dismiss, the Court accepts all well-pleaded factual allegations as true and draws all reasonable inferences in favor of the non-moving party. See *Goldstein v. Pataki*, 516 F.3d 50, 56 (2d Cir. 2008). However, conclusory allegations are not entitled to be assumed true. *Ashcroft v. Iqbal*, 556 U.S. 662, 680-681 (2009) Moreover, to survive a motion to dismiss, a complaint must contain "enough facts to state a claim for relief that is plausible on its face." *Bell Atl. Corp. v. Twombly*, 550 U.S. 544, 570 (2007).

Additionally, in a defamation case, these standards must be applied consistently with the First Amendment protections famously put forward in *New York Times v. Sullivan*, 376 U.S. 254 (1964) and its progeny. Thus, in "defamation cases, Rule 12(b) (6) not only protects against the costs of meritless litigation, but provides assurance to those exercising their First Amendment rights that doing so will not needlessly become prohibitively expensive." *Biro v. Conde Nast*, 963 F. Supp. 2d 255, 279 (S.D.N.Y. 2013); see also *Michel v. NYP Holdings, Inc.*, 816 F.3d 686, 702 (11th Cir. 2016) ("[A]pplication of the plausibility pleading standard makes particular sense when examining public figure defamation suits. In these cases, there is a powerful interest in ensuring that free speech is not unduly burdened by the necessity of defending against expensive yet groundless litigation.").

As noted, the complaint here alleges, in a single count, the tort of defamation. "Defamation is the injury to one's reputation either by written expression, which is libel, or by oral expression, which is slander." *Idema v. Wager*, 120 F. Supp. 2d 361, 365 (S.D.N.Y. 2000) (citing *Morrison v. Nat'l Broad. Co.*, 19 N.Y.2d 453, 458 (1967)). The specific elements of this tort are set forth in applicable state law, here the law of

New York. "Under New York law, a plaintiff must establish five elements to recover in libel: 1) a written defamatory statement of fact concerning the plaintiff; 2) publication to a third party; 3) fault (either negligence or actual malice depending on the status of the libeled party); 4) falsity of the defamatory statement; and 5) special damages or per se actionability (defamatory on its face)." *Celle v. Filipino Reporter Enterps. Inc.*, 209 F.3d 163, 176 (2d Cir. 2000).

As to the third element, plaintiff because she is a public figure, must under federal law "surmount a much higher barrier" and establish by clear and convincing evidence that the Times acted with "actual malice," that is, with knowledge that the statements were false or with reckless disregard of their falsity. *Philadelphia Newspapers, Inc. v. Hepps*, 475 U.S. 767, 773, 775 (1986). "Though a state-based cause-of-action, the elements of a libel action are heavily influenced by the minimum standards required by the First Amendment." *Celle*, 209 F.3d at 176.

In its pending motion, the Times advances three bases for dismissing the Complaint: first, that the challenged statements are not "of and concerning" plaintiff; second, that the challenged statements are not provably false; and third, that plaintiff has not adequately plead actual malice. . . . The Court considers each in turn:

1. Whether the Statements are "Of and Concerning" Mrs. Palin

For purposes of the law of defamation, statements alleged to be defamatory are "of and concerning" a plaintiff where "'the allegedly defamatory content refer[s] to the plaintiff' such that those knowing the plaintiff 'understand that [she] was the person meant.'" *Gilman v. Spitzer*, 538 F. App'x 45, 47 (2d Cir. 2013) (quoting *Brady v. Ottaway Newspapers, Inc.*, 84 A.D.2d 226, 228 (1981) and *Geiser v. Petrocelli*, 616 F.2d 636, 655 (2d Cir. 1986). That is, a statement is "of and concerning" a plaintiff if it "could have been understood by a reasonable reader as being, in substance, actually about" the plaintiff. *Kirch v. Liberty Media Corp.*, 449 F.3d 388, 399 (2d Cir. 2006) (emphasis in original).

Here, the editorial in issue stated that "Sarah Palin's political action committee" circulated the SarahPAC Map. Compl. Ex. 1 at 2 (emphasis added). The Times argues that plaintiff's claim of defamation is "directed" at plaintiff's political action committee, SarahPAC, and not plaintiff herself. Mot. to Dismiss at 6-10. "Under the group libel doctrine, a plaintiff's claim is insufficient if the allegedly defamatory statement referenced the plaintiff solely as a member of the group." *Church of Scientology Int'l v. Time Warner, Inc.*, 806 F. Supp. 1157, 1160 (S.D.N.Y. 1992), aff'd sub nom *Church of Scientology Int'l v. Behar*, 238 F.3d 168 (2d Cir. 2001).

However, the group libel doctrine is inapplicable where, as here, "'the circumstances of the publication reasonably give rise to the conclusion that there is a particular reference to the member.'" Id. (quoting Restatement (Second) of Torts § 564A(b)). Three circumstances permit the inference that the challenged statements would be understood by a reasonable reader as being about plaintiff in particular. First, the political action committee is not mentioned by name. Second, plaintiff is referenced by name. Third, the reference describes plaintiff's relationship to the political action committee as possessive. . . [T]he Court finds, for purposes of this motion to dismiss, that the allegedly defamatory statements are of and concerning plaintiff. *Three Amigos SJL Rest., Inc. v. CBS News Inc.*, 15 N.Y.S.3d 36, 41 (N.Y. App. Div. 2015), aff'd 28 N.Y.3d 82 (2016).

2. Whether the Statements are Provably False

Falsity is a necessary element of a defamation action. *Buckley v. Littell*, 539 F.2d 882, 889-894 (2d Cir. 1976); *Gross v. New York Times Co.*, 82 N.Y.2d 146, 152-153 (1993). Therefore, "a statement of opinion relating to matters of public concern which does not contain a provably false factual connotation will receive full constitutional protection." *Milkovich v. Lorain Journal Co.*, 497 U.S. 1, 20 (1990). Here, however, although the offending paragraphs quoted above contain various assertions of opinion, a reasonable reader could well view them as asserting that there was a "direct" "link" between the SarahPAC Map and the Loughner shooting. Indeed, according to Mr. Bennet's testimony, it was the receipt by the Times of communications from readers complaining about such an assertion that led Bennet to order the corrections thereafter made.

If these readers were reasonably reading the sentences here at issue to suggest that, as a factual matter, distribution of the SarahPAC Map was directly causally linked to Loughner's shooting, then, as even the Times appears to concede, that is a factual statement that can be proved false, and, according to the complaint, has already been so proven, since, among other things, there is no evidence that Loughner ever saw the SarahPAC Map. . . . But even if, on the Times' somewhat strained reading, the statements here at issue should be read to suggest no more than that the SarahPAC Map helped foster "political incitement" (albeit seemingly directed at the specified incumbents), which in turn was "direct[ly]" and "clearly" linked to Loughner's shooting, these are still factual assertions that can be demonstrated to be false and, according to the complaint, were made in reckless disregard of their falsity. . . .

As to the first assertion, that circulation of the SarahPAC Map helped foster political incitement, this is akin to the kind of factual assertion that juries in effect have to resolve regularly in false advertising cases that assess the effect of a given advertisement on consumers. See *Johnson & Johnson* Merck Consumer Pharm. Co. v. Smith Kline Beecham Corp.*, 960 F.2d 294, 297-298 (2d Cir. 1992); *Mylan Pharm., Inc. v. Proctor & Gamble Co.*, 443 F. Supp. 2d 453, 459-460 (S.D.N.Y. 2006). As to the second assertion, that the political incitement directed at the incumbents was directly linked to Loughner's shooting, the Times argues that this is really an assertion about an individual's motivation to act, which, it claims, can never be proved false. . . . But, as the courts have so often noted, "the state of a man's mind is as much a fact as the state of his digestion," *Siegelman v. Cunard White Star Ltd.*, 221 F.2d 189, 198 (2d Cir. 1955), though such mental states are often proved or disproved circumstantially. Indeed, the Times itself stated in its published correction that "An earlier version of this editorial incorrectly stated that a link existed between political incitement and the 2011 shooting of Representative Gabby Giffords. In fact, no such link was established." . . . As this very statement suggests, the link in question can, as a factual matter, either be "established," i.e., proved, or disproved.

That the offending statements appeared in an editorial, which by its nature presents an overall opinion or opinions, is relevant, but hardly dispositive. See *Brian v. Richardson*, 87 N.Y.2d 46, 52 (1995). Unlike statements in cases relied upon by the Times that voiced editorial opinions about connections that "appeared to be" or "could well happen," see, e.g., *Immuno v. Moor-Jankowski*, 77 N.Y.2d 235, 255 (1991), the statements here complained of stated unequivocally that there was a "direct" and "clear" link between the SarahPAC Map and the Loughner shooting, albeit a link created by intermediating political involvement. A reasonable reader could well infer that the Times was in possession of objective evidence that the SarahPAC Map incited Mr. Loughner's shooting, whereas, according to the complaint, the Times had no evidence of either a direct or indirect link.

In short, some or all of the statements here at issue are fact-laden statements that can be proven false, and the complaint adequately alleges evidence sufficient to enable a reasonable juror to find them false if the juror so chose.

3. Actual Malice

Public figures who seek damages for defamatory statements must, however, do more than prove that the statements about them were false. They must also prove by "clear and convincing evidence" that the statements were made with "actual malice"—that is, with knowledge that the statements were false or with reckless disregard as to their falsity. *Sullivan*, 376 U.S. at 279-280; *Masson v. New Yorker*, 501 U.S. 496, 508 (1991); *Biro v. Conde Nast*, 807 F.3d 541, 544-545 (2d Cir. 2015). Reckless disregard can be established by "evidence of an intent to avoid the truth," *Harte-Hanks Comms., Inc. v. Connaugnton*, 491 U.S. 657 (1989), evidence that the defendant "entertained serious doubts as to the truth of his publication," *St. Amant v. Thompson*, 390 U.S. 727, 731 (1968), or evidence that the defendant acted with a "high degree of awareness of [a statement's] probable falsity," *Garrison v. State of Louisiana*, 379 U.S. 64, 74 (1964). See *Dongguk Univ. v. Yale Univ.*, 734 F.3d 113, 124 (2d Cir. 2013). But even then, a defamation complaint by a public figure must allege sufficient particularized facts to support a claim of actual malice by clear and convincing evidence, or the complaint must be dismissed.

Here, as already mentioned, the complaint fails on its face to adequately allege actual malice, because it fails to identify any individual who possessed the requisite knowledge and intent and, instead, attributes it to the Times in general. This will not suffice. "When there are multiple actors involved in an organizational defendant's publication of a defamatory statement, the plaintiff must identify the individual responsible for publication of a statement, and it is that individual the plaintiff must prove acted with actual malice." *Donqguk Univ.*, 734 F.3d at 123; see *Sullivan*, 376 U.S. at 287 ("[T]he state of mind required for actual malice would have to be brought home to the persons in the [defendant's] organization having responsibility for the publication of the [statement].")

But even assuming, in light of the evidentiary hearing, that the complaint should now be construed as asserting actual malice on the part of Mr. Bennet — the primary if not the sole author of the sentences in question and the Times' editorial page editor — plaintiff still fails to meet the actual malice standard. That standard is grounded in "a profound national commitment to the principle that debate on public issues be uninhibited, robust, and wide-open, and that it may well include vehement, caustic, and sometimes unpleasantly sharp attacks on government and public officials." *Sullivan*, 376 U.S. at 270. *Sullivan* and succeeding cases "have emphasized that the stake of the people in public business and the conduct of public officials is so great that neither the defense of truth nor the standard of ordinary care would protect against self-censorship and thus adequately implement First Amendment policies." *St. Amant*, 390 U.S. at 731-732. "[S]peaking out on political issues is a core freedom protected by the First Amendment and probably presents the 'strongest case' for applying 'the *New York Times [v. Sullivan]* rule.'" *Schatz v. Republican State Leadership Comm.*, 669 F.3d 50, 51 (1st Cir. 2012) (quoting *Harte-Hanks*, 491 U.S. at 666 n. 7, 686-687)).

Coupling this protective overlay with the more technical requirement that a public figure, in order to survive a motion to dismiss a claim of defamation, must allege specific facts that plausibly evidence actual malice in a clear and convincing manner, it is plain that plaintiff has not and cannot meet this standard, even with the benefit of the facts brought forth by the evidentiary hearing. To put the matter simply, Bennet—as the undisputed testimony shows—wrote the putatively offending passages of the editorial over a period of a few hours and published it very soon thereafter. Shortly after that, his mistakes in linking the SarahPAC Map to the Loughner shooting were called to his attention . . . and he immediately corrected the errors, not only in the editorial itself but also by publishing corrections both electronically and in print . . . . Such behavior is much more plausibly consistent with making an unintended mistake and then correcting it than with acting with actual malice.

Plaintiff's response is, first, to posit that the Times in general, and Mr. Bennet in particular, had a motive to defame Mrs. Palin. As to the Times in general, the complaint alleges that "there is existing hostility toward Mrs. Palin" and "her name and attacks upon her inflame passions and thereby drive viewership and Web clicks to media companies." . . . As to the alleged "hostility," it goes without saying that the Times editorial board is not a fan of Mrs. Palin. But neither the fact of that opposition, nor the supposition that a sharp attack on a disfavored political figure will increase a publication's readership, has ever been enough to prove actual malice. See, e.g., *Harte-Hanks*, 491 U.S. at 665 ("[A] newspaper's motive in publishing a story—whether to promote an opponent's candidacy or to increase its circulation—cannot provide a sufficient basis for finding actual malice."). For "it is hardly unusual for publications to print matter that will please their subscribers; many publications set out to portray a particular viewpoint or even to advance a partisan cause. Defamation judgments do not exist to police their objectivity." *Reuber v. Food Chem. News, Inc.*, 925 F.2d 703, 716 (4th Cir. 1991).

Here, moreover, as previously noted, it is not the Times' collective knowledge and intent that is relevant but rather Mr. Bennet's. As to hostility, the best that plaintiff can muster is that Mr. Bennet has a long association with liberal publications and that his brother is the Democratic senator from Colorado who was endorsed by Congresswoman Giffords' political action committee in his 2016 election and whose opponent was endorsed by Mrs. Palin in that same election. . . . If such political opposition counted as evidence of actual malice, the protections imposed by *Sullivan* and its progeny would swiftly become a nullity.

As for the alleged economic motive, there is not a shred of factual support, either in the complaint or in the evidentiary hearing, for the supposition that considerations of attracting readership ever entered Mr. Bennet's mind when he was drafting this particular editorial. Indeed, if that were his goal, one would have expected him to mention Mrs. Palin's name more than once in the editorial or use her name in the social media promoting the editorial, neither of which was done. . . .

In her complaint, plaintiff also relies on her allegations that the Times cited "no source" for the challenged statements and failed to conduct an adequate investigation into their veracity, allegations that plaintiff now suggests apply to Mr. Bennet as well. . . . As to the Times in general, this allegation is undercut by the fact that the original draft of the editorial that Ms. Williamson sent Mr. Bennet, as well as the version published, included a hyperlink to an article that described in some detail the SarahPAC Map and its circulation and concluded that there was no proven link between that circulation and the Loughner shooting. . . . "The hyperlink is the twenty-first century equivalent of the footnote for purposes of attribution in defamation law." See *Adelson v. Harris*, 973 F. Supp. 2d 467, 484 (S.D.N.Y. 2013). The inclusion of this article through the hyperlink shows, first, that the Times did do some research before publishing the editorial (despite the very limited time available) and, second, that the allegation of actual malice is even more improbable because the Times included as a hyperlink an article undercutting its own conclusions.

Once again, however, it is Mr. Bennet's knowledge and intent that are ultimately at issue so far as actual malice is concerned, and Mr. Bennet testified that he himself did not read the hyperlinked article when rewriting the editorial nor do any further investigation of his own (though he was copied on a communication sent by the researcher that he had directed to find and examine prior Times editorials regarding Mrs. Palin and the Loughner shooting). . . . But it is well-established that supposed research failures do not constitute clear and convincing evidence of actual malice, even of the "reckless" kind. Indeed, in *Sullivan* itself, the Supreme Court recognized that the editorial advertisement there at issue contained facts contradicted by earlier news stories printed in the New York Times. 376 U.S. at 287. The Court held that the existence of these prior stories did not establish actual malice in part because failure to investigate "supports at most a finding of negligence in failing to discover the misstatements." Id. at 288.

Similarly, failure to comply with journalistic policies . . . cannot establish actual malice absent allegations supporting an inference of reckless disregard. *See, e.g.,* *Harte-Hanks,* 491 U.S. at 665 ("[A] public figure plaintiff must prove more than an extreme departure from professional standards" to demonstrate actual malice).

Alternatively, plaintiff argues that Bennet actually knew, or recklessly disregarded, that his editorial statements were false, because of prior articles in the Times and the Atlantic (where Bennet was editor-in-chief for many years) that he presumably read and that disclaimed any link between the SarahPAC Map and the Loughner shooting. At the evidentiary hearing, Bennet testified that he did not remember reading any of these articles or, if he did read them when they appeared years earlier, he did not have them in mind when he wrote the editorial. . . . Plaintiff's position is that either Mr. Bennet, contrary to his testimony, read and remembered these sources, in which case he knew the challenged statements were false, or else, consistent with his testimony, he did not read and/or remember these sources, in which case he acted with willful blindness in publishing the editorial. . . .

But these kinds of lawyers' arguments do not substitute for the requisite factual showing. The fact is that all these articles appeared years earlier, and there is no reason to suppose that, even if Bennet had read them at the time, he would necessarily remember their conclusions, especially since, as the complaint itself notes, there were also articles that appeared shortly after the Loughner shooting that drew contrary conclusions. . . . As the Supreme Court stated in *Sullivan,* "The mere presence of stories in the files does not, of course, establish that the Times 'knew' the [publication at issue] was false." 376 U.S. at 287.

Plaintiff argues, however, that Bennet's failure, at the very time he was preparing the editorial, to read . . . the hyperlinked [article is] evidence of reckless disregard. As for the hyperlinked article, however, the inclusion of the article along with the editorial cuts against any inference of actual malice. If Bennet purposely failed to read it because he knew it would undercut his thesis, why would he not have removed the hyperlink, which he had full power to do [?]. . .

As for the editorials emailed to Ms. Williamson and copied to Mr. Bennet by the Times' researcher, Bennet knew by the time he rewrote the editorial that Ms. Williamson had likely reviewed them, so there was little incentive for him to read them as well. . . . Plaintiff claims that, if Bennet had read them, he would have seen that at least two of them contradicted his erroneous statements. . . . But this is doubly wrong: it does not matter what they contained unless his failure to read them reasonably suggests reckless disregard, which it does not; and, in any event, they do not contradict his thesis nearly as much as plaintiff suggests. . . .

So Bennet, even if he had read these articles (which he claims he did not), would not automatically have been led to conclude that his editorial was erroneous. . . .

We come back to the basics. What we have here is an editorial, written and rewritten rapidly in order to voice an opinion on an immediate event of importance, in which are included a few factual inaccuracies somewhat pertaining to Mrs. Palin that are very rapidly corrected. Negligence this may be; but defamation of a public figure it plainly is not.

For the foregoing reasons, the Court grants defendant's motion to dismiss [with prejudice].

Chapter 15

Privacy

The development of a common law right of privacy was heralded at the end of the 19th century by an influential article in *Harvard Law Review* by Professor Samuel Warren and future Supreme Court Justice Louis Brandeis:

> This development of the law was inevitable. The intense intellectual and emotional life, and the heightening of sensations which came with the advance of civilization, made it clear to men that only a part of the pain, pleasure, and profit of life lay in physical things. Thoughts, emotions, and sensations demanded legal recognition, and the beautiful capacity for growth which characterizes the common law enabled the judge to afford the requisite protection, without the interposition of the legislature.

> Recent inventions and business methods call attention to the next step which must be taken for the protection of the person, and for securing to the individual what Judge Cooley calls the right "to be let alone." Instantaneous photographs and newspaper enterprise have invaded the sacred precincts of private and domestic life; and numerous mechanical devices threaten to make good the prediction that "what is whispered in the closet shall be proclaimed from the house-tops." For years there has been a feeling that the law must afford some remedy for the unauthorized circulation of portraits of private persons; and the evil of the invasion of privacy by the newspapers, long keenly felt, has been but recently discussed by an able writer. The alleged facts of a somewhat notorious case brought before an inferior tribunal in New York a few months ago directly involved the consideration of the right of circulating portraits; and the question whether our law will recognize and protect the right to privacy in this and in other respects must soon come before our courts for consideration.

> Of the desirability—indeed of the necessity—of some such protection, there can, it is believed, be no doubt. The press is overstepping in every direction the obvious bounds of propriety and decency. Gossip is no longer the resource of the idle and of the vicious, but has become a trade, which is pursued with industry as well as effrontery. To satisfy a prurient taste the details of sexual relations are spread broadcast in the columns of the daily papers. To occupy the indolent, column upon column is filled with idle gossip, which can only be procured by intrusion upon the domestic circle. The intensity and complexity of life, attendant upon advancing civilization, have

rendered necessary some retreat from the world, and man, under the refining influence of culture, has become more sensitive to publicity, so that solitude and privacy have become more essential to the individual; but modern
enterprise and invention have, through invasions upon his privacy, subjected
him to mental pain and distress, far greater than could be inflicted by mere
bodily injury. Nor is the harm wrought by such invasions confined to the
suffering of those who may be made the subjects of journalistic or other
enterprise. In this, as in other branches of commerce, the supply creates the
demand. Each crop of unseemly gossip, thus harvested, becomes the seed of
more, and, in direct proportion to its circulation, results in a lowering of
social standards and of morality. Even gossip apparently harmless, when
widely and persistently circulated, is a potent for evil. It both belittles and
perverts. It belittles by inverting the relative importance of things, thus
dwarfing the thoughts and aspirations of a people. . . .

It is our purpose to consider whether the existing law affords a principle
which can properly be invoked to protect the privacy of the individual; and,
if it does, what the nature and extent of such protection is.

S. Warren & L. Brandeis, *The Right to Privacy*, 4 Harv. L. Rev. 193, 195–97 (1890).

As with most of torts, Dean William Prosser has done much to organize and classify the subject of privacy:

[The] law of privacy comprises four distinct kinds of invasion of four different interests of the plaintiff, which are tied together by the common name,
but otherwise have almost nothing in common. . . . [T]hese four torts may
be described as follows:

1. Intrusion upon the plaintiff's seclusion or solitude, or into his private
affairs.

2. Public disclosure of embarrassing private facts about the plaintiff.

3. Publicity which places the plaintiff in a false light in the public eye.

4. Appropriation, for the defendant's advantage, of the plaintiff's name or
likeness.

. . . .

W. Prosser, *Privacy*, 48 Cal. L. R. 383, 389, 407 (1960). *See also* Restatement (Second)
of Torts § 652.

Problem

Sally, a college student, attended the festivities in New Orleans during Mardi Gras.
When a young man with a video camera said, "lift your top," she obliged. He then
gave her a string of beads. Sally was surprised to find that she is being pictured on a
TV ad for an on-line video called, "Naked Ladies of Mardi Gras" (download price
$19.95) produced by One Night Production and that she is pictured in the video with
her top lifted. Sally acknowledges that she had a lot to drink, many other cameras

were there, and other women were lifting their tops. Discuss Sally's suit against One Night Productions.

A. Intrusion

Nader v. General Motors Corp.

Court of Appeals of New York, 1970
255 N.E.2d 765

Fuld, Chief Judge

On this appeal, taken by permission of the Appellate Division on a certified question, we are called upon to determine the reach of the tort of invasion of privacy as it exists under the law of the District of Columbia.

The complaint, in this action by Ralph Nader, pleads four causes of action against the appellant, General Motors Corporation, and three other defendants allegedly acting as it agents. The first two causes of action charge an invasion of privacy, the third is predicated on the intentional infliction of severe emotional distress and the fourth on interference with the plaintiff's economic advantage. This appeal concerns only the legal sufficiency of the first two causes of action, which were upheld in the courts below as against the appellant's motion to dismiss. . . .

The plaintiff, an author and lecturer on automotive safety, has, for some years, been an articulate and severe critic of General Motors' products from the standpoint of safety and design. According to the complaint—which, for present purposes, we must assume to be true—the appellant, having learned of the imminent publication of the plaintiff's book "Unsafe at any Speed," decided to conduct a campaign of intimidation against him in order to "suppress plaintiff's criticism of and prevent his disclosure of information" about its products. To that end, the appellant authorized and directed the other defendants to engage in a series of activities which, the plaintiff claims in his first two causes of action, violated his right to privacy.

Specifically, the plaintiff alleges that the appellant's agents (1) conducted a series of interviews with acquaintances of the plaintiff, "questioning them about, and casting aspersions upon [his] political, social . . . racial and religious views . . . ; his integrity; his sexual proclivities and inclinations; and his personal habits" (Complaint, par. 9[b]); (2) kept him under surveillance in public places for an unreasonable length of time (par. 9 [c]); (3) caused him to be accosted by girls for the purpose of entrapping him into illicit relationships (par. 9[d]); (4) made threatening, harassing and obnoxious telephone calls to him (par. 9[e]); (5) tapped his telephone and eavesdropped, by means of mechanical and electronic equipment, on his private conversations with others (par. 9[f]); and (6) conducted a "continuing" and harassing investigation of him (par. 9[g]). . . .

Turning, then, to the law of the District of Columbia, it appears that its courts have not only recognized a common-law action for invasion of privacy but have broadened the scope of that tort beyond its traditional limits. Thus, in the most recent of its cases on the subject, *Pearson v. Dodd* (410 F. 2d 701, *supra*), the Federal Court of Appeals for the District of Columbia declared (p. 704):

> "We approve the extension of the tort of invasion of privacy to instances of *intrusion*, whether by physical trespass or not, into spheres from which an ordinary man in a plaintiff's position could reasonably expect that the particular defendant should be excluded." . . .

Quite obviously, some intrusions into one's private sphere are inevitable concomitants of life in an industrial and densely populated society, which the law does not seek to proscribe even if it were possible to do so. "The law does not provide a remedy for every annoyance that occurs in everyday life." (*Kelley v. Post Pub. Co.*, 327 Mass. 275, 278.) However, the District of Columbia courts have held that the law should and does protect against certain types of intrusive conduct, and we must, therefore, determine whether the plaintiff's allegations are actionable as violations of the right to privacy under the law of that jurisdiction. . . .

. . . .

The classic article by Warren and Brandeis *(The Right to Privacy*, 4 Harv. L. Rev. 193) — to which the court in the *Pearson* case referred as the source of the District's common-law action for invasion of privacy (410 F. 2d, at p. 703) — was premised, to a large extent, on principles originally developed in the field of copyright law. The authors thus based their thesis on a right granted by the common law to "each individual . . . of determining, ordinarily, to what extent his thoughts, sentiments and emotions shall be communicated to others" (4 Harv. L. Rev., at p. 198). Their principal concern appeared to be not with a broad "right to be let alone" (Cooley, Torts [2d ed.], p. 29) but, rather, with the right to protect oneself from having one's private affairs known to others and to keep secret or intimate facts about oneself from the prying eyes or ears of others.

In recognizing the existence of a common-law cause of action for invasion of privacy in the District of Columbia, the Court of Appeals has expressly adopted this latter formulation of the nature of the right. (See, e.g., *Afro-American Pub. Co. v.Jaffe*, 366 F. 2d 649, 653, *supra.*) Quoting from the Restatement, Torts (§ 867), the court in the *Jaffe* case (366 F. 2d at p. 653) has declared that "[liability] attaches to a person who 'unreasonably and seriously interferes with another's interest in *not having his affairs known to others*'" (Emphasis supplied.) And, in *Pearson*, where the court extended the tort of invasion of privacy to instances of "intrusion," it again indicated . . . that the interest protected was one's right to keep knowledge about oneself from exposure to others, the right to prevent *"the obtaining of the information* by improperly intrusive means" 410 F. 2d, at p. 704; emphasis supplied. . . .

It should be emphasized that the mere gathering of information about a particular individual does not give rise to a cause of action under this theory. Privacy is invaded only if the information sought is of a confidential nature and the defendant's conduct was unreasonably intrusive. Just as a common-law copyright is lost when material is published, so, too, there can be no invasion of privacy where the information sought is open to public view or has been voluntarily revealed to others. (Restatement, 2d, Torts, Tent. Draft No. 13, § 652B, comment c.) In order to sustain a cause of action for invasion of privacy, therefore, the plaintiff must show that the appellant's conduct was truly "intrusive" and that it was designed to elicit information which would not be available through normal inquiry or observation.

... At most, only two of the activities charged to the appellant are, in our view, actionable as invasions of privacy under the law of the District of Columbia .... However, since the first two counts include allegations which are sufficient to state a cause of action, we could—as the concurring opinion notes ... —merely affirm the order before us without further elaboration. To do so, though, would be a disservice both to the judge who will be called upon to try this case and to the litigants themselves. In other words, we deem it desirable, nay essential, that we go further and, for the guidance of the trial court and counsel, indicate the extent to which the plaintiff is entitled to rely on the various allegations in support of his privacy claim.

. . . .

Turning, then, to the particular acts charged in the complaint, we cannot find any basis for a claim of invasion of privacy, under District of Columbia law, in the allegations that the appellant, through its agents or employees, interviewed many persons who knew the plaintiff, asking questions about him and casting aspersions on his character. Although those inquiries may have uncovered information of a personal nature, it is difficult to see how they may be said to have invaded the plaintiff's privacy. Information about the plaintiff which was already known to others could hardly be regarded as private to the plaintiff. Presumably, the plaintiff had previously revealed the information to such other persons, and he would necessarily assume the risk that a friend or acquaintance in whom he had confided might breach the confidence. If, as alleged, the questions tended to disparage the plaintiff's character, his remedy would seem to be by way of an action for defamation, not for breach of his right to privacy. (*Cf. Morrison v. National Broadcasting Co.*, 19 N Y 2d 453, 458–459.)

Nor can we find any actionable invasion of privacy in the allegations that the appellant caused the plaintiff to be accosted by girls with illicit proposals, or that it was responsible for the making of a large number of threatening and harassing telephone calls to the plaintiff's home at odd hours. Neither of these activities, howsoever offensive and disturbing, involved intrusion for the purpose of gathering information of a private and confidential nature.

As already indicated, it is manifestly neither practical nor desirable for the law to provide a remedy against any and all activity which an individual might find annoying. On the other hand, where severe mental pain or anguish is inflicted through a deliberate and malicious campaign of harassment or intimidation, a remedy is available in the form of an action for the intentional infliction of emotional distress—the theory underlying the plaintiff's third cause of action. But the elements of such an action are decidedly different from those governing the tort of invasion of privacy, and just as we have carefully guarded against the use of the prima facie tort doctrine to circumvent the limitations relating to other established tort remedies (*see Morrison v. National Broadcasting Co.*, 19 N.Y.2d 453, 458–459, *supra*), we should be wary of any attempt to rely on the tort of invasion of privacy as a means of avoiding the more stringent pleading and proof requirements for an action for infliction of emotional distress. (*See, e.g., Clark v. Associated Retail Credit Men*, 105 F. 2d 62, 65 [Ct. App., D.C.].)

Apart, however, from the foregoing allegations which we find inadequate to spell out a cause of action for invasion of privacy under District of Columbia law, the complaint contains allegations concerning other activities by the appellant or its agents which do satisfy the requirements for such a cause of action. The one which most clearly meets those requirements is the charge that the appellant and its codefendants engaged in unauthorized wiretapping and eavesdropping by mechanical and electronic means. The Court of Appeals in the *Pearson* case expressly recognized that such conduct constitutes a tortious intrusion (410 F. 2d 701, 704, *supra*), and other jurisdictions have reached a similar conclusion. In point of fact, the appellant does not dispute this, acknowledging that, to the extent the two challenged counts charge it with wiretapping and eavesdropping, an actionable invasion of privacy has been stated.

There are additional allegations that the appellant hired people to shadow the plaintiff and keep him under surveillance. In particular, he claims that, on one occasion, one of its agents followed him into a bank, getting sufficiently close to him to see the denomination of the bills he was withdrawing from his account. From what we have already said, it is manifest that the mere observation of the plaintiff in a public place does not amount to an invasion of his privacy. But, under certain circumstances, surveillance may be so "overzealous" as to render it actionable. Whether or not the surveillance in the present case falls into this latter category will depend on the nature of the proof. A person does not automatically make public everything he does merely by being in a public place, and the mere fact that Nader was in a bank did not give anyone the right to try to discover the amount of money he was withdrawing. On the other hand, if the plaintiff acted in such a way as to reveal that fact to any casual observer, then, it may not be said that the appellant intruded into his private sphere. In any event, though, it is enough for present purposes to say that the surveillance allegation is not insufficient as a matter of law.

. . . .

We would but add that the allegations concerning the interviewing of third persons, the accosting by girls and the annoying and threatening telephone calls, though insufficient to support a cause of action for invasion of privacy, are pertinent to the plaintiff's third cause of action—in which those allegations are reiterated—charging the intentional infliction of emotional distress. . . .

---

1. Restatement (Second) of Torts §652B (Intrusion) provides:

One who intentionally intrudes, physically or otherwise, upon the solitude or seclusion of another or his private affairs or concerns, is subject to liability to the other for invasion of his privacy, if the intrusion would be highly offensive to a reasonable person.

2. *Pavesich v. New England Life Ins. Co.*, 50 S.E. 68 (Ga. 1905), involved an unauthorized use of plaintiff's picture in an advertisement and was the first case to recognize the privacy cause of action. The court declared that the "right of privacy has its foundation in the instincts of nature," and is therefore an "immutable" and "absolute" right "derived from natural law." *Lake v. Wal-Mart*, 582 N.W.2d 231 (Minn. 1998) (quoting *Pavesich*).

Pearson v. Dodd

United States Court of Appeals for the District of Columbia Circuit, 1969
410 F.2d 701, *cert. denied*, 395 U.S. 947

J. Skelly Wright, Circuit Judge:

This case arises out of the exposure of the alleged misdeeds of Senator Thomas Dodd of Connecticut by newspaper columnists Drew Pearson and Jack Anderson. . . . [T]he court denied partial summary judgment on the theory of invasion of privacy. . . . We affirm the District Court's denial of summary judgment for invasion of privacy . . .

The undisputed facts in the case were stated by the District Court as follows:

". . . On several occasions in June and July, 1965, two former employees of the plaintiff, at times with the assistance of two members of the plaintiff's staff, entered the plaintiff's office without authority and unbeknownst to him, removed numerous documents from his files, made copies of them, replaced the originals, and turned over the copies to the defendant Anderson, who was aware of the manner in which the copies had been obtained. The defendants Pearson and Anderson thereafter published articles containing information gleaned from these documents."

I

The District Court ruled that appellants' six newspaper columns concerning appellee, which were attached to appellee's complaint, did not establish liability for the tort of invasion of privacy. That tort, whose historical origin lies in the famous Warren and Brandeis article of 1890, is recognized in the District of Columbia. It has always been considered a defense to a claim of invasion of privacy by publication, however, that the published matter complained of is of general public interest. The columns complained of here gave appellants' version of appellee's relationship with certain lobbyists for foreign interests, and gave an interpretive biographical sketch of appellee's public career. They thus clearly bore on appellee's qualifications as a United States Senator, and as such amounted to a paradigm example of published speech not subject to suit for invasion of privacy.

Indeed, appellee has not urged with any vigor on appeal the theory that appellants' publications in themselves tortiously invaded his privacy. Rather he has argued that the District Court misapprehended his privacy claim, which went rather to the manner in which the information in the columns was obtained than to the matter contained in them.

Appellee proceeds under a branch of privacy theory which Dean Prosser has labeled "intrusion," and which has been increasingly recognized by courts and commentators in recent years. Thus it has been held that unauthorized bugging of a dwelling, tapping a telephone, snooping through windows, and overzealous shadowing amount to invasions of privacy, whether or not accompanied by trespasses to property.

Unlike other types of invasion of privacy, intrusion does not involve as one of its essential elements the publication of the information obtained. The tort is completed with the obtaining of the information by improperly intrusive means.

. . . .

We approve the extension of the tort of invasion of privacy to instances of intrusion, whether by physical trespass or not, into spheres from which an ordinary man in a plaintiff's position could reasonably expect that the particular defendant should be excluded. . . . The protection should not turn exclusively on the question of whether the intrusion involves a technical trespass under the law of property. The common law, like the Fourth Amendment, should "protect people, not places."

The question then becomes whether appellants Pearson and Anderson improperly intruded into the protected sphere of privacy of appellee Dodd in obtaining the information on which their columns were based. In determining this question, we may assume, without deciding, that appellee's employees and former employees did commit such an improper intrusion when they removed confidential files with the intent to show them to unauthorized outsiders.[19]

Although appellee's complaint charges that appellants aided and abetted in the removal of the documents, the undisputed facts . . . established only that appellants received copies of the documents knowing that they had been removed without authorization. If we were to hold appellants liable for invasion of privacy on these facts, we would establish the proposition that one who receives information from an intruder, knowing it has been obtained by improper intrusion, is guilty of a tort. In an untried and developing area of tort law, we are not prepared to go so far. A person approached by an eavesdropper with an offer to share in the information gathered through the eavesdropping would perhaps play the nobler part should he spurn

---

19. Appellants have argued that appellee's employees and former employees committed neither conversion nor trespass nor invasion of privacy, because their actions are privileged by a public policy in favor of exposing wrongdoing. See Restatement (Second) of Agency § 395, Comment f (1958):

> "An agent is privileged to reveal information confidentially acquired by him in the course of his agency in the protection of a superior interest of himself or of a third person. Thus, if the confidential information is to the effect that the principal is committing or is about to commit a crime, the agent is under no duty not to reveal it. . . ."

And compare Code of Ethics for Government Service, House Doc. No. 103, 86th Cong., 1st Sess. (1958): "Any person in government service should: . . . (IX) Expose corruption wherever discovered."

the offer and shut his ears. However, it seems to us that at this point it would place too great a strain on human weakness to hold one liable in damages who merely succumbs to temptation and listens.

Of course, appellants did more than receive and peruse the copies of the documents taken from appellee's files; they published excerpts from them in the national press. But in analyzing a claimed breach of privacy, injuries from intrusion and injuries from publication should be kept clearly separate. Where there is intrusion, the intruder should generally be liable whatever the content of what he learns. An eavesdropper to the marital bedroom may hear marital intimacies, or he may hear statements of fact or opinion of legitimate interest to the public; for purposes of liability that should make no difference. On the other hand, where the claim is that private information concerning plaintiff has been published, the question of whether that information is genuinely private or is of public interest should not turn on the manner in which it has been obtained. . . .

Here we have separately considered the nature of appellants' publications concerning appellee, and have found that the matter published was of obvious public interest. The publication was not itself an invasion of privacy. Since we have also concluded that appellants' role in obtaining the information did not make them liable to appellee for intrusion, their subsequent publication, itself no invasion of privacy, cannot reach back to render that role tortious.

. . . .

———————

1. The cause of action for invasion of privacy need not involve a physical trespass. *See Roach v. Harper*, 105 S.E.2d 564 (W. Va. 1958). In *Vernars v. Young*, 539 F.2d 966 (3d Cir. 1976), liability for intrusion was imposed on a corporate executive who opened and read employees' personal mail that had arrived at the office. In *Pinkerton National Detective Agency, Inc. v. Stevens*, 132 S.E.2d 119 (Ga. Ct. App. 1963), the surveillance employed by the insurance company was sufficiently intrusive to be "highly offensive to the reasonable person." However, in *I.C.U. Investigations v. Jones*, 780 So. 2d 685 (Ala. 2000), the videotaping of a worker's compensation claimant urinating in his front yard was held not sufficiently offensive or objectionable to constitute intrusion.

2. In *Bartnicki v. Vopper*, 532 U.S. 514 (2000), the Supreme Court held that the First Amendment barred liability for a media defendant that accurately broadcast the contents of a private conversation between a union official and union members about a teacher's strike that had been illegally obtained by others.

3. The wide availability of tiny, unobtrusive, and remotely operable cameras and recording instruments has vastly increased the potential for surreptitious video and audio surveillance of others. When does such surveillance constitute intrusion? *See Hernandez v. Hillsides, Inc.*, 97 Cal. Rptr. 3d 274, 211 P.3d 1063 (2009) (employer's surreptitious video surveillance of employees in workplace to discover who was using employer's computers to access pornography was not "highly offensive"). The

development of digital social media has also greatly expanded the ability of individuals to publish the products of that surveillance on digital media. One particular problem has been the widespread publication of sexually explicit images and videos. Many states have enacted "revenge porn" laws that provide potential criminal punishment for publishing intimate images of another individual that were knowingly taken or posted without the other person's knowledge or consent. The terms of the statutes vary from state to state. For an example, see N.J. Stat. Ann. 2C:14-9 (2015).

How should these developments affect tort liability? In *Bollea v. Gawker*, the professional wrestler known as "Hulk Hogan" successfully sued Gawker, LLC, for posting a surreptitiously obtained video recording of him engaging in a sexual liaison. The case was ultimately settled for $31 million. Shortly thereafter, Gawker went out of business. *See* Sidney Ember, *Gawker and Hulk Hogan Reach $31 Million Settlement*, New York Times (Nov. 2, 2016).

4. In *Taus v. Loftus*, 151 P.3d 1185 (2007), the California Supreme Court upheld a claim for intrusion. The plaintiff was an individual who as a child, many years before, had been the subject of a psychological case study that had figured prominently in a national debate over the validity of recovery of repressed memory. The authors of the original study, who favored the idea of recovery, had referred to the plaintiff only as "Jane Doe." The defendants, who opposed the idea of recovered repressed memory, were able to use various facts disclosed in the original study, plus information revealed by the original authors in scholarly presentations on the subject, to discover the true identity of the plaintiff. Using that information, they were then able to obtain various additional facts about the plaintiff that had not been revealed in the initial study. In a subsequent publication, while still referring to the plaintiff as "Jane Doe," they disclosed these additional facts to challenge the claims of the original authors that the "recovered" memory was in fact valid. The court rejected all but one of the privacy claims based on the defendants' research, ruling that they had only used information that had been obtained from others or from public sources, including court records. However, the court ruled that one claim, based on allegations that the defendants had obtained information from the plaintiff's former foster mother by misrepresenting the nature of their interest in the case, could go forward. The court reasoned that the former foster parent might not have been willing to disclose the facts if she had been aware of the true motives of the defendants. Justice Moreno dissented, arguing that the plaintiff had no reasonable expectation of privacy in facts about her life that were possessed by a third party.

Galella v. Onassis

United States Court of Appeals for the Second Circuit, 1973
487 F.2d 986

J. Joseph Smith, Circuit Judge:

Galella is a free-lance photographer specializing in the making and sale of photographs of well-known persons. Defendant Onassis is the widow of the late President,

John F. Kennedy, mother of the two Kennedy children, John and Caroline, and is the wife of Aristotle Onassis, widely known shipping figure and reputed multimillionaire. John Walsh, James Kalafatis and John Connelly are U.S. Secret Service agents assigned to the duty of protecting the Kennedy children. . . .

Galella fancies himself as a "paparazzo" (literally a kind of annoying insect, perhaps roughly equivalent to the English "gadfly.") Paparazzi make themselves as visible to the public and obnoxious to their photographic subjects as possible to aid in the advertisement and wide sale of their works.

Some examples of Galella's conduct brought out at trial are illustrative. Galella took pictures of John Kennedy riding his bicycle in Central Park across the way from his home. He jumped out into the boy's path, causing the [Secret Service] agents concern for John's safety. The agents' reaction and interrogation of Galella led to Galella's arrest and his action against the agents; Galella on other occasions interrupted Caroline at tennis, and invaded the children's private schools. At one time he came uncomfortably close in a power boat to Mrs. Onassis swimming. He often jumped and postured around while taking pictures of her party, notably at a theater opening but also on numerous other occasions. He followed a practice of bribing apartment house, restaurant and nightclub doormen as well as romancing a family servant to keep him advised of the movements of the family.

After detention and arrest following complaint by the Secret Service agents protecting Mrs. Onassis' son and his acquittal in the state court, Galella filed suit in state court against the agents and Mrs. Onassis. Galella claimed that under orders from Mrs. Onassis, the three agents had falsely arrested and maliciously prosecuted him, and that this incident in addition to several others described in the complaint constituted an unlawful interference with his trade.

Mrs. Onassis answered denying any role in the arrest or any part in the claimed interference with his attempts to photograph her, and counterclaimed for damages and injunctive relief, charging that Galella had invaded her privacy, assaulted and battered her, intentionally inflicted emotional distress and engaged in a campaign of harassment.

. . . .

Certain incidents of photographic coverage by Galella, subsequent to an agreement among the parties for Galella not to so engage, resulted in the issuance of a temporary restraining order to prevent further harassment of Mrs. Onassis and the children. Galella was enjoined from "harassing, alarming, startling, tormenting, touching the person of the defendant . . . or her children . . . and from blocking their movements in the public places and thoroughfares, invading their immediate zone of privacy by means of physical movements, gestures or with photographic equipment and from performing any act reasonably calculated to place the lives and safety of the defendant . . . and her children in jeopardy." Within two months, Galella was charged with violation of the temporary restraining order; a new order was signed which required that the photographer keep 100 yards from the Onassis apartment and

50 yards from the person of the defendant and her children. Surveillance was also prohibited.

. . . .

After a six-week trial the court dismissed Galella's claim and granted relief to both the defendant and the intervenor. Galella was enjoined from (1) keeping the defendant and her children under surveillance or following any of them; (2) approaching within 100 yards of the home of defendant or her children, or within 100 yards of either child's school or within 75 yards of either child or 50 yards of defendant; (3) using the name, portrait or picture of defendant or her children for advertising; (4) attempting to communicate with defendant or her children except through her attorney.

. . . .

Discrediting all of Galella's testimony the court found the photographer guilty of harassment, intentional infliction of emotional distress, assault and battery, commercial exploitation of defendant's personality, and invasion of privacy. Fully crediting defendant's testimony, the court found no liability on Galella's claim. Evidence offered by the defense showed that Galella had on occasion intentionally physically touched Mrs. Onassis and her daughter, caused fear of physical contact in his frenzied attempts to get their pictures, followed defendant and her children too closely in an automobile, endangered the safety of the children while they were swimming, water skiing and horseback riding. Galella cannot successfully challenge the court's finding of tortious conduct.

Finding that Galella had "insinuated himself into the very fabric of Mrs. Onassis' life . . ." the court framed its relief in part on the need to prevent further invasion of the defendant's privacy. Whether or not this accords with present New York law, there is no doubt that it is sustainable under New York's proscription of harassment.

Of course legitimate countervailing social needs may warrant some intrusion despite an individual's reasonable expectation of privacy and freedom from harassment. However the interference allowed may be no greater than that necessary to protect the overriding public interest. Mrs. Onassis was properly found to be a public figure and thus subject to news coverage. Nonetheless, Galella's action went far beyond the reasonable bounds of news gathering. When weighed against the *de minimis* public importance of the daily activities of the defendant, Galella's constant surveillance, his obtrusive and intruding presence, was unwarranted and unreasonable. If there were any doubt in our minds, Galella's inexcusable conduct toward defendant's minor children would resolve it.

Galella does not seriously dispute the court's finding of tortious conduct. Rather, he sets up the First Amendment as a wall of immunity protecting newsmen from any liability for their conduct while gathering news. There is no such scope to the First Amendment right. Crimes and torts committed in news gathering are not protected. . . .

———————

What do you think of the solution adopted by the court? Under what circumstances should individuals be able to seek injunctive relief (as opposed to the typical tort remedy of damages) to prevent invasions of privacy? Note the court's reliance on New York law proscribing harassment as support for its decision.

Shulman v. Group W Productions, Inc.

Supreme Court of California, 1998
955 P.2d 469

WERDEGAR, JUSTICE.

In the present case, we address the balance between privacy and press freedom in the commonplace context of an automobile accident. . . .

FACTS AND PROCEDURAL HISTORY

On June 24, 1990, plaintiffs Ruth and Wayne Shulman, mother and son, were injured when the car in which they and two other family members were riding on interstate 10 in Riverside County flew off the highway and tumbled down an embankment into a drainage ditch on state-owned property, coming to rest upside down. Ruth, the most seriously injured of the two, was pinned under the car. Ruth and Wayne both had to be cut free from the vehicle by the device known as "the jaws of life."

A rescue helicopter operated by Mercy Air was dispatched to the scene. The flight nurse, who would perform the medical care at the scene and on the way to the hospital, was Laura Carnahan. Also on board were the pilot, a medic and Joel Cooke, a video camera operator employed by defendants Group W Productions, Inc., and 4MN Productions. Cooke was recording the rescue operation for later broadcast.

Cooke roamed the accident scene, videotaping the rescue. Nurse Carnahan wore a wireless microphone that picked up her conversations with both Ruth and the other rescue personnel. Cooke's tape was edited into a piece approximately nine minutes long, which, with the addition of narrative voice-over, was broadcast on September 29, 1990, as a segment of *On Scene: Emergency Response.*

The segment begins with the Mercy Air helicopter shown on its way to the accident site. The narrator's voice is heard in the background, setting the scene and describing in general terms what has happened. The pilot can be heard speaking with rescue workers on the ground in order to prepare for his landing. As the helicopter touches down, the narrator says: "[F]our of the patients are leaving by ground ambulance. Two are still trapped inside." (The first part of this statement was wrong, since only four persons were in the car to start.) After Carnahan steps from the helicopter, she can be seen and heard speaking about the situation with various rescue workers. A firefighter assures her they will hose down the area to prevent any fire from the wrecked car.

The videotape shows only a glimpse of Wayne, and his voice is never heard. Ruth is shown several times, either by brief shots of a limb or her torso, or with her features blocked by others or obscured by an oxygen mask. She is also heard speaking several times. Carnahan calls her "Ruth," and her last name is not mentioned on the broadcast.

While Ruth is still trapped under the car, Carnahan asks Ruth's age. Ruth responds, "I'm old." On further questioning, Ruth reveals she is 47, and Carnahan observes that "it's all relative. You're not that old." During her extrication from the car, Ruth asks at least twice if she is dreaming. At one point she asks Carnahan, who has told her she will be taken to the hospital in a helicopter: "Are you teasing?" At another point she says: "This is terrible. Am I dreaming?" She also asks what happened and where the rest of her family is, repeating the questions even after being told she was in an accident and the other family members are being cared for. While being loaded into the helicopter on a stretcher, Ruth says: "I just want to die." Carnahan reassures her that she is "going to do real well," but Ruth repeats: "I just want to die. I don't want to go through this."

Ruth and Wayne are placed in the helicopter, and its door is closed. The narrator states: "Once airborne, Laura and [the flight medic] will update their patients' vital signs and establish communications with the waiting trauma teams at Loma Linda." Carnahan, speaking into what appears to be a radio microphone, transmits some of Ruth's vital signs and states that Ruth cannot move her feet and has no sensation. The video footage during the helicopter ride includes a few seconds of Ruth's face, covered by an oxygen mask. Wayne is neither shown nor heard.

The helicopter lands on the hospital roof. With the door open, Ruth states while being taken out: "My upper back hurts." Carnahan replies: "Your upper back hurts. That's what you were saying up there." Ruth states: "I don't feel that great." Carnahan responds: "You probably don't."

Finally, Ruth is shown being moved from the helicopter into the hospital. The narrator concludes by stating: "Once inside both patients will be further evaluated and moved into emergency surgery if need be. Thanks to the efforts of the crew of Mercy Air, the firefighters, medics and police who responded, patients' lives were saved." As the segment ends, a brief, written epilogue appears on the screen, stating: "Laura's patient spent months in the hospital. She suffered severe back injuries. The others were all released much sooner."

The accident left Ruth a paraplegic. When the segment was broadcast, Wayne phoned Ruth in her hospital room and told her to turn on the television because "Channel 4 is showing our accident now." Shortly afterward, several hospital workers came into the room to mention that a videotaped segment of her accident was being shown. Ruth was "shocked, so to speak, that this would be run and I would be exploited, have my privacy invaded, which is what I felt had happened." She did not know her rescue had been recorded in this manner and had never consented to the recording or broadcast. . . . Asked at deposition what part of the broadcast material she considered private, Ruth explained: "I think the whole scene was pretty private. It was pretty gruesome, the parts that I saw, my knee sticking out of the car. I certainly did not look my best, and I don't feel it's for the public to see. I was not at my best in what I was thinking and what I was saying and what was being shown, and it's not for the public to see this trauma that I was going through."

Ruth and Wayne sued the producers of *On Scene: Emergency Response*. . . . The first amended complaint included two causes of action for invasion of privacy, one based on defendants' unlawful intrusion by videotaping the rescue in the first instance and the other based on the public disclosure of private facts, i.e., the broadcast.

Defendants moved for summary judgment, contending primarily that their conduct was protected by the First Amendment because of the broadcast's newsworthy content. . . .

The trial court granted the media defendants' summary judgment motion, basing its ruling on plaintiffs' admissions that the accident and rescue were matters of public interest and public affairs. Those admissions, in the trial court's view, showed as a matter of law that the broadcast material was newsworthy, thereby vesting the media defendants' conduct with First Amendment protection. The court entered judgment for defendants on all causes of action.

The Court of Appeal reversed and remanded for further proceedings, but on limited grounds and as to some causes of action only. First, the Court of Appeal held plaintiffs had no reasonable expectation of privacy in the events at the accident scene itself. According to the lower court, "Appellants' accident occurred on a heavily traveled public highway. . . . The videotape itself shows a crowd of onlookers peering down at the rescue scene below. Appellants could be seen and heard by anyone at the accident site itself and could not have had a reasonable expectation of privacy at the scene in regard to what they did or said. Their statements or exclamations could be freely heard by all who passed by and were thus public, not private." Once inside the helicopter, however, the court next reasoned, plaintiffs *did* have a reasonable expectation of privacy; the helicopter was essentially an airborne ambulance, and an ambulance in emergency medical use is considered a private space, both by social tradition and by analogy to a hospital room, which was deemed private *in Noble v. Sears, Roebuck & Co.* (1973) 33 Cal. App. 3d 654 [109 Cal. Rptr. 269, 73 A.L.R.3d 1164].

As to Ruth's cause of action for publication of private facts (limited to the broadcast of events recorded inside the helicopter), the Court of Appeal concluded triable issues of fact existed on the element of offensiveness and on a defense of newsworthiness. With regard to plaintiffs' claims of intrusion, also as related to the recording of events in the helicopter, the Court of Appeal, citing *Hill v. National Collegiate Athletic Assn.* (1994) 7 Cal. 4th 1 [26 Cal. Rptr. 2d 834, 865 P.2d 633], held the trial court . . . should have conducted an analysis balancing plaintiffs' privacy rights against defendants' First Amendment interest in recording the rescue. The Court of Appeal therefore remanded for further proceedings as to both plaintiffs' cause of action for intrusion and as to Ruth's cause of action for publication of private facts.

We conclude the Court of Appeal's judgment should be affirmed except insofar as it remanded for further proceedings on Ruth's private facts claim. . . . Summary judgment thus was proper as to both plaintiffs on the private facts cause of action.

As to intrusion, the Court of Appeal correctly found triable issues exist as to whether defendants invaded plaintiffs' privacy by accompanying plaintiffs in the helicopter. Contrary to the holding below, we also hold triable issues exist as to whether defendants tortiously intruded by listening to Ruth's confidential conversations with Nurse Carnahan at the rescue scene without Ruth's consent. Moreover, we hold defendants had no constitutional privilege so to intrude on plaintiffs' seclusion and private communications.

DISCUSSION

. . . California courts have recognized both of the privacy causes of action pleaded by plaintiffs here: (1) public disclosure of private facts, and (2) intrusion into private places, conversations or other matters.

We shall review the elements of each privacy tort, as well as the common law and constitutional privilege of the press as to each, and shall apply in succession this law to the facts pertinent to each cause of action.

I. Publication of Private Facts

. . . .

A few words are in order at this point regarding the right of privacy secured by article I, section 1 of the California Constitution. The Court of Appeal, citing *Hill v. National Collegiate Athletic Assn., supra,* 7 Cal. 4th at pages 37–38 *(Hill)*, equated the judicial balancing undertaken in delineation of the common law right of privacy to the balancing of interests this court has prescribed for evaluating claims raised under our state's constitutional right of privacy. Defendants attack the Court of Appeal's adoption of *Hill's* balancing test in the common law tort context, arguing that under the *federal* Constitution newsworthiness is a complete bar to liability, rather than merely an interest to be balanced against private or state-protected interests.

We agree with defendants that the publication of truthful, lawfully obtained material of legitimate public concern is constitutionally privileged and does not create liability under the private facts tort. As discussed above, however, a certain amount of interest-balancing *does* occur in deciding whether material is of legitimate public concern, or in formulating rules for that decision. To that extent, the Court of Appeal's analogy to *Hill* was not in error.

. . . .

II. Intrusion

Of the four privacy torts identified by Prosser, the tort of intrusion into private places, conversations or matter is perhaps the one that best captures the common understanding of an "invasion of privacy." It encompasses unconsented-to physical intrusion into the home, hospital room or other place the privacy of which is legally recognized, as well as unwarranted sensory intrusions such as eavesdropping, wiretapping, and visual or photographic spying. (See Rest. 2d Torts, § 652B, com. b., pp. 378–379, and illustrations.) It is in the intrusion cases that invasion of privacy is most clearly seen as an affront to individual dignity. "[A] measure of personal isolation and personal control over the conditions of its abandonment is of the very essence of personal freedom and dignity, is part of what our culture means by these concepts.

A man whose home may be entered at the will of another, whose conversations may be overheard at the will of another, whose marital and familial intimacies may be overseen at the will of another, is less of a man, has less human dignity, on that account." . . .

[T]he intrusion tort has received less judicial attention than the private facts tort, and its parameters are less clearly defined. The leading California decision is *Miller v. National Broadcasting Co., supra*, 187 Cal. App. 3d 1463 *(Miller)*. *Miller*, which like the present case involved a news organization's videotaping the work of emergency medical personnel, adopted the Restatement's formulation of the cause of action: "One who intentionally intrudes, physically or otherwise, upon the solitude or seclusion of another or his private affairs or concerns, is subject to liability to the other for invasion of his privacy, if the intrusion would be highly offensive to a reasonable person." (Rest. 2d Torts, § 652B; *Miller, supra*, 187 Cal. App. 3d at p. 1482.)

As stated in *Miller* and the Restatement, therefore, the action for intrusion has two elements: (1) intrusion into a private place, conversation or matter, (2) in a manner highly offensive to a reasonable person. We consider the elements in that order.

We ask first whether defendants "intentionally intrude[d], physically or otherwise, upon the solitude or seclusion of another," that is, into a place or conversation private to Wayne or Ruth. (Rest. 2d Torts, § 652B; *Miller, supra*, 187 Cal. App. 3d at p. 1482). "[T]here is no liability for the examination of a public record concerning the plaintiff, . . . [or] for observing him or even taking his photograph while he is walking on the public highway. . . ." (Rest. 2d Torts, § 652B, com. c, pp. 379–380; . . .). To prove actionable intrusion, the plaintiff must show the defendant penetrated some zone of physical or sensory privacy surrounding, or obtained unwanted access to data about, the plaintiff. The tort is proven only if the plaintiff had an objectively reasonable expectation of seclusion or solitude in the place, conversation or data source. (Rest. 2d Torts, § 652B, com. c, p. 379; . . .).

Cameraman Cooke's mere presence at the accident scene and filming of the events occurring there cannot be deemed either a physical or sensory intrusion on plaintiffs' seclusion. Plaintiffs had no right of ownership or possession of the property where the rescue took place, nor any actual control of the premises. Nor could they have had a reasonable expectation that members of the media would be excluded or prevented from photographing the scene; for journalists to attend and record the scenes of accidents and rescues is in no way unusual or unexpected. *(Cf. Pen. Code, § 409.5, subd. (d), 409.6, subd. (d)* [exempting press representatives from certain emergency closure orders].)

Two aspects of defendants' conduct, however, raise triable issues of intrusion on seclusion. First, a triable issue exists as to whether both plaintiffs had an objectively reasonable expectation of privacy in the interior of the rescue helicopter, which served as an ambulance. Although the attendance of reporters and photographers at the scene of an accident is to be expected, we are aware of no law or custom permitting the press to ride in ambulances or enter hospital rooms during treatment without the patient's consent. (See *Noble v. Sears, Roebuck & Co., supra*, 33 Cal. App. 3d at p. 660 [accepting, subject to proof at trial, intrusion plaintiff's theory she had "an exclusive right of occupancy of her hospital room" as against investigator]; *Miller, supra*, 187 Cal. App. 3d at pp. 1489–1490. . . . Other than the two patients and Cooke, only three people were present in the helicopter, all Mercy Air staff. As the Court of Appeal observed, "[i]t is neither the custom nor the habit of our society that any member of the public at large or its media representatives may hitch a ride in an ambulance and ogle as paramedics care for an injured stranger." (See also *Green v. Chicago Tribune Co., supra*, 675 N.E.2d at p. 252 [hospital room not public place]; *Barber v. Time, Inc., supra*, 159 S.W.2d at p. 295 ["Certainly, if there is any right of privacy at all, it should include the right to obtain medical treatment at home or in a hospital . . . without personal publicity."].)

Second, Ruth was entitled to a degree of privacy in her conversations with Carnahan and other medical rescuers at the accident scene, and in Carnahan's conversations conveying medical information regarding Ruth to the hospital base. Cooke, perhaps, did not intrude into that zone of privacy merely by being present at a place where he could hear such conversations with unaided ears. But by placing a microphone on Carnahan's person, amplifying and recording what she said and heard, defendants may have listened in on conversations the parties could reasonably have expected to be private.

The Court of Appeal held plaintiffs had no reasonable expectation of privacy at the accident scene itself because the scene was within the sight and hearing of members of the public. The summary judgment record, however, does not support the Court of Appeal's conclusion. . . . The videotapes (broadcast and raw footage) show the rescue did not take place "on a heavily traveled highway," as the Court of Appeal stated, but in a ditch many yards from and below the rural superhighway, which is raised somewhat at that point to bridge a nearby crossroad. From the tapes it appears unlikely the plaintiffs' extrication from their car and medical treatment at the scene could have been observed by any persons who, in the lower court's words, "passed by" on the roadway. Even more unlikely is that any passersby on the road could have heard Ruth's conversation with Nurse Carnahan or the other rescuers.

Whether Ruth expected her conversations with Nurse Carnahan or the other rescuers to remain private and whether any such expectation was reasonable are, on the state of the record before us, questions for the jury. We note, however, that several existing legal protections for communications could support the conclusion that Ruth possessed a reasonable expectation of privacy in her conversations with Nurse Carnahan and the other rescuers. A patient's conversation with a provider of medical care in the course of treatment, including emergency treatment, carries a traditional and legally well-established expectation of privacy.

. . . .

Ruth's claim, of course, does not require her to prove a statutory violation, only to prove that she had an objectively reasonable expectation of privacy in her conversations. Whether the circumstances of Ruth's extrication and helicopter rescue would reasonably have indicated to defendants, or to their agent, Cooke, that Ruth would desire and expect her communications to Carnahan and the other rescuers to be confined to them alone, and therefore not to be electronically transmitted and recorded, is a triable issue of fact in this case. As observed earlier, whether anyone present (other than Cooke) was a mere observer, uninvolved in the rescue effort, is unclear from the summary judgment record. Also unclear is who, if anyone, could overhear conversations between Ruth and Carnahan, which were transmitted by a microphone on Carnahan's person, amplified and recorded by defendants. We cannot say, as a matter of law, that Cooke should not have perceived he might be intruding on a confidential communication when he recorded a seriously injured patient's conversations with medical personnel.

We turn to the second element of the intrusion tort, offensiveness of the intrusion. In a widely followed passage, the *Miller* court explained that determining offensiveness requires consideration of all the circumstances of the intrusion, including its degree and setting and the intruder's "motives and objectives." The *Miller* court concluded that reasonable people could regard the camera crew's conduct in filming a man's emergency medical treatment in his home, without seeking or obtaining his or his wife's consent, as showing "a cavalier disregard for ordinary citizens' rights of privacy" and, hence, as highly offensive. (*Miller, supra*, 187 Cal. App. 3d at p. 1484.)

We agree with the *Miller* court that all the circumstances of an intrusion, including the motives or justification of the intruder, are pertinent to the offensiveness element. Motivation or justification becomes particularly important when the intrusion is by a member of the print or broadcast press in the pursuit of news material. . . . [T]he First Amendment does not immunize the press from liability for torts or crimes committed in an effort to gather news[. T]he constitutional protection of the press does reflect the strong societal interest in effective and complete reporting of events, an interest that may—as a matter of tort law—justify an intrusion that would otherwise be considered offensive. . . .

In deciding, therefore, whether a reporter's alleged intrusion into private matters (i.e., physical space, conversation or data) is "offensive" and hence actionable as an invasion of privacy, courts must consider the extent to which the intrusion was, under the circumstances, justified by the legitimate motive of gathering the news. Information-collecting techniques that may be highly offensive when done for socially unprotected reasons—for purposes of harassment, blackmail or prurient curiosity, for example—may not be offensive to a reasonable person when employed by journalists in pursuit of a socially or politically important story. . . .

The mere fact the intruder was in pursuit of a "story" does not, however, generally justify an otherwise offensive intrusion; offensiveness depends as well on the particular method of investigation used. At one extreme, "routine . . . reporting techniques" such as asking questions of people with information ("including those with confidential or restricted information") could rarely, if ever, be deemed an actionable intrusion. At the other extreme, violation of well-established legal areas of physical or sensory privacy—trespass into a home or tapping a personal telephone line, for example—could rarely, if ever, be justified by a reporter's need to get the story. Such acts would be deemed highly offensive even if the information sought was of weighty public concern; they would also be outside any protection the Constitution provides to newsgathering.

. . . .

On this summary judgment record, we believe a jury could find defendants' recording of Ruth's communications to Carnahan and other rescuers, and filming in the air ambulance, to be "highly offensive to a reasonable person." With regard to the depth of the intrusion . . . , a reasonable jury could find highly offensive the placement of a microphone on a medical rescuer in order to intercept what would otherwise be private conversations with an injured patient. In that setting, as defendants could and should have foreseen, the patient would not know her words were being recorded and would not have occasion to ask about, and object or consent to, recording. Defendants, it could reasonably be said, took calculated advantage of the patient's "vulnerability and confusion." . . . Arguably, the last thing an injured accident victim should have to worry about while being pried from her wrecked car is that a television producer may be recording everything she says to medical personnel for the possible edification and entertainment of casual television viewers.

For much the same reason, a jury could reasonably regard entering and riding in an ambulance—whether on the ground or in the air—with two seriously injured patients to be an egregious intrusion on a place of expected seclusion. Again, the patients, at least in this case, were hardly in a position to keep careful watch on who was riding with them, or to inquire as to everyone's business and consent or object to their presence. A jury could reasonably believe that fundamental respect for human dignity requires the patients' anxious journey be taken only with those whose care is solely for them and out of sight of the prying eyes (or cameras) of others.

Nor can we say as a matter of law that defendants' motive—to gather usable material for a potentially newsworthy story—necessarily privileged their intrusive conduct as a matter of common law tort liability. A reasonable jury could conclude the producers' desire to get footage that would convey the "feel" of the event—the real sights and sounds of a difficult rescue—did not justify either placing a microphone on Nurse Carnahan or filming inside the rescue helicopter. Although defendants' purposes could scarcely be regarded as evil or malicious (in the colloquial sense), their behavior could, even in light of their motives, be thought to show a highly offensive lack of sensitivity and respect for plaintiffs' privacy. (*Miller, supra*, 187 Cal. App. 3d at p. 1484.) . . .

CONCLUSION

. . . .

The intrusion claim calls for a much less deferential analysis. In contrast to the broad privilege the press enjoys for publishing truthful, newsworthy information in its possession, the press has *no* recognized constitutional privilege to violate generally applicable laws in pursuit of material. Nor, even absent an independent crime or tort, can a highly offensive intrusion into a private place, conversation, or source of information generally be justified by the plea that the intruder hoped thereby to get good material for a news story. Such a justification *may* be available when enforcement of the tort or other law would place an impermissibly severe burden on the press, but that condition is not met in this case.

In short, the state may not intrude into the proper sphere of the news media to dictate what they should publish and broadcast, but neither may the media play tyrant to the people by unlawfully spying on them in the name of newsgathering. Summary judgment for the defense was proper as to plaintiffs' cause of action for publication of private facts (the second cause of action), but improper as to the cause of action for invasion of privacy by intrusion (the first cause of action).

DISPOSITION

The judgment of the Court of Appeal is affirmed except insofar as the Court of Appeal reversed and remanded for further proceedings on Ruth Shulman's cause of action for publication of private facts.

GEORGE, C. J., and KENNARD, J., concurred.

KENNARD, JUSTICE, concurring.

. . . .

The free flow of truthful information, however, is also a fundamental value of our society, embodied in the First Amendment to the federal Constitution. As the plurality opinion notes, the United States Supreme Court has not yet attempted to fashion a general rule striking a balance between our competing interests in preserving a sphere of personal privacy and in unfettered publication of truthful information. Because of the complexities of the problem, crafting a general rule in this area would not be an easy task. The authors of two prominent constitutional law treatises, for example, take opposite views on whether the First Amendment permits a cause of action for truthful publication of private facts. Professors Rotunda and Nowak would not allow the cause of action: "[I]n light of later constitutional cases, and given the general [First Amendment] rationale articulated by the Supreme Court over the years, the state should always recognize that truth is a defense in a defamation or right of privacy action. . . ." Professor Tribe, on the other hand, takes the view that the First Amendment permits the cause of action: "[W]hen government acts to limit the untrammeled gathering, recording, or dissemination of data or statements about an individual, of course it inhibits speech—but it also vindicates the individual's ability to control what others are told about his or her life. Such control constitutes a central part of the right to shape the 'self that any individual presents to the world." (Tribe, American Constitutional Law (2d ed. 1988) § 12–14, p. 887.)

MOSK, J., concurred.

CHIN, JUSTICE, concurring and dissenting.

. . . .

I dissent . . . from the plurality's holding that plaintiffs' "intrusion" cause of action should be remanded for trial. The critical question is whether defendants' privacy intrusion was "*highly* offensive to a reasonable person.'" . . . As the plurality explains, "the constitutional protection of the press does reflect the strong societal interest in effective and complete reporting of events, an interest that may—as a matter of law—justify an intrusion that *would otherwise be considered offensive*". . . . I also agree with the plurality that "Information-collecting techniques that *may be highly offensive* when done for socially unprotected reasons—for purposes of harassment, blackmail or prurient curiosity, for example—*may not be offensive to a reasonable person* when employed by journalists in pursuit of a socially or politically important story" . . . (italics added.)

. . . .

Ruth's expectations notwithstanding, I do not believe that a reasonable trier of fact could find that defendants' conduct in this case was "highly offensive to a reasonable person," the test adopted by the plurality. Plaintiffs do not allege that defendants, though present at the accident rescue scene and in the helicopter, interfered with either the rescue or medical efforts, elicited embarrassing or offensive information from plaintiffs, or even tried to interrogate or interview them. Defendants' news team evidently merely recorded newsworthy events "of legitimate public concern" . . . as they transpired. Defendants' apparent motive in undertaking the supposed privacy invasion was a reasonable and nonmalicious one: to obtain an accurate depiction of the rescue efforts from start to finish. The event was newsworthy, and the ultimate broadcast was both dramatic and educational, rather than tawdry or embarrassing.

. . . .

———————

Is this a valid case of intrusion or should plaintiff be asked to develop a thicker skin? Should truth be a defense?

Desnick v. American Broadcasting Companies, Inc.

United States Court of Appeals for the Seventh Circuit, 1995
44 F.3d 1345

POSNER, CHIEF JUDGE.

The plaintiffs—an ophthalmic clinic known as the "Desnick Eye Center" after its owner, Dr. Desnick, and two ophthalmic surgeons employed by the clinic, Glazer and Simon—appeal from the dismissal of their suit against the ABC television network, a producer of the ABC program *PrimeTime Live* named Entine, and the program's star reporter, Donaldson. The suit is for trespass, defamation, and other torts arising out of the production and broadcast of a program segment of *PrimeTime Live* that was highly critical of the Desnick Eye Center. . . .

In March of 1993 Entine telephoned Dr. Desnick and told him that *Prime-Time Live* wanted to do a broadcast segment on large cataract practices. The Desnick Eye

Center has 25 offices in four midwestern states and performs more than 10,000 cataract operations a year, mostly on elderly persons whose cataract surgery is paid for by Medicare. . . . Entine told Desnick that the segment would not be about just one cataract practice, that it would not involve "ambush" interviews or "undercover" surveillance, and that it would be "fair and balanced." Thus reassured, Desnick permitted an ABC crew to videotape the Desnick Eye Center's main premises in Chicago, to film a cataract operation "live," and to interview doctors, technicians, and patients. Desnick also gave Entine a videotape explaining the Desnick Eye Center's services.

Unbeknownst to Desnick, Entine had dispatched persons equipped with concealed cameras to offices of the Desnick Eye Center in Wisconsin and Indiana. Posing as patients, these persons—seven in all—requested eye examinations. Plaintiffs Glazer and Simon are among the employees of the Desnick Eye Center who were secretly videotaped examining these "test patients."

The program aired on June 10. Donaldson introduces the segment by saying, "We begin tonight with the story of a so-called 'big cutter,' Dr. James Desnick. . . . In our undercover investigation of the big cutter you'll meet tonight, we turned up evidence that he may also be a big charger, doing unnecessary cataract surgery for the money." Brief interviews with four patients of the Desnick Eye Center follow. One of the patients is satisfied ("I was blessed"); the other three are not—one of them says, "If you got three eyes, he'll get three eyes." Donaldson then reports on the experiences of the seven test patients. The two who were under 65 and thus not eligible for Medicare reimbursement were told they didn't need cataract surgery. Four of the other five were told they did. Glazer and Simon are shown recommending cataract surgery to them. Donaldson tells the viewer that *PrimeTime Live* has hired a professor of ophthalmology to examine the test patients who had been told they needed cataract surgery, and the professor tells the viewer that they didn't need it—with regard to one he says, "I think it would be near malpractice to do surgery on him." Later in the segment he denies that this could just be an honest difference of opinion between professionals.

An ophthalmic surgeon is interviewed who had turned down a job at the Desnick Eye Center because he would not have been "able to screen who I was going to operate on." He claims to have been told by one of the doctors at the Center (not Glazer or Simon) that "as soon as I reject them [i.e., turn down a patient for cataract surgery], they're going in the next room to get surgery." A former marketing executive for the Center says Desnick took advantage of "people who had Alzheimer's, people who did not know what planet they were on, people whose quality of life wouldn't change one iota by having cataract surgery done." Two patients are interviewed who report miserable experiences with the Center—one claiming that the doctors there had failed to spot an easily visible melanoma, another that as a result of unnecessary cataract surgery her "eye ruptured," producing "running pus." A former employee tells the viewer that Dr. Desnick alters patients' medical records to show they need cataract surgery—for example, changing the record of one patient's vision test from 20/30 to 20/80—and that he instructs all members of his staff to use pens of the same color in order to facilitate the alteration of patients' records.

One symptom of cataracts is that lights of normal brightness produce glare. . . . Donaldson tells the viewer that "the Desnick Center uses a very interesting machine, called an auto-refractor, to determine whether there are glare problems." Donaldson demonstrates the machine, then says that "Paddy Kalish is an optometrist who says that when he worked at the Desnick clinic from 1987 to 1990, the machine was regularly rigged. He says he watched a technician tamper with the machine, this way"—and then Kalish gives a demonstration, adding, "This happened routinely for all the older patients that came in for the eye exams." . . .

The second class of claims in this case concerns, as we said, the methods that the defendants used to create the broadcast segment. There are four such claims: that the defendants committed a trespass in insinuating the test patients into the Wisconsin and Indiana offices of the Desnick Eye Center, that they invaded the right of privacy of the Center and its doctors at those offices (specifically Glazer and Simon), that they violated federal and state statutes regulating electronic surveillance, and that they committed fraud by gaining access to the Chicago office by means of a false promise that they would present a "fair and balanced" picture of the Center's operations and would not use "ambush" interviews or undercover surveillance.

. . . .

No embarrassingly intimate details of anybody's life were publicized in the present case. There was no eavesdropping on a private conversation; the testers recorded their own conversations with the Desnick Eye Center's physicians. There was no violation of the doctor-patient privilege. There was no theft, or intent to steal trade secrets; no disruption of decorum, of peace and quiet; no noisy or distracting demonstrations. Had the testers been undercover FBI agents, there would have been no violation of the Fourth Amendment, because there would have been no invasion of a legally protected interest in property or privacy. "Testers" who pose as prospective home buyers in order to gather evidence of housing discrimination are not trespassers even if they are private persons not acting under color of law. . . . The situation of the defendants' "testers" is analogous. Like testers seeking evidence of violation of antidiscrimination laws, the defendants' test patients gained entry into the plaintiffs' premises by misrepresenting their purposes (more precisely by a misleading omission to disclose those purposes). But the entry was not invasive in the sense of infringing the kind of interest of the plaintiffs that the law of trespass protects; it was not an interference with the ownership or possession of land. . . .

What we have said largely disposes of two other claims—infringement of the right of privacy, and illegal wiretapping. The right of privacy embraces several distinct interests, but the only ones conceivably involved here are the closely related interests in concealing intimate personal facts and in preventing intrusion into legitimately private activities, such as phone conversations. As we have said already, no intimate personal facts concerning the two individual plaintiffs (remember that Dr. Desnick himself is not a plaintiff) were revealed; and the only conversations that were recorded were conversations with the testers themselves.

. . . The defendants did not order the camera-armed testers into the Desnick Eye Center's premises in order to commit a crime or tort. Maybe the program as it was eventually broadcast was tortious, for we have said that the defamation count was dismissed prematurely. But there is no suggestion that the defendants sent the testers into the Wisconsin and Illinois offices for the purpose of defaming the plaintiffs by charging tampering with the glare machine. The purpose, by the plaintiffs' own account, was to see whether the Center's physicians would recommend cataract surgery on the testers. By the same token it was not to injure the Desnick Eye Center, unless the public exposure of misconduct is an "injurious act" within the meaning of the Wisconsin statute. Telling the world the truth about a Medicare fraud is hardly what the framers of the statute could have had in mind in forbidding a person to record his own conversations if he was trying to commit an "injurious act."

---

1. Was the defamation count prematurely dismissed?

2. *Sanders v. ABC*, 978 P.2d 67 (Cal. 1999), makes clear that the use of technology may "contribute to the offensiveness of an intrusion." Employees of a telepsychic marketing company, whose workplace conversations had been covertly videotaped by an undercover television news reporter, who had secretly taken a position with company, sued the reporter and broadcaster after the video tapes were aired. The court held that an "employee who lacks a reasonable expectation of complete privacy in a workplace conversation, because it could be seen and overheard by coworkers (but not the general public) may nevertheless have a claim for invasion of privacy by intrusion based on a television reporter's covert videotaping of that conversation."

3. In *Food Lion v. Capital Cities/ABC*, 194 F.3d 505 (4th Cir. 1999):

> Two ABC television reporters, after using false resumés to get jobs at Food Lion, Inc., supermarkets, secretly videotaped what appeared to be unwholesome food handling practices. Some of the video footage was used by ABC in a Prime Time Live broadcast that was sharply critical of Food Lion. The grocery chain sued Capital Cities/ABC . . . for the program. . . . Food Lion did not sue for defamation, but focused on how ABC gathered its information through claims for fraud, breach of duty of loyalty, trespass, and unfair trade practices. Food Lion won at trial.

The Court of Appeals held: (1) alleged acts of fraud by undercover reporters who obtained jobs with chain did not proximately cause damages; (2) reporters breached duty of loyalty owed to chain under North Carolina and South Carolina law by using hidden cameras; (3) breach of duty of loyalty vitiated reporters' consent to enter chain's stores, so that they could be held liable for trespass; (4) misrepresentations could not support claim under North Carolina Unfair and Deceptive Trade Practices Act; (5) First Amendment did not bar recovery for fraud and breach of duty of loyalty; but (6) chain could not recover for damages resulting from broadcast of news programs.

The award of $2.00 for trespass by the two reporters was upheld. Other damages were reversed.

B. Public Disclosure of Private Facts

Sidis v. F-R Pub. Corp.

United States Court of Appeals for the Second Circuit, 1940
113 F.2d 806

CLARK, CIRCUIT JUDGE.

William James Sidis was the unwilling subject of a brief biographical sketch and cartoon printed in *The New Yorker* weekly magazine for August 14, 1937. . . . He brought an action in the district court against the publisher, F-R Publishing Corporation. His complaint stated three "causes of action": The first alleged violation of his right of privacy. . . . Defendant's motion to dismiss the first two "causes of action" was granted, and plaintiff has filed an appeal from the order of dismissal. Since a majority of this court believe that order appealable, for reasons referred to below, we may consider the merits of the case.

William James Sidis was a famous child prodigy in 1910. His name and prowess were well known to newspaper readers of the period. At the age of eleven, he lectured to distinguished mathematicians on the subject of Four-Dimensional Bodies. When he was sixteen, he was graduated from Harvard College, amid considerable public attention. Since then, his name has appeared in the press only sporadically, and he has sought to live as unobtrusively as possible. Until the articles objected to appeared in The New Yorker, he had apparently succeeded in his endeavor to avoid the public gaze.

Among The New Yorker's features are brief biographical sketches of current and past personalities. In the latter department, which appears haphazardly under the title of "Where Are They Now?" the article on Sidis was printed with subtitle "April Fool." The author describes his subject's early accomplishments in mathematics and the wide-spread attention he received, then recounts his general breakdown and the revulsion which Sidis thereafter felt for his for his former life of fame and study. The unfortunate prodigy is traced over the years that followed, through his attempts to conceal his identity, through his chosen career as an insignificant clerk who would not need to employ unusual mathematical talents, and through the bizarre ways in which his genius flowered, as in his enthusiasm for collecting streetcar transfers and in his proficiency with an adding machine. The article closes with an account of an interview with Sidis at his present lodgings, "a hall bedroom of Boston's shabby south end." The untidiness of his room, his curious laugh, his manner of speech, and other personal habits are commented upon at length, as is his present interest in the lore of the Oka-makammessett Indians. The subtitle is explained by the closing sentence, quoting Sidis as saying "with a grin" that it was strange, "but, you know, I was born on April

Fool's Day." Accompanying the biography is a small cartoon showing the genius of eleven years lecturing to a group of astounded professors.

It is not contended that any of the matter printed is untrue. Nor is the manner of the author unfriendly; Sidis today is described as having "a certain childlike charm." But the article is merciless in its dissection of intimate details of its subject's personal life, and this in company with elaborate accounts of Sidis' passion for privacy and the pitiable lengths to which he has gone in order to avoid public scrutiny. The work possesses great reader interest, for it is both amusing and instructive; but it may be fairly described as a ruthless exposure of a once public character, who has since sought and has now been deprived of the seclusion of private life.

. . . .

1. . . . Under the first "cause of action" we are asked to declare that this exposure transgresses upon plaintiff's right of privacy. . . .

All comment upon the right of privacy must stem from the famous article by Warren and Brandeis on *The Right of Privacy* in 4 Harv. L. Rev. 193. The learned authors of that paper were convinced that some limits ought to be imposed upon the privilege of newspapers to publish truthful items of a personal nature. "The press is overstepping in every direction the obvious bounds of propriety and of decency." . . . Warren and Brandeis, supra at page 196.

Warren and Brandeis realized that the interest of the individual in privacy must inevitably conflict with the interest of the public in news. Certain public figures, they conceded, such as holders of public office, must sacrifice their privacy and expose at least part of their lives to public scrutiny as the price of the powers they attain. But even public figures were not to be stripped bare. "In general, then, the matters of which the publication should be repressed may be described as those which concern the private life, habits, acts, and relations of an individual, and have no legitimate connection with his fitness for a public office. . . . Some things all men alike are entitled to keep from popular curiosity, whether in public life or not, while others are only private because the persons concerned have not assumed a position which makes their doings legitimate matters of public investigation." Warren and Brandeis, supra at page 216.

It must be conceded that under the strict standards suggested by these authors plaintiff's right of privacy has been invaded. Sidis today is neither politician, public administrator, nor statesman. Even if he were, some of the personal details revealed were of the sort that Warren and Brandeis believed "all men alike are entitled to keep from popular curiosity."

But despite eminent opinion to the contrary, we are not yet disposed to afford to all of the intimate details of private life an absolute immunity from the prying of the press. Everyone will agree that at some point the public interest in obtaining information becomes dominant over the individual's desire for privacy. Warren and Brandeis were willing to lift the veil somewhat in the case of public officers. We would go further, though we are not yet prepared to say how far. At least we would permit limited scrutiny of the "private" life of any person who has achieved, or has had thrust upon him, the questionable and indefinable status of a "public figure."

William James Sidis was once a public figure. As a child prodigy, he excited both admiration and curiosity. Of him great deeds were expected. In 1910, he was a person about whom the newspapers might display a legitimate intellectual interest, in the sense meant by Warren and Brandeis, as distinguished from a trivial and unseemly curiosity. But the precise motives of the press we regard as unimportant. And even if Sidis had loathed public attention at that time, we think his uncommon achievements and personality would have made the attention permissible. Since then Sidis has cloaked himself in obscurity, but his subsequent history, containing as it did an answer to the question of whether or not he had fulfilled his early promise, was still a matter of public concern. The article in *The New Yorker* sketched the life of an unusual personality, and it possessed considerable popular news interest.

We express no comment on whether or not the news worthiness of the matter printed will always constitute a complete defense. Revelations may be so intimate and so unwarranted in view of the victim's position as to outrage the community's notions of decency. But when focused upon public characters, truthful comments upon dress, speech, habits, and the ordinary aspects of personality will usually not transgress this line. Regrettably or not, the misfortunes and frailties of neighbors and "public figures" are subjects of considerable interest and discussion of the rest of the population. And when such are the mores of the community, it would be unwise for a court to bar their expression in the newspapers, books, and magazines of the day.

. . . .

———————

1. The Restatement 2d § 652D (Publicity) provides:

One who gives publicity to a matter concerning the private life of another is subject to liability to the other for invasion of his privacy, if the matter publicized is of a kind that

(a) would be highly offensive to a reasonable person, and

(b) is not of legitimate concern to the public.

2. In *Sidis*, why did the public need to know of the facts which were so painful to the plaintiff? Why was there a "legitimate intellectual interest" as opposed to "trivial and unseemly curiosity"?

Haynes v. Alfred A. Knopf, Inc.

United States Court of Appeals for the Seventh Circuit, 1993
8 F.3d 1222

POSNER, CHIEF JUDGE.

Luther Haynes and his wife, Dorothy Haynes née Johnson, appeal from the dismissal on the defendants' motion for summary judgment of their suit against

Nicholas Lemann, the author of a highly praised, best-selling book of social and political history called *The Promised Land: The Great Black Migration and How It Changed America* (1991), and Alfred A. Knopf, Inc., the book's publisher. The plaintiffs claim that the book libels Luther Haynes and invades both plaintiffs' right of privacy. Federal jurisdiction is based on diversity, and the common law of Illinois is agreed to govern the substantive issues. The appeal presents difficult issues at the intersection of tort law and freedom of the press.

Between 1940 and 1970, five million blacks moved from impoverished rural areas in the South to the cities of the North in search of a better life. Some found it, and after sojourns of shorter or greater length in the poor black districts of the cities moved to middle-class areas. Others, despite the bally-hooed efforts of the federal government, particularly between 1964 and 1972, to erase poverty and racial discrimination, remained mired in what has come to be called the "urban ghetto." *The Promised Land* is a history of the migration. It is not history as a professional historian, a demographer, or a social scientist would write it. Lemann is none of these. He is a journalist and has written a journalistic history, in which the focus is on . . . the actual migrants. Foremost among these is Ruby Lee Daniels. Her story is the spine of the book.

. . . .

When we meet her, it is the early 1940s and she is a young woman picking cotton on a plantation in Clarksdale, Mississippi. . . . Ruby had married young, but after her husband had been inducted into the army on the eve of World War II she had fallen in love with a married man, by whom she had had a child. The man's wife died and Ruby married him, but they broke up after a month. Glowing reports from an aunt who had moved to Chicago persuaded Ruby Daniels to move there in 1946. She found a job doing janitorial work, but eventually lost the job and went on public aid. She was unmarried, and had several children, when in 1953 she met "the most important man in her life." Luther Haynes, born in 1924 or 1925, a sharecropper from Mississippi, had moved to Chicago in an effort to effect a reconciliation with his wife. The effort had failed. When he met Ruby Daniels he had a well-paying job in an awning factory. They lived together, and had children. But then "Luther began to drink too much. When he drank he got mean, and he and Ruby would get into ferocious quarrels. He was still working, but he wasn't always bringing his paycheck home." Ruby got work as a maid. They moved to a poorer part of the city. The relationship went downhill. "It got to the point where [Luther] would go out on Friday evenings after picking up his paycheck, and Ruby would hope he wouldn't come home, because she knew he would be drunk. On the Friday evenings when he did come home . . . he would walk into the apartment, put on a record and turn up the volume, and saunter into their bedroom, a bottle in one hand and a cigarette in the other, in the mood for love. On one such night, Ruby's last child, Kevin, was conceived. Kevin always had something wrong with him—he was very moody, he was scrawny, and he had a severe speech impediment. Ruby was never able to find out exactly what the problem was, but she blamed it on Luther; all that alcohol must have gotten into his sperm, she said."

Ruby was on public aid, but was cut off when social workers discovered she had a man in the house. She got a night job. Luther was supposed to stay with the children while she was at work, especially since they lived in a dangerous neighborhood; but often when she came home, at 3:00 a.m. or so, she would "find the older children awake, and when she would ask them if Luther had been there, the answer would be, 'No, ma'am.'" . . . After only a few months, Luther ruined everything by going out and buying a brand-new 1961 Pontiac. It meant more to him than the house did, and when they couldn't make the house payment, he insisted on keeping the car even though she hadn't enough money to buy shoes for the children. The family was kicked out of the house. . . .

Meanwhile Luther had lost his job in the awning factory "that he had for a decade, and then bounced around a little. He lost jobs because of transportation problems, because of layoffs, because of a bout of serious illness, because of his drinking, because he had a minor criminal record (having been in jail for disorderly conduct following a fight with Ruby), and because creditors were after him." He resumed "his old habit of not returning from work on Fridays after he got his paycheck." One weekend he didn't come home at all. In a search of his things Ruby discovered evidence that Luther was having an affair with Dorothy Johnson, a former neighbor. "Luther was not being particularly careful; he saw in Dorothy, who was younger than Ruby, who had three children compared to Ruby's eight, who had a job while Ruby was on public aid, the promise of an escape from the ghetto, and he was entranced." The children discovered the affair. Kermit tried to strangle Luther. In 1965 Luther moved out permanently, and eventually he and Ruby divorced.

. . . .

After divorcing Ruby, Luther Haynes married Dorothy Johnson. He is still married to her, "owns a home on the far South Side of Chicago, and has worked for years as a parking-lot attendant; only recently have he and Ruby found that they can speak civilly to each other on the phone."

. . . .

The major claim in the complaint, and the focus of the appeal . . . is invasion of the right of privacy. . . .

Even people who have nothing rationally to be ashamed of can be mortified by the publication of intimate details of their life. Most people in no wise deformed or disfigured would nevertheless be deeply upset if nude photographs of themselves were published in a newspaper or a book. They feel the same way about photographs of their sexual activities, however "normal," or about a narrative of those activities, or about having their medical records publicized. . . . The desire for privacy illustrated by these examples is a mysterious but deep fact about human personality. It deserves and in our society receives legal protection. The nature of the injury shows, by the way, that the defendants are wrong to argue that this branch of the right of privacy requires proof of special damages.

But this is not the character of the depictions of the Hayneses in *The Promised Land*. Although the plaintiffs' claim that the book depicts their "sex life" and "ridicules" Luther Haynes's lovemaking (the reference is to the passage we quoted in which the author refers to Ruby's "devastating imitation" of Luther's manner when he would come home Friday nights in an amorous mood), these characterizations are misleading. No sexual act is described in the book. No intimate details are revealed. Entering one's bedroom with a bottle in one hand and a cigarette in the other is not foreplay. Ruby's speculation that Kevin's problems may have been due to Luther's having been a heavy drinker is not the narration of a sexual act.

. . . .

The branch of privacy law that the Hayneses invoke in their appeal is not concerned with, and is not a proper surrogate for legal doctrines that are concerned with, the accuracy of the private facts revealed. It is concerned with the propriety of stripping away the veil of privacy with which we cover the embarrassing, the shameful, the tabooed, truths about us. . . . The revelations in the book are not about the intimate details of the Hayneses' life. They are about misconduct, in particular Luther's. (There is very little about Dorothy in the book, apart from the fact that she had had an affair with Luther while he was still married to Ruby and that they eventually became and have remained lawfully married.) The revelations are about his heavy drinking, his unstable employment, his adultery, his irresponsible and neglectful behavior toward his wife and children. So we must consider cases in which the right of privacy has been invoked as a shield against the revelation of previous misconduct.

Two early cases illustrate the range of judicial thinking. In *Melvin v. Reid*, 112 Cal. App. 285, 297 P. 91 (Cal. App. 1931), the plaintiff was a former prostitute, who had been prosecuted but acquitted of murder. She later had married and (she alleged) for seven years had lived a blameless respectable life in a community in which her lurid past was unknown—when all was revealed in a movie about the murder case which used her maiden name. The court held that these allegations stated a claim for invasion of privacy. The Hayneses' claim is similar although less dramatic. They have been a respectable married couple for two decades. Luther's alcohol problem is behind him. He has steady employment as a doorman. His wife is a nurse, and in 1990 he told Lemann that the couple's combined income was $60,000 a year. He is not in trouble with the domestic relations court. He is a deacon of his church. He has come a long way from sharecropping in Mississippi and public housing in Chicago and he and his wife want to bury their past just as Mrs. Melvin wanted to do and in *Melvin v. Reid* was held entitled to do. Cf. *Briscoe v. Reader's Digest Ass'n*, 4 Cal. 3d 529, 93 Cal. Rptr. 866, 483 P.2d 34, 43 (Cal. 1971). In Luther Haynes's own words, from his deposition, "I know I haven't been no angel, but since almost 30 years ago I have turned my life completely around. I stopped the drinking and all this bad habits and stuff like that, which I deny, some of [it] I didn't deny, because I have changed my life. It take me almost 30 years to change it and I am deeply in my church. I look good in the eyes of my church members and my community. Now, what is going to happen now when this public reads this garbage which I didn't tell Mr. Lemann to write? Then all this is going to go down the drain. And I worked like a son of a gun to build myself up in a good reputation and he has torn it down."

. . . .

Luther Haynes did not aspire to be a representative figure in the great black migration from the South to the North. People who do not desire the limelight and do not deliberately choose a way of life or course of conduct calculated to thrust them into it nevertheless have no legal right to extinguish it if the experiences that have befallen them are newsworthy, even if they would prefer that those experiences be kept private. The possibility of an involuntary loss of privacy is recognized in the modern formulations of this branch of the privacy tort, which require not only that the private facts publicized be such as would make a reasonable person deeply offended by such publicity but also that they be facts in which the public has no legitimate interest.

The two criteria, offensiveness and newsworthiness, are related. An individual, and more pertinently perhaps the community, is most offended by the publication of intimate personal facts when the community has no interest in them beyond the voyeuristic thrill of penetrating the wall of privacy that surrounds a stranger. The reader of a book about the black migration to the North would have no legitimate interest in the details of Luther Haynes's sex life; but no such details are disclosed. Such a reader does have a legitimate interest in the aspects of Luther's conduct that the book reveals. For one of Lemann's major themes is the transposition virtually intact of a sharecropper morality characterized by a family structure "matriarchal and elastic" and by an "extremely unstable" marriage bond to the slums of the northern cities, and the interaction, largely random and sometimes perverse, of that morality with governmental programs to alleviate poverty. Public aid policies discouraged Ruby and Luther from living together; public housing policies precipitated a marriage doomed to fail. No detail in the book claimed to invade the Hayneses' privacy is not germane to the story that the author wanted to tell, a story not only of legitimate but of transcendent public interest.

The Hayneses question whether the linkage between the author's theme and their private life really is organic. They point out that many social histories do not mention individuals at all, let alone by name. That is true. . . . But it would be absurd to suggest that cliometric or other aggregative, impersonal methods of doing social history are the only proper way to go about it and presumptuous to claim even that they are the best way. Lemann's book has been praised to the skies by distinguished scholars, among them black scholars covering a large portion of the ideological spectrum. . . . Lemann's methodology places the individual case history at center stage. If he cannot tell the story of Ruby Daniels without waivers from every person who she thinks did her wrong, he cannot write this book.

Well, argue the Hayneses, at least Lemann could have changed their names. But the use of pseudonyms would not have gotten Lemann and Knopf off the legal hook. The details of the Hayneses' lives recounted in the book would identify them unmistakably to anyone who has known the Hayneses well for a long time (members of their families, for example), or who knew them before they got married; and no more is required for liability either in defamation law. . . . Lemann would have had to change some, perhaps many, of the details. But then he would no longer have been writing history. He would have been writing fiction. The nonquantitative study of living persons would be abolished as a category of scholarship, to be replaced by the sociological novel. . . . Reporting the true facts about real people is necessary to "obviate any impression that the problems raised in the [book] are remote or hypothetical." *Gilbert v. Medical Economics Co., supra*, 665 F.2d at 308. And surely a composite portrait of ghetto residents would be attacked as racial stereotyping.

The Promised Land does not afford the reader a titillating glimpse of tabooed activities. The tone is decorous and restrained. Painful though it is for the Hayneses to see a past they would rather forget brought into the public view, the public needs the information conveyed by the book, including the information about Luther and Dorothy Haynes, in order to evaluate the profound social and political questions that the book raises. . . .

Does it follow, as the Hayneses' lawyer asked us rhetorically at oral argument, that a journalist who wanted to write a book about contemporary sexual practices could include the intimate details of named living persons' sexual acts without the persons' consent? Not necessarily, although the revelation of such details in the memoirs of former spouses and lovers is common enough and rarely provokes a lawsuit even when the former spouse or lover is still alive. The core of the branch of privacy law with which we deal in this case is the protection of those intimate physical details the publicizing of which would be not merely embarrassing and painful but deeply shocking to the average person subjected to such exposure. The public has a legitimate interest in sexuality, but that interest may be outweighed in such a case by the injury to the sensibilities of the persons made use of by the author in such a way. Restatement (Second) of Torts, *supra* 652D, comment *h*. At least the balance would be sufficiently close to preclude summary judgment for the author and publisher.

The judgment for the defendants is

AFFIRMED.

------

1. In *Doe v. Berkeley Pub.*, 496 S.E.2d 636 (S.C. 1998), plaintiff sued a newspaper after it ran a truthful report that the plaintiff was sexually assaulted while in jail. The court held that "the commission of a violent crime between inmates of a county jail is a matter of public significance, as a matter of law."

2. In *Gilbert v. Medical Economics Co.*, 665 F.2d 305 (10th Cir. 1981), plaintiff anesthesiologist accused of causing two serious injuries sued defendant after an article reported her history of psychiatric and related personal problems. Even though

she conceded that the event itself was newsworthy, plaintiff claimed the intrusions were actionable. The court held for defendant; the facts were connected to the article by the "rational inference that plaintiff's personal problems were the underlying cause of the malpractice."

3. In *Sipple v. Chronicle Publishing Co.*, 201 Cal. Rptr. 665 (Ct. App. 1984), plaintiff thwarted an assassination attempt on President Ford and received a great deal of media coverage including stories that disclosed his homosexuality. The court held for the defendants, finding that the article was "prompted by 'legitimate political considerations,' i.e., to dispel the false public opinion that gays were timid, weak and unheroic figures and to raise the equally important political question whether the President of the United States entertained a discriminatory attitude or bias against a minority group such as homosexuals."

In a non-media case, *Ozer v. Borquez*, 940 P.2d 371 (Colo. 1997), plaintiff associate brought suit against a partner of his law firm who told everyone in the entire firm that plaintiff had AIDS; plaintiff, who was gay, had not disclosed his homosexuality to anyone in his firm, and he had asked the partner to keep his sensitive medical condition in confidence. Verdict for plaintiff.

C. Constitutional Privilege

The Florida Star v. B.J.F.

Supreme Court of the United States, 1989
491 U.S. 524

Justice Marshall delivered the opinion of the Court.

Florida Stat. § 794.03 (1987) makes it unlawful to "print, publish, or broadcast . . . in any instrument of mass communication" the name of the victim of a sexual offense. Pursuant to this statute, appellant The Florida Star was found civilly liable for publishing the name of a rape victim which it had obtained from a publicly released police report. The issue presented here is whether this result comports with the First Amendment. We hold that it does not.

I

The Florida Star is a weekly newspaper which serves the community of Jacksonville, Florida, and which has an average circulation of approximately 18,000 copies. A regular feature of the newspaper is its "Police Reports" section. That section, typically two to three pages in length, contains brief articles describing local criminal incidents under police investigation.

On October 20, 1983, appellee B.J.F. reported to the Duval County, Florida, Sheriff's Department (Department) that she had been robbed and sexually assaulted by an unknown assailant. The Department prepared a report on the incident which identified B.J.F. by her full name. The Department then placed the report in its pressroom. The Department does not restrict access either to the pressroom or to the reports made available therein.

A Florida Star reporter-trainee sent to the pressroom copied the police report verbatim, including B.J.F.'s full name, on a blank duplicate of the Department's forms. A Florida Star reporter then prepared a one-paragraph article about the crime, derived entirely from the trainee's copy of the police report. The article included B.J.F.'s full name. It appeared in the "Robberies" subsection of the "Police Reports" section on October 29, 1983, one of 54 police blotter stories in that day's edition. . . . In printing B.J.F.'s full name, The Florida Star violated its internal policy of not publishing the names of sexual offense victims.

On September 26, 1984, B.J.F. filed suit in the Circuit Court of Duval County against the Department and The Florida Star, alleging that these parties negligently violated § 794.03. . . . Before trial, the Department settled with B.J.F. for $2,500. The Florida Star moved to dismiss, claiming, *inter alia*, that imposing civil sanctions on the newspaper pursuant to § 794.03 violated the First Amendment. The trial judge rejected the motion. . . .

At the ensuing daylong trial, B.J.F. testified that she had suffered emotional distress from the publication of her name. She stated that she had heard about the article from fellow workers and acquaintances; that her mother had received several threatening phone calls from a man who stated that he would rape B.J.F. again; and that these events had forced B.J.F. to change her phone number and residence, to seek police protection, and to obtain mental health counseling. In defense, The Florida Star put forth evidence indicating that the newspaper had learned B.J.F.'s name from the incident report released by the Department, and that the newspaper's violation of its internal rule against publishing the names of sexual offense victims was inadvertent.

At the close of B.J.F.'s case, and again at the close of its defense, The Florida Star moved for a directed verdict. On both occasions, the trial judge denied these motions. He ruled from the bench that § 794.03 was constitutional because it reflected a proper balance between the First Amendment and privacy rights, as it applied only to a narrow set of "rather sensitive . . . criminal offenses." App. 18–19 (rejecting first motion); see *id.*, at 32–33 (rejecting second motion). At the close of the newspaper's defense, the judge granted B.J.F.'s motion for a directed verdict on the issue of negligence, finding the newspaper *per se* negligent based upon its violation of § 794.03. *Id.*, at 33. This ruling left the jury to consider only the questions of causation and damages. The judge instructed the jury that it could award B.J.F. punitive damages if it found that the newspaper had "acted with reckless indifference to the rights of others." *Id.*, at 35. The jury awarded B.J.F. $75,000 in compensatory damages and $25,000 in punitive damages. Against the actual damages award, the judge set off B.J.F.'s settlement with the Department.

The First District Court of Appeal affirmed in a three-paragraph *per curiam* opinion. 499 So. 2d 883 (1986). In the paragraph devoted to The Florida Star's First Amendment claim, the court stated that the directed verdict for B.J.F. had been properly entered because, under § 794.03, a rape victim's name is "of a private nature and not to be published as a matter of law." *Id.*, at 884, citing Doe *v. Sarasota-Bradenton Florida Television Co.*, 436 So. 2d 328, 330 (Fla. App. 1983) (footnote omitted). . . .

II

The tension between the right which the First Amendment accords to a free press, on the one hand, and the protections which various statutes and common-law doctrines accord to personal privacy against the publication of truthful information, on the other, is a subject we have addressed several times in recent years. Our decisions in cases involving government attempts to sanction the accurate dissemination of information as invasive of privacy, have not, however, exhaustively considered this conflict. On the contrary, although our decisions have without exception upheld the press' right to publish, we have emphasized each time that we were resolving this conflict only as it arose in a discrete factual context.

The parties to this case frame their contentions in light of a trilogy of cases which have presented, in different contexts, the conflict between truthful reporting and state-protected privacy interests. In *Cox Broadcasting Corp. v. Cohn*, 420 U.S. 469 (1975), we found unconstitutional a civil damages award entered against a television station for broadcasting the name of a rape-murder victim which the station had obtained from courthouse records. In *Oklahoma Publishing Co. v. Oklahoma County District Court*, 430 U.S. 308 (1977), we found unconstitutional a state court's pretrial order enjoining the media from publishing the name or photograph of an 11-year-old boy in connection with a juvenile proceeding involving that child which reporters had attended. Finally, in *Smith v. Daily Mail Publishing Co.*, 443 U.S. 97 (1979), we found unconstitutional the indictment of two newspapers for violating a state statute forbidding newspapers to publish, without written approval of the juvenile court, the name of any youth charged as a juvenile offender. The papers had learned about a shooting by monitoring a police band radio frequency and had obtained the name of the alleged juvenile assailant from witnesses, the police, and a local prosecutor.

. . . .

We conclude that imposing damages on appellant for publishing B.J.F.'s name violates the First Amendment, although not for either of the reasons appellant urges. Despite the strong resemblance this case bears to *Cox Broadcasting*, that case cannot fairly be read as controlling here. The name of the rape victim in that case was obtained from courthouse records that were open to public inspection. . . . Significantly, one of the reasons we gave in *Cox Broadcasting* for invalidating the challenged damages award was the important role the press plays in subjecting trials to public scrutiny and thereby helping guarantee their fairness. *Id.*, at 492–493. That role is not directly compromised where, as here, the information in question comes from a police report prepared and disseminated at a time at which not only had no adversarial criminal proceedings begun, but no suspect had been identified.

Nor need we accept appellant's invitation to hold broadly that truthful publication may never be punished consistent with the First Amendment. Our cases have carefully eschewed reaching this ultimate question, mindful that the future may bring scenarios which prudence counsels our not resolving anticipatorily. . . . Respecting the fact that press freedom and privacy rights are both "plainly rooted in the traditions and significant concerns of our society," we instead focused on the less sweeping issue "whether the State may impose sanctions on the accurate publication of the name of a rape victim obtained from public records—more specifically, from judicial records which are maintained in connection with a public prosecution and which themselves are open to public inspection." *Ibid.* We continue to believe that the sensitivity and significance of the interests presented in clashes between First Amendment and privacy rights counsel relying on limited principles that sweep no more broadly than the appropriate context of the instant case.

In our view, this case is appropriately analyzed with reference to such a limited First Amendment principle. It is the one, in fact, which we articulated in *Daily Mail* in our synthesis of prior cases involving attempts to punish truthful publication: "[I]f a newspaper lawfully obtains truthful information about a matter of public significance then state officials may not constitutionally punish publication of the information, absent a need to further a state interest of the highest order." 443 U.S., at 103 . . . .

Applied to the instant case, the *Daily Mail* principle clearly commands reversal. The first inquiry is whether the newspaper "lawfully obtain[ed] truthful information about a matter of public significance." 443 U.S., at 103. It is undisputed that the news article describing the assault on B.J.F. was accurate. In addition, appellant lawfully obtained B.J.F.'s name. Appellee's argument to the contrary is based on the fact that under Florida law, police reports which reveal the identity of the victim of a sexual offense are not among the matters of "public record" which the public, by law, is entitled to inspect. Brief for Appellee 17–18, citing Fla. Stat. §119.07(3)(h) (1983). But the fact that state officials are not required to disclose such reports does not make it unlawful for a newspaper to receive them when furnished by the government. Nor does the fact that the Department apparently failed to fulfill its obligation under §794.03 not to "cause or allow to be . . . published" the name of a sexual offense victim make the newspaper's ensuing receipt of this information unlawful. Even assuming the Constitution permitted a State to proscribe *receipt* of information, Florida has not taken this step. It is, clear, furthermore, that the news article concerned "a matter of public significance," 443 U.S., at 103, in the sense in which the *Daily Mail* synthesis of prior cases used that term. That is, the article generally . . . involved a matter of paramount public import: the commission, and investigation, of a violent crime which had been reported to authorities.

. . . .

When a State attempts the extraordinary measure of punishing truthful publication in the name of privacy, it must demonstrate its commitment to advancing this interest by applying its prohibition evenhandedly, to the smalltime disseminator as well as the media giant. Where important First Amendment interests are at stake, the mass scope of disclosure is not an acceptable surrogate for injury. A ban on disclosures effected by "instrument[s] of mass communication" simply cannot be defended on the ground that partial prohibitions may effect partial relief. Without more careful and inclusive precautions against alternative forms of dissemination, we cannot conclude that Florida's selective ban on publication by the mass media satisfactorily accomplishes its stated purpose.

III

Our holding today is limited. We do not hold that truthful publication is automatically constitutionally protected, or that there is no zone of personal privacy within which the State may protect the individual from intrusion by the press, or even that a State may never punish publication of the name of a victim of a sexual offense. We hold only that where a newspaper publishes truthful information which it has lawfully obtained, punishment may lawfully be imposed, if at all, only when narrowly tailored to a state interest of the highest order, and that no such interest is satisfactorily served by imposing liability under § 794.03 to appellant under the facts of this case. The decision below is therefore

Reversed.

---

1. Compare the constitutional privilege presented in *The Florida Star* with the "fair comment" privilege discussed in the defamation chapter.

2. What rule do you gather from *Cox, Florida Star* and *Oklahoma Publishing*? How is your conclusion different from the holding in *Florida Star*?

D. False Light

Cantrell v. Forest City Publishing Co.

Supreme Court of the United States, 1974
419 U.S. 245

Mr. Justice Stewart delivered the opinion of the Court.

Margaret Cantrell and four of her minor children brought this diversity action in a Federal District Court for invasion of privacy against the Forest City Publishing Co., publisher of a Cleveland newspaper, the *Plain Dealer*, and against Joseph Eszterhas, a reporter formerly employed by the *Plain Dealer*, and Richard Conway, a *Plain Dealer* photographer. The Cantrells alleged that an article published in the *Plain Dealer Sunday Magazine* unreasonably placed their family in a false light before the public through its many inaccuracies and untruths. The District Judge struck the claims relating to punitive damages as to all the plaintiffs and dismissed the actions of three of the Cantrell children in their entirety, but allowed the case to go to the jury as to Mrs. Cantrell and her oldest son, William. The jury returned a verdict against all three of the respondents for compensatory money damages in favor of these two plaintiffs.

The Court of Appeals for the Sixth Circuit reversed, holding that, in the light of the First and Fourteenth Amendments, the District Judge should have granted the respondents' motion for a directed verdict as to all the Cantrells' claims. 484 F.2d 150. We granted certiorari, 418 U.S. 909.

In December 1967, Margaret Cantrell's husband Melvin was killed along with 43 other people when the Silver Bridge across the Ohio River at Point Pleasant, W. Va., collapsed. The respondent Eszterhas was assigned by the *Plain Dealer* to cover the story of the disaster. He wrote a "news feature" story focusing on the funeral of Melvin Cantrell and the impact of his death on the Cantrell family.

Five months later, after conferring with the Sunday Magazine editor of the *Plain Dealer*, Eszterhas and photographer Conway returned to the Point Pleasant area to write a follow-up feature. The two men went to the Cantrell residence, where Eszterhas talked with the children and Conway took 50 pictures. Mrs. Cantrell was not at home at any time during the 60 to 90 minutes that the men were at the Cantrell residence.

Eszterhas' story appeared as the lead feature in the August 4, 1968, edition of the *Plain Dealer Sunday Magazine*. The article stressed the family's abject poverty; the children's old, ill-fitting clothes and the deteriorating condition of their home were detailed in both the text and accompanying photographs. As he had done in his original, prize-winning article on the Silver Bridge disaster, Eszterhas used the Cantrell family to illustrate the impact of the bridge collapse on the lives of the people in the Point Pleasant area.

It is conceded that the story contained a number of inaccuracies and false statements. Most conspicuously, although Mrs. Cantrell was not present at any time during the reporter's visit to her home, Eszterhas wrote, "Margaret Cantrell will talk neither about what happened nor about how they are doing. She wears the same mask of non-expression she wore at the funeral. She is a proud woman. Her world has changed. She says that after it happened, the people in town offered to help them out with money and they refused to take it." Other significant misrepresentations were contained in details of Eszterhas' descriptions of the poverty in which the Cantrells were living and the dirty and dilapidated conditions of the Cantrell home.

The case went to the jury on a so-called "false light" theory of invasion of privacy. In essence, the theory of the case was that by publishing the false feature story about the Cantrells and thereby making them the objects of pity and ridicule, the respondents damaged Mrs. Cantrell and her son William by causing them to suffer outrage, mental distress, shame, and humiliation.

II

In *Time, Inc. v. Hill*, 385 U.S. 374, the Court considered a similar false-light, invasion-of-privacy action. The New York Court of Appeals had interpreted New York Civil Rights Law §§ 50–51 to give a "newsworthy person" a right of action when his or her name, picture or portrait was the subject of a "fictitious" report or article. Material and substantial falsification was the test for recovery. 385 U.S., at 384–386. Under this doctrine the New York courts awarded the plaintiff James Hill compensatory damages based on his complaint that Life Magazine had falsely reported that a new Broadway play portrayed the Hill family's experience in being held hostage by three escaped convicts. This Court, guided by its decision in *New York Times Co. v. Sullivan*, 376 U.S. 254, which recognized constitutional limits on a State's power to award damages for libel in actions brought by public officials, held that the constitutional protections for speech and press precluded the application of the New York statute to allow recovery for "false reports of matters of public interest in the absence of proof that the defendant published the report with knowledge of its falsity or in reckless disregard of the truth." 385 U.S., at 388. Although the jury could have reasonably concluded from the evidence in the *Hill* case that Life had engaged in knowing falsehood or had recklessly disregarded the truth in stating in the article that "the story re-enacted" the Hill family's experience, the Court concluded that the trial judge's instructions had not confined the jury to such a finding as a predicate for liability as required by the Constitution. *Id.*, at 394.

The District Judge in the case before us, in contrast to the trial judge in *Time, Inc. v. Hill*, did instruct the jury that liability could be imposed only if it concluded that the false statements in the Sunday Magazine feature article on the Cantrells had been made with knowledge of their falsity or in reckless disregard of the truth. No objection was made by any of the parties to this knowing-or-reckless-falsehood instruction. Consequently, this case presents no occasion to consider whether a State may constitutionally apply a more relaxed standard of liability for a publisher or broadcaster of false statements injurious to a private individual under a false-light theory of invasion of privacy, or whether the constitutional standard announced in *Time, Inc. v. Hill* applies to all false-light cases. *Cf. Gertz v. Robert Welch, Inc.*, 418 U.S. 323. Rather, the sole question that we need decide is whether the Court of Appeals erred in setting aside the jury's verdict.

III

At the close of the petitioners' case-in-chief, the District Judge struck the demand for punitive damages. He found that Mrs. Cantrell had failed to present any evidence to support the charges that the invasion of privacy "was done maliciously within the legal definition of that term." The Court of Appeals interpreted this finding to be a determination by the District Judge that there was no evidence of knowing falsity or reckless disregard of the truth introduced at the trial. Having made such a determination, the Court of Appeals held that the District Judge should have granted the motion for a directed verdict for respondents as to all the Cantrells' claims. 484 F.2d, at 155.

The Court of Appeals appears to have assumed that the District Judge's finding of no malice "within the legal definition of that term" was a finding based on the definition of "actual malice" established by this Court in *New York Times Co. v. Sullivan*, 376 U.S., at 280: "with knowledge that [a defamatory statement] was false or with reckless disregard of whether it was false or not." . . . In a false-light case, common-law malice—frequently expressed in terms of either personal ill will toward the plaintiff or reckless or wanton disregard of the plaintiff's rights—would focus on the defendant's attitude toward the plaintiff's privacy, not toward the truth or falsity of the material published. See *Time, Inc. v. Hill*, 385 U.S., at 396 n. 12. See generally W. Prosser, Law of Torts 9–10 (4th ed.).

Although the verbal record of the District Court proceedings is not entirely unambiguous, the conclusion is inescapable that the District Judge was referring to the common-law standard of malice rather than to the *New York Times* "actual malice" standard when he dismissed the punitive damages claims. . . .

Moreover, the District Judge was clearly correct in believing that the evidence introduced at trial was sufficient to support a jury finding that the respondents Joseph Eszterhas and Forest City Publishing Co. had published knowing or reckless falsehoods about the Cantrells. There was no dispute during the trial that Eszterhas, who did not testify, must have known that a number of the statements in the feature story were untrue. In particular, his article plainly implied that Mrs. Cantrell had been present during his visit to her home and that Eszterhas had observed her "[wearing] the same mask of non-expression she wore [at her husband's] funeral." These were "calculated falsehoods," and the jury was plainly justified in finding that Eszterhas had portrayed the Cantrells in a false light through knowing or reckless untruth.

The Court of Appeals concluded that there was no evidence that Forest City Publishing Co. had knowledge of any of the inaccuracies contained in Eszterhas' article. However, there was sufficient evidence for the jury to find that Eszterhas' writing of the feature was within the scope of his employment at the *Plain Dealer* and that Forest City Publishing Co. was therefore liable under traditional doctrines of respondeat superior. Although Eszterhas was not regularly assigned by the *Plain Dealer* to write for the *Sunday Magazine*, the editor of the magazine testified that as a staff writer for the Plain Dealer Eszterhas frequently suggested stories he would like to write for the magazine. When Eszterhas suggested the follow-up article on the Silver Bridge disaster, the editor approved the idea and told Eszterhas the magazine would publish the feature if it was good. From this evidence, the jury could reasonably conclude that Forest City Publishing Co., publisher of the Plain Dealer, should be held vicariously liable for the damage caused by the knowing falsehoods contained in Eszterhas' story.

It is so ordered.

Mr. Justice Douglas, dissenting.

. . . Freedom of the press is "abridged" in violation of the First and Fourteenth Amendments by what we do today. . . .

A bridge accident catapulted the Cantrells into the public eye and their disaster became newsworthy. To make the First Amendment freedom to report the news turn on subtle differences between common-law malice and actual malice is to stand the Amendment on its head. Those who write the current news seldom have the objective, dispassionate point of view—or the time—of scientific analysts. They deal in fast-moving events and the need for "spot" reporting. The jury under today's formula sits as a censor with broad powers—not to impose a prior restraint, but to lay heavy damages on the press. The press is "free" only if the jury is sufficiently disenchanted with the Cantrells to let the press be free of this damages claim. That regime is thought by some to be a way of supervising the press which is better than not supervising it at all. But the installation of the Court's regime would require a constitutional amendment. Whatever might be the ultimate reach of the doctrine Mr. Justice Black and I have embraced, it seems clear that in matters of public import such as the present news reporting, there must be freedom from damages lest the press be frightened into playing a more ignoble role than the Framers visualized.

---

1. The Restatement 2d § 652E (False Light) provides:

One who gives publicity to a matter concerning another that places the other before the public in a false light is subject to liability to the other for invasion of his privacy, if

(a) the false light in which the other was placed would be highly offensive to a reasonable person, and

(b) the actor had knowledge of or acted in reckless disregard as to the falsity of the publicized matter and the false light in which the other would be placed.

2. What does the Court say about "malice" as applied to privacy? How do the constitutional and common law concepts of "malice" differ?

Lake v. Wal-Mart Stores, Inc.

Supreme Court of Minnesota, 1998
582 N.W.2d 231

Blatz, Chief Justice

Elli Lake and Melissa Weber appeal from a dismissal of their complaint for failure to state a claim upon which relief may be granted. The district court and court of appeals held that Lake and Weber's complaint alleging intrusion upon seclusion, appropriation, publication of private facts, and false light publicity could not proceed because Minnesota does not recognize a common law tort action for invasion of privacy. We reverse as to the claims of intrusion upon seclusion, appropriation, and publication of private facts, but affirm as to false light publicity.

Nineteen-year-old Elli Lake and 20-year-old Melissa Weber vacationed in Mexico in March 1995 with Weber's sister. During the vacation, Weber's sister took a photograph of Lake and Weber naked in the shower together. After their vacation, Lake and Weber brought five rolls of film to the Dilworth, Minnesota Wal-Mart store and photo lab. When they received their developed photographs along with the negatives, an enclosed written notice stated that one or more of the photographs had not been printed because of their "nature."

In July 1995, an acquaintance of Lake and Weber alluded to the photograph and questioned their sexual orientation. Again, in December 1995, another friend told Lake and Weber that a Wal-Mart employee had shown her a copy of the photograph. By February 1996, Lake was informed that one or more copies of the photograph were circulating in the community.

Lake and Weber filed a complaint against Wal-Mart Stores, Inc. and one or more as-yet unidentified Wal-Mart employees on February 23, 1996, alleging the four traditional invasion of privacy torts—intrusion upon seclusion, appropriation, publication of private facts, and false light publicity. Wal-Mart denied the allegations and made a motion to dismiss the complaint under Minn. R. Civ. P. 12.02, for failure to state a claim upon which relief may be granted. The district court granted Wal-Mart's motion to dismiss, explaining that Minnesota has not recognized any of the four invasion of privacy torts. The court of appeals affirmed.

Whether Minnesota should recognize any or all of the invasion of privacy causes of action is a question of first impression in Minnesota. . . .

Today we join the majority of jurisdictions and recognize the tort of invasion of privacy. The right to privacy is an integral part of our humanity; one has a public persona, exposed and active, and a private persona, guarded and preserved. The heart of our liberty is choosing which parts of our lives shall become public and which parts we shall hold close.

Here Lake and Weber allege in their complaint that a photograph of their nude bodies has been publicized. One's naked body is a very private part of one's person and generally known to others only by choice. This is a type of privacy interest worthy of protection. Therefore, without consideration of the merits of Lake and Weber's claims, we recognize the torts of intrusion upon seclusion, appropriation, and publication of private facts. Accordingly, we reverse the court of appeals and the district court and hold that Lake and Weber have stated a claim upon which relief may be granted and their lawsuit may proceed.

. . . .

We decline to recognize the tort of false light publicity at this time. We are concerned that claims under false light are similar to claims of defamation, and to the extent that false light is more expansive than defamation, tension between this tort and the First Amendment is increased.

False light is the most widely criticized of the four privacy torts and has been rejected by several jurisdictions. Most recently, the Texas Supreme Court refused to recognize the tort of false light invasion of privacy because defamation encompasses most false light claims and false light "lacks many of the procedural limitations that accompany actions for defamation, thus unacceptably increasing the tension that already exists between free speech constitutional guarantees and tort law." Citing "numerous procedural and substantive hurdles" under Texas statutory and common law that limit defamation actions, such as privileges for public meetings, good faith, and important public interest and mitigation factors, the court concluded that these restrictions "serve to safeguard the freedom of speech." Thus to allow recovery under false light invasion of privacy, without such safeguards, would "unacceptably derogate constitutional free speech." The court rejected the solution of some jurisdictions — application of the defamation restrictions to false light — finding instead that any benefit to protecting nondefamatory false speech was outweighed by the chilling effect on free speech.

We agree with the reasoning of the Texas Supreme Court. Defamation requires a false statement communicated to a third party that tends to harm a plaintiff's reputation. False light requires publicity, to a large number of people, of a falsity that places the plaintiff in a light that a reasonable person would find highly offensive. The primary difference between defamation and false light is that defamation addresses harm to reputation in the external world, while false light protects harm to one's inner self. Most false light claims are actionable as defamation claims; because of the overlap with defamation and the other privacy torts, a case has rarely succeeded squarely on a false light claim.

Additionally, unlike the tort of defamation, which over the years has become subject to numerous restrictions to protect the interest in a free press and discourage trivial litigation, the tort of false light is not so restricted. Although many jurisdictions have imposed restrictions on false light actions identical to those for defamation, we are not persuaded that a new cause of action should be recognized if little additional protection is afforded plaintiffs.

We are also concerned that false light inhibits free speech guarantees provided by the First Amendment. As the Supreme Court remarked in *New York Times Co. v. Sullivan:* "Whatever is added to the field of libel is taken from the field of free debate." Accordingly, we do not want to:

> create a grave risk of serious impairment of the indispensable service of a free press in a free society if we saddle the press with the impossible burden of verifying to a certainty the facts associated in news articles with a

person's name, picture or portrait, particularly as related to nondefamatory matter.

Although there may be some untrue and hurtful publicity that should be actionable under false light, the risk of chilling speech is too great to justify protection for this small category of false publication not protected under defamation.

Thus we recognize a right to privacy present in the common law of Minnesota, including causes of action in tort for intrusion upon seclusion, appropriation, and publication of private facts, but we decline to recognize the tort of false light publicity. This case is remanded to the district court for further proceedings consistent with this opinion.

Affirmed in part, reversed in part.

———

1. What about consent or assumption of risk by the plaintiffs that the photographs would be shown to others? What if they forgot these pictures were on the roll of film?

2. Was the plaintiffs' assumption that the pictures would not be passed around reasonable? Do individuals who engage in "sexting" (electronic transmission of sexually suggestive or revealing messages or images) have a reasonable expectation that the recipients of their "sexts" will not retransmit them to others?

3. How does the court draw the distinction between defamation and false light? Is it valid? Note that in many jurisdictions, courts have ruled that the false light version of the tort of privacy is subsumed in (and therefore subject to the same rules as) the tort of defamation. *See, e.g., Denver Publishing Co. v. Bueno*, 54 P.3d 893 (Colo. 2002) (concluding that false light claims are subsumed in defamation). *But see Franchise Tax Bd. v. Hyatt*, 335 P.3d 125 (Nev. 2014) (recognizing false light privacy tort under Nevada law).

E. Appropriation

Zacchini v. Scripps-Howard Broadcasting Co.

Supreme Court of the United States, 1977
433 U.S. 562

Mr. Justice White delivered the opinion of the Court.

Petitioner, Hugo Zacchini, is an entertainer. He performs a "human cannon-ball" act in which he is shot from a cannon into a net some 200 feet away. Each performance occupies some 15 seconds. In August and September 1972, petitioner was engaged to perform his act on a regular basis at the Geauga County Fair in Burton, Ohio. He performed in a fenced area, surrounded by grandstands, at the fair grounds. Members of the public attending the fair were not charged a separate admission fee to observe his act.

On August 30, a free-lance reporter for Scripps-Howard Broadcasting Co., the operator of a television broadcasting station and respondent in this case, attended the fair. He carried a small movie camera. Petitioner noticed the reporter and asked him not to film the performance. The reporter did not do so on that day; but on the instructions of the producer of respondent's daily newscast, he returned the following day and videotaped the entire act. This film clip, approximately 15 seconds in length, was shown on the 11 o'clock news program that night, together with favorable commentary.

Petitioner then brought this action for damages, alleging that he is "engaged in the entertainment business," that the act he performs is one "invented by his father and . . . performed only by his family for the last fifty years," that respondent "showed and commercialized the film of his act without his consent," and that such conduct was an "unlawful appropriation of plaintiff's professional property." App. 4–5. Respondent answered and moved for summary judgment, which was granted by the trial court.

The Court of Appeals of Ohio reversed. The majority held that petitioner's complaint stated a cause of action for conversion and for infringement of a common-law copyright, and one judge concurred in the judgment on the ground that the complaint stated a cause of action for appropriation of petitioner's "right of publicity" in the film of his act. All three judges agreed that the First Amendment did not privilege the press to show the entire performance on a news program without compensating petitioner for any financial injury he could prove at trial.

Like the concurring judge in the Court of Appeals, the Supreme Court of Ohio rested petitioner's cause of action under state law on his "right to publicity value of his performance." 47 Ohio St. 2d 224, 351 N.E. 2d 454, 455 (1976). The opinion syllabus, to which we are to look for the rule of law used to decide the case, declared first that one may not use for his own benefit the name or likeness of another, whether or not the use or benefit is a commercial one, and second that respondent would be liable for the appropriation, over petitioner's objection and in the absence of license or privilege, of petitioner's right to the publicity value of his performance. *Ibid.* The court nevertheless gave judgment for respondent because, in the words of the syllabus:

> "A TV station has a privilege to report in its newscasts matters of legitimate public interest which would otherwise be protected by an individual's right of publicity, unless the actual intent of the TV station was to appropriate the benefit of the publicity for some non-privileged private use, or unless the actual intent was to injure the individual." *Ibid.*

We granted certiorari . . . to consider an issue unresolved by this Court: whether the First and Fourteenth Amendments immunized respondent from damages for its alleged infringement of petitioner's state-law "right of publicity." Insofar as the Ohio Supreme Court held that the First and Fourteenth Amendments of United States Constitution required judgment for respondent, we reverse the judgment of that court.

I

. . . .

There is no doubt that petitioner's complaint was grounded in state law and that the right of publicity which petitioner was held to possess was a right arising under Ohio law. It is also clear that respondent's claim of constitutional privilege was sustained. . . . The court preferred the notion of privilege . . . reasoning that "since the gravamen of the issue in this case is not whether the degree of intrusion is reasonable, but whether First Amendment principles require that the right of privacy give way to the public right to be informed of matters of public interest and concern, the concept of privilege seems the more useful and appropriate one."

II

The Ohio Supreme Court held that respondent is constitutionally privileged to include in its newscasts matters of public interest that would otherwise be protected by the right of publicity, absent an intent to injure or to appropriate for some non-privileged purpose. If under this standard respondent had merely reported that petitioner was performing at the fair and described or commented on his act, with or without showing his picture on television, we would have a very different case. But petitioner is not contending that his appearance at the fair and his performance could not be reported by the press as newsworthy items. His complaint is that respondent filmed his entire act and displayed that film on television for the public to see and enjoy. This, he claimed, was an appropriation of his professional property. The Ohio Supreme Court agreed that petitioner had "a right of publicity" that gave him "personal control over commercial display and exploitation of his personality and the exercise of his talents." This right of "exclusive control over the publicity given to his performances" was said to be such a "valuable part of the benefit which may be attained by his talents and efforts" that it was entitled to legal protection. It was also observed, or at least expressly assumed, that petitioner had not abandoned his rights by performing under the circumstances present at the Geauga County Fair Grounds.

The Ohio Supreme Court nevertheless held that the challenged invasion was privileged, saying that the press "must be accorded broad latitude in its choice of how much it presents of each story or incident, and of the emphasis to be given to such presentation. No fixed standard which would bar the press from reporting or depicting either an entire occurrence or an entire discrete part of a public performance can be formulated which would not unduly restrict the 'breathing room' in reporting which freedom of the press requires." 47 Ohio St. 2d, at 235, 351 N.E. 2d, at 461. Under this view, respondent was thus constitutionally free to film and display petitioner's entire act.

The Ohio Supreme Court relied heavily on *Time, Inc. v. Hill*, 385 U.S. 374 (1967), but that case does not mandate a media privilege to televise a performer's entire act without his consent. . . .

Time, Inc. v. Hill, which was hotly contested and decided by a divided Court, involved an entirely different tort from the "right of publicity" recognized by the Ohio

Supreme Court. As the opinion reveals in *Time, Inc. v. Hill*, the Court was steeped in the literature of privacy law and was aware of the developing distinctions and nuances in this branch of the law. The Court, for example, cited W. Prosser, Law of Torts 831–832 (3d ed. 1964), and the same author's well-known article, *Privacy*, 48 Calif. L. Rev. 383 (1960), both of which divided privacy into four distinct branches. The Court was aware that it was adjudicating a "false light" privacy case involving a matter of public interest, not a case involving "intrusion," 385 U.S., at 384–385, n. 9, "appropriation" of a name or likeness for the purposes of trade, *id.*, at 381, or "private details" about a non-newsworthy person or event, *id.*, at 383 n. 7. It is also abundantly clear that *Time, Inc. v. Hill* did not involve a performer, a person with a name having commercial value, or any claim to a "right of publicity." This discrete kind of "appropriation" case was plainly identified in the literature cited by the Court and had been adjudicated in the reported cases.

The differences between these two torts are important. First, the State's interests in providing a cause of action in each instance are different. "The interest protected" in permitting recovery for placing the plaintiff in a false light "is clearly that of reputation, with the same overtones of mental distress as in defamation." Prosser, supra, 48 Calif. L. Rev., at 400. By contrast, the State's interest in permitting a "right of publicity" is in protecting the proprietary interest of the individual in his act in part to encourage such entertainment. . . . Second, the two torts differ in the degree to which they intrude on dissemination of information to the public. In "false light" cases the only way to protect the interests involved is to attempt to minimize publication of the damaging matter, while in "right of publicity" cases the only question is who gets to do the publishing. An entertainer such as petitioner usually has no objection to the widespread publication of his act as long as he gets the commercial benefit of such publication. Indeed, in the present case petitioner did not seek to enjoin the broadcast of his act; he simply sought compensation for the broadcast in the form of damages.

. . . .

There is no doubt that entertainment, as well as news, enjoys First Amendment protection. It is also true that entertainment itself can be important news. *Time, Inc. v. Hill.* But it is important to note that neither the public nor respondent will be deprived of the benefit of petitioner's performance as long as his commercial stake in his act is appropriately recognized. Petitioner does not seek to enjoin the broadcast of his performance; he simply wants to be paid for it. Nor do we think that a state-law damages remedy against respondent would represent a species of liability without fault contrary to the letter or spirit of *Gertz v. Robert Welch, Inc.*, 418 U.S. 323 (1974). Respondent knew that petitioner objected to televising his act but nevertheless displayed the entire film.

We conclude that although the State of Ohio may as a matter of its own law privilege the press in the circumstances of this case, the First and Fourteenth Amendments do not require it to do so.

Reversed.

1. Many television news shows, in addition to reporting the day's events, have features on various local activities, coming television attractions, lives of celebrities, and the like. Are they news or entertainment?

2. How important to the court's decision was the fact that Zacchini had asked defendant not to film his performance? In *PETA v. Bobby Berosini Ltd*, 895 P.2d 1295 (Nev. 1995), *overruled on other grounds, Las Vegas Downtown Redev. Agency v. Hecht*, 940 P.2d 127 (1997), the court rejected a privacy claim brought by a prominent animal trainer who had been surreptitiously filmed mistreating his animals backstage by members of an animal rights organization.

3. The Restatement 2d §652C (Appropriation) provides:

> One who appropriates to his own use or benefit the name or likeness of another is subject to liability to the other for invasion of his privacy.

Midler v. Ford Motor Co.

United States Court of Appeals for the Ninth Circuit, 1988
849 F.2d 460

JOHN T. NOONAN, CIRCUIT JUDGE:

This case centers on the protectibility of the voice of a celebrated chanteuse from commercial exploitation without her consent. Ford Motor Company and its advertising agency, Young & Rubicam, Inc., in 1985 advertised the Ford Lincoln Mercury with a series of nineteen 30 or 60 second television commercials in what the agency called "The Yuppie Campaign." The aim was to make an emotional connection with Yuppies, bringing back memories of when they were in college. Different popular songs of the seventies were sung on each commercial. The agency tried to get "the original people," that is, the singers who had popularized the songs, to sing them. Failing in that endeavor in ten cases the agency had the songs sung by "sound alikes." Bette Midler, the plaintiff and appellant here was done by a sound alike.

Midler is a nationally known actress and singer. She won a Grammy as early as 1973 as the Best New Artist of that year. Records made by her since then have gone Platinum and Gold. She was nominated in 1979 for an Academy award for Best Female Actress in *The Rose*, in which she portrayed a pop singer. *Newsweek* in its June 30, 1986 issue described her as an "outrageously original singer/comedian." *Time* hailed her in its March 2, 1987 issue as "a legend" and "the most dynamic and poignant singer-actress of her time."

When Young & Rubicam was preparing the Yuppie Campaign it presented the commercial to its client by playing an edited version of Midler singing "Do You Want To Dance," taken from the 1973 Midler album, "The Divine Miss M." After the client accepted the idea and form of the commercial, the agency contacted Midler's manager, Jerry Edelstein. The conversation went as follows: "Hello, I am Craig Hazen from

Young and Rubicam. I am calling you to find out if Bette Midler would be interested in doing . . . ?" Edelstein: "Is it a commercial?" "Yes." "We are not interested."

Undeterred, Young & Rubicam sought out Ula Hedwig whom it knew to have been one of "the Harlettes" a backup singer for Midler for ten years. Hedwig was told by Young & Rubicam that "they wanted someone who could sound like Bette Midler's recording of [Do You Want To Dance]." She was asked to make a "demo" tape of the song if she was interested. She made an a capella demo and got the job.

At the direction of Young & Rubicam, Hedwig then made a record for the commercial. The Midler record of "Do You Want To Dance" was first played to her. She was told to "sound as much as possible like the Bette Midler record," leaving out only a few "aahs" unsuitable for the commercial. Hedwig imitated Midler to the best of her ability.

After the commercial was aired Midler was told by "a number of people" that it "sounded exactly" like her record of "Do You Want To Dance." Hedwig was told by "many personal friends" that they thought it was Midler singing the commercial. Ken Fritz, a personal manager in the entertainment business not associated with Midler, declares by affidavit that he heard the commercial on more than one occasion and thought Midler was doing the singing.

Neither the name nor the picture of Midler was used in the commercial; Young & Rubicam had a license from the copyright holder to use the song. At issue in this case is only the protection of Midler's voice. The district court described the defendants' conduct as that "of the average thief." They decided, "If we can't buy it, we'll take it." The court nonetheless believed there was no legal principle preventing imitation of Midler's voice and so gave summary judgment for the defendants. Midler appeals.

The First Amendment protects much of what the media do in the reproduction of likenesses or sounds. A primary value is freedom of speech and press. *Time, Inc. v. Hill*, 385 U.S. 374, 388, 87 S. Ct. 534, 17 L. Ed. 2d 456 (1967). The purpose of the media's use of a person's identity is central. If the purpose is "informative or cultural" the use is immune; "if it serves no such function but merely exploits the individual portrayed, immunity will not be granted." Felcher and Rubin, *"Privacy, Publicity and the Portrayal of Real People by the Media"* 88 Yale L.J. 1577, 1596 (1979). Moreover, federal copyright law preempts much of the area. "Mere imitation of a recorded performance would not constitute a copyright infringement even where one performer deliberately sets out to simulate another's performance as exactly as possible." Notes of Committee on the Judiciary, 17 U.S.C.A. § 114(b). It is in the context of these First Amendment and federal copyright distinctions that we address the present appeal.

Nancy Sinatra once sued Goodyear Tire and Rubber Company on the basis of an advertising campaign by Young & Rubicam featuring "These Boots Are Made For Walkin'," a song closely identified with her; the female singers of the commercial were alleged to have imitated her voice and style and to have dressed and looked like her. The basis of Nancy Sinatra's complaint was unfair competition; she claimed that the song and the arrangement had acquired "a secondary meaning" which, under California law, was protectible. This court noted that the defendants "had paid a very substantial sum to the copyright proprietor to obtain the license for the use of the song and all of its arrangements." To give Sinatra damages for their use of the song would clash with federal copyright law. Summary judgment for the defendants was affirmed. If Midler were claiming a secondary meaning to "Do You Want To Dance" or seeking to prevent the defendants from using that song, she would fail like Sinatra. But that is not this case. Midler does not seek damages for Ford's use of "Do You Want To Dance," and thus her claim is not preempted by federal copyright law. Copyright protects "original works of authorship fixed in any tangible medium of expression." 17 U.S.C. § 102(a). A voice is not copyright-able. The sounds are not "fixed." What is put forward as protectible here is more personal than any work of authorship.

Bert Lahr once sued Adell Chemical Co. for selling Lestoil by means of a commercial in which an imitation of Lahr's voice accompanied a cartoon of a duck. Lahr alleged that his style of vocal delivery was distinctive in pitch, accent, inflection, and sounds. The First Circuit held that Lahr had stated a cause of action for unfair competition, that it could be found "that defendant's conduct saturated plaintiff's audience, curtailing his market." That case is more like this one. But we do not find unfair competition here. One-minute commercials of the sort the defendants put on would not have saturated Midler's audience and curtailed her market. Midler did not do television commercials. The defendants were not in competition with her.

California Civil Code section 3344 is also of no aid to Midler. The statute affords damages to a person injured by another who uses the person's "name, voice, signature, photograph or likeness, in any manner." The defendants did not use Midler's name or anything else whose use is prohibited by the statute. The voice they used was Hedwig's, not hers. The term "likeness" refers to a visual image not a vocal imitation. The statute, however, does not preclude Midler from pursuing any cause of action she may have at common law; the statute itself implies that such common law causes of action do exist because it says its remedies are merely "cumulative." *Id.* § 3344(g).

The companion statute protecting the use of a deceased person's name, voice, signature, photograph or likeness states that the rights it recognizes are "property rights." *Id.* § 990(b). By analogy the common law rights are also property rights. Appropriation of such common law rights is a tort in California. *Motschenbacher v. R.J. Reynolds Tobacco Co.*, 498 F.2d 821 (9th Cir. 1974). In that case what the defendants used in their television commercial for Winston cigarettes was a photograph of a famous professional racing driver's racing car. The number of the car was changed and a wing-like device known as a "spoiler" was attached to the car; the car's features of white pinpointing, an oval medallion, and solid red coloring were retained. The driver, Lothar Motschenbacher, was in the car but his features were not visible. Some persons, viewing the commercial, correctly inferred that the car was his and that he was in the car and was therefore endorsing the product. The defendants were held to have invaded a "proprietary interest" of Motschenbacher in his own identity. *Id.* at 825.

Midler's case is different from Motschenbacher's. He and his car were physically used by the tobacco company's ad; he made part of his living out of giving commercial endorsements. But, as Judge Koelsch expressed it in *Motschenbacher*, California will recognize an injury from "an appropriation of the attributes of one's identity." *Id.* at 824. It was irrelevant that Motschenbacher could not be identified in the ad. The ad suggested that it was he. The ad did so by emphasizing signs or symbols associated with him. In the same way the defendants here used an imitation to convey the impression that Midler was singing for them.

Why did the defendants ask Midler to sing if her voice was not of value to them? Why did they studiously acquire the services of a sound-alike and instruct her to imitate Midler if Midler's voice was not of value to them? What they sought was an attribute of Midler's identity. Its value was what the market would have paid for Midler to have sung the commercial in person.

A voice is more distinctive and more personal than the automobile accoutrements protected in *Motschenbacher*. A voice is as distinctive and personal as a face. The human voice is one of the most palpable ways identity is manifested. We are all aware that a friend is at once known by a few words on the phone. At a philosophical level it has been observed that with the sound of a voice, "the other stands before me." D. Ihde, Listening and Voice 77 (1976). A fortiori, these observations hold true of singing, especially singing by a singer of renown. The singer manifests herself in the song. To impersonate her voice is to pirate her identity. *See* W. Keeton, D. Dobbs, R. Keeton, D. Owen, Prosser & Keeton on Torts 852 (5th ed. 1984).

We need not and do not go so far as to hold that every imitation of a voice to advertise merchandise is actionable. We hold only that when a distinctive voice of a professional singer is widely known and is deliberately imitated in order to sell a product, the sellers have appropriated what is not theirs and have committed a tort in California. Midler has made a showing, sufficient to defeat summary judgment, that the defendants here for their own profit in selling their product did appropriate part of her identity.

REVERSED AND REMANDED FOR TRIAL.

———————

1. Why no recovery in copyright? Why did Nancy Sinatra lose her case? Does the California Statute preclude Midler's suit? If damages are the market value of Midler's voice, who won? Does this make a case for punitive damages?

2. When are videos circulated on YouTube actionable?

3. In *White v. Samsung Electronics America, Inc.*, 971 F.2d 1395 (1992), *cert. denied*, 508 U.S. 951 (1993), the court upheld a right of publicity claim brought by *Wheel of Fortune* game-show star Vanna White. The case involved an advertisement by the defendant that used a robot that was dressed and styled to resemble the plaintiff. The ad was set as though it occurred in the 21st century, and its message was that the defendants' products would still be in use then even though the star of the current show would be replaced by a robot. (Ironically, the ad was for a videocassette recording device (VCR), which is a product that was long-gone by the 21st century, while the plaintiff is still hosting her long-running game show.) Over a vigorous dissent, the court rejected the defendant's argument that the ad was not an appropriation of the plaintiff's likeness but rather a parody. Is conscious resemblance by an artificial figure enough to generate a right of publicity? Should it be?

4. In *ETW Corp. v. Jireh Publishing, Inc.*, 332 F.3d 915 (6th Cir. 2003), the court held that defendant's marketing of an artistic print featuring the likeness of professional golfer Tiger Woods at the Masters golf tournament was protected by the First Amendment from a right of publicity claim. The court reasoned that the artist's rendition contained "significant transformative elements" which made it "especially worthy of First Amendment protection and also less likely to interfere with the economic interest protected by Woods' right of publicity." Over a strong dissent, the court both distinguished and noted its disagreement with much of the reasoning in *White*.

Index

[References are to sections.]